Sep 8
1969

HOOVER WAR LIBRARY PUBLICATIONS—NO. 1

Fall of the German Empire
1914-1918

VOLUME I

HOOVER WAR LIBRARY PUBLICATIONS—No. 1

FALL OF THE GERMAN EMPIRE

1914-1918

VOLUME I

Selected and Edited by

RALPH HASWELL LUTZ

Translations by

DAVID G. REMPEL *and* **GERTRUDE RENDTORFF**

1969

OCTAGON BOOKS

New York

Reprinted 1969

by special arrangement with Stanford University Press

OCTAGON BOOKS
A DIVISION OF FARRAR, STRAUS & GIROUX, INC.
19 Union Square West
New York, N. Y. 10003

LIBRARY OF CONGRESS CATALOG CARD NUMBER: 71-89977

Printed in U.S.A. by
TAYLOR PUBLISHING COMPANY
DALLAS, TEXAS

PREFACE

THESE TWO volumes of contemporary German sources, covering the period from the outbreak of the World War to the collapse of the German Empire, form the first of a contemplated series of publications on the reorganization of Germany since 1914. Since the German Revolution not only destroyed the Bismarckian Empire but altered the life and institutions of the German people, a knowledge of the fundamental causes of the revolution, the details of its progress, and its immediate results in the development of democratic control is essential to an understanding of contemporary Germany and of those political and social problems which have resulted from the defeat of the Empire in the World War. The purpose of the research in German history here bearing fruit has therefore been to investigate the causes of the collapse of the German Empire, the fundamental historic movements of the German Revolution, and the reorganization of the nation under the Weimar Constitution.

These materials of German history from 1914 to 1918, a large portion of which have not hitherto been translated or published, very definitely increase our knowledge of the underlying causes of the collapse of German imperialism during the World War. For those interested in this historic period they present materials not generally accessible, since the documents included are, with important exceptions, to be found only in special libraries. The two volumes, in my opinion, enable students to overcome many material ostacles to their research, to go beyond secondary authorities with respect to a number of objectively presented war problems, in general to penetrate behind the ordinary narrative of German history, and thus to vitalize their study by immediate contact with primary sources. It is not out of place to remark further that they give the meaning of a number of little-known technical terms and they indicate methods of historical investigation.

The body of materials here drawn upon, collected in Germany since 1919, includes: *Verhandlungen des Reichstags,* 1914–1918, and other official documents of the Reich and the Federal States; the Moenkemoeller and Leipzig collections of war and revolutionary materials; the Herron Papers; the Kanner Papers; official and unofficial collections of captured political, military, and naval documents; the war-time files of the *Norddeutsche Allgemeine Zeitung, Deutscher Reichsanzeiger, Berliner Tageblatt, Vorwärts,* and other daily papers and periodicals; personal and partisan pamphlets; personal memorabilia and documents of statesmen and soldiers; *apologia;* annals; selected secondary accounts; and proclamations and posters. They do not include additional confidential materials concerning numerous war problems which have been secured and are held under restrictions which preclude their publication before about the middle of the century.

Materials previously translated and made accessible to students have been included only when necessary to an understanding of hitherto unpublished documents. The originals or authentic copies of all documents which are included in these volumes are now in the Hoover War Library of Stanford University.

Of those materials not included, the most important are those collected by the Parliamentary Investigating Commission of the German National Assembly and the German Reichstag and published by the Fourth Sub-committee of the Parliamentary Investigating Commission for War Guilt in the series entitled *The Causes of the German Collapse in the Year 1918.* Permission was secured in 1928 from the Foreign Office, the Reichstag, and the Deutsche Verlagsgesellschaft für Politik und Geschichte to publish an English translation of a selected list of all documents of the Parliamentary Investigating Commission provided that the selection was not biased, the translations were literally accurate, the editor omitted all personal interpretations, and the strictly scientific character of the original compilation was maintained. The selection from this mass of historical materials for the period following 1914 has been approved by the Parliamentary Investigating Commission, and translations of them have been prepared in Berlin under the supervision of Dr. Eugen Fischer, Executive Secretary of the Commission. It is planned to publish this volume of documents on the German Collapse in 1933.

The subject of German responsibility for the outbreak of the war, which falls only partially within the scope of this study, has been very briefly presented in the second chapter. Other subjects, notably Submarine Warfare, the Navy, and the problems of War

Diplomacy, owing to insurmountable difficulties of selection, have been less fully presented than they deserve.

The historical materials in these volumes are divided into the following seven parts: The Empire at War, War and Peace, the Armed Forces of the Empire, War Diplomacy, Social Democracy, Economic Conditions, and the Collapse of the Empire. Each part is subdivided into chapters, each of which in turn is headed by a brief introductory note indicating the historical importance of the materials in the chapter. The documents included in each chapter have in general been presented in chronological order, and they are numbered consecutively throughout the volumes. The sources of all materials cited are given in footnotes. Abridgments have been made in these materials, often tediously long debates and memoranda, where space could be saved without distorting the sense or suppressing the truth; these omissions have in every case been indicated. My editorial explanations are inclosed in brackets, while parentheses are used only as in the original. A formal bibliography is not included in these volumes, the bibliographical footnotes being considered adequate. A chronology of German history from the beginning of the 1914 crisis to November 11, 1918, is appended to the second volume.

Official German war-time publications, including publications of the Kriegspresseamt, were made available by the generosity of the German Government. Valuable materials were secured from the Weltkriegsbücherei at Stuttgart-Berg, the Prussian State Library and the Central Office for the Investigation of the Causes of the War in Berlin, the Reichsarchiv at Potsdam, the Bibliothèque et Musée de la Guerre at Château de Vincennes, France, the Commission for Relief in Belgium Educational Foundation of New York City, and the Carnegie Endowment for International Peace, of Washington, D.C.

The major portion of the material in these volumes has been translated by Mr. David G. Rempel and Miss Gertrude Rendtorff at the Hoover War Library. Certain documents have been severally translated by Dr. Max E. Petersen, Mrs. Ramia I. Giese, and other translators at Berlin and Stuttgart. These translations of official documents, Reichstag debates, and publications of the daily press have wherever possible been compared with those in the *Daily Review of the Foreign Press,* together with its numerous confidential supplements, which was issued during the World War by the British

General Staff through the War Office, London. In an attempt to maintain uniformity I have revised the translations, and I assume responsibility for them as they stand.

Wherever possible, the form of each contemporary source has been followed. But in the many cases where the literary form of the originals was distinctly inferior, no attempt has been made to employ in translation English of a corresponding grade. Variations in the translation of official titles of individuals and of offices of state, and the inclusion of many German terms such as "Fraktion" are indications of the unsolved problems of the editor.

Translations of diplomatic, military, and naval documents which were made available officially during the World War by the governments of the United States, Great Britain, and Germany, and by the General Staffs of the American and British Expeditionary Forces have here been reprinted verbatim. A number of Commission for Relief in Belgium documents have been reprinted with the permission of the Commission for Relief in Belgium Educational Foundation. The Carnegie Endowment for International Peace also granted permission to include documents appearing in the Endowment's translation entitled *Preliminary History of the Armistice*.

To many statesmen, soldiers, and scholars I am indebted for valuable information concerning this period of German history. The officials and staff of the Hoover War Library and those of the Weltkriegsbücherei have also rendered valuable aid, and I wish to express my thanks and gratitude to them. Dr. Esther Caukin Brunauer has aided me materially in the selection of materials. Miss Bernice Miller and Miss Doris Dorcy have rendered important services as research assistants and typists. Professor William Hawley Davis, editor of the Stanford University Press, has made many valuable suggestions and numerous welcome verbal changes.

R. H. L.

STANFORD UNIVERSITY, CALIFORNIA
August 8, 1932

TABLE OF CONTENTS

Part I—The Empire at War

Part III—The Armed Forces of the Empire

Chapter X. The Army 583

PART IV—WAR DIPLOMACY

Fall of the German Empire
1914-1918

Part I
The Empire at War

CHAPTER I

THE OUTBREAK OF THE WORLD WAR

INTRODUCTORY NOTE

THE WAR between Austria and Serbia, which commenced July 28, 1914, developed into a conflict between the two great alignments of European powers when on July 30 the Tsar of Russia signed the ukase for the general mobilization of the Russian Army. On July 31 the Imperial German Government, in an ultimatum to Russia, demanded the cessation of this mobilization and simultaneously proclaimed the threatening danger of war, which meant mobilization.

At 3:30 P.M., July 31, an ultimatum was sent to France informing the French Government of the ultimatum to Russia and asking if France intended to remain neutral in a Russo-German war. This was followed by a declaration of war against France, on August 3.

At 7:00 P.M., August 2, the German representative in Brussels presented an ultimatum to the Belgian Minister for Foreign Affairs and demanded a reply within twelve hours. The Belgian Government refused to accept the proposals for a German military advance into Belgian territory. At 6:00 A.M., August 4, Germany notified the Belgian Government that she was going to act by force of arms, and two hours later her troops crossed the frontier. At 2:00 P.M., August 4, Great Britain sent an ultimatum to Berlin and asked for a satisfactory reply by midnight. At midnight no satisfactory answer had been received, and Germany and England were at war.

On August 4, Kaiser Wilhelm II in the speech from the Throne and Chancellor von Bethmann-Hollweg in his statement to the Reichstag presented the official version of the outbreak of the war. The entire nation responded to this call to arms in the firm conviction that the Empire was fighting a just war in self-defense.

3

1. THE KAISER'S SPEECH FROM THE BALCONY OF THE ROYAL PALACE, BERLIN, JULY 31, 1914[1]

A momentous hour has struck for Germany. Envious rivals everywhere drive us to legitimate defense. The sword has been forced into our hand. I hope that, if my endeavors up to the very last moment should not succeed in bringing the adversaries to reason and in preserving peace, we may wield the sword, with God's help, so that we may sheathe it again with honor. War would demand enormous sacrifices from the German people, but we would show the enemy what it means to attack Germany. And so I commend you to God. Go now into the churches, kneel before God, and implore His help for our brave army.

2. IMPERIAL PROCLAMATION OF STATE OF SIEGE, JULY 31, 1914[2]

We, Wilhelm, by the Grace of God, German Emperor, King of Prussia, etc., ordain upon the basis of Article 68 of the Constitution of the German Empire, in the name of the Empire:

The territory of the Empire, with the exception of the territory of the Kingdom of Bavaria, is hereby declared to be in the condition of war (*Kriegszustand*).

This ordinance takes effect on the day of its proclamation.

Given under Our Own Hand and Imperial Seal at the *Neues Palais,* July 31, 1914.

WILHELM I. R.

von Bethmann-Hollweg

3. THE KAISER'S SPEECH FROM THE BALCONY OF THE ROYAL PALACE, BERLIN, AUGUST 1, 1914[3]

I thank you from the bottom of my heart for the expression of your affection and your loyalty. When it comes to war, all parties cease and we are all brothers. This or that party has attacked me in peace time, but I forgive them now whole-heartedly. If our neighbors do not concede us peace, then we hope and wish that our good German sword comes out of this war victorious!

[1] *Norddeutsche Allgemeine Zeitung,* August 2, 1914, evening edition, p. 1.

[2] *Deutscher Reichsanzeiger und Königlich Preussischer Staatsanzeiger,* July 31, 1914, p. 1.

[3] *Frankfurter Zeitung,* August 2, 1914, II, 1.

4. PROCLAMATION OF A GARRISON COMMANDER, AUGUST 1, 1914[4]

PROCLAMATION

His Majesty the Emperor and King has proclaimed the state of siege over the territory of the Empire.

The executive power is herewith transferred to me.

More detailed ordinances will, if necessary, be announced in the future.

v. TAYSEN, Major and Garrison Commander

JENA, August 1, 1914

5. PROCLAMATION OF THE ELEVENTH ARMY CORPS COMMANDER, AUGUST 1, 1914[5]

TO THE POPULATION OF THE 11TH ARMY DISTRICT

His Majesty the Emperor has proclaimed the state of siege over the territory of the Empire. The reasons for this measure are not fears that the population might possibly fail to observe its duty to the Fatherland but solely to expedite the rapid and equal carrying through of the mobilization. The rapidity and safety of our advance demands a unified and clear-sighted direction of the whole executive power. No one who observes the law and follows the ordinances of the authorities will be restricted in the pursuit of his occupation by the increased rigidity of the law due to the state of siege. I am confident that the entire population will gladly and unreservedly support the military and civil authorities and therewith make it easier for us to do our highest duties to the Fatherland. Then it will also be possible to maintain the old glory of the XI Army Corps and the Army and to keep it in honor in the eyes of the Emperor and the nation.

The Commanding General
VON PLÜSKOW

CASSEL, August 1, 1914

[4] German War Poster, Hoover War Library.
[5] *Ibid.*

6. GENERAL MOBILIZATION, AUGUST 1, 1914[6]

I order the German Army and the Imperial Navy to be placed on a war footing in accordance with the plans of mobilization for the German Army and the Imperial Navy.

August 2, 1914, is fixed as the first day of mobilization.

WILHELM I. R.

von Bethmann-Hollweg

BERLIN, August 1, 1914

7. SUMMONS TO REPORT, AUGUST 1, 1914[7]

His Majesty the Emperor has ordered the

MOBILIZATION

of the Army and the Navy

I. The first day of mobilization is August 2, 1914
    The second day of mobilization is August 3, 1914
    The third day of mobilization is August 4, 1914
    The fourth day of mobilization is August 5, 1914
    The fifth day of mobilization is August 6, 1914
    The sixth day of mobilization is August 7, 1914

The calendar days of the following days of mobilization can be determined from this.

II. All officers and the rank and file of those on leave, including the substitute-reservists (*Ersatz-Reservisten*) who have been served with the war-order, have to report at the place and time given on the war-orders. Those who have a pass-notice (*Passnotiz*) remain at home for the time being.

III. All substitute-reservists who have not been served with a war-order must stay at home after the eighth day of mobilization, to receive the order to report to a substitute-troop division (*Ersatz-Truppenteil*).

IV. All privates of the entire furloughed rank, as well as all privates of the reserve and the first and second *Landwehr,* who are not in possession of a war-order or a pass-notice, have to go *at once* to the nearest Head-Reporting office in order to fix the date of their report. The 14-day time-limit given in peace time for reporting is abolished.

---

[6] *Deutscher Reichsanzeiger,* August 1, 1914.
[7] German War Poster, Hoover War Library.

From this is excluded only the person who is expressly freed from reporting in case of mobilization.

V. *Anyone failing to comply with the above order is subject to punishment under martial law.*

VI. Practices and control-meetings already announced will not take place.

VII. The conduct-money is to be obtained from the respective troop division, and not from the local authorities.

VIII. All men who are called to arms have, in order to reach their place of report, to get *free railroad passage,* without buying a ticket and without previous inquiry at the ticket window, solely by showing the conductor the war-order or other military papers. In case of absence of military papers, an oral statement to that effect shall suffice without exception.

IX. The peace-time train schedule ceases the night between the second and third day of mobilization. From the morning of the third day of mobilization to the sixth day, the trains will go according to the military train schedule, which is being announced in the more important papers, at the railroad stations, and through public notices.

(Seal)

The Commanding General of the
XIX (2. K. S.) Army Corps

8. THE SPEECH FROM THE THRONE IN THE WHITE HALL OF THE ROYAL PALACE, BERLIN, AUGUST 4, 1914[8]

Today in the White Hall of the King's Palace in Berlin at one o'clock noon, the solemn opening of the Reichstag by the Kaiser took place.

Preceding the opening, a service was held at 12:30 in the cathedral for the Reichstag members of the Evangelical Church, and in St. Hedwig's Church for members of the Catholic Church.

After the religious ceremony the members of the Reichstag gathered in the White Hall and took their position in the center of the hall opposite the throne. Then, led by the Chancellor, the members of the Bundesrat entered and took a position to the left of the throne.

Dr. v. Bethmann-Hollweg then announced the Kaiser, who upon entering the White Hall was greeted by three "Hochs," and took his position before the throne. Thereupon His Majesty accepted from the hand of the Chancellor, Dr. v. Bethmann-Hollweg, the speech from the throne and, with helmet on, read:

[8] *Deutscher Reichsanzeiger,* August 4, 1914, p. 1; *Verhandlungen des Reichstags,* No. 1, August 4, 1914, pp. 1–2.

"Honored gentlemen, at a time of such importance I have assembled the elected representatives of the German people about me. For nearly half a century we have been allowed to follow the ways of peace. The attempts to attribute to Germany warlike intentions and to hedge in her position in the world have often sorely tried the patience of my people. Undeterred, my Government has pursued the development of our moral, spiritual, and economic strength as its highest aim, with all frankness, even under provocative circumstances. The world has been witness that during the last years, under all pressure and confusion, we have stood in the first rank in saving the nations of Europe from a war between the great powers.

"The most serious dangers to which the events in the Balkans had given rise seemed to have been overcome—then suddenly an abyss was opened through the murder of my friend the Archduke Franz Ferdinand. My lofty ally, the Emperor and King Franz Josef, was forced to take up arms to defend the security of his empire against dangerous machinations from a neighboring state. The Russian Empire stepped in to hinder the allied monarchy from following out her just interests. Not only does our duty as ally call us to the side of Austria-Hungary, but it is our great task to protect our own position and the old community of culture between the two Empires against the attack of hostile forces.

"With a heavy heart I have had to mobilize the army against a neighbor with whom it had fought side by side on many a battlefield. With unfeigned sorrow I saw broken a friendship which had been faithfully preserved by Germany. The Imperial Russian Government, yielding to the pressure of an insatiable nationalism, has taken sides with a state which through its sanctioning of criminal attacks has brought the evils of this war. That France, too, should have taken sides with our enemy could not surprise us; too often have attempts to come to a more friendly relationship with the French Republic failed because of her old hopes and old resentments.

"Honored gentlemen, what human insight and power could do to equip a people for these uttermost decisions has been done with your patriotic assistance. The hostility which has been making itself felt in the East and in the West for a long time past has now broken out in bright flame. The present situation is the result of an ill will which has been active for many years against the power and the prosperity of the German Empire.

"No lust of conquest drives us on; we are inspired by the unalterable will to protect the place in which God has set us for ourselves and all coming generations. From the documents which have been submitted to you, you will see how my Government, and especially my Chancellor, have endeavored even to the last moment to stave off the inevitable. In a defensive war that has been forced upon us, with a clear conscience and a clean hand we take up the sword.

"I issue my call to the peoples and stocks of the German Empire that with their united strength they may stand like brothers with our allies in order to defend what we have created through the works of peace. Following the example of our fathers, staunch and true, earnest and knightly, humble before God, but with the joy of battle in the face of the enemy, we trust in the Almighty to strengthen our defense and guide us to good issue.

"Honored gentlemen, the German people gathered about their princes and leaders are today looking to you. Come to your decisions quickly and unanimously. Such is my most earnest wish."

His Majesty added to that:

"You have read, gentlemen, what I have said to my people from the balcony of the castle. Here I repeat: I know no more parties, I only know Germans. [*Loud cheers.*] As proof that you are strongly resolved to hold with me, through thick and thin, through want until death, without difference of race and difference of religion, I challenge the leaders of the parties to step forward and to pledge me their word."

The leaders of the parties did so under loud and protracted applause. Thereupon the Chancellor stepped forward and declared the Reichstag opened.

After renewed cheers, uttered by the Bavarian Minister von Lerchenfeld-Köfering and in which he was joined by the others, the assembly sang with enthusiasm "Heil Dir im Siegerkranz," to which the Kaiser listened standing. Amidst continued cheers His Majesty left the hall with a "Thank you" to all sides, and shaking hands with many members as he left.

9. SPEECH OF THE IMPERIAL CHANCELLOR, DR. VON BETHMANN-HOLLWEG, IN THE REICHSTAG AUGUST 4, 1914[9]

A stupendous fate is breaking over Europe. For forty-four years, since the time we fought for and won the German Empire and our position in the world, we have lived in peace and have protected the peace of Europe. In the works of peace we have become strong and powerful, and have thus aroused the envy of others. With patience we have faced the fact that, under the pretense that Germany was

[9] *Verhandlungen des Reichstags,* No. 1, August 4, 1914. This journal is designated in the original according to the sessions of the Reichstag. For convenience of reference in this work the session will be indicated as "No —."

desirous of war, enmity has been awakened against us in the East and the West, and chains have been fashioned for us. The wind then sown has brought forth the whirlwind which has now broken loose. We wished to continue our work of peace, and, like a silent vow, the feeling that animated everyone from the Emperor down to the youngest soldier was this: Only in defense of a just cause shall our sword fly from its scabbard. [*Hearty applause.*]

The day has now come when we must draw it, against our wish, and in spite of our sincere endeavors. Russia has set fire to the building. [*Stormy shouts: "Quite right!" "Very true!"*] We are at war with Russia and France—a war that has been forced upon us.

Gentlemen, a number of documents, composed during the pressure of these last eventful days, are before you. Allow me to emphasize the facts that characterize our attitude.

From the first moment of the Austro-Serbian conflict we declared that this question must be limited to Austria-Hungary and Serbia [*"Quite true!"*], and we worked with this end in view. All Governments, especially that of Great Britain, took the same attitude. Russia alone asserted that she had to be heard in the settlement of this matter.

Thus the danger of a European crisis raised its threatening head. [*"Very true!"*]

As soon as the first definite information regarding the military preparations in Russia reached us, we declared at St. Petersburg in a friendly but emphatic manner that military measures against Austria would find us on the side of our ally [*hearty applause*], and that military preparations against ourselves would oblige us to take counter-measures [*renewed hearty applause*] ; but that mobilization would come very near to actual war.

Russia assured us in the most solemn manner of her desire for peace [*stormy shouts: "Hear! hear!"*], and declared that she was making no military preparations against us. [*Commotion.*]

In the meantime, Great Britain, warmly supported by us, tried to mediate between Vienna and St. Petersburg. [*"Hear! hear!"—Hearty applause.*]

On July 28 the Emperor telegraphed to the Tsar asking him to take into consideration the fact that it was both the duty and the right of Austria-Hungary to defend herself against the pan-Serb agitation, which threatened to undermine her existence. [*Hearty approval.*] The Emperor drew the Tsar's attention to the solidarity of the interests of all monarchs in view of the murder at Sarajevo. [*"Hear! hear!" and "Very good!"*] He asked for the latter's personal assistance in smoothing over the difficulties existing between Vienna and St. Petersburg. About the same time, and before receipt of this telegram, the Tsar asked the Emperor to come to his aid and to induce Vienna to moderate her demands. The Emperor accepted the rôle of mediator.

But scarcely had active steps on these lines begun when Russia mobilized all her forces directed against Austria [*hearty shouts: "Hear! hear!" "Unheard!"*], while Austria-Hungary had mobilized only those of her corps which were directed against Serbia. [*"Hear! hear!"*] To the north she had mobilized only two of her corps, far from the Russian frontier. [*Renewed: "Hear! hear!"*] The Emperor immediately informed the Tsar that this mobilization of Russian forces against Austria rendered the rôle of mediator, which he had accepted at the Tsar's request, difficult, if not impossible.

In spite of this we continued our task of mediation at Vienna and carried it to the utmost point which was compatible with our position as an ally. [*Hearty shouts: "Hear! hear!"*]

Meanwhile Russia of her own accord renewed her assurances that she was making no military preparations against us. [*Great excitement. Shouts of disgust.*]

We come now to July 31. The decision was to be taken at Vienna. Through our representations we had already obtained the resumption of direct conversations between Vienna and St. Petersburg, after they had been for some time interrupted. [*Lively, "Hear! hear!"*] But before the final decision was taken at Vienna the news arrived that Russia had mobilized her entire forces and that her mobilization was therefore directed against us also. [*"Hear! hear!"*] The Russian Government, who knew from our repeated statements what mobilization on our frontiers meant, did not notify us of this mobilization, nor did they even offer any explanation. [*"Hear! hear!"*] It was not until the afternoon of July 31 that the Emperor received a telegram from the Tsar in which he guaranteed that his army would not assume a provocative attitude toward us. [*"Hear! hear!"—Laughter.*] But mobilization on our frontiers had been in full swing since the night of July 30–31. [*"Hear! hear!"*]

While we were mediating at Vienna in compliance with Russia's request, Russian forces were appearing all along our extended and almost entirely open frontier, and France, though indeed not actually mobilizing, was admittedly making military preparations. What was our position? For the sake of the peace of Europe [*thumping the desk in excitement and in a raised voice*] we had, up till then, deliberately refrained from calling up a single reservist. [*Hearty applause.*] Were we now to wait further in patience until the nations on either side of us chose the moment for their attack? [*Many shouts: "No, no!"*] It would have been a crime to expose Germany to such a peril. [*Stormy, protracted applause.*] Therefore, on July 31 we called upon Russia to demobilize as the only measure which could still preserve the peace of Europe. [*"Quite right!"*] The Imperial Ambassador at St. Petersburg was also instructed to inform the Russian Government that in case our demand met with a refusal we should have to consider that a state of war (*Kriegszustand*) existed.

The Imperial Ambassador has executed these instructions. We have not yet learned what Russia answered to our demand for demobilization. [*"Hear! hear!" and great excitement.*] Telegraphic reports on this question have not reached us even though the wires still transmitted much less important information. [*"Hear! hear!"*]

Therefore, the time limit having long since expired, the Emperor was obliged to mobilize our forces on the first of August at 5:00 P.M. [*Hearty applause.*]

At the same time we had to make certain what attitude France would assume. To our direct question whether she would remain neutral in the event of a Russo-German war France replied that she would do what her interests demanded. [*Laughter.*] That was an evasion, if not a refusal. [*"Very true!"*]

In spite of this, the Emperor ordered that the French frontier was to be unconditionally respected. This order, with one single exception, was strictly obeyed. France, who mobilized at the same time as we did, assured us that she would respect a zone of, ten kilometers on the frontier. [*"Hear! hear!"—Right.*] What really happened? Aviators dropped bombs, and cavalry patrols and French infantry detachments appeared on the territory of the Empire! [*"Hear! hear!"*] Though war had not been declared, France thus broke the peace [*"Quite right!"*] and actually attacked us. [*"Very true!"*]

Regarding the one exception on our side which I mentioned, the Chief of the General Staff reports as follows: "Only one of the French complaints about the crossing of the frontier from our side is justified. Against express orders, a patrol of the 14th Army Corps, apparently led by an officer, crossed the frontier on August 2. They seem to have been shot down, only one man having returned. But long before this isolated instance of crossing the frontier had occurred, French aviators had penetrated into Southern Germany and had thrown bombs on railway lines. [*Lively "Hear! hear!"*] French troops had attacked our frontier guards on the Schlucht Pass. Our troops, in accordance with their orders, have remained strictly on the defensive." This is the report of the General Staff.

Gentlemen, we are now in a state of necessity (*Notwehr*) [*lively approval*], and necessity (*Not*) knows no law. [*Stormy applause.*] Our troops have occupied Luxemburg [*applause*] and perhaps have already entered Belgian territory. [*Renewed applause.*]

Gentlemen, that is a breach of international law. [*"Hear! hear!"*—*Right.*] It is true that the French Government declared at Brussels that France would respect Belgian neutrality as long as her adversary respected it. We knew, however, that France stood ready for an invasion. [*"Hear! hear!"*—*Right.*] France could wait; we could not. A French attack on our flank on the lower Rhine might have been disastrous. [*Lively approval.*] Thus we were forced to ignore the rightful protests of the Governments of Luxemburg and Belgium. [*"Quite right!"*] The wrong—I speak openly—the wrong we thereby commit we will try to make good as soon as our military aims have been attained. [*Applause.*]

He who is menaced as we are and is fighting for his highest possession can only consider how he is to hack his way through (*durchhauen*). [*Enthusiastic applause in entire House.*]

Gentlemen, we stand shoulder to shoulder with Austria-Hungary.

As for Great Britain's attitude, the statements made by Sir Edward Grey in the House of Commons yesterday show the position assumed by the British Government. We have informed the British Government that as long as Great Britain remains neutral our fleet will not attack the northern coast of France, and that we will not violate the territorial integrity and independence of Belgium. These assurances I now repeat before the world [*"Hear! hear!"*], and I may add that, as long as Great Britain remains neutral, we would also be willing, upon reciprocity being assured, to take no warlike measures against French commercial shipping. [*Applause.*]

Gentlemen, so much for the facts. I repeat the words of the Emperor: "With a clear conscience we enter the struggle." [*Applause.*] We are fighting for the fruits of our works of peace, for the inheritance of a great past and for our future. The fifty years are not yet past during which Count Moltke said we should have to remain armed to defend the inheritance that we won in 1870. Now the great hour of trial has struck for our people. But with clear confidence we go forward to meet it. [*Stormy applause.*] Our army is in the field, our navy is ready for battle—behind them stands the entire German nation [*protracted enthusiastic applause in entire House; the Reichstag rises*], the entire German nation [*to the Socialists*], united to the last man. [*Renewed enthusiastic applause.*]

Gentlemen, you know your duty and all that it means. The proposed laws need no further explanation. I ask you to pass them quickly. [*Stormy applause.*]

10. SPEECH OF THE PRESIDENT OF THE REICHSTAG, DR. KAEMPF, AUGUST 4, 1914[10]

Gentlemen, the seriousness of the situation, as to which no one among us can have deceived himself, found expression in all its extent and magnitude in the words of the Chancellor.

We find ourselves facing powerful enemies who threaten us on the right and on the left, who without declaration of war have invaded our territory, and who have forced upon us a war for the defense of our country. We are conscious that the war into which we were forced is a defensive war; but at the same time its highest spiritual and material possessions are at stake for Germany. It is a war of life and death [*hearty applause*], a struggle for our existence [*repeated hearty applause throughout the entire House*].

The moment in which the Reichstag, in view of the outbreak of the war, prepares to vote those laws which are to establish the secure foundations for the war itself and for the economic life of the nation is a solemn and profoundly serious one, but at the same time a forever great and exalting one. [*Applause.*] Heavy burdens must be placed upon the entire nation, and heavy sacrifices must be demanded of every individual. However, there is not one in the whole German Empire who does not fully comprehend what is at stake and who does not cheerfully take upon himself these burdens and make these sacrifices for the Fatherland. [*Hearty applause.*]

The enthusiasm which sweeps like a storm across the country is our witness that the entire German people are resolved to sacrifice life and property for the honor of their country. [*Hearty applause.*] Never have the people been more united than they are today. Those, too, who are professed opponents of war, hasten to the standards, and their representatives in the Reichstag approve unhesitatingly the means necessary for the defense of the country. [*Hearty applause.*] Thus the entire German people stake their lives for the expiation of the wrong done to us in this war which has been forced upon us.

In this we know ourselves at one with the Governments of all the Federal States. All of us, Governments and people, have but one thought: the honor, the welfare, and the greatness of the German Empire. [*Hearty applause.*]

Thus the people, old and young, go into this holy war conscious of their strength and full of enthusiasm. From the eyes of our sons and brothers gleams the old German courage of battle. [*Lively applause.*] We see the commanders of our army and navy at their great tasks, thoughtfully but joyously confident of victory.

[10] *Verhandlungen des Reichstags,* No. 1, August 4, 1914, p. 7.

The unanimity of the entire nation, the strength of our people in arms, the cool-headedness of the army and navy command, all this assures us of victory in this war which we are waging in defense of our honor and the greatness of our Fatherland. [*Prolonged stormy applause from all sides of the House.*]

11. HAASE'S SPEECH IN THE REICHSTAG, AUGUST 4, 1914[11]

Gentlemen, upon instruction from my party I have the following statement to make:

We are standing before a fateful hour. The consequences of imperialistic policy, through which an era of competitive armaments was ushered in and the antagonism between nations was intensified, have swept over Europe like a tidal wave. The responsibility for this rests with the champions of this policy [*"Very true!"—Social-Democrats*]; we refuse it. [*Applause from the Social-Democrats.*] Social-Democracy has fought this ominous development with all its might, and even in these last hours it has endeavored to secure peace through impressive demonstration in all countries especially in cordial agreement with our brothers in France. [*Hearty applause from the Social-Democrats.*] Its efforts have been in vain.

Now we are facing the grim fact of war. We are threatened by the horrors of hostile invasion. Today we do not have to decide whether for or against war, but solely about the question of means necessary for the defense of our country. [*Hearty approval by the bourgeois parties.*] Now we must think of the millions of our fellow-countrymen who, without guilt of their own, have been drawn into this doom. [*"Very true!"—Social-Democrats.*] Our fervent wishes accompany our brothers who have been called to the colors, irrespective of party. [*Hearty applause on all sides.*] We also think of the mothers who must surrender their sons and of the women and children who are deprived of husband and father and who, besides their anxiety for their loved ones, are threatened by the horrors of starvation. And there will soon be tens of thousands of wounded and mutilated soldiers. [*"Very true!"*] To help them all, to alleviate this immense distress—this we regard as our compelling duty. [*Hearty approval by the Social-Democrats.*]

Much, if not all, is at stake for our people and its freedom in the future, in case victory should be on the side of Russian despotism sullied with the blood of the best of its own people. [*Lively shouts: "Very true!"—Social-Democrats.*] It is necessary to ward off this danger, to render secure the civilization (*Kultur*) and the independence of our own

[11] *Verhandlungen des Reichstags*, No. 1, August 4, 1914, pp. 8–9.

country. [*Applause.*] And we shall do what we have always maintained: in the hour of danger we do not leave the Fatherland in the lurch. [*Hearty approval.*] In so doing we feel ourselves in agreement with the International, which at all times has recognized the right of every people to national independence and self-defense [*"Quite right!"—Social-Democrats*], just as we, in agreement with it, condemn every war of conquest. [*"Very true!"—Social-Democrats.*]

We demand that, as soon as the aim of protection shall be attained and the enemies be inclined toward peace, the war be ended by a peace which shall render possible friendship with our neighbors. [*Applause by Social-Democrats.*] We demand this not only in the interest of that international solidarity which we have always championed but also in the interest of the German peoples themselves. [*"Very good!"—Social-Democrats.*] We hope that the cruel school of the war sufferings will awaken in additional millions the abhorrence of war and win them over to the ideal of socialism and of peace among nations. [*Hearty applause by the Social-Democrats.*] Guided by these principles we vote for the war credits asked for. [*Hearty applause by the Social-Democrats.*]

12. THE IMPERIAL CHANCELLOR'S WORDS AT THE CLOSE OF THE SESSION OF AUGUST 4, 1914[12]

Gentlemen, at the close of this brief but solemn session, but one brief word. It is not the great importance of your decisions which gives this session its significance, but the spirit which prompted you to make them —the spirit of a unified Germany, the spirit of unconditioned and unreserved mutual confidence, even unto death. [*Applause.*] Whatever the future may have in store for us, the 4th of August 1914 will be to all eternity one of the greatest days of Germany. . . . .

13. THE ROYAL PRUSSIAN DECREE OF AMNESTY[13]

We, Wilhelm, by the Grace of God, King of Prussia, etc., in view of the self-sacrificing love of the Fatherland which the whole nation is displaying in the war which has been forced upon us, do unto all persons who, up to the present day, have

(1) For *lèse majesté* against their own ruler or against a federal Prince (paragraphs 94–101 of the Criminal Code) ; for hostile action against friendly states in the sense of paragraphs 103–104 of the Criminal

---

[12] *Verhandlungen des Reichstags*, No. 1, August 4, 1914, p. 11.
[13] *Norddeutsche Allgemeine Zeitung*, August 5, 1914, I, 1.

Code; for offenses and misdemeanors in the exercise of civic rights (paragraphs 105–109 of the Criminal Code); for resistance to the authority of the state (paragraphs 110–122 of the Criminal Code); for offenses and misdemeanors against public order in the sense of paragraphs 123–138 of the Criminal Code; for insults in cases provided for by paragraphs 196–197 of the Criminal Code; for offenses in the sense of paragraph 153 of the Industrial Regulations; for punishable actions committed through the press or punishable under the Press Law of May 7, 1874 (*Imperial Law Gazette,* page 65), or under the Law of Public Meetings of April 19, 1908 (*Imperial Law Gazette,* page 151)

Been condemned to a fine, to arrest, to confinement within a fortress up to two years, inclusive, or to imprisonment up to two years, inclusive; or

(2) For theft or embezzlement (paragraphs 242–248 of the Criminal Code, paragraph 138 of the Military Code); for fraud in the sense of paragraph 264a of the Criminal Code; for criminal appropriation in the sense of paragraphs 288–289 of the Criminal Code; for malversation in the sense of paragraph 370 of the Criminal Code; or for an action punishable under the law relating to poaching of April 15, 1878 (*Collection of Laws,* page 222)

Have been condemned to a fine, or to arrest or to imprisonment up to three months, inclusive:

Grant remission of such penalties as shall have not yet been carried out, together with all costs in arrears and the enjoyment of all civic rights which they may have forfeited.

If penalties have also been inflicted on account of one and the same act under a provision which does not fall within the scope of this decree, remission of such penalty is also granted if it can be established under the law with which this decree is concerned. In the case of punishment resulting from conviction for another punishable offense full remission is granted of the punishment inflicted for the offense within the scope of the present decree.

If for the same act a fine had been inflicted as well as loss of liberty, a fine is to be remitted only if the punishment involving loss of liberty comes within this decree.

In the case of sentences pronounced by a tribunal exercising jurisdiction in common with other Federal States this decree finds application in so far as we possess the right of amnesty in the particular case under agreements made with the Governments concerned.

Our Ministry of State is to provide for the prompt publication and execution of this decree.

WILHELM R. . . . .

BERLIN CASTLE, August 4, 1914

14. "EUROPE'S HOUR OF DESTINY," EDITORIAL IN *VOR-WÄRTS*, ORGAN OF THE SOCIAL-DEMOCRACY[14]

The terrible catastrophe which we have foreseen and whose approach we have tried to prevent with all our might seems to be at hand; we are face to face with the world war. A state of war has already been proclaimed in Germany and, according to the statement of the Commander-in-Chief of the Marches, this is merely the first step toward a general mobilization.

At any minute the final decision may come and the last bit of hope we may have had for the maintenance of peace is about to be extinguished. Wilhelm II himself spoke last Friday night and his words reflected the seriousness of the situation. Unless his efforts to preserve peace are destined to be successful in the last moment, war is inevitable.

That peace may after all be maintained is, at the present moment, all the more unlikely as all nations are engaged in a feverish preparation for war and, consequently, are nervous and excited. At such a moment calm and sensible negotiations are exceedingly difficult. And yet the country that could at this moment preserve its self-control the longest would render to the whole civilized world a service which later generations would gratefully remember.

For even now peace might be maintained if a compromise could be formulated that would be satisfactory to both Austria and Russia.

The stipulations of such an agreement, however, must take into account the actual political situation and must not overlook the rôle played by Russia. This view, which we have presented more than once recently, found in the *Berliner Tageblatt* an exponent in the person of Walter Rathenau, one of the leading industrialists of our time.

According to the semi-official *Lokalanzeiger*, the Emperor has actually, though in vain, used his good efforts to persuade Russia to accept, in the last hour, a satisfactory basis for further negotiations; but Russia has answered by mobilizing her army.

This Russian mobilization does not appear to us to offer a sufficient reason why serious, earnest, and patient negotiations on the basis of an honest endeavor for peace should not be continued. Nobody knows whether or not Russia considered it necessary to continue her rapid preparations for war for the very reason that the *Lokalanzeiger*, by a very strange mistake, had published the German order for mobilization before it was authorized to do so (*Fälschlicherweise*). But even the fact that Russia has actually mobilized her armies need not make Germany nervous, because Russia, on account of the organization of her army and because of the vastness of her country, needs infinitely more

[14] *Vorwärts*, No. 207, August 1, 1914.

time for the purpose of mobilization than Germany. Even now there is time for negotiations which could avert from civilized Europe this terrible catastrophe, especially from Germany, which, according to the words of Wilhelm II himself, would be forced to make enormous sacrifices in "Blut und Gut" if fate is inexorable.

As for us, we are even now unable to accept this war as unavoidable. For no state, no group of powers can with surety count on victory, laurels, political triumphs. All parties must be ready and willing to accept a fair compromise, if only the right way can be found. And according to our opinion the more difficult and complicated the situation the greater the glory for the statesman who, by means of his energy, tenacity, and clear-headedness, will be able to avert the terrible fate from the nations, above all, from his own nation, which is so terribly involved in the turmoil.

Walter Rathenau asks that the demands of both contesting parties be made public. This will probably not be done before August 4, when, in case the war breaks out, the Reichstag will convene.

At that time the Reichstag will be informed of the official German interpretation of the situation, which will probably be explained by official documents. France and Russia may likewise be expected to give their versions from their respective points of view. Which one of these statements will come nearest the facts only the future will tell, only the objective historian will prove.

Today, when the declaration of war is imminent, and when independent public opinions have ceased to exist, such inquiries into the question of war guilt are of value; today academic discussions as to what might have been done or not done are useless.

Today, in this last most critical hour, there remains but the one question: how may war be averted even now? We can but state once more our position—a position which millions and millions of Germans are holding with us—by solemnly urging those on whom the responsibility rests to exert all their energy, all their prudence and wisdom, in order that peace may be preserved.

The socialistic proletariat of all countries, in contrast to all Governments, is passionately working in this behalf.

If, nevertheless, the hideous specter should become reality, if the bloody torrent of a war of nations should sweep over Europe—one thing is sure: Social-Democracy bears no responsibility for the coming events.

_____

These words had just been written when the telegraph brought the following momentous announcement:

BERLIN, July 31. The *Norddeutsche Allgemeine Zeitung* says: "After the negotiations undertaken by request of the Tsar himself have been terminated by the Russian Government by ordering the general mobilization of the Russian army and navy, the Government of His Majesty the Emperor has informed St. Petersburg today that the German mobilization must be expected unless Russia, within twelve hours, stops her preparations and gives definite assurances that they will not be resumed. Simultaneously the French Government has been addressed regarding its attitude in case of war between Germany and Russia."

15. SOCIAL-DEMOCRACY AND THE WAR[15]

In today's session of the Reichstag the Social-Democratic "Fraktion" voted the war credits demanded by the Government. At the same time it outlined its stand as follows:

[*Vorwärts* then prints Haase's statement of August 4 in the Reichstag; see above, Document 11.]

16. THE BAN ON SOCIAL-DEMOCRATIC LITERATURE REMOVED[16]

Comrade Stadthagen, representing *Vorwärts,* is in receipt of the following communication from the War Office:

"Referring to your letter of the 17th inst. the War Office informs you that section 3 of the ordinance of the War Office, dated 24.1.1894, prohibiting the subscription to and the distribution of revolutionary or Social-Democratic literature, as well as the dissemination of such literature in military barracks or other buildings used for military purposes, has been repealed as far as Social-Democratic literature is concerned, if published after 31.8.1914.

"The Ministry of War takes the occasion to state that this repeal has been made in the expectation that nothing will be published which might endanger the spirit of loyalty in the army. If this should not be the case every Chief Command (*General-kommando*) is empowered to put the ordinance in force again.

"Nothing but a literal copy of the above communication in the press without any comments will be permitted by the War Office.

"VON FALKENHAYN"

[15] *Vorwärts,* Special Edition, No. 210a, August 4, 1914.
[16] *Ibid.,* No. 239, September 2, 1914.

17. THE IMPERIAL MANIFESTO OF AUGUST 6, 1914[17]

Since the foundation of the Empire it has been for forty-three years my strenuous endeavor, and that of my predecessors, to preserve the peace of the world and to promote by peaceful means our vigorous development. But our adversaries were jealous of the success of our work.

All open and latent hostility on the East and on the West and beyond the sea we have borne till now in the consciousness of our responsibility and power. Now, however, an attempt is being made to humiliate us. We are expected to look on with folded arms whilst our enemies are arming themselves for a treacherous attack. They will not suffer that we maintain resolute fidelity to our ally, who is fighting for his position as a Great Power and with whose humiliation our power and honor would equally be lost.

So the sword must decide. In the midst of perfect peace the enemy takes us by surprise. Therefore, to arms! Any dallying, any temporizing would betray the Fatherland.

What is at stake is whether the Empire which our fathers founded anew shall or shall not subsist, whether German power and German life shall or shall not subsist. We shall resist to the last breath of man and horse, and shall fight out the struggle even against a world of enemies. Never has Germany been subdued when it was united. Forward with God, who will be with us as He was with our ancestors!

WILHELM

BERLIN, August 6, 1914

18. THE EMPRESS AUGUSTE VICTORIA TO THE WOMEN OF GERMANY[18]

Obeying the summons of the Emperor our people are preparing for an unprecedented struggle which they did not provoke and which they are carrying on only in self-defense.

Whoever can bear arms will joyfully fly to the colors to defend the Fatherland with his blood.

The struggle will be gigantic and the wounds to be healed innumerable. Therefore, I call upon you women and girls of Germany, and upon all to whom it is not given to fight for our beloved home, for help. Let everyone now do what lies in her power to lighten the struggle for our husbands, sons, and brothers. I know that in all ranks of our people

[17] *Deutscher Reichsanzeiger,* August 6, 1914.
[18] *Ibid.*

without exception the will exists to discharge this high duty, but may the Lord God strengthen us in our holy work of love, which summons us women to devote all our strength to the Fatherland in its decisive struggle.

The organizations primarily concerned, to whom our support is above all things needful, have already sent out notices as to the mustering of volunteers and the collection of gifts of all kinds.

AUGUSTE VICTORIA

BERLIN, August 6, 1914

19. KAISER WILHELM II TO THE OBERBÜRGERMEISTER OF BERLIN, AUGUST 16, 1914[19]

The progress of military operations compels me to remove my headquarters from Berlin. My heart prompts me, in bidding farewell to the citizens of Berlin, to return my deepest thanks for all the manifestations and proofs of love and affection which these great and fateful days have brought to me in such abundant measure. I rely fully on the help of God, on the gallantry of the army and the navy, and on the unconquerable resolution of the united German nation in the hour of danger. Victory will not fail our righteous cause.

WILHELM I. R.

BERLIN, the Palace, August 16, 1914

[19] *Norddeutsche Allgemeine Zeitung,* August 17, 1914, I, 1.

CHAPTER II

THE QUESTION OF WAR GUILT

INTRODUCTORY NOTE

THE QUESTION of War Guilt, the *Kriegsschuldfrage*, has been debated since the outbreak of the World War in August 1914. In Germany it has led to the development of a national movement. The German Government has replied to the accusation of almost exclusive war guilt by publishing the great collection of documents from its diplomatic archives entitled *Die Grosse Politik der Europäischen Kabinette, 1871–1914*.

The Allied and Associated Powers inserted in the Treaty of Versailles the following pronouncements:

ARTICLE 227: The Allied and Associated Powers publicly arraign William II of Hohenzollern, formerly German Emperor, for a supreme offence against international morality and the sanctity of treaties.

A special tribunal will be constituted to try the accused, thereby assuring him the guaranties essential to the right of defence. It will be composed of four judges, one appointed by each of the following Powers: namely, the United States of America, Great Britain, France, Italy, and Japan.

In its decision the tribunal will be guided by the highest motives of international policy, with a view to vindicating the solemn obligations of international undertakings and the validity of international morality. It will be its duty to fix the punishment which it considers should be imposed.

The Allied and Associated Powers will address a request to the Government of The Netherlands for the surrender to them of the ex-Emperor in order that he may be put to trial.

ARTICLE 231: The Allied and Associated Governments affirm and Germany accepts the responsibility of Germany and her allies for causing all the loss and damage to which the Allied and Associated Governments and their nationals have been subjected as a consequence of the war imposed upon them by the aggression of Germany and her allies.

These clauses, which Germany was forced in 1919 to accept, have created a great post-war literature and a national movement against the charge of special war guilt. Article 227 was never carried out. Article 231 as a pronouncement of the sole guilt of Germany has "no moral right nor judicial validity."

20. ADDRESS OF REICHSPRÄSIDENT VON HINDENBURG ON THE WAR GUILT QUESTION SEPTEMBER 18, 1927[1]

The Tannenberg national monument is devoted primarily to the memory of those who fell fighting for the freedom of their country. But their memory and the honor of my still living comrades adjure me, in this hour and at this spot, to declare solemnly: The accusation that Germany is responsible for this greatest of all wars we hereby repudiate —all classes of the German people unanimously repudiate it. It was not out of envy or hate or desire of conquest that we drew the sword. The war, on the contrary, with all the terrible sacrifices demanded from the whole nation, was the extreme measure resorted to in preservation of our existence against a host of enemies. With clean hearts we marched out to defend the Fatherland, with clean hands the German Army wielded the sword. Germany is ready at any moment to prove this fact before impartial judges.

21. THE PROCLAMATION OF THE GERMAN GOVERNMENT CONCERNING THE WAR GUILT QUESTION AUGUST 29, 1924[2]

BERLIN, 29–8–24   Official

On the occasion of the passing of the laws relative to the London Agreements, the Chancellor of the Reich, on behalf of the German Government, issues the following proclamation:

"With the resolution it has passed today, the Reichstag has set its seal to the London Agreements. Therewith a decision has been taken which cannot but be of determinant importance for the destinies of Germany for years to come. The Government feels itself impelled to

[1] *Deutsche Allgemeine Zeitung,* quoted in *Die Kriegsschuldfrage,* October 1927, p. 931.

[2] W. T. B. Nachtausgabe, 75. Jahrgang, Nr. 1768, quoted in *Die Kriegsschuldfrage,* September 1924, pp. 337–38.

express its thanks to all those members of the Reichstag who have contributed to this result. All who have had a share in this decision have had to overcome grave misgivings and in many cases have even had to put aside their personal convictions in order to attain the acceptance of the London Agreements. Hard though it may have been for each individual to come to this decision, no choice was left him if the way to a better future was to be opened for our country.

"The German Government cannot and will not allow this momentous occasion to pass, an occasion on which the Government is taking upon itself such grave obligations in execution of the Treaty of Versailles, without clearly and unequivocally affirming its stand on the question of Germany's responsibility for the war, a question which has since 1919 lain heavy upon the soul of the German people.

"The statement imposed upon us by the Treaty of Versailles under the pressure of overwhelming force, to the effect that Germany had by her attack precipitated the World War, contradicts the facts of history. The German Government therefore declares that it cannot recognize the statement in question. The German nation justly demands its liberation from the burden of this false accusation. As long as this demand remains unsatisfied and as long as one single member of the comity of nations is branded as having committed a crime against humanity, no real understanding and no true reconciliation is to be achieved among the nations.

"The German Government will take occasion to bring this declaration to the notice of foreign governments."

(*Signed*) MARX, German Chancellor

BERLIN, 29th of August, 1924

22. THE OFFICIAL RAISING OF THE WAR GUILT QUESTION
SEPTEMBER 26, 1925[3]

(*a*) THE PRESENTATION OF THE GERMAN VERBAL DECLARATION IN LONDON AND PARIS

On the afternoon of September 26, 1925, the German Ambassadors von Hoesch in Paris and Dr. Sthamer in London presented to the Governments of these countries the German Note of acceptance of the Locarno Conference. At the same time the German Ambassadors were instructed to make certain declarations to this Note, and submit them in written form, *i.e.*, not directly as a Note, but as a Verbal Declaration.

[3] *Die Kriegsschuldfrage,* October 1925, pp. 700–707.

The content of this declaration, which is reproduced below, refers to the war guilt question and the evacuation of the Cologne Zone. Herr von Hoesch submitted the Note on September 26 to the Secretary-General of the Quai d'Orsay, M. Berthelot, since M. Briand happened to be absent from Paris. When Dr. Sthamer announced in London that the German Government expected to publish the Verbal Declaration, he met with the most energetic opposition of Chamberlain. That Berthelot too was alarmed about this German proposal has now become known. The Paris correspondent of the *Berliner Tageblatt* telegraphed about it on September 30 [*Berliner Tageblatt,* September 30, 1925, No. 463] :

"According to the description of a well-informed person, 'Berthelot almost fell off his chair,' when he heard the entirely unexpected declarations and was informed that they were to be published. He begged to be permitted to discuss this matter with Briand, whom he had already informed on Saturday over the telephone."

For the time being, Berlin awaited the result of this discussion between Briand and von Hoesch. That there was no intention of giving in, in any way whatsoever, as regards the war guilt question was evident in Paris from the leading editorial of the Sunday evening *Temps* [September 27, 1925], which emphasized in the sharpest form imaginable the war guilt of Germany as resulting from Article 231 of the Versailles Treaty. The editorial read :

"One does not demand of Germany a new admission of her responsibility for the war as a condition for her admission into the League of Nations, but this guilt of Germany is contained in the following terms in Article 231 of the Treaty of Versailles: 'The Allied and Associated Governments affirm, and Germany accepts, the responsibility of Germany and her allies for causing all the loss and damage to which the Allied and Associated Governments and their nationals have been subjected as a consequence of the war imposed upon them by the aggression of Germany and her allies.' Not a single recantation must attenuate the effects of this recognition of its culpability made by Germany in signing the Treaty of Versailles; it is not within the authority of any power to suppress this Article 231 of the Treaty, which plainly justifies our right to obtain from the nations who are responsible for the war, the reparations imposed upon them by the Allies."

The interview between Briand and Herr von Hoesch, during which the latter submitted to the French Foreign Minister the German Verbal Declaration, took place from 5 : 00 to 6 : 00 P.M. on September 28. No agreement was reached as to the treatment of the questions, particularly the war guilt question, raised by the declaration.

In Berlin upon receipt of the Ambassador's report about his inter-

view with Briand, Chancellor Dr. Luther, in view of the seriousness of
the situation, called a meeting of the Cabinet at 9:00 P.M. on September 28. This session lasted until 1:00 A.M. That very night Herr
von Hoesch received further instructions. In the forenoon of the following day [September 29], just before the meeting of the French
Ministerial Council took place, the Ambassador went to Briand. The
discussion was very short. Evidently Herr von Hoesch had instructions
to inform them that the German Government had to insist on the publication of the Verbal Declaration. About 5:00 P.M. a second meeting of
Briand and the Ambassador took place, during which Briand handed to
Herr von Hoesch the answer of the French Government to the German
Note and the German Verbal Note.

22. (b) THE GERMAN VERBAL NOTE

BERLIN, September 25, 1925

At the moment when the Ministers of the Governments concerned
are at the point of meeting for important discussions about the strengthening of peace between their countries, the German Government holds
it necessary to announce in all clearness to the Allied Governments its
attitude upon two questions which are very closely connected with the
purpose of those discussions. In the exchange of notes that preceded,
the Allied Governments made the conclusion of a Security Pact dependent upon Germany's entrance into the League of Nations. The German
Government has not objected to the linking of the two problems; however, it feels itself thereby obliged to come back to a point which,
in connection with the League question, it has already expressed in its
Memorandum of September 1924 to the Governments represented in
the Council of the League.

From this Memorandum it repeats the declaration that a possible
entrance of Germany into the League of Nations be not construed as an
acknowledgment of the assertions made to substantiate Germany's
international obligations, which assertions constitute a moral burden for
the German nation. It believes that in this sense the public statement
of August 29, 1924, by the German Government of that time, serves the
purpose of understanding and the sincere reconciliation of the nations,
and on its part it expressly adopts this announcement with the desire
thereby to create a state of mutual respect and inner equality, which
forms a condition for the success of the confiding discussion now held
in prospect. The purpose of understanding and reconciliation aimed at
would be further impaired if it would not be possible, prior to Germany's entrance into the League and the negotiation of a Security Pact,

to resolve the quarrel which still divides Germany and the Allied countries. And that is the evacuation of the northern Rhineland zone and the conclusive determination of the German disarmament questions.

As long as the present condition of protracting the occupation of great German territories continues, which condition the German people feel as unjust, so long will it be impossible to restore the confidence of peaceful development upon which depends the effectiveness of the international agreements planned. The Government of the Reich hopes that the Allied Governments will receive these announcements in the same spirit of loyalty in which they were made, and that they recognize in them the sincere wish to smooth the way for the realization of the now proposed great work of peace.

22. (c) THE ANSWER OF THE FRENCH GOVERNMENT

PARIS, September 29, 1925

The Government of the Republic has been happy to receive the response by which the German Government expresses its consent to the meeting of the Locarno conference.

It assumes that the consent carries with it no reservations.

The Verbal Declaration simultaneously delivered by the German Ambassador refers to two questions which cannot in any way enter into the negotiations at Locarno, as they have no relation whatever to the discussion of the Pact of Security.

As to the first of these matters the French Government considers the question was settled by the Treaty of Versailles, which, as the Government has clearly indicated in its notes, cannot in any way be modified by the Security Pact.

As to the evacuation of the Cologne Zone and the question of German disarmament with which it is bound up, the French Government reiterates that it rests with Germany alone to hasten the solution of the question by the execution of its engagements, and the French Government can do nothing more in connection therewith than to refer to the Allied Note of May 30, 1925.

The French Government assumes that the German Government is in accord on this point, namely: The verbal observations formulated in the German supplementary memorandum are not to be considered as reservations or conditions in any way preliminary to the conference.

22. (*d*) THE ANSWER OF THE BELGIAN GOVERNMENT

BRUSSELS, September 29, 1925

The Belgian Government is happy to receive the Note with which the Government of the Reich accepts the extended invitation to the Conference of Locarno on the coming 5th of October. It notes with satisfaction that this acceptance does not carry any reservations. In answer to the declarations, which Your Excellency added to the handing of the Note, without, however, appending to them the condition of the German acceptance, the Belgian Government believes it may confine itself to the following observations:

In regard to the evacuation of the Cologne Zone and the question of German disarmament the Belgian Government permits itself to observe that it depends upon the Reich alone to hasten the solution it desires by carrying out the obligations of which it was reminded by the Note of July 4, 1925.

As regards the question of war guilt, that is not being raised through the project of the Pact. Besides, so far as Belgium is concerned, the issue was settled not only by the Treaty of Versailles but also by the declaration of Chancellor Bethmann-Hollweg in the Reichstag on August 4, 1914.

22. (*e*) THE ANSWER OF THE ITALIAN GOVERNMENT

ROME, September 30, 1925

As "Stefani" reports, the Italian Government, which at the same time as the other Allies received information about the participation in the Security Pact Conference and the supplementary verbal declarations, has been informed of the exchange of opinion between the Allied Governments regarding the answer to be given to Germany. Since the Security Pact is to be based upon the complete respect for the treaties made, it is not possible to discuss the questions raised by Germany. The answer which the Italian Government sent to the German Government was worded accordingly.

22. (*f*) THE ANSWER OF THE ENGLISH GOVERNMENT

YOUR EXCELLENCY:

His Majesty's Government received with pleasure the acceptance by the Government of the Reich of the proposal for a conference on October 5 at Locarno. His Majesty's Government notes with satisfaction that the acceptance is given without reserve.

In reply to the declaration which Your Excellency made to me at the same time I have the honor to take note of the assurance of Your Excellency that the questions therein raised do not constitute conditions preliminary to a meeting of Foreign Ministers. These questions have, in fact, no relation to the negotiations for a Security Pact and have formed no part of the preliminary exchange of views.

As regards that part of the declaration which deals with Germany's entry into the League of Nations, His Majesty's Government notes with satisfaction that the German Government raises no objection to this essential condition of any mutual pact. The question of Germany's responsibility for the war is not raised by the proposed Pact, and His Majesty's Government is at a loss to know why the German Government has thought proper to raise it at this moment. His Majesty's Government is obliged to observe that the negotiation of a Security Pact cannot modify the Treaty of Versailles or alter their judgment of the Pact.

As regards the evacuation of the Cologne Zone, I have the honor to repeat that the date of that evacuation depends solely on the fulfilment of Germany's disarmament obligations, and that His Majesty's Government will welcome the performance of those obligations as permitting the Allies at once to evacuate the northern zone. I have the honor to be, with the highest consideration,

Your Excellency's obedient servant (for the Secretary of State),

(*Signed*) VICTOR WELLESLEY

23. WHAT BÜLOW WOULD HAVE DONE IN THE SUMMER OF 1914[4]

T. W. [Theodor Wolff] : . . . . Prince Bülow has, of course, always rejected the accusation that the German Government of 1914 willed the war and deliberately brought it about as a malicious invention. He has never concealed his views concerning the thoughtlessness and giddiness of the policy of that year. . . . . Since it is not contrary to his wish and, moreover, since it will be helpful in the just appraisal of his character, I hereby reproduce that part of his letter in which he expresses his attitude toward that catastrophic policy of 1914.

"I can hardly find anything more absurd than the *Vaticinationes ex eventu* in which German 'historians' indulge after the unhappy outcome of the World War. However, I should like to state truthfully and definitely the following:

"1. I would not have given Austria full power of attorney for her procedure against Serbia; rather would I have demanded a prompt

[4] *Berliner Tageblatt,* October 29, 1929, pp. 1–2.

examination of her ultimatum. At any rate, after the ultimatum had lain on the table of the Foreign Office for twenty-four hours prior to its dispatch, I would have stopped the whole action with the strongest pressure and the greatest severity.

"2. Never and under no circumstances would I have permitted Austria, upon a hasty examination of the Serbian Note, to declare it insufficient, to sever diplomatic relations with Serbia, and to begin military action. Serbia had accepted practically all of the Austrian demands. We were obliged to recognize this, with gratitude for the wise peace efforts of all Powers and the good will of all the Serbs, and at the same time to propose that the two Austrian demands—which were rather dubious—not yet accepted by Serbia should be submitted for study and decision to the Hague Tribunal.

"3. I would not have declared war upon Russia and France; for thereby we placed at first Rumania, then Italy *ex nexu foederis.* That was a great blunder on the part of Bethmann and v. Jagow. Even our friends in Italy are at a loss to understand this *lourde bêtise,* although they pardon us by saying that in the summer of 1914 we did not sin out of malevolence but out of simple-mindedness. It really is and remains hard to explain. Ballin has assured me that Bethmann insisted upon our declaration of war against Russia because he believed that that would be the only way to drag in Social-Democracy, upon whom Tsarism, which our Left hated so much, would have the same influence as a red cloth upon a certain quadruped animal.

"4. Naturally, I would never have permitted our march into Belgium as long as Belgian neutrality had not been violated by our enemies.

"5. I would have insisted that all our naval units be used immediately after the outbreak of the war and that *à tout risque et péril.* I am in doubt as to whether I would have permitted the U-boat war. At any rate, in no case would I have permitted it at the time and in the manner which unfortunately was the case.

"6. In 1915 I would have exploited the appointment of Sturmer in order to come to an arrangement with the Russians, to whom I gladly would have left all the Poles and Lithuanians. Never would I have restored Poland. That was the greatest of the mistakes during the war.

"7. In 1916 I would have exerted everything in order to come to a peace with England. I would not have permitted the silly peace resolution of the Reichstag, and still less the lachrymose peace letter of the Kaiser to Bethmann. I would have made an end to the well-intentioned, but clumsy zigzag journeys of the childishly awkward Erzberger. I would have had the English informed, at the latest prior to our last offensive, through a serious intermediary, such as the King of Denmark, or the Pope, or the King of Spain, or the King of Sweden, that I was ready to relinquish Belgium without any mental reservation, condition, or servitude *nettement et clairement*. If absolutely necessary, I would also have considered a 'combination' with French Lorraine. If there was no peace inclination in England, which I doubt, there was no reason for us to give in to Wilson so clumsily; rather should we have tightened the reins at home, as was being done in France, and fought to the last drop of blood. It could not have been worse than that which happened to us after our capitulation."

24. KAISER WILHELM II TO SECRETARY OF STATE FOR FOREIGN AFFAIRS VON JAGOW[5]

July 28, 1914

YOUR EXCELLENCY:

After reading the Serbian reply, which I received this morning, I am convinced that the wishes of the Danube Monarchy have, on the whole, been acceded to. The few reservations that Serbia makes in regard to individual points could, in my opinion, be settled by negotiation. But a capitulation of the most humiliating kind is therein announced *orbi et urbi,* and through it every cause for war falls away.

Nevertheless, the piece of paper, like its contents, is to be given only limited value so long as it is not translated into deeds. The Serbs are Orientals; therefore they are given to lying, are false, and are masters of procrastination. In order that these beautiful promises may become truth and fact, a *douce violence* must be exercised. This would have to be arranged in such a way that Austria receives a death-pledge (Belgrade) for the enforcement and carrying out of the promises, and should occupy and retain it until the terms had actually been complied with. This is also necessary in order to give the army—now for the third time mobilized unnecessarily—the external *satisfaction d'honneur* of an ostensible success in the eyes of the world, and to enable it to feel that it had at least stood on foreign soil. Without this, the abandonment of a campaign might give cause to a very bad feeling against the Monarchy, which would be highly dangerous. In case Your Excellency shares my view, I propose that we say to Austria: "Serbia has been forced to retreat in a very humiliating manner, and we congratulate you. Naturally, every cause for war has vanished. However, a guaranty that the promises will be carried out is necessary. That could be achieved by means of a temporary military occupation of a portion of Serbia, similar to the way we kept troops stationed in France in 1871

---

[5] Karl Kautsky, *Die deutschen Dokumente zum Kriegsausbruch,* II, 18–19.

until the billions were paid." On this basis, I am ready to mediate for peace in Austria. Proposals or protests to the contrary on the part of other nations I should refuse absolutely, especially as all of them are appealing to me more or less openly to help in maintaining peace. This I will do in my own way, and as sparingly of Austria's national feeling and of the honor of her arms as possible. For the latter has already been appealed to on the part of the highest War Lord, and it has to respond to the appeal. Consequently, it is absolutely necessary for it to receive a visible *satisfaction d'honneur;* this is the prerequisite of my mediation. Therefore Your Excellency will submit to me a proposal along the lines sketched out, which will be communicated to Vienna. I have had Plessen write along the lines sketched above to the Chief of the General Staff, who is in complete accord with my views.

WILHELM I. R.

25. THE WAR AND THE NATIONS[6]

All the nations are unanimous in affirming, and all with equal fervor, that they did not want the war, that they were forced into it, that they were acting only in extreme self-defense when they chose to fight. To a certain degree that may be true of all of them. Not one of the five great military nations now engaged in a struggle for life or death was blind to the meaning of modern warfare and to what is at stake for each of them.

The truth probably is that all "wanted" peace, but that each one was also counting on war, a war in which they were to deal the first blow. But we find still other assertions. We hear that the common people of England did not want the war, do not want it now, and, instead of being in sympathy with it, view it with repugnance. We hear that the declaration of war came as a painful surprise to the people of France, that there is no war-enthusiasm, that the masses of the people are in a depressed state of mind. We hear that great masses of peasants in Russia are positively desperate when they are called to the ranks; we hear the same also from Serbia, where the common people are in rebellion against the irrational policy of the war agitators at Belgrade. And how was the feeling in Germany? The fact that today everywhere in Germany the grim determination prevails that we must defend ourselves against our enemies and preserve the independence and freedom of the Fatherland, does not do away with the fact that before the outbreak of the war, the mood of an overwhelming majority of the people, if we exclude the eternally clamoring nationalists and all those interested in arma-

[6] *Vorwärts,* No. 224, August 18, 1914, p. 1.

ments, was pacifistic, that the German people did not rush into the war because of some foolish delusion. Today we hear the echoing war cries all over Europe, and yet it is a fact that everywhere the people were content to live in peace, to enjoy the blessings of a peaceful development, and that before the World's War began there was no indication anywhere among the common people of a desire for the bloody struggle that is going on. The nations were peace-loving, they did not long for war; and yet it has broken out and we experience it in all its horror! How can we explain this? How can we comprehend it?

The answer is simple: because the people of a nation do not determine their own fate. And this fundamental fact is not affected by any particular type of government. France is a republic where the people apparently rule with sovereign power, but the people were not even asked whether they desired to make a pact with the despotic state of Russia, and it has never learned the contents of this agreement; war was decided upon before the Chambers had been convened. The British Empire is ruled by Parliament, but this all-powerful Lower House did not learn of the agreements with France and Russia until a few hours before the war was declared. Peace and war in their nature are worlds apart, yet to pass from the state of peace to a state of war may be a matter of only a few hours. Before the common people of England or of France, who by their numbers possess great voting power, could say anything, before they had any adequate realization of the extent of the danger, the war was upon them. A handful of politicians, as a matter of fact, a clique of wire-pullers, had decided matters before the people could rise up and resist. But now when the die is cast, when war is upon us, then indeed there is an end to all doubt and irresolution. For no matter how we got into the war, whether it came, so to speak, as a necessary part of an evolution, or whether it was brought about thoughtlessly, whether it is a just or an unjust war (to use expressions that do not exactly fit a world even such as this), now that the war has come it must be carried through to the end even by those who oppose it because of their convictions and moral ideals, their philosophy of life.

For the laboring class does not hold itself apart or beyond the state; the laboring class does not place itself outside of the nations; on the contrary, through the capitalistic process it is being transformed more and more into the most significant factor in the state. Therefore the fate of the nation and of its manifestation, the state, is of the greatest importance and for the future development of the laboring class. However, all this by no means contradicts the underlying idea of Socialism, the solidarity of labor that knows no barriers; it does not do away with the glowing ideal of the internationalism of civilization (*Kultur*). And surely the divine right which the international concedes to every nation

we will not deny to our own nation. War is the "last resort," the means
of despair resorted to by the capitalistically organized states, but it is
by the works of peace that humanity goes onward and upward; these
works alone will reveal the full ability and genius of a people. We are
not faint-hearted; with all our might we will fight this war to the end,
hoping that we may then find the road clear that leads to the spiritual
and moral perfecting of mankind.

26. SPEECH OF THE IMPERIAL CHANCELLOR TO THE
MAIN COMMITTEE OF THE REICHSTAG[7]
NOVEMBER 9, 1916

. . . . Gentlemen! The full debates which have taken place in the
Main Committee during the course of the last few weeks have, in
the end, always turned on questions regarding the prosecution and the
termination of the war. On the enemy's side they usually speak only
of the prosecution of the war. But Lord Grey has also spoken about
peace in his speech at the banquet given to the Foreign Press Association. The British Minister then said that there was only one thing which
deserved to be kept in mind—namely, that one could not revert too
often to the consideration of the origin of the war, because that origin
would have its influence on the conditions of peace. Lord Grey added
that if it were true that the war was forced upon Germany then it was
only logical that Germany should demand safeguards against future
attack. This is, in any event, a remarkable admission. Naturally, it
was quickly followed by an assertion contradicting the German representation of the origin of the war. "The truth is," Lord Grey proceeded,
"that the war was not forced on Germany, but Germany forced the
war on Europe."

In view of the fundamental importance which Lord Grey again
recently attached to the question of peace conditions, and which we
too have attached to it, I am obliged again to state facts in order to
dispel the clouds with which our enemies endeavor to disguise the real
situation. In reply, I can only repeat what is known. The act which
made war inevitable was the Russian general mobilization which was
ordered on the night of July 30–31, 1914.

Russia, England, France, and the entire world knew that this step
must have made further waiting impossible for us. Even in England
people are beginning to understand the fateful significance of the Russian mobilization. The truth is coming to light. An English professor
of world fame wrote some time ago that many people would think dif-

[7] *Norddeutsche Allgemeine Zeitung,* November 10, 1916, I, 1–2.

ferently about the end of the war if they were better informed about its beginning, especially about the facts of the Russian mobilization. No wonder, then, that Lord Grey, in his recent speech, could not pass the Russian mobilization unnoticed, but felt himself obliged to speak of it. He could no longer deny that the Russian mobilization preceded the German and Austrian mobilization, but as he desires to remove all blame for the war from the Entente, he makes a daring endeavor by means of quite a new version of the case to represent the Russian mobilization as Germany's work.

Lord Grey's explanation is that Russia ordered her first mobilization only after a report had appeared in Germany that Germany had ordered a mobilization, and after this report had been telegraphed to Petrograd. Alluding to the alleged falsification of the Ems dispatch in 1870, Lord Grey added that at the moment chosen by Germany we maneuvered to provoke another country to take defensive measures, and that then these defensive measures were answered by us with an ultimatum which made war inevitable.

It was about two and a quarter years before Lord Grey discovered this interpretation, which is as new as it is objectively false, of the cause of the war. The occurrence to which he alluded is well known. The document which forms the basis of his proof is an extra edition of the Berlin *Lokalanzeiger*.

You will remember, gentlemen, perhaps, that on Thursday, July 30, 1914, in the early afternoon, the *Lokalanzeiger* in an extra edition issued a false report that the Emperor had ordered mobilization. You also know that the sale of this extra edition was at once stopped by the police and the available copies were seized. I can also declare that the Foreign Secretary immediately informed the Russian Ambassador, and simultaneously all the other Ambassadors, by telephone, that the news issued by the *Lokalanzeiger* was false. The Russian Embassy was also informed as soon as possible from the *Lokalanzeiger*'s office that there had been a mistake. I can further confirm that the Russian Ambassador, immediately after the issue of the extra edition, telegraphed a cipher message to Petrograd which, according to the Russian *Orange Book,* read as follows:

"I learn that an order for the mobilization of the German Army and Fleet has just been published."

But this telegram, after Herr von Jagow's telephonic explanation, was followed by a second telegram *en clair* which read as follows:

"Please consider my last telegram cancelled (*nichtig*). Explanation follows."

A few minutes later the Russian Ambassador sent a third cipher telegram which, according to the Russian *Orange Book,* said that the

German Foreign Minister had just telephoned to him that the news of the mobilization of the army and fleet was false and that the extra edition in question had been seized.

The immediate intervention of Herr von Jagow, the Secretary of State for Foreign Affairs, in order to rectify the false news—an intervention which, in the official Russian *Orange Book,* is confirmed by the telegram of M. Sverbeieff, the Russian Ambassador—of itself contradicts the assertion of Lord Grey that we intentionally desired to deceive Russia for the purpose of bringing about a mobilization. I can, however, also confirm that, according to investigations of the Imperial Postal Administration about the times of dispatch of the Russian Ambassador's three telegrams, these must have arrived in Petrograd almost simultaneously. Thus the Russian Government can have been only for a short time under the false impression that Germany had ordered a complete mobilization. At any rate, the correction of the false report had taken place before Russia, in its turn, ordered complete mobilization. Gentlemen, we do not have to fear any tribunal. I can further prove that the new version is invented entirely by Lord Grey.

The Russian Government itself, which, after all, must be best acquainted with the reasons for its mobilization, never had an idea of explaining its fateful step by appealing to the *Lokalanzeiger*'s extra edition. Lord Grey, I assume, will not desire to reject the Tsar as a witness. On Friday, July 31, at two o'clock in the afternoon, when the mobilization order had already been issued to all the Russian forces, the Tsar telegraphed in reply to the Kaiser's last appeal for peace:

"It is technically impossible to discontinue our military preparations, which have become necessary owing to Austria-Hungary's mobilization." No mention of the *Lokalanzeiger*. No mention of the German mobilization. I only recall *en passant* that the reference of the Tsar to the alleged mobilization of Austria-Hungary could be no reason for a Russian general mobilization. Austria-Hungary, at the time when a general mobilization was ordered in Russia, had placed only eight army corps on a war footing with a view to the conflict with Serbia. As early as July 29, Russia had already answered this measure with the mobilization of thirteen army corps. After July 29 Austria-Hungary had taken no further military measures which could have furnished Russia with any grounds for a general mobilization which was equivalent to a declaration of war.

Only after the general mobilization had taken place in Russia did Austria-Hungary, on the morning of July 31, also proceed to a general mobilization. We, ourselves, even then, exercised forbearance and patience to the utmost limits of consideration for our own existence and our duty toward our allies. As far back as July 29, when Russia mobilized against Austria-Hungary, we could have mobilized. The text of our Treaty of Alliance with Austria-Hungary was known and nobody could have considered our mobilization aggressive. We did not do it.

But to the news of the Russian general mobilization, we at first replied only with the announcement of a state of affairs threatening danger of war which did not yet signify mobilization. We informed the Russian Government, and added that mobilization must follow if Russia did not cease every war measure against us and Austria-Hungary within twelve hours, and give us a definite declaration about this. We gave Russia, thereby, even when war appeared, owing to her fault, already inevitable, another chance to come to her senses and even at the last moment to preserve peace. By this delay we also gave Russia's Allied friends the world-historical opportunity to influence Russia in favor of peace.

It was in vain. Russia left us without a reply, and England persisted in silence toward Russia. France, through the mouth of her Premier, in the evening of July 31, simply denied to our Ambassador the fact of the Russian mobilization, and ordered her own mobilization some hours earlier than we ourselves proceeded to mobilize.

Moreover, as regards the alleged defensive character of the Russian complete mobilization, I will here emphatically declare that on the outbreak of war in 1914 a general instruction of the Russian Government issued in 1912 for the contingency of mobilization was in force, which, word for word, contains the following passage by the All Highest:

"It is ordered that the announcement of mobilization is at the same time an announcement of war against Germany."

Against Germany! In 1912, against Germany!

It is incomprehensible how, in view of these documented facts, Lord Grey can come before the world and his own country with the story of a maneuver by which we enticed the pacific Russian into mobilization against his own will by grossly deluding him about our own measures. No! The truth is Russia would never have decided on the fateful step had she not been encouraged to it from the Thames by acts of commission and omission.

I recall the actual situation at the time when Russia issued the order for a general mobilization. The instructions which I gave our Ambassadors in Vienna on July 30 are known. In those instructions I urged on the Austro-Hungarian Government an immediate understanding with Russia, and urgently and emphatically declared that Germany did not desire, through disregard of our advice, to be drawn into a world conflagration. Lord Grey also well knows that I retransmitted to Vienna with the most peremptory recommendation the mediation proposal which he made to our Ambassador on July 29 and which appeared to me a suitable basis for the maintenance of peace. I, at that time, telegraphed to Vienna:

"Should the Austro-Hungarian Government refuse all mediation we are confronted with a conflagration in which England would go against us, and Italy and Rumania, according to all indications, would not be with us; so that with Austria-Hungary, we should confront three Great Powers. Germany, as the result of England's hostility, would have to bear the chief brunt of the fight. The political prestige of Austria-Hungary, the honor of her arms, and her justified claims against Serbia could be sufficiently safeguarded by the occupation of Belgrade or other places. We, therefore, urgently and emphatically ask the Vienna Cabinet to consider the acceptance of mediation on the proposed conditions. Responsibility for the consequences which may otherwise arise must be extraordinarily severe for Austria-Hungary and ourselves."

The Austro-Hungarian Government acceded to our urgent representation by giving its Ambassador in Berlin the following instructions:

"I ask your Excellency most sincerely to thank Herr von Jagow, the Secretary of State of Foreign Affairs, for the information given through Herr von Tschirschky and to declare to him that, despite the change in the situation which has since arisen through the Russian mobilization, we are quite ready to consider the proposals of Sir Edward Grey for a settlement between us and Serbia. A condition of our acceptance, of course, would be that our military action against Serbia shall meanwhile proceed, and that the English Cabinet shall induce the Russian Government to bring to a standstill the Russian mobilization directed against us, in which case we, as a matter of course, will at once cancel our defensive counter-measures in Galicia, forced upon us."

This I contrast with the moves made by Lord Grey: On July 27, 1914, he replied to a remark of the Russian Ambassador in London that among Austrian and German circles the impression prevails that England would remain quiet, as follows: "This impression is being set aside by the orders we issued to the first fleet."

On July 27 Lord Grey informed the French Ambassador of his confidential warning to our Ambassador in London, namely, that Germany must anticipate quick English decisions, i.e., its participation in the war.

Could Lord Grey suppose that such a disclosure would serve peace? Must not France have regarded this disclosure as a promise of military assistance in case of war? Must not France thereby have been encouraged to give Russia a promise of unconditional war support which Russia had for days urgently demanded? Must not Russia have been strengthened to the utmost in her bellicose intention by the certainty of a Franco-British Alliance?

The Russian reply to Lord Grey's morning conversation was, in fact, not long in coming. On the evening of the same day, July 29, M. Sazonoff instructed the Russian Ambassador in Paris to express his sincere thanks for the declaration made to him by the French Ambassador that Russia could rely fully on the support of her ally, France.

Russia, therefore, during the night of July 30, faced the fact of Austro-Hungarian compliance due to our influence, which gave an open road to the maintenance of peace. She was simultaneously faced with the certitude of Anglo-French support, disclosed by Lord Grey to M. Paul Cambon, which alone gave her the possibility of war. She chose mobilization, and, with it, war.

Who now is to blame for this fateful decision? We, who with the greatest emphasis recommended to the Vienna Cabinet utter complaisance and the acceptance of the English proposal for mediation, or the British Cabinet, which in a critical hour held out to France and Russia a prospect of its support? Lord Grey did not speak of these decisive things, but on the other hand he turned the attention of his audience to minor things. The resort to the Hague Tribunal, which the Tsar proposed, seems at first sight very important, but it was proposed after the Russian troops had already been put in motion against us. His own conference proposal (I have repeatedly pointed out this in the Reichstag) Lord Grey set aside in favor of our mediation.

And Belgium? Before a single German soldier had set foot on Belgian territory, Lord Grey explained to the French Ambassador, after the latter's report to his Government, that in case the German Fleet should enter the Channel or pass from the North Sea with the intention of attacking the French coast or the French Fleet, or disturb (*beunruhigen*) the mercantile fleet (I repeat the word disturb, gentlemen), the British Fleet would interfere and give its protection in such a manner that from this moment England and Germany would be in a state of war. Can he who declared that our fleets putting to sea would be a *casus belli* still seriously maintain that the violation of Belgian neutrality was the sole cause of England's entering the war against her will?

And, finally, with regard to the statement that in order to keep England out of the war we made a discreditable proposal to the British Government to shut its eyes to the violation of Belgian neutrality and allow us a free hand to take the French colonies, I challenge Lord Grey to investigate the real facts in his *Blue Book* and in his documents. In an earnest endeavor to localize the war, I assured the British Ambassador in Berlin on July 29, that on the condition of England's neutrality we would guarantee France's integrity. On August 1, Prince Lich-nowsky asked Lord Grey whether in the event of Germany's undertak-ing to respect the neutrality of Belgium England would also undertake to observe neutrality. He further held out the prospect that in the event of English neutrality the integrity not only of France but also of the French colonies might be guaranteed. On my instructions he gave an assurance that we were ready to give up the idea of an attack against France, if England would guarantee the neutrality of France. At the last moment, further, I promised that so long as England remained neutral our Fleet would not attack the French northern coast, and on the condition of reciprocity would undertake no hostile operations against French merchant ships. Lord Grey's sole reply to this was that he must finally decline all promise of neutrality; he could only say that England wished to keep her hands untied.

If England had given this declaration of neutrality, she would not have been exposed to the contempt of the whole world but would have gained merit for having prevented the outbreak of the war. I ask here, too, who willed the war—we, who were prepared to give England every imaginable security for France and Belgium, or England, which declined all our proposals and refused even to indicate the way for the preserva-tion of peace? Gentlemen, I repeat, all these things have been so often explained by the German Government, partly in my speeches and partly in official publications, that now that the war has raged for over two years it goes against my nature to reiterate these reflections. But this is no question of controversy. We all have the greatest interest in dis-sipating as thoroughly as possible the belief which again and again has been artificially fed that Germany has been the aggressor. And if Lord Grey's opinion is accurate that the recognition of the real causes of war is of great importance regarding its termination and peace conditions, then also my words refer to the future.

Lord Grey finally dealt exhaustively with the period after peace and with the establishment of an international union to preserve peace. On that subject, too, I will say a few words. We never concealed our doubts whether peace could be lastingly insured by international organizations such as arbitration courts. I will not discuss here the theoretical side of the problem, but in practice now and in peace we shall have to define our attitude toward the question. When after the termination of the war the world will fully recognize its horrible devastation of blood and treasure, then through all mankind will go the cry for peaceful agree-ments and understandings which will prevent so far as is humanly possible the return of such an immense catastrophe. This cry will be so strong and so justified that it must lead to a result. Germany will honorably co-operate in investigating every attempt to find a practical solution and will collaborate toward its possible realization, and that all the more if the war, as we confidently expect, produces political conditions which will do justice to the free development of all nations, small as well as great.

In that case the principle of right and of free development must be made to prevail not only on the Continent but also at sea. Of that Lord Grey, of course, did not speak. The guaranty of peace which he has in mind appears to me to possess a peculiar character devised especially for British wishes. During the war, the neutrals, according to his desire, will have to remain and patiently endure every compulsion of British world domination on the seas. After the war, when England, as she thinks, will have beaten us, when she will have made a new arrangement of the world, then neutrals are to combine as guarantors of the new English arrangement of the world.

To this arrangement of the world will also belong the following: From a reliable source we know that England and France already in 1915 guaranteed to Russia territorial rule over Constantinople, the Bosphorus, and the western shores of the Dardanelles, with its hinterland, while Asia Minor was to be divided among the Entente Powers. The English Government avoided replying to the questions which were asked in Parliament on this subject, but certainly these plans of the Entente are also of interest for the international peace union which later is to guarantee them. These are the annexation intentions of our enemies, to which also must be added Alsace-Lorraine; while I, in the discussions of our war aims, never indicated the annexation of Belgium as our intention.

Such a policy of force cannot form the basis for an effective international peace union, and it is in the strongest contrast to Lord Grey's and Mr. Asquith's desired ideal state, where right governs might and all states form a family of civilized mankind and can freely develop themselves, whether big or small, under the same conditions and in accordance with their natural capabilities. If the Entente wishes seriously to take up this position, then it would consequently act upon it; otherwise the most exalted words about peace, union, and harmoniously living together in an international family are mere words (*Schall und Rauch*).

The first condition for the development of international relations by means of an arbitration court and the peaceful liquidation of conflicting antagonisms would be that henceforth no aggressive coalitions should be formed. Germany is ready at all times to join the union of peoples and even to place herself at the head of such a union which will restrain the disturber of peace.

The history of international relations before the war lies clearly before the eyes of the entire world. What brought France to Russia's side? Alsace-Lorraine. What did Russia want? Constantinople. Why did England join them? Because Germany in peaceful work had become too great for her. What did we desire? Grey says that Germany with her first proposal of the integrity of France and Belgium desired to purchase England's permission to take what she wanted of the French colonies. Even the most harebrained German did not entertain the idea of attacking France for the purpose of seizing her colonies. It was not that which was fatal to Europe, but that the English Government favored French and Russian predatory aims unattainable without a European war.

As against this aggressive character of the Entente, the Triple Alliance has always found itself in a defensive position. No honorable observer of affairs can deny that. Not in the shadow of Prussian militarism did the world live before the war, but in the shadow of the policy of isolation which was to keep Germany down. Against this policy, whether it appears diplomatically as encirclement, militarily as a war of destruction, economically as a world boycott, we have from the beginning been on the defensive. The German people wages this war as a defensive war for the safety of its national existence and for its free development. We never pretended anything else; we never intended anything different. How otherwise could this display of gigantic forces, this inexhaustible heroism determined to fight to the last be explained! There is no precedent for it in all human history. Confronted by the obstinacy of the enemy's will to war, by the calling up of military material and auxiliary forces from all parts of the world, our resistance hardened to still greater determination. However England may still supplement her strength—and there is a limit even to England's command of strength—it is predestined to fail before our will to live. This will is unconquerable, imperturbable. We wait for our enemies to recognize this, confident that this recognition has to come.

27. MEMORANDA BY DR. HEINRICH KANNER OF CONVERSATIONS WITH GERMANS CONCERNING THE LEGEND OF THE CROWN COUNCIL OF POTSDAM

(a) CONVERSATIONS WITH DR. NAUMANN,[8] JUNE 30, 1915, AND NOVEMBER 1, 1915

When questioned in regard to Bulgaria, Naumann expressed little confidence and meant that a very wrong policy had been pursued

[8] Kanner Papers, I, 84, 98–104.

toward her. Bulgaria had wished to attack Serbia in November in order to get Macedonia. Unwittingly, Bulgaria had been persuaded differently at that time. When asked why, Naumann said on account of Rumania. Out of fear of a Rumanian attack, it had been considered desirable to keep Bulgaria neutral in order to use her as a club against Rumania. . . . . In general, a wrong policy had been pursued toward Bulgaria. In order to make sure of her, the attempt should have been made to draw her into the war as soon as possible. Instead of that Bulgaria had been held back. This was the more foolish, because the delay in presenting the Serbian ultimatum had been allowed expressly on Bulgaria's account. When asked how that was to be understood, Naumann said that the ultimatum, as was "known," had been decided upon already on July 5, but that it had not been handed over until July 23, in order to give Bulgaria time. Asked to be more specific, Naumann said, that Bulgaria had been informed about the plans against Serbia from the very beginning and her co-operation had been secured. However, when on July 5 the decision was made, Bulgaria had declared she was not sufficiently ready and had therefore begged to be given more time. This explains the delay until July 23. When asked what really had taken place in Potsdam at 5 : 00 P.M. on July 5 and whether it was true that an Austro-Hungarian delegate had been invited to that Crown Council, Naumann replied that it really was not a Crown Council in the usual meaning of the term, for in a Crown Council, usually the only participants were the Ministers under the chairmanship of the Kaiser. In this case, a counsel had taken place between the highest civil and military German authorities, under the chairmanship of the Kaiser, and in the presence of five Austrian delegates. To the question what really had been decided upon at that meeting, Naumann said, with an expression of regret: To give Austria a free hand in regard to Serbia. When asked whether at this meeting there had been produced certain evidence material, Naumann replied that it was hardly probable that evidence material had been submitted, rather only assertions of evidences existing. Questioned as to the nature of these evidences, Naumann said, that on that date the whole affair had been presented from the Austrian side in such a way as to show that the Serbian Crown Prince had been the plotter of the assassination of the Austrian Archduke. Asked whether or not evidences of Russian cognizance had been produced, Naumann claimed to have heard only about Serbia. Naumann also denied that the text of the Note to Serbia was submitted to this Crown Council. The discussion had confined itself to a general approval of Austria's attitude.

(In the presence of Professor Singer) :

We mentioned that, as far as our knowledge went, on July 3, 1914, the decision had been made in Vienna to undertake a military action against Serbia, and we requested Naumann to supplement our information with that of his. Thereupon he recounted again what he had told us previously: On July 5, a meeting took place at Potsdam under the Chairmanship of the Kaiser and in the presence of five Austro-Hungarian delegates who had come to Berlin for this purpose. These were: The Minister of Foreign Affairs, Count Berchtold; the Chief of the General Staff, Baron Conrad; the Minister of War, Krobatin; and two more whose names Naumann had not found out. Asked whether Forgach and Hoyos had been those two persons, he answered that he had not heard these two names in that connection. Asked further whether it might have been the Austrian Premier, Count Stürgkh, and the Hungarian Premier, Count Tisza, he replied that that seemed probable; however, neither had he heard their names in that connection. On the German side, as far as his knowledge went, were Bethmann-Hollweg and Jagow. He supposed that also the former Chief of the German General Staff, Moltke, and the Minister of War, Falkenhayn, as well as the Chief of the Navy Department, Tirpitz, had been there. He had not heard that; he only regards that as self-evident. He questioned Zimmermann's presence, since he is regarded as merely an official.

27. (b) CONVERSATION WITH COUNT LEYDEN
FEBRUARY 16, 1916[9]

. . . . Thus we came to talk about the war in general. Count Leyden voiced in unminced terms his disapproval with the fact that the Serbian Note to Austria's ultimatum had not been accepted. Upon the basis of that Note the war could easily have been avoided. He could not understand why that had not been done, and he expressed the view that the war had been willed.

I told him, thereupon, that I too had had occasionally the same suspicion, since during the fateful days between Austria's ultimatum and Serbia's reply I had heard high functionaries in Vienna say that they expected and wished a negative answer from Serbia. This remark seemed to fit Count Leyden's train of thought. However, he interrupted my exposition, turning suddenly to me as if undecided whether to trust me or not; then he queried whether I was informed about the preliminary history of the war. I told him then that I believed I

[9] Kanner Papers, I, 59–74.

knew a few things, for example, about the war council at Potsdam on July 5. He wished to know more about it, and I told him that, as far as I was informed, in this war council, at which the Austro-Hungarian functionaries were also present, it was decided to give Austria a free hand regarding Serbia. Count Leyden listened attentively, assented, and said: "That's true, and the Kaiser then went away"—here Count Leyden laughed—"in order to procure an alibi. Isn't that true?" he asked. However, I expressed my astonishment that one could have embarked upon a war with such ease. Count Leyden replied that of course Berlin too was surprised about the text of the Serbian Note. I asked whether Berlin really had not known the text of the Note, which he affirmed resolutely. I expressed my great surprise about that, and could not believe it possible. Count Leyden said that he understood the events very well. Already during and after the Balkan War Vienna had continually complained that Berlin had hindered Austria's active participation' in the affairs of the Balkans. . . . . Berlin, plagued by these perpetual complaints, now decided to give in.

27. (c) CONVERSATION WITH PROFESSOR JAECKH
SEPTEMBER 14, 1916[10]

I now came back to the origin of the war and reminded Jaeckh of the Crown Council of July 5, 1914, about which he had talked to me on previous occasions. He recalled it. I then said that it was inconceivable to me that Germany should not have known the content of the Serbian Note through which Germany had been forced into the greatest of all wars. Jaeckh replied that that was not quite correct. "We"— here again he identified himself with the leading men—"knew what was going on. Austria's demands were submitted to us at the Crown Council, and assented to." I asked why the long delay with the declaration of war. Did they really wait until the district judge in question was ready with the evidence of the *Princip Case?* Jaeckh said that that was not the case at all. He then pondered for a second, calculating mentally, and then said: "Yes, it was ten days after the Crown Council took place when I myself read these demands formulated in written form. Of course, we knew only the demands, not the phraseology of the Serbian Note. This we did not want to know. Naturally you understand that this was on account of certain considerations. We wished to be able to say that we had not known the wording of the Note, which was true.". . . .

[10] Kanner Papers, III, 297–306.

27. (d) CONVERSATION WITH HERR VON GERLACH[11]
JANUARY 7, 1917

. . . . Gerlach told me that the night before he had attended a banquet in honor of the American Ambassador Gerard and that he had sat near Professor Niemeyer. He said that a debate about the war guilt question had ensued between them and that he, Gerlach, had asserted that although Germany could not be accused of a *dolus* for this war, it could not be cleared of a *culpa lata*. To this Niemeyer had given a heated reply and said Germany, according to his exact information, bore a *dolus* share of guilt for the war. To substantiate this, his assertion, he said he knew that the war had been decided upon at Potsdam on July 5, 1914. Present at this conference, which took place at the command of the Kaiser, were Conrad, Falkenhayn, Tirpitz, and Moltke. I told Gerlach that I was very much interested in this remark, since I had heard from a reliable source elsewhere about this alleged Crown Council; but that so far I had always been under the impression that the statesmen too were present at this meeting. Gerlach replied that Niemeyer had mentioned only the military men. When asked as to Niemeyer's source of information, Gerlach said that Niemeyer frequently visited the Foreign Office and was in the position to procure valuable information. Also as Chairman of the International Law Association, Niemeyer had had business with the Foreign Office. . . . .

27. (e) CONVERSATIONS WITH REGIERUNGSRAT MARTIN[12]
JANUARY 8, 1917, AND AUGUST 19, 1917

. . . . Scarcely had I introduced myself to Martin, when he started to talk about things which interested me greatly, namely, about the preliminary history of the war. According to his view there is no doubt that Germany wanted the war. He said that from the day of the assassination of the Archduke, Tschirschky had been in daily communication with Berchtold and Tisza. Conrad was in Potsdam already on July 4, where, under the chairmanship of the Kaiser, he talked with Moltke, Falkenhayn, and Tirpitz. There they decided upon war. Upon my remark that I had heard elsewhere that the meeting took place on July 5, he replied that it was possible that Conrad was still in Potsdam on July 5 and had another conference, but this he did not know. He insisted upon July 4. Asked whether and what statesmen were present,

[11] Kanner Papers, III, Part 2, pp. 11–16.
[12] *Ibid.*, pp. 8–10.

he declared resolutely that no statesmen had been present. The war had been decided upon solely by the military men. . . . . That the Berlin Foreign Office did not know the text of the ultimatum before it was dispatched, is certainly not true. Berlin and Vienna were in constant communication after Conrad's visit. Tirpitz knew the text of the ultimatum already on July 12. The Berlin Foreign Office had not only seen the ultimatum but also corrected it; but, of course, only privately, not officially. This had been decided upon beforehand, in order that they might have an alibi later on if needed. Martin even declared that he knew who in Berlin had corrected the ultimatum and what corrections had been made. Upon my doubting questions Martin added that something of those events had at that time seeped through in the *Frankfurter Zeitung,* whose Berlin correspondent, Stein, was very intimately acquainted with Hammann and doubtless found out everything from him. A few days after July 4 there appeared a Berlin dispatch in the *Frankfurter Zeitung* in which it was indicated that this time Austria would make conclusive settlement with Serbia. Two days later there appeared another dispatch in the same paper, again calling attention to the seriousness of the situation. (Indeed, the second morning edition of the *Frankfurter Zeitung* of July 11, 1914, page 1, column 4, has a correspondence which Martin might have meant; also in the second morning edition of July 17, 1914, page 1, column 1, it says expressly that the ultimatum will be sent the following week.)

. . . . I asked about the Crown Council on July 5, 1914. He still thinks that it was held, but holds that the details as published in the *Times* are false. When I reminded him that he had placed the date of the Crown Council at July 4, he replied that it seemed that conversations had taken place on both days, July 4 and 5. Upon my question as to the source of his information about the Crown Council, he answered with the following story: On the day in question—whether the 4th or 5th of July, he left open—a friend of his, a very high official, whose name he could not disclose to me, had dined at the best restaurant in Potsdam. The name of the restaurant his friend had not disclosed; however, Martin had suspected that it was the "Stadt Königsberg." While there, his friend had seen a group of Austrian and German officers enter the restaurant, among whom he believed he recognized Archduke Friedrich and Archduke Albrecht. Martin, however, thinks that in the case of Archduke Friedrich there was a mixup in names. Also he had seen Conrad in that group. The officers had gone into a private room, and for the time being Martin's friend had not ascribed any special importance to the incident. But afterwards the proprietor of the restaurant had come to him and asked him: "Listen, is it really possible that we may go to war with Russia?" Martin's informer then had asked the proprietor how he happened to get such an idea. The proprietor replied that there was a group of officers in the next room and the waiter who was serving them said that the officers talked continually about a war with Russia. Martin believes that those men were members of the so-called Crown Council and possibly also a few other officers who had joined them afterwards. As often happens, the gentlemen did not take any notice of the waiter and talked absolutely unrestrainedly in his presence. The waiter had not understood details of the conversation, except that about war with Russia. Martin says that the incident had aroused the curiosity of his informer, who had decided to find out more about the matter, and thus he had heard about the Crown Council. . . . .

28. DR. MÜHLON'S MEMORANDUM[13]

Toward the middle of July 1914, about the 15th, I had, as was often the case, a conversation with Dr. Helfferich, at that time Director of the Deutsche Bank in Berlin and actually representative of the Chancellor. The Deutsche Bank had declined to support certain great transactions with Bulgaria and Turkey in which the Krupp firm for commercial reasons (delivery of war materials) took a great interest.

Finally Dr. Helfferich gave me the following reason which justified the attitude of the Deutsche Bank: The political situation had become threatening. At all events the Deutsche Bank must wait before engaging herself any further in foreign affairs.

The Austrian leaders had just been with the Emperor. Vienna will send, within a week, a very sharply worded and short-termed ultimatum to Serbia which will contain demands such as punishment of a number of officers, dissolution of political associations, a commission of inquiry to be sent to Serbia by the Dual Monarchy and composed of her officials; in a word, a number of definite and immediate compensations will be demanded. In the case of their non-fulfilment Austria-Hungary will declare war on Serbia.

Dr. Helfferich added that *the Kaiser had energetically approved* of these actions of Austria-Hungary.

He, the Kaiser, said that he considered an Austro-Hungarian conflict with Serbia as an internal concern between the two countries and that he would allow no other state to meddle in this concern. If Russia should mobilize, he would mobilize also. But in his case, mobilization meant immediate war. This time there was to be no hesitation.

[13] Herron Papers, "Germany," Document VI B. Herron's translation of the German document which Mühlon presented to him.

The Austrians were very satisfied with this determined attitude of the Kaiser.

When, upon this, I said to Dr. Helfferich that these sinister revelations strengthened my growing fears of a world war and made it a certainty, he replied that it looked exceedingly like it. Possibly Russia and France would still think better of it. It was certain that the Serbians deserved a proper lesson.

This was the first news I had of the discussions between the Kaiser and his Allies. I knew Dr. Helfferich's particularly intimate relations with personalities who were bound to know the truth, and that his declaration could therefore be counted upon. That is why I immediately let Mr. Krupp von Bohlen und Halbach know after my return from Berlin; Dr. Helfferich had expressly stated that I might do this. (At that time it was proposed to offer him a post in the Boards of Control of the Krupp firm.)

Von Bohlen seemed horrified that Dr. Helfferich should be in possession of such knowledge; he remarked that persons in the Government never could hold their tongues completely, and then told me what follows:

He himself had seen the Kaiser within the last few days. The Kaiser had spoken to him also of the discussions with the Austrians and their result; he, von Bohlen, had, however, considered the matter to be so secret that he would not even have dared to mention it to his Board of Directors. But since I was already informed he could now tell that the declarations of Helfferich were quite correct.

It would seem that the latter was acquainted with more detail than he himself was. The situation was in truth very serious. *The Kaiser had told him personally that he would declare war at once if Russia were to mobilize.* This time everyone should see that he, the Kaiser, would not retreat. In fact the Kaiser's constant reiteration that this time no one would be able to reproach him with indecision produced an almost comic effect.

On the very day announced to me by Helfferich, Vienna's ultimatum to Serbia appeared. I was then again in Berlin and said to Helfferich that I thought the tone of the ultimatum absolutely monstrous. Dr. Helfferich suggested that it only sounded so in the German translation. He said that he had seen the ultimatum in French and in that form it could in no way be called exaggerated. *On this occasion Dr. Helfferich told me that the Kaiser had started on his journey to the north merely as a blind,* that the length of the journey had been greatly diminished, and that the Kaiser would remain within calling distance and in constant touch with the capital.

It now remained to be seen how things would develop. It was to be hoped that the Austrians, who did not in the least count upon Serbian acceptance of the ultimatum, would act quickly before the other powers had time to interfere. The Deutsche Bank had taken all necessary precautions and was prepared for all happenings. Thus it had returned the gold for general circulation. It was quite easy to do this unobserved, and the gold was accumulating day by day in a most satisfactory manner.

As soon as the Vienna ultimatum to Serbia had appeared, *the German Government declared that Austria-Hungary had acted entirely on her own, without the knowledge of Germany.*

Any attempt to reconcile these declarations with the occurrences mentioned above could lead to but one explanation; the Kaiser must have already taken his decision without the co-operation of his government, and during the discussions with the Austrians the Germans must have refused to fix the exact wording of the ultimatum, for I have just shown that the contents of this ultimatum were well known in Germany.

Mr. Krupp von Bohlen, with whom I discussed this German declaration which was to all intents and purposes a lie, was also very dissatisfied with it, as in so serious a matter Germany had no right to give a free hand to a state like Austria-Hungary; the duty of the leading statesmen would have been to demand of the Kaiser as also of his Allies that the Austrian claims and the ultimatum to Serbia should be discussed in detail and settled together, and that the exact program for both states should be determined before anything further was done. Whatever point of view one adopted, there was no sense in giving oneself into the hands of the Austrians and thus bringing the country into possible situations which had in no way been foreseen. It would have been better to put certain conditions to these obligations. In short, Herr von Bohlen considered the German denial of all foreknowledge, *even if there were the slightest grain of truth in this assertion,* to be a great blunder and opposed to the very elements of diplomacy.

He told me that he intended to speak to Herr von Jagow (at that time Secretary of State in the Ministry of Foreign Affairs), who was a particular friend of his, and to explain his view to him.

As a result of this discussion Herr von Bohlen acquainted me with the following: Herr von Jagow had repeatedly declared to him that he had taken no part in the wording of the Austro-Hungarian ultimatum and that Germany had never demanded to do so. When Herr von Bohlen objected that such a thing was quite incomprehensible, Herr von Jagow replied that he had of course in his quality of diplomat thought of making such a demand. But the Kaiser *had already been so decided at the time when Herr von Jagow was called in* to take part in the discussion, that it was too late for any measures *to be taken* according to diplomatic custom.

The situation had, in fact, been such that no further stipulations or clauses could be inserted.

Finally he (Jagow) had thought that this omission would have one advantage: The good effect that would be made at Petrograd and Paris by the German declaration that the German Government had had no part in the working out of the Vienna ultimatum.

29. DISTORTIONS AND FACTS[14]

Some papers have printed the letter of Dr. Mühlon, to an anonymous correspondent, which was recently described in the Main Committee of the Reichstag by the Vice-Chancellor as the utterance of a diseased brain. This has given the full text of the letter an undeserved publicity. So we are compelled to return to this affair.

Mühlon claims to base his tale on communications from two gentlemen. Written statements by these two gentlemen prove that what really happened was this:

In July 1914, Mühlon, then a director of the firm of F. Krupp, a joint-stock company, had an interview with Dr. Helfferich, at that time a director of the Deutsche Bank. The latter told him that the Deutsche Bank felt obliged to move very slowly in some big deals which it had long been negotiating with Krupp's, in consequence of the threatening political situation produced by the Sarajevo murders. Similarly, early in July, at a meeting of the Krupp directors, called to provide the firm with raw materials and foodstuffs, Herr Krupp von Bohlen und Halbach declared that the political situation was so serious, after the murder of the heir-apparent and his wife, that he thought it expedient to provide against all eventualities.

In his letter Mühlon decorated this plain story with tales which went to prove that Germany was responsible for the war. Both Dr. Helfferich and Herr Krupp von Bohlen und Halbach dismiss these tales as fanciful and irrelevant. In the Main Committee of the Reichstag the Chancellor's deputy added that on examination the statements of the two gentlemen—so far as they could be tested—had shown that the words put in their mouths could not have been spoken, as they were in flat contradiction to the facts.

These five points are certain: 1. Before the outbreak of war, rumors were current about a supposed council of war, or Crown Council (*Kronrat*), or conference under the Kaiser's presidency—at which Austro-Hungarian delegates took part—on Sunday, July 5. There is no foundation for these rumors; neither on July 5 nor on any other day was such a council held.

[14] *Norddeutsche Allgemeine Zeitung,* March 22, 1918, II, 1.

2. The negotiations with Austria-Hungary in the crisis caused by the Sarajevo murders were conducted solely by the Chancellor and the Foreign Office. The duly constituted authorities bear complete responsibility in all respects for the conduct of the negotiations.

3. From the beginning, the policy of the Imperial Government was directed to the maintenance of peace, in full accordance with the intentions of the Emperor. Of course, peace could not have been bought by the betrayal of Austria-Hungary; nor ought it. The Imperial Government allowed no doubts on this point to spring up on either side, because it was convinced that in difficult situations the best policy is clearness and openness.

4. To the same extent the Imperial Government left the Russian Government no room for doubt that a Russian mobilization would be followed by an immediate German mobilization and, necessarily, by war.

5. Within the limits imposed by the alliance and the duty of self-preservation, the Emperor and his Government did all that man could do, up to the last moment, to avert the catastrophe; as has often enough been made clear. The Sukhomlinov trial has proved to the hilt who are responsible for the world-conflagration, even to doubters who are not satisfied with German assertions and documents.

30. MEMORANDUM BY DR. KANNER OF A CONVERSATION WITH PRINCE LICHNOWSKY, MARCH 27, 1916[15]

. . . . It is impossible today to oppress a nation with a strong national feeling, as Vienna thinks it can do. That is the case with the Serbians. Already your [Austria's] whole policy during the Balkan war was a mistaken one. At the Ambassadors' Conference in London we unitedly worked to preserve the peace of Europe. Grey did a particularly great service. At that time all of these questions existed. Serbia wished to have a port on the Adriatic, which should have been given to her . . . . and peace would have been established. But today I do not know whether you will be able to retain Bosnia. It seems questionable to me. Bosnia really is the source of all these entanglements.

I [Dr. Kanner] replied that it certainly was peculiar that Prince Bismarck, who always was an enemy of the Hapsburgs, should have made them a present, Bosnia, one which had proved to be a Danaian present. This remark apparently struck the Prince unfavorably. He protested that it had not been a Danaian present. Bismarck did not mean it as such at all. You need to understand Bismarck rightly. He

[15] Kanner Papers, III, 114–28.

was a great statesman until '71. Everything he did up to that time was excellent. He was a natural fighter, and as long as it was necessary to fight for the unification of Germany he was in his place. Later on he committed grave errors. Much could be said about that; however, his greatest mistake was apparently his greatest triumph, the Berlin Congress. Here was laid the foundation of all subsequent European entanglements. But Bismarck did not have any bad intentions against Austria. What actuated him at this conference were various positive and personal motives. Above all, he wished to render a service to England. Austria he had never understood rightly. He knew France and Russia well, but never Austria. In Austria he saw, even after '71, only what he had been used to seeing at Frankfurt—Prussia's rival. And in later times too, he was always actuated by the fear that Austria could destroy the unity of Germany, his creation. During all his life he saw in Austria only the Austria of Schmerling. On that account, too, he persecuted the Austrian Old-Liberals, because he saw in them the representatives of Schmerling's views. But he never had a correct understanding of Austria's peculiarities and its national difficulties. Likewise he misunderstood the Balkan question. He believed, just as do your statesmen at this very day, that the times have not changed and that one could shift nationalities back and forth just as of old. He did not notice how these nationalities have risen to independence and suffer themselves no longer to be handled just as pawns, as in general he strongly underrated the importance of the Balkans. That is why he did not think of any difficulties when he gave Bosnia to Austria. Another mistake was that at the Berlin Congress he reduced Greater Bulgaria. Events have shown that his creation was untenable. The Bulgarians would not suffer to be separated, but Bismarck did not comprehend that. Greater Bulgaria, as conceived by Russia, meant to him a Russian satrapy, in which he saw danger. Added to that was the rivalry with Gortschakov, who, too, did not have any conception of the internal life of the Balkan peoples, otherwise he would not have left Bosnia's capital to Austria. Besides, Bismarck had a personal inclination to Andrassy. That is the way everything happened. (During these observations I had the feeling that Lichnowsky, although he did not say a thing about it, also regarded the German-Austrian Alliance as one of Bismarck's mistakes.)

I said that according to this one could justly assert that the Berlin Congress was the source of this war. Lichnowsky replied that that was correct, only that the present war could have been avoided; even in its last stage, if only Berlin had exerted some pressure upon Austria. However, it seems that your statesmen wanted the war; otherwise their whole attitude would be inconceivable. The Serbian Note was something monstrous. At that, Serbia really accepted all the important points of the Austrian demands. It was almost unbelievable to what an extent Serbia complied. It rejected only points 5 and 6, wishing to discuss them. That should have been done, for your diplomacy would then have scored a great success. I told the Serbian envoy, who came to me greatly agitated, to accept the Austrian ultimatum, in order to avoid further complications for the moment. I told him what of it if they dissolved their organization, the Narodna Obrana, for they could organize another one under a different name. At that, the Austrian officials are not so terrible. They will submit documents to you, but you will be able to talk with them. But in Austria, Lichnowsky said, they wished to give in only when it was too late. That is shown by the last Berchtold statement, expressing willingness to negotiate with Russia. Then he asked whether in Austria there had been any thought at all that this Serbian affair might result in a European war. I answered this question with a resolute "no," telling Lichnowsky how in July 1914 the prevailing opinion in all responsible quarters in Vienna had been to the effect that the whole affair meant only a punitive expedition against Serbia and that the Great Powers would not join in, as I had warned in my article of July 4. They did not wish to listen to me. Lichnowsky replied that he knew it. The Serbian *Blue Book,* too, contained it. I said that the following day, July 5, a Crown Council took place at which we decided upon war. Whereas in Berlin Austria was being accused of having willed the war, informed circles in Vienna said that Germany wished the war. . . . .

When asked about the plans of a *rapprochement* between Germany and Austria, Lichnowsky said that this *Mitteleuropa* idea was sheer idiocy. He was disgusted that such a propaganda was permitted and said that after the war we need only one commercial interest, namely, that we should enjoy the most-favored-nation privileges everywhere. That is what we should aim at, and not at isolation from the rest of the world.

He then asked what political plans were being made in Vienna. I explained that the general opinion was the annexation of Serbia and Montenegro on one side and that of the Poles on the other side, and that there existed different tendencies such as Dualism, Trialism, Quadralism, etc. At first he listened quietly, then said in a provoked tone that he doubted the possibility of Austria's annexing Serbia. The difficulty in the path of such an annexation was being underestimated. The rumor regarding the independence or the restoration of the Polish Kingdom he regarded as a thoughtless phrase. How was the whole affair conceived? If we wish to restore the Polish Kingdom we would have to include within it not only Galicia but also Pomerania. Not only that; the kingdom would be unable to exist and, just as Serbia is clamoring for a port in the Adriatic, it would have to call for an outlet on the Baltic. The erection of such a kingdom and supplying it with an outlet to the sea would mean for us the loss of Pomerania; we also would have to give it Courland and East and West Prussia. Lichnowsky meant that the understanding of the Three Powers who committed the crime against Poland was a prerequisite for any such arrangement. . . . .

We then talked about the Kaiser, and Lichnowsky said that he is not a balanced mind. Lichnowsky, who had become quite excited, finally remarked that it would be best if we [Germany] had a republic. . . . .

I was ready to leave, but at the door we got to talking about peace conditions. I indicated that now, after the colonial and naval policies had proved a fiasco, it would be possible to formulate the conditions of peace between England and Germany, and that this was the time to do it. Prince Lichnowsky agreed with this last point and, to my surprise, he then proceeded to state what were apparently his own ideas about peace. He said that at the beginning of the war we had announced that we had been attacked and that we had taken to the sword only as a matter of defense (this he said in an ironical tone) and that we did not wish anything else except to make ourselves safe against the possibility of such a recurrence in the future. This, Lichnowsky said, is our war aim, a negative war aim, but the sole one which so far has been pronounced from official place. How then is this negative war aim to be realized? An all-round limitation of armaments of all European countries, he said; and then asked whether that was not true. Then I took leave of him.

31. PRINCE LICHNOWSKY'S STATEMENT ON THE
ORIGINS OF THE WAR[16]

. . . . Since the Crimean War, however, the opposition between Russia and Austria has never disappeared. The greatest military power in the world, the German Empire, has stood behind Austria-Hungary ever since the Berlin Congress. And since Bismarck's time, and against what he intended, she has made use of the Alliance, concluded as a result of the Congress, and of the friction between Germany and Russia, as a kind of blank check, on which to draw in the Eastern interests of the Allies.

Bismarck had already only lukewarmly supported Russia at the Congress and had deprived her of the full fruit of victory more under the influence of personal irritation than from material considerations.

---

[16] *Berliner Tageblatt,* January 8, 1918.

He had also helped Count Andrassy to the "occupation" of so-called Turkish, but what was ethnographically far more Serbian, territory, and our attitude later on, with regard to the annexation of Bosnia, which destroyed Serbia's dreams of a future, led to a still further estrangement from our Eastern neighbor and traditional friend, whose neutrality had made the successes of 1866 and 1870–71 possible. The recall of the reassurance treaty was followed by the Russo-French fraternization, supplemented still further, after Algeciras, by the British-Russian understanding.

Whilst a far-reaching interpretation of the Alliance enabled our Austro-Magyar friends, with our help, to oppose the Serbian aspirations for unity, which were supported by Russia, our aspirations, on the other hand, to a dominant position on the Bosphorus supported by military missions, which were intended to strengthen the Turks' power of resistance, aroused the displeasure of the Tsarist Government. The Fleet and Algeciras on the one side and Serbian and Turkish policy on the other created the state of feeling out of which the Entente grew.

Then, at the London Conference of Ambassadors, the creation of Albania was pressed through with our help, with the intention of cutting Serbia off from the Adriatic. Through this Serbia found herself under the necessity of pressing southward and taking possession of the Vardar line, in order to gain access to the sea at Salonica, in conjunction with a friendly Greece. And, finally, when Count Berchtold, who would never really recognize the peace of Bucharest, wanted to set about the revision of the treaty, with the support of the Alliance, Russia's opposition led to the World War, which now confronts us with the task of finding a fresh and, it is to be hoped, a permanent basis for our future relations with Russia. . . . .

32. THE PUBLICATION OF LICHNOWSKY'S MEMORANDUM[17]

T. W. [Theodor Wolff] : In the summer of 1916, having rejected several other drafts, Count Lichnowsky wrote a memorandum under the title "My Mission in London." . . . . He did not intend the document for publication but only for a few persons whom he knew personally. He had made five or six typewritten copies, of which he sent one to Ballin, one to Herr von Gwinner, and one to me. Each of the persons named kept the dangerous present under lock and key in his desk. But a fourth copy lost its way and fell into hands for which it was not intended. . . . . Lichnowsky undoubtedly had been imprudent; however, it is ridiculous to talk about a betrayal of official secrets. . . . . How this fourth copy got out, is quite romantic. . . . .

[17] *Berliner Tageblatt*, March 25, 1918, pp. 1–2.

I got to know the officer [Hauptmann von Beerfelde] who "borrowed" the memorandum and then sent written copies to state officials and politicians, some years before the war. He belongs to an old noble family, and his career was watched with sympathy by General von Moltke. He was an enthusiastic student of the philosophy of religion and of theosophy, a thoroughly manly, but mystical, type. . . . . After hard war experiences he felt a strong call to devote himself wholly to the cause of peace and gave himself up to a pacifism, which is quite incompatible with the wearing of the uniform. Late one evening he called on me. He was very much excited, and told me he had had copies made of a memorandum of Lichnowsky's which had been lent to him, and had sent it, without asking the author's permission, to "the leading men." No logic could convince him that his action was illegal, senseless, harmful. . . . .

33. STATEMENT OF VON PAYER IN THE MAIN COMMITTEE OF THE REICHSTAG ON THE MEMORANDA OF PRINCE LICHNOWSKY AND DR. MÜHLON[18]

We are mainly concerned with a memorandum of August 14, 1916, by Prince Lichnowsky, who represented the German Empire in London from 1912 to 1914—it is dated August 1, 1916, and relates to our foreign policy from the time of Prince Bismarck—which the Prince has committed to writing, in connection with a description of his activities in London. With regard to its origin and publication, he wrote himself on the 5th instant to the Imperial Chancellor as follows:

"Your Excellency is aware that purely private memoranda, which I wrote in the summer of 1916, have found their way to the public, through an unprecedented breach of confidence.

"In explanation of the matter allow me to make the following statement:

"The question is mainly of subjective observations on our general foreign policy since the Berlin Congress. I regarded the policy of turning away from Russia and extending alliances to Oriental questions, which has since been pursued, as the real root of the war. In connection with this, I briefly examined our Moroccan and naval policy.

"My London mission, of course, could not be left out of the question, all the more as I felt the necessity of putting down the details of my experiences and impressions there, for the sake of the future and for my own justification, before they escaped my memory.

"I thought I could show these memoranda, intended only, so to

[18] *Norddeutsche Allgemeine Zeitung,* March 19, 1918, II, 1.

speak, for the family archives, which I had written from memory, without documentary material or notes from the time of my official activity, to a very few political friends in whose judgment I had as much confidence as in their reliability, on being assured of their secrecy.

"Unfortunately, without my knowledge, one of these gentlemen gave my memorandum to an officer in the political department of the General Staff who was very much interested in the questions touched on and with whom I am not acquainted. This officer, completely failing to recognize the far-reaching consequences of his step, made copies of the memorandum and sent them to a number of persons mostly unknown to me.

"When I heard of the mischief done, it was unfortunately too late to be able to call in all the copies sent out. I therefore placed myself at the disposal of the then Imperial Chancellor, Dr. Michaelis, and intimated to him my most sincere regret for the whole painful affair. In constant touch with the Foreign Office, I have since endeavored to prevent the further publication of my opinions, unfortunately without the desired success.

"Your Excellency will permit me to renew in this form my already verbally expressed most profound regret at the extremely annoying occurrence.

"With sincere respect,

"Your Excellency's most obedient,

"(*Signed*) LICHNOWSKY"

"His Excellency the Imperial Chancellor, Count Hertling"

In the meanwhile the Prince has tendered his resignation, which has been accepted and, as he certainly had no evil intention—it was more a question of imprudence—no further proceedings have been taken against the Prince. Some of his representations and assertions must, however, be contradicted in the Main Committee. That applies particularly to the assertions as to the political occurrences in the last months before the outbreak of war. The Prince had no personal knowledge of these occurrences. He appears to have received incorrect information from a third, wrongly informed party, which possibility the Prince has himself admitted.

A key to the mistakes and false conclusions of the memorandum may perhaps also be found in the Prince's remarkable overestimation of his own merits, which is accompanied by a downright hatred of those who did not recognize his services as he expected. In more than one place he hints that professional considerations did not primarily influence their decisions but rather the question whether their attitude would be advantageous or detrimental to him, agreeable or disagreeable. In harmony with this characteristic, a remarkable regard for the foreign diplomatists runs through the whole memoir, particularly for the English, who are portrayed with positive affection, and, in contrast to this, an equally remarkable irritation against almost all the German statesmen. The result was that in not infrequent instances the Prince had regarded the most ardent enemies of Germany as her friends because they were on good terms with him personally. When he so misjudged people, it is no wonder that the Prince came to false conclusions in his imagination. Thus he himself admits that at first he attached no far-reaching importance to the murder of the heir to the Austrian throne and took it amiss that in Berlin the position was differently estimated. This mistake alone explains the Prince's not having had a clear understanding of the subsequent events and their significance.

In particular it appears from the memoir that as early as in the summer of 1914, as well as when he wrote the memoir, the Prince was of opinion that in spite of the murder of the heir to the Austrian throne peace might have been maintained through the influence of the German Government on Austria if it had only turned England's love of peace sufficiently to account; if this had been done, a military attack on the part of Russia would hardly have been likely. How mistaken such a policy would have been is now convincingly established by the evidence of the Sukhomlinov trial.

The alleged facts to which the Prince appealed in order to justify his policy were individually to a great extent in direct contradiction to the truth, which can be established by actual facts. The speaker demonstrated this in detail. Thus it is with regard to the Prince's assertion that Count Moltke urged war, with regard to the Crown Council held in Potsdam on July 5, 1914, and with regard to the sending of an Austrian protocol respecting the alleged Crown Council to Count Mensdorff in London, which protocol contained a supplementary note: "It would not matter if a war with Russia were to result from this." All these statements were demonstrably false. Equally the statement that the then State Secretary for Foreign Affairs was in Vienna in July 1914 and the statement that Count Pourtales had reported that Russia would not move under any circumstances. How unfounded were the Prince's complaints that no effort was made, in accordance with his suggestion, to put an end to the Serbian crisis by a conference, is now unmistakable, and the proceedings of the Sukhomlinov trial have shown how unfounded were his reproaches that Germany had replied to the Russian mobilization with an ultimatum and a declaration of war. It was just the same with the assertion that the German Government had refused all England's proposals of mediation. Sir Edward Grey's last proposal of mediation was urgently seconded in Vienna by Berlin, as appears from the instructions which the Imperial Chancellor read in the Main Committee on November 9, 1916. Unfortunately for the Prince, he composed his memoir three months too early. How little foundation there is for the Prince's reproach that German policy was not peaceloving is proved by an incident he relates himself in the memoir. At that time, in consequence of a telephonic misunderstanding, the Prince had reported from London that Sir Edward Grey had asked him whether Germany would not attack France if she remained neutral in a Russo-German war. Immediately after the arrival of this telegram, the Emperor's well-known telegram to the King of England was sent from Berlin, in which Germany offered to agree to the English proposal if England would guarantee France's unconditional neutrality with all her forces. That the Prince's communication was a mistake does not detract from the value of the German step. When the memoir speaks of an understanding with England, it must be pointed out, in order to avoid mistakes, that this had related only to the Bagdad railway and to the Portuguese colonies; in view of the conditions in Europe at that time, particularly in view of England's firm adherence to the Entente policy as evinced in the negotiations over the Anglo-Russian Naval Agreement, it can readily be understood that, contrary to the Prince's assertion, a general understanding with England had not been assured.

The object of the memorandum as a whole was obvious. It was to show the reader how much better and more discerning the policy of the author had been and how he would have secured peace for the Empire if his advice had been taken. No one will blame the Prince for holding this belief in itself. He is also at liberty to make his own comments on the occurrences and on his attitude toward them. But then it was absolutely incumbent on him to take care that they should not be made public, and, however small the circle of readers he had in view, it was still his duty not to assert anything contrary to the facts known to him and to examine the material of the facts reported to him. As things are now, the memorandum, the intention of which was merely to prove that the course of the world's history was only wrongly guided, because otherwise people would have been jealous of his, the Prince's, success, will do harm enough, amongst both the ill-disposed and those who are superficial. The memorandum has no historical value, nor is it intended to serve the interests of actual truth, but merely the subjective objects of an individual.

The remaining question was of a circular in the form of a letter sent to a number of persons by a Dr. Mühlon, at present residing in Switzerland, and who at the time of the outbreak of war was a member of the Krupp board of directors; many copies had since been made of the letter, and its genuineness had not been disputed so far. The date of its composition was not known. According to the letter, Dr. Mühlon occupied a distinguished position with two well-known gentlemen in succession in the second half of July 1914, and he now relates alleged utterances of theirs from which he draws the conclusion that in July 1914 the German Government did not want peace. The two gentlemen had stated in writing that in the case of Dr. Mühlon it was a question of a man suffering from nerves who, as early as at the time of his activity at Essen, could not go into a place where several gentlemen with whom he was not acquainted were assembled and who, after he left the board of directors, had repeated nervous breakdowns and had to devote a long period exclusively to his recovery. They did not credit him with any intention of injuring the Fatherland; the statements alleged to have been made by them, from which Dr. Mühlon thought to draw his conclusions, disposed of any such idea. They could only describe his memorandum as pathological. He must have jumbled up things he had heard from others or, later on, that which he had imagined, with the purport of the conversations which actually took place. A subsequent examination of the assertions said to have been made by these gentlemen, as far as they could be actually checked, had shown that the alleged statements could not have been made, as they were absolutely contrary to the facts. It was also almost incompatible with the assertions made in the letter that, before the outbreak of war, Dr. Mühlon, a declared representative of pacifist ideas, should have been in the service of the Foreign Office abroad for a long time before the war, although, as he now asserts, he knew, as early as 1914, that the German Empire was at that time helping to bring about war. He had also not given up his further activity in the interest of the Empire in May 1917 out of consideration for the position of the German Government at that time but because in 1917 he had given up all hope that the Government of the day was in earnest as regards peace. Under all these circumstances no greater weight could be attached to Dr. Mühlon's narrations than has been attached to them by the two gentlemen who are supposed to have made the alleged statements, namely, that they are the utterances of a diseased mind.

34. STATEMENT OF VON JAGOW CONCERNING LICH- NOWSKY'S MEMORANDUM, MARCH 23, 1918[19]

. . . . When I was appointed State Secretary in January 1913 it seemed to me that a German-English *rapprochement* was desirable and an understanding upon these points where our interests touched, and sometimes even crossed; and this I deemed feasible. At least it was my intention to work in this sense. One of the chief points in which we

[19] *Norddeutsche Allgemeine Zeitung,* March 23, 1918, II, 1–2.

were then interested was the Mesopotamian Asia Minor question, the so-called Bagdad policy, which had become for us a question of prestige. If England insisted on excluding us from there it appeared to me that a conflict would be avoided with difficulty. I took up the question of an understanding concerning the Bagdad railway in Berlin as soon as it was possible. We were met in a conciliatory manner by the English Government, and an agreement had almost been reached just previous to the outbreak of the World War.

At the same time there were negotiations concerning the Portuguese colonies which were initiated by Metternich and subsequently carried on by Baron Marschall and later by Prince Lichnowsky. Other questions, such as the East Asiatic, I thought of bringing up later when those questions which I thought most important, such as the Bagdad railway, had been settled and thereby an atmosphere of greater confidence created. The question of the Fleet I also put aside, as an understanding on this point seemed to me extremely difficult in view of former experiences.

The Albanian Question

I can pass over the evolution of the Albanian question as it was previous to my taking up office. In a general way, however, I would remark that such complete disinterestedness in Balkan questions as Prince Lichnowsky seems to advocate does not seem to me possible. It would even have been contrary to the Central Alliance policy if we had ignored the really vital interests of one of the parties concerned in it. We also had asked Austria for support in the Algeciras question, and the attitude of Italy at that time had caused us some apprehension. Russia also stood by the side of France, though she has absolutely no interests in Morocco. Finally, it was our business as the third party in the Alliance to support those measures which were calculated to facilitate a compromise between the divergent interests of our Allies and to prevent a conflict between them.

It further appeared to me impossible to abandon the Triple Alliance policy with reference to such questions as touched our Allies. Italy would thereby in Eastern questions have been driven completely into Entente currents, and Austria would have been handed over to Russia. The Triple Alliance would have been practically sacrificed by such an action, and without any support we also would have been unable to realize our interests in the East. That we have great economic interests there to protect, even Lichnowsky will not deny. Economic interests today are no longer to be treated apart from political.

The assertion made by Prince Lichnowsky that in Petrograd the independence of the Sultan was desired is one which he really ought to substantiate, for it is in contradiction to all the former traditions of Russian policy. And if we had not been able to avail ourselves of Marschall's great influence in Constantinople we should hardly have been able to protect our economic interests in Turkey in the manner we desired.

Prince Lichnowsky further speaks contrary to historical facts when he asserts that we drove Russia, "our natural friend and best neighbor, into the arms of France and England by our Oriental and Balkan policy." It was Gortchakov's Russian policy, gravitating toward *revanche*-seeking France, which forced Bismarck to enter into alliance with Austria-Hungary. By his alliance with Rumania he turned the key in the door which barred Russia's southward pressure. Lichnowsky condemns the basic principles of Bismarck's policy. Our efforts at a *rapprochement* with Russia failed—Björkö bears witness to this fact—or remained ineffective, as also the so-called Potsdam agreement. Russia was not always our "best neighbor"; in the reign of the Empress Elizabeth, as now, she strove for East Prussia with the intention of extending her Baltic coast and thus insuring her supremacy in the Baltic Sea. The Petersburg "window" was opened wider little by little by the incorporation of Esthonia, Livonia, Courland, and Finland, and was to have included Aaland. Poland was made a jumping-off ground against us. The Pan-Slavism which more and more governed Russian policy was directly anti-German.

We put no pressure on Russia to abstain from her policy of expansion in Asia, but tried only to guard against her incursions into Europe and her envelopment of our Austro-Hungarian allies.

The Ambassadors' Conference

We no more desired war on Albania's account than did Sir Edward Grey. That is why, in spite of our unfortunate experiences at Algeciras, we consented to a conference. The merit of a "conciliatory attitude" at the conference must not be denied to Sir Edward Grey. But it is going a little too far to say that "he in no wise ranged himself on the side of the Entente." He certainly often urged Petersburg to make concessions and found "principles of accord" (*Einigungsformeln*) suitable to this end. But really he represented the Entente, as he could no more leave his associates in the lurch than could we. Nor did he wish to do so. On the other hand, the assertion that we adopted without exception the standpoint prescribed for us by Vienna is absolutely untrue. We played, as did England, a conciliatory rôle, and urged concession and moderation upon Vienna far more than Lichnowsky seems to be aware of or at any rate admits. Vienna thereupon made a variety of most far-reaching concessions (Dibra and Djakowa). If Prince Lichnowsky, who always wanted to be wiser than the Foreign Office and who obviously allowed himself to be strongly influenced by the Entente representatives, was unaware of this, at least he might abstain from making false assertions now. When indeed in Vienna the necessary degree of compliance had been reached, then we naturally had to represent the Austrian standpoint at the conference. Ambassador Szögyéni himself did not belong to the extremists. In Vienna his attitude was far from being consistently approved of. That this ambassador with whom I had daily dealings consistently harped on the refrain of *casus foederis* is quite unknown to me. It is true that Lichnowsky was never regarded in Vienna as a friend of Austria, even before those days. Nevertheless, I received many more complaints concerning him from the Marquis San Juliano than from Count Berchtold.

THE BALKAN CONFERENCE AND THE SECOND BALKAN WAR

The occupation of Scutari by King Nikita brought the whole conference into contempt and was a provocation of all the contracting Powers.

Russia in no wise was forced "to give way everywhere before us." On the contrary, she more than once obtained "satisfaction for Serbian wishes"; some towns and strips of land were even allotted to Serbia which might be regarded as purely or mainly Albanian. Prince Lichnowsky says "the result of the conference was a fresh humiliation for Russian pride," and there was much "annoyance" in Russia over it. It is not our business to support all unjustifiable claims of the overweening pride of a power absolutely unfriendly to us at the expense of our allies. Russia has no vital interests on the Adriatic, but our allies have. Had we adopted the Russian standpoint, as apparently Lichnowsky would have liked us to do, the result would have been humiliation for Austria-Hungary and thereby indirectly the weakening of our group. Lichnowsky is apparently always anxious that Russia should escape humiliation; that of Austria evidently is a matter of indifference to him.

When Lichnowsky asserts that our "Austrophilia was not calculated to promote Russia's Asiatic interest," it is not quite clear to me what he means thereby. After an unsuccessful diversion toward East Asia— in the Japanese war we favored Russia without receiving any thanks!— Russia turned once more to her East-European policy (the Balkans and Constantinople) with renewed energy (the Balkan Union, Buchlau, Iswolski, etc.).

The sly Cretan, Venizelos, with the "Ribbon of the Red Eagle," thoroughly understood how to throw dust in the eyes of our Ambassador. Unlike King Constantine and Theotoki, he was always friendly to the Entente. His present attitude has shown this disposition in the clearest light. But Herr Danew was thoroughly in favor of Petersburg.

That Count Berchtold betrayed a certain leaning toward Bulgaria, in the differences between that country and Rumania, is true. That we "naturally agreed with him" in this is, however, false. It was thanks to us that King Carol obtained satisfaction at the peace of Bucharest. If in the peace of Bucharest, in which we favored the wishes and interests of our ally Rumania, our policy deviated somewhat from that of Vienna, nevertheless the Austro-Hungarian Cabinet most certainly did not believe—as Prince Lichnowsky asserts—"that it could count on our support in a revision of the treaty." That San Juliano warned us "as far back as the summer of 1913 that we would become involved in a world war" because at that time the idea of "armed intervention in Serbia" had found favor in Austria is unknown to me. As little am I aware that von Tschirschky—who, it must be admitted, was somewhat pessimistic by nature—uttered a warning as early as the spring of 1914 that there would soon be war. Concerning certain "important events" which Lichnowsky hints at, I was in ignorance as much as he himself! Events such as the English visit to Paris, the first paid by Sir Edward Grey to the Continent, must have been known to the Ambassador, and we certainly communicated to him the secret Russo-English naval agreement; but he would not believe in it.

In the affair of Liman von Sanders we made a very far-reaching concession to Russia by giving up the general's command over Constantinople. I will admit that this point of the agreement concerning the military mission was politically inopportune.

Colonial Agreement

When Lichnowsky flatters himself that he had succeeded in giving the agreement a form corresponding to our wishes, the merit of this should not be taken from him; but it certainly required strong pressure at different times to induce him to represent with sufficient emphasis certain others of our wishes.

Lichnowsky's statement that he received power for the final conclusion of the agreement after he had previously asserted that the agreement had fallen through is obviously a contradiction, the explanation of which must be left to the Prince himself. But his assertion that we delayed publication because the agreement was a public success for himself which we did not wish him to enjoy is a preposterous insinuation. It can only be accounted for by his self-centered conception of things. The agreement would have missed its practical and moral effect—one of its chief objects was to create a better atmosphere between England and ourselves—if its publication had been greeted by attacks on "perfidious Albion" in our Anglophobe press and in the parliament. This would undoubtedly have resulted from the immediate publication of the so-called Windsor Agreement, considering the home situation then prevailing. And the outcry against England's perfidy which would have been raised in view of the inner contradiction between the text of the Windsor Agreement and our own agreement would hardly have been dispelled in the case of our public opinion by the assurance of England's *bona fides*. With justified prudence, we intended to delay publication to a suitable moment when the danger of unfriendly criticism should be less acute; if possible, we meant to publish it simultaneously with the Bagdad agreement, which was on the point of being signed. The fact that between England and ourselves two great agreements had been concluded would have favored the acceptance of the first-named, and would have helped us over the slight blemishes in the Portuguese agreement. It was our consideration of the effect likely to be produced by the agreement, which was intended to improve our relations with England but not to produce new friction, which caused the delay in its publication.

It is true that we were also influenced, although naturally in a secondary manner, by hoped-for economic interests which we sought at that time to gain in the Portuguese colonies and which, naturally, would have been made harder to realize had the other agreement been made public. Possibly Lichnowsky was not in the position to see from London all the sides of this question, as we were, but he ought to have trusted our judgment and been content to remain quiet, instead of showing up his want of understanding by accusations and insinuations of personal motives. With English statesmen he certainly would have found an appreciation of our arguments.

The speeches of the Ambassador excited much annoyance at home. It was necessary, in order to create a better atmosphere, in which alone the *rapprochement* sought for would be produced, that German public opinion should have confidence in our English policy and our Ambassador in London. This fact Lichnowsky did not properly appreciate, in spite of his being generally so susceptible to public opinion, for he saw everything through his London spectacles. His complaints of the attitude of the Foreign Office are so unsupported that they are not worth going into. I would only state that the Prince was not left in ignorance of "most important things" in so far as they concerned his mission. On the contrary, I gave the Ambassador more extensive information than had previously been the custom. My own experiences as Ambassador induced me to do this. Lichnowsky was in the habit of trusting more to his own impressions and judgment than to the communication and instructions of the Central Authorities. The sources of our information I had not always the occasion or the authority to communicate. In this respect very definite considerations weighed, especially the fear of compromising those sources. The memorandum of the Prince is the best vindication of the prudence exercised in this respect.

Event of War

It is not true that in the Foreign Office the information that England would under all circumstances protect France found no credence.

Serbian Crisis

In Konopischt [on the occasion of the visit of the Kaiser to the Austrian heir to the throne] no plans were made for an active policy against Serbia. The Archduke Ferdinand was not, as is often supposed, in favor of a policy which would lead to war. During the London Conference he always advocated moderation and the avoidance of war.

The "optimism" of Prince Lichnowsky was hardly justified, as he may have since convinced himself after reading the disclosures of the Sukhomlinov case. Moreover, the secret Russo-English naval agreement, of which, as I said, he had been informed, might have made him more skeptical. The mistrust expressed by the Imperial Chancellor and the Under-Secretary of State was, unfortunately, well founded. How can these facts be reconciled with the assertion that we, relying on the report of Count Pourtales that Russia "would under no circumstances take action," would not believe in the possibility of war? Moreover, Count Pourtales, as far as my recollection goes, never made any such report.

We were bound to consider Austria-Hungary as justified in deciding to take action against the continued provocations engineered by Russia (Herr von Hartwig), which had their climax in the murder of Sarajevo. In spite of previous agreements and compromises to avoid threatened conflicts, Russia would not give up her policy, which aimed at the complete exclusion of Austrian influence, and naturally also of ours, in the Balkans. Russian agents inspired by Petersburg continued their intrigues. The prestige and existence of the Danube Monarchy were at stake. Either the monarchy had to lower its sails to Russo-Serbian intrigue, or it had to issue a *quos ego* even at the risk of war. We could not leave our Allies in the lurch. If it was desired to exclude altogether the *ultima ratio* of war, the alliance should never have been concluded. Added to this, it was clear that Russian military preparations (for instance, the completion of railways and fortifications in Poland, for which money was lent by *revanche*-breathing France, and which were to be finished in a few years) were directed especially against us. But in spite of this, in spite of the ever more clearly and obviously aggressive tendency of Russian policy, the idea of a preventive war was far from us. We decided to declare war on Russia only in view of the Russian mobilization and to prevent a Russian invasion.

Our letters exchanged with the Prince—only private letters were in question—I have not at hand. Lichnowsky pleaded for the abandonment of Austria. I answered, as far as I can remember, that we, apart from our treaty obligation, could not sacrifice our Allies for the sake of the uncertain friendship of England. If we sacrificed our one reliable ally we ran the risk of finding ourselves later isolated in the presence of the Entente. It is possible that I wrote that "Russia was becoming ever more anti-German, and we must just take the risk of it"; it is also possible that, in order to stiffen Lichnowsky's nerves and to prevent him from giving expression to his views in London, I wrote that there might be a "row," and that "the firmer we held by Austria, the sooner would Russia give way"; that our policy was not based upon reports which excluded the possibility of war I have already said. I considered that war at that time was avoidable but was fully aware, as we all were, of the serious danger of it.

We could not agree to the English proposal for a conference of Ministers, as it would doubtless have led to a serious diplomatic defeat for us. For even Italy was friendly with Serbia, and is, in view of her Balkan interests, opposed to Austria. Even Lichnowsky admits the "confidential Russo-Italian relations" existing at that time. The best and most feasible way out was the localization of the conflict, an understanding between Vienna and Petersburg. In this sense we worked with all our energy. That we "insisted upon war" is an absurd assertion, which has been sufficiently refuted by the telegrams, published in the *White Books,* from the Kaiser to the Tsar and King George (Lichnowsky, of course, knows only of the "really too humiliating" one addressed to the Tsar), as well as by the instructions sent by us to Vienna. The most remarkable caricature occurs in the sentence, "When finally Count Berchtold decided to give way, we replied to the Russian mobilization, after Russia had for a whole week waited and negotiated in vain, by an ultimatum and declaration of war."

Were we expected to wait until the mobilized Russian Army had poured over our frontier? Possibly the reading of the Sukhomlinov case may by now have impressed even Lichnowsky with the feeling, *"Oh si tacuisses!"* On July 5 I was absent from Berlin. The statement that I was in Vienna "shortly after to talk it all over with Berchtold" is false. I returned on July 6 from my honeymoon to Berlin, and from then I did not move until the break-up of the great Headquarters on August 15. As State Secretary I was in Vienna only once before the outbreak of war; that was in the spring of 1913.

ENGLISH DECLARATION OF WAR

The confusing dispatch which Prince Lichnowsky sent on August 1 (I have not the text with me) he glosses over as a "misunderstanding," and appears even to blame us for having made the "receipt of the message in Berlin the basis for far-reaching actions without awaiting the text of the conversation." War with England hung on minutes; immediately after the receipt of the dispatch the decision was taken to make an eleventh-hour effort to avoid war with England and France. His Majesty sent the well-known telegram to King George.

The contents of Lichnowsky's message could not be interpreted otherwise than as we did. Prince Lichnowsky's representation contains so many incorrect or distorted versions of the facts that it is not surprising that his conclusions also should be mistaken. It is positively grotesque to charge us, as does Lichnowsky, with having sent an ultimatum to Petersburg on July 30 on the mere mobilization of Russia, with having declared war on Russia on July 31 although the Tsar had pledged his word that he would not move a man so long as negotiations continued, and with having thereby deliberately annihilated the possibility of a peaceful solution. In the conclusion he seems almost to identify himself with the standpoint of our enemies.

The Ambassador charges us with pursuing a policy of identification "with Turks and Austro-Magyars," and with having subordinated our point of view to "those of Vienna and Pest." We may fairly report that he could see things only through London spectacles and exclusively from the point of view of that *rapprochement* with England which he sought *à tout prix* to bring about. He appears also to have completely forgotten that the Entente was made much more against us than against Austria.

I also pursued a policy directed toward an understanding with England, because I was of the opinion that this was the only way out of the unfavorable situation into which we had been brought by the unequal division of power and by the weakness of the Triple Alliance. But Russia and France pressed for war. We were bound by our agreement with Austria, and our position as a Great Power was threatened with hers. *Hic Rhodus, Hic Salta!* But England, which was not equally bound to Russia and which had received from us far-reaching assurances regarding the indulgent treatment of France and Belgium, drew the sword.

I do not intend to adopt the theory now widespread amongst us that England was the originator of all the intrigues leading to the war; on the contrary, I believe in Sir Edward Grey's love of peace and his genuine desire to arrive at an understanding with us. But he had allowed himself to become too deeply entangled in the network of Franco-Russian policy—he could find no way out—and therefore failed to do that which had been in his power, namely, prevent the World War. The war was not popular among the English people; therefore Belgium had to serve as a battle cry.

"Political marriages for life and death," as Prince Lichnowsky observes, are not possible in a society of nations. But "isolations are equally impossible under the conditions at present existing in Europe." European history has been made up of coalitions, some of which resulted in the avoidance of armed outbursts while others merely led to violent collisions. The loosening and dissolving of the old ties which no longer correspond to all conditions is only then indicated when new combinations are achievable. This was the object of the policy of *rapprochement* with England. So long as that policy did not offer reliable guaranties we could not abandon the old securities and the obligations which they carried with them.

The Moroccan policy had led to a political defeat. In the Bosnian crisis this had fortunately been avoided, as also at the London Conference. A new diminution of our prestige was intolerable for our position in Europe and the world. The prosperity of states, their political and economic successes, rest upon the prestige which they enjoy in the world.

The personal attacks contained in the memorandum, the incredible insinuations against and abuse of other persons condemn themselves. The perpetually recurring suspicion that everything happened because he, Lichnowsky, was begrudged any success tells of wounded vanity and disappointed hopes of personal success. The effect is painful.

In conclusion, I should like to refer to the memorandum of Prince Bismarck of 1879, quoted by Hermann Oncken in his work *Central Europe; Old and New,* wherein the idea is developed that the German Empire must never allow matters to reach the point where Germany would remain isolated on the European Continent between Russia and France, beside an Austria-Hungary prostrated and deserted by Germany herself.

JAGOW

CHAPTER III

PROPAGANDA

INTRODUCTORY NOTE

A T THE outbreak of the World War the official propaganda was conducted by the Press Bureau of the Imperial Foreign Office, the affiliated telegraph agencies, and foreign press bureaus. The official versions of the causes of the war and the war aims of the belligerents were circulated throughout the world. The Government also established centers of propaganda in neutral states, notably Switzerland and Holland. The Imperial Government, which had taken the offensive in the propaganda war as well as in the conflict of arms, had thereby a distinct initial advantage over the propaganda of the Allied Governments.

"When the war came," the great historian Lamprecht said in December 1914, "everyone who could write obtained the largest possible goose quill and wrote to all his foreign friends, telling them that they did not realize what splendid fellows the Germans were, and not infrequently adding that in many respects their conduct required some excuse. The effect was stupendous." This unorganized, unofficial propaganda forced the Government to take energetic measures to control public opinion at home and to supervise all the propaganda work in neutral, allied, and enemy countries.

The chief topics of the home propaganda were: the war of self-defense against the encircling policy of the Entente; the certainty of victory and the consequent necessity of fortitude (*Durchhalten*); the violations of the laws of land and naval warfare by all the enemies; the historic mission and high culture of Germans (*Deutschtum*); the need for national expansion; and the proclamation that German victory would be for the good of the world. These themes were used also in the attempt to control neutral opinion. Elaborate explanations also were made for those acts of war which have interfered with the rights of neutrals, as the sinking of neutral vessels, the use of mines, and the adoption of unrestricted submarine warfare. The advantage which would come to all neutrals from the

72

freedom of the seas was also stressed. The control of opinion in Austria-Hungary, Bulgaria, and Turkey, the allies of Germany, was successful, and emphasis was placed upon their common interests and great future. Finally, the chief topics of the propaganda in enemy countries were: proclamation of the certainty of German victory; proclamation of disaffection between the Entente powers due to their divergent war aims; encouragement of nationalist and revolutionary movements within the British and Russian Empires; attempts to inflame anti-patriotic or defeatist opinion in all Entente states; encouragement of pacifism in enemy and neutral countries.

35. THE WAR AGAINST THE FRENCH GOVERNMENT[1]

FRENCH SOLDIERS!

The Germans are only making war against the French Government, which is sacrificing you and your country to the egotism of the English. Your commerce, your industry, and your agriculture will be ruined by this war, whilst the English alone will derive enormous profit from it.

You are pulling the chestnuts out of the fire for the English.

The news spread by your Government that the Russians are near Berlin is false. On the contrary, the Russians have been beaten in two great battles. One hundred and fifty thousand Russians have been captured, and the rest have been driven in rout from German territory.

36. THE FORGED "ARMY ORDER BY THE GERMAN EMPEROR"[2]

"It is my Royal and Imperial command that you concentrate your energies, for the immediate present, upon one single purpose, and that is that you address all your skill and all the valor of my soldiers to exterminate first the treacherous English and walk over General French's contemptible little army.

"HEADQUARTERS, Aix-la-Chapelle, August 19"

[1] Collection of German Propaganda, Hoover War Library.
[2] *The Times,* October 1, 1914.

37. THE MANIFESTO OF THE GERMAN UNIVERSITY PROFESSORS AND MEN OF SCIENCE[3]

TO THE CIVILIZED WORLD!

As representatives of German Science and Art, we hereby protest to the civilized world, against the lies and calumnies with which our enemies are endeavouring to stain the honour of Germany in her hard struggle for existence—in a struggle which has been forced upon her.

The iron mouth of events has proved the untruth of the fictitious German defeats, consequently misrepresentation and calumny are all the more eagerly at work. As heralds of truth we raise our voices against these.

It is not true that Germany is guilty of having caused this war. Neither the people, the Government, nor the "Kaiser" wanted war. Germany did her utmost to prevent it; for this assertion the world has documentary proof. Often enough during the 26 years of his reign has Wilhelm II shown himself to be the upholder of peace, and often enough has this fact been acknowledged by our opponents. Nay, even the "Kaiser," whom they now dare to call an Attila, has been ridiculed by them for years, because of his steadfast endeavours to maintain universal peace. Not till a numerical superiority which had been lying in wait on the frontiers, assailed us, did the whole nation rise to a man.

It is not true that we trespassed in neutral Belgium. It has been proved that France and England had resolved on such a trespass, and it has likewise been proved that Belgium had agreed to their doing so. It would have been suicide on our part not to have been beforehand.

It is not true that the life and property of a single Belgian citizen was injured by our soldiers without the bitterest self-defense having made it necessary; for again, and again, notwithstanding repeated threats, the citizens lay in ambush, shooting at the troops out of the houses, mutilating the wounded, and murdering in cold blood the medical men while they were doing their Samaritan work. There can be no baser abuse than the suppression of these crimes with the view of letting the Germans appear to be criminals, only for having justly punished these assassins for their wicked deeds.

It is not true that our troops treated Louvain brutally. Furious inhabitants having treacherously fallen upon them in their quarters, our troops with aching hearts, were obliged to fire a part of the town, as a punishment. The greatest part of Louvain has been preserved. The

---

[3] *An die Kulturwelt!; To the Civilized World* (Manifesto of the Ninety-three German Intellectuals); A. Morel-Fatio, *Les Versions Allemande et Française du Manifeste des Intellectuals Allemands dit des Quatre-Vingt-Treize.*

famous Town Hall stands quite intact; for at great self-sacrifice our soldiers saved it from destruction by the flames. Every German would of course greatly regret, if in the course of this terrible war any works of art should already have been destroyed or be destroyed at some future time, but inasmuch as in our love for art we cannot be surpassed by any other nation, in the same degree we must decidedly refuse to buy a German defeat at the cost of saving a work of art.

It is not true that our warfare pays no respect to international laws. It knows no undisciplined cruelty. But in the east, the earth is saturated with the blood of women and children unmercifully butchered by the wild Russian troops, and in the west, dumdum bullets mutilate the breasts of our soldiers. Those who have allied themselves with Russians and Serbians, and present such a shameful scene to the world as that of inciting Mongolians and Negroes against the white race, have no right whatever to call themselves upholders of civilization.

It is not true that the combat against our so-called militarism is not a combat against our civilization, as our enemies hypocritically pretend it is. Were it not for German militarism, German civilization would long since have been extirpated. For its protection it arose in a land which for centuries had been plagued by bands of robbers, as no other land had been. The German army and the German people are one, and to-day, this consciousness fraternizes 70 millions of Germans, all ranks, positions and parties being one.

We cannot wrest the poisonous weapon—the lie—out of the hands of our enemies. All we can do is to proclaim to all the world, that our enemies are giving false witness against us. You, who know us, who with us have protected the most holy possessions of man, we call to you:

Have faith in us! Believe, that we shall carry on this war to the end as a civilized nation, to whom the legacy of a Goethe, a Beethoven, and a Kant, is just as sacred as its own hearths and homes.

For this we pledge you our names and our honour.

ADOLF VON BAEYER,
Professor of Chemistry,
Munich

PROF. PETER BEHRENS,
Berlin.

EMIL VON BEHRING,
Professor of Medicine,
Marburg.

WILHELM VON BODE,
General Director of the Royal Museums,
Berlin.

ALOIS BRANDL,
Professor, President of the Shakespeare Society,
Berlin.

LUJU BRENTANO,
Professor of National Economy,
Munich.

PROF. JUSTUS BRINKMANN,
Museum Director,
Hamburg.

JOHANNES CONRAD,
Professor of National Economy,
Halle.

FRANTZ VON DEFREGGER,
Munich.

RICHARD DEHMEL,
Hamburg.

ADOLF DEISSMANN,
Professor of Theology,
Berlin,
Berlin.

PROF. WILHELM DÖRP-
FELD,
Berlin.

FRIEDRICH VON DUHN,
Professor of Archae-
ology,
Heidelberg.

PROF. PAUL EHRLICH,
Frankfort on the Main.

ALBERT EHRHARD,
Professor of R. Catho-
lic Theology,
Strassburg.

KARL ENGLER,
Professor of Chemistry,
Karlsruhe.

GERHARD ESSER,
Professor of R. Catho-
lic Theology,
Bonn.

RUDOLF EUCKEN,
Professor of Philos-
ophy,
Jena.

HERBERT EULENBERG,
Kaiserswerth.

HEINRICH FINKE,
Professor of History,
Freiburg.

EMIL FISCHER,
Professor of Chemistry,
Berlin.

WILHELM FOERSTER,
Professor of Astron-
omy,
Berlin.

LUDWIG FULDA,
Berlin.

EDUARD VON GEB-
HARDT,
Dusseldorf.

J. J. DE GROOT,
Professor of Ethnog-
raphy,
Berlin.

FRITZ HABER,
Professor of Chemistry,
Berlin.

ERNST HAECKEL,
Professor of Zoölogy,
Jena.

MAX HALBE,
Munich.

PROF. ADOLF VON
HARNACK,
General Director of the
Royal Library,
Berlin.

GERHARDT HAUPT-
MANN,
Agnetendorf.

KARL HAUPTMANN,
Schreiberhau.

GUSTAV HELLMANN,
Professor of Meteor-
ology,
Berlin.

WILHELM HERRMANN,
Professor of Protestant
Theology,
Marburg.

ANDREAS HEUSLER,
Professor of Northern
Philology,
Berlin.

ADOLF VON HILDE-
BRAND,
Munich.

LUDWIG HOFFMANN,
City Architect,
Berlin.

ENGELBERT HUMPER-
DINCK,
Berlin.

LEOPOLD GRAF KALCK-
REUTH,
President of the Ger-
man Confederation
of Artists,
Eddelsen.

ARTHUR KAMPF,
Berlin.

FRITZ AUG. V. KAUL-
BACH,
Munich.

MAX KLINGER,
Leipsic.

PAUL LABAND,
*Professor of Jurispru-
dence,*
Strassburg.

MAXIMILIAN LENZ,
Professor of History,
Hamburg.

LUDWIG MANZEL,
*President of the Acad-
emy of Arts,*
Berlin.

SEBASTIAN MERKLE,
*Professor of R. Catho-
lic Theology,*
Wurzburg.

FRIEDRICH NAUMANN,
Berlin.

WILHELM OSTWALD,
Professor of Chemistry,
Leipsic.

ALBERT PLEHN,
Professor of Medicine,
Berlin.

ALOIS RIEHL,
*Professor of Philos-
ophy,*
Berlin.

MAX RUBNER,
Professor of Medicine,
Berlin.

THEODOR KIPP,
*Professor of Jurispru-
dence,*
Berlin.

ALOIS KNOEPFLER,
*Professor of History of
Art,*
Munich.

KARL LAMPRECHT,
Professor of History,
Leipsic.

MAX LIEBERMANN,
Berlin.

JOSEF MAUSBACH,
*Professor of R. Catho-
lic Theology,*
Munster.

EDUARD MEYER,
Professor of History,
Berlin.

ALBERT NEISSER,
Professor of Medicine,
Breslau.

BRUNO PAUL,
*Director of School for
Applied Arts,*
Berlin.

GEORG REICKE,
Berlin.

KARL ROBERT,
*Professor of Archae-
ology,*
Halle.

FRITZ SCHAPER,
Berlin.

FELIX KLEIN,
*Professor of Mathe-
matics,*
Goettingen.

ANTON KOCH,
*Professor of R. Catho-
lic Theology,*
Munster.

PHILIPP LENARD,
Professor of Physics,
Heidelberg.

FRANZ VON LISZT,
*Professor of Jurispru-
dence,*
Berlin.

GEORG VON MAYR,
*Professor of Political
Sciences,*
Munich.

HEINRICH MORF,
*Professor of Roman
Philology,*
Berlin.

WALTER NERNST,
Professor of Physics,
Berlin.

MAX PLANCK,
Professor of Physics,
Berlin.

PROF. MAX REINHARDT,
*Director of the German
Theater,*
Berlin.

WILHELM RÖNTGEN,
Professor of Physics,
Munich.

ADOLF VON SCHLATTER,
*Professor of Protestant
Theology,*
Tübingen.

AUGUST SCHMIDLIN,
*Professor of Sacred
History,*
Munster.

GUSTAV VON SCHMOL-
LER,
*Professor of National
Economy,*
Berlin.

REINHOLD SEEBERG,
*Professor of Protestant
Theology,*
Berlin.

MARTIN SPAHN,
Professor of History,
Strassburg.

FRANZ VON STUCK,
Munich.

HERMANN SUDER-
MANN,
Berlin.

HANS THOMA,
Karlsruhe.

WILHELM TRÜBNER,
Karlsruhe.

KARL VOLLMÖLLER,
Stuttgart.

RICHARD VOSS,
Berchtesgaden.

KARL VOSSLER,
*Professor of Roman
Philology,*
Munich.

SIEGFRIED WAGNER,
Bayreuth.

WILHELM WALDEYER,
Professor of Anatomy,
Berlin.

AUGUST VON WASSER-
MANN,
Professor of Medicine,
Berlin.

FELIX VON WEINGART-
NER

THEODOR WIEGAND,
Museum Director,
Berlin.

WILHELM WIEN,
Professor of Physics,
Wurzburg.

ULRICH VON WILAMO-
WITZ-MOELLENDORFF,
Professor of Philology,
Berlin.

RICHARD WILLSTÄTTER,
Professor of Chemistry,
Berlin.

WILHELM WINDEL-
BAND,
*Professor of Philos-
ophy,*
Heidelberg.

WILHELM WUNDT,
*Professor of Philos-
ophy,*
Leipsic.

38. MEMORANDUM BY DR. KANNER OF A CONVERSATION WITH PROFESSOR SIEPER, JULY 13, 1915[4]

. . . . Dr. Sieper, who at once made a very favorable impression upon me, told me that he had just dictated to his stenographer the

[4] Kanner Papers, I, 17–26. *Germany of Today,* by George Stuart Fullerton, Ph.D., LL.D., professor of philosophy in Columbia University, 1904–17 (The Bobbs-Merrill Co., Indianapolis, 1915), was, however, obviously written by the author himself and not by Dr. Sieper. In his preface, Professor Fullerton states: "In this little volume I have brought together a collection of facts that may easily be verified by anyone who has access to a public library. He who cares to do so may wholly overlook any expressions of opinion which I have permitted myself, and may confine his attention exclusively to the facts adduced. They have been sifted with much care and have been submitted to the criticism of experts. I believe them to be accurate."

translation of a book which he had written upon the request of the Foreign Office. The book was destined for the United States, and was to enlighten the Americans to the fact that Germany really is a democratic state and that their views about Germany are erroneous. He said that this work was not the same sort of propaganda literature which had been used so far and which had done more harm than good. The mistake of the previous propaganda literature had been that Germany had been discussed as if addressing Germans alone, and thereby a very bad impression had been created upon the neutrals. That literature always bragged about our advantages, as we may do amongst ourselves; however, neutrals do not understand such language. The Foreign Office now realized its mistake in issuing that kind of literature and called upon Dr. Sieper to write a different work. Dr. Sieper wrote this book in collaboration with a simon-pure American, Professor Fullerton, who is in Germany as an exchange professor. The real author of the book is Professor Sieper. Professor Fullerton, according to Dr. Sieper, has only given the book an American *niveau*. However, as author is given only Professor Fullerton's name. The book is being published simultaneously in America and in Germany, the English version being by Professor Fullerton in order that the style may be smooth. Of course, the Americans must not find out that the book was written in Germany and by a German, otherwise it would be doomed to failure from the beginning. . . . .

Dr. Sieper describes the conditions in the Foreign Office as being very confused. First of all, the Navy Department goes contrary to the Foreign Office, and *vice versa;* the actions of one are being constantly opposed by the other. Their struggles are frequently reflected in the press. Dr. Sieper says that in this Tirpitz has the edge over Bethmann, because he had an excellently organized press at his command. In the Foreign Office itself different tendencies are exerting themselves. Dr. Sieper says that Bethmann-Hollweg is very weary of the struggle. . . . . Dr. Sieper speaks in very disparaging terms about the inadequate command of the English language that the German statesmen have. He thinks that many misunderstandings between England and Germany, as well as Germany and America, are due to that fact. . . . .

Dr. Sieper was very pessimistic about Germany's economic condition. He thinks there might be danger of financial bankruptcy for Germany after the war. There could be no thought of a war indemnity, and so the enormous costs of the war would have to be paid by increased taxation. . . . .

39. THE *CONTINENTAL TIMES* ACCOUNT OF "THE TRUTH
ABOUT THE GERMAN NATION," FEBRUARY 25, 1916[5]

Partisanship in this war is determined by many factors—by birth, by self-interest, by personal prejudice, ignorance or sentiment. If we would realize how utterly contemptible the human intellect may become during these times of international stress, we need only observe how few are the voices lifted in the camps of the partisans against the prevailing madness, error or iniquity. . . . . The greater credit is therefore due to those men who defend a cause, a people or a principle solely out of their love for objective truth, for abstract justice, or sheer, cold fact. . . . . From the very beginning the German cause and the world-conquering German idea have had few better or more skilful defenders than Professor George Stuart Fullerton. . . . .

"The Truth about the German Nation" is a bold title, and the book, despite its value and accuracy, is written in a style that might almost be called cold were it not redeemed by a deep and simple sincerity. A subdued but luminous intensity may be felt in it, the scholar's desire so to present the truth that not only all men may but that all men *must* believe.

. . . . To many the work will have all the value of a circulation—to all it will bring a clear picture of the inner constitution of a great power now obscured by the clouds and smoke of international fury and misrepresentation. . . . .

Professor Fullerton belongs emphatically to that class of enlightened Americans who are pro-German in their sympathies because they have realized the immense significance of the message which Germany bears to the world—and in particular its value to our own country in its present state of development. These clear-sighted scholars are the wholesome counteracting force against the reactionary and sterile Anglicism of such men as Professor Eliot, bent on bolstering up the crumbling structure of British ideals, theories and traditions, which needed but the shock of war to make plain their inner decay. . . .

[5] *The Continental Times* ("A Journal for Americans in Europe"), No. 1244, February 25, 1916, p. 3.

40. REVOLUTIONARY PROPAGANDA IN THE RUSSIAN ARMY[6]

Imperial German Legation
  Military Attaché

Sofia, February 5, 1915

Military Report No. 64

Attached is a report concerning the inner conditions of Russia in 1915, prepared by Dr. Tranjen, who has been mentioned by me already in previous reports and has in the meantime been bound to the local Imperial Legation for our purposes. He will go immediately to Bucharest in order to work out a program of action with the Russian Revolutionary Committee there.

It is proposed to prepare revolutionary leaflets for circulation in Russia. These will be distributed to the new recruits in order to bring the revolutionary propaganda into the ranks of the fighting army. The sending of emissaries is also envisaged. They will, according to present plans, also be available for military intelligence.

(*Signed*)   Baron von der Goltz
Major and Military Attaché

41. THE NATIONAL GROUPS AND THE IMPERIAL CHANCEL-LOR—MEMORANDUM OF GENERALLANDSCHAFTS-DIREKTOR KAPP—KÖNIGSBERG PR.[7]

Not Intended for Publication

Table of Contents

Königsberg, Prussia, May 1916

[6] Collection of German Military Documents, Hoover War Library.

[7] Collection of German Manuscripts, Hoover War Library.

I. The Fundamental Discontent with the Political Direction in the Best Circles of the German People

The outbreak of the World War forged together a united and combative people. Confidence in the German arms and willingness to bear

The people will fight indefatigably until an advantageous peace is assured.

all burdens became the general battle cry. The war has lasted since then longer than many expected. A hard struggle has strained all our energies. As a result of this, have our unity against the enemy, our self-sacrificing spirit, and our confidence been shattered? Absolutely not! Only small fractions of radical fanatics or unprincipled weaklings stand aside. Certainly there exists a deep desire for peace in the people, certainly there are scoldings and complaints about economic mistakes, but the conviction is almost unanimous that the struggle must be cheerfully continued until an advantageous peace is secured. Indeed the length and severity of the war have resulted in stronger and louder conviction that after all the achieved sacrifices and suffered losses the war must be fought out to a victorious conclusion. Rather bend all our energies to the utmost toward this goal, than suffer ourselves to become enervated prematurely and thus cause all our previous heavy sacrifices to be in vain.

Active discontent and distrust dominate, however, without question the most faithful-minded groups of our people and specifically those

Discord among precisely the most faithful of our people.

who possess the most political instinct or political training; not because they have any doubts regarding the nation, the army, the navy, or the victorious prosecution of the war, but because they are firmly convinced that the political direction which we have in this war, despite its good intention to further the best interests of the country, lacks decision and clearness of will. It is not a question of unity in the prosecution of the war, as many wish to believe; but apprehension prevails that the political direction is not possessed of that energy which pervades the German people.

Although this discontent has been widely disseminated among the people, it remains nevertheless concealed from many eyes. His Majesty

The operation of the censorship.

the Emperor and King is also not informed of the existence and extent of it. Free criticism of our public affairs, which in times of peace is open to everyone by speech and writing, and which moreover is accustomed to reach the ear of the ruler, has been completely suppressed since the outbreak of the war by the censor. Only what is acceptable to the Government, corresponds to their wishes and purposes, is printed in the newspapers, so that there are now really only semi-official newspapers. Nowhere does any room remain for the assertion of one's rights or the expression of differing opinions. The discussion of war-and-peace aims is expressly forbidden by law, which, according to the constant complaint of national circles, is administered less to their advantage than to that of the political radical press such as the *Berliner Tageblatt* and the *Frankfurter Zeitung*. To be sure, a strong censorship is absolutely necessary in a war. Its present administration creates the impression, however, according to the opinion of the two most faithful- and national-minded groups of the people, that it is used less in the service of the cause of the Fatherland, than in personal protection against attacks, which because of their policies in the fields of politics and economics have been directed against the men who at present occupy the leading positions of the state. Thus the prevailing discontent is further strengthened. A people, like the German, which has withstood *Censorship should* so brilliantly and faithfully the struggle for exis- *not be moderated.* tence imposed upon it, has, within the limits which the interest of the Fatherland seems to demand, a justifiable claim to take part through consultation and assistance in the decisions concerning its fate. An understanding government would in this instance be less inclined to stand on its infallibility and omniscience and be rather more liberal- than more narrow-minded.

This is indeed absolutely necessary in order to liberate the powerful but slumbering forces in our people for a great national policy and by *The Government* these means again and again to arouse our high *needs, for the dura-* idealistic ardor, which the Government cannot dis- *tion of a long war, a* pense with if, as a result of the long duration of *public opinion which* the war, the enormous sacrifices of blood and *is supported by uni-* treasure and the severe discomforts and sufferings *versal confidence.* of all sorts are not to cause the longing for peace among the weak and faint-hearted to become ever stronger and thus threaten to weaken the German people's will to victory and to the destruction of the enemy. The war can still last a long time. There exists a great difference between the two tasks: "to defeat the enemy," and "to force the enemy to sue for peace." We have accom- *The enemy has been* plished the first, but not yet the second. We pro- *defeated but has not* fess too much the erroneous belief that the enemy *yet been forced to* has indeed been defeated and therefore must sue *make peace.* for peace. All friends of Germany must do their utmost to destroy this error and to fan anew into flame in the entire nation the holy conviction that the enemy must be fought with all our energy until he is forced to make peace. On that account the Government must rally around it all groups of our people who are inspired by this will. The Government must avoid everything which tends to create in these groups a lack of confidence and well-grounded discontent.

Now, anyone affirming that the prevailing lack of confidence in the people toward the political direction is due to a momentary, in fact an

The discontent is not artificial; confidence in the political direction has been lost.

artificial, agitation, or that it is held essentially by only a few shouters and a misled following, is either unbelievingly unaware of the frame of mind of the widest and most faithful ranks of the people or else deliberately misconstrues the truth. Whoever makes such assurances in the highest places and allows the inference to be drawn that a large part of this sentiment is "made" by a few disgruntled persons, misconstrues the events and negatives the spirit which animates those social ranks which are devoted to the Kaiser and the Empire with all their heart. It is also absolutely wrong to assume that all this is due to the controversy regarding the U-boat war, which has held the foremost place lately. The U-boat question was only the culminating factor which brought to an eruption that which had occupied for some time the hearts of all who felt themselves knit together by the success and destruction of Crown and Fatherland, namely, the feeling, that the political direction, as evidenced previous to and at the outbreak of, the war, and still in the course of the war, is not able to cope with its tasks and that above all it apparently lacks political instinct.

In the face of this, the Chancellor appeals to the necessary unity of the nation, which should stand behind him with confidence. The watch-

The watchword, "Unity."

word "unity" begins to play for us the same unfortunate rôle as did once in 1806 the words "quiet is the citizen's first duty," which is an inglorious memory in the history of Prussia. The "unity" demanded by the Chancellor means: be silent, keep quiet, believe and hope everything, but lock your worries in this greatest, most beautiful, and darkest hour in German history in your breast; wait patiently for whatever will happen; do not disturb the Governmental circles. Theirs, not yours, is the task to determine the history of the Fatherland. The Government alone possesses the necessary insight and perspective of what becomes the Fatherland. It would make a bad impression upon the enemy if disunity came among us.

The Chancellor demands confidence. Does he have a right to it? We do not want to delve into the past too much. However, it has been

A change in Chancellorship would in no way give an impression of weakness.

hard for us from the beginning to have this confidence in the Chancellor who at the opening of this war, and to his own complete surprise, stood helpless before the collapse of that thought which dominated, weighted, and hampered his policy, the thought—upon an impossible paper basis—of reaching an understanding with England. The difficulty of such a confidence was still further enhanced when at the beginning of the war the words of guilt against Belgium escaped the Chancellor's lips and when by so doing, as he admits himself today, he deprived himself of freedom of decision as regards the fate of Belgium. No injustice happened to Belgium. Belgium has herself caused and deserved her fate, as was soon afterwards shown by our Government. However, our confidence in the

The illusion of an understanding with England kept alive even during the war.
Chancellor stood the severest trial when we were involuntarily impressed with the fact that the illusion of an understanding with England unfortunately dominated our policy even during the war. And that in spite of the fact that this illusion collapsed so miserably at the beginning of the war and—what is more—that between our arch-enemy England and ourselves weapons alone should speak.

Everyone may fail at times; but a leading statesman who in an eventful time has committed a mistake, who, moreover, even today lacks

The inability of the present political direction to conclude a good peace.
a clear understanding of the necessary war aims, who does not determine political events but on the contrary allows himself, through the force of circumstances which are independent of his will, to be forced to embarrassing decisions, such a man, if he had political sense, should have realized the inadequacy of his powers of statesmanship and should have told himself that he is not the man who can speak with the defeated enemy.

Bismarck has stabilized German authority in the sphere of foreign policy to such a degree that, in spite of what has happened in the past, we would be willing today to forgive the political direction, to acknowledge its greater insight which it so often claims for itself, and to follow it confidently upon roads which to us seem incorrect. Readily would the German consent to be led in this great war, even at the sacrifice of his own favored dreams, by a Government which pursues its aim decisively. The happenings of the last weeks, however, make that impossible for the national circles. More and more they find their worst fears confirmed.

It is a misconstruing of facts when the national groups are being

The distrust is based not upon rumors but upon facts.
accused of hurling unfounded accusations, which are founded upon pure rumors. There can be no talk of rumors, for the facts are before the eyes of everyone who can see and wants to see. We wish solely to let the facts speak and presently to call attention to the course of the U-boat warfare.

II. America and Our Government

A twelvemonth has the German nation—always put off with empty hopes—been waiting for the energetic use of this decisive weapon. But

Retreat all along the line before America.

in vain. The German nation does no longer believe the assurances of the political leadership that the imperative thing is not indecision, rather the sober weighing of all motives which come into consideration. Now it has recognized that it is not courage but vacillation which for more than a year has not made use of this weapon, but has again and again hampered its use. In the so eagerly awaited German answer to "the last word" of Wilson, our political leadership has retreated all along the line. America has actually achieved what it wanted to achieve for England. For now the rules of cruiser warfare will also be applied to the U-boat warfare in the English war area, owing to the latest German promises. Yet if this new U-boat weapon be used effectively, these rules are not at all suitable. In a war where our very existence is at stake, in which everything that international law was—protection of private property

Germany's renunciation of the sole weapon against England.

and of unarmed persons—was torn to pieces long ago, in which the rights of neutrals under the leadership of England have been brutally violated by our enemies, are we to refrain from the effective use of the sole weapon which we have against our arch-enemy, just because there is no written international law for it? And that in truth, only because our enemies do not have that weapon of defense; yet it is a weapon which we cannot sacrifice. Where powerful pride alone and fearless energy would have been able

Sacrifice of our national prestige.

to bring the only solution suitable to German honor, we retreat under the sacrifice of our national prestige in inglorious indecision before America. The United States has given up its neutrality long ago and, as a secret ally of England, does not want an understanding commensurable with our legitimate interests but wishes complete submission to humiliating demands which it asserts with an imperious mien. This fact is not the least altered by reservations, for the assertion of which, as before, we will not have stamina; is also not changed by the timid protests of the German answer to the impudent interferences of America and our declared enemies.

With arrogant pride the American Government accepts the German promises concerning the question of the U-boat policy as something

The insulting note of America is submissively accepted.

self-evident. However, it at the same time in a challenging answer insultingly rejects the German claim that America, in acknowledgment of the German accommodation, henceforth summon England to observe the commonly accepted principles of international law. And although the German Government, in its Note of May 4, 1916, in case of nonfulfilment of its claims establishes the existence of a new state of affairs "for which it reserves for itself full freedom of decision," it accepts the unequivocal rejection in the American answer apparently without any further protestations.

Can the German people have further confidence in a political leadership which has so far sacrificed German honor? The weakness which is so apparent in our conduct of war against England as well as in our attitude toward America has caused us incalculable damage in the entire world, and that in spite of all our victories on land. "The spirit of conciliation," and the "sober consideration of pertinent factors," and the appeal to "Germany's might," these and other points of view which were extolled by proponents of an understanding with America, in truth only veil our defeat. It might be said that in this connection only one sentiment prevails in the entire German nation: the sentiment that the limits to retreat which are drawn by our honor have finally been overstepped. The entire nation has decided not to advance any longer along this road; it refuses to follow, if it is presumed that it will stand any more insults to the country's honor.

The nation is determined not to advance any longer along this road.

Just a while ago it was said: we won't let this precious weapon be wrung from our hands. The end of it is: we suffer this weapon to be seized from our hands. Will it not be easy now for America, through the repetition of its threats, to wrest from us everything that has been achieved with such sacrifice of blood and goods, so that in the end we shall be left impoverished and deprived of all our successes? That and nothing else would be essentially the result of American peace intervention, upon which many base their idle hopes. It started with little weaknesses, it has ended with the greatest. The world must believe that Germany, although victorious on all fronts, although financially stronger than all her foes, although powerful and determined to succeed also in the economic war, for unknown reasons, perhaps, has lost her nerve, and is compelled to give up. What fools our enemies would be—and the present American Government belongs to our enemies—if they did not threaten us with the danger of war with the tenth enemy, for they firmly believe that if the war continues long enough victorious Germany will have to surrender. Instead of showing cool firmness, our political direction constantly swings to and fro between strong words which it does not follow up with deeds. And it is this unintelligible and weak position of our Government which prolongs the war, which sacrifices human lives and

America has wrested from us the U-boat weapon.

We do not need to fear a war with America.

billions of material goods, until the moment when all this enormous expense will be futile. What can America do to us if it really comes to a break?

The loss of German ships, totaling 600,000 tons, which are in American harbors and those of her colonies, together with, as we are being

Loss of German tonnage.

told, the 500,000 tons which are to be found in South American and other American harbors, is not, regrettable as it may be, of significance in the struggle against English tonnage nor for the outcome of the war.

At any rate it does not matter when our national honor is at stake. In this war of unprecedented dimensions, which will decide our position as a world power, only decisive factors may determine our policy. Complications and unpleasantness are in the wake of every great, responsible step. To achieve victory they must be taken into the bargain. Everything else is immaterial. Our future depends upon victory.

Our Department of Foreign Affairs itself does not seriously believe that Holland and Denmark, in case of a breach with the United States,

Effect of a break with America upon neutrals.

would be active against us. The importance of imports from these countries is being overestimated; much more important is the food policy in the interior, which, if sensibly conducted, would enable us to hold out economically. However, as that policy is being handled at present it might force us under certain circumstances to conclude a premature peace. Life and death really do not depend upon the Dutch-Danish imports. It is clear, however, that in case of a somewhat effective U-boat war the two countries would be almost forced to increase trade with us.

The American question is not decisive for Rumania, but on the contrary, the military position in the East. The newest development in the Balkans has already brought it about that Rumania, for good or evil, has to range herself somehow with us. And that will be the case especially, if Russian successes do not materialize. If the American Government can, unpunished, treat the German Empire on the same footing as an exotic Negro Republic, that will influence Rumania and other neutrals more unfavorably than if, in guarding our national prestige, we had let it come to a break with America.

The much-feared financial support cannot help our enemies. If our U-boats blockade England, then American money can buy for her

America's capital against us.

neither foodstuffs and raw materials nor munitions. Whether or not American money will flow to our enemies to the extent predicted by the "understanding politicians" is at least questionable. And such a support has, for our opponents, an unpleasant side to it too; for certainly the money is not being donated.

The manufacture of munitions for the Allies will hardly be increased through the entrance of America into the war. The future, then, is replete with possibilities which will compel America for the time being to take care of herself. And as far as that is concerned, our highest military command need not be worried much about increased shipments of munitions to the Allies. Certainly, it will not be the deciding factor. Yet upon the decision of the U-boat question everything now depends.

The shipment of troops would only further increase the tonnage shortage of England. Already out of the total of 17,800,000 registered English tons, 5,300,000 tons, that is, about a third, *Dispatch of Ameri-* are being used by the navy. If we consider only *can troops to the* the 8,000,000 tons which alone really come into *English front.* consideration for trade along European routes, then the percentage which is continually used for war purposes is still further increased. Under such circumstances, should America have to make increased claims upon English ships, it might even become an ally dangerous for England. Finally, in a land that does not know compulsory military service and which commands only a small standing army it is not so simple to raise troops. Before such assistance can be rendered, the war in Europe, if we are only willing to use our weapons unscrupulously, must be over. Not the last piece of gold but the last piece of bread in England will determine the war!

The honor and the future of Germany are closely inter-related. It is a dangerous error to believe that England and America any longer are two different concepts to us. If we wish to main-*Solidarity of Amer-* tain ourselves against them, we must face both of *ica and England.* them in the present struggle. The American Government wishes our defeat and England's victory, and we cannot count upon its good wishes if we want to secure a decisive success over England. The Chancellor's abandonment of the U-boat warfare leaves only two possibilities open: either he knows a different means of defeating England, which, of course, is not the case; or the Chancellor himself knows that neither war to exhaustion nor victory on land are able to give us a real victory over England. Logically, *Chancellor does not* therefore, the only thing remaining is that the *believe in victory* Chancellor forego this success and continue to *over England; he* fool himself with the illusion that England will *will not gain it.* agree to a useful understanding. This is the crux of the problem: The Chancellor does not believe in the victory over England, and therefore he will not gain it.

Has the German Government found the courage, or will it find the courage, after Lansing has refused any negotiations whatsoever with England regarding its observation of the rules of international law, to take back its concessions concerning the use of the U-boats? We give up the hope that that will happen. The way the Chancellor has trans-

The freedom of action reserved by the German Government.

lated his words into action on previous occasions shows that he will not ask anyone to believe in the freedom of action which he reserves for himself. And it did not take long to be announced officially that it was not supposition but expectation which caused the German concessions regarding the U-boat to be made. And thereby the reservation made is stripped of every legal significance. We find ourselves now in the unpleasant position that any inadvertent torpedoing, which is unavoidable by the very nature of the U-boat weapon, will either bring us new humiliations or will bring us to war with the United States under circumstances which will formally place us in the wrong position.

How did it happen that we suffered ourselves to get maneuvered into such an unfavorable position with respect to America?

III. The Chancellor's Attitude toward the U-Boat Question

When in February 1915 Germany declared the waters around England a war area, with the intention of employing the U-boats inconsider-

For a year we have been retreating step by step before America.

ately and of keeping England from the sea, before the protest of America the German Government soon retreated. It is clear now, from the American Sussex Note, that the American Government from the very first day was of the opinion that the use of the U-boats, because of the character of the ships employed and the methods of attack necessitated by their use, was irreconcilable with what the American Government calls the "fundamental precepts of humanity embodied in international law." Instead of proudly calling attention to the new right of the new weapon, instead of on her part protesting against the ignominious and the war-prolonging munitions- and arms-trade of the United States of America, so contrary to all precepts of humanity, the German Government submissively promised to restrict the U-boat war. And at each sinking of a ship it gave an expression of regret, with new promises which could not be observed because their observance is physically impossible if the U-boat weapon

Now we face the danger of a war or the heavy sacrifice of our honor.

is to be used as it should be and as our interests and the peculiarities of the weapon dictate that it should be. Even if in consideration of Bulgaria a giving-in was necessary, it was imperative from the beginning, for the eventuality of a German victory in the Balkans, to pave the way for a return to the full use of this weapon. Instead of that—new promises. Thus the German Government has formally placed herself in the wrong and through constant giving-in has put herself and the American Government in a position which must end either in war or in a heavy sacrifice of our honor and prestige.

This failure with America will necessarily undermine the people's confidence in the wisdom of our political leadership. But even prior to this its priggish tactics had been enough to arouse even the most sluggish. At first, by way of re-capitulation, the memorial of February 8, 1916, was intended to create the impression that the in-tensification of the U-boat war so long expected had actually taken place. Whoever questioned that the content of the memorial had anything to do with such an intensification was branded as being unpatriotic. Gradually the truth leaked out that really the intensive U-boat warfare was not being waged any more. Then the tactics changed. Whereas the representative of the highest military leadership, in a regular press conference, declared it a lie that the U-boat warfare should not be waged with all energy, and that political considerations in any way played a part in this purely military question, the Chancellor told the press representatives that there were political as well as military considerations which prevented the sharp use of the U-boats. It may be that this divergent presentation of the U-boat question was due to the divergent opinion on the part of the military authorities. But was the whole occurrence conducive to the creation of confidence? And indeed it did not deserve confidence, as the succeeding developments show. After political and military considerations had been advanced in unintelligible combinations, the following motivation was finally victorious: of course the political leadership would, without any sentimentality, favor an inconsiderate application of the U-boat weapon if only there was an assurance of a decisive success; unfortunately, such a prerequisite did not exist. This opinion naturally became audible only after the retirement of Admiral von Tirpitz and Admiral von Capelle had taken place.

The memorial of February 8, 1916; misleading the people about the weakened U-boat war.

Supposed ineffectiveness of the U-boat war.

Indeed, the only method by which a justification for the omission of a vigorous U-boat warfare could be gained was by the assertion of its probable ineffectiveness. For it is impossible that considerations for neutrals could have been the deciding factors when it was certain that by means of a sharp U-boat war a decisive military success could be secured against England.

Who then had to answer this decisive military question?

Certainly not the political leadership! It has only aroused lively astonishment that the Chancellor deemed it right to make full military declarations of a very doubtful sort and pronounce purely military judgments about the conduct and success of the U-boats to irresponsible representatives of the press.

The deciding voice in this question rested solely with the responsible navy men—the Chief of the Admiralty Staff and the Secretary of

The two competent authorities decided in favor of an inconsiderate U-boat war.

the Navy Department—while the Chief of the Navy Cabinet does not belong there at all. That Admiral von Tirpitz, on the basis of his nearly twenty years' experience as leader of the Imperial Navy Department and as the creator of our navy and our U-boat weapon, and with his accurate knowledge of its material and foundation, was of the opinion that by means of a rigorous U-boat war a decisive success against England could be scored, is certain. It is equally well known today that he was not invited to the deciding consultations in March of this year, whereas precisely the question as to the number and kind of U-boats available, a question touching immediately upon his province, should have been the basis of every decision. The Admiralty Staff, the other responsible and competent board of the navy, has—that is equally certain—also expressed the same opinion that through the U-boat warfare a decisive victory over England could be achieved in six months at most. Not known, but for that matter unimportant, is whether the Chief of the Admiralty Staff in the last minute gave in for political reasons, which allegedly did not play any rôle at all. The deciding fact is this: the two responsible military authorities have given the decided opinion that a complete success could be expected with certainty from a sharp U-boat campaign.

What considerations and what kind of material were the basis of this supposition naturally is not known to us in detail and does not need

Facts that speak for the effectiveness of the U-boat weapon.

further discussion, for not our judgment of that is significant but the judgment of the responsible authorities. Besides, restraint in this respect is advisable. However, in connection with U-boat proposals in the Reichstag, there have been given in the Ways and Means Committee before two hundred persons detailed disclosures concerning the number and kind of U-boats, which disclosures naturally and deplorably have by now started their journey through the German and probably also foreign publicity in the most varied forms. It will therefore be permissible, on the basis of the commonly known facts, to offset by means of a few statements the misrepresentations current in the public:

1. It is a fact that today we have appreciably more capable U-boats than a year ago—thanks to the energetic organization and concentration of the building activity during the war.

2. It is certain that each month, thanks to the same fact, brings extraordinary growth of first-class material.

3. It is a distortion of the actual situation if, in juxtaposition to the available U-boats, the boats in the Mediterranean, the Baltic, and other places are not counted in; for it is evident that the basis of success is concentration of forces, and that only those detachments which are absolutely necessary should be maintained.

4. It is a falsehood that the temporary small boats, through the building of which a rapid increase and some portable material was to be achieved, are not serviceable. On the contrary, they perform very good services off Flanders and a few other stations.

5. It is an offense against the truth to say that besides a few big boats we have only these small ones of lesser value. For in truth at present we have developed, besides numerous big boats and the above-named small ones, the construction of which is discontinued, an extraordinarily useful middle type, armed with torpedoes and artillery, and of large cruising radius. A large number of this type are under construction.

6. It is a falsehood to assert that the U-boat war of 1915 had shown the impossibility of achieving a decisive success. For the political direction has actually from the first day heavily hampered its being carried out. Gradually it made the U-boat war entirely impossible.

What extraordinary effect, however, can be expected from a sharp U-boat war, is shown by the considerable results of the restricted U-boat war of April 1916, even if the results stand by 225,000 tons below a decisive effect. But then that is precisely due to the restriction of the use of the weapon. Were these restrictions to fall and a concentrated sharp U-boat war to be conducted against England, a triple increase of the present results, soon even a crushing effect, could be achieved, according to authentic calculations.

7. Justice is not done to all the results of a rigorous U-boat war, if one merely calculates the number of tons, the destruction of which in definite periods may be assumed, and then contrasts this number with the remaining tonnage. For, first of all, in that way the decisive psychological factor is being overlooked. The expected effective working of the U-boat war would create such an uncertainty that all continued sea intercourse would be hampered to a much greater extent than the calculated loss of tonnage indicates. Besides, the above-mentioned mechanical conception entirely disregards the fact that even the purely numerical reduction of tonnage would surely mean an intolerable injury to the economic life of England, above all, through the reduction of imports, and an injury to England's financial strength through the reduction of her exports. It must never be forgotten that for Germany sea trade is only one important phase, whereas for England it is the life nerve.

But, as was said, our main point is that the Chancellor again and again refused a sharp U-boat war, although the only two competent military authorities definitely assured him of success against England. The lamentable result remains that we renounced the application of the sharpest weapon against England. The Chancellor allowed political considerations to win over the military points of view, either under extortionate pressure from the American Government or because he held his own military views to be more appropriate than those of experts—in so far as he allowed the latter to say anything.

The Chancellor brought about a restriction of the U-boat war because of political reasons.

IV. The War Aims of the Chancellor

The retreat before America and the renouncing of the U-boat weapon is more than a marine-strategic incident. It is the renunciation of the victory over England and is an evil omen for the coming peace negotiations. It could indeed be a prelude to surrender of territories and a general retreat. Of what use is it then still to talk about war aims and, looking East and West, to weigh the German conquests? Upon the embarked route not even that goal can be reached which hovers constantly before the Chancellor. For the rest, in the delimitations which the Chancellor has set to his aims in the West, there is the same submissiveness toward England which exists in his attitude toward the U-boat question and which we refuse to accept. And for the following reasons: first, because we firmly believe in victory; and, second, because we know that our future depends upon it and therefore we must achieve more than the Chancellor has set as his aim.

Renunciation of victory over England.

The Chancellor's war aims in the West.

The Chancellor has spoken with entire clearness that Belgium, which earlier he had indicated as a pledge in hand, will be surrendered—although only in return for real guaranties, so that it will not become again an outpost of our enemies—but surrendered, and that is the deciding thing! In the future too there shall exist a Belgium alongside of us. That is an impossible result if we weigh the losses of this war and wish to continue the increasingly difficult struggle with the Anglo-Saxons. The guaranties demanded by the Chancellor, even if they be "real," cannot in this respect help us at all. For he has in view only negative guaranties against the plans of our enemies. What we, however, need are positive guaranties for our future development as a world power. We can obtain such guaranties, however, only if we do not deliver Belgium but under some form, above all by the retention of the

coast, take her under political, economic, and military control. That is
exactly what the Chancellor does not want. In England, then, his
declarations have found an immediate echo which must fill all patriots
with anxiety. The danger of a foul peace with England, which indeed
can be the only possible result of the described procedure, is in the immediate future.

The Chancellor has not spoken about France. We wish, therefore,
to omit it and will only briefly discuss the East.

As for the East the Chancellor has wished to indicate far-reaching
aims which would satisfy the national elements. But he did not succeed
in this, since here too, we fear, he was not clear
The Chancellor's war aims in the East. himself concerning what our interests demand.
With the exception of the negative boundary
guaranties, he has presented as his aim only the
liberation from the Tsarist yoke of all the non-Russians between the
Baltic and the Volhynian marshes as well as that of giving the Poles a
new and better future, as had been indicated by him before.

With these war aims we Germans have nothing to do. We do not
fight for the Poles or for other foreigners. We do not fight against the
Russian reaction. We fight against the Russian
The Chancellor's war aims are not worth the sacrifices. danger to our country and for the safeguarding
of the future of our nation. The declaration of
the Chancellor was intended primarily for foreign
consumption and for others like the incorrigible Democrats who confuse
domestic politics with the conduct of the war, but it will convince
neither group that we are shedding our blood for something else. The
territorial changes which we want to secure in the East must be adjusted
to our interests alone, and in the Chancellor's sketching we are not able
to see the safeguarding of even these interests.

V. THE WRONG FOOD POLICY OF THE GOVERNMENT

The same indecision and weakness which governs our foreign policy
shows itself also in our inner state life. That is apparent especially in
the question of feeding the people. Here it is the
Indecision of the po- litical direction in re- gard to food policy. fear of the great mass of consumers in the large
cities and industrial centers which has driven
the Government into a most ungratifying State-
Socialism. The fixing of prices is not left any longer to the economic laws of supply and demand, but out of a misunderstood hu-
manitarianism, the justifiable interests, according
State-Socialism for fear of the masses. to social points of view, of the producers are
set aside and prices are fixed by administrators.
In the same way the distribution of foodstuffs is no longer left to

trade, the natural distributor between food production and food consumption, but is carried out by bureaucratic organizations.

The result of this highly questionable State-Socialism in the field
of foodstuff provisioning is a serious endangering of the people's feeding. Even if, owing to good weather conditions
and the expected good crop, the need of foodstuffs is lessened, it will be only a passing relief.
By a further pursuing of the hitherto prevailing
principles the old need will make itself felt again
with the advancing of the season and the gradual exhaustion of the supplies. Through it our inner power of resistance is being threatened and
the blind, thoughtless yearning for peace by governing and governed is
continually being nourished, so that in the end, whether we wish it or
not, we shall be forced to a premature peace.

*The result is thought-
less yearning for
peace among governing
and governed alike.*

This danger and want in the matter of feeding the people need not
be; it is artificially brought about. It has been possible to destroy all
the thousands and thousands of age-old natural
relationships which bind together producer and
consumer, as well as the surplus-producing provinces on one side and the thickly populated industrial regions like the Rhineland, Saxony, and the
large cities on the other side. In short, one has put aside big business
and divided Germany into a large number of isolated states, separated
by means of duty barriers, which one laboriously tries to unite by artificial means from the center. But what is worse still is that even small
business has been killed. Broken are the innumerable short connections which lead back and forth between city and country, between
producing and consuming ranks. Without these boundless, numerous
connections the millions in the cities cannot be nourished. That which
is supposed to take the place of free trade, the bureaucratic, public
provisioning through state institutions, syndicates, etc., cannot do justice
to even one-third of this necessary work. Because of that an artificial
need is at our door, for free trade even today would be able to solve
the problem.

*This want is pro-
duced artificially by
the exclusion of
free trade.*

This policy arises out of a confused State-Socialism, which believes
it is able to do everything through public service. To our nation's great
disadvantage this problem will bankrupt it, and after the war investigations will have to be made in order to determine how much destruction
and rotting of foodstuffs, and how many expenditures were caused by
this provisioning of the people out of public funds.

The basis of this policy is a false economic conception of trade
which, unfortunately, has its inception in the German higher institutions
of learning. It holds the speculative earnings of trade to be usury and
believes that it has to protect the nation against them. It therefore

believes that it has to eliminate the usurious middleman. In truth, honest trade is thereby eliminated while usury proper alone retains the field. Such a view arises also out of a perverted conception of the natural laws of price-fixing. As if bureaucratic arbitrary action were empowered to fix the price, and as if the free will of usury could be combated by the law of the state! This policy started with the idea that the hideous worm of war usury had to be combated. But it happened as with many other things—one achieves exactly the opposite of what one wants. At the present time usury is flourishing more than ever. That is due to this: the sole successful enemy of usury is honest, free competition of the many small retail dealers in the open market. If they are excluded, then the dishonest usurer, who circumvents all laws, has the field to himself, the more so since the authorities never succeed in entirely dispensing with the big trader. The surest means of combating usury are, then, not maximum prices and public distribution—that we ought to have learned by this time—but an open market, dependable inventories, and abundant competition. By means of the arbitrary fixing of maximum prices one actually achieves only a complete disorganization of the natural system of prices which is the regulating power of pro-

That slogan, "Organization." duction as well as of distribution. With true childish self-praise they call it "German Organization," and it really is the most complete disorganization and disarrangement of the market that has been achieved with this system of maximum prices.

Besides this they fear that "the prices will run away," that the rich will snatch away foodstuffs from the poor. In truth that is a super-

Fear of exorbitant prices. stition. For to do that the rich would have to eat twenty times more than they can stand. All these measures spring from the fear of the masses and their prejudices. They wish to please the masses, and yet by these very wrong measures that have been imposed they bring the people to the

Fear of favoring the rich. verge of starvation. The abominable queue standing on the streets which deprives the poor women of their time and strength, and which in time must bitterly antagonize the nation, is a necessary result of this system of artificial price-fixing. Truly, the nation pays dearly for the maximum-priced goods.

Therefore one has to fear that the hour will soon arrive when the nation will turn against its false friends in justified wrath. In reality

Policy of a bureaucracy. it is the policy of petty officialdom, so short-sighted, as the insight of petty officials in the intricacies of political economy usually is; because they have never traded, they do not know what an indispensable rôle trade plays in political economy.

Unfortunately, this fundamentally wrong policy not only harms trade but—and that is by far the greater damage—it also hampers production.

Damage to production. The idea has been spread that Germany has been in a stage of siege and has had to manage its household accordingly. That might have been barely true in the first year of the war, as long as we had to manage on the existing stores of the first crop. But as soon as we approached the second harvest it should have been the extreme endeavor to raise production to the highest possible degree. This should have succeeded and would have provided from crop to crop for the needs of the German nation on the area at our disposal. God had decided to send us a new affliction through the crop failure in grain and fodder in 1915. However, it should have been our duty to exert all our forces of production, whereby the nation can aid powerfully if it submits to the necessary price increases. With the help of our great potato and beet production we could, to a large degree at least, replace imported foods. And with a little saving in consumption on the part of the whole nation, which could have been achieved by raising the whole price-range, the provisioning of the nation from crop to crop could have been improved and safeguarded to an increasing degree if only production and trade had been given the necessary freedom.

Instead of that, the State-Socialists succeed in introducing on every farm and estate a kind of forced management, and do not see that *Forced management on the farms.* thereby they hinder production. The farmer does not understand and tolerate this system of maximum prices, of expropriations and supervisions; he feels that along this road in the end he will be made the slave of the city consumer. The prohibition of domestic slaughter which prohibits *Prohibition of home slaughter the acme of insanity.* the hard-working men and the laboring women from slaughtering the product of their labor for their own use, is the acme of insanity. It is an unbearable vexation, the heavy consequences of which cannot be comprehended by the narrow-minded, paid officials in the cities.

It is high time that a fundamental change of system be undertaken in our food-provision policy; if not, calamity will result. It is possible even today, solely through the freeing of the natural trade forces and production, to exorcise the threatening ghost of want in the cities, because this want is an artificial one, created by the faulty policy of the Imperial Government.

The danger exists now, after the need has been recognized, that there must be a continuation of the forced regulations of our economic life. They even clamor for a general as economic dictator! They believe that one can and must arrange the economic life of the nation in a manner

similar to the provisioning of the army in order to bring army and nation within one great military organization. That
*The new economic
dictator.* is an exceedingly dangerous error. The provisioning of the army in war is dependent entirely upon
an existing free national economy, which can give something and which
continually reproduces anew. The provisioning of the army in war by
a strong executive power cannot be managed otherwise than where
there is plenty. At all past times it was a freely
*National economy
organized like
military provisioning
system.* managing nation which had to maintain the war.
Were one to dissolve the free economic life of the
nation into the army provisioning system, then
the war strength of the nation would soon be
crippled. For every public management, if it goes beyond its limits,
squanders; the greater it is, the more it resembles a horseman who, if
he is too heavy, smothers his beast of burden, the nation.

We really need an economic dictator, but not one who out of his own
head wishes to dictate all the movements of national economy—there is
no such man, even if he be a superman—rather
*Necessity of freeing
the national economy.* we need an economic dictator, who has the power
of conviction to counteract the boasting State-
Socialism of today, one who can come forth as the liberator of the
economic life, and who, with a few necessary exceptions, tears down
the heap of regulations in order that the producing ranks may again
produce and the consuming ranks may obtain something.

That of course cannot be done with one jerk; rather it will be
necessary to retreat from one article to another along the way we have
come. The beginning will have to be made where
*Gradual retreat
to free trade.* the need is greatest, for example, with meat and
milk. One will soon notice that thereby one will
be ready to follow a law which is rooted in fact. It is possible to
erect for the care and solicitude of free trade a scale of products,
according to their necessity. Milk, for example, because it *is* so perishable, needs very close care, which only the small interested party can
give. Meat is equally perishable. Its useful quality is dependent to a
large degree upon its treatment. . . . . The provisioning of potatoes too
is defective, because it is handled by public officials and because they
always work by schematization. . . . .

With free trade goes the free fixing of prices. The laws for expropriations, public distribution, and maximum prices will have to be
abolished for each article the circulation of which
*The effect of free
trade upon the
fixing of prices.* is to be re-established. It will then be necessary,
in order to meet the prevailing fear and prejudice,
that the producer and seller shall be able, by
means of keeping the goods off the market, to raise price levels at will.

Probably the plagued consumer might give up that prejudice as soon as he learns how compulsory fixing of prices of such articles as meat and milk have driven them entirely off the market. He will now be glad that they are again on the market, even if at higher prices. . . . .

If this road be followed, we shall live to see milk and butter in the cities and to watch the meat markets open again. Then there cannot be any more talk about real want. Of course the prices will be high for the time being, but very soon they will drop. All well-earning circles of the German nation, especially also the hard-laboring ones, will be able to pay these prices. On the other hand, the height of the prices as determined by free trade will exert a saving influence in domestic economy which is indispensable for surviving through the war. For

Public and private aid to those who need.

those who cannot pay these prices the support of the community and free philanthropy will provide necessities, and with less expense than under the present system because the enormous number of officials will decline. It will be found that the number actually to be supported will be surprisingly small. Already the doing away with the queue-standing will give incalculable economic advantage by saving time for the women and mothers. Besides that it will be a moral and political benefit. If we get a good crop, the milk and hog production will rise. The small producers, if they are secure from price-fixing and see profitable prices offered, will eagerly raise goats, hogs, and chickens. In short, the blessings of free trade, as in peace times, which we in the confusion of the war and misled by a false national economy misunderstood and did not observe, will slowly reappear. . . . .

As far as grains and flour are concerned, as already told, the return to free trade is not so urgent. But here, too, it will be profitable to give up the system of expropriation and price-fixing during the next economic year and, following the example of Frederick the Great as well as the fundamentals of Kanitz's proposal, to establish a system of warehouses which will safeguard the needs of the army and the monthly reserves for the civil population and at the same time stabilize the prices from one harvest to another.

Certainly, it remains always wrong, if the foreign policy is being determined by the food-provisioning policy, so that the success of the

A wrong food policy may force Germany to a premature and unsatisfactory peace.

war and victory efforts cannot be awaited without fear. The nation will have to suffer through decades for a premature and timid peace. But it would be an immeasurable disaster if the mistakes of the food policy should be disclosed and if these should be responsible for such a premature peace. Then, to be brief and sharp, it would be our own Government which in the end forced us to peace through starvation. Therefore, let us change this policy ere it is too late. As yet there is time! When the nation sees that the need will be less from week to week under a better policy, it will cast aside all narrow prejudices, will again take courage, and will be ready to follow a strong government to a final victory.

The moment has come when that has to happen. The new harvest approaches and before it is here all farmers and honest butchers and *The food policy must be changed prior to the next harvest.* dairymen—90 per cent of whose businesses are closed—must be assured beyond doubt that the time of the naïve persecution of honest trade is past, and that again they may count on the product of their labor. The safeguarding of the right food-provisioning is at present a problem which for the outcome of the war is almost more important than the taking of Verdun. If we pursue as devastating an economic policy as before, we shall soon have to seek peace, and exactly then our enemies will refuse it, because they will see that we constantly grow weaker. All victories of arms will then be of *We must prepare for an indefinite period; thereby we shall force the conclusion of peace.* no avail. On the contrary, if we adopt a better economic policy, bettering our provisioning with each harvest so that we shall not be forced at all to conclude a peace on account of hunger, in short, if we arrange ourselves for an indefinite period of war, we shall have peace the quicker and shall be the victors. A compulsory state management, such as we have carried on so far, would have been possible for the duration of a short war and without the pernicious effects that we observe at present. But the longer the war lasts the more we approach a condition in which the same economic laws demand attention as they do in peace times.

VI. The True Problems of a Strong Government

These are the five main causes of the present distrust, in large and devoted circles of the nation, of the political leadership:

Reasons why the people cannot have confidence in the political leadership. 1. The renunciation of the application of a weapon against England which the responsible experts declared as absolutely successful, and therewith the renunciation of the victory over England.

2. The prolonging of the war by not using the weapons in our hands, rather, through negotiations and surrender of our honor, by allowing ourselves to be drawn into an ever more unfavorable position.

3. In the midst of the war and even the beginning of negotiations, an already publicly announced willingness to surrender Belgium upon

negative guaranties and therewith the renunciation of the absolutely necessary strengthening of our position.

4. The setting up of war aims in the East which are not adjusted to our military, economic, and national interests but which in an unintelligent way, by implicating internal political considerations, place before us as our object the liberation of foreigners.

5. The complete breakdown of our food policy and the resulting compulsion, in spite of all our military successes, to conclude a premature and unsatisfactory peace.

The Chancellor, as solely responsible for the hitherto prevailing policy, under such conditions cannot count any longer upon the confidence of the national elements. He also has no right formally to claim this confidence just because at the moment he represents the political leadership. For not "unity" as such has value, but only the unity which stands behind a firm, clear will as support and mainstay.

A determined political leadership would even today have behind it more than ever a united, self-sacrificing nation. Whoever today believes *Even today the nation would follow enthusiastically a strong political leadership.* in the political leadership does so out of ignorance of the situation and current happenings, or else for political reasons, or out of the too weak, natural disinclination to make great decisions. A clear and firm political leadership, however, would find for its great aims and responsible decisions a mighty response and a strong mainstay in the oppressed hearts of the best of the Fatherland. And in the entire nation, which really longs for such leadership, it would find an irresistible, sure-of-victory, fellow combatant. Under the existing conditions the economic wants operate with a double heaviness and lead to an increasing estrangement which would recede into the background if the Government would rise to an energetic foreign and domestic policy; the mutual depression and the depression against the political leadership would result in exasperation solely against the enemy. Today the monarchy, to which the nation rallied willingly at the outbreak of the war, is drawn into the vortex of the day's struggle. And this through the guilt of the political leadership which, although it alone and solely was being attacked, tried to use the Kaiser's powers as commander as a shield in the U-boat matter, and in its turn suspected honest and devoted patriots of wishing to interfere with the Kaiser's inalienable rights.

Danger to the monarchy from a foul peace. According to Article II of the Imperial Constitution the Kaiser must conclude the peace. In exercising this personal prerogative our Imperial Master acts simultaneously as counsel for the entire German nation. Our brave nation, which in this struggle for its national existence has borne incomparable sacrifices with never-wanting, self-denying inspiration, expects the most of this peace. It dares not be deprived of the reward for these sacrifices. It has a valid claim to the magnificence whose development is opened by the victories of our arms. Should it be disappointed in its lofty expectations, the destructive results to our internal political life and their reaction upon the Reich's foreign policy would be enormous. An irremediable reduction of the Kaiser's position and with it a weakening of the prestige of the Government would take place which would immensely strengthen the parliament and would endanger the future of the German Empire. The flaming national enthusiasm, which in these great days of mutual need has so powerfully affected the whole German nation, would disappear powerless and useless in the sand. Internally and externally the Empire idea would suffer great injury.

On the other hand, the more glorious the peace the higher the price of victory for all the sacrifices of the Fatherland, the freer and mightier the development of the German nation. A strong, *Enhancement of the* popular Empire of highest splendor will arise *Kaiser's prestige* which will empower Germany to the greatest *through a splendid* political, economic, and cultural productivity. In *peace.* this expected powerful national development our nation will surpass itself, will grow with its historically destined purposes in inner maturity and political insight. Quarreling and discord in the interior will cease, and in self-sacrificing surrender intellectual and political leaders of our nation will give their will and power for the interest of the Fatherland. Through concentration and reorganization of the political parties our desultory political life will recover. Under the reaction and reflected light of such a peace our Government will grow stronger, its representatives will truly become the leaders of the nation. They will not let themselves be forced in their decisions by the exigencies of the day but will be above external influences and mass suggestions. They will tackle with strong hands the external and internal problems which a great upward-aiming nation with undreamed-of future possibilities will place before them. Only then shall we escape from the democratic swamp into which we should undoubtedly be drawn after a lukewarm peace. Only then will the political conscience of our people be sharpened and their feeling of responsibility and duty in the sense of a sane and free development be awakened and enlivened so that we may look into the future without worry about our own internal political development. The yardstick, with which the present historical developments are to be measured, is such a mighty one that before it everything of bygone centuries and millenniums shrinks into nothingness. Recent developments require of our generation an entirely new and unaccustomed power of imagination and greatness of conception. If our nation is great in the conduct of war and small in the making of peace, if it is unable in Germany's fatal hour to rise to the height and power which is demanded of it, then Germany will probably have forever spurned its destiny of introducing a new and happy epoch of humanity.

How the purging effect of war and that precious word of the Kaiser which is so sacred to the nation—"I no longer know any parties, only Germans"—did weld the entire nation together to a mighty union at the beginning of the war! It is all the more painful that through the policy of the present Government we are sinking from the height of inspiration back into the barren quarrel of the professional ranks where each regards the other as an enemy, and also back into the sober indifference of everyday life, uninspired by a ray of ideal fire. Thus it happens when there are no great aims put before the eyes of the people! Therefore it is the sacred duty of a Government, which can and will lead, to put before the nation the prospect of an honorable and advantageous peace as the price of victory for its enormous efforts and sacrifices; and above all to show it the program of a freely conceived and truly popular internal policy in line with its moral forces.

The Government must keep alive the enthusiasm of the people.

VII. THE DEMANDS OF INTERNAL POLICY

Here, in the first place, stands the consideration of the sound policy of protection of our national labor. The systematic strengthening of our internal market and the safeguarding of our economic independence from foreign countries are the great aims that lend themselves here. An appropriate protection of the nation's labor is one of the most important assumptions for the creation and maintenance of an internal market which is able to buy. The value of our external trade relations for Germany's well-being and powerful position cannot and ought not to be belittled under any circumstances. The growing development of this intercourse, however, has in the immediate past wrongly led to the undervaluing of the importance of the internal market to industry and trade. More important than export is the internal disposal. In the hour of danger the internal economic power is the only certain security of our economic and military preparedness. At no time has the correctness of this sentence been proved to such a degree as just in the course of this World War. This is being realized even by those who formerly were accustomed to see the security of the Fatherland mainly in the nursing of our foreign relations and in the negotiation of international agreements. In a new regulation of our trade policy, the consideration of an increased protection of the nation's labor as the prime requisite of a closed, self-sufficient domestic economic

Care and strengthening of the internal market.

field ought never to be lost sight of. As the most recent developments particularly and convincingly teach, this law of our commercial-
Reorganization of   political decisions holds not only for our agricul-
our trade policy.   ture but equally for the two other great resources
                             for earning a livelihood of German political econ-
omy, namely, industry and trade. This commercial-political problem
ought not to be solved after the war; rather its regulation must take
place at the same time as peace negotiations are being carried on and
must actually be prepared during the war. Commercial-political questions are questions of might in the same way as the political. Under
pressure of our military successes the attempt must be made here, too,
to achieve the most. Besides that, the reorganization of our commercial
policy lends itself as an effective weapon for the strengthening of our
economic and external political influence. Precisely at this time, when
the economic and political inter-relations of the countries all over the
world face a change the like of which the world has never seen, our
system of commercial treaties possesses increased practical significance.
Here is offered, if we are victorious in this war, a most important means
of intervening determinedly in the history of the nations in a direction
A customs-union   where Germany calls into existence a customs-
of European con-   union of European Continental countries on the
tinental countries.   basis of the most-favored-nation principle. This
                             union must have far-reaching political ramifica-
tions (defensive and offensive alliances; securing of the rights of neutrals) as a counter-weight against the English, American, and Russian
economic fields. . . . .

In the field of our internal-political and social-political developments
there are the questions of country and urban settlements, connected
with which are the carrying out of the problems of our population
policy: the city dwelling reform; the giving of credit on real estate in
cities; the new regulation of the maintenance costs of public schools
and the law of dwellings support; in short, all endeavors which are
aimed at a sound and strong development of our middle classes in
country and city. They open for legislature and administration, after
peace has been concluded, new and fine duties. A fine statesmanship,
which gives full play to the rights of economic self-determination and
the sense of responsibility of the individual, besides a successful foreign
policy, will aid most effectively to maintain the elevating powers of the
war for our nation in its resistless climbing work. Under the living influence of this great time it will be possible to overcome all difficulties
which previously were in the way of the solution of these great problems. The more freely all these blessings will be given our nation as
justified reward for its self-sacrificing spirit in war and the more
liberally they will be made, the more easily will it be convinced that the

last and highest aim lies not in exaggerated constitutional demands for the introduction of a radical suffrage law in Prussia. And so much the more easily will it be possible to bring about a Prussian suffrage reform on the basis of a direct, open, automatically working, plural vote by raising the voting age within the limits of the common interests of the state. In discussing the inner political development of the German people, to be pursued after conclusion of peace, the importance has been wrongly placed upon the suffrage demands and their realization. The basis of a truly political freedom is the economic independence and the economic self-determination of the individual. Its safeguarding is its most complete security for a sound inner political development that corresponds to the interests of the state.

A sound reform of the Prussian suffrage.

A real government has the duty after the war to advance in a leading and deciding way in all fields of our public life. It must take the initiative and indicate the ways to be embarked upon. Permeated with a sense of responsibility, it must, immediately after the war has been concluded, come forward with a comprehensive plan. To preserve its reputation it must not let the reins be taken from its hands by the political parties; otherwise it is to be feared that unity of action will be destroyed, that the government will be driven to the defensive by the unreasonable demands of political parties, and that because of the arising political complications general dissatisfaction and disillusionment will take place instead of improvement, as had been hoped. Immediately, therefore, the elaboration of a government program, to be formulated before peace is concluded, must be begun, a program which has as its object the reorganization of our internal political conditions.

Necessity of immediately formulating comprehensive program of internal policy.

VIII. Conclusion

If such great objects of foreign and internal policy were again placed before the eyes of the nation, it would rally with new inspiration around the Monarch by whom it expects to be led to victory. Stronger in their foundation would Throne and Empire come out of the heavy affliction. That and nothing else is the glowing wish of all who today are filled with anxiety and who have to remain in that anxiety as long as a system whose pernicious effects are visible to everyone is not being changed. The Fatherland is in danger! Therefore it is the right and duty of every German to break this oppressive silence before it is too late.

(*Signed*) KAPP
Generallandschaftsdirektor

KÖNIGSBERG IN PRUSSIA, May 20, 1916

42. GOVERNOR-GENERAL VON BISSING'S INSTRUCTIONS TO THE MILITARY LAW-OFFICERS, SEPTEMBER 29, 1916[8]

. . . . It remains for me, in the name of the Governor-General, to call the gentlemen's attention to the following duty: You know that the enemy countries are endeavoring to brand us as barbarians and violators of international law and that they base their accusations unscrupulously upon whatever news they get hold of. The situation dictates fear that our discussions, too, could give malevolent people basis for suspicion; therefore the gentlemen are being requested to regard as absolutely confidential everything that is being discussed here. More particularly are the gentlemen being requested not to publish in the press anything that is being discussed here without the prior consent of the Governor-General thereto in each individual instance. . . . .

43. A SUPPRESSED PAMPHLET SECRETLY CIRCULATED IN 1917[9]

(a) THE MEXICAN ENTR'ACTE, MARCH 6, 1917

HAMBURG

You know that I do not participate in the favorable opinion which one generally has of State Secretary Zimmermann. I would not like therefore to withhold from you my view of the Mexican coup of our Foreign Minister which meanwhile has become known. Really every word which one says about the matter is too much. But as political ignorance in the Reichstag applauds, one must be clear.

Zimmermann had to reckon with the possibility that the offer could come by a long, dangerous, and roundabout way into American hands; even that in Mexico itself the offer could still be betrayed to America. He had, therefore, to make clear to himself the effect of this offer upon the American attitude. With some little acumen he had to say to himself that disposal of American territory in favor of disorganized and despised Mexico would also mean a mortal insult to American pride. This would with one blow silence our friends over there, suffocate pacifist movements, and call forth a united enthusiasm for war with Germany, for his coup strikes particularly at the Southern and Western States in which we enjoy the most sympathy.

[8] *Protokolle der Tagung Richterlicher Militärjustizbeamter in Brüssel*, A.M., 29–30 September 1916, *samt einigen vorbereitenden gutachten*, A.M.G. (14079), p. 14.

[9] Friedrich Bendixen, *Politische Briefe aus der Ära Bethmann-Zimmermann 1916–1917*, N.O., Hamburg, September 1917. (15366.)

If one with all cunning wishes to provoke America to enter the war, one cannot do it better than we do it. First we allure her by yielding, to risk her coming so far toward us that she can hardly go back; then we disregard her by the suddenness of the U-boat war; next we commit the dishonesty of remaining silent about the American note of May 10, 1916, which the newspapers had considered then as an agreement and now as a sign of indissoluble differences of opinion, and thus expose ourselves in the part of the unfair opponent. After all that, instead of combating Wilson's message, as I proposed in February, we fight and thus place spiritual weapons in the hands of our friends the pacifists; we induce the newspapers to write moderately against America, in order to appear patient and meek before the world; but secretly we promote the taking away of American Federal Territory—if this does not help to bring America to a boiling-point against cowardly, insincere, and insidious Germany, what remains to be done?

It is exceedingly bitter to make oneself clear. In what a hateful light we must appear to our enemies in consequence of the policy we are pursuing. But for the understanding of our political position this knowledge is indispensable. Wilson needs all his power of resistance against the popular influences in order to save peace. He feels himself to be laboring under the most terrible embarrassment. With the letter to our Ambassador in Mexico he is able to set the whole land in an enthusiastic war-mood. But that is what he wishes to avoid. He wants peace, but he is not able to stand the caprices of the Wilhelmstrasse forever. After Zimmermann's latest performance I no longer believe that Wilson remains master of his determinations and that peace with America can be maintained.

But was then this proposal of alliance to Mexico justified at least internally? We have an ambassador who in any case has more political understanding than Zimmermann, Herr von Eckardt, a Balkan specialist; wherefore the wisdom of the Foreign Office sent him to the land of the Aztecs. He also has proved his acumen there, in that he was the first of the foreign diplomats who foresaw the victory of Carranza in the Revolution and had himself accredited to him. Instead of giving him directions, the Foreign Office could have allowed him to work calmly and have waited for his report. The gentlemen in the Wilhelmstrasse listen usually so attentively to the advice of our diplomats abroad, if their names are for instance Bernstorff or Kuehlmann, exhorting them to extreme caution. Perhaps Herr von Eckardt would have found out that without political concessions one can get much from the Mexican rulers if one only puts money in their purses. That would certainly have suited us better than to have burdened ourselves with obligations toward these somewhat dubious gentlemen.

Then it is really grotesque to treat Mexico as a state of equal standing and capable of an alliance with us, and to bind ourselves in future negotiations with America to a preceding agreement with that wild country. Who is there then who could offer us any guaranties? Or did we want to break and keep our promises as we could? Military cooperation is not to be thought of. However, we could offer money only if we could bring it there. Then Carranza would be a kind of bloodhound for us as to payment, but not an ally. And he is to conquer Texas and Arizona? Also California and Louisiana? And to want to win Japan through Mexico? Is that really the only way to the ear of the Mikado? But Japan longs for nothing better than that the Americans should be involved in the European War, and therefore she would guard herself against frightening Wilson by an approach to us. I am all the more convinced that America can assure herself of Japan's benevolent neutrality in the easiest manner or has already done so.

In every direction this Mexican action seems to me to prove completely the ineptitude of the Secretary of Foreign Affairs.

43. (b) AMERICAN INTERVENTION AND RUSSIAN REVOLUTION, APRIL 4, 1917

HAMBURG

You want to hear my voice, so I will tell you what I think about America and Russia. The noble Wilson has drawn the sword certainly in the conviction that he is doing what is necessary and has no other choice. The opposition in Congress will not be numerous enough to be able to interfere, and so Fate takes its course. Whatever could have been done from our side to secure this result we have honestly done. However, I will not enumerate the mistakes by which we have brought Americans upon our necks.

Eduard Meyer's work, *The American Congress and the World War,* which has just appeared, is very interesting. It contains the negotiations in Congress of February and March, 1916. Congress, by a large majority, was of the opinion that the nation should not intervene on behalf of Americans who sailed upon the armed commercial ships of the belligerent states, and wanted to warn them openly. It approved in other words the German point of view, which agreed with Lansing's note of January 18, 1916, according to which armed merchant ships were to be regarded as warships. But Wilson refused the warning and identified the honor of the nation with the right of Americans to travel unmolested on such ships. He threatened to resign, and Congress gave in, in order not to make the negotiations with Germany more difficult for the

President, but only after Wilson had given the assurance that before breaking off diplomatic relations the matter should be laid before Congress. The President broke this promise in that on April 18, 1916, without previously consulting Congress, he sent Germany the ultimatum concerning which he came into violent collision with Senator Stone. But Germany's compliance freed him from his embarrassment. These negotiations in Congress did not become known in Germany. But Bernstorff must have known of them, and it is difficult to understand that this diplomat, in spite of this, ardently advised compliance. Whether the Congress would have accommodated itself to the President, if the attitude of Germany had justified the supposition that she would remain immovable upon the Lansing note of January 18, 1916, which was so welcome to her—even at the risk of a diplomatic break—I doubt. When Congress, in an unprecedented manner, renounced its right to express its real opinion, it surely made this sacrifice only in view of the almost certain gain which Wilson could make from the German weakness of character; and this supposition was not erroneous.

Wilson's message of today shows the man *in puris naturalibus*. He knows no more about the origins of the war than the average reader of the Anglophile press and contrives already in his message of the 3d of February of this year, to set the German people in opposition to the German Government, "the dynasty and some ambitious men." A sneer from all German newspapers should answer him so that all America should listen dumbfounded. But our Government will probably muzzle the press again, as on the 4th of February, when nothing could have helped us more than the most violent language against Wilson and his God-forsaken Government. But we remained as ever in the position of the naughty boy who has stolen the apple: either a stupid excuse as in the Sussex case or an intimidated waiting as if we expected to be scolded and then beaten. So piteously we stand there! But Wilson concludes from the silence of the press that the German people consider him right but that in its enslavement it dares not say anything, and against the logic of this reasoning there is little to be objected to. What is disconcertingly illogical in our policy is that it misleads the whole world. The rule that one should presuppose the most reasonable from one's opponent has no value against us. Take for example, the torpedoing of the Dutch ships on the 22d of February. We had already warned them against going out and had refused any absolute guaranty; what was to be done after the torpedoing? We deny our guilt and offer "neighborly" (who is laughing there?) compensation, which in effect, of course, is a confession of guilt, and calls forth the most disgraceful charges. A few days ago a Dutchman told me that if we had denied absolutely all responsibility and compensation no excitement whatever would have occurred in Holland. But that by the way. In Congress our best defender was Senator MacLemore of Texas. Our friends in Texas will be no longer exactly enthusiastic about us, after the publication of the Zimmermann instruction to our ambassador in Mexico. The prospect of being sold to Mexico, as thanks for their friendliness to Germany after an unhappy ending of the war, is somewhat desolate. I do not expect immediate ill effects from America's intervention—at most for America itself, which with an active export of provisions and even without that will experience a gigantic rise in prices and hardship among the lower classes. The second great event, the Russian revolution, is an enormous problem, which for many a year will confront us with the problem of its destiny. To see in it merely an English feint is as unhistorical as if one would make single persons responsible for the World War. From our standpoint the event is more advantageous than from the English, as it concerns the further development of the World War. For the future, the republic (or the United States of Russia) promises us, as well as the English in India, something good. I do not believe that the Cadet-Government will last. In such revolutions, radicalism triumphs until it is relieved again by Tsarism. But this presupposes national unity, which is lacking in Russia. The revolution in France unified the nation, which had grown together in the previous centuries and had disposed of the peculiarities of the provinces. In Russia the iron band of the autocracy held together the originally foreign and centrifugal powers. Should it be broken, Russia will disintegrate from the inside. The fall of the Tsar certainly does not yet signify the dissolution of the band. The bureaucracy, the *chin,* is the power which holds the whole together, and all depends on whether this or a new central force presses the *chin* into its service before people and *zemstvo* destroy it.

The Russian urge for expansion is by wise judges not considered truly Slavic. The Slav has not the inclination for world-mastery but for division into peoples. It is the Mongolian influence (*Einschlag*) which produces the conqueror in the Muscovite. I would not like to consider such ethnological speculations significant. But it is certain that the Russian ceases to be a danger to his neighbors when his vast country is no longer governed by a unified principle. It is difficult to imagine the consequences which would result for Germany's future if, after this war, France's military and national strength were broken and Russia ceased to be a dangerous neighbor. Does disarmament then follow? And shall then the wonderful training of our people for order and devotion to duty cease? Or a shortening of the period of service to about six months? What colonizing tasks arise for us particularly in the East? . . . .

44. RUSSIAN PROPAGANDA IN THE GERMAN ARMY; PROCLAMATION TO THE GERMAN SOLDIERS[10]

The Provisional Government has fallen; the power is now in the hands of the Russian People, and the New Government considers the immediate conclusion of peace as its foremost duty.

We have taken every measure so that the text of our peace terms should be distributed among the belligerent powers. We now charge you soldiers to stand by us in the fight for peace and Socialism; for Socialism alone can give to the Proletariat a lasting peace. It alone is in a position to heal all wounds which the war has inflicted.

Soldiers, Brothers! The shining example which your leader Liebknecht has given you, the struggle which you have been carrying on in your assemblies and in the press, finally the revolutionary spirit in the German people, assures us that your Battalion of Workers are girded for the fight for freedom.

Brothers! If you support us, the cause of freedom is assured. All other powers will agree to a righteous and democratic peace.

If you stand by us in the fight for Socialism, then the spirit of your organization and your experience will help to bring about a universal Socialistic victory. Our soldiers have laid down their arms, it is now for you to follow this standard of peace.

May Peace Triumph!

May the Socialistic and International Revolution Live!

For the Council of People's Commission

(*Signed*) LENIN

TROTSKI

PETROGRAD, December 5, 1917

45. RUSSIAN PROPAGANDA IN THE GERMAN NAVY[11]

TO THE SAILORS OF THE BALTIC FLEET AND ALL OPPRESSED PEOPLES

Do you hear our voice, and do you hear the cries and groans of our brothers, the soldiers who are drowning in their own blood, and the sailors who are meeting their death day by day in the misty sea and the cold depths of the seas and oceans? Do you hear the heartbreaking lamentations and the despairing sobs of mothers, brothers, and children

[10] *Secret Summary of Intelligence,* American Expeditionary Force, General Staff No. 97, April 16, 1918, p. 395.

[11] Collection of German Military Documents, Hoover War Library.

through Europe which is drenched in blood? Do you not see the approaching shadow of the black specter of famine and his bony hand?

If you hear and you see all this, why do you keep silent?

Give your answer to our cry and to the appeals of your brothers. Follow the example of the Russian people . . . . rise up like a hurricane, tear off the fetters of bondage, overthrow the thrones of tyrants, and free yourselves from the god you have made with your own hands— Capitalism.

With a fury of haste turn your cannons and machine guns and let loose a hail of shells, of lead, and of shrapnel. . . . .

Therefore raise boldly the standard of revolt. Leave the sepulcher of the trenches; make an end of the despots.

46. FRENCH MILITARY PROPAGANDA[12]

We could have bombarded the open city of Berlin, killing innocent women and children; we shall be satisfied, however, to give the following message to the German people.

The French Aviators

To the People of Berlin

Today, already, it is known by many thinking Germans that the war was brought about by the military advisers at the court of Berlin and Vienna. There are no official lies nor excuses which will erase the plainly proved fact from the world that the German Government, together with the Austrian Government, had fully planned and wanted this war, which was made inevitable.

This is a fact which nobody in the whole world doubts except the Germans themselves. The German people were blinded by lies and deceit to urge them to make a war which they really did not want. A war of defense and a war for liberty this war was called, which in reality was nothing else than a long-prepared-for war of conquest and robbery.

How long shall this slaughter last?

How many times has peace been promised to you? First in 1914, then in 1915, and each time for Christmas; then after the capture of Warsaw; then after taking Serbia; and again and again was peace promised to you. This time you were told that peace would come after the capture of Verdun. There are mountains of your own people lying dead before Verdun. At this place there is an unheard-of gamble with

---

[12] Collection of French Military Documents, Hoover War Library.

the lives of the Germans going on; the dead are numberless—but they will not bring you peace.

The Allies have everything. They don't know anything about bread cards, fat cards, nor meatless days. The products of the entire world are at their disposal and arrive incessantly. Their military force is increasing continuously. Your soldiers know the French Army, the courage and determination of the French soldiers. The military power of England is growing daily; she just adopted conscription in her empire of 50,000,000 people.

Every one of her powerful colonies will be faithful to her to the utmost and help her in every way possible. Russia gets up new armies all the time, putting them at the disposal of the Allies. The Russian army is well equipped now with ammunition and fighting material.

Germany has lost the sympathy of all the neutral nations on account of the crime she committed in drowning the many innocent women and children who traveled on the passenger boats and by her merciless conduct of the war. The number of her enemies is increasing daily.

The Allies are determined to fight to the last.

You are fighting for your steel kings, your junker and agrarian lords. *We* fight for the liberty of all nations against the might of a military caste. We want the punishment of the guilty ones; we want to make any such bloodshed impossible in the future. And we will have arrived at this goal when the German people themselves will have the right to determine about war or peace.

47. ACCOUNTS OF AMERICAN INTERVENTION:

(a) LES RAISONS DE M. WILSON,
11 AVRIL 1917[18]

Dans le message qu'il a adressé au Congrès, pour justifier sa décision de participer à la guerre contre l'Allemagne, M. Wilson se dit, une fois de plus, le defenseur du Droit et de l'Humanité. On trouvera plus loin le résumé essentiel de ce document que nous livrons au jugement de l'Histoire. Mais, des aujourd'hui, l'on peut affirmer que les raisons humanitaires invoqués par le président des États-Unis ne sont pas ses motifs décisifs.

On est mal placé pour défendre la morale outragée, lorsqu'on a tout fait pour couvrir politiquement l'enrichissement d'une industrie vivant de l'anéantissement du genre humain! C'est ce qu'a fait M. Wilson.

---

[18] *Gazette des Ardennes* (Journal des pays occupés paraissant quatre fois par semaine), No. 378, Charleville, le 11 Avril 1917.

Toute sa politique a profité en première ligne aux gros métallurgistes américains qui fournissent canons et munitions à l'Entente, alors que le "defenseur de Droit" n'a pas bronché lorsque l'Angleterre, au mépris des principes reconnus en matière de blocus et de contrabande de guerre, interdit *tout trafic* neutre vers l'Allemagne.

Cette politique, si elle manqua d'équité, fut d'autant plus fructueuse en profits.

Les États-Unis se sont enrichis par la guerre dans des proportions vraiment impressionnantes. L'afflux d'or, joint à la production aurifère nationale, a porté le stock du métal jaune des États-Unis à 2,636,009,564 de dollars, soit plus de 13 milliards de francs. (au 1er janvier 1917.)

Les Américains ont traversé une periode d'incroyable prospérité. Ils ont pu racheter la plus grande partie de leurs titres nationaux, notamment leurs obligations de chemins de fer, placées à l'Étranger. ... L'industrie américaine a atteint ainsi un degré de prospérité inconnu jusqu'à ce jour. ...

Que se passerait-il notamment si l'Allemagne et ses alliés l'emportaient sur le groupe des débiteurs de l'Amérique? Ayant permis que celle-ci s'engageât à fond dans l'aventure, le président Wilson se voit entraîné plus loin qu'il ne l'avait sans doute prévu tout d'abord. Son intervention prouve qu'il apprécie dûment la force des Puissances centrales et qu'il craint leur victoire. L'empêchera-t-il? C'est une autre question.

Les partisans de l'Allemagne ne sont pas seuls à juger ainsi la politique wilsonnienne. Il n'y a pas longtemps, le correspondant américain du *Petit Journal* en exposait les motifs dans un article dont voici la substance, d'après le résumé qu'en a donné la *Belgique*:

La guerre des sous-marins renforcée, n'a été que le prétexte. Au-delà des considérations professorales de M. Wilson, il faut chercher la cause de la rupture dans la situation financiére des États-Unis. Le directeur d'une des grandes banques de New York s'est tout récemment exprimé à ce sujet comme suit:

"Dans la seule année 1916, nous avons vendu aux alliés pour plus de 10 milliards de francs, le maximum de ce qu'était vendable aux billigérants. Nous avons fourni des munitions, du blé, de la viande, du cuir, du coton. ... Les 'farmers' de l'Ouest se sont enrichis; les industriels de l'Est ont fait des affaires brillantes; ... Et il en est ainsi dans toutes les branches de l'activité industrielle des États-Unis.

"... *Nous en sommes arrivés au point que, pour les États-Unis le papier des Alliés n'a de valeur que s'il est gagé par la victoire. ... Les Alliés doivent triompher à tout prix, si nous voulons être payés. ...*"

Pour juger le côté moral de cette politique d' "affaires," donnons la parole à un socialiste américain résidant à Berne, lequel s'exprime ainsi dans l'organe socialiste suisse *Berner Tagwacht,* qui n'est nullement hostile à l'Entente :

"Le Rôle que l'Amérique a joué dans cette guerre couvrira la grande république d'une honte éternelle. Nous sommes à proprement parler les vautours du monde, engraissés et enrichis par le plus affreux des carnages humaines. ... Mais ce qu'il y a de plus écoeurant dans toute l'histoire, c'est qu'en même temps, nous voulons garder l'auréole de la sainteté, et que notre Président veut souvenir que nous defendons l'humanité et la dignité humaine! ..."

Le jugement est sévère, mais il frappe juste. ...

Faut-il s'étonner que le peuple américain ait accepté de suivre son président dans la voie de la guerre? Nous croyons que cette attitude de l'opinion publique s'explique par le fait que la grande majorité de peuple américain est apparantée à l'Angleterre, tant par le sang que par la mentalité, et qu'elle a subi depuis le début de la guerre l'influence de la propagande tendancieuse partant de Londres. ...

... En declarant la guerre, M. Wilson a jeté son masque. Il descend à son tour dans l'arène, aprés s'être trop longtemps contenté d'y lancer ses flèches meurtrières, sans courir luimême le risque des combattants. ...

47. (*b*) L'AIDE AMÉRICAINE, 17 JUIN 1917[14]

Il est intéressant de constater que, chaque fois qu'une puissance se trouve entraînée dans la guerre aux côtés de l'Entente, le formidable appareil de la propagande alliée est mis en mouvement pour fêter sur tous les tons l'importance de l'aide nouvelle. Le but est clair : Il s'agit de nourrir chez les peuples alliés l'espoir en cette "victoire" toujours promise et toujours remise.

Il en fut ainsi lorsque l'Italie, puis lorsque la Roumanie, rompant les accords qui les liaient aux Puissances centrales, entrèrent perfidement dans la guerre contre la "barbarie," le "militarisme," etc. Aujourd'hui, nous voyons l'histoire se répéter à propos de l'intervention américaine.

Rappelons les brillants articles dans lesquels la presse parisienne fêta l'arrivé des Italiens et des Roumains. ... Rappelons aussi les espoirs qui saluèrent l'entrée en guerre du Portugal. Aujourd'hui le "poilu" français sait à quoi s'en tenir sur l'aide de cet allié.

On lui dit d'attendre les Américains. Mais trop de désillusions l'ont rendé nerveux, le "poilu." C'est pourquoi la propagande officieuse de l'Entente force la note comme jamais, pour que le poilu patiente un

---

[14] *Gazette des Ardennes,* No. 416, June 17, 1917.

hiver encore, en attendant les Américains, qui apporteront la victoire—
l'année prochaine!

À lire les radiogrammes de Lyon, il semble que la France soit sou-
dain déchargée de tout le poids de la guerre. "L'oncle Sam paye tout!"
Cela rappelle certains restaurants chics, où la carte n'indique pas les
prix. On ne les trouvera que plus tard, sur l'addition finale!

En attendant, les informations publiées au sujet de l'aide militaire
américaine sont pleines de contradiction. Le 12 Juin, à 5.h. 30 du matin,
le radiogramme de Lyon donnait un aperçu des forces de l'armée
américaine. À part une serie importante de troupes auxiliares de tous
genres, cette armée comprendrait également des troupes combattantes.
Mais le radiogramme de Lyon 12 Juin, 8 heures du soir, donne des
chiffres bien différents. D'aprés cette information l'Amérique enver-
rait provisoirement neuf régiments de génie et en fait de troupes *combattantes,* une division de soldats exercés, forte de 20,000 hommes. Le
même radiogramme laisse entendre que cela portera, à bref délai, à
100,000 hommes le chiffre des Américains combattant dans les rangs
de l'Entente.—Les "poilus" seront sans doute étonnés d'apprendre qu'il
y a aujourd'hui déjà tant d'Américains parmi eux!

Le fait est que les chiffres du matin différent sensiblement de ceux
du soir, de sorte que nous préférons attendre, en réservant notre jugement, comme nous avons attendu lorsque sont venus les Italiens, les
Roumains, les Portugais. ... [*sic*]

48. THE INTERCEPTED GERMAN WIRELESS MESSAGE OF
APRIL 20, 1917

(*a*) THE BRITISH FOREIGN OFFICE TO THE COMMISSION
FOR RELIEF IN BELGIUM[15]

No. 82433/X   FOREIGN OFFICE, S.W.1
                                                    April 25th, 1917

SIR: With reference to your letter of the 17th instant and Mr. Poland's subsequent verbal communications relative to the proposed release
of the Relief vessels temporarily detained at Halifax, I am directed by
Lord R. Cecil to transmit, for your information, copies of an intercepted
German Wireless message of the 20th instant [Document 48*b*] and of
an Admiralty Press Communiqué [Document 48*c*], now under issue,
denying the allegations therein contained.

---

[15] This and the other related documents (48*b*–48*e*) are in the Archives of the
Commission for Relief in Belgium, Hoover War Library.

2. Apart from the very serious situation created by the loss of the vessels and cargoes whether by mine or torpedo, His Majesty's Government are reluctantly constrained to infer, from the absence of any expression of regret or apology by the German Government for mistakes made by their naval officers, and in view of the justification which has apparently been advanced, that the outrages are clearly quite deliberate and will if possible be continued.

3. The position is receiving the very serious consideration of His Majesty's Government, of whose final decision in the matter I shall advise you as soon as possible. For the present, His Majesty's Government, as at present advised, are forced to the conclusion that, in existing circumstances, they would not be justified in granting facilities for additional Relief vessels to proceed on their voyages unless and until reliable evidence had been adduced that the German Government have no intention of sinking such vessels.

48. (b) THE INTERCEPTED MESSAGE

From Graudens, Berlin   April 20th, 1917
To United Press, New York

France's recent protest against sinking Relief Ship caused German Admiralty's suspicion because formerly France not much pleased with Relief work which eased German Government's responsibility towards feeding of Belgians. Today German submarine reported real reason French and English fitting boats as submarine traps painting boats like relief ships as prescribed by German Admiralty. When said submarine approached false relief ship latter opened fire. This French trick despicable because under pretense of charitableness construct new "Baralong" case. Admiralty reports submarines returned since April 13 reported ninety-three thousand tons sunk in Channel, Atlantic, and North Sea.

48. (c) ADMIRALTY PRESS COMMUNIQUÉ, APRIL 22, 1917

22d April 1917

The German official wireless message of 20th April accuses the French and British Governments of employing vessels for the attack of submarines under the ruse of the distinctive markings carried by Belgian Relief ships. The allegation is entirely untrue, and is absolutely without the shadow of foundation.

It is merely a variation of the equally groundless assertion that the Hospital Ships of the Allies are used for purposes other than those sanctioned by the Hague Convention, and is evidently intended as a pretext for torpedoing Belgian Relief ships at sight, and thus further reducing the mercantile tonnage of the world.

48. (d) THE BRITISH FOREIGN OFFICE TO THE COMMISSION FOR RELIEF IN BELGIUM, MAY 15, 1917

. . . . With reference to your letter of the 7th instant to Sir H. Daly, forwarding a copy of a telegram received from the Rotterdam Office of the Commission for Relief in Belgium, I am directed by Lord Robert Cecil to transmit to you herewith a copy of a telegram which has been sent to His Majesty's Minister at The Hague for the information of the Netherland Government, and for transmission to the Netherland Minister in Berlin.

You will observe that His Majesty's Government deny the German statement as to the misuse of the Commission's distinctive marking of vessels, and that they state that the assurance already given to the Commission holds good at the present time. . . . .

48. (e) TELEGRAM FROM THE BRITISH FOREIGN OFFICE (EN CLAIR) TO SIR W. TOWNLEY (THE HAGUE), MAY 12, 1917

No. 1225 . . . .

London Office of Commission for Relief in Belgium have received following telegraphic message from their Rotterdam Office: (Begins.)

Note Verbale to Dutch Legation Berlin, dated April 29th states German Government has received submarine report that submarine trap bearing marks of the C.R.B. has been discovered. This opens up serious possibilities. Please arrange have officially denied and previous guarantee confirmed. (Ends.)

Please inform Netherland Government for communication to the Netherland Minister at Berlin that the German allegation is absolutely devoid of truth; and that the German statements, originally made in the German wireless of April 20th, were categorically denied in a statement issued to the press here on April 22d, as follows:

"The German wireless message of 20th April accuses [see Document 48c, above]."

His Majesty's Government long ago gave the C.R.B. a categorical assurance that they would never use the Commission's distinctive marks for any other ship, and that guarantee holds good today.

49. THE KRIEGSPRESSEAMT CONFERENCE,
AUGUST 7 TO 10, 1917[16]

Major Stotten, Chief of the Kriegspresseamt [War Press Office], opens the session at 9 : 10 A.M.

Chairman : Gentlemen, ... The purpose of our gathering is, first of all, just as at our previous meeting, to give you, gentlemen, new material for your activity and to give you an opportunity to relate to us your experiences. . . . .

Deutelmoser, Director in the Foreign Office, reports about the general political situation : It was my intention to give you a comprehensive talk about the general political situation. To my regret that will be impossible for me to do, owing to the fact that the filling of the Imperial offices, particularly the Foreign Office, took longer than was anticipated, and that as a result I have not yet been able to get directions from my new chief, His Excellency v. Kühlmann. Therefore I must confine myself to a few brief words and refrain from all details.

First of all, I may emphasize again what the Chancellor put forward as his program when he took charge of his office. The two main points of this program are : maintaining firm unity at home, and strong resistance toward the enemy. . . . .

Whoever in the face of the magnificent deeds which our soldiers and U-boats are performing under the leadership of the greatest military leaders of the present still doubts our military victory, cannot be helped. . . . .

I believe that the present moment would be the poorest possible for the further evidencing of peace desires, which are always interpreted abroad as an imperative need of peace for us. We do not further the cause of peace by attempting to approach it in an imposing manner. . . . . Peace, in so far as it can be furthered at all by political means and not obtained by force of arms, must be approached very cautiously. That is the only thing politics can do in this respect. But it has done that already, for our enemies know that they can have an honorable peace from us. If they, in spite of that, still refuse to extend their hand, that shows that they are not yet weary enough for peace. What the enemy people think about it is a different thing. We have to confine ourselves to those people who are leaders in their governments and who dictate the policies for those nations. . . . . The worst thing we could do would be to give them the impression that we are running after peace. Peace will come as soon as the enemy realizes that he needs it

---

[16] Kriegspresseamt, *Bericht über die Tagung vom 7 bis 10 August 1917 in Berlin.*

more than we. Therefore, everything must be avoided which might give the wrong impression, that we need peace more than they do. . . . .

Chairman: . . . . Things being as they are it is evident that today we will have to forego a discussion about the political situation. . . . . I should like to touch briefly upon a question which, I assume, interests you a great deal, too. In our activity of enlightening the people, when we constantly have to urge the people to hold out and to sustain their hopes and confidence, it is natural that the question should arise what we shall tell the people will be the reward of their great sacrifices and continual new efforts. The question might arise how far our work is being impaired by the well-known decision of the Reichstag. I cannot take an unreserved attitude on this question, because it is not within my competence. However, I should like to give you my opinion.

It is known that the decision, according to those who sponsored it, was intended for political effect, and, the situation at the moment being what it is, it would be a mistake to take an open hostile attitude toward that decision. It is also undesirable for the reason that our work of informing the people must be kept out of politics completely. On the other hand, I am convinced that there is no reason for us to be pessimistic because of that decision. . . . . Should peace finally come, let no one believe that we will face it with hands tied while our opponent has complete liberty, ... therefore, I believe that we can look with confidence toward peace. How the latter will look, once it comes, will, of course, depend upon the situation in which peace finds us militarily, politically, and economically. We shall hear reports about our economic position which will give you confidence that we can face the future calmly and full of hope. I shall not go any deeper into these questions, for the reason that they are beyond my competence. This I should like to impress upon you particularly for the entire work of enlightenment: Gentlemen, keep out of internal politics! Our work has nothing to do with politics.

AFTERNOON SESSION

Professor Wiedenfeld, member of the Scientific Commission of the War Department, reports about "Procuring of Raw Materials."

After the report, the question being asked why certain breweries are still allowed to keep their copper boilers and the breweries do not have to report them, Professor Wiedenfeld answers that the Government confiscates at first only those copper boilers which can be spared. Also that the whole policy of mobilization of metals aims, first of all, to take those things for which a substitute of iron or of another metal, not yet scarce, can be found.

Major Meyerhoff (Repr. Gen. Com. X.A.-C.) asks information about a rumor current both at home and at the front, namely, as to whether the church bells in the occupied territory were to be confiscated, as had been done at home. He says that that has caused great bitterness among the people.

Professor Wiedenfeld says that the situation in the occupied territories is not as simple as at home. For one thing, the majority of the people, both in the East and the West, are Catholic. Therefore, negotiations would have to be carried on not only with the highest authorities of the congregation, and of the country, but also with the Pope. In both Germany and Austria the church authorities of all denominations adjusted themselves to this necessity, which attitude was also approved by the Pope. On the other hand, there were certain doubts about the occupied territory, for naturally we cannot hold it against the clergy of those districts that they do not take the same attitude as did ours at home. Their patriotic feeling is against us, naturally. At the same time transportation facilities also were lacking in order to do that immediately. But now the decision has been made to treat those territories the same as has been done at home.

Dr. Hertel (Repr. Gen. Com. XIV. A.-C.) asks whether monuments will be spared while church bells have been confiscated.

Professor Wiedenfeld: The monuments which would really bring us considerable quantities of copper and tin, because they consist of bronze, are, first, few in number, and, second, are such pronounced pieces of art that we cannot take them on that account. By far the most of the monuments which appear to us as being of bronze contain so little copper and tin that it is not worth mentioning. . . . . The expense of labor, coal, and transportation, etc., must be in proportion to the result of metal gained, and that is not the case with the monuments. . . . .

Follows report by Dr. Herbig: "Our Coal Provisioning."

Major Warnecke: . . . . In my opinion the coal question is the most important determining factor of the sentiment of the people for the coming winter. I have been urged on all sides to use all my efforts that the population may not hunger and freeze at the same time. Therefore, I should like to know what percentage of the total coal consumption goes for house-heating purposes. I have been told by various people that it is between 10 and 14 per cent of the total. If now we have to reduce our total consumption by 10 per cent, that would mean about 1 to 2 per cent reduction for house-heating purposes. Gentlemen, that is such a small amount that it would not pay at all. The important thing is this: if the worker comes home from work and does not find a warm room, nor a warm meal, then the output of the factory suffers much more than if the factory were given a little less coal. . . . . Then I wish to emphasize that coal should be given only to such industries as are absolutely necessary for the waging of the war. . . . .

Professor Förster, University of Frankfurt A.M.: A point which causes a great deal of surprise among the population is the impression that different parts of our country are treated differently in regard to provisioning with coal and foodstuffs. Unfortunately in the matter of foodstuffs the German Reich is again divided into numerous Federal States, with some of them erecting barriers against the export of food products. Particularly Bavaria. Now, I read with great bitterness that Bavaria makes great claims upon coal. In such a case I would say that if a Federal State draws such a sharp barrier in one field, then it would be justifiable to withhold from it something in other fields, and in that way achieve an adjustment of differences.

Dr. Herbig: We estimate the total coal demand at between 190 to 210 million tons, about 20 to 30 million tons of that total for house consumption, i.e., about 10 to 15 per cent. After all not such a negligible amount. And we take the attitude that many small amounts make a big amount. . . . . But there is no intention to take from the poor man his coal for fuel or his gas for cooking. . . . . The emphasis is entirely upon saving wherever possible. . . . .

As regards barriers between different Federal States, I may only say that we wish to prevent that as much as possible. Certainly I can say in the name of the Imperial Commissioner of Coal that he does not know any internal boundaries. . . . .

Lieutenant Grim (A.O.K. Woyrsch): I should like to call attention to the many strikes which the war has brought us. Particularly noticeable has the effect been in the field of coal production. Therefore I should like to raise the question whether it would not be possible to use our enlightenment activity particularly among those circles which produce the coal, and to call these people's attention to the fact that they harm their classes first of all by the strikes. It might be possible also occasionally to threaten with compulsory measures, by threatening to reduce their own home consumption.

Major Warnecke: I think that is a very good suggestion, one which the gentlemen should avail themselves of.

Dr. Herbig: The labor policy is a very ticklish question. . . . . Gentlemen, I have had twelve years experience in the Saar region, which has a very quiet and patriotic population; but this one thing I have learned, namely, that one has to be very careful. . . . . In my opinion it would be a mistake to express a threat in this sense: "Well, then we shall hold you responsible and reduce the amount of coal for your own needs." Much as I approve the thought underlying it, I beg you for tactical reasons not to let such words escape your lips.

Dr. Kempkes (lawyer Repr. Gen. Com. VII A.C.) : The one thing that is lamentable is that we have no basis for enabling us to say what the coal provisioning will be and for how long a period. This the people demand to know.

The question of threats against the laboring population I regard as fraught with the greatest danger. If you say, however, tell the workers in your propaganda that by striking they only harm themselves, then I say that that is self-evident. I mention this only so as not to give rise to the conception that this has not yet been done in the broadest way. Our entire work of enlightenment goes in that direction. But to go farther and to express such threats, or even only to indicate that one could entertain such thoughts, would be very dangerous.

One more question I should like to raise. If the coal situation is such that everything must be done to improve the situation, would it then not be appropriate to reduce the coal consumption of the railroads? That could be done by stopping all pleasure trips, in that anyone wishing to travel would be required to have a permit from the authorities, the permit to be given only in case of urgent necessity. . . . .

Captain Kleisinger (Repr. Gen. Com. XVIII A.C.) : I should like to mention still another point on which possibly we could get some information. It has been often discussed that there are only very few people who really know how to heat a stove. This holds also with regard to war industries. The furnaces are operated by inexperienced stokers, for the experienced ones are all in the field. It now has been suggested that these latter be given furlough or be exchanged for the inexperienced ones. A further suggestion has been that special firing courses be organized to train stokers. I also should like to know whether any publication of the *Presseabteilung* or any other paper publishes something about the method of heating. . . . .

SECOND DAY, WEDNESDAY, AUGUST 8, 1917

FORENOON SESSION

Chairman: Major Stotten opens the session.

Director Reifs reports about "The Condition of Our Paper Market."

Dr. von Hieber: I take the privilege of making a little suggestion to the reporter. He says that the question of how to save still more paper is one of the chief problems of the bureau [the War Economic Bureau, division of German newspapers]. Then I should like to call attention to the great mass of professional and club publications which serve solely the interests of a particular profession or organization. Should one-third of these be discontinued, a great amount of paper could thereby be saved.

Director Reiss: . . . . In regard to the professional publications I should like to say that our bureau wishes to close only as few of them as possible. And you must further think of the typesetters, professional organizations, etc., which need their publications as much to maintain the morale of their members as do the newspapers. I think, therefore, that we should gain nothing by such a procedure.

Professor Dr. Reinke (Kiel): We all agree that the problem of enlightenment of the German people is among the most important problems of the fourth year of war. It can and will aid in raising the sentiment, the confidence of victory, and the desire for victory among the great masses of the nation. It will aid in strengthening the nerves of the people and in keeping public opinion sound. But the solution of this problem can be left only partly to the newspapers, for they are predominantly party papers, and party papers find it always very bitter to place their interests after those of the Fatherland. I have in mind only a positive enlightenment in an objective sense. The weight of happenings must be realized, positively, in simple and unadorned words; negatively, for example, in emphasizing the English and French lies and audacities.

And now I beg to be permitted to make a few proposals. First, in regard to the press. I think it is important that our papers bring, besides reports from our General and Admiral Staffs, also a group of foreign reports, signed by the News Bureau of the Foreign Office. In this respect I think that not enough has been done for our public, for only if such reports are officially marked do the newspapers of all shades of opinion reprint them regularly. We cannot permit the editors of the newspapers to make résumés for themselves from other official reports, such as the Wolff's Bureau or the *Norddeutsche Allgemeine Zeitung.* No, the résumés must be handed to them exactly as the General Staff and the Admiral Staff report about the events of the front on land and sea. I think that such reports would often achieve the same aim which in England the Ministers try to achieve by their cross-country journeys.

My second proposal is to work intelligently through public notices. Here it is a question of short but strong words which go straight to the heart of the people and steel their desire for victory. The nation thirsts for such enlightenment. It cannot be expected to gather it from the newspapers. . . . . One should not dwell only upon news in such notices. Such important questions as the war aims of the enemies or the Kaiser's peace proposal of 1916 can be treated again and again. Everything depends upon vividness and the wording, in order to create impressions. One must hammer these facts into the people's heads. That can be achieved only by repetition. Do not be misled by cries of artificially made sentiment.

Lastly, I should like to emphasize the importance of frequently hoisting the flags. . . . . The nation is thrilled by the sight of flags. Old and young are proud of them. . . . . Of course, it must not be carried to extremes, which would result in indifference. . . . .

THIRD DAY, THURSDAY, AUGUST 9, 1917

Major Warnecke opens the session.

Professor Abderhalden: Gentlemen, I should like to relate a few common things about the problem of enlightenment. Each one of us had his own experiences, and I think it will be best if everyone relates those and then we may discuss them together.

At first I should like to make a little suggestion. I would regard it as very important that the Kriegspresseamt should organize a division to which one could address questions, and that it be so organized that there would be a list of experts in all the different fields. I am convinced that it would be easy to find experts in almost any field who would be willing to answer every single request for information. . . . .

Second, in order to be able to work, one must know the prevailing sentiment of the particular group among which one works. One must know the sources of their sentiment, and it is very difficult to determine that. Those who must enlighten or who wish to do so must be very well informed. They must know even the most intimate matters.

I think that enlightenment in regard to the food question is the most important problem. Yesterday it was said that not enough interest existed. I cannot understand that. Of course it depends upon the way one enlightens. In Halle three-day courses were given to preachers, teachers, etc., and they were very well attended. The interest was very great, and those men spread the information gained among the great masses. I find that such courses should be given frequently. Of course, in these courses I do not propose the counting of calories and the evidencing that the nourishment given is sufficient; rather I always emphasize that the food as such is good but that the quantity is very small. One must not try to lie to those people, for they notice it at once. . . . .

Major Warnecke: In regard to the speaker's suggestion that a food-information bureau be established in the Kriegspresseamt, I wish to say that it is not intended for that. Those questions must be sent directly to the War Food Department, whose province it is to deal with food questions. As regards his suggestion of organizing more food courses, I can only approve of that. . . . .

We now take up the question of organization. I should like to read a few proposals of Professor Stephinger:

1. All enlightenment organizations, now existing or still to be cre-

ated, should be uniformly integrated, and be divided and regulated upon the basis of functions.

That is being done by all enlightenment officers in their respective districts.

2. In the executive committees to be created, the Government and the people, i.e., consumers and producers, workers and officials, and housewives should be represented.

Conditions are different for each district. I doubt whether it would be wise to have Government representation in all committees. The reverse, I think, wherever the committees organize and work on their own initiative. It is much better, and possibly also more effective, when the thing is unofficial. With the less show the thing is done, the more effective it is. . . . .

4. These committees must refrain from every official activity and occupy themselves only with economic questions.

That, I think, is the chief point of the entire work of enlightenment. That is the assumption upon which every successful work of this nature is based. But we must be sure that we pursue constructive tendencies, not destructive.

Our purpose is not to represent war aims, nor to represent measures of the Government. Our sole purpose is to enlighten; where false impressions have been created, to remove them; to help the people with advice where they are completely lost. On the one hand, you are to advise; on the other hand, to raise public confidence; and particularly not merely with patriotic phrases, for you will not get anywhere with them, but with facts. And the material we give to you shall, in the first place, serve to inform you, and is not to be scattered among the masses. . . . .

General Superintendent Möller thinks it might be well to use wall posters, possibly every two weeks or every four weeks, which would briefly summarize the results of the various offensives. Or, now that winter is at hand, with concerts, lectures, etc., in the larger cities. It might be well to furnish each auditor, upon leaving the meeting place, with pamphlets, sheets, etc., telling what great men have said about the Fatherland, or any other worth-while subject. . . . .

And one thing more, we must know what is happening among the people, how they live, what they say, and what they think. The last is often very difficult to find out. For that purpose I would suggest the distribution at meetings of questionnaires drawn up by the Kriegspresseamt or other suitable organizations, these questionnaires to be distributed with the request that everyone fill them out as well as he can and that it be left to each one to decide whether he wishes to sign his name or indicate his occupation. It has been my experience to gain in this way information which I should not have been able to obtain in any other way.

The chief thing, in his own mind and in his dealings with others, for each enlightenment worker, is not to adopt a superior attitude. He must place himself upon the same level as the one whom he wishes to enlighten. Another thing, we must realize that those we wish to enlighten are no longer children and the mere display of authority will get us nowhere. . . . . One must leave the people to decide as much as possible for themselves. We like everyone who is of the same opinion as ourselves; we respect those who have different opinions, but we never despair of those who are far off from ours. We cannot do this work without a good dose of idealism, of a clear and sound optimism.

Colonel Kittel (Repr. Gen. Com. XIX A.C. War Department division): Yesterday evening was mentioned the organization of the XIX Army Corps, which is attached to the Leipzig branch of the War Department, and the doubt was expressed whether this organization would function as well with other corps which are directly subordinated to the general command. To answer that question and to dispel any doubts, I should like to say the following: . . . . Our organization is very large, comprising about five hundred people, and has its own district representatives, who as a rule are elderly gentlemen, mostly from industry, who know their districts very well. They act as our so-called confidential agents. . . . . We are also in the position to exert pressure upon the local press, particularly the small. . . . . We alone have also worked through the means of the poster. Via neutral states we obtained a great number of English recruiting posters and French war posters, and both we and the artist whom we called in for advice were really astonished to see how much our enemies have achieved in the use of the poster.

We distributed the poster, "England's Intention," prepared by the Kriegspresseamt, to the extent of 20,000 copies, so that not a factory or workshop in our district was omitted. We have been told that the effect of the poster among the workmen was extraordinary. We are having others printed, for example: "This I did for you, what are you doing for me?" . . . . We also distributed the map "Should They Win" in every saloon, hangout, etc. . . . . .

We also arranged entertainment evenings where, after the opening songs by first-rate choirs or musicians, a speaker makes a short enlightening speech. As far as I am able to judge we scored very good results. . . . .

We have also speakers who are prepared to speak upon any imaginable subject, so that in case of demand, for example, the threat of a strike in any industry, we can dispatch an expert to handle the situation.

REPORT ABOUT THE SESSION ON APRIL 20 TO 21, 1917

Lieutenant Dr. Henning (abridged) : . . . . To find subject material
for our speeches it is only necessary for us to mix with the people and
listen, for instance, to the talk in the street car, on the railroad, or in
the saloon or bar. Then we readily notice what is the matter. If in
individual cases we are not equipped to discuss in detail certain subjects,
the information sections of the Foreign Office and the War Department are always willing to supply the necessary information. The
latter publishes the *Economic Statements,* in which there is a wealth of
suitable material. . . . .

Of course, besides this subject-matter, first in consideration comes
what the Kriegspresseamt and its allied organizations publish. Of the
latter, which comprise all ranks of the people from the associations of
scientists and artists to the labor organizations, women's clubs, etc., I
wish to mention only the following: the Information Bureau of the
United Organizations, which publishes the *Communications* (Berlin,
No. 24, Friedrichstr. 136) ; the "Kulturbund" (Berlin, N.W. 7, Unter
den Linden 38), which distributes books and pamphlets in great numbers, such as *The Strength of the German People after Two Years of
War* (Leipzig, Teubner, 1916) and Max Cohen's *The People and the
War* (Berlin, Hobbing, 1916) ; and the Catholic People's Union in
Munich-Gladbach, which publishes excellent propaganda literature.

Of the material prepared by the Kriegspresseamt the *German War
Weekly Review* (D.K.W.) is the most familiar to you. . . . . Besides the
lectures of the D.K.W., it will be profitable for you to read the news
of the foreign press (N.d.A.), which reflects the sentiment of the enemy
and neutral countries. In your speeches you will always be confronted
with the task of encouraging your listeners to hold out. That will be
easy, if you remind your audiences of the enemy war aims. And those
you can find at all times in the enemy press. . . . . The maps entitled
"Should They Win," which supplemented No. 21 of the D.K.W., can
be used with the same success as the pamphlet under the same title by
W. Schmidtbonn. Valuable also is *The Destruction of Germany,* by
Dr. J. Neumann-Frohnau, published in 1915 by Carl Curtius, Berlin. . . . .

Of the many pamphlets and individual writings which are prepared
for the Kriegspresseamt by scientists, writers, Reichstag deputies, politicians, and speakers, I need mention only a few: *Woe to the Defeated,*
by Stresemann, *The German Worker and the War* and *Holding Out
until Victory,* by H. Priebe. Very important is *What Does England
Have Against Us?* by the Information Bureau of the United Associations, because it contains very important statistical data which may serve

as a supplement to *Germany, Facts and Figures, a Statistical Cordial,* by D. Trietsch (Lehmann, Munich).

The Kriegspresseamt has published in great numbers a small study, *The Origin of the World War,* which contains a clear statement of the historical development of its causes and the outbreak of the war. This, together with the pamphlet likewise so entitled by Hans Altmann (Leipzig, Teubner) and the *New Supplements to the History of the Development of the World War 1914* by Valter, is a rich source for anyone having to speak about this subject, which our enemies veil so systematically. . . . . At present the Kriegspresseamt is occupied with preparing a synopsis of the most important war literature. . . . . In order to remain in contact with the spirit which prevails at the front and to fight against defeatism it is valuable to get a field paper, for example, the excellently edited *Feldgrauen,* with pictures, published by the 50th Infantry Division.

In conclusion, special attention must be called to the "Letters from Germany." These are letters of complaint sent from home to the front and which fell into the hands of the enemy, who assembled and distributed them in France. They were also dropped from airplanes behind our front. . . . .

Lieutenant Weutscher expressed the opinion that in order to allay the internal dissatisfaction it was necessary to further the internal-political "neutrality," to bring about a neutral understanding between the different classes. Particularly important, he thought, was it to straighten out diplomatically the differences between city and country, to tell the city men about the many difficulties of the farmer and to tell the latter of the heavy work of industry. Tolerance should be every-where the first condition of a successful influence upon the people. Attention should also be called to the dangerousness of spreading rumors, gossip, and premature peace possibilities. . . . .

Chairman : . . . . Slogans are one means by which the Entente works so extraordinarily successfully and in which we have not succeeded at all. The only useful slogan we have is "The Freedom of the Seas"; others we have none. I should like to arrange a contest and offer a prize for really appropriate slogans. I should be very much obliged to you if you would support us in that and would help us to express briefly certain existing ideas in pregnant words, words which illumine them like a flash of lightning. . . . .

I return briefly to the matter of pamphlets and in that connection to the employing of artists. The attempt has been made to approach the artists with the suggestion that they place their services at the disposal of this enterprise. Actually a great number of artists belong to that group of people who survey the war only critically. That the lead-ing minds of the nation—to which the artists belong under any condition—can do a great deal for the sentiment of the people, is beyond doubt. Therefore, I should like to advise you, gentlemen, to try to get the artists of your district to co-operate with you. . . . .

The Bavarian Minister of War recently suggested to us that we should make more use of the placard. In England entire houses have been covered with war loan posters. We are convinced that the artistic poster is very effective, for the war loan poster by Erler had very good results. We shall, therefore, order a number of posters. However, we shall have to use some restraint, since artistic postering is very expensive, and post them only in places where they will be most effective, e.g., in railroad depots, factories, and labor dining-rooms. Also we shall have to use only good subject-matter for posters. . . . .

The question has been asked whether military authorities should participate in this work of informing the civil population by themselves giving speeches. Gentlemen, one cannot generalize about it. The military authorities, in general, have questioned its advisability for reasons of discipline. We are informed by some military authorities that military speakers have spoken with wonderful success at meetings regarding war loan subscriptions. On the other hand, I recognize the danger of letting soldiers speak at meetings. If we speak of soldiers, we do not think of the pre-war soldier, but in the field-grey uniform at present you find all classes of people represented. We must also not forget that the uniform enjoys a tremendous authority and that the word of a man, particularly if he comes from the lower army ranks and is decorated with the cross of the first class, sounds entirely different from that of a civilian giving a high-sounding speech. Of course, it is rather questionable whether to send soldiers into meetings of Social-Democrats who have an entirely different political philosophy and where a speaker of different views is simply yelled out of the building. I think, though, that in smaller places, where the individual is well known to everyone, it would be valuable, but probably not in the larger cities. . . . .

50. GENERAL VON KUHL'S ORDER CONCERNING OFFICER WAR CORRESPONDENTS SEPTEMBER 24, 1917[17]

Ia I.N.O. No. 27442. . . . . The intelligent development of the activity of the O.K.B. (Officer War Correspondents) is in the present situation of our people an effective means of maintaining and strengthening the interest of the homeland in the progress of the war.

V.S. d. O.K.

Distribution . . . . 125 copies. v. KUHL

[17] Collection of German Military Documents, Hoover War Library.

51. SPEECH OF LANDSBERG IN THE REICHSTAG AGAINST
THE PAN-GERMAN PROPAGANDA OF THE VATER-
LANDS-PARTEI, OCTOBER 6, 1917[18]

Landsberg: Gentlemen, on numerous occasions we have heard the
bench of the Federal Council express the principle that the army must
be kept free from the agitations of the political parties. The introduction of political agitation into the army has always been looked upon as
dangerous. It is a matter of opinion whether in peace time this theory
has always been practiced; in any case the principle has repeatedly been
emphasized that the introduction of political movements into the army
must not be allowed under any circumstances. This principle appears
to be abandoned in war time, although not entirely. A circular from the
Social-Democrats of Greater Berlin to the readers of *Vorwärts* in uniform was prohibited; also a brochure by Deputy Stücklen. The Pan-
German agitation, however, is regarded with favor. Pan-German
agitations are introduced into the army through innumerable channels,
and with the distinguished co-operation of the same authorities, who
have always maintained that the army should have no politics. We
know that the Fatherland Party, with its fine name, is a Pan-German
institution. [*"Quite right!"—Social-Democrats.*] The Pan-German
League, the Defense League, the Navy League, the Colonial League,
the East Mark League, the independent committees for a German
peace, they are always the same men: nothing is changed but the name.
[*"Very true!"—Left and Center.*] If one did not know that the Pan-
German Union was behind this party institution, it would be recognized
by the arrogance of the party name. One recalls the disagreeable way
in which that side, even before the war, often designated the opponents
of their extravagant position as enemies of their country. They maintained that Pan-Germans alone had the right to decide what was German
and what was patriotic (*Vaterländisch*). [*"Quite right!"—Social-
Democrats.*] By their choice of a name they tried to convey that they
alone defended the interests of the Fatherland. And at the head of this
party there are men *who hitherto*—I will use parliamentary language—
have not suffered through the war. [*"Quite right!"—Social-Democrats.*]
I do not assert that the Fatherland Party is *a party of persons having
an interest in the war. Many idealists have been caught in the net of*

[18] *Verhandlungen des Reichstags*, No. 122, October 6, 1917, pp. 3714–23.
This was in connection with the following interpellation by the Social-
Democratic Party: "Is it known to the Chancellor that orders have been issued
by deputy chiefs of the General Command by which the right of coalition and
meeting is treated in a one-sided manner in favor of Pan-German propaganda?
What does the Chancellor intend to do to check these abuses?"

this party. [*"Quite right!"—Social-Democrats.*] They ask: Are the sacrifices that have been made to be in vain? What an extraordinary idea: *The sacrifices have been made to save Germany. And that is to be regarded as useless?* Can one shed one's blood in a nobler cause than the deliverance of one's country? [*"Very good!"—Social-Democrats.*] We give place to none in love of our country. [*Applause from the Social-Democrats.*] Our love for our Fatherland is so great that we do not want to pursue Courland and Longwy-Briey at the risk of losing Germany. You must see clearly that without allies, Germany, however great her power—the question must be put in this way—cannot dictate peace to the world. [*"Very good!"—Social-Democrats.*] The time appointed for the realization of definite hopes is postponed again and again, just as an insolvent debtor renews the bills he has drawn and cannot meet. The people's necessities of life are spoken of. They consist of something very different from the ore districts of Longwy-Briey and Courland. When one sees the picture drawn of all that Germany must have in order to exist, one wonders that we could get on so well for forty-three years. The prophecy that the Empire would be ruined unless some particular conquest were made by the sword should also be accepted with caution. The idealists in the Fatherland Party should ask themselves what we really could do with these conquered territories.

We have not the gift necessary for moral conquests. [*"Very good!"* —Social-Democrats.*]

Certainly we should improve the educational system, build railways, etc., but the population would remain anti-German, because we always forget quite a trifle, namely, that other nations also have a soul. [*"Very good!"—Left.*] We can only maintain ourselves in the future if we can break up the enemy alliance. The best means of consolidating this alliance would be German territorial conquests. [*"Quite right!"—Left.*] I speak thus to the idealists in the Fatherland Party. I must speak otherwise to the men who, because the war furthers their material interests, will not be restrained from active agitation which must serve to prolong the war. No doubt they may have to bear sufferings, but they are other people's sufferings. [*"Very good!"—Left.*] They buy up newspapers, and spend enormous sums on the creation of an atmosphere in which a war profiteer is really happy. . . . . The gentlemen have learned that a good elbow thrust is more serviceable than gentleness of spirit and elevation of mind. They bring these business experiences into politics. Among their resources are occasional threats not to subscribe to war loans unless the Government makes satisfactory statements. [*"Hear, hear!"—Left.*] One can only wonder that they still supply material for the war although it threatens to end in a peace of renunciation. [*"Very good!"—Left.*] But they are altruistic enough for that! [*Laughter.*] When a man who has been under fire says the war should not end without German conquests, respect for the man would prevent my passing any judgment on his views. [*"Very good!"* —*Left.*] But I should like to cry shame on the men whose conditions of life are favorably influenced by a prolongation of the war, as is shown by the daily quotation of dividends, and who at the same time agitate for conquests. [*Disturbance on the Right; applause from the Left and Center.*] I hope [*turning to the Right*] you have the feeling which alone can enable you to understand this appeal. [*On the Left: "No."*] They have created a fund of millions to corrupt the soul of the German people. [*Great disturbance on the Right and cries of: "Unheard of!"* *Von Westarp: "Agitator!"*] You are an expert on agitation. They want to repress efforts to increase the political influence of the people. Ostensibly they want to avoid internal discord. [*Loud applause on the Left. Ebert, Socialist: "It is their only business."*] They want to disgust the German people with parties; State and people are to be one. This war, however it may end, must result in want and misery. The gentlemen know this very well, and therefore they put forward war aims in which they do not believe themselves in order that they may afterward make the Reichstag majority responsible for all the misery which stands to the credit of the war. [*"Quite true!"*—*Left.*] The Liberals who have joined the Fatherland Party did not understand [*laughter from the Right*] this. It is not long since one of these men, Ludwig Thoma, was to be tried by the Supreme Court of Justice in Leipzig by desire of the Conservatives for high treason because the French made use of pre-war illustrations from *Simplicissimus* in pamphlets to demonstrate German barbarity. [*"Hear, hear!"*—*Left.*] He has now been pardoned. The case of Ludwig Thoma shows that a clever man and an excellent novelist can be at the same time a very poor politician. [*"Very true!"*—*Left.*] Freiherr von Wangenheim's suggestion that controversial matters should be dropped now should have given the Liberals in the Fatherland Party food for reflection. If we stand for greater freedom even now during the war, it is because we look on democracy as the source of the greatest and most powerful force, because we want to increase the German people's will for victory. The Fatherland Party should be conspicuous for its conscientious pursuit of one aim and self-effacement. It seems that conscientious pursuit of one aim is to apply to the Conservatives and self-effacement to the Liberals among its members. [*Laughter.*] A flood of vituperation has been poured on the Reichstag. "Whining for peace," "cowards," "paid foreign agents," and so forth. Scheidemann is said to be in English pay. [*Laughter and protests from the Social-Democrats.*] These people cannot understand anyone taking an active part in politics for any other object than money. The Reichstag has been called an "idiot

asylum," and the Reichstag resolution an "ignominy peace resolution."
And when Riga fell the tactful remark was made that the majority were
depressed at this military success. [*Shouts from the Left.*] The
Deutsche Tageszeitung, the German paper in which morality touches its
nadir [*applause on the Left, and an uproar on the Right*], continually
speaks of the "Hunger Peace Majority." It seems that a not inconsiderable portion of the class whose interests are represented by the
Deutsche Tageszeitung are not very much troubled by the idea of their
own people starving. [*Continuous uproar on the Right. Von Westarp:
"Shameless!"*] I am surprised at your anger. [*Von Kreth: "We are
not so callous!" Laughter on the Left.*] The fact that all the necessities
of life disappear from the markets as soon as maximum prices are fixed
should give food for reflection. It was not for nothing that Herr v.
Heydebrand went to the trouble of warning his class comrades in the
House of Deputies. [*Von Westarp: "Class Comrades?"*] I know, Herr
von Westarp, that you are not very good at interrupting. The German
Reichstag will proceed from vituperation to the order of the day. If
the gentlemen of the Fatherland Party think that war can be waged not
only against the whole world but also against the majority of the German people, we will not dissuade them from that. They might, however,
consider how far they have brought about inclination for war among
the peaceable German people. The feeling in favor of war was immensely increased in America by an article in the *Alldeutschen Blättern*
in which Herr v. Strantry invited the thirty million German-Americans
to come into the war on Germany's side and not to forget Canada. He
exhorted them also to form themselves into an independent state with
the Irish. Here we laughed at such absurd rubbish, but in America they
foamed with anger. Bethmann is right—the war has intensified the Pan-
German want of intelligence to the point of absurdity. The Pan-German
Union was founded to protest against the Zanzibar agreement which
gave Heligoland to Germany. This agreement was the greatest sacrifice
of German interests, according to the Pan-Germans, and necessitated
an organization of all true patriots. Had the Pan-German agitation been
successful at that time, the English would now erect a monument in
Trafalgar Square to commemorate the founders of the Pan-German
Union. [*"Very good!"—Social-Democrats.*] No greater satisfaction
could be given to those in favor of prolonging the war in foreign countries than the appointment of a Pan-German as Chancellor [*Cries of
"Herr Kapp!"*]—or, better still, Count Reventlow. The German people
do not want this atmosphere of hate. [*Laughter from the Social-
Democrats and the Left.*] The Reichstag majority of July 19 have been
reproached with having represented the position as desperate. That is
a dangerous falsehood. [*"Quite right!"—Social-Democrats.*] Great as
is our longing for peace, we continue to repeat that we would not pur-

chase it at the price of Germany's mutilation or oppression. [*Applause from the Social-Democrats.*] But neither will we impose the yoke on other nations against whom we are defending ourselves. [*"Very good!"* —*Social-Democrats.*] If anyone believes that Germany cannot exist without a war indemnity, that is a mammonist idea. We have the courage to tell the nation that after the war it will have to work terribly hard; we also have confidence, however, that the nation will pull through this period. [*"Very good!"*—*Social-Democrats.*] We refuse to play, like the gambler, for increasingly high stakes at the risk of the loss mounting up to a gigantic figure. Barnum methods could hardly go further than they have been followed by the Fatherland Party. The pastor of Niederschönhausen asked how anyone could stand before God if he did not belong to the Fatherland Party! [*Laughter from the Social-Democrats.*]

We protest against this agitation on the part of the authorities on behalf of the Fatherland Party. From all parts of Germany appeals for help come from unfortunate people who have been compelled by their superiors to join the Fatherland Party. In a large number of places the town halls have been turned into centers of agitation for the Fatherland Party. Legal officials agitate for it. They should rather concern themselves with the coal and food supply. [*Applause.*] In Hanover they have the good taste to call on the people to fight the enemy at home and abroad. The business office of the Fatherland Party in Breslau is in the official building of the Provincial Administration; in Potsdam it is in the Royal Government building. [*"Hear, hear!"*] In Breslau was circulated a proclamation signed: "Postmaster Linde and 78 officials." This "and" is really delightful. Which is the most surprising, the lack of pertinence of the 78 officials or the impertinence of the superior? In Hamburg, Herr Traub [*"Hear, hear!"*], Herr v. Liebert, and Herr v. Graefe spoke. Herr v. Liebert spoke of a "Cowardice Resolution." He must have forgotten that some friends belonging to his "Fraktion" voted for it. No prohibition was issued against Herr v. Liebert speaking, but when a reply was to be made at a workmen's meeting, the permission which had been given was withdrawn. [*Indignation among the Socialists.*] . . . .

Information comes from all sides that the military superior officers recruit members from among the soldiers. Soldiers are ordered to attend Pan-German meetings, as, for instance, at Freiburg in Saxony. [*"Hear, hear!"*] The poor devils even have to pay the contribution out of their 53 pfennigs per day. The soldiers are requested only to give their civilian profession in this connection. They want to obliterate all trace of the cheat. We have further information that agitation of this kind is being conducted by the inspectors of the 10th Army Corps Prisoners of War Camp, by almost every military bureau in Hanover, the 14th Jäger Battalion, the staff of the 346th Infantry Regiment, the 2d Landsturm Infantry Battalion, Insterburg, and even in Macedonia. A certain Lieutenant Berg agitated in Crossen. When only a third of the troops responded he called the remainder "wretched fellows." Which is the more deserving of this description, a subordinate who resists a superior's unreasonable demand or a superior who abuses his power? In the chemical department of the Ministry of War a notice was also sent round asking people to join the Fatherland Party, and everyone signed, as they knew what they would risk by not doing so. Such notices were sent round the headquarters in the Mark by request of the commanding officer ["*Hear, hear!*"], and circulated in the offices of the High Command. Herr Backmeister, a virtuoso of the Fuhrmann orchestra [*laughter*], was engaged in Cologne for a meeting under the auspices of the Acting General Command. .... In the 7th Army Corps district, a certain Pastor Krüger was put up to give lectures; he had the audacity to assert that when the soldiers heard the news of the Peace Resolution they were angry that the Reichstag could not be flogged. The study of theology apparently does not always have an elevating effect. [*Laughter.*] .... In another case a number of ready-made speeches were supplied for use, with a notice stating that the use of these in case of necessity might be regarded as a national service. [*Great excitement from the Left.*] .... It is really high time that we should get out of the suffocating atmosphere of a state of siege, for it breeds a corruption which bodes ill for the future. ["*Very good!*" —*Left.*] On the Western front Deputy Traub delivered at least fourteen lectures; Herr Mumm was sent to the East. Which front will complain that the other is more favored? Discussions are not allowed at the meetings. So they want a peace in accordance with the soldiers' wishes, but the wishes are not to be expressed. Recently Herr Max Bewer was allowed to visit the Western front. Judging by his public statements, the whole year is one long day of roses to him. [*Great merriment on the Left.*] In his speeches he spoke against the "eternal peace twaddle," and invited the Emperor to kick the political starvelings, Scheidemann and Erzberger, out of doors. Superior military officers were present and did not object; on the contrary, the series of meetings was completed. The Censor, however, prohibited the publication of reports of these lectures. ["*Hear, hear!*"—*Left.*]

Even those who are ill are not left in peace; there has been the same activity in the hospitals. In Mainz anyone who spoke publicly in favor of restoration of the *status quo ante* was declared to be guilty of high treason. .... It was said in a prisoners' camp that Erzberger and Scheidemann ought to be in a lunatic asylum; on another occasion a major spoke of "Scheidemann and the other clowns." .... A cheery captain took the cake when he expressed his surprise that no one had yet shot down Scheidemann. [*Laughter on the Left.*] I do not hold any official quarter responsible for these extravagances. People must be perverse indeed to relish such idiotic abuse. But the whole of this propaganda is arranged in high quarters (*von oben*). Army orders before us prove this, and therefore politics have been introduced into the Army. . . . . It is done on quite definite principles, as to which the War Minister will perhaps give us some information. [*"Very good!"—Social-Democrats.*]

One more word as to the War Press Bureau. . . . .

A physician, Professor Zimmermann, approached Field-Marshal v. Hindenburg with a suggestion that the medical men could best get at the sick and convalescents in the hospitals. Zimmermann said the Social-Democrats in the Army had no idea what Scheidemann wanted and that the middle classes must be got at through the purse to win them over to the right peace. [*"Hear, hear!"—Left.*] The War Press Bureau comments on this that Professor Zimmermann's suggestion appears thoroughly worth consideration. . . . . This whole propaganda is admittedly directed against our resolution of July 19. . . . . Ostensibly they want to fortify the soldiers' courage. That is neither possible nor is it necessary in the case of the men fighting in Flanders and the victors of Riga. Everything is political which concerns the state, and there is nothing which could possibly be more political than the question of the conditions under which peace shall be concluded. Politics can be tolerated in an army only when it feels itself politically absolutely united; this may tend to fortify its courage. It is not the case in our army, in which all parties are represented, and agitation against the Reichstag majority must be offensive to the supporters of those parties, and result in general discontent calculated to lower their military efficiency.

Ambition for annexations is augmented by distance from the front. This agitation is likely to create a feeling among the soldiers that among their superiors there are men who want to prolong the war for objects over and above defense. That is an immense danger. . . . . The policy of the Reichstag majority is also that of the Imperial Chancellor. He stated that in the plainest words in the answer to the Papal Note. The Imperial Chancellor has hitherto been a blank sheet. It is the duty of the German Empire and the Imperial Chancellor to remove the sting from the enemy bees, to whom every budding Pan-German agitation is honey. The reply to the Papal Note was good work; *may the sword not spoil what the pen has made good.* [*Laughter on the Right.*] The Imperial Chancellor must announce that he is taking steps against this agitation. We are giving him an opportunity of showing that he will not allow the direction of affairs to be taken out of his hands, as he said. The welfare of the Empire will depend to a very great extent on his attitude. [*Hearty applause from the Social-Democrats.*]

52. LA DOMINATION BRITANNIQUE EN INDE

Par William Jennings Bryan, Ancien Secrétaire d'État des
États-Unis d'Amérique[19]

"Qu'est-ce que la vérité?" demanda jadis Pilate. Et il n'attendit point a la réponse à la question. Celle-ci a été posée plusieurs fois et les réponses ont beaucoup varié. L'énigme me revint à la mémoire lorsque je lus, au-dessus du portail du Palais de Justice à Aligarh, en Inde, la devise: "La justice est la force de l'empire Britannique."

Aucun empire, aucun gouvernement, aucune société ne peuvent avoir d'autre source permanente de force. Des chefs hindous citent les paroles de Lord Salisbury: "L'injustice acculera les plus puissants à la ruine"; et, tous, nous le croyons volontiers. Wendell Phillips exprima la même pensée avec autant de vigueur et encore plus d'éloquence (je cite d'après mémoire): "Vous pouvez bâtir vos capitoles jusqu'à ce qu'ils atteignent le ciel, mais s'ils sont fondés sur l'injustice le pouls d'une simple femme les fera crouler. ...

Pire que le Despotisme Russe

Le gouvernement de l'Inde est tout aussi arbitraire et aussi despotique que ne le fut jamais le gouvernement de la Russie; et à deux points de vue, le premier est encore pire. D'abord, il est entre les mains d'un peuple étranger, tandis que les fonctionnaires en Russie sont des Russes. Ensuite, il dépense en dehors du pays une grande partie des impôts; le gouvernement russe, au contraire, dépense chez lui l'argent obtenue du peuple. ...

L'Inde et la Politique Coloniale

Que personne ne s'avise à citer l'exemple de l'Inde en faveur d'une politique coloniale! Sur les bords du Gange et de l'Indus l'Anglais— malgré ses nombreuses bonnes qualités et nonobstant ses importantes contributions à l'avancement de la civilisation — a une fois de plus démontré combien il est impossible à l'homme d'exercer sagement et équitablement le pouvoir sur un peuple sans défense, lorsque aucune responsabilité ne s'attache à l'exercice de sa charge. L'Anglais a, sans doute, conféré quelques bienfaits à l'Inde, mais le prix qu'il a exigé pour eux a été énorme.

Tandis qu'il se vante d'avoir apporté la paix aux vivants, il a donné

---

[19] Collection of German Propaganda, Hoover War Library. *British Rule in India* was translated into French, Italian, Spanish, Portuguese, Dutch, German, Arabic, Turkish, Hindu, and Urdu. The English edition stated: "The sending of this publication out of the United States *prohibited* by President Wilson."

à des millions la paix du tombeau; tandis qu'il fait volontiers valoir l'ordre établi par lui parmi des tribus guerrières, il a appauvri le pays par un pillage légalisé. "Pillage" est, certes, un gros mot; mais aucune subtilité de langage ne pourrait servir à rendre le systéme actuel moins inique.

Combien cela durera-t-il avant que la conscience purifiée des habitants chrétiens de l'Angleterre entende la supplication qui monte vers eux de l'Inde enchaînée, avant qu'elle consente à appliquer à la plus grande colonie anglaise ces doctrines de fraternité humaine qui ont donné à la race anglo-saxonne le prestige dont celle-ci jouit?

53. "AMERICA, ONCE THEY WERE MORE FORTUNATE"[20]

Wilson once more opened his big mouth. As we all know he seems to feel like a pocket edition of God Almighty and decides upon what conditions a lasting peace is to be concluded for all peoples. Of course, it is twaddle when a nation, which so far has performed only the basest stock-market jobberies and has not shown a cent's worth of bravery, all of a sudden aims to play the rôle of a big world power. Let Wilson first of all raise and train his 5,000,000 soldiers which he has promised to the world; and then let him inoculate in those men a sacred patriotic feeling instead of that detestable worship of the dollar. Until then his "Wild West" fighters need not concern us. . . . .

54. GERMAN MILITARY PROPAGANDA[21]

(a) THERE COULD HAVE BEEN AN END TO ALL BOMBING

if your ministers had not rebuked our attempts to have a conference in a neutral country.

1. YOUR MINISTERS TELL YOU YOU ARE FIGHTING FOR BELGIUM

Your labor leaders declared that if Germany would give up Belgium they would decidedly be against the continuation of the war.

a) Count Hertling, Imperial Chancellor, declared he would agree to Belgium's freedom (speech, 12-7-18).

b) Dr. Solf, State Secretary, repeated this declaration (speech, 20-8-18).

c) Dr. v. Payer, Vice-Chancellor, said: "The Government does not intend to annex Belgium" (speech, 12-9-18).

DO YOU STILL BELIEVE YOU ARE FIGHTING FOR BELGIUM?

[20] *Liller Kriegszeitung*, No. 109, June 22, 1917, p. 1.
[21] Collection of German Propaganda, Hoover War Library.

2. Your Ministers Tell You You Are Fighting for a League of Nations

Your labor leaders demanded a league of nations and national self-determination.

a) Count Czernin, Austrian minister, agreed (speech, 2-4-18).

b) Prince Max v. Baden expressed his sincere hopes that a league would be formed (speech, 22-8-18).

c) Dr. v. Payer, Vice-Chancellor, agreed (speech, 12-9-19).

d) Mr. Erzberger, M.P., not only agreed, but did his utmost for its realization.

DO YOU STILL BELIEVE YOU ARE FIGHTING FOR A LEAGUE OF NATIONS?
OR WHAT ARE YOU FIGHTING FOR?

Do you think you can destroy Germany? If so . . . . try it.

Do you think America will attain what Russia could not manage with Rumania's help in 1914, 1915, 1916, 1917?

Do you think America has gained the predominance in shipbuilding and has seized the world's commerce for your sake?

54. (*b*) SPILLING YOUR BLOOD FOR ALSACE-LORRAINE, THE TRUTH

What do you know about Alsace-Lorraine?

Do you know that its proper historic name is Elsass-Lothringen?

Do you know that most of the territory which Germany is supposed to have "robbed" from France in 1870 was actually robbed from Germany by an invasion of the armies of that French tyrant, Louis the Fourteenth, in the very midst of peace, in 1674 and 1681? That adjoining pieces of pure German territory were forcibly "annexed" by France during the French Revolution?

These were among the most brutal and lawless robberies in all history, for in race, speech, family names, architecture, dress, everything that makes nationality, these provinces and their population are GERMAN.

Today 85 per cent of this population speaks German even after the long French occupation.

IN 1870 GERMANY MERELY TOOK BACK HER OWN PROPERTY AND PEOPLE—and not even all the stolen property, for originally Verdun, Toul, and Nancy (Nanzig) were German soil.

Read your own historians. Read what the English newspapers of the period said of the absolute justice of Germany's action—to mention but a few, *The Times* of September 7th, 1870, the *Saturday Review* of September 10th, the *Daily News* of September 20th!

The French clamor dishonestly for the "de-annexation" of Alsace-Lorraine. Well, this "de-annexation" was made by Germany in 1870.

During French rule the provinces were poverty-stricken, backward, their inhabitants the butts of the French. During the forty-eight years of German rule the provinces have flourished, industry has revived, the people have become prosperous and well educated—though French spies and agents constantly sought to stir up trouble. France was happy, rich, and strong without these two German lands. But her "Revanchards" continued to breed hatred and revenge—not because of Alsace-Lorraine but because of the well-merited thrashing France received in 1870.

If the French are so sure that the Alsace-Lorrainers wish to become French, why do they object so furiously to a popular vote? If they are not sure and wish once more to rob these lands—and such is the case—how can they or their allies still have the monstrous impudence to prate of the principle of "self-determination of nationality"?

To the rabid French Jingoes Alsace-Lorraine is merely an excuse for their senseless and criminal war of *revanche*. Germany did not "attack" France, as you have been told, but asked her whether she were for war or peace. France, tied body and soul to Tsaristic Russia, returned a threatening answer. She wanted war—had wanted it ever since 1870!

And now you are to shed your blood to help the robbers of German soil to recover their former booty! For this British blood is to flow in torrents! To aid in repeating one of the crimes of history!

Listen to what a great English historian, E. A. Freeman, says:

"The Kingdom of Germany has suffered large dismemberments. In the sixteenth century the three Lotharingian Bishoprics of Metz, Toul, and Verdun were won by a mixture of force and fraud."

"Alsace sounds as if it had been a French province from all eternity; the Teutonic Elsass suggests ideas altogether different."—*Select Historical Essays,* "The Franks and the Gauls."

And now, thanks to a Lying Press, to tyrannous Dictators and unscrupulous Demagogues, Englishmen are dying in their thousands to help Poincaré and the Tiger Clemenceau to repeat the crime of Louis the Fourteenth and to give them an excuse for having what—only sacrificed hundreds of thousands of Frenchmen.

They are dying to help these madmen sow the certain seed of future bloody wars!

54. (c) DEAR PALS

Now here I am right in among the Jerries and have got a palliasse and blanket; that's more than you've got anyway. And I've found Jerry is quite a sport, and he don't mind sharing anything he's got with you. I know there's been a lot of mud thrown by the papers over there, but there's nothing to it as I've seen.

And now I've had time to think it over, it seems to me it's about time this damned comedy was cut out. What the hell's the use of keeping this up; we'll never get Germany to jump off the blooming fence, and this fighting-for-France dope is a damned foolish thing. Tell you what it is, fighting for Belgium and France, lads: I've been out here since 1914 and I've been in Belgium, I've been in Flanders, and in this last push down at Soissons; and if you think this country's worth fighting for, I don't. We'll freely give it to them any day and apologize for the state they find it in. If I'd known before I came out what a hole Belgium and France is, I'd never have volunteered to come. Let 'em fight for their own; they want it, not us. If they want Alsace-Lorraine back, let 'em get it. That's not our squabble; let 'em squabble between their two selves if they want Alsace-Lorraine.

They've been telling us all along that we're fighting against Prussian militarism. Say, Bill, can you tell me what that is? I should like to know; I've never come across it yet. They keep on shoving it down our throats about militarism as though it was Old Nick himself, but they've never told us what it really is. If it means fighting the Jerries, well, he's only a man same as us. When you were at work in your shop, at the bench or down in the pit, were you ever troubled by Prussian militarism? I'm blowed if I knew anything about it till this war started. All I troubled about was raking in the quids at week-end.

Then there's the Yanks! What the hell did they want to shove their noses into this business for? They're coming over here with all their swank about "Where's your God-damned shooting gallery?" But I "guess" and "calculate," as they say, they'll jolly soon find their "shooting gallery," and not a drawing-room shooting match, either. Stick them in the trenches up to their waist in mud and water and see how long they'll be shouting about carrying on the war! It seems to me they'll only keep things going another 2 years where it might have finished this year. And why are they doing it? Because it would be a pity to leave off now that the gun and ammunition manufacture is in full swing and the big pots are raking in all the brass.

Say, Bill! D'you recollect the duds they sent us over from America in 1914 and '15? Do you remember the S.A.A. stuff we used to get, that made a big kick and a bang and only dropped out of the muzzle?

What did they care, as long as they were paid for it! Was the Yanks after anything else but the Almighty Dollar?

And then don't you forget while we're losing ships and keep on building new ones to have them sent down to the bottom soon after, the Yanks are building ships as fast as they can; but they're not sending them out carrying ammunition across; they leave us to do that; they're just waiting till the war is over, then they'll start pinching our trade—in fact they're starting now. The American industry is up to full pitch turning out goods to flood the world with after the war, while our factories are all wasting valuable time and material turning out guns and ammunition, to go to the devil and to do the devil's work, and British workmen have been throwing their lives away for four years, and don't even know what for. What shall we get for it afterward? Supposing you or I went home with a leg off or crippled some way, what are they going to give us for it? Most likely the workhouse or sommat like that.

It's all right for the big pots to tell us we're fighting for the flag, for the motherland, or for liberty and all that! But give me back the liberty I enjoyed before the war, and I'm contented.

It's all right talking about fighting for Alsace-Lorraine, Bill, as the Froggies want, but what do I care if they drive us out of France? But let 'em come to that little island of ours; then the lads in blue will be able to have a go. Jerry knows as well as us they can't dig us out of there!

Now let's see this damned rotten business done with soon; I've no mind to sit around here another two years or so wasting my time, and you're doing the same, and what's worst of all, we don't know what for.

Ain't life worth more to you than rotting in a shell-hole at the end?

Hoping you'll come out of this all right,

Your old pal
JACK

54. (d) NEVER SAY DIE!

Don't die till you have to!

WHAT BUSINESS HAVE YOU TO DIE FOR FRANCE? FOR ALSACE-LORRAINE, OR FOR ENGLAND IN FRANCE?

Isn't it better anyhow to live than to die, no matter for how "glorious" a cause? Isn't it better to live and come back to the old folks at home, than to rot in the shell-holes and trenches of France?

You have had to hear many high-falutin' words about "liberty," "humanity," and "making the world safe for democracy"; but honest, now, aren't these catchwords merely sugar coating to the bitter pill of making you spend wretched months far from home? Do you really believe those German soldier boys in their faded grey uniforms on the other side of "No Man's Land" are hot on the trail of your liberties?

Just like you, they want the war to end with honor so they can go back to their home folks. All they want is a chance to live and let live.

And so, if it should happen to you to fall into their hands you will find that they will treat you fair enough on the principle of "live and let live." Why run any more chances than you have to? You might as well be a free boarder in Germany till the war is over. You don't want to die till you have to!

54. (*e*) THE BETTER PART OF VALOR

Are you a brave man or a coward?

It takes a brave man to stand up for his principles. Cowards stand behind leaders and die, imagining that by so doing they become heroes.

The motive of an act is its measure. If you think the war is hell and that you as a citizen of the United States of America have no business to be fighting in France for England, you are a coward to stay with it. If you had the courage to face criticism you would get out and over the top in no time to a place where there is some likelihood that you may see home again.

What business is this war in Europe to you anyhow? You don't want to annex anything, do you? You don't want to give up your life for the abstract thing, "humanity."

If you believe in humanity and that life is precious, save your own life and dedicate it to the service of your own country and the woman who deserves it of you.

Lots of you fellows are staying with it because you are too cowardly to protest, to assert your own wills. Your wills are the best judges of what is best for you to do. Don't ask anyone's opinion as to what you would better do! You know best what is the right thing to do. Do it and save your life! Germany never did any harm to you; all the newspaper tales of wrongs were printed to inflame you to the fighting pitch— they were lies; you know you can't believe what you read in the papers.

If you stay with the outfit, ten chances to one, all you will get out of it will be a tombstone in France.

54. (*f*) TO THE COLORED SOLDIERS OF THE U.S. ARMY

Hello boys, what are you doing over here? Fighting the Germans? Why? Have they ever done you any harm? Of course, some white folks and the lying English-American papers told you that the Germans ought to be wiped out for the sake of humanity and democracy. What is Democracy? Personal Freedom, all citizens enjoying the same rights socially and before the law! Do you enjoy the same rights as the white people do in America, the land of Freedom and Democracy? Or aren't you rather treated over there as second-class citizens? Can you go into a restaurant where white people dine; can you get a seat in a theater where white people sit; can you get a Pullman seat or berth in a railroad car, or can you even ride, in the South, in the same street car with white people? And how about the law? Is lynching and the most horrible cruelties connected therewith a lawful proceeding in a democratic country?

Now, all this is entirely different in Germany, where they do like colored people, where they treat them as gentlemen and not as second-class citizens. They enjoy exactly the same social privileges as every white man, and quite a number of colored people have mighty fine positions in business in Berlin and other big German cities.

Why then fight the Germans only for the benefit of the Wall Street robbers to protect the millions they have lent to the English, French, and Italians? You have been made the tool of the egotistic and rapacious rich in England and in America, and there is nothing in the whole game for you but broken bones, horrible wounds, spoiled health, or— death. No satisfaction whatever will you get out of this unjust war. You have never seen Germany; so you are fools if you allow people to teach you to hate it. Come over to see for yourself. Let those do the fighting who make profit out of this war; don't allow them to use you as cannon food. To carry the gun in their service is not an honor but a shame. Throw it away and come over to the German lines. You will find friends who help you along.

54. (g) HOW TO STOP THE WAR

Do your part to put an end to the war! Put an end to your part of it. Stop fighting! That's the simplest way. You can do it, you soldiers; just stop fighting and the war will end of its own accord. You are not fighting for anything anyway. What does it matter to you who owns Metz or Strassburg; you never saw those towns nor knew the people in them, so what do you care about them? But there is a little town back home in little old United States you would like to see, and if you keep on fighting here in the hope of getting a look at those old German fortresses you may never see home again.

The only way to stop the war is to stop fighting. That's easy. Just quit it and slip across "No Man's Land" and join the bunch that's taking it easy there waiting to be exchanged and taken home. There is no disgrace in that. That bunch of American prisoners will be welcomed just as warmly as you who stick it out in these infernal trenches. Get wise and get over the top.

There is nothing in the glory of keeping up the war. But think of the increasing taxes you will have to pay; the longer the war lasts the larger those taxes at home will be. Get wise and get over.

All the fine words about glory are tommyrot. You haven't any business fighting in France. You would better be fighting the money trust at home instead of fighting your fellow soldiers in grey over here where it doesn't really matter two sticks to you how the war goes.

Your country needs you, your family needs you, and you need your life for something better than being gassed, shot at, deafened by cannon shots, and rendered unfit physically by the miserable life you must live here.

The tales they tell you of the cruelties of German prison camps are fairy tales. Of course you may not like being a prisoner of war, but anything is better than this infernal place with no hope of escape except by being wounded, after which you will only be sent back for another hole in your body.

Wake up and stop the war! You can if you want to. Your government does not mean to stop the war for years to come, and the years are going to be long and dreary. You better come over while the going is good.

54. (h) LIFE, LIBERTY, AND HAPPINESS

So long as the Administration is determined to keep the war going there is only one way for you to get out of this miserable fix and that is for you to stop fighting. You can do this honorably. As a free-born American citizen you have the right to LIFE, LIBERTY, AND THE PURSUIT OF HAPPINESS. The American constitution guarantees to you these rights. Exercise them!

Get out and dash to safety! If you don't, you stand a very slim chance of ever seeing Broadway or the old home again.

The Wall Street millionaires may like this war, because they are becoming billionaires. But you will have to pay for it all, my boy, PAY FOR IT WITH YOUR BLOOD AND TAXES and the tears of your loved ones at home.

If you were fighting on your own soil against a foreign foe it would be another matter, but what are you doing in Europe? France is not your country, neither is Belgium nor Alsace-Lorraine. Are you satisfied that you are in the full enjoyment of your "inalienable rights to life, liberty, and the pursuit of happiness" as promised to you by the AMERICAN BILL OF RIGHTS?

The years will be lean and weary and the work will be hard and long for you, and the longer the war lasts the longer will be the debt which you will have to pay to the money magnates of Wall Street for the munitions you are shooting away.

Don't give up your life till you have to and don't give any more labor for the benefit of the money trust! Quit it!

55. WHERE DID THIS HAPPEN: AMERICA OR MECKLENBURG?[22]

"A little while ago this shocking case happened in Blackville, South Carolina." A negro working in the fields, on the estate of Jonathan F. Parker, was discovered by the overseer to have pulled ears from the cut corn and put them in a sack. The nigger admitted that he wanted to make malt coffee out of the corn. With blows from his whip the overseer forced the black to carry the sack with its contents to the farm buildings, where he threatened to shoot him if he tried to escape. Mr. Parker was furious with the negro and threatened to have him prosecuted and sent to prison. The nigger, however, implored him not to, and Mr. Parker consented on condition that the black agree to take a thrashing. The man, terrified, made no objection. A fire, however, broke out in the neighborhood, and attention was distracted from the delinquent. But Mr. Parker did not forget his honorable resolution. He went next day with the reaper into the park and there had him stripped to the skin. That done, he was made to stretch his arms round a suitable tree and his hands were tied together with a leather strap. In this position Mr. Parker laid on the negro with his hunting-crop, giving him some fifty strokes on his naked body. The poor wretch tried to jump around the tree in his agony, so Mr. Parker tied another leather strap round the tree and the black's body, and set to work again. Pain made the negro scream; he was forbidden to scream and told that if he did he would be gagged. Directly after the flogging, the nigger, though the skin of his back was torn to pieces, was sent to work again.

The case today was tried before a Blackville jury. They seemed to regard the whipping described to them as an everyday sort of occurrence, for they sentenced Mr. Parker to one month's imprisonment and his overseer to a fine of ten dollars.

"Thoroughly American!" our whole German press will exclaim. "Such a thing could only have happened in that arch-hypocrite Wilson's happy land of freedom! That's the moral standard of former slave-owners. That's American justice! Thank God, things are different with us!"

22 *Vorwärts,* January 27, 1918, p. 2.

But one moment, please! we have a slight correction to make; apparently we have made a blunder in the scene of action. Profuse apologies! It did not happen in South Carolina, but in Mecklenburg. The place is not called Blackville, but it is the Roggow estate near Neu-Bukow. The culprit's name is not Mr. Jonathan F. Parker; he is a Mecklenburg *Junker* . . . . ; his accomplice is no overseer, but a gamekeeper. And the victim is no negro but a white agricultural laborer called W——, a reaper. Finally, the court which pronounced the light sentence is not a Blackville "jury," but the court at Neu-Bukow. Otherwise the affair happened precisely as we have described it above.

It is no mere accident that this revolting incident should have occurred within that very Federal State whose constitution—if such a word may be used in this connection—has remained stationary since the sixteenth century.

. . . . [This *Junker's*] conduct is a disgrace to the German nation. How can this disgrace be wiped out? Only if its cause is removed. Down with the lawlessness of Mecklenburg and all such things everywhere! Down with the tyranny of the big landowners dwelling east of the Elbe!

56. THE MILITARY REPRESENTATIVE AT THE FOREIGN OFFICE TO THE CHIEF OF INTELLIGENCE, GREAT GENERAL HEADQUARTERS[23]

BERLIN, 14th of June, 1918

Herewith are being forwarded four copies of *Merkblatt No. 92*, entitled "France Bleeds to Death for England."

57. GREAT GENERAL HEADQUARTERS TO ARMY HEADQUARTERS, MAY 17, 1918[24]

Merkblatt No. 88, entitled "The German Defensive Offensive," is being forwarded herewith:

14th of May, 1918

(1) The goal of the German Defensive Offensive is the destruction of the power of the enemy armies, the annihilation of their units, and of their material, and thus the breaking of the enemy's will to war. The progress of the Battle in the West up to the present time has now, to a high degree, achieved this purpose. . . . .

[23] Collection of German Military Documents, Hoover War Library.
[24] *Ibid.*

58. THE CONFERENCE OF EDITORS OF TRENCH PAPERS AT MÉZIÈRES-CHARLEVILLE, AUGUST 1, 1918[25]

Publicity Bureau attached to
General Staff of the Field Army
Headquarters, Mézières-Charleville

B.-No. 11208 L   HEADQUARTERS, September 1, 1918

Enclosed for your information the Minutes of the Conference of the Editors of Trench Papers, held August 10.

(*Signed*) VON GLEICHEN
Captain and p.t. in charge of the
Intelligence Bureau of the Army

Copies to be sent to:
Nodohl der Heeresgruppen der Westfront..... 1 copy
Nodohl der Armeeoberkommandos........... 2 copies
Abteilung IIIb ⎫
Leiter der Armeezeitungen ⎬................. 1 copy each
Feldpressestelle ⎭
Reserve ....10 copies

MINUTES OF THE CONFERENCE OF THE EDITORS OF THE TRENCH
PAPERS, MÉZIÈRES, AUGUST 10

Present:
Major Kroeger .... Abteilung IIIb
Major Piper .... Kriegspresseamt
Hauptmann Freiherr von Gleichen.... Leiter der Feldpressestelle
Oberleutnant Flach .... Feldpressestelle
Leutnant v. d. Goltz.............. Feldpressestelle
Leutnant Winand .... Feldpressestelle
Rittmeister v. Seydlits .... IIIb West
Oberleutnant Flesche .... Genkdo Marinekorps
Leutnant Ebert .... A.O.K. 1
Leutnant Reinmann .... A.O.K. 2
Leutnant d. r. Esche.............. A.O.K. 3
Oberleutnant Strunk .... A.O.K. 4
Oberleutnant Wittich .... A.O.K. 5
Hauptmann Joho .... A.O.K. 7
Oberleutnant Deubner .... A.O.K. 19
Oberleutnant Gluth .... A.A. B.
Leutnant Bubendey .... A.A. C.

[25] Collection of German Military Documents, Hoover War Library.

The meeting was opened by Major Kroeger. Today's meeting, he said, was called in accordance with instructions received from the Quartermaster-General to the effect that in future the trench papers must be used more vigorously and efficiently to keep up the morale of the troops which lately seems to have been affected by the ever-increasing enemy propaganda, by the not altogether favorable conditions at home, and by the momentary change in the military situation at the Western front.

The Quartermaster-General is personally deeply interested in the growth of the trench papers. In order to be fully informed as to their functions he has had, a few days ago, a lengthy conference with First Lieutenant Flach.

On this occasion, he (the Quartermaster-General) outlined his views of the scope and function of the trench papers, stressing the following points: They must serve to enlighten the soldiers, in a manner adapted to their way of thinking, discussing such questions as the great demands of the present day, the economic needs and the causes which have brought this about, the war aims of our enemies, etc. The soldiers must be addressed in vigorous words. The time of masking the situation and of soothing words has passed.

The purpose of today's meeting is to clarify, by means of a general discussion, some of the most urgent problems. Only unrestrained discussion of the actual conditions can acquaint all with the knowledge gained from personal experience and thus help us to discover the means for remedying them.

The trench papers owe their existence to the initiative of some highly intelligent officers at the time when trench warfare began. At that time, their main purpose was to furnish entertainment. But now they have grown to be extremely important factors in imparting instruction and enlightenment. As has been emphasized in previous conferences, the Supreme Command does not wish to insist on uniformity. On the contrary, it is realized (by the Supreme Command) that all papers should retain their individual character stamped upon them by the individuality of their editors at the time of their foundation. The trench papers are not to compete with the daily press. They are to be supplements serving the needs of the soldiers and speaking to them in their own language. Thus the trench papers are valuable factors in helping the soldiers to understand the demands of the time (*Vaterländischer Unterricht*).

The editors must maintain the closest possible contact with the intelligence officers of the Supreme Command and with L.V.U. and O.K.B. of the army. Wherever such a contact does not yet exist it must be established immediately. But the Supreme Command of each Army (*Armee Oberkommando*) is to remain not only responsible for the trench papers but also for the civic instruction (*Vaterländischer Unterricht*) and for the activities of officers serving as war correspondents, as has been expressly ordered by the Supreme Command of the combined armies (*Oberste Heeresleitung*).

The Supreme Command of the combined armies will undertake to establish a central bureau whose express duty it will be to facilitate the close co-operation of the four organs just enumerated, and it requests that the junior intelligence officer attached to each army be designated by name. This officer will then be placed in charge of this function.

The publicity bureau (of the Supreme Command) will continue, as far as possible, to support the efforts of the trench papers, and whenever this bureau is unable to fulfill the wishes of the papers it will forward them to the Supreme Command either directly or through the Supreme Commands of the several armies. These wishes will be given careful attention, but one should keep in mind that unreasonable demands should not be made.

Speaking in behalf of the Supreme Command and representing Abteilung III*b* Major Kroeger expressed the hope that if all trench papers would co-operate in the spirit of mutual confidence and good will, such as expressed by the Quartermaster-General, the trench papers would continue to make progress along the road entered.

Point 1 of the Order of the Day

Distribution of the Papers

The discussion reveals disagreement regarding the question of free distribution versus payment. The majority decides in favor of free distribution. But it is admitted that even papers not distributed free of charge have steadily gained in circulation and are enjoying great popularity even among troops that have been recently detached from armies where free distribution is customary.

Major Kroeger: The question cannot be settled with absolute uniformity. The method of distribution must be solved by the managers of the papers themselves. They must convince the authorities, either directly or by N.O.S., of the value of the service performed by the papers. Under no condition must the papers remain unused and undistributed at the bureaus. Officers of A.O.K. going to the front may be able to assist in controlling the distribution.

Account must be taken of the constant changes in relocating the armies. Divisions sent back for rest and recruiting camps must be carefully considered. The papers must be obtainable at the railway stations where soldiers on furlough assemble.

A.O.K. 1 complains that the railway bookstores are not always willing to co-operate.

Major Kroeger promises that the matter will receive attention.

Point 2 of the Order of the Day

Economic Questions

A.A.C. stresses the danger of arousing the thought that peace is imminent.

Major Kroeger: This danger may be avoided. Presenting their material in a manner understood by the common soldier the paper should be an antidote against complaints received at the front from the families at home. The trench papers should discuss such questions as enforced collection of clothes, raw materials, rations, and housing.

A.O.K. 7: Since the trench papers are looked upon as being official, great care must be taken as to form and place of the matters discussed. Stories are suggested as being a suitable form for bringing out the necessity of thrift, collecting all sorts of materials, use of trains transporting soldiers on furlough, saving of clothes, etc.

A.O.K. 4: When economic questions were given increased attention in our papers the soldiers declined to read them. Officers of the educational staff and inquiries received by the papers testify that the soldiers are especially interested in the question of homesteads and settlements.

A.O.K. 1: The soldier wants to be entertained. He wants to laugh. He does not care for theoretical discussions. His own personal experience often contradicts what he has read. Information bureaus have proved to be of the greatest practical value; they have been developed from the "letter boxes" and now co-operate with the trench papers.

First Lieutenant Flach: Demands for reprints prove that discussions illustrated by statistics are most popular. It is not necessary to use the mask of narration (stories).

Major Kroeger: The trench papers must not be propaganda. A middle course must be adopted. Since spring the enemy propaganda dropped by aviators (Northcliffe, by balloon) has become so clever and so voluminous that special attention is demanded. What countermeasures are to be taken and by whom?

A.O.K. 4: Enemy propaganda dropped by aviators has recently increased twenty times. That depression is actually caused by it is confirmed by the reports received from the divisions and by a conference of the officers of the educational staffs. Effective political propaganda, such as Lichnowsky's, greatly attracts the soldiers.* [*My London Mission was distributed as A.P. No. 86 by balloon.]

Major Kroeger: Soldiers known to be in the possession of enemy propaganda must immediately be set right by the captains of their companies. In this the trench papers must give their assistance. It is most important that immediate action be taken in such cases without waiting for orders or instruction.

A.O.K. 4: Captains of companies are rarely able, unaided, to counteract enemy propaganda. Our own troops must be given powerful propaganda literature and such matter should also be dropped over the trenches of the enemy.

A.O.K. 5: Our own *Gazette des Ardennes* does not stand comparison with English propaganda.

Major Kroeger: The *Gazette* is exerting its influence, slowly but surely, but only on the French. The Supreme Command intends to leave to the individual armies the decision regarding measures to be taken in individual cases, but it also intends to issue orders giving general directions. The rewarding of soldiers who report the finding of enemy propaganda has proved to be effective and will be continued.

Lieutenant Winand: Considering the number of men in arms, 400,000 copies of our trench papers are wholly insufficient to play an important part. Publicity carried on by the field press is incapable of protecting us; it cannot do the work alone.

Major Kroeger: Quite correct! Our field press is merely a means; it must be raised to a higher level.

POINT 3 OF THE ORDER OF THE DAY

Information concerning the Military Situation and How to Procure the Material for Such Information

Major Kroeger: The Supreme Council furnishes the (central) War Publicity Bureau with the necessary orientation. In future, the intelligence bureaus of the several armies will also receive similar information in case of important events.

A.O.K. 7: Orientation received by the intelligence bureaus is very satisfactory. Together with the material received from the officers serving as war correspondents and from the War Publicity Bureau it is perfectly sufficient.

A.O.K. 2: Direct orientation would be preferable.

Major Kroeger: In particular cases editors may request by telephone or by wire material from the intelligence bureau of their own army, such material to be used for information, not to be published verbatim.

A.O.K. 1: Cologne is the only place where the actual daily material can be obtained over the telephone.

Major Kroeger: Wireless telegraphy may help out; contact with Akonach necessary for this.

A.O.K. 1: It is desirable that the intelligence bureaus of the several armies might be used as central receiving stations for all new information, this information to be relayed to the editors.

Captain Baron von Gleichen: This proposal was discussed in Berlin but not adopted, as it would necessitate a complete reorganization of the service. Brussels and Strassburg, branch stations of W.T.B., are easily accessible sources of information.

Major Kroeger: In future the intelligence bureaus of the several armies are to receive orientation from the Supreme Command direct. Editors of trench papers may turn to them. When it is desired that certain information be spread rapidly the intelligence bureaus will be used as agencies.

POINT 4 OF THE ORDER OF THE DAY

Supply of Paper

Major Kroeger: The intelligence officers of the several armies do not serve as depots for the distribution of paper.

Paper of better quality for the printing of pictures is desired by several editors.

Major Kroeger: [Translation of this short passage is omitted, as the German text does not seem to make sense; apparently the meaning is that Major Kroeger offers to use his influence with the authorities].

POINT 5 OF THE ORDER OF THE DAY

Question of Personnel

A.O.K. 7 and Marines: [Express] Complaints that the investigating commission has acted too rigorously.

Major Kroeger: Abteilung III believes (i.e., I am expressing the opinion of Abteilung III when saying . . . .) that the Supreme Command of each army is entitled [has authority] to insist that, in the interest of the papers, indispensable men be retained (i.e., not be sent to the front).

POINT 6 OF THE ORDER OF THE DAY

Co-operation with the Directors of the Educational Staff and with the Officers acting as War Correspondents

Captain Baron von Gleichen: Since O.K.B. maintains contact with the troops constantly and is best acquainted with their spirit it would be advisable to pay attention to its activities; the material sent out by it should be given more space in the trench papers. The troops like to see themselves mentioned in the papers. The example set by Armies 1, 3, and 7 should be followed. "Memorial tablets" should be reproduced in the papers and should be sent to the publicity bureaus and to the troops themselves. These tablets serve to inspire the soldiers; they send them home and have them framed.

A.A.C.: Our printing-presses are insufficient.

Major Kroeger: The printing might be done elsewhere.

A.O.K. 7 stresses the quality and importance of the memorial tablets; they must be reproduced.

Major Piper asks to have such tablets sent to him.

Captain Baron von Gleichen wishes to learn how the material sent to the papers by [Abteilung] III*b* is liked.

General satisfaction [is expressed].

Major Kroeger: The intelligence bureaus of the several armies and of the War Office are always ready to answer questions and to supply material.

Lieutenant Winand: Whenever there are problems deserving special attention the Publicity Bureau would like to receive suggestions.

Major Kroeger: The longer the war lasts the more difficult becomes the work of the trench papers. Some of the old and experienced editors have been called home; the economic needs are increasing. To adjust the tone of the papers to the spirit of the soldiers and to carry out simultaneously the orders coming from Headquarters is assuredly not an easy task. But where there is a will there is a way.

If the Supreme Command of every army is willing to co-operate with the intelligence bureaus and with Abteilung III*b*, we shall succeed, in spite of the enemy propaganda and in spite of the influences from home, in keeping up the morale of our troops until the war has been carried to a victorious end.

[Major Kroeger uses here the vague and guarded expression *"Einflüsse der Heimat,"* evidently anticipating the "Stab-in-the-Back" legend.]

Afternoon Session

Lieutenant-Colonel Nicolai: It is the duty of the trench papers to strengthen the morale of the troops. In order to do so they must relieve the soldiers of worries regarding their families at home as well as regarding their own future. Any exaggerated fears that they may have concerning the economic situation at home must be set right. They must be fully informed of what has been done for the benefit of the soldiers and their families. It is the duty of the Intelligence Bureau to aid the trench papers not only with articles ready for print but also with material.

It is also the duty of the trench papers to comment upon the events at the front in such a way that all sentimentality is avoided, that the common interest in the Fatherland is emphasized and thus the soldiers are encouraged and strengthened. They should appeal not only to those who are timid, but also to those who are strong and courageous. What is true must not be denied, but attention should not be called unnecessarily to events that are apt to have a bad effect on the morale.

To bring this about it is advisable to direct the attention of our soldiers more than before to what is going on in the enemy's camp: his war losses, his anxieties regarding the future. It should be pointed out that conditions over there are, in many ways, worse than with us. That holds true especially regarding the latest effects of the war: England is losing the political and economic world supremacy, while America is gaining; France is made dependent on England and is weakened by being the battleground. It must be pointed out again and again that our enemies are resorting to unfair means, that their aim is to crush Germany. Our soldiers must be made to realize that they are fighting for their very existence, for the future of the Fatherland and of their children.

As a rule political questions should not be discussed in the trench papers. If it must be done, such questions must be treated in a purely objective manner. Actual information should be used to counteract the poisonous propaganda of (certain) political parties.

Papers published daily are generally more effective than papers published at intervals. But the daily papers must retain the highest standards. It would be better to have papers published rarely but of excellent quality rather than mediocre dailies.

The circulation of the papers must be adjusted to the needs of the troops; it must be changed if the troops stationed in the district served by a paper are changed. In exceptional instances papers of districts in which the number of troops has greatly diminished may be used to help out other districts where large contingents are located. The intelligence bureaus might assist in making arrangements for the uniform and even distribution of the papers along the whole front.

The circulation of the papers among the troops needs improvement. They must be accessible to the greatest possible number of soldiers. They must be posted in public places; they must be obtainable in all soldiers' homes, at the railway depots, etc. Hospitals, recruiting camps, and similar places should be especially considered. To manage the shipping of the papers properly is difficult, but just as the troops are always provided with foodstuffs and provisions a way must be found to provide for their intellectual needs.

The editors of the trench papers must not be exclusively absorbed by the business of editing; they must try to understand the spirit of the common soldiers. Only thus will they know how to speak to them and to exert the proper influence. The trench papers must not be a foreign body in the army; they must be an organic part of it. In order to assure themselves that they conduct their papers properly the editors should pay attention to the opinion of their superior officers and to the commanding generals. A closer contact between the editors and the Supreme Commands of the several armies is desirable. The Supreme Command of the combined armies intends to emphasize the importance of the trench papers and will advise the Commanders of the several armies to support the papers. The War Publicity Bureau should constantly examine the trench papers, and wherever there is room for improvement it should suggest the proper remedies.

The Supreme Command of the combined armies has decided that, in future, it will supply the editors with information regarding the situation; general directions will also be furnished. But the editors must never be content to wait for such information, thereby losing the right moment for action. Directions from Headquarters must be the exception. The editors must know for themselves what to do and must act to the best of their knowledge.

59. NORTHCLIFFE PROPAGANDA[26]

A.P. 1

We are not waging an aggressive war against the German people. .... The destruction or the dismemberment of the German people was never one of our war aims, either at the beginning or today. Against our will, and wholly unprepared, we were forced into this war; we were forced into it in defense of the international law of Europe which was broken and in justification of the sacred treaties upon which European society rested and which were violated by Germany in a most cruel manner by the invasion of Belgium. We had to go to war or see Europe approach destruction and brutal strength triumph over international law and international justice. .....

We have not taken part in this war in order to disturb the constitution of the Empire, although we regard that militaristic autocratic constitution in the twentieth century as a terrible anachronism. ....

[26] Great Britain, Department of Propaganda in Enemy Countries, A.P. (Air Post), 1, 20, 40, 45, 65, 83.

A.P. 20

By Balloon (*Durch Luftballon*)

Seid Ihr Bayern ein Freies Volk?

(Are You Bavarians a Free People?)

No, you are not! Why? Because you are subjected by the instigator of the war.

Why are you in the war? Why are you fighting? Must you defend your borders? Why then are you fighting? Because you are a free people only in a limited sense; in reality you are only, as history shows, an instrument for carrying out the Prussian desires. You are forced to fight against innocent women, children, and old people; to murder and burn all that comes your way, to serve the Prussian militarists and Junkers. . . . . Ask yourselves why? What for? . . . .

All you can say now is that you are slaves! When your eyes are opened you will cry out:

"We want to be free citizens of Bavaria, and serve our King. We want to be free from Prussian influence."

The sooner you come to this view the sooner will peace come. . . . . Down with the instigator of the war, and Prussian militarism!

A.P. 40

By Balloon (*Durch Luftballon*)

Does It Pay?

Tomorrow you will probably be killed! Why? Because your Kaiser wants it! Does it pay?

At home your wives and children and mothers are starving.

Will your death help them? Are you going to death for that reason? . . . .

Why then are you offering up your life? . . . . Are you certain it pays?

A.P. 45

A Question of Bread

How long will it be before Germany has sufficient bread?

Why is it that England is never forced to distribute her bread in rations?

In England everybody eats as much bread as he wishes.

In Germany the bread ration is lowered continually. . . . .

How is it with the activity of the submarine boats?

. . . . Hindenburg has claimed that the U-boats would play their rôle. Have they done this?

. . . . They have not forced England to her knees. They have not prevented the transport of troops and cannon to France.

A.P. 65

By Balloon (*Durch Luftballon*)

German Troops!

You are being dragged again to the slaughter bench. The ghastly months of Verdun are being re-enacted. . . . . Your General Staff itself admits that the loss "in several places was more than usual." . . . . This means that it was terrible.

Reports of German officers found bear this out. Whole companies were destroyed to the last man; whole regiments were wiped out to a very few men. Some divisions lost 70 per cent, many 50 per cent of their number. . . . .

A few weeks ago a great annexationist deputy, the National-Liberal Stresemann, admitted inadvertently in the Reichstag that the war had already cost Germany two and one-half millions in dead.

Two and one-half million dead! A few more weeks at this rate and three million Germans will have given their lives for the mad plans of the Prussian Militarists.

A.P. 83 . . . .

The Result of the German July Offensive and the French Counter Offensive

From July 15 to 18 the German armies moved forward toward Paris. . . . .

From July 18 to 29 the German armies retreated. Since then further retreats are taking place.

They had crossed the Marne. Now they crossed it again in all haste. . . . . All the territory which they had gained they had to give up again. They left behind . . . . 33,400 prisoners of war, 400 cannon, thousands of machine guns, and a large quantity of war supplies. The war correspondent of a neutral paper, the *Morgenbladet* at Christiania, writes: "The German July offensive . . . . has ended in a woeful defeat. In no small measure this must be ascribed to the Americans."

No wonder that the German Emperor said to Karl Rosner . . . . : "The worst days of the war for Germany are still to come."

60. THE NORTHCLIFFE PROPAGANDA BUREAU IN HOLLAND[27]
(Duplicate)

Foreign Office
Intelligence Section A.N.
Secret 667   BERLIN, June 25, 1918

TO THE MILITARY REPRESENTATIVE AT THE FOREIGN OFFICE

According to a report received here, the newly established Propaganda Bureau of Lord Northcliffe in Holland, which is in close connection with the English Legation in The Hague, is henceforth to direct the political propaganda against the Central Powers. This Bureau plans to purchase various restaurants and hotels on the Dutch-German border, particularly on the line from Nijmegen to Maastricht, in order to be able to expedite their propaganda literature from these points to Germany without hindrance. According to one estimate, this Bureau has been organized with a fund of about two million dollars which will be exclusively used for political propaganda. . . . .

61. ORDER OF 15TH INFANTRY DIVISION ON ALLIED PROPAGANDA, AUGUST 12, 1918[28]

15TH INFANTRY DIVISION   August 12, 1918

On the afternoon of August 9, propaganda tracts of a seditious character, probably dropped by hostile aviators, were distributed along the road from Bac d'Arblincourt to the canal by German soldiers (wearing fatigue coat and black cap) to passing soldiers.

Everyone will be strictly warned that all tracts, whether loose leaves or packets tied up with string, dropped by hostile airplanes or found, will be immediately turned over to Headquarters with a statement of the place where they were picked up. It should be explained to the men by citing the above example how much damage they may cause by thoughtlessly distributing these tracts, and that they are liable to severe punishment.

Every man in whose hands such a tract has been placed is in duty bound to ascertain the name and unit of the distributor and to report it.

[27] Collection of German Military Documents, Hoover War Library.

[28] *Summary of Information,* American Expeditionary Force, General Staff, III, No. 157, September 5, 1918, p. 1054.

62. GENERAL ORDER OF THE 18TH ARMY
AUGUST 29, 1918[29]

18TH ARMY   August 29, 1918

ARMY ORDER

The enemy begins to realize that we cannot be crushed by blockade, superiority of numbers, or force of arms. He is therefore trying a last resort: while engaging to the utmost his military force, he is racking his imagination for ruses, trickery, and other underhand methods, of which he is the past master, to induce in the minds of the German people a doubt in their invincibility. He has founded for this purpose a special ministry, "The Ministry for the Destruction of the German Confidence," at the head of which he has put the most thoroughgoing rascal (*der geriebenste Schurke*) of all the Entente, Lord Northcliffe. He has been given billions for use in influencing the opinion in the interior of the country and at the front by means of paid agents, the assassination of ambassadors, and all the other ways in favor with the Entente. The method employed by Northcliffe at the front is to distribute through aviators a constantly increasing number of leaflets and pamphlets. The letters of German prisoners are falsified in the most outrageous way; tracts and pamphlets are concocted to which the names of German poets, writers, and statesmen are forged, or which present the appearance of having been printed in Germany, and bear, for example, the title of the "Reclam" set, when they really come from the Northcliffe press, which is working day and night for this sole purpose. His thought and aim is that these forgeries, however obvious they may appear to a man who thinks twice, may suggest a doubt, even for a moment, in the minds of those who do not think for themselves, and that their confidence in their leaders, in their own strength, and in the inexhaustible resources of Germany may be shattered. Fortunately, Northcliffe, "the Minister of Destruction of German Confidence," forgets that German soldiers are neither Negroes nor Hindus, nor illiterate French, English, or Americans, incapable of seeing through such machinations.

Explain these infamous attempts to your young and inexperienced comrades and tell them what our mortal enemy expects of them and what is at stake.

Pick up the leaflets and pamphlets and give them to your com-

[29] *Summary of Information,* American Expeditionary Force, General Staff, III, No. 171, September 19, 1918, p. 1126.

manders for transmission to the High Command, which will be able to make valuable deductions from them as to the aims of our enemies. You will thus help the Command, and you will also help to hasten the hour of victory.

VON HUTIER
Infantry General and Army Commander

63. A HINDENBURG MANIFESTO TO THE GERMAN PEOPLE
SEPTEMBER 2, 1918[30]

We are engaged in a severe battle with our enemies. If numerical superiority alone were to guarantee victory then Germany would long since have lain crushed on the ground. The enemy knows, however, that Germany and her allies are not to be vanquished by arms alone. The enemy knows that the spirit which inspires our troops and our nation renders us unconquerable, and has, therefore, along with the battle against German arms, waged war against the German spirit. He wants to poison our spirit, and believes that the German arms will be blunted if the German spirit is corroded. We should not treat lightly this plan of the enemy.

He wages his campaign against our spirit with various weapons. He drenches our front not only with a drum-fire of artillery but also with a drum-fire of printed paper. His airmen throw, besides bombs which kill the body, leaflets which are intended to kill the soul. Our field-greys on the Western front handed in of these enemy leaflets 84,000 in May, 120,000 in June, and 300,000 in July—an enormous increase. Ten thousand poisoned arrows per day in July. Ten thousand times daily the attempt to take away from each and all belief in the justice of our cause and our strength for and confidence in final victory. We may at the same time calculate that a great number of enemy leaflets have not been found by us. The enemy, however, is not satisfied merely with assailing the spirit of our front. He wants above all to poison the spirit of those at home. He knows what resources of strength for the front there are at home. His aëroplanes and balloons, it is true, do not carry leaflets far into the homeland, from which the lines are remote where the enemy is vainly struggling for victory by arms; but the enemy hopes that many a field-gray will send home the leaflet which so harmlessly fluttered down from the air. At home, then, it passes from hand to hand. It is discussed at the beer-table, in

---

[30] *Norddeutsche Allgemeine Zeitung,* September 5, 1918, I, 1.

families, in workrooms, in factories, and in the streets. Unsuspectingly many thousands imbibe the poison, and for thousands the burden which war in any case lays on them is thereby increased and their will to and their hope in the victorious issue of the war is removed. All these in turn write to the front about their doubts, and Wilson, Lloyd George, and Clemenceau rub their hands. The enemy attacks the home spirit also in other ways. The most insane rumors, calculated to break our internal power of resistance, are set in circulation. We discover them simultaneously in Switzerland, Holland, and Denmark. From there they spread in waves over all Germany, or they arise simultaneously, accordant in their senseless details, in the remotest parts of Germany, in Silesia, East Prussia, and the Rhineland, and from there pass over the rest of the country. This poison takes effect on men on leave and flies in letters to the front, and again our enemies rub their hands. The enemy is clever. He knows how to compound the powder for each victim. He entices fighters at the front. One leaflet said:

"German soldiers, it is a disgraceful lie that the French ill treat German prisoners. We are not brutes. Come to us confidently. Here you will find considerate treatment, good food, and peaceful shelter." As to this, ask the brave men who with unutterable difficulty have succeeded in escaping from enemy captivity. In barbed-wire enclosures, without a roof, induced by hunger and thirst to make traitorous statements, or forced by blows and threats of death to betray their comrades, spat at by the French population on their way to hard labor, bespattered with filth, and robbed of everything—this, in reality, is the paradise conjured up by the enemy.

Reproductions of original letters from prisoners are also thrown down in which German prisoners describe how well off they are. Thank God, there do exist decent, human, prison camp commanders in England and France. They, however, are the exception, and the letters which the enemy throws down are only of three or four varieties. He sends them, however, multiplied in many thousands of copies.

The enemy intimidates the faint-hearted thus: "Your fight is hopeless. America will finish you. Your submarines are of no use. We construct more ships than you sink. Your trade is destroyed. We shall cut you off after the war from raw materials. Then Germany's industries must famish. You shall never see your colonies again." Such is the tone of his leaflets, sometimes menace and sometimes cajolery.

What are the facts? In the East we have forced peace, and we are strong enough to do so in the West also, despite the Americans. But we must be strong and united. That is what the enemy fights against with his flysheets and rumors. He wants to deprive us of our belief, confidence, will, and strength. Why is the enemy still ever seeking for allies in the fight against us? Why does he try to force nations which are still neutral into war against us? Because we are a match for him. Why does he incite black and other colored people against German soldiers? Because he wants to annihilate us.

To others, again, the enemy says: "You Germans, your form of Government is wrong. Fight against the Hohenzollerns and against capitalism. Help us, the Entente, to give you a better constitution." The enemy knows what strength resides in our State and our Empire. But just for that reason he combats them.

The enemy also endeavors to open up old wounds in the German body politic. With his leaflets and rumors he endeavors to sow dissension and mistrust among the Federal States. We seized on Lake Constance many thousands of leaflets which were sent to Bavaria and were intended to stir up feeling against the North Germans. The German Empire, which was the dream of Germans for centuries, and which our fathers won for us, that is what they want to destroy, and to condemn Germany to the powerlessness of the Thirty Years' War.

The enemy also wants to shake our loyalty to our allies. He does not know the German character and the value of a German's word. He himself sacrifices his allies. Whoever is England's ally dies as a consequence.

And, finally, the enemy sends not the least dangerous of his poisoned arrows dipped in printer's ink when he uses statements made by German men and newspapers. Statements in German newspapers are wrested from their context. As to statements of Germans which are reproduced, remember there have always been traitors to the Fatherland, witting and unwitting. They mostly dwell in neutral countries in order not to be obliged to share our battles and deprivations, or to escape being executed as traitors. Neither should partisans of extreme party views claim to speak for the generality of the German people. It is our strength, but also our weakness, that even in war we allow free expression to every opinion. We have also tolerated thus far the reproduction in our newspapers of enemy army *communiqés* and speeches of enemy statesmen, which are at the same time weapons of attack against the spirit of the German Army and people. This is strength because it shows that we know our strength. But it is also weakness because it permits the enemy's poison to enter our midst.

Therefore, German Army and German Home, if one of these poisoned morsels in the form of a leaflet or rumor comes to your ears or eyes, remember it comes from the enemy and that nothing comes from the enemy of any service to Germany. That is what everyone must say to himself, no matter to what class or party he belongs. If you meet anyone who may be in name or origin German but in heart is in the enemy's camp, keep him at a distance and despise him. Hold him

up to public scorn so that every other true German also may despise
him. Be on your guard, German Army and German Home.

VON HINDENBURG
Field-Marshal General

GENERAL HEADQUARTERS
September 2, 1918

64. NEWS-SHEET OF THE 18TH ARMY[31]

No. 10   A.H.Q., October 6, 1918

> In support of the brave!
> In encouragement of the faint-hearted!
> In enlightenment of the doubting!

TO THE GERMAN ARMY AND THE GERMAN NAVY

For months past the enemy has been storming our lines with immense efforts of strength and without any pause in the fighting. You
have to endure and defy the numerically far superior enemy during
weeks of struggle, often without rest.

Therein lies the greatness of the task which confronts you, and
which you fulfil.

Troops of all German tribes are doing their duty and defending the
Fatherland heroically on foreign soil.

The position of my fleet, in asserting itself against the combined
enemy naval forces and assisting the army in its hard struggle by their
untiring work, is a difficult one.

The eyes of those at home are turned to the deeds of the army and
navy with pride and admiration.

I thank you on my own behalf and on that of the Fatherland.

In the midst of the severest struggle the Macedonian front has
collapsed. Your front is unbroken, and will remain so.

In agreement with our allies I have decided once more to offer the
enemy peace.

But we shall only extend our hand for an honorable peace. We owe
that to the heroes who have given their lives for the Fatherland; we
owe that to our children.

Whether there will be a cessation of hostilities is still uncertain.
Until then we must not flag. We must, as hitherto, do our utmost to
hold our own untiringly against the enemy assault.

[31] Collection of German Military Documents, Hoover War Library.

The hour is grave.

However, in reliance on our strength and on God's gracious help, we feel ourselves strong enough to defend our beloved country.

GREAT HEADQUARTERS
October 5, 1918   WILHELM I. R.

Everyone's initiative and co-operation is being sought!
Communications via field-mail to A.O.K. 18, Division V.U.

(To be passed from hand to hand)

CHAPTER IV

CENSORSHIP

INTRODUCTORY NOTE

THE OUTBREAK of the World War forced the immediate establishment of the censorship. From the standpoint of national safety it was necessary to control wireless communications, telegrams and cables, postal communications, printed publications. A rigid censorship was also essential from a military standpoint to prevent the enemy from securing valuable information.

To the Headquarters of the Army Corps Districts was assigned the task of administering the censorship regulations established by the Central Government. The censorship regulations for the press of Hamburg, for example, illustrate: the news which could not be published; the attitude which was to be taken toward certain questions; the inspired articles which could not be printed. Under these instructions and the system of preventive censorship, the corps commanders were able to prevent any discussion of questionable subjects, any criticism of the supreme command, any severe criticism of the civil government, and any allusion to military information.

Especially interesting are the instructions which insisted that the issues of all periodicals should not reveal any noticeable traces of censorship.

This press censorship, although as efficient as the French and British censorships, was not severe enough to prevent numerous indiscretions by the German socialist and even bourgeois press.

The postal censorship exercised an almost absolute control of this channel of communication and rendered invaluable aid to the military work of counter-espionage.

More suppressed pamphlets circulated secretly throughout the Empire during the war than in any other belligerent power. The censorship failed to close this channel of communication with an iron hand, and the inevitable result was that the revolutionary propaganda of the enemy thus entered Germany.

65. WARFARE AND THE PRESS[1]

The Chief Command in the Marks, that is, the military authority into whose hands, since the proclamation of martial law, the entire executive power and therewith the control of the press has passed over, makes the following announcement:

BERLIN, August 8 (W.T.B.)

In spite of many instructions and warnings, and although attention has been called again and again to the regulations (together with the article of the Penal Code referring to them) issued for the press, a number of newspapers have not considered it necessary to act according to these orders. The press is reminded once more, and for the last time, that according to the Proclamation of July 31, 1914, the printing of news regarding military affairs is prohibited. All military and naval matters, which include those relating to the allied armies, also all pictures and maps of similar content which the newspapers wish to print, must first be submitted, as follows:

For all matters of a military character to the Commander-in-Chief of the Marks, and for all matters of a naval character to the Reichsmarineamt. (Intelligence Bureau.)

We emphasize particularly that the printing of military and naval matters, which was accessible to everyone in times of peace, is prohibited during war time unless the censorship has made an exception.

Of course it is not permissible to give to the enemy a professional criticism of his military operations from our point of view, or to elucidate the mistakes he has made from a technical or tactical standpoint.

All news communicated by Wolff's Telegraph Bureau can be published only in literal reproduction and if the source is clearly stated. (W.T.B. is sufficient.)

During the last few days the High Command has in a number of cases warned editors of newspapers both in person and in writing and called their attention to existing regulations, and from now on measures of force will be resorted to against the transgressors. Public warnings have not been lacking.

In addition to this Wolff's Telegraph Bureau gave out the following:

BERLIN, August 8. In spite of repeated general warnings and references to the notice of the Imperial Chancellor prohibiting the publishing of military news, the *Tägliche Rundschau für Schlesien und Posen* has published such news. Further editions of this paper have been suppressed by the proper General Command.

[1] *Vorwärts*, No. 215, August 9, 1914.

From the standpoint of the General Staff such regulations and measures are quite comprehensible. For the press it signifies a great handicap in the performance of its service toward the reading public, a service which, during decades of peace, they have taken as a matter of course. At present the press and especially the press of the opposition is bound hand and foot, for in the publishing of and commenting upon news it is under the supervision of a military board.

In the *Militärwochenblatt* of September 2, 1913, there is an article on "The Importance of the Press in Times of War." The article first describes the conditions under which war reporting was done during the wars of the last century, including the last two wars in the Balkans. The following conclusions are drawn:

"As we have admitted that the press wields great power the military authorities will be obliged to consider it as an important factor in time of war. The question of the reporting of war news gains in importance as the means of transportation and the means of spreading news are developed. (Among these of late, especially wireless telegraphy and the telephone.) In the future we cannot expect to receive such full and extended war news as was given out during recent wars. To find the proper balance between what should be published in order to keep up a healthy popular morale and what must necessarily be suppressed in the news will always be an important problem for the military authorities."

With these principles in mind it must be evident to every intelligent reader that he cannot expect that the newspaper he reads will maintain, in its news service, articles, and editorials, the peculiar attitude which has characterized it in time of peace. If then at this time many of our readers are puzzled by the attitude of *Vorwärts,* they should remember that their paper, without giving up its fundamental standpoint, is, after all, much limited in its freedom of action. It is extremely difficult for the editors of a socialistic labor paper to combine the duty of protecting the interests of the laboring class with the task of conforming with the regulations of the military authorities.

66. INDEPENDENCE OF THE PRESS[2]

The appeal of Baron von Zedlitz concerning the necessity for the expression of one's opinions in the press finds characteristically general approval in the conservative press. In the *Tag* the conservative Professor Reinke, of Kiel, complains of "the not all too cheerful situation, when one finds one's daily paper filled with extracts from foreign newspapers under strong suppression of one's own work." Of course, in such a situation, those newspapers suffer much which try to form their

[2] *Vorwärts,* January 30, 1915, pp. 6–7.

attitudes not by whims but by a clear conviction gained in times of peace and confirmed in times of war.

As to the discussion of peace, Reinke demands, in agreement with v. Zedlitz, the following:

"Certainly the opinions about the attainable war aims differ, of course, widely; perhaps every brain pictures to itself a different result. Yet, all of us, up to the Chancellor, are at one in the will and desire to see Germany safeguarded against future attacks. There scarcely can be a permanent exclusion of a free expression of opinions concerning these war aims, nor concerning the various possible solutions of this problem.

"The public opinion in Germany at the beginning of the war has proved to be mature; and one should not silence it during the war. Even our diplomacy can profit by a sensibly restricted discussion in the press, as the public opinion of a people, of whom the highest demands are being exacted in all fields, expects to be enlightened in due time about important questions by official agencies, and the people, as a matter of course, do not desire to dull permanently the reflex of this light."

Further, Reinke will leave it to the Government to determine when the right time for a public discussion has come; but he, too, thinks this discussion necessary in the interest of Government:

"All of us have the desire to furnish to the leading statesmen timely information about the sentiment of the people as a basis for fundamental principles for their action. . . . .

"An objective press, which either brings forth the truth or searches for it, would be the ideal condition. Particularly if it is able to reflect openly the opinion of the people, or of large groups thereof, we must welcome it; for it, too, will presently promote a policy of the people, not that of the armchair."

67. *ARBEITERZEITUNG* OF DORTMUND UNDER CENSORSHIP[3]

The *Arbeiterzeitung* in Dortmund received the following ordinance from the General Command in Münster:

MÜNSTER, April 24, 1915

Registered
To the Editor and Publisher of the Dortmund
Arbeiterzeitung, *Dortmund:*

In your number of April 22, 1915, you published a comment on an article of Professor Brentano under the heading, "Against the Big

[3] *Vorwärts,* May 1, 1915, p. 9.

Talk," and adopted, as the chosen title shows, some of his statements, the publication of which is contrary to the prohibition of the discussion of war aims during the party truce (*Burgfrieden*).

As regards the latter point, you are to be especially reprimanded for stating that there are parties which are particularly interested in the continuance of a war fever among large numbers of the people. These parties are said to be especially those which are interested in an aggravation of the economic struggle among the nations. The animosity caused by the war is said to be already utilized as an effective means of promoting special interests. Such unfounded statements are apt to poison seriously the public life of the German people. On account of a similar statement I gave you a formal warning as early as March 20, 1915.

The attacks upon large numbers of the people who regard the annexation of Belgium as vital to the interest of the Fatherland have also been positively prohibited ever since your article, "The Future of Belgium," appeared in the number of March 26, 1915. (Rf. long distance call of March 27, 1915.)

Because your attitude is no guaranty of future avoidance of encroachments of the kind reprimanded, I decree a censorship of your newspaper. The local police is charged with the execution of the censorship. You are prohibited from publishing a text different from the censored one or from making known, in any form whatsoever, any suppressed passages or changes of the text.

It is left to you to publish this ordinance verbatim without any additions. Every different kind of publication and every kind of comment on the ordinance and on the underlying facts are prohibited.

The General in Command
BARON V. GAYL

68. ESTABLISHMENT OF THE WAR PRESS OFFICE[4]

The last number of the *Armeeverordnungsblatt* publishes the following ordinance:

In consequence of the enlargement of the Supreme Censorship Office, ordered by His Majesty the Kaiser and King, an agency called Kriegspresseamt (K.Pr.A.) has been established in Berlin. It is directly controlled by the General Staff and has been set up:

1. To facilitate co-operation between the General Staff and the authorities at home with regard to the press;

2. To give information to the authorities and to the press;

3. To take care of the uniform application of the censorship.

[4] *Norddeutsche Allgemeine Zeitung,* October 17, 1915, II, 2.

The principles of the central authorities concerning the application of censorship will be forwarded to the Censorship Agencies (*Oberzensurstelle*) by the Kriegspresseamt.

69. THE CENSORSHIP IN THE FREE AND HANSEATIC CITY OF HAMBURG, 1915–1917[5]

LIST OF DOCUMENTS

	1915	J.-Nr.	
Ia	Feb. 17	1550	Espionage
Ib	Feb. 17	1550	Military operations not to be published
II	Mar. 4	2130	Raw materials (Cf. XIb, XIIe, XVIIIa)
III	Mar. 15	2375	Reports of military or political affairs
IV	Mar. 20	2437	Reports of military or political affairs
V	no date	2375	Memorandum for the press
VIa	May 14	3663	German colonies and expansion beyond Europe
VIb	May 14	3663	Austria, a victim of Germany
VIc	May 14	3663	Bread and rice supply
VId	May 14	3663	Economic exploitation of Belgium (Cf. Xb)
VII	May 17	3746	Italy about to enter the war
VIII	May 26	3868	"Lusitania" (Cf. XVIIIa, XIX)
IX	Aug. 6	5624	Belgian archives
Xa	Aug. 15	5828	Reprinting war reports of the enemy
Xb	Aug. 15	5828	Exploitation of occupied territories
XIa	Aug. 28	6018	Censorship (Cf. XVI, XXb)
XIb	Aug. 28	6018	Oil and grease market
XIc	Aug. 28	6018	Pacifists in Stuttgart
XId	Aug. 28	6018	Peace and war aims (Cf. VIa, XIIb, XIIf)
XIe	Aug. 28	6018	Amendment of military laws (Cf. XIg, XIId)
XIf	Aug. 28	6018	Rumania, England, and France
XIg	Aug. 28	6018	Military laws
XIh	Aug. 28	6018	American cotton
XIIa	Sept. 7	6214	Military bill
XIIb	Sept. 7	6214	War aims of Social-Democrats
XIIc	Sept. 7	6214	Functions of Kriegspresseamt

[5] Hamburg-Polizeibehörde, *Zensur-Anordnungen,* February 17, 1915—February 5, 1917. The *Zensur-Anordnungen* include orders of the Central Intelligence Bureau (*Oberzensur*) of the Representative General Staff, Berlin, and orders of the Commanding General (*Armee-Oberkommando*) of the 9th Army Corps.

	1915		J.-Nr.	
XII*d*	Sept.	7	6214	Landsturm
XII*e*	Sept.	7	6214	Raw materials
XII*f*	Sept.	7	6214	Polish question
XII*g*	Sept.	7	6214	Polish question
XII*h*	Sept.	7	6214	Persia
XIII*a*	Sept.	15	6381	America (Cf. XIII*c*, XVII*b*, XXIV*c*)
XIII*b*	Sept.	15	6381	Oriental affairs
XIII*c*	Sept.	15	6381	Rumania, Japan, America
XIV	Oct.	1	6601	Speeches of Kaiser (Cf. XXIII)
XV	Nov.	29	7410	The press and the food situation (Cf. XX*b*)
XVI	Dec.	11	7415	Censorship
XVII*a*	Dec.	15	7420	Session of Reichstag
XVII*b*	Dec.	15	7420	Military attaché, Washington, recalled
XVIII*a*	Dec.	31	8071	Raw materials
XVIII*b*	Dec.	31	8071	Reprinting war reports of enemy
XIX	Jan.	14	111	American note
XX*a*	Jan.	26	120	Speeches of commanding generals
XX*b*	Jan.	26	120	Criticism desired by Government
XXI	Feb.	25	123	America
XXII*a*	May	19	1020	Ambassador Gerard
XXII*b*	May	19	1020	"Battle of the Marne"
XXII*c*	May	19	1020	"America and We"
XXII*d*	May	19	1020	German note to the U.S.A.
XXIII	Nov.	21	7011	Speeches of Kaiser (Cf. XIV)
XXIV*a*	Feb.	5	124	Supreme Command not partisan
XXIV*b*	Feb.	5	124	U-boat warfare
XXIV*c*	Feb.	5	124	Addresses to Kaiser urging U-boat warfare

I*a*
Stellvertretendes Generalkommando
  IX Armeekorps
Abteilung Id, No. 19626

ALTONA, February 17, 1915. J.-Nr. 1550/15.IV.M.

Without permission of the General Staff of Army III*b*, Berlin, no news of any kind must be printed referring to undertakings alleged to have been made by spies, for instance, the case of Corporal Tison, who is said to have been sent to the French socialists.

VON ROEHL, General of Artillery

I*b*   February 17, 1915

Discussions in the press regarding the plans of the Austrians in the Carpathian Mountains and the probable course of our military operations in the East are prohibited.

VON ROEHL, General of Artillery

II   March 4, 1915. J.-Nr. 2130/15.IV.M.

Supplementing our order of December 27, 1914—I*d*, No. 55681 (discussion of the scarcity of raw materials to be avoided), I make the following anouncement:

Such press notices are prohibited only in so far as they refer to materials necessary for our economic warfare and for the equipment and armament of our troops. To this class belong: grease, chemicals, saltpeter, wool, cotton, flax, hemp, hides, substances used for tanning, metals such as nickel, aluminum, copper, brass, zinc, tin, lead, antimony; also tin plate, graphite, rubber, resin, copal. The intention was not to prohibit reports regarding materials raised at home in sufficient quantities or of minor importance for the manufacturing of war equipments, such as coal, pig iron, aluminates.

Above all, no lists must be published revealing the change in prices or the volume of trading in the raw materials listed before.

VON ROEHL, General of Artillery

III

FREIE UND HANSESTADT HAMBURG
(Police Department)

Very Secret . . . .

HAMBURG, March 15, 1915. J.-Nr. 2375/15.IV.M.

By order of the General Command of the 9th Army Corps I herewith send you the enclosed Memorandum (*Merkblatt für die Presse*) with the request that the instructions contained therein be observed most closely. You are admonished to keep the Memorandum strictly secret.

Books and pamphlets are subject to the same censorship as newspapers. Any offense against these orders will be punished severely. I call your attention to the fact that it is your duty to submit to the General Command all articles touching upon military and political affairs *before* they are published. In case you desire to publish letters received from the front which touch upon naval affairs, such letters should first be submitted to the Intelligence Bureau of the Department of the Navy, Berlin.

You are requested to acknowledge the receipt of this letter and of the enclosed Memorandum on the enclosed formula, which you will return immediately to the Department of Police, Abteilung IV.

CHIEF OF POLICE DR. ROSCHER

IV

FREIE UND HANSESTADT HAMBURG
(Police Department)

Secret . . . .

HAMBURG, March 20, 1915. J.-Nr. 2437/15.IV.M.

Your attention is called to the order making the publication of all accounts of our military operations subject to the permission of the Chief of Staff of our Field Army. This order applies not only to detailed reports of our operations that are still going on but also of operations that have already been brought to an end.

The permission of the Chief of the General Staff may be obtained by applying to the Intelligence Bureau of the General Staff, Berlin.

DR. ROSCHER, Chief of Police

A MEMORANDUM FOR THE PRESS

V   (No date) J.-Nr. 2375/15.IV.M.
Secret

I

The Military Command, in referring to the "Prohibition of Publications about Troop Movements and Means of Defense," issued by the Chancellor, turns in this eventful time to the press as that organ whose works are being spread far beyond the confines of the Reich.

The history of late wars is rich in examples of how easily inadvertent reports may disclose to the enemy the marching up of the country's forces and thereby give the course of the war a turn destructive to the Fatherland.

The perfection of news transmission during the last few years has increased the danger of doing injury to the Fatherland by such publications.

More than ever are we being watched by our political adversaries; every inadvertent publication is being flashed to them in a thousand ways. Even reports which appear harmless often suffice to give the enemy an accurate picture of our military situation. If we wish to secure for ourselves favorable prospects for a war, then our military measures must be kept secret before the enemy as well as our own country.

Of course, uncertainty and doubt will be felt particularly heavily at this time, but the welfare of the Fatherland demands the sacrifice of strict discretion in all questions pertaining in any way to the German Army and Navy or to the military power of the Allies. Disclosures of military events in all other countries, too, must be refrained from until the clarification of the political affairs, since we do not know what attitude these countries will adopt toward us. As soon as this clarification takes place the press will be informed thereof.

If the press is conscious of its heavy responsibility and the consequence of its reports, it will not light-heartedly become an ally of our enemy. It will give thanks to the War Command when the latter informs it as to what publications would be injurious to the Fatherland. By refraining unselfishly from every report of a military character it will spare the military and naval authorities the necessity of taking legal action against it, the strictest enforcement of which in cases of violations of this prohibition is demanded by interests of state.

The War Command will in its turn do everything to satisfy the legitimate demand of the nation for news. If these reports will have to be at first rather meager, it will be best for the realization of the patriotic effort of the press if it enlightens the nation about the reasons for and the necessity of secrecy and reminds it of its duty.

Through the Press Bureau of the Great General Staff and the Admirals Staff of the Navy reports will be sent out as often as possible to the Generals in Command and the Commanders of Naval Stations for delivery to the publishers of their respective districts. This will be the surer and quicker way for all publishers to get in possession of news than by despatching their own reporters, who can be admitted to the theater of war in only very limited numbers and with restricted freedom of movement.

All requests of the press are to be directed to the local Generals in Command—in case of their removal to the front, to their representatives—to the Commanders of Naval Stations, in Berlin to the Press Bureau of the Great General Staff, Berlin N.W. 40, and to the Admirals Staff of the Navy, Berlin W. 10, Königin Augustastr. 38/42.

II

It is impossible to say beforehand all that which in case of war should be kept secret in the interest of the Fatherland. Tact and insight of the representatives of the press will enable them to form a judgment from the following statements in what matters silence is being dictated until further notice.

Measures the disclosure of which could be injurious to the Fatherland and be of value to the enemy:

1. Formation of troops for the protection of boundary, coast, and islands. The guarding of harbor entrances and mouths of rivers.

2. Measures for the protection of railroads, canals, buildings, etc., and the formation of troops assigned for it.

3. The appearance of our own airships or aëroplanes.

4. Data as tò the course of mobilization, the calling of reserves and the Landwehr, and the arriving of ships.

5. The placing of new troop formations and their description.

6. The arrival of detachments in the border districts for the preparation of the quartering of troops.

7. Building of ramps at railroad stations in the border districts by railroad troops and civilians.

8. The establishment of warehouses in the border districts and the purchasing of provisions by the military and naval administrations.

9. The shipment of troops and military authorities, of artillery, munitions, mines, and torpedoes from the garrisons, and the direction of their journey.

10. The journeying or marching through of troops of other garrisons and the direction of journey or march.

11. Arrival of troop divisions from the interior at the border and the naming of the station of their disembarkment and their quarters.

12. Strength and kind of troops advancing toward the frontier.

13. Naming of border districts where there are no troops or from which troops have been withdrawn.

14. Names of the higher leaders, where used, and possible changes in command.

15. Information as to departure and arrival of the higher military authorities at Great Headquarters.

16. Journeys and destination of Princes and other personalities, accompanying the army, as well as the place of their stay upon arrival at the front.

17. Delays of railroad shipments through accidents or the depreciation of railroads and bridges.

18. Work being done on fortresses, coast and inland defenses, in government or private shipyards and other establishments, entrusted with military consignments.

19. The making ready of rolling stock and laborers for purposes of the army or the navy.

20. The launching and damaging of warships.

21. Place of stay and movements of warships.

22. Arrival and sailings of ships of commerce.

23. The preparation and erection of barriers and supplying of ships with mines.

24. Changes of sea code and the extinction of lighthouses.

25. Damaging of ships and their repairs.

26. The garrisoning of places of naval information.

27. Making ready, equipping, and impressing of ships of the merchant marine for naval purposes; change of their crews.

28. The preparing of docks.

29. Publication of letters from people belonging to the army or navy without the consent of the military authorities at home.

30. Publication of lists of losses prior to their release by the military authorities.

The above refers to the allied armies and navies. Publications concerning them in the above sense are forbidden even in the eventuality of an outbreak of war. What countries are to be regarded as "allies" will be announced.

What other information the publishers should be able to find out after the outbreak of war through their foreign correspondents about the armies and navies of our enemies may be published only after the military authorities shall release such publications, since otherwise it will be easier for the enemy to draw conclusions as to our countermeasures. However, in order to utilize in time all reports from abroad, the publishers who come in possession of such reports would earn the praise of their country if they wire them—giving the source of the information—immediately to Great Headquarters in Berlin, in case the information deals with army affairs, or to the Admirals Staff of the Navy in Berlin, in case of naval affairs. The expenses entailed hereby will be borne by the Army and Navy Administrations.

It is desirable that none of these statements under II of this memorandum be published.

As far as is possible every publisher in the Reich has received a copy of this memorandum.

The publication of a forbidden military report in one paper does not absolve other publishers from the observance of the secrecy injunction of the Chancellor.

Supplement to the Memorandum for the Press

It must be emphasized that the attitude of the press and its observance of the rules laid down in the "Memorandum for the Press" so far deserves and finds full appreciation. In spite of that it must be noted that certain papers use now and then a language which is not adapted to the importance of the time. This circumstance forces the War Command, in order to supplement the "Memorandum for the Press," to formulate the following regulations, the observance of which during the duration of the state of war is urgently recommended. The War Command is convinced that the hitherto patriotic attitude of the press is evidence that the press endeavors also in the future to prevent unintentional injuries to our great cause.

1. A questioning of the national sentiment and determination of any German, any one party or newspaper is highly detrimental, because it impairs the impression of German unity and energy.

2. German victory means liberation for many foreign peoples from Russian despotism and English world-hegemony, and does not signify oppression. It would be injurious to our cause if German papers should express a contrary view.

3. The language used against the enemy countries may be harsh. However, an insulting and belittling tone is no sign of power. The purity and greatness of the movement which has gripped our nation demands a dignified language.

4. The foreign policy of the Chancellor, conducted upon instructions from His Majesty the Kaiser, must in this critical moment not be interfered with or hindered by covert or overt criticism. To doubt its firmness injures the prestige of the Fatherland. Confidence in it must be strengthened, and, like the confidence in the military leaders, it too must not be shaken.

5. Demands for a barbaric conduct of war and the annihilation of foreign peoples are repulsive. The army knows where severity and leniency have to prevail. Our shield must remain clear. Similar clamors on the part of the inciting press of the enemy are no excuse for a similar attitude on our part.

ROYAL MINISTRY OF WAR

VI*a*   May 14, 1915. J.-Nr. 3663/15.IV.M.

Military considerations demand that the press should refrain from discussing the question whether the German Colonial Possessions will be retained or lost or whether any territories outside of Europe might be acquired from foreign powers. Lectures discussing this topic in public are not desirable. Such lectures must not be reported nor should the papers express their own attitude.

VI*b*   May 14, 1915

It is highly desirable that the German press, when arguing the causes which brought about the war, should point to Serbia as the decisive factor. German war literature (for instance, the very title of a whole series of publications, *"The German War"*) has greatly helped persons in Austria who, in good faith or with malicious intent, wish to make it appear that Austria has been made the victim of Germany in the war. All polemics must be avoided, but it must be stressed that the aim of the war is to preserve Austria, an aim which is greatly in the interest of Germany. This will serve to counteract or, at least, to weaken from the very beginning the malicious agitation which is expected to break out in Austria after the war.

VI*c*   May 14, 1915

The bread supply is absolutely sufficient. The recent inventory of the rice supply was made merely to ascertain the amount of rice stored but not accessible to the retailers. Only stores kept for the sake of speculation will be affected. The retail trade will not be interfered with. The price has been fixed in order to encourage import. There is a good chance to profit by importing.

VI*d*   May 14, 1915

It seems necessary to call renewed attention to the order issued to the press March 9, 1915, to the effect that, at present, articles discussing the economic exploitation (*Ausnutzung*) of the occupied territories are not desirable. Such articles, therefore, should not be printed. There is no telling to what an extent and in what manner the enemy might use such discussions in order to hurt us.

VII   May 17, 1915. J.-Nr. 3746/15.IV.M.

In case of war with Italy everything must be avoided that might stir national passion or produce race hatred. Only the present Government should be held responsible for the war, not the Italian people.

VIII   May 26, 1915. J.-Nr. 3868/15.IV.M.

English press notices concerning a note alleged to have been addressed by the United States to Germany regarding the sinking of the "Lusitania" were obviously written with the purpose of increasing ill feeling in the two countries. The German press is to be induced to express hatred and, in return, such expressions are to be used to arouse animosity in America. We trust that it will suffice if we call the attention of our press to this so that the English machinations will fail to produce the desired result. If a note should really be received from the U.S.A., it would be advisable for the press to delay expressing its position until it has communicated with the Foreign Office.

IX   August 6, 1915. J.-Nr. 5624/15.IV.M.

The archives of the Ministry of Foreign Affairs, Brussels, have been carefully examined. Very interesting documents have been found received from the (Belgian) ambassadors in London, Paris, and Berlin, covering the last few decades. Beginning tomorrow, these documents will be published as supplements by the *Norddeutsche Allgemeine Zeitung* in their original French text and in translation. Short extracts will also be published by the same paper. The whole series is later to be published in pamphlet form. The papers are requested to print these extracts or to make extracts for themselves and to refer frequently to the supplements of the *Norddeutsche Allgemeine Zeitung*.

X*a*   August 15, 1915. J.-Nr. 5828/15.IV.M.

There is no uniformity in the German press regarding the official war reports of our enemies. Many papers reprint them in full, while others publish merely extracts. Reports apparently particularly unfavorable to our cause are sometimes omitted. The Supreme Command of the Army, however, holds that unabbreviated reprinting of the official reports of the enemy is desirable, exceptions to be made only when the cost of printing or technical difficulties stand in the way.

The complete reprinting of *all* reports spread by our enemies can do all the less harm as our own war reports are absolutely reliable and enable everyone to form a correct opinion for himself. The fear is expressed by some that the enemy's official war reports might create anxiety, but one should keep in mind that actual facts cannot be concealed. Truth will win out.

X*b*   August 15, 1915

The sale and utilization of raw materials (wood, etc.) shipped from the occupied countries is still being discussed in the papers, mostly in mercantile papers. The press is reminded of the order prohibiting the publication of reports containing information regarding the economic exploitation of the occupied territories.

XI*a*   August 28, 1915. J.-Nr. 6018/15.IV.M.

It has become necessary to warn all newspapers, magazines, etc., not to refer to censorship (preventive censorship, suppression of papers, etc.). Such items will be permitted only in rare and exceptional cases. When a paper has been ordered to stop publication it may advise its readers of the fact by means of extras or in some such way. But this must be done in an inoffensive manner and the causes leading to the suppression must not be stated.

XI*b*   August 28, 1915

All reports and price quotations referring to the German market in oil and grease must in future be omitted in the daily papers and in the technical press.

XI*c*   August 28, 1915

Any future reference to the criminal procedure instituted against certain persons in Stuttgart for having distributed a manifesto advocating peace is prohibited. The penalty pronounced may be published but must not be discussed.

XI*d*   August 28, 1915

As the manifesto of the National-Liberal Party of August 15 (demanding the annexation of Belgium) has been reprinted in many papers I am forced to remind the press with all seriousness of the orders issued for its direction.

These orders prohibit, for the present time, any discussion of the peace question and of our war aims. In case a discussion of these topics is desired by a paper, the article intended for publication must be first submitted for approval to the General Command or the Commanding Officer of the garrison.

If transgressions of these orders should again occur I shall have to use the most severe measures.

XI*e*   August 28, 1915

Any discussion of the Military Law of the Empire (*Reichsmilitärgesetz praemissis praemmittendis*) is undesirable. It is in the interest of the Government that the law be passed quietly.

XI*f*   August 28, 1915

It would be desirable if the press would show more restraint in its tone toward Rumania and if all threats were to be omitted. Rumania's attitude is still wavering, it is true, but there is no fear that she will join our enemies.

The change in the Greek Cabinet does not mean a complete change in the political attitude of that country. The report may be published without fear that it will cause anxiety.

An exhaustive study made of the French press proves that considerable ill feeling exists between France and England. It is not desirable that the German press take notice of this study or comment upon the animosity between England and France.

The press notice of "Havas," according to which an attaché of the Department of Commerce, acting in behalf of Germany, has attempted to coerce Rumania in order to make possible the shipment of armament to neutral Bulgaria, is, according to our information, not based on facts.

XI*g*   August 28, 1915

The Federal Council will receive today a bill to amend the Reichsmilitärgesetz and also a bill proposing to amend the law of February 2, 1888, regulating military service. These bills must not be mentioned in the press.

XI*h*   August 28, 1915

The Southern States of the U.S.A. are using pressure to force the President to permit the export of cotton from America to Germany. We are much interested in the import. If negotiations with America are to be successful and if England is not to interfere at the last moment, the press must not discuss the problem of cotton.

XII*a*   September 7, 1915. J.-Nr. 6214/15.IV.M.

Concerning the proposed amendment of the Militärgesetz discussions in the press must be limited to what has been actually said by members of the Cabinet or by deputies in open session.

XII*b*   September 7, 1915

The Social-Democratic Party is about to make a public announcement of its position on the question of war aims and the agitation for annexations. The sentence concerning the restoration of Belgium must be eliminated before the statement is published. The press is forbidden to continue any further discussion of the party's principles.

XII*c*   September 7, 1915

The Central Intelligence Bureau of the Supreme Command (*Kriegspresseamt*) has been instructed to keep the censors informed of the military and political situation, and the censors will thus be enabled to carry out their duties more intelligently (*mit mehr Verständnis*). The press will also be supplied by this newly created Bureau more plentifully than before with military information (*Deutsche Kriegsnachrichten, Nachrichten der Auslandspresse, Deutsche Kriegswochenschau*) and will thus be enabled to understand better the spirit of the directions given by the censors.

The new Bureau has been given special power and will serve to transmit to the censors the direction of the central authorities whose earnest desire is that censorship be administered with justice and uniformity. The Bureau is made finally responsible for the strict observance of the directions.

It is expected that the new organization, together with the contemplated centralization of the censorship, will greatly help to improve the relation between the press and the censor.

XII*d*   September 7, 1915

The rumor that the period of service for the Landsturm is to be extended is absolutely without foundation. An official denial is neither intended nor desired. However, it is advisable that editors should contradict the rumor in case inquiries are made.

XII*e*   September 7, 1915

A renewed request is made calling for caution in commenting upon the lack of raw materials, sequestration of such materials, or other retardations in business undertakings. This should be kept in mind when meetings of boards of directors of industrial companies are reported or when annual statements of such companies are reported.

XII*f*   September 7, 1915

The Chancellor's speech of August 19 has led to inquiries as to the treatment of the Polish question by the press. Attention is called to the order prohibiting any public discussion of our war aims, an order which covers the discussion of events that, in future, may occur in the East. The Chancellor alluded to the Polish question for the only reason that he could not very well pass over so important an event as the capture of

Warsaw without touching the future of Poland. Poland's future cannot be definitely settled until the war has come to an end. Several eventualities must be considered. To discuss these at the present moment would not be expedient; the reaction of such a discussion on Austria must be considered. The attitude of the press must be determined by the consideration that a friendly attitude on the part of Poland will be of great importance for us at the time when the final settlement will be made.

XII*g*   September 7, 1915

Military reasons demand that our press forego discussing the war aims. As regards Poland, it cannot be immaterial for us whether the population of that large territory which, at present, is stretched out between us and our victorious armies, shows a friendly or hostile disposition. The German press should avoid anything that might antagonize the Polish people or that might induce them to turn toward Russia instead of against Russia in order to gain freedom.

It should also be kept in mind that any detailed discussion of the Polish question is impossible without bringing in our own domestic politics and without arousing party against party. How great this danger actually is, is proved by the vigor with which certain papers demand that the question be opened for public discussion. If opinions did not differ to such a degree, there would be no reason for such a demand. But if the discussion were to be permitted at this early date the quarrel of the parties would surely be carried by the papers into the conquered countries and would affect the Polish people.

It is hardly necessary to point out how pleased our enemies would be to discover something that might be taken for a symptom indicating the disintegration of our inner solidarity, and that at a time when our armies are so victorious.

XII*h*   September 7, 1915

News regarding German intrigues (*Machenschaften*) in Persia should be printed only with the special permission of the Foreign Office or the Supreme Command. If the papers are not willing to suppress such news by their own volition, they must consult these bureaus before publishing news of that kind.

XIII*a*   September 15, 1915. J.-Nr. 6381/15.IV.M.

Military considerations make it desirable that any article likely to impair our relations with the U.S.A. be omitted. Such articles should not be printed.

XIII*b*
                                    September 15, 1915

The Intelligence Bureau in charge of Oriental Affairs believes that the German press when discussing Oriental affairs does not always strike the right note. The use of the "Correspondence" edited by the Bureau is recommended; it will be sent to interested editors upon request and free of charge.

XIII*c*
                                    September 15, 1915

For the time being unfriendly articles against Rumania are to be omitted.

According to our information in Japan also a change of front is noticeable. The astounding military achievements of our armies are admired and recognized. Feeling toward England is growing less and less friendly. The wish to reach a lasting understanding with Russia is constantly increasing. As regards our attitude toward Japan the press should observe the following directions: It is in the interest of Japan to resume relations with Germany. But if we were to take the initiative it would be considered weakness on our part, and this policy is therefore not advisable. It will be best for us to wait quietly and watch developments without interference by press articles.

Pamphlets written in very poor English and printed on yellow paper have been recently found enclosed in newspapers mailed to America. Destruction of bridges and sabotage of railways are urged in these pamphlets. Such activity is utterly scandalous (*ganz grober Unfug*) and should be branded as such by the press. It can only undermine our standing.

XIV   October 1, 1915. J.-Nr. 6601/15.IV.M.

The press is again reminded that reports of the speeches and remarks of the Emperor must be submitted to the Supreme Council for examination and approval. In future, orders-in-council and telegrams of His Majesty will also be covered by this order.

XV   November 29, 1915. J.-Nr. 7410/15.IV.M.

Referring to the statement of the Ministry of the Interior regarding the food situation and the rise of prices I wish to express on my own behalf to the entire press of my district my earnest expectation that, in future, all possible moderation will be used when measures of the

Government are criticized. The belief of the Ministry of the Interior that public criticism has already reached the point of becoming a national danger is shared by me. I, therefore, shall not tolerate under any condition that a considerable part of the press of my district shall continue its attitude toward the questions referred to above, inasmuch as the Federal Council is using its utmost energy to amend abuses that have been found to exist in the management of our economic affairs. At this very moment orders are again to be issued serving this purpose and there is no reason why the people should look into the future with anxiety and distrust. If this order is not strictly observed I shall take severe measures.

XVI   December 11, 1915. J.-Nr. 7415/15.IV.M.

The wish has been frequently expressed by the German press that, in a greater measure than heretofore, it might be allowed to reprint dispatches and items of the *Nachrichten der Auslandspresse,* published by the Intelligence Bureau, Berlin, Department of Foreign Affairs. This wish can be fulfilled only if the management of the *Nachrichten der Auslandspresse* can be relieved of the trouble and the loss of time due to the fact that all articles to be reprinted must first be submitted to the local censor. The Intelligence Bureau is willing to make a new departure. All news published by the *Nachrichten der Auslandspresse* will in future be submitted to the Central Intelligence Bureau (*Oberzensurstelle*), which will decide whether or not it may be published. Every item will be numbered consecutively. The numbers borne by those articles which may be published by the press without further censorship will then be communicated to the Wolff Bureau. This agency will then send to the papers, together with the *Nachrichten der Auslandspresse,* the list of numbers of the items released for publication.

In order to enable the local censors to assure themselves that none but articles released for general publication are reprinted, any item taken from *Nachrichten* must be marked N.D.A.

As a matter of principle, the Central Intelligence Bureau will release only such articles as may be printed in full without changes or additions. Under certain conditions extracts from articles taken from the *Nachrichten der Auslandspresse* may be reprinted, but only by special permission of the local censor. Such permission will be restricted to articles written by the editors themselves with the use of the material furnished by the N.D.A., provided they contain nothing objectionable. Only passages taken from articles not released for general publication by the Central Bureau may be reprinted verbatim.

XVII*a*   December 15, 1915. J.-Nr. 7420/15.IV.M.

Reliable reports of the approaching session of the Diet are not objectionable. Speeches made in the Diet, however, should be discussed only in so far as the Chancellor will refer to them.

XVII*b*   December 15, 1915. J.-Nr. 7420/15.IV.M.

The criminal proceedings against Kramář are about to begin in Vienna. The official report of the Press Bureau (*Korrespondenzbureau*) may be published, but further reports are undesirable and will not be permitted.

Reports referring to the alleged recall of the Military and Naval Attachés, Washington, are undesirable and will not be permitted.

Details concerning the proceedings instituted against certain Hapag [Hamburg-American Line] employees are likewise prohibited.

XVIII*a*   December 31, 1915. J.-Nr. 8071/15.IV.M.

Any press notices concerning the hoarding of copper (*Kupfer-Verkleidungen*) or the amount of copper at hand in Germany or in the allied countries are prohibited.

XVIII*b*   December 31, 1915

As a matter of principle the official war news of our enemies referring to the operations on land may always be reprinted in full. However, when public interest demands that especially glaring misstatements be disproved, or when an especially favorable opportunity is offered for effective refutation, it is advisable to print a critical comment together with the enemy reports. In case our own official war reports or those of our Allies do not furnish sufficient basis for such corrections, the General Staff is ready to supply needed information upon request.

Unofficial news gathered from hostile or neutral sources must be examined before publication with regard to the effect it may have on public opinion in Germany. It must neither arouse false hopes nor create unnecessary anxiety. It must also be considered whether such items might impair our military operations. If news taken from foreign papers is reprinted by the German press the enemy might be led to think that its authenticity is confirmed by that fact, and he might draw valuable inferences.

When referring to naval operations, all official and unofficial reports of our enemies must always be submitted to the Intelligence Bureau of the Navy. All articles, dispatches, and letters printed in foreign papers that touch upon naval affairs are subject to censorship.

The official war reports of Turkey are to be treated on exactly the same basis as the reports issued by the German or Austro-Hungarian Headquarters, i.e., they are to be reprinted in full.

Other reports of military operations of Turkey may be printed provided they were mailed in Turkey, as that will prove that they have been examined by the Censor. News referring to Turkish operations, when gathered from Turkish papers, may be printed unconditionally. But any news regarding alleged military operations (of Turkey) in the future or alleged preparations for a renewed attack on the Suez Canal is absolutely prohibited.

XIX   January 14, 1916. J.-Nr. 111/16.IV.M.

Publication and discussions of the text of the second Ancona Note are prohibited until the note has actually been printed in the Vienna papers.

XXa   January 26, 1916. J.-Nr. 120/16.IV.M.

It is requested that all press news of conversations with commanding generals of the German army and of all their speeches, letters, telegrams, and orders be submitted to the Central Intelligence Bureau. This procedure is so much the more advisable as the authenticity of such reports must always be established before the question can even be considered whether or not it will be expedient to release them.

Such examinations are obligatory even when the speeches, etc., contain no statements in conflict with the orders of the Censor.

XXb   January 26, 1916

Military as well as political considerations demand that the food question be discussed in the press in the proper spirit. Errors made here are bound to react not only on the people directly, in that they undermine our national solidarity, but also indirectly, in that they strengthen the morale of our enemies.

For the guidance of the press of this district the following directions are recommended:

1. A certain increase in the price of victuals, caused by the rise in the cost of production, is the inevitable result of the war. It affects not only us but also our enemies and most of the neutral countries. Scarcity of food due to the high prices does not in itself prove that mistakes have been made that might have been avoided. It is the patriotic duty of the press to convince the people that they must be willing to adjust them-

selves to a reasonable increase in prices. The burden will be borne more willingly if the press points out frequently that the economic difficulties at home are nothing when compared with the troubles and dangers that our heroic troops are facing for the sake of the Fatherland.

2. Even the most efficient administration can reduce prices only to the point demanded in the interest of the preservation and stimulation of our economic productivity. It would be imprudent and unreasonable to insist that the price of all victuals, even of such as are scarce, be reduced to such a low level that no one would be forced to retrench.

3. Even if prices should rise to a level that the poorer classes would need the aid of the state in procuring the necessities of life, agriculture and commerce should not be criticized without good reason. Criticism, under present conditions, is quite natural but for that very reason one should not indulge in thoughtless and malicious generalities. The common interest of all classes and of all occupations must always be considered.

4. We owe it to our troops, who in the present war are meeting demands such as no army has ever faced in the history of the world, that no sickly sentimental or malicious complaints be sent to the army in the field, causing worry and anxiety among soldiers when the actual conditions at home do not justify it. It is the duty of the press to scrutinize all complaints, even when they are warranted, and then to decide whether public criticism is really required or whether there may not be some other way to obtain redress. The war demands mutual confidence and co-operation between the press and the authorities, who are always ready to give information and assistance.

Victuals absolutely needed to maintain the army and the people are available in sufficient quantities. The fear that the enemy may starve us is groundless. Wherever there is momentary need it is caused by the difficulties of distribution and transportation. Such difficulties are never insurmountable. Occasional complaints should never induce anyone to doubt this consoling fact. Exaggerated, frivolous, or malicious reports are doubly harmful; they not only lead to speculation and profiteering but they also cause timid people to make hasty and unwarranted sales, thereby contributing to the rise in prices.

6. Agriculture and commerce are vital organs of our economic life. They must be protected not only for their own sake but also in the interest of the whole nation. Their right to make reasonable profits must not be disputed. To attack these organs of our economic life by general accusations is unjust and unpatriotic.

7. Our discussions of our economic situation are watched by the foreign press, especially in the enemy countries, with a degree of attention which we can hardly realize. But there is a simple explanation for

this. The armies of our enemies have had no success worth mentioning, while we, on our various fronts, are constantly gaining. It is therefore quite natural that our enemies are trying to find consolation in the thought that by strangling us economically they will obtain what they have failed to obtain by force of arms. Nothing is more certain than that any discussion in the German press contributing to this hope will serve to prolong the war. Whoever discusses our food situation in public incurs not only a political but also a military responsibility, so great that the Censor is justified in undertaking to share this responsibility with the author.

8. This does not mean that it will be necessary or even desirable to suppress public discussion of the economic situation in any way. On the contrary, the press must retain the right of free expression, restricting itself only by observing the "truce" (*Burgfrieden,* interparty agreement) and by considering the effect that public criticism might have on the enemy.

Nor shall the press be restricted when criticizing the Government. As a matter of fact, our Government needs criticism and desires it so long as public confidence is not shaken by constant and destructive criticism apt to obstruct the efficient execution of the measures intended to relieve the economic situation.

It is a matter of prime importance that the good will [patriotism] of political opponents be not questioned so long as there is no absolute proof to the contrary. But when cases of profiteering are proved, the severest censure will not be strong enough.

XXI   February 25, 1916. J.-Nr. 123/16.IV.M.

All reports and discussions referring to our relations with America are to be submitted for examination to the General Command of this district.

There is reason to assume that all controversial questions at present pending between us and America will be settled in a thoroughly satisfactory manner. The negotiations carried on to bring this about must not be disturbed by inopportune press discussions. Firm determination is required and everything must be avoided that might be interpreted as a sign of weakness. But the press must not assume a provocative attitude. In discussing the stricter blockade (*Blokadeverschärfung*) planned by England and the so-called "Lansing Demands," the press may touch upon the U-boat question as it has direct bearing on these matters. Stress may be laid on the fact that in the U-boats we possess a very effective weapon and that we shall always be able to make such energetic use of them as circumstances demand. But it is not advisable to make detailed proposals or demands. At the present time, it is not in the German interest to question the conciliatory attitude of the American Government or to accuse it of conscious partisanship in favor of our enemies. By so doing the press would only aid the English effort to induce America to join her side or to use America's help for her own benefit. Personal attacks upon Wilson or Lansing must also be avoided. Political as well as military considerations demand the strictest objectivity in tone and content. Such an attitude is quite in accordance with that proud self-confidence to which we are entitled by our military and naval strength.

These instructions must be strictly obeyed.

XXII*a*   May 19, 1916. J.-Nr. 1020/16.IV.M.

The attacks made by Martin, a journalist, against the American Ambassador Gerard must not be published.

XXII*b*   May 19, 1916

The *Süddeutsche Konservative Korrespondenz,* Karlsruhe, has sent out a discussion of a book, *The Battle of the Marne,* published by Mittler & Son, Berlin. Reprinting of this discussion is not permitted.

XXII*c*   May 19, 1916

The article printed in the *Kreuzzeitung* (No. 217, April 29), "America and We," must be neither printed nor discussed.

XXII*d*   May 19, 1916

It is the patriotic duty of the press of this district to observe the following directions when discussing the German note to the U.S.A.:

"The well-known reasons making it advisable for us to keep America from entering the war continue to prevail. In consequence, the German answer has been drawn up in such terms that a break on the part of Germany has been avoided. The purpose of the note is to settle the German relations with America, at least for a period of time (*auf absehbare Zeit*), and to make sure that the war will be carried to a successful end without interference on the part of America.

"Consequently, the press must avoid all discussions not in accordance with this aim. There is no foundation for the statement that our enemies would prefer the U-boat war to be carried on with less ruthlessness rather than win the active assistance of America.

"Dependable information received from London and Paris makes it clear that the authorities there fervently hope that a break between Germany and the U.S.A. will soon occur, as this would mean a prolongation of the war and, together with that, would offer the possibility of improving their military situation.

"The war has lasted twenty-one months. Throughout this period Germany has demonstrated to the world and to the generations to come the glory of her army. Our wish to avoid adding a new enemy to the ring of our adversaries cannot and must not be misinterpreted by anyone!"

XXIII   November 21, 1916. J.-Nr. 7011/16.IV.M.

All references to His Majesty the Emperor, whether he be at home or at the front, so far as they are not prohibited, must be submitted to the Censor. This order covers speeches, orders-in-council, telegrams, and other manifestoes of the Emperor.

Excepted are all telegrams and reports of the official war correspondents, which must be submitted to the Central Intelligence Bureau, Berlin, as before.

Not permitted are:

1. Reports, based on fact or on rumor, regarding the movements of the Emperor, unless such reports are based on official reports.

2. Reports dealing with the extent of the military activities of the Emperor, or changes in these activities, as, for instance, the rumor that he has assumed the Supreme Command of all armies of the Central Powers.

Pictures of the Emperor showing His Majesty while taking active part in military activities must be submitted to the Central Intelligence Bureau, Berlin, before they can be reproduced.

Pictures showing the Emperor when not taking part in military activities must be submitted to the local censor.

Publishers undertaking the publication or distribution of the pictures are charged with the responsibility of procuring permission.

Previous orders not in accordance with the present order are invalidated.

XXIVa   February 5, 1917. J.-Nr. 124/17.IV.M.

It is the urgent wish of the Supreme Command not to be involved in partisan controversies and not to be drawn into political quarrels, as this would seriously interfere with the conduct of the war. Articles and public lectures likely to have such an effect are prohibited.

XXIV*b*   February 5, 1917

In several papers articles have recently been published directly or indirectly demanding ruthless U-boat warfare. This has been done in a tone approaching an attempt to coerce the Supreme Command.

I am ordered by the Supreme Command to remind all papers of my district of the order of the Censor demanding that all articles dealing with U-boat warfare be first submitted to the Censor.

As this order is demanded in the interest of the army, and as it is obviously necessary that the orders of the Censor be strictly observed, any offense will be severely dealt with.

XXIV*c*   February 5, 1917

The addresses sent from many parts of the country to His Majesty the Emperor and King in response to His "Proclamation to the German People" (January 12, 1917) have been discussed by the *Alldeutsche Blätter* (No. 4, January 20, 1916, under the caption: *Alldeutsche Umschau,* paragraph 2). The same topic has been discussed by Otto Eichler, paragraph 1, caption: "129th Week of the War," *Berliner Neueste Nachrichten,* No. 37; also *Deutsche Zeitung,* No. 37. The indicated paragraphs of these articles must not be reprinted.

70. CENSORSHIP OF DIPLOMATIC DISPATCHES[6]

.... ARMY CORPS, MARCH 23, 1916

TO THE CHIEF OF THE REPRESENTATIVE GENERAL STAFF
OF THE ARMY, BERLIN

The Chief Command has the honor to send herewith a copy of a report, intercepted at the post supervision, Foreign Station . . . . written by the . . . . Minister . . . ., Petersburg, dated March . . . ., 1916, which was opened there in a way that could not be detected and in the same manner closed and forwarded without delay.

The Royal Ministry of War has received a communication similar to this with the report annexed for the information of the Foreign Office, also the Chief of the General Staff of the Field Army.

On the part of the Representative Chief Command, the

Chief of Staff
LIEUT.-COL. . . . .

[6] Collection of German Military Documents, Hoover War Library.

71. CENSORSHIP OF THE WITHDRAWAL ON THE
WESTERN FRONT, APRIL 28, 1917[7]

(1917)   TELEGRAM
Very urgent!

War Surveillance Commission, Budapest

ss dd War Press 375 -66/63 -15 4/28 N.-

Upon wishes of the German H. A. C. let the press be confidentially informed that for tactical reasons the Ancre front will soon be drawn back. The preparations and the cross-plowing of the ground are progressing finely. Newspapers must retain articles to this effect until announcement follows.

To War Surveillance Office, Vienna, and to War Surveillance Commission, Budapest.

War Press Command E
No. 2262

72. STATEMENT OF DR. PFLEGER AGAINST THE
CENSORSHIP[8]

. . . . Gentlemen, the complaints about the application of the laws of the state of siege, particularly those of the censorship, show that measures are often being taken which are partly unintelligible and harmful and which have often a rather comical result. . . . . Other complaints—and these are to be taken more seriously—deal with the inconsiderateness, such as complete suppression, sometimes meted out to newspapers. [*"Quite right!"—Left.*] Gentlemen, the publishing business is a commercial enterprise, and if a newspaper is being suppressed for four to six weeks or even longer, that means that that business is completely ruined. [*"Quite right!"—Center.*] In the Budget Committee such outrageous cases were cited to us that it is regrettable that the suppression of newspapers is not made dependent upon the consent of the Chancellor. . . . . In the last debate a promise was made that the discussion of economic questions would be allowed. And yet papers have been suppressed because they criticized economic measures. . . . . One paper was suppressed on account of an article on the butter question and of a well-founded criticism on the use of bread-corn for the distillation of spirits. . . . . If the censorship be conducted on more

[7] Collection of Hungarian Documents, Hoover War Library.

[8] *Verhandlungen des Reichstags,* No. 53, May 24, 1916, pp. 1236–42.

liberal principles as regards criticism of economic measures, many of the present evils would not exist. . . . . Especially regrettable is the supersensitiveness of many censors as regards criticism of measures of a provincial or local character. . . . .

73. WHAT IS THE CENSORSHIP FOR NOW?[9]

The time has come to withdraw a forgotten sentinel who has remained in place ever since the beginning of the war. We still have the censorship. But we probably have it only because nobody has bothered himself to think about the reason for it.

The censorship is one of the instruments of a war in which victory is attained very quickly. In all cases, when action alone decides, doubt, scruples, and spiritual influences which endanger the success should be repressed. But just as one could never have pictured the war except as a brief and painful occurrence, so one could never regard the censorship as anything but a temporary measure.

It is not otherwise that it can be brought to bear upon public opinion. For free discussion springs up involuntarily again and again in a country in which it is customary. We ask: Is there any thought about the war and other attendant questions which the people do not know and which the people do not discuss? Let us mention first the enemy's notes and the enemy's war bulletins. They contain most frank remarks about the rulers, governments, and conduct of the war of the Central Powers. Before the war, even one-tenth of its contents would have been enough to bring down upon every editor who would have published it long terms of imprisonment. Today, however, everybody can read it in the *Norddeutsche Allgemeine Zeitung!*

Next, the proceedings of the parliament. Even during the war, these are unrestricted; and the records of the debates of the Reichstag and the Landtag contain, in fact, every thought which the people entertain. . . . .

And what about the press itself? There, too, the old experience has been confirmed that censorship can only turn the stream of public opinion into other channels but cannot stop them entirely. And, finally, the necessity of a public discussion becomes evident time after time. In spite of the party truce, there is no lack of animated discussions between different political opinions. Differences between capital and labor, between town and country, appear necessarily in all discussions about measures of war economy. There is an unrestrained public debate about war aims, even about war methods.

[9] *Vorwärts,* January 18, 1917, pp. 1–2.

There is no doubt that the German press would have had much the same aspect, even if no censorship had existed.

Moreover, we have seen the German peace offer made and have experienced its refusal by our enemies. For the whole world, thus, it has become evident that Germany is forced to wage a war of defense against hostile intentions of conquest. Thus, the need of continuing our defense . . . . is self-evident to all the people. Everybody knows that everything which is being done is being done only because there is no choice. . . . .

Someone may raise the following objection: If the German press is permitted to say exactly what it wishes to say, and if its text is not dictated by the authorities but by cold facts, what, then, is the use of a repeal of the censorship?

The answer is: The repeal of the censorship is doubly necessary because we must show the annexationists abroad that they have to do not only with a German Government and a public opinion which is created by it, but also with the people themselves, who despise wars of conquest, whichever side wages them. . . . .

74. STATEMENT OF HERR MÜLLER-MEININGEN IN THE REICHSTAG AGAINST THE ACTIVITIES OF THE WAR PRESS BUREAU[10]

. . . . In the debate on the auxiliary service we were given binding assurances as to the administration of the laws relating to a state of war. None of them have been fulfilled. A rational decree was issued relating to the right of assembly on September 25, but the decree came very late, only just before the Reichstag met. The former satisfactory relations between the *General Kommandos* and the trade unions have become worse and worse. [*"Quite right!"—Left.*] The question of importance now is that the decree of September 25 should be properly carried out. After all, there is only one way of insuring the absolute homogeneity of the administration. The Highest Army Command must call the heads of the *General Kommandos* together and explain to them that they must alter their practice. Otherwise the state of affairs will more and more tend to bring about a collision with the trade unions. . . . . No human being has anything to say against the protection of true military interests. A poor editor who gives information as to any movement of troops is punished, but when the Imperial Chancellor discloses the most serious occurrences in the navy, the knowledge of which in

[10] *Verhandlungen des Reichstags*, No. 126, October 11, 1917, pp. 3885–92.

foreign countries might bring to us infinite harm, nothing happens.
. . . . [*Hearty approval from the Left.*] My attitude toward pacifism
has always been skeptical, but it is an injustice to outlaw the leader of
this school of thought so absolutely, and this at a time when those at
the head of Imperial affairs are making concessions to pacifism. Meetings at which hatred and love are to be spoken of are prohibited and
complaints are dismissed without any justification. People who represent just the same ideas as those contained in the answer to the Papal
Note are gagged. Thus martyrs are created. . . . . The activity of the
War Press Bureau, which has suddenly so immensely increased, is far
less harmless. Formerly these authorities employed about ninety officers; now they employ several hundred. We must have more light
thrown on the establishment and construction of this bureau. [*Applause
on the Left.*] It appears to be the center of a worse system of secret
bribery than ever. [*"Hear, hear!"*] The editors of the German press
are robbed with the greatest lack of consideration. At the same time a
pressure is put on the press, which threatens to become a very great
danger. [*"Very good!"—Left.*] Remember the evil effect of the Press
Department of the Admiralty under v. Tirpitz. [*"Quite right!"—Left.*]
But things appear to be far worse in the War Press Bureau. . . . . It
is not unheard of that this War Press Bureau should directly incite a
one-sided literary activity, calculated to disturb the peace in the most
one-sided way. [*"Hear, hear!"*] The War Press Bureau offered an
article entitled "Scheidemann's Following" to an important South German paper. This article stated that the Social-Democratic Majority
Party could not now reckon on more than 706,000 votes, and added that
this was a remarkable majority of the people. [*"Hear, hear!"—Left.*]
[*Interruption: "That is the work of the War Press Bureau."*] Those
are calculations of a general nature put forward by the Independent
Social-Democrats in the interest of their party. [*"Hear, hear!"*] . . . .
The newspaper to which the article was sent naturally forwarded the
article and the letter to the Bavarian War Ministry. . . . . I ask the
Imperial Chancellor what his attitude is toward activity of this kind on
the part of the War Press Bureau. . . . . When such a spirit prevails
in the censorship and the War Press Bureau, the wildest indiscretions
on the part of the Pan-Germans as regards our Allies, and especially as
regards Vienna, are not to be wondered at. But they have proceeded
against other parties in the most unheard-of way. For instance, the
publication of a Hindenburg birthday article, full of admiration and
love, by Friedrich Naumann, was prohibited because there was something in it about proud, superman, armchair warriors who might abuse
the Field-Marshal. . . . . Who would deny that we have a breed of
snakes in our midst, or that there are armchair warriors full of super-

man pride? . . . . A progressive newspaper recently said that the expression used day after day by the German Conservative Press, "Hunger Peace Majority," applied not only to the Reichstag Majority but also to the Imperial Government and the Highest Army Command. On this the following notice was issued by the Censor:

"The article suggests that the Highest Army Command agreed with the resolution of the Reichstag Majority. I must again call attention to the prohibition against drawing the Highest Army Command into political debates, and should regret having to take strong measures in case of a repetition of the offense."

When, therefore, in contradiction to the daily assertions of the Conservative Party that, notwithstanding the express declaration of the Imperial Chancellor, the Highest Army Command did not agree with the Reichstag policy, a newspaper confirms what the Chancellor himself said on this point, the Censor comes along and suppresses this paper. A more drastic and shameless attitude to adopt against the policy of the Chancellor himself cannot be imagined. . . . . Is the Imperial Chancellor going to tolerate indefinitely the slander that he is pursuing a double policy? If he is going to put up with this, and if obstacles are actually to be thrown in the way of any announcement to the contrary, then everything is at stake for the Imperial Chancellor, even his good name. A policy in which the Government, the Army Command, and the representatives of the people are absolutely united must be established once for all. . . . .

75. AN INTERCEPTED AND DECIPHERED BRITISH WIRELESS[11]

Wireless Message Rotterdam to London. Received September 21, 1918 . . . . English No. 124 deciphered by *Kriegsnachrichtenstelle, Gruppe, Berlin.* . . . . 2—10—1918. [Beginning of message.] To Upbraiding—perhaps the Air Ministry, London—Nr. 662. . . . . The agent in Zeebrugge reports that a —1— cm. gun is located — yards to the side of — inberghe. A —1— cm. gun is located fifty yards to the west of a house at La Panne. . . . . Maxse. [End of message.]

. . . . To the *Zentralpolizeistelle,* Belgium.

[11] Collection of German Military Documents, Hoover War Library.

CHAPTER V

REVISION OF INTERNAL POLICIES

INTRODUCTORY NOTE

THE PRESSURE in the Reichstag during the war for the revision of internal policies (*Neuorientierung*) is first noted in the debates of March 10, 1915. In the debate on internal political conditions, April 5–6, 1916, all parties except the Conservative Party advocated a freer Germany and a more centralized Empire.

76. THE PRESSURE IN THE REICHSTAG FOR A REVISION OF INTERNAL POLICIES

(a) HAASE'S SPEECH IN THE REICHSTAG, MARCH 10, 1915[1]

Gentlemen, the idea that actuated the Social-Democratic Party at the outbreak of war was that it is our duty to do everything for the protection of our own country. [*Applause from Social-Democrats.*] These endeavors are not thwarted by public criticism; on the contrary, they are strengthened by criticism of the right sort. The Social-Democratic Party has never thought of asking for any presents in return for its vote of August 4 and December 2. It is not considering and has never considered its vote as a trade transaction. But we cannot approve of the Government on the whole presenting nothing but the budget to a Reichstag gathering in the eighth month of a war that has upset the whole world. The sacrifices which our people are bearing are overwhelming. Our brothers in the field, facing death every moment, are doing their duty with an almost superhuman strength [*"Quite right!"*— *S.D.*], all of them equally; and under such circumstances the Government must no longer evade its task of seeing to it that the amount of political rights should be equal to the amount of the duties. [*Hearty assent from S.D.*] It is quite unbearable that all citizens, without difference of class, party, religion, and nationality, are not being granted full equality. [*Renewed assent by S.D.*]

[1] *Verhandlungen des Reichstags*, No. 4, March 10, 1915, pp. 45–48.

Gentlemen, the workmen's organizations have supplied more than 20 army corps from amongst their members. [*"Hear, hear!"—S.D.*] On the battlefields and at home they have done great things, as the Government itself has acknowledged, and now is a session of the Reichstag to pass, without doing away with the exceptional regulations concerning the rights of coalition which are directed against them? What we ask for is equality in all respects [*"Quite right!"—S.D.*], not only as a reward for the immense sacrifices but also as the fulfilment of an undeniable claim. [*"Quite right!"—S.D.*] Gentlemen, it is always being put forward that our chief care must be not to lower the sentiment of our brothers in the front ranks who are doing wonders in bearing privations and sufferings; but those who want to act thus must first see to it that our brothers, when they come home, are not looked upon one day longer as citizens of lesser rights in empire, state, and parish. [*Hearty assent by S.D.*] Nothing will hurt the masses more deeply than consciousness of the fact that those who on account of the war are restricted in their earning power will on that account be marked as citizens of lesser rights. [*"Quite right!"—S.D.*] There is no more room within the German Empire for class suffrage.

If the Government will actively set its mind to it, it will, with the aid of our people, overcome all obstacles. The more openly and decisively it acts, the more easily it will reach its goal. Something could be achieved immediately, without parliamentary discussion, if the Bundesrat would approve such measures as, for example, that regarding the Reich Law of Association. [*"Quite right!"—S.D.*]

We shall again put forward a motion to that end, and if the Government will maintain its reluctant and evasive position, the soldiers coming back from the war, together with those of their comrades who stayed at home, will claim their rights impetuously. [*"Quite right!"—S.D.*] We must not close our eyes to the fact that after the blood and health of hundreds of thousands of men have been sacrificed for the protection of the Empire, the fight for equal rights and the democratization of organizations will be continued with more stress than ever. [*Assent by S.D.*]

With growing discontent we are watching the restrictions and even the destruction of the liberties already won, for instance, the rights of association and assemblage, as also those of the press. The present state of affairs is not based on the constitution of our Empire. The latter only allows the declaration of the state of war in case the public safety of one of the Federated States is threatened. But hardly anyone would venture to say that in the whole German Empire the public safety is in danger. Our people have waited in vain for the end of the state of siege in the interior of the Reich, as was promised at the outbreak of the war; but the restrictions on the contrary have been rather increased and have caused growing discontent, the importance of which the authoritative circles evidently do not grasp. [*"Quite right!"—S.D.*] In various districts even the closed meetings must be sanctioned and supervised by the police and the speakers are obliged to submit their manuscripts for approval to the Censor, before the meeting is allowed to be held.

How the censorship is being handled! The fate of political lectures and papers is laid in the hands of censors who have never before had anything to do with politics and accordingly have no understanding of the matter. The reasons for which newspapers have been prosecuted and prohibited indeed defy all description. Out of the overwhelming mass of examples, to which we shall again refer in the Budget Committee, I shall only pick out one of the latest facts:

In the *Koenigsberger Volkszeitung* of February 22, 1915, the Masurian victory is described in the most vivid colors. The ingenious strategy of Hindenburg is praised and it is further mentioned that the quality of the troops has also helped toward the military success and that the right of coalition has not been without effect. The article closes with the following words:

"Not only did Hindenburg gain a victory over the Grand Duke Nicolaievitch, but also did universal suffrage and the right of coalition triumph over absolutism." [*"Quite right!"—S.D.*] One would not have marveled if the writer of this article had received a letter of acknowledgment, but in fact because of that article the paper was suppressed for three weeks. [*"Hear, hear!"—S.D.*] One could really think that one dare not attack the Russian absolutism; that the legal institutions of our Empire, universal suffrage and the right of coalition, which are contrary to absolutism, must not be praised any more. [*"Quite right!"—S.D.*] The central courts of appeal of the Reich and of Prussia have in this case, as well as in a number of other cases—as I must expressly admit—intervened in a conciliatory way, and some days later the suppression of the paper I mentioned was canceled. But the damage done has not been repaired. The free interchange of views has received a blow; writers are discouraged. Many of the censors seem to lack the consciousness that the suppression of a newspaper will often cause material damages which can never be made good and which will throw many persons out of work.

Lately the censorship has prevented the literal publication of the speech on the potato question which our colleague Wurm made in the City Hall. [*"Hear, hear!"—S.D.*] I am quite convinced that no representative body of the people will put up with this interference with the rights of the parliament. [*"Quite right!"—S.D.*]

Gentlemen, the reference to the so-called "party truce" frequently becomes a nuisance. The party truce, as it has been proclaimed, requires that, in the political struggle, attacks against parties or religions in a hateful personal form should be avoided; but it should not lead to a denial of principles or to the renunciation of a Weltanschauung. It would be a misfortune for our people if the party truce should lead us to the peace of a cemetery. [*"Quite right!"*—*S.D.*]

When *Vorwärts* was suppressed, the Censor expressly permitted that during the party truce every newspaper should be able to discuss all happenings of public life and of the world in the light of its Weltanschauung. Only under this reservation did *Vorwärts* declare that it would not touch on the theme "Class Struggle and Class Hatred" during the war. It gave assurance that it would abstain from every hateful polemic against any class, which, by the way, it had done even before its suppression.

Gentlemen, the question arises now whether the newspapers have actually been given full scope of expression. Nobody will be able to assert that. Week after week new regulations are being given out. Only yesterday meetings for women were forbidden [*"Hear, hear!"*—*S.D.*], an action which demands the same criticism. The Chancellor wants the German people to be a free people. The condition just described is not worthy of a free people and should be cleared away immediately. A free people deserve free speech. [*Hearty assent by S.D.*] This is especially requisite as soon as the war approaches its end. The German people should not allow themselves to be pushed aside when the fateful question of their future is being settled. [*Hearty assent by the S.D.*] They have the right to take part in discussions and preparations.

Gentlemen, in all countries dread of the war makes itself felt more every day. It is natural that the longing arises everywhere to put an end to the terrible butchery of the nations. To express this is not a sign of weakness and can least of all be looked upon as such by us. For our military successes are indisputable; our social life, stimulated by the war industry, has been revived in a surprising manner; our finances have proved themselves to be strong. It is just the strong who may first hold out the hand of peace. My party as representative of international socialism has always been the peace party, and it knows that this is the case for the Socialists of other countries as well. Our desire is for a lasting peace, such a one as does not include new difficulties and does not contain seeds of future quarrels. That can be obtained if the nations do not oppress each other [*approval by S.D.*] and if the peoples see the advantage of the peaceful exchange of culture. The delusion that the German people can be annihilated has been destroyed. [*"Quite right!"*—*S.D.*] Our people are not to be annihilated any more than any other nation which defends its independence and self-reliance with all its strength. Until the bloody struggle has come to a close, we in Germany have the great task to fulfil that in any case the feeding of the people be made safe. Our people cannot be forced to their knees by hunger; that is our conviction. The food will have to be regulated without regard to special interests. Up to now much has been done amiss. We cannot save the Government this reproach. My "Fraktion" has already in the middle of August, and since then, continually drawn the attention of the Government to taking the necessary measures in conformity with this proposal. A timely embargo on wheat would have greatly increased our store of food. The high prices of bread-grains, which have gone far beyond the famine prices of 1891, were not necessary. The timely slaughter and conserving of pigs would have saved great quantities of potatoes for human food. The unfortunate idea of establishing economical housekeeping by raising the price of potatoes deserves the strictest condemnation. [*Hearty assent by S.D.*]

The task of the Government is to make safe what food we have for the people, and to distribute it appropriately at moderate prices to the consumer. No interest should come before that of the consuming population. [*Approval by S.D.*] He who withholds food with the intention of profiteering should be dealt with severely and should be held in contempt by everybody. [*Applause by S.D.*] At a time when our best people are dying on the battlefields it is more than ever our duty to prevent the population which remains behind from becoming weak by underfeeding. It is more than ever our duty to see to it that a healthy, strong generation grows up. Besides other regulations, as for instance weekly assistance for women during confinement, it is necessary to procure food at moderate prices for the whole population, especially for the poorer classes. The increase of prices, which is not to be avoided anyhow, makes it a duty also to raise the money for this purpose. At the same time the law concerning the maintenance of military persons and their survivors will have to be amended. The details of all these measures will be discussed in the Budget Committee and, if necessary, will be discussed at the second reading of the Budget.

Gentlemen, the enormous expenditures which confront the state, as the Secretary of Finance just mentioned, will demand great sources of income. It is not unjust to demand that those who increase their fortune in this time of great need should give up a large part of their increment. [*"Quite right!"—S.D.*] The Secretary of Finance will be pleased to examine closely the law for property taxes, which is very suitable for this purpose. [*"Very true!"—S.D.*] The effect would be embittering if the speculators and contractors who have coined money through the misery of our people should get off wholly unmolested. [*"Very true!"—S.D.*] Gentlemen, never before has the Reichstag had its ordinary session in such difficult times as now. It has great tasks to accomplish. We shall strive to the end that effective and successful work may be rendered and that these tasks may be brought to a favorable solution. [*Lively applause by S.D.*]

76. (b) DR. SPAHN'S SPEECH[2]

Deputy Dr. Spahn (Center) : Gentlemen, in the name of the rest of the parties of this House, with the exception of that of the Poles, I have briefly to declare the following : in themselves the declarations of the honorable speaker preceding me would not compel us to an expression at this hour; for the views which underlie them have been partly discussed at the December session, or they will, in so far as they have not done so already, find their discussion and decision in the Budget Committee, to which I propose to refer the entire estimates and also those of the occupied districts, thus furnishing an opportunity to consider them more carefully.

However, one point necessitates a counter remark in spite of the wording of the declarations, namely, the remark of the previous speaker about the peace, which, as it was made, might easily lead to misunderstandings abroad. [*Lively protests by the S.D.*]

Gentlemen, we have to explain this : the German people, too, do not wage war for the sake of war, but for the sake of peace [*"Very good!"*] ; for a peace which secures for the German labor a free world competition and more powerful development than ever before [*"Bravo!"*], and which will offer the Reich a lasting protection against atrocious attacks upon the foundations of its greatness. [*Renewed "Bravo!"*] The achievement of this aim requires further victorious battles, which the German nation is ready to fight until their completion. [*Lively assent.*]

76. (c) SEYDA'S SPEECH[3]

Deputy Seyda : Gentlemen! In the name of my "Fraktion" I have to declare the following : in so far as we can analyze the estimates in advance, they do not contain any points as to which we are compelled to differ on principle. However, we deem it necessary to repeat our previous demand, at the present moment, too, that all exceptional measures in the Reich as well as in the Federal States should be lifted during the war. [*"Quite right!"—Poles and S.D.*] We reserve the right during the course of further debates to bring out more in detail that this demand corresponds not only with justice but also with the expressed interests of the Reich. [*"Quite right!"—Poles and S.D.*]

[2] *Verhandlungen des Reichstags,* No. 4, March 10, 1915, p. 48.
[3] *Ibid.,* p. 48.

76. (d) SPEECH OF DR. DELBRÜCK IN THE REICHSTAG
MARCH 10, 1915[4]

Dr. Delbrück (representing the Chancellor, Minister of State, Secretary of the Interior): Gentlemen, the subject mentioned by Deputy Seyda would not have been the cause for me to speak. Deputy Seyda wants the repeal of the emergency laws, which he believes to be inflicting a wrong on that section of the people which he represents. He wants them to be repealed during the war. Gentlemen, there is no law of the country known to me that would be likely to prejudice the rights particularly of the German population of Polish extraction [*shouts from the Poles*], with the exception perhaps of paragraph 12 referring to the forming of associations. I have already pointed out to you, on another occasion, that the Chancellor and the Federated Governments doubtless recognize that the great events which the war has brought will put us face to face with the necessity of examining to what extent our internal politics require re-orientation. But, gentlemen, it has also been pointed out several times that the Chancellor and the Federated Governments are of the opinion that such an examination would not be possible during the war. [*"Quite right!"—Right.*] In consideration of this all differences of opinion which now exist and which have separated the several sections and parties of our people should, as far as possible, not be discussed as long as our soldiers are fighting at the front. [*"Quite right!"—Right.*] The Federated Governments must stand by this principle.

As regards the speech of member Haase, I greatly regret it [*"Quite right!"—Right*], and in my opinion it is not likely to promote unity, which nobody is more willing to preserve than the Government. Also this speech may give rise to and may spread inaccurate and misleading interpretations about the attitude and sentiment of the Government, not only in our own country but also beyond our frontiers. Herr Haase has also demanded in general the repeal of the emergency laws, which, as he alleges, have been issued against a certain part of the population only. But, gentlemen, if member Seyda asserts that paragraph 12 is prejudicial to his party only, it cannot affect you anyhow. [*Shouts from S.D.*] Herr Haase has demanded particularly the removal of the emergency law with reference to the right of coalition. I am unaware that emergency laws exist in regard to the coalition right. [*Laughter by S.D.*] Nor are there emergency laws which are directed against a particular political party. We may possibly have some laws which limit the freedom of individuals. We shall always and must always have such

[4] *Verhandlungen des Reichstags,* No. 4, March 10, 1915, pp. 48–50.

laws; for no state and no public community can exist without certain constitutional limitations upon the freedom of the individual. [*"Quite right!"—Right.*] But we have no laws in the German Empire which place a particular limitation on the freedom of a certain part of the people. Regarding this point, you will see that the demands of Herr Haase are not justified, and I most decidedly reject them [*applause from the Right*] in order to avoid giving the erroneous impression to foreign countries that there are such laws in the German Empire. It is true that there are different kinds of opinions concerning the administration of some of the laws. [*"Aha!"—S.D.*] Regarding this (*to the Social-Democratic Party*) many complaints have been put forward on your part, several of them have been examined, and it has been established that they were unfounded. [*Laughter by S.D.*] But, gentlemen, I should like to state expressly that not only the Government but also the governments of the separate states have taken great pains to prove during this great war, by their administration of the laws, that they are equally fair to all parties. [*"Quite right!"—Center and Right. Denial from S.D.*] The Governments are fully aware of the duty which they owe to a nation which fights at the frontiers with such unity, with such bravery, for the safety of the Fatherland. [*Applause from Right, Near Left, and Center.*] I should like to state expressly, too, that, as long as the war lasts, the Government of this Empire and the Federal States is and will be carried on from this point of view. [*Shouts from S.D.: "And afterward?"*] Herr Haase also thought that the existing liberties would be still more curtailed. That sounds as if we used the state of war for limiting the lawful liberties of the German nation. [*Shouts from S.D.*] That is not the case; the state of war, which is bound to increase the limitation to a certain extent of the liberties of the individual, the liberties of the press, and the right to form associations, is a temporary state of affairs. It is, however, a constitutional restriction which has been provided, and the limitation upon certain liberties for the duration of the war is on a lawful basis. However, Herr Haase is of the opinion that there are no reasons for ordering a state of siege. I must dispute this point of view also; one cannot carry on a great war on four fronts and grant the same liberty to the press and to assemblies and allow all kinds of processions as in peace times. We want a censor; we must be in a position to prevent our diverse opinions and points of view from passing across the frontier, as they might be misunderstood in foreign countries and do us damage there by being misrepresented and misused by our enemies [*"Quite right!"*] in the manner well known to you, and especially in order to inflame their population and above all the neutral countries against us. That is one of the reasons, besides the most important and decisive military reasons, why the state of siege has been proclaimed. It must be kept up in the full consciousness of the great responsibility which the Chancellor bears for the maintenance of the state of siege. But, gentlemen, with this responsibility, the Chancellor's responsibility for what happens under the state of siege comes to an end. The Chancellor is responsible only to the extent that the state of siege must not be ordered unless constitutional necessities for ordering it do arise; and if they do arise the Chancellor must also see that the state of siege is not maintained any longer than these conditions exist.

What the military officials, in whose hands the executive power has been placed by the state of siege, think fit to do on the strength of their authority, is outside the competence of the Chancellor [*"Hear, hear!"*— *S.D.*], and is also above the criticism of this House as long as it is being done according to the constitution of the country.

Herr Haase has further pointed out that mistakes had been made by the military authorities, but he has also expressly stated that in such cases the Government and the governments of the Federal States have successfully interposed, and this proves that nothing is further from the intention of the Government and the Federated Governments than to limit the liberties of the people, the liberties enjoyed by them in peace time, beyond the most necessary restrictions. The fact that we have intervened successfully proves that in military circles also there is no intention to limit anybody's rights except as it is absolutely necessary. Otherwise they would not have taken the advice of the civil authorities in the numerous cases where intervention by the civil authorities occurred, nor would they have altered the decisions which they had previously made.

Well, gentlemen, nothing is more incorrect than to assert that we have a government of terror which limits the liberties of the individual and the justified free utterance of opinion more than is necessary. Herr Haase having pointed out that it was not even permitted to copy *in extenso* the speech of one of his party members about the potato question, I wish to remind him of the freedom with which on the whole all mention of the food question at meetings and in the press has taken place without any limitation. [*Contradiction by S.D.*] Gentlemen, I, of course, cannot discuss speeches which have not yet been made, but I believe you will admit that that part of the press, I mean of all parties, which has criticized the measures I have taken within my *ressorts* has not been affected by the Censor.

With this I conclude. The measures which the military commanders have taken respecting the limitation of personal liberty and the free expression of opinion are, as the complaints show, being used against the organs of all parties alike. So here, too, the apprehension that there exist emergency laws or that the laws are being administered to the disadvantage of a single party or a single "Fraktion" only is without foundation. Gentlemen, I will limit myself to these explanations. I presume that the deliberations of the Committee will give an opportunity to discuss the several demands about which Herr Haase has spoken. There are in his statement a series of wishes which I think are well worth considering, wishes which I know have also been the cause of discussions and considerations already among the Federated Governments, as also of the various other parties. I have therefore no reason for discussing these things any further. Herr Haase, or one of his friends, interrupted me at the beginning of my speech, when I spoke of the conduct of the Government during the war, with the words, "And what will happen afterward?" Gentlemen, I can only refer to what I have replied to member Seyda at the beginning of my statements: The Federal States are convinced of the necessity of acting after the war according to the changed circumstances which the war will have brought. They are convinced that it is their duty to examine how far there is cause for suitable alteration of our views on politics. If I am not mistaken, it was pointed out yesterday by the representatives of the different parties in the Reichstag that these explanations of the Government will have to be taken seriously and that the Government has the obligation to redeem the promises which it has given concerning this, also after the war. Gentlemen, if the other parties have confidence in such an attitude of the Government, we can also demand that the same confidence in the Government be shown by your side during these serious times. For, gentlemen, only if this confidence exists, are we in a position to conduct the war to that end toward which we are aiming, namely, to a victory which will save us from invasions similar to that we have to fight now, to a victory which gives us the possibility of reaping the fruits of our industry in the future without having them disputed in the way it is being done now.

76. (e) DR. JUNCK'S SPEECH, AUGUST 27, 1915[5]

Deputy Dr. Junck (National-Liberal): Gentlemen, I have no intention of provoking one of those entertaining debates about the Imperial law concerning the right of association which has occupied us every year. Against that law we involuntarily assumed a belligerent attitude, so to say, and got ready to shoot. [*Mirth.*] That attitude we may now leave to others, and I have the task merely of indicating the attitude of my political friends toward this difficult bill.

It concerns itself with three groups of decisions: first, about the conception of the political association, whereby the trade unions chiefly come into consideration; second, about the language question; and, finally, about the so-called youth paragraph.

---

[5] *Verhandlungen des Reichstags,* No. 20, August 27, 1915, pp. 386–87.

Regarding the infringement of Article 3 of the law, which paragraph concerns itself with the conceptions of a political association, I think I am justified in saying that we co-operated seriously in order to bring about a progress. If it will be successful in restricting the conception of the political association, then it will be given only in case its purpose is to discuss political subjects at meetings; and if it will be successful—in this I agree with the reporter—in observing this new decision of definition in actual practice, then youth would thereby be freed from a barrier which at present restricts their joining certain associations. I wish to name only singing and gymnastic clubs, which until now were often treated as political associations. I am emphasizing this now because when discussing the youth paragraph later on a few special remarks will have to be added to it.

The new Article 3 also makes exception of professional and social organizations from the Law of Association, whereby, in the first place— why should it not be spoken?—we think of the trade unions. We are ready to approve this change, which we greet joyously. We do not misconstrue the fact that this legal change, too, belongs to the great province of new orientation of our internal policy which the Honorable Chancellor has promised for the time after peace has been concluded. However, if we now approve this single decision, it is because we wish to extend a hand to those who are ready to go with us. We wish to show that we seriously mean to co-operate in the recreating of our national life. ["*Bravo!*"] We know how hard the proscription of professional organizations under the Law of Association has been felt among the affected groups, particularly the workers in these organizations. Whether this feeling was always correct or whether it was often exaggerated I do not wish to discuss at present. It is enough that it exists, and we are therefore ready to help. We know that the trade unions in particular proved themselves national-minded in this war, for which they deserve the thanks of the entire nation, and that they have proved their worth during a period now open to conclusive judgment.

We further believe that the excepting of professional organizations from the Law of Association really corresponds to the true intention of the lawgivers not only of the Reichstag but also of the Federal Government, which, through the present Chancellor, gave at that time an explanation promising much. Finally, we joyously take this opportunity to make a real step forward.

Gentlemen, for youth, too, something substantial is to be won; for now they could be members of professional organizations. In these organizations, and if need be, also in public meetings, the youth would be able to inform themselves about the conditions of their work and would discuss them, even if at times they reached over into the province of legislation. We do not hold that as unauthorized; on the contrary, we know that the child of the unpropertied masses is thrown into the vortex of life much earlier than the child of the propertied ranks, which are in the position to hold the child longer under their care. And of course this latter fact also conditions a longer dependence upon the home. In other words, he who possesses means is in the fortunate position of being able to prolong the golden youth of his child. For the unpropertied masses it is necessary that their youths may be able to inform themselves in the circle of their own comrades about labor conditions and to debate upon those problems. So here, too, the first proposal which I wish to become law offers a material remedy and progress.

But so much the more are we surprised to see that the majority of the commission is being set upon to abolish also Article 17, and therewith the last restraint which keeps youths from political organizations and public meetings. In this we shall refuse to follow, and that out of deepest and sincerest conviction. We are of the opinion that thereby we would not really serve our youth. [*"Quite right!"—National-Liberals.*] We all strive for the ability of our youth to bear arms, not only in the physical and military senses but also in the spiritual sense. This ability will be better obtained at other places than in the unpleasant atmosphere of public meetings. We do not see any reason why immature boys in meeting halls should take places away from someone else and join the rhythm of "Bravo!" and "Quite right!" [*Mirth and shouts.*] But, gentlemen, we all know what happens at such times. I am convinced that if we should ask our teaching ranks we should receive an almost unanimous answer that our youth do not belong there. [*"Quite right!"*] Finally, we are men enough, as fathers and older brothers, to judge that our youth would not be helped that way. Accordingly we reject this change of the law.

We must also reject the encroachment upon the language decisions of the Association Law. And here we have the urgent desire to express our views clearly and unequivocally. Gentlemen, there is no talk among us about an overestimation of the material importance of Article 12 of the Association Law. I think also that I am not going too far in assuming that we, in case things take such a turn as we expect, shall be willing to co-operate in a revision of the language legislation. I wish to avoid the use of the somewhat worn phrase "well-intentioned examination" and to assert that we shall whole-heartedly and clear-mindedly approach this important question when its time has arrived. But we cling to our assertion that its time has not yet come. Under the language restriction fall also parts of our Fatherland which are still occupied by the enemy.

Concerning the language of the Poles we heard with joy the tributes and admiration which the Chancellor recently paid to the energy and passion with which the Polish nation pursues its national aims. We readily join in this admiration. We, too, wish that the Poles may achieve the aim which they have in view. But here I permit myself to make the reservation, concerning which we are probably agreed, that German territory, of course, does not come into consideration. [*"Quite right!"*] We are not in the position at this moment, where as yet all things are in a state of flux, to abolish a legal decision which in its time was the storm center of a very passionate political struggle. We are not disposed to abolish a single link of a legislation which the Government built up with our support and co-operation. We are also convinced that large groups of our nation would misunderstand a sudden retreat on this point and view it as a relaxation of national energy. Besides that—I wish to be quite frank—should the moment of a "revaluation of all values" of the internal policy come, we do not wish to stand there as players who have played all their trumps before their time.

In truth, I can only beg that you do not weigh down the ship of this law with ballast which possibly will prevent the ship from entering the harbor, or better, since the law probably will be approved without our votes, with ballast which would compel us to leave the ship before it entered the harbor. We would not be in a position—I say that definitely—to vote for the whole law if the paragraphs about the language and youth are abolished. Failing that, we are forced to vote against the entire law, to our great sorrow, because we would willingly have participated in the vote of confidence concerning the trade unions and have participated in the voting at the second reading. Should the law stand on account of overloading, then we shall not be guilty, but those who at the deciding moment do not have enough self-restraint [*laughter by S.D.; "Quite right!"—Left*] to confine themselves to what it is possible to achieve. [*"Bravo!"—National-Liberals.*]

77. THE DEBATE IN THE REICHSTAG ON INTERNAL POLITICAL CONDITIONS, APRIL 5-6, 1916

(a) EBERT'S SPEECH[6]

. . . . Gentlemen, unfortunately no improvement has taken place in the handling of the state of siege and the press censorship, although at the last session all parties sharply condemned the many encroachments and mistakes made in this field. Conditions here are getting worse, and call for the sharpest criticism. [*"Quite right!"—S.D.*]

[6] *Verhandlungen des Reichstags,* No. 39, April 5, 1916, pp. 859–60.

I shall not go into details at present; that will be done from our side on a different occasion. However, at present we must emphatically protest against the unjustified infringements of the right of assemblage which take place almost everywhere in the Reich. Thus meetings which wished to discuss the tax plans of the Government have been frequently broken up. That happened in spite of the fact that the Government at our last session told the Reichstag that such meetings were not to be prevented. The Government has readily intervened in cases of complaint and at times has been successful. But into what a degrading rôle has the Reich Government been reduced, when the military authorities honor so little its parliamentary declarations or even frustrate them! [*"Quite right!"—S.D.*] These one-sided encroachments upon the internal policy are not the affair of the military authorities and must finally be made impossible. [*Renewed approval from the S.D.*] Rightly does our population regard these continued encroachments as senseless chicanery [*"Quite right!"—S.D.*]; they achieve the opposite of what was intended, and contribute appreciably to the embitterment of our population. My party friends will at this session again propose the repeal of the state of siege.

In this connection I must briefly touch upon the Coalition Law. I shall not go back to the changes decided upon here last spring. We regard those decisions of the Reichstag as entirely justified and their execution as necessary as before. I refer to a declaration which the Government gave at this place on January 18 through Ministerial Director Dr. Lewald. In that declaration we read among other things:

"It must be legally established that trade unions and the corresponding organizations of employers are not being treated as political associations if they occupy themselves with such social-political and economic-political affairs as are connected with their proper sphere of achieving more favorable wage and labor conditions or for preserving and furthering their professional interests. The Federal Governments have declared themselves in agreement with this attitude of the Reich Government. I am therefore empowered to declare that a bill will accordingly be submitted to the Reichstag." [*"Hear, hear!"—S.D.*]

Gentlemen, that is a clear and binding declaration, and what is especially gratifying is the fact that the Federal States have agreed to it. At the same time that proposal has not reached us to this very day. [*"Hear, hear!"—S.D.*] In view of the simplicity of the matter this seems to us very strange. In the name of my friends, I therefore urgently request the Reich Government to comply with its declaration as soon as possible and to submit to us the bill. [*"Very good!"—S.D.*] And accordingly we work on the assumption that the government project comprises all trade unions, particularly those of the farm workers, who have had to suffer most from the current harassing. [*"Quite right!"—S.D.*]

Gentlemen, the Honorable Chancellor said in this place in December 1914:

"It is a liberation and blessing that this whole mess and dirt has finally been swept away, that the man alone counts, one as much as the other."

In the prospective measures about the Coalition Law it matters only about the removal of mess and dirt. But all the more must we demand of the Government to remove it as soon as possible. [*"Very good!"—S.D.*]

"Gentlemen," the Chancellor said, "the man alone counts, one as much as another." I believe I may assume that the last speech from the Throne in Prussia with the promise of a suffrage reform comes somewhat nearer to that thought; of course, in a rather indefinite form. [*"Quite right!"—S.D.*] Nevertheless, Herr v. Heydebrand called this very cautious promise of a suffrage reform entirely irresponsible, and blessed the three-class suffrage as the right idea. [*"Hear, hear!"—S.D.*] Gentlemen, repeatedly we have declared here that we do not demand any counter-gift for the services we have rendered the Fatherland in this hour of danger. Our attitude toward the defense of the Fatherland must not be the object of a political bargain. But, gentlemen, anyone believing he is able carelessly to set aside the lessons of this war will suffer terrible disappointments! [*"Quite right!"—S.D.*] In a speech from the Throne there is, among others, the following sentence: "In the tremendous experience of this war a new generation grows up." I will leave the sense of that sentence undecided. However, I am firmly convinced that the masses who will return from the trenches will be moved by a strong self-consciousness [*"Very true!"—S.D.*]; they will be filled with the firm wish that the state for which they sacrificed their lives shall not be the tool of a small privileged class. [*Lively applause from the S.D.*]

Gentlemen, this new trench generation, which in the long months of the war constantly faced death, death which knew neither classes nor exceptions—this new trench generation will not suffer its political life to be squeezed into the wire barricades of a three-class suffrage system. [*"Very true!" "Bravo!"—S.D.*]

Gentlemen—and with this I conclude—the new generation demands liberty and civil equality [*"Quite right!"—S.D.*], and it will, if necessary, know how to get them. [*Lively "Bravos!" from the S.D.*] Therefore, the hour of peace must be the hour of civil equality. [*Lively applause from S.D.*]

77. (b) PAYER'S SPEECH[7]

. . . . Permit me to mention briefly a few points which bear upon our internal political conditions. The Honorable Ebert who spoke before me said true and warm words yesterday about the sentiments and wishes of those who today are still in the trenches but who wish to return home as equally privileged citizens. ["*Quite right!*"—*Left.*] May these words not escape the attention of the Imperial Government. I should like to recommend them for most serious consideration, and that at the earliest possible moment, before it is too late. ["*Quite right!*"—*Left.*] We have said often enough what we think of the censorship, and have nothing to add to it. We have no great faith in the protracted debates about the censorship and the individual restrictions to be imposed upon it. All that has little practical value. As long as we have the Censor we must use him as he is. To make him palatable is a misguided undertaking. We have to accept that he is hard to digest [*mirth*] and hope that he soon will be entirely superfluous. ["*Very good!*"—*Left.*] Therefore, without illusions we shall co-operate with all attempts which in spite of this are directed toward bringing about an improvement in the situation. But here, too, we believe that action has contributed more toward an improvement of conditions than all the debates in the Reichstag and its committees, namely, the Chancellor's act of announcing yesterday in this place the war aims of the Imperial Government. The Imperial Government having expressed itself about the war aims, even only within the limits it did, I regard it as impossible that the same Imperial Government will prevent the common man from expressing himself about the war aims. ["*Quite right!*"—*Left and Right.*] Once the war aims have been given for public discussion, there will be enough for the public to occupy itself with for several months. [*Humorous approval.*]

Gentlemen, quite rightly did the Chancellor yesterday call attention to the difficulties of providing food. He expressed his admiration for the willingness to sacrifice and surrender with which the poor and less-propertied population have adapted themselves to this hard time. Knowing as we do the actual condition of affairs, we only can join in such a conviction, and in future discussions, which doubtless will take place in this House, we on our part shall co-operate to remedy those conditions. But one hint I cannot spare the Federated Governments after the Chancellor's speech, namely, this, that these sufferers would suffer much more willingly if they had and could have the conviction that these sacrifices were and must be an imperative result of our economic

[7] *Verhandlungen des Reichstags,* No. 40, April 6, 1916, pp. 865–66.

position during the war. [*"Quite right!"—Left.*] The confidence of the numerous small consumers has been shaken, not because of the inadequacy of individual organs and individual mistakes in the execution— no—it began to waver to the extent in which the government measures failed in control and unity [*"Quite right!"—Left*] and to the degree with which one began to feel that the many mistakes occurring were due to those who had a greater understanding of the maintenance of one-sided interests of professions and social ranks than of the common welfare. [*Lively "Bravo!" from the Left.*] And the confidence of the small producers too, which are also numerous, has been destroyed by one stroke with the subsequent raising of the maximum prices. This was decreed as premium for avarice on the part of some and as punishment for the loyal behavior of those who lived up to their obligation toward society. [*Lively approval from the Left.*]

. . . . I wish to conclude with an urgent request which I have to address to the Federated Governments and which refers to the project for the Coalition Law, which project is to enable professional and special organizations to safeguard their rights against unlawful application of the existing law. I should like to request that this question be given every consideration, for this reason: that the Federated Governments have given a solemn promise in this House, which they must keep. [*Lively approval from the Left.*] They have declared that a "proposal accordingly" would soon be submitted; "soon"—that was January 18 of this year. At that time the firm accepted the check drawn on their account, and they now must pay it, irrespective of whether or not there exist differences of opinion among the partners as to the nature of the payment. [*"Very good!"—Left.*] If they do not redeem the check, they lose their credit. [*Renewed approval from the Left.*]

But even on material grounds it is necessary that an immediate remedy be provided for improving existing conditions. The promise was regarded among the people—and not without some basis—as the first payment on the great new orientation which was to come in the course of time and must come. Without distinction of person and without regard to political views the entire nation has placed its life and health at the disposal of the whole. The professional organizations, which are the bone of contention, have been particularly useful co-workers in economic and political questions. [*"Quite right!"—Left.*] The Imperial Government itself has admitted that the interpretations of these measures about political organizations by the courts and administrative authorities have not always left a sufficient degree of freedom to the professional organizations which they need for the realization of their economic and welfare purposes. Once that is admitted, the necessary consequences must follow; at least as long as one is dependent upon the future co-operation of these organizations. [*"Quite right!"—Left.*]

Gentlemen, at a time when the Government must claim so much confidence from the nation, and where so much depends upon the confidence which the Government enjoys in the nation, one should not artificially produce distrust and pour water upon the mills of those who are only too ready to tell the nation that after the war things will look much worse and as unliberal as ever before, that all promises are only so much bunk, and that, therefore, one couldn't be too radical and international. [*"Quite right!"—Left.*] Whoever favors the spread of such attitudes among the people creates a great misunderstanding. This the Federated Governments must remember. Also a passive attitude would have the same effect. The Federated Governments must rid themselves of the thought that the things which matter in the project are only matters of detail and correction. No, that completely recedes before the political significance of the matter. If the Government does not reckon with that, it commits a grave error. [*Lively approval from the Left.*]

77. (c) STRESEMANN'S SPEECH[8]

. . . . The idea of a "Central Europe," however, presents not only an economic but also a political problem. On it is imprinted the profound understanding between Germany and her allies; in it is impressed the deeply significant idea of making the present political union into an economic one for all times. If we turn our eye to Bismarck and learn from him, the greatest statesman of all times, and ask ourselves when Bismarck proved himself to be the greatest and most ingenious statesman, we see that it was in the hour of the bitter struggle with his King. It was at the time when by the Peace of Nicolsburg he laid the foundation that the enemy of that time could become the ally of the future [*"Quite right!"*] that he used all the powers of his genius and will against a restless exploitation of the victory and so created the possibility of bringing the defeated to the side of the victor. However, what was right at that time toward the allied and consanguineous Austria cannot be applied to France, England, or Russia. [*"Quite right!"*] Bismarck's train of thought was to make secure the relationship of two racial stocks which up to that time had formed the German Reich in order that in the future they could again form a united political community but in a different form. Strong new relationships have been created with Austria, Hungary, Bulgaria, and Turkey. We are glad of this co-operation at home and abroad and are determined to maintain

---

[8] *Verhandlungen des Reichstags*, No. 40, April 6, 1916, pp. 871–72.

it for the future. In such a sense can result a political Central Europe which could and will be of great economic and political importance for our future development.

That our own economic future is difficult I have emphasized on a previous occasion. It is already very difficult to bear, but it shows one ray of light. By all the struggles and by the entire transformation of the economic conditions, we have had no social conflicts in the Reich, hardly any strikes, and no tests of strength between the state and employers and between employers and employees. Our Ministers have not gone to the workers and begged them to do overtime work in order to produce the war necessities; rather employer and employee have done everything to meet the demands. The professional organizations of officials and foremen, the trade unions and other trade organizations have not been surpassed in their patriotism by any other group of the German people. This I wish to express here. For this reason and because we regard the project as essential we approve the demand that professional organizations be freed from political restraints. In this project we see one of the steps in the process of new political orientation which shall bring to us the development of all our institutions in a liberal sense; and that in the Reich as well as in the Federal States. ["*Bravo!*"—*Left.*] If there is anything at all that has crystallized out of this war, it is the Empire thought (*Reichsgedanke*). We can no longer talk about the life of a Federal State as being a life unto itself. It reflects upon Reich legislation, as Reich legislation reflects upon the Federal States. In this sense the suffrage question in the Federal States is a German question. We regard it as such and shall co-operate in the realization of the ideas expressed by us. We strive for a Greater Germany—we confess that openly—but as a liberal party we also aim for a more liberal Germany. We believe that the German monarchy, which is deeply rooted in history, cannot be better anchored than as it builds itself up upon the confiding attachment of a free and self-conscious nation. If a nation deserves confidence, it is the German nation of the present. It has given life and property for the Fatherland's future. May its unexcelled self-sacrificing spirit be rewarded with the achievement of external and internal freedom! [*Lively approval from the Left.*]

77. (d) WESTARP'S SPEECH[9]

Count v. Westarp: . . . . Today it is necessary to concentrate all our efforts, all our thoughts upon this one aim: to carry this war through

[9] *Verhandlungen des Reichstags*, No. 40, April 6, 1916, p. 872.

to a final victory. [*"Bravo!"—Right.*] That is the answer of my political
friends to a part of the declarations, particularly regarding the right of
association and the Prussian suffrage question, made by various speakers
before me. Those are not questions which are directly connected with
the war, and we mean that anything which detracts from the one great
aim should recede at this time! [*"Quite right!"—Right. Objection
from the Left.*] This the more since, according to our conception, the
formulation of the suffrage right is not a function of the Reichstag
but of the Federated Governments and Parliaments. [*"Quite right!"
—Right.*] Therefore, I dismiss those subjects without discussing
them. . . . .

The Chancellor at this time did not fail to go into details as on
former occasions. I have a few things to add to what he said about
Belgium and the Flemish people. I agree that the Flemish people under
German influence would be more able to develop their Netherlandish
characteristics than under Belgian influence. As regards the Belgian
question, we, too, agree with the Chancellor, namely, that Belgium shall
not again become an outpost, a vassal state of England and France. . . . .

The Polish question is doubtless one of the most difficult questions
to be solved after this war. The Chancellor said that we would solve it
together with Austria. If that happens, then the brotherhood in arms,
which united us with Austria, will be a guaranty that in the solution of
the Polish question the interests of both Germany and Austria will find
full consideration. It will be a guaranty that in the future, too, these
countries will face common dangers together.

What the Chancellor said about colonies and our colonial policy we
fully subscribe to and so have nothing to add to it. . . . .

77. (e) WERNER'S (GIESSEN) SPEECH[10]

. . . . I spoke of the "fostering treatment" which the Imperial Government employs against a certain portion of our press. As against that
stands the all too lenient treatment of press organs which, at least until
now, certainly did not have the monarchy in their escutcheon. . . . .
The *Berliner Tageblatt* and its people, the *Frankfurter Zeitung* and its
supporters, are granted free speech. When will the rest of free Germans
be granted free speech? The depression howlers have liberty of speech,
they may express their negative war aims. But the rest of our nation,
which profess different views, have not been allowed to speak until now.
If the depression howlers are given an opportunity to proclaim their
war aims, to profess a belief in a peace in which there are neither van-

---

[10] *Verhandlungen des Reichstags,* No. 40, April 6, 1916, p. 876.

quished nor victors, then the Nationalists too must have an opportunity to express their opposite views in public. [*"Quite right!"—German "Fraktion."*]

However, it seems as if in the German Reich there are gradually developing two different concepts of right. . . . . The censorship conditions under which we live show us that against the Nationalist papers and their supporters extremely sharp measures are being taken, whereas the newspapers of the Left, particularly the Jewish, are being shown great leniency. . . . .

If this is to be the new orientation of our policy, that everything lowest be placed highest, that the positive elements of our nation be placed under exceptional laws, then we refuse to accept it. . . . . If the press of those parties which are hostile to agriculture and not particularly friendly to the middle classes is constantly attacking the farmers and the middle classes, we do not deny anyone the right to do so. We do not deny that among those two classes there are base elements. But if such elements are being attacked, it is not just to condemn the entire farming element and the middle classes. At the same time the attacked side must be given an opportunity to defend itself. . . . .

In connection with the question of taxation we protest against the continued tax exemption of military doctors, military officials, and officers. It arouses extraordinary bitterness among the population that people who are permitted to continue their civil profession, as is the case with many doctors, are in the position to draw a big military salary and thus build up a small fortune. [*"Quite right!"—German "Fraktion."*] . . . .

We further wish that as to the tax question there should not enter a one-sided burdening of the independent middle classes. What some time ago appeared in a paper about the earning capacity of the middle class seems to be quite substantiated, namely, that the new tax projects of the Government pass by the armored towers of capitalism and attack and scatter the moderate properties of the middle class. Not enough consideration is being shown them. . . . .

Besides that, it is necessary that the small and middle people be extended further credit terms. Also, there must be a better regulation of lifting the load from the severely suffering house-owners, who are often considered great capitalists, whereas in reality they are recruited from small and middle-class people [*"Quite right!"—German "Fraktion"*]—an extraordinarily valuable part of the German middle class. The latter is condemned to proletarianization if appropriate measures are not undertaken during the war and beyond the war. [*"Quite right!" —German "Fraktion."*]

Loan societies have been created, but they extend loans—although that is not in their statutes—only upon goods current in the market. It is a fact that thereby such industries as the porcelain and building-material industries are suffering a great deal, because they cannot receive any loans upon their products.

The Chancellor spoke yesterday about our war aims. Previously he had emphasized and expanded the statement that we need military and political security for our Fatherland. We add that we also need security for the population. What our nation has lost in German and Germanic outposts since 1648 we must try to regain as much as possible. In this sense we particularly salute the Chancellor's reference to the Flemish people.

If we wish for a peace of any worth to us, it must be not only an honorable peace but also one which promises to last for a while. A peace which is based solely upon international agreements, without giving to us, as the Chancellor says, "real guaranties," would be of very doubtful value to us.

This I wish to emphasize from my Pan-German standpoint: we not only have, as the Chancellor thinks, the duty of freeing non-Russian peoples from the Russian whip, but also from the German standpoint we must refuse to wander about the world as police officials guarding the rights of small nations. We do not have the right to interfere in the internal affairs of other countries in so far as we are not fighting against them or are conducting peace negotiations with them. We have rejected and shall always refuse to urge the German Reich, for example, to interfere with Rumania's internal political conditions, as Herr Ledebour repeatedly has done when he asked the Reich Government to call Rumania's attention to the treaty of 1878. Those who have been in Russia and Rumania know exactly what the basis of the Russian and Rumanian exceptional measures are. Those laws certainly have not been issued by those governments for their pleasure but because of a very great political necessity. . . . .

But because we wish that the German should be the focal point of our future political work, we are not satisfied with what the Reich Government has promised to do for the Germans abroad. The Foreign Office has assured Germans abroad that at the conclusion of peace all their demands for restoration of their former rights will be considered. But that alone cannot be satisfactory to Germans abroad. We believe that a much more extensive promise should be made to them. . . . .

Gentlemen, the Chancellor also touched upon the Polish question. But a regulation of the Polish question without solving the question of the Jews from the East seems to us precluded. It is impossible for us to regard a peace as salutary which does not close the present borders of the Reich to Jewish immigration. [*Approval from the Right; dis-*

approval and unrest from the Left.] . . . . At any rate, gentlemen, I believe that even those who do not agree with us on the Jewish question will readily forego a further coming of Jews. If we really have "unlearned" what "sentimentality" is, then for us Germans there can only be German interests. Paper treaties do not help us a bit, and the "real guaranties" must be of such a nature that they will be lasting. International understanding will in no way be of any use to us. It is based upon a lack of international comprehension, for even you [*to the Social-Democrats*] are probably clear among yourselves that it is the national thought which in this time is victorious, not the international idea. [*"Quite right!"—Right.*] The gentlemen of the Social-Democracy have probably realized from the attitude of their party comrades abroad that for them national welfare is most important and that, accordingly, national blood is doubtless thicker than the water of the international. [*"Very good!"—Right.*] The modern ideal, born of the convulsions of the French Revolution, is the constitutional state with a national basis. This development of the nation state is not yet concluded, and this war shows the correctness of this statement, particularly in eastern Asia, as well as in the Balkan States and Italy.

That the "union of states" did not carry off the victory over the "nation union," about that we will be able to talk in greater detail after the war when once the Austrian conditions will have crystallized and can be discussed in public. But for all those who have learned anything from history, particularly from the development of the last hundred years, for them there is no doubt that the multi-nation state will some time break down and that the future will belong to the nation state which is organically built up from the bottom to the top with a reasonable freedom of advancement and expression for all who are morally, intellectually, and physically fit. Certainly the future of Central Europe will not belong to the *homunculus medi-europaeus,* who escaped from the retort of a liberal politician whose name has been mentioned very much lately. Intensely as we wish from our own standpoint the formation of one great strong economic territory from Berlin to Bagdad and beyond it, just so surely do we know that the future belongs to a racially determined Germanic Central Europe. For us Germans there can be nothing else. The German can be helped only through Germans, and accordingly our endeavor in the future must be to dedicate all our energies to the German and his state and to serve him alone. [*Applause from the German "Fraktion."*]

77. (f) HAASE'S SPEECH[11]

Gentlemen, according to the decision of the Committee on Rules, questions of internal and external policy, in particular also the proposals for the U-boat war, are to be considered jointly. I should first like to indicate the parliamentary significance of the proposals made; their content and political bearing I shall touch upon in a different connection.

The prerogative of the parliament is certainly not broadened by these proposals, but it finds an appreciable recognition, and particularly from those parties who consistently have refused to do so, namely, the Conservatives. At the most recent reform of the standing rules, when the parliament was given the right by interpellations to put the proposal that the Reichstag agreed or did not agree with the views of the Chancellor, the Conservatives adopted a very sharp attitude toward it. And now, gentlemen, they wish to give the Chancellor the responsibility for the conduct of war and at the same time to lend expression to their dissatisfaction. That is the good prerogative of the parliament, which in London, Paris, and even in the Duma at Petersburg has been used during the war—at times very energetically—but which prerogative still has to fight for its recognition in Germany. I remind you, gentlemen, of how you behaved in this hall when some time ago my party colleague, Ledebour, made use of this right. [*"Quite right!"—Social-Democratic Labor Group.*] The *Kreuzzeitung* has frankly admitted that through the proposals an influence should be exerted upon the decisions of the conduct of the war. "And in this," that paper continues, "the fact is revealed that the highly desired confidence is not there any longer to the degree which would be necessary to refrain from every attempt at such an influence." [*"Hear, hear!"—S.D.L.G.*]

The proposal, therefore, was to include also a vote of non-confidence toward the Government, but, as the committee states that the proposal contains neither an expression of confidence nor non-confidence, an expression of confidence is precluded by this cool reserve. [*"Quite right!" —S.D.L.G.*] The gentlemen, of course, make the fine distinction that their criticism directs itself only against the political, not the military, leadership, and thereby they wish to escape the accusation of having intervened in the powers of command of the highest war lord. Gentlemen, these two sides of the conduct of the war cannot be kept separate. [*"Quite right!"—S.D.L.G.*] The political point of view—that is our conviction, too—must by all means always be the determining factor in the conduct of the war [*"Very true!"—S.D.L.G.*], and in this we are supported by the undisputed authority, Clausewitz, who said:

[11] *Verhandlungen des Reichstags,* No. 40, April 6, 1916, pp. 881–89.

"The subordination of the political point of view to the military would be illogical; for politics have produced the war. [*"Very true!"* —S.D.L.G.*] Politics are the intelligence, war only the instrument, and not the reverse. Therefore, the only thing possible is the subordination of the military point of view to the political."

Gentlemen, if the Government clings to this maxim, it certainly does not deserve to be reproached for it. It would be a tragedy to leave politics also to the military authority.

Now the champions of the proposal have experienced the grief of being accused of having broken the confidential unity of the people, which they have preached again and again in this House. The press charged that their attitude bordered on treason. [*"Hear, hear!"*— S.D.L.G.*] Herr Dr. Müller-Meiningen has in a well-known article expressed his indignation, that the "proposers of this proposal lend their support in the face of a world of enemies to an unprecedented political spectacle [*"Hear, hear!"*—S.D.L.G.*] which under the circumstances could become very dangerous to our Fatherland." He compared it to Catiline [*mirth*] and concluded with the words: "The nation today wishes no speeches which could cause quarrels among us, but only the sacred unity for victory. [*"Quite right!"*] He who disturbs it is a traitor to the future of the German people, irrespective of whether he stands Left or Right, by Liebknecht or by Heydebrand." [*Shout from the Right, "Haase!" Great mirth.*] Yes, Herr Oertel, I shall come to that immediately.

In the first month of the war many basked in the belief, in spite of previous experiences, that now no one in Germany would dare to accuse the members of another party of being men without a country. When on August 26, 1915, Colleague Bauer made a speech in this House in which he called attention to the abuses taking place in the war provisioning, he was accused of having humiliated Germany before the outside world and thus of having injured Germany's prestige. Now even the Conservatives and the National-Liberals are placed on the bench of the accused.

Therefore, I was not the least surprised—and now I come to that, Herr Oertel, which you expect—when the bourgeois press heaped the most indecent accusations upon me after my speech of March 24. [*"Very good!"*—S.D.L.G.*] .... But then I know that the absurd false thought that a criticism of domestic conditions helps the interests of foreign countries cannot be eradicated from the brain of narrow fanatics. [*"Quite right!"*—S.D.L.G.*] I believe that with this assertion I can leave this subject. [*"Very good!" and laughter.*] If the parliament is not to become a bloodless phantom, then every conviction must be allowed to be expressed there. [*"Quite right!"*—S.D.L.G.*] When the cited speech of Mr. Snowden was delivered in London, the Lower House listened to him with the greatest interest, although his views deviated from those held by the majority of the House. The same thing happened a short while ago in Rome when my party comrade, Turati, hurled his accusations in the face of the war baiters and confirmed his own socialistic creed; in the same way the Duma behaved during the speeches of Chkeidze [Nikolai] and Chkhenkeli [Akakii], about which also our bourgeois press reported with satisfaction. And I probably may assume that we do not wish to be left behind as far as parliamentary polemic customs are concerned. [*"Very good!"*— *S.D.L.G.*] Gentlemen, no one of us thinks to disclose secrets to the world. But we must reserve the right to discuss all happenings in the light of our convictions. [*"Very true!"*—*S.D.L.G.*]

Turning now to the question of internal policy, I can only establish the fact that it does not offer anything gratifying. All parties have attacked the food-provisioning policy. That the great masses suffer great wants cannot be disputed; the patience of the people is heavily taxed. I do not fail to realize for a moment that the ruling society, if it does not wish to abdicate, is not in a position to remedy this situation entirely, for an economic order which is based upon the striving for profit cannot by its very nature serve the interests of the whole. But the Government could improve things by energetic interference. Already it has been indicated what influences are working against it. . . . . Gentlemen, it is no exaggeration to assert that never yet has the struggle for the golden calf been conducted so shamelessly as in this time of great need. . . . .

Yesterday the Chancellor spoke of the great moral reserve which enables the German people to maintain the enormously improved standard of life which has come into being in the last decades. Large groups of the labor and middle classes, however, did not participate in the raising of the standard of life; others, of course, have done so, as we have always admitted. But even these better-situated circles have been forced away below the previous level. And in what way should the great masses restrict themselves still more? Prices of food products are as a rule beyond their means. . . . . The well-to-do and the rich—that we admit openly—are subjected to some restrictions and annoyances at this time. However, anyone having money is still in a position to buy sufficient food materials and sweets. [*"Very true!"*—*Right.*] The poor and those with lesser means suffer want again and again, as is being admitted on all sides. [*"Quite right!"*—*S.D.L.G.*] The differences between various classes become more apparent than ever. The enormous raising of prices on foodstuffs requires the monetary aid given to soldiers' dependents to be correspondingly raised. [*"Very good!"*—*S.D.L.G.*]

I shall come back to what we have to say about the treatment of soldiers and the complaints regarding the payment order.

But now I must turn to a chapter which belongs to one of the most unpleasant in this time of war. The censorship rules and all ringing appeals do not mean a thing to us as long as the state of siege is not being lifted and constitutional conditions are not restored. [*"Quite right!"—S.D.L.G.*] When we hear that Germany is the sanctuary of freedom, that we wish to rescue freedom for our people, that we even have the task of bringing freedom to other peoples, that calls forth in us a sharp dissonance. [*"Very true!"—S.D.L.G.*] What has become of the promise that the state of siege would be abolished after the completion of mobilization? What has become of the promise that the censorship would apply only to military reports, that a political censorship would never take place? . . . . Gentlemen, briefly at least I would like to remind you that the "safety-arrest" (*Schutzhaft*) is being employed in an incredible manner, which leaves the victims of this military procedure no legal guaranties. . . . .

I have to call attention to still another dark spot. Last year when it became known that all the letters to lawyer Classen, the chairman of the Pan-German League, were being intercepted, all parties protested unanimously. Professor Bornhak declared such a measure legally unpermissible; yet it holds for a greater number of people, Social-Democrats and others, whose reliability cannot be doubted. It is regrettable to announce that closed letters are being opened, closed again, and then delivered to the addressee. [*"Hear, hear!"—S.D.L.G.*] A black cabinet exists therefor. We lack a parliamentary expression, ... for calling such a condition by its proper name.

The reform of the Coalition Law becomes almost a tragi-comedy. [*"Very good!"—S.D.L.G.*] The bill was to come in December. Then it was announced that the reporter became ill. To our great joy we have seen him well since. [*Laughter by S.D.L.G.*] But the bill did not come. It was then to be submitted in March. In vain did we search for it in the orders of the day. . . . . And if among the individual groups of people existed the hope that after the enormous sacrifices brought by them civil equality would be given them, that hope has been thoroughly shattered. Gentlemen, we know, of course, that rights are never being given the people, but that they must conquer them in bitter struggle. [*Assent by S.D.L.G.*] The attitude of the Government has only strengthened us in this belief. The passage about suffrage in the last speech from the Throne moves in meaningless words, which are much less satisfactory than the declarations in the Prussian speech from the Throne in 1908. Again they work according to the formula; they wash the fur without making it wet. A hundred years ago Frederick

William III spoke clearer words about the liberties and rights of all
ranks than occur in the present Prussian speech from the Throne.
[*"Very good!"—S.D.L.G.*]

Gentlemen, just as dark as the sky of internal policy is that of
external policy. The Chancellor lifted one veil from his program. At
least one part of his war aims appears in sharp contrast. Never has he
been as outspoken as yesterday. He said that never would Germany
voluntarily deliver the Poles, Baltics, Lithuanians, and Latvians to
reactionary Russia. What shall become of Poland? The answer to this
question is missing. We, of course, are emphatically against a plan
which would result in another partition of Poland. [*"Quite right!"*—
S.D.L.G.] The partitions of Poland are recorded on dark pages of
history, and it would be indefensible should that chapter be enriched
with another one. [*"Quite right!"—S.D.L.G.*] However, if the Polish
people are to become independent, then we are agreed to it. But the
Polish people must decide for themselves in what constitutional form
they wish to realize their independence. [*"Very good!"—S.D.L.G.*]
We ask further: What shall become of the Baltics, Latvians, and Lithuanians? Are they to be joined with a state, and to which? The population of the territory has not until the war expressed the wish for
joining with Germany. The strong Social-Democratic Party of Latvia
has always and also of late expressed its opposition to a separation from
Russia. It wishes to obtain liberty within the fold of the Russian
Empire and has committed heroic acts for that purpose. Whether the
majority now wish something different must first be shown. I know
this much, that if these peoples are promised liberation from reactionary
Russia they must recall the time when they themselves fought for liberation and were then disavowed by Germany as beggars and plotters.
[*"Very good! Very true!"—S.D.L.G.*]

Gentlemen, *Beneficia non obtruduntur.* We must not force good
acts upon a racial stock and bestow benefits upon it if it does not desire
them. [*"Very good!"—S.D.L.G.*] It is said that we would give this
people a chance for progress if it belonged to Germany. Well, gentlemen, a people which has proved its worth to such an extent in the
past must itself decide how it best wishes to achieve its development.
[*"Quite right!"—S.D.L.G.*] We stick unfalteringly to our principles
against annexations. [*"Very true!"—S.D.L.G.*] But this principle is
also a command of political wisdom. [*"Quite right!"—S.D.L.G.*] The
traces of Alsace-Lorraine should be a deterrent! What Marx, Engels,
Bebel, and Liebknecht predicted in 1870 has become the bitter truth.
France was driven into Russia's arms by the policy of that time, which
was partly carried out against Bismarck's wishes. [*"Very true!"*—
S.D.L.G.]

Gentlemen, do you wish to drive Russia into the arms of England for the future by means of a similar shortsighted policy? [*Shouts: "Is already in English arms!"—Great merriment.*]

Gentlemen, if you shout, "Is already!" you yourself know best— you have written and said so of late—that such alliances do not last forever [*"Very true!"—S.D.L.G.*], that they are held together by interest. And it depends on whether or not you wish to create conditions through which they will be chained to each other for a long time to come. [*Lively approval from the S.D.L.G.*]

We must again turn to the Chancellor's declarations concerning Belgium. Certainly it shall not become a vassal state of England and France, and surely it has no desire to do so. We, however, do not wish it to become a vassal state of Germany; we do not wish it to become a vassal state at all. Of course, Belgium must not be permitted to become an economic and military bulwark against Germany; but neither must it become a German stronghold against the West. We wish the Flemish people a development suitable to their peculiarities, but we fool ourselves if we think that even a considerable minority wishes to sever the political community with the Walloons. What does it mean, what the Chancellor said in this connection, that even as regards Belgium there was no *status quo ante?* We demand the political restoration of Belgium, and not only that, but also its political and economic independence. [*Lively approval from S.D.L.G.*]

Gentlemen, we all know well that right and justice during a war are at low ebb. But we raise our demand from a sense of right. We are also of the opinion that only if Germany is willing to make good the wrong done to Belgium [*lively shouts from Right; countershouts from S.D.L.G.*] will we be able before long to come to a peace, a peace which promises to be lasting. Gentlemen, you surely will allow me to repeat the words which the Chancellor himself said in this House! [*"Very good!"—S.D.L.G.*]

Gentlemen, on April 29, 1913, I declared in the Budget Committee —I support myself upon the report of the *Norddeutsche Allgemeine Zeitung* which is reprinted in the Belgian *Grey Book:*

"Many Belgian circles view with alarm a possible war between Germany and France, because they fear that Germany will not respect Belgian neutrality." [*"Hear, hear!"—S.D.L.G.*] At that time, April 29, 1913, according to the *Norddeutsche Allgemeine Zeitung,* Secretary of State v. Jagow answered that Belgium's neutrality had been established by international agreements and Germany was determined to observe those agreements. [*"Hear, hear!"—S.D.L.G.*] After a group of my party friends and a member of the Progressive People's Party had issued warnings against a violation of Belgian neutrality, the War Minister declared:

"Belgium does not play a rôle in the substantiation of the war measures; rather does its foundation lie in the circumstances of the East. Germany will not lose sight of the internationally guaranteed neutrality of Belgium." [*"Hear, hear!"—S.D.L.G.*]

Gentlemen, it therefore was a surprise when on August 4, 1914, the report was made here that our troops probably had already entered Belgian territory and to raise our voice against it was not possible. But the open explanation of the Chancellor left at least room that that which had been against the law of nations would be repaired as much as was humanly possible. The Chancellor said at that time:

"Our troops have occupied Luxemburg, possibly already entered Belgian territory. Gentlemen, that is against the rules of international law. But we were compelled to disregard the justified protests of the Luxemburg and Belgian Governments. The injustice—I speak quite plainly—the injustice which we have done thereby we shall try to make good as soon as our military purpose has been achieved. [*"Hear, hear!"—S.D.L.G.*] We did it in self-defense; and necessity knows no law!"

Gentlemen, we cannot recognize the principle, "Necessity knows no law!" [*"Very true!"—S.D.L.G.*] But in numerous circles the Chancellor at that time was praised for his proud and honest words. And he was ill-advised when on December 2, 1914, he tried to circumscribe his explanation. [*"Very true!"—S.D.L.G.*]

The Social-Democrats at that time at once declared that the documents found in Belgium could not lead to justification of another opinion than that announced by the Chancellor on August 4. And now, gentlemen, if it is not yet clear to anyone what the Chancellor meant yesterday when he spoke about Belgium, the speeches of the bourgeois parties placed the Chancellor's views in the proper light. Herr Spahn at once drew the conclusion from the Chancellor's words that Belgium would come into our hands militarily, politically, and economically. [*"Hear, hear!"—S.D.L.G. "Quite right!"—Right.*]

Gentlemen, you shout "Quite right!" Then you probably will also admit that this garbled form of annexation is much worse than the open, and that a nation which has led an independent political life will find it more difficult to bear than the loss of a strip of land. [*Lively assent by S.D.L.G.*] What you wish is nothing less than that its sovereignty in the most important questions be removed. [*"Quite right!"—S.D.L.G.*]

Herr Dr. Spahn, you shake your head. I have before me a petition which at this very hour is being circulated in Bavaria and which bears the signatures of well-known persons from all parties except the Social-Democrats. Among them, for example, is the signature of the "gymnasium" teacher, Bauer, executive member of the Progressive People's

Union in Würzburg. [*"Hear, hear!"—S.D.L.G.*] I notice further the following names: agricultural counsellor, Beck, member of the Lower House, chairman of the Bavarian Agricultural Executive Committee of the Union of Farmers; George Behringer, Nuremberg, district leader of the Christian Building Workers' Union; Dr. Brandmeier, chairman of the Munich local association of Bavarian "Real" School Teachers Association; Fritz Müller, member of the Chamber of Deputies in Zweibrücken; Dr. v. Cassel, mayor of Bayreuth, chairman of the Liberal Union of the Chamber of Deputies [*"Hear, hear!"—S.D.L.G.*]; and then a number of members of the Christian trade unions as well as professors. [*Laughter and shouts from the Right: "What is in it?"*] Here you probably find an explanation of the thought which Herr Spahn has not yet expressed—clearly on my behalf. It is about Belgium:

"By rejecting a political disfranchisement of the two Belgian peoples, the German Reich must take over the military defense of the country against the plottings of the Western Powers. . . . . [*sic*] In the interest of an undisturbed development the German Reich must be given the foreign political representation of Belgium." [*"Hear, hear!"— S.D.L.G.*]

Gentlemen, does a state still have its sovereignty, if it no longer has an external representation because it has transferred this representation to someone else?

Gentlemen, that writing shows in general with what plans the higher circles occupy themselves.

Among other things it goes on to say that the French iron ore districts, situated near our former boundary, belong commercially and economically to Germany. [*"Hear, hear!"—S.D.L.G.*]

As regards Russia, not only is the demand being put forward that as much as possible Russia be driven out of the territories not inhabited by Great Russians but it is also demanded that the Baltic provinces and the southern governments (provinces) be joined to the German Reich. [*"Quite right!"—Right. "Hear, hear!"—S.D.L.G.*]

This demand is put forward against England—the improvement of our military position through the winning of useful bases opposite the English coast for our navy and air fleet. [*Shouts from the Right: "Quite right!" "That is self-evident."*] Yes, gentlemen, it is exactly what I wish to establish, that you too are of these views—securing our sea power through naval bases as counterweight against England's former rule of the sea.

The Chancellor has said that the "German people have no land hunger." Yes, does he not know the war literature? Does he not know that again and again it is being explained that we need colonization land and that through this war we must secure this land for our surplus population under any conditions. On March 20, 1916, the Pan-German League, specifically the local group at Cologne, sent to a number of persons a statement accompanied by an article of Adolf Bartels with the title: "One Thing Is Necessary." In it, he says:

"Do not deceive yourself. The old humanitarian ideal is gone forever. [*"Hear, hear!"—S.D.L.G.*] We want the one thing which is necessary, land, in order to become a greater nation." [*"Quite right!"*—*Right.*] And it concludes with the shout, "Land, land, land!" [*"Very good!"—Right. Laughter among the S.D.L.G.; laughter, Right.*]

I understand your conception very well, even if I disapprove of it. But that you still can become indignant about the destructive will of others, is hard to comprehend after that. [*"Hear, hear!"—S.D.L.G.*]

In contrast to Dr. v. Payer I would like to mention that the Chancellor's speech did not bring us closer to peace; it rather removed us from it. [*Renewed approval by S.D.L.G.*] All the statesmen chant peace. Whoever still has a human feeling in his breast wishes to get out of this gruesome slaughter. This cannot be doubted. However, platonical peace wishes do not bring us a step nearer to peace. It depends upon the will to act, and that seems to be lacking in all the statesmen. They have run into a *cul-de-sac* and cannot come out of it. Since they cannot come out of it, and since they do not find the road to peace, it will therefore have to be the nations who take their fate into their own hands who shall make an end to the most terrible of wars. [*Lively shouts; "Quite right!"—S.D.L.G.*]

Gentlemen, toward the questions of peace and war, we take an attitude exactly opposite to yours. And thereby is indicated also our attitude to the proposals for the U-boat war. . . . .

Gentlemen, what an ambiguous and opalescent word, this of a "peace which guarantees Germany's future"! Well, who does not want a secure future for Germany? [*Shouts from the Left.*] But the pivotal point is: along what road to achieve that aim? What is to be understood under the "real guaranties" and "securities," which are held necessary to safeguard the future? There the opinions part and each one may have his view of the resolution. It permits the unrestricted U-boat war, and only during the negotiations shall the justified interests of neutrals be discussed. Gentlemen, we demand something entirely different. We want those principles which have been laboriously obtained in the field of international law to be observed. [*"Very true!"*— *S.D.L.G.*] That particularly non-combatants, men, women, and children, even if they are on enemy merchant ships, be not torpedoed and abandoned to destruction. [*"Very true!"—S.D.L.G. Shouts from the Right: "And you they wish to starve!"*]

Gentlemen, we demand further that our Government, as was demanded already in December by the Social-Democratic "Fraktion," seek peace, make a peace proposal ["*Very true!*"—*S.D.*], that it do everything to bring about an understanding among the nations. Of course I am very well aware, as I have already said, of the fact that our Government will hardly be in a position to do that, since like all other statesmen it wishes a peace whereby it can dictate to the other party the peace conditions. [*Shouts from the Right.*] But, gentlemen, just as little as we want to let the other group place its foot upon our neck, just so little should we attempt by prolonging the war to exhaust the other group so that we can simply dictate to it our peace conditions *quand même.* ["*Very true!*"—*S.D.L.G. Shouts from Right.*] Only if this is being openly said [*mirth at the Right*] is a basis being created for peace negotiations. ["*Quite right!*"—*S.D.L.G.*] . . . .

Gentlemen, when it comes time to formulate peace conditions, it is time to think of another thing than war aims, namely, the heavy armament burden, which the nations have borne so long and which will weigh upon them more heavily later on. ["*Quite right!*"—*S.D.L.G.*] Gentlemen, I know very well that capitalism, as long as it exists, will again create the danger of war. But it must not be lost sight of that the experiences of this war will bring the adherents of capitalism, probably not to their senses nor to the humanitarian ideal—certainly not that—but possibly to the realization that their interests are better guarded without war than by war. ["*Quite right!*"—*S.D.L.G.*] Then the capitalists within a country will not cut each other's throats in competition but will unite in trusts and syndicates. Also the capitalists of different countries will attempt an understanding without appealing to the sword. The combinations will serve the purpose of exploiting them. But at least the danger of war between big industrial countries will be lessened.

Added to that is another very important factor. Even if the nations again decide for armament races, will it be realizable? Will it be possible to raise the funds for those aims? Should not this reason produce the thought, whether it would not be possible to limit armaments by means of international agreements? That thought cannot be a Utopian one, for England and Germany in the past made the attempt to come to an agreement at least in regard to naval armaments. If that attempt failed, it was not because it was practically unrealizable, for then the practical statesmen would not have tackled it, but only because of the fact that in the prevailing atmosphere of suspicion such a thought could not ripen. ["*Quite right!*"—*S.D.L.G.*] Should the atmosphere once be cleared, then it will be quite possible. ["*Very true!*" —*S.D.L.G.*] That at least would be something worth while that could come to the nations out of this war. A strip of land, whichever it may be, can never compensate for the bloody victims of even a day. [*Stormy approval from S.D.L.G.*] If you would ask the civilian and military population whether they would like to continue fighting if there were the prospect of winning land in the East, or whether their arms should be laid down for a peaceful competition of nations, then I am sure that ninety per cent or more would be in favor of making an end, of concluding peace. [*Stormy approval by S.D.L.G. Lively protests and laughing by the other parties. Renewed applause by the S.D.L.G.*]

Gentlemen, if you pay no heed to this, then events will go beyond your control, and, if all signs do not deceive, the motto of the Communist Manifesto will live again: Proletariat of the world, unite! Unite for the high purpose of giving the bleeding nations peace! [*Stormy applause and handclapping by S.D.L.G. Hissing at the Right. Bell of the Chairman.*]

77. (g) VON JAGOW'S STATEMENT[12]

Von Jagow, Minister of State, Secretary of State of the Foreign Office: Gentlemen, Deputy Haase has brought up the old Belgian stories. When I gave that declaration, I had to regard Belgium as a neutral country. When the Chancellor made his declaration on August 4, he could not know that Belgium had already taken position. Only subsequently it has been proved, and thoroughly proved, that the guilt was with the Belgians. [*Lively approval.*]

Gentlemen, how such expressions, as made by Deputy Haase, exert an influence abroad, I shall show you by reading, with the Chairman's approval, a paragraph from *L'Oeuvre*. It says there:

"The last Reichstag session equals a victory of our arms. [*Lively shouts: "Hear, hear!"*] If in France a deputy had said only one-fourth of what Herr Haase did say, his colleagues would have stoned him immediately." [*Lively applause and "Hear, hear!" Laughing and shouts by S.D.L.G.*]

77. (h) SCHEIDEMANN'S SPEECH[13]

Gentlemen, at the head of my speech I should like to place a sentence expressed here yesterday by the Chancellor: "For Germany, not for a foreign piece of land, do Germany's sons bleed and die." [*"Bravo!"*

---

[12] *Verhandlungen des Reichstags,* No. 40, April 6, 1916, p. 889.
[13] *Ibid.,* pp. 889–96.

"*Quite right!*"] That was a confirmation of a sentence from the beginning of the war: "We are not driven by lust of conquests." That was
an underlining of the sentence: "It is not land greed that actuates us."
To me that was a new and clear answer to all kinds of visionaries.
[*"Quite right!"*] Not all have derived this from the Chancellor's speech.
. . . . The gentlemen, Stresemann and Count v. Westarp, drew conclusions from it which do not agree with what the Chancellor said. Should
the Chancellor subsequently confess himself to the aims of Count v.
Westarp, aims whose realization would delay a possible early peace,
then, I may say it with confidence, the Chancellor, Dr. Spahn, and
Count v. Westarp will have to continue the war alone. [*"Quite right!"*
—*S.D.*] If attention was called to pamphlets in which all kinds of
demands are being put forward, I wish to remind them that we had
similar pamphlets also in times of peace. [*"Quite right!"—S.D.*]

I would also have liked it had the Chancellor expressed himself so
clearly that there would have been no other explanation than the one
he gave. [*"Quite right!"*] But one has to do violence to his expressions if one wishes to distil out of them brutal intentions of conquest
and oppression. [*"Very true!"*] If freeing the Poles from Tsarism
succeeds, then the whole civilized world will be glad of it! [*Applause.*]
Of course, it will be a hard nut to crack, to come to an agreement
with the Poles, suitable to them and their neighbors. [*"Quite right!"*
Laughter.]

If it will be possible to secure for the Flemish people in the peace
treaty the possibility of fostering their own culture upon the basis of
their own language, then, I ask, is that violence? [*"Very good!"*] We
would be decidedly against any violence that possibly could happen.
[*Applause.*]

The Chancellor has said, "The Europe which will come out of this,
her greatest of all crises, will be in many respects different from the old
Europe." And at another place he said, "History does not know the
status quo ante after such terrible happenings."

Gentlemen, one must be a political imbecile [*mirth*] to believe that
a whole continent can be in flames, that millions are being killed, that
inestimable material goods can be destroyed—and that after all this, not
a single border-stone may be shifted. [*Protracted stormy applause.*] A
border-stone placed there by a long-decayed diplomat! [*Mirth.*]

No, gentlemen, I have no great admiration for the living diplomats,
and no one must ask me to remain in veneration before the diplomats
out of the time of the Holy Alliance. [*Mirth.*]

Gentlemen, this war is also a revolution, a revolution of such far-
reaching import that its results cannot be foreseen at all. Our task must
be to make an end of this struggle as soon as possible. When this war

is continued even a day longer than the attitude of the enemies demands, or for capitalistic interests, then we must resolutely oppose it. [*"Quite right!"*] We know that our Government is fundamentally ready to enter peace negotiations. But we also know that the statesmen of the enemy countries so far have not been willing to listen to it. [*"Quite right!"*]

Only a few words about the U-boat question. For very good reasons did we vote for the U-boat resolution. We are not responsible for the different things which some have tried to read out of or into that resolution. . . . . It (the U-boat) is therefore to be used. That I hold for granted; for the means which we appropriated for the protection and defense of our country, we surely do not regard as things not to be used. [*"Very good!" Mirth.*]

Gentlemen, it would be very pleasing to me if we could place the U-boats and guns in museums and exhibition halls. Unfortunately the English do not permit that as yet. [*"Very good!" Mirth.*]

For the time being we must protect our skin. I should like to know what our party comrade, Albert Thomas, the French Minister of Munitions, would say if the proposal were made to him that he should procure munitions and arms all right, but that he should also take care that they do not harm the enemy. [*"Very good!" Mirth.*] There can be no talk about that. We must protect ourselves with the U-boat, in order that our wives and children be not abandoned to starvation. [*Stormy applause.*]

What else does the U-boat resolution contain? It says further that the U-boat is to help us to win for Germany a satisfactory peace. Certainly no one could object to that! [*"Very good!"*] We have repeatedly explained what we understand under such a peace. I shall come back to that later on.

But the resolution also says—and without this we should not have voted for it—that the legitimate interests of the neutral states must be observed. That was the deciding factor for us. . . . .

Equally evident is it that we cannot approve Bernstein's resolution (No. 258). I should like to say this about that resolution. It rejects the inconsiderate U-boat war. We do the same. According to the proposal of the commission, such a war is not to take place at all. Such a U-boat war is impossible after the joint proposal [*"Hear, hear!"—S.D.*], in which it expressly says that the legitimate neutral rights are to be observed. One cannot observe those rights, if one torpedoes their ships without consideration.

When now proposal No. 258 demands, further, that also enemy merchant ships which are armed and which have the order to ram our U-boats and fire upon them be spared, we cannot approve of that.

["Quite right!"—S.D.] The tendency of paragraph 2 of proposal No. 258 agrees completely with what we have professed before. That is known and needs no elucidation. The formulation of the proposal, however, is not acceptable to us. It demands immediate opening of negotiations on the part of Germany, although it is well known that enemy statesmen so far have rejected every thought of peace. Further, it fails to announce what we regard as assumptions for a peace, namely —and here I come to that which I lightly touched upon before—the inviolability of the Reich, its political independence, and freedom of its economic development. ["Quite right!"] In view of all this we cannot approve proposal No. 258.

In spite of the fact that we had to reject much that had been expected of us with regard to the conduct of the war, I shall say again at this time that we have very great sympathy for a certain tendency which contains many attacks and proposals. This tendency aims to realize and expand certain parliamentary rights hitherto disputed. According to many proposals it is being demanded that the parliament have even a consultatory right concerning the manner of conducting the war. . . . . Is that being (turning to the Right) disputed? It cannot be disputed, for the conduct of the war is an entity in itself in which belong the aërial as well as sea warfare. The one or the other shall, let us say—in a restricted or unrestricted way—be carried out. Quarreling ensues. The Reichstag shall decide in this quarrel; but that means, the Reichstag shall take a position concerning the conduct of the war. That is a clear fact. A number of gentlemen who now demand influence upon the conduct of the war have rapidly learned according to a better method. When a change in the war salary ordinance was demanded, we were being told: keep your fingers off, because there is an intervention in the powers of the Highest Command! ["Hear, hear!"] Now we are being asked to help decide special questions in the conduct of the war! Would not that be an intervention in the powers of the Highest Command? We are the most resolute champions and defenders of parliamentary rights. But I confess openly that we have not the thought of helping to decide what shall be done on the battlefield or in a sea battle. [Laughter.] . . . . I am of the opinion that in those questions one can have greater confidence in the strategic knowledge of Hindenburg and Falkenhayn. ["Quite right!"—S.D.]

But, as was said, in the struggle for the increasing of the people's rights Herr Heydebrand shall always find us at his side. ["Quite right!" —S.D.] Gentlemen, as first target for the common attack, I would propose the big house in Prince Albrecht Street. [Mirth.] Thereto we must direct the first torpedoes; there we must effect a breach, in order to create the opportunity to illumine it thoroughly. . . . .

It was recently said in a German paper that if an attempt had been made to exert an influence upon the conduct of the war it was because of lack of confidence: "We have no confidence any more!" If that comes from a certain group, then it is a pithy sentence, which reminds us of other sentences that came formerly from the same group but which I am not going to name here intentionally. I am no optimist in political things, particularly as regards our internal conditions. But when certain circles lose confidence in the Government, then I ask: does not the nation possibly have reason to get a little fresh hope? [*"Very good!"—S.D.*] . . . . To the Government I dare to say that it must be sure that it can well afford to lose the confidence of small groups, but that it will be lost and the entire country will be abandoned to the greatest turmoil if the nation itself loses confidence. [*"Quite right!"—S.D.*]

I have spoken about the Prussian Landtag. It protested against consultatory right in regard to the conduct of the war and the foreign policy. I think I am not wrong in assuming that the gentlemen who sit in the Prussian Lower House do not care a bit if the Reichstag has no word at all on Reich questions. Rather they would like to see Germany's foreign policy directed entirely from Prince Albrecht Street. [*"Quite right!"—S.D.*] It is one of the most urgent tasks of the promised new orientation policy of the Reichstag to illumine thoroughly the Prussian Lower House. If Prussia demands the right to take part in determining the conduct of the war, then we shall reverse the spear, in order to convince the gentlemen that the Reich will look into the affairs, let us say, of Mecklenburg and Prussia. [*"Quite right!" Mirth.*] . . . .

The Reich Government is responsible for my having to be quite outspoken about the question of the Reich Coalition Law. According to the report made to us in the rules committee it "cannot be foreseen" when the bill supplementary to the Reich Coalition Law will reach the House. [*Lively shouts; "Hear, hear!"—S.D.*] The difficulties which have arisen are supposed to lie in the fact that the Prussian Government demands [*shouts from the S.D.: "Again and again Prussia"*] that this bill confine itself only to those labor categories which come under Article 152 of the Trade Regulation, and particularly that it exclude farm laborers. [*Renewed shouts; "Hear, hear!"—S.D.*] If the Reich Government gives in, it will place itself in sharpest contradiction with its repeated declarations. [*"Quite right!"—S.D.*]

Already at the Reichstag session of March 20, 1915, the Secretary of State of the Interior Department said that the trade unions do not enjoy the right place in our legal life and that it is necessary to remedy this situation. In the commission which we installed these words condensed themselves into the most definite declarations of Ministerial-

Director Dr. Lewald, and later on to equally clear and unequivocal declarations of the representatives of the Federated Governments in this House. I have these important declarations at hand but shall not read them. They can be reduced to this: the Government has always taken the attitude that no category of laborers, of whatever nature, should occupy itself with political affairs, and that no organization, of whatever nature, should become a political organization when the affairs about which a legal regulation is being sought are such as to affect the economic welfare of the members of the organization concerned or the relatives of the occupations concerned. [*"Hear, hear!"—S.D.*] The administration of justice, however, had wrongly and contrary to the unanimous legislative view brought a mistake into the law. [*"Hear, hear!"—S.D.*] A bill correcting this mistake was to have been submitted to us at an early date. [*"Hear, hear!"—S.D.*]

Now all of a sudden this solemn promise is to have lost its validity, merely because Prussian "gentlemen" do not want it. The Reich Government now expects of us almost a monstrosity. The coupling of the Reich Coalition Law with Article 152 of the Trades Regulation is legally misguided and logically senseless. This the Reich Government, too, has recognized, in that it has not indicated with a single word in Dr. Lewald's explanation, which I cited above, that the supplementary bill was to confine itself only to those categories of workers mentioned in Article 152 of the Trades Regulation. All rural legal restraints of the right to strike—also the Prussian law of April 24, 1854, which forbids farm laborers to agree to quit work—remain in force, according to this bill. It confines itself to entirely unimportant promises exclusively in the field of the Coalition Law. That the latter is to be sharply distinguished from Article 152 no one has told us more clearly than the Secretary of State of the Department of the Interior in his Reichstag speech of December 10, 1912. The Reich Government admits that it always took the attitude that discussion of the social-political affairs of the professional organizations is non-political.

The Government admits that the courts have wrongly accepted the opposite. This injustice is now to be rectified for those workers coming under Article 152, but is to remain for all other groups. If that happens, it means that a wrongly accepted standpoint, as expressly admitted by the Government and which until now has worked to the disadvantage of the laborers, is to be legalized for a definite group of laborers. And shall the trade unions give their approval to such a state of affairs? The Government has expressed its gratitude to the trade unions for their unexcelled accomplishments in this war. Shall the reward be impairment of the legal rights of large labor groups? What worker could still have confidence if the trade unions were calmly to accept such presumptions? The Christian and Hirsch-Duncker trade unions certainly do not deviate in this from the independent trade unions.

One more word to mark this entire logical nonsense. It often happens that in the same trade unions are united the most varied groups of workers; for example, the transport trade union, which comprises, on one side, chauffeurs, coach drivers, and domestic servants, and, on the other side, street-car employees and inland shippers. If the first groups should approach the Reichstag with a petition regarding an improvement of their situation, that would not be a political affair. If the second groups do the same, it suddenly would become a political matter. Gentlemen, you see that that is an impossible state of affairs. [*Lively approval by S.D.*]

If we fully realize what that means, then we must say to ourselves it is impossible for the Government to expect such things of us from essential motives.

Gentlemen, there are no essential motives; the fact is that there are influential men who fear that certain insignificant rights might be given the laboring masses in return for their very heavy sacrifices endured in the war. That is to be prevented. . . . . I beg all of you, in particular the gentlemen of the Government, to realize fully how embittered the labor class must become if even these insignificant privileges should be withheld, and when such a procedure would make clear that the small and degrading police struggle, which we have discussed here annually before the war, should also be continued after the war.

We therefore demand of the Reich Government that it resolutely oppose all difficulties raised by Prussia. It must not take lightly the Prussian machinations. It could easily lead to a terrible explosion. [*"Quite right!"—S.D.*] Gentlemen, there is a limit to everything. We have heard here very promising words about a "new orientation." The emphasis that the recent speech from the Throne placed upon the suffrage-reform promise of the speech from the Throne of 1908 has stirred a great fury. But, gentlemen, here too let the Government be on its guard. The German people do not sacrifice hundreds of thousands of their sons for a pre-March Prussia. [*"Quite right!"—S.D.*] . . . . To oppress foreign peoples is a crime of the worst kind; but to graduate the rights of their own people according to the content of the pocketbook is worse than a crime. It is an imbecile thing to do; an imbecility which will be bitterly revenged. [*"Very good!"*]

I should like to insert at this point a few words about occurrences in the Imperial territories (*Reichsländer*). I protest emphatically against the way in which certain military commanders regard their position in these territories. It is natural that certain difficulties should arise out of the fact that Alsace-Lorraine is partly a war area, but what certain military authorities are doing there serves only to arouse the loyal majority of the population against Germany. . . . .

Up to the present day the breaking down of the German nation is the greatest hope of our enemies. . . . . We have often laughed about the many threats being sent to us from abroad. But what matters at present are not the threats of the enemy press but that we now have to recognize that the English President of the Board of Trade, Runciman, openly and officially announced in the House of Commons that an economic war would be ruthlessly conducted against Germany after the close of the war. Now it is: no separate peace with Germany. After the war it is to be: no separate commercial peace with Germany—we ruin the Reich in unison. . . . . Gentlemen, we must not forget that we actually fight for our existence, for the future of our children. [*Lively approval.*] For these reasons we must not only thank the men at the front but must do everything to insure that the determination and the courage of the women at home in the struggle against all kinds of enemies be not lowered. [*"Very true!"—S.D.*] The final settlement with those who make life difficult for our soldier families will come after the war [*"Very good!"—S.D.*], but then in unrestricted and inconsiderate fashion. [*Lively approval from the S.D.*]

Gentlemen, I said previously in my speech of March 18, 1915: "To wage war we need, besides arms and munitions, also bread and freedom!" Therefore, away with censorship and state of siege. [*"Quite right!"—S.D.*] I shall not go into details. . . . . At this moment I wish only to remind you what Herr Ebert said about all the malice and imbecility of various officials. He said that the central authorities tried as much as possible to repair those conditions. But, gentlemen, the damage which hundreds of censors, mayors, district councils, etc., do, not even the strongest central authority can repair. [*"Quite right!"—S.D.*] Gentlemen, if you do not wish to bring the entire nation against you, make an end of this state of affairs. I demand the immediate abolition of the state of siege, and recommend this: write on each of your office doors the well-known words of Cavour about the state of siege—words which for propriety's sake I shall not cite here.

Gentlemen, above all the most important: When shall there be peace?

On December 9 of this year I expressed the thought that all nations long for peace. In this conviction I have been strengthened in the meantime. Of course since then many absurd speeches have been made in Petersburg, London, Rome, and Paris—very inciting speeches. But, gentlemen, I ask you in all honor and all conscience: have we heard at home only speeches of pure love and mildness? What absurdities have been preached and written among us! Anyone reading the newspapers knows how many "home-warriors" make daily conquests upon their paper battlefields, which are saturated with their expensive ink. [*Laughter.*] But besides lamentable speeches we have heard also very gratifying expressions from abroad. [*"Quite right!"—S.D.*] Gentlemen, we have heard words of peace from all enemy capitals except Paris, where official representatives, unfortunately also certain of our party circles, have demanded again and again that France and Belgium must be first cleared as preliminary to any peace discussion. It is not necessary to add that that is an impossible attitude. [*"Quite right!"*] What could only be the result of negotiations is here demanded as a condition to negotiations. [*"Quite right!"—S.D.*] Translated into our position that would mean: first give up all your colonies and open all sea routes to Germany, and then negotiate. [*"Bravo!"*] Gentlemen, in this manner we would have to continue the war forever. Therefore, I say that that is impossible. Negotiations must be opened as soon as possible, for it is my firmest conviction that the beginning of negotiations is also the end of the war. [*"Quite right!"—S.D.*] . . . .

The whole war probably would have been impossible had democracy been more developed in those countries which are now at war. [*"Very good!"—S.D.*] Gentlemen, do not misunderstand me, I will not [*Deputy Dr. Liebknecht: "But you play into the hands of the war instigators!" Excited shouts and laughter.*]—Gentlemen, I will not say [*Deputy Dr. Liebknecht: "Shame on you!" Merriment and violent shouts!*]— . . . . But, gentlemen, please calm yourselves! . . . . Do not misunderstand me. I know what led to the war. We have said it here expressly enough. We know the imperialistic motivations, and we have always fought them. You know that we expressly rejected the responsibility for the policy which moved in an imperialistic direction. I beg to be understood. I do not really say that the diplomats made the war! No, they probably did not do that; but they were not able to prevent the war. [*"Quite right!"*] The nations would have been able to do that had they, upon the basis of democratic rights, been able to intervene more strongly; if they had had a word to say. Therefore I say whoever wishes to prevent wars in the future must fight for democracy and against secret diplomacy. [*"Quite right!"—S.D.*]

Gentlemen, the whole war with the West, the war between Germany, France, England, is madness. It is a boundless crime against humanity. [*"Quite right!"—Left.*] Whoever has not lost the last trace of brains and humanity must use all his forces in order that we soon may come to an end. [*"Quite right!"—S.D.*] Let not anyone deceive himself into thinking that this war cannot be prolonged through various circumstances. It can. My colleague Ebert said yesterday that fundamentally we have given up nothing. We are what we were, and we remain what we are [*"Quite right!"—S.D.*] ; Socialists and Democrats! [*"Quite right!"*]

The German people wish an early peace, as doubtless do all nations which are involved in this war. We demand that an end be made of the war as soon as the enemies are inclined to peace. That we have declared here many times. That we are against every oppression of other peoples is as self-evident to us as is our demand that Germany's inviolability, political independence, and freedom of economic development be safeguarded in the peace treaty. I believe that we should be a step nearer peace if it had been possible to prompt our party comrades in France to talk in their parliament as we have done, if they too had told their Government to take a step in order to come nearer the aim. Unfortunately that did not happen. I confess it with regret.

I close. We know our duties as Germans and Socialists. We shall do our duty. [*Lively "Bravos" by the S.D.*]

78. DISCUSSION IN THE MAIN COMMITTEE OF THE REICHS-TAG ON IMPERIAL REFORMS, MARCH 3, 1917[13a]

The Main Committee of the Reichstag began yesterday [March 3] the discussion of the budget of the Empire for the fiscal year 1917–18 with the estimates of the Chancellor and the Imperial Chancery.

Present were Secretaries of State Dr. Helfferich, Zimmermann, Dr. Lisco, and Count von Roedern, as well as Undersecretary of State Wahnschaffe.

A Social-Democratic Deputy demanded a redivision of electoral districts in view of the great shifting of the population during the war. He contended that the rural population, which is receding in numbers, should not be privileged any longer at the expense of the industrial population.

A speaker of the Progressive Party wished that in the coming elections the discriminations against other nationalities in the mixed-population districts should be excluded. The Polish and the Danish Germans had done their full duty in this war. The introduction of proportional representation in the eastern and northern part of the country would bring about an improvement in the situation.

A speaker of the Social-Democratic Labor Group demanded the changing of the election procedure and the application of the proportional-representation system in the larger electoral districts with the retention of the present number of deputies. To introduce proportional representation only into the mixed-population districts would not be appropriate, for a struggle for the mandates from the border places would still take place, in so far as the system was not changed uniformly for the entire country.

[13a] *Norddeutsche Allgemeine Zeitung,* March 4, 1917, I, 3.

A speaker of the Social-Democratic "Fraktion" predicted that the Government and the bourgeois parties would, in the present discussions, be confronted with the question as to whether they were ready to grant equal rights in the matter of suffrage. He said that the number of Reichstag Deputies could not remain at four hundred.

Thereupon the estimates of the Chancellor and the Imperial Chancery were accepted.

79. THE DEBATE IN THE REICHSTAG ON INTERNAL REFORMS, MARCH 29, 1917

(a) DR. SPAHN'S SPEECH[14]

Gentlemen, ... The Prussian Herrenhaus has of late repeatedly taken the opportunity to occupy itself with our affairs. As chairman of the I. Commission, which was hit hardest by these accusations, you must permit me to say a few words by way of retaliation. Yesterday it was said that the German nation deserves a better parliament than this Reichstag, and shortly ago they accused the Reichstag of having exceeded its constitutional prerogatives by demanding, without the approval of the Bundesrat, a share in the executive power, which was revolutionary. As proof was cited the Economic Advisory Council in the Imperial Office of the Interior. . . . .

At the beginning of the war the Reichstag deemed it advisable to transfer its legislative powers, in so far as they pertain to economic war measures, to the Imperial Office of the Interior and the Bundesrat. That was a great accommodation. ["*Quite right!*"] We could have demanded that the innumerable announcements of the Bundesrat should have first received our approbation. We believed that it was in the interest of the Fatherland that the Bundesrat be empowered to regulate those measures as circumstances demanded. . . . .

It was with the approval of the Bundesrat that we created the Economic Advisory Council in the Imperial Office of the Interior. Furthermore, with the Bundesrat's approval we were empowered to meet, during the recess of the parliament, as the I. Commission of the Reichstag, in order to receive information from the Chancellor about the military and political situation. . . . . Between the Bundesrat and the Commissions there has never been any quarrel. The Praesidium of the Herrenhaus allowed those accusations to be made without any regard for us. If that had not happened, I should have remained indifferent to the allegations; but the Praesidium was in duty bound to guard the rights of the Reichstag ["*Quite right!*"], and therefore I feel myself obliged

Verhandlungen des Reichstags, No. 95, March 29, 1917, pp. 2831–35.

to say to the Praesidium that the Herrenhaus should sweep in front of its own house and leave us in peace [*lively "Bravo!"*]. . . . .

Gentlemen, the Chancellor said in his speech before the Abgeordnetenhaus that he was of the opinion that the experiences of this war must lead to a reorganization of our internal political life. He declared imperative a reform of the Prussian suffrage. As legislators the Prussian suffrage does not affect us. [*Shouts.*] Technically we have nothing to do with it. It interests us as Germans, this I confess. [*"Quite right!"*] But as such it does not come within our competence, and therefore I should not go into it, the more so since no electoral reform bill is under discussion. But I am interested in it as a Prussian. I wish to emphasize this because my political friends in the Abgeordnetenhaus have always endeavored to bring about such a reform. I hope that they will be able to meet those steps which the Chancellor may take in this direction and may co-operate with him to remove this thorny question. In a proposal before us and in the discussions which already have taken place here, particularly in the I. Commission, mention has also been made about the question of the Reichstag suffrage, more especially the question of the division of Reichstag electoral districts. I do not recognize the necessity of these changes to the extent of the discussions which have taken place, but I should not like to go into this question. I do not hold it necessary, nor advisable, to allow discussion about it to take place at this moment. It is not an imperative question for any one party, and can be dropped during the war.

The Chancellor said also in that speech that he wished a "strong policy toward the outside as well as the inside," and as a basis of policy he recognized the necessity of the political equality of the whole nation in all of its ranks. That is a basis. His thoughts about the future realization of this remained unspoken. We fully approve of this basic thought, which can find application also here in the Reich. With it we also in the Reichstag shall be ready enough to strive for the creation of a strong and young nation. . . . . Gentlemen, we shall succeed in maintaining a strong state and a strong nation if we succeed in preserving in each individual a strong sense of duty and honest work, a spirit of generosity and a strong sense of responsibility before himself and his neighbor, and before God and His eternal laws. [*"Bravo!"—Center.*]

Gentlemen, the Chancellor in his speech before the Abgeordnetenhaus stressed particularly the care of the laboring masses. In regard to the social policy, which is connected with this care, I should like once more to emphasize the remarks of Herr Giesberts made here just a few days ago. Thereby I shall avoid going into the details of this question. I emphasize particularly his remark about the importance of the "moral and religious factor of the social question." [*"Bravo!"—Center.*] If one has perused the war literature to any extent, one finds himself prompted to remark that the atmosphere which we breathe and in which we move does not flow from Kant or Hegel, but from Christianity. [*Shouts from the Left.*] It is Christ's sun which enlightens our mind, and upon this Christian character of our nation is based the progress of our state and nation. [*"Quite right!"—Center.*]

Gentlemen, we have before us a number of resolutions regarding our internal policy. I shall not go into any one of them except in regard to the proposal of Dr. Albass, which proposes that for each individual state there be prescribed a constitutional government with a representative body. I must ask whether the question of competence is not in point. . . . .

79. (b) NOSKE'S SPEECH[15]

. . . . Gentlemen, the discussion about German internal political questions becomes livelier from day to day. The Chancellor, too, participated in this debate in his Reichstag speech of February 27 and in the Abgeordnetenhaus on March 17. The necessity of a thorough reorganization of conditions in Germany, in the cities as well as in the individual states, becomes constantly more imperative. [*"Quite right!"—S.D.*] Justice must be done to the masses of the people as soon as possible. [*Lively approval by S.D.*] The Imperial Government recognizes this necessity. The Chancellor said on March 17 in the Abgeordnetenhaus: "That was well said, but it does not mean acting." I add: The interest of the Empire demands that the electoral reform be begun immediately. [*Lively approval by S.D.*] Hesitation might cause irreparable damage. [*"Quite right!"—S.D.*] . . . .

Gentlemen, not only will a reformation of Europe come out of this war but also one of the whole world. But there are groups in our country who shout loudest for the most far-reaching changes of our borders and who would like to continue the war until world empires be brought to a collapse, and yet who fight in unconceivable delusion against any change or reform in the Reich and the individual states. [*"Quite right!"—S.D.*] Thus world history cannot be and is not being written. [*"Very good!"—S.D.*]

Herr Dr. Spahn just now rejected the attacks of the Prussian Herrenhaus. I would take no notice of what was said in that House if there were not a real danger that these speeches may be heard beyond the border and there create the impression that out of that Chamber sounds the language of the German nation and German life. [*Cheers and shouts.*] . . . . Gentlemen, the chief arguments of our enemies in creating sentiment against Germany were the German illiberality and

---

[15] *Verhandlungen des Reichstags*, No. 95, March 29, 1917, pp. 2835–42.

the hostility of the German governmental system toward freedom. [*"Quite right!"—S.D.*] . . . . Therefore, the world is filled with prejudices and antipathies against Germany. [*"Very true!"—S.D.*] Of course, that is not the cause of the war. . . . . The moral factors, however, which speak against Germany are very great.

Gentlemen, the Russian revolution is being used in France and in England also as a thrust against the reactionary Prussianism. There they compare German conditions and the defunct Tsarist régime on the same basis, pronounce them in the same breath. [*Shouts from the Right.*] . . . . This much at least is true, that it will become increasingly difficult for reactionaries to maintain the present system if Germany is to be surrounded by democracies not only in the West, North, and South, but also in the East. [*"Quite right!"—S.D.*] That will compel even the most obstinate ones to an adjustment. The question now is in what form the transformation shall take place. M. Ribot, the newest of French Premiers, recently expressed the hope that the Russian revolution would serve as an example to other countries. There cannot be any doubt as to the country to which this referred. We German Social-Democrats have received such advice often during the war. German Social-Democracy was asked to incite a revolution when on the East the Russian armies and in the West the millions of French and English soldiers of all colors stormed our borders. Compliance with such advice would have meant the defeat of our country [*"Quite right!"—S.D.*], would have meant endless suffering for our nation, and not least for our workers. [*"Quite right!"—S.D.*]

The French Socialistic party of the Chamber of Deputies recently sent a congratulatory telegram to the Russian Socialists, which says: "May this revolution, of which you always spoke as a condition for a democratic progress and a conclusive peace, indicate the road to the Proletariat and Socialists of Germany and Austria-Hungary. Now they are confronting that decision." To that I say: We keep the same coolness of mind and sober judgment which guided us in all our decisions during the war. [*"Quite right!"—S.D.*] What has to be done in Germany, we ourselves know. What they have in store for our nation and our country in case of our defeat, that the statesmen of the Entente have said clearly enough in their answer to the German peace proposal of December 12 last. . . . .

Gentlemen, we place the future security of our nation and country above all our wishes, demands, and future efforts. This alone was what caused us again and again to vote for the war appropriations, and that in spite of the fact that many things were happening in Germany also during the war which did not meet with our approval, rather which demanded our severest criticism. Today, I think, one may recall that we Social-Democrats have not forgotten at all the injustice done to us previously. [*"Quite right!"—S.D.*] . . . . That brings back the memory of the Socialist Law, the Penitentiary Bill, the efforts to abolish the right of coalition, and finally also the speeches about the men without a country. Gentlemen, those memories are not erased with a few pleasing words [*lively approval from the S.D.*], and in judging the internal political occurrences during the war which are not pleasing to the governing and propertied classes let them consider that these are the fruits of theirs and their fathers' sin. [*"Very good!"—S.D.*]

Gentlemen, regarding the speed with which the Conservatives wish to carry out reforms, their speaker said on February 27 the following: "Important practical problems will so occupy us after peace has been restored that then too, just as now during the war, we should take heed not to throw unnecessary questions and points of dispute into public discussion." The Conservatives would like a proclamation of a "Burgfrieden" for all times. That would suit them! [*"Quite right!"—S.D. Laughter from the Right.*] . . . .

Now the Government would like to introduce the new orientation process with negligible reforms. To keep the Center in good humor, it says—and we shall gladly welcome it, were the rumors to materialize—that finally one exceptional law shall fall, namely, the Jesuit Law, for the abolition of which we have fought as long as it existed. The Secretary of State for the Interior recently promised the Center a far-reaching parity in the matter of filling offices. But we ask: Why not a thorough re-orientation, once a beginning is made with trivialities? I should like to mention only casually that the Prussian Poles were promised a new orientation at the beginning of the war. Finally after two and one-half years the representative of the Minister President said in the Herrenhaus that the Government would deliberate as to whether or not the language paragraph, etc., could be removed from the law of dispossession. Why in the world should an old injustice last one day longer after its abolition has been recognized? Hopes of the future and future promises, which we have heard so often, are beautiful enough, but surely practical acting by the Government would be more in order. [*"Quite right!"—S.D.*] Unfortunately, Prussia has not done a thing so far to make moral conquests; rather it often destroys what good feeling there is. . . . .

We cannot admit that it is necessary to wait for the beginning of this process of new orientation until the end of the war. [*"Quite right!"—S.D.*] Surely the entire complex of the pending questions cannot be solved overnight. But what can be done at once, must no longer be delayed. . . . . Certainly the war does not prevent the people from being burdened by excessive taxes. [*"Quite right!"—S.D.*] Why then should progress alone not materialize [*"Very good!"—S.D.*], and why should that be the case only in Germany? England changes its suffrage system in the midst of the war [*"Hear, hear!"—S.D.*], extends the suffrage right, and also wishes to give limited suffrage to women. In such a case, my political friends say, let the Chancellor learn from the enemy. [*Lively shouts; "Very good!"—S.D.*]

. . . . We have demanded a redivision of electoral districts. The constitution of the Reichstag prescribes such a redivision. [*"Hear, hear!"—S.D.*] We therefore do not demand a reform, no fundamental change, but only that the Chancellor observe the constitution of the German Empire. [*Lively approval by the S.D.*] . . . .

Finally, the Chancellor should immediately take up the reform of the electoral systems of the individual states. [*"Very good!"—S.D.*] If the German statesmen knew the art of handling people, then there would be no three-class suffrage system in Prussia, not to mention at all the medieval arrangements of Mecklenburg. [*"Very good!"—S.D.*] . . . . Gentlemen, what a Junker said yesterday in the Herrenhaus is a gross insult and challenge to the disfranchised masses, that in Prussia there exists every liberty except that of stealing and murder. [*"Hear, hear!"—S.D.*] . . . .

It is not true that suffrage reform is impossible in time of war. The Conservative *Post* recently wished to instruct us that now a majority in favor of universal suffrage could not be found in the Prussian Landtag. Well, we often thought of that, without, however, giving up our demand for it. What cannot be achieved with the Landtag and the Herrenhaus will some day be realized without them. [*Lively approval from the Left.*] . . . .

If one asks why the Chancellor hesitates, then one gets the answer that a handful of Conservatives who fear to lose their privileged status in state and society is opposed to it. [*"Very true!"—S.D.*] Herr Chancellor, these people comprise only a very small fraction of the German and the Prussian people! [*Shouts from the Right.*] In order to humor them the Chancellor sees—without doing anything about it—how the dissatisfaction of the people constantly grows. That we regard as a policy fraught with danger. [*"Very true!"—S.D.*]

There is nothing to prevent the Federal Governments from bringing in a project whereby all individual representative bodies should arise out of equal, universal, secret, and direct suffrage. . . . .

We are indifferent to the discussion as to whether this or another Chancellor would be more amenable to the demands of a reform policy. At what pace Germany will be modernized does not depend upon the will of individual persons; that will depend upon the will and the strength of the masses of the people, who do not beg payment for good behavior but who demand their rights. [*"Very good!"—S.D.*] It did not require much prophetic gift to say the words which Deputy Haussmann said at this place on March 2: "If the Government and bourgeois majority reject a new orientation, then we shall face the bitterest struggle after the war." That we also say, not as a threat but as a fair warning, and say it calmly yet not the least bit less emphatically. [*"Quite right!"—S.D.*]

The German nation should after the war be enabled to use all its energy and strength for the nursing of the wounds sustained by millions of people and the whole structure of society. [*"Quite right!"—S.D.*] The Government should spare us from every political quarrel. Therefore, we demand of the Chancellor: create now a new road for a free people in a new period and spare us the quarrels after the war when we have better things to do. [*"Bravo!"—S.D.*] Unfortunately, so far we have not been able to get the impression that the Government and the majority of the Reichstag are willing to rise to the occasion and bring about the reforms which are urgently needed for the interests of Germany. The people must continue to give the Fatherland all that is necessary for its security; certainly not for the interest of Junkers and capitalists but only to save its own skin.

But, gentlemen, be sure of it, that if once the danger is passed and nothing has been done by that time, we shall know how to obtain for the people what they claim; if it cannot be obtained in a peaceful way, then we shall claim it in a sharp and determined fight! [*Lively applause by the S.D.*]

79. (c) STRESEMANN'S SPEECH[16]

. . . . Gentlemen, in going over now to the internal political questions, permit me to remind you that the struggles for a constitution began in Germany at a time when a great war drew to its conclusion and in which the Prussian and the German people expected from the war not only a liberation from foreign oppression but also a rejuvenation of their own political and intellectual life. Those were the wars of liberation of 1813 and 1815. At that time the King of Prussia gave his word that he would give the people a constitution. At that time, it was Russia's influence which in the form of the Holy Alliance restricted Prussian constitutional development. We should have been spared much of the bitterness in Prussian-German history if Russian reaction had not dominated Prussia. Gentlemen, upon reading yesterday's debates of the Herrenhaus there come to my mind the conditions of that time and the gentlemen who at that time wished Prussia's rejuvenation. The gentlemen of the Right just a while ago confirmed with "Very true!" that in the last resort it was military absolutism which had made Prussia and Germany great. I do not know where history confirms this con-

[16] *Verhandlungen des Reichstags,* No. 95, March 29, 1917, pp. 2851 ff.

ception. [*"Quite right!"—Left.*] I do not wish to picture the year 1806 as solely a breakdown of military absolutism; it possibly was through a breakdown of diplomacy that Prussia at first waged this war without any coalition. But let us not close our eyes to the fact that it was the turning away from the former character of Prussian militarism which doubtless decided the successes of the struggles of 1813 and 1815. [*"Quite right!"—National-Liberals.*] Scharnhorst, the man who gave us the people's army in which we all confess our confidence, wrote to Frederick William III at that time: "It is not always the standing armies which have saved Throne and Crown; most generally it has been the love and enthusiasm of a nation for its King and Fatherland." That was the man who made an end to the idea which possibly after all was military absolutism. And I can think of another man who served Prussia only one year but who in that year did a work which was to last more than a century—that man was von Stein. If I think of today's particularistic forces, I am reminded of the words of von Stein: "I know only one Fatherland, and that is Germany [*"Bravo!"—Left*], and, therefore, I am devoted only to it, not any one part of it!" [*Renewed "Bravo!"*] . . . . Gentlemen, it sounds very well: Hands off of old Prussia! Often it is not being realized in Prussia that the greatness of Prussia and what it has done for German history is being fully appreciated even when one criticizes the internal institutions of Prussia. [*"Quite right!"—N.L.*] . . . . But, gentlemen, the times of Frederick the Great are gone. Today the Emperor cannot be at all the personal leader of the ship of state in the same sense as was possible then. Today many a thing that you call the prerogative of the Emperor and many a thing that is done in the name of the King has become a mere formula. [*"Quite right!"—N.L. and S.D.*] Today that which is covered by the name of Emperor and King often enough is only the result of the views of a small circle which chances at the moment to be in an advisory position about the Kaiser and the King. [*"Very good!"—N.L. and S.D.*]

Therefore, one should not say that this old Prussia must remain as it once was. It is no longer the old Prussia. It is possible that the Herrenhaus did not even give a true picture of the economic and intellectual forces of Prussia at the time when it was founded. And who criticized the Herrenhaus most bitterly? Long before that was done by a Liberal, Bismarck did it. It was also such a Conservative historian as Treitschke, a man who was averse to any demagogy and who would have nothing to do with democracy, who pronounced the bitterest judgment ever made about the Prussian Herrenhaus.

Hands off of old Prussia! That also means—do not undermine our constitution as it stands today, neither attack the Prussian Herrenhaus! Well! are we then supposed to pass over blindly all the great economic developments which have taken place since? Are we to shut our eyes to the fact that the economic forces of the Prussia of today are entirely different ones than purely agricultural? Shall we stand aside now that this great and mighty labor movement has set in, which has been a foundation of our national life thanks to the World War, and when an undermining of this national life would mean the endangering of the entire state? [*"Quite right!"—N.L. and S.D.*]

Gentlemen, it is impossible to blindfold oneself in this respect. It is intolerable not only that now the Herrenhaus wishes to preserve the existing order of things but also that a member of the Herrenhaus can voice in so tense an atmosphere his views about the suffrage reform without any regard to the number of people he insults. [*"Quite right!" —N.L. and Left.*] It is unendurable when a member of the Herrenhaus thinks that he has to tell the Reichstag that the German people deserve a better Reichstag and then talks about the installation of an Imperial Superhouse to control the Reichstag. Gentlemen, a control over this Reichstag which, when the war began, narrowed its prerogatives with the knowledge that for the time being all that mattered was to strengthen the powers of the Government is unthinkable. This Reichstag, which did not inquire whether difficulties for itself would arise out of that or whether that would limit its right of criticism—rather it gave the Government much power in order to enable it to bring this war to a victorious conclusion. [*"Very good!"—N.L., Left, and S.D.*]

Gentlemen, this "military absolutism" is a very dangerous term. My political friends are of the opinion that much that we have suffered under the law of the state of siege is unbearable, that it is impossible for the individual to tolerate it any longer. During the discussions over Alsace-Lorraine and cases of arrests we hear already particulars which from a merely human standpoint often benumb the blood in our veins [*"Quite right!"—N.L.*], particulars showing how little understanding was shown by many military authorities for the magna charta of personal liberty. We heard full details of how the individual was brushed aside without any consideration, as if together with his duties as citizen the constitution did not guarantee him the right of his person. Gentlemen, the need of protecting personal liberty against arbitrary action is impressed upon us with such a force that I cannot understand how in the face of the difficulties which might arise one can still appeal to military absolutism as a cure for all ills. Do not undervalue this one thing, and do not misunderstand it: the nation likes the Army, it worships the victorious war leaders, but it does not want military absolutism. [*Lively approval by N.L.*]

Gentlemen, it is a lamentable fact that the Prussian Minister of Agriculture too, without provocation, thought it necessary to avenge himself on the Reichstag. He was attacked by Deputy Scheidemann, and had to even his score with him. That is his clear right. [*"Quite right!"—N.L.*] But on this occasion there was no reason for his saying about the Reichstag: "Thank God, the Reichstag is not yet in a position to depose Prussian State Ministers." First of all, Herr Scheidemann is not the whole Reichstag. . . . .

The Chancellor defended the Reichstag against these attacks and we are grateful to him for it. [*"Bravo!"—Left.*] We view with regret that today there are again being manifested particularist tendencies. We fight them, whether they arise in the South or in the North. If anything arises greatly strengthened out of this storm of war, it will be the German national thought. [*"Quite right!"*] . . . . What the Federal States mean to us [National-Liberals] is this: we wish to preserve their cultural centers for the German intellectual life; we shall co-operate in any way to help them to rehabilitate themselves after the war. But we shall leave no doubt about this: First comes the Reich, and the national thought we place higher than the federal feeling. [*"Quite right!"—N.L.*]

Also we shall leave no doubt about the fact that a new era demands its new rights. . . . . We are glad of what the Chancellor said in the Abgeordnetenhaus about the reorganization of our internal affairs. But we are of the opinion that one does not have to wait for that until after the war. [*"Quite right!"—Left.*] I know that this is in conflict with our former attitude. But I may say this: when at the beginning of the war we agreed with the Chancellor that such reforms must be post-poned until after the war we always hoped that the war would come to a speedy conclusion. Now, however, we are facing the fact that the war has brought us the greatest economic changes, demands unprecedented sacrifices of us, and finally forces us to face questions of clarification. Then, too, we cannot see why these problems should not be solved during the course of the war. [*"Bravo!"—N.L. and Left.*] Therefore, it is the opinion of my political friends and my "Fraktion" that the time has come to begin a reorganization of affairs in Germany and the Federal States. [*Repeated lively applause by N.L. and Left.*]

I think that in this respect we find ourselves in agreement with the Chancellor. I believe that the Chancellor also has changed his view. Whereas he formerly told us that all this could take place only after the war, his representative in the Herrenhaus, Herr von Breitenbach, said that the Government was considering whether the Polish Dispossession Law could be changed. I do not think that in such an important question the words "have under consideration" are meant to be merely formal. That can only mean that in that field we enter upon reorganization. If that can be done during the war, there is no reason why it cannot be done in other fields. [*Lively approval from the N.L. and Left.*] We cannot see why the question of the position of the parliament in the leading Federal States to the Reichstag should not be solved. Or the question of a suffrage reform. Of course, gentlemen, not in the sense of the proposals, á la Bernstein and friends, that each one of us should print his program and bring it in as a proposal. No, far be it from us that we should want to study at this time the programs of all the parties in regard to their constitutional questions. But we regard it as the duty and the task of the parliament to take up those political and constitutional questions which the present now prescribes—Noske's proposal of redividing electoral districts, and others.

It is, however, also necessary to study the system of proportional representation in order to find out whether it does not suit our political life of the present in a way entirely different from the system of district election, which presupposes a relationship between deputy and district. The latter has somewhat lost its importance in a parliament which deals with the great questions of foreign policy, economic policy, social legislation, and constitutional laws, in not all of which the interest of the individual district comes into consideration. [*"Quite right!"—N.L.*] Of course, we would be averse to introducing a scheme which regards the whole Reich as one electoral district. Yet it seems to us important to discuss the question of how far the present injustices could be removed by a system which treated the provinces of Prussia and the individual Federal States of the Reich as great electoral districts, which in their turn would send the Deputies to the Reichstag. We shall also have to study the question of the responsibility of the Imperial Ministers, the reorganization of the position of the Secretaries of State, possibly in a way such as England has, where the Secretaries of State, too, follow the directions of the Prime Minister but are individually responsible for what happens in their departments. Finally we shall have to study how the relationship of parliament to the Government is to be placed upon a different basis.

My political friends have never demanded the parliamentary system as a party program. We have very lively disputes about that within our own ranks. But the experiences of the World War must prompt us to a reconsideration of our governmental system. It also seems to me questionable whether we have the right to look down, as it were, upon the democratically governed countries as if they were not in the position to solve the problems which they have before them. [*"Quite right!"* —N.L.] The debates of the Herrenhaus revealed an awe of the concepts of a parliamentary system, of the strengthening of the rights of the parliament. They said that that endangered the rights of the crown and would lead to a republic. At best even among our bourgeois circles it is said that that would be a system of dead uniformity, a system of attorney government, which in the end would lead to internal rottenness and decay. Well, if that were true, then France would have broken down long ago in this war. [*Lively approval from the Left.*] If that were true, then we should not have to fight so for our very life with England. [*Renewed approval from the Left.*] If that were true, then things could not have come out in such a way that England is successful in building up a great system of alliances with all kinds of nations, whereas we see nations fighting us with whom we have been allied for more than three decades, so that in the end we had lost the war diplomatically even before it began militarily.

No, gentlemen, things are such that we had to learn in this war that the parliamentary system forms after all a tie between people, government, and state. I would have held it impossible in times of peace that such a system could endure a war which would shake the state to its very foundations. It seems to me that the political and diplomatic amateurs who came forth from this system were not inferior to our seasoned diplomats in diplomatic skill. [*"Quite right!"—Left.*] We have also been compelled to see that they were destined to successes in the organization of their own countries which forced us to exert great effort in order not to let victory slip out of our hands. [*Approval.*]

Gentlemen, I beg you to permit me to call attention to what our esteemed leader, Bassermann, has repeatedly said in our circles when speaking of these matters. That is, the great contrast of the last few decades which exists in Germany between the mighty development of our economic forces and our intellectual potentialities in the interior on one side and the—always lagging behind—political successes on the other side. Germany has experienced this magnificent economic development in the last few decades: it now holds second place in world trade; it is the first industrial country of the world. Its captains of industry are personalities of the first class, ... our technique, our chemistry, our intellectual achievements—all are on top. Therefore, we do not lack personalities in Germany, but in spite of the fact we see that, counterbalancing this brilliant development which finally aroused the envy of others, the political advantages are practically all on the side of our enemies. We see that they knew, far better than we, how to win for themselves sympathy. We see that they knew how to encircle us, so that today we are fighting a war for existence. If in contrast to the brilliant internal development we still see political defeat toward the outside and inside, a constant growth of the radical elements in spite of our exemplary social policy, then there must, somewhere, be a mistake in the political system. [*"Very true!"—Left.*] And in such a case one has to search once in a while for things that need to be changed. In such a case one does not get by with the sentence, "Hands off of old Prussia!" [*"Very good!"—Left.*]

Gentlemen, many speakers have pointed out today the mistakes made. We too have expressed them before. Here they are: a failure to understand the mental sentiment of other nations and of our own, failure to understand the effect of political measures; brilliant department ministers who do excellent administrative work but who often lack the political view. I have been told that the Entail Law was a masterpiece juristically, but politically it was at the moment the most imbecile thing. [*"Very true!"—Left.*] If we had a closer connection between parliament and Government, then it would have been easiest—and this has nothing to do yet with the parliamentary system—for the Chancellor sometime to invite the party leaders and say to them: "I intend to submit, in the near future, to the parliament, some fundamental bills; but before I do that I should like to talk with you in order that I may evaluate their political effects." Should such a co-operation develop, ... then I see in it no impairment of the rights of the Government and the Crown. . . . . Gentlemen, no one can assert that Germany is not ready for such a strengthening of parliamentary rights. The war has given us a lesson here too. Just a few words about the Progressive proposal concerning the suffrage in the Federal States. The details of their suffrage we shall have to leave to the parliaments of those states. But, gentlemen, for me and my political friends there is no doubt but that the Prussian suffrage is a German question [*lively applause from the Left*]; it cannot be solely evaluated from the Prussian point of view. . . . . The National-Liberal Party, and particularly its Prussian parliamentary "Fraktion," has demanded this reform for years; it will co-operate in this and expects from it a liberation of forces in the interior. I may refer you to the attitude of my political friends, who also recently took the initiative with the proposal of Herr Friedberg in the matter of reforming the Herrenhaus. We wish a reorganization of things, and as a basis of such reorganization we demand the equality of all parties in state and administration. We always have professed that political opinion must not be a hindrance in state or administration. . . . . We must break with the attitude that, for example, a man cannot hold an Imperial office just because he is a Socialist. . . . .

79. (*d*) COUNT WESTARP'S SPEECH[17]

Gentlemen, ... I feel that at this moment the questions of our internal political future are relegated into the background by the more pressing needs of the war. Therefore, I shall not go into such a detailed discussion of them as did the speakers before me. Nevertheless my

[17] *Verhandlungen des Reichstags*, No. 95, March 29, 1917, pp. 2857–64.

friends and I doubt very much whether such a discussion at this moment serves the good of the country. [*"Very true!"—Right.*] . . . . At the head of the program of new orientation stands the question of the Prussian suffrage and the reorganization of the Prussian Landtag. But in this we are and shall remain of the opinion that that is an internal affair of Prussia [*"Quite right!"—Right; restlessness and shouts from the Left*], discussion of which here in the Reichstag is of no use and will not serve the cause. [*Renewed shouts from the Left.*]

. . . . Vigorous attacks were made today against the Herrenhaus and against individual speeches given there. . . . . I do not quarrel with the speakers' unquestionable rights to protest against those speeches. What I wish to warn them against and what does not seem right to me is the personal underrating of the gentlemen who spoke in the Herrenhaus. I beg you not to forget this one thing—that they are trustworthy men with an unstained past, with great achievements in the positions they hold, and that those gentlemen have a political worry over a policy of the Reichstag which according to their belief would lead to a democratization and, consequently, to injury to the interests of the Fatherland. . . . . We also were told today that, now that Russia too had entered the ranks of democratically governed countries, it was time for Germany also to join that group. No, gentlemen, I am of the opinion that a comparison of our country with the fate of our enemy countries has irrefutably proved the opposite. [*"Quite right!"—Right. Protest from Left and S.D.*]

Herr Stresemann expressed the thought whether or not the political and diplomatic failures with which we entered the war necessitate an attempt on our part to approximate the governmental system of our enemies, particularly the systems of England and France. I believe that Herr Stresemann thereby did not fully appreciate the great difficulties which arose for Germany owing to the fact that she entered the ranks of the world powers as a novice who first had to gain ground against enmity, jealousy, and ill will. . . . .

Gentlemen, it is wrong . . . . to accuse us Conservatives of not wishing to co-operate in the exercising by the parliament of the rights which are granted to it in the constitutional monarchy, and that we do not see in such an exercise of those rights a great value for the progress of the country. We participate in the matter of legislating in the control over the budget, and those rights we wish to maintain to the fullest extent. But what we do not wish is a struggle for the extension of those rights. We wish to maintain a strict separation between legislation and administration. We do not wish the parliamentary régime in the sense that the Emperor be obliged to select his Ministers from the Majority parties. [*Shouts from the Left.*] . . . .

80. RIDERS TO THE BUDGET OF 1917
(a) MOTION NO. 730[18]

to the second reading of the bill regarding the establishment of the budget of the Empire for the fiscal year 1917. (Drucksachen Nos. 618, 654.)

The budget for the Imperial Chancellor and the Imperial Chancery

Annex II: Ordinary budget. Current expenses

Chapter 3, Title 1

Albrecht and party members: Be it resolved that the Reichstag decide to organize a commission for the preliminary discussion of reforms which aim at the political reconstruction of the German Reich. To this commission are to be submitted the pertinent proposals and resolutions introduced into the Reichstag.

BERLIN, March 28, 1917
    Albrecht . . . . Ebert . . . . Scheidemann . . . .

80. (b) RESOLUTION NO. 735[19]

to the second reading of the bill regarding the establishment of the budget of the Empire for the fiscal year 1917. (Drucksachen Nos. 618, 654.)

The budget for the Imperial Chancellor and the Imperial Chancery

Annex II: Ordinary budget. Current expenses

Chapter 3, Title 1. (Imperial Chancellor)

Bassermann and party members: Be it resolved that the Reichstag decide to create a special commission consisting of 28 members (Constitutional Committee) for the study of constitutional questions, in particular the composition of the representative body and its relation to the government.

BERLIN, March 28, 1917
    Bassermann . . . . Stresemann . . . .

[18] *Verhandlungen des Reichstags,* No. 321, "Anlagen zu den Stenographischen Berichten," p. 1402.

[19] *Ibid.,* p. 1406; *Verhandlungen des Reichstags,* No. 314, "Sachregister," pp. 6703–4.

This resolution with the addition, "To this commission are to be submitted the pertinent proposals and resolution introduced in the Reichstag," was accepted in individual voting by 228 to 33 votes, with 5 abstaining. Motion 730 was withdrawn.

80. (c) RESOLUTION NO. 736[20]

to the second reading of the bill regarding the budget of the Empire for the fiscal year 1917. (Drucksachen Nos. 618, 654.)

The budget for the Imperial Chancellor and the Imperial Chancery

Annex II: Ordinary budget. Current expenses

Chapter 3, Title 1. (Imperial Chancellor)

Dr. Ablass and party members: Be it resolved that the Reichstag request the Imperial Chancellor to work immediately to the end that a constitution be created in all German Federal States with a representative body that is based upon universal, direct, equal, and secret suffrage.

BERLIN, March 29, 1917
Dr. Ablass . . . . v. Payer . . . .

81. RESOLUTIONS REGARDING CONSTITUTIONAL QUESTIONS[21]

Chairman: Prince of Schoenaich-Carolath has the floor for a point of order.

Prince of Schoenaich-Carolath: Mr. Chairman, I would like to say the following in regard to our resolution No. 735. We bring to it an addition from motion No. 730, so that our resolution shall read:

Be it resolved that the Reichstag decided to create a special commission consisting of 28 members (Constitutional Commission) for the study of constitutional questions, in particular the composition of the representative body and its relation to the government.

And this is the addition from No. 730:

To this commission are to be submitted the pertinent proposals and resolutions introduced in the Reichstag.

[20] *Verhandlungen des Reichstags,* No. 321, "Anlagen zu den Stenographischen Berichten," p. 1406.
[21] *Verhandlungen des Reichstags,* No. 96, March 30, 1917, pp. 2932–36.

Chairman: Deputy Scheidemann has the floor for a point of order.

Scheidemann: After the declaration by Prince of Schoenaich-Caro-lath I withdraw in the name of my "Fraktion" our resolution. . . . .

Prince of Schoenaich-Carolath: In the name of my political friends I withdraw our motion for an individual vote. . . . .

Ledebour: In the name of my political friends I wish to say that we agree with the submission of our resolution to the planned Com-mission. But I wish again to call attention to the fact that points B and G of our resolution are not to be included, since they do not deal with constitutional questions. In our opinion these two points must first come to a vote, before it is decided that our resolution and all the others are to be submitted to the Constitutional Commission.

Chairman: Do I understand you aright that you wish to see a vote taken only upon points B and G? The other points are constitutional questions. [*Is affirmed.*] . . . .

Count von Westarp: I do not think it permissible that motions be changed after the discussion is closed. . . . . But I shall not raise any objection.

Dr. Müller (Meiningen): I assume that our motion No. 736 will therefore be submitted to this commission. I should like to establish definitely whether that is the wish of the House.

Chairman: No. 736 shall be submitted to that commission. . . . .

Hirsch: Gentlemen, I signed the motion 735, but after the course of the debate I and other political friends are not in a position to vote for it. [*"Hear, hear!"*]

Prince of Schoenaich-Carolath: Things being as they are now I again bring up our motion for an individual vote. [*"Bravo!"*] I beg that you put the question of seconding.

[*Commotion. Bell of the Chairman!*]

Chairman: . . . . We shall now take the vote about the combined motion 735 and 730. Its phraseology you know. It has been proposed to vote individually. . . . .

[*Is done.*] . . . .

Gentlemen, the vote is as follows: Yes, 228; no, 33; abstained, 5; voided, 1. Total, 267.

The combined motion No. 735 and 730 is accepted.

We come now to vote upon points B and G (Drucksachen No. 690). First, point B reads: "To work for the speedy conclusion of peace upon the basis of rejecting any kind of annexations by all warring countries."

Will the gentlemen who wish to vote for it rise? . . . . That is the minority. Point B is rejected.

We now come to point G, which reads: "To take care that all punishments accrued for political crimes be immediately suspended."

Will the gentlemen who wish to vote for it rise? . . . . That is the minority. Point G is rejected.

The rest of the motion No. 690 will be submitted to the Constitutional Commission.

We now come to a vote on the motion No. 736 by Dr. Ablass, etc. Herr Dr. Müller (Meiningen) has proposed that this motion, too, be submitted to the Constitutional Committee.

Since no objections are being raised, that is done.

82. THE APPOINTMENT OF A CONSTITUTIONAL COMMITTEE[22]

By a vote of 228 to 33, with 5 abstaining, the Reichstag passed by roll call a motion, introduced by the National-Liberals, to appoint a special committee of twenty-eight members (*Verfassungsausschuss*) for the examination of constitutional questions especially in regard to the structure of the representative body of the nation and its relationship to the government. The Reichstag also passed a Social-Democratic motion to send to this committee these motions and resolutions introduced in the Reichstag.

83. THE NEXT DEMAND[23]

In an article which has been published in various party newspapers, Comrade Eduard David asked as the next demand of the reform a revision of the electoral districts. He points to the really incredible inequalities existing in the division of the electoral districts, according to which, for instance at the election of 1912, the district Teltow-Beeskow-Charlottenburg had 1,315,601 inhabitants with 339,256 qualified electors, whereas the district Schaumburg-Lippe had only 46,652 inhabitants and 10,709 electors. These two extreme cases show how far the Reichstag franchise has failed to secure a state of equality on account of the increase of population since 1869. . . . .

84. GERMAN PARLIAMENTARISM IN THE PAST AND THE FUTURE, BY PROFESSOR MAX WEBER (HEIDELBERG)[24]

. . . . III. Administrative Publicity and Political Responsibility

Officialdom has worked brilliantly in all routine tasks, i.e., tasks which were definitely delimited by experts, in which it had to show

---

[22] *Vorwärts*, No. 89, March 31, 1917.   [23] *Ibid.*, No. 84, March 26, 1917.

[24] *Frankfurter Zeitung*, June 24, 1917, I, 1–2.

its sense of responsibility, its objectivity, and its power of mastery of organization problems. It has completely failed where it has been occupied with political questions. This is no matter of chance. On the contrary, it would be surprising if aptitudes which are entirely foreign to each other should meet in one person or in the same organization. It is not the business of an official to engage in politics. It is, of course, the duty of the heads of officialdom, who prescribe the tasks of the latter, to solve political problems, and the duty of the parliament to control those powers. Not only problems assigned to the highest central authorities, but any purely technical question in the lower offices may become politically important. Politicians must provide the counterpoise to the rule of officialdom. However, the desire for power of the highest officials of a bureaucracy is opposed to such a counterpoise.

The position of authority of all officials is based . . . . upon knowledge of two kinds. First there is the technical knowledge, using the word "technical" in its widest sense, obtained in professional training. Whether such knowledge is represented in parliament, or whether deputies are in the position to gather information privately from specialists, is a matter of chance and a private affair. But never does that offer parliament that systematic cross-examination (on oath) of experts together with officials of the department concerned before a parliamentary commission, as is guaranteed by control and a comprehensive questioning. The Reichstag has no power to compel such information; constitutionally it is therefore condemned to ignorance.

But the official's position of authority is not founded on technical knowledge alone. Added to that are the concrete facts which largely determine the official's attitude, namely, the knowledge of the service itself (*Dienstwissen*), acquired by means of the departmental apparatus and which is accessible to him alone. Only one who can secure this factual knowledge independently of the good will of the official may on particular occasions effectively control the administration. . . . . Here too the Reichstag has no power to compel information on oath. Intentionally it is placed beyond the position to acquire the knowledge necessary for controlling the administration; i.e., beside ignorance, it is also condemned to unacquaintance. . . . .

The insulting manner in which administrative chiefs often reply to criticisms and attacks of members of parliament is only possible because the absence of the right of interpellation denies parliament the means of constantly securing for itself that knowledge of facts and the viewpoints of experts which alone give it a continuous co-operation with and influence upon the direction of the administration. . . . . The integrity of English officialdom and the high state of political education of the English people depend to a large extent upon that right. . . . . Seldom and

certainly not in countries where people enjoy a parliamentary training
is there such an ignorant attitude of the public in relation to officialdom
as in Germany. . . . . Publicity in administration, obtained through effective parliamentary control, is therefore the necessary prerequisite
for all fruitful parliamentary work. We too have now entered upon
that road. . . . . But an indispensable guaranty for such a further development is the right of parliament to secure, whenever needed, the
requisite technical and service information.

A sole objection, and one worthy of consideration, which political
scientists raise against such a development is the fact that the Reichstag
in the formulation of its rules of procedure is absolutely autonomous
and that therefore a temporary majority could so arrange matters that
it would be impossible to ascertain facts unpleasant to it. . . . . Certain
legal norms should be set up as guaranties of dependability. . . . . Other
guaranties too are necessary. As long as there are competing industries
in various countries, it will be necessary to protect their secrets at least
against tendencious publications, particularly military-technical secrets.
Finally, matters of foreign politics too must be protected against such
publicity. For it is of course an error of individual littérateurs, derided
at this very moment by the facts themselves, that foreign policy, which
is roughly a practical compromise between the interests of the belligerent countries, can be conducted by the public proclamation, after the
fashion of the highest bidder in the auction room, of sham "principles,"
instead of by practical negotiation. Certainly, it is with entirely different
means than the ideas of such dilettanti-littérateurs that we have to lay
the axe to the root of the mistakes of our past.

And here a word may be said about publicity in foreign affairs—for
it is exactly upon this point that the limits of the capacity of the rule of
a pure officialdom are demonstrated and, moreover, the terrible price
that we have had to pay for tolerating it is revealed.

. . . . For more than a decade, from the Kruger telegram to the
Morocco crisis, it has been our experience that the political Government
of Germany has partly tolerated, because of overzealous Court officials
or telegraph agencies, partly, however, connived at, the publication of
purely personal utterances of the Monarch upon questions of foreign
policy. Proceedings are in question which were of the very greatest consequence for the kind of orientation given to world-policy, and in particular for the formation of the world coalition against us. The Kruger
telegram, the warning against the yellow peril, the speech at Damascus,
the speech at Tangier—the list could be very much lengthened. Notice
particularly that there is no question here of the justice of the attitude
taken up by the Monarch. That is a matter of opinion. In many of these
cases at least it is quite possible that the diplomatic communication of

his energetic personal attitude (in the proper form) might have had a good political effect upon the Governments to which they were made. But the incredible thing was the open publication, for tolerating or causing which the political leaders of Germany bear the responsibility. For there is—and this seems to be forgotten among us—an absolutely enormous difference between the case when a leading politician (Prime Minister or even President of the Republic) publicly, as in parliament, makes no matter how angry a declaration and the case when he allows a personal utterance of the Monarch to be published and then "covers" this with a gesture as cheap as it is stagy. The truth is that a public statement of the Monarch is withdrawn from unsparing criticism at home and thus it covers the statesman who misuses it from unsparing criticism of his own behavior. But foreign countries do not halt there; they go straight to the Monarch. Politicians can and must go, when a situation changes and the required attitude has shifted accordingly. The Monarch must remain. With him, however, remain his words also. In vain he makes the attempt, being now personally and publicly so engaged, to withdraw them as the situation changes. The passions and the point of honor of the nation are awakened. Stupid demagogues like the Pan-Germans have an easy game; at home and abroad they hold fast permanently to the words once spoken, and the situation becomes fixed and inelastic.

This behavior of our leading politicians was irresponsible and without precedent in the policy of all great powers. A public action from this quarter was permissible only if the intention was to act seriously, and immediately. But neither in the case of the Boers, nor against the Mongols, nor against the Sultan of Morocco did we really intend to have recourse to arms, and in the two first cases we had neither invitation nor means to do so; and yet our leading politicians suffered it that through a public intervention of the person of the Monarch a practical understanding with England over the interests of both sides in South Africa and with France over those in North Africa was made impossible, because our attitude now appeared to be fixed like a point of honor and yet finally it had to be given up. The inevitable result was heavy defeats that still burn in the soul of every German, and serious and permanent harm done to our interests. But, above all, the most dangerous impression, that Germany, after using the strongest outward gesture, would take care to withdraw, because of this belief, which certainly contributed to determine the attitude of English policy in July 1914, must be traced to the same source.

This unnatural world-coalition against us was also largely brought together by the same incredible blunders. And not that alone. They are still at work in the world. The swindle which is now being played throughout the world with the talk of German "autocracy" is a swindle —but the possibility of it is politically anything rather than a matter of indifference. Who has made it possible for our enemies, who believe in it no more than they do in other fairy tales about Germany, to carry on this swindle with success? Who brought the enormous hatred of a whole world—politically by no means indifferent—upon the head of this Monarch? Who made it possible that the masses in foreign countries very often seriously believe that Germany is yearning for "liberation," and that if they held out long enough that feeling would finally make its way out to the open? Who induced the incredible madness of the present position, which makes any practical action difficult, impossible?

The rule of Conservative officialdom did this, which in decisive moments put men with the spirit of officials in places where politicians belong, that is, people who have learned in the political struggle to estimate the value of the publicly spoken word and who, above all, have the politician's sense of responsibility and not that of an official. They are two very different things.

But in all this the worst has not been said. Of nearly all those men who have had the guiding of our policy in their hands during the dangerous decade we have mentioned, it is known, and can, if necessary, be proved, that they in private (not only once, but over and over again) have disclaimed the material responsibility for the decisive publication of acts for which they accepted the formal responsibility. If one asked in astonishment why the statesman involved and for the moment deprived of the necessary powers to prevent the publication had not resigned, one usually heard: "Another would have been found." But would another have been found if the political leader had had to bear the responsibility as the responsible head of a strong parliament? Here one can sense the abyss which separates the official's sense of responsibility from that of the politician. For those in question were not incapable or uneducated—some of them are diplomats of the highest distinction—but they lack that which, in the purely political sense of the word, is called character. It was not an accident that they lacked this, but because of the structure of the state, which has no use for character.

What is one to say to this state of affairs, unprecedented in a great power throughout the world? To the state of affairs in which an equerry or a telegraph agency, or whoever it may be that takes the liberty, can publish abroad things of supreme importance for foreign policy, and thereby fix our policy bunglingly for decades while the leading politician accepts it with a shrug of the shoulders and lets it pass over his head with a few *soi-disant* noble gestures? And that in a state in which in domestic affairs, in the interests of the power of the heads of the administration, the "service secret" figures as the pearl of the official's obligations? And what are we to say to the further fact that there is no body which has the power to drive immediately out of their posts the politicians who suffer these things against their own convictions? And what, finally, to the fact that, in spite of these things which are visible to every eye there are still littérateurs to be found who represent that the state structure which has functioned thus in points that are politically decisive has "been brilliantly successful"? As we have said before, the service duties of officers and officials have been more than brilliant, where this quality is decisive. But in the politicians' province the rule of officialdom has for decades past not merely failed, but in order to cover itself it has diverted the odium of its own politically characterless and vacillating behavior to the Monarch personally, and has helped create the constellation of the world which is directed against us, which could have cost him only his Crown but Germany its whole political future. Any state structure which prevents this is better than the present incredible condition of affairs. It must cease. . . . .

CHAPTER VI

SUBMARINE WARFARE

INTRODUCTORY NOTE

THE DECLARATION of unrestricted submarine warfare, on February 4, 1915, immediately involved the Empire in a diplomatic controversy with the United States. The sinking of the "Lusitania," May 7, 1915, then brought about a crisis which threatened to involve America in a war with Germany. The Imperial decision to limit submarine warfare followed.

The Supreme Command, which had reluctantly accepted this decision, raised the issue again at the time of the attack on Verdun and later on the rejection of the German peace offer. At Pless, Ludendorff and Hindenburg forced the Imperial Government to recommence unrestricted submarine warfare, and thus sealed the fate of an Empire which held within its grasp a peace by understanding through American mediation. The Reichstag and the majority of the nation ratified this fateful decision.

Zimmermann summed up the point of view of the Supreme Command and the Foreign Office in the statement: "We are convinced that we can win." At the very moment when President Wilson was working for a peace without victory, a settlement which would have maintained the integrity of the German Empire, the politico-military directorate adopted a policy which added America to the list of Germany's enemies. On January 26 President Wilson presented his peace plan to the Senate and offered to act as mediator for a peace by understanding. On January 29 Chancellor von Bethmann-Hollweg telegraphed the German terms of peace to Bernstorff with instructions to deliver them to President Wilson. Then on January 31 Bernstorff presented the declaration of unrestricted submarine warfare, and the peace-without-victory plan collapsed. President Wilson immediately broke off diplomatic relations with Germany and declared, "This means war."

The news of President Wilson's decision reached Berlin late on

February 3, when the National-Liberal Party under Stresemann's leadership was approving the new submarine policy and denouncing the *Flaumacher* who had warned against it. An analysis of the German press reveals the general determination to carry out the unrestricted submarine warfare and to place the responsibility for war upon Wilson.

85. DR. DERNBURG'S ESTIMATE OF SUBMARINE WARFARE[1]
MARCH 28, 1916

Dernburg spoke at first in a more or less conventional way about the general political situation. . . . . I then changed the conversation to Tirpitz's retirement and the U-boat war. Dernburg answered in a half-hour exposition during which I had hardly a chance to make a remark. The exposition, in the course of which Dernburg cited from memory all kinds of figures, calculations, and particulars which I found difficulty in following and retaining, gave me the impression that he related to me an already prepared statement about the U-boat warfare. From insinuations during the conversation that followed I found out that he actually had prepared a memorandum, presumably for the Chancellor. I noticed that he was very well informed about this question, and that he knew many things which must not come into the open and that he could not tell even privately. Well, the fact is, that this extremely coherent exposition was indeed prepared for the Chancellor. . . . .

Dernburg began by stating that he could not tell me the exact number of U-boats at Germany's disposal but could give me some figures which show that the U-boat war could not bring about a result which would mean England's starvation. He said that 4,800 ships enter and leave English ports each month, i.e., 160 ships per day. We should have to sink every single one of these ships, and to do that would require a tremendous U-boat fleet. From the known figure of U-boats sunk Dernburg drew the conclusion that we did not have such a great U-boat fleet at our disposal. Dernburg continued that England possesses 20,000 ships. What effect then shall we produce by sinking a few hundred, or several thousand, ships! . . . .

England's dependence for her food supply upon foreign countries, he said, was greatly exaggerated. Her production is not as negligible as we imagined. That was true in respect to grain as well as cattle. Dernburg then cited figures of the English grain crop and the amount of cattle, and came to the conclusion that English per capita production

[1] Kanner Papers, III, 99–113.

amounts to 75 per cent of the per capita production of Germany, i.e., English dependence upon imports in this respect was only 25 per cent greater than that of Germany.

The size of the English fleet, totaling 12,000,000 tons, must be considered also, he said. That makes about 100 kg. per head a year. And if we assume that under the stress of the U-boat war the English will limit themselves to the same rations as we—which they will certainly do —then they will need about 4,000,000 tons of bread a year for the people. Since they themselves produce at least one-fourth of that amount, an importation of 3,000,000 tons a year will suffice for England. Therefore, to bring in that amount only one-fourth of the English merchant marine needs to make one voyage a year. And that we cannot prevent.

In order to cut off English imports from abroad entirely, we would have to blockade not only all English ports but also Spanish and Portuguese ones and those on the French west coast. . . . .

Dernburg cited a number of other figures, made involved calculations, etc., the gist of the whole exposition being that the U-boat war was a failure in so far as it would not and could not produce the results expected of it in Germany. . . . .

86. THE SUSSEX PLEDGE, MAY 4, 1916[2]

AMBASSADOR GERARD TO THE SECRETARY OF STATE

(Telegram)

No. 3848   AMERICAN EMBASSY, BERLIN, May 4, 1916

Following is the text of the note handed to me both in German and English at 5:30 this afternoon by Secretary of State for Foreign Affairs:

"FOREIGN OFFICE, BERLIN, May 4, 1916

"The undersigned, on behalf of the Imperial Government, has the honor to present to His Excellency the Ambassador of the United States, Mr. James W. Gerard, the following reply to the note of April 20 regarding the conduct of German submarine warfare:

"The German Government has handed over to the proper naval authorities for further investigation the evidence concerning the 'Sussex,' as communicated by the Government of the United States. Judging by results that this investigation has hitherto yielded, the German

---

[2] United States, Department of State, *Diplomatic Correspondence with Belligerent Governments Relating to Neutral Rights and Duties, European War, No. 3,* pp. 302–6. Hereafter cited as U.S., *European War.*

Government is alive to the possibility that the ship mentioned in the note of April 10 as torpedoed by a German submarine is actually identical with the 'Sussex.' The German Government begs to reserve further communications on the matter until certain points are ascertained which are of decisive importance for establishing the facts of the case. Should it turn out that the commander was wrong in assuming the vessel to be a man-of-war the German Government will not fail to draw the consequences resulting therefrom.

"In connection with the case of the 'Sussex,' the Government of the United States has made a series of statements, gist of which is the assertion that this incident is to be considered as one instance for the deliberate method of indiscriminate destruction of vessels of all sorts, nationalities, and destinations by German submarine commanders. The German Government must emphatically repudiate this assertion. The German Government, however, thinks it of little avail to enter into details in the present stage of affairs, more particularly as the Government of the United States has omitted to substantiate this assertion by reference to concrete facts. The German Government will only state that it has imposed far-reaching restraints upon the use of the submarine weapon solely in consideration of the interests of neutrals, in spite of the fact that these restrictions are necessarily of advantage to Germany's enemies; no such consideration has ever been shown to the neutrals by Great Britain and her Allies.

"The German submarine forces have had, in fact, orders to conduct submarine warfare in accordance with the general principles of visit and search and destruction of merchant vessels as recognized by international law, the sole exception being the conduct of warfare against the enemy trade carried on enemy freight ships that are encountered in the war zone surrounding Great Britain; with regard to these no assurances have ever been given to the Government of the United States; no such assurance was contained in the declaration of February 8, 1916. The German Government cannot admit any doubt that these orders have been given and are executed in good faith. Errors have actually occurred; they can in no kind of warfare be avoided altogether, and allowances must be made in the conduct of naval warfare against an enemy resorting to all kinds of ruses, whether permissible or illicit. But, apart from the possibility of errors, naval warfare, just like warfare on land, implies unavoidable dangers for neutral persons and goods entering the fighting zone. Even in cases where naval action was confined to their ordinary forms of cruiser warfare, neutral persons and goods have repeatedly come to grief. The German Government has repeatedly and explicitly pointed out the dangers from mines that have led to the loss of numerous ships. The German Government has made several proposals to the Government of the United States in order to reduce to a minimum for American travelers and goods, the inherent dangers of naval warfare. Unfortunately the Government of the United States has decided not to accept these proposals; had it accepted, the Government of the United States would have been instrumental in preventing the greater part of the accidents that American citizens have met with in the meantime. The German Government still stands by its offer to come to an agreement along these lines.

"As the German Government has repeatedly declared, it cannot dispense with the use of the submarine weapon in the conduct of warfare against enemy trade. The German Government, however, has now decided to make a further concession in adapting the methods of submarine warfare to the interest of the neutrals; in reaching this decision the German Government has been actuated by considerations which are above the level of the disputed question.

"The German Government attaches no less importance to the sacred principles of humanity than the Government of the United States. Again, it fully takes into account that both Governments have for many years co-operated in developing international law in conformity with these principles, the ultimate object of which has been always to confine warfare on sea and on land to the armed forces of the belligerents and to safeguard, as far as possible, noncombatants against the horrors of war.

"But, although those considerations are of great weight, they alone would not, under the present circumstances, have determined the attitude of the German Government.

"For, in answer to the appeal made by the United States Government on behalf of the sacred principles of humanity and international law, the German Government must repeat once more with all emphasis that it was not the German but the British Government which, ignoring all accepted rules of international law, has extended this terrible war to the lives and property of noncombatants, having no regard whatever for the interests and rights of the neutrals and noncombatants that through this method of warfare have been severely injured.

"In self-defense against the illegal conduct of British warfare, while fighting a bitter struggle for her national existence, Germany had to resort to the hard but effective weapon of submarine warfare. As matters stand, the German Government cannot but reiterate its regret that the sentiments of humanity which the Government of the United States extends with such fervor to the unhappy victims of submarine warfare are not extended with the same warmth of feeling to the many millions of women and children who, according to the avowed intentions of the British Government, shall be starved and who, by their sufferings, shall force the victorious armies of the Central Powers into ignominious capitulation. The German Government, in agreement with the German people, fails to understand this discrimination, all the more as it has repeatedly and explicitly declared itself ready to use the submarine weapon in strict conformity with the rules of international law as recognized before the outbreak of war, if Great Britain were likewise ready to adapt her conduct of warfare to these rules. The several attempts made by the Government of the United States to prevail upon the British Government to act accordingly have failed because of the flat refusal on the part of the British Government. Moreover, Great Britain has ever since again and again violated international law, surpassing all bounds in outraging neutral rights. The latest measure adopted by Great Britain, declaring German bunker coal as contraband and establishing conditions under which alone English bunker coal shall be supplied to neutrals, is nothing but an unheard-of attempt, by way of exaction, to force neutral tonnage into the service of the British trade war.

"The German people knows that the Government of the United States has the power to confine this war to the armed forces of the belligerent countries in the interest of humanity and the maintenance of international law. The Government of the United States would have been certain of attaining this end had it been determined to insist against Great Britain on its incontestable rights to the freedom of the seas. But, as matters stand, the German people are under the impression that the Government of the United States, while demanding that Germany, struggling for her existence, shall restrain the use of an effective weapon, and while making the compliance with these demands a condition for the maintenance of relations with Germany, confines itself to protests against the illegal methods adopted by Germany's enemies. Moreover, the German people know to what a considerable extent its enemies are supplied with all kinds of war material from the United States.

"It will therefore be understood that the appeal made by the Government of the United States to the sentiments of humanity and to the principles of international law cannot, under the circumstances, meet with the same hearty response from the German people which such an appeal is otherwise always certain to find here. If the German Government, nevertheless, has resolved to go to the utmost limit of concessions, it has not alone been guided by the friendship connecting the two great nations for over a hundred years, but it also has thought of the great doom which threatens the entire civilized world should this cruel and sanguinary war be extended and prolonged.

"The German Government, conscious of Germany's strength, has twice within the last few months announced before the world its readiness to make peace on a basis safeguarding Germany's vital interests, thus indicating that it is not Germany's fault if peace is still withheld from the nations of Europe.

"The German Government feels all the more justified to declare that the responsibility could not be borne before the forum of mankind and history if, after twenty-one months' duration of the war, the submarine question under discussion between the German Government and the Government of the United States were to take a turn seriously threatening the maintenance of peace between the two nations.

"As far as it lies with the German Government, it wishes to prevent things from taking such a course. The German Government, moreover, is prepared to do its utmost to confine the operations of war for the rest of its duration to the fighting forces of the belligerents, thereby also insuring the freedom of the seas, as principle upon which the German Government believes, now as before, to be in agreement with the Government of the United States.

"The German Government, guided by this idea, notifies the Government of the United States that the German naval forces have received the following orders: in accordance with the general principles of visit and search and destruction of merchant vessels recognized by international law, such vessels, both within and without the area declared as naval war zone, shall not be sunk without warning and without saving human lives, unless these ships attempt to escape or offer resistance.

"But neutrals cannot expect that Germany, forced to fight for her existence, shall for the sake of neutral interest restrict the use of an effective weapon if her enemy is permitted to continue to apply at will methods of warfare violating the rules of international law. Such a demand would be incompatible with the character of neutrality, and the German Government is convinced that the Government of the United States does not think of making such a demand, knowing that the Government of the United States has repeatedly declared that it is determined to restore the principle of the freedom of the seas, from whatever quarter it is violated.

"Accordingly, the German Government is confident that, in consequence of the new orders issued to its naval forces, the Government of the United States will now also consider all impediments removed which may have been in the way of a mutual co-operation toward the restoration of the freedom of the seas during the war as suggested in the note of July 23, 1915, and it does not doubt that the Government of the United States will now demand and insist that the British Government shall forthwith observe the rules of international law universally recognized before the war as they are laid down in the notes presented by the Government of the United States to the British Government on December 28, 1914, and November 5, 1915. Should the steps taken by the Government of the United States not attain the object it desires to have the laws of humanity followed by all belligerent nations, the German Government would then be facing a new situation, in which it must reserve itself complete liberty of decision.

"The undersigned avails himself of this occasion to renew to the American Ambassador the assurances of his highest consideration.

"VON JAGOW"

Foreign Office informs me note will be given out here to the German newspapers and American correspondents late tomorrow afternoon.

GERARD

87. MEMORANDUM BY DR. KANNER OF A CONVERSATION WITH PROFESSOR JAECKH, SEPTEMBER 14, 1916[3]

. . . . Thus the conversation turned to the U-boat theme. I gave Jaeckh to understand that I was informed about its chief problems, namely, the insufficient number of U-boats. Without mentioning any figures, he said that we have too few U-boats to cut off England. Then, too, one has to consider their limited technical capability, for only one-third of the U-boats we have can be active at any one time. But even if that were not the case, it would be impossible to bring England to her knees, as the common expression goes. . . . . I said that absolutely false ideas as to the number of U-boats prevail among the general public, and even among the educated people. Jaeckh confirmed that, and expressed himself in very sharp language against the followers of Tirpitz. I replied that Tirpitz himself is responsible for the spread of such rumors and that he is exploiting a patriotic lie, which it is impossible for Bethmann-Hollweg to repudiate. Jaeckh assented to that and said that Tirpitz is a great liar in general. It is characteristic of Tirpitz that even in his official reports he has always given false figures about the number of U-boats available. Only after Capelle came in was the actual number of U-boats known, a number much lower than that given by Tirpitz. I expressed my surprise to Jaeckh about this, and asked him if Tirpitz had given false figures to the Kaiser also, and whether or not the latter had found out about it. Jaeckh's reply was that the Kaiser has known for a long time that Tirpitz is a liar. "I myself," he added, "know about a case which happened a year before the war when Tirpitz told another lie to the Kaiser and the latter said that it was almost im-

[3] Kanner Papers, III, 297–306.

possible to believe that Tirpitz could refrain from lying. Kiderlen-Wächter, too, had complained about Tirpitz's mendacity. . . . ."

Jaeckh, who during the conversation always identified himself with the Foreign Office, said that Tirpitz always caused "us" trouble. Through even his first announcement of the U-boat war he had caused the Foreign Office a great embarrassment. There suddenly appeared an interview in which he announced the U-boat war without having conferred about it with anyone else. The Foreign Office was simply stunned. Even the Admiral's Staff did not know about it. Then, too, the announcement was a great mistake, above all, because it promised too much and thus created expectations which could never be achieved by the U-boat warfare.

. . . . Thereupon, I remarked that the sentiment for the unrestricted submarine warfare seemed to me so strong that it might be undertaken in spite of the reasons which speak against its adoption. Jaeckh did not think it improbable. I said that formerly I had heard that the unrestricted U-boat warfare was to begin this fall, but now I hear that it is not to start until next spring, because of the belief that at that time England will have to bring out its grain; Jaeckh said that of course there would be a delay, but largely on account of the presidential campaign in the United States. For the President is an entirely different man after the election than before it; after the election he is freer. Were we now to announce the unrestricted U-boat warfare, war with the United States would be highly probable. Under the new President it may not come to that.

88. ZIMMERMANN'S INSTRUCTIONS TO VON ECKHARDT SENT THROUGH VON BERNSTORFF, JANUARY 19, 1917[4]

BERLIN, January 19, 1917

On the 1st of February we intend to begin submarine warfare unrestricted. In spite of this, it is our intention to endeavor to keep neutral the United States of America.

If this attempt is not successful, we propose an alliance with Mexico on the following basis: That we shall make war together and together make peace. We shall give general financial support, and it is understood that Mexico is to reconquer the lost territory in New Mexico, Texas and Arizona. The details are left to you for settlement.

You are instructed to inform the President of Mexico of the above in the greatest confidence as soon as it is certain that there will be an

---

[4] *Congressional Record,* March 1, 1917, p. 4596.

outbreak of the war with the United States, and suggest that the President of Mexico, on his own initiative, should communicate with Japan suggesting adherence at once to this plan; at the same time, offer to mediate between Germany and Japan.

Please call to the attention of the President of Mexico the fact that the employment of ruthless submarine warfare now promises to compel England to make peace in a few months.

ZIMMERMANN

89. BERNSTORFF TO LANSING, JANUARY 31, 1917[5]

GERMAN EMBASSY, WASHINGTON, January 31, 1917

MR. SECRETARY OF STATE:

Your Excellency were [was] good enough to transmit to the Imperial Government a copy of the message which the President of the United States of America addressed to the Senate on the 22nd instant. The Imperial Government has given it the earnest consideration which the President's statements deserve, inspired as they are by a deep sentiment of responsibility. It is highly gratifying to the Imperial Government to ascertain that the main tendencies of this important statement correspond largely to the desires and principles professed by Germany. These principles especially include self-government and equality of rights for all nations. Germany would be sincerely glad if, in recognition of this principle, countries like Ireland and India, which do not enjoy the benefits of political independence, should now obtain their freedom. The German people also repudiate all alliances which serve to force the countries into a competition for might and to involve them in a net of selfish intrigues. On the other hand, Germany will gladly co-operate in all efforts to prevent future wars. The freedom of the seas, being a preliminary condition of the free existence of nations and the peaceful intercourse between them, as well as the open door for the commerce of all nations, has always formed part of the leading principles of Germany's political program. All the more the Imperial Government regrets that the attitude of her enemies who are so entirely opposed to peace makes it impossible for the world at present to bring about the realization of these lofty ideals. Germany and her allies were ready to enter now into discussion of peace and had set down as basis the guaranty of existence, honor, and free development of their peoples. Their aims, as has been expressly stated in the note of

---

[5] U.S., *European War,* No. 4, pp. 403–7.

December 12, 1916, were not directed toward the destruction or annihilation of their enemies, and were, according to their conviction, perfectly compatible with the rights of the other nations. As to Belgium for which such warm and cordial sympathy is felt in the United States, the Chancellor had declared only a few weeks previously that its annexation had never formed a part of Germany's intentions. The peace to be signed with Belgium was to provide for such conditions in that country, with which Germany desires to maintain friendly neighborly relations, that Belgium should not be used again by Germany's enemies for the purpose of instigating continuous hostile intrigues. Such precautionary measures are all the more necessary as Germany's enemies have repeatedly stated not only in speeches delivered by their leading men but also in the statutes of the economical conference in Paris that it is their intention not to treat Germany as an equal, even after peace has been restored, but to continue their hostile attitude and especially to wage a systematical economic war against her.

The attempt of the four Allied Powers to bring about peace has failed owing to the lust of conquest of their enemies, who desired to dictate the conditions of peace. Under the pretense of following the principle of nationality our enemies have disclosed their real aims in this war, viz., to dismember and dishonor Germany, Austria-Hungary, Turkey, and Bulgaria. To the wish of reconciliation they oppose the will of destruction. They desire a fight to the bitter end.

A new situation has thus been created which forces Germany to new decisions. Since two years and a half, England is using her naval power for a criminal attempt to force Germany into submission by starvation. In brutal contempt of international law the group of Powers led by England does not only curtail the legitimate trade of their opponents but they also, by ruthless pressure, compel neutral countries either to forego altogether every trade not agreeable to the Entente-Powers or to limit it according to their arbitrary decrees. The American Government knows the steps which have been taken to cause England and her Allies to return to the rules of international law and to respect the freedom of the seas. The English Government, however, insists upon continuing its war of starvation, which does not at all affect the military power of its opponent, but compels women and children, the sick and the aged to suffer for their country pains and privations which endanger the vitality of the nation. Thus British tyranny mercilessly increases the sufferings of the world indifferent to the laws of humanity, indifferent to the protests of the neutrals whom they severely harm, indifferent even to the silent longing for peace among England's own Allies. Each day of the terrible struggle causes new destruction, new sufferings. Each day shortening the war will, on both sides, preserve the life of thousands of brave soldiers and be a benefit to mankind.

The Imperial Government could not justify before its own conscience, before the German people and before history, the neglect of any means destined to bring about the end of the war. Like the President of the United States, the Imperial Government had hoped to reach this goal by negotiations. After the attempts to come to an understanding with the Entente-Powers have been answered by the latter with the announcement of an intensified continuance of the war, the Imperial Government—in order to serve the welfare of mankind in a higher sense and not to wrong its own people—is now compelled to continue the fight for existence, again forced upon it, with the full employment of all the weapons which are at its disposal.

Sincerely trusting that the people and Government of the United States will understand the motives for this decision and its necessity, the Imperial Government hopes that the United States may view the new situation from the lofty heights of impartiality and assist, on their part, to prevent further misery and avoidable sacrifice of human life.

Enclosing two memoranda regarding the details of the contemplated military measures at sea, I remain, etc.,

(*Signed*) J. BERNSTORFF

(Inclosure 1)

MEMORANDUM

After bluntly refusing Germany's peace offer, the Entente-Powers stated in their note addressed to the American Government that they are determined to continue the war in order to deprive Germany of German provinces in the West and the East, to destroy Austria-Hungary, and to annihilate Turkey. In waging war with such aims, the Entente-Allies are violating all rules of international law, as they prevent the legitimate trade of neutrals with the Central Powers, and of the neutrals among themselves. Germany has, so far, not made unrestricted use of the weapon which she possesses in her submarines. Since the Entente-Powers, however, have made it impossible to come to an understanding based upon equality of rights of all nations, as proposed by the Central Powers, and have instead declared only such a peace to be possible which shall be dictated by the Entente-Allies and shall result in the destruction and humiliation of the Central Powers, Germany is unable further to forego the full use of her submarines. The Imperial Government, therefore, does not doubt that the Government of the United States will understand the situation thus forced upon Germany by the Entente-Allies' brutal methods of war and by their determination to destroy the Central Powers, and that the Government of the United States will further realize that the now openly disclosed intentions of the Entente-Allies give back to Germany the freedom of the action which she reserved in her note addressed to the Government of the United States on May 4, 1916.

Under these circumstances Germany will meet the illegal measures of her enemies by forcibly preventing after February 1, 1917, in a zone around Great Britain, France, Italy, and in the Eastern Mediterranean all navigation, that of neutrals included, from and to England and from and to France, etc., etc. All ships met within that zone will be sunk.

The Imperial Government is confident that this measure will result in a speedy termination of the war and in the restoration of peace which the Government of the United States has so much at heart. Like the Government of the United States, Germany and her allies had hoped to reach this goal by negotiations. Now that the war, through the fault of Germany's enemies, has to be continued, the Imperial Government feels sure that the Government of the United States will understand the necessity of adopting such measures as are destined to bring about a speedy end of the horrible and useless bloodshed. The Imperial Government hopes all the more for such an understanding of her position, as the neutrals have, under the pressure of the Entente Powers, suffered great losses, being forced by them either to give up their entire trade or to limit it according to conditions arbitrarily determined by Germany's enemies in violation of international law.

(Inclosure 2)

MEMORANDUM

From February 1, 1917, all sea traffic will be stopped with every available weapon and without further notice in the following blockade zones around Great Britain, France, Italy, and in the Eastern Mediterranean.

In the North: The zone is confined by a line at a distance of 20 sea miles along the Dutch Coast to Terschelling fire ship, the degree of longitude from Terschelling fire ship to Udsire, a line from there across the point 62 degrees North 0 degrees longitude to 62 degrees North 5 degrees West, further to a point 3 sea miles South of the Southern point of the Faroe Islands, from there across point 62 degrees North 10 degrees West to 61 degrees North 15 degrees West, then 57 degrees North 20 degrees West to 47 degrees North 20 degrees West, further to 43 degrees North, 15 degrees West, then along the degree of latitude 43 degrees North to 20 sea miles from Cape Finisterre and at a distance of 20 sea miles along the North coast of Spain to the French boundary.

In the South: The Mediterranean.

For neutral ships remains open: The sea West of the line Pt. del'Espiquette to 38 degrees 20 minutes North and 6 degrees East, also North and West of a zone 61 sea miles wide along the North African coast, beginning at 2 degrees longitude West. For the connection of this sea zone with Greece there is provided a zone of a width of 20 sea miles North and East of the following line: 38 degrees North and 6 degrees East to 38 degrees North and 10 degrees East to 37 degrees North and 11 degrees 30 minutes East to 34 degrees North and 11 degrees 30 minutes East to 34 degrees North and 22 degrees 30 minutes East.

From there leads a zone 20 sea miles wide West of 22 degrees 30 minutes Eastern longitude into Greek territorial waters.

Neutral ships navigating these blockade zones do so at their own risk. Although care has been taken that neutral ships which are on their way toward ports of the blockade zones on February 1, 1917, and have come in the vicinity of the latter, will be spared during a sufficiently long period it is strongly advised to warn them with all available means in order to cause their return.

Neutral ships which on February 1 are in ports of the blockaded zones can, with the same safety, leave them if they sail before February 5, 1917, and take the shortest route into safe waters.

The instructions given to the commanders of German submarines provide for a sufficiently long period during which the safety of passengers on unarmed enemy passenger ships is guaranteed.

Americans, en route to the blockade zone on enemy freight steamers, are not endangered, as the enemy shipping firms can prevent such ships in time from entering the zone.

Sailing of regular American passenger steamers may continue undisturbed after February 1, 1917, if

a) the port of destination is Falmouth;

b) sailing to or coming from that port course is taken via the Scilly Islands and a point 50 degrees North 20 degrees West;

c) the steamers are marked in the following way, which must not be allowed to other vessels in American ports: On ship's hull and superstructure 3 vertical stripes 1 meter wide each, to be painted alternately white and red. Each mast should show a large flag checkered white and red, and the stern the American national flag.

Care should be taken that, during dark, national flag and painted marks are easily recognizable from a distance and that the boats are well lighted throughout;

d) one steamer a week sails in each direction with arrival at Falmouth on Sunday and departure from Falmouth on Wednesday;

e) the United States Government guarantees that no contraband (according to German contraband list) is carried by those steamers.

90. SPEECH OF THE IMPERIAL CHANCELLOR TO THE MAIN COMMITTEE OF THE REICHSTAG, JANUARY 31, 1917[6]

On December 12 last year I explained before the Reichstag the reasons which led to our peace offer. The reply of our opponents stated clearly and precisely that they decline peace negotiations with us and that they want to hear only of a peace which they dictate. This decides the whole question of the guilt for the continuation of the war. The guilt falls on our opponents alone. Just as certain stands our task. The enemy's conditions we cannot discuss. They could be accepted only by an utterly defeated people. It therefore means fight.

President Wilson's message to Congress shows his sincere wish to restore peace to the world. Many of his maxims agree with our aims— namely, the freedom of the seas, the abolition of the system of balanced power (which is always bound to lead to new complications), equal rights to all nations, and the open door. But what are the peace conditions of the Entente? Germany's defensive force is to be destroyed; we are to lose Alsace-Lorraine and our Ost-Marken; the Danube Monarchy is to be dissolved; Bulgaria is again to be cheated of her national unity; and Turkey is to be pushed out of Europe and obliterated in Asia. The destructive designs of our opponents cannot be expressed more strongly.

We have been challenged to fight to the end. We accept the challenge. We stake everything, and we shall be victorious.

By this development of the situation the decision concerning submarine warfare has been forced into its last acute stage. The question of the U-boat war, as the gentlemen of the Reichstag will remember, has occupied us three times in this Committee—namely, in March, May, and September last year. On each occasion I expounded exhaustively the pros and cons of the question. I emphasized on each occasion that I was speaking pro tempore, and not as a supporter in principle, nor as an opponent in principle, of the unrestricted employment of U-boats, but in consideration of the military, political, and economic situation as a whole, always proceeding from an inquiry into the question whether an unrestricted U-boat war will bring us nearer to a victorious peace

[6] *Norddeutsche Allgemeine Zeitung,* February 1, 1917, I, 1.

or not. "Every means," I said in March, "that is calculated to shorten the war is the most humane." "Even the most ruthless means, that leads us to victory, and to a speedy victory," I then said, "must be employed." . . . .

I also said: "As soon as I, in agreement with the Supreme Army Command, reached the conviction that ruthless U-boat war would bring us nearer to a victorious peace, then the U-boat war would be made."

This moment has now arrived.

Last autumn the time was not yet ripe, but today the moment has come when with the greatest prospect of success we can dare this enterprise. But we dare not wait for a moment.

Where has there been a change?

First, the most important fact: The number of our submarines has very considerably increased as compared with last spring, and thereby a firm basis has been created for success.

The second co-decisive reason: The bad wheat harvest of the world. This already confronts England, France, and Italy with serious difficulties. We firmly hope to increase these difficulties, by means of an unrestricted U-boat war, to the point of unbearableness.

The coal question, too, is a vital question in war. Already it is critical, as you know, in Italy and France. Our submarines will render it still more critical.

To this must be added, especially as regards England, the supply of ore for the manufacture of munitions in the widest sense and of timber for coal mines.

Our enemy's difficulties in this matter are rendered still more acute by the increased lack of enemy cargo space. In this respect time and the U-boat cruiser warfare have prepared the ground for a decisive blow. The Entente suffers in all its members from lack of cargo space. It makes itself felt in Italy and France not less than in England.

If we may now venture to estimate the positive advantages of an unrestricted U-boat war very much higher than last spring, the dangers which arise for us from the U-boat war have correspondingly decreased since that time. . . . .

A few days ago Marshal von Hindenburg described to me the situation as follows: Our front stands firm on all sides. We have everywhere the requisite reserves. The spirit of the troops is good and confident. The military situation as a whole permits us to accept all consequences which an unrestricted U-boat war may bring about, and, as this U-boat war, everything considered, is the means by which to injure our enemies most grievously, it must be begun.

The Admiralty Staff and the High Seas Fleet entertain the firm conviction, a conviction which has its practical support in the experiences of the U-boat cruiser warfare, that Great Britain will be brought to peace by arms.

Our allies agree with our views. Austria-Hungary adheres to our procedure in practice also. Just as we lay a barred zone around Great Britain and the west coast of France, within which we shall try to prevent all shipping traffic to enemy countries, Austria-Hungary declares a barred zone around Italy.

To all neutral countries a free path for mutual intercourse is left outside the barred zone.

To America we offer, as we did in 1915, safe passenger traffic under definite conditions, even with certain English ports.

No one among us will close his eyes to the seriousness of the step which we are taking. That our existence is at stake everyone has known since August 4, 1914, and this knowledge has been bloodily emphasized by the rejection of our peace offer. When in 1914 we had to seize the sword against the Russian general mobilization, we did so with the sense of deepest responsibility toward our people and conscious of the resolute strength which says, "We must, and therefore we can." Endless streams of blood have since been shed, but they have not washed away the "must" and the "can."

In now deciding to employ the best and sharpest weapon we are guided solely by a sober consideration of all the circumstances that enter into the question and by a firm determination to help our people out of the distress and disgrace which our enemies contemplate for them. Success lies in a Higher Power, but as regards all that human strength can do to enforce success for the Fatherland you may be assured, gentlemen, that nothing has been neglected. Everything in this respect will be done.

91. SPEECH OF COUNT HERTLING IN THE FINANCE COMMITTEE OF THE BAVARIAN LANDTAG, FEBRUARY 1, 1917[7]

In the Bundesrat Foreign Relations Committee questions were discussed with absolute freedom, and its recommendations were followed to a considerable extent. . . . . At all events, the Committee had been heard before the German peace proposal was announced—a proposal to which it gave its vigorous support. There have never been any illusions in Berlin as to the difficulty of the war, and it is quite impossible to speak of any weakness in the attitude toward England. There is no foundation for the talk of a separate peace with Russia, and the people

[7] *Münchener Neueste Nachrichten*, February 2, 1917.

must not be deceived by the rumors of a strong peace movement in France. As for the unrestricted U-boat warfare, the people are wrong to expect that America's attitude will be one of indifference, but the time for weighing pros and cons is over now. There is only one possibility of a speedy and successful end of the war, and that is the ruthless prosecution of the U-boat campaign, which the Chancellor today supports just as strongly as the High Military Command.

War aims depend on the military situation; therefore it is not advisable to say much about them now. Naturally, there must be guaranties for the security and development of the Empire, but he too rejects an outspoken policy of annexation. His confidence in the successful issue of the war is firm as a rock.

92. OFFICIAL REVIEW OF THE GERMAN PRESS ON THE SEVERANCE OF DIPLOMATIC RELATIONS WITH AMERICA[8]

EXCLUSIVELY FOR DEPARTMENTAL USE

Headquarters for Foreign Service Newspaper Control
German and Austrian Press

1. Foreign Policy

AMERICA

Severance of Diplomatic Relations

Wilson attempts once more to restrain our arms by employing the strongest means of peaceful pressure at his disposal, announcing at the same time resort to war in case the first means should fail. We regret the incident, since in all probability it will compel us to oppose American sea intercourse in the forbidden zone and thereby the war will be made more terrible.

But Mr. Wilson and his advisers should not think that their steps have made us waver even for a moment, that they could paralyze even for a second our decision to make full use of the weapon which we have recognized as necessary in order to bring about victory and peace. Let not America fool herself about the fact that Mr. Wilson's step also makes our hands free. (*Kölnische Zeitung,* February 5 and 6.) If Wilson knows the character of the German people, he must also know that in such a struggle their strength will increase tenfold. A few weeks

---

[8] Collection of German Documents, Hoover War Library.

ago Wilson declared that he wished a peace without victory, that he did not wish the destruction of the German people. Therefore, not until we have a disavowal by overt acts of all statements of his previous messages shall we believe that he will join in a struggle whose avowed aim is our destruction. (*Tag*, February 5.) There is no necessity to become faint-hearted on account of America's decision. Practically it will alter the situation very little. The unfriendly attitude of America cannot impair the firm will of our people to save our Fatherland from the distress and insult which our enemies have intended for it. On the contrary, the more evident it becomes where Germany's secret enemies are entrenched, the better it will be for us and our weapons. (*Bayrische Staatszeitung*, February 5.) Of course, America's entrance into the war would temporarily mean a great moral as well as material help to our enemies and, contrary to Wilson's proclamation, it would thus prolong the war. However, American participation will not be decisively important. Far be it from us to be "hostile-minded" toward the Americans. We only demand that they respect our blockade. If Wilson does not wish a hostile conflict, as he says in his messages, he has the power to prevent it. (*Neue Preussische Zeitung*, February 5.) To the United States, which has always moved very close to the threshold of war, this condition of veiled enmity and apparent neutrality was agreeable and profitable. To us, such a condition would, in time, have become highly dangerous, even suicidal; therefore, our unreserved decision has cut the knot at the last moment. (Hoetzsch in the *Neue Preussische Zeitung*, February 7.) Anyone who observed Wilson during the war with uncolored glasses will not be surprised by his action now. Since his re-election he has the power in his hand which, as presidential candidate last year, he did not have. (H. R. in *Tägliche Rundschau*, February 5, 6, and 7.) All in all, the severance of diplomatic relations on the part of the United States does not come as a surprise to Germany and the German people. It does not destroy any hopes, nor does it invalidate any calculation. On the contrary, it creates clarity and places the firmness and the irrevocability of the German decision in a light which we Germans greet with a solemn, but by no means reduced, satisfaction. Enough Notes have been exchanged. (C. R., *Deutsche Tages-Zeitung*, February 5.) Germany's position has not been endangered and become weaker on account of the disappearance of the former "moral pressure"; on the contrary, in view of the conditions and events of the last two years it has become incomparably stronger. (C. R., *Deutsche Tages-Zeitung*, February 7.) It will now come to a showdown as to whether America will pursue an American or an English policy. With complete calmness we await the events that will come. Should it come to war, then America's losses will undoubtedly not be less than those it inflicts on us. If this realization is not yet completely choked in America by her jingoists then it may possibly serve to induce a compromise which Germany has proposed for some time: We restrict the U-boat warfare to cruisers, and America guarantees us the importation of food products. This should be distinctly in the interest of America. We are the last ones to take lightly America's entrance into the war. America has great reserves of supplies and man power, and it is well for us not to belittle this fact. Berlin has naturally debated all this, and there is now no return. In this the entire German nation agrees. (*Rheinisch-Westfälische Zeitung,* February 5.) .... To anyone as convinced as we and the leading men in Germany are as to the decisive effectiveness of the unrestricted U-boat war the threats of increased loans and shipments of ammunition are mere words. The deciding factor in all these questions rests with the U-boat war on merchant ships. It alone matters, and upon that assumption it is being waged. (*Hamburger Nachrichten,* February 5 and 7.) .... America draws conclusions from its former attitude and retains the position it has occupied for a long time. Germany accepts this step with a compassionate shrug of the shoulders. It really takes it without regret as something self-evident. (*Dresdener Anzeiger,* February 5.) .... And as for us, we can be satisfied if the future, too, will reveal to us the true picture of Wilson, one which we have suspected and have seen for some time. However, to our conviction that Wilson's idea of a perpetual peace was an unfulfilled dream, has been added another, namely, that Wilson would be the last to guarantee this peace forever. (*Germania,* February 5 and 7.) .... A Hindenburg does not suffer himself to be knocked out even by a Wilson, and it will not happen for the second time that a German Secretary of State of the Navy will have to resign on account of a Wilson blow. (*Kölnische Volkszeitung,* February 6.) .... The fact that the German-American relations have reached the breaking-point cannot change in the least the unrestricted U-boat war and the calm confidence of our people. No one must or will misunderstand the seriousness of the step which the American Government felt it had to take; however, no one must be misled by this new threat into doubting the strength of our nation. Let everyone tell himself that, had it not been necessary, our leaders would not have taken the decision, however fraught with danger it may be. (*Frankfurter Zeitung,* February 5.) .... With a bold step, President Wilson has changed from a champion of peace and the arbiter of the world to a partisan of England. This step is convincing evidence that this friend of England regards England's position as endangered. America has given us many evidences of ill will. If she intends to give us extreme evidence, then we shall accept it with sincere regret, but in cold blood, as the last result of a policy which so long ago ceased to be

neutral. (*Münchener Neueste Nachrichten*, February 5 and 6.) . . . . We
have often regretted that Germany did not present in time to the United
States the token of friendship of formal and binding acknowledgment
of the Monroe Doctrine. Even today we believe that that would have
been advisable, since it would have closed many a hole to denunciations
against Germany. (*Weser Zeitung*, February 6.) The attitude which
the Social-Democrats adopted prior to January 31 is well known. For
the rest it is evident that German Social-Democracy will not desert its
own people in an hour of distress. The voices of the masses are, of
course, not determining the result of the U-boat war as such. However,
heavy storms are also in store for the country at home, and it will take
the united will of millions to break their force. (*Vorwärts*, February 5.)
. . . . A new blood-dripping epoch of the greatest and most devastating
of all wars is approaching. Should there still be a last possibility of
sparing mankind an increase and prolongation of this terrible struggle,
then we would demand with the utmost emphasis that it be utilized in
every possible way by those who hold the destinies of nations in their
hands. (*Leipziger Volks-zeitung*, February 5.) . . . . The step which
Wilson took on February 3 is very grievous. However, it will be
advisable to view the said turn calmly and not let the President, whose
noble ideals were praised even in the official Notes until lately, be pictured as a man suddenly possessed by war-mania. (*Wiener Arbeiter-
Zeitung*, February 7.) Just for the reason that we do not expect a
decisive result from an American declaration of war, we may freely
confess a wish which we like to clothe, with a few changes, in the words
of Wilson's message: "May it be God's will, that we shall not be forced
to defend our right to freedom, justice, and an unmolested life through
acts of injustice on the part of the American Government." (*Pester
Lloyd*, February 5.)

93. DR. SPAHN'S SPEECH IN THE REICHSTAG, FEBRUARY 27, 1917[9]

. . . . Gentlemen, in consideration of the many writings sent to me
regarding the U-boat war, I must once more go briefly into our attitude on this question. The attitude of my "Fraktion" has not met full
comprehension among our party members. As the Chancellor indicated, the importance of the weapon was not fully understood at the
beginning of the war. That came only after the initial successes, and
since then the perfecting of it has been most energetically carried on.
At the first detailed discussion in the Ways and Means Committee about

[9] *Verhandlungen des Reichstags*, February 27, 1917, pp. 2380–81.

the U-boat question, the members of the Commission, so far as they belong to our party, were under the impression that this weapon could be used unrestrictedly only in case heavy damage to England could certainly be achieved, but that the enlightenment given us did not establish convincingly such a certainty. Not only did the technical naval questions have to be considered but also the condition of the land forces and certain political factors. The conduct of the war is the task of the highest military authorities; the disposal of war means is the business of the Emperor, and for the manner of carrying out the Emperor's disposals the military authorities are responsible to him. At that time we deemed it necessary only to demand of the Chancellor, who is responsible to us, that the recognition of this weapon in international law and the development of it be not restricted through agreements with other countries.

When in September 1916 we had again to occupy ourselves with the question of the U-boat war, the following declaration was made on October 7, in the Ways and Means Committee, in the name of all the members of the Center "Fraktion":

"The Chancellor alone is responsible to the Reichstag for the political decision about the conduct of the war. The decision of the Chancellor will have to rely mainly upon what the Highest Military Command has resolved. Should the decision be in favor of the ruthless U-boat war, the Chancellor can be sure of the concurrence of the Reichstag."

Therein was the imputation that should the Chancellor decide against it his decision should not come in question for the waging of such a U-boat war. We recognized the justification of the U-boat war. For if England used against us the hunger blockade, then we were justified in warding off that weapon with every means at our disposal, that means not being contrary to international law, in order to bring about that success which the opponent wished to achieve against us. . . . .

We are not waging the U-boat war because we believe the enemy will be victorious on land and because we therefore find ourselves in a dubious position, but because we hope by its means to end the war more quickly. . . . .

94. THE IMPERIAL CHANCELLOR'S SPEECH IN THE REICHSTAG, FEBRUARY 27, 1917[10]

Gentlemen, while our soldiers at the front stand under drumfire in the trenches, and our submarines, defying death, hasten through the seas, while we at home have absolutely no other task but to produce cannon, ammunition, and food and to distribute victuals with justice in the midst of this struggle for life and the future of our Empire,

[10] *Verhandlungen des Reichstags*, No. 83, February 27, 1917, pp. 2374-79.

intensified to the extreme, there is only one necessity of the day which dominates all questions of policy, both foreign and internal—to fight and gain victory. [*Hearty applause.*]

The overwhelming majority by which the Reichstag last week voted the new war credits has announced to all the world our irrevocable resolve to fight until the enemy is ready for peace. [*Hearty applause.*] As to the form of this peace, since discussion of war aims was permitted much has been written in the press and said at public meetings. In the Prussian House of Deputies, too, a short and incidental discussion has taken place as to what increase of territory, if any, and what other securities peace must bring us.

Decisive as these questions are for our future and deeply as they quite rightly move us, I hold it premature for me to take a personal part in such debates. [*"Quite right!"—Left.*]

To make promises or formulate detailed conditions would, in my position, be unproductive and hazardous. Enemy leaders have done this abundantly. They gave extravagant assurances to each other, but they only succeeded by this in involving themselves and their nations more deeply in the war. [*"Quite right!"—Left.*] Their example does not tempt me. [*"Very good!"*] What I can declare to be the tendency and aim of our conditions, I have declared repeatedly—to terminate the war by a lasting peace which grants us reparations for all wrongs suffered and guarantees the existence in the future of a strong Germany, that is our aim. [*Hearty applause.*]

Gentlemen, in reference, too, to the great problems of internal policy, I wish to limit myself to general remarks. As in the case of war aims, so too with reference to the shaping of our internal political relations, opinions vary. "Neuorientierung?" It is not a pretty word. [*"Quite right!"—Left.*] Today I use it for the first time, and it may easily create a false impression. As though it depended on our preference whether we should adopt a Neuorientierung or not! No, gentlemen! The new era and the new nation are here! [*Cries of "Quite right!"— Left.*] The war has created them. [*Repeated applause from the Left.*] A race that has been shaken like ours by appalling experiences to the inmost fibers of its being, a people of which it can be said, in the striking words of the field-grey poet, that "her poorest son was also her truest" [*hearty applause from the Left*], a nation that has realized daily in a thousand ways that only her whole strength could meet and overcome the peril from without—that, gentlemen, is a living force that no party program either on the Right or the Left can confine or turn aside from its course. [*Applause from the Left.*] Where political rights have to be created anew, there is no question of repaying the people for what they have done [*hearty applause*]—that conception has always struck me as humiliating—but only of finding out the right political and civic expression for the true nature of that people. [*"Very true!"*]

Important political, intellectual, economic, and social tasks face us in the war. We can solve them only if the whole strength, by the united use of which alone we can win this war, continues to operate in peace—if that strength is given the openings by which it can continue to operate gladly and joyfully. [*Hearty applause from the Left.*] We cannot regulate this by party cries—it demands the internal forces of the state. And this demand will continue. [*"Very good!"*] If anyone objects that after the wars of liberation a hundred years ago the hopes of a reformation in favor of the people of the internal life of Germany were deceived, he overlooks entirely the difference of the forces involved. [*"Quite right!"*] The times have gone by when governments were ruled by the policy of cabal and the influences in favor of liberty were more or less cosmopolitan. Then the spirit of nationality shone only in a few. Today, standing above class or party, it embraces the whole people [*"Quite right!"—Left*], and fuses them into an inseparable unity.

Just as good Conservatives rejoice to recognize the value of our monarchical institutions, so I think all sensible representatives of the rights of the people know how to estimate their true value. [*"Very good!"—Right.*] The Briands and Lloyd Georges and the like wish to make the world believe that their object is to deliver Germany from Prussian militarism and to give the German people democratic liberties. Well, if we are to be liberated, we will see to it ourselves. [*"Quite right!"*] And as for militarism, we all know—even Mr. Lloyd George knew it before the war—that our geographical position, in the words of Frederick the Great, always gives us the warning, "Toujours en vedette!" Nothing can make our watch more effective than institutions based on the firm grounds of monarchy, than a monarchy rooted in the widest classes of the people, and drawing its strength from this unfailing spring—the love of free men. [*Hearty applause.*] That and nothing else is the meaning and the essence of the German conception of the Emperor and of the Prussian conception of the King. [*Loud applause.*]

Gentlemen, from the future I turn to the conditions of the present. My last speech delivered to the assembled Reichstag, on December 12, 1916, contained the proposal of Germany and her allies to enter into peace negotiations. Our action met with the warmest welcome among the neutral states. That welcome was expressly stated in the well-known proposals of the President of the United States, in the action of the Swiss Confederacy, and that of the Scandinavian Kingdoms.

But among our enemies the embittered war-passions of their rulers were stronger than the people's cries for peace.

Their answer was ruder and more presumptuous than any sensible person in our country or in neutral countries could have imagined. [*"Quite right!"—Left and Right.*] The effect produced by this document of barbarian hatred and of derision is manifest to the whole world. Our alliances and our front stand firmer, and the German nation is more united and more resolute than ever. [*"Bravo!"*]

As to the blockade, gentlemen, which we in union with Austria-Hungary have established round England, France, and Italy, I have spoken to you already in the Main Committee on January 31. On the issue of the Note then published in which we announced the blockade, we received from neutral states replies containing reservations, objections, and protests.

We by no means undervalue the difficulties caused to neutral shipping, and we therefore try to alleviate them as much as possible. For this purpose we also attempt to supply, within the limits of our power, neutral states with raw materials needed by them, such as coal and iron. But we also know that all these difficulties, after all, are caused only by England's tyranny of the seas. We will and shall break this enslavement of all non-English trade. [*Hearty applause.*] We will meet halfway all the wishes of neutrals that can be complied with. But in our endeavor to do so we never can go beyond the limits imposed upon us by the irrevocable decision to reach our aim of the establishment of a barred zone. I am sure that later a moment will come when neutrals themselves will thank us for our firmness [*"Quite right!"*]; for the freedom of the oceans which we gain by fighting is of advantage to them also. [*"Quite right!"*]

One step further has been made by the United States of America. President Wilson, after receiving our Note of January 31, brusquely broke off relations with us. Authentic communications giving reasons for his step have not reached me. [*"Hear, hear!"*] The former United States Ambassador here in Berlin communicated to the Secretary of Foreign Affairs only verbally in breaking off relations between great nations living in peace, an act probably without precedent in history. [*"Quite right!"*] As all official documents are lacking, I am forced to rely upon doubtful sources, that is, upon the Reuter Office's version of the contents of the Message delivered by President Wilson on February 3 to Congress.

In this version the President is reported to have said that our Note of January 31 suddenly and without previous indication intentionally withdrew the solemn promises made in the Note of May 1916 and that therefore there was no other choice compatible with dignity and honor left to the United States Government than that announced in its Note of April 20, 1916, in the event of Germany refusing to change her submarine method. If these arguments are correctly reported by Reuter, then I must decidedly protest against them. [*"Quite right!"*— *Right.*]

For more than a century friendly relations have been carefully promoted between us and America. We honored them—as Bismarck once put it—as an heirloom from Frederick the Great. Both countries benefited by them, both giving and taking. Since the beginning of the war things have changed on the other side of the water. Old principles have been overthrown. On August 27, 1913, during the Mexican troubles, President Wilson in a solemn message to Congress declared that he intended to follow the best usages of international law by prohibiting the supplying of arms to either of the Mexican parties at war against each other. [*Lively shouts of "Hear, hear!"*] One year later—1914— these usages were apparently no longer considered good. Countless war material has been supplied by America to the Entente, and while the right of American citizens to travel to the Entente countries without hindrance, the right to trade with France and England without hindrance, even through the midst of the battlefield of the seas, and even the right of such trade as has had to be paid for with German blood— while all these rights were jealously guaranteed, the same right of the American citizen in regard to the Central Powers did not seem to be as worthy of protection and as valuable. They protested against some measures of England which were contrary to international law, but they submitted to the conditions so established.

Their objection as to lack of respect makes a strange impression. [*"Quite right!"*] With equal decisiveness I must protest against this objection that we, by the manner in which we withdrew the assurances given in the Note of May 4, 1916, offended the honor and dignity of the United States. From the very beginning we had openly and expressly declared that these assurances would be invalid under certain conditions. [*"Quite right!"*]

I ask you, gentlemen, to remember the end of our Note of May 4, 1916, in which we agreed in carrying on the submarine war to observe the rules of the "guerre de course." . . . . The Government of the United States in its Note of May 10 confirmed the receipt of our Note of May 4. It is true that they expressed in that Note the opinion that we did not intend to make the maintenance of our newly announced policy in conducting submarine warfare dependent on the result of diplomatic negotiations between the United States and any other Government; but this was so absolutely contrary to what we in our Note had said clearly and without any possibility of misunderstanding that a reply on our part would have changed nothing as to the positions maintained on the two sides. [*"Quite right!"*] But nobody, probably even in America, could or can doubt that already the conditions upon which we made the regaining of our full liberty of decision to depend were fulfilled. [*"Quite right!"*]

England did not abolish the isolation of Germany, but on the contrary intensified it in the most reckless fashion. [*"Quite right!"*] Our adversaries were not made to respect the principles of international law universally recognized before the war, nor to follow the laws of humanity. The freedom of the seas which America wanted to restore in co-operation with us during the war has been still more completely destroyed by our adversary, and America has not hindered this. All this is common knowledge. Even at the end of January, England issued a new barred zone declaration for the North Sea, and since May 4 nine months have already passed. Could it, then, be surprising to anybody that on January 31 we considered that the freedom of the seas had not been re-established and that we drew conclusions from this? [*"Quite right!"*]

But the case is of more than formal importance. We who were ready for peace by mutual understanding now fight for life against an enemy who from the beginning put his heel upon the recognized laws of nations. The English starvation blockade, our peace offer, its rejection by the Entente, the war aims of enemies purporting our destruction, the speeches of Mr. Lloyd George also are all known in America. I should fully understand it if the United States as the protector of international law had cared for its re-establishment on equal lines in regard to all belligerents, and if, wishing to restore peace to the world, she had taken measures for enforcing the end of bloodshed. But I cannot possibly consider it a question of life and honor for the American nation to protect international law in a one-sided fashion against us alone.

Our enemies and American circles which are unfriendly to us thought that they could point out an important difference between our course of action and that of the English. England, it has been said, destroys only material values which can be replaced but Germany destroys human lives which it is impossible to replace. Well, gentlemen, why did the English not endanger American lives? Only because neutral countries, and especially America, voluntarily submitted to English orders and because the English therefore could obtain their object without using force. [*"Quite right!"*] What would have happened if the Americans had valued unhampered passenger and goods traffic with Bremen and Hamburg as much as that with Liverpool and London? If they had done so we should then have been freed from the painful impression that, according to American ideas, submission to English power and control is compatible with this neutrality, but a recognition of German measures of defense is irreconcilable with this neutrality. [*"Quite right!"—Center, and National-Liberals.*]

Gentlemen, let us consider the whole question. The breaking off of relations with the United States and the attempted mobilization of all neutrals against us do not serve to protect the freedom of the seas proclaimed by the United States; they must rather have the result of encouraging the attempt to starve Germany and of increasing bloodshed.

We regret the rupture with a nation who by her history seemed predestined to work together with us, not against us, for common ideals. But since our honest desire for peace has encountered only hostile ridicule on the part of our enemies, there is no more "going back," but only "ahead" is possible for us.

That England would represent the intensified use of submarine warfare as the greatest crime in the history of the world could be foreseen. [*"Quite right!"—National-Liberals.*] England regards herself simply as the predestined ruler of the seas and the general benefactor of the whole of mankind. The whole of international law with its rules for maritime warfare is unconditionally binding for others—for England only so far as her own interests allow. Lord Lytton declared the laws of naval policy were the concern of England. Who intrusted them to England? Who supervises her? Every opponent who will not submit to the British habit of extending or compressing the laws of justice and morality according to the elastic demands of political, economic, or military necessity is represented as a traitor to humanity and relegated to the ranks of Huns or pirates.

Before the war when no anxiety could prevail as to the German submarines, the case was different. It is worth while to notice the opinion of a British naval authority, Sir Percy Scott, given on July 17, 1914, and therefore shortly before the outbreak of war. There had been objection to his view that the future of naval warfare rested with the submarines, and that submarines, owing to the nature of their construction, could not take prisoners, but only annihilate. This would be an offense against the laws of humanity and a reversion to barbarism. In his reply in the *Times* Sir Percy put the following case: An island, depending on imports for its food supplies, becomes involved in war. The enemy regards it as his task to cut off its supplies. Accordingly, he establishes a mine and submarine blockade about the island and informs all neutrals that such a blockade has been established and that any ship approaching it does so at its own risk of destruction by mines and submarines. [*"Hear, hear!"*] In fact, exactly our position. This is Sir Percy's judgment in his own words: "Such an announcement would be entirely in order, and if British or neutral ships disregard them and attempt to break the blockade, it could not be assumed that they were serving peaceful purposes. If they were sunk, it could not be regarded as a reversion to barbarism, and designated as piracy in its worst forms." [*"Hear, hear!"*] Exactly the point of view which we maintain, only our position is strengthened and justified by the fact that it was the island itself which began the methods of starvation and forced us to retaliate in self-defense. It seems to me that the *Kölnische Zeitung* hit the nail on the head, when, after reprinting the *Times* article of July 17, 1914, it remarked: "If the position today in respect to the submarine war were reversed, England would say unanimously today what Sir Percy Scott said then." But I repeat, gentlemen, in answer to the campaign of calumny that England is waging against us today, and I emphasize it, our present submarine war is a reply to the hunger-blockade which England has exercised against us since the beginning of the war.

The rulers of England lulled themselves with the hope that the war would not cost them too dear. The work on land they would, in accordance with past precedents, leave to their Allies, and Albion needed only her proud fleet to force the German people as a whole to capitulate through starvation without her having to suffer any loss of men. For England the recipe is not new. I would remind you, gentlemen, of the notorious concentration camps in which England confined the wives and children of the gallant Boer warriors and of the inhuman treatment dealt out to them there with the express purpose of diminishing by their sufferings the power of resistance of their husbands in the field. As was admitted in the English Parliament, this measure, which will form an eternal blot on the English name, had in fact the opposite effect. It had the result of increasing the opposition of the Boers and of prolonging the war. It is a strange irony of history that the present Prime Minister, Lloyd George, who now is insatiable in the violent expressions in which he attacks German barbarism, that same Mr. Lloyd George in his day asserted in the English Lower House the fact that from 15,000 to 16,000 women and children had been sacrificed to English cruelty. [*Lively cries of "Hear, hear!"*] For example, according to his account the mortality of children under twelve years old in the concentration camps amounted to 41.6 per cent. The actual death rate was far higher. Mr. Chamberlain, then English Colonial Secretary, who endeavored to defend the Government's policy, admitted that the death rate of children in the Orange Free State was temporarily 55 per cent. These conditions were the result of a systematic policy of extermination, according to which the unfortunate women and children were insufficiently supplied with food, not perhaps because there was lack of food but for deliberate reasons. [*"Hear, hear!"*] In the same way all sanitary considerations were neglected. I take these facts not from any partial propaganda writings but from the official report of the proceedings in the English Lower House in which these facts were established.

Now, gentlemen, England wishes in the present war to employ on a large scale the methods which she then practiced on a small scale. In the Boer War it was a question of 150,000 women and children, of whom from 15,000 to 16,000 according to Mr. Lloyd George's account, that is about 12 per cent, fell victims to the barbarous methods of English warfare. In the present war, the whole German nation, with a population of close upon 70,000,000, including women and children, the aged and infirm, is to be forced to capitulate by hunger and deprivation in order that England may thus win a victory that she cannot enforce by arms. [*"Quite right!"*] It was England who from the beginning wanted to make this war not a war of army against army but of nation against nation. [*"Very true!"*] And after she did so, after her leaders had replied to our offer of peace only with scorn and mockery, then, for the German will for defense, nothing was left but Goethe's word, according to which rudeness must be met with rudeness. [*"Bravo!"*]

England seems to realize the danger the U-boat war will have for her. Lloyd George's speech testifies to that. Of course, the British Government is forced to soothe the people with the assurance that they will soon be masters of the submarine war. We shall wait and see. [*"Quite right!"*] Meanwhile I am able to declare that the successes in submarine warfare already obtained much surpass the expectations of our navy. [*Applause.*] I can, of course, give no definite figures. We established the barred zones hardly four weeks ago, and included within these four weeks is the period of grace allowed for such ships as were on their way on February 1 and therefore could not be warned. The reports from a large proportion of our submarines have not yet been received because they are still on their way. But wherever reports have been made the success is great. Our enemies, of course, admit only part of their losses. If all these are added together, then the figures published by us to date in our newspapers—which are only part of the sinkings—demonstrate that we can be more than satisfied with the results obtained. [*Applause.*] The reports made by our enemies as to ships which have broken the blockade, of which they particularly boast, are no disappointment for us.

As is generally known, we did not declare a blockade but only established a definite barred zone within which ships have to count on immediate attack. That individual ships escape is therefore obvious. But that does not change the total success. This success we shall be able to obtain partly by sinking and partly by discouraging neutral shipping, a success which has already happened in the widest sense. [*"Bravo!"*] Thanks to the incomparable bravery of our submarine crews we are entitled to await with full confidence further developments, which will be increasingly important. [*Hearty applause.*]

One short word in conclusion. After the refusal of our peace offer, our Kaiser, in his message of January 12, expressed his confidence that the strength of every German man and woman would be doubled by holy scorn of the lust for power and passion for destruction announced once more by the rulers of the enemy. How justified this confidence was the German people in all its parts and in every way demonstrated— on the battlefield, in the sphere of labor, and in willing endurance.

Hard winter is behind us, hard especially for the poor population. Difficulties of railway traffic have increased the difficulties in supplying victuals and fuel. The heroism of our women and children, the spirit of patriotism, so unflinchingly maintained, has already shattered the English policy of starvation. [*Applause.*]

Gentlemen, since my last speech the military situation has hardly been changed. Everywhere our fronts have been made stronger and our brave soldiers look with full confidence upon their leaders, who are accustomed to victory, strengthened in their haughty confidence by the scornful refusal of our readiness for peace. Safely protected on the land fronts by the genius of our Supreme Army Command [*applause*], victorious on the water and many times more prepared for the submarine war than a year ago, we confidently look toward the coming months. [*Applause from the Right.*]

The army that faces the foe and the army at home are equally animated by the unbending will not to suffer our Fatherland to fall into dishonor and be compelled to renounce her freedom. This will, preserved and strengthened a thousandfold in danger and death, makes us invincible. It brings us victory.

95. THE HIGH MILITARY COMMAND AND THE U-BOAT WAR[11]

We hear that in the conversations held in Berlin between the High Command and members of the Reichstag, General Ludendorff made the following statement, among others, as to the U-boat war: The desire which primarily determined the High Command in conducting the U-boat war was to hit the enemy war economy and especially the production of munitions. The Western armies have experienced an important relief through the submarines. The enemy output of munitions has been diminished and the submarines have fulfilled this task. The cooperation of navy and army is thus demonstrated to be exemplary, in accordance with the stupendous conditions of the World War in which we still stand with both feet.

[11] *Norddeutsche Allgemeine Zeitung,* July 19, 1917, I, 1.

The Highest Army Command further expects from the U-boat war that it will break the war efficiency of England by diminishing freight-space on the sea and by the consequences arising from this. The fulfilment of this second desire also will come and with it, in spite of America, the ending of the World War and the peace which the High Command also desires.

96. LUDENDORFF'S STATEMENT CONCERNING AMERICA AND THE U-BOAT WAR[12]

.... If the prospect of American help had not opened out, the Western European Powers would certainly have been more inclined to make peace. Since the U-boat war gave America the pretext to enter the war, this question is tantamount to a question whether or not the U-boat war was the right policy. Regarding this, my conviction is unchanged. The U-boat war was right. It has accomplished what we expected. . . . . It was not a question of starving England within a few months, but of making her inclined toward peace. That was to be attained by the diminution of tonnage which England has at her disposal more than by actual starvation. Not less important for England is the question of the supply of coal and pit props. There our U-boat hit the enemy on his tenderest spot. . . . .

97. DISCUSSION OF SUBMARINE WARFARE IN THE MAIN COMMITTEE OF THE REICHSTAG, MAY 11, 1918

(a) STATEMENT OF ADMIRAL VON CAPELLE[13]

I should like first to express the thanks of the navy for the appreciation of the navy and its activity expressed by the reporter, and I should like specially to thank him for and entirely to associate myself with the appreciation he expressed of the Imperial dockyards, the private shipyards, and all the contractors for submarine requisites. The unrestricted U-boat warfare was the commencement of a very strong offensive against the Entente at sea. The results are known to you from the publications of the Admiralty Staff. The reports for April are also good up to now. Of course there have also been losses. Such a strong offensive at sea as this cannot be carried on without losses. But the main thing is: "During the unrestricted U-boat warfare the additions to the U-boats at the front have exceeded the number of losses. Our offensive

[12] *Vorwärts*, December 3, 1917, 1–2.
[13] *Norddeutsche Allgemeine Zeitung*, May 12, 1918, I, 5–6

at sea is stronger today than at the beginning of the unrestricted U-boat warfare [*"Hear, hear!"*], and that gives us a sure prospect of final success." The U-boat warfare becomes more and more a struggle between what the U-boats accomplish and what is accomplished in the way of building new ships. Up to now the monthly figures giving the number of vessels sunk have always been several times higher than the figures giving the number of new ships built; even English Ministers and the whole press admit that. An appeal to the English workmen in the shipbuilding yards, which was distributed widely in the English shipbuilding yards, appears to me particularly significant. This appeal is as follows: "The construction of merchant ships amounted in March to 161,000 tons, or to 30 ships of 5,000 tons each. But the Huns sank 810 [*applause*] ships during the same period. Workmen! you can and will prevent the Huns from starving us out." This appeal does not appear to have had any great success, for according to the most recent publications of the English Admiralty, circulated by Reuter, the construction of ships went down from 192,000 tons in March to 111,000 tons in April, or, reckoned in ships, from 32 to 22. That means a decline of 50,000 tons, or 40 per cent. America has so far built little, and has fallen far short of expectations. Even if an increase is to be reckoned on in the future, this increase will be entirely used up by America herself. Added to the sinking by U-boats, there is also the considerable decline in tonnage through accidents at sea and ships becoming unserviceable. One of the best-known big English shipowners stated at a meeting of the Chamber of Shipping that the losses of the British merchant fleet through accidents at sea, owing to the conditions created by the war, were three times as great as in peace time. He added: "I think I am not mistaken in saying that our whole construction of new ships since the beginning of the war has merely sufficed to cover the losses through accidents at sea, without there being any question of the losses caused by the enemy." [*"Hear, hear!"*] The average decline in world tonnage in peace time through accidents at sea and ships becoming unserviceable was 800,000 gross tons, including the marine losses of the Quadruple Alliance. You may now consider for yourselves what this decline signifies. In his great speech on the offensive in the West the English Prime Minister, Lloyd George, said that even if the land war were lost the war at sea would still be very far from ending.

We must wait and see whether the English people make this threat their own. If they do, our U-boats will continue to do their duty and will surely not fail to succeed. [*Enthusiastic applause.*] Our opponents will then see that our U-boats hold out longer. Gentlemen, as far as is at all possible, i.e., in so far as the other imperative needs of the army and navy allow of it, the whole of the war industries suitable for the purpose will be placed at the service of U-boat construction. Provision will be made that for years to come there shall be no interruption of any kind in the regular supply of new U-boats. We have therefore every reason to regard our U-boats with trust and confidence [*applause*], and can safely reckon on their achieving their object, in conjunction with our victorious army. [*Enthusiastic applause.*] Gentlemen, I should like to refer to one more point. You will have read in this morning's papers that the English have made a fresh attack on Ostend. The English reports assert that this attack was crowned with success. In answer to this, I affirm that, as appears from the Admiralty Staff official announcements, the English blockading ship was sunk outside the waterway [*"Hear, hear!"*] ; consequently the attack may be described, like the former attack, as a failure. [*Applause.*]

97. (b) KAPP'S SPEECH[14]

At the conclusion of peace under no circumstances must we be induced to agree to the creation of any restrictions of an international nature against the employment of U-boats in war which would conflict with the special uses of this modern weapon of warfare and impose on us an irremediable hindrance in our relation to England and the protection of our interests and means of defense. We may be quite certain that England, with the gracious assistance of President Wilson, will advance claims of this kind at the conclusion of peace. I point therefore to the excellent remarks of Geheimrat Wilhelm v. Siemens as to the liberty of the seas, where the U-boat, in union with the High Seas Fleet, is pointed to as the means for the maintenance of German naval power. We not only need this arm as a retaliation for the ruthless starvation blockade of our enemies, but it is a newly created weapon of naval warfare which must be used as such. [*"Quite right!"*] Any possible attempts of our enemies, therefore, to limit our right to the use of this weapon must be unconditionally rejected. [*Enthusiastic assent on the Right.*] It is a welcome fact that all parties are agreed as to continuing the unrestricted U-boat war under all circumstances. All parties are also agreed that as far as can be humanly foreseen the U-boat war will lead to final success. This unanimity will produce a much stronger impression on foreigners than any peace offensives, which, after all, will be construed only as an expression of weakness. [*"Quite right!"—Right.*]

[14] *Norddeutsche Allgemeine Zeitung,* May 12, 1918, I, 6.

97. (c) STRESEMANN'S SPEECH[15]

The last speaker's utterances can only provoke us to a debate on international politics and the various contentious issues involved in them. I will not allow myself to be drawn into this trap. It is far more important for our judgment of the position as a whole to emphasize the fact that all parties, including the Social-Democrats, are united in standing for the unconditional continuance of the unlimited U-boat war. With equal unanimity we agree to the short statement of the Secretary of State to the effect that all the larger Reichstag parties will oppose any attempt that may be made at the peace negotiations to take from our hands by any kind of conditions the submarine weapon. [*Lively applause.*] The services of our navy have shown how false was the view that the conception of militarism in any way extinguishes responsibility and initiative.

97. (d) VOGTHERR'S SPEECH[16]

As a matter of course we do not agree to the declaration as to the ruthless U-boat war. We have never given up our opposition in principle to its employment. Even today, after fifteen months, it is impossible to see how it has brought us nearer to the end of the war. Meanwhile we continue to destroy tonnage which we shall need bitterly after the war to supply us with raw materials. We have often read Herr Kapp's speech during the last year, though it is better and more intelligently put even in the *Deutsche Tageszeitung*. His view on peace conditions we can regard with indifference. In my opinion we shall be very glad if we can get peace in the West soon on quite different terms, if the only point at issue is the surrender of this method of war. The prohibition against the reading of Independent-Socialist journals by sailors is a humiliation to those troops. In the matter of the public prosecution of Dittmann, Haase, and myself, Herren von Capelle and Michaelis have not found themselves in a position to draw the necessary inferences from their big words. The action against Frau Zietz has had to be abandoned after a seven months' examination of a number of men in the navy. In spite of the utter bankruptcy of this proceeding, welcomed by the vanished Chancellor, Dr. Michaelis, and Herr von Capelle—to which Count Hertling has raised no objection—even today no one is ashamed to regard as absolutely without rights, even in war time, soldiers who belong to our party.

[15] *Norddeutsche Allgemeine Zeitung,* May 12, 1918, I, 6.
[16] *Ibid.*

Part II
War and Peace

CHAPTER VII

WAR AIMS

INTRODUCTORY NOTE

ALTHOUGH the Empire unsheathed the sword to wage a war of national defense, the military victories of 1914–15 called forth vast plans of annexation and domination. As early as the spring of 1915 large groups in Germany were bent upon annexations. Belgium was to be joined in some way to the Empire. The Six Economic Associations demanded, in addition to Belgium, the Briey and Calais districts, as well as the fortresses of Belfort and Verdun; colonial possessions commensurate with Germany's population and economic power; a strategic and economic frontier-zone in the Baltic lands; and a war indemnity. In the summer of 1915 the King of Bavaria declared that the Empire must have a direct outlet from the Rhine to the sea.

At the same period Naumann wrote in his great work, *Mitteleuropa:* "We shall emerge from the War as Mid-Europeans." Meanwhile Rohrbach in *Das Grössere Deutschland* explained that the Bagdad Railroad would give the Empire control of a vast empire from the North Sea to the Red Sea and the Indian Ocean.

The general war aims of the annexationists may be grouped as follows: (1) The maintenance and protection of the Empire; (2) the formation of Middle Europe on the largest possible scale; (3) the destruction of the interference of Britain in continental politics and especially of her balance-of-power policy; (4) the extension of German frontiers and influence so that she can never again be subjected to an encircling policy; (5) the establishment of the freedom of the seas not only for Germany but for all the minor naval powers.

98. OUR WAR AIMS[1]

In the latest number of the *Preussische Jahrbücher* Dr. Delbrück, the editor, voices in very sensible words his opposition to certain de-

---

[1] *Vorwärts,* October 1, 1914, p. 5.

mands for annexation which have been repeatedly made even within the circle of his close political friends. Commenting upon the conditions which should guide Germany in making peace he writes:

"Complete security against a defeated enemy resuming warfare at a favorable opportunity is to be found in complete and permanent subjugation. Such was the policy of the Romans, and in this manner they gradually established a world empire. Such a world empire, however, for the good of mankind, is impossible in modern times.

"A middle course would be to demand the cession of large territories, to retain fortified places of strategic importance, and to strangle the enemy economically. Such was Napoleon's method, especially in 1807, when dealing with Prussia. He took half of our kingdom, retained the fortresses along the Oder River, limited the size of our army, and demanded a war indemnity so large that we were unable to pay it in many years. His method did not prove to be successful. It might, however, have been successful if Napoleon had conquered the rest of the world, i.e., if Napoleon had followed the Roman example. As he was not able to do so, only six years elapsed before Prussia rose again; it was then seen that the terrific economic pressure imposed upon us by the French had awakened in us moral energies that were not only equal to the pressure exerted but even exceeded it.

"May God forbid that Germany will enter the path of the Napoleonic policy, after the victory which we expect. Wars without end would be the consequence. However heavily we might chain other nations, we cannot keep them in fetters forever. Europe stands united in this one conviction: it will never submit to a hegemony enforced upon it by a single state."

. . . . The view presented here by Professor Delbrück certainly deserves earnest consideration even though we may differ in details. It is singular in its calmness and in that it renounces claims that might make the discussion of the conditions on which peace must be based exceedingly difficult.

99. ONCE MORE: OUR WAR AIMS[2]

The article of Professor Delbrück of the University of Berlin quoted at length in *Vorwärts* not only has been severely criticized, as we have mentioned before, in the *Deutsche Tageszeitung* (a criticism which the Saturday edition of that paper repeats and enlarges on) but *Die Post* and the *Tägliche Rundschau* also violently raise their voices in protest. *Die Post* says:

"Our diplomacy everywhere gives way to the impudent demands of

[2] *Vorwärts,* October 4, 1914, p. 3.

our 'friends' and all over the world the Germans are despised and derided. That was the diplomacy of the 'balance of power,' and we are merely to go on with it after the war. We reject such a philosophy of history and such diplomacy! The phrase, a 'European balance of power,' is used merely to cover the supremacy in Europe of our enemies. Only some professors of history and some German pre-war diplomats have believed in this idol and offered sacrifices to it, but we will no longer be fooled by this phrase and we refuse any longer to be made the scapegoat of the European balance of power."

The *Tägliche Rundschau* calls Delbrück's treatise "an insipid song of the blessings of political moderation." His statements were all called "soft" (*Windelweicheit*) ; he is accused of "elementary mistakes in historical thinking"; he is blamed for "wanting to put obstacles in the path of world history that the enemy is forcing Germany to travel." *Die Post* does not even shrink from such an expression as "crime against the good cause of Germany," because Delbrück (as *Die Post* states) would make the world believe that our statesmen may intend to follow Napoleon's policy. What the *Deutsche Tageszeitung* had merely insinuated is here expressed very distinctly: "Professor Delbrück is subservient to our enemies in foreign countries in a way which would be reprehensible even under ordinary circumstances and which today is positively criminal." Delbrück is supposed to have created in foreign countries the impression that chauvinism is rampant in Germany.

The *Tägliche Rundschau* contrasts Delbrück's statements with some sentences written forty-four years ago in the same *Preussische Jahrbücher* during the Franco-German War by Professor Treitschke, Delbrück's predecessor. In so doing the *Tägliche Rundschau* makes it apparent that the war must not be brought to an end without the acquisition of new territory or without a "strengthening of our frontier," to use Treitschke's words. The *Rundschau* adds that today the "price" of peace paid by the enemy must be higher than that paid forty-four years ago.

The *Tägliche Rundschau* and other papers of the same kind seem to overlook the fact that Professor Delbrück, in quietly and seriously discussing the possibility of peace, merely advocated common sense and political moderation; and in defining as the aim of the war the demand "that on land the balance of power must be maintained as it is and that on the sea a similar balance must be attained," Professor Delbrück, we repeat, in reality demanded exactly what Emperor William formally proclaimed at the beginning of the war. In his address from the Throne on August 4 he said: "We are not driven by lust for conquest; we are filled with the grim determination to retain for ourselves and for all coming generations the place that God has given us."

We have previously stated that one need not be in full agreement with Professor Delbrück's propositions. We, too, believe that the hour has not yet come when the details of a peace treaty may be discussed. But the fundamental thought of Delbrück, which is also the fundamental thought underlying the Emperor's speech from the Throne on August 4, must be our guiding star today and forever: no greed for conquest! Wise moderation is needed to make possible a permanent peace and the growth of the spirit of conciliation among the nations. Professor Delbrück deserves recognition for having given renewed expression to this thought.

Incidentally, in view of the formal truce agreed upon by our political parties, on what ground will the papers mentioned justify their attacks on Professor Delbrück?

100. EXTENSION OF TERRITORY AT THE CONCLUSION OF PEACE?[3]

Contrary to assurances of the Chancellor that the present war will be waged as a war of defense, Deputy Dr. Oertel in the *Deutsche Tageszeitung* directs very sharp attacks against a lecture of Professor Anschütz. In this lecture the latter said that extension of German territory in Europe is undesirable from a purely political point of view provided it is not demanded for military reasons. Even this very general limitation that the itch for territories desirable from an economic point of view must not influence the question of annexations meets opposition from the conservative representative. Dr. Oertel writes:

"But it has been generally and repeatedly demanded with great firmness that the peace justify the great sacrifices which have been made by the German army and by the German people, and that the peace, if possible, secure the future of the Reich and the German nationality. That is the way German princes, Germans of almost all parties, almost without exception the German newspapers, and the legitimate representative bodies of the German people have expressed themselves. To renounce on principle every extension of territory in Europe which is not demanded and does not accord with military reasons, would not be compatible with this solemnly and generally proclaimed opinion of the people."

Dr. Oertel is decidedly mistaken in stating that the whole people agree with him and that the "legitimate representative bodies of the German people" (the Parliaments, no doubt) had expressed that agreement. On the contrary, exactly the opposite view has been expressed

[3] *Vorwärts*, January 30, 1915, p. 7.

by the largest parties of the Reichstag in agreement with the great majority of the people.

Dr. Oertel is furthermore mistaken in writing that opposition to the extension of territory can become very dangerous for the Reich and the peace negotiations. Here also, it seems to us, the attitude of the Social-Democratic Party and its parliamentary group is in the interests of the Reich and of a permanent peace. We can prove it in detail if discussion, which is demanded also by Representative Dr. Oertel, is permitted.

101. DISCUSSION OF THE CONDITIONS OF PEACE[4]

In *Der Tag,* C. Raschdan continues his arguments about the necessity of a public discussion of the conditions of peace. He writes:

"In the newspapers there is a constant increase of argument by well-known politicians who deem it desirable and even necessary that discussion of the conditions under which Germany would make peace —which discussion so far has been prevented or at least restricted by the censorship—be permitted. In a magazine a distinguished party leader has expressed his anxiety over the present situation as comparable with an overheated boiler the safety valve of which is closed and the explosion of which is not impossible. Nobody can misunderstand the importance and significance of this problem. . . . .

"Certainly the present state of affairs, when something of such concern to us all cannot be discussed, is difficult to bear, especially by those ardently interested in the future of our country. For these men are poignantly conscious that in the multitude of possibilities which present themselves in the stress of great events, important and significant things may escape the most experienced and best advised statesmen, and that the often beneficial influence of public opinion may be completely lost through mere rapidity of development. Today, such is the state of affairs in which we are living that we deal with the question of the conditions of peace as with a mysterious family affair, as with the 'ghost in the house, of which one speaks only in private.' "

Raschdan, of course, does not believe that the day for the discussion of the conditions of peace has come. His real grounds for such a belief are that the desires revealed by free discussion may prove too extravagant and fantastic and may do only harm:

"Among the disadvantages of these public discussions one must list not only the confusion which might result from them among us Germans in regard to our present unanimity but also their effect on foreign

[4] *Vorwärts,* February 5, 1915.

countries and especially on neutrals. It does not seem appropriate here to elaborate this discussion and submit details. At present I only want to have it understood that our relation to our enemies should not be considered and judged completely from the point of view of the fortunate victor. We shall gain the victory in this struggle; but we are victorious only because from the very beginning even our children have recognized that we are fighting for our existence, and because everybody—soldier and civilian—fights for a higher cause than our enemies. But this incomparable and unprecedented readiness for sacrifices and its good results must not lead us to exaggerations harmful to our cause. . . . . The discussion of different conditions of peace as such seems to be inappropriate today, because of the extravagance of the programs and their effect at home and abroad."

We believe we are in a position to assert that saner voices also will not be lacking; Raschdan's objection therefore seems to us untenable.

102. ADDRESS OF DEPUTY HEINE (S.D.) IN STUTTGART[5]

If I am today to speak about Germany's future and Social-Democracy, then I have nothing more at heart to express than my agreement with the Chancellor when he said that the aim of the war is to be a free people. A prerequisite to our becoming a real free people is peace. Social-Democracy is the party which fights for peace among nations. . . . . We are not chauvinists; we are not so-called "rah-rah" patriots. It is contrary to German character to be chauvinistic. We simply defend our Fatherland, our economic life, our existence, our German civilization, the independence and integrity of the Reich.

In this we do not wish to weaken. We must hold out, as the Chancellor said. We do not wish to crush the whole world but rather to secure a lasting and honorable peace. Of course, this confession of our desire for peace is unsatisfactory to many. Unfortunately there is a large group of pacifists, so much ridiculed, often unjustly, who expect of Social-Democracy special efforts for peace. Our love and longing for peace are beyond doubt. However, the time has not yet come to demand peace, and every inopportune step is evil and produces the opposite of what we wish to achieve. This lesson we learned from the London Conference. . . . . Among us, too, there are people with fantastic peace plans. . . . . If we want peace, then we must, for the time being, trust German arms, the German field-marshals, the German people, and the men who are doing wonders at the front. Today the army is the nation and the nation the army. [*Lively applause.*]

[5] *Vorwärts,* February 25, 1915.

Let us also place confidence in the Emperor's love for peace and his determination to achieve it. Twice in recent years he preserved peace by his personal intervention. Of importance also is the Government's proclamation, clearly bearing the imprint of the Chancellor, published today in all newspapers, warning the public not to discuss the conditions of peace at the present time. We can agree completely with this proclamation. The war is, on our part, no war of conquest. If necessary, Social-Democracy will support the Kaiser and the Chancellor, the question being that of securing an honorable peace that does not involve the dangers of a new war. . . . .

103. A CONSERVATIVE ACCOUNT OF THE PETITION OF
THE SIX ECONOMIC ASSOCIATIONS[6]
MARCH 10, 1915

The Agrarian League, the German Peasants League, the Central Union of German Industrialists, the League of Industrialists, the Hansa League, and the German League of Middle-Class Citizens have addressed a joint petition to the Reichstag in which the latter is asked to beg the Chancellor to do his utmost to permit discussion of peace terms in order that public opinion concerning peace negotiations may express itself in time. The petition closes with the following sentences:

"If free discussion as to the object and the conditions of peace is allowed, it will appear that, with quite trifling exceptions, the whole people, irrespective of party, and in the field as well as at home, is possessed by a single strong will. This will is to hold out to the very end, so that our German Fatherland shall emerge from its fight for existence, which has been forced upon it, greater and stronger, with secured frontiers in the West and the East, and with the European and colonial extensions of territory necessary for the security of our sea power as well as for military and economic reasons. Without these extensions of territory, our common goal—the ending of the war in such a way that a repetition of our struggle is practically out of the question—cannot be attained.

"It is toward the permanent interest of Germany and therefore the well-being of our German Fatherland that this united and strong will expresses itself as that of the whole German nation, united in self-sacrifice and standing with indomitable energy behind a Government representing this will."

[6] *Deutsche Tageszeitung*, March 11, 1915.

104. AN OFFICIAL ACCOUNT OF THE PETITION[7]

THE DAY'S POLITICAL REPORT

BERLIN, March 12

In a joint petition of the Agrarian League, the German Peasants League, the Central Union of German Industrialists, the League of Industrialists, the Hansa League, and the German League of the Middle-Class Citizens, it is being demanded of the Chancellor that discussion of peace conditions be permitted as soon as possible. The petition considers that the drafters of the article against the immediate release of public discussion about future peace conditions were ill informed about the wishes of the great masses of our people, and in turn it calls attention to the common strong will to persist in this war until the end.

This counterview proves nothing against our exposition, since we too have no more eager wish than to maintain to the utmost this single and powerful will of the people unbroken and secure against misunderstanding on the part of our enemies and of neutrals. The question, however, is rather whether the impression of complete unanimity in fighting through will continue if we begin to talk about the reward for all the sacrifices we have made and about gratifying the six great unions as to the best form for the treaty of peace before we have finally conquered. This talking will be disputing. It is a happy thing that six great leagues, otherwise not always united, which embrace millions of businesses, great and small, appear absolutely united in the interest of the Fatherland. We consider, however, that their polemic against a decision of the highest military and civil authorities is untimely, because freedom *inter arma* to discuss matters would not accelerate victory in the field. And that is what matters.

105. THE PETITION OF THE SIX ECONOMIC ASSOCIATIONS OF MAY 20, 1915[8]

The Agrarian League, the German Peasants League, the Christian German Peasants Unions, the Central Union of German Industrialists, the League of Industrialists, and the League of Middle-Class Citizens in the German Empire have on May 20, 1915, forwarded the following petition to the German Chancellor: . . . .

"EXCELLENCY!

"Together with the whole German people, those occupied in business pursuits, whether in agriculture or manufacture, in handicrafts or trade,

[7] *Norddeutsche Allgemeine Zeitung,* March 13, 1915, I, 1.

[8] *Eingabe der 6 Verbände; l'Humanité,* August 11, 1915.

are determined to endure to the end, notwithstanding every sacrifice, in this struggle for life and death which has been forced upon Germany, in order that Germany may emerge stronger in its external relations, assured of a lasting peace, and thus also assured of further national, economic, and cultural development at home.

"Since the whole German people recognizes these aims as its own, and has given tangible proof of its willingness to make sacrifices for their achievement, the rumors recently circulating in town and country were bound to be most disquieting. These rumors (confirmed, apparently, by certain announcements in the press) were to the effect that preliminary steps were being taken to prepare the way for peace negotiations, and, in particular, for a separate peace with England, based on certain English wishes and demands.

"Hence universal satisfaction has been caused by the declaration of the *Norddeutsche Allgemeine Zeitung* that no competent judge would dream of sacrificing Germany's favorable military position in order to conclude a premature peace with any one of her enemies.

"Even if the military situation were more unfavorable, or more doubtful than it is, it should make no difference to our determination—unless, indeed, we are to lose sight of the aims in home and foreign policy which His Majesty the Emperor has himself proclaimed. These aims can be attained only by achieving a peace which will bring us better security for our frontiers in East and West, an extension of the foundations of our sea power, and the possibility of an unchecked and strong development of our economic resources; in short, those extensions of power, alike in politics, in the army, in the navy, and in our economic life, which will guarantee to us a stronger position in the world.

"Any peace which does not bring us these results will make a speedy renewal of the struggle inevitable under circumstances essentially less favorable to Germany. Therefore, no premature peace! For from a premature peace we could not hope for a sufficient prize of victory. Also no half-hearted peace, no peace which does not include complete political exploitation of those ultimate military successes which we expect to obtain!

"For it must be realized that the security of our future international position and our power to utilize the present self-sacrificing spirit of the German people for the settlement of those questions of domestic policy which will arise on the return of peace alike presuppose the complete exploitation of our military position for increasing Germany's power abroad. Assuredly our people would understand concessions wrung from them by a military situation so desperate as to oppose insuperable obstacles to any resistance however determined and self-sacrificing; but they would not tolerate concessions at the conclusion of peace not justified and necessitated by the military situation. Concessions of this kind would be fraught with the most fatal consequences for the domestic peace of our Fatherland, since they might lead to the same result as a premature withdrawal from the conflict, and our soldiers would discover, on returning home, that the only reward for their splendid endurance was a crushing burden of taxation. Hundreds of thousands have given their lives; the prize of victory must correspond to the sacrifice.

"The following memorandum was drawn up on March 10 of this year and addressed to Your Excellency by the Agrarian League, the German Peasants League, the Central Union of German Industrialists, the Industrialists League, and the League of Middle-Class Citizens in the German Empire. The memorandum, to which the Christian German Peasants Unions, who are also signatories to the present Petition, have given their adhesion, explains in detail the requirements which, the necessary military successes being assumed, must in the opinion of the undersigned associations be fulfilled in order to secure for Germany that political, military, and economic position which would enable her to look forward with confidence to the possibilities of the future. The memorandum was as follows:

" 'The undersigned corporations have carefully considered what measures are required to give effect to the formula which has so often been heard during the last few months, viz., that this war must be followed by an honorable peace corresponding to the sacrifices which have been made and containing in itself a guaranty for its continuance.

" 'In answering this question, it must never be forgotten that our enemies continue to announce that Germany is to be annihilated and struck out of the ranks of the Great Powers. Against such aims treaties will afford us no protection; for treaties, when the proper moment comes, would once more be trodden under foot. We can look for safety only in a serious economic and military weakening of our enemies sufficient to insure peace for as long a time as can be foreseen.

" 'We must demand a colonial empire adequate to satisfy Germany's manifold economic interests; we must safeguard our future policy in matters of customs and commerce; and we must secure a war indemnity to be paid in a form suitable to our requirements! But our chief aim in the struggle which has been forced upon us is, in our opinion, to strengthen and improve the foundations on which Germany's position in Europe rests, in the following directions:

" 'To provide the necessary security for our influence at sea and to secure our future military and economic position as against England, Belgium, owing to the close connection of Belgian territory (which is economically of such importance) with our main manufacturing districts, must be subjected to German Imperial legislation, in both military and tariff matters and also in regard to currency, banking, and postal arrangements. Her railways and canals must be incorporated in our transport system. In general, the government and administration of the country must be so managed that the inhabitants shall exert no influence on the political fortunes of the German Empire; there must be separation of the Walloon and of the predominantly Flemish territory; and all economic and industrial undertakings and real estate, which are so vital to the government of the country, must be transferred to German hands. We must consider the question of French territory from the same point of view; that is to say, the extent to which it affects our position toward England. Hence we must regard it as a matter of vital importance, in the interests of our future influence at sea, that we should hold the French coastal districts from the Belgian frontier approximately as far as the Somme, and thus secure access to the Atlantic Ocean. The Hinterland, which must be acquired with them, must be so delimited as to secure to us the complete economic and strategic exploitation of those Channel ports which we gain. Any further acquisitions of French territory, apart from the necessary annexation of the iron-ore district of Briey, must be determined solely by military and strategic considerations. After the experiences of this war, it may be regarded as self-evident that we cannot in the future leave our frontiers at the mercy of hostile invasion by allowing our opponents to retain those fortified positions which threaten us, in particular Verdun and Belfort and the Western slopes of the Vosges which lie between them. The acquisition of the line of the Meuse and the French Channel coast would carry with it possession not only of the iron-ore district of Briey mentioned above but also of the coal country in the departments of the Nord and Pas-de-Calais. These annexations also, as is self-evident after our experiences in Alsace-Lorraine, must be so arranged that the population of the annexed districts shall be precluded from exercising political influence on the fortunes of the German Empire; and all the economic resources of these districts, including both large and medium-sized estates, must be transferred to German hands on such terms that France shall compensate and retain their owners. As to the East, the determining consideration must be that the great addition to our manufacturing resources which we anticipate in the West must be counterbalanced by an equivalent annexation of agricultural territory in the East. The present economic structure of Germany has shown itself so fortunate in this war that it is hardly too much to say that every German is convinced of the necessity for maintaining it for as long a time as we can foresee.

" 'The necessity of strengthening the sound agricultural basis of

our economic system, of making possible a German agricultural colonization on a large scale, of restoring the German peasants who are living
abroad—especially those settled in Russia and at present deprived of
their rights—to the territory of the Empire, so that they may take part
in the economic life of Germany, and, lastly, of greatly increasing the
numbers of our population capable of bearing arms implies a considerable extension of the Imperial and Prussian frontiers in the East by
annexation of at least parts of the Baltic Provinces and of those territories which lie to the south of them, while at the same time we must
keep in mind the object of making our eastern German frontier capable
of military defense. The restoration of East Prussia requires a better
safeguarding of its frontiers by placing in front of them other districts;
nor must West Prussia, Posen, and Silesia remain frontier marches
exposed to danger as they now are.

   " 'With regard to the granting of political rights to the inhabitants
of the new districts and the safeguarding of German economic influence,
what has already been said about France applies also. The war indemnity to be paid by Russia will have to consist to a large extent of the
cession of land. Of course these demands depend on the hypothesis
that military results will enable them to be carried out. But in view of
what we have already achieved we confidently rely on our army and its
leaders to gain a victory which will guarantee the attainment of these
ends. We must pursue these ends not from a policy of conquest but
because it is only by attaining them that we can secure that lasting peace
which all classes of German people want in return for their sacrifices.
Moreover, in our opinion, a voluntary surrender of hostile territories,
in which so much German blood has been spilled and so many of our
best and noblest have found a grave, would do violence to the sentiments
of our people and to their conception of an honorable peace. In the
future, as in the past, the want of harbors directly on the Channel
would strangle our activity beyond the seas. An independent Belgium
would continue to be a *tête de pont* to England, a point from which to
attack us. If the natural line of fortifications of France were left in
the hands of the French, there would be a permanent menace to our
frontier; and Russia, if she emerged from the war without loss of
territory, would underestimate our ability and power to prevent her
doing injury to our interests, while, on the other hand, failure to win
new agricultural territories on our eastern frontier would diminish the
possibility of strengthening the defensive power of Germany against
Russia by a sufficient increase of the German population.'

   "We have the honor to draw Your Excellency's attention to the
views expressed above, which are not confined to the undersigned associations but are widely held, possibly with occasional variations in detail,

in many German circles which have not as yet publicly expressed them, and at the same time to inform you that we have simultaneously communicated this petition to the Ministries of the various Federated States.

"As a supplement to this memorandum, we must here lay stress on the fact that the political, military, and economic objects which the German people must strive after in the interests of the security of their future are inseparably connected with one another. It is clear, to start with, that the attainment of our great political objects depends on the offensive power and the successes of our army. But our actual experiences in this war prove, beyond any doubt, that our military successes, particularly in a long war, and their further exploitation depend to a large extent upon the economic strength and ability of our people. If German agriculture had not been in a position to secure the food of the people despite all the efforts of our enemies, and if German manufacturers, German inventive genius, and German technical skill had not been able to render us independent of foreign countries in the most different spheres, then, notwithstanding the brilliant successes of our victorious troops, we should have had to give way eventually in the struggle which has been forced upon us, if indeed we should not have been defeated already.

"Hence it follows that even those demands which seem at first sight to possess a purely economic significance must be viewed in the light of the urgent necessity for the greatest possible increase of our national strength, and also from a military standpoint.

"This applies with special force to the demands set forth in the memorandum both (a) for the acquisition of territory suitable for agricultural settlement and (b) for the appropriation of the iron-ore district of the Meurthe and the Moselle, of the French coaling districts in the Departments of the Nord and Pas-de-Calais, and also of the Belgian coalfields.

"The acquisition of sufficient territory suitable for agricultural settlement is indispensable (a) in order to broaden the agricultural basis of our national resources and thus to maintain that happy balance in our whole economic life which has been recognized as so necessary in the present war, and (b) in order to strengthen our military power by safeguarding the sources of our national strength which depend upon a vigorous agricultural policy and, more especially, by assuring the increase of our population.

"In the same way, acquisitions such as that of the iron-ore and coal districts mentioned above are demanded by our military necessities and not by any means in the interests only of our manufacturing development. This is clear from the following facts and figures:

"The monthly production of pig iron in Germany has risen once more, since August 1914, to nearly 1,000,000 tons; that is, it has nearly doubled. The monthly output of steel has risen to more than 1,000,000 tons. There is, however, no excess of pig iron or steel; on the contrary, there is a deficiency in Germany, and an even greater deficiency in neutral countries. The output of shells calls for both iron and steel, in quantities of which only a few persons originally had any conception. For cast-iron shells alone—the inferior substitute for drawn and cast-steel shells—at least 4,000 tons of pig iron have been used daily during the last few months. The exact figures are not at the moment before us; but this much is certain, that, unless the output of iron and steel had been doubled since the month of August the continuation of the war would have been impossible.

"As a raw material for the production of these quantities of pig iron and steel, minette is being employed more and more, for this ore alone can be obtained in this country in greatly increasing quantities.

"The output of the other iron-ore districts of Germany is very limited, and the overseas imports, even of the Swedish ores, are so difficult to procure that in many places, in addition to Luxemburg and Lorraine, minette at the present time covers 60 to 80 per cent of the output of steel and pig iron. If the output of minette were interrupted, the war would be as good as lost.

"But how do matters stand as regards the supply of minette in this or in the future war?

"If the fortress of Longwy, with the numerous surrounding French blast-furnaces, were given back, then in another war, with a few long-range guns, the following works in Germany and Luxemburg could be ruined in a few hours:

Works	Kilometers from Longwy
Rodingen	7
Differdingen	10
Esch	16–17
Oettingen	21
Rümelingen	21
Düdelingen	25

By this destruction alone it may be estimated that 20 per cent of the German output of pig iron and steel would be lost.

"But a glance at the map shows us further that, e.g., Jarny (the 'Phoenix' minette pits) lies at a distance of 13 to 15 kilometers from Verdun, and that the western mining concessions near Landres and Conflanz are not more than 26 kilometers at most from Verdun. Today we are bombarding Dunkirk from a distance of 38 kilometers. Does anyone believe that the French, in the next war, would neglect to place long-range guns in Longwy and Verdun and would allow us to continue the extraction of ore and the production of pig iron?

"Incidentally it may be remarked that the extensive production of steel from minette offers at the same time the one and only possibility of providing German agriculture with the necessary phosphoric acid for the manufacture of the now excluded phosphates.

"Hence the security of the German Empire in a future war imperatively demands the possession of the whole minette-bearing district of Luxemburg and Lorraine, together with the fortifications of Longwy and Verdun, without which this district cannot be held.

"The possession of larger supplies of coal—and, in particular, of coal rich in bitumen, which is found in great quantities in the basin of northern France—is at least as decisive for the result of this war as the possession of iron ore.

"Belgium and North France together produce over forty million tons.

"Even today, as the British prohibition of coal exports (enacted on May 15) shows us, coal is one of the decisive means of political influence. The neutral manufacturing states must do the bidding of that belligerent which can guarantee a supply of coal. We cannot do this at present to a sufficient degree, and are today already compelled to fall back upon the Belgian coal supply in order not to let our neutral neighbors become entirely dependent upon England.

"It is quite probable that the systematic increase of the Belgian coal output, even during the present war, will prove a weighty factor in the determination of various neighboring states to remain neutral.

"That coal, which produces coke and gas, at the same time supplies the basis of our most important explosives is presumably well known, as is also the importance of coal in the production of ammonia.

"In benzol, moreover, it offers the only substitute for petrol, of which we are short; and, finally, it supplies coal-tar, which yields (a) the oil fuel so indispensable for the navy; (b) anthracite oil, the most serviceable substitute as yet obtainable at home for lubricating oil; and (c) naphthalene, the probable base of synthetic petroleum.

"It may in this connection be remarked that we should probably be unable to develop our destroyer and submarine warfare to the requisite intensity without an abundance of liquid fuel. The course of the war has so clearly proved the superiority of oil fuel over ordinary coal-firing in torpedo-boats that we should be guilty of unpardonable folly if we failed to base our future conduct on this experience. If our hostile neighbors secure the possession of the oil wells, Germany must take care to secure for herself the necessary supplies of gas-producing and bituminous coal and must in time of peace develop these until they constitute inexhaustible sources of oil, benzol, toluol, ammonia, and naphthalene; and that, not merely in order to increase our prosperity in time of peace, but as an indispensable part of our equipment for war.

"To recapitulate: the realization of the war aims, which are proposed above with a view to our permanent economic security, will also guarantee our military strength and consequently our political independence and power; moreover, we shall thus secure an extended field for our economic activity, which will afford and guarantee increased opportunities for work and thus benefit our working classes as a whole."

[Signed by the Associations]

106. BELGIUM'S SPIRITUAL UNITY[9]

Obviously the press, which is closely connected with Pan-German circles, emphasizes intentionally the difference between the Walloons (Belgians of French descent) and the Flemish people (Belgians of German descent). It exaggerates to a certain degree in stating that the Flemish people have been suppressed entirely by the Walloons and that their rights have been restored only recently by the German Government. There did indeed exist an antagonism between the Walloons and the Flemish people, but it was not so great that one could call it an impassable gulf. Impartial observers of Belgium know that right now in the war the whole Belgian people form a stronger unit than ever before. . . . .

107. IMPERIALISM[10]

Although one generally concedes that imperialism is the fundamental cause of the present war, the imperialistic idea is agitating right now for new adherents. Something like an intoxication is sweeping through all bourgeois classes. Even circles which hitherto kept entirely aloof from politics have become very ardent followers of the imperialistic policy. Former opponents of imperialism are now discovering all sorts of good sides to this modern form of economic development— just at the moment when this development in reality shows most clearly its contradictions and evils.

Even in the proletarian ranks rise those who apologize for imperialism and who plead not guilty or at least extenuating circumstances. These apologists are most dangerous when they substantiate their pleading, like the students of modern criminology, by the statement that the

[9] *Vorwärts,* March 27, 1915, p. 3.
[10] *Ibid.,* March 29, 1915, pp. 1–2.

defendant must "necessarily" act that way. The modern criminologist may rightly make that statement, for he proposes also a better method of punishment. The modern apologists for imperialism think they have done their duty by proving the causal law of imperialism necessary. After all, they will let matters develop until something happens and the imperialistic type of economic life is replaced by a different one. Because of the fact that the whole economic life goes through our human consciousness, we need, besides the technical and economic changes, a simultaneous transformation of consciousness in order to overcome imperialism. To prepare and carry it out is the duty of the opposition's policy.

Among the bourgeoisie, however, there is no such policy. Only those who believe in a finished system like the socialistic theory, as a basis of judgment on the present economic and social order and as a means of bringing about a new form of social life, can oppose the imperialistic idea effectively. Mere criticism of the single errors of imperialism is worthless. As long as one acknowledges the capitalistic system, such criticism will necessarily be reactionary. This is clearly proved by a pamphlet (*"Der englische Gedanke in Deutscheland. Zur Abwehr des Imperialisms"*) in which Ernst Müller-Holm attempts to criticize imperialism from a bourgeois point of view. However striking his single arguments against a policy of expansion and colonial policy are, his proposals as a whole are reactionary utopian ideas. . . . .

108. DALLWITZ AGAINST THE "TWOFOLD CIVILIZATION" IN THE IMPERIAL PROVINCES OF ALSACE AND LORRAINE[11]

At a festival in honor of the Second Chamber of the Landtag, Governor von Dallwitz of the Imperial Provinces made an address in which, among other things, he said:

"Quite apart from the actual military events, the war has caused a quick succession of more or less satisfactory occurrences of various kinds within the boundaries of our country. Among the first mentioned I list the easy and orderly progress of the mobilization, even in the districts which are situated on the enemy's boundaries, and especially the voluntary enlistment of so many patriotic and self-sacrificing young men. On the other hand, I regret to have to mention certain preposterous affairs, the nature of which appears from merely mentioning the names of Weill and Wetterle and others. They are an evidence of the confusion which has been created in many heads by the foolish play with the strange and nothing less than grotesque idea of the so-called 'twofold civilization,' which had been so much in vogue before the war,

[11] *Vorwärts,* April 11, 1915, p. 5.

and by the idle talk, which approaches the same character, of the 'mediatory rôle of the borderland.'

"Gentlemen, however many wounds the war may have afflicted on Alsace and Lorraine, however hard the sacrifices and burdens which have been imposed upon them, our country will, as I hope with confidence, derive from this source the permanent benefit of seeing itself purged of the tendencies and efforts which usually are hidden under these vague phrases and loose slogans and of having it generally understood that just the western borderland of the Reich—on account of its geographical situation and its historical past—is called upon and obliged to be a strong and unshakable bulwark of purely German civilization and feeling."

109. THE FIRM THREAT[12]

In a fieldpost letter, published in one of the party newspapers of Germany, we find a polemic against the well-known article of the three comrades, Bernstein, Haase, and Kautsky, which, as is known, is chiefly directed against the different plans of conquest which at present are being professed by many German circles. The Chancellor's organ, too, drew attention to them last Sunday. This letter arouses our interest for three reasons:

(1) Its author, who in the meantime has been called to the colors, is the chief editor of the *Chemnitzer Volksstimme*, the paper that publishes this letter and has become more chauvinistic perhaps than any other party paper in Germany.

(2) What this paper previously so vehemently denied, the famous Manifesto of the Party Directorate, has in the meantime been declared to be the demand of the party, not only that of individual members.

(3) The letter offers the opportunity to call attention to a fundamental error of thought; without any mental reservation we avail ourselves of this opportunity to disclose that error.

In our French reporter's description of the "bad feeling in France," the opinion is being expressed "that the majority of the French people do not long for anything more intensely than the speedy conclusion of this human slaughter." If, however, these wishes for peace do not come to the surface, or if, being expressed by individuals, they do not find an echo among the masses, then the chief responsibility lies with those proclamations that threaten to destroy France's first-class position, to tear asunder her national state organism, and to bleed her white economically. Our *Chemnitz* comrade thinks otherwise. He has in store a regular program of revenge and annexation: "Once all enemy attacks

12 *Arbeiter Zeitung* (Vienna), July 8, 1915, pp. 1–2.

have been repulsed, then our enemies will be made to suffer for having attacked Germany. To grant those bandits a pass so that they can jump at our throat whenever they wish to do so, without running the danger of being held responsible for it, would be not policy but suicidal insanity. Right now we should tell our enemies that their game is lost and that they will have to pay dearly for each day they hesitate longer to throw up the sponge. Only by means of such severe threats shall we be able to hasten the re-establishment of peace which we have begged in vain of our enemy's justice and love for peace."

This Flemish comrade of Chemnitz not only adopts the most extravagant annexationist program but also thinks that proclaiming it loudly and energetically would be the best means of bringing the enemy to reason. The more one threatens them, the more fearful the threats are, the sooner will they give way and sue for peace. In short, the lonely Fleming thinks that the surest, in fact the only, means of instilling the longing for peace in the enemy is the threat of having to pay dearly for it. One need not take these ridiculous speeches of conquest too seriously; however, the question as to what could strengthen the wish for peace in France and what would enliven the desire for war deserves closer examination. For even the most ardent dreamer of conquests will be unable to stem the peace.

The test as to whether or not the restoration of peace has been accelerated by the "strong threat" with a "dear peace" has been actually made. Even before the comrade in the "Flanderic loneliness" had risen to the decision to have the enemy "smart," a similar program of annexation was published in the Reich, and that by people who probably will impress the army more than the Flemish letter-writer. We reported about the latter program in great detail at an earlier date; however, in order to study the effects of these penitence programs we must recall its provisions again. It was in May that a group of large industrial associations—the Agrarian League, German Peasants League, Westphalian Peasant League, Central Union of German Industrialists, the League of Industrialists, and the League of the German Middle Classes—submitted to the Chancellor a petition in which they discussed what, in their opinion, constitutes an "honorable peace, one which would do justice to the sacrifices already made and would contain a guaranty of its durability." They came to the following conclusions:

[The provisions of this petition are given above.]

. . . . It is of great interest to watch how this program has affected France. It reached France via Switzerland and has produced there exactly the opposite effect from the one the Chemnitz correspondent thought it would have. It has not strengthened the wish for peace;

rather it has added new fuel to the receding and dying enthusiasm for war.

The *Berliner Tageblatt* says of it that the Socialist *Humanité* accompanied its publication with an editorial in which it made use of that petition to revive the weary ones and to combat and convert war-weary party members. "No Frenchman and no Socialist remains indifferent in the face of such danger," it declares. And at the same time proof is being looked for in this event for the "préméditation des classes régnantes de l'Allemagne." Significant also is the fact that M. Gabriel Hanotaux, the former Foreign Minister, and Mr. Georges Clemenceau, the former Premier, assert that the Chancellor mentioned the war aims in the petition. This, of course, is a lie; but in the light of the comrade's conception a remarkable lie, for the consent of the Chancellor would assuredly still more increase that fear, whereas the French politicians think that the consent of the leading statesman would only serve to increase the war madness. Thus we see that exactly the reverse is true of what they would like to make us believe. The "firm threats" are not only not likely to advance the desire for peace in France, but rather the effect would be that the war-agitators will continue to have the big word in Paris and that the determination to guard themselves against a "peace" which would strike a mortal blow to their country would only grow all over France.

. . . . With Social-Democratic views such a peace has, of course, nothing in common. But it is too much that they wish to make us believe that thereby the cause of peace is being served. Against that we protest. It remains a fact that the courageous proclamation of the Party Directorate which longs for an honorable peace, which it can obtain only if it considers the vital condition of every nation, came forth from the right understanding of the situation and that it is on the right road to the goal. And this goal, irrespective of the braggings audible from abroad, is and remains the aim and hope of all European peoples.

110. VOICES FOR AND AGAINST A POLICY OF ANNEXATION
JULY 11, 1915[13]

No. 63 P.-A.   BERLIN, July 11, 1915
Strictly confidential

PRINCE HOHENLOHE TO BARON BURIAN

The Vienna *Arbeiterzeitung* of July 8 publishes under the title, "The Firm Threat," a large part of a memorandum submitted on May 20 of

---

[13] Collection of Austrian Documents, Hoover War Library.

this year to the Imperial Chancellor by the Agrarian League, the German Peasants League, the Westphalian Peasant Union, the Central Union of Industrialists, the League of Industrialists, and the German Middle-Class Union.

The extract published in the *Arbeiterzeitung* agrees verbally with the text of the memorandum which you know and represents one of the innumerable programs of annexation which are being eagerly discussed all over Germany. At the same time this program of the organizations mentioned above is by no means the most extravagant; for there are people who, besides the territories named for annexation in this program, mention also the entire Baltic provinces, Gibraltar, and Suez; and, as I was told yesterday by a gentleman who had just returned from a similar meeting, even parts of South America are being designated as objects for annexation.

These meetings, in which ground was prepared for the most exorbitant policy of annexation, have increased particularly in the last weeks, owing undoubtedly to the effect of our military successes. The press of all party shades, too, occupied itself with the discussion of war aims, and one must acknowledge that in spite of the repeated assurances of the Government that the moment had not yet come to formulate precisely the war aims, voices nevertheless reached the public uninterruptedly, and those which demanded far-reaching plans of annexation were much more numerous than those opposed to such a policy.

This is the more remarkable as I know very well from my discussions with the Chancellor and the Secretary of State that these officials are averse to these plans of annexation. If, nevertheless, they have failed to adopt more drastic measures against these excesses, it is probably due to their hope that these unofficial voices, expressing as they do complete confidence in Germany's victory and their far-reaching expectations, will not fail to produce a certain effect upon the enemy countries.

It is doubtful if the competent authorities by such a procedure will reach the expected result. Rather must it incite the enemies to the utmost resistance.

Naturally, there are also voices which express themselves decisively against every policy of annexation and condemn these annexationist views most energetically.

At the head of the anti-annexationists is Prince Hatzfeldt-Trachenberg, who, surrounded by a staff of liberal politicians and journalists, exerts every effort to impress upon the Government the damages of such a policy of annexation. The Prince tells me that a memorandum is being prepared to be submitted to the Chancellor, signed by himself and his friends, among whom are great scholars, like Professors Harnack, Kahl, Dernburg, and others. This memorandum is to prove that great and influential circles of Germans emphatically reject all these annexationist fantasies.

The Prince, too, was responsible for the so-called "Belgian Conferences" which recently took place in the building of the Prussian Abgeordnetenhaus, at which meetings a decisive attitude was adopted against annexations in general and that of Belgium in particular. Resolutions to that effect were handed to the Chancellor.

It is significant that this entire group thereby considered it unnecessary to obtain in advance the Chancellor's approval, which would seem to be the first requisite; rather it turned to Field Marshal Hindenburg for the approval of its views, on the supposition that the public will have more confidence in this national hero than in the Chancellor.

Accordingly Prince Hatzfeldt addressed a letter to von Hindenburg in which he explains his and his friends' opposition to every policy of annexation, in that they regarded the war as one of preservation only and not of conquest. Von Hindenburg replied that those were exactly his views too.

In order to advise the Field Marshal politically and also in order to influence him in the desired direction, this group, to which belong also Count Monts and the one-time German Ambassador in London, Count Metternich, sent Prince Hatzfeldt a number of times to Eastern Headquarters.

I doubt, however, whether Field Marshal Hindenburg, although a national hero, will ever play a political rôle; for one thing, since he hardly will have the ambition to do so, and, for another, since, even if he had the ambition, the antagonism which prevails between him and Great Headquarters would possibly make such a move impossible. The most recent visit of the Kaiser to Hindenburg in Posen has not altered the situation in the least.

As was said, the Government does not express itself officially about war aims and states that it would be best if these two conflicting views were to balance each other, so that neither one of them will become too strong at the moment. It thinks that the day has not yet arrived for the Government to come forward with a well-defined peace program.

Much, undoubtedly, can be said in favor of such an attitude; however, on the other side arises the question how the desired clarification of the situation is to be obtained which will make it possible for the Government to disclose its views.

Herr von Jagow told me recently when we spoke about similar affairs that for the time being all that matter are the military accomplishments and that only later on will it be possible to think about the basis of peace. To this I answered that, after all, sooner or later one must make a decision as to the things one is aiming at in order to make them known to the military leaders for their realization, but that, once this decision has been reached in a general way, it will be possible to sketch the general outlines of the peace conditions.

This, however, makes as little impression upon the Secretary of State as upon the other responsible authorities, because—and possibly not without reason—not one of them dares to fix such a plan, even in gross contour. Of course, to do that it would be necessary to know for sure the internal conditions and sentiment of our enemies. This, however, we know not at all as regards Russia and only to a limited extent in general.

It is therefore left to the military authorities to decide in each case what is to take place. Accordingly the final aims of the whole struggle change kaleidoscopically according to the military situation on the different fronts.

Yet in the long run it is impossible to continue the war for the sake of the war; and in the end the Foreign Office will have to come out of its reserve and take an attitude toward the whole complex of the war-aims question, among which the decision about Belgium is undoubtedly the most knotty. Not only Germany's interests but also those of her allies will sooner or later make it imperative for the German Government to make a decision.

111. PROCLAMATION OF KAISER WILHELM II
AUGUST 1, 1915[14]

To the German People

A year has passed since I had to call the German people to arms. A period more sanguinary than any hitherto has come over Europe and the world. My conscience is pure before God and history: I have not willed the war. After a decade of preparation, the union of powers, for whom Germany had become too strong, thought that the moment had come to humiliate the Reich, which loyally stands by its ally Austria-Hungary in its just cause, or to crush it in an all-powerful ring.

It was not lust for conquest that drove us into the war, a fact which I proclaimed a year ago. When in those days of August all men fit for military service rushed to the colors and the troops marched to the struggle of defense, following the example set by the unanimous vote of the Reichstag, every German on the earth felt that he had to fight for the supreme good of the nation, for life and liberty. What we had to expect if a foreign power had succeeded in determining the fate of our people and of Europe the afflictions of my loved province of East

[14] *Norddeutsche Allgemeine Zeitung*, August 1, 1915, II, 1.

Prussia have proved. The consciousness of the struggle forced upon us has brought about the miracle—political conflicts subsided and former enemies began to understand and to appreciate each other. All fellow-men were imbued with the spirit of loyal comradeship.

Full of thanks, we may say today: God has been with us. The hostile armies which boastfully promised to march into Berlin in a few months have been driven far back to the West and East with mighty blows. Numerous battlefields in various parts of Europe, sea struggles remote and near, testify what German wrath and German military science are able to do in self-defense. No violation of international laws by our enemies could shake the economic foundation of our warfare. State and community, agriculture, industry and commerce, science and technique vie with one another to soften the calamities of war. Full of understanding for the necessity of interference in free commerce, entirely devoted to the care of our brothers afield, the population at home did its utmost to ward off the common danger.

With deep gratitude the Fatherland thinks today and forever of its soldiers, of those who face the enemy undaunted by death, of those who return wounded or ill, of those in particular who rest in foreign soil or at the bottom of the sea, weary of the struggle. Like the mothers and the fathers, the widows and the orphans, I mourn for the beloved ones who have died for the Fatherland.

Internal strength and unified national will in the spirit of the creators of the Reich warrant a victory. The dikes, which they have built, anticipating that we should some day have to defend what we won in 1870, have braved the greatest flood of world history. After these unparalleled proofs of personal ability and national vigor, I entertain the cheerful confidence that the German people, sustaining the chastenings of the war, will vigorously march forward upon the well-tried, old path and the new course of civilization we have confidently embarked upon.

Great trial inspires us with awe and courage. We shall persevere without hesitation in our heroic deeds and hardships until peace comes, a peace which affords for us the future necessary military, political, and economic securities and fulfils the conditions for the unhindered development of our activities at home and on the free sea.

Thus we shall endure with honor the great struggle for Germany's right and liberty, however long it may last, and be worthy of our victory unto God, whom we pray to bless our arms as before.

WILHELM I. R.

GREAT HEADQUARTERS, July 31, 1915

112. DECLARATION OF THE NATIONAL-LIBERAL CENTRAL COMMITTEE ON AUGUST 15, 1915[15]

The Central Committee of the National-Liberal Party declares in agreement with the proceedings of the Directing Board and the State Chairmen on May 16 that the war can end only in a peace securing us militarily, politically, and economically against a new attack. This is to be done by extending our boundaries in the East and West and in our colonies, thus justifying the sacrifices which the German people have made so far and have decided to continue making until victory is achieved.

The Central Committee heartily and unanimously thanks its chairman, Deputy Bassermann, for his efforts—supported by the confidence of the whole party—to put through these national war aims.

The Central Committee will back unanimously every Government which pursues this aim with unyielding firmness.

113. AN EXPLANATION OF THE PROGRESSIVE PEOPLE'S PARTY[16]

The Reichstag "Fraktion" of the Progressive People's Party has occupied itself in a searching declaration with the problems which confront the Reichstag in the course of the current and most important events. It has carefully examined the existing demands as to future boundaries, raised in consideration of the aim of the war, and after a conscientious study it has reached the conclusion that the time has not yet come for the formulation of a definite program with comprehensive demands as to the ending of the war. The party is as much opposed to a fundamental rejection of territorial conquests as it is to boundless annexation plans, but it holds it to be imperative that by means of military and economic measures and by a necessary enlargement of territory conditions be created for the peaceful competition of nations which will secure the development of German national energies and the German nation at home as well as upon the free sea. The unanimous expectation was expressed that the Reich Government would at the proper moment and with the confidential co-operation of the Reichstag bring about an open discussion of the basis of peace. The "Fraktion" also stated the firm conviction that nation, army, and navy, being aware of the historical importance of these great struggles, will

[15] *Vossische Zeitung,* August 16, 1915, II, 2.
[16] *Deutsche Tageszeitung,* August 18, 1915, p. 3.

hold together unswervingly and will exert every ounce of power to obtain an honorable and enduring peace. The party is ready to support the Government, which, according to the words of the Kaiser of July 31, 1915, makes it its task to advance steadily along old and well-proved roads.

114. THE FIGHT OVER WAR AIMS[17]

The recent controversy between the *Norddeutsche Allgemeine Zeitung* and the press of the Right has, contrary to the Chancellor's intentions, deepened the animosity and irritation of the opponents of the Chancellor. Since an open discussion of the essential differences has been prevented, the discussion has been carried on for the most part in a manner which will surely make an impression equally strange at home and abroad. In reality, the Chancellor's point of view is not very different from that of his bourgeois opponents. But in spite of all that, it is easily understood that the controversy has been carried on in quite an irritated manner; for nothing arouses such profound ill feeling as the variety of external conditions under which the controversy is being conducted.

The attempt has been made to justify the suppression of discussion of war aims out of consideration for foreign countries. But there is certainly no one who denies that the present controversies in Germany must give to foreign countries a much falser and thus more dangerous picture than would be the case if the discussion were not restricted at all. . . . .

115. THE ENTENTE'S CAPACITY TO PAY[18]

In the Committee of Commerce and Industry of the Reichstag were considered petitions of the industrial associations of Württemberg and Saxony, requesting the Government to ascertain at the peace negotiations the demands against the enemy countries as well as the debts to those countries and to settle accounts with them. The petitions were handed over to the Government for consideration. Other measures demanded but in regard to which it was left undetermined whether the Government or the Chambers of Commerce should decide were also submitted to the Government for consideration.

[17] *Vorwärts,* July 14, 1916, p. 1.
[18] *Ibid.,* August 21, 1916, p. 3.

116. THE SOCIALIST PRINCIPLES FOR THE CONCLUSION OF PEACE, AUGUST 16, 1915[19]

The Reichstag "Fraktion" and the Party Committee considered the question of war aims in a joint session on August 14, 15, and 16. The conference was opened with reports from Comrades David and Bernstein. The two *rapporteurs* submitted leading points which were to form the basis of the discussion. The two bodies voted separately on the following questions of peace:

For the protection of the national interests and rights of our own people and in consideration of the vital interests of all nations, the German Social-Democratic Party endeavors to establish a peace which will guarantee a lasting peace leading the European nations to a closer legal, economic, and cultural association. Accordingly, we lay down the following principles for the conclusion of peace:

1. The maintenance of the political independence and integrity of the German Reich requires us to reject all demands of our enemies which aim at the encroachment of its territorial rights. This refers also to the demands for re-annexation by France of Alsace-Lorraine, no matter how it is done.

2. In order to secure the free economic development of the German people, we demand:

the "open door," that is, equal rights for economic activity in all colonial territories;

the insertion of the most-favored-nation clause in the peace treaties of all belligerent powers;

the promotion of economic co-operation by removing customs and traffic barriers as far as possible;

the equalization and improvement of social-political institutions in the meaning of the Internationale;

the freedom of the seas guaranteed by international treaties. For this reason, prisage is to be abolished, and the straits of importance to international traffic are to be internationalized.

3. In the interest of Germany and the economic development in the Southeast, we reject all the war aims of the Allies pointing to the weakening and destruction of Austria-Hungary and of Turkey.

4. Remembering that the annexation of territories with foreign populations is against the right of self-determination and that, besides, the internal unity and strength of the German national state is only thus weakened and its political relations to the foreign countries greatly

[19] *Vorwärts*, August 24, 1915, p. 5.

prejudiced, we oppose the shortsighted politicians' plans of conquest which have this aim.

5. The terrible misery and destruction which this war has afflicted on mankind have won over the hearts of millions to the ideal of a world peace, which will be secured permanently by institutions of international law. To strive for this aim must be regarded as the supreme moral duty of all those who are called upon to co-operate for the conclusion of peace. We demand, therefore, that a permanent International Court of Arbitration be established. All future conflicts between nations must be submitted to it.

We feel obliged to let our readers know that for well-known reasons we are not permitted to publish the full contents of the peace program of our party leaders.

THE EDITORS OF "VORWÄRTS"

117. WAR AIMS AND "INDEPENDENT PATRIOTIC ASSOCIATION"[20]

[Reply of Professor Dr. Wilhelm Kahl, Chairman of the Independent Patriotic Association, to an attack of the National-Liberal *Westfälische Politische Nachrichten* of August 10 in regard to Kahl's attitude on the question of war aims. He writes:]

". . . . I am taken to task in a somewhat surprising manner because I am one of the signers of a memorial to the Chancellor which does not suit the author. As was to be expected, I reject this meddling with my own decisions. I was able to sign the memorial which is objected to by the author because it only tends to bring about a peace 'which offers a firm foundation for the strategic needs, the political and economic interests of the country, and the unrestrained exercise of its initiative at home and on the free sea.'

"Everything else is a question of degree and depends particularly on circumstances which so far cannot be surveyed. Therefore the resolution of August 15, 1915, of the Central Committee of the National-Liberal Party corresponds literally to this mode of expression. Assuming erroneously that I took part in this resolution, I am asked today for an explanation as to whether it means objection to or agreement with the memorial. If, however, I have fundamental misgivings with respect to the annexation of states which up to the present time have been politically and historically independent—for this alone is in question and not the extension of territory for military, political, and economic security, which everyone desires—then these scruples are based

[20] *Tägliche Rundschau*, August 25, 1915, I, 1–2.

upon cool, deliberate, and nationalistic considerations and principles of international and constitutional law, and not upon sentimental weakness or an attitude 'which would result in robbing the German people of the fruit of their victory.'

"Influenced by Bismarck's school, not only by his writings but also by personal intercourse with him, I have learned to appreciate the German national state and also the great principle that no decision of international importance shall be taken which renders impossible the political and cultural reconciliation of its people. I esteem every dissenting opinion and would be afraid of judging its worth from a moral point of view; that would be tantamount to accusing it of lack of understanding for the happiness and the security of our Fatherland. But I demand the same for myself. It is a blot on our present age that there are Germans who do not shrink from attacking publicly a fellow-citizen who advocates a different and perhaps moderate opinion about the peace conditions by calling him boldly and arbitrarily an underminer of public will, a sentimental dreamer, and goodness knows what else. There is no appreciation for our having reached in the course of the war a position where we can speak about the conditions of peace which we hope to impose upon our enemies. On the contrary, the controversy among the citizens is fanned by base imputations and personal defamations. I protest against this on behalf of myself and many others. . . . ."

118. WAR AIMS OF THE GERMAN CONSERVATIVE PARTY[21]

The Inner Committee of the German Conservative Party met recently in Berlin for a discussion of the general political situation.

The unparalleled achievements of our army and navy, the brave co-operation of our allies, and our favorable military situation on all fronts were mentioned with most grateful recognition and ardent thankfulness. The hope was also expressed that the marvelous success of our arms might finally break the gigantic power of the Russian enemy and permanently guarantee the national security of the German people in the East.

The Inner Committee of the Conservative Party feels at the same time conscious that of all the great tasks which the World War has created for the German people that which we have considered most important has first to be taken into consideration, namely, the DEFEAT OF ENGLAND, WHO HAS BROUGHT ABOUT THE WAR AND WHO WILL NEVER CEASE TO THREATEN AND INJURE OUR POSITION IN THE WORLD AND OUR FUTURE DEVELOPMENT.

[21] *Deutsche Tageszeitung,* September 28, 1915, p. 1.

The Inner Committee feels that it is at one with the whole Conservative Party and the whole German people in refusing to shrink from any further sacrifice necessary to carry on the war until a permanent, honorable peace which secures the foundation of the German future is achieved. The Committee will, of course, support all annexations necessary for this purpose.

119. WAR POLICY IN THE REICHSTAG[22]

On Wednesday took place the "great" session which was supposed to bring a settlement of the internal differences of opinion as to various problems of the war, i.e., the conduct of the war, and other problems which must not be discussed in the press. And it can be said that here an almost complete agreement was reached. . . . .

However, those who might have expected from this session, in which the Chancellor requested the floor again for a Government speech, an acceleration of the coming of peace or at least the prospect of provisional peace negotiations were deeply disappointed. In the Wednesday session there was no question of any perceptible prospect of an international reconciliation apart from a few expressions of pacific desire on the part of the speaker of the Social-Democratic majority. These, however, by their formulation and their underlying principles showed so little understanding of the only possible way toward international reconciliation that they fall considerably short of Scheidemann's statement which he thought necessary to set forth four months ago in describing the motives of a Social-Democratic peace interpellation at that time. The effect of these Social-Democratic statements on the proletarian masses at home and abroad will naturally reflect this, but of course it will not tend to dampen the war passion. . . . .

The German Chancellor thus declared that a peace based on the *status quo* will be out of the question for Germany, and that the victorious Central Powers must stipulate conditions which provide for a material strengthening of the German position and, of course, a corresponding weakening of the enemy's position.

That his attitude was approved by the bourgeois parties goes without saying. But it struck us as strange that he did not arouse by his disclosures, the completeness of which can scarcely be surpassed, any kind of serious opposition from the speaker of the Social-Democratic majority! For though Comrade Ebert, who asked for the floor on behalf of the majority, protested against the annexationistic statements of the speaker of the Center Party, Spahn, he had to be persuaded by a shout from Liebknecht to state some reservations to the Chancellor's state-

[22] *Vorwärts,* April 6, 1916, p. 1.

ments. Reservation—not even criticism! For Ebert passed by the
Chancellor's explanations, which at this time had but one meaning and
which were free from any far-fetched interpretation, with the extenuating remark that von Bethmann-Hollweg's statements certainly should
be taken with his former pronouncements that Germany will not sub-
jugate any foreign nation, a statement to which we have given our
adequate comment above. . . . .

The French, English, and Russian Government delegates have certainly made haughty and foolish speeches which could not promote any
peaceful reconciliation. It is a source of the greatest pleasure to us that
there has arisen in England and France a strong opposition, especially
of the proletariat, against the unreasonable and criminal plans of destruction; or at least against high-sounding phrases of such plans. But
it must affect these bourgeois and proletarian elements of the sensible
opposition like a shower of cold water, when they read, after Herr v.
Bethmann-Hollweg's address, the statements of the Social-Democrat
Ebert. These statements ring with self-satisfaction to a degree really
not to be expected from the speaker of a state which before the war was
the leading Socialist country!

And, in addition, all countries will be convinced of the fact that
this is the limit of the present Government's wisdom and of their policy
of diplomacy, and that the people themselves must take in hand their
own future in order to save at least some fragments of the former
European civilization.

120. STRESEMANN'S SPEECH IN THE REICHSTAG
ON FOREIGN AFFAIRS[23]

Dr. Stresemann: With a feeling of justified satisfaction the Chancellor yesterday characterized the military-political situation, and he was
the interpreter of all our sentiments when he said that there were not
words enough to express that feeling of gratitude which we have toward
the deeds of our armies. From the platform we have repeatedly sent
our greetings to our troops on land, on sea, and in the air. . . . . Gentlemen, we are fighting this war in all corners of the earth and what our
armies have performed in the twenty months of war can worthily be
compared with what we had been taught in history about the Greeks
and the Romans. We should like to express the wish that in the future
in all of Germany's schools more will be done to inform our youth concerning von Moltke and Hindenburg than concerning Caesar and Alexander [*lively approval*], so that what a nation has done in a struggle

[23] *Verhandlungen des Reichstags*, No. 40, April 6, 1916, pp. 866–70.

for existence both at and behind the front may be held before their eyes. ["*Bravo!*"] Mentioning the name of Hindenburg, permit me to express this: when Field Marshal von Hindenburg tomorrow celebrates his fiftieth military jubilee, the entire German nation comes to him with congratulations and is animated with only one sentiment—that a benevolent destiny may long preserve for us this man with all his geniality and creative powers, this man who liberated East Prussia. [*Lively "Bravo!"*]

Gentlemen, the Chancellor has also justifiably emphasized that what is being done economically behind the front also cannot be overestimated. We all know that those who are well off today must forego many things, but suffer as yet no wants. We know, and appreciate the more, what the sacrifices mean to our middle class, our laborers, employees, and officials. Economically we have become almost an isolated state. It would be foolish to try to deny it, since our entire legislation evidences it. We see it in the reduction of bread consumption and of meat consumption, and in the restriction of raw materials. We see it in industry, which has to place so many restrictions upon itself that it has come to a partial shut-down. Now the Paris Conference has decided to further sharpen this "strangling of Germany," as they call it. That compels us on our part, too, to use all means at our disposal to their full extent in order to safeguard Germany's peace and future. Among these means we have a sharp weapon to curb English insolence, a means to strike at the root of English political economy; and we demand that everything be done to reach that goal. Gentlemen, when the Main Committee of this House, in complete approval and agreement with our conception, has decided that the justified interests of neutrals must be observed, we hold that as self-evident. The justified interests of neutrals our Government so far has observed to the minutest degree. Never has any neutral state been able to complain that Germany has attempted to interfere with its vital interests. And never will that happen in the future. But what we wish on our part is that unjustified demands of neutrals be rejected. ["*Quite right!*"] I agree with what my colleague von Payer said about the United States of America, which has interpreted the concept of neutrality in a way that is irreconcilable with the German conception of the essence of neutrality. ["*Quite right!*"] For example, we cannot regard as justified the demand to make pleasure trips in the war area on armed ships. The Government will have our complete support in the justified effort to let the neutrals feel as little as possible the difficulties of the resulting situation and the protection of legitimate neutral interests. But we also hope that each unjustified demand will be opposed.

The chief thought that at times actuated us in making proposals about the U-boat question in this House has been expressed in the decision of the Main Committee which has been accepted by a great majority. We further hope that it is in the meaning of this decision that the method we once advocated will insure the future of our Fatherland which we all hope for. That enabled us to vote for the decision submitted.

Having previously often admitted that the blockade of our enemies has placed us in a difficult economic position, I wish also to emphasize, on the other side, that there is probably no one among us who assumes that thereby Germany will ever be brought to surrender. We heard the sharp words of criticism of the Honorable von Payer about certain occurrences in our economic organization. We do not deny those criticisms. We, too, see many things that should be criticized. But one thing we must not forget: we deputies often stand too close to things; we see the mistakes and the folds of the new dress.

If once the history of this war is written, the manner in which we succeeded in safeguarding the reorganization and preservation of the economic strength of the Reich in the face of this strangulation will be hailed as a great achievement of German organization and German science. [*"Quite right!"—National-Liberals.*] In all our justifiable criticism we must not forget that.

Our honorable colleague Ebert yesterday gave expression to the wish for peace which is present in Germany and other countries. He added that in the face of our military and political situation no one could misconstrue such a desire as a sign of weakness. I am firmly convinced that the words of Herr Ebert are far from being misconstrued among the German peoples, that they cannot be misinterpreted, and that they were prompted by a high patriotic sentiment. Whether or not that is the case abroad I refrain from saying. However, we cannot change the fact that the sentiments which we express are being ascribed to wrong motives. In expressions of such peace desires I see no signs of weakness. The desire for peace that exists in the world is certainly adequate to the height of the nations' cultures. So much is being destroyed in this war that the question should be raised whether or not it is right that the greatest efforts of the human brain should be solely devoted to destruction.

We also hear warning voices of a "certain Europeanism" which put before us the Europe-America problem, i.e., what shall be the relation between the two continents after the war. If we take no account of all that the enemies have done to us, and if we once more visualize the concept of the whole of Europe, then we must recognize this at least: after this war, Europe will be a convulsive and bleeding body. Opposed to it stands America, not only unweakened, but greatly strengthened, for which Goethe's words, "America, you are better off than our continent, the old one!" have never been more appropriate than now. Each new month brings new records of American exploitation of the present war condition. Among the German people there prevails a great agitation about this conception of American neutrality which is symbolized so clearly in material desires. There is a blending of humanitarian ideals with repugnant hypocrisy, a mixture of election interests and the fate of nations. ["*Quite right!*"] Von Payer very rightly said that among the German people were strong sympathies for the young, rising nation on the other side of the ocean. And our present a   ion is not directed against the American people but toward that one-.   conception of neutrality, that exploitation of a certain war junc.   which is so shamelessly—one is almost tempted to say licentiously—evident in all the business desires of certain American circles.

We can indemnify and rebuild destroyed provinces in Europe, but the lost intelligence of hundreds of thousands who in the future probably would have been our collaborators in new great ideals, on great new works of culture, science, and technique, we cannot claim back. Therefore, we fully honor the ethical character of the peace desires expressed yesterday by Herr Ebert. However ethically founded those sentiments may be, they must endure the strong realities of the life of nations. The International, the union of nations in the intellectual field —I am not speaking of the political International—I think, has been shipwrecked in both the narrower and the broader sense. It will not easily recover, and an understanding among the nations in the future will be equally difficult to restore. If a nation, like the German, that has contributed so much to civilization, is now being branded as Hun and Barbarian, it will not be easy to build the bridge to those who now call us by those names. I would regret it if all these ties were to be cut, but now I wish to emphasize this: if any one nation can stand intellectual isolation, it is the German nation. For this German nation has given the world much more than the world has given back to it in cultural things. ["*Quite right!*"] I believe, therefore, that we should not thrust ourselves into the coming understanding among nations but should let the rest look somewhat to us and realize what they will miss if they break association with German culture.

The peace desire itself, according to the conception of my friends, must be circumscribed by the principle of achieving the freedom of our country and the security of our future. The experiences of the war have convinced us that the security of our future is assured only by Germany's strengthening in the East and the West. In complete agreement with the Chancellor, we too see in an unassailable Germany the best peace guaranty for Europe and the world. I know that there are

other views—views which go out from the primary point—that peace
is best secured by rejection of world-political expansion, by means of
understanding and accommodation to other people. Such a view before
this war I should have regarded as debatable, but not after the experiences of the present war.

For have we not for decades pursued a policy of world-political
resignation for the sake of peace? When have we actually expressed
a desire for world-political expansion? When have we taken advantage
of the difficulties of other people in order to increase Germany? When
Russia was engaged in a life-and-death struggle with Japan, the Tsar
could remove the last regiment from the East-Prussian border because
he was sure of Germany's peace desires. When England fought a war
for existence, or at least for its prestige, with the Boers, were we the
ones to capitalize its embarrassment? We did not recognize Morocco as
a reason for war; we have looked on while all North Africa was being
divided; in recent decades we saw the growth of a great French colonial
Empire—Tunis, Algeria, Morocco—we saw how Italy took Tripoli; we
saw how Russia and England divided Persia into spheres of interest.
Always we kept peace; the world could always depend upon the Kaiser's
and the German nation's love of peace.

Where is the gratitude for all of this? The thanks are a world of
enemies, hatred and passionate aversion toward Germany, partly even
among neutrals.

If one thus awakes from a beautiful dream, one dare not dream it
again. [*"Quite right!"*] At least in the future one dare not believe
that the forgoing of world position, accommodation, and understanding
are guaranties of lasting peace. [*Lively approval!*] No, gentlemen,
above this war against us stand the words: *"Propter invidiam."* They
begrudged us the Reich and its economic development. They loved us
and were friendly to us, and we had sympathies in the world, as long
as we were politically impotent, as long as we were a nation of poets and
thinkers. When "Michael the Dreamer" became "Michael the Sea-
farer," when the political unification and the development of our economic strength came, when Hamburg and Bremen became what they
are, when the Rhineland-Westphalia region developed the great foundation of its economic strength, when we created the seaports for the
German world trade that insured Germany's economic position in the
world, then began the economic struggle even before the clash of arms
came. England's whole history shows this struggle against us. The
English patent law shows it, for it is more than a protective duty: it is a
prohibitive duty. The struggle is further shown by the law about navigation subsidy and the "Imperial preference." I still think of the words
which the director of one of our greatest shipping companies once

expressed in a speech before the war. He said that nothing showed so much the turn of events as the action of England, which for a century had been the strongest pillar of free trade and free competition, in using its taxes for subsidizing strong shipping companies, only in order to have the glory of claiming the fastest ship in the world as its own, only to regain the blue ribbon of the sea. Therein was evidenced her first uneasiness about Germany's growing economic strength. It is that which fanned the war and which the enemies fight for. They wish not only to destroy Prussian militarism but also to tear down Germany's entire economic strength, and thereby—as Herr Ebert justly emphasized —they strike at the root of the life interests of the German laboring class.

Gentlemen, because that is true, because we believe that we have learned that lesson from past history, we see the guaranty of a lasting peace only in a strong, unassailable position for Germany. Therefore, we thank the Chancellor for what he said yesterday about the safeguards in the East and the West. The Chancellor indicated that we would not oppress any nationalities but also we would not suffer that racial stocks be further oppressed by other nations. In this connection he spoke about the Baltic Germans. Gentlemen, I regard the Baltic provinces as German-Baltic country, as a land of German culture. It may be shown that the Baltic Germans are outnumbered by the Esthonians and the Latvians. If you accept pure numbers, then that may be true; but not alone the numerical strength determines the character of a country. Rather it is determined by that racial stock which has given the imprint of its culture and intellect to the entire country [lively approval]—our Baltic Germans. They have retained this German character in Libau, in Mitau, in Riga, in Dorpat, and in the entire country, in spite of the fact that the Tsar broke his word and abolished their constitutional institutions. It is often not sufficiently realized among the German people what a wealth of German intellectual life existed in past centuries and still exists in the Baltic provinces, how the intellectual life reacted back upon our own. It is often not realized how many professors at Germany's higher institutions of learning received their training at Dorpat, where the second German fraternity was founded. There they feel and think German. If we give up the Baltic, then the last trace of Baltic freedom and independence would be obliterated under a process of Russification which would set in in a manner that would make us greatly responsible to those who under continued oppression kept true to Germany. [Lively approval.]

Gentlemen, the Chancellor further spoke about the bonds which unite us and the Flemish people in the fact that they too are a Teutonic branch. Previously I had to report here about a petition of the Young-

Flanders organization which gave expression to the same thought that the Chancellor expressed here yesterday, namely, that Flanders shall in the future live its own life and that it will not be subjected to a further process of Belgification. These, therefore, are not wishes suggested by us; they are sentiments which exist in Flanders itself, as we also have been told by colleagues who have had the opportunity to work there.

We are agreed that the program of the Chancellor shall be carried out as announced. However, we must supplement it in one respect, namely, that besides the cultural interests, besides the racial connections which compel our consideration, the Belgian question still contains great political problems. If we wish Belgium again to become a glacis for our enemies, then not only must the *status quo ante* be excluded but German military, political, and economic supremacy must be safeguarded. [*"Quite right!"*] We must demand this the more—and in that we hope to be in agreement with the Chancellor—since on previous occasions he declared the achieving of the freedom of the seas to be Germany's war aim.

Here, too, the experiences of this war must be taken into serious consideration. We have seen how in this World War declarations of international law have been violated and broken like threads. If today the freedom of the seas be guaranteed to us by international agreements, their freedom would not be safeguarded. [*"Quite right!"*] We have the freedom of the seas during peace time; that has never been protested. The freedom of the seas first becomes practical when the nations start fighting each other. And if in such a contingency it is guaranteed only by international agreements, that is no security. Was Greece secure from shameless demands of the Entente? Do we not see that other neutral states constantly appeal to agreements and their rights if they are being violated? And never of any avail? No, gentlemen, the freedom of the seas which we need for our world-economic position, which we need in order to be able to breathe, can be insured only by Germany's might on the sea. It can be safeguarded only if we have access to the sea. It further can be secured only by our having naval bases in the wide world to protect our navy in case of danger. Our navy should never again be confronted with the unhappy situation with which our cruisers met at the beginning of the war—they had to sink, since there was no other honorable course.

These are war aims which have nothing to do with an oppression of other nations, which take complete cognizance of the life of other nations, but which finally also have as their basis Germany's interests, and which want to safeguard its future following the innumerable sacrifices made by its people.

Gentlemen, on the other side also things demand an agreement as to an economic war aim. I see such an aim in the safeguarding of the freedom and participation of Germany's creative forces. We have been the champions of this freedom, which the enemies have shamelessly suppressed in this war. I wish merely to indicate how systematically England went about to suppress German property. It will forever be a blemish upon the record of English business that England not only demanded the liquidation of German enterprises in foreign lands but also demanded that the books which gave the results of this liquidation be burned, in order not to have to give the unfortunate loser a receipt as to what he had possessed.

We were not the ones who started the war against the civilian population and the struggle against economic enterprises. It was England which placed civilian populations in concentration camps; it was Russia which directed its legislation against German property in Russia. Mr. Goremykin said literally: "We fight the war against not only the German Empire but against everything German." The Portuguese theft of ships is booked not to the Lisbon account but to that of London. [*"Quite right!"*] That is only a link in the chain of this plan to destroy what German enterprise built up during the last few decades. [*"Quite right!"*]

What have we done in the face of such acts? Our legislation did not suffer itself to be provoked but only followed step by step the enemy procedure. That holds in respect to civilian population as well as to economic undertakings. The German custodians who have been assigned to administer foreign property administer it like their own property. They are faithful men, who protect the interests of the English and French firms as if they were German governmental officials placed in German firms. Once upon a time honesty and faith in international intercourse were more important than all written law. When England destroys such a conception, then Germany too must give up its passivity. [*"Quite right!"*]

We demand that our government protect German property in enemy countries. We agree and are glad that the Chancellor announced yesterday that he will protect German property in Russia. We hope that he will use all the forces of Germany to protect German property everywhere. We are not helped by being told that legal remedies will be restored after the war. No, gentlemen, before the war the German business man seldom sought his right before foreign courts. The foreigner knew that in German courts his right was just as much protected as that of the native. The German in foreign countries, if he could not come to an agreement with his debtors, would rather erase the whole account than go into a foreign court. [*"Quite right!"*] And now when billions of German property are in danger, we are being told that the Foreign Office will resort to all legal remedies; that means giving German industry and business stones instead of bread. [*"Quite right!"*] We know how the people's passions have been fanned, how the destruction of German property is being considered abroad as almost a patriotic duty. How then shall we believe that we shall again have the properties which have been invested abroad out of confidence in the German Government if the German Reich does not assume their protection to the same extent as that the Chancellor promised to the property of the Germans who are subjects of enemy countries? Since we are speaking of Germans abroad, I should like to take this opportunity to express our thanks to those who, under the most trying circumstances, have practically without exception been true to their old home. [*Lively "Bravo!"*] That holds true not only of the German-Americans but also of all German men and women all over the world. In the face of a hostile world they showed by sentiment and act that their hearts belonged to their Fatherland. Thus they have created a basis for the future community of culture of a nation of 100,000,000 people. If they were in the minority—and therefore, could not come into the open with their ideas—that does not alter one bit the thanks which we owe them and which we hereby express. [*"Bravo!"—National-Liberals.*]

Gentlemen, our economic future is in closest relation with our political development as a world power. I am glad that in this respect I fully agree with a member of the Social-Democratic "Fraktion," Herr Cohen, who in his recent article in the *Glocke* indicated the close relationship existing between political might and economic development. We are often inclined to view England's position towards Germany in absolute numbers, which show us that English foreign trade is probably equal to German. Gentlemen, that is not the right state of affairs. If one wishes to compare correctly, one has to go back to the sources from which they flow, and then we see that in 1912, from England's total exports of 9,993,000,000 marks, 3,830,000,000 marks' worth went simply to English colonies and protectorates. That means that more than one-third of the total English exports is based solely upon the political position of England. In the same year we exported to our colonies 51,000,000 marks' worth. If we subtract that from our total export and do the same in the case of England, i.e., consider only the field of world competition, we compete with England on equal footing and are not hampered by English preference duties or by the mighty political strength of England, for the last pre-war year shows German exports to be 9,000,000,000 as against 6,000,000,000 for English. That in itself is a pleasing number. But it shows England how important economically developed colonial possessions are for the political economy of the mother country, and how important it is for us to regain a great colonial empire which in the course of time can be developed as a basis of Germany's political economy, as to both exports and imports. Therefore, we believe that the maintenance of German colonial possessions is a necessity not only from the standpoint of prestige but also from the standpoint of our economic life.

The speaker before me discussed the measures which the enemy countries have threatened to use against us after the war. We hear a great deal about the Entente forming an economic bloc. Whether or not it will come to pass seems to me doubtful. Geographic continuity is necessary for such a bloc. France and Russia cannot conclude an economic bloc, for between them is situated the German Reich and it will always be easier to export from Upper Silesia to Russia than from France to Russia. At any rate, we cannot undervalue the following basic thought: In the future we shall have to reckon with the fact that the thought of Greater Britain, expressed once upon a time by Cecil Rhodes and the Chamberlainists, might become a reality, namely, a Greater Britain, politically united, and also economically closely bound together by means of common tariffs. We shall have to reckon with the fact that strong boycott movements against us will be manifested in France, that Russia's inclination toward an economic-political autocracy will further increase, and that the tremendous strengthening which the United States has unfortunately experienced during this war will give her a preponderance against us and, to a greater extent, against Great Britain in this struggle for world markets. Gentlemen, above all that, we must demand the re-establishment of the basis of free economic competition.

In this chapter belongs the demand for protection of German claims abroad. To it also belongs the important question of the regulation of the transition period from war to peace. Herr Ebert has already touched upon it, but he spoke chiefly about the securing of employment opportunities. I should think that equally important is the entire transformation of our condition today as an isolated state into one of free world competition, which cannot be brought about without a period of transition. Equally important are the questions of raw materials and the re-establishment of our monetary values. I am convinced that the Federated Governments are already occupied with this question. But in one respect I am opposed to what the speaker before me said, namely, when in speaking about commercial-political questions he said that that was finally the business of the Government and must be secured by it. I should urgently request that in this regulation the co-operation of trade and industry should not be undervalued [*lively approval from the National-Liberals*], in order that there may not be a repetition of many happenings which we at present lament, and when still more difficult problems need to be solved. We must beware of opening up our foreign market in this period of transition for the importation of foreign goods. Should we be poor in raw materials, or if for a few months we should not be in a position to manufacture at all, the throwing open of our internal market would lead to a closing of our industries, since England and France would flood us with goods. It would also mean the further depreciation of our currency and in the end the stabilization of our economic defeat after the military victory. [*"Quite right!"—National-Liberals.*] I am convinced that if the trade unions once direct their attention to this question, particularly the trade unions of the textile workers, for example, they would find that the quota of foreign imports does not contain any hidden protective tariff efforts but that it is only a safeguarding of this period of transition.

Gentlemen, if I do not regard the entire enemy economy as being able to bring us in the end to terms, it is due to the knowledge that the German market represents the purchasing power of a nation numbering 70,000,000 people. Things are so arranged that not only they need our goods outside but also they need our market for their goods. And a nation with such a tremendous purchasing power and economic strength cannot be covered simply with a tariff war, since the tariff war could possibly injure the attacking party more than the attacked one.

To this question also belongs the problem of a "Central Europe," the problem—regarding it first from the economic standpoint—of a customs understanding with our allies. What essentially does it mean? It proceeds from the fundamental truth that people cannot fight together on the battlefield and then later on fight each other economically. It is further based upon the thought that the customs understanding can be of the greatest economic strengthening for both participants. Finally it proceeds from the train of thought that if the enemies realize their intention, if they form their economic bloc and attack us, such an attack can best be warded off if it is opposed by one great economic field with a 120,000,000 population than if opposed singly and individually. With these limitations this idea needs every encouragement.

However, I must make a very decisive front against those extremists who believe that our economic development should take only an Eastern trend. No, things are not arranged that way. Our future does not lie in the East, and the struggle for world markets we will not give up [*"Quite right!"—Left, Center, and Right*] ; for if we give it up, England's purpose has been achieved. [*Renewed approval.*] With the first ship that leaves Cuxhaven and Bremerhaven this struggle for world markets begins anew and will be carried on with all the German business man's intensity and joy of producing. [*Lively approval.*] The world was our field and will be so in the future. What we can offer the East is the investment of German capital, in order to give it a better opportunity to open up its resources; and when afterwards their purchasing power increases through this investment of capital, our future generations will enjoy a greater growth of export to them. For the present things are not such that a "Central Europe" could and should be so conceived as if it were the fundamental trend of a future economic development. That it cannot be and shall not be. . . . .

121. SOCIAL DEMOCRATIC ANNEXATIONISTS[24]

Only recently did the Party Committee direct itself again against annexations. In spite of all that, it is known that several members of the old party, as well as various Social-Democratic writers, are by no means disinclined to put into effect demands for annexation. They are joined by the *Chemnitzer Volksstimme,* which writes as follows in a leading article:

"What the German people need is the security of their country and the guaranteeing of its potential economic development. It is silly to quarrel at this moment about how this can be achieved in all of its details. Scheidemann, as the authorized speaker of the Social-Democratic Party, has said in the Reichstag that it would be foolish to assume that this war will come to an end without a border stone being moved. One should keep from blaming the Social-Democratic Party because our attitude might have an unfavorable effect abroad. What the peoples are able to do is no longer a matter of doubt in the belligerent countries. Mighty words no longer make an impression. The thing that fills the foreign countries with respect is our strong will to sacrifice for Germany's future everything necessary—even our life and our fortune. For this purpose the German Social-Democracy will spare nothing."

The same paper, however, states in another place that the Social-Democratic Party is an opponent of annexation; but this opposition is not and cannot be taken seriously—as statements of different bourgeois papers show—if individual party members and party newspapers state again and again that they are not averse to boundary changes. Certain papers have even stated that the Chancellor dare not renounce annexation for reasons of "statesmanship," in order to have more trumps in his hand at the time of peace negotiations! An opposition to annexation is of political meaning only if it is adhered to in practice and is not merely advanced as a principle upon the realization of which one does not place great importance.

[24] *Vorwärts,* July 28, 1916.

122. RESOLUTIONS OF THE SOCIAL-DEMOCRATIC PARTY
AUGUST 11, 1916[25]

COMRADES!

Two fatal years are behind us. Millions of sturdy human lives have been destroyed; many hopes have failed; and countless achievements of civilization have been ruined. Is this struggle that devastates countries and annihilates peoples—the worst calamity that has ever befallen civilized humanity—to continue still longer? . . . .

The will for peace, which is as strong among the people of enemy countries as in Germany, will undoubtedly be weakened and set back when, like the chauvinistic annexationists in the countries of the Entente, influential German circles set forth war aims and propagate plans of conquest which will incite the people of those countries to the strongest resistance.

It seems to be the right time for the German people to take a free and unhampered position in regard to these plans of conquest the realization of which would furnish the seeds of new wars and which are more than likely to prolong the war.

The repeal of martial law demanded for a long time by the Social-Democratic Party has not yet been secured. Besides, the permission to discuss war aims has not yet been granted. In spite of all that, desires of certain circles for annexation have again and again been made public and have been used to create a feeling in the enemy's countries.

On August 1 there took place in numerous German cities meetings of the "National Committees for a Victorious and Honorable Peace" in which most of the speakers discussed problems connected with war aims, probably in an annexationistic manner. After this, it is the clear duty of the Government to allow the general discussion of war aims. We have, therefore, in a memorial to the Chancellor, again demanded permission to discuss war aims.

We ask the party organizations to hold public meetings during the next few weeks in which they will take their stand on war and peace aims. We also request that preparations be made for the signing of a petition in which there is demanded a peace which will make friendship of neighboring peoples possible and which will secure territorial integrity, independence, and freedom of economic development for our country.

COMMITTEE OF THE SOCIAL-DEMOCRATIC
PARTY IN GERMANY

BERLIN, August 11, 1916

[25] *Vorwärts,* August 11, 1916, p. 1.

123. GEORG BERNHARD, "HINDENBURG AND SCHEIDEMANN"[26]

. . . . Herr Scheidemann has declared in several speeches and newspaper articles that both the French and the Belgians could even today get back the territories which we have wrested from them. In saying this Herr Scheidemann referred to the Chancellor's word that he had never intended to annex Belgium. . . . . We are the last ones to deny Herr Scheidemann the right to express his views about the war aims. Nor can we join the chorus which sees the world coming to an end just because the war aims of a Social-Democrat could agree with those of the Chancellor. However, we demand to know whether Scheidemann has a right to declare authentic his interpretations of the Chancellor's aims. For in this lies the danger of Scheidemann's agitation—the whole world believes that Scheidemann speaks, if not upon instruction, at least with the silent approval of the Chancellor.

If Scheidemann were merely expressing his own views, it would be a welcome sign that public discussion is at last being permitted. It would indeed be a good thing for the official voice to be silent while such discussion went on. The views of the public, freely expressed, would guide, but not bind, the Government. However, Scheidemann has unfortunately not failed to strengthen the effect of his words by harping upon the agreement of his views with those of the Chancellor, and so has placed the latter in a position which should have been avoided by all means.

We agree essentially with Herr Scheidemann's views that the overwhelming majority of the German people, with few exceptions, wishes for nothing more longingly than for peace. We surely know what peace means, for we have learned to know what war does. But we also know that it does not depend upon us at all to make peace. And we regard it as extremely dangerous to spread illusions among the German people that the Chancellor, at any time, could open the gates to the paradise of a lasting peace. Nothing is farther from the truth, ... and anyone who read with what scorn the English press rejected the peaceful intentions of the last speech of the Chancellor will know that. . . . .

It is so easy to speak to the nation at this time of peace. It is so welcome to them, and may be so effective hereafter for the winning of votes. We are all now feeling the burdens of war so heavily that it is no wonder if for citizens as for soldiers the word peace sounds more insinuating than ever. But one must also think of the other side of the case. We have reached a critical stage of the war. Our enemies are

[26] *Vossische Zeitung,* November 20, 1916, I, 1.

beginning to realize that the war which they are waging is hopeless and that the longer the war which they have stirred up continues the more clearly its madness is shown. They are slowly acquainting themselves with the sacrifices which they will have to make if Germany resolutely uses her strength. Therefore they are launching peace-wishes, trying to stir up the neutrals to intervention. They know that the German people also want peace, and they are hoping, by speech and writing, to make the German people weak, to induce them to barter their future for the sake of a speedy peace. This would mean the spoiling of our military successes by diplomacy. It would mean the ruin of our development, driving us into bankruptcy.

. In this most dangerous epoch it is necessary to remain cool and to keep one's nerves. However, Scheidemann's agitation serves only to weaken the nerves of the German people instead of strengthening them. We regret sincerely to have to say that, for we are convinced from personal knowledge of Scheidemann's personality that he is animated by a passionate longing to help his nation; but his activity has a different effect from what he believes and wishes.

124. AIMS OF PAN-GERMAN–CONSERVATIVE CIRCLES[27]

. . . . We all desire peace, but an honorable peace, worthy of the struggle, not a Social-Democratic peace dictated by Herr Scheidemann, nor any peace made up according to an American prescription from the English pharmacy, which must necessarily be damaging to us. The Democratic peace-politicians, who are today forcing themselves to the front, try to represent the case as if the "Pan-German–Conservative circles"—the comprehensive catchword applied to everything that is not Socialistic or Democratic—desired to prolong the war and to stand in the way of a reasonable peace. This is the same unworthy poisoning of national opinion which induced the same people in time of peace to accuse everyone who supported German defensive armament of desiring to bring on a war or to increase the profit of munition contractors for the sake of his selfish interests. The gentlemen have shown themselves as more or less guilt-burdened, illusionary politicians without whose agitation we would have entered this war better armed and therefore ended it sooner. Their peace policy during the war, too, is based upon illusions and cannot, accordingly, shorten the war; rather will it prolong the war or at least damage its victorious conclusion, since it weakens the will to victory in the army at home. We wish a secured peace, not a contractual armistice, which would have to be followed by a new war,

[27] Collection of German Documents, Hoover War Library.

since every party would just be looking for the proper moment to achieve its aim. We suffer a heavy distress; but our enemies do not fare better. . . . . Whenever our enemies are ready for peace, we shall have been so long before. However, since they are not, the distress of the coming months and Hindenburg's fist must bring them to readiness, not paper and oratorical peace offers from those superfluous persons who during two years of war have not yet attained a clear insight into the character and aims of our enemies.

125. STATEMENT OF LEDEBOUR IN THE REICHSTAG ON WAR AIMS[28]

He who votes for the credits gives a blank check for the use, at the Government's pleasure, of the means thus granted. A party which by voting this credit gives the Government the strongest possible vote of confidence thereby takes on itself a share in the responsibility for the war aims of the Government and the measures which the Government thinks good for the realization of its war aims. [*"Very good!"*— *S.D.L.G.*] We are again unable to give the Government this vote of confidence. [*"Quite right!"*—*S.D.L.G.*] Our reasons for that are that all peoples long for an immediate, durable peace. All Governments allege that they are seriously striving to bring about peace. The facts are not in agreement with the lip profession. [*"Very true!"*—*S.D.L.G.*] The peace proposal of the Imperial Government itself is not in accordance with what is demanded in such a proposal. [*"Very true!"*— *S.D.L.G. Laughter.*] Its lack of content diminishes its value. [*Laughter.*] An empty offer of peace contradicts in particular our demand that in any such pronouncement all annexations should be renounced. [*"Very true!"*—*S.D.L.G.*] The Imperial Government demands, in fact, acquisitions of territory in the East and the West, and it is a question, further, of acquiring districts of alien population. [*"Very true!"*— *S.D.L.G.*] The boasting about victory which is never absent from a speech of the Chancellor or from a monarchical proclamation [*"Very true!"*—*S.D.L.G.*] is in full accordance with these schemes of annexation—it was not dropped even at the time of the peace offer. [*"Very true!"*—*S.D.L.G.*] We hold firmly to the principle of the right of the nations to self-government. . . . . The fact that the Ten in their Notes have intimated their adherence to extravagant schemes of conquest cannot weaken our judgment on the attitude of our own Government. [*Stormy laughter.*] Our opposition, however, to the war policy of our own Government gives us the full right to express the urgent desire

[28] *Verhandlungen des Reichstags*, No. 82, February 23, 1917, pp. 2366–67.

that our Socialist friends in the countries of the Ten [*renewed stormy laughter*] may follow the happy example which has everywhere been set by the protagonists of Socialism by fighting with determination against the peace-balking devices of their own rulers. [*"Quite right!"*— *S.D.L.G. Shouts from Right.*] We Socialists must wage the same fight in all countries against the imperialistic efforts of capitalism. The recent rounding out of a Polish state is also in conflict with the principle of the right of nations to self-government. It ought to have left the Polish people [*laughter*] the decision as to the form to be assumed by the Polish state. [*"Quite right!"*—*S.D.L.G. Laughter.*] The prejudicing of this war aim must make the conclusion of peace more difficult. Further, we cannot accept a share of responsibility for the methods of the German conduct of war. We demand the cessation of the ruthless U-boat war. [*Stormy laughter.*] It is as inconsistent with the laws of humanity as the English starvation scheme. The ruthless U-boat war has unfortunately given the war-mongers and war contractors in the United States the desired pretext for forcing their Government to a rupture with Germany. Our attitude in principle to the U-boat war gives us, however, the assurance that we shall find a hearing when we urgently ask our comrades in America and all friends of peace there to continue undistracted their efforts to prevent even at the last hour the entrance of the United States into the war, and the consequent limitless extension of the butchery of the people. [*"Very good!"*—*S.D.L.G.*] We are also in outspoken opposition to the domestic policy of the Government. [*"Quite right!"*—*S.D.L.G.*] For two and a half years the Government has been consoling the people with empty, unbinding promises. Where is the improvement of the franchise for the Empire and the individual states? [*"Quite right!"*—*S.D.L.G. Great excitement at Right.*] Yes, in the Empire, too. The objection that war time is not appropriate for legislative changes is refuted by the Prussian Government itself by the introduction of the Entail Bill. . . . . The state of siege is still not raised, and the free expression of public opinion is increasingly restricted. . . . . We appeal to the tormented peoples to work with us for a lasting peace resting on mutual understanding. [*Applause by S.D.L.G.*]

126. THE SOCIAL-DEMOCRACY AND LIBERATED RUSSIA[29]

The belief that Germany is waging a war of conquest has become so rooted among our opponents as a result of the foolish war-aims debate that the words of the latest German governmental declaration will perhaps not even now succeed in uprooting it.

[29] *Vorwärts*, April 15, 1917, p. 1.

But in Russia they ought to reflect that the German party which is strongest and has the richest future, the Social-Democracy, with all sharpness and decisiveness, rejects every policy of conquest and supports a peace which does violence to no one and guarantees the peoples their right to decide their own destiny.

We have grounds for the assumption that the German Government as well recognizes this point of view today as justified, and honestly desires to bring the war to an end in negotiations in which the Powers meet as complete equals in right and in which every thought of the cession of territory under forcible compulsion is to be excluded.

Further, the Czernin proposal makes it possible to take up negotiations without at once ending the war. Thus it is in the power of our opponents to continue the war if they should find the proposals of the Central Powers humiliating and inconsistent with their own interests.

This very circumstance, together with the fact that the governments of the Central Powers, in obedience to the pressure of their own peoples, are striving for peace, may give all genuine friends of peace abroad the certainty that the Central Powers would enter upon negotiations with the firm intention of bringing them to a good issue, honorable for all.

The German Government would not dare to bring back war from a conference on the ground that they had not been able to put through this or that demand for annexation. The only case in which the German people would take on itself the terrible burden of a yet longer war would be that of the opponents wishing to make the return of peace contingent on terms which are inconsistent with its honor and freedom.

But every government would be in the same situation. If the negotiations are once begun, they must lead to the same goal, since that is what the will of all peoples demands.

Every opponent will find the mass of the working people in Germany ready to fight so long as it is obliged to fear having to pay for any weakening in the struggle by permanent oppression and misery. But every friend of peace can count on its support when it is a question of fighting against imperialist ambitions and giving the world a peace which gives all peoples freedom.

The German people desires to live in friendship with the liberated Russian people. It therefore desires no peace which will kindle the longing for revenge on one side or the other. Russia is Germany's enemy only as a helper in the schemes which aim at Germany's dismemberment and annihilation. The freedom of the Russian people, however, has a loyal ally in the working masses of the German people.

127. THE INDEPENDENT COMMITTEE FOR A
GERMAN PEACE[30]

The Social-Democratic Party has published a resolution demanding a peace without annexation and without indemnity. In his concluding speech after the deliberations, the leader of the party [Scheidemann] spoke of "preposterous demands" of the "annexationists," a "handful of people whom one cannot take seriously." If the Independent Committee for a German Peace allowed these utterances to go into the world uncontradicted it would make itself partly responsible for one of the worst falsifications of history that has ever been attempted. The Independent Committee has never put forward preposterous demands. This is an accusation which is not made truer by constant repetition. If the demands of the Independent Committee are preposterous, so are the Imperial Chancellor's. Scheidemann attempts to show that on certain points the Independent Committee goes beyond what the Chancellor himself has defined as our war aim in the Reichstag. This holds also in regard to the demands of the "United Organizations." The Committee asks the securing of our frontiers East and West. Is East Prussia to be again exposed in the future to the fortress-chain of Warsaw-Kovno? Is Belgium to remain an open gate of invasion in the immediate neighborhood of our most important industrial area, without whose secure possession we cannot wage war at all? Are we for all time to go without the extended land-colonization with which we simply cannot dispense? A peace without an increase of power and a war indemnity is equivalent to "distress and oppression," which, according to their statement, the leaders of the Social-Democrats desire to keep away from the German people. Our workers will have to call us to account if we are obliged to suffer the results of such a peace. The governments of the Central Powers have declared that they do not desire to interfere in Russia's internal evolution. There is no one in Germany and Austria-Hungary who does not approve that declaration. But is the statement of the Social-Democrats that they greet the victory of the Russian Revolution with "passionate sympathy" consistent with this? Can anyone on God's earth know that there may not emerge from the Russian Revolution conditions which are in the highest degree perilous for the stable prosperity of our nation? In the face of this situation, there is at the present hour only one task for the Central Powers—Victory! The Social-Democrats make demands which go far beyond the Easter message. The Independent Committee has never intervened in regard to domestic evolution. It has always represented the view that there ought

[30] *Neue Preussische Zeitung,* April 23, 1917.

to be no conflict about the furnishing of the house so long as its stability is not assured. Now, too, it is of the opinion that changes which cannot be achieved without conflict are inadvisable so long as millions of our best have to offer their breasts to the enemy for the Fatherland. We are at one with the Social-Democracy in the decided repudiation of our opponents' assertion "that the continuance of the war is necessary in order to force Germany to receive free institutions." But we raise the most decided protest when it asserts that we should "help to secure the lasting stability of the future world-peace by acceding to a super-state organization and consenting to a compulsory court of arbitration." This would be equivalent to the establishment of an Anglo-American management of the world. Wilson, in his message to Congress, has adopted the assertion of Germany's lack of freedom in a ruder form than any other of our enemies. As against the declaration of the Social-Democracy we expect, as indispensable, that our Government will publicly state its position. The Social-Democratic resolution does not represent the thoughts of the German people, and the Government is in duty bound to make it known that it is not on this basis that it seeks for the unity so often recommended and preached.

THE INDEPENDENT COMMITTEE FOR A GERMAN PEACE

BERLIN, April 22, 1917

128. ADDRESS OF THE IMPERIAL CHANCELLOR TO THE REICHSTAG, MAY 15, 1917[31]

Gentlemen, the interpellations which have just now been brought forward demand from me a definite, detailed statement regarding the question of our war aims. To make such a statement at the present moment would not serve the interests of the country. [*"Quite right!"*— Left.] I must, therefore, decline to make one. [*Applause from the Left.*]

Since the winter of 1914–15 I have been pressed first on one side and then on another to make a public statement of our war aims, if possible with details. [*Shouts from the Right of "Not Details!"*] They are being demanded of me every day, Herr Roesicke. [*Denials from the Right.*] To force me to speak, various parties and tendencies have interpreted my silence on declarations of war aims, as giving my assent to their programs. When giving permission for a free discussion concerning our war aims, I expressly declared that the Government could not and would not take part in any controversy. I protested against any positive conclusions whatever as to the Government's attitude being

[31] *Verhandlungen des Reichstags,* No. 109, May 15, 1917, pp. 3395–98.

drawn from the Government's silence. [*"Hear, hear!"—Right.*] I now repeat this protest in the most emphatic manner. [*"Bravo!"—Left and Center.*]

What I was able to say at any time about our war aims I have said here publicly in the Reichstag. They were fundamental principles—they could not be more than that [*cheers*]—but they were sufficiently clear to exclude identification with other programs which have been made public. [*Approval.*] I have adhered to these fundamental principles until now. They also found solemn expression in the peace offer made conjointly with our allies on December 12, 1916. [*Cheers.*] The supposition which has recently arisen that some differences of opinion existed between us and our allies regarding the question of peace belongs to the realm of fable. [*Loud cheers by the German "Fraktion," Center, National-Liberals, and Left.*] I expressly state this now with the conviction that I am also expressing the opinion of the leading statesmen of the powers allied to us. [*Renewed applause.*]

Gentlemen, I thoroughly and completely understand the passionate interest of the people in our war aims and the conditions of peace. I understand the demand for a precise statement which was addressed to me today from the Right and the Left. But in a debate on war aims the only guiding line for me is an early and satisfactory conclusion of the war. [*Loud cheers.*] Beyond that I cannot do anything. If the general situation obliges me to maintain an attitude of reserve, as is the case at present, I will maintain this reserve, and no pressure from either Herr Scheidemann or Herr Roesicke will force me to depart from my path. [*Cries on the Left, "Roesicke began it," and laughter.*]

I will not allow myself to be led astray by the speech with which Herr Scheidemann, at a time when the drumfire is being heard on the Aisne and at Arras, believed he could disseminate among the people the possibility of a revolution. [*Stormy applause from Right, Center, and Left.*]

Gentlemen, the German people, like myself, will fail to understand this speech. But just as little will I allow myself to be diverted from my course by Herr Roesicke's attempt to represent me as treading the paths of Social-Democracy. I will not allow myself to be forced into the paths of either party [*hearty applause by National-Liberals, Center, Progressive People's Party, and German "Fraktion"*], either by the Left, or by you [*turning to the Conservatives.*] No, gentlemen, certainly not; my paths are entirely those of the German nation, whom alone I have to serve, whose sons, one and all, are fighting for the life and being of the nation, standing firm about their Kaiser, whom they trust and who trusts them. [*Applause.*] Gentlemen, the Kaiser's words of August will live on; they have not been falsified nor proved falsely stamped by the course of time. Herr Roesicke, who has here put on airs as the special guardian of those words [*"Very good!"—Left*] will be able to read the necessary answer to his question whether the Kaiser's word still holds good in the Kaiser's Easter message, countersigned by me. [*"Quite right!"—Left.*]

I trust that the reserve which I must exercise—and it would be unscrupulousness on my part if I failed to exercise it—will find the support of the majority of the Reichstag and also of the people. [*Approval by Center, National-Liberals, Progressive People's Party.*] For the past month unparalleled battles have been raging on the Western front. The whole people, with all its feelings and anxieties, its thought and its thanks, is present with its sons out there, who, with unexampled tenacity and contempt of death, are resisting the attacks daily renewed by the British and the French. [*Loud cheers.*]

Even today I see no readiness for peace on the part of Great Britain and France and no abandonment of their excessive aims of conquest or economic destruction. Who, then, were the strong ones whose governments openly stood up last winter before the world in order to bring this insane slaughter of nations to a conclusion? Were they in London or Paris? The most recent declarations which I have seen from London state that the war aims which were announced two years ago remain unaltered.

Even Herr Scheidemann does not believe that I could answer this declaration with a *beau geste*. Does anyone believe, in view of the state of mind of our Western enemies, that they could be induced to conclude peace by a program of renunciation? [*"Very true!"*] It comes to this: Shall I immediately give our enemies an assurance which would enable them to prolong the war indefinitely without danger of losses to themselves? Shall I inform these enemies that, come what may, we shall under any circumstances be the people which renounce—we shall not touch a hair of your heads; but you, who want our lives, may without any risk continue to try your luck? Shall I nail down the German Empire in all directions by a one-sided statement which comprises only one part of the total peace conditions, renounces the successes gained by the blood of our sons and brothers, and leaves everything else in a state of suspension? [*"Quite right!"*] No! I reject such a policy. [*Prolonged cheers.*] I will not pursue a policy which would be the basest ingratitude toward the heroic deeds of our people before Arras and on the Aisne. It would permanently weigh down our people, to the humblest worker, in all conditions of life, and would be equivalent to surrendering the future of our Fatherland.

On the other hand, perhaps I ought to lay down a program of conquest? I decline to do that also. [*Cries on the Right: "Why do you say that to us?" Laughter on the Left.*] If it has not been demanded, then we are of one opinion. I say again, I also decline to lay down a program of conquest. We did not go to war, and we are not fighting now against almost the whole world, in order to make conquests, but only to secure our existence and firmly to establish the future of the nation. A program of conquest is as little helpful in achieving victory and ending the war as a program of renunciation. On the contrary, in doing so I should only be playing the game of the hostile rulers and making it easier for them further to dupe their war-weary peoples into an immeasurable prolongation of the war. That also would be base ingratitude toward our warriors before Arras and on the Aisne.

As regards our Eastern neighbor, Russia, I have already spoken recently. It seems as if new Russia has renounced her violent plans of conquest. Whether or not Russia will act or can influence her allies in the same direction I am unable to estimate. Doubtless Great Britain, with the assistance of her other allies, is doing her utmost to keep Russia in the future also harnessed to Britain's war chariot [*loud cries of "Hear, hear!"*] and to oppose Russian wishes for the speedy restoration of world peace. If, however, Russia desires to prevent further bloodshed of her sons and renounces for herself all violent plans of conquest, if she wishes to restore the permanent relations of peaceful life side by side with us, then it surely results as a matter of course that we, since we share this desire, will not prevent the establishment of permanent relations in the future, and will not render their development impossible by demands [*loud and prolonged cheers*] which would not be in accordance with the ideal of the freedom of nations and would lay the germ of enmity in the Russian nation. I do not doubt that an agreement aiming exclusively at a mutual understanding could be obtained which would exclude every thought of oppression and leave behind no sting of discord. [*Loud cheers.*]

Our military position has never been so good since the beginning of the war. [*Cheers.*] The enemy in the West, in spite of their most terrible losses, cannot break through. Our U-boats are operating with increasing success. [*Cheers.*] I will not employ any fine words about them. The deeds of our U-boat men speak for themselves. [*Loud applause.*] I think that even the neutrals will recognize this. As far as is compatible with our duty toward our own people, who come first, we take into account the interests of the neutral states. The concessions which we made to them are not empty promises. That is so in regard to our neighbors on the frontier, Holland and Scandinavia, as well as those states which, because of their geographical position, are greatly exposed to enemy pressure. I am thinking in this connection especially of Spain, which, in loyalty to her noble traditions, is endeavoring under great difficulties to preserve her independent policy of neutrality. We thankfully recognize this attitude, and have only one wish, namely, that the Spanish people may reap the reward of their strong independent policy by a development of their power and further prosperity. [*Loud applause.*]

Thus time is on our side. In full confidence we can trust that we are approaching a satisfactory conclusion. Then the time will come when we can negotiate with our enemies about our war aims, regarding which I am in full harmony with the Supreme Army Command. [*Loud cheers.*] Then we shall attain a peace which will bring to us liberty to rebuild what the war has destroyed in unimpaired development of our strength, so that from all the blood and all the sacrifices an empire, a people, will rise again strong, independent, unthreatened by its enemies, a bulwark of peace and labor. [*Prolonged cheers.*]

129. THE PAN-GERMAN LEAGUE TO THE CHANCELLOR[32]

To His Excellency the Imperial Chancellor Herr Dr. von
Bethmann-Hollweg

Great Headquarters   Bamberg, May 5, 1915

I have the honor to submit to Your Excellency, at the instance of the General Directorate of the Pan-German League, a conspectus of those demands regarding the political aim of the war the realization of which appears to my political friends and to widest circles beyond the Pan-German League a necessity for the security of our people in the future. That military attainment, actual and possible, must be the measure of negotiation is clear to my political friends, but just as clear is it that military undertakings (the continued efficacy of our army assumed) must be directed to political war aims.

In giving into Your Excellency's hand the guiding principles of the General Directorate, I regard myself as impelled by my conscience to say another word on the consequences of a result of the war not in accordance with the needs of the German people.

Feeling in the broadest circles of our people is today embittered, even to the point of desperation. This is not the place to investigate the cause of this phenomenon which conflicts with the greatness of our people's achievement. Be it said merely that there is far too much evidence that the Imperial Government has set up too narrow a war aim, and that precisely the most loyal and politically trustworthy circles are compelled to perceive in this fact a renunciation of the full use of our certain victory.

[32] *Vorwärts*, May 22, 1917, p. 1.

My conscience commands me to utter a warning against such a renunciation; it would be the most disastrous political error, and its immediate consequence would be revolution. The word must be uttered. When one considers what a burden of debt will rest upon the Empire after the war, it is clear that taxation must increase to gigantic proportions if the war result is inadequate. Place oneself in the position of the returning warriors, each one of whom definitely stakes his hopes on some reward; instead of this reward they find, on their homecoming from the field, a considerably increased burden of taxation. A tremendous disappointment and embitterment will be the result; there will be no check, and the people, disappointed after all its achievements, will rise. The Monarchy will be endangered, even overthrown, and thereby the fate of our people will be sealed.

Your Excellency, these are no imaginations of a trouble-crazed brain nor the anxieties of a single individual. Thus speak, thus think, thus fear countless brave men who unconditionally support the Monarchy, but who know what is going on in our people.

In the face of such a prospect there is one certainly effective lightning-conductor—a peace which fulfills in every direction the needs of the people, a war result which satisfies the spirit of our people and fills it with pride and joy. That such a peace can be wrested no one of the people doubts; and I as an old soldier carry the certainty in me that with firm will and unshattered nerve we can and shall achieve militarily what must be aimed at politically.

Our nation is at stake! The monarchical foundation of the Empire and the Federal States is at stake. For that reason I implore Your Excellency, in complete agreement with my political friends, to counteract the terrible dangers by winning a peace which will bring our people what it deserves and what it can claim. The tragedy of our people collapsing after the tremendous achievements must not become a reality.

Further, I beg Your Excellency to note that I am commissioned to submit copies of "War Aim Demands" and of this, my letter, to the High Governments of the Federal States.

Your obedient, etc.,

(<i>Signed</i>) BARON V. GEBSATTEL</div>

130. THE CHANCELLOR'S REPLY TO VON GEBSATTEL[33]

BERLIN, May 13, 1915

I have the honor of notifying Your Excellency of the receipt of your letter on May 6 of the present year. The war-aim demands put

[33] *Vorwärts,* May 22, 1917, p. 2.

forward by the Pan-German League will remain to be estimated after the complete overthrow of all our enemies. For the moment, interests of foreign policy and national defense, which must take precedence of all other considerations, forbid detailed examination of their material content.

Your Excellency ventures in your letter accompanying these demands of the Pan-German League to state that feeling in the broadest classes of our people is embittered, even to the point of desperation, because the Imperial Government has set up too narrow a war aim and would renounce full use of our certain victory. Moreover, you do not shrink from declaring that the people, disappointed after such achievements, would rise and overthrow the Monarchy, unless, as the one effective lightning-conductor, a peace is achieved which in every direction satisfies the necessities of the people, i.e., as understood by the P.G.L.

My reply is this: I admit the merit which the Pan-German League gained before the war by heightening the national will to power and by combating the international fraternity idea. But, unfortunately, the League united to this national will so much lack of political insight that even in the period before the war it often impeded political business and forced into antagonism every Government which does not want to have its windows broken.

The war and its experiences have made the national will to power, the raising of which forms the *raison d'être* of the P.G.L., the common property of the German people; but instead of removing the lack of political insight in the circles of the P.G.L., the war and its experiences —as I gather from Your Excellency's letter—have increased this lack of insight to the point of grotesqueness. The loyal monarchical circles which Your Excellency desires to represent would most grossly violate their duty to the Crown if, instead of waiting until the Government considers the moment for plain speaking to have arrived, they were to attempt to stir up disquiet among the people about a limp and timid policy which does not exist and of which there is no evidence. According to Your Excellency's words, this disquiet is said to have risen to embitterment and even to the point of desperation and threatening hints of revolution. In this there are only two possibilities: Either this assertion is true, and in that case responsibility falls on those who, instead of opposing, have stirred up this feeling, in spite of all the unmistakable declarations of the Government, through lack of political judgment and national discipline; or it is false, in which case I am compelled to recognize in it a menace and the attempt of a minority to subject to their will the leaders summoned by the Crown to conduct the business of the Empire. I am confident that Your Excellency, as an old soldier, will understand my frank speaking as demanded from the standpoint of discipline by the times, and that you will contribute your utmost not to impair the pride and joy of the people in the prize of victory which it will win.

There is no objection to the publication by the P.G.L. of this correspondence. For my part, I reserve its publication for such an opportunity as may seem favorable.

Respectfully, etc.,

(*Signed*) Dr. v. Bethmann-Hollweg

131. MEMORANDUM OF THE AUSTRIAN MINISTRY OF FOREIGN AFFAIRS CONCERNING THE ADMINISTRATIVE DIVISION OF BELGIUM, JUNE 18, 1917[34]

Vienna, June 18, 1917

K. and K. Ministry of the Imperial and
Royal House and Foreign Affairs
56314/9
Request of the Military Government of
Belgium Concerning the Prepara-   *Confidential*
tion of Economic Agreements

To the Royal Hungarian Ministerial Präsidium at Budapest

Upon the initiative of the German Military Government in Belgium an especially constituted commission has been occupied for some time with the study of the question of what measures of organization were to be taken in order to prepare the way for dividing Belgium administratively into a Flemish and a Walloon part. From the reports of the K. and K. Commissioner to the said government it seems that the idea of this division of Belgium is finding increasing favor among the Flemish population.

One of the leading men of the Flemish movement approached the K. and K. Commissioner with the request for detailed information in regard to the manner in which the one-time centralized form of government in Austria-Hungary had been decentralized in the sense of a dualism. One of his questions asks for information as to the way in which our two governments handle preparation of international economic agreements.

In view of the fact that we too have an interest in the movement

[34] Collection of Austrian Documents, Hoover War Library.

for the administrative division of Belgium, the K. and K. Ministry of Foreign Affairs would like to oblige the Commission entrusted with the study of this question by supplying the requested information.

The K. and K. Ministry of Foreign Affairs, therefore, has the honor of requesting the Royal Hungarian Ministerial Präsidium to report as soon as possible how it wishes to answer the question in regard to the preparation of international economic agreements.

For the Minister:

IPPEN M.P.

132. STATEMENT OF DERNBURG ON WAR AIMS[35]

NEUMUENSTER, July 1

At the convention of the Progressive People's Party of Schleswig-Holstein, held at Neumuenster, Herr Dernburg, the ex-Colonial Minister, enunciated the following war aims, which he declared to be his own views and consequently did not bind his party in any way:

1. Annexations of free peoples, used to autonomy and self-government, like Belgium, I reject. This does not exclude our further promotion of the separation of the different national stocks, the Flemings and the Walloons, if one of them asks for it, and does not exclude our allowing such guaranties to be given us in the future evolution of Belgium as in all human calculation make it improbable that any other power will exercise there a greater influence than ourselves.

2. The acquisition of portions of France, for instance of Briey and Longwy, I personally reject. Naturally I am equally little prepared to make concessions on the question of Alsace-Lorraine.

3. If the High Command on grounds of military technical nature asks for certain changes of frontier here and there which are indispensable for the defense of our country, which is always in a position of peril in the center of Europe, my demands do not oppose this.

4. As for our war aims in the East, we must await the development of Russia. As regards the interests of our allies in the South and the Southeast, it is for them to say what they ask. It is no part of my business to interfere there. They have remained loyal to us, as we to them, and this relation we will maintain, loyalty for loyalty.

5. We ask for the return of our stolen colonies, and we ask that they should receive those extensions about which in 1914 we had almost agreed with England.

[35] *Vossische Zeitung*, July 2, 1917, II, 3.

6. We ask that all the aims set forth by the Paris Economic Congress for world trade should be given up.

7. We ask for the freedom of the seas, the conclusion of the hegemony of a single power on the world-sea, and especially the restoration of and respect for international law in time of peace and war. The sea is the property of no single nation. It is the highway of all.

133. TIRPITZ TO BASSERMANN, JULY 17, 1917[36]

To my joy I see in the newspapers that the National-Liberal Party, loyal to its traditions, has rejected the peace resolution, which is pernicious both at home and abroad and a tactical mistake even if we were obliged to strive for a peace without indemnities—precisely in that case we should have to behave in just the opposite way. But we absolutely do not need to strive for such a peace, and ought not to do so, but must hold firmly to the confidence expressed in the utterances of Field Marshal Hindenburg. Neither passing aggravations in our food anxieties nor anxieties in this connection about the future ought now to induce us to lose nerve and to grasp at a peace which imperils our future, and particularly that of our working class, since the unswerving stubborn continuance of the U-boat war will bring us, not indeed today or tomorrow, but surely and in due time, success. Recalling our long years of common work for the aims indicated to the German people by their Kaiser, I appeal to you, honored Bassermann, to do everything to prevent the resolution.

v. TIRPITZ

134. A TIRPITZ TELEGRAM TO DR. SPAHN[37]

Dr. Spahn, Reichstag, Berlin

Recalling the long and sympathetic co-operation of the Center in working for the world-position and sea-power of Germany founded by our Kaiser, I think it my duty to express to Your Excellency my opinion that the contemplated war-aim resolution in its present or any similar shape must have a most harmful effect both at home and abroad for our whole future. In my opinion it is not to be expected that a peace feeling which is to our advantage will be promoted abroad. Besides, even if we were compelled to strive for a peace without indemnities and guaranties, the present resolution would be the most unsuitable means

[36] *Deutsche Zeitung,* July 18, 1917, p. 1.
[37] *Ibid.,* July 19, 1917, p. 2.

to it. Precisely in that case we should have to adopt a different method. But we absolutely do not need to strive for such a peace. Let us hold firm to the confidence expressed in the utterances of Field Marshal Hindenburg. Neither temporary aggravation of the food anxieties, nor anxieties in this connection about the future, ought to induce us to lose nerve or to grasp at a peace which imperils our future, and particularly that of our working class, since the unswerving, stubborn continuance of the U-boat war will bring us, not indeed today or tomorrow, but surely and in due time the success for which, according to numerous pronouncements of Your Excellency, we are fighting. I hope you have now recovered.

VON TIRPITZ

135. STATEMENT OF IMPERIAL CHANCELLOR MICHAELIS TO THE MAIN COMMITTEE OF THE REICHSTAG, AUGUST 21, 1917[38]

After I was called to the post of Imperial Chancellor, my immediate task regarding foreign policy was to take up relations with the leading statesmen of the countries allied with us. With Bulgaria and Turkey this could, unfortunately, be done only in writing. On the other hand, with the statesmen of the Austro-Hungarian monarchy I have repeatedly been able to enter into an exchange of views, first at Vienna, and then at Great Headquarters, and finally when Czernin visited Berlin. In mutual confidence we joined hands for further work. The Alliance stands firm, unbreakable. It is in conformity with the closest relations that exist between us and our allies that we have agreed to a continuous exchange of views. As regards our enemies, their number has increased since the adjournment of the Reichstag by three—namely, Siam, Liberia, and China. These countries have no convincing reason for enmity against us. They acted solely under the pressure of the Entente and the United States, which latter country has great influence over Liberia and China. We have made it clear to these countries that we shall bring them to account for damage done to German interests in defiance of international law. Regarding our relations with our allies, complete uniformity exists not only politically, but also regarding all warlike measures, which is in contradiction to the situation existing among our enemies. For this our special thanks are due to the Supreme Army Command. Our success is in accordance with this uniformity.

I have asked Field-Marshal von Hindenburg to inform me of the present military situation. He answered in the following telegram:

[38] *Norddeutsche Allgemeine Zeitung*, August 22, 1917, II, 1–2.

"Nothing proves the effect of our submarine campaign more than the tenacity, despite losses, with which the English and French continue their exasperated attempts to force us down by military measures on the West front in the course of this year. With the greatest concentration of material and man-power, after the most careful preparation, the English have attempted now for the second time within a short period to force an entry into our position in Flanders. Strong forces, both of the English and of their allies, were held in readiness to follow up the break-through in order to proceed to the conquest of the coast of Flanders and the destruction of the submarine bases. Both times gigantic enemy assaults failed with the heaviest losses. Despite the reckless sacrifice of men's lives, the enemy did not proceed beyond the field of craters in front of our positions. For the same reason as in Flanders, yesterday, August 20, the French also began an attack on a great scale near Verdun. Our artillery counter-measures considerably delayed here the beginning of the enemy attacks. During the artillery battle our infantry showed its excellent attacking power by successful counter-thrusts. Here also the French succeeded in capturing only some unimportant portions of the crater-field, suffering great losses in doing so. These successes have been achieved by the unequaled attitude of our brave troops, and by superior leadership. The enemy's secondary attacks at Lens, on the Aisne, and in western Champagne brought him no advantage despite his massed concentration, owing to the more developed and more active methods of fighting of our troops. Full of confidence we can look forward to further developments of the fighting, which may certainly bring small local successes, owing to the enemy's superiority of man-power, but it will have no effect on the military situation, which is favorable for us.

"In the East, both in defense and in attack, our troops have gained new victories. Everywhere the enemy's mass attacks have collapsed with heavy losses. Our own attack overlapped the enemy positions and crushed in a rapid and victorious advance large parts of the Russian Army. Wide tracts belonging to our faithful ally were reconquered. The army again proved what will-power and absolute determination to win are able to accomplish even against a numerically superior enemy. If this enemy superiority on the battlefield imperatively called for an increased effort and sacrifice of life and blood, the labor accomplished daily and hourly on quiet fronts should not be forgotten. The nerve-wearing vigilance and the harder tasks in extended positions demand here also of large parts of our army their most loyal fulfillment of their duty. In the fourth year of the war, moreover, all privations of home comforts are manfully and willingly borne, and everywhere heroic deeds prompted by the firm will to victory are accomplished.

"In the Balkans and Asia, German troops are fighting side by side with our faithful and brave Bulgarian and Turkish allies; there also a faithful watch is kept. A glance at all fronts shows that at the beginning of the fourth year of the war we stand in a more favorable position than ever from a military point of view."

Our success on land corresponds with our success on sea. In July, according to the latest information, 811,000 tons were sunk by us. Contemplating these results on our side and the failures on the enemy side, it appears incomprehensible that our opponents until now have shown not even the beginning of any idea pointing at peace, not to mention a peace which includes renunciation. I was able to show recently by information on the Franco-Russian secret treaty what far-reaching war aims France cherished and how England supported French desires for German land. Only recently a member of the British Cabinet declared there would be no peace until the German armies were thrown across the Rhine. I am now able to show further arrangements made by the enemy regarding their war aims, some details whereof have already been made known to the Committee on an earlier occasion.

I will proceed in chronological order. On September 7, 1914, the enemy coalition decided to conclude only a joint peace. On March 4, 1915, Russia made the following peace demands, whereof England approved by a note dated March 12 and France by a note of April 12, namely, that Russia should receive Constantinople, with the European shore of the Straits, the southern part of Thrace as far as the Enos-Media line, the islands in the Sea of Marmora, and also Imbros and Tenedos, and on the Asia Minor side, the peninsula between the Black Sea, the Bosphorus, and the Gulf of Ismailia, as far as the River Sakario in the East. This basis being laid down, negotiations continued during 1915 and 1916. In the course thereof Russia obtained the promise of the Armenian vilayets of Trebizond and Kurdistan; France claimed Syria with Adana and Mersina and the hinterland extending northward as far as Sivas and Kharput; England's share was to be Mesopotamia. The rest of Turkey in Asia was to be divided between the English and the French spheres of interest. Palestine was to be in some way internationalized, and other districts inhabited by Turks and Arabs, including Arabia proper and the holy places of Islam, were to be formed into a special Federation of States under British suzerainty. When Italy entered the war and demanded her share of the booty, fresh negotiations were opened up which in no way indicated renunciations. I think that as to these we shall have further details, which will be published later. With such far-reaching enemy war aims, it is reasonable that Balfour should have recently stated he did not consider it advisable to make a detailed statement on the war policy of the Government. Those are the fundamental facts as they appear to us at the present moment when we envisage the possibility of concluding peace.

It is comprehensible that in view of our enemies' attitude, the position is taken by our press that it is impossible for us to come forward with a new peace offer. The situation is well depicted, for instance, by *Vorwärts,* which wrote on August 19 that at no period of the war was it so clear that the prolongation is unavoidable and that the blame for it solely and exclusively falls upon our enemies. The reply to our hand, extended for peace, was the menacing shake of the boxer's fist. At this moment there is only one possibility—a fight for our lives. I believe these utterances represent the general feeling of our people.

In the situation as depicted by me there has now come the Pope's Peace Note, the contents whereof I may assume to be known. The basic idea thereof corresponds with the position which the Pope occupies in virtue of his whole personality and with the charge that he has as the head of Catholic Christianity. The Pope in developing his ideas emphasizes that might and arms must be replaced by right and moral law. On this basis he develops his proposals as to arbitration and disarmament, and he also arrives at further deductions as to the period following the conclusion of peace. Regarding the material contents of the papal note, I can take up no final and detailed position before coming to an understanding with our allies. I can only speak quite generally, and should like to do this in two directions. I must first oppose the idea that the decision of the Pope has been influenced by the Central Powers. I can state that the Pope's note as it became known through the press is the spontaneous decision of the head of the Catholic Church.

Secondly, although I must reserve taking up any position regarding the details of the note, I can even now say that it corresponds with our repeatedly manifested attitude and our policy since December 12, 1916, sympathetically to welcome every attempt to bring the idea of peace into the international misery of war, and that we especially welcome the Pope's step, which in my opinion is born of a serious endeavor toward justice and impartiality. I summarize as follows: firstly, the note has not been induced by us, but is the product of the spontaneous initiative of the Pope; secondly, we welcome with sympathy the efforts of the Pope to bring about the conclusion of the war by a lasting peace; thirdly, regarding our reply, we are in consultation with our allies, but the consultation is not yet concluded. At present I cannot dwell further on the material points of the Pope's note, but I am prepared to come into contact with the Committee in a special manner, which must be agreed upon, regarding the further negotiations until our reply is ready. I express the hope that this common labor may bring us nearer to the goal which we all have in mind, namely, an honorable peace for the Fatherland.

136. MANIFESTO OF THE GERMAN VATERLANDS-PARTEI, SEDAN DAY, 1917[39]

Large sections of the German public are not in agreement with the attitude of the present Reichstag majority regarding the most vital questions of the Fatherland. They consider the endeavor to place conflict on constitutional questions in the foreground as a danger to the Fatherland and an advantage to the enemy, especially now, when the fate of the Empire is at stake. They do not consider that the Reichstag elected before the war really any longer represents the will of the German people. Who is there that does not long for peace with all his heart? *Nervous and weak peace manifestoes,* however, only postpone peace. Our enemies, bent on the destruction of Germany, see signs only of collapse in them. And this, too, at a time when, according to our Hindenburg, *our military situation is better than ever.* If we convince the enemy that he can have an honorable peace by negotiation at any moment, he will have nothing to gain and everything to lose by continuing the war. In the light of past events, our Government is in a dilemma. *Without strong support from the people the Government by itself cannot master the situation.* For a strong imperial policy it needs a strong instrument. Such an instrument must be provided in the form of a large party based on all sections of the Fatherland.

The German Empire should now be not split by party strife but united in the will to victory! Calling to mind with gratitude our first beloved Emperor of undying memory and his iron Chancellor, who united the German peoples, devoted to a titanic struggle against *destructive party strife,* against which Otto von Bismarck appealed before God and the people, the undersigned men of East Prussia, true to the traditions of their forebears, *have founded the*

GERMAN VATERLANDS-PARTEI

to guard and shield the German Fatherland in this gravest hour of German history from the evil of disunion and division.

The German Vaterlands-Partei aims at welding together the whole energy of the Fatherland without distinction of party politics. It consists of patriotic individuals and associations. It will support and defend a strong Government which can reflect the signs of the times, not in weak concessions at home and abroad, but in a resolutely German and unshakable belief in victory.

The German Vaterlands-Partei will not enter into rivalry with

[39] *Norddeutsche Allgemeine Zeitung,* September 12, 1917, p. 4.

patriotically minded political parties. *With these* it will work hand in
hand for the confirmation of the will to conquer and to overcome difficulties. *The German Vaterlands-Partei* is a party of union. *It does not,
therefore, contemplate setting up its own parliamentary candidates.*
When peace is proclaimed it will dissolve. We want no internal strife.
We Germans are apt too easily to forget the war in internal quarrels.
Not for a moment does the enemy forget them! The Germans united
in the German Vaterlands-Partei pledge themselves to do everything to
preserve internal concord until the conclusion of peace. *However any
individual may view vexed questions of internal politics, the decision of
these is to be postponed till after the war.* Then our heroes will have
returned from the battlefield and will be able to co-operate in the
internal construction of the Empire. Now victory is all that matters!

We do not live, as our enemies falsely pretend, under autocratic
absolutism, but surrounded by the blessings of a constitutional state
whose social activities put to shame all the democracies of the world,
and which has given the German nation the strength to defy the enormously superior power of the enemy. *German freedom stands heaven-
high above the unreal democracies and all their vaunted blessings,*
which English hypocrisy and Wilson prate of in order thereby to destroy Germany, which is impregnable against their weapons. We will
not further England's interests.

We know, and all the Germans in the world know, that it is not for
Germans, as for the English, a matter of business! *England, the originator of the world conflagration, is in a critical position.* We are victorious on land and on sea! Hit in her most vital spot by the submarine
campaign, England is placing her last hopes on German unrest and disunion. The time is not far off when her pride will be humbled, if we
can only endure and withstand deceitful peace-kites!

We know, and the enemy knows too, how much Germany has to
thank the Kings of Prussia of the House of Hohenzollern for her military education. In the existence of the Emperor the enemy sees the
chief obstacle to the defeat of Germany. By means of cunning and
lies they want to encourage Germany's sons to *abandon their* Imperial
Chief. They know not the meaning of German loyalty nor how the
German Federal Princes and races stand by the Emperor and the
Empire with blood and iron to their last breath. They do not know
that to us Germans military training is *no sacrifice but our greatest
pride.*

We will have no starvation peace! In order to attain a speedy peace
we must strengthen our nerves for endurance as Hindenburg bids. *If
we willingly bear with distress and deprivation, the German people will
gain a Hindenburg peace,* which will adequately repay the price of

victory, terrible sacrifice, and exertion. Any other peace means a devastating blow to our future development. The stunting of our position in the world and accompanying intolerable burdens would destroy our commercial situation and all the prospects of our working classes. Instead of exporting valuable wares, Germany would then again see her sons emigrate in large numbers.

The Founders of the German Vaterlands-Partei have requested His Highness the Archduke John Albert of Mecklenburg and the Grand Admiral von Tirpitz to become the leaders of the party.

To all who subscribe to these views we appeal to join the German Vaterlands-Partei. Anyone wishing to help is welcome. The aims of the party must be realized at once. Not a moment is to be lost.

Germany's salvation, honor, and future is at stake!

Königsberg in Prussia, on the Day of Sedan, 1917

137. A HINDENBURG STATEMENT FROM GENERAL HEADQUARTERS, SEPTEMBER 25, 1917. W.T.B.[40]

I have been informed by the War Minister that it has been frequently asserted in an unauthorized quarter that, according to statements made by myself and General Ludendorff, threatening economic collapse and exhaustion of military resources are forcing us to peace at any price.

I do not desire that our names should be connected with such utterly false assertions.

I declare, in full agreement with the Imperial Government, that we are equipped in both the military and the economic sense for further fighting and victory.

von Hindenburg

138. STATEMENT OF THE BRANDENBURG PROVINCIAL BRANCH OF THE GERMAN VATERLANDS-PARTEI, NOVEMBER 3, 1917[41]

The national movement inaugurated by the German Vaterlands-Partei is ever increasing with torrential force. Every day multitudes of men and women of our province join its ranks. This has caused the undersigned to found a provincial branch for the province of Branden-

[40] *Norddeutsche Allgemeine Zeitung,* September 26, 1917, II, 1.
[41] *Neue Preussische Zeitung,* November 8, 1917, p. 4.

burg on November 3 in Berlin. The provincial branch will gather the
existing local groups into one, will help to form new local groups in
town and country, and will afford members who have no local group in
their neighborhood an opportunity for affiliation.

The Vaterlands-Partei is a great bond of union which permits everyone to retain his political convictions, which never interferes in internal
politics and party organizations, and which will cease to exist on the
day when peace is concluded. Away with all internal quarrels among the
German people! The enemy welcomes and promotes this, our unfortunate inheritance, in order to wrest victory from us at the eleventh
hour. The Vaterlands-Partei desires to restore a party truce (*Burgfrieden*) and unity of the domestic front in the sense desired by Hindenburg, and to rekindle the burning enthusiasm of August 1914.

Our opponents call us prolongers of war. That is a mistake. No
German wishes to prolong the horrible murder of peoples. But every
section of the German people is coming to recognize that each offer of
peace has added to the enemies' confidence of victory, that each diplomatic retreat and renunciation has increased their greed. Three months
and a half have passed since July 19. We have had no reply other than
scornful rejection and practical demonstration of an intensified will to
destroy. The course is now clear. Even the Reichstag is no longer
bound by its peace resolution; rather is that superseded, like Count
Czernin's peace program, by the enemy's rejection of it.

Therefore, away with all weakness, and away with all blissful credulity in view of our enemies' determination to destroy us. After the
forcible occupation of Riga and Oesel, after the incomparable stroke of
genius in the break-through from the Isonzo to the Tagliamento, with
its immeasurable military and political results, and considering the in-
flexible resistance of our heroes on the Western front, we at home have
really now only one duty—not to jeopardize the victorious issue by our
behavior. It is not for Germany and her allies but for the enemy to
speak now if they want to negotiate. We can afford to wait for that
after the brilliant results of the Seventh War Loan, and knowing that
our economic supplies are assured. Russia is done for, and Italy will
soon be done for, too. France has half bled to death in England's
service and England herself is full of apprehension and is fighting our
submarines, watch in hand. Let us show ourselves worthy of the glorious heroism of our united defensive forces; let us help our gallant men
on land, on water, and in the air, by silence and endurance, in unity
and in confidence.

We are not fighting for what is a matter of course, namely, that
original territory which from ancient times was German, such as Alsace-
Lorraine, should continue to belong to the Empire; we are fighting for

the necessary guaranties for Germany's position in the world. In particular, Belgium must not again become a vassal state of England. Our sons and grandsons must dwell in safety in a proud, free country; our workmen must not be compelled to cross the sea, but must earn an ample living under flourishing home administration.

Every friend of the Fatherland is welcome in our ranks, every genuine inhabitant of the Mark, man or woman. Do not come alone. Bring friends and comrades.

New members should send in their names and subscriptions to the office of the Provincial Branch (*Landesverein*) of the German Vaterlands-Partei for the Province of Brandenburg, at the Potsdam branch of the Deutsche Bank, unless they are affiliated with a local association. The minimum annual subscription is Mk. 1. Donations are also urgently needed in the interest of the cause.

All local associations are requested to send the names of their committees and lists of their members to the offices of the provincial branch.

THE BRANDENBURG PROVINCIAL BRANCH OF THE
GERMAN VATERLANDS-PARTEI
THE EXECUTIVE COMMITTEE

139. CHANCELLOR VON HERTLING'S SPEECH IN THE MAIN COMMITTEE OF THE REICHSTAG ON THE FOURTEEN POINTS OF PRESIDENT WILSON, JANUARY 24, 1918[42]

Gentlemen, when I last had the honor to speak before your Committee—that was on January 3—we were faced by an incident which had occurred at Brest-Litovsk. At the time I expressed the opinion that we should await the settlement of this incident with equanimity. The facts have corresponded with the expectation. The Russian Delegation has again arrived at Brest-Litovsk, and negotiations have been resumed and continued. The negotiations are progressing slowly. They are exceedingly difficult. I have referred, on a previous occasion, to the exact circumstances from which these difficulties arise. Indeed many times there were reasons to doubt whether the Russian Delegation was in earnest about its peace negotiations, and all sorts of wireless messages with remarkably strange contents which were going around the world tended to strengthen this doubt. Nevertheless, I hold firmly to the hope that we shall in the near future conclude a favorable agreement with the Russian Delegation at Brest-Litovsk.

[42] *Norddeutsche Allgemeine Zeitung*, January 25, 1918, I, 1.

Our negotiations with the representatives of the Ukraine are more favorable. Here also there still are some difficulties to be overcome, but the prospects as I regard them are favorable. We hope in the near future to arrive at a settlement with the Ukraine which will be to the interest of both sides and which should also be advantageous in so far as its economic aspect is concerned.

One important result could already be recorded on January 4 at ten o'clock in the evening. As you all know, the Russian Delegation, at the end of December, made the proposal that we send an invitation to all the participants in the World War asking them to take part in these peace negotiations. As a basis for this the Russian Delegation submitted certain proposals of a very general character. We, at the time, agreed to the proposal for inviting participators in the war to the negotiations, with the condition, however, that this invitation should be limited to a clearly defined period. On January 4, at ten o'clock in the evening, this period expired. No answer had been received. The result is that we are bound no longer in any way so far as the Entente is concerned, that we have a clear road in front of us for separate negotiations with Russia, and also that, obviously, we are no longer bound in any way, as far as the Entente is concerned, to the proposals for a general peace which have been submitted by the Russian Delegation.

Instead of the then anticipated reply, which failed to come, two announcements have, as we all know, been made in the meantime by the enemy statesmen—the speech by the English Minister, Mr. Lloyd George, of January 5; and the message of President Wilson of the day after. I freely admit that Mr. Lloyd George has changed his tone. He no longer employs abuse, and thus appears to wish to establish again his claim to ability as a negotiator, of which I had previously despaired. All the same, I cannot go as far as the many opinions from neutral countries which claim to read in the speech of Mr. Lloyd George a sincere desire for peace and even a friendly spirit. It is true that he declares that he does not wish to destroy Germany and that he has never wanted to destroy her. He even finds expressions of respect for our economic, political, and cultural position; but among them there is no lack of utterances, and between the lines there is always present the idea that it is his duty to sit in judgment on guilty Germany for all sorts of crimes.

This is a spirit, gentlemen, with which, naturally, we can have nothing to do, and in which as yet we can observe no trace of a sincere desire for peace. We are supposed to be culprits over whom the Entente is now sitting in judgment. That forces me to pass in review the conditions and incidents which preceded the war, even at the risk of again repeating what has long since been known.

The establishment of the German Empire in the year 1871 put an end to the old state of dismemberment; by uniting its peoples the German Empire, in short, attained that position which corresponded with its economic and cultural achievements and the claims founded thereon. Prince Bismarck crowned his life's work by the alliance with Austria. It was a purely defensive alliance and was from the very first day regarded and desired as such by the high contracting parties. In the course of decades never has the slightest thought of its misuse for aggressive purposes cropped up. The defensive alliance between Germany and the adjacent Danube Monarchy, united with us by the traditions of centuries and common interests, should serve especially to maintain peace.

But Prince Bismarck was often reproached with being haunted by the nightmare of coalitions, and the events of the times that followed have shown that it was not a mere terrifying phantom. The danger of enemy coalitions which threatened the allied Central Powers often made its appearance. The dread of coalitions became a reality, owing to the hemming-in policy of King Edward. The German Empire, struggling upward and increasing in strength, stood in the way of English imperialism. This British imperialism only too readily found support in the French longing for revenge and in the Russian struggle for expansion; and so plans for the future developed which were dangerous for us.

Germany has always been faced with danger of war on two fronts owing to her geographical position. It now became more and more clearly visible. An alliance was concluded between Russia and France, whose inhabitants were more than double those of the German Empire and Austria-Hungary. France—Republican France—lent to Tsaristic Russia milliards for the construction of strategic railways in the Kingdom of Poland which were to facilitate an advance against us. The French Republic called up its last man for three years' military service. Thus France, together with Russia, created for herself an armed force up to the limits of her capacity. Both pursued aims which our enemies now characterize as imperialistic. It would have been neglect of duty if Germany had merely looked on quietly and also if we had not attempted to create for ourselves an armament with the object of protecting ourselves against future enemies. I may perhaps remind you of the fact that I myself, as a member of the Reichstag, have often spoken about these things, and that on the occasion of new army budgets I have always pointed out that the German nation, in agreeing to these armaments, merely wished to pursue a policy of peace and that these armaments were forced upon us for defense against the danger threatening us from our enemies. It does not seem that these words were in any way heeded by foreign countries.

And now, as to Alsace-Lorraine—which is once again referred to by Mr. Lloyd George. Once again he speaks of the injustice which Germany committed against France in the year 1871. Alsace-Lorraine —I do not say this to you, you do not need this information, but abroad there still seems to be ignorance about these things—Alsace-Lorraine, as is known, includes for the most part purely German territory, which was detached from the German Empire by centuries of continuous violation and breaches of right, until finally in 1789 the French Revolution swallowed up what was left. At that time they became French provinces. When, therefore, in the War of 1870, we demanded back the regions which had been wantonly wrested from us, that was not conquest of foreign territory but was in reality what today is called disannexation, and this disannexation was expressly recognized by the French National Assembly and the Constitutional representatives of the French nation at that time, March 29, 1871. And in England people at that time spoke very differently from what they do today.

I can refer to a classical witness. He is no other than the celebrated English historian and author, Thomas Carlyle, who in a letter to the *Times* in December 1870 wrote as follows: "No nation ever had such a bad neighbor as Germany possessed in France during the last four hundred years. Germany would be mad if she did not think of erecting a frontier wall between herself and such a neighbor"—I draw attention to the fact that for my part I am not repeating the very sharp terms Carlyle used against the French in this connection—". . . . and if she does not erect for herself such a frontier wall when she has the opportunity to do so, I know of no natural law and no Heaven-sent decree on the strength of which France, alone among the dwellers of the earth, should not be obliged to return a portion of stolen territories when the owners from whom they were wrested have a favorable opportunity to get them back." Prominent English press organs expressed themselves in the same sense. I may mention for instance, the *Daily News*.

And now, gentlemen, I come to President Wilson. Here also I admit that the tone has changed. It appears that the unanimous rejection of the attempt of Mr. Wilson, at the time of the reply to the papal note, to sow discord between the German Government and the German nation has done its work. It is possible that this unanimous rejection led Mr. Wilson to the right road, and perhaps a beginning has been made, because now there is at least no longer any question of the suppression of the German nation by an autocratic Government, and the former attacks against the House of Hohenzollern are not repeated. I will not go into the distorted representations of German policy which are even yet to be found in Mr. Wilson's message, but I will discuss in

detail the points which Mr. Wilson brings forward. There are no less
than fourteen points in which he formulates his peace program, and I
beg you to have patience if I bring forward these fourteen points for
discussion, as briefly as possible.

The first point: No Secret International Agreements! Gentlemen,
history records that we were the first to be able to declare ourselves in
agreement with the most extensive publicity of diplomatic agreements.
I remind you of the fact that our defensive alliance with Austria-Hungary has been known to all the world since the year 1889, while the
offensive agreements of our enemies have had to be disclosed during the
course of this war, chiefly by the publication of the Russian secret
documents. The full publicity also given to the negotiations at Brest-
Litovsk proves that we were in a position to consent readily to this
proposal, and to declare the publication of negotiations as a general
political principle.

The second point: The Freedom of the Seas. Complete freedom of
navigation on the seas in war and peace is also put forward by Germany
as one of the first and most important demands for the future. Here,
therefore, there is no difference of opinion whatever. The restriction
mentioned by Mr. Wilson toward the end is incomprehensible and
seems superfluous. It should therefore be suppressed. It would, however, be important in a high degree for the future freedom of the seas
if claims to strongly fortified naval bases on important international
shipping routes, such as England maintains at Gibraltar, Malta, Aden,
Hongkong, or on the Falkland Islands, and at many other points, were
renounced.

The third point: The Abandonment of All Economic Restrictions
Which Hinder Commerce in an Unnecessary Manner. With this we
wholly agree. We also condemn an economic war which would inevitably bring with it causes for future warlike complications.

The fourth point: The Limitation of Armaments. As has already
been declared by us on previous occasions, the subject of the limitation of armaments is a matter quite suitable for discussion. The financial situation of all the European States after the war should further its
satisfactory solution in a most effective manner. [*"Quite right!"*] It
will be seen that, as to the first four points of the program, agreement
could be reached without difficulty.

The fifth point: The Amicable Arrangement of All Colonial Claims
and Disputes. The practical carrying out of the principle laid down by
Mr. Wilson will, in this world of realities, meet with some difficulties.
In any case I believe that, for the time being, it may be left to the
greatest colonial empire—England—to determine how she will come to
terms with her ally regarding this proposal. We shall have to talk

about this point of the program at the time of the reconstruction of the colonial possessions of the world, which has also been demanded unconditionally by us.

The sixth point: The Evacuation of Russian Territory. The Entente States having refused to join in the negotiations within the period agreed upon by Russia and the four Allied Powers, I must decline, in the name of the latter, any subsequent interference. The question here involved is one which alone concerns Russia and the four Allied Powers. I cherish the hope that, under the conditions of the recognition of the right of self-determination for the nations within the western boundaries of the former Russian Empire, it will be possible to be on good relations with these nations, as well as with the rest of Russia, for whom we urgently wish a return of guaranties which will secure a peaceful order of things and the welfare of the country.

The seventh point: The Belgian Question. As far as the Belgian question is concerned it has been declared repeatedly by my predecessors in office that at no time during the war has the forcible annexation of Belgium by the German Empire formed a point in the program of German politics. The Belgian question belongs to a complicity of questions the details of which will have to be regulated during the peace negotiations. As long as our enemies do not unreservedly adopt the attitude that the integrity of the territory of our allies offers the only possible foundation for peace negotiations, I must adhere to the standpoint which up to the present has always been taken, and must decline any discussion of the Belgian question until the general discussion takes place.

The eighth point: The Liberation of French Territory. The occupied parts of France are a valuable pawn in our hands. Here also forcible annexation forms no part of the official German policy. The conditions and mode of the evacuation, which must take into consideration the vital interests of Germany, must be agreed upon between Germany and France. I can only once again expressly emphasize that there can never be any separation of the Imperial Provinces. We will never permit ourselves to be robbed by our enemies of Alsace-Lorraine, which in the meantime has become more and more closely and internally allied with German life, which is developing economically more and more in a highly satisfactory manner, and where more than eighty-seven per cent of the people speak the German mother tongue.

The ninth, tenth, and eleventh points: The Italian Frontiers, the Question of Nationality in the Danube Monarchy and the Balkan States. As regards the questions dealt with by President Wilson under these clauses, they embrace questions of paramount importance to the political interests of our ally, Austria-Hungary. Where German interests are concerned we will guard them to the utmost, but the reply to President Wilson's proposals in connection with these points I would prefer to leave in the first instance to the Foreign Minister of the Austro-Hungarian Monarchy. A close connection with the allied Danube Monarchy is a vital point of our policy today and must be a guiding line for the future. The faithful comradeship in arms which proved itself so brilliantly during the war must continue to have its effect also in peace, and we on our part will bring everything to bear in order to bring about for Austria-Hungary a peace which takes into account her justified claims.

The twelfth point: Turkey. Also in connection with the point which concerns our brave and powerful ally, Turkey. I should like in no way to forestall the attitude of Turkish statesmen. The integrity of Turkey and the security of her capital which is closely connected with the questions of the Straits are important and vital interests also of the German Empire. Our ally can, in this respect, always rely on most explicit assistance.

The thirteenth point: Poland. It was not the Entente—which found nothing but meaningless words for Poland and before the war never mediated on her behalf with Russia—but the German Empire and Austria-Hungary which freed Poland from the Tsaristic régime which was restricting her national individuality. Therefore, it must be left to Germany and Austria-Hungary and Poland to come to an agreement about the future organization of that country. We are, as has been proved by the negotiations and declarations of the last year, well under way with the task.

The fourteenth point: The League of Nations. In regard to this point I am sympathetic, as is shown by my previous political activity toward any thought which for the future excludes all possibility and probability of wars and tends to promote a peaceful and harmonious co-operation among nations. If the conception of the "League of Nations" mentioned by President Wilson demonstrates under further development and after a trial that it really was conceived in a spirit of complete justice to all, and with complete freedom from prejudice, the Imperial Government will be gladly prepared—after all the other questions in suspense have been settled—to investigate the principles of such a national union.

Gentlemen, you are conversant with the speeches of Mr. Lloyd George and the proposals of President Wilson. I must repeat what I said at the beginning. We must now ask ourselves, whether out of these speeches and proposals a really earnest and honest desire for peace appears before us. They contain certain principles for a general peace which we also admit, and could form points of departure and of aim for negotiations. Where, however, concrete questions are concerned—points which are of decisive importance to us and to our allies—there the wish for peace is less perceptible. Our enemies do not wish to "destroy" Germany, but they cast furtive and covetous glances toward parts of our lands and those of our allies. They speak with respect of Germany's position, but the idea that we are culprits who must do penance and promise reformation repeatedly makes itself apparent. This is the usual tone of the victor to the vanquished. This also is the tone of a man who points to all our former statements of willingness for peace as mere signs of weakness. From this standpoint, from this conception, the leaders of the Entente will first have to free themselves.

In order to make this easier for them I should like to remind them exactly how the situation really stands. May they believe me when I state that our military situation was never so favorable as it is now. [*"Bravo!"*] Our highly gifted army leaders face the future with undiminished confidence in victory. Throughout the whole army, in the officers and in the men, lives the unbroken joy of battle. I remind you of the words which I spoke on November 29 in the House. I repeatedly expressed willingness for peace, and the spirit of reconciliation which is revealed by our proposals must not be regarded by the Entente as a license permitting an indefinite lengthening of the war. Should our enemies force us to prolong the war, they will have to bear the consequences resulting therefrom. If the leaders of the enemy powers are really inclined toward peace, let them revise their program once again, or, as Mr. Lloyd George said, introduce another reconsideration. If they do that and come forward with fresh proposals, then we will examine them carefully, because our aim is no other than the re-establishment of a lasting general peace. But this lasting general peace is not possible so long as the integrity of the German Empire, the security of her vital interests and the dignity of our Fatherland are not guaranteed. Until that time we must quietly stand by each other and wait. As to this purpose, gentlemen, we are united. [*Lively applause.*]

In regard to the methods and the "modalities" there may be differences of opinion. But let us shelve all these differences. Let us not fight about formulas, which always fall short in the mad course of the world events, but, acting above divisive party controversies, let us keep our eyes on the mutual aim, the welfare of the Fatherland. Let us hold together the Government and the nation, and victory will be ours. A good peace will and must follow and must come. The German nation bears in an admirable manner the sufferings and the burdens of the war, which is now in its fourth year. In connection with those burdens and sufferings I think especially of the sufferings of the small artisan and the lowly paid official. But you all, men and women, will carry on and will see it through. With your political knowledge you do not allow yourself to be fooled by carefully hatched phrases; you know how to distinguish between the reality of life and promising dreams. Such a nation cannot go under. God is with us and will be with us also in the future. [*Lively applause.*]

140. OTTO PFEFFER: "THE STATE OF FLANDERS"[43]

On January 20, the Council of Flanders published a resolution according to which it decided, on December 22, 1917, for complete independence of the country; as a consequence it is laying down the mandate which it received on February 4, 1917, and is submitting to new elections. Thereby has been reached a historical landmark, not in Germany's Flemish policy but in the Flemish movement. This must be strongly emphasized. This Council, although an outcome of the war, has been no more engineered by Germany than the Flemish movement itself. The policy found and is finding a support in the founding of a Flemish University at Ghent and in the separation of administration. Both arrangements are long-standing wishes of the Flemings, and it is necessary for us to get it straight that separation has long been both a Flemish and a Walloon claim. . . . .

What is characteristic of the decision of the Council of Flanders at this time is its complete independence from German influences. It is an act of strong confidence on the part of the leaders of the Flemish movement in the sound political sense of the Flemish people.

The principal reasons for the resolution are probably to be found in the following three points: first, in the recognition that even from the reformed Belgian Government, on account of its tendency to centralization, nothing is to be hoped for the Flemings; next, the extraordinary strengthening of the movement, as it has found expression recently, *inter alia,* in the adherence of the two Flemish leaders in Holland, Franz v. Cauwelaert and Camille Huysmans, to the program of the Nationalist Activist Flemish Party in the occupied territory; and, lastly, in the characteristic of the time—that is, the adoption of the idea of the right of self-determination of nations.

What is its aim and foundation? From the statement of the Council and the commentaries of the press it seems that complete severance from Walloon territory is aimed at, which is tantamount to the dissolution of Belgium.

If Meert's saying that *"Flamands et Wallons sont des réalités,*

---

[43] *Münchener Neueste Nachrichten,* February 3, 1918, p. 1.

Belges est une étiquette" is going to be applied, that shows that there is
an aim to get at reality. The aim is based upon the feeling of the community of interest among the 4,000,000 Flemings in Belgium, upon the
expectation to win over the pacifists also (who up to now would accept
nothing "from the enemy," or were fearful of their position on the
return of the Government from Havre), and convince them that Flanders is culturally, politically, and economically quite capable of sustaining the burdens of a modern state. . . . . Everything Flemish as against
French will be promoted, and in the economic sphere a policy will be
adopted contrary to the close union with Great Britain desired by the
Belgian Government, and consequently in opposition to the economic
war after the war. . . . .

The political aspect is not so clear. Certainly complete independence
of a national kind is aimed at, but how far things have progressed in
this direction and how far so radical a solution can be carried through is
for the time being uncertain.

According to the Flemish papers, a state of Flanders with its own
government and parliament might be called into existence at any
moment. There should therefore be elections now for a Constituent
Assembly, so that in February there should be in existence a body completely representative of the Flemish people of the five provinces in
place of the former Belgian Provincial Councils.

A democratic expression of all those Flemings who are ready to
recognize the new state could thus be quickly obtained. But there would
still be many political problems to solve. The *Antwerp Eendracht* asks,
for instance, whether one should prefer a personal union with the
Walloons, an alliance, a federal state, or a confederate state. These
are matters for the Flemings to decide.

We fully understand when the Flemings assert that they know very
well Germany's interest in seeing Flanders a Flemish country but that
the interests of Flanders alone are determining their present action and
future aims.

Things having reached their final stage, we must await the result
of the elections. But one thing is certain today: the Flemings have
shown their firm resolve to maintain with a strong hand what has been
achieved, and to rely on the national feeling in such a way as, for the
welfare of all Flemings, will reduce to a minimum, if not completely
obviate, the danger of the repeal of the separate administration by the
Belgian Government when peace comes.

141. STATEMENT OF THE SECRETARY OF COLONIES, DR. SOLF, ON THE NECESSITY OF GERMAN COLONIAL POSSESSIONS[44]

If before the war the necessity for German colonial possessions was still considered doubtful in not a few economic circles and political groups, the war, with all its unwelcome economic consequences, has yet had one good result: it has insistently and, as I hope, convincingly set before the eyes of doubters the economic necessity of a German colonial realm. The economic status of the German people has during the last few years stood, and still stands, subject to a deficiency in colonial raw materials and luxuries. There is not a single industrial concern in Germany and not a single household which has not come to perceive the want of cotton, wool, and other fibrous stuffs, of leather, guttapercha, of oils and fats used in technical manufacture, of fat for cooking, of coffee, tea, cocoa, fodder, and so forth.

In earlier times, in the times of closed economic states, economic life aimed almost entirely at satisfaction within the limits of one's own country, and only a few luxuries, which made no excessive demands on cargo-space, were brought from overseas; whereas during the last few decades our economic life, in consequence of the vast extension of steamboat and railway traffic, with its lower freights and great holding capacity, is more and more freeing itself from local preoccupations for the supply of raw materials and replacing them by import from abroad. The foreign imports were a necessary condition of the increase in our population, which within the last fifty years has made possible almost a doubling of the German people. The increase in population has had, in its turn, as a result, a rise in the demand for foreign articles, and thus, both as cause and as effect, has led to German economic life becoming more and more dependent upon the import from abroad of raw materials and food. This dependence is now established by the development of economics and the increase of the population, and will not admit of any retrogression.

In the first period of the war the effect of this cutting off of supplies was limited to a few branches of economic life, but it has more and more made itself felt and exposed the German people to serious shortage and in many departments to actual want and privation. In the first place, the million German workers who earned their living in the textile industries came to realize, as a result of the closing of the factories,

---

[44] *Norddeutsche Allgemeine Zeitung,* February 11, 1918, II, 3. Dr. Solf wrote this statement as an introduction to a special pamphlet on Colonies for the *Deutsche Kriegswochenschau.*

their dependence on overseas supplies. Other industries soon followed. Still more has the daily household life of every individual suffered from the want, most of all, of soap-fats, caused directly by the lack of raw material for margarine and indirectly by the lack of fodder, which, previously, in the form of milk, butter, lard, and meat, had formed the food of the people. Under the lack of tea, coffee, and cocoa, the German people, though they could have borne the absence of these as luxuries in themselves, have been heavily tried in view of the general simplification and retrenchment of daily housekeeping. The only reason why the cutting off of the importation of cotton, wool, and other fibrous material and of hides did not lead to a catastrophe in the clothing of our population was that in a country like ours, where there is such a high average of material outward *Kultur,* there was a large superfluity of clothes, linen, and shoes remaining over from peace time that could be drawn upon as from a reserve. The effect of the cutting off of the overseas imports might be followed up in yet many other details; I pass by this, since every individual has sufficiently felt the effect for himself, and since many among those who previously used cotton products and edible fats without a thought, as a matter of course, may now have been brought to reflect on the origin of these wares. The end of such a train of thought will generally have been: "Imports from overseas."

What will happen when the war is over? The goods which we have drawn from countries with similar climatic conditions, such as bread and grain for fodder, we shall have in future to try to secure for ourselves by improvements in our agricultural methods and by the cultivation of our commercial relations with neighboring, and especially with allied, states. It is a different matter with wares which require different climatic conditions. Whoever looks for salvation on the day after the conclusion of peace and thinks that everything will settle back into the old ways which were barred by August 1, 1914, will probably be grievously disappointed. England and her allies threaten us with an ɔmic war following the war of weapons, and are making all their preparations to bring all the raw material of the world under their control. Assuming the worst, that it may come to an economic war in the acute form thus threatened, where shall we obtain the colonial raw material native to territories now for the most part in the hands of our present enemies? Those neutral countries overseas which are not under enemy control do not suffice to cover our requirements. And even if from business interests our present enemies at a later date should allow their surplus in raw material to fall to us, do you suppose that it will not come to us burdened with export duties or other such imposts as will make our industrial competition and the maintenance of our industrial army of workers impossible? In this case it is only a colonial territory of our own which can deliver us from the burden of economic pressure of our enemy. Our colonies before the war contributed indeed only a small portion of our requirements in raw materials. But the point is not so much that we should obtain all our raw materials from our own colonies as that we should be able to fight an enemy trust in the world's raw materials market. For that purpose experience shows that a comparatively small amount of untaxed materials is enough; and if we succeed by intensive labor and, if possible, by extension of our colonial possessions in raising our colonial production of raw materials, which was small before the war but rapidly increasing, we may then hope to be able to meet the enemy trust with the assistance of other raw materials which, as I have said, are not under the enemy's control. Without production of our own we should stand defenseless against the enemy.

But even if the economic war in its threatened form does not materialize, if commerce by means of commercial treaties can be secured, and producer and merchants from business motives allow personal and political sympathies and antipathies to sink into the background, there is still one thing that must be clearly recognized. Even before the war was visible the tendency to destroy the general free economics of the world by the creation of large closed economic areas, self-sufficing both as to the supply of their own raw material and in the sale of their finished products. Among the imperialistic aims of Greater Britain, even before the war, the creation of such a self-contained world system of economics held first place. In this English system the colonies were to be more closely fitted into the English world economics and combined with the homeland in a joint customs system against the other economic areas. Russia and the United States with their gigantic areas of territory stretching over different climatic zones contain within themselves the premises for such a development. Even France in its great compact colonial Empire has similar possibilities for development. Japan seeks them for herself in China. That is a development which we never promoted before the war. On the contrary, we made it our object through the commercial-political position of our protectorates to prevent it. This development, however, has not been interrupted by war economics but has become still more sharply accentuated. Sooner or later, in one place more sharply, in another in looser forms, it will assert itself yet more strongly and will do away with the effects of our commercial treaties and all industrial and mercantile efficiency. Germany's economic position must permanently languish if she does not connect herself with this development and does not at the same time secure an overseas territory or supply corresponding to and sufficient for her economic strength, one which also later on may offer a secure market for a part of her finished goods. This today can happen only in Africa, where political boundaries are still in the making. But after this war the boundaries in Africa, too, will be definitely established, possibly for many years to come. If we wish to keep pace in the future with the other economic powers, then at the peace negotiations every influence must be exerted that our colonial needs in Africa may be satisfied. What this peace fails to give us in Africa will be lost for us for a long time, possibly forever. . . . .

Finally, our position as a civilized nation (*Kulturvolk*) demands that we do not leave the labor, costs, and honor of civilizing the world entirely to the other civilized nations. Our participation in the raising of the level of uncivilized peoples and in the opening up of the tropical territories is not only a claim which we must raise with our enemies but also our duty to Germanism and humanity. The moral and the constructive work which Germany has shown in this war demands a field of endeavor beyond our borders.

142. STRESEMANN'S SPEECH IN THE REICHSTAG, FEBRUARY 27, 1918[45]

Gentlemen, the pending conclusion of peace with Russia will have a decisive influence upon the further course of the World War. It means the defeat of our greatest military enemy in this war. . . . . These [the peace negotiations at Brest-Litovsk] will have the immediate effect that Rumania will be compelled to sue us for peace. Therewith begins the liquidation of this war in the Balkans and the reorganization of political conditions there. That also means that the attempts at unification on the part of our valiant ally, Bulgaria, approach their realization. [*"Bravo!"*—*National-Liberals and Right.*] . . . . Our joy about this peace in the East is enhanced by the reports of the latest victories of our glorious armies in the Baltic provinces and our intended liberation of old German cities there. . . . .

I am gratified that the new peace terms will provide better opportunities for German trade than did the earlier proposals. Their new proposals also provide a distinction between Esthonia and Livonia on the one hand and Courland on the other.

Against this distinction we have the view not only of German but also of Lettish circles that the Balticum is a unit which in any event cannot be split up as at present it seems to be. One cannot in that way separate Courland from Esthonia and Livonia. The countries belong absolutely together. Completely independent state formations are here

[45] *Verhandlungen des Reichstags*, No. 135, pp. 4189–99.

impossible. They must find someone to lean on. They cannot live an isolated life between West and East. Financially and economically they would not be in a position to do so. We hope that it is in us that they have found and will find those on whom they will lean. . . . .

In a view of our whole situation I should regard a fresh peace offer as a mistake. [*"Quite right!"—National-Liberals and Right.*] The Chancellor certainly has no idea of one. Yet his invitation to the Belgian Government makes me feel certain misgivings. [*"Quite right!"—National-Liberals and Right.*] I think that within this formulation the defense of German interests is possible. But I must protest here against Herr Trimborn, who repeatedly referred to the papal note in connection with Belgium. According to that, Belgium is to be restored to independence. Such a formulation in the sense of complete independence toward anyone whatever would be something less than the *status quo ante,* since the *status quo* forbade Belgium to make a defensive or offensive alliance against Germany. If we restore Belgium, it must be established that this cannot mean any sort of freedom to take part in any way in any sort of military or economic actions against Germany. [*"Quite right!"—National-Liberals and Right.*] Therefore, in the possible event of negotiations with Belgium, I prefer by far the point of view of Count Hertling to that of the papal note. But, gentlemen, my chief concern is against the taking of the Belgian question out of the whole complex peace question. It is precisely if annexation of Belgium is not to take place that Belgium is our most important pledge, especially against England. The restoration of Belgium before the conclusion of peace with England seems to me an impossibility. [*"Quite right!"—National-Liberals and Right.*] It would put England in a position to play at the general peace conference the one and only big trump which she still has against Germany, namely, the territories she has occupied, and the far greater trump of shutting Germany off from the seas. [*Lively assent from the National-Liberals.*] . . . .

Scheidemann said that the Flemish question in Belgium is a question which does not concern us and is to be settled between the Flemings and Walloons. I wish to point out that Bethmann-Hollweg and Michaelis gave quite definite assurances to the leaders of the Flemish movement, and as long as these are not withdrawn—Chancellor Hertling has had no occasion to withdraw them—they exist also for the present Government. [*"Quite right!"—National-Liberals and Right.*] Anyone who attaches importance to our not being surrounded by the hatred of the world after the war ought to be the last person to treat such promises as non-existent. [*Applause from National-Liberals and Right.*]

I turn to the Rumanian question. I must say that Rumania does not deserve any consideration from us. [*"Quite right!"—National-*

Liberals and Right.] A demented aristocracy hurled their country into ruin, and the country now has to pay for it. . . . . Nor need we take any consideration for the new king who broke his faith. He has forfeited his inheritance, and will himself have to settle with his people whether he still possesses the authority which will enable him to remain on the throne. . . . . I ask whether we feel ourselves bound as against Rumania to renounce a war indemnity? . . . . Naturally, the indemnity should not be put on the table in twenty-lei pieces. We are thinking of economic concessions. The manner in which Rumania is to pay this indemnity to us is a matter to be decided at the negotiations. But I demand that Rumania restore our costs of this adventure, precipitated by the Rumanians. Of course, they cannot pay for the blood that has been shed, but they must pay for our material expenses. [*Great applause from National-Liberals and Right.*]

We must recover our colonies in order to be able to carry on again our old life as a colonial power. [*"Quite right!"—National-Liberals and Right.*] The English General Smuts has asserted that England has never militarized the natives. One stands amazed at the assertion, after England has sent a whole army of blacks to Europe. . . . . The English have not given up the old scheme of the domination of the line from Cairo to Capetown. They put a high value on German East Africa. . . . . The German people send warm greetings to the brave fighters of German East Africa who are now continuing the struggle on Portuguese territory. [*"Bravo!"—National-Liberals.*] . . . . The English assert that the stubborn defense of East Africa is due to the fact that Germany was aware of the pre-eminent importance of that colony. Had we had larger ideas before the war, we should not have lost our colonies. . . . . It would be a good thing if we could have a reassuring statement that there is no thought of giving up our position as a Colonial Power. [*"Quite right!"—National-Liberals and Right.*]

In the decisions of the Allied Socialists in London we find the demand for an independent Poland reaching the sea, for the separation of Arabia, Armenia, Mesopotamia, and Palestine from the Turkish Empire, for an independent South Slav State, and a referendum as to the future allegiance of Alsace-Lorraine. [*"Hear, hear!"—National-Liberals.*] In the face of this how can one expect to obtain peace by resignation on our part? If the Socialists among our opponents still stand for such aims, what about the Imperialists? [*"Quite right!"—National-Liberals.*] . . . . The conclusion of peace with Russia will be an example to show our enemies that no eternity will ever bring back to them what they have rejected at the critical moment. There is a great difference between our first peace terms and the present ultimatum. The fault is with those who refused to come to an understanding with

Germany and have therefore had to feel her power. We have the same possibility also in the West. Perhaps what has happened will have an educational effect there too.

Gentlemen, I now turn to questions of internal policy. . . . . The Vice-Chancellor here has developed a program to the fundamentals of which we agree. Out of the whole complex of this program I shall mention today only two questions. In connection with the bill for the establishment of Labor Councils my political friends demand that Employers Councils, too, should be created. . . . .

I now come to the question of the Prussian Franchise, which Vice-Chancellor von Payer rightly described as a German question. That is the result of the leading position of Prussia in the Empire, which must be maintained. . . . . Differences with the smaller Federal States do not affect the vital nerve of the German Empire. A direct contradiction between Imperial and Prussian policy is in the long run intolerable. . . . . Certainly the equal franchise in Prussia smooths the way for democratization. But if the equal franchise is wrecked now, then I fear a much more comprehensive democratization will come than my own friends desire. [*"Quite right!"—National-Liberals.*] The Reichstag is confronted with great tasks after the war. If the question of the Prussian franchise is not settled, then the next Reichstag will have a composition that is not favorable for the solution of tasks. . . . . What is at stake in the matter of foreign policy we all know. We can only obtain what is necessary if we hold together. [*"Quite right!"—National-Liberals, Center, and Right.*] A rejection of the equal franchise is impossible without the severest crises. The National-Liberal Reichstag "Fraktion" almost unanimously takes the view that the introduction of the universal equal franchise into Prussia is absolutely necessary. [*Lively assent from National-Liberals, Center, and Left.*]

143. ANOTHER ELUCIDATION ABOUT BELGIUM[46]

On Thursday and Friday the Chancellor spoke about Belgium in the Reichstag. Thursday's elucidation—treated as confidential—seemed to the Social-Democrats to be ambiguous and unsatisfactory. Friday the Chancellor then gave a further explanation which sounded more definite, was more agreeable to the Social-Democrats, but created the strong dislike of Count Westarp. This second elucidation, too, was to be confidential for the time being, yet the Government had to realize that the confidential giving of explanations about Belgium could not have the effect—that of furthering peace—desired by the Left. Accordingly,

[46] *Vorwärts*, July 15, 1918.

Friday's explanation was published by W.T.B. and yesterday discussed by the entire press.

The Right now demanded in its press [*Kreuzzeitung*, July 14], and possibly at another place also, that Thursday's explanation also be made public. The *Norddeutsche Allgemeine Zeitung* of Sunday now supports this wish, following, as it says, a suggestion from the Reichstag that for the sake of coherence the presentations of the Chancellor's speech of July 11, which treated the same subject, be published. Thursday's explanation of the Chancellor, in regard to Belgium, according to the official paper, reads:

"Gentlemen, as far as the West is concerned, Belgium now as before holds the foreground. That we shall not take Belgium for a protracted period has been the intention from the very beginning of the war. The war for us, as I have also said on November 29, has from its inception been one of defense and not a war of conquest. That we marched into Belgium was a necessity thrust upon us by the exigencies of the war. Equally forced upon us by the war was the necessity of Belgium's occupation. That we introduced in Belgium civil administration corresponds essentially to the Hague land-war provisions. Accordingly we have introduced there German administration in all fields, and I believe it has not been to the disadvantage of the Belgian population. Belgium in our hands is the dead-pledge for future negotiations. A dead-pledge means the safety against certain dangers which are warded off by having such a dead-pledge in the hand. This dead-pledge, therefore, one surrenders only after the dangers have been removed. The dead-pledge of Belgium, therefore, means for us: In the peace negotiations, as I have said before, we must safeguard ourselves against Belgium becoming again the advance ground of our enemies; and that not only in the military sense, gentlemen, but also in the economic. We must safeguard ourselves against being strangled economically after the war. Belgium through its relations, position, and development is essentially dependent upon Germany. If we enter into close economic relations with Belgium, that is entirely to Belgium's advantage as well. If we succeed also in obtaining an understanding with her upon political questions which touch upon vital economic interests of Germany, then we have the sure prospect of having the best guaranty against future dangers which could threaten us by way of Belgium and England and France. Kühlmann, too, agreed to this."

The official declaration in this case proceeds like a film being unwound from the wrong end. One sees the latter, Friday's explanation, first, and that which preceded, Thursday's explanation, last. This has created a wrong and misleading impression. Thursday's explanation now appears as the authentic interpretation of Friday's explanation, whereas the reverse holds true. In so far as there seems to be a discrepancy between Thursday's and Friday's explanations, that which was said Friday, of course, stands. Could the Thursday explanation create the suspicion that Germany wishes to swallow Belgium, to incorporate it both economically and politically, then such a suspicion was rejected on Friday through the assurance that we did not intend to hold Belgium under any circumstances.

How the Right now expects to operate further is evident from a release of the *Deutsche Tageszeitung,* which, in conjunction with the *Kreuzzeitung,* demands the publication of Thursday's explanation. In it Count Reventlow writes:

"The publication of the Chancellor's Friday explanation proceeded involuntarily, as probably did the entire utterance in the Main Committee, which is the last result of Kühlmann's appearance there and which forced Count Hertling to act contrary to his view that now is a time for action, not words. But after it is once published one cannot stop in the middle of the road. It is necessary that the country and the outside world know the Chancellor's expressions in his speech of July 11. The danger exists that the Chancellor's Friday explanation will be construed as an entirety in itself; yet it belongs to the continuity and connection of previous declarations and must be studied and valued as such. The Chancellor's speech is the connecting link thereto. Its publication together with the two explanations would have been the only right thing; its supplementary publication now is an imperative demand."

Already yesterday we said that the Right would make the attempt to give Friday's explanation the opposite interpretation, to blow it until it will be like a hollow egg. The instrument for this interesting endeavor it thinks to have found in the Chancellor's Thursday explanation.

We also said yesterday that the importance of Friday's explanation depends upon the Government's protecting itself against all efforts to belittle the message and also upon the seriousness of its intention not to hold Belgium under any form, never to allow its becoming anyone's vassal, Germany's either. If such doubts are allowed to exist, they attack the honor of the German Government and thereby also the honor of the German people, which it represents externally.

War prolongers abroad, of course, will make common deed with the war prolongers here and declare that Hertling's speech on Friday was only an attempt to fool, that his actual intention was revealed in Thursday's explanation, from which one must not read the wish of a "leaning" separate peace with Belgium, although one could do so. The Right apparently supports the attempt of the enemy to brand German politics as false, double-dealing, and treacherous. The dangerousness of such an attempt the Government dare not overlook and it will not be able to shun its duty to oppose it strongly. Far more important than the value of German money is the value of the German word. It is very sad that there are people who do not find the simplest fundamentals of honesty compatible with their "German importance," and we "men without a country" of yesterday have to tell them that we do not understand their conception of "national honor." The "national honor" according to our conception demands honesty, clearness, loyalty to the given work, and if it once has been said that Belgium's independence will be restored, then only that peace is to be called honorable which fulfills that promise without hesitation.

CHAPTER VIII

PEACE PROPOSALS

INTRODUCTORY NOTE

URING the World War the Central Powers attempted at various opportune periods to end the war by diplomacy. In the first phase of the war Chancellor von Bethmann-Hollweg tried to make peace with England but was never able to remove the Belgian obstacle. The political parties and public opinion in general were opposed to the complete restoration and indemnification of Belgium and were largely responsible for the failure, in the spring of 1915, of the mission of Colonel House and of the Anglo-German conversations at The Hague.

After the fall of Bucharest the Central Powers made their great peace offer of December 12, 1916, which was rejected by the Allied Powers. The peace diplomacy of Germany was then fundamentally altered by the entrance of the United States into the war and the outbreak of the Russian revolution. The Czernin memorandum illustrates the new peace policy of Austria-Hungary, whose ultimate aim was to induce Germany to sacrifice Alsace-Lorraine for the sake of a general peace. In July 1917 the Social-Democratic Party, the Progressive People's Party, and the Center Party united upon a peace resolution, which was adopted by the Reichstag.

In August 1917 Pope Benedict XV addressed a peace note to the belligerents. The reply of the Imperial Government to the Pope on September 19, 1917, failed to make a definite statement concerning Belgium. At this time the civil and military directors of the Empire did not utilize the Reichstag resolution and missed a diplomatic opportunity.

The peace negotiations at Brest-Litovsk from December 1917 to March 1918 revealed another abandonment of the July resolution for a peace by understanding. Chancellor von Hertling, however, carried on a public debate with President Wilson on the "Fourteen Points" and the "Four Principles."

In March 1918 Colonel von Haeften attempted peace conversations with American groups at The Hague. He acted without the previous knowledge of the Supreme Command, as well as without formal instructions from the Foreign Office, and his negotiations were fruitless. However, his memorandum to von Kühlmann, June 3, 1918, contained a correct estimate of the situation. Especially important was the increasing effect of the hunger blockade upon the desires of the Allied and Associated Powers for a peace by understanding.

On June 24, 1918, Foreign Minister von Kühlmann declared in the Reichstag, in accordance with the Memorandum of Colonel von Haeften, that the war could not be ended entirely by military means. The General Staff, which secured von Kühlmann's immediate dismissal, was, however, forced, after the military reverses of July 15–August 8, to inform von Kühlmann's successor, von Hintze, that the war must be ended by diplomacy. This was followed by the historic demand which led to the sending of the first note to President Wilson.

144. MEMORANDUM BY KANNER OF A CONVERSATION WITH ZIMMERMANN, OCTOBER 25, 1915[1]

. . . . I then asked Zimmermann how affairs stood with America. He replied that things are beginning to get better with the Americans. "Mr. Wilson," he said scornfully, "has recently married"; and then added laughingly that doubtless Wilson would now have more important things to do than to write us Notes. I said thereupon that if relations with America were now that favorable, could one not assume that America would now attempt to mediate between the warring states? Zimmermann then grew furious and said at the top of his voice: "What! Mr. Wilson should bring us peace? To that we absolutely refuse to assent. After all Mr. Wilson has done to us shall we accept his mediation? Not a trace of it! Rather—" and here he raised his voice to a piercing tone, turned his head in the direction of the window, and pronouncing every word distinctly said, "rather will I hang myself on this window frame than consent to Wilson bringing us peace."

I said that among the people, however, there was a frequent expectation that peace would come soon and that people often speak of Christmas as the possible time when peace negotiations will begin. . . . . Zimmermann looked at me smilingly, as if he wished to say that he had not realized that I, too, was so naive. After a brief interval he said: "Yes, that is the way people talk. Christmas is a family and a peace feast, and

[1] Kanner Papers, II, 328–36.

therefore people think that there must be a peace. That is the only basis for such a view." I thereupon asked once more whether there were really no serious reasons for the expectation of an early peace. He repeated that there was nothing in sight.

145. KAISER WILHELM II TO THE IMPERIAL CHANCELLOR, OCTOBER 31, 1916[2]

New Palace, 31.10.16

My dear Bethmann :

Afterwards I thoroughly reflected upon our conversation; it is clear that the peoples of our enemies, who are under the influence of the war psychosis and who are bound in madness and hatred by lies and falsehoods, do not have men who have the capacity or the moral courage to pronounce the liberating word. Making the peace proposal is a moral act necessary for relieving the world, including the neutrals, from the burden which weighs upon all. For the commission of such an act a ruler is necessary who has a conscience, who feels himself responsible before God, who has a heart for his and the enemy peoples, and, finally, who, irrespective of the intentional misinterpretation of his move, has the desire to free the world from its suffering. I have the courage to do it. Trusting God I shall risk it. Submit the notes to me at an early date and make everything ready.

(*Signed*) Wilhelm I. R.

146. BEGINNING AND END[3]

The Main Committee of the Reichstag listened yesterday with the greatest attention to the Chancellor's words. . . . .

When will it come to an end? If all people of Europe should think as the great mass of the German people thinks, then it would end today. Peace at any price? No! But war, continuous war for conquest? Even less! A defeat, partition of the country, slavery under the yoke of the enemy? Never! But a peace of reconciliation, which gives all nations, great and small, the right of living their own life immediately rather than tomorrow!

That is the way ninety-nine Germans out of a hundred think today. When the other nations come to think the same, we shall have peace. The Chancellor's address of yesterday is, perhaps, a step toward the desired goal!

[2] *Norddeutsche Allgemeine Zeitung,* January 15, 1917.
[3] *Vorwärts,* November 6, 1916.

What the German Government intends to do is now fairly clear. What belongs to France shall remain French; what belongs to Belgium shall remain Belgian; what belongs to Germany shall remain German. That is what the Chancellor said yesterday, using different words than Scheidemann but speaking no less clearly. Poland shall be freed from Russia and shall depend on the Central Powers. The Chancellor consented to the idea of an International Court of Arbitration advocated by Wilson and Grey. In doing so, he expressed himself so strongly that one cannot doubt his honesty.

147. SPEECH OF THE IMPERIAL CHANCELLOR IN THE REICHSTAG, DECEMBER 12, 1916[4]

Gentlemen, the reason why the Reichstag was not adjourned for a long period, and why your President was given discretion to fix the date for the next plenary session lay in the hope that fresh favorable events would soon occur in the field. The hope has been fulfilled almost more quickly than had been expected.

I will be brief. Actions speak.

Rumania's entry into the war was to have destroyed our position and that of our allies in the East, and simultaneously the great offensive on the Somme was to have pierced our Western front, while renewed Italian attacks were to have paralyzed Austria-Hungary. The situation was serious. With God's help, our splendid troops have created a state of affairs which gives us complete security, a greater security than ever before. [*Lively applause.*] The West front stands. It not only stands but is equipped, in spite of the Rumanian campaign, with greater reserves of men and material than was previously the case. [*"Bravo!"*] Most careful precautions were taken against all Italian diversions; and while on the Somme and in the Carso drum fire thundered and the Russians stormed against the eastern frontiers of Transylvania, Field-Marshal Hindenburg, by leadership of unparalleled genius, and with troops which in emulation of their allies one and all have turned the impossible into the possible in what they have achieved in marching and in the fight [*lively applause*], captured the whole of western Wallachia and the enemy capital. [*Lively assent.*] And Hindenburg does not rest. The military operations are proceeding. [*"Bravo!"*] At the same time, by strokes of the sword, a firmer foundation has been laid for our economic needs. [*"Bravo!"*] Great stocks of grain, food, oil, and other goods have fallen into our hands in Rumania. Their transportation has begun. In spite of scarcity we should have come through with our own

4 *Verhandlungen des Reichstags,* No. 80, December 12, 1916, pp. 2331–32.

resources, but now our economic safety stands beyond all question. [*"Bravo!"*]

To the great happenings on land the heroic deeds of our submarines are a worthy complement. [*"Bravo!"*] From the specter of famine which they intended to invoke against us, our enemies themselves will not again be free. [*"Bravo!"*]

When his Majesty the Emperor, after the termination of the first year of war, addressed his people in a public proclamation, he said: "To live through a great experience makes [men] reverent and strong in heart." Never have our Emperor and our nation thought otherwise. Nor do they now. Leadership of genius and achievements of unprecedented heroism have created facts as firm as bronze. When the enemy counted on internal weariness, there too he was deceived. In the very midst of the pressure of the fight without, the German Reichstag has helped to create a new defensive and offensive arm, the Law for Patriotic Auxiliary Service. Behind the fighting army stands the nation at work. [*"Bravo!"*] The giant strength of the nation is at work for the one common aim. Not a beleaguered fortress, as our enemies have imagined, but one powerful and firmly disciplined camp, with unexhausted resources—*that* is the German Empire [*"Bravo!"*], firm and faithful in its union with the battle-tested brothers in arms who fight beneath the Austro-Hungarian, the Turkish, and the Bulgarian flags. Undistracted by the speeches of our enemies, which falsely attributed to us, now schemes of world conquest, now desperate cries of anxiety for peace, we have gone forward, always ready to defend ourselves and to strike for our nation's existence, for its free and secured future, always ready, on these terms, to stretch out the hand for peace. For our strength does not make us deaf to our responsibility before God, before our own nation, and before mankind. [*"Bravo!"*] Our previous declarations of readiness for peace have been evaded by our opponents. Now we have gone a step farther.

By our Constitution it was on his Majesty the Kaiser personally that on August 1, 1914, was laid the gravest decision which a German has ever had to make—the order for mobilization. During these long and heavy years of war the Emperor has been moved by the single thought how to prepare peace again for a safeguarded Germany after the struggle has been victoriously fought. No one can better testify to this than I, who bear the responsibility for all the actions of the Government. Swayed by a deep moral and religious sense of duty to his people and beyond them to humanity, the Emperor holds that the moment has come for an official action for peace. His Majesty, therefore, in complete agreement and in common with his high allies, has decided to propose to the hostile Powers that we enter into peace negotiations.

[*Lively applause. Commotion.*] This morning I handed to the representatives of the Powers who are watching over our rights in hostile states, to the representatives of Spain, to the United States of America, and to Switzerland, a note to this effect, addressed to all the hostile Powers, with the request that it be forwarded. The same procedure is being adopted today in Vienna, Constantinople, and Sofia. The other neutral states and his Holiness the Pope have also been informed of the step we are taking.

Following is the text of the note:

"The most terrible war which history has ever witnessed has been raging almost two years and a half over a great part of the world. This catastrophe, which the tie of a common civilization of a thousand years was not able to prevent, is striking at humanity in its most precious achievements. It threatens to lay in ruins the spiritual and material progress which was the pride of Europe at the beginning of the twentieth century.

"Germany and her allies, Austria-Hungary, Bulgaria, and Turkey, have shown in this struggle their unconquerable strength. They have won mighty successes over adversaries superior in number and in war material. Their lines stand unshakable against the ever-repeated attacks of the armies of their enemies. The latest onslaught in the Balkans has been speedily and victoriously beaten down. The most recent events show that a further continuation of the war will not avail to break their power of resistance, but that rather the situation as a whole justifies them in the expectation of further successes.

"It was to defend their existence and their freedom of national development that these four allied powers were forced to take up arms. Even the glorious deeds of their armies have in no way altered that fact. They have always held firmly to the conviction that their own rights and justified claims stand in no contradiction to the rights of other nations. They do not aim at shattering or annihilating their opponents.

"Supported by the consciousness of their military and economic strength and ready, if need be, to continue the struggle, which has been forced upon them, to the bitter end, yet at the same time prompted by the desire to avoid further bloodshed and to make an end of the atrocities of war, the four allied powers propose to enter forthwith into peace negotiations. The proposals which they will bring with them to these negotiations and which have for their object the guaranteeing of the existence, honor, and freedom for development of their nations offer, they are convinced, an appropriate basis for the setting up of a lasting peace.

"If in spite of this invitation to peace and reconciliation the struggle should go on, the four allied powers are determined to wage it to the victorious end. But they solemnly decline all responsibility for this before humanity and history.

["The Imperial Government has the honor, through the good offices of Your Excellency, to request the Government of . . . . to bring this communication to the knowledge of the Government of . . . ."]

["*Bravo!*"][5]

Gentlemen, in August 1914 our enemies raised the issue of the World War, the question of power. Today we put forward the question of peace, a question of humanity.

The tenor of the reply of our enemies we await with the calm which is given us by our external and internal strength and by our clear conscience. [*"Bravo!"*] If our enemies decline and desire to take upon themselves the world-burden of all the horrors that will ensue, then in the humblest homes every German heart will burn anew with sacred wrath against enemies who for the sake of their plans of conquest and annihilation prefer no cessation of the human slaughter.

In a fateful hour we have made a fateful decision. It is drenched with the blood of hundreds of thousands of our sons and brothers who have given their lives for the security of home. In this struggle of the peoples, which has unveiled all the terrors of earthly life but also the greatness of human courage and human will in a fashion never seen before, the wit of man and the hand of man cannot avail to the very end. God will judge. We intend to follow our path without fear and with unbowed heads, determined for war, ready for peace. [*Stormy applause, Left and Center.*]

148. THE PEACE PROPOSAL, DECEMBER 12, 1916[6]

MR. CHARGÉ D'AFFAIRES:

The most formidable war known to history has been ravaging for two and a half years a great part of the world. That catastrophe, that the bonds of a common civilization more than a thousand years old could not stop, strikes mankind in its most precious patrimony; it threatens to bury under its ruins the moral and physical progress on which Europe prided itself at the dawn of the 20th century. In that strife Germany and her allies, Austria-Hungary, Bulgaria, and Turkey, have given proof of their indestructible strength in winning considerable successes at war. Their unshakable lines resist ceaseless attacks of their enemies' arms. The recent diversion in the Balkans was speedily

---

[5] The peace proposal was published, precisely as here quoted by the Chancellor, in the *Norddeutsche Allgemeine Zeitung* for December 13, 1916, p. 1.

[6] United States, *European War*, No. 4, pp. 305–6. The document stands there in the English version here given.

and victoriously thwarted. The latest events have demonstrated that a continuation of the war cannot break their resisting power. The general situation much rather justifies their hope of fresh successes. It was for the defense of their existence and freedom of their national development that the four allied powers were constrained to take up arms. The exploits of their armies have brought no change therein. Not for an instant have they swerved from the conviction that the respect of the rights of other nations is not in any degree incompatible with their own rights and legitimate interests. They do not seek to crush or annihilate their adversaries. Conscious of their military and economic strength and ready to carry on to the end, if they must, the struggle that is forced upon them, but animated at the same time by the desire to stem the flood of blood and to bring the horrors of war to an end, the four allied powers propose to enter even now into peace negotiations. They feel sure that the propositions which they would bring forward, and which would aim to assure the existence, honor, and free development of their peoples, would be such as to serve as a basis for the restoration of a lasting peace.

If, notwithstanding this offer of peace and conciliation, the struggle should continue, the four allied powers are resolved to carry it on to a victorious end, while solemnly disclaiming any responsibility before mankind and history.

The Imperial Government has the honor to ask through your obliging medium the Government of the United States to be pleased to transmit the present communication to the Government of the French Republic, to the Royal Government of Great Britain, to the Imperial Government of Japan, to the Royal Government of Rumania, to the Imperial Government of Russia, and to the Royal Government of Serbia.

I take this opportunity to renew to you, Mr. Chargé d'Affaires, the assurance of my high consideration.

von Bethmann-Hollweg

To Mr. Joseph Clark Grew,
    Chargé d'Affaires of the
        United States of America   Grew

149. REPLY OF THE IMPERIAL GOVERNMENT TO PRESIDENT WILSON, DECEMBER 26, 1916[7]

With reference to the esteemed communication of December 21, Foreign Office No. 15118, the undersigned has the honor to reply as

---

[7] *Ibid.,* p. 327.

follows: To His Excellency the Ambassador of the United States of America, Mr. James W. Gerard.

The Imperial Government has accepted and considered in the friendly spirit which is apparent in the communication of the President, noble initiative of the President looking to the creation of basis for the foundation of a lasting peace. The President discloses the aim which lies next to his heart and leaves the choice of the way open. A direct exchange of views appears to the Imperial Government as the most suitable way of arriving at the desired result. The Imperial Government has the honor, therefore, in the sense of its declaration of the 12th instant, which offered the hand for peace negotiations, to propose the speedy assembly, on neutral ground, of delegates of the warring States.

It is also the view of the Imperial Government that the great work for the prevention of future wars can first be taken up only after the ending of the present conflict of exhaustion. The Imperial Government is ready, when this point has been reached, to co-operate with the United States at this sublime task.

The undersigned, while permitting himself to have recourse to good offices of his Excellency the Ambassador in connection with the transmission of the above reply to the President of the United States, avails himself of this opportunity to renew the assurances of his highest consideration.

Zimmermann

150. TO MY ARMY AND MY NAVY![8]

In unison with the rulers allied to me I proposed to our enemies to enter into immediate peace negotiations. The enemies have declined my offer. Their lust for power contemplates the destruction of Germany.

The war goes on!

The heavy responsibility before God and men for all the future terrible sacrifices, which my desire wished to spare you, falls upon the enemy governments.

In righteous indignation over the enemy's insolence and in the desire to defend our most sacred possessions and to secure for the Fatherland a happy future, you must harden into steel.

Our enemies did not want the conciliation which I offered them. With God's help our weapons shall force them to it.

Wilhelm I. R.

Great Headquarters, January 5, 1917

[8] *Norddeutsche Allgemeine Zeitung,* January 6, 1917, II, 1.

151. COMMUNICATION OF THE LABOR UNIONS TO THE IMPERIAL CHANCELLOR, JANUARY 16, 1917[9]

The Chancellor received the following communication of January 16:

"On December 12, 1916, Your Excellency proclaimed in the Reichstag the peace offer of Germany and her allies. This was unanimously supported among the ranks of the laborers and employees in Germany. This is proved by the favorable reception of the announcement of the peace offer in a conference attended by eight hundred representatives of the trade-union and employee organizations, which took place on the same day in Berlin.

"Germany's enemies declined the offer of peace. The suggestion of peace made by the President of the United States of America has also been refused by them.

"The Entente's answer to this peace note discloses war aims which can be fulfilled only after a complete defeat of Germany and her allies.

"Its fulfillment would necessarily lead to Germany's economic ruin and to the destruction of the livelihood of many hundred thousands of laborers and employees and their families.

"The unreasonable demand of the Entente could have been set forth only under the assumption that Germany's military and economic power has already been broken.

"Considering our position on the battlefields, it need not be mentioned that Germany's military power has not been broken. Furthermore, her economic power has not been exhausted. We do not deny that the separation of Germany from international markets and the insufficient regulation of the distribution of all food supplies at hand in Germany have brought misery upon large parts of the working people. In view of the future, which threatens the German people if the enemy war aims are carried out, it is absolutely necessary to secure the just distribution of the food supply at hand. Then the difficulty can be met; and all the easier because all of us will be conscious that it bears on all classes of the German people to the same degree.

"The Entente's answer removes every doubt that Germany wages a war of defense. In the full understanding that the existence of our country and of its people is at stake, we shall urge forward all powers of the working classes to the utmost.

"On December 12 the Governments of Germany and her allies proposed to put an end to the great bloodshed by peace negotiations. They

---

[9] *Vorwärts*, No. 19, January 20, 1917.

declared that their own rights and well-founded claims are not contradictory to the rights of other nations.

"The existence, honor, and freedom of development of the people shall be secured and, thus, the foundation for a permanent peace shall be laid.

"Germany's enemies refuse to carry on peace negotiations on this basis. They force the peoples, long eager for peace, to continue the destruction of human life and of the achievements of civilization.

"Under these circumstances, we declare that it is our solemn duty to work more than ever before for the existence of our country.

> "General Committee of the Trade Unions in Germany
> "P. Legien
> "General Association of Christian Trade Unions
> "A. Stegerwald
> "Association of the German Trade Unions
> "Gust. Hartmann
> "Association of the Merchants' Unions
> "Eisner
> "Association for a Uniform Right of Employees
> "S. Aufhäuser
> "Association for Technical Unions
> "Dr. Höfle"

152. SCHEIDEMANN'S ESTIMATE OF WILSON'S PEACE MESSAGE, JANUARY 22, 1917[10]

"The door to peace is not only closed but barred with such care as though its reopening were dreaded. The Entente answer will rouse the jingoes in all countries to renewed activity. Behind it lurks a veritable detestation for negotiations. The enemy rulers evidently believe that its patter is indispensable to the vigorous prosecution of the war. They did not fear the reasonableness of the German peace conditions; why did they not meet our delegates, listen to the wicked German war aims, and then proclaim all over the world that Germany's conditions were irreconcilable with the dignity and security of their own peoples? The gentlemen feared that their patter could not be kept up at the conference

---

[10] *Vorwärts*, January 25, 1917, p. 1. Attached to the item is the following: "Comrade Scheidemann gave an interview last Monday [January 22] to the American journalist, R. Swing, of the *Chicago Daily News*. The interview, which is placed at our disposal, will also interest the German public. Wilson's new peace message was not yet known at the time of the interview.—The Editors."

table. In my view, they are right. Just picture to yourself the Rumanian delegate rising and demanding guaranties of its neutrality against Austrian attacks; Italy pleading for the sanctity of treaties; the Russian delegate, somewhat ashamed, asserting that the Tsar had drawn the sword solely for the protection of small nations; or Lloyd George repeating his boxer interview: 'First I knock you out, and then march into the peace league!' They are right; such talk thrives only in an atmosphere of war fever. Could we win free of these vague phrases, we should be free of war. Our German war rhetoric, too, might be none the worse for a little combing."

When asked if he saw a prospect of early peace, he said:

"Alas! no, after what we have experienced, I foresee a long war, with great suffering for all nations. But peace will come the sooner for the President's note. This is the third time that my friends and I have looked to America to throw its moral preponderance into the scale of the people. The first time was in February 1915 when Wilson sent his identical note to Britain and Germany insisting on security for noncombatants at sea, thus requiring us to renounce the declared U-boat war, and at the same time uplifting his voice for noncombatants on land by requiring England to abandon her hunger blockade. . . . . The second time was in the summer of 1915 when he informed Germany that he would fight uncompromisingly for the freedom of the seas, whichever side might impair it. And now the third time, here he is, no longer occupied merely with the methods of warfare but presenting to the whole world his conception of an early and a lasting peace.

"I rejoice to find that Wilson's note of December 18 is regarded in other belligerent countries as a grave and important step. I have here an extract from the *Nation:*

" 'Since Wilson's speech in May, America has become more than a mediator. Every new *démarche* of President Wilson is an acceptance of Grey's invitation to set about the securing of peace. Every Note from Washington is not a platonic exercise, but an actual move in the war game.'

"But the value of Wilson's action is shown not so much by its welcome from the moderate as by the ill-mannered rage which it excites in the bellicose. Europe is not yet exhausted; there are many more war plans to be carried out; and to them Wilson's intervention is inopportune. It may be that in a year or two the bellicose in all lands would welcome it, but now it disturbs them. They are afraid of the outbreak of reconciliation; that is what underlies the Entente answer. Northcliffe called for help, Reventlow answered promptly, and they worked jointly against any understanding between the Moderates. The Entente in its note is acting as an *agent provocateur* on German policy."

What, in your opinion, does the Entente expect from the Chancellor?

"They would like the Chancellor or, better still, a man more after their own heart in his place to declare a program of mutilation and annexation—such conditions as the Navy League recommends, and as all the Chancellor's enemies would fain force upon him."

And will he not give way to them?

"I cannot speak in his name, but I feel confident that he will not. In Germany, as in all countries, there are masses who are amenable to reason but can be worked up to a righteous frenzy; and Lloyd George has stirred them up. If the Entente had let our delegates come and state our terms or had announced moderate terms of their own, the chauvinists would have shrieked in organized chorus: 'Without the Flemish coast Germany is besieged.' But a mighty and unexpected accession of support would have been gained for our program: Justice for Germany in a free Europe, Belgium for the Belgians, France for the French, Poland for the Poles and not for the Russians."

Would this program have found support on the Conservative side?

"I may mention Delbrück and his associates. It was Delbrück who, before the French victory on the Marne, when we stood before Paris, declared the annexation of Belgium incompatible with the interests of Europe and Germany. And in his last article, which went through the whole German press, he says there are now scarcely any advocates of the annexation of Belgium to Germany, a compromise is impossible, and only complete independence remains, leaving the integrity, sovereignty, and honor of Belgium intact."

But are you sure that the German Government would have been disposed for moderation, if the Entente had been ready to state moderate terms?

"I can only repeat what I said at Munich: If a proposal for a conference had been sent to us, and the German Government had refused even to hear the enemy's terms, the masses in Germany would have risen as one man."

I asked Scheidemann how strong the Moderate Party in Germany is.

"There are Extremists and Moderates in every party, even in ours; and the numbers fluctuate from day to day, according to the attitude of the enemy. It is Northcliffe's and Reuter's greatest triumph to mislead the English public as to German public opinion. . . . . Wilson's proposal for a League of Peace will have great effect in all countries on those who have been for continuing the war in order to insure peace for generations to come."

You think there is a strong movement for peace in England?

"How strong it is, I don't know. President Wilson helps it, and the authors of the Entente answer fear it. . . . . The whole world wishes to find a cure for the armament fever. They all like to have the feeling of security. Europe's men wish to go back to work again. This peace league contains a great force of attraction. Large numbers of people have come to the realization that it does not pay to sacrifice millions of human lives for the extension of territorial possessions."

You don't share in the view that the consideration of this League must be postponed till after the war?

"Not at all. The peace terms themselves will be modified if an agreement is reached as to the practicability of the enforcement of peace. This idea should be discussed in every country. I am just starting on a political tour which will bring me to many a Pan-German outpost, and in every speech I shall deal with the theme of territorial security and a League of Peace. . . . ."

If there is so widespread a readiness for peace, why need the war go on?

"That is a problem of leadership. You must not forget that the great military campaign of 1917 is already under way. The generals on both sides will not have their finely thought-out plans disturbed; the war machine is going full steam ahead. It requires more than one man's power to stop it, a force for which the workers in all countries are yearning and which in the last resort will be supplied by Socialism. And then the war will soon be over."

153. SPEECH OF SCHEIDEMANN IN THE REICHSTAG, FEBRUARY 27, 1917[11]

The feelings of Social-Democrats today are very different from those of December 12. Although our hopes of an early peace are shattered, as a Socialist I still consider that that day was one of the proudest and happiest of my life. . . . .

The Governments of the Central Powers did not specify to the hostile Governments the terms which they were prepared to offer to the proposed conference. Hence a great controversy has arisen as to whether these proposals really agreed with those of the Social-Democrats. Such a controversy seems to me very idle; at such conferences the question is not how they begin but how they end [*"Quite right!"*— *Social-Democrats*]; and I am firmly convinced that the result of such a conference, whether it happens sooner or later, will not differ essentially from those repeatedly outlined here by my friends as the proper German peace program. [*"Quite right!"*—*Social-Democrats.*] At the same time, I remain of the opinion that a still clearer expression of this

[11] *Verhandlungen des Reichstags*, No. 83, February 27, 1917, pp. 2386–93.

inevitable result in the second German note would have done more good than harm. It is true that after our previous experiences we must reckon with the possibility that a clearly expressed renunciation of all thoughts of conquest would have increased still more the energies of hostile war parties. [*"Quite right!"—Social-Democrats.*] But it would also certainly have given powerful support to the peace movement, and of course our whole policy must be directed to that end. [*"Very true!"—Social-Democrats.*] We shall be told today that our work has not succeeded. To that I reply: If today we were facing the same situation, we should act exactly as we acted then. [*"Quite right!"—Social-Democrats.*] If we can only attain the peace for which the world is longing, there must appear in every land a strong movement against all policies of unlimited conquest and against fighting to the bitter end, a movement which will show the Government the way to the necessary self-limitation. Otherwise there will be no end of it. When the enemy in their notorious answer to Wilson recklessly exposed their policy of conquest, they aroused once more in our country the firm will to defend ourselves. There was only one feeling in the people—better anything than such a peace. [*"Quite right!"—Social-Democrats.*] It is always wise to judge other nations by one's own—the differences are not so great as war-phrases strive to paint them. So I ask, if we had laid down such a program in the opposite direction, should not we have kindled the same will for self-defense in them?

When the peace offer was made we saw our task to be that of doing our best to bring about a conference in a reasonable time, and, further, doing our best to save our Government from being forced by the annexationists into demands which would once more make the realization of peace doubtful. The answer of our enemies to President Wilson blotted out our calculations. Everyone expected them not to accept the German offer of a conference without hesitating and dallying, without emphasizing their own strength, and without attempts to review our terms in advance. But even on their side there are few who expected so brutal a statement of demands, so mad a program of conquest in mockery of facts. Whatever may be said on their side of the frontier about the origin of the war, they will never wash away the new stain of blood-guiltiness which they have incurred by their brutal reception of the peace offer. [*"Quite right!"—Social-Democrats.*]

In view of this expression of their will, what could we do? . . . . The Social-Democrats thought that the great successes won by our previous methods could, without a change of method, without drawing in a further power on the side of our enemy, be secured until the desire for peace made itself felt among them too. . . . . To stick to the defense of our country, to cling to the desire for peace and to be ready to discuss with the enemies on the basis of a program, acceptable to all—that was the policy which we regarded as the right one. Our policy did not prevail. Much as we lament it, we realize the fact none the less. On the day when the enemy's conquest-program was published, one of the papers that has always opposed us most bitterly wrote an article entitled "Thanks to Lloyd George." . . . . They were right to thank him, for the war-prolongers work into each other's hands. In fact, the submarine war was decided by the Allied Conference at Rome. But now that the course has been adopted, we, too, only hope with all our hearts that it may bring us peace as soon as possible.

. . . . We could have wished that the Chancellor had before the voting of the credits given a declaration of the general policy of the German Government. The Chancellor, too, had spoken about war aims and said that he would not go into details; he had often spoken on the subject and took back nothing. His last words on the subject were those of December 12, in which he announced his readiness for peace. I have not been able to find that the Chancellor feels himself at variance with the speech of the Hungarian Premier. Count Tisza, too, has repeatedly declared that he stands by the peace offer of December 12, and the explanatory note to neutrals states that "we are still ready for peace, we are still ready for negotiations, and if the war continues, it is not our fault, but exclusively that of the enemy." Count Tisza's own words are:

"We are waging this war, because we must wage it to defend our life against attack. We will wage it against all enemies and in all circumstances as long as it is necessary for the preservation of our life, our liberty, and our essential interests, and not a moment longer. In this all our allies are agreed. If the Quadruple Alliance were to conclude with a peace of this kind that its enemies seek to enforce, such a peace could by no possible settlement be made permanent. Only a peace that arouses no thoughts of revenge in any quarter can be permanent."

These wise expressions met with the greatest favor in Germany; also with objections—not numerous but violent. . . . . We agree with Count Tisza that the war must not last a minute longer than is necessary for the safety of our Fatherland and the guaranteeing of our existence. ["*Quite right!*"—*Social-Democrats.*] The peoples of the world who suffer under this war just as much as we do must know that it is only the obstinacy of their own Governments which is responsible for their and our suffering, and that they can have peace the day they wish to have it. . . . .

154. POLITICAL REPORT OF THE DAY, APRIL 5, 1917[12]

A certain phrase in Mr. Wilson's speech must particularly be pointed out. To our people in their severe struggle for existence and freedom the President would represent himself as the bringer of true freedom. What servility of soul does he believe the German people possess when he thinks it would allow its freedom to be given it from the outside? We know sufficiently well the freedom which our enemies have in store for us. In the name of freedom England will throw us into the old impotency; in the name of freedom France will snatch from us lands of German blood; in the name of freedom their ally, Tsarism, dragged women, children, and the aged into Russian captivity. The German people has become clear-sighted in the war. It sees in President Wilson's words of peace nothing but an attempt to loosen the firm bonds between the people and princes of Germany in order that we may become an easier prey to our enemies.

We ourselves know that the important task which remains to us to solve is the consolidation of our external power and also of our freedom at home. The words which the Kaiser, in the memorable days of August 1914, spoke to the people and the Reichstag already contained a program which assumed shape more and more as the speeches of the Chancellor described it more distinctly. In the heat of the war the Kaiser never forgot the questions of the new national orientation. When recently in the Reichstag words favorable to a Socialist monarchy were spoken, they also were signs that there is confidence between the people and the Kaiser.

The common road which the Kaiser and the people tread leads to the goal, not of autocracy, as Wilson says, but of rooting a popular kingship of the Hohenzollerns firmly in the German earth. For this purpose our strength has grown in the storm.

155. CZERNIN'S MEMORANDUM, APRIL 12, 1917[13]

In April 1917—a year and a half ago—I sent to Kaiser Karl the following exposition, which was sent by him to Kaiser Wilhelm with the observation that he shared my estimate of the situation:

Will your Majesty permit me, with the frankness granted me from the first day of my appointment, to submit to your Majesty my responsible opinion of the situation?

It is quite obvious that our military strength is coming to an end.

---

[12] *Norddeutsche Allgemeine Zeitung*, April 6, 1917, I, 1.

[13] *Reichspost* (Vienna), No. 573, December 12, 1918, morning edition, pp. 2–3. Italics as in the original.

To enter into lengthy details in this connection would be to take up your Majesty's time needlessly.

I allude only to the decrease in raw materials for the production of munitions, to the thoroughly exhausted human material, and, above all, to the dull despair that pervades all classes owing to under-nourishment and that renders impossible any further endurance of the sufferings from the war.

Though I trust we shall succeed in holding out during the next few months and shall maintain a successful defense, I am nevertheless quite convinced that another winter campaign would be absolutely out of the question; in other words, that *in the late summer or in the autumn an end must be put to the war at all costs.*

Without a doubt, it will be most important to begin peace negotiations at a moment when the enemy has not yet grasped the fact of our waning strength. If we approach the Entente at a moment when disturbances in the interior of the Empire reveal the coming breakdown, every step will have been in vain and the Entente will agree to no terms except such as would mean the absolute destruction of the Central Powers. To begin at the right time is, therefore, of extreme importance.

I cannot here ignore the subject on which lies the crux of the whole argument. That is, the *danger of revolution* which is rising on the horizon of all Europe and which, supported by England, is demonstrating a new mode of fighting. Five monarchs have been dethroned in this war, and the amazing facility with which the strongest Monarchy in the world was overthrown may help to make us feel anxious and call to our memory the saying, *exempla trahunt.* Let it not be said that in Germany or in Austria-Hungary the conditions are different; let it not be contested that the firmly rooted monarchist tendencies in Berlin and Vienna exclude the possibility of such an event. This war has opened a new era in the history of the world; it is without example and without precedent. The world is no longer what it was three years ago, and it will be vain to seek in the history of the world a parallel to the happenings that have now become daily occurrences.

The statesman who is neither blind nor deaf must be aware how the dull despair of the population increases day by day; he is bound to hear the sullen grumbling of the great masses, *and if he be conscious of his own responsibility he must pay due regard to that factor.*

Your Majesty has seen the *secret reports from the governors.* Two things are obvious. The Russian revolution affects our Slavs more than it does the Germans, and the responsibility for the continuation of the war is a far greater one for the monarch whose country is united only through the dynasty than for the one where the people themselves are fighting for their national independence. Your Majesty knows that the

burden laid upon the population has assumed proportions that are unbearable; your Majesty knows that the bow is strained to such a point
that any day it may be expected to snap. But should serious disturbances occur, either here or in Germany, it will be impossible to conceal
the fact from the Entente, and from that moment all further efforts to
secure peace will be defeated.

*I do not think that the internal situation in Germany is widely dif-
ferent from what it is here. I am only afraid that the military circles in
Berlin are deceiving themselves in certain matters.* I am firmly convinced that Germany, too, like ourselves, has reached the limit of her
strength, and the responsible political leaders in Berlin do not seek to
deny it.

I am firmly persuaded that, if Germany were to attempt to embark
on another winter campaign, *there would be an upheaval in the interior
of the country* which, to my mind, would be far worse than a peace concluded by the monarchs. If the monarchs of the Central Powers are
not able to conclude peace within the next few months, it will be done
for them by their people, and then will the tide of revolution sweep
away all that for which our sons and brothers fought and died.

I do not wish to make any *oratio pro domo,* but I beg your Majesty
graciously to remember that I, the only one to predict the Rumanian
war two years ago, spoke to deaf ears, and that when I, two months
before the war broke out, prophesied almost the very day when it would
begin, nobody would believe me. I am just as convinced of my present
diagnosis as I was of the former one, and I cannot too insistently urge
you not to estimate too lightly the dangers that I see ahead.

Without a doubt, the American declaration of war has greatly ag-
gravated the situation. It may be many months before America can
throw any noteworthy forces into the field, but the moral fact, the fact
that the Entente can count upon fresh forces, brings the situation to an
unfavorable stage for us, because our enemies have more time before
them than we have and can afford to wait longer than we, unfortunately,
are able to do. It cannot yet be said what course events will take in
Russia. I hope—and this is the vital point of my whole argument—that
Russia has lost her motive power for a long time to come, perhaps forever, and that this important factor will be made use of. I expect,
nevertheless, that a Franco-English, probably also an Italian, offensive
will be launched at the first opportunity, though I hope and trust that
we shall be able to repulse both attacks. If this succeeds—and I reckon
it can be done in two or three months—we must then, before America
takes any further military action to our disadvantage, make a more
comprehensive and detailed peace proposal and not shrink from the
probably great and heavy sacrifices we may have to make.

Germany places great hopes on the U-boat warfare. I consider such hopes deceptive. I do not for a moment disparage the fabulous deeds of the German sea heroes; I admit admiringly that the tonnage sunk per month is phenomenal, but I assert that the success anticipated and predicted by the Germans has not been achieved.

Your Majesty will remember that Admiral von Holtzendorff when last in Vienna told us positively that the unrestricted U-boat warfare would bring England to her knees within six months. Your Majesty will also remember how we combated the prediction and declared that, though we did not doubt the U-boat campaign would seriously affect England, yet the looked-for success would be discounted by the anticipated entry of America into the war. It is now two and a half months (almost half the time stated) since the U-boat warfare started, and all the information that we get from England is to the effect that the downfall of this, our most powerful and most dangerous adversary, is not to be thought of. If, in spite of many scruples, your Majesty yielded to Germany's wish and consented to allow the Austro-Hungarian Navy to take part in the U-boat warfare, it was not because we were converted by the German arguments but because your Majesty deemed it absolutely necessary to act with Germany in loyal concert in all quarters and because we were firmly persuaded that Germany, unfortunately, would never desist from her resolve to begin the unrestricted U-boat warfare.

Today, however, in Germany the most enthusiastic advocates of the U-boat warfare begin to see that this means to victory will not be decisive, and I trust that the mistaken idea that England within a few months will be forced to sue for peace will lose ground in Berlin too. *Nothing is more dangerous in politics than to believe the things one wishes to believe;* nothing is more fatal than the principle not to wish to see the truth and to fall a prey to utopian illusions from which sooner or later a terrible awakening will follow.

England, the motive power in the war, will not be compelled to lay down her arms in a few months' time, but perhaps—and here I concede a limited success to the U-boat scheme—perhaps England in a few months will ask herself whether it is wise and sensible to continue this war *à l'outrance,* or whether it would not be more statesmanlike to set foot upon the golden bridges the Central Powers must build for her, and then the moment will have come for great and painful sacrifices on the part of the Central Powers.

Your Majesty has rejected the repeated attempts of our enemies to separate us from our allies, in which step I took the responsibility because your Majesty is incapable of any dishonorable action. But at the same time, your Majesty instructed me to notify the statesmen of the German Empire that our strength is at an end and that *after the close of the summer Germany must not reckon on us any longer.* I carried out these commands, and the German statesmen left me in no doubt that for Germany, too, another winter campaign would be impossible. In this one sentence may be summed up all that I have to say:

We can still wait some weeks and try if there is any possibility of dealing with Paris or Petersburg. If that does not succeed, then we must—and at the right time—play our last card and make the extreme proposals I have already hinted at. Your Majesty has proved that you have no selfish plans and that you do not expect from your German ally sacrifices that your Majesty would not be ready to make yourself. More than that cannot be expected.

Your Majesty, nevertheless, owes it to God and to your peoples to make every effort to avert the catastrophe of a collapse of the Monarchy; it is your sacred duty to God and to your peoples to defend those peoples, the dynastic principle, and your throne with all the means in your power and to your very last breath.

With deepest respect,

CZERNIN

VIENNA, 12 April 1917

156. THE PART TO BE ASSIGNED TO THE SOCIAL-DEMOCRATS AT THE PEACE CONFERENCE: BARON VON BRAUN TO COUNT CZERNIN[14]

No. 47 P   DRESDEN, April 26, 1917

It is generally conceded that the Social-Democrats will be allowed to play an important part in the peace conferences, especially the one with Russia. As a result of this, some circles are greatly perturbed, fearing that this might lead to incisive changes in the internal affairs of Germany in the future, particularly if the Social-Democrats should actually succeed in bringing about a peace with Russia. On the other hand, many merely shrug their shoulders, saying: If the Social-Democrats are unable to establish peace, who is there to do it?

In a conversation I recently had with the foremost official of the Saxon Ministry for Foreign Affairs, I was told the following:

"Scheidemann and his gang have recently turned more toward the Left, partly in order to retain their influence within the body of the Social-Democrats who otherwise might be won over by the radical element, and partly in order to avoid the danger of being considered too

[14] Collection of Austrian Documents, Hoover War Library.

much in sympathy with the existing Government when the time for peace conferences has actually arrived. The Government treats the Social-Democrats with extreme caution, as indeed it is forced to do, considering the present situation. The Government also must prepare for a time when it will have to use the Social-Democrats as a tool in the peace conferences.

"Ambassador von Leipzig, when asked whether or not the German Government will permit delegates of the German Social-Democrats to attend the Stockholm conference, was inclined to believe that the majority Social-Democrats might be permitted to do so, but, he thought, the radicals would certainly not be permitted to attend.

"Count Vitzthum, the Secretary of [the Saxon] State, whom I visited, surprised me by expressing a totally different opinion. According to him, no German Social-Democrat, no matter to what "Fraktion" he may belong, will be permitted to go to Stockholm. All Federal States, he informed me, had been advised by the Reich to forward to Berlin any application for passports made by members of the Social-Democratic party. He [Count Vitzthum] declared himself firmly opposed to the idea of permitting the Social-Democrats to play a decisive part in the peace conferences, inasmuch as Russia had refused to conclude a separate peace."

By this statement Count Vitzthum seemed to wish to indicate that if the Social-Democrats had been successful in bringing about a separate peace with Russia, they might have been considered entitled to take part in the peace conferences with the Entente.

It seems to be commonly accepted that the recent unrest in Germany, especially the strike in the munitions factories, must be traced to the Russian revolution. The unrest is believed to have been caused not so much by famine and need as by political motives and the spirit of internationalism. It is significant that the press has announced that agents working in the interest of England are attempting to create dissatisfaction in Germany, thus preparing the revolution. I was recently told that a strike of the munitions workers in all countries might bring the war to its natural end.

157. BETHMANN-HOLLWEG TO CZERNIN, MAY 11, 1917[15]

In accordance with your Majesty's commands I beg most humbly to submit the following in answer to the enclosed *exposé* from the Imperial and Royal Minister of Foreign Affairs of the 12th ultimo.

Since the *exposé* was drawn up, the French and English on the Western front have carried out the predicted great offensive on a wide

[15] Collection of German Documents, Hoover War Library.

front, ruthlessly sacrificing masses of men and an enormous quantity of war material. The German Army checked the advance of the numerically superior army; further attacks, as we have every reason to believe, will also be shattered by the heroism of the men and the iron will of their leaders.

Judging from all our experiences hitherto in the war, we may regard the situation of our allied armies on the Isonzo with the same confidence.

The Eastern front has been greatly relieved, owing to the political upheaval in Russia. There can be no question of an offensive on a large scale on the part of Russia. A further easing of the situation would release more men even if it were considered necessary to have a strong barrier on the Russian frontier to guard against local disturbances owing to the revolutionary movement. With the additional forces, the conditions in the West would become more favorable for us. The withdrawal of men would also provide the Austro-Hungarian Monarchy with more troops for the successful carrying out of the fighting on the Italian front until the end of the war is reached.

In both allied monarchies there is an ample supply of raw material for the manufacture of munitions. Our situation as regards provisions is such that with the greatest economy we can hold out until the new harvest. The same applies to Austria-Hungary, especially if her share of supplies from Rumania is taken into consideration.

The deeds of our navy rank beside the successes of the army. When Admiral von Holtzendorff was permitted to lay before His Apostolic Majesty the plans for the U-boat war, the prospects of success for the stringent measure had been thoroughly tested here and the expected military advantages had been weighed against the political risk. We did not conceal from ourselves that the infliction of a blockade of the coasts of England and France would bring about the entry of the United States into the war and consequently the defection of other neutral states. We were fully aware that our enemies would thus gain a moral and economic renewal of strength; but we were, and still are, convinced that this disadvantage of the U-boat war is far surpassed by its advantages. The largest share in the world struggle which began in the East has now been transferred to the West in ever-increasing dimensions, where English tenacity and endurance promote and strengthen the resistance of our enemies by varied means. A definite and favorable result for us could be achieved only by a determined attack on the vital one among the hostile forces, that is, England.

The success obtained and the effect already produced by the U-boat war exceed all calculations and expectations. The latest statements of leading men in England concerning the increasing difficulty in obtaining provisions and the stoppage of supplies, as well as corresponding comments in the press, not only include urgent appeals to the people to put forth their utmost strength but bear also the stamp of grave anxiety and testify to the distress that England is suffering.

The Secretary of State, Helfferich, at a meeting of the Main Committee of the Reichstag on the 28th ultimate gave a detailed account of the effects of the U-boat war on England. The review was published in yesterday's *Norddeutsche Allgemeine Zeitung*. I beg herewith to refer to the enclosed.

"According to the latest news, the Food Controller, Lord Rhondda, owing to the inadequate supply of corn, has been compelled to specify a new allotment of cargo space. This is already so restricted that more room for corn can be secured only by hindering the conduct of the war in other ways. Apart from abandoning overseas traffic, vessels could be released only by cutting down such imports as absorbed much space. England requires great transport facilities not only for provisions but also for the import of ore to keep up war industries and for pit props to enable the coal output to be kept at a high level. In view of the ore needed for England and the wood available within the country, it is not possible to restrict the cargo space in these two instances. Already, after three months of the U-boat war, it is a fact that the shortage of cargo space caused by the U-boats reduces the living conditions of the population to an unbearable extent, and paralyzes all war industries, so much so that the hope of defeating Germany by superior stores of munitions and by a greater number of guns has had to be given up. The lack of transport facilities will also prevent the larger output of war industries in America from making up for the lesser output by England. The speed with which the U-boat war has destroyed vessels precludes the possibility of building new vessels to furnish adequate cargo space. More vessels have been destroyed in a month of U-boat war than the English dockyards have turned out in the last year. Even the thousand much-talked-of American wooden vessels, if they were there, would cover the losses of only four months. But they will not come before it is too late. English experts on the subject have already said quite openly that there are only two ways of counteracting the effect of the U-boats: either by building vessels faster than the Germans destroy them or else by destroying the U-boats faster than the Germans can build them. The first has proved to be impossible, and the U-boat losses are far less than the building of new ones."

England will also have to reckon on a progressive rise in the loss of tonnage.

The effects of the U-boat war on the people's provisions and on all private and government activities will also be felt more and more.

I anticipate, therefore, the final results of the U-boat war with the greatest confidence.

According to secret and reliable information, Prime Minister Ribot recently stated to the Italian Ambassador in Paris that France was faced with exhaustion. This opinion was expressed before the beginning of the last Franco-English offensive. Since then, France has sacrificed life to a terrible extent, which will keep on mounting until the offensive ceases.

The French nation is certainly doing marvelous things in this war, but the Government cannot sustain the enormous burden after it reaches a certain limit. A reaction in the temper of France, which is kept up by artificial means, is inevitable.

As regards our own internal situation, I do not underestimate the difficulties presented by the inevitable results of the severe fighting and the exclusion from the seas. But I firmly believe that we shall succeed in overcoming these difficulties without permanently endangering the nation's strength and general welfare, without any further crisis, and without menace to government organizations.

Although we are justified in viewing the total situation in a favorable light, I am nevertheless in complete agreement with Count Czernin in pursuing the aim of bringing about as speedily as possible an honorable, and, in the interests of the Empire and of our allies, a just peace. I also share his opinion that the important factor of the weakening of Russia must be exploited, and that a fresh tentative offer for peace must be put forward at a time when both political and military initiative are still in our hands. Count Czernin estimates that a suitable time will be in two or three months, when the enemy offensive will be at an end. As a matter of fact, in view of the French and English expectations of the decisive success of their offensive, and the Entente not having lost all hopes of Russia resuming her activities, any too pronounced preparations for peace would not only be doomed to failure but would put new life into the enemy by revealing the hopeless exhaustion of the Central Powers' forces. At the present moment a general peace could be brought about only by our submission to the will of the enemy. A peace of that nature would not be tolerated by the people and would lead to fatal dangers for the Monarchy. It appears to me that quiet, determination, and caution as regards the outside world are more than ever an imperative necessity. The development of affairs in Russia has hitherto been favorable to us. Party disputes are kept more and more within the narrow limits of peace-and-war questions by political, economic, and social exigencies, and the impression grows every day that the party which makes for peace with the Central Powers will be the one to remain in power. It is our solemn duty carefully to follow and encourage the process of development and disruption in Russia and to sound the country, not with too obvious haste, but with expert skill sufficient to lead to practical peace negotiations. The probability is that Russia will avoid all appearance of treachery toward her allies and will endeavor to find a method which will practically lead to a state of peace between herself and the Central Powers but will outwardly have the appearance of a union of both parties as a prelude to the general peace.

As in July 1914 we entered unreservedly into a loyal alliance with Austria-Hungary, in like manner when the World War is at an end we shall find a basis for terms which will guarantee a prosperous peace to the two closely united monarchies.

158. MILITARY REPRESENTATIVE IN THE INTELLIGENCE SECTION OF THE FOREIGN OFFICE TO GENERAL HEADQUARTERS, MÉZIÈRES-CHARLEVILLE, JULY 29, 1917[16]

.... *Berner Tageblatt,* 28 number 348 editorial note on the rejection of the peace resolution in the English Lower House: it becomes all the more apparent that owing to the guilt of England we shall not have peace for a long time. . . . .
Letter book number 28748–14532.

159. MICHAELIS TO CZERNIN[17]

BERLIN, August 17, 1917

According to our agreement, I take the liberty briefly to lay before you my views of our discussions of the 14th and 15th instant and would be extremely grateful if your Excellency would be so kind as to advise me of your views concerning my statements.

The internal economic and political situation in Germany justifies me in the firm belief that Germany herself would be able to stand a fourth year of war. The bread-corn harvest promises better than we thought five or six weeks ago and will be better than that of the previous year. The potato harvest promises a considerably higher yield than in 1916–17. Fodder is estimated to be much less than last year; but by observing a unified and well-thought-out economic plan for Germany herself and the occupied territories, including Rumania, we shall

[16] Collection of German Military Documents, Hoover War Library.
[17] *Ibid.*

be in a position to hold out in regard to fodder, as was possible in the very dry year 1915.

There is no doubt that the political situation is grave. The people are suffering from the war, and the longing for peace is very great; however, there is no trace of any general and really morbid exhaustion, and when food is controlled any work done will be no worse than it was last year.

This economic and political prospect can be altered only if the condition of the allies, or of the neutrals, under pressure from the Entente, should become very much worse. It would be a change for the worse for us if our allies or the neutral states, contrary to our expectations and hopes, were to experience such shortage as would cause them to resort to us. To a certain extent, this is already the case; a further increase of their claims would greatly prejudice our economic position and in certain cases endanger it. It must be admitted that the situation in the fourth year of the war in general is more difficult than in the third year. The most earnest endeavors, therefore, will be made to bring about a peace as soon as possible.

Nevertheless, our genuine desire for peace must not lead us to come forward with a fresh peace proposal. That, in my opinion, would be a great tactical error. Our *démarche* for peace last December found sympathy in the neutral states, but it was answered by our adversaries raising their demands. A fresh step of the kind would be put down to our weakness and would prolong the war; and peace advances must, therefore, come now from the enemy.

The leading motive in my foreign policy will always be the watchful care of our alliance with Austria-Hungary which the storm of war has made still stronger, and a trusting, friendly, and loyal co-operation with the leading men of the allied Monarchy. If the spirit of the alliance—and in this I know your Excellency agrees—remains on the same high level as heretofore, even our enemies would see that it was impossible for one of the allies to agree to any separate negotiations offered to him unless he states beforehand that the discussion would be entered into only if the object were a general peace. If this were clearly laid down, there could be no reason why one of the allies should not listen to such a proposal from the enemy and with him discuss preparations for peace.

At present no decided line of action can be specified for such a proceeding. Your Excellency was good enough to ask me whether the reinstatement of the *status quo* would be a suitable basis on which to start negotiations. My position as to this matter is as follows: I have already stated in the Reichstag that Germany is not striving for any great changes in power after the war and is ready to negotiate, provided the enemy does not demand the cession of any German territory; with such a conception of the term "reinstatement of the *status quo*," that form would be a very suitable basis for negotiation. This would not exclude the desired possibility of retaining the present frontiers, and by negotiation, bringing former enemy economic territory into close economic and military conjunction with Germany—this would refer to Courland, Lithuania, and Poland—and thus securing Germany's frontiers and giving a guaranty for her vital needs on the Continent and overseas.

Germany is ready to evacuate the occupied French territory, but must reserve to herself the right, *by means of the peace negotiations, to the economic exploitation of the territory of Longwy and Briey,* if not through direct incorporation, then by a legal grant to exploit. We are not in a position to cede to France any noteworthy districts in Alsace-Lorraine.

I should wish to have a free hand in the negotiations in the matter of *connecting Belgium with Germany in a military and economic sense.* The terms that I promulgated, taken from notes at the Kreuznach negotiations—the military control of Belgium until the conclusion of a defensive and offensive alliance with Germany, and the acquisition of Liége (or a long-term lease thereof)—were the maximum claims of the Supreme Military and Naval Command. The Supreme Military Command agrees with me that these terms or similar ones can be secured only if peace can be enforced on England. But we are of the opinion that a vast amount of economic and military influence must be brought to bear in Belgium in the matter of the negotiations and would perhaps not meet with much resistance there, because Belgium, as the result of economic distress, will come to see that her being joined to Germany is her best guaranty of a prosperous future.

As regards Poland, I note that the confidential hint from your Excellency to give up Galicia and enroll it in the new Polish state is subject to the ceding of portions of Alsace-Lorraine to France, which, as a counter-sacrifice, must be considered out of the question. The development of Poland as an independent state must be carried out in the sense of the proclamation of November 5, 1916. Whether this development will prove to be an actual advantage for Germany or will become a great danger for the future will be tested later. There are already many signs of danger, and what is particularly to be feared is that the Austro-Hungarian Government cannot notify us now during the war of her complete indifference to Poland and leave us a free hand in the administration of the whole state.

It will also remain to be seen whether, in view of the danger caused to Germany and also to her relations with Austria-Hungary, through Poland's unwillingness to accept the situation, it would not be more desirable politically for Germany, while retaining the frontier territory as necessary for military protection, to grant Poland full right of self-determination, also with the possibility of being joined to Russia.

The question of annexing Rumania, according to the Kreuznach debate of May 1, must be considered further and solved in connection with the questions that are of interest to Germany respecting Courland, Lithuania, and Poland.

It was a special pleasure to meet you, dear Count Czernin, here in Berlin and to discuss openly and frankly with you the questions that occupy us at present. I hope in days to come there may be an opportunity for a further exchange of thoughts enabling us to solve problems that may arise and to carry them out in full agreement.

With the expression of my highest esteem, I remain your very devoted

MICHAELIS

160. AMERICA'S ANSWER TO THE POPE[18]

The Government of the United States has been the first to answer the Peace Note of the Pope. The new discussion of the conditions in accordance with which the great butchery of men can be ended is thereby opened.

The American Note is a document showing foresight and skill. With passionate accusations it directs itself alone against the *system of government* prevailing in Germany, to which it assigns the blame for all the horrors in the world. But from the German people, says America, she wants to exact no retribution, since Germany has herself suffered much in this war, which she did not want.

That is doubtless a very just remark. The German people did not want this war, and it has suffered very much in the course of it. The anxiety lest *yet worse* should be inflicted on it keeps it watchfully on the defensive. Yes, *on the defensive,* for though you may blame others a hundred times with having attacked to conquer, the German *people* is fighting only to defend itself.

The American Government has repeatedly declared that it cherishes no enmity toward the German people. But it owes us the proof of this contention, which it could furnish only by announcing as its will that the German people shall not *be plundered* and made to pay tribute to its enemies. This point, which is of decisive significance for the German people, it cautiously evades. It neither supports the wishes of its allies for conquest and compensation, nor expressly abandons them. But in

---

[18] *Vorwärts,* September 1, 1917.

France people will notice that it does not speak of these things. The single word "satisfaction" which it uses opens a wide field for interpretations.

In one respect, however, the American Note is clear. It refuses to negotiate with Germany as long as *the present system of government* subsists. It demands that the will of the German people shall stand behind the will to treat (*Vertragswillen*) of the German Government. A certain part of the German press will hasten to assert that it would be unworthy of the German people to give such pledges. We think, on the contrary, that it would be unworthy of them *to refuse* them.

The German people is fighting this hardest of all fights not for the rights of single families, and not for a particular form of government, but for its *own existence*. In this sense Social-Democracy stands for the defense of its country, and in no other. Social-Democracy refuses, in her efforts after *altered constitutional* conditions, to use means which might weaken the power of the country to defend herself. But she has not abandoned these efforts themselves.

It would be an unbearable thought that the men out there were fighting not for the preservation of the Empire but to maintain a state of things not worth maintaining. It would be unbearable to think that a single mother's son should fall, not for the rights of people, but for privileges of separate classes of the people such as today exists nowhere else in the world. This thought must not arise, and the circumstances which nourish it must be cleared away. . . . .

161. REPLY OF THE IMPERIAL GOVERNMENT TO THE PAPAL NOTE, SEPTEMBER 19, 1917[19]

Your Eminence has been good enough to transmit, together with your letter of August 2 to the Emperor and King, my most gracious Master, the Note of His Holiness the Pope in which His Holiness, filled with grief at the devastation of the World War, makes an emphatic peace appeal to the heads of the belligerent peoples. The Emperor has deigned to acquaint me with Your Eminence's letter and to entrust the reply to me.

His Majesty has been following for a considerable time with great respect and sincere gratitude His Holiness's efforts in a spirit of true impartiality to alleviate as far as possible the sufferings of the war and to hasten the end of hostilities. The Emperor sees in the latest step of His Holiness fresh proof of his noble and humane feeling, and cherishes

[19] *Norddeutsche Allgemeine Zeitung*, September 22, 1917, II, 1.

a lively desire that, for the benefit of the entire world, the Papal appeal may meet with success.

The effort of Pope Benedict XV to pave the way to an understanding among all peoples may the more surely reckon on a sympathetic reception and the whole-hearted support from His Majesty, seeing that the Emperor, since taking over the Government, has regarded it as his principal and most sacred task to preserve the blessing of peace for the German people and the world.

In his first speech from the Throne at the opening of the German Reichstag on June 25, 1888, the Emperor promised that his love of the German Army and his position toward it should never lead him into temptation to cut short the benefits of peace unless war were a necessity forced upon us by an attack on the Empire or its allies. The German Army should safeguard peace for us, and, should peace nevertheless be broken, it would be in a position to win it with honor. The Emperor has fulfilled the promise he then made by his acts during twenty-six years of happy rule, despite provocations and temptations.

In the crisis which led to the present world conflagration, His Majesty's efforts were up to the last moment directed toward settling the conflict by peaceful means. After the war had broken out, against his wish and desire, the Emperor, in conjunction with his high allies, was the first solemnly to declare his readiness to enter into peace negotiations. The German people supported His Majesty in his keen desire for peace.

Germany sought within her national frontiers the free development of her spiritual and material possessions and outside the imperial territory unhindered competition with nations enjoying equal rights and equal esteem. The free play of forces in the world in peaceable wrestling with one another would have led to the highest perfecting of the noblest human possessions. A disastrous concatenation of events in the year 1914 absolutely broke off all hopeful course of development and transformed Europe into a bloody battle arena.

Appreciating the importance of His Holiness's declaration the Imperial Government has not failed to submit the suggestion contained therein to earnest and scrupulous examination. Special measures, which the Government has taken in closest contact with representatives of the German people, for discussing and answering the questions raised prove how earnestly it desires, in unison with His Holiness, that the peace resolution of the Reichstag on July 19 may find a practical basis for a just and lasting peace.

The Imperial Government greets with especial sympathy the leading idea of the peace appeal wherein His Holiness clearly expresses the conviction that in the future the material power of arms must be superseded by the moral power of right. We are also convinced that the sick body of human society can be healed only by fortifying its moral strength of right. From this would follow, according to His Holiness's view, the simultaneous diminution of the armed forces of all states and the institution of obligatory arbitration for international disputes.

We share His Holiness's view that definite rules and the sure safeguarding of a simultaneous and reciprocal limitation of armament on land, on sea, and in the air, as well as of the true freedom of the community of the high seas are the things in treating which the new spirit that in the future should prevail in international relations should first find hopeful expression. The task would then of itself arise to decide international differences of opinion, not by the use of armed forces, but by peaceful methods, especially by arbitration, the high peace-producing effect of which we, together with His Holiness, fully recognize.

The Imperial Government will in this respect support every proposal compatible with the vital interests of the German Empire and people.

Germany, owing to her geographical situation and economic requirements, has to rely on peaceful intercourse with her neighbors and with distant countries. No people, therefore, has more reason than the German people to wish that instead of universal hatred and battle a conciliatory fraternal spirit should prevail among nations.

If the nations are guided by this spirit it will be recognized to their advantage that the important thing is to lay more stress upon what unites them in their relations. They will also succeed in settling individual points of conflict which are still undecided in such a way that conditions of existence will be created satisfactory to every nation and that thereby a repetition of this great world catastrophe may appear impossible.

Only on this condition can a lasting peace be founded which would promote an intellectual *rapprochement* and a return to the economic prosperity of human society. This serious and sincere conviction encourages our confidence that our enemies also may see a suitable basis in the ideals submitted by His Holiness for approaching nearer to the preparation for future peace under conditions corresponding to a spirit of reasonableness and to the situation in Europe.

(*Signed*) (Name of the Imperial Chancellor)

His Eminence
The Secretary of State of His Holiness
Pope Benedict XV,
Lord Cardinal Gasparri, Rome

162. SPEECH OF PRINCE MAX VON BADEN IN THE FIRST CHAMBER OF BADEN, DECEMBER 14, 1917[20]

At the end of July 1914 the French people desired to follow the lead of Jean Jaurès, who wanted the whole weight of France thrown into the scale for peace. The jingoes ordered the murder of Jean Jaurès. The French Government successfully mastered the revolutionary spirit of the people by publishing Germany's announcement of war danger, without making known the general mobilization of Russia. According to English reports the German act of self-defense against Russia thus appeared as an attack on France. Naturally, the French people now turned away from the enemies in their midst in order to protect their country. In this manner the desire for war was awakened in the French people, by fraud. The speaker then went on to say that in the decisive hour the English people were equally helpless in the hands of their Government. He spoke sharply against Wilson for reviving all the old 1914 Entente battle cries and for undertaking a crusade against Germany, as the destroyer of peace, in the name of humanity, freedom, and the rights of small nations. Those are great names, and we must not deceive ourselves. They appeal to the idealism of millions. I put this question to you: Has the President of the United States any right to play the part of universal judge? President Wilson has no right to fight in the name of humanity, for he allowed a great number of American peace industries to be changed into workshops for death and destruction at a time when America was at peace with Germany. He carefully kept within this *formal right* of providing our enemies with munitions, whilst he gave up without a struggle America's *humanitarian* rights to care for our non-combatants, especially the weak and the sick. President Wilson also allowed the care of our *prisoners of war in Russia,* which America had undertaken, to be neglectfully and heartlessly conducted. Under the old régime thousands of our prisoners of war perished miserably without America ever exercising its great power to force an improvement. He also allowed our compatriots to suffer every form of cruelty, torture, and shame in France.

President Wilson had no right to speak in the name of democracy and freedom, for he was the powerful war helper of Tsaristic Russia and turned a deaf ear to the calls for help of the Russian democracy, saying that it must be given a chance to discuss peace terms or at least not to order an offensive, in order that it might consolidate its freedom. High-minded, honorable gentleman! Even if I deny the enemy's slightest claim to occupy the position of judge, I do not wish to deny that we

[20] *Norddeutsche Allgemeine Zeitung,* December 18, 1917, I, 3.

should criticize ourselves. We are well aware that there was also a German lack of freedom, but it was not to be found in the institutions of the German Empire; it lay more in a certain spiritual attitude of broad sections of the people.

The enemies say that autocrats force their will upon a resisting people and take upon themselves the absolutely grotesque rôle of wishing to liberate the German people from these tyrants. This moves us to laughter. The fault, on the contrary, lay in the fact that many Germans were only too willing indolently to face the authorities without desiring to be personally responsible for the cause of the Fatherland. The war came as a great awakener. Everywhere the hidden forces of the people have showed themselves and all the submerged possibilities of our history have risen again to the surface. On the field of battle our people have learned how many and varied are the forces which have united to form our strength. The people in arms will return with newly steeled strength and also with strengthened rights.

We have the right to expect everything for our German future from the great united will which found its origin in the field. The spirit of our political reformers, Stein and Hardenberg, is beckoning to us with warning and with promise from the past. The fulfillment of the promise will be determined solely by the character of the people themselves. There is no doubt that the longer the war lasts, the harder will be the rebirth, not only with us, but with the enemy. He also is losing his best blood. Who can find this a theme for rejoicing? It may be impossible for Europe to find balm enough to close its awful wounds.

It looks today as if the war would be fought to the point of the final exhaustion of Europe. This is the wish of America and of the French and English governments. They boldly spurn the general aims of humanity because in them they see the pillars which will support the great uniting bridge between the peoples. . . . . [sic]

We must not let Lloyd George and M. Clemenceau deceive us. The unity which they speak of behind their lines does not exist. There are powers at work in France and England which do not want a forced peace but only a peace consistent with the honor and security of their countries. From this situation arises a double duty for us: that we gather all our national strength for the severe struggle which we still have to face; and that we simultaneously strive to clarify the spirit with which we intend to approach the ordering of things in a way contrary to the methods of the enemy Governments. If clarity is to be attained, we must not hesitate to wage a war of opinions in Germany. To muffle or hide the contrary opinions which inevitably arise, even in war time, would be to institute a false and deceiving unity at home. Real unity demands that people should discuss their problems, avoiding withal a contemptuous or provocative spirit. Gentlemen, we know that with a little good will this is possible. When our Emperor was able to speak the redeeming word on August 1, 1914, "I know no parties, I know only Germans," German history reached a high point indeed. Behind us were decades of bickering. It is with a deep sorrow that we have had again to see our sons fighting among each other with the same poisoned weapons as before. Recollection of the great feeling of solidarity during the first months of the war should bid us take heed anew to the Kaiser's word, in rightful understanding. Truly there are parties, but we are all Germans.

Gentlemen, I have come to the end. Those who direct the history of peoples have a terrible responsibility. All who are living through the war must help bear this burden at home, with their senses awake and with burning hearts. Everywhere healing powers are coming together, everywhere we are tired of the moratorium of the Sermon on the Mount. Humanity is longing for its prophecies to be fulfilled before the war has come to an end. The lately deceased Christian, Sir William Byles, who coined this terrible phrase about the Sermon on the Mount becoming a dead letter, was not thinking of the inevitable horrors of the field of battle but of the heathenish way of thinking indulged in almost proudly by so many of the higher intellectual men of all countries during the war.

We must turn from this war-coarsening before war stops, and we can well follow the guidance of the best spirit in the army. A Christian soldier is as much imbued with the spirit of the Red Cross as with the spirit of Mars. He considers it as much a breach of duty not to spare a defenseless enemy as not to try and annihilate the enemy. From England we hear similar voices which tell us how English priests learned to respect the enemy from the fighting troops, which will not stand the dictates of the shouting press at home. From this feeling originated the Hague agreement on the exchange of prisoners. The scheme has not yet been carried out; it still needs enlarging.

In the appeal of the "Office for the Information and Help of Germans Abroad and of Foreigners in Germany" there is a sentence which I would quote here: "In war also the love of the enemy is the sign of those who are faithful to their Lord." I should like to add to this, "It is also the sign of those who are faithful to Germany."

It has been stated that hate is necessary for an energetic prosecution of the war. A German princess has made the following reply to this assertion: "The love of country is enough for any sacrifice." Power alone cannot assure our position in the world, which we consider our right. The sword cannot destroy the moral resistance which has been raised against us. If the world is to become reconciled to the greatness of our power, it must feel that a world conscience is behind that power. I agree with this statement. To satisfy this demand we need only open the gates of our innermost beings, for through the whole German spiritual history shines out our feeling of responsibility to all mankind. This sign can be written in truth on Germany's standards: *In this sign you will conquer.*

163. OFFICIAL REPORT OF AN INTERVIEW GIVEN BY PRINCE MAX VON BADEN TO DR. MANTLER, DIRECTOR OF W.T.B., CONCERNING THE SITUATION[21]

The Prince said: This peace is important in many respects. I believe that the foundation of the Ukraine will prove a factor of lasting pacification in European history. There were two ways out of the Russian Revolution: the one leading to order, toleration, and freedom; the other back to officially ordered murder and massacre. The Russian foreign nationalities were resolved to tread the first path and are now fighting for their existence against the representatives of the other tendency. Germany had to decide either for peace with the Bolsheviks, with the sacrifice of the nationalities which are putting their affairs in order, or for peace with those border peoples who ask only to be able to consolidate themselves decently. I rejoice at the decision that has been taken. In so far as they consist of idealists, the Bolsheviks are fighting for an idea: the destruction of nations. Wherever citizens of different classes and standing combine their forces for the sake of a national task, they want to break up and undo these forces. That applies to Finland as much as to Germany or France or England. They aim at nothing more nor less than preparing Finland's fate for the whole of Europe.

It has ever been Germany's historic task to be a bulwark against the destructive forces threatening from the East. This we did in 955 at Lechfelde, in 1241 at Liegnitz, and in 1914 at Tannenberg. Hindenburg's victories were not only Germany's victories but Europe's. Anyone who has not understood that does not understand the real grounds for our anger with England. I cannot forget with what satisfaction Great Britain pictured in 1914 and 1915 how the Russian steam-roller would crush Germany.

Vigilance is necessary again now against the great danger threatening from the East. There is the risk of a moral infection. When cholera and plague are threatened—and these dangers are not merely of the past—all civilized states have to adopt joint preventive measures. Sick Russia of today's sole ambition is to carry her disease into all healthy

21 *Norddeutsche Allgemeine Zeitung,* February 16, 1918.

states and into states which are regaining health. It is time to be clear as to the preventive measures which are necessary.

First Trotsky proclaims a world-destiny which he wants to bring about. One must fight ideas with ideas. To Trotsky's world-disorder, which is destructive of liberty, we must oppose a world-order which protects liberty. Germany must confidently state that she is taking the happiness and rights of other peoples under her national direction. We must have a good name not only within our own borders. In this Germany must not forego her moral consideration in the world. That would be striving for a peace of renunciation.

As a second measure of safety it is necessary that we should make our German organism as sound and capable of resistance as possible. All the requisite conditions for this exist. We have behind us a national advance without parallel, a joint exertion of strength, joint suffering, and unprecedented experiences of danger and salvation, such as must weld a people together, even if it were not so united a structure as the German. But there are forces at work today which design to slacken the German organism, forces which place themselves at the service of the diplomatic offensive, which our enemies pride themselves on having undertaken for the destruction of our domestic front. I am thinking first of those groups on whom the feeling of August 4 made no impression, who have long been working to destroy belief in the justice of the German cause and to put Germany in the wrong, both at home and abroad. Despondent and embittered elements have joined them, as was unavoidable in a war lasting so long. But the great mass of the German working people protest with a strong and sound instinct against the attempt to weaken Germany's defensive power.

Therefore I regret the agitation, which aims at branding and isolating wide circles of our people as unpatriotic. There must be strife in every country over the war aims; but I should like to take every opportunity of repeating what I said in Karlsruhe: in our internal differences we must cease always accusing our political opponents of unpatriotic motives; such accusations should not be made aloud, even as weapons in the war of words.

That is an offense against the front and the feeling prevailing there. No qualified person should stand aside from the task of keeping this general national feeling alive at home also; otherwise we imperil our immunity against the Eastern infection. I have an English paper before me which reports that the English trade unions have asked the old Tory leader, Lord Lansdowne, to address them. This is a national necessity which the old parties in Germany also should be eager to develop.

The third and most effective preventive measure would, of course, be peace.

I asked the Prince what he thought of the prospects of a general peace. He answered:

"The key to the position is in the hands of the Anglo-Saxon peoples. It is very difficult to see clearly. Reports from America are very contradictory. I will not anticipate the Chancellor's reply to President Wilson, but will point out only that in his last speech the President did not speak as a world-judge.

" 'The United States has no desire to interfere in European affairs or to act as arbiter in European disputes. She is quite ready to be shown that the solutions she has suggested are not the best or the most enduring. They are merely her own provisional sketch of principles and of the way in which they should be applied.' These words are significant; everything would be gained if once the people get so far as to speak to one another without any claim to infallibility but rather in a Christian spirit. The American papers give another picture than that which we get from Wilson's speech. It is as though Reuter had placed all his hackneyed material for agitation at the disposal of the Americans. The delight in war shown by the American press reminds one of the feeling in the Entente countries in the years 1914 and 1915.

"It is likewise difficult to form a clear, matter-of-fact idea of the views now prevailing in England. Lord Northcliffe and Reuter regard it as their special task to show Germany an England with whom there can be only a war of life and death. Certainly, other voices are heard, but the real decisive question remains: What is the comparative strength of the conflicting tendencies? This question I am unable to answer. One thing is certain: the Versailles War Council has once more proclaimed a decision by force of arms alone. There are many serious parallels between the situation today and that at the end of 1916. Then, also, there were strong currents in England (the *Morning Post* revealed that they reached into the Cabinet and even gave the names of their opponents) which favored a peace of understanding; of course, only a peace which was compatible with England's honor and safety. Lloyd George saw threatened his great offensive in which he so rejoiced as War Minister, and made the knock-out speech which summoned the war passions of all countries to his help. So the campaign of 1917 came about. Today there are men of all parties in England looking for a way out—a public conversation between statesmen has just been going on, as in 1916, in the conversations between Grey and Bethmann over the League of Peace. The Versailles Council meets and rejects the idea of negotiations, and England takes the field for the reconquest of Alsace-Lorraine."

Here I objected that in neutral quarters it had repeatedly been pointed out that Lloyd George had changed; in respect to Alsace-

Lorraine, he had used the word "reconsideration" as opposed to the former announcement of war *à outrance,* contained in the demand for restoration. The Prince answered:

"Palliating symptoms of that kind have been pointed out to me by neutral friends also. I was reminded of the speech to the trade unions, and of the earlier Glasgow speech in which he proposed making the colonies the subject of a conference. I had no faith in this. Lloyd George has become once and for all, in the history of the world, the exponent of the knock-out militarism, of the inexorable will to destroy. When such a man suddenly appears to be looking for a bridge between himself and his adversary, two interpretations present themselves unavoidably. The first, England is so weak that Lloyd George is unwilling to take on himself a further continuation of the war; the second, Lloyd George wants to fool the German and English supporters of a peace of understanding, in order to facilitate the war, the continuation of which he desires. I rejected the first interpretation at once. This claim of seeing signs of weakness in the opponent belongs to those illusions which prolong the war again and again. How often have the enemies seen in Germany signs of approaching breakdown! We do not wish to be guilty of the same mistake. The moral resources of a nation whose war is a people's war are almost inexhaustible. But the second interpretation, the one involving dishonesty, I regard as correct, and events have shown that I was right. For a few short weeks Mr. Lloyd George donned the sheep's clothing of the pacifist only to discard the troublesome garment with unseemly haste at the first opportunity. How are we otherwise to explain the great haste with which the operations in London and at Versailles were carried through? Lord Robert Cecil did not even wait until he had read Count Hertling's speech before declaring that it was unacceptable as a basis of peace. Yet its main program was:

"1. The integrity of German state territory, and of the state territories of her allies, as also renunciation on principle of economic war.

"2. It was not Germany's intention forcibly to incorporate the conquered territories.

"3. We are prepared to negotiate as regards everything else.

"But to negotiate is precisely what the enemy does not want. This fear of the conference table is the infallible test of the war aims for which the enemy Governments are striving. . . . . Only those who must fear that the negotiations will expose the unfairness of their own and the fairness of the enemy demands must shrink from a conference as the guilty shrink from legal proceedings.

"Mr. Lloyd George and M. Clemenceau have therefore decided in favor of the campaign of 1918. The feeling of responsibility toward humanity would have demanded that one should not let loose hell again this year before an honest attempt had been made to see if the differences between the belligerents had not already disappeared or if negotiations might bridge them over. I consider it likely, even very likely, that this attempt would have failed; but a huge burden would have been lifted from every conscientious man—the conditions would have been made clear. In a certain sense they are already clear. Mankind is to enter upon this year's campaign, which must be the bloodiest of all, because it has been so decided at Versailles."

I asked the Prince if Lord Lansdowne's letter did not appear to show a way out. He answered:

"To speak of peace, pure and simple, sounds well. The conception is correct that, as a preparation for peace, an agreement upon certain general aims must be reached, aims which stand out from the multitude of special aims which are not those of any one nation but are to a certain extent those of all nations. Every public discussion in this matter is advantageous. (1) I will begin with a demand which is deeply rooted in the history of the German people, the freedom of the seas. The basic principle involved in the freedom of the seas is that on sea and on land non-combatants should be spared the injuries of war; no fresh wars of starvation should be waged. The sure establishment of freedom of the seas would mean more than the giving to coming wars of a more humane form—it would be a guaranty of peace, for the prospect of being able to misuse sea-power unpunished is one of the greatest temptations to war. (2) The world must not be divided into two groups of powers which outbid each other in the matter of armaments. The aim which must be our guide is that which the Chancellor accepted in November 1916—the co-operation of nations to prevent future wars. But the moral conditions for this will be brought about only when a change of disposition has entered into the life of the nations, when the various nations aim at co-operation instead of antagonism. (3) The first sign of this change of disposition would be a general avowal of commercial peace. Peace must not be a continuation of war carried on by other means. (4) The groups of colored people must also not be looked upon merely as a means to an end. Their right to be an end themselves must be recognized, as has been demanded. The opening up of Africa must take place according to the fundamental principles of a feeling of responsibility toward the black races and of consciousness of the solidarity of the white races.

"These aims are the aims of humanity. They will be pursued unceasingly in all countries. He who stands by them will be the victor. He who denies them will be defeated."

164. SPEECH OF SCHEIDEMANN IN THE REICHSTAG, FEBRUARY 26, 1918[22]

Even without the information Under-Secretary of State von dem Bussche has just given us, it would be impossible to go into the general political situation in this debate without thinking of Russia's great tragedy, on the fifth act of which the curtain will probably fall in a day or two. The Imperial Chancellor informed us yesterday that the Russian Government had accepted the German peace conditions.

It is not our intention, the intention of German Social-Democracy, that—I say this quite openly—Russia's fate should be what it is now. We fought in order to defend our Fatherland against Tsarism and we are still fighting the Entente plans for conquests. We were fighting just as little for the dismemberment of Russia as for the suppression of Belgian independence or to get Longwy or Briey. [*"Quite right!"*— *Social-Democrats.*] We consider it necessary to proclaim to all the world that the policy which has been pursued toward Russia is not our policy. The Imperial Chancellor's former announcement here that he would stand for the right of self-determination of peoples was received with applause. That he did not add at that time that the right of self-determination of the Russian border nations excluded their voluntary reassociation with Russia was no doubt an act of diplomatic caution. Such caution, however, is likely to call forth equal caution on the other side. After the Russian Government had agreed to the German proposals at Brest-Litovsk the release of the Russian border countries from Russia appeared unavoidable. We doubt whether anything profitable for the future of the German nation was attained by this. [*"Quite right!"—Social-Democrats.*] Frankly we fear the contrary. Meanwhile there is nothing to be gained by making empty protests against things which we endeavored but were not strong enough to prevent. But we regard it as our duty to say here that these countries ought not to be brought into a relationship with Germany which they themselves perhaps do not wish. We further regard it as our duty to say once more, at the eleventh hour, that conditions should not be created which must finally make the outbreak of the idea of *revanche* in Russia unavoidable. [*"Quite right!"—Social-Democrats.*]

If our views had no effect on the Eastern policy, if a course was taken against our advice which we were convinced would not be for the benefit of our people, Russian Bolshevism had its fair share in this development of affairs. It completely disarmed Russia, after Tsarism had lost its battles, and showed not the slightest interest in preserving

22 *Verhandlungen des Reichstags*, No. 134, February 26, 1918, pp. 4162–67.

the Russian Empire, at all events not at the beginning. In so doing it played into the hands of all separatist designs. If it now asks that we should try to repair the consequent injury by a revolution, it asks too much of us. We are still at war in the West, and the Bolshevist recipes have not proved so good that their application to Germany can be recommended. If the German workmen were now to attempt to save Russia, and if Germany were thereby reduced to the same condition as Russia, could we hope that the English and French would follow their lead and save Germany? One's faith would have to be very great to cherish this confidence. We feel painfully that we have not the power to arrest a development which we regard as evil. But we do not wish to attain power under conditions which would compel us to conclude a peace with the Entente such as Trotsky and Lenin are now concluding with the Quadruple Alliance. [*"Very good!"—Social-Democrats.*] There is not one in this House who wishes that. The nature of the conclusion of peace with the Ukraine and Russia makes the political situation more complicated as regards the West. England, as was to be expected, has refused to recognize the Ukraine peace. Wilson has adopted the point of view that all peace questions should be solved together at a general conference of the Powers. On the other hand, the conclusion of peace in the East creates accomplished facts. I regard the idea that the Entente will recognize these facts as too optimistic, so long as they are not compelled to do so. We Social-Democrats adopt the position that the arrangement made in the East ought not to be an insurmountable obstacle in the way of a general peace. The happiness this arrangement is to give us is of a highly doubtful nature. Or have you observed anywhere among the German people joy and satisfaction that Lithuania, Courland, Poland, and perhaps other countries are to be more or less "voluntarily" attached to us? Oh, no; the German people rejoice in the thought that at least a portion of the longed-for peace is there, and they hope that the remainder will soon follow. [*"Very true!"—Social-Democrats.*] They regard the contemplated "attachments" with great dissatisfaction and distrust. A conclusion of peace of another nature in the East might perhaps have gained us more tranquillity and security. [*"Very true!"—Social-Democrats.*]

Some of you are of the opinion that the West will be ready for a peace of understanding if only it fares tolerably well itself; that it takes no further interest in Russia. I sincerely hope that you may prove to be right, but a condition of this is that the German Government shall be prepared for a real peace of understanding such as the Reichstag majority wishes and such as the Imperial Chancellor also wishes, and not a peace such as is to be concluded with Russia. When one sees what has happened in Courland, Lithuania, etc., and what many wish shall happen in Flanders, the similarity is striking. The statement the Imperial Chancellor made recently in the Main Committee as regards the West was, unfortunately, not so compellingly unequivocal that it could not finally be explained somewhat as the Brest-Litovsk statement of December 25 was explained on December 27. In foreign countries people still believe in the designs of the German Government on Belgium and on Longwy and Briey, and, unfortunately, after the experience we have already had we cannot say offhand with absolute certainty that this belief is entirely mistaken. That can be stated only by the Government itself, and we expected such a statement, aye, we ought to demand it quite definitely in the present debate. The Imperial Chancellor said plainly yesterday that he accepted the four principles of a general peace proposed by Wilson and that he is therefore prepared to enter into peace negotiations on the basis proposed by Wilson. We sincerely welcome this announcement. [*Lively assent.*] But the significance of this will be fully evident only if one keeps in view what Wilson said in direct connection with the enumeration of the four points he had formulated, namely:

"As far as we can judge, those principles that we regard as fundamental are already accepted everywhere as imperative except among the spokesmen of the military and annexationist party in Germany. If they have been rejected anywhere else, the objectors have not been sufficiently numerous or influential to make their voices audible. The tragic circumstance is that this one party in Germany is apparently willing and able to send millions of men to their death to prevent what all the world now sees to be just."

Now, gentlemen, this one party of which Wilson speaks is fortunately no longer of decisive importance in this country. [*Laughter from the Independent Socialists.*] The Imperial Chancellor does not intend, as his speech of yesterday has shown, to pursue a policy with the minority against the will of the German people. [*"Quite right!"—Left.*] Neither can the curious reception accorded to Herr v. Payer by the Extreme Right be very well interpreted as meaning that he had shown any inclination to make concessions to the Right. [*Joyous assent.*]

In accepting Wilson's four points, the Chancellor should also have made clear to the whole world the meaning in general of his statements regarding Belgium and the West. Whoever accepts Wilson's points must, of course, renounce every plan of conquest and oppression. As Count Hertling said yesterday, we wish to live in peace and unity with Belgium. But that can take place only if its independence is completely restored. Therefore, the Flemings and Walloons must themselves solve their political differences. The Chancellor has expressed the wish that a discussion about Belgium in a narrower circle take place. We welcome it . . . . and hope that it will lead to peace. Do what you can, Herr Chancellor, to preserve the life and health of hundreds of thousands, and to stem the hatred and death of hundreds of thousands.

To those armchair conquerors and might-politicians, I wish to say this: they cannot impose their imperialistic program permanently on the East and the West without first reducing the West to the same degree of impotence and consequent readiness to accept unconditional terms of peace as Russia. Such an attempt would mean a trial of strength which would be dangerous for Germany if it failed and also dangerous for Germany if it succeeded. For that would mean a peace which would turn the whole world into a vast military camp. And to preserve such a peace, our impoverished and war-weary nation would have, in the future, to bear the most terrific armament burden. . . . .

Should the coming peace be no real peace but only a time of preparation for fresh wars, it will bring about the realization of the Bolshevist dreams, a world revolution. [*"Very true!"—Social-Democrats.*] You, gentlemen, would be unable to prevent that. There is a degree of disappointment which no people can endure. [*"Very true!"—Social-Democrats.*] We are convinced that we show our patriotism best by warning you against thinking only militarily, and not politically. [*"Very true!"—Social-Democrats.*] No state in the world, not even the strongest, can live permanently without peace. Where are our friends? Yesterday there were still the Poles, so we were told; but what has become of this friendship? In Austria-Hungary there is great ill feeling with regard to the fresh military measures against Russia in which Austria is not taking part. [*"Hear, hear!"*] And the majority of the people are openly hostile to us. . . . .

Instead of that we have recently had to read a speech in which the world was informed that we should be willing to conclude peace with it but it must first recognize that we had conquered. It is long since we have read anything the tone of which was so unsatisfactory and the purport of which so impolitic as this speech. [*Renewed lively assent on the Left.*] This is perhaps a favorable time to remind members that all parties in this House, the Conservatives speaking through Herr v. Heydebrand in November 1908, recommended rather more reserve in that quarter. [*"Very good!"—Social-Democrats.*]

At a time when peace and war currents among our enemies are wrestling so violently with one another as at present, every word which is spoken from authoritative quarters should be weighed. [*"Very true!"*] As this was, unfortunately, not done, I must state most decidedly here, on behalf of the large section of the people we represent, that we do not share the views which were expressed in that speech [*"Bravo!"—Social-Democrats*], but decidedly reject them. [*Renewed "Bravo!"*] We do not wish any humiliation of the enemy or any peace of might (*Machtfrieden*) which can be won and maintained only by gas grenades; we want a peace based on freedom, friendship, and mutual trust between the nations. If the people once for all give us the decisive power, which we do not possess today, we shall do everything possible to bring about such a real peace. [*"Bravo!"—Social-Democrats.*] . . . .

165. *"WHY DID WE* HAVE TO GO TO VERSAILLES?"
BY OSCAR MÜLLER[23]

A book has just been published by Reimar Hobbing, Berlin, which, under the caption given above, attempts to furnish a solution for the most important political problem of our policy—the responsibility for the breakdown. We reproduce here the chapter in which are summarized the results of the investigation made.

"This short account of the history of the war begins at that point where the first serious talk about peace made its appearance, at a time of the first expectation of and belief in peace and the first intellectual struggle for it. The account can end there, where it became clear that we could hope only for a peace which bore all the marks of defeat, disgrace, and oppression. . . . . Now that after the Peace of Versailles Germany against her will wears a crown of thorns, which is supposed to be the symbol of guilt for the war, the debate in Germany turns unrestrainedly to the question as to who of us is responsible for the peace. I do not like to participate actively in such an infamous and questionable enterprise, but it is necessary to refute the following assertions:

"1. That the Peace Resolution of July 19, 1917, prevented Germany from winning in that it strengthened the will for war of the enemy and weakened the will for victory in our own nation.

"I believe I have shown that the decision of the Reichstag was imperative for internal reasons, that it did justice to the external situation, and that it could have been a success if the Government had followed a decisive and unambiguous policy at the first favorable opportunity, namely, the peace efforts of the Pope of August 2, 1917. I believe, further, to have shown that the tragic fate of the German victories over Italy and Russia and the external success of the great offensive in the West psychologically excluded a later exploitation of that peace instrument.

"2. That the breakdown of Germany had become unavoidable only

[23] *Deutsche Allgemeine Zeitung,* July 25, 1919, evening edition.

with the Revolution and that, therefore, the responsibility lay with the parties which became bearers, heirs, or executors of the Revolution.

"I bring an unbiased judgment against that on the basis of the following facts: that the military success of the great offensive did not materialize in spite of the unreserved sacrifice of our nation's strength; that the military leadership had miscalculated the measure of what could be achieved militarily, but particularly politically; and that it did not comprehend the final cause of the breakdown of our entire war position, namely, the dissolution of our alliances. Whether the Revolution could have been avoided through immediate acting, no one can say; at any rate it is to be regarded not as the mother but as the child of the breakdown.

"Of course, with these absolutely foolproof assertions one does not remove every basis for the belief that Germany's war policy in itself was bad, wrong, and unsatisfactory from the very beginning. But this view is less dangerous than those precise provocatory accusations, which, seasoned with personal distrust of individual parties and persons, furnish this acrimonious debate. That criticism regards it as a calamity that the war aroused in Germany the powers and the demands of democracy, and that these latter received a gradual development during the war, until the Revolution brought their final realization. From this final stage the Conservatives draw the conclusion that the policy which at the beginning of the war began the pact with liberalism and which ended with capitulation to the democratic and social revolution had been fraught with danger. It will never be possible to convince the chief representatives of this opinion, the Prussian Conservatives, of the error in their view; but when they attempt to spread such false assertions among the masses, then it is necessary to oppose them resolutely. . . . .

"It was the ill fate of Germany that it was given this task at a time of internal unpreparedness, expressing itself in the sterility of political inventiveness on the part of individuals and of parties. This was a task which only an entirely mature people, led by mature leaders, could have successfully brought to an end. We did not lack the physical and moral strength to bring the war to a successful end; rather we lacked the most patent sign of maturity, namely, the recognition of limits and of what was possible. The struggle for the recognition of these two filled the second half of the war. Once we were near the goal. Then the guilty ones—those who are the accusers of today—remained the victor, and we had to go to Versailles."

166. THE REVELATIONS CONCERNING THE PEACE PROPOSALS OF 1917

(a) THE POLITICAL DISCUSSION AT WEIMAR[24]

An element of conflict in the great political discussion in the National Assembly has been in the air for some time. It was well known that great differences existed in the committees, particularly the Tax Committee, differences which pressed for a public airing. The differences lay in the attitude of the two parties of the Right, particularly the German Nationalists, which in these committees had taken an attitude of energetic opposition to the Government, and within the latter more especially to the Minister of Finance, Erzberger, and his tax policies. It was self-evident that the debate about the political program of the Government offered to both sides the best opportunity for open attacks and counter-attacks. Today's afternoon session of the National Assembly marked the beginning of the struggle. After a protracted speech by Deputy Frau Dr. Bäumer, Herr von Graefe, who is usually drafted by the German Nationalists when they wish to make a sharp attack, spoke in behalf of the latter. At its very opening the speech contained sharp polemics against the program of the Government, which he accused of containing nothing new and of being in the final analysis only a compilation of ancient party speeches. Herr von Graefe denied that there was a Republican majority among the German people or even in the National Assembly. Also a part of the party which today tolerates the Republic, he said, had, prior to November 9, been an opponent of the abolition of the monarchy, and one certainly could assume that it had not changed its conviction over night. He said that the Social-Democrats had exploited the longing of the people for peace and bread through a wicked agitation, that longing which was ready to extend the hand to anyone who promised it peace and bread. The speaker then tried to prove that Social-Democracy was responsible for the disintegration of the army and thereby for the loss of the war. After that there had been no fear to present, as an armistice, the capitulation, through which we were deprived of all our weapons. And now those who are responsible for such a disarming are facing the bankruptcy of their policy. Then von Graefe made personal attacks upon Erzberger, whom he accused of former professions of annexationism. V. Graefe concluded with a motion which contained a vote of non-confidence in the Government.

The answer to this attack was given by Minister Erzberger with the usual repartee. The Government would accept the combat which the German Nationalists announced and would prosecute it without consideration. The guilt for the loss of the war lies with the extreme Right, which had been the pace-setter of the war. Guilty also were the Kaiser and the heads of the Federal States, who had left the scene ignominiously. If he personally was being accused of once having pursued policies different from the present ones, that was due to the credulity which he had shown toward what the Government and the Right had preached again and again to the nation. Ever since 1915 he had worked for peace, but at that time he had still believed in the Government's explanation of an attack by the enemy and a violation of neutrality of the Belgians. Today he knew that all that had been a fairy tale, and he had learned his lesson. At any rate, he had always tried to work in the interest of the Fatherland.

And who was it, really, that irresponsibly precipitated Germany for four years from one illusion into another? That was due to the fact that Germany for four years had had not a political Government but a military dictatorship. More than once there had been a possibility of peace, but the Right, together with the military clique, had always forestalled a realization of these opportunities. They were also the ones who, under the leadership of Dr. Helfferich, organized the aspirations of big industry upon Belgium. Erzberger read an official report according to which big industrialists under the leadership of various firms and persons, among whom was Herr Hugenberg, wished to acquire for German capitalism great industrial establishments in Belgium. Wilson's desire for peace had been sabotaged in 1916 through the announcement of the U-boat warfare. That was a fact which could not be contested. Minister Erzberger then took up the discussion of the statements of Count Wedel in the *Hamburger Nachrichten,* contrary to which he maintains that he had been in Vienna upon official business. The report of Count Czernin would be published in a few days. In its conclusion this report had read that Austria had reached the end of her strength and the German statesmen had left Count Czernin convinced that for Germany, too, a winter campaign was impossible. This report had been placed at his—Erzberger's—disposal with the sole condition that he keep silent about its origin; and it was a lie and a slander to assert that he had acted in the interests and upon the instruction of Austria. Erzberger then went into a discussion of the peace proposal which had been made to Germany in July 1917 through the Pope. For four weeks this proposal had been left unanswered and even then the answer had said that at present no clear answer could be given. Thereby the peace movement broke down entirely. For two years the nation had been misled. The battle cry of the parties was: "No peace, no liberty!" At that time also had been founded the Fatherland Party, which had succeeded in destroying all hopes of peace. Every attempt for the renewed service of good offices had been destroyed with military clubs. When things finally had reached such a stage that an utter defeat was sure, the present Majority parties were pushed to the front. And the only mistake which these made was that they did not let Ludendorff himself conclude the armistice. In that case, of course, there would have been a second Sedan. At present it had been possible at least to bring back the armies. Two things he wished to establish: first, that the peace resolution of the Reichstag would have been a success if it had been applied to the subsequent policy; second, that the collapse was solely brought about by lack of insight on the part of the Right and of the Highest Army Command. Erzberger concluded his speech with the assurance that the Government's patience toward these misstatements of the Right had reached an end. Never would the Right be absolved of its guilt, whether before the people, before history, or before their own consciences.

Erzberger's speech provoked many stormy interruptions on the part of the Nationalists, which in turn were answered by counter-attacks from the Left and the Center. The speech was followed by a whole series of personal remarks, among them by Graefe, Hugenberg, etc., to which Erzberger once more answered briefly.

166. (b) ERZBERGER'S SPEECH ON PEACE PROPOSALS[25]

. . . . In 1916 Wilson actively tried to bring about peace. Just ask Count Bernstorff. Why was Count Bernstorff, for weeks after his return from Washington, not allowed to report to the highest authority? ["Hear, hear!"] Wilson's peace work was sabotaged by the proclamation of the unrestricted U-boat warfare. . . . . In his Democratic Germany Count Bernstorff gives an account of his efforts at mediation and establishes that they were crossed by the U-boat declaration and so the war was lost for us. . . . . It cannot be denied that the Highest Military Command misjudged our military position and thus failed to realize the right moment for the conclusion of peace. [Continued interruptions from the Right.] These are undisputed facts. Herr Count Graefe occupied himself with an account of Count Wedel in the Hamburger Nachrichten. I am grateful to Count Wedel for his coming out with that account. [Shouts from the Right: "Well, well!"] In his article he affirms two things: The necessity of concluding peace in 1917 and the possibility of doing so. . . . . Those are the great political facts which Herr Wedel's article contains. [Lively approval from the Left and the Center.] Up to this hour, however, you [to the German Na-

[25] Verhandlungen der Nationalversammlung, No. 66, July 25, 1919, pp. 1931–45.

tionalists] have always disputed such a possibility. In this connection I should like to remind you of my words of July 1917, which have often been misused yet which are based upon the possibility of concluding peace. At that time I said that one could arrive at peace terms after a few hours' discussion with Lloyd George. . . . . I shall not go into a discussion of the qualities of Count Wedel. [*Shouts from the Right: "This method, too, we know!"*] I only indicate this, that as late as September 28, 1918, he wired the Imperial Government an encouraging telegram about the breakdown of Bulgaria. . . . . I shall not say much about the fact that Dr. Stresemann of the present German People's Party also demanded the removal of Count Wedel from his post. . . . . Contrary to Count Wedel's assertion, I maintain that I was in Vienna upon official business. Of Count Czernin's report Herr Wedel has said only this one sentence: "It did not make the impression upon Headquarters that had been hoped for." I cannot read the report in its entirety, but it will be published in a few days, and then everyone may judge for himself whether this report could be disposed of with such a meaningless sentence. [*Erzberger then reads excerpts from this report.*] This report was placed at my disposal on the sole condition that I do not disclose its origin. I feel myself duty-bound to be discreet and shall not disclose the name of the transmitter. [*These assertions give rise to a great commotion.*] And now Count Graefe dares to say that I have been bribed by Austria. [*Heated denials from the Right.*]

Chairman Fehrenbach: Count Graefe did not say that, although he used an expression which I rather wish I had not heard.

Erzberger: I ask Count Graefe whether he meant to say with his innuendoes that I had been bribed by Austria or that I stood in Austria's pay, or did he intend in any way to insinuate that I had taken my stand on the question of peace after being prompted or influenced by Austria? I do not need to wait for the answer, but declare in advance: Anyone daring to affirm either one of these sentences, I stamp as a mean liar and blackmailer. [*Applause.*] In compliance with the condition to make use of the report in a way which would further the peace, and actuated by the conviction that the final determining factor to wage war is not the power of the strongest but that of the weakest ally, I informed my party friends at Frankfort A.M. of its contents, and I am absolutely sure that nothing leaked out of this circle. [*Denial from the Right.*] Who asserts the opposite? You, Herr Hugenberg? You just wait, for you are just the right one for me. [*Laughter.*] Count Graefe asserts that a certain paper on the Rhine had reported about it. But he was so shy as not to disclose the name of the paper. I'll tell you: it was the *Rheinische Westfälische Zeitung.* [*Merriment.*] Is anyone simple enough really to believe that that paper was informed

by me or by the Center? Or, for example, is there not a possibility—
I do not assert it, but is it possible, anyway—that the Highest Military
Command, which also possessed the report, directed it to this paper?
And even if the Entente received information of this report, as Count
Wedel intimates, the former did not give up its readiness in 1917 to
conclude peace. . . . .

Count Wedel also said that Czernin had caused me to come to
Vienna to give an account. False! I did not journey to Vienna. My
discussion took place in a Berlin hotel in September 1917. It is also not
true that I had realized my mistake and confessed it. . . . .

Now I come to a point—and I am sorry to have to express this;
however, it must be said in order to prevent a poisoning of public
opinion—namely, that our Government prevented the possibility of
bringing about a peace by understanding [*lively shouts of "Hear,
hear!"*] with the hearty co-operation of the gentlemen of the Conservative Party. [*"Hear, hear!"—Center and Left. Shouts from the
Right.*] Now that Czernin's report is known to both sides there is no
longer any need to be silent about it. I must now also disclose the name
of Herr Deputy Schiffer and tender him my apologies for not having
asked in advance for his consent. In April 1917 I had a discussion in
the Foreign Office with Secretary of State Zimmermann, in which
Herr Schiffer and Count Westarp also participated. Herr Schiffer had
heard rumors that in Vienna there was a strong desire for peace, and
he came to the conclusion that Germany should take a step in that
direction, and that it would be better if a concerted action with Austria
should be made. To that the leader of the Conservatives said that it was
immaterial whether or not Vienna concluded a separate peace, for then
it would be so much easier for us to fight alone. [*Lively shouts: "Hear,
hear!" and great excitement. Shouts from the Right.*] Just wait, a great
deal more is coming. Do you really think that we shall stand your abus-
ing us all the time and not come forward with the truth? This whole
attitude agrees fully with the program of the Conservative Party. The
proclamation of the Executive Committee of the Conservative Party
of April 28, 1917, says:

"The resolution of the Social-Democrats, which demands that peace
be concluded within the near future at a common Peace Conference and
which should be based upon the demands of the Social-Democratic
International without annexations and indemnities, would bring our
Fatherland to the verge of the abyss should it be realized. That would
deprive us of the possibility of concluding a peace that would do justice
to the glorious deeds of our victorious armies and the fleet and which
would enable us to heal the wounds inflicted by the war by means of
sufficient indemnities. We can support only such a victorious German

peace." ["*Hear, hear!*"] I have shown already what this party said in spite of our warnings and in spite of our evident weakening, and in spite of the fact that it was clear to every intelligent observer that the last German weapon, the U-boat warfare, could not bring about the results promised and hoped for.

Affairs moved on. I shall not dwell upon the nature of the answer Germany sent to Vienna. The moment will come when this too will be published. The German people shall know the entire truth. Then it will be seen who the guilty ones are.

Then came the days of the Peace Resolution. Before I undertook any action I had repeatedly consulted the former Chancellor von Bethmann about the necessity of taking some measure against the Pan-Germans, stating that our nation had to be persuaded to give up the exaggerated aims and be brought back to the formula of August 4. I spoke also with other Secretaries of State [*shouts from the right: "Resolution?"*] about taking some kind of action. I talked with Dr. Helfferich before the debate in the Main Committee and called his attention to the fact that the calculations about the U-boat war were wrong. . . . . It is a complete misunderstanding that on July 6 I spoke for the first time in this sense. Already on July 4 I spoke for the first time in great detail about it, and on July 6 I only expanded upon it. At the same time I aimed at an agreement between the parties.

[Erzberger then quotes from his speech of July 6, 1917, to be found below, Document 439 in Volume II.]

Gentlemen, that was the chief content of my speech of July 6, 1917. I believe that many of you, who have heard this for the first time, must say to himself: Well, did we live in a madhouse in 1917? [*"Very good!"—Majority parties.*] Is there anyone today who dares question the correctness of even a single one of these sentences or these arguments? [*Lively approval from the Majority parties. Shouts—"Yes, sir! Herr Traub!"*] Well, I have already said that there are incorrigible ones. The session was over. The Chancellor was not present. He called me up in the afternoon and said that I had attacked him from the rear. I said that I had told him in advance that such action would come. I had verbally told the Chancellor before:

"Herr Deputy Roesicke has bothered your Excellency for months with the question: 'How does the Chancellor expect to finish the war without an unrestricted U-boat war?' and now I shall ask Herr Roesicke: 'How do you expect to finish the war after the fiasco of the U-boat war has been established?'" To this the Chancellor answered on July 6: "Yes, I admit it; but then I understood it differently." That is the course of events of July 6. [*Shouts from the Right.*] . . . .

But what was the situation at that time? How did Herr Stresemann understand this move? [*"Very good!"—Social-Democrats.*] That has been entirely forgotten. On July 9 . . . . Herr Stresemann said that "it was wrong to assume that the responsibility for the situation in which we found ourselves could all be laid at the feet of Erzberger and that the Reichstag had completely lost its equilibrium owing to Erzberger's speech. Already at the opening of the session there had been doubt as to whether the Social-Democrats would vote for new appropriations, and that this doubt weighed so heavily upon the entire situation that it pressed for an immediate solution. That Herr Erzberger's speech really was only a cross-section of the sentiment which prevailed in the entire German nation [*"Hear, hear!"—Social-Democrats*], that we were approaching the end of this gigantic struggle or at least could approach it. Finally that we had to draw up a balance sheet of our entire world situation and therefore had to ask ourselves to what consequences this situation forced us. [*"Hear, hear!"—Social-Democrats.*] Stresemann questioned that Erzberger's calculations indicated "a lost battle." There was a crisis in all parliaments of the world. . . . . The gist of Erzberger's speech had been that we should approach the discussion about the U-boat warfare in a sober and dispassionate way; that if we could not definitely establish how soon England could be defeated, it was well to think of whether we should get more favorable peace conditions the next year. This was the thesis of the discussion and it would not have caused such a great storm had not other considerations entered in. [*Lively shouts. "Hear, hear!"—Social-Democrats.*]

Thus Stresemann expressed himself on July 9, the same man who subsequently became the strongest opponent of the peace resolution of the Reichstag.

What attitude did the leader of the Conservatives take? Upon a question from the Commission to Count Westarp, "What position do the Conservatives take and are they willing today to conclude a peace upon the *status quo ante?*" Count Westarp said: "No!" [*"Hear, hear!"—Majority parties.*] Thus in July 1917 the leader of the Conservatives rejected a peace which should uphold the old boundaries of the Reich, which was not to impose any war indemnities upon Germany, which was to retain our colonies and which would have secured us equal economic opportunity. The entire Conservative "Fraktion," with the exception of two votes, I believe, rejected it. . . . .

The Peace Resolution obtained the majority in the Reichstag. I shall not discuss here how this resolution was strangled at its very inception by the Government of the day with the unfortunate words "as I understand it." Would you [*to the Right*] dare say that we had not had success with that resolution, you who together with the military authorities killed the resolution? . . . .

Then came the Pope's Note of August 1. On August 21, the Chancellor made a speech in the Main Committee, the basic thought of which was "the prospects for peace are rather slim." The allies wished peace in order to prevent another winter campaign. That is a fact. The battles of the allies in Flanders, at Verdun, and on the Meuse aimed solely—as Michaelis said—to prepare Germany for a peace late in 1917. The Pope's Peace Note contained concrete proposals. There was an opportunity to apply the resolution of the Reichstag. That did not take place. By the strong opposition on the part of the Highest Army Command, Michaelis was unable to make the necessary declaration about Belgium. We discussed the answer in the committee. Ebert, then as Deputy, now the President of the Reich, and I demanded of the Chancellor that in his answer to the Pope he give a clear declaration regarding Belgium. The Chancellor refused and said that such a declaration would be sent in a different form. We could not be sure that that would happen. And what happened?

On August 30, 1917, the Chancellor received a communication from the Apostolic Nuncio at Munich. It reads:

"Your Excellency! I have the great honor herewith to transmit to Your Excellency a copy of a telegram which His Excellency the Ambassador of the King of England handed to His Eminence the Papal Secretary of State. The French Government agrees with these views expressed in a similar telegram. [*"Hear, hear!"*]

"His Eminence is eager to continue effectively those efforts for a speedy attainment of a just and lasting peace, which the Imperial Government has shown such conciliatory readiness to accept. Therefore, His Eminence has charged me to call Your Excellency's attention particularly to the point relative to Belgium:

"(1) A positive declaration regarding the views of the Imperial Government with respect to the complete independence of Belgium and the indemnification of Belgium for the damages done during the war [*"Hear, hear!"*] ;

"(2) An equally definite statement of the guaranties which Germany demands for its economic, political, and military independence. His Eminence thinks that in case this declaration is satisfactory, then an important step will have been taken toward the further development of the negotiations. The English Ambassador here mentioned has already informed his Government that the Holy See will reply to the communications made in the aforementioned telegram as soon as it receives, through me, the answer of the Imperial Government.

"It may be permitted me to give expression to my firm conviction that if by using your influence in All-Highest quarters on behalf of the Papal proposal and for this peace work a conciliatory reply be obtained which can open up the prospect of peace negotiations, Your Excellency will gain the eternal thanks of the Fatherland and the whole of humanity.

"Your devoted, etc., etc.,

"(*Signed*) Eugen Pacelli, Archbishop of Sardi

"Papal Nuncio"

What do we have here? An official step of a neutral power. . . . . The Holy See undertook a step, not upon its own initiative, but expressly upon the request of the English Government, and it transmitted this telegram upon the expressed authorization of the French Government. . . . . What was the essence of what was demanded of Germany in order to facilitate the continuation of the peace negotiations? A precise declaration regarding Belgium! I cannot at this moment disclose the content of the English Ambassador's Note, since the consent of the Holy See has not as yet been obtained. It is sufficient to mention the accompanying letter of the transmitter, which was dated August 30, 1917. The answer of the German Government to the official note of the Pope had not, as yet, been dispatched. This letter was a parallel step. And what happens in Berlin? One would not think it could be possible! For almost four weeks no answer was given. [*Great noise at the Left and Center. Stormy shouts of indignation. Great commotion.*] . . . . Gentlemen, I understand your excitement . . . . but I cannot spare this bitter medicine. I can go yet a step farther. A writing of the Chancellor's, dated September 24, neglects to make such a declaration . . . . it begins with the words:

"I have the honor to acknowledge the receipt of Your Excellency's writing of August 30 and beg you to accept my sincerest thanks for the kind transmission of the interesting information."

Since the writing, too, will be published within the next few days, I shall read to you only the concluding paragraph. It reads:

"If today under the existing circumstances we are not yet in a position to comply with Your Excellency's request to make a declaration about the views of the Imperial Government regarding Belgium and the guaranties desired by us, it is not because the Imperial Government is fundamentally averse to making such a declaration or because it underestimates the decisive influence of such a declaration upon the question, or because it believes its views and the guaranties which seem to it absolutely imperative could form an insurmountable barrier to peace, but only because it thinks that certain preliminary conditions which comprise an absolutely necessary prerequisite for the making of such a declaration, seem not to have been cleared sufficiently. [*Shouts from the Left and counter-shouts from the Right.*]

"To clarify these, will be the effort of the Imperial Government, and it hopes, should circumstances favor its endeavors, to be able in the near future to give Your Excellency information about the views and necessary demands of the Imperial Government.

"(*Signed*) MICHAELIS"

I repeat the facts which are hereby established: For almost four weeks a Government, whose people are in greatest need, does not answer an official move on the part of a neutral. And four weeks later comes the declaration that it is impossible at present to give a clear answer. [*The German Democrats: "Has it not yet been given!"*] As far as I know it has never been given. But, gentlemen, listen further. At the end of September I was in Munich. The Papal Nuncio is a personal friend of mine of long standing. I did not know of the content of the German answer, since I too was told only that an affirmative answer would be given. At the time of my visit the Nuncio came to me, with tears in his eyes, saying: "Everything is lost, even your poor Fatherland." That made an end to this peace move. And this is the tragedy of our nation: There was a possibility of concluding peace. . . . . Thus the honest will of the Reichstag to bring about a peace by understanding, of compromise and without annexations and indemnities, was brought to naught in September 1917. . . . . Our Government forced the Entente to fight to the utmost, until our nation bled to death. Shall I remind you of that December 25, 1917, when that same Government, which soon afterwards concluded the Brest-Litovsk Peace, offered a peace to the whole world? Shall I remind you of the caricature of December 27, 1917, when our Government, without having received an answer from the whole world upon its peace offer, made exactly the opposite demands of Russia?

Thus things went on until the offensive of March 1918. Every attempt to reason in Germany and to save what still could be saved, was knocked down with military clubs. . . . .

The recently published notes of Secretary of State Hintze show that on July 25 General Ludendorff answered with a determined "Yes" to von Hintze's question whether the present offensive would definitely defeat the enemy. On August 13 Ludendorff confessed to von Hintze that he was not so sure that the present offensive would force the enemy to sue for peace. Then came the Crown Council of August 14. The documents, with all the negotiations that led to the armistice, will be laid before the National Assembly this week; . . . . therefore, I shall not tax your patience at this time with details. But of one thing I must remind you; on the second Sunday in September a number of deputies from the Majority parties—I do not recall the names of all of them, but they were of all those parties which had accepted the Reichstag Resolution—met with the Chancellor and demanded the immediate commencement of peace negotiations, owing to the fact that alarming reports had come from Vienna. We were told to wait a while. Then came the resistless military defeat at the end of September.

And what was the situation at that time? You [*to the Right*] speak again and again that the turning-point came on November 9. No! The turning-point came on September 30. At that time the different party leaders—only one member from each party was present, and he had to promise to divulge nothing of what had been discussed—were told that everything was gone, that further military resistance was useless, and that an immediate peace must be concluded. One dispatch after another was sent from headquarters to Berlin; if a new government was not being formed immediately, if peace was not offered that very night, then it was impossible to guarantee that the front could hold another twenty-four hours. . . . .

And now comes Herr v. Graefe and says that the blame for this defeat rests upon the undermining of the army. . . . . Two things brought on the collapse: on one side, the length of the war; and, on the other side, the great abuses and grievances in the army. . . . . Herr v. Graefe asserts also that on October 25 the situation was still such that the German nation could have been saved, for a dispatch had come from Hindenburg which called for military resistance. Gentlemen, what an illusion! On October 28, Austria concluded its armistice. On the forenoon of that day we consulted other military leaders besides Ludendorff, who threatened to retire if other generals were to be called in. After he was gone we consulted two other experienced military leaders, who at first gave us a somewhat more encouraging picture of the possibility of Austria's capitulation; and these two generals also recognized that there could be no thought of military resistance. Things went on. On November 6, in the forenoon, I was assigned the task of capitulating on November 8. This was upon the proposal of and under the approval of the Highest Army Command. In the face of these facts Herr v. Graefe dares to say that we committed an historical lie when speaking of the armistice. . . . .

Through this historical account of the course of the events I have established the following: (1) that the Peace Resolution should have been and would have been a success if its fundamental principles had found unequivocal application at the first opportunity, namely, at the time of the Pope's Peace Note; (2) that the collapse of Germany did not come as a result of the Revolution but was conditioned by continual deception by the army as to things that could be achieved militarily and politically and by blindness toward the consequences of the dissolution of the coalition.

It was not the Peace Resolution which paralyzed Germany's power of resistance; rather that took place owing to the catastrophic lack of political insight with which the Conservatives and the Highest Military Command were smitten and with which they intimidated and terrorized the Government and the people. . . . .

166. (c) LUDENDORFF'S EXPLANATION OF THE PACELLI-MICHAELIS CORRESPONDENCE[26]

After the course of yesterday's debate at Weimar, it was natural that the persons whom Erzberger attacked—above all the Highest Army Command and Dr. Michaelis—should express themselves upon the cardinal question of the debate, namely, the Pacelli-Michaelis correspondence. The Highest Army Command does it in the following statement, published today by the *B.Z.* from an "authoritative source" of the Army Command. It is published in the name of Ludendorff:

"The writing of Nuncio Pacelli and the answer to that by former Chancellor Michaelis which was published in this morning's papers became known to Ludendorff for the first time today. He has never heard of them before. In a suggestive and secret way the Highest Military Command was informed at the end of August and the beginning of September 1917 that England was attempting a sounding out of such feeling. Entirely independent of this, General Ludendorff was informed at the beginning of August by Colonel von Haeften, on the basis of reports he had received from pacifist circles of neutral countries, that England, at this moment, would welcome an open German declaration regarding Belgium. The General believed that in both cases it concerned the same question, and stated on both occasions his agreement to such a declaration. A number of discussions then took place about the Belgian question. Also, a Crown Council took place on September 11. In the course of these discussions an agreement was reached upon a formula as regards Belgium. A few days later Dr. Michaelis had a meeting with Dr. Helfferich and Secretary of State Kühlmann. Colonel von Haeften, Director Deutelmoser, and a representative of the Kriegspresseamt were present at this meeting. In it, Dr. Michaelis suggested that public opinion at home and at the front should be prepared for a considerable restriction of the demands which were current in many circles as regards Belgium. For unknown reasons von Kühlmann spoke strongly against such an undertaking. General Ludendorff in these days persuaded Dr. Michaelis to refrain from a projected

[26] *Deutsche Allgemeine Zeitung,* July 26, 1919, II, 1.

speech in connection with war collections, so as not to endanger any possible negotiations. On September 20 Colonel von Haeften, who likewise knew nothing of Pacelli's writing, had an audience with Secretary of State von Kühlmann, during which, upon the request of Deputy Konrad Haussmann, he asked the former to make a public statement regarding Belgium. Kühlmann declined. Colonel von Haeften reported accordingly to the Highest Military Command. General Ludendorff subsequently asked the Chancellor or the Secretary of State what had become of the supposed English sounding. He received an evasive answer."

166. (d) CZERNIN'S STATEMENT[27]

GRUNDLSEE, July 27; 4:10 P.M.

In order to comply with the numerous requests of the press, I beg you to publish the following lines: So far as I am able to judge from the notices in the press, the speech of Erzberger does not give an exhaustive picture of the events. Many extremely important events are not even mentioned. As a result a false picture of the whole is created. As concerns my report of April 1917, mentioned by Erzberger, in which I advised putting an end to the war by territorial concession on the part of the Central Powers, I may say that it was intended solely for the two Emperors and the Imperial Chancellor. There existed at that time the well-founded hope of achieving a peace by understanding, even if at the cost of sacrifices. By an irresponsible party and without my knowledge this report was given to Herr Erzberger, who did not keep it secret. However, I must expressly state that Herr Erzberger acted in good faith and was firmly convinced that he acted in accordance with the intentions of his employers when he revealed the strictly secret facts. Through Erzberger's procedure the content of this report became known to our enemies. Anyone reading it can imagine the results. The representation of Count Wedel, as far as I am aware of it, is therefore fully correct. For the rest, I could substantiate my version, as well as many things not even mentioned, with documents in my possession. I learned that my report had been given to Erzberger only when it was too late. The facts now discussed between Erzberger and Count Wedel, however, are only links in a whole chain of an irresponsible policy, carried on sub rosa, the entirety of which I only discovered one year later and which prompted my resignation. My book about the World War which will be published in the near future, will, in so far as I deem it advisable, clarify these political events, and will bring out the truth, supported by documents.

[27] *Deutsche Allgemeine Zeitung*, July 28, 1919, evening edition, p. 1.

166. (e) HELFFERICH'S STATEMENT[28]

Although von Kühlmann's statement up to this moment is not available and, further, the content of the English telegram to Rome has not yet been published, Dr. Helfferich thinks that he can already definitely establish that there was no talk about an English peace proposal. Helfferich is of the opinion that:

(1) This telegram "was nothing else than the attitude of the Foreign Office to the peace note which the Pope sent to all belligerent countries on August 1."

Helfferich says further in the *Kreuzzeitung* that

(2) The contents of the telegram did not in the least constitute an offer of peace. It was scarcely to be distinguished from the insolent answer which the Entente Powers gave to Wilson's Peace Note on January 10, which answer raised a storm of protest from all parties in Germany and also from Herr Erzberger.

(3) The earnest wish of the Pope to bring about peace indeed prompted him to make the almost hopeless attempt to further the cause of peace by finding out what Germany's views were regarding Belgium.

(4) The Chancellor and the Secretary of State of the Foreign Office made Pacelli's letter, in which the German Government was asked to state its attitude toward the Belgian question, an opportunity for getting the Kaiser, in the Crown Council of September 11, to come to a decision which would give them an absolutely free hand as regards the restoration of Belgian territorial integrity and complete Belgian sovereignty, in order to succeed in introducing and carrying through the peace negotiations.

(5) The Chancellor and the Secretary of State for Foreign Affairs, although being inclined to believe in the—not actually manifested—English initiative in consequence of the Nuncio's report, were skeptical as regards the sincerity of the British will for a peace by understanding, owing to the phraseology of the dispatch of the Foreign Office and other information. Before we gave a statement as to our giving up Belgium, it seemed necessary, first of all, to examine this British desire for understanding. For reasons as stated by Michaelis, and also owing to the indiscretion of Herr Erzberger, this examining was attempted by a means other than that provided by the Vatican. The neutral diplomat who was chosen for this purpose was informed that conditions relative to peace negotiations were: the maintenance of our pre-war possessions, including the colonies; the refraining from war indemnities and from an economic war after the present war, i.e., the program of the July Resolution.

[28] *Deutsche Allgemeine Zeitung*, July 28, 1919, II, 1.

(6) The attempt to verify England's desire for peace and its readiness to conclude peace gave a negative result.

166. (f) STATEMENT OF THE FORMER GERMAN AMBASSADOR IN VIENNA, COUNT WEDEL[29]

Herr Erzberger has denied in Weimar that Count Czernin caused him to come to Vienna in order to report to him about the use he had made of this report. A letter of Count Czernin's, which is in my possession, says: "Some time ago Erzberger got knowledge of my report and committed the gravest indiscretion. He came to Vienna, summoned by me, in order to account to me for his procedure. He was very much downcast at the time and realized his colossal mistake."

Not only do the Hohenlohe letters about this affair exist, but also other convincing documents. Herr Erzberger should think of that. Secretary von Kühlmann, too, knows the truth.

167. STATEMENT OF MICHAELIS ON THE "ENGLISH PEACE-FEELER"[30]

Former Imperial Chancellor Michaelis asks us to publish the following explanation concerning the attacks of Minister Erzberger in the National Assembly of July 25, 1919:

The official documents about the treatment of the Nuncio Pacelli's writing to me of August 30, 1917, are not accessible to me. According to my personal notes I have to say the following concerning the treatment of the so-called "English peace-feeler":

The document was submitted to me at the beginning of September. I discussed it with the Secretaries of State and the Ministers, and journeyed to meet the Kaiser, who, if I am not mistaken, returned September 9 from a trip to the front, in order to report to him.

I begged the Kaiser to hold a Crown Council in the presence of the Highest Army and Navy Command. Such a meeting took place on September 11 at the Bellevue palace. The result of the deliberation was condensed to the following note, which the Kaiser personally signed:

"The annexation of Belgium is questionable. Belgium could be restored. The coast of Flanders, though, is very important and Zeebrugge should not fall into English hands. But not merely the Belgian coast

---

[29] *Deutsche Allgemeine Zeitung*, July 28, 1919, II, 1.

[30] *Neue Preussische Zeitung*, July 27, 1919.

is to be held. A close economic union of Belgium and Germany must be brought about. In that Belgium itself has the greatest interest."

About the further treatment of the peace-feeler Secretary of State v. Kühlmann agreed that through an absolutely reliable person a sounding could be made as to whether or not on the English side there was indeed a will to abandon the former position involving exaggerated peace aims—unquestionably that, according to our knowledge—and to negotiate upon an acceptable middle course. The letter of the Papal Nuncio did not contain any convincing proofs in this direction. The danger existed that there was the intention to cause Germany to make accommodating declarations without giving up their own extravagant attitude, and that thereby the negotiations would be shifted to our disadvantage.

The choice of intermediary fell upon an outstanding neutral diplomat who was in close personal contact with v. Kühlmann and who seemed to be particularly well qualified to undertake the necessary sounding. His mission was circumscribed, together with the announcement of Germany's attitude, in the following way:

A presumption for negotiations with England was the recognition: (a) that our borders should remain intact; (b) that our colonies would be given back; (c) that no reparations would be demanded; (d) that an economic war would be refrained from.

In agreement with His Excellency v. Kühlmann, I held this way to be the most correct one, because the pursuit of these first peace threads seemed to be possible only under absolute confidence. The negotiations by way of the Papal See did not offer this security. Already upon the receipt of the Nuncio's writing it was shown that Deputy Erzberger had been informed about the coming of the writing before I was. An indiscretion through him, however, had to be avoided by all means. On that account we could adopt only an attitude of waiting toward the Nuncio and give him later on only an answer consisting of generalities.

That each indiscretion bore the greatest danger for the preparing of negotiations, the further course of the negotiations has shown. The deliberations of the Crown Council and their aims did not remain secret. The bellicose parties in Germany, England, and France seized the opportunity, and the result was that the representative of the English Government publicly denied that a peace proposal had been made on the part of the English Government. I eagerly embraced the idea of achieving peace by foregoing concessions regarding Belgium, and brought it about that a unified attitude toward this question prevailed in responsible circles. I exerted myself to select the proper way for the pursuit of the first stimulus. If the plan failed it was due to the fact that our enemies did not wish it.

SAAROW, July 26, 1919   (*Signed*) MICHAELIS

168. THE DEBATE IN THE NATIONAL ASSEMBLY AT WEIMAR ON THE PEACE EFFORTS OF JULY 1917, JULY 28, 1919

(a) MÜLLER'S SPEECH[31]

. . . . At the session of July 26, Herr Erzberger reported the step which the Papal Nuncio made on August 30, 1917, and Chancellor Michaelis's answer to it on September 24. At present so much is being written about these two messages that I have ordered that all these writings, which are available at the Office, be collected and issued as a White Book, and then be placed at the disposal of the National Assembly. Today I shall confine myself to the following statements. We have, in the meantime, established that the Pacelli writing, dated August 30, reached Berlin only on September 5, which reduces the period of Germany's delay in answering Pacelli's writing to 19 days. On September 24, Michaelis sent his answer. The request of the English Government accompanied Pacelli's writing as a supplement, and it was without date. Translated, it reads as follows:

"We have not yet had an opportunity to consult with our allies regarding the Note of Your Eminence, and are unable to answer the proposal made by Your Eminence concerning the terms of a lasting peace. In our opinion there does not exist a probability of coming nearer to this aim as long as the Central Powers and their allies have not officially announced their war aims; also what restorations and indemnities they are ready to agree upon and by what means in the future the world could be protected against the recurrence of the horrors under which it suffers today. [*"Aha!"—Right.*] Even concerning Belgium— and on this point the Powers have admitted themselves to be wrong —we have never heard a definite statement about their views as to restoration of its complete independence and reparation for the damages inflicted upon it by them. [*"Hear, hear!"—Left.*]

"Your Eminence is doubtless aware of the declarations made by the allies in reply to President Wilson's Note. [*"Aha!"—Right.*] Neither Austria nor Germany has ever made such an equivalent statement. An attempt to bring the belligerent countries to an agreement seems to be fruitless as long as we are not clear about the point where their opinions differ."

It is evident from this writing that the Belgian question was the cardinal problem of the peace question, and only a clear answer on this

---

[31] *Verhandlungen der Nationalversammlung*, No. 68, July 28, 1919, pp. 2006–12. Müller was Minister of Foreign Affairs.

question respecting the restoration of Belgium and its independence could bring us closer to peace. . . . .

In this connection it is also necessary above all to elucidate the fact why the Foreign Office did not give more attention to the Pacelli writing. One other statement I should like to make today, namely, that, besides this step, another move was made. The Foreign Office made connections with a neutral diplomat, who in turn was to sound out the English. This step was taken before September 5, 1917, thus before the Note of the Papal Nuncio arrived in Berlin.

As we now notice from the reports of Chancellor Michaelis, a Crown Council took place on September 11. Details concerning this meeting unfortunately cannot even yet be found.

As to the mediation of neutrals I am in a position to state that it was by a Spanish diplomat. The members of the former Reichstag know the book which appeared under the title: *Documents from the Russian Secret Archives, in so far as they have appeared up to July 1, 1918,* which was given to the members of the Reichstag. I am referring to the report of the Russian Chargé d'Affaires in London, of September 23 [October 6], 1917. Regarding this move the report says:

"Balfour had a meeting with the representatives of the High Allied Governments of France, Italy, America, Japan, and Russia, and gave us the following strictly confidential information: The Spanish Minister told the English Ambassador in Madrid, that 'a person in a very high position in Berlin' had expressed to the Spanish Ambassador in Berlin a desire to enter into negotiations with England. The Spanish Government rejected a 'mediation,' but 'deemed it not appropriate to withhold from England this declaration of Germany's readiness.' The English Ambassador answered that he did not know what attitude his Government would take toward Germany's statement but that in order to make a discussion of the peace proposals by the Allies at all possible these conditions would have to differ sharply from the demands of Germany which are expressed in the German press. After the receipt of the report of its Ambassador, the English Government faced the alternative either to leave Germany's declaration unanswered or else to answer it with the utmost caution. The first alternative would have given the German Government the opportunity to use England's refusal for the enhancement of its own prestige at home, and, what was still more important, to strengthen the already too great disintegrating agitation in Russia; the latter alternative could have been interpreted that England desired the complete destruction of Germany and was taking Russia and the other Allies in tow."

Therefore the British Government gave the following answer through its Ambassador in Madrid:

"The Government of His Majesty would be ready to receive a communication which the German Government would wish to make to it regarding peace. It would make this information a subject of discussion with its allies." This was to be transmitted verbatim.

In view of the urgent necessity to observe the utmost and greatest caution in the relations with our enemy, who does not hesitate to distort words and principles, the English answer was worded very briefly. In the discussion at today's meeting of the Ambassadors, we reached the unanimous conclusion that Germany's aim—the entire maneuver we ascribe to Kühlmann—consists of tempting the Allies to a discussion of peace conditions with Germany. The present German attempt confirms the fears expressed in my telegram of 7.20.9 No. 761. We agreed that Germany be told that if through the present brief communication the negotiations should begin, we expect a clear statement of its war aims, and in no case shall we agree to separate negotiations of one of our Allies with Germany, nor to collective negotiations, until we have decided whether or not the entire war aims of Germany are acceptable to us. It was unanimously decided that today, more than ever, unity was needed among the Allies. Undoubtedly, Germany turned towards England, because the latter, at present, doubtless, occupies the chief position in the Alliance.

In the following paragraph this is said about the position:

"Under the impression of the recent English victory in Mesopotamia and the great success on the Western front a great change of sentiment has taken place in the army and at home in favor of the conviction of the final victory. On the other hand, all evidences show that the spirit in the German Army has been correspondingly lowered."

From these statements we see how at that time the Allied Governments regarded the whole situation. They were sure of their cause. They had America on their side and, as Lloyd George once said, time was working for them. Therefore they demanded precise statements concerning the German war aims.

As concerns Germany, it is a fact that the Michaelis Government at that time did not inform the party leaders of the Pacelli writing nor of the English supplement; second, that the party leaders were promised that a precise statement about Belgium would be made; and, third, that the answer of Michaelis to the Pacelli writing is just the opposite of a precise answer. . . . .

168. (b) BAUER'S SPEECH[32]

. . . . Ladies and Gentlemen: The truth above everything! The war-lies must not be followed by peace-lies. ["*Quite right!*"—*S.D.*] The

[32] *Verhandlungen der Nationalversammlung*, No. 68, July 28, 1919, pp. 2017–22.

attempt of the former rulers to throw all blame upon the Republic we oppose with a determination which the nation expects of a People's Government. Herr Erzberger revealed recently the secret exchange of notes with the Papal Nuncio in which the former rulers refused to make a clear statement about their views regarding Belgium. This revelation brought forth a statement by the former Chancellor Michaelis and an explanatory note in the name of General Ludendorff. It is being announced in the name of Ludendorff that the General had given his consent to a statement about Belgium and that an agreement concerning Belgium had been reached in the Crown Council of September 11, 1917. Herr Michaelis prefaced this announcement with a statement of Wilhelm II which summarized the results of this Crown Council. This statement reads as follows:

"The annexation of Belgium is questionable. Belgium could be restored. The coast of Flanders, though, is very important and Zeebrugge must not fall into English hands. But not merely the Belgian coast is to be held. A close economic union of Belgium and Germany must be brought about. In that Belgium itself has the greatest interest."

This remark looks very innocent at first sight; but what lurks behind it you shall soon see.

Besides this, Michaelis names four conditions preliminary to negotiations with England: (a) that our borders remain intact; (b) that our colonies be given back; (c) that no indemnities be demanded; (c) that there be no economic war.

In contrast with these two statements, which make it seem almost enigmatical that our readiness to restore Belgium, which Herr v. Kühlmann regarded as an absolutely necessary condition of every move for peace, was not expressed, I submit to you two letters dating from those days. One by Michaelis, dated September 12, 1917, i.e., the day after the meeting of the Crown Council, and addressed to Field-Marshal von Hindenburg; the second letter, dated September 15, 1917, is Hindenburg's answer, which is supplemented with a memorandum by Ludendorff. After you know the content of these writings, you will understand why a request for a precise statement regarding Belgium did not receive a precise answer. Herr Michaelis writes:

"BERLIN, September 12, 1917

"HIGHLY ESTEEMED GENERAL FIELD-MARSHAL!

"After the conclusion of yesterday's discussions under the Chairmanship of His Majesty, I feel the urge to express my thanks to you and General Ludendorff for the far-sighted and militarily unbiased support you gave me in the matter of circumscribing discreet war aims in the eventuality that we should soon come to peace negotiations, possibly in the fall or spring of next year.

"As demands of the Highest Army Command, which in your opinion must absolutely be retained, I include in our plans of negotiations that both of you demand, in the first place, Liége and a piece of territory for the protection of our western industry; that with a really close economic union of Belgium and Germany both of you expect a condition which will show the Belgians the futility of drifting into warlike differences with us in the future for purely egotistical and economic reasons; and that, therefore, when Belgium shall have complied with all our demands for the securing of an economic union—which naturally would take several years after the opening of peace negotiations— the military security can be dropped. Liége would therefore be demanded only as a pledge and only for the time being.

"I now have an urgent request to make to Your Excellency. When —as is to be expected—a visitor comes to headquarters (I myself have, for example, persuaded Count von Westarp to go once to Kreuznach) who belongs to a partisan annexationist group and knows little or nothing about the great relationships existing between the Central Powers and therefore is still inclined to regard peace as undesirable, will you not in such cases, inform him of your ideas, so that thus, perhaps, the extreme demands may be brought within bounds. [*"Hear, hear!"*]

"Accordingly, Count Westarp's demands went much farther than those about which you will get some more information.

"One must make those people realize what designs the enemies had toward us, and what we achieve. Instead of destruction and territorial conquests: In the West the intactness of our borders and the sure promise of using the raw materials in the defeated territories [*"Hear, hear!"*], favorable economic and transportation terms upon railroads and waterways, privileged places in the harbor of Antwerp; influence upon the part of the Flemish people who look toward Germany; the imposition of reparations for the damages done to us; the exclusion of English influence from the coast of Flanders and Northern France; and the demand for the restoration of our colonies eventually as an object for adjustment."

To this Hindenburg answered:

"GREAT HEADQUARTERS, September 15, 1917

"HIGHLY ESTEEMED CHANCELLOR!

"I have the honor to acknowledge to Your Excellency the receipt of your writing of September 12. In compliance with Your Excellency's request I shall help to enlighten leading men about our views regarding

Belgium, as to which there now exists clearness in the event that we get peace this year.

"I do not deceive myself that the matter of giving up the coast of Flanders will be received in the navy and other patriotic circles as a heavy blow which can be alleviated only if the compensations for the navy, which you, too, have recognized, become reality. I and General Ludendorff see those compensations in the form of bases within and outside of our colonial Empire.

"To two points of Your Excellency's writing I have to add a few explanations:

"1. The economic connection of Belgium with Germany will not be possible without pressure upon Belgium even after the conclusion of peace. [*Lively shouts by the Majority parties: "Hear, hear!"*] For this purpose it will be necessary to occupy it for several years [*"Hear, hear!"—Majority parties*], necessary for military reasons even if England and America leave France.

"The German position in Liége must exert an influence beyond the several years of occupation. Its chief purpose is the immediate military protection of the industrial territory of the Lower Rhine and Westphalia. Only if we are and remain in Liége, the undisputed masters of the situation [*"Hear, hear!"—Majority parties*], can we make the necessary military and administrative regulations. I can, therefore, not imagine that we could leave Liége at any conceivable and stipulated period of time." [*"Hear, hear!"—Majority parties.*]

And this Herr Michaelis calls discreet war aims! A yardstick for the war aims which the Right and the Fatherland Party have entertained! We read further in Hindenburg's writing:

"2. The 'imposition to bear the burden of the heavy damages done by us to the neighbors' will hardly be conceived by anyone as an important gain. The heavy damages which we inflicted upon the neighbors were unavoidable necessities of the war. The understanding that a reparation for that could come into the question must not be presupposed by our military position. This we must not make public to the outside world.

"As far as I can understand our psychology, I believe I doubt the validity of the statement that the fact that the enemy wished to cut us to pieces and did not succeed in doing it will be in a way a compensation for not possibly achieving our war aims. In the accompanying memorandum General Ludendorff has brought together his statements in Berlin and expanded those in respect to Longwy-Briey, agriculture, and overseas trade. The memorandum agrees completely with my views.

"(*Signed*) VON HINDENBURG"

[Bauer then read extracts from Ludendorff's memorandum, dated September 14, 1917, the document given below on pp. 464–68.]

Ladies and Gentlemen: From these writings it is clear why no satisfactory answer was given to the peace proposal of the Entente. In view of the increasing participation of the United States in the war, no neutral power would have accepted and transmitted such a completely unsatisfactory proposal about Belgium.

Among the principles which Michaelis gives as preliminary conditions for the opening of negotiations with the Entente, there is not included the most important one which condemned all negotiations to failure: the partly open, partly hidden annexation of Belgium. ["Very true!"—Majority parties.] . . . . Ladies and Gentlemen! This material will suffice. I refrain from further conclusions. Only one thing more should I like to say. Who was standing behind the Fatherland Party and who furnished the immense sums of money for this annexationist madness, which at that time had obtained a foothold in Germany? [Lively approval by the Majority parties. Denial and shouts from the Right.] At a time when we were already facing internal collapse, when women and children by the thousands were starving in the big cities and industrial places [renewed approval by Majority parties and denial from the Right], at that moment every attempt to arrive at a sane peace was branded as treason. All men, who exerted their best powers in order to show the outside world that Germany was not annexationist mad, that it wished to conclude an honorable and understanding peace, all these men were branded as "enemies of the Fatherland" and were actually being threatened with violence. [Stormy approval by the Majority parties. Heated denials by the Right.] That was your [to the Right] work, Herr Traub and Herr Graefe, particularly your work, for which the German people will ever call you to account. . . . .

[After Bauer had finished, Erzberger once more replied to the attacks of the Right, denouncing them with particular vehemence.]

169. FOREIGN REVELATIONS CONCERNING THE PEACE PROPOSALS

(a) RIBOT ON ERZBERGER'S REVELATIONS, 1919[33]

VERSAILLES, July 28. Ribot told a representative of Le Temps that he had to make certain reservations regarding the correct reproduction of the statements concerning Erzberger's revelations published in Echo de Paris. Ribot permitted Le Temps to print the following:

[33] Deutsche Allgemeine Zeitung, July 29, 1919, evening edition, p. 3.

It is true that the French and English Governments had come to an agreement not to answer the Pope's Note before Germany had declared the reparations and guaranties she was ready to give. The English Ambassador at the Papal Court was requested to avail himself of the opportunity to explain to Cardinal Gasparri that no serious move could be made as long as the Central Powers had not revealed their views, particularly with regard to Belgium. When the French Government received word of the instructions sent to the English Ambassador, it expressed the wish that this diplomat be instructed to include France in his answer for the British Government. The English Ambassador undertook the commission to leave Cardinal Gasparri a note in the course of this interview which was to be regarded as only quasi-official. Cardinal Gasparri felt himself justified in transmitting the dispatch— which has just been published—to the Papal Nuncio in Munich. According to the views expressed by the French Government to the English Government it might be dangerous to enter into premature discussions. Therefore, the English Government gave its representative at the Papal Court corresponding instructions. To that alone this affair is to be traced back. What is to be emphasized especially is that Germany, being requested by the Vatican to state unequivocally its views regarding Belgium, hesitated to do so. It is clear that in August and September of 1917 Germany was not at all ready to restore to us Alsace-Lorraine and to guarantee the complete independence of Belgium.

169. (b) THE CONVERSATION BETWEEN CARDINAL GASPARRI
AND COUNT SALIS[34]

Pichon's *Petit Journal* gives the following details of the conversation that took place between Cardinal Gasparri and the English Ambassador at the Vatican, Count Salis:

The Cardinal felt that the oral statement of the English Ambassador would insure little success for the Papal Peace Note; therefore he requested the English diplomat, who had held his *Aide-Mémoire* in his hand, to leave this document with him, so that he could reproduce exactly its content. Thereupon Count Salis took the scissors from the Cardinal's desk and clipped off the heading of Balfour's letter, in order that the document should lose its diplomatic value. Gasparri then sent the *Aide-Mémoire* to Nuncio Pacelli. Therefore, continues the *Petit Journal,* it concerned itself with a number of misunderstandings which possibly were interesting for the diplomatic history of the war but which did not give Germany the right to speak about a peace proposal. Should

[34] *Ibid.,* July 30, 1919, evening edition, p. 2.

she do so nevertheless, then she would act in bad faith. France had only formally joined the English *démarche*, and that with hesitation and scruples.

169. (c) STATEMENT OF THE PAPAL NUNCIO, ARCHBISHOP PACELLI[35]

Weimar, July 30 (W.T.B.). From authentic sources we learn the following: From the official statement by the Papal Nuncio Archbishop Pacelli, we learn that the Nuncio did not inform Herr Erzberger of the content of the Nuncio's letter to Herr Michaelis in 1917. This fully corroborates Herr Erzberger's statement. Herr Erzberger has repeatedly explained in the National Assembly that although he knew in 1917 of the fact of the correspondence, he did not know the content of the Nuncio's letter and that of Michaelis' answer. However, both the Nuncio and Michaelis, each independent of the other, had forced Erzberger to give his word of honor not to disclose even the existence of the correspondence.

170. COLONEL B. SCHWERTFEGER, "THE PEACE-FEELER OF 1917"[36]

Through yesterday's disclosures at Weimar the high tide of the revelations reached its peak. The Belgian question, the cardinal point of the whole war, is again placed in the center of discussion. Writings were disclosed which show that in the summer of 1917 leading German circles were not yet willing to make a frank statement regarding Belgium. Whether such a declaration at that time would have meant—or would, at least, have made possible—the paving of the way for peace negotiations, must as yet be held questionable as far as the documents which so far have been revealed are concerned. At least the thought, that the Entente at that moment would not yet have given up its far-flung war aims, cannot be rejected. On the other hand, the German Government should not have left untried any possibility which gave the slightest promise to put an end to the war upon any acceptable conditions. From the just-published second volume on the World War by Helfferich, we know that Bethmann-Hollweg always took this attitude, and even at times when our military position took a turn for the better he tried to bring about an end of the war as soon as possible. His suc-

---

[35] *Deutsche Allgemeine Zeitung,* July 30, 1919, evening edition, p. 2.
[36] *Ibid.,* July 29, 1919, evening edition, p. 1.

cessor, Herr Michaelis, in his letter of September 12, 1917, to Hindenburg, in which he expressed his views regarding Belgium, has probably striven for the same aim but was doubtless more subjected to the military views of the Highest Army Command than his predecessor. It remains open to question whether he clearly foresaw the whole bearing the Belgian question had in connection with the waging of the war and the war aims of the Entente and whether he could estimate its decisive importance accordingly. Certain is it that to him, too, a circumscribing of the extreme German annexationist demands seemed to be absolutely desirable. . . . .

[Schwertfeger then discussed Hindenburg's and Ludendorff's views with regard to Belgium, both of which are given above.]

Indeed, the industrial region of the Lower Rhine and Westphalia formed the most acute part of our Western front. If we were met with reverses there, or, as has been mentioned occasionally, had been compelled to begin the two-front war with an offensive against Russia, then it would have been easy for a French attack, via Belgium, to occupy this region and completely paralyze Germany's power of resistance. From the military standpoint it was natural that this consideration should be much emphasized, in the manner of Moltke after the war of 1870. Thus, the Highest Army Command doubtless acted in accordance with its duty when it placed its expert views at the disposal of the political branch of the Government. Of course, these views could be of value only as departmental views, and it is a familiar experience that the representatives of individual departments demand more than enough rather than less. But it was the task of the political branch, to include and subordinate the wishes of the Highest Army Command within the frame of the entire policy. The Government alone is responsible for it if this did not take place, for the prosecution of the war is the instrument of the policy and not the reverse.

Up to this very day, large groups in Germany are still regrettably unenlightened about the connection of the Belgian problem with the outcome of the war. The insufficient enlightenment about it did indeed keep the Government for a long time in an oppressive dependence upon public opinion. The precipitous and hasty publication of the Belgian documents of 1914 revenged itself in that it created in Germany a belief that Belgium, long before the war, had already come to a more or less pronounced offensive agreement with the Entente. And thus it was the most dangerous and important link in the chain of encircling Germany. Accordingly, great groups of Germans, and even the great masses, regarded it throughout the war as almost a moral duty not to relinquish the defeated Belgium after the conclusion of peace. Gradually different interests connected themselves with this conception, and

in time it became such a force that at first its strength was underestimated. Neither did the responsible authorities attempt to restrict it.
All statements of the German Government regarding its views about
Belgium, no matter how moderate and justified they appeared, were of
no avail as long as the daily press produced countless articles, proclaiming the most fantastic war aims in respect to Belgium. The ghost which
had been precipitously conjured up in 1914 could not be driven away,
and so the greatest obstacle to the achievement of peace developed out
of the Belgian question. An actual result from the German offers of
peace could be expected only in the case where public opinion in Germany had been unreservedly informed about the state of affairs in the
Belgian question and thus the mistakes previously committed had been
rectified. But this the Government of that time failed to do.

171. LUDENDORFF'S MEMORANDUM, SEPTEMBER 14, 1917[37]

GREAT HEADQUARTERS, September 14, 1917

First Quartermaster-General

In the *pourparler* in Berlin our position and that of the enemy were
discussed. I myself feel obliged to return once more to them and to
express in written form the train of thought in which I moved. I have
here expanded my views in regard to Longwy-Briey, agriculture, and
overseas trade. According to the reports of the representatives of the
departments, our internal situation is in a difficult position in regard to
fodder and coal. The lack of coal is unfortunately due to conditions
of previous months. Our financial condition is extraordinarily strained.
The Reichstag majority has made our internal state of affairs rather
unsatisfactory. The labor question and also that of "Ersatz" have become more acute. These internal difficulties can be overcome only by
firm administration on the part of the present Government. That is
possible. Austria-Hungary is chained to us for the coming months, for
reasons which I need not expound here. Bulgaria, too, becomes more
accommodating since the French have scored some local advantages
west of Lake Ochrida. We are sure of the Turks for the time being.
It is unnecessary for me to dwell upon the facts that our military position is strengthened and that the U-boat warfare is working. In contrast to this the position of the Entente is much more difficult. Russia
is drifting toward internal dissolution, and thus disappears as an important opponent. Her internal conditions are bound to lead to a crisis
in the matter of fuel- and food-provisioning. These conditions will

[37] *Deutsche Allgemeine Zeitung,* July 31, 1919, p. 3.

react upon Rumania. Affairs in the East have taken a decisive turn in our favor. The rest of the Entente Powers have no longer been able to count strongly upon Russia and Rumania. Our alliance does not show similar symptoms.

Italy apparently counts upon a success in the 12th Isonzo battle which will be withheld from her. The internal conditions thus drive her toward a crisis. Her lack of coal must become very great.

That the new Ministry in France will be for some time more wary than the previous one is not to be assumed. The opposite is to be expected. France also fears a coal crisis. All recent news from France proves that the U-boat warfare is working, that the question of food is serious, and that the English Government has to contend with great social difficulties. The demand for peace in England is growing. I do not need to dwell upon that *in extenso*. Should England undertake [peace] moves, it will be a sign that she no longer believes in victory. And from this there is no long step to the conviction that she can but lose.

The Entente's hope since the breakdown of Russia is America. This cannot be underestimated, but also must not be overestimated. At this moment England seems to fear that the leadership will go to America.

Italy's relation with the Entente may be overlooked. At any rate there is great friction between the Entente Powers. So far the year 1917 has not brought any great military successes to the Entente. Only Mesopotamia has been won by England. The great military successes both on land and on sea belong to us.

I draw this conclusion: Our military position is more favorable than that of the Entente; our alliance is firmer; internal difficulties among us are fewer than among the Entente Powers. In spite of this, I too am of the opinion that a peace before winter is desirable for us and that it will give us the most essential things which we need for the security of our later economic development and which will place us in such an economic and military situation that we can calmly face a future defensive war.

The mainsprings of our military and economic resistance lie—aside from the army and the navy—in our agriculture, our natural resources, and our strongly developed industries. Without Rumania and other occupied territories we should have been placed in a highly serious food situation. Even with Rumania it has been serious enough. It would become still more acute, if, as we must hope, we shall also have to provide for Belgium. This at present we cannot do. Therefore, we must receive an enlargement of our territory. This we can find only in Courland and Lithuania, which offer good agricultural possibilities. By holding Poland we must, for military reasons, shift Lithuania's border over Grodno to the south and extend Prussia's boundary to the east and west. Only then we shall be able to defend Prussia. At certain places in the Province of Posen, too, the boundary is militarily unfavorable. Whether or not with Courland we shall be able to exert an attracting influence upon the Baltic Provinces, must be left to future political development.

How a better future food reserve would influence our relations with neutral countries may be just mentioned here. Grain and potatoes mean power as much as coal and iron. Our natural resources and our industries are situated along the border as unfavorably as possibly could be. The Government and the Reichstag, even before the war, recognized the difficult position of the Upper Silesian basin, and took appropriate measures to defend it. This is still unsatisfactory, for we must guard Upper Silesia by territorial extension. This could be facilitated by liquidating the industries, which are in enemy possession, and placing them in German hands.

In the west we have two great centers, the iron-ore basin of Alsace-Luxemburg, with the Saar basin, and the industrial territory of the Lower Rhine–Westphalia, which is going to extend more and more toward Belgian and Dutch borders. The danger which threatens these areas has not been evidenced during this war, since we beat the Entente to it by our offensive. Besides, the importance of these industrial districts was not recognized at all in the beginning. Now there is no doubt about it, and we shall have to reckon with the fact that the Entente will do everything to gain these territories. Should this materialize we should never be in a position to wage a defensive war; economically too, we should be done for; the internal political consequences I need not mention.

The defense of these two districts is for us a question of life and death. We must here secure all that our position entitles us to and all that is obtainable in any way. If we achieve nothing, our position will be precarious, and in such a case it would be preferable to continue to fight and not to think of peace as yet. We must keep in mind that that which we do not achieve must be adjusted in peace time with great expense (aerial defense, maintenance of air-fleets, strong border patrol) in so far as such an equalization is possible at all.

The Lorraine iron-ore basin demands territorial aggrandizement toward the west. The greater it is, the easier will be the defense. The keeping of the border as prior to the war would have as a result that every political disturbance would have its reaction upon the industries with their large laboring-masses. By an opening of hostilities their operation would be paralyzed and exposed to destruction. In the territories which we will gain mines are located. This, in the first place, would permit greater economizing of our ores in peace time. Since the German ore reserves are rather limited, this point is not unimportant. But above all such a land accretion would be a guaranty that the mines now in German hands would also be able to operate in time of war, provided they have immediate military defense. Of course this territory remains greatly endangered through artillery and airplanes and will require great defensive measures, since we cannot shift our border up to the Meuse.

But more imperative is the undisturbed maintenance of the territory of the Lower Rhine and Westphalia. What the coast of Flanders means to this territory for an aerial attack upon England, but to a still greater degree, the Meuse line at Liége means to this industrial district. We must retain in our possession both sides of the Meuse southward to St. Vith. To achieve this I see, so far, only one means, namely, that of incorporating those territories in the German Empire. Whether or not there exists any other way, I shall leave unanswered. None seems to have been found, at least for the time being.

The possession of the Meuse line alone is not sufficient to give the industrial district the necessary security. We must push the English-Belgian-French Army back still farther. That can be done only if we can bind Belgium so closely to us economically that she will seek a political union also with us. The economic union will not materialize without strong military pressure—extended to occupation—and without taking possession of Liége. Belgium's neutrality is a phantom which in practice cannot be counted upon. Only with the occupation of all of Belgium and the holding of the coast of Flanders could we have complete security, especially if the building of a tunnel from Dover to Calais becomes a reality. In spite of all of England's difficulties we cannot achieve this at present. The question now is whether we must continue the war to achieve that purpose. That, I think, would be necessary if England should retain a strip of territory (Calais) in France. If they do not do it, then in my opinion there is no need to continue the war into the winter in order to possess the coast of Flanders. Such action upon England from off the coast of Flanders we must then obtain in a roundabout way. I regard this as possible if Belgium, divided into Wallonia and Flanders, can be united with Germany economically, and when, in time, she herself takes up defensive measures against France and England, and when, after the conclusion of the occupation, she maintains her own army and navy.

The result of uniting Belgium with Germany will be that through a policy which clearly pursues its aim Holland will be attracted to us, particularly if its colonial possessions should be guaranteed by an alliance of ours with Japan. Thereby we get again at that part of the coast which lies opposite England and thus we realize that aim which the navy is now already trying to achieve. In regard to England we shall obtain a position which will enable us in the next war to maintain our trade. This, the third great aim, we must not lose sight of.

To this belong, besides Russia, market places across the ocean in South America, a colonial Empire in Africa, and firm strongholds within and outside of the colonial Empire. Particularly if we now give up the coast of Flanders, then the navy has a right to demand bases elsewhere as compensation, as the Chancellor himself has said, in order to enable it to keep the highways of the sea open for Germany by the nearest routes, and thus to maintain its imports. The more we fall short of this aim, the greater becomes the need of capital which we must invest—without bearing interest—in raw material in Germany.

In passing it may be said that Denmark, closely united with us by favorable commercial treaties, would greatly enhance our maritime position and commercial freedom.

CHAPTER IX

CONVERSATIONS WITH HERRON

INTRODUCTORY NOTE

THE FOLLOWING documents have to do with the efforts of certain German representatives to secure a negotiated peace through contact with President Wilson or the American Government. They reveal the very confidential and intimate diplomatic work of Dr. George Davis Herron, who was regarded by an influential German group first as a correct interpreter of Wilson and later as a confidential spokesman for America whose prophecies invariably became true. In December 1917 Herron commenced to report regularly to the American legation in Berne concerning the visits of German representatives. From his outpost at Geneva he proclaimed a crusade and *la guerre a l'outrance* against a Germany which might attempt to subdue all Europe. On January 17, 1918, Ambassador Sharp informed Herron that the substance of his first report had been cabled to Washington and that the State Department had approved his position. Herron was also, during this period, in communication with the British Foreign Office.

The conversations between Dr. de Fiori and Herron, taken down by a "confidential stenographer," covered two hundred typewritten pages. They were later verified by the principals and copies were sent to (1) the King of Bavaria, (2) the Imperial Chancellor, (3) the State Department, and (4) the British Foreign Office. Professor Edgar Jaffé published on November 22, 1918, in the *Münchener Neueste Nachrichten* and the *Berliner Tageblatt,* his revelation of an American peace offer, to which Herron replied. The subsequent controversy was concerned with the Jaffé-Herron conversations, which are completely reported in the following documents.

Finally these documents reveal the very confidential and intimate diplomatic work which Herron did and show also that he acted in all good faith. Concerning the victors who dictated the Treaty of Versailles he wrote: "Not all the things wherein Wilson erred nor any of the things he lacked can any wise atone for the guilt of the peacemakers, or cancel the scarlet issues of their perjury."

After the signing of the Treaty of Versailles, Herron wrote the following observations, which are explanatory and more or less essential to an understanding of the documents:

I

1. At the outset of any serious examination of these documents on the part of student or historian, it should be kept in mind 'that the military operations of the Great War always had their diplomatic and psychical equivalent or counterpart. Among all the belligerents, a continuous search for peace through negotiation and compromise was carried on—but always, on the part of each belligerent save America only, with the idea of securing special advantages for itself. The intensities and ramifications of this inner struggle,—of the strife of nation against nation for the procurement of concessions and terms of peace behind the scenes,—little of all this was known, and still less was understood, by the peoples at home or upon the fields of battle. . . . .

2. There never was a time, after the first Battle of the Marne, when a tolerable peace might not have been had if there had been any adequate intelligence or morality resident in the men in places of power. That such a peace was not arrived at, sooner or later, before the victory which resulted in the present general ruin of the world, was always due to either stupidity or corruption—sometimes both—on the part of the governments—or rather of one government or another.

3. It was inevitable that Switzerland, not only because of her central geographical position, nor only because of her necessary neutrality toward all belligerents, but because of her historical toleration and hospitality toward the political missioners of all nations, should become the field of these inner operations of the war. Indeed, it may be well said that Switzerland was the war's real psychic center. Certain it is that the war's noblest visions and efforts, its most spiritual manifestations and determinations, marched beside its vilest intrigues and dirtiest phases amidst the cities and secret meeting places of the Helvetian Confederation. Switzerland literally swarmed with the emissaries of all the considerable tribes and nations of the earth. And each of the belligerents had a host of agents (of one sort and another) which has never been numbered. The estimate of five thousand is probably not too high for the number of Germany's varied actors, including the highest diplomatic missioners and the lowest spies. The number in the employ of England would run up into very many hundreds. The same would be the case with France, with Austria, with Italy, to say nothing of the intriguing hordes of the lesser powers.

Among the greater powers, each department of state would have its representatives, and these would often be unacquainted with the representatives of other departments of state. The British War Office, for instance, had its own set of intelligence officers in Switzerland, and the British Foreign Office had another set. The agents of these respective departments would often be unknown to each other. Each would be carrying on its own inner operations or espionage toward the enemy. But not only this; it sometimes happened that the agents of one department of a particular government were engaged in actively spying upon the agents of another department of the same government. This was true alike of Germany, of England, and of France; and also true, alas! of agents sent out by the American government. But this kind of intrigue—carried on within the boundaries of Switzerland by the agents of one department of a government against another department of the same government,—was not at all confined to intelligence officers or to lower orders of spies; it was carried on by the representatives of the heads of government. General Ludendorff, for instance, had his own representatives in Switzerland watching over and working against the representatives of the German Chancellor. . . . .

4. For obvious reasons, the inquiries, initiatives and movements toward peace had to be carried on by unofficial persons; it might happen, though rarely, that a diplomatic personage would "unofficially" participate. Naturally, members of belligerent governments could not meet for the discussion of peace and at the same time carry on war. The persons carrying on the "conversations"—as all such initiatives and discussions came to be termed—might previously have been members of their respective governments, or they might be prospective members of some future governments. But generally, except in the case of France, the missioners or messengers were men with little previous diplomatic experience and without official connection with their governments. They were, however, apt to be men of intellectual and moral authority in their respective countries. England, for instance, would "send" General Jan Smuts or Dr. Seton-Watson, or even a distinguished University mathematician. Or possibly Lord Robert Cecil would come on such an errand while the government professionally closed its eyes. From Germany and Austria almost invariably came men of the highest personal worth— men of great intellectual standing and most serious character, but who were children as regards the world of war and of diplomacy. Nearly always these were from the great universities, though with them would sometimes be such as Erzberger, a Catholic Archbishop, or Scheidemann the Socialist, or General Count Montgelas of the Army. . . . .

Two points regarding the "negotiators" must be kept in mind:

A. The fiction always had to be maintained that they were not "sent" by their respective governments. The meetings, if they became known,

were due to accident; or to past personal friendships between unac-
knowledged personalities who actually represented their governments;
or to the personal initiative of one or more of the participants. The
governments alike considered that they must be in a position to deny
any knowledge of such negotiations in case of information leaking
through to the public.

For instance, it was arranged with me that discreet duplicates of my
reports to our State Department should be sent to the British Foreign
Office, providing only Mr. Balfour and Sir William Tyrrell should read
them. At the time of the Bavarian "conversations" between Dr. de
Fiori and myself—conversations included in the German documents—
the British Foreign Office telegraphed me, through the chief of the
British Intelligence Service in Geneva, to know if the documents in
question might be personally submitted to the Prime Minister, Lloyd
George. . . . .

B. This dualism could result in nothing but ultimate and increasing
evil, as one now sees, viewing the matter retrospectively.

In the first place, the peoples who were making the enormous sacrifices and fighting the battles were kept in complete ignorance of each
other's real fears and reasons and purposes—in complete ignorance of
essential things that stupendously mattered—indeed, of the real or inner
and psychic centers and motivating forces of the war. It was only by
being kept in ignorance,—and by being hypnotized with continuous
falsehoods—that the peoples were reduced to the state of mind essential
to the indefinite continuance of the war. And this ignorance of what
really happened, especially of what caused this or that to happen, continues until this day. The most of what has been written about the war,
whether by members of the Peace Conference or others, is substantial
fiction and largely irrelevant. The most of it is in the nature of personal
apology, or else of propaganda. . . . .

C. One other result of these "conversations" must be kept in mind.
That is, the tragedy ensuing to men of deep and urgent good faith,—to
men who had no other thought than getting humanity out of its scrape,
—who thus found their good faith bridled and saddled and ridden to
goals the exact and fearful opposite of what they themselves pursued.
For instance, I, as one of those destined to carry on these "conversations," and acting according to my instructions, did my best to undermine
the *morale* of German resistance. I convinced the German emissaries,—
because I myself was convinced,—that the principles pronounced by
President Wilson—the famous Fourteen Points—would be precisely
and comprehensively carried out. I did my best to make these Germans
believe in Wilson. They did believe in him. I acted in all good faith—
with a good faith that now seems naive. . . . .

II

My own part in these inner phases of the war came about in ways not altogether known to myself, and I found myself very profoundly and responsibly involved before I quite knew what had happened. Almost immediately upon the outbreak of war, I had conceived of writing an interpretation of it that would appeal to American understanding. I was then in Florence, but soon thereafter removed to Geneva, where I felt myself more in the center of the conflict. There I wrote the interpretation I had in mind, and it was published in New York, London, Geneva and Florence, in a little volume entitled: "The Menace of Peace."

At this time, the moral credit of America was very low in Europe. Even in Geneva, which claims to be the mother of American institutions, it was felt that America's only interest in the war was financial—was a question of how to make the largest profits out of all the belligerents. The name of Woodrow Wilson was a byword in London, Paris, Geneva and Rome. The American colony in each of the cities did its best, by every manner of gossip, to discredit the President. Clémenceau had referred to Wilson in a speech in Paris in most contemptuous terms. The Northcliffe press was proclaiming that the thing to be done was to keep Wilson out of the war and get him to mind his own business. The word of Roosevelt was everywhere taken as authority on Wilson's political purposes and character. I then took it upon myself to contribute what I could to the interpretation of Wilson and America in Europe. Different journals at this time had asked me to write about Wilson and America, such as the *Journal de Genève, La Semaine Littéraire* of Geneva, *La Gazette de Lausanne, Le Temps* of Paris, *L'Epoca* of Rome, and *Die Neue Zuericher Zeitung*. I was also writing for some of the more advanced weekly journals in London, such as *The New Age*. Some of these articles were published in a little volume entitled: "Woodrow Wilson and the World's Peace." An address I gave to the theological students of Geneva was published in a little volume entitled: "Germanism and the American Crusade." These volumes were published in French in Geneva at the same time they were published in America; and before being published in book form, they appeared in the different European journals for which they were written, and were widely copied and discussed in the German and Austrian press.

The result of it all was, that *I really did make Europe believe in Wilson,* and to what proved to be an amazing degree—to a degree, indeed, far beyond any hope or expectation I had when my erstwhile purely private and journalistic propaganda began. Thus there grew up the legend, which no effort or denial of mine was ever able to counteract or diminish, that I was Wilson's personal spokesman and interpreter in Europe, and his intimate friend. All my words were invested (especially in the mind of Middle Europe) with an authority that they in no wise possessed—their only original authority consisting of the faith they promulgated, the truth they proclaimed. But the State Department afterwards came to regard this legend as a valuable asset, and decided to capitalize it to the utmost of its possibilities.

But I must here go back a little before giving a further account of how I became involved in the inner negotiations carried on during the war. Because of friendships I had with different men in Italy, and afterwards with Serbian representatives in Geneva, I often found myself, during the early part of the war, in a mediatory position between spokesmen of these nations. These representatives would sometimes meet in my house in Geneva, and I would try to get them to some sort of agreement. Then the Italian Legation at Berne had become a post of great diplomatic importance because of the war. At its head was the accomplished Marquis Paulucci di Calboli, now the Italian Ambassador in Madrid. Next to him was the Marquis Durazzo, one of the ablest and noblest of the younger Italian diplomats. Associated with these were Baron Russo, now Chef de Cabinet of the Ministry of Foreign Affairs under Mussolini, and Count Pignatti, who is now the First Secretary of the Legation at Berne. There was also Professor G. A. Borgese, who had special charge of the Italian propaganda, and also Dr. Giulio Caprin, now literary editor of the *Corriere della Sera*. These were all greatly troubled by the apparent ignorance of the Government in Rome regarding the importance of the conflict between Italy and the Yougo-Slavs over the Adriatic territories. It was felt that the Pact of London, and especially the lack of all conciliatory policy toward the Yougo-Slavs on the part of Baron Sonnino, was damaging the cause of Italy in America and England. Marquis Paulucci and Marquis Durazzo therefore urged upon me, in the summer of 1917, to go privately to Rome, armed with letters from them, and see if I could not bring about a change of attitude on the part of members of the Government. It was a somewhat curious and delicate mission—a rather extraordinary position for an American to find himself in. I, an American citizen, was persuaded to go to Rome as a missioner of an Italian Embassy to the Italian Government. The mission, of course, had to be conducted with the utmost discretion and privacy.

But, in the providence of events, the mission turned out to be an altogether different one from that upon which I started. Stopping in Milan and Florence on the way, I finally arrived in Rome but a short time before the disaster of Caporetto, which threatened to engulf the whole Italian nation and to end in Germany's encampment upon the heights of Genoa. Naturally, the issue between Italy and the Southern Slavs became for the moment unimportant. De Martino, who was then Under-Secretary of Foreign Affairs, convinced me that I ought to go to Paris and see what could be done toward persuading Americans in authority there to bring about an American declaration of war against Austria. It was felt by many in Rome that nothing else could save Italy. From this feeling, however, Sonnino must be decidedly excepted. He regarded American participation in the war as of no consequence whatever; and, indeed, always spoke of it derisively. It was impossible for Sonnino, either then or afterwards, to take Woodrow Wilson seriously, or to regard him as other than a sentimental schoolboy.

So it turned out that instead of going to the Italian front, as I had expected to do, I went to Paris. Even so, this was not due in the first place to persuasion in Rome, but because there was no way of getting through to Geneva except by the way of Paris. Soon after my arrival in Paris, Ambassador Sharp called together the available Americans in positions of authority, including some members of our General Staff and Admiral Niblack of the Navy, with Robert Woods Bliss and others of the Embassy. Colonel House was just leaving for America, but made an appointment with me over the telephone. The appointment, however, was countermanded, though Colonel House says he never knew how, and that it was certainly not by his authority. Anyhow we missed each other. But to the twenty-five authoritative Americans gathered together behind closed doors I presented the whole Italian situation quite nakedly, and what I conceived to be the causes of the disaster, with the urgent reasons for an American declaration of war against Austria, and with what seemed to me the still more urgent reasons for sending a part of the American Army to the Italian Front. Ambassador Sharp reported the whole matter to Washington. The American declaration of war against Austria came, though how much or how little my presentation of the matter had to do with the declaration I never knew.

At this time, however, it was known that my opinions about the things of the war had personal influence with the President. He had expressed himself to different men as feeling that I had a singular grasp of all the elements of the war and of his own personal mind concerning it. It also happened, at this time, that President Wilson was relying largely upon Ambassador Sharp, rather than upon Mr. Page in London, for information. Mr. Sharp therefore asked that I keep him informed regarding the interior European situation as I should see it in Switzerland, especially in Geneva, which had become the crossroads of the world as well as the psychic crossroads of the war. It was understood that whatever I should write, Mr. Sharp would use in his own communications to the President and the State Department. To this I agreed, though with considerable reluctance and with many questionings and heart-burnings. On my return to Geneva, at the end of November 1917, I felt deeply that my conversations with the Germans, Austrians and Bulgarians who came to talk with me, and my report of these conversations to Mr. Sharp and indirectly to the President, placed me in a position of very serious moral responsibility without any collateral power or authority to procure the seizure of any opportunity that might arise for peace or for changing the course of things.

However, I began to write to Mr. Sharp, as the first two letters constituting the German documents will show. But the fact that I had communicated with Mr. Sharp became known to the American Legation at Berne—presumably through friends of members of the Legation in the State Department at Washington. I should say, here, that the Legation at Berne consisted at this time of a group of the very ablest young men in the diplomatic service. Without going into the question of the individual or collective ambitions of this group, or its wisdom or ethics upon one occasion and another, it must be said that the group made itself by far the most useful as well as serious and reliable American diplomatic center in Europe. The services rendered by these young men to the American Government are not yet a matter of history, but they were by far and away the most important rendered to the State Department and the President by any diplomatic center during the war. The American Minister, Mr. Stovall, was absent in America at the time of my return to Geneva, and the beginning of my correspondence with Mr. Sharp. At the head of the legation was Mr. Hugh R. Wilson, and associated with him were Mr. Frederic Dolbeare, Mr. Allen Dulles, Colonel William Godson, Mr. Loring Dresel, and afterwards several other young men of the diplomatic service, including Mr. Herter, now secretary to Mr. Hoover at Washington. Mr. Wilson came to see me first, at the beginning of December 1917, to talk about my visit to Italy, incidentally raising the question, however, of the diplomatic ethics of Mr. Sharp in conscripting the services of an American citizen residing in Switzerland, when such services should rightly be rendered in cooperation with the Legation in Switzerland rather than with the Embassy in Paris.

Soon after Mr. Wilson came to me with the desire and the proposition that I receive the various missions that came to Switzerland from Germany, Austria and Bulgaria and elsewhere, and carry on the conversations or negotiations with them on behalf of the State Department and the Legation; the Legation would dispatch all my reports (coded, of course) to Washington. Such was the beginning of the reports contained in the documents which follow.

There remains to be explained my relation to the British Government in the conduct of these negotiations. At the beginning of my work in Geneva, I became acquainted with Commander (afterwards Sir) Hugh Whittall, who was in charge of the highly-organized and efficient British Intelligence Service in Switzerland. He frequently received from the British War Office telegrams asking him to "inquire what Professor Herron thinks" of this or that matter, with the request to reply by telegraph. Neither Commander Whittall nor myself ever knew whence or where or why these telegrams began, except that they came from his chief in the War Office at London. The telegrams and my responses were numerous; but I don't know how many and I have no record of them. And to get copies of them out of the British War Office would probably be impossible.

Now during this time, and for that matter throughout the war, there was continuous strife between the British War Office and the British Foreign Office, in some cases each having its own intelligence service on the same field and each working at cross-purposes with the other.

One morning early in 1918, I received a visit from Mr. J. O. P. Bland, at that time connected with the Information Department of the British Foreign Office. Mr. Bland, let it be said in passing, was the chief British specialist and authority on China and Far Eastern Affairs, and had negotiated some of the principal British transactions in China. He had also written different books on China and the Far East—books which were the chief source of authority in British governmental circles. Mr. Bland stated that he had been sent to arrange with me, if possible, to send to the British Foreign Office papers or reports of the same order I had been sending to the American State Department or to President Wilson. The British Foreign Office knew of these reports through occasional duplicates furnished by officials somewhere in our State Department. In answer to my questions as to why the British Government should wish such papers from me, in the face of a highly-organized intelligence department, and both these in addition to frequent special missioners, such as General Smuts and others, he replied that my contact with German intellectuals and others was such as to enable me to furnish a synthetic view of the situation that could not be obtained elsewhere. I referred the matter to the State Department through the legation at Berne and received a somewhat noncommittal reply, but with the implication that the State Department would be just as well satisfied if I did not respond favorably to the British request. However, as I had come to feel that various intrigues were occurring in the Legation and the State Department to prevent the President from getting the whole truth of what I sent, I finally agreed to the request of Mr. Bland upon the pledge that only Mr. Balfour and Sir William Tyrrell should read my papers, and that any initiative or action taken because of them should be only in conjunction with the State Department, or preferably President Wilson directly. Whether these conditions were strictly carried out or not, I have no means of knowing. Mr. Balfour said to me in Paris, with at least seeming sincerity, that my reports were the only ones he read during the war, and that I had done much toward shaping the British Foreign Office policy toward Germany. Sir William Tyrrell wrote me a letter to the same effect. Once the British Foreign Office telegraphed to know if the documents concerning the Bavarian negotiations with Dr. de Fiori might be laid before Lloyd George, then Prime Minister.

This much I must say in this connection, that so far as my observation and experience go, I gained the impression that the British diplomatic tradition or practice is more honorable than that of other nations —that is, so far as diplomacy can be said to have any elements of essential honor.

172. DR. HERRON'S REPORT OF A CONVERSATION WITH HAUSSMANN AND MEINL, DECEMBER 28, 1917[1]

I have had two or three experiences in German mentality and method recently, about one of which I would especially ask your opinion and advice: it is a typical instance of German procedure, and is also indicative of Germany's determination to procure a peace that shall be to her advantage before America can reach Europe in adequate force.

A former Dutch Departmental Chief in the Ministry of Justice, Dr. B. de Jong van Beek en Donk, now settled at Bern and equipped with everything necessary for his work, is carrying on an urgent propaganda for a German peace. He asked a British military attaché,—who is also my intimate friend—for an introduction to me and made an appointment at my house. When he sent up his card, I went down to find him accompanied by Mr. Haussmann, the leader of the Progressive or Liberal Party of Germany, and for thirty years a member of the Reichstag and one of the most influential German politicians; also by Mr. Meinl, one of the most powerful financiers of the Austrian Empire and very close to the Emperor Charles. I let them speak for an hour without interruption. The substance of their speech and query was as follows:

I. Germany and Austria are very anxious for peace. They have learned many lessons by the war, and now want to resume normal relationship with the world, and enter a league of nations.

II. But, of course, Germany is now in a position of great military

---

[1] Herron Papers, Hoover War Library, I. Germany; Document II (Herron to Sharp).

advantage, with every reason to expect still further military gains, and must not be expected to make too many concessions.

III. America is naturally a pacifist nation, engaged in a war that is unnatural to her people, and ought to be the first to persuade the Allies to come to terms with Germany.

And the substance of my reply was:

I. If Germany really wants peace, all she has to do is openly to transmit her request to the Allies through any neutral agency acceptable to them, and to state specifically and unreservedly her terms, so that the Allies can consider them. She does not need to be undermining the world with subterranean intrigues, nor to be besieging unofficial individuals such as myself.

II. That her present military advantage affords her no basis whatever for negotiating a peace; it only gives her an opportunity to take the initiative. If she wants peace, she can never obtain it by assuming the rôle of the victor, or by seeking it by her present indirect methods.

III. That she is laboring under an utter delusion as regards America. It is true that we are a pacifist nation. Germany compelled us to declare war even though war is against our national desires and temperament. But it is thereby all the more certain that, having once drawn the sword, we will never sheathe it until either the thing called Germanism or ourselves is destroyed. The deeper we become involved in the war, the more certainly shall we become a nation of crusaders, the war taking on a distinctly religious character. Even if all Europe be temporarily subdued by the German sword, America will not make peace with a victorious Germany—not if the war lasts twenty or a hundred years. At least, I said, such is my personal opinion as to the feeling of my countrymen.

In fine, I seized the opportunity that had been forced upon me by these men to preach to them the meaning of the present world-crisis according to American understanding of it. I think they were considerably subdued.

The discussion then went on for another hour, finally resolving itself into this question on the part of my visitors: If Germany now takes the initiative, if Germany makes a great *beau geste,* proposing what she would regard as definite and generous terms of peace, what would be the attitude of President Wilson and the Government at Washington? Germany might be ready now to take this initiative, so they said, if she knew in advance that she would not be turned down by America.

I naturally told the gentlemen that the only way for them to ascertain the attitude of America was to make their proposition; in that manner and no other would they find out. I knew no more than they what reply Washington would make. And even if I, individually, had an opinion on the subject, I had absolutely no authority to express it. Furthermore, the mere fact of their wanting such advance information was evidence that the terms of peace they had in mind were of doubtful value.

The discussion continued for about three hours, with still another question: Would I undertake to find out, through the Paris Embassy or elsewhere, the probable American attitude—that is, would I transmit the inquiry to you to transmit to Washington? I immediately pointed out to them the impossibility and the absurdity of the position in which they were trying to place me, and the impudence of the thing they asked of me. They were asking me as an individual to ask the chief of my country, or its supreme authorities, a question which it would be to the interests of their Emperor or his prime minister to have answered, but which question neither the Kaiser nor his Minister would directly ask. I stated distinctly that, if Kaiser William and Chancellor Hertling wished to know what President Wilson and Secretary Lansing would think in certain circumstances, their business was to transmit their inquiry (through a neutral power) directly to our President and our Secretary of State. They certainly had no right, I declared, to come to me with any such question. Let them come, I explained, with the question written and signed by their Kaiser or his Chancellor if they wished it transmitted to Paris and Washington. I thought of course the obvious improbability and irregularity of such proceeding closed the discussion.

And yet they left me this last interrogation: "Suppose we do come to you with a mandate signed by either the Kaiser or Chancellor Hertling—a confidential mandate, of course, predicating a confidential answer—inquiring as to the probable attitude in Washington if Germany should take the initiative in proposing definite and generous terms of peace, would you take or transmit that imperially signed and confidential question?"

I submit this whole interview to you, asking your immediate and urgent judgment about the matter. If the utterly incredible thing should happen; if these men, who are powerful personalities, after all, should, as the Americans say, "call my bluff," should I transmit the question to you, or should I flatly refuse to receive both the question and the men? I certainly should have refused to see them in the first place, had I known they were coming as they did, or what they had to propose. I suppose they sought me out rather than some other American for the reason that I have written so much for the German Press in defense and interpretation of President Wilson and America's action, that I am to their minds an available or obvious person to see unofficially; or possibly they imagine that I possess some personal power or authority which I do not in the least possess.

You will easily understand why I come to you for advice rather than to our Legation here. I have great admiration for Hugh Wilson and his conduct of our affairs. He is exceptionally well poised and trustworthy and competent. But he is young in experience and in years, and you are rich in experience and in the service of democracy. You are also rich in faith, and you are close to the President. I need and I trust your judgment as to what I had best do. I am betimes greatly troubled about it. I do not want to shirk any duty, but I am very averse to some of these situations. Besides, I am as far as possible from being a diplomat in temperament or desire or capacity. I am only a dreamer, and want nothing of the world except its deliverance and a chance to write my dreams. I feel much like a child, if not a fool, in these positions in which I am caught unaware by officials and missionaries of Germanism. What shall I do?

I would ask that you kindly request the Legation at Bern, when you send your sealed reply, please to send it on to me, for the short distance between Bern and Geneva, by a courier, as I have been repeatedly informed by both the British and American Secret Service that the Swiss post office is absolutely unsafe.

Let me now say, in conclusion, that I have searched hopefully but in vain since I last saw you for any ray of light in the German darkness, or for any sign of repentance in the German people as a whole. Since their recent victories in Italy and Russia, Switzerland is swarming with highly-placed Germans; they are everywhere, and it is impossible to avoid them, even if one would. I have listened to their talk with aching heart, hoping and hoping for some sign of moral reason, some sense of humanity. Even among those who pretended to be moderate a short while ago, who made upon me the impression of thinking Germany wrong, I now find nothing but impudence and arrogance, and moral insensibility—a moral insensibility, a nonchalant brutality, that defies all understanding or psychological analysis. It gives me moments of black despair as to the near human future.

Nor do I see the slightest chance, now, of a democratic revolution in Germany. Six months ago, it seemed possible that something might happen among the German people—seemed as if they might take some step toward their own emancipation. But they won't—they won't—except under the scourge of that overwhelming military defeat which they now believe themselves secure against.

The Germans now absolutely believe they have Europe in their hands. Their complete victory over France and England is, to their minds, no longer in doubt. They confidently expect to defeat France and England before America can prevent it.

So, as I see it, two long terrible highways open out before mankind.

One, an utter German domination of Europe, Asia and Africa, and the extinction of hope and freedom for who knows how many years—the divine method of purging us of our materialism. The other, the consecration and equipment of America for the long and hard struggle of sweeping that Germanism and all that it means from the face of the earth. Between these two I can see no middle way.

It may be—and I pray and even trust that it may—that He who is the actual Lord of our earth, who proved His Kingship by His service and sacrifice, has somewhere in the shadows some divine dénouement, unforeseen by us as yet, that shall be for the redemption, the freedom and the joy of all peoples. If it be so, let Him come quickly.

With all best wishes for you for the New Year, mingled with our mutual prayers and wishes for the imperilled world, I remain, dear Mr. Sharp,

Faithfully yours,

(Signed) George D. Herron

P.S. If there is anything in my letter, especially about the interview and about Germany, which you think would be of any interest or value, you are of course at liberty to transmit such to Washington or elsewhere.

173. MEMORANDUM OF CONVERSATION WITH COUNT MONTGELAS, FEBRUARY 28, 1918[2]

Count Montegeles came yesterday and remained from 2:00 until 11 o'clock, though I had to excuse myself betimes to see other people.

He has presented a much more serious situation than I had anticipated, and seems to be a much larger man than I expected. I feel that I must get his presentation before you as quickly as possible, and that it is one that ought at least to be considered by our Government.

He says that this is the first time he has talked with any other than a German, as he has felt that his position in the army required that much loyalty from him, even against his convictions. He has discussed the matters which he presented to me only with Prince Hohenlohe and Mr. Muehlon, but Mr. Muehlon persuaded him it was his duty to place confidentially before me his view of Germany's purposes and probabilities.

I cannot peer closely enough into the future to know how far his terribly dark outlook is correct. I know that it agrees with what I have seemed to see increasingly as an European possibility, these last few

[2] Herron Papers, I, Document IX.

weeks. At any rate, I must present you the possibility which Count Montegeles presents to me, and leave it to your judgment as to how immediately and urgently you present it to our Government.

The Count is, as you know, one of the three or four important Germans in Switzerland who are against the present German Government and who labour for the redemption of Germany. He has long been an intimate friend of Mr. Muehlon, who declares for his utter integrity of conviction and purpose. Mr. Muehlon also says that he was one of the ablest of the German Generals and that absolutely the only thing that has ever been against him is his liberal tendencies. The charge against him when he was relieved of his command was that of "an exaggerated sense of justice toward the enemy." I judge him to be a very much abler man than his brother of the German Legation. It is partly on account of his brother's position, which he does not want to imperil, that he has hesitated about speaking to anyone, but he feels it now his duty to humanity to place before the American Government the European situation as it appears to him.

1. The Count affirms, and with profoundest feeling and deliberate conviction, based upon his knowledge of Germany's present purposes and powers and secret weapons, that a complete European catastrophe is at hand. In two months Prussia will be in practical possession of Europe, he believes, unless some moral or political initiative of America intervenes. The danger to France and England is far greater than they realize, and the position of the neutral countries is far graver than they have knowledge of. He does not believe there is any earthly power can prevent the approaching German offensive from being successful. It is only a question of a very few weeks till France and Italy will be overwhelmed and new submarine inventions are in rapid preparation which will still further endanger England and prevent America from getting her troops and their supplies to France.

2. But even if the offensive fails to break through, but simply leaves the military status quo on the Western front, Germany's political propaganda and domestic situation are now so well organized that the catastrophe will come anyhow. He declares that we can have no idea, outside of Germany, how the whole German people are sustained with lies. There are even Generals in high command on the Western front who have been fighting there for 3 and 4 years, who today absolutely believe Belgium invaded Germany first. The Socialist leaders also are utterly ignorant of the beginnings of the war. They are still convinced that the war began as a resistance to a Russian invasion. The whole German population is more and more saturated with a fanatical idea of self-defense. No matter what miseries they may have to pass through, the German people will go on unto the end. The Count declares that they

have reached the point where they will kill their own fathers and mothers for the sake of saving food for the army, if the State commands it. It is an absolute delusion to hope for anything in the nature of a revolt in Germany. There is not one ray of light, he declares, in the German darkness.

3. The Prussian political program is to subsidize and stimulate all the subversive elements in the different countries in order to create Bolshevik efforts and appearances, and to make way for a separate peace with the different nations and divisions of nations. It is through this method that Russia is now absolutely in her hands, and the organization for this accomplishment is much more complete throughout the whole of Europe than France or England at all appreciates. The separate peace with each country, or division of a country, will not be difficult. Germany can always assemble the members of a fictitious government where she wills. The Ukraine peace is an example of what she is preparing to do throughout Europe. The signers of the Ukraine peace in no sense really represent the Ukraine people The peace was signed by some Jewish traders and a boy 20 years old. Governments of the same sort will be set up by Germany in Rumania, in what is left of Poland, in Courland and Lithuania, and a separate peace made with each. Then Serbia and Belgium will next be provided with governments that will also sign a separate peace. Finally, Italy will be broken and disorganized and brought to the same position. France, Germany believes, will come next. The continent of Europe will then be in Prussian hands with England and America left to carry on the war and that without means of communication with each other.

4. The neutrals will also be forced to make new terms with Germany. Switzerland is already practically in German hands. He deplores the failure of American wheat to reach Switzerland. Even at great sacrifice, it is a matter of vast importance that the Allies should not leave Switzerland to the bounty of Germany. Yet this is just what is happening. Germany has laid before the Swiss Government, already, a plan for supplying wheat from the Ukraine; and, in default of American wheat, Switzerland will accept this plan. He says he knows intimately the mind of the Swiss staff and he believes that General Willey is conniving with the German staff in a program to have French troops in Alsace forced into Switzerland, in the coming offensive, and that this will be made a pretext for a German invasion and for making the Swiss people feel that Germany is defending them against France. The next step will be that Germany will demand that Switzerland prohibit all anti-German propaganda and that such men as Muehlon and himself and even Prince Hohenlohe will have to be surrendered to the German Government.

5. He points out the fact that, as the European situation now stands, Germany actually outnumbers the Allies. With her armies on the Eastern front so largely reduced, and with the Slavic soldiers that she can conscript, the armies that Germany can now command actually outnumber the combined armies of England, France, Italy, and America. With the population of Russia and Asia to draw upon, Germany will have behind her peoples to the number of two or three hundred millions as against the allied populations.

6. He also points out that this approaching catastrophe of a Prussian Europe is not so much a Prussian military victory as a moral and diplomatic failure on the part of the Allies. Time after time, when the tide might have been turned, the Allies have invariably (and apparently inevitably) either done the wrong thing or failed to do the right thing; he takes as an instance the escape of the "Goeben" and its entrance into the harbor of Constantinople. This one thing is so important that he insists that it is the "Goeben" that won the war. If she had only been captured, or the English ships had pursued the "Goeben" straight into the harbor of Constantinople, as they had an international right to do, Turkey could never have joined the side of Germany.

Again, when Serbia was in a position to strike Bulgaria and knew perfectly well Bulgaria's intentions, France and England prevented her, and to this all the Serbians agreed; and thus Germany won an enormous military advantage in the destruction of Serbia and the encircling of Salonika.

Another instance is the method of reaching Salonika. At the outbreak of the war the Albanians were in power in Constantinople, and the 40 Albanian members of the Turkish Government were the only force that could oppose Enver Pasha and the German designs. The Albanians were absolutely loyal to England and France. Dr. Adamidi was then a member of the Turkish Government, and leader of the Albanian group. He went to England to tell the Government the dangers of Turkey's joining with Germany, and tried to get the English Government to act at once. He also explained to them the necessity of building a road direct from Valona to Salonika, thus using the route via Brindisi instead of the long Mediterranean route. If that had been acted upon, Germany never could have reached Constantinople. Nothing was done about it for two years. The Albanian contingent in Constantinople was broken up and dispersed. And so on, one count after another. Count Montegeles declares our Allied diplomacy has blindly worked for a German victory, quite as much as the Germans have done by their foresight. He also makes a very heavy count against us as Americans for not taking up our leadership in the matter sooner; in fact, he feels that everything we do is done from one to two years too late.

(You understand that I am faithfully presenting for your consideration and the consideration of our Government the situation as it appears to Count Montegeles, and not as it appears to me. It is his view that I want considered at this time, though I largely agree with him.)

7. At the present moment, he sees only two possible doors of European escape from this overwhelming catastrophe of a complete German dominion. One is through Austria. But he fears even that is too late. He declares that in Berlin they would even welcome the effort of Austria for a separate peace, as that would give them the excuse for immediately occupying Vienna. He believes Austria to be now helplessly in Germany's hands. No less, he would urge that our last resources should be exhausted in trying to build a bridge between Vienna and Washington.

Another possibility would be that the President should instantly respond to Hertling's ostensible acceptance of the four principles of peace propounded by the President and ask why then, if Germany accepts those principles, is she marching upon a defenseless Russia and making a separate peace with different divisions of that country. The President should also say, Count Montegeles thinks, that he assumes it as a matter of course that Germany will annul each separate peace she has made, in order to take up the question of the general and inclusive peace in which all nations would participate. He thinks such a course would give America a moral advantage.

8. I took up with the Count, as I had previously taken up with Mr. Muehlon, the question of what would be the effect upon the German people if the Allies, under American initiative, should form the League of Nations now. Suppose, I propounded, the Allies should, by their representatives assembled, form the Constitution of the Society of Nations, and, without naming any one nation, invite all the nations of the world to join; and that the Allies, and such neutrals as would, should immediately give their assent and constitute themselves the Society of Nations, proceeding with their organization as if Germany did not exist, but with the place left at the table for Germany whenever she should choose to accept the conditions and sign the Constitution.

When I presented this question to him, just as I had presented it to Mr. Muehlon, he declared, after much reflection, that he believed that it was still possible to win a moral victory over the German people, even in default of a military victory on our part, by this instant formation of the League of Nations. For the League thus to exist, with reciprocity between all its members, with an international tribunal established for the settlement of all disputes, and for Germany to be outside the doors of the League, being regarded by the League as an outlaw among nations,—this, he believes, would have an overwhelming effect upon even German mentality.

I have talked with you considerably, dear Mr. Wilson, about this immediate establishment of a League of Nations. I have intended to formulate my thought of the matter more fully before presenting it to you, but I feel it is urgent to raise the question, even in this incidental way, at the conclusion of this report. I am profoundly convinced that it is the most urgent matter that can come before the attention of our Government; that the most immediate action that should command our Government is this very Society of the Nations. I wish it could be urged upon our President and our State Department with sufficient appeal and authority. Our President should not lose a day in taking the initiative in convoking the representatives of the Allies for the formation of this Society. I believe it to be the supreme defense, and mayhap the only defense, that can finally prevail against the Prussianization of Europe, if not of the world. . . . .

174. MEMORANDUM OF CONVERSATION WITH HERMANN VON BOETTICHER, MARCH 12, 1918[3]

Le Retour
26, Chemin des Cottages
Geneva, Switzerland

12th March, 1918

I am almost daily beset with a somewhat new and puzzling type of German messenger whose riddle I cannot clearly read. I present the riddle to you and you can judge for yourself if the reading thereof may have an interest to our Department of State.

The type of messenger to which I refer differs widely from such high-minded and entirely honest Germans as Dr. Mühlon, Dr. Sturmer, or Count Montegeles. On the other hand, the type cannot be classified with the spies.

It is strange, it seems paradoxical indeed, that at the moment when Germany is manifesting a brutal and arrogant self-confidence she also is sending out so many skilful and ingenious pleaders on her behalf. None of the Allies—least of all America—would so abase themselves, even in direct defeat and discouragement. Yet the German Government through its army of diplomats—each one of whom is a moral curiosity, if not a monstrosity—is daily whining at our doorsteps.

Does this mean that Germany is really as assured of victory as she pretends? Or does it mean that she plans to make victory doubly sure? Or is it simply an inevitable manifestation of the nature of The Beast?

---

[3] Herron Papers, I, Document XII.

I must prelude the particular instance I wish to present to you by recalling to your mind two previous instances which I have told you about in conversation, but have never included in any written report.

The first of these is the case of my being invited to the apartment of a rather well-known German literary woman, residing in Berne,— supposedly because her opposition to German militarism made it impossible for her to reside in her own country. You will remember that, on entering her salon, I found myself face to face with the German Minister, who proceeded to inform me that he knew America very well; that America was wholly pacifist and would never fight; and that Germany need not, therefore, take our President's proclamations into account. I asked him why he should then take the trouble to meet me there and impart his knowledge, and I vocally marvelled in his presence at his impenetrable ignorance of America. After doing my best to enlighten him as to the meaning of America's entrance upon the war, and doing all I could to put the general fear of God into his heart, I abruptly left the room.

The second instance I spoke to you about was that of a Polish lady of ancient family, who came to my home ostensibly to talk about the wrongs of Poland, but whom I soon discovered to be a very skilful and highly paid agent of the German Government.

She explained to me the great mistake that the President had made in demanding so much for Posen. The Province of Posen she declared to be three-fourths German and only one-fourth Polish and should, therefore, not be included in the restored Kingdom of Poland. The Austrian Poles would be much more contented to be erected into a Federal State of the Austrian Empire.

The people of the Balkans were all impossible and would inevitably exterminate each other. The only trustworthy people among them—or bordering them rather—were the Turks. The Bulgars were fairly tolerable, but even they must not have much consideration.

In consonance with these two instances is the one I am about to narrate.

On Saturday morning, Dr. Oscar Levy telephoned to know if he could come to speak of a German poet who wished to be presented. Dr. Levy is one of the most eminent of German literary men, being the literary executor and biographer of Nietzsche, and having lived in London for 14 years by choice. He has sincerely and urgently warned the world against Prussian militarism for many years, notwithstanding the fact that he is Prussian by birth and that his brother is an officer of the German General Staff. He is thoroughly trusted by both France and England.

He did not wish to make himself responsible for the young poet who asked for presentation, but told me frankly he believed the man was coming to me with the knowledge at least of the German Minister. He thought it might be no less advisable that I receive the said inquirer, as it would give me some insight into the present German mind and method.

The name of the young man is Hermann von Boetticher. Before America's entrance upon the war, he had been for two years in New York and Washington working, so he avows, in the interest of the German democracy. He names different Americans with whom he co-operated—among them Dr. Frank Bohn, who is the very able and devoted leader of the American movement for the promotion of democracy in Germany.

Some time before the American declaration of war, Herr von Boetticher sailed for Germany by the way of Holland, but was taken from the steamer and interned in France for two years. He was then permitted to reside in Switzerland, where he has been now for some months. He is here in one sense as a French prisoner, and yet he confesses to be working in the German Legation, and is in what I infer to be a somewhat intimate connection with the personnel of the Legation. He came to me ostensibly as an earnest advocate of German democracy but if he had been shrewder he would not have assumed—as he did assume in the opening of his conversation—my acquaintance with such men as Dr. Mühlon and Count Montegeles.

The professed objects of his visit were:

1. To point out how America and the Allies were constantly working against the democratic movement in Germany by their diplomatic methods instead of making connections with it that would enlighten and encourage it. If we had permitted the Stockholm Conference to take place, the German social democrats would have learned for the first time about the origin of the war and the determination of the democracies of America and England and France to continue the war unto the complete overthrow of Governmental Germany.

If the Allies had accepted the invitation of Russia to discuss peace, the representatives of the Allies would have had an opportunity to enlighten the democracy of Germany, for the discussions would have been public and have been held in a neutral country.

If President Wilson would confine his answers to Germany to an appeal to German democracy, and not condemn the Kaiser and discuss the surrender of Alsace-Lorraine, again the German democracy would have been in the way to be won.

He declares that the whole diplomatic policy of the Allies is such as to drive German democracy into the arms of the Prussian militarists and into an unnatural loyalty to the Kaiser.

All this he developed at considerable length and with a great deal of sophistry. He wished to appeal to the President to take a new attitude toward Germany in order to encourage a democratic revolution. He presented me with a letter addressed to the President which he had been waiting two months to deliver, but could hitherto find no channel that he considered trustworthy. I enclose the letter to you because of your very healthy sense of humor, but I do not think you will find it worth while forwarding it to the State Department.

2. Herr von Boetticher declares that there is an enormous spirit of division and revolt in Germany which only the diplomatic conduct of the Allies prevents from manifesting itself. He says that in the Legation at Berne there are many in high authority who constantly discuss the madness of the Kaiser and the absolute necessity of his dethronement as the only hope of Germany. Germany is held together, and the military party kept in power, and the Kaiser still reigns, because the Allies will neither receive nor make any overtures that look toward the discussion of peace. We could afford to leave territorial questions in abeyance, and discuss peace on the basis of something that he calls the President's four principles,—for we would find an almost immediate and complete political revolution taking place in Germany upon the signing of such a peace.

3. He affirms that, as a result of the hardening of the German heart by the diplomatic conduct of the Allies, Germany is making both economic and military preparations for a 20 years' war, if such should be necessary: with her possession of the Roumanian and Russian oil fields and the Russian and Roumanian wheat lands and with Bulgaria and Turkey now well in hand, Germany can carry on the war indefinitely.

He does not understand that this continual affirmation on the part of such as himself, coupled with persistent and manifold plans for such interviews as his with me—he does not see that all this constitutes an essential refutation of Germany's ability to carry on war indefinitely. If she is so amply and unquestionably prepared, why do her messengers of intrigue and entreaty sit upon our doorsteps? None but the German Government would stoop to such undignified and servile proceedings as even the Germans of high governmental authority stoop, to say nothing of her thousands of academic and literary agents. German university professors of high standing accept the most degrading offices of interview and intrigue. Even Herr von Boetticher is a writer and poet of very considerable reputation, and his family is one of the most ancient of German families.

I have presented this interview as an instance of Germany's increasing method of conquest. She has her missionaries in every one of the Allied countries. I have come to believe this method of psychic penetration and moral assault is more dangerous to the human future than the might of the German armies. She is literally undermining the resisting power of Europe; preparing the nations for a universal Bolsheviki as a prelude to a universal Prussian dominion.

175. REPORT OF A CONVERSATION WITH PROFESSOR EDGAR JAFFÉ, MARCH 26, 1918[4]

GENEVA, March 26, 1918

By means of a four days' visit from Professor Doctor Edgar Jaffé, of the University of Munich, I have been able to obtain what I believe to be a pretty accurate account of Germany's present inner condition and of the purposes of her Government in Europe, and especially in the East.

I do not need to tell you about Professor Jaffé, but doubtless something should be said for the information of our State Department. Naturally, being at such distance from the centre of the European crisis, our Government cannot know as to the standing of individuals who are not immediately connected with governmental operations, though of course the names and achievements of such men as Lammasch and Foerster and Jaffé will be well known to the President and to Mr. Lansing.

Professor Jaffé is one of the best known of continental social economists, and is the first authority of Germany in his own special sphere of banking and finance. I think he is so recognized in England also. He was professor at Heidelberg for a long time, but some nine years ago was transferred to Munich. He is also editor of the principal sociological review of Germany. After the occupation of Belgium he was sent to that unhappy country as a commissioner, with the special duty of organizing the financial and banking systems upon the German model. The condition of Belgium so astonished him and appalled him that he refused to serve, and with a number of other conscientious German officials resigned and came home. When the Government began the economic reorganization of Germany with reference to the war, he was the member who outlined the financial system which has since been put into operation throughout the Empire, and by which Germany is largely able to sustain herself. In one capacity and another he has been until quite recently a constant advisor of the Imperial Council. He has been much in the confidence of Helfferich and Kühlmann, as well as of Bethmann-Hollweg. For years prior to the war he had deplored the

[4] Herron Papers, I, Document XIII.

course of things in Germany, but when the war actually came he felt that there was no course to take but to try to guide things within as well as possible, and hope for a better future. One might say that his is the attitude of Erasmus, but that is not quite correct, for on different occasions he has been very courageous in his opposition to the military party, and he and Professor Foerster have done their best to gather up such resisting power as was left in the so-called democracy of Germany.

I shall have to explain why he has put the condition of Germany before me so frankly and fully. We have been for many years very close friends, and there has been between us a rather unique spiritual intimacy. Professor Jaffé is known to the world only as an economist and statistician, or as an authority on banking and financial theory, but behind the man who is publicly known is one who has inwardly suffered much over the prospect of Europe, and especially of Germany, these many years past, and who has gone through tremendous psychological crises in getting himself extricated from both the German philosophy and German imperialism; and it is this inner man with whom I have long been intimate. We have met in many different places of Europe, and together pondered the deep things of human history, for years before the present catastrophe. We talked much about its possible approach. All this is merely to explain how it comes about that Professor Jaffé would now speak to me so intimately about his own country. We are not respectively a German and an American, but friends who have together peered into the human future for these many years.

I know exactly what the British diplomat would say concerning the report I am about to make. He would swear upon his soul that Professor Jaffé has been sent by von Kühlmann to perpetrate the subtle and most strategic sort of camouflage; that Jaffé's errand to me is nothing else than a finer piece of the usual German propaganda; that the German Government hopes through me to reach the President with a presentation of German invincibility. I can quite see how, to judge by Germany's conduct and by experiences, so far as Jaffé's visit is concerned it is easy to come to this conclusion, but I do not for a moment believe that such men as Professors Foerster and Jaffé and Lammasch are either consciously or unconsciously guilty of fulfilling any agency of deception for their respective governments or countries. Professor Lammasch has shown something like the heroism of Socrates in his recent solitary defiance of both the Austrian and German Governments, and bids fair to joining the company of Socrates. Professor Foerster has shown extraordinary courage for a man of his temperament, defying as he has the whole military power of Germany; I have known Professor Jaffé so uniquely and intimately and in ways that so touch the very centre and integrity of a soul, that I would stake my own soul upon his absolute sincerity in all that he has to do with me. It is true that one who tries to deal directly with the best that is in man will often get either ludicrously or tragically fooled. Surely no one ought to know that better than myself. On the other hand, one who assumes only the worst in man dealing with great crises and questions, will not merely sometimes but always be fooled. All European diplomacy is both deceiving itself and its peoples and advancing from confusion to confusion, because it is today absolutely sceptical and cynical. If British diplomacy has anything to show for itself since the beginning of this terrible war than blunder after blunder, than stupidity piled upon stupidity, I am innocent of any knowledge of it. The history of the past four years surely does not show this diplomacy as leading in the path of either practical statesmanship or sensible political strategy, to say nothing of the incredible diplomatic ignorance with which every European and South-Eastern question has been dealt.

But now, after this rather unwarrantable prelude, let me take up the question of Germany as viewed by one of the few men who still strive for the redemption of the German name.

"I have come to you this time," said Professor Jaffé in substance, "not upon any mission from Germany, but solely because I want to talk with you somewhat as we used to talk in the old days, and to learn if you see any ray of light in the darkness. It looks like a Prussian victory, and as a German I deplore such victory as the ruin of Germany as well as the doom of European civilization." A German victory will result, according to Professor Jaffé, in either: (a) a European Bolsheviki, the condition of Russia spreading out and submerging the whole continent; or (b) a complete Prussian domination that will establish a material tyranny from which there can be no escape for at least two or three or four generations.

To enlarge upon the first alternative, Professor Jaffé admits that Germany is seeking or encouraging the subversive influence that will lead to such a Bolsheviki, believing that she will be the ark of the Lord, so to speak, that will outride and thereafter organize the dry land. He believes, however, that the pan-German and military parties are mistaken in this, but considers that Germany, he declares, will inevitably be swallowed by the flood if it submerges the rest of Europe. Not even the nerves of Germany can hold out against such an encircling catastrophe. The end of it all will not be what one can call revolution, but a complete eclipse of the whole superstructure of society. The institutional nerves of Europe will give out. There will be nothing left whereby social or political economic life can function. He considers that in a year, or in a year and a half at the farthest, Europe will suddenly go to pieces as a result of the present strain. There will be a universal condition of hysteria, or if not hysteria, a complete exhaustion of European nerves. Organized life will cease to exist. He doubts if even a German victory can prevent this engulfing catastrophe. It can very well immediately follow upon a German victory as well as take place in the midst of the tension of the war without any decisive issue.

Now as to the other alternative, if Germany does win the war, which he is now convinced is the inevitable issue of the conflict if Europe holds together and if Germany can then still hold Europe together long enough to initiate her program.

The result will be the iron domination of which I have spoken, and from which the nations will not for a long time be able to extricate themselves. The reason lies in the thorough and evilly scientific program which Germany has so carefully and comprehensively prepared for such an eventuality. It is a program of immediate and swift economic penetration and control. It is illustrated by the method wherewith she is already in practical possession of Switzerland. Her agents are everywhere buying up everything, even to the corner newsstands. The German approaches the little merchant in a mountain village, or the lace-maker in St. Gall, or even the small newspaper or manufacturer in the French cantons. The first question is: "How is your business since the war began? Bad? Why, what is the matter? What is your business worth?" The price is named, and generally an exaggerated one. "No matter, here's your check for what you ask. Take your money and I will take your business." The same process is going on all through the Austrian states, all through Bulgaria, all through Greece. It is also taking place throughout Italy through the agencies and in the names of subsidized Italian agents. A vast deal of this has taken place even in France through subsidized and traitorous French agents. More than European nations suspect Germany has already accomplished her economic conquest as well as her psychic penetration, while the military conquest is still being pursued and undecided; and granting a final German military victory, the economic and administrative machinery will be so completely prepared for instant operation throughout the whole of Europe that it will be clapped upon the continent, so to speak, before the general treaty of peace shall have been signed.

Furthermore, Professor Jaffé is of the opinion that this economic conquest is probably assured even in case of an Allied military victory, unless the victory is so complete as to result in the complete destruction of the present German system and in the extinction of the Prussian State. The President and Mr. Lansing will remember Napoleon's lament, one of his chief regrets indeed, that he did not extinguish the Prussian State when he had the opportunity, as he believed therein lay the chief peril to the future of Europe.

I will now take up Germany's program, which I asked Professor Jaffé to give me fully and frankly.

I. On the East and the North and the South Germany's first plan is to form a number of small states, each of which will become more or less related to the Empire politically, and absolutely possessed by the Empire economically, but absolutely separated from any representation in either the Prussian Diet or the Imperial Reichstag. Lithuania and some three or four other such smaller states will be carved out and placed under the headship of members of the Hohenzollern family and be given a sort of quasi-autonomy or limited self-government. But their railways, their postal systems, and their military, will be under German ownership and administration, and they will be economically bound by a comprehensive Zollverein. Finland will have an apparent independence, but be made practically a German protectorate, and given the Aaland Islands, which Sweden had expected. It is possible that even Petrograd may be made the outpost of an enlarged but dependent Finland. The Baltic will become absolutely German waters, and thus Sweden and Norway and Denmark will ultimately be compelled to come into the German system. Prussian Poland will be retained and enlarged, but a small sovereign Poland may be worked into a Kingdom as a member of the Hapsburg system, the present Emperor being crowned King of Poland. Ukrainia and the Russian State, which will still be large, will necessarily be recognized as independent, but will be made economically or commercially dependent on Germany through a system of comprehensive and drastic treaties, and be so enclosed that they have no outlet except by German consent. Roumania will be compelled to give up Dobroudja and her mountain passes into Transylvania, but be permitted to annex Bessarabia and given a shadowy independence, but essentially be made a part of the German system. Her foreign affairs will be absolutely in German hands, as well as her railways, her oil fields, and she will be permitted to sell her wheat only to Germany. Thus by this essential incorporation of Roumania in the German system, Germany will be absolutely independent of the rest of the world so far as her wheat and oil are concerned. Bulgaria is already economically in Germany's hands, and so is the Austro-Hungarian Empire. Through this economic conquest and penetration the political independence of these two, and of all the Balkan States, will be but nominal. Serbia will also be made a member of this Prussianized Austrian system. To Turkey will be restored provinces like Batoum, that she lost in her last war with Russia, and she will have Palestine and Syria and Arabia restored to her. If Germany wins in the present offensive on the west and succeeds in the subjection of France to her Prussian military occupation, she will afterwards fulfill her promise of taking Egypt and turn it over to the Turks nominally. She will thus have her own way clear to East Africa through the Suez Canal, and cut England's connection with India. She then plans the economic penetration of, and control of Persia, and in fact the whole of Western Asia up to India. All this is her immediate program in case she wins the war. India and China will be left for the future to decide.

As to Siberia, Germany does not care for that vast domain at present. It is outside her immediate ambitions. She would be quite willing to grant Siberia to Japan on the basis of an agreement with Japan as to the division of Asia.

It is interesting here to note the opinion that prevails through Germany as to the intervention of Japan in Siberia. Not a word has been said, so I am informed against this Japanese intervention in the German press. In German political circles it is commonly spoken of as a desirable event. Germany believes or pretends to believe that she can come to an arrangement with Japan that will be highly satisfactory to both Japan and Germany. Personally I do not believe for a moment that Japan would betray her Allies. However imperious her imperialistic purposes are, I am convinced that Japan has a high and chivalrous sense of national and international honour. As to whether Germany's conception of Japan is true, or has any foundation, Professor Jaffé has no opinion.

The result of this organization of Eastern Europe and Western Asia, bringing all the vast territories of ancient empires into her political system, would be that Germany would render herself wholly and permanently independent of North and South America. So far as she is henceforth concerned, Columbus need never have set sail. The American continents for her no longer exist, and until such time as she had subdued the old world North and South America would be ruled off the planet.

Germany's program granted, she would have unlimited raw materials to draw upon from the East and have practically an exhaustless market in which to sell her goods.

This is Germany's present actual program. Professor Jaffé does not believe that even in case of an overwhelming German victory the program will be permanently, or even for a long time successful. He does not believe that Russia is finished. It is true that now Russia is utterly disintegrated. There is not a shadow of social organization left. The whole structure of Russia's society has dissolved and disappeared. But Professor Jaffé believes that notwithstanding this disintegration and notwithstanding the iron hand wherewith she shall be grasped, Russia will yet rise and surprise the world, and not be so long about it as would now seem. He thinks that within five years the unique and indestructible soul of Russia will find itself and will again gather its body together, and that Germany will not be able to prevent the resurrection. He even thinks that just because the new society of Russia must rise right out of the human soul, it may be that Russia is to give the new society of Europe, German conquest or no German conquest. He also believes that despite every effort to prevent it, the Russian influence will soon begin to profoundly affect the German people.

I have spoken especially of Turkey, because the end of that so-called empire is obvious to anyone, as well as to Professor Jaffé. It will remain nominally Turkish, but the whole administration, both civil and military, will soon become altogether German, and for all practical purposes the Turkish lands will be component parts of the German system.

II. As to the West, Professor Jaffé is certain that if Germany is victorious in the present offensive, there will be no further discussion about the restoration of Belgium and of the occupied portions of France, and this he deplores much more than the German program in the East, for something might be said as to the value of a German organization and administration of the East for a time; whereas the German occupation of the West means the destruction of a civilization which the Professor admits is infinitely superior to Germany's, at least in all its spiritual or intellectual aspects. If Germany is victorious, there is no question of her surrendering anything that she has gained. She will not only keep Belgium and the parts of France already occupied, but will extend her annexations to Calais. This he believes to be absolutely certain, granted a German victory. She might grant a shadowy independence to Belgium, but it would be a very dependent sort of independence, leaving Belgium practically in her hands, with Holland surrounded and ripe for picking any time Germany chooses to reach for the fruit. Italy Professor Jaffé already regards as coming to Germany, whichever way the war ends, unless it end in the overwhelming German defeat of which I have already spoken. He considers that Italy's whole gravitation is towards Germany, that the sympathies of both her socialists and her financiers are pro-German. This he also especially deplores, as Germany will call out and develop all the worst features of Italian life and character.

III. (a) Taking up now the inner condition of Germany, Professor Jaffé says that there is not the slightest hope for even any further democratic resistance, much less a democratic movement or revolution. Every democratic initiative or effort has been successfully and completely stamped out. The Socialist Party has not produced a single initiative or leader, and even the Socialist Minority has now practically given up the struggle. German militarism is in complete and unshakable command of the situation. Germany is wholly and scientifically governed by an iron military dictatorship, whose hold upon the Empire is complete. What he says of the Emperor in this connection is curiously interesting and astonishing. He declares that Kaiser William now figures only in the world of Germany's enemies. In Germany herself he has been completely set aside, or rather swept aside as an incompetent fool. In Germany no one ever speaks of him. He has practically ceased to exist. He is not even formally consulted in Berlin. He has been so completely ignored and pushed aside that he scarcely ever attempts to interfere, or if he does, he is treated as an annoying child who gets under foot or in the way. The only function he has left is that of making his speech about Germany and God, which the Germans themselves have come to regard as the harmless absurdities of a religious maniac. The stock of the Hohenzollern dynasty is indeed at its lowest ebb, but the military party will not make or suggest any change of dynasties as such a change might unsettle themselves.

The power of the military party was enormously strengthened by events in Russia. The military party is able to say that where Kühlmann and the diplomatists failed and would have conceded away enormous German interests, they, the militarists, succeeded and made Germany the master of the East.

(b) The economic position of Germany has enormously improved. As compared with a year ago there is now a plenty of everything. Notwithstanding contrary reports, Germany has obtained vast supplies of cereals from Roumania, as well as of cattle and meat and oil, and has obtained many things from the Ukraine, even a very considerable quantity of cotton which had there been stored. Even butter is now to be had in ample quantities, and a great deal of milk can be so sterilized as to be shipped from Roumania and the Ukraine. There is therefore no longer any question of the conquest of Germany by starvation. So far as food and other supplies go, Germany is in a comfortable condition to carry on the war indefinitely.

(c) Furthermore, besides the great fields of supply that have been opened to her in the East, the whole resources of German science, or such resources as were not occupied in the invention of new and deadlier instruments and munitions of war, have been made and put into operation, whereby Germany is already becoming one vast manufactury, and every inch of soil intensively cultivated and chemically raised to the nth degree of productivity. Even if Germany should be so far defeated as to be compelled to carry on a defensive war for a long period of years, she is becoming so intensely and comprehensively organised that she will soon be capable of entirely sustaining herself, and will also become as one vast and impregnable fortress, through which it would take long years and altogether new instruments of war to break.

IV. It is of interest to notice here the relation of Germany to the recent initiative of the Austrian Emperor through Professor Lammasch, and the effort to reach America, or rather President Wilson, through the conversations between Professor Lammasch and myself. Germany was perfectly aware of the conversations and the desire of the Emperor and those who had his confidence to come to some understanding with America whereby Austria might reorganize herself and escape Prussian domination. The German Foreign Office did not know the details of what passed between Professor Lammasch and myself, but had no trouble in taking for granted the general trend of the conversations, and knew very well what lay behind them. The practical ultimatum which Germany presented to the Austrian Foreign Office was almost immediate. Germany had no intention whatever of allowing Austria to take the reins of her own power into her own hand much less permit her to take any initiative of her own or take the lead in any proposals for peace. Besides, Germany is altogether hostile to the program of a confederation of the states under the Hapsburg crown. Once the United States of Austria have taken the place of the old and purely Hapsburg Austro-Hungarian Empire, then all manner of democratic tendencies would be let loose and the whole Prussian system endangered. The final result of the plan of Professor Lammasch and Emperor Charles, namely the reorientation of Austria with the western and democratic powers, would be inevitable.

Germany is furious with Austria, and has compelled the Austrian Government to renounce Professor Lammasch and reinforce Czernin. The German fury is directed especially against Lammasch, as he is supposed to have inspired the Emperor's program, being altogether the strongest personal influence in the Imperial household. Indeed Germany is decided to hound Professor Lammasch to his death, and Professor Lammasch seems to anticipate some such issue of the struggle in his recent declaration at Salzburg that he will fight for the new Austria to his death.

Professor Jaffé declares the proceeding of Germany in this respect to have been the climax of diplomatic folly. It was Germany's best chance, and she will never have another as good, to end the war by negotiation, taking the attitude of graceful consideration of the interests of her Allies.

V. However unimportant diplomatically, but significant as a matter of German governmental psychology, is a revelation which Professor Jaffé made to me regarding the procedure of the German Foreign Office towards myself. I report it for its possible pedagogical utility; besides, if it serves no other purpose, it may add to the gaiety of the State Department in these most solemn times.

Because of my legendary position as an interpreter of President

Wilson's mind, with which apparently I have some telepathic or occult communication, it seems that besides my house and all my steps being under the constant guardianship of previous German spies, I am honored with a great deal of attention and mental scrutiny at the German Foreign Office. The method of von Kühlmann is this. Professors Jaffé and Foerster, and other Germans who personally know me or have recently seen me, are called in one by one to hear me utterly discredited as an American authority or human being. Then one or two or three new men are called in, such as Hausmann for instance, and are told that I am the one person who must be seen and whom the man or men must make an impression upon if they are to reach the President. Then these new men are sent to Switzerland to see me. They go first to Count Romberg who tells them, yes, I am the person they must see, and what intermediaries are to be chosen. The meeting takes place. The sole and invariable information which each man is able to take back to Berlin consists of my personal opinion of Germany and my ever increasing emphasis of the fact that no matter how long it takes or what the cost in American life and resources, nor even if Germany is able to subdue all Europe in her dominion, will America make peace with a victorious Germany or Americans consent to live in a world which Germany dominates. Then the new men are told that during their absence the Foreign Office has discovered that I am a person whose opinion has utterly no value or authority, and I am discredited. The whole process begins again. Another man is chosen, or perhaps another two or three, and the same process is gone through, with the same information to the disgusted Foreign Office, and the same effort made to discredit me.

Professor Jaffé tells me also that from now on a continuous and sinister effort will be made to so discredit me as to destroy my supposed influence against Germany here in Switzerland, and through the European press, to which I have contributed.

The German Foreign Office knows precisely, Professor Jaffé says, what my position is, knows that it is absolutely unofficial and purely personal, and that makes them all the more anxious about it and makes it more puzzling to them as to just how to deal with the matter, except to deal with it through some Satanic process. He declares it absolutely impossible for the German Foreign Office to do anything in a straightforward or honourable way, or to conceive that anything has ever been done in a straightforward or honourable way in the past, or ever can be so done in the future.

VI. I think I have synthesized with perfect accuracy my noble and distinguished friend's view of Germany, and the whole European situation. I have had to push his presentation into my own language, of course, and to clothe it in my own modes of expression, but I have been careful to state as exactly as possible what he sees and says. I also felt morally obliged, because of our long-standing intimate friendship to tell him I would like to make a personal report of his point of view to my Government. To this he quite unhesitatingly agreed, only naturally desiring that if perchance any public use of this report should be made, his name should be withheld, as that would make his position in Germany, already difficult enough, still more difficult. I am at perfect liberty to use his name in this report, however, which I am presuming you will wish to make to the Department of State.

Again I hear the British or Italian diplomat say: "Of course. It was to get this German presentation of her present position and power before the President that Professor Jaffé was sent to Mr. Herron by von Kühlmann"; and again I would say I do not for one moment believe it. I would put my judgment concerning Professor Jaffé against that of all the diplomats in Europe. I am most certain that von Kühlmann would never send Professor Jaffé to lay bare the German imperialist program in the East or to confess Germany's program in the West in case of her victory, and Professor Jaffé would never be allowed another hour of liberty, even if he were allowed to live, if it were known that he had frankly and fully disclosed the actual program of the German military power or government.

VII. In conclusion let me say that I believe that Professor Jaffé has revealed to me with absolute accuracy the imperialistic program of Germany, which reaches out to the early inclusion within its scope of the entire continents of Europe and Africa and all that part of Western Asia which I have already named, with the eventual domination of the rest of the world. I must also say, if I am unreservedly honest in my report of this world-situation, that I am convinced Germany is nearer to the accomplishment of her purpose than she has been at any moment since the war began. One source of Germany's success lies in the utter lack, even after these four years of unimaginable murder and misery, of any real leadership or perspective or large statesmanship in Europe. Out of all the military and political men who have to do with the situation, there is not a single man of European size. There is not one authoritative man among the Allies who really knows what to do, who really sees an hour ahead. Germany is the one force that knows exactly what she wants and keeps persistently at it through both success and failure, but the rest of Europe is simply drifting, drifting into a kind of blind fatalism, or to change the figure, Europe is staggering like a drunken man on the brink of a precipice. Beside all that, I am constantly discovering that the Allies are acting behind each other's back, in spite of all their loud proclamations of unity, and that each of them is trying to checkmate the others in some direction or other.

The only hope of Europe, the only hope of these three continents, is in America and in our President's faithful and undeviating adherence to his world program. I hope that I am not presumptuous in praying devoutly that he may ever more emphatically, even imperiously, pursue his own diplomacy, nor be influenced by the Allies, however tactfully and wisely he pursues it.

There seem to me only two possibilities of politically circumventing Germany and to that degree reinforcing the long and terrible military struggle that may lie before us. One way lies through the immediate organization of the Society of Nations, organizing it as though Germany did not exist, and inducing all the Allied nations and as many of the neutrals as possible to adopt an early and complete constitution and to enter into a mutual compact to obey it. This Professor Jaffé admits, as well as do Doctor Mühlon and Count Montgelas and Professor Foerster, would create a feeling of anxiety and shame among at least the common peoples of Germany and would tend to embarrass the mastery of the military power. The second way lies, though it is a very dim way at present, through Austria. Notwithstanding the complete defeat at the hands of Germany of our recent effort and hope in that direction, the Austrian door should still be kept open. If we had any way of giving military protection to Austria, I believe we could have her absolutely on our own terms. There may yet come the possibility, though a very small one at best, of yet organizing Austria and the Balkans, including even Italy, against Germany.

In this connection I ought to say that Professor Jaffé admits that President Wilson has struck a considerable moral blow even in the moment of Germany's triumph by his insistent attitude and words of good will toward Russia. This has now been supplemented by the profoundly wise and courageous declaration of our Ambassador, Mr. Francis. It is in just this attitude that President Wilson's statesmanship is so far above anything that the Allies have manifested as to seem superhuman in comparison. It is the very highest political and moral strategy on the part of America to continue to count Russia as an Ally and to so declare to the world. The President's attitude in this respect has filled the German Foreign Office with both fury and bewilderment.

176. REPORT OF A CONVERSATION WITH PROFESSOR QUIDDE AND DR. DE JONG VAN BEEK EN DONK, APRIL 19, 1918[5]

GENEVA, April 19th, 1918

Notwithstanding the discouraging response I gave to their request for an interview, Professor Quidde and Dr. de Jong van Beek en

[5] Herron Papers, I, Document XIV.

Donck appeared yesterday afternoon. Their conversation was as curious and puzzling as it was extraordinary and impertinent.

Professor Quidde is from the University of Munich, and is the head of the peace societies of the German Empire. He is a member of the Bavarian Upper House and a friend of Count Hertling. He was active and eminent in peace propaganda, according to the German understanding of peace, before the war; and he is now actively engaged in efforts to procure a peace that shall be to the satisfaction of Germany. He declared that he was speaking on behalf of the friends of peace in Germany, who were only biding their time. He also let it be understood that, in a sense, he represented the German Foreign Office. But he speaks more especially, I imagine, for the Crown Prince Rupprecht of Bavaria, who recently put himself in somewhat active opposition to his father the King, and to the Prussian military party.

I expressed my open and instant astonishment that Germany should begin now a new peace offensive in the midst of her present overwhelming military campaign. But Professor Quidde was urgent and excited in his insistence that soon, probably within a month,—and this no matter which way the battle goes in France,—there will come the moment when the peace party will assert itself, and the German Government be ready to consider peace. He wished me to prepare the President for the approach of such a moment and to urge that he take quick advantage of it. When I inquired as to what kind of peace he thought might be approaching, and as to precisely what he wished our President to take advantage of, it turned out to be nothing but the common tedious and treacherous plan for a German peace: the question of Alsace-Lorraine must not be discussed; Germany must not be asked to renounce anything in advance regarding Brest-Litovsk and the succeeding treaties. Concerning these treaties, the Allies must bring them into court; they might, perhaps, wrest concessions from Germany. In fine, Germany must have all she wanted and give practically nothing in return; and woe to our President if he does not seize the promised proffer of the opportunity to beg Germany to make peace! And woe to the whole family of man as well!

According to Professor Quidde, the present Western offensive is presented to the German people, and is so regarded by them, as the final movement for peace; it is not military in its ultimate purpose. I could not but exclaim as to what an extraordinary peace proceeding this seemed (to non-German mortals) to be, and I expounded to him the fact that, so far from producing a reconciliating effect upon America, it was simply preparing our national will for indefinite war. We are now expecting, I explained, to fight for five years at least, and probably for ten years, as we now clearly understand that there can be no sanity or health in the house of the world until the Prussian military power,—probably the Prussian State also,—is absolutely extinguished. So far as we can now see, Germany can only be negotiated with by the sword. Every day that Germany pursued her present path of ferocious conquest and diplomatic perfidy is simply steeling the American arm and consecrating the American mind to the destruction of all that Germanism means—to the full and final banishing of the immemorial Prussian terror and torture from the heart of Europe. The time was near, I affirmed, when America would resolve to fight until she could impose her own conditions upon Germany or be herself destroyed. If Professor Quidde and Germany called the remorseless slaughter of probably two or three million men a peace offensive,—if they fancied the far-firing gun which was killing babies and their mothers in the birth-beds of Paris to be a method of conciliation,—they were making the most monstrous and mysterious mistake that the mind of men and nations was ever capable of.

The eminent messenger then descended at once to that curious and repellent whine so characteristic of the whole German mentality, and especially of the arrogance with which it always begins its pourparlers. It is difficult to restrain one's expression of disgust after repeated contact with this mentality. Professor Quidde's manner, like that of all his hither-coming predecessors, was at first imperious and pompous; but, when I dealt with him as I felt it behoved an American citizen to deal, he became humble and servile *ad nauseam*.

The whole trouble about Germany, I was to learn, lay in the fact that President Wilson was always misinformed. If each step the President had taken had been a little different, a little more to the right, a little more to the left, a little more conciliatory, then the world could have had peace long ago. Poor Germany is now so wantonly misunderstood! The way in which this pitiful and peaceful people was being forced to continue the war,—continue it because the Allies, and above all our President, had constantly rejected the pleading hands stretched forth to them and to him, even into this last daring effort of Count Hertling,—this was an occasion for tears which Professor Quidde exhibited to me as a melting specimen of the tears of the whole German nation.

I remarked to him, with a rather brutal frankness I fear,—how marvellous it all seemed to me—this curious blending of ostentatious arrogance and dog-like servility which he and all his predecessors manifested, along with an appalling lack of capacity for moral responsibility: "How comes it, Professor Quidde, that you do not seem to see any moral responsibility on the part of Germany; that you put the whole responsibility for all you have done and are doing upon the

Allies; that you come asking the American President to take upon himself the responsibility of saving you from yourselves? Your psychology presents to me, I must say, the most inscrutable problem of human history."

No less, the interview closed with the entreaty that I urge the President to make ready for the opportunity, sure to present itself soon, of procuring peace with Germany. And this entreaty trailed Professor Quidde's departure down my doorstep, even though I had used language I am sure he will not hear this side of the Day of Judgment.

Now as to the part of Dr. de Jong in this interview. He declared, in common with Professor Quidde, that if the President had only supported Holland in the move she was ready to make, a short while ago —namely, an inquiry on the part of the Government of Holland as to whether Germany, represented by Count Hertling, would be ready to submit the Russian treaties, and even Alsace-Lorraine, to a peace congress that would assemble on the basis of the four principles laid down by the President—that if this had been done, there would have been a favorable response on the part of Germany, and the offensive would not have taken place. To my question as to why, in the heaven's name, Germany did not say so instead of writing in one month the death-roll of a million of men,—the response to this question was naught but the usual unintelligible shuffle and whine, the usual shift and evasion of responsibility.

But now, the messengers asked, was it not possible for Holland to try again, for the President this time to encourage Holland, foreknowing that Germany might even yet give a favorable response? It was useless to make these men see the puerility and shame of the question they were putting, even though I was obviously ashamed at being the unwilling listener to such pitiable verbal jugglery from the lips of grown men.

And here the interview closed. If these men possessed any known mentality now prevailing on this harassed globe except that of Germany, I should expect that neither of them would ever wish to look upon my face again, but being German-minded, they very likely will be sitting on my doorstep when I waken tomorrow morning.

Please pardon me, dear Mr. Wilson, that I have been unable to keep my disgust out of the memorandum I am now presenting to you. And above all, do not let my manner of presentation keep from you the momentous importance of the fact—and do not let it delay you in communicating the fact to our Government—that Germany is about beginning a vastly organized and penetrative peace offensive as the parallel to her military offensive in France. She is preparing to reach the mind of America—especially of the President—by the time she reaches

Calais. This preparing campaign for peace will be as unprecedented and as massed as her campaign in Flanders. Professor Quidde has fired the first gun. The peace forces are on the march from Berlin, from Munich, from Sofia and Constantinople. And this campaign for peace may be more menacing to the whole family of man than the German march upon England. We shall need strong trenches to withstand the assault. I am building mine now—for I am receiving news and authoritative hints from many directions.

When Germany mounts her guns in Calais, and these begin dropping bombs upon Westminster,—if such a dark day be before us,—upon that day must America be prepared to say to Germany: "Your last opportunity to discuss terms of peace is gone forever. Henceforth we will talk with you no more. Either all that has made you what you are we shall destroy, or we shall be destroyed by you. But either the Germany that now is or America must leave the world. The same planet cannot house us both. Either we shall meet destruction at your hands, or you will take unconditionally the terms we impose." This, and nothing less is the answer America must be prepared to return to Germany's triumphant demand, if it so be, in the providence of the divine progress, such German triumph be awhile permitted.

177. THE QUIDDE INTERVIEW

(a) REPORT OF MAY 11, 1918[6]

Le Retour
26, Chemin des Cottages
Geneva, Switzerland   May 11, 1918

Edleman has just brought me your message. I will try to tell you briefly what happened, and ask Osuky personally to explain to you more fully.

I. Whittall telephoned that Professor Delmar would like to meet me, and brought him at an appointed time. I knew Delmar was of the Daily Mail, and the Northcliffe news service, but supposed him making a personal call, as he professed himself a great admirer of my books. I also took it for granted he was a member of the British Legation family. Whittall brought up the Peace Offensive, and the anger of the German Press at me for having—according to the Germans—killed it. We discussed Quidde also. Whittall, you remember, had asked for a duplicate of my memorandum on the Quidde interview, and I had given it with your approval: so it was natural enough to discuss it.

[6] Herron Papers, I, Document XV.

Delmar said he wanted to inform his paper about the Peace Offensive, and I agreed it ought to be widely known and gave him general information of German methods. But I not only told him he must not use me in the matter, but that he was not to use *any of the names of persons who had held interviews with me,* as that would put me in the position of revealing confidential matters, even if my name were not used. In fine, I thought I was talking with a typical English gentleman, and that he was only seeking color and perspective for a general article on German propaganda methods. I never dreamed of such a dispatch as appears in the papers; never dreamed of my name, or that of Quidde and Solf, being used; and I am simply stupefied over what has happened—stupefied and humiliated beyond measure.

The dispatch has gone all over the world, and there is no recalling it. The Geneva papers have been fine about it, and have sent word to me that they will not publish a word of comment without first consulting me. But Geneva, of course, is an incident.

II. Whittall professes himself as astounded as myself, and has made many apologies, and has verified to the letter the circumstances as I have given them, and has called Delmar to account. But, (a) he excused the matter somewhat on the ground that both Ding-Dong and Quidde had talked so much about it—had complained so much about my attitude and the repulse I had given them—that the affair had already in fact become public property—known to the man in the street. Anybody, he says, could have picked up the matter without having seen me at all.

Then, (b) notwithstanding the apology, Whittall and his associates are obviously elated over the publication, declaring it will do no harm but untold good. He apologises profusely, yes, but no less rejoices in the results of this flagrant breach of confidence on the part of Delmar.

And (c) Whittall's explanation is this: The dispute between Lord Robert Cecil and Balfour. You have probably followed this. Cecil had announced the German Peace Offensive, possibly having read the memorandum I gave to Whittall. Balfour flatly denied it: so one of the usual British Governmental muddles arose. The Northcliffe Press is backing Cecil. Whittall opines that Delmar, in order to back his party, and support Northcliffe, took the risks involved in the unexpected violation of confidence. The report of Quidde's interview with me was published to confirm Cecil's statement: it was a dastardly thing to do, but all things connected with European diplomacy are becoming fouler and fouler.

Besides that, (d) it may be that the British Government has determined to bring American initiative, American interchange of opinion with the enemy, to an end; and that they have chosen this method of doing it. If so, I have certainly been trapped—trapped by my confidence in the good faith of these men—and have proved conclusively my unfitness for the work I have been trying to do.

Upon this subject, Edleman has some decided opinions, and I have asked him to put them into writing; to accompany this, which I am sending by Osuky.

III. What about it all? The thing has gone broadcast; and I was asked by the Associated Press to say yes or no by 11 o'clock. I did not like to act without consulting you, so took the risk of telephoning you. It was that or act on my own responsibility. Unfortunately, you had not seen the papers, so needless words on my part followed, and I very well understand your anxiety and impatience over the matter.

So far as I can see, the matter stands as follows:

(a) It is purely a question of veracity between Quidde—and the German Legation doubtless—and myself. The American Legation is not involved, nor the American Government. I am not named in any diplomatic or official sense; nor is there any hint of my filling any such capacity. I am only named as a disciple of President Wilson, whom the peace messengers had to reach through me, and failed. Is this true or not? The Germans and I have to fight it out. The American Legation is not called upon either to own or disown me. I am not in a position, as I see it, where I have to be dishonored by both the German Government and my own.

The only thing that might arise, in extreme need, would be for the Legation to say that it was a matter between the Germans and myself, but that, though the matter was personal and not official, the Legation knows me to be an honorable man who would not report a thing at the time if it were untrue.

(b) I do not see how, if the issue is forced, I can remain silent. I can't serve the cause by submitting to dishonours. *The report in the papers is true to the letter.* To deny or evade it would be to play into Germany's hands. I do not need to debate the matter—I need only to affirm it by a simple query, when Germany denies it, and let people take their choice.

In conclusion, I am profoundly hurt and humiliated over this incident, which may be more than incidental in the end. I am hurt and humiliated, first, because the substance of a confidential memorandum, intended for our State Department and the President, should have been made public—even though the public knows nothing of the existence of such a document; and second, because this essential betrayal has come about in the house of our friends, our Allies, in order to serve party ends and to effect a diplomatic blockade of Americanism—of the penetration of Woodrow Wilson's ideal.

Already, the feeling and the attacks of Germany against me were becoming so constant and vindictive that it was clear the German Government had given up hope of reaching America through me, and would forbid any further intercourse with me.

I have been aware, too, for a good while of being closely watched by the British Foreign Office with the determination to stop all interchange between Austria and Germany and ourselves; that is, England does not want American influence in Europe—other than military help.

So it looks to me as if Germany and England together had ended any further usefulness—if I have ever been useful—in the work I have been doing.

And the fact that I could be so entrapped is a demonstration of my unfitness for the work.

177. (b) REPORT OF MAY 24, 1918[7]

GENEVA, May 24th, 1918

Mr. Edwards came to see me yesterday. He states that the earlier information (for which it seems Mr. Delmar was responsible) about the conduct of Sir Horace in the Quidde affair is altogether incorrect. It turns out, on the contrary, that Sir Horace was truly indignant about it, and that the Foreign Office in London was equally if not still more indignant, as a result of Sir Horace's presentation of the matter. It is surmised, also, that London communicated its indignation to Washington, so that any danger of misunderstanding between the two governments over the incident is eliminated. This was the one danger to be avoided, whatever else might happen.

The State Department, and more especially the President, should always be told the truth, for they will thereby the more wisely interpret the Alliance; thereby the President will be better able to bring the Alliance to American terms and will guide it towards his goal of world-democracy.

I am only referring to this matter again in order to exonerate Sir Horace of any such conduct as was baldly attributed to him in the first days of this affair. I do this the first moment I know about it, because I would not have any shadow of question or doubt affect your cordial relations with him. Except for clearing everybody that it is possible to clear, I should be profoundly thankful not to have to speak or to think of the matter again—all the more so since there is no use trying to reconcile the contradictory statements concerning its origin made by even the same person. I have been glad, however, to clear in your mind as well as in mine any question of duplicity on the part of either Sir Horace Rumbold or Sir Hugh Whittall.

Only one thing seems absolutely certain, both to myself and to my British friends here; that the whole thing was deliberately planned beforehand by the Northcliffe crowd in London, and that Delmar was sent back here to accomplish, in one way or another, the thing that he did accomplish. Another thing certain is, that the Northcliffe people had access to my memorandum and took the contents thereof as their basis of action. Delmar, as Whittall himself distinctly remembers, knew all about the Quidde affair and the contents of my memorandum before he came to see me at all.

You need have no apprehension about my receiving any of these Germans again, either now or at any time, under the former conditions. Very likely I have taken the efforts of these months both too seriously and with a somewhat absurd sincerity as well as with a too high and persistent hope. However that be, I should not again be willing to undertake any such staggering responsibilities without some proportionate responsibility behind me.

I have just received this morning the first word from the matchless Ding-Dong, and a most impudent word it is. He informs me that it will be impossible for him to see me any more, either alone or in the company of his German friends, unless I am able to prove to him I am not responsible for the action of the Daily Mail.

Of course, I shall pay no attention to his impudence and I think I can survive the calamitous loss of his lugubrious company.

178. PROFESSOR QUIDDE'S STATEMENT CONCERNING HIS CONVERSATION WITH DR. HERRON[8]

By its report on the "Peace Offensive" which I am alleged to have undertaken on behalf of the German Government by a visit to the American Professor, Dr. Herron, in Geneva, the *Daily Mail* has again done honor to its old reputation as the *Daily Liar*.

The *Norddeutsche Allgemeine Zeitung* having already made the statement that I "had received no commission of any sort, either from the Chancellor or from the Foreign Office, for the above-named American," I, for my part, consider it important to confirm that the remainder of the report is equally incorrect.

It is only true that I spent some days in the middle of April in Switzerland—not on a political mission (unfortunately!), but to arrange about some financial interests with a society in Berne—and that

8 *Berliner Tageblatt*, May 14, 1918, I, 3.

on this occasion I visited Professor Herron, in the company of Dr. de Jong van Beek en Donk, the former having, in answer to my Dutch friend's inquiry, expressed a wish to see me.

Everything else is a lie, pure invention, or in its purport, a direct inversion of the truth. First, and foremost, I have made no kind of peace proposals, either for transmission to President Wilson or in any other way, nor have I therefore had any refusal. There was no indignation and no scene such as the report describes; on the contrary, we parted with the regret that, owing to the time for my departure having arrived, our intercourse had to be prematurely interrupted.

That I have given no sort of reason to lead people to suppose that I had been commissioned by the Imperial Chancellor or the Foreign Office is so obvious that I need say no more as to the nature of the report.

BERLIN, May 13, 1918 L. QUIDDE

179. FOERSTER TO MUEHLON, MUNICH, JUNE 4, 1918[9]

I take advantage of a sudden opportunity to send you an uncensored letter, and I am writing during the few moments I can dispose of.

I very often think of you, and mentally have a conversation with you; and frequently I ask myself if I was wrong to leave Zurich? If this leaving,—so hard for myself and for my family—has been a failure? If there is no hope here? If I am no more suitable for here? If the German people cannot be saved from its hardness of heart? . . . . I don't dare till now to decide: there are such grand dispositions and traditions, that cne should think they can break through this present hardness.

I would like to say a few words about what could be done from the other side to favor this breaking through; and what mistakes have been done in the matter. In doing so, I am guided by impressions I received in conversations with the finest types of both parties, Catholic and Liberal.

If I oppose to those persons the ambiguity of our Government, they complain for their part that the Entente too is equivocal; and that the Entente should speak once in a quite concrete manner about the German Colonies, and about Alsace, and should loudly disavow the claims for the left bank of the Rhine. I always answer: "You forget that this ambiguity is only an echo of your own. If you desire to continue the old state of the world, if you stand to your violence-peace in the

---

[9] Herron Papers, I, Document XXIII. Dr. Herron's own translation of the German letter.

East, you cannot expect that England will support you and all your explosives as a colonial neighbor or even will contribute to it."

So I speak to our people; and to the Ententists I would say: "If it is true that your point of view as to the colonial question depends entirely upon the existence of an honest *new* Germany, why don't you say it plainly, clearly, as evidently as a schoolbook, in some such way as this: 'If the German people profess so *undoubtedly* the moral foundations for a league of nations (e.g., by the complete restoration of Belgium and by the transmission of the eastern question to the peace congress) *that we may trust to it,* then it is evident that we will give back everything. But to establish such a confidence, other means are needed than speeches of the Chancellor or resolutions of the Reichstag. It requires *concrete pledges,* engagements that leave the abstractions behind them and that clearly show the triumph of the principle of right over the will for power and for "safety." But if the German people intends to perpetuate the old state, we are compelled to infer from that all the consequences, and to adhere firmly to all the safeties we hold in hand. If the German people would have pronounced itself as clearly and as *exhaustively* to the principle of right, as it has been done by President Wilson in reference to Germany, there would be for us no further reason for distrust. If thus we cannot till now speak clearly on the colonial question, it is not our fault, but it depends upon the fact that the German people maintains a total unclearness about *the situation of the peoples after the war.* And yet *everything* depends upon that.' "

If the Entente would speak like that, it would be a great help to the reasonable elements in our country.

The same thing should be done in relation to the economic war. On that subject there is an awful confusion. Here also the Entente should speak quite frankly and say: "We condemn every economic war after the war; we are even disposed to favour in any way the reconstruction of the world-economy of the Central Powers, first by . . . ., [*sic*] second by . . . ., third by . . . ., if the German people is undecided to make a concrete use of the Wilsonian principles on all the questions concerning the conclusion of peace. *If* it does not happen, then we are obliged to . . . ."

I think that such a precision is extremely necessary, instead of the way in which today an economist of the Entente declared himself opposed to the economic war after the war, and that tomorrow a politician declares: " 'Raw materials' is a word that the German will no more find in any dictionary." Such a pellmell is of service to no others than to our prolongers of the war.

By all means I do not make any proposition to the Entente; I only take note of her intentions as I know them and I say: "Do express clearly the *alternatives;* in order that the public opinion here may exactly know how her attitude to those questions will be answered." People on the other side do not think enough upon our censorship and of our servile press; they give too numerous arguments to those who here wish to obliterate the real state of things; they do not imagine how little knowledge one has here about the real intentions of the enemy.

One must confess that now Erzberger stands very uprightly; but in order to support him and his surroundings, a new declaration of the Entente on the scopes of the war is necessary, in order to trouble the work of the incitors on our side.

This time there is no intoxication of victory; the number of people is increasing who realize that no military success can save us from a terrible bankruptcy; but that we must come to terms with the owners of the sources of the raw material we need—that is an acknowledgment to be skilfully helped from the other side.

180. MEMORANDUM CONCERNING A NEW GERMAN PEACE INITIATIVE, JUNE 14, 1918[10]

GENEVA

On June 6th I received from Professor Foerster of Munich a letter asking me to receive a special friend of his, bringing "very valuable information as to the interior political condition of Germany." The letter had been personally taken across the frontier by a private courier. The same day, the expected gentleman telegraphed from Zurich and arrived here on the evening of the 7th. He proved to be a Bavarian, and a friend of Count Hertling as well as of Professor Foerster. He had been for thirty-five years connected with the Vienna *Neue Freie Presse,* however, and only since the beginning of the war had he lived at his original home in Munich.

After informing me as to the present condition of Professor Foerster, who is permitted to go only from his home to the University and give his lecture and return, and that always under military guard, Dr. de Fiori, the gentleman in question, proceeded to state his errand. I discerned, in a very few moments, that the friendship between Professor Foerster and myself was being used for ends that Professor Foerster himself was probably quite unaware of, and that I was witnessing the beginning of a serious effort on the part of a responsible party in Germany to open a door toward peace.

Dr. de Fiori began by a rather too profuse apology concerning the

[10] Herron Papers, I, "Herron to Balfour," June 14, 1918, Document XXV–A.

Quidde affair, taking the attitude that the German Foreign Office owed me an apology rather than I the German Foreign Office. He said that Count Hertling had summoned Professor Quidde to his presence and roundly rebuked him for mismanagement of the whole affair, and for taking with him to such an interview so indiscreet and irresponsible a person as Dr. de Jong van Beek en Donk. He used a German expression concerning Professor Quidde which means, literally translated, "a mad old hen." He inquired as to what really happened, and I informed him that nothing happened that could be taken seriously. Professor Quidde had come to me in a somewhat excited state; had named four conditions on which he thought Germany would make peace; had complained somewhat bitterly that President Wilson would not give Germany a chance for peace when she wanted it; and had asked that the President be informed that within a month an opportunity would arise for peace with Germany, and begged that the President be asked to seize the opportunity and to present it to the Allies. I had merely replied that, so far as I knew, America had no desire whatever for peace with the German Empire as it is now constituted; but that if Germany wished to propose peace, there was nothing whatever to prevent her. The normal diplomatic way was open. She could very easily apply to the Allies, through the Government of Switzerland or that of another neutral power, for the opening of negotiations, stating the terms upon which she was willing to proceed. It was a waste of time for her to be sending messengers to unofficial individuals such as myself.

After this mutual explanation concerning the Quidde affair, Dr. de Fiori proceeded straightway to his errand; and I must say he stated it with unusual frankness for a German. He at once stated that what he should present to me he wished to have conveyed verbatim to the President; he also stated that the substance of our interview would be conveyed directly, and as literally as possible, to the German Chancellor. I asked him if he was aware that he was speaking to one who had absolutely no authority, personal or official, to conduct negotiations of any kind, or to utter anything other than his own individual convictions. He affirmed that he understood this perfectly, and upon the basis of that understanding he would proceed. I then proposed to him, that, in view of the seeming seriousness of his errand, and of his statement that our conversations were to be reported to the Chancellor, we ought to have present with us a confidential stenographer, and our respective statements verified before the conversations should end. To this he unhesitatingly agreed; and, at the conclusion of several interviews, he affirmed the correctness of the statements and answers which I am herewith sending.

At the outset, before proceeding to definite questions and propositions, Dr. de Fiori put before me as deftly as he could, and by implication so far as possible, the present political condition of Germany. I shall try to synthesize this as briefly as possible.

Germany is now ruled, and with little or no resistance, by a small military and junker class, whose chief is von Ludendorff. The Kaiser is regarded by this ruling party as a fool, and has been completely set aside, so far as the Councils of Government are concerned. Nor does the Chancellor greatly count, many of the most important decisions and actions being taken without reference to him. The Government of Germany is practically that of a Pretorian Guard, and von Ludendorff is the executive and generally the originator, of its decrees. But it is absolutely necessary to this junker and military caste to retain the dynasty.

Ludendorff is Germany's evil genius at the present time. Neither he nor his party desires peace, but would rather prefer war for years to come. Ludendorff loves war for its own sake, and actually believes that Germany, if she persists, can conquer the world and rule it more efficiently and permanently than ever it was ruled by Rome.

One the other hand, there is a growing liberal movement in Germany, not yet articulate or formed into a party, that perceives that the war will be the ruin of Germany. This party embraces many intellectuals and former political persons, but receives no sympathy whatever from socialist leaders such as Scheidemann, all of whom are now thoroughly identified with the German Government. This liberal movement, having yet no organs of expression in Germany, is therefore unable to function itself. None the less it is now resolved upon making an effort toward the initiation of a program for peace, believing that the moment is near when it may be able to mobilize the German people in such numbers and authority as to force the hand of the military party. The German liberals hope, working at first through personal conversations or pourparlers, to obtain such encouragement, if not assurance, from the Allies, especially from America and England, as will stimulate and sustain them in their efforts.

It is evident, from what Dr. de Fiori implied more than directly stated, that this liberal movement is looking to the Crown Prince of Bavaria to lead it when the moment for definite action arrives. The Crown Prince has joined issue with his father, the King, and is bitter in his condemnation of the sacrifice of Bavaria for the enhancement of Prussia. He has written letters, and has held conversations with liberal leaders in Bavaria, which have not only encouraged, but have even urged their procedure. Dr. de Fiori stated that the liberals could count upon Chancellor Hertling, if they could come to him in sufficient force, and that probably even Hindenburg would not oppose them. Hindenburg, he says, does not love war for its own sake, and loves the German people more than war; and he would throw all his influence on the side of what the German liberals would consider a reasonable peace.

Dr. de Fiori said, at the close of his prelusive survey of the German situation, that he hoped a result of our conversations, after they were reported to the Chancellor, would be that I would be asked to listen to much more important persons than himself, implying the possibility that the Bavarian Crown Prince might be among the three or four who would come, providing a secure incognito could be devised.

Before stating his proposition, however, there are one or two important incidents of recent history which should be set forth. His statements, or revelations, cannot be verified, of course; but I believe Dr. de Fiori to be truthful in them, as I believe him to be honest, though uncomprehending, in his peace proposals:

(a) Concerning the peace of Brest-Litovsk. The most of the German people believed Brest-Litovsk to have been a colossal and costly blunder. Chancellor Hertling was honest, he says, in his acceptance of President Wilson's Four Principles, even though the Chancellor was awkward and reticent in his acceptance. He had no knowledge of what was planned concerning Russia by the military party, and was in fact not consulted or considered in the negotiations at all. General Hoffmann himself protested vehemently against the treaties unto the last, declaring to the Government at Berlin that by such treaties Germany was laying up disaster for herself, and that it was impossible for them to shut off the Russian people from the sea or permanently control them in the interests of Germany. He refused to sign the treaty until he was compelled to do so by military order from the General Staff. But though most of the German people are appalled at Brest-Litovsk, believing it to be the basis of future wars and endless troubles, yet now that the treaty has been signed, they accept it as inevitable, and will make no effective complaint unless aroused by future developments or leadership.

(b) Dr. de Fiori raised the question as to why all effort toward peace through America, or for the detachment of Austria, had come to an end, when there did seem to be, months ago, the possibility of a bridge between Austria and the Allies. How came it that the really heroic and comprehensive effort of Professor Lammasch and his friends had failed? I asked Dr. de Fiori if he was aware that Berlin served a substantial ultimatum upon Vienna, threatening immediate occupation if the efforts of Professor Lammasch were not immediately ended and disowned. He said, yes, that it was pretty generally guessed or known that the Austrian door, if such it should be called, was abruptly closed by military Germany; that even if Germany had wanted peace she did not propose to have the initiative taken by Austria or to permit any assertion or action that looked toward Austrian independence. He said that this practical ultimatum, however, was served over the head of Chancellor Hertling, who even today had no actual knowledge of what happened.

(c) This naturally led to the Czernin and Clémenceau disputations, and the publication of Kaiser Karl's letter. Dr. de Fiori, speaking for others as well as himself, and speaking very deliberately, said that the publication was adroitly and carefully planned by Czernin, in conjunction with Berlin. Both Czernin and Berlin knew of the letter and its contents, and were determined to use the same for the destruction of Kaiser Karl's authority; and, also they wished to close the Austrian door once and for all. Czernin and his Emperor had been in bitter and continuous opposition to each other, and Czernin's opposition had developed into hatred and into an actual betrayal of the Austro-Hungarian ruler. Especially when the Emperor sent Professor Lammasch to Switzerland, and after his return from the conversations with me, in the house of Dr. Muehlon at Guemligen, Czernin laid the whole situation before the German military party, and then the action which resulted in the publication of the Emperor's letter was agreed upon. Count Czernin precipitated the dispute with Clémenceau for the purpose of forcing the publication. As far as Czernin and the German Oligarchy were concerned, a trap was laid for Monsieur Clémenceau, and into the trap he walked.

Germany is, of course, quite unaware that the Allies would now prefer the independence of the nationalities, now in revolt against the Hapsburg crown, to the continuation of the Austro-Hungarian Empire as a province, or as a parcel of provinces, become vassal to the German Crown. It is Austria herself that has been entrapped, and Germany that will ultimately be outflanked by the action of Czernin and Berlin.

Now taking up definitely the propositions of Dr. de Fiori and his answers to my questions concerning them.

Our conversations lasted through three days. We had four different meetings in my home, each of which lasted three to four hours. The propositions, as well as the questions and answers, were taken down stenographically; at the conclusion of the conversations they were edited and verified by us together, and reduced to such brevity as the subjects discussed made permissible.

181. COPY OF DR. W. ROBERT DE FIORI'S FIRST REPORT TO THE IMPERIAL CHANCELLOR[11]

I. BELGIUM

De Fiori: The re-establishment and restoration of Belgium is a condition of peace *sine qua non*. Outside the more fanatical members of the Oligarchy, there are no two minds in Germany about the evacuation and independence of Belgium. But this must be preceded by a settlement of all pending questions of a commercial or economic nature. A very important question for us, for instance, is the mouth of the Rhine, as well as the navigation of the Scheldt. The Rhine is a German river, and yet the mouth of it is in the hands of other countries than Germany. Some arrangement could be made which would satisfy Germany and all elements of conflict removed by giving other and reciprocal advantages to England.

Herron: Would only the relations between Belgium and Germany be considered, and would the powers assembled in the Peace Congress treat Belgium as a state whose arrangements must be imposed upon her, or made for her by other sovereignties than her own? Or would Belgium be left as a sovereign state, politically free in fact, and also free to make her own arrangements between England and herself, between France and herself, as well as with Germany?

De Fiori: Yes, absolutely independent—but, after all, the pending questions which I have raised must be settled first.

Herron: I fear the German conception of independence is as incomprehensible to an American as the American conception of independence is incomprehensible to a German.

De Fiori: Perhaps so; but Germany must know that her economic freedom is assured, and that her economic arrangements with England must be agreed upon, before she can conclude peace.

Herron: Will France be wholly evacuated? Does Germany mean to make any territorial changes? Does she mean to keep Briey and Longwy?

De Fiori: I believe Germany will evacuate France and not put her hands upon Briey and Longwy; but she might ask economic concessions concerning the Briey-Longwy region.

II. ALSACE-LORRAINE

De Fiori: I tell you quite privately, and in parentheses, that early in the war Bethmann-Hollweg seriously planned some corrections of the

[11] Herron Papers, I, Document XXV–B.

frontier. He was ready to give the western part of Lorraine—that is, the French speaking part—back to France as a token of friendship and as an inducement to peace. But now, of course, since our military successes and the ascendancy of the military party, no one in Germany thinks of giving any part of Alsace-Lorraine to France.

It goes without saying that Germany is ready to give of her own accord autonomy to Alsace-Lorraine as a federated state of the German Empire. Therewith Alsace-Lorraine will have the right to arrange her inner life according to her own liking, but she therefore takes over the duties which, according to the Constitution of the Empire, the other states of the Confederation fulfil. The Empire will have no right to meddle in the inner questions of the new state. This would bring about a solution of the question of nationality. There would be French schools and French professors in the French parts of Alsace and the University of Strasbourg would take up its old form, resuming the constitution it had anciently until 1864. Strasbourg University would have, as it had from 1680 to 1864, the same life as the German Universities.

We must not forget that Alsace-Lorraine is a kind of "gray zone." It is not a closed unity, but a border-land between two great peoples. It ought to become again, as it was under the old Empire, a bridge of understanding. I believe the Reichstag would agree to a free competition between France and Germany, if the ancient condition of Alsace-Lorraine could be restored. An agreement would have to be made concerning the commerce in coal, potash and iron between France and Germany. These economic and political and linguistic arrangements would destroy all difficulties—all the hatred and jealousy that have grown out of the inequality between France and Germany in economic access to Alsace-Lorraine.

Herron: Do you mean that Germany would agree to absolute free trade between France and Alsace-Lorraine? In fine, do you mean that France would have the same economic advantages in Alsace-Lorraine that Germany has?

De Fiori: Yes, I believe we can admit this very easily, because we do not have to fear French competition. Our people are so much more active, our industries so much more developed than those of France, that we can very well give to France full freedom of competition. (America may take advantage of this argument, but she must not speak publicly about it.) Germany can fear nothing if she leaves her customs frontiers open. France has a right to develop her industries again as before 1870; and, with this understanding she can freely do so, and we shall not lose economically by granting all this to her.

There are so many half-fabrics that come from France to Alsace, such as cotton, for instance. Cotton was shipped to Alsace and printed there and sent back to the French market. This process can very well be taken up again. Then if the potash supply is divided equally between France and Germany, France will have immense industrial means on hand, equal in fact to those of Germany.

To resume, to Alsace we would give independence, freedom of administration and of education, nationalization of the schools, re-establishments of the old order at the University, equal access to iron, coal and potash, and free commerce.

Herron: Exactly what do you mean by an autonomous state? I observe that you call it an independent state within the German Empire. Would you reconstitute Alsace-Lorraine as a kingdom, such as Saxony or Bavaria for instance? Would you choose a prince for them, say a member of the House of Hohenzollern, or would you constitute them into a Hanseatic State like Hamburg? Or would the peoples of Alsace-Lorraine be free to choose their own form of government, and their own laws and governors?

De Fiori: It would be better if Alsace-Lorraine took on the form of a Hanseatic State; but this is a secondary question. I believe that Bavaria would not pursue her dynastic interests in Alsace, and that the states of Southern Germany, and even the liberals of Prussia, would make no opposition to having the new state constituted according to the Hanseatic mode.

This would be the best possible solution for the Alsatians themselves. If Alsace-Lorraine were given back to France, her individuality would be swallowed up. As a free state, independent of both Germany and France, she would lead the poor life of Luxembourg. If she were a state within the German Confederation, she would (a) always have the Rhine between herself and Germany; (b) she could restore and keep her old Franco-German individuality; (c) having her own constitution and her free commerce, she could resume her old relations with France, even though remaining a political unit of the German Empire. The Alsatians would have the same possibility of moving back and forth from France that they had before 1870. In fine, we should make out of Alsace-Lorraine a German state, whose business it would be to build a bridge between Germans and Celts; to dissolve the old conditions of dissension between the two races; and to be the medium of friendship between the lands to the east and the lands to the west of the Rhine.

Herron: Suppose the Allies would not consider peace on any such a basis as you propose. Suppose that neither America nor England nor France would consent to the continuance of a German Alsace-Lorraine under any form whatever. Do you think that, as a last surrender to peace, Germany would agree to the creation of Alsace-Lorraine into an independent and sovereign state, such as Belgium was before the war? I do not mean to intimate for a moment that the Allies would consent to any other solution than that of the return of Alsace-Lorraine to France. I am only asking this question in order to ascertain what would be the last mind of Germany, her last concession to peace, short of which concession she would prefer to continue the war indefinitely.

De Fiori: If you put the question so categorically, I would have to say nothing is impossible, and that everything is relative. If you should ask me if I have the courage to put this question to Germany, I should say no. But if you asked me whether there might come a state of mind that was favorable to such a solution, I would ask you to think what we lose. To ask Germany to renounce Alsace-Lorraine today, after all that has happened, seems to me very hard. If we Germans want peace, you would require us to say that peace is worth more to the world than our possession of Alsace-Lorraine. You require us to make the sacrifice for the sake of peace. That would take a long time. If we are to have peace quickly I believe the form that I have proposed is the only one which could be accepted in Germany today, and even so that there would be opposition.

Herron: Why does Germany consider that the possession of Alsace-Lorraine is more important to her than the peace of the world, and how comes it that Germany, after having precipitated this immeasurable catastrophe upon the world, expects that the Allied nations, large and small, accept all the sufferings and ravages that Germany has put upon them, and in addition to that make all the sacrifices and concessions requisite to peace, while Germany shall make no sacrifices, no concessions, and receive no punishment and admit of no wrong?

De Fiori: But the question of Alsace-Lorraine is different. It is our hereditary country. It was a part of our Empire. It is rooted in all our feelings, in the heart of the German people. If since 1870 there have been deplorable conditions, we ourselves are now sorry. But we do not want to make Alsace-Lorraine an apple of discord any more. We want to keep it because it is German, and belongs to Germany. But all the conflicts which made it an object of quarrel must not be any more. Germany would offer to France to remove all causes of quarrel, and this would be an immense moral satisfaction to France. There would thus be no more strife of interests between France and Germany. Alsace-Lorraine was ours till the time of the French Revolution, and the peasant was more German then than he is now. The country has always been our own flesh and blood. The world should not demand that we sacrifice one of our members, when we are ready to eliminate all reasons for discord between ourselves and France and to make the country a platform on which two great peoples may clasp hands with each other.

Herron: Why did not Germany do this in 1913? Why does she think only to make this effort, after the uncountable misery she has inflicted upon France?

De Fiori: This question makes our discussion much more difficult.

Herron: Would Germany consent that the people of Alsace-Lorraine decide their future for themselves by a plebiscite conducted by a neutral state?

De Fiori: In twenty years?

Herron: Now.

De Fiori: Impossible. There are many men in Germany who are convinced that Alsace-Lorraine would decide for Germany if we give everything I have proposed to you. But the plebiscite cannot be now. That would be impossible.

Herron: Why should Germany refuse or hesitate now? You say the people of Alsace-Lorraine are German. You have had half a century in which to indoctrinate them, to impose your will upon them, and thousands of the old French families have long ago emigrated. You have had fifty years of advantage and France fifty years of disadvantage. Why do you hesitate to let the people of Alsace-Lorraine decide for themselves? Germany certainly does not show much confidence in the quality of her justice, of her administration of Alsace-Lorraine, if she fears now, after fifty years of opportunity of exercising their administration, she is not willing to let the Alsatians say what they think of German rule.

De Fiori: America did not enter the war for Alsace-Lorraine. If Germany admits that in principle Alsace-Lorraine shall be a free state within the borders of the Empire, we do not fear that there will be a new war over the question, especially if the League of Nations be established. Then perhaps in twenty years Alsace-Lorraine may decide whether she will continue with Germany or go back to France. It might be she would decide neither for the one nor the other, but decide for her sovereign independence.

Herron: No, America did not go to war for Alsace-Lorraine, but Alsace-Lorraine is fundamentally involved in the purpose for which America went to war, and that is to establish the right of the peoples to dispose of themselves. This is the very basis of a permanent peace, of a stable civilization, of the Society of Nations. Alsace-Lorraine is the European symbol of the issue between Germany and civilization. It is only Germany that has regarded Europe as a sphere of conquest during these last hundred years. This is Germany's fourth war of conquest in Europe, her fourth effort toward world-dominion in the last half-century. The German possession of Alsace-Lorraine symbolizes the principle of Prussian expansion and dominion, and is the precise antagonism of the principle which America has entered the war to establish. There has not been a time since Charlemagne, if I read history aright, when the peoples of Alsace-Lorraine were willingly a part of Germany. They have always been French from choice and in affection. Why should America have gone to war if she consents, for the sake of peace, to the negation of the very principle for which she went to war, and that in the instance of the very first application of the principle?

De Fiori: We shall give Alsace-Lorraine the same constitution that England gives Ireland.

Herron: Will you? England has put the whole decision as to Ireland's future into the hands of the Irish themselves, and has not even asked to be present at the deliberations of the Irish convention. Ireland has not been obliged to furnish a single soldier to fight for the existence of Great Britain against the German assault. It is not England's fault if the Irish have not been able to agree among themselves. She has granted the Irish the right of disposing of themselves as a state of the British Empire. You have just refused, in speaking for Germany, to give the people of Alsace-Lorraine any voice or part in disposing of their own future. You admit only the right of the German Empire to dispose of their destinies, and yet you now say that Germany will do for Alsace-Lorraine all that England will do for Ireland. Here is a complete contradiction. Which do you really mean, your first refusal or your present proposition?

De Fiori: If Alsace-Lorraine becomes a state of the German Confederation the same as Bavaria, then she will have in coming years perhaps as much as Ireland will have.

Yet it is the truth that Alsace-Lorraine is today even more independent than Ireland. She has her own provincial legislature, her own representation in the Federal Council, and self-administration in technical matters. The only difference between Alsace-Lorraine and the other states of the German Confederation is that she is administered as an imperial territory and is therefore under the Prussian rod, bringing with it a discipline that does not correspond with her feelings and her traditions. But if she becomes a federal state, she will then have complete home-rule within the Empire.

Herron: Your statements and your contradictions are alike interesting, but you have not answered my question. Would Germany agree to go as far with regard to Alsace-Lorraine as England would go with Ireland?

De Fiori: I can answer this question only by another question. How far should England go with Ireland according to America?

Herron: But your other question is no answer to my question. I ask you to state explicitly whether or no you would contract with America to give exactly as much freedom to Alsace-Lorraine as England is now ready to give to Ireland?

De Fiori: I do not believe that England will ever give Ireland more than we do Alsace-Lorraine. We shall certainly go as far as human reason and the existence of the German State can permit.

If I had to decide personally, I would say to France: "See if you yourselves can agree with Alsace-Lorraine." Even the French and the Alsatians perpetually abuse each other. I do not believe that there would be agreement between France and our Rhine province, even if France were given a free hand.

It is true we have done a great moral wrong to Alsace-Lorraine. The world has judged us for it. But this is the guilt of the Prussian junkers, not of the German people. Give the German people freedom from war so that they can begin to take their own inner problems in hand, and they will destroy the junkers. Then Germany will be quite different from what it appears to President Wilson. Then the Alsace-Lorraine peoples will be as well off as the Bavarians. Let me tell you in parentheses and quite secretly that we in Bavaria always think and speak of Prussia as an enemy country.

Herron: Then why do you not liberate yourselves from Prussia? I will take up this question, since you have refused to answer my last question concerning Alsace-Lorraine and Ireland.

De Fiori: Even the Prussians themselves will have to be liberated from their junkers. We Germans of the other states will accomplish this liberation if once we are free from the heavy material cares of the war. But we feel that President Wilson, having a mission to fight for right, ought to see that he is fighting against the junkers and not the German peoples. He ought to trust us a little. I am ready to bring you men of great position who will tell you this. This current for freedom from Prussia is now powerful in Germany, and it ought not to be thwarted by the continuance of the war for secondary things, thus hindering the liberal development of the German people.

III. POLAND

De Fiori: As you know, Secretary Lansing has agreed to the program initiated at Rome; and, previous to the Rome Congress, President Wilson proclaimed an independent Poland. The Allied Governments have now declared to the Poles that the Polish question can only be settled if Poland becomes an independent and sovereign state with access to the sea. Now this access to the sea can be granted without territorial dislocations. There is a possibility of giving Poland the freedom of her flag on German rivers, and a free access to the sea through Lithuania.

Herron: Do you mean a really independent Poland?

De Fiori: An absolutely independent Poland and Podolia, which under Russia was called the Government of Warsaw and Minsk.

Herron: I take it that you mean only that part of Poland which belonged to Russia shall be erected into a so-called Polish Kingdom, and that those parts of Poland which are held by Prussia and Austria shall remain still subject to the Central Empires. In other words, you propose to give away something that did not belong to you, and to keep everything that you have previously made forcibly yours. It seems to me this is a mere caricature of a Polish state that you propose. What about Prussian Poland and Dantzig? What about Austrian Galicia?

De Fiori: Austria cannot exist without Galicia. I will not say that Galicia should not take a special position. But the province really forms an economic unity with Austria, and the economic life of Austria depends upon Galicia.

If we wish to create a foundation for the future regulation of Europe, it is terrible now to ask too much as a result of this one war. If a small Poland is created, with free access to the sea, it can develop in a quiet and orderly evolution. The Polish nation will really be existing in full unity, even if parts of it still belong to Germany and Austria. The principal necessity is that Poland shall again have recognition as a nation, with access to the sea. All the further development is a matter of the peaceful common mission of the peoples of Europe.

Herron: And what if Austria should break to pieces? What if the nationalities within the Austro-Hungarian Empire should together rise and together declare their independence?

De Fiori: The way to Austrian federation cannot be stopped. Germany wanted to prevent it because she wished to keep the control of Austria-Hungary in the hands of the Austrian Germans, and because she took advantage of the false tactics of Lloyd George and Clémenceau. We should indeed have had no Pan-Germanists in Germany today if Lloyd George and Clémenceau had only co-operated with us in our efforts toward peace. The Pan-Germans exist and prevail today because of the false tactics of the Allies, and they will be overcome when the German peoples are convinced that they may have a righteous peace.

Herron: But I ask again (and this time I leave out the question of Poland), what would Germany do in case Austria should begin to dissolve in a revolution of the different nationalities against the Monarchy?

De Fiori: It would be a crowning misfortune for Europe.

Herron: But I ask again, what would Germany do? Would she occupy Prague and Vienna?

De Fiori: I do not believe it is to the interests of the advocate of peace to weaken Austria too much. If Austria should fall to pieces, the ferment that today threatens her inner life would extend on international waves that would engulf the whole of Europe. There would only be more covetousness and more international difficulties and more wars.

You cannot give independent political existence to the Poles, to the Czechs, to the Roumanians, to the Slovaks, to the Serbs, to the Lithuanians, to the Lettish people, without touching and wounding the interests of other peoples. The interests of those who have for hundreds of years belonged to the Austro-Hungarian Monarchy are involved in the perpetuation of that Monarchy. Nor do these peoples really cry for the Monarchy's destruction, but for its reorganization.

Austria must gain back her inner peace. She can have a central administration and still give her peoples independence and freedom inside the Monarchy, and so become a model state for the peoples and a guarantee for the general peace of Europe. I believe we shall do our best for the world to give a new spirit to the Austrian central bureaucracy—to open the eyes of Kaiser Karl so that he may understand all the needs of these peoples.

Herron: But why, then, did Germany swiftly and brutally shut the door that Kaiser Karl and Professor Lammasch tried to open toward Federalism and peace?

De Fiori: But you must not blame the German peoples for the faults of their rulers.

Herron: But the German peoples have not manifested to the world anything that indicates a difference between them and their rulers. And besides, you have not answered my question.

De Fiori: Do you think the Austrian door is altogether closed? Do you think it impossible that America might still open that door?

Herron: I know nothing about what is at this moment in the minds of the Allied Governments. I know nothing of the present attitude of Washington toward Austria. But I have a personal conviction that Germany has closed the Austrian door forever, and that there no longer exists an Austrian question. I imagine, furthermore, that it will henceforth be impossible for even Germany, in her last extremity, to create an Austrian question. There exists now, I consider, only the question of the freedom and sovereignty of the respective nationalities under the Austro-Hungarian yoke. From what I read, I should guess that the deliverance and integration, the sovereignty and self-government of these enslaved peoples is all that now interests the Allies, so far as they think of Austria.

IV. Serbia

Herron: What does Germany propose to do with Serbia?

De Fiori: The question might better be put: "What will Austria do?" Germany is not directly interested, and would only support Austria's interests in Serbia. Germany is not opposed to Serbian independence. It is the Hungarians who oppose it. If I may say so, the conflict with Serbia is a question of pigs. Serbia had to buy from Austria all her machines and industrial products, and was not allowed to export her pigs to Hungary, because Hungary wanted no competition from Serbia, preferring to raise and to export her own pigs. It was Hungary who was bent upon the subjection of Serbia. If Austria-Hungary had treated Serbia decently, the Serbian problems would never have become so sharp. If now a victorious Austro-Hungary should come to pass and be able to decide as to the future of Serbia, she would make out of Serbia a kind of "hotel dépendance." This is not the desire of the German politicians, however. They would gladly re-establish Serbia in its former frontiers, and give the Serbs a port on the Adriatic. If Germany herself has freedom of action she will stand for the independence and restoration of Serbia.

Herron: You ignore the fact that Serbia was an essential and avowed part of the pan-German program; that it was Germany and not Austria that originally forced the war with Serbia; that the subjection of Serbia is almost the first condition of the Hamburg-to-Bagdad program.

De Fiori: Oh, we will never have peace if we do not keep territorial questions in their subordinate place.

V. Yougo-Slavia

De Fiori: There are two kinds of Southern Slavs, those who belong to Austria and those who do not, and the future of each depends upon the settlement of all Balkan questions at the peace conference. Each of the Slav nations in Austro-Hungary must have home rule, of course, and also the Istrians and Croatians and Dalmatians, and the Italians of Trieste as well. These peoples cannot be separated, for they are too much intermingled. But we must find a solution for their differences in equality of races, equality of languages, equality of communal administration, so that they shall agree among themselves. But if you insist on settling all these questions before the conference, we shall not have peace for a hundred years.

Herron: But we shall never have peace till we have settled these questions. For what else did Germany go to war except to give these questions a German solution? For what else have the Allies and America gone to war except to give to those questions a just and democratic solution?

Let me add here, in passing, that the Pan-Germans would have done far better for their program, if they had united the Yougo-Slavs and sought their friendship, instead of first seeking to subject them through war and then of purchasing the help of Bulgaria. In building a greater Bulgaria, Germany has raised up her strongest future enemy in Europe. Bulgarians and certain powerful Hungarians and the New Turks are today planning a pan-Turanian alliance against Germany, to become effective after they have gained all that is possible from their alliance with Germany. The Bulgarians are expecting to appropriate the Constantinople-to-Bagdad plan for themselves. They are planning to take over the exploitation of the Turkish territories of Asia Minor and the whole German idea in Asia, in fact. While Bulgaria is Germany's Ally she is doing her utmost to undermine the influence of Germany in all the Allied countries. The worst reports of German atrocities ever made in America have been made not by the Belgians, but by the Bulgarians. It is curious that the German military party is unaware of how Bulgaria is filling the world with intrigues against Germany.

De Fiori: Oh, we can settle with Bulgaria when once we have peace with the Allies.

Herron: Does the German military party want peace?

De Fiori: No, not short of complete victory, and it believes that it will achieve complete victory by fighting on. It is a madness, that is true, but we, the German peoples, must go on with the military party so long as we do not get any encouraging word from the Allies. The Allies must make the German people know that they do not need to fear for their bread, that they do not need to dread an economic isolation, if once they have peace.

VI. General Questions and Answers

Herron: But we are leaving Serbia and the Balkans and coming back to Germany. Since this is the case, I would ask you: "Does the military party of Germany expect to gain the hegemony of Europe and to establish a complete European dominion?"

De Fiori: Yes. There is no use in denying the truth about the German military purpose.

Herron: But the peoples, you say, want peace. What kind of peace?

De Fiori: Each of the German peoples is an honest and peace-loving people, but full of belief in authority and kept under the spell of discipline and tradition. The technique of the modern German Bureaucracy has reached the stage of what we might call an absolute mechanical despotism. Yet each of these peoples already pulls at its chains. If the Germans were convinced that they could have free access to the necessities of a peaceful existence, namely, colonies, raw materials, free commerce, freedom of contact with England and America— then these Germans would break their chains and make war no longer.

Herron: What assurance do the German peoples want in order to enable them to break their chains, and to whom do they look for this assurance?

De Fiori: They look to President Wilson. I am convinced that the politicians and papers that speak of an intrigue or conspiracy between President Wilson and England to destroy Germany are telling lies. Our press is not an expression of the conscience of our people. It is only an echo of the war party, of the great General Staff.

The assurance can be given. If I wish to give persons with whom I desire to live in friendship and peace the assurance of my friendship and peace for them, convincing them they have nothing to fear from me, I can find the right form for this assurance. So if President Wilson has the right mind toward Germany, he will find the right form of giving assurance to the German people. Instead of using great catchwords, he should try to reach the heart and the head of the German peoples with the simplest means. He ought to make them know that America desires to live in peace with them, provided they are reasonable.

On our side we would say to you of America that you have nothing to fear. We are ready to give you everything that will assure your future and that will end this terrible war. If America wants to destroy militarism, it has only to offer peace to the German peoples, and the German peoples will destroy their own militarism.

America can do this. It does not matter about the form in which it is done. That is a detail. America must not forget in what a pathological state Europe is today. She can heal this state without any sacrifice to herself, and it is only America which can do this great thing before the world and before God.

Herron: But Germany began the war. If she wants peace why does she not take the initiative herself? Why does she put the moral responsibility upon our American President?

De Fiori: The German people cannot take the initiative. But America can. America has a mission; and if America sends the honest message of one pacifist people to another pacifist people, such as the Germans really are, and speaks frankly about the peace that ought to be both in the interests of the German people and of the world, then the coalition of the financiers and the junkers will be destroyed. All the liberal leaders in Berlin and in Munich, and men as different as Scheide-mann and Erzberger, as different as Haase and Haussmann from Chan-cellor Hertling,—all agree that if President Wilson were to speak the right word to the German people he could create a new order of things and dissolve the power of the military party. He will do a greater his-toric deed by a peaceful word, a deed which will constitute a foundation for the freedom of the German peoples, and win a greater victory than could ever be won by the Allied armies. We the German peoples are bound. We have not the means clear to deliver ourselves. But President Wilson can deliver us by a clear proclamation concerning the intentions of America and the Allies as regards our commerce, our colonies, our economic future.

Herron: The Germans all seem to be Marxians! You believe only in the material foundations of society, in the material solution of even spiritual questions, to say nothing of all political and social questions.

De Fiori: We say openly that everything with us depends upon freedom for our economic expansion throughout the world. If we can force peace with France and Italy today, and with England tomorrow, then we shall have permanent peace in Europe. But even then the continent is not a world market to us and the questions of our existence are not settled; and we are aware that we can never force America to come to our terms, and that it is only through peace with America that we can become again what we were and go on with our spiritual and material development. But we can hold Europe against America, and we have the East open to us. So if America will not offer us peace, we must fight on because we have no other choice.

Herron: You believe, then, that Germany will be victorious in France?

De Fiori: The General Staff does, the military party does, and most of the German peoples have believed so until recently, but my personal conviction is that it is not possible to work out strategically the program of the military party in such a way as to insure a permanent victory or a permanent possession of the things we fight for.

VII. As to Germany's Last Terms

Herron: If Germany faces a clear and unevadable choice between peace upon terms that will be acceptable to the Allies and an indefinite war with America,—if Germany were convinced that America would continue the war regardless of the time element, even if France had been rendered powerless and English communication with France and America had been greatly crippled if not sundered,—if Germany knew that despite her possible or achieved victory over Europe she must reckon upon continual war with America until America's power to fight were destroyed or the German power competely overthrown,—what then, standing face to face with such choice, would be Germany's last terms of peace, her last concession for the sake of peace, beyond which terms and concession she would not go, preferring to fight on until her extinction or the defeat of America should decide?

De Fiori: The answer to this question does not depend upon whether or not Germany faces such a choice, but upon the conditions of peace which the United States of America would make possible. Let America formulate the fundamental demands for a just peace, in which the needs of Germany shall be assured, and the war will be finished at once. President Wilson himself, with his sense of justice, will know it is impossible for Germany to surrender until she has been offered terms of peace. He will also admit that he himself, in declaring war on Germany, has renounced his right to judge of what is just concerning Germany.

Herron: But how, in heaven's name, Dr. de Fiori, do you expect our President to take upon himself the responsibility of giving peace to Germany, when you declare that he has renounced all capacity to be a judge of what is just to Germany?

De Fiori: Let me go on. The main condition for a durable settlement is the antithesis of a solution through the power of arms. Such a solution can only end in the suppression of the spiritual and economic welfare of the defeated party. The achievement of the President's peace program at the cost of the cultural and economic influence of Germany in the world would mean the destruction of Germany first, and second, the plunging of all Europe into infinite destruction and misery. For it is clear beyond any doubt that Germany will die fighting rather than surrender herself and make peace without conditions.

And it is not to be thought or said that Germany would succumb under any circumstances, however desperate the struggle with America. For the advantages are all on Germany's side. Her means are not at all exhausted. She can make war for ten years more. Her technique, her science, her spirit of invention, sharpened through tragical need, would give her unexpected strength. And finally let it be said that God, who as you yourself have said in one of your little books is not neutral, will certainly stretch his hands protectingly over the German peoples, who certainly are not the least fruits of his creative power. If Mr. Wilson wants to find acceptance for his program for a world peace fulfilled, that is, fulfilled within the restricting wisdom of man and inside of human possibilities,—then the German people will respond to his voice and agree to his program for an honest peace among the peoples of Europe.

I would say that the European conditions are so difficult and tangled that they do not now permit of drastic solutions. Not political surgery is needed for Germany, but the cleansing spirit of a mildly working physician. And this President Wilson can be.

But I repeat, Germany can go on with the war. Her intensive agriculture, developed to the *n*th degree, will render her economically independent. The East is open to her, and she can indefinitely increase the productive capacity of the Ukraine and of Roumania and Turkish countries. She has abundant supplies of raw materials to draw upon, and she has invented a new substitute for cotton, besides. The Allies cannot compete with Germany, nor can America, in the technique of war or in chemical and mechanical invention.

If Germany is offered peace only by force and on the terms of the Allies, she will go on fighting. She will die standing rather than kneeling. And does America believe she can execute her program for the Society of Nations, that she can give Europe a new order of things, by bringing unimaginable misery upon Europe through continuing the war against Germany;—a war of ten, yes, of fifty, even of a hundred years duration? Does America believe that such a war, even if fought for the freedom of the peoples, would be worth while? Does America believe that she can heal Europe by killing the European peoples?

Let me say again that all territorial questions are secondary and can be settled, if complete economical arrangements with England concerning the world markets can be achieved. If we can settle with England as to an equal freedom with her in economic and colonial expansion through the world, and as to the navigation of the seas and the coaling stations and so forth upon which that navigation depends, and settle all these world questions with England not only theoretically but in practice,—then we can have a permanent world peace without further American sacrifice or an American continuance of the war.

VIII. Concluding Conversation

De Fiori: And now? What have you to say? I have spoken. I will listen to you.

Herron: You understand that I hold no diplomatic position, no secret commission, that I speak only as an American citizen, whose opinion you have asked? I do not speak for anyone but myself; the only authority I have is such as may reside in the truth of what I say, but I speak as one conversant with the mind and feeling of the American people.

De Fiori: I understand, and I shall not fail to report exactly what you say to Count Hertling, perhaps even explaining the whole thing to him myself in person.

Herron: These conversations between us would be useless if I did not speak to you with the utmost frankness and sincerity. I do not wish to be brutally rude. I do not wish to hurt your feelings as a German anxious for a new life for your people. But I must tell you exactly what I think. I must express my true personal convictions about your proposals, without any concealment or evasion. Otherwise there is no possible use in your having come to me, and no possible good can come from my having listened to you.

Let me say to you at once that I see not the slightest hope for peace, or the smallest ground on which to base peace discussions, in anything you have said to me in the course of these three days. Let me speak wholly from the standpoint of an American citizen representing the average American mind.

I. When the European war began, America was largely a pacifist nation. We were laboring under the high delusion that war between civilized peoples was at an end. And when our delusion was dispelled, when we were compelled to believe in the reality of the catastrophe that had overtaken the world, our population was charged with large sympathies for Germany and with a considerable expectation of a German triumph. But, in the course of the war, the attitude of the American people, so far as its pro-German sympathies are concerned, was entirely changed. This was due not to any propaganda on the part of England or France; both England and France were deplorably deficient in their efforts to make us understand what the war was about. It was Germany herself that taught us to understand Germany. The German propaganda in America, the German diplomatic intrigues in Mexico and Japan and South America, the German espionage and German-American disloyalty, in fact, everything that Germany said and did,—all produced in us a psychological revolt against all things German and a national horror of German "Kultur."

Without wishing to discuss this attitude with you, I must insist upon the basic fact that the American people has come to look upon Germany as the enemy of that kind of civilization, that kind of political and social and moral culture, for which America stands. Rightly or wrongly, and unchangeably too, we have come to feel that Germanism is the enemy of the human race. We have come to feel that the globe is not habitable so long as the present German power exists. The human race is not worth perpetuating, nor can it look forward to any desirable or decent future, so long as the German governmental power or system, so long as the German idea is left undestroyed, or is not made helpless. We have come to feel that the disarming of the German idea, that the destruction of the German power, that the cleansing of the world of everything that Germanism means,—is a literal divine mission which we as a nation must fulfil or ourselves spiritually perish.

But even that is but the negative or preparatory phase of our mission. We feel that we must make the world the sphere of democratic and self-governing nations, federated together in a world society wherein war hath no place. Making the world safe for democracy is no mere phrase with us. It is the burden which history and which all the deferred hopes of mankind have laid upon us. Whether Germany believes it or not, we have gone to war for this ideal; we are at war with Germany because Germany stands squarely in the way of its realization,—for which realization we believe we as a nation exist, for which realization we believe humanity exists. We expect to get nothing out of a victorious war except the joy and the human prospect that shall accrue to us through the liberation of mankind from the German menace, including in itself as it does the menace of all the wrong and despotic forces of the past.

Make no mistake about the increase and the permanence of the American mind and feeling about Germany. Remember that we are still a pioneer people. America is still young, made up of political and religious refugees from different parts of the world, made up of many kinds of adventurers, and capable of being so absolutely seized by an idea and a determination as to make us a nation of high fanatics. Once we are thoroughly involved in the war, once we begin to pay our part of the price of Germany's overthrowing, nothing can stop us. There will come a time, should the war continue, when we should refuse to discuss peace with you at all. We should feel that the peace of the world and the existence of the German power constitute such a contradiction that there is only an abyss between them and no ground whatever for discussion. Either mankind must altogether give up the hope of peace, of a peaceful progress, or banish the last remnant of the German power from the human midst. The German idea and the world idea which the democratic nations have accepted as their sign in the heavens,—these two cannot stay together in the same world. The world will have to give up one or the other.

We are already so sure of this, we Americans, that the war against you is becoming with us a religious war. We actually believe that we have gone to war for the salvation of humanity. You may argue that the belief is wrong, but it is there, and it is ineradicable. We are possessed of exactly the same spirit, though modernized of course, that possessed the first crusades. And we are expecting no short or easy victory. We are preparing for indefinite war, and we are resolved not to sheathe the sword until Germanism is destroyed, until the Prussian military state is extinguished, or until we ourselves are destroyed.

II. Germany has also convinced America that she still considers no peace except a peace based upon the acknowledgment of a German victory. Your Kaiser has precisely and repeatedly stated this in his speeches. Your great Hindenburg has stated the same. So have your journals, your professors, your socialist leaders, and in fact most of your spokesmen. And thoughtful Americans are everywhere saying in reply,—and they are saying it to their English kinsmen and the France that has suffered martyrdom at your hands,—that we prefer death for ourselves and our children, we prefer extinction for ourselves as a nation, to living in a world that has become a German dominion and on terms dictated by the German power and penetrated and possessed by your German "Kultur." It is what Germany herself has said and done that has caused us to face and to deliberately make this choice of extinction rather than preserve life on Germany's terms. I am telling you this in order that you may consider, and if possible persuade your rulers to consider, what manner of America you are at war with.

III. The American people is also entirely convinced that it would be useless to sign a negotiated peace with Germany, because such a treaty would have no validity, would be wholly worthless indeed. We are convinced that a treaty with Germany has no value whatever, except Germany be rendered powerless to break it. This is a hard saying, but your masters have taught us that it is true. You might wish to debate the saying, but with us it has been so constantly and consistently verified as to become undebatable. We do not believe that a peace with the Germany that now is would have the value of the paper upon which it is written; of the ink expended in signing it, so long as the present mind and power of Germany endures. I repeat to you, that until you are rendered powerless to break the treaty of peace which you sign, your whole history is the proof that you will not respect your pledged word on the instant when you find some advantage in violating it. I do not refer merely to the crime and perjury involved in your invasion of Belgium. I do not refer merely to your pretended acceptance of our President's Four Principles at the time you were planning the destruction of Russia in order that you might erect a German dominion upon the ruins. I do not refer to your firing upon Paris on the very hour when the Allies, graciously acceding to the Pope's request on your behalf, abstained from firing on Cologne. I mean that the present German Empire has been built upon a foundation of triumphs procured through the perfidy and perjury and rapacity of your rulers, and in fulfilling the pursuit of your "Kultur."

I think that you ought to know this is the way America looks at you, the way that the whole civilized world looks at you. Even if you say the viewpoint is wrong, you must reckon with the fact that Germany is, whether she will or no, a pariah and outcast among the nations. Your rulers seem to have no realization of this, and all that you do in the progress of the war, and all your methods of seeking peace through personal intrigue, are increasing your evil position in the world.

IV. I think Germany very much underestimates the power of American organization and the perseverance of the American people in the war. Even our school children are organized; all our social and religious activities are mobilised; all our inventive power and material and mechanical resources are consecrated unto a war of indefinite duration. In time, we shall be able to relieve France of the continuance of the sacrifice she has made for humanity, and to take our place beside our Anglo-Saxon kinsmen in bearing the burden of your continued assault upon civilization and the human soul.

V. One thing that seems to put the possibility of a righteous peace with you out of consideration is the fact that every one of you who comes seeking peace seems to have no sense of moral responsibility regarding that peace. You come, each of you and all of you, seeming to place the whole responsibility for giving peace to Germany upon President Wilson. Or you say if Monsieur Clémenceau had done this or Lloyd George had done that, or if America had done something else, or England pursued a different course, you could have had peace. But always, just as you have gone around all my questions to you and really answered none of them, so Germany pursues her intrigues for a peace that shall be proposed by President Wilson or someone else, and a peace that shall enable her rulers to appear before their peoples as unconquered. Not one of you has made, in any of your conversations with me, a single proposition or tentative that was not immoral, or that showed anything that seems to me a capacity for national morality, even among those who call themselves liberals. How comes it that you put all moral responsibility for ending this world war which you began upon those you make against? These peace efforts of yours only serve to convince us that an overwhelming German defeat alone can clear the ground for the creation in you of a capacity for a true national or an international morality, without which a peace between Germany and the democratic nations is no peace, but a preparation for universal darkness and destruction.

VI. Now every day that the war continues is deepening in the American people this feeling that Germanism is the last great enemy of a true human progress or evolution. And all your military achievements are only increasing our purpose against you. Win as many victories as you can; every victory the German armies now win is but heaping up the ruin of Germany. Every advance of the German armies into France or Russia is but more deeply decreeing Germany's doom. However many your victories, however far your armies may yet march, you will get no peace by them. The more completely you consecrate

America's whole national being to your ultimate overthrow, the more surely you make impossible any peace except that which shall finally be imposed upon you by the democratic armies. The world will not now nor ever give you peace at the point of your sword. By the sword you have drawn you can only perish. If you want peace, sheathe your sword, withdraw your armies within your own frontiers, make restitution and reparation for all the savage evil you have done, so far as such restitution and reparation are mortally possible. And then ask for peace upon the basis that every question raised by the war, and that without conditions or reservations, shall be submitted to the Peace Congress or to the tribunal erected by the Society of Nations. It is you who have drawn the sword against civilization, against democracy, against freedom, against humanity. And it is you who must withdraw the sword, and withdraw it while there is yet time, if you are to have peace and not ultimately perish.

There is a greater might abroad in the world today than the might of arms, and against this might the German power is helpless and will be finally ground to dust. Until Germany learns that her armies are helpless no matter what victories they may win, until Germany learns that her armies and her victories can win no peace for herself,—until then the war must go on.

De Fiori: But why must the German people suffer for what their rulers have done?

Herron: Because they have given no evidence that there is any difference between them and their rulers. The distinction which you, and which even good men among the Allies make, as to the difference between the German Government and the German peoples, is altogether a delusion. You have done exactly as your rulers told you to do; you have never repudiated them; you have never risen against them; there are no martyrs, save Liebknecht, among you for democracy; even your socialist leaders are, as you yourself say, among the most confirmed in the idea of a German peace won through a German victory. As long as the German peoples give no evidence that they are other-minded than their rulers, it is futile for such as you to plead for such discrimination on our part.

De Fiori: But is there no way by which we of the German liberals may move toward peace?

Herron: I have just pointed out the way. It is perfectly open and obvious. There is nothing to prevent Germany from obtaining peace except the German mind itself. You have only to ask Switzerland or another neutral country to convey in a regular way your proposals to the Allies' Governments, if you have any. Or if I am speaking to you as a representative of a German liberal movement, I would say that you have only to persuade or compel your Government to take the course of action I have indicated. And surely Germany is in a position, because of her present military advantage, to state definitely her terms of peace, without any humiliation on her part. She has now an opportunity that may never come again. If you Germans want peace, why doesn't your Government, frankly and fully, without equivocation, state exactly your terms, and ask the Allies to consider them. Now is your time, perhaps the last chance you will ever have, to make the great gesture that may do somewhat to redeem Germany in the eyes of the world. Instead of seeking peace through subterranean methods, propose a peace that will make possible the Society of Nations; propose a peace that will eliminate conflict between nations, and not a peace that will be merely a veiled German dominion. Give to the world some evidence of sincerity and of fellowship with civilization by taking this initiative now. I see no choice between your taking this initiative upon yourselves and your settling down to a condition of permanent war between yourselves and the Anglo-Saxon world, entrenched upon the soil of France and consecrated by the almost Messianic sacrifice of the French people.

De Fiori: But this means the ruin of the world, the suicide of the race.

Herron: But it is Germany that has precipitated this ruin, and unless Germany is prepared to take the moral responsibility of saving the world from further ruin through her own self-redemption, I do not see that there is anything else for America to do but to march all her millions and all her resources against Germany. Certainly the world will be ruined in any case; indeed, the world was already well-nigh ruined before the war began, because of the penetration and dominance of the German mind. If the democratic nations have to face the choice between physical ruin at Germany's hands and moral ruin through Germany's power, I think the physical ruin will be the wise and instant choice.

De Fiori: But is it not the duty of America to speak some word that will help and encourage the German liberals?

Herron: What else has President Wilson done? Since that August day of 1914 in which you began your assault upon the world, what else has he done but seek to evoke some sign or action that would indicate a better Germany? President Wilson has proposed the Society of Nations as the hoped-for issue of the world war. He has spoken of a world-constitution wherein the rights and the liberties and the duties of all peoples should be signed and guaranteed. In this Society Germany would be, with every other nation, protected in all her just rights and powers. Let Germany sincerely and unequivocally, without conditions or reservations or afterthoughts, propose now to accept the President's idea of the Society of Nations. Let Germany automatically end the war by asking President Wilson to convoke the Society of Nations, with an authoritative and unequivocal assurance that she is prepared to accept the program.

De Fiori: Is this a personal suggestion of yours, or do you know if President Wilson would now propose this program if he were officially assured of a sincere response from the Central Powers?

Herron: I want to again emphasize that I have no authority whatever to speak for the President upon this subject. But on the other hand, I have a profound personal conviction that not only our President, not only America, but the Allies as well, would be ready to propose and enter the Society of Nations if assured beforehand that Germany would unconditionally enter the Congress of Peace, accept the constitution that should be agreed upon for the Society of Nations, and accept the judgments of the tribunal of that congress or that Society of Nations upon all questions raised by the war, including Alsace-Lorraine and the treaties she has made with Russia.

De Fiori: Let me again explain to you that Count Hertling was sincere in accepting the President's Four Principles and in hoping to prepare the way for a Society of Nations. But why did the Allies let ten days go by without coming to the table of peace with Russia, discussing only, of course, the questions at issue between Russia and Germany? We could then have really concluded peace without annexing any part of Russia. But the Allies committed a great error and enabled our military party to get the upper hand in the negotiations. The German people had firmly decided to execute the decision of the Reichstag and to give a real peace to Russia. We really went to Brest-Litovsk with this decision in mind. The military peace was the result of the absence of the Allies from the negotiations, and also the consequence of the absolute impossibility of negotiating properly with the Bolsheviki.

Herron: But if we debate the words of Chancellor Hertling and the peace of Brest-Litovsk, we shall go on indefinitely. I personally am convinced,—and you did not deny it yesterday at the dinner table,—that the Petrograd pronouncement for peace without annexations and without indemnities was really a Berlin program for peace without the surrender of Alsace-Lorraine, without granting anything to Poland, and without making any restitution to Belgium or to France.

I am sorry to conclude our conversations in this way. I assure you that I am deeply hurt within myself to have had to say the things that I, as an American, have said to you as a German. But I can do nothing else. I should not be honest with you, nor with the peace movement of those who call themselves liberals, if I spoke other words than I have spoken. There is no use in looking for peace where there is no peace.

The world has reached the parting of ways, I think; it must choose between a peace that is based upon freedom and righteousness among the
nations, or else meet with possible extinction. Germany precipitated this
day of judgment, and in this judgment Germany must be the first to
be judged. I do not think there is anything more to say.

De Fiori: No, there is nothing more to say. I shall try to report all
our conversations exactly as they have taken place. I know you have
spoken honestly, and if, as I hope, they lead to some better promise,
you will see me again with much more important men than myself.

182. MEMORANDUM CONCERNING DR. MUEHLON'S INTERPRE-
TATION OF DR. DE FIORI'S MISSION, JUNE 27, 1918[12]

Dr. de Fiori is the highly paid personal agent of General Ludendorff. Dr. Muehlon makes the statement upon his own absolute knowledge, he declares, and not upon hearsay or rumor. He has kept himself
accurately informed of de Fiori's proceedings for the past four or five
months. A month previous to the actual interview, Dr. de Fiori had
applied to Dr. Muehlon to arrange for a meeting with me, and Dr.
Muehlon had refused—in fact had taken steps to prevent the meeting—
preferring it should wait until the hoped-for failure of the German
offensive in France; in case of which failure, the military party for
which Dr. de Fiori is acting would be likely to reveal its idea of peace
more fully.

Ludendorff, Dr. Muehlon says, practically carries on his own personal government of Germany. He has formulated his own peace program, quite without reference to the nominal German government. His
power in Germany for the moment is supreme. He desires to keep the
dynasty as a symbol, as a necessity; but he also plans for a supreme
personal political power for himself. He has his own personal cabinet,
his own personal agents; and the military and pan-German party is so
incarnated in Ludendorff's authority and power, that neither Chancellor
Hertling nor the German Kaiser dares interfere. Ludendorff holds the
diplomats and politicians of Germany, as well as the Reichstag, in quite
obvious derision. He fully believes himself able to make a much better
peace for Germany than they. He is confident, indeed, that he can procure a peace that is essentially German, even in case of the failure of the
great offensive in France.

Dr. Muehlon considers de Fiori's mission as the beginning of a new
offensive that is especially of Ludendorff's initiative. And it is the success or failure of these peace manoeuvres during the summer months,
that will put Ludendorff's power to its ultimate test.

[12] Herron Papers, I, Document XXV–C.

For this reason, Dr. Muehlon urges that I be accessible to each new German messenger, and that I say to each the precise thing I said to Dr. de Fiori. "Make convincingly clear to each one," he said, "that any thought of peace by compromise or negotiation, so far as America is concerned, is sheerest delusion. Convince each one that America has long ago abandoned any thought of peace with Germany except through a complete victory over the German Empire, and the destruction of the Prussian autocracy." "You have taken exactly the right course," continued Dr. Muehlon, "in declaring that America does not want peace with existing Germany, or upon any terms that Germany has to propose. America expects peace only through triumphal war, and is preparing to wage that war for fifty years, if necessary. Every time you convince a German peace messenger of this, you are doing the one thing that can now be morally or politically done, by a non-German, to undermine the authority of Ludendorff. Hold fast to this American weapon; and to the opportunity which the Germans themselves are putting into your hands to wield it."

As to what may result from this initial effort of Ludendorff, made through his agent Dr. de Fiori, remains to be seen. Dr. Muehlon says that Dr. de Fiori gave out in Zurich that he had gone to the mountains for a holiday, and then took the night express for Berlin, immediately at the close of his conversations with me. He travels with a military passport signed by Ludendorff, and is quite independent of either the German Foreign Office or the German Legation in Switzerland. The result of his initial effort may be that Ludendorff will wait awhile, to see what the result of the next drive toward Paris will be. Or it may be that de Fiori will soon return to Switzerland accompanied by persons of greater significance than himself.

Taking up now the interior condition of the Central Empires, as presented by Dr. Muehlon:

I. During the past few weeks, he has received a number of secret visits from persons of high place and authority in the German Government, including, so he implied, an imperial minister. These have one and all substantially said to him: "We now see that you are entirely right in what you have said and done; but we cannot do and say the same ourselves; for that would mean certain ruin. We have been obliged to denounce and discredit you publicly, so far as our authority goes in Germany, but we want you to know that we do not individually hold any such opinion as we have expressed publicly. We also want you to know that the German people do not believe the things that we have had to say about you in the press and in the Reichstag. We are helpless to make any move or to speak any word toward change until Germany has suffered such a military reverse as shall weaken the power of Ludendorff."

Dr. Muehlon gathers, from all of these increasing official visitations, that there is a potential opposition to the military party and to the pan-Germanist conception that has not existed before. He for the first time believes that a political revolution in Germany is possible. This political revolution depends (*a*) upon the German people being absolutely convinced of the impossibility of achieving any compromise peace through American mediation; and (*b*) upon the Allies holding fast, through whatever stress, until America has reached France in a force sufficient for taking the offensive. Dr. Muehlon conceives that, when faced with these two tremendous and invincible facts, the German people will break down.

II. While convinced that this breakdown of the German people and their institutions is infinitely preferable to the perpetuation of existing Germany, Dr. Muehlon no less views such an issue of the war with great apprehension. He says that, knowing the psychology of the German people as he does, he foresees a reaction, once the reins of restraint are loosened or cut, that may be violently disastrous to Europe. The very stolidity and docility that have kept the German people in their present place, holding them to such prolonged and unthinking obedience to their masters, may have for its rebound or reaction a dissolution of every vestige of authority. The reaction would be equal to the antecedent action. It is quite possible, Dr. Muehlon thinks it even probable, that the whole German nation might dissolve in a sudden and universal and uncontrollable hysteria—in a national Saturnalia of murder and of every kind of crime. It would be a diabolic deluge, he said, that would not be confined within the German frontiers. . . . .

183. MEMORANDUM TO MR. J. O. P. BLAND OF THE BRITISH
FOREIGN SERVICE CONCERNING DR. MUEHLON,
JULY 21, 1918[13]

GENEVA, July 21st, 1918

First of all, let me thank you for the letter of Sir William Tyrrell, and especially for conveying to me the knowledge of Mr. Balfour's appreciative interest in my memoranda. Since I regard Mr. Balfour as the first of living Englishmen, and, above all, as the one who most thoroughly and intelligently apprehends the great purpose of our President, his gracious thought of my very incidental services can only be precious to me.

But what I wish to write to you especially about, at this moment,

---

[13] Herron Papers, II, Germany, Document XXX.

is your opinion (and also the opinion of the Foreign Office, if I understand you rightly) concerning Dr. Mühlon. I do this the more freely and frankly, since you ask for my mind upon the subject. I agree with you that the matter is important. There might come a crisis or an opportunity wherein our decision as to the integrity or non-integrity of Dr. Mühlon would be very vital indeed.

Let me at once say that, so far as my conviction counts, Dr. Mühlon's loyalty to our cause, his devoted determination to destroy the old Germany and make way for the new, is beyond question or doubt, and without qualification or reservation. I have been in pretty close touch with him since January, and the effect of my contact has been a steady growth of my confidence in both his sincerity and his ability. I think I know something of human psychology; I have studied all the human types I have met here very carefully; and especially with regard to Doctor Mühlon I have mustered whatever powers of analysis I have. I have watched him especially, because I believe him destined to play a very important part in the future of Germany. I do not believe that you, or Mr. Balfour, or anyone, could come in personal contact with the man without arriving at my conclusion—without coming not only to trust, but greatly to admire his spiritual quality and his mental apparatus; without estimating him, indeed, as an unusual human potentiality.

A criticism which one might make is, that Dr. Mühlon is neurasthenic and consequently "temperamental." His neurasthenia, or "temperament," *does* affect the color of his horizon, according to his condition of nerves, or the impression made upon him by the last person with whom he has talked. I mean by this that he may be very hopeful one day, very doubtful the next day, and very depressed on the third. But these temperamental changes never affect his principles. They have only to do with the immediate prospect of the fulfilment or failure of those principles. He has never deviated from his declaration and determination that the existing order of things in Germany must be destroyed, either by the Allied armies from without or by a German revolution from within. He has also steadfastly stood against any consideration of a negotiated peace, or any compromise with Germany on the part of the Entente. If the Entente should consider peace on any other terms than Germany's unreserved confession of fault and unconditional surrender, then the Entente and America would be traitors to their cause, to themselves and to mankind—and to Germany also. Such is Dr. Mühlon's unchanging attitude toward the war during the half-year wherein I have held occasional but earnest and lengthy converse with him. At a meeting of leading Opposition Germans and Austrians at his château at Gümligen, yesterday and the day before, he insisted upon the two following principles as fundamental to the organization of the Opposition into a working association here in Switzerland.

I. Germany must be so completely defeated that she admits her defeat, and that the German peoples behold the falsity and impotence of their military past, before the question of peace can come into the field. The only other alternative to this is, that the German people shall rise and accomplish the necessary overthrow of the present military society by domestic revolution. But until Germany is compelled, either from within or from without, to confess her sin candidly before the world, and to sue for peace unconditionally, no peace must be accorded to Germany by the Entente. Such he demands as the fundamental principle which the Opposition he has gathered must accept.

II. He also demands that the Opposition shall be so comprehensive and so radical in its manifesto that it shall include all the republican following that groups itself about the *Freie Zeitung* and Dr. Schlieben.

I have this program, in substance, from himself. He has just dismissed his friends in a thoroughly friendly way, to call them together again when they are ready to agree to these two fundamentals.

There is one point especially, so Whittall tells me, that has been made much of in London government circles—namely, the visits of persons of high governmental position in Germany to the Gümligen château.

Now I have been perfectly aware of these visits: Dr. Mühlon has twice discussed them with me: and I feel that he has acted for the best interests of our cause.

It is true that important personages from Berlin, members of the government, also Count Romberg the German Minister at Bern, have come to Dr. Mühlon's château to argue, to persuade or to confess. He has received these visitors in order that he might tell them the truth as he sees it—in order that he might, as St. Paul would say "convict them of sin, of righteousness and of judgment to come." He knew they could not move him: he believed he could move them.

In some cases he *did* move his visitors. Some frankly confessed that Dr. Mühlon was right—that Germany was hasting to her ruin; but they also confessed that they had not the spiritual nerve to pass into open opposition to the existing military government. In cases where Dr. Mühlon failed to enforce any moral conviction, he *did* put the fear of America—since the fear of God was impossible—into the hearts of the most stubborn of his visitors.

Dr. Mühlon did highly right in opening his doors and his mind to these messengers. I do not see how his course can be questioned: it deserves only the highest commendation. And such commendation, so far as I am concerned, I have given him.

And now let me say, in this connection, that I think it is time your governmental chiefs should be warned against the deplorable and disastrous growth of the really venal cult of suspicion now rampant in Switzerland, and likely to be ruinous to sobriety or responsibility of judgment regarding certain men and events. It has been the business of the omnipresent German agents, since the beginning of the war, and especially during the past year, to sow deeply throughout Switzerland the seeds of suspicion between the Allies and Opposition Germans, and also between representatives of the Allies in their relations to each other. The seeds which the Germans have thus sown are bearing a malign and appallingly bountiful harvest. Switzerland is rotten with the presence of these innumerable suspicion-sowers and suspicion-reapers. Everywhere, the most sordid and atrocious accusations are swarming, and to such an extent that we are living here in a sphere of the uncleanest imaginable cynicism. It is not merely that Germany has done her utmost to break down the confidence of the Allies in such men as Mühlon and Lammasch; it is that all the best Intelligence Services, all the peoples connected with Allied Legations, are unwittingly baffled by this diabolically occult German propaganda of suspicion.

I have deplored the difficulties which these low traffickers in suspicion have placed in the way of the altogether admirable and efficient services of Commander Whittall. Certainly, the British Empire could not have, either in one of its critical outposts or in its most menaced home-center, a more loyal, more intelligent, more honorable and high-minded servant. I have known several instances—of which I have never spoken to him—of how deeply he has become an object of both German animosity and Latin jealousy. His work is constantly interfered with; he has been compelled to give up agents whom I believe to be objects of vindictive misrepresentation; and all through the insistent meddling of men who may be working for the Entente with their miserable best intention, but who are in effect exactly carrying out Germany's propaganda of suspicion and disruption.

In this respect, our Latin friends are especially guilty. The different men of both the French and Italian services are constantly warning everybody against everybody—they frequently warn me even against each other. During this year, wherein I have been acting as a sort of watchman on the walls of Europe, I have met the representatives of everything that can claim to be not only a nation, but a tribe: and I have found among most of these some sort of faith towards humankind and toward each other; but I must confess that, among the Frenchmen in Switzerland engaged in their country's service, I have found not one who spoke well of another, or who had anything but suspicions to offer concerning the servants of the other Allies; and I have found the Italians are but little better. In this work of discrediting not only the agents of the enemy, but of England and Italy and America and all the lesser Allies as well, the agents of France in Switzerland seem to revel; and some of these suspicion-mongers, I assure you, are types that most faithfully accord with their vicious labors—dishonoring the fair fame of France, and the spiritual splendor of her matchless armies. It seems never to occur to these agents that it is worth while seeking for something trustworthy. They have no interest in fidelity or good faith. Their sole and eager interest seems to be in hunting out actions and persons to whom suspicion can be attached, in hunting out bad faith and false motives. It is impossible to interest these people in anything that is good.

Thus the Latin Intelligence Services are acquiring an almost vulturous appetite for the rotten. And Switzerland is demoralized with hundreds of agents of these Services—most of whom are parasites, some of whom are the lowest pothouse blackguards.

Now you know, dear Mr. Bland, that once the appetite for evil report is in a man, his opinions are not only worthless; they may, if seriously acted upon, be dangerous to the last degree. The man who highly trusts some people may, betimes, be disastrously fooled. But the man who is clamorously distrustful of all persons is a fool all the time; and anything that he says about men or circumstances is more than irresponsible: it is to be shunned as one shuns the venom of the viper.

It is time, I repeat, that we should be warned as to the disastrous judgments that may be formed from this sort of intelligence—judgments based upon these rapidly increasing charges and counter-charges and suspicions—judgments based upon the word of agents who make suspicion-mongering a profitable profession. By listening to these charges, we not only develop the worst sort of credulity; we are deliberately submitting ourselves to the German hypnosis; we are accepting the evil spell which the Germans have cast over us by their creation of this inferno of calumny. Besides that, we not only are likely to do irreparable wrong to highly honorable men—to men whose only thought is to serve disinterestedly, even if sometimes awkwardly—but we also deprive our cause of services that might be most desirable, and formative at most critical moments.

As to your fear that my expression of confidence in Dr. Mühlon might have an effect upon the military situation at Washington, I can assure you that fear is utterly groundless. I have carefully abstained, in all memoranda, from any meddling in military matters, for which matters I know well enough I have no competence. In only one instance, that of Dr. Mühlon, have I even reported a military suggestion.

But let me say to you personally what I have not said in any memorandum; I believe the suggestion of Dr. Mühlon—which I am certain he made in all good faith—was tremendously right. Six weeks ago, or a month ago even, if the Italians could have been reinforced by the maximum of 200,000 English and American troops, with the sort of leadership that would have gone with these troops, Austria could have been irremediably smashed, and even the march to Vienna could have begun. Germany would then have been compelled to let Austria go, or else take away a large body of troops from the offensive in France. In either case, an irreparable and possibly decisive blow would have been dealt to Germany. To have dealt this blow would have been, on the part of the Entente the highest strategic wisdom, and would have produced the most immediate practical military results. Time after time, the German Empire could have been successfully attacked on the South-Eastern flank—if attacked in sufficient force. But the opportunities have all been passed by, or at most comparatively played with. So we are sacrificing hundreds of thousands where tens of thousands might have been sufficient.

So much for my only and perhaps unpardonable intrusion into the military situation. I must lay upon you the responsibility for provoking it.

In conclusion, let me assure you again that no incidental word of mine concerning the military view of Dr. Mühlon, or of any other man, will have the slightest effect upon America's dispositions of her forces.

I fear I have greatly presumed upon your request for my thought of Dr. Mühlon, but I have said (aside from the military parenthesis) only what I feel needs to be said, and said immediately and forcefully.

184. SECOND INTERVIEW WITH DR. DE FIORI: BAVARIAN PEACE OVERTURES, JULY 8, 1918[14]

(a) OPENING CONVERSATION

Dr. de Fiori, of Munich, with whose tentative and indefinite proposals my memorandum of June 14th was concerned, returned on July 1st, much sooner than I expected, and this time with a definite and quasi-official proposition for the initiation of peace overtures.

Before proceeding with the narrative of his return to Germany and his consequent interviews, and the commission on which he had returned to Geneva, I would say that he asked at the outset that I verify his report of our previous conversations. He read it to me carefully, from beginning to end, and I must say that it was astonishingly correct; as Dr. Mühlon had assured me it would be. I called his attention to the

[14] Herron Papers, I, Documents XXV–E and F.

fact that he had softened some of my expressions somewhat and that he had added here and there a flourish about the glory and splendor of German science and the like. He agreed that this was true, but insisted that I must remember that the conditions of the German Nation are wholly pathological. He had to prepare his report for sick minds. He said frankly that the mind of the German Government is a mind diseased, and that the mind of the German people is in a like condition. So long as his report of my statements was substantially exact, he felt that he was justified in resorting to a few phrases, or a few modifications, "in order to make sure that the bitter medicine would be swallowed."

After I had confirmed the accuracy of his report, he then proceeded with the narrative of his return to Germany, and of the remarkable interviews that resulted in his knocking again at my doors.

When he left Geneva, on the night of the last interview as reported in my previous memorandum, it was with the intention of proceeding directly to Berlin, where Dr. Mühlon told me he had gone. By the time he had reached the frontier, he decided to go first to Munich, to confer with Professor Foerster and also with the Bavarian Minister of War, Colonel Sondenburg, who is Dr. de Fiori's immediate chief and special friend. I should say that Professor Foerster is, in a sense, a member of the Bavarian Government, or rather of the King's Council. He occupies what is known as the "Royal Chair" in the University of Munich, the occupant of which can only be chosen by the King. It is through the protection of Professor Foerster by the King of Bavaria that the German Imperial Government has been prevented from taking severer measures than have been taken against the Professor, because of his odd utterances and actions. Professor Foerster and Dr. de Fiori went very carefully over the report of the conversations with me, and together they planned a program of action. Dr. de Fiori took his report to the Minister of War and left it with the word that he was at the Minister's disposal and would wait in Munich before proceeding to Berlin. Professor Foerster called upon the Minister President, and set before him his knowledge of myself personally, reaching back through a previous intimate friendship, making clear to the Minister President that he must not put me in a class with the various German professors who come on missions to Switzerland, nor must he think of me as a diplomatic agent, or engaged in any intrigue against Germany, with which intrigue Kühlmann had charged me. Professor Foerster informed him that he must try to conceive of an American who ardently cared about humanity, who was devoted to the person and the cause of President Wilson, and whose words must be taken as sincere and true. With that, Professor Foerster and Dr. de Fiori waited the result. Within a few hours the Minister of War sent for Dr. de Fiori, who found the Minister profoundly moved, and even agitated. "The words of Mr. Herron are true," he said. "This is the literal truth of what Germany must face regarding America. Either we must force Prussia to make peace, or Germany is ruined. In the end America will not only defeat us, but destroy us, if we do not make acceptable terms now. There is not a moment to lose." The Minister of War then had copies of the report made, to put into the hands of the various members of the Bavarian Government, and first of all in the hands of the Minister President, and the Crown Prince Rupprecht. The Crown Prince was so deeply impressed with the report that he himself took it to his father, the King, and convinced the King as to the truth of the report, and of what must be expected from America. On the morning of the third day the Minister President telephoned for Dr. de Fiori, and demanded of him to know where and when the War Minister had had an opportunity to have an interview with Professor Herron. "It is not Colonel Sondenburg, but myself who has had the interview," replied Dr. de Fiori. "But Colonel Sondenburg speaks continually as if he had had an interview," replied the War Minister. Colonel Sondenburg was then called, and said: "Yes, this report has had such an extraordinary psychological effect upon me that I am constantly laboring under the impression that I myself have seen and talked with Professor Herron."

By that time the minds of the King and the Crown Prince and other Ministers were known, and an informal meeting of the whole Bavarian Government was held, including the King, the Crown Prince, the Minister President, the Minister of War, the Bavarian Chief of Staff, and others. Not to delay too long on the details which Dr. de Fiori gave me, I would say that the result of this and following consultations between the different personalities mentioned, including Professor Foerster also, was an approximate agreement among them upon the terms of peace wherewith Bavaria might approach other federal states of the German Empire, and might so organize them as to compel Prussia and Ludendorff and the Kaiser to take definite steps toward peace. A somewhat free sketch of the terms of peace upon which Bavaria could proceed to take such an initiative, was drawn up and agreed upon by the members of the Bavarian Government. Dr. de Fiori was then charged to return to me with those proposals and not to proceed to Berlin.

It would seem, according to this, that there is a considerable reassertion of independence on the part of the Bavarian Government and people. It was decided among them that it would be just as well to let Berlin remain in a state of doubt and anxiety as to what Bavaria thought. The Minister President had copies of the report made and sent to Chancellor Hertling and to the Great General Staff. Chancellor

Hertling was so greatly impressed that he had some fifteen or sixteen copies made for his own special followers in the Reichstag. Dr. de Fiori states that certain phrases in von Kühlmann's speech to the Reichstag, especially the words about the impossibility of a conclusion of the war being reached by military means, were taken verbally from his (Dr. de Fiori's) report. The report was read by Ludendorff and the General Staff, but what these thought, Bavaria does not know, or did not at the time of Dr. de Fiori's return. Just as he was starting back to Geneva, he received a telegram from Berlin, asking why he did not come, but as Dr. de Fiori's responsibility is directly to the Bavarian Minister of War, and only indirectly to Ludendorff, he returned to Geneva according to the will of the Bavarian Minister; on whom the responsibility to the Great General Staff rests. He was very frank about explaining his position to me, and his explanation clears up the statement of Dr. Mühlon referred to in my previous report regarding Dr. de Fiori's relation to Ludendorff. I am convinced that Dr. de Fiori was telling me the truth, and besides my personal conviction I have the word of Professor Foerster, whose personal word would be unquestioned the world over, that I can depend upon whatever Dr. de Fiori tells me concerning these matters.

Before presenting the peace proposals, I must try to make as clear as I can the psychology of their presentment, I must try to define, if such definition is possible, in what sense they are and are not official. They are official in the sense that they are the propositions which the Bavarian Government will proceed to act upon, if it receives the necessary encouragement or assurance. "If I were speaking to a diplomatic body," said Dr. de Fiori, "I could not speak to that body officially. But speaking as a man of honor to a man of honor, I would say to you that I am authorized by Bavaria to lay these propositions before you, and Professor Foerster has already vouched for the truth of what I say. I understand that naturally, if we wish to know the mind of the Chief of your Government concerning so important a matter, then it is the business of the Chief of our Government to formally make inquiry through a neutral power. But the German Kaiser will not at present make any such inquiry, or take any such step, until he is forced to do so. The King of Bavaria cannot take such a step, as Bavaria is a federal state of the German Empire, and has no authority to directly address the President of the United States. For him to formally take such a step would be equivalent to an act of rebellion on the part of Bavaria against the Empire. Nor can the Bavarian Minister President, or the King, or anyone representing him, address you as an American citizen upon such a subject. But all these are questions of diplomatic technique. If Bavaria wishes to break through the difficulties of her situation and force open a door toward peace, and to take an initiative within the German Empire toward bringing Germany to the threshold of that door, there is absolutely no other way open to Bavaria than the way we are now taking. Unofficially, it is true, but morally and actually, we wish to know if you can give us your word that President Wilson would consider favorably the opening of peace discussions upon the basis of the proposals we present to you. Since we are not presenting these propositions directly to him, we naturally cannot ask him to speak to us. But if you can only say to me that you believe President Wilson would look with favor upon these proposals as a basis of discussion, then Bavaria will proceed to act."

"You understand," he continued, "that there is no thought whatever of any separate discussion with America. We understand that the discussion must be with all the powers of the Entente together. But believing, as we do, that it is with America we must fight in the end, if the war continues, and believing that it is America that must arbitrate between England and Germany in the end, we feel that it is necessary to know first of all if President Wilson would look with favor upon our procedure, before we take an initiative that would result in an official proposition to the Allies as a whole. We ask, I repeat, as a point of departure, your word and no more. If you can say to us now, or in a few days, that you are personally convinced that the President would look with favor upon our action, we will proceed. We need only a word, some word of assurance or even encouragement. If you cannot, or will not, give this, then, of course, there is nothing to be done. Bavaria must not proceed so to unite the federal states of the Empire as to bring pressure to bear upon the Pan-Germans and the Imperial Government, and then have the overtures rejected."

The following is the memorandum submitted by Dr. de Fiori:

"The restoration of Belgium; contracts concerning the liberty of German navigation on Scheldt and Rhine; elevation of Alsace-Lorraine to a free confederate state with complete home-rule; equal free trade with France and Germany; contracts for the custom-free exchange of coal, potash and iron between Germany and France; (personally, I put here complete freedom of press, of language and school, and in all national and political things). I attract your attention to the fact that the representation—that is, the parliamentary representation of the new German confederate state—would not stand on any other basis than it does now, because they have now already the direct right of vote for the Landtag in Alsace-Lorraine.

"Self-administration for all the Austrian peoples, including the Germans, according to the principles agreed upon with Professor Lammasch; self-administration for the Italian provinces, with Trieste as capital and free port; repeal of all existing differential contracts in favor of Trieste, which are greatly to Italy's damage; reorganization of the traffic of Trieste with the Lombardy and Venice, like before 1859; wherewith Trieste would remain, and would have to remain, a completely Italian city. Under the term self-administration of Trieste, I understand also the political and police administration, so that the state and not the monarchy would have the right to hinder in any way the political intercourse with Italy. The political relations of the territory of administration of Trieste with Italy would therefore be the same as those of the Canton of Ticino with Italy. Self-administration of Dalmatia, Bosnia and Herzegovina; self-administration for all non-Magyar peoples of Hungaria.

"Complete restoration of Serbia, with free access to the Adriatic, perhaps Durazzo becoming a Serbian port, and the Serbian part of Albania going to Serbia.

"Restoration of Poland in full freedom and independence. I do not mean that Galicia should go to Poland, nor that Prussia should give Posen. (I avoid these questions on purpose, because they would create confusion. I personally and confidentially would say that it would be a great injustice to leave Posen with Prussia, if Posnanian Poland would not get complete self-administration like Alsace-Lorraine.) Poland should receive freedom of the flag on Weichsal and Memel, and a free access to the East Sea, through Lithuania. Reopening of the peace of Bucharest and the peace of Brest-Litovsk.

"All the Balkan questions should be referred to the peace conference for their final settlement. America should mediate between England and Germany in all questions of the colonies: also in all German-English questions of the Balkans, till a satisfactory arrangement was arrived at. (Return to the policy of contracts, which already before the war was on its best way.)

"Disarmament; the Society of Nations."

Dr. de Fiori insisted again and again that these terms must not be considered as final. They represent what he called "the middle ground of discussion." Bavaria could not think of how far she would be willing to go for the moment, but upon what terms she could so organize the federal states as to bring sufficient pressure to bear upon the Prussian and Imperial Governments. If the German Government could at all be brought formally to propose peace discussions to the Allies, approximately upon the basis here proposed, and it became apparent to Germany that her rights and interests would receive reciprocal consideration at the hands of the Entente, Dr. de Fiori considered that Germany would probably then go further than was proposed by his memorandum, for the sake of achieving a durable peace.

All this was narrated and proposed to me on the evening of Dr. de Fiori's return. I then proposed to him that we should have present in subsequent conversations the same confidential stenographer who had reported our previous conversations, so that there would be no mistake in the words that either of us might use. To this he readily agreed. I will therefore now present the verbatim conversations that took place between us, and afterwards present my own observations and conclusions.

184. (b) SECOND CONVERSATION

Herron: You have stated that you regard your memorandum as a basis of discussion, and not as the ultimate of what Germany might do for the sake of peace. You will remember that I asked you in our previous interview as to how much you thought Germany might, as a last resort, concede concerning Alsace-Lorraine. Suppose America were so pledged to France that no discussions of peace could proceed except upon the basis of the renunciation of Alsace-Lorraine upon the part of Germany, Alsace-Lorraine being returned to France, or as a compromise, being erected into a sovereign and independent state such as Switzerland. I do not pretend to say or know what the nature of America's pledge to France is, but I know that the American people would be against any compromise that would be contrary to French wishes, or be in the least disappointing to the French people. You must remember that we Americans owe a debt to France of more than a hundred years standing, and that the payment of this debt is with us a point of honor, fulfilling a wish that is traditional with every American schoolboy. You must take account of this as an element in our continuation of the war, or our consent to peace.

De Fiori: My opinion is that America has not made any such pledge. If America had given such promise, then Professor Lammasch could not have suggested, as I understand from Professor Foerster he suggested, that Alsace-Lorraine become a confederate state.

I believe that America ought not to put this question before the general consideration of peace. And then, according to my present opinion, it would be quite impossible to bring Germany to a separation from Alsace-Lorraine. As I said before, Alsace-Lorraine would be better conditioned as a confederate state in the German Empire than as an independent state. She could be a kind of peaceful advocate of French interests inside of Germany. Her moral independence would be greater than if she were an independent state like Luxembourg. If there were a difference of opinion between Germany and France, and Alsace-Lorraine were an independent or foreign state, she could not influence Germany. But if she were a confederate state within the German Empire, she could use her influence as a member of the family, and as such she could speak with weight.

As an example, take the present case of Bavaria. If Bavaria should succeed in initiating this program of understanding, it would be the position of Bavaria in the Federation which would make this success possible. But if Bavaria were a foreign state, it would have just as much influence as Switzerland or Holland, and no more. Furthermore, if the King of Bavaria, or the head of Alsace-Lorraine as a federated state, in a confidential talk with the generals of the Kaiser should say: "We cannot do what you want," then this refusal would never be known to the public, but nevertheless what Prussia wanted would certainly be rendered impossible.

Still more, if Alsace-Lorraine remains with Germany, then everything that has to do with the armament and disarmament of the German people would be decided in a democratic sense, for with the addition of Alsace-Lorraine the states of South Germany will be able to form a complete counterbalance to Junker Prussia. The strengthening of the South German States means the return of the German peoples to the views and the policies which in olden times brought them the sympathy of the civilized world. It would develop their true culture, and enable them to withstand the pressure of the Prussian system.

These are reasons which, quite aside from sentimental views, should convince America and France that the cause of the freedom of the people is stronger if Alsace-Lorraine becomes and remains a free confederate state of the German Empire. The new state will play a much more important rôle in helping on your democratic program for the world by this plan than by becoming a small, independent state, with no other rôle to play than that of a bag of grain between two millstones.

Herron: Let me say first of all, in answer to what you have said, that there was never any agreement between Professor Lammasch and myself regarding Alsace-Lorraine. As mutual believers in the Society of Nations, we discussed all the problems of the war. But we certainly never imagined ourselves competent to say what Germany would or would not do. Professor Lammasch may naturally have expressed an opinion about Alsace-Lorraine, as I suppose pretty nearly every other citizen of the world has done, but our discussions had to do with the future of the Austrian peoples, and not with Germany except incidentally.

De Fiori: Continuing then, I would say that if the French could only let go of the thought of disannexation from Germany and annexation to France, then they would have Germany on their side, and Prussia would be overcome. And what I say in this respect is very important. In the Reichstag, the Social-Democrats, the Polish members of the Reichstag and the Alsatians vote together. The Alsatians vote with the democratic majority. If you take away Alsace, the democratic parties are not in majority any more. Would it not be an immense political advantage, I ask you, if we let Alsace-Lorraine become a democratic state within the German Empire? Once she was a vassal state of our Empire. Then she was a province of France. Then she became a Prussian penitentiary. But now, full of French culture, Alsace-Lorraine might become a redeeming element in German life and contribute to the sane evolution of the whole German people. You must consider this question historically, and not merely from an immediate military or political point of view. From the historical standpoint, the old idea of Alsace-Lorraine as the ambassador of France inside of Germany, if this idea were realized, would dissolve the Alsatian problem forever.

I say this aside from the fact that I can find no other solution. Alsace-Lorraine is too small to become an independent sovereign state. If she is returned to France, she will become merely a province, and lose all her individuality. If she remains in the German Empire, with full freedom and complete home-rule, she will become a strong helper of the democratic element, in company with the South German States, against Prussia. Germany needs this Alemannic influence of Alsace-Lorraine. Even the Alsatian deputy said to me: "We do not want to be separated from Germany. We do want to be an independent state within the Confederation." The Landtag thinks in the same way, with a majority of five to six, and the deputies of Alsace-Lorraine, mind you, receive the mandate through a general, direct vote. That this Landtag of the Alsatians is intolerable to Prussia is evidenced from the fact that it is not now permitted to meet. But even so, the deputies of Alsace-Lorraine say they do want to remain within the German Empire, but as a free and independent German state, and not as a Prussian penitentiary.

Herron: I understand your point of view, and what you conceive to be the historical logic of the present situation. Still, you have never come down to my precise question. Supposing for the moment that America is pledged to France as to the return of Alsace-Lorraine (and I would suppose the same thing about England if I were an Englishman), I ask you again, is peace with Germany absolutely impossible upon any other basis than that of the retention of Alsace-Lorraine in some form or other within the German Empire? Supposing good conditions of peace were made, that promised protection to Germany in all that she had a right to ask, would Germany still prefer to go on with the war rather than discuss a peace upon the basis of the return of Alsace-Lorraine? Do you think this is an undebatable question, so far as Germany is concerned? Would she be willing under any circumstances to submit the question to the Peace Congress, or turn it over to the Tribunal of the Society of Nations, to be investigated and decided after all parties and interests were fully heard and considered? Will you give me a categoric answer to that question?

De Fiori: It is possible that America may have given this promise. But it is not excluded, it is not humanly unthinkable that America should have given the promise without really understanding the true question of Alsace-Lorraine. It sometimes happens that two completely right men conclude a contract under assumptions on the part of one of them of things that are not true, or that one of the parties finds himself damaged through the contract and desires to have it nullified. I would say that America stands in such a relation toward France, she has pledged herself to something which the Alsatian people themselves do not want. If America can be convinced that she has done this, then the promise is not valid, or at least can be reconsidered.

May I say again that I am convinced that we shall give Alsace-Lorraine just as many rights as England will give to Ireland. I say this because I am sure that England will never consent to Irish separation from the British Empire. They may give Ireland home-rule, but not separation.

If separation were a condition of peace, and if England should consent to the separation of Ireland from the British Empire for the sake of peace, then I think Germany might consent to the same regarding Alsace-Lorraine. Whatever England gives to Ireland, Germany will also give to Alsace-Lorraine.

Herron: You are the only German representative with whom I have spoken, except Professor Foerster, who did not state categorically that Alsace-Lorraine was purely a German domestic question, and could not be brought before the table of peace. This was the attitude of Haussmann in both the interviews he sought with me.

De Fiori: Of course, I do not take any such view. I do take the view that the question might be settled prior to the peace congress, and settled in such a way, with such a prior and privately arranged agreement between Germany and America and the Entente, that the question need not come before the peace congress. If we settle beforehand that Alsace-Lorraine is to be a free confederate state within the Empire, having full freedom of making connections with France exactly in accordance with her liking, and if we come to the conference with the question settled in this Hippocratic method, then of course the question is settled thoroughly and well, and what remains is a mere matter of form. It is not unthinkable to give America and the Entente guaranties concerning Alsace-Lorraine, binding herself prior to the peace congress, so that the question need not be discussed at the conference.

The Irish question is important to America also, and it is likely that there have been conversations between America and England concerning the Irish problem. But the Irish question will not come up at the peace congress. And why may not the same thing happen with regard to Alsace-Lorraine? England has probably promised that Ireland shall have home-rule inside the British Empire. Why may not Germany do for Alsace-Lorraine what England has done for Ireland, Germany even giving guaranties and voluntarily binding herself?

If the initiation of peace depends first of all on the question of Alsace-Lorraine, and if peace discussions can begin upon the basis that Alsace-Lorraine shall be made a confederate state, then I have no doubt that the other federal states of the Empire will agree to it—I mean other states than Prussia, of course.

Other answer I cannot give to you. I believe you can wholly separate Alsace-Lorraine only by bringing Germany to her knees. You can get Alsace-Lorraine away only by force. And even then, the separation would be against the will of the present peoples of Alsace-Lorraine.

Herron: What do you consider the principal question to be answered prior to peace discussions?

De Fiori: The principal question is this: What is England's mind about our position in the Society of Nations? How does England mean to settle her differences with us? Will she grant to us the same position as other nations in the new international régime? Is she ready, with the help of America, to come to an agreement with us in all other questions than the question of Alsace-Lorraine? If so, then the question of Alsace-Lorraine is secondary.

War is often made for one set of differences in fact, while made for another set of differences in theory. The great questions of interest between Germany and England are the real cause of this war, and not Alsace-Lorraine. We must know whether England is ready to arrange a peace of understanding with us. If England were ready for this, then why should we not be ready to give the people of Alsace-Lorraine what they want, whatever that might prove to be in the end?

What does America think of our position in the Society of Nations? Would all the votes be against us, except our own and the votes of Austria? Would Germany be alone in all the juridical questions, in all the colonial differences that have to be settled?

Herron: I cannot go into a detailed answer at this moment, as it is already past the hour of luncheon. I can only say to you that about

America's impartiality in the Society of Nations there need be no shadow of doubt. If Germany had unconditionally accepted membership in that Society, placing herself upon an equality therein with England and France and Italy and America, exacting no prior conditions for herself, then America would just as jealously guard the rights of the German people as she would guard the rights of the American, or the English or the French or Italian.

184. (c) THIRD CONVERSATION

Herron: Before we proceed with our mutual questions and answers, let me say that it is at least a hopeful sign to me that when you went back to Germany you told those in authority and told them honestly what I had said to you. I imagine this is the only time I have been truthfully reported in Germany, except in the conversations I had with Professor Foerster at the beginning of last September. In very important instances the whole value of the interview, so far as I was concerned, was lost. Let me take one example. Haussmann has been to me twice. The last time, in the month of February, we spoke together for the larger part of the night. I said to him many of the things concerning America's mind about the war that I said to you in our last interview. He seemed greatly moved, saying the next morning that he felt I had spoken truly, and that he would go before certain members of the Reichstag with my words, and try to secure a majority in favor of asking the Government to make peace on the basis of President Wilson's proposal for the Society of Nations. By the time he had reached Berlin, if I am correctly informed, as I believe I am, his courage failed him entirely, and those who sit in the high places still cherished their illusions that America had not seriously gone to war with Germany. This conversation took place in February at the home of Dr. Muehlon in Guemligen. I am profoundly thankful that you have reported my presentation of America, as both Professor Foerster and Dr. Muehlon have assured me you would do.

De Fiori: I have told them everything quite honestly and literally and prefaced it all with my personal conviction concerning the truth of what you had said, in addition to your own personal sincerity in the matter. And what you said is already now known to the important members of the Government in Berlin, not to the Government only, but to the leading men of Parliament, as a consequence of having been communicated by the Chancellor of the Empire.

Herron: You must understand that your question places me in a position of grave responsibility. I must have time for profound and faithful reflection before I can take it upon myself to express an opin-

ion upon the subject concerning which you ask my opinion. If I decline
to give any answer whatever to your question, even in that I take a
tremendous responsibility upon myself.

Your first words when you came to me last evening were a declaration that I had it in my power to open the door unto peace, and unto
what you considered a peace of both understanding and justice,—a
peace also that would lead to the Society of Nations and mutual disarmament. Even if your supposition were true, I should have to think
well before I should open the door of which you speak. If I could
certainly foresee that through that door would pass a really changed
and repentant Germany, a Germany that would not take advantage of
a negotiated peace to prepare to spring upon the world a few years
hence, when mayhap Germany would have more rapidly recovered
from the war than France and England; if I could foreknow that there
would issue forth from such a peace a Germany that would consecrate
her efficiencies to the service of humanity, and not to a Prussian might
and a Prussian dominion over the world, if I could be sure such a
peace were not giving unto Germany a vaster and still more predatory
opportunity, but that on the contrary Germany would sincerely choose
the Society of Nations and a federated world, with fellowship and co-
operation among all peoples,—then, so far from hesitating I would not
only thank God for the opportunity of opening that door, but would
verily give a thousand lives, if I had them, for the privilege of so
doing. But so far as I am able to see at this moment, the opening of
such a door as you propose, a door opening unto what you deem to
be a peace of understanding, would within a few years eventuate in a
catastrophe so much greater than the one we are now in the midst of
as to make our present war seem as the dress-rehearsal that came
before the presentation of the real drama.

But let me see if I have an exact understanding of your question.
I understand that the principal personages of Bavaria wish to know,
and that you are making the inquiry on their behalf, if President Wilson would consider the proposals you have presented to me as a sufficient basis for the discussion of peace between the Central Powers and
the Entente and America. You do not ask, as you say, any word from
President Wilson in answer to your question, at least not directly. You
ask for my honest opinion as to whether the President would or would
not favor the consideration of these terms of peace. If I could give
you some personal or confidential encouragement in this direction, if
I could express to you a positive opinion that the President would look
favorably upon the terms you propose as a basis of discussion, then
Bavaria would proceed to use her influence upon the other confederate
states, with the purpose of uniting them in an effort to compel Prussia

to accept these terms, with the result that the Imperial Government would then formally and regularly propose to America and her Allies the opening of negotiations for peace according to these initial proposals. Have I thus stated your mission and your question correctly?

De Fiori: Exactly, perfectly.

Herron: I wish to raise once again the question as to your method of procedure. We are agreed that the proper presentation of such a question would be for the Chief of your nation to transmit the inquiry to the Chief of my nation through a neutral power, even if the question were to be kept wholly confidential. I understand, of course, that at present your Kaiser would not ask any such question, and would not be prepared to discuss peace on the terms you suggest, but I am not yet clear that it is impossible for the King of Bavaria to transmit such a question to our President, especially since the question would be wholly confidential.

De Fiori: But such a question could never be kept secret, or confidential, if once it were transmitted through a neutral power.

Herron: But if the King of Bavaria would put his question into writing, and I would undertake its transmission to the President, then the doubt as to the certain secrecy of a neutral power is removed. And I can assure you that whatever else may or may not be counted upon in this world, the honor of our President can be counted upon even unto the last extremity.

De Fiori: Before I could say whether such a course were possible or not, I should have to return to Munich. Today I can only tell you this. In Munich there is the desire to prepare the way for a peace of understanding. But it lies in the nature of the case that Bavaria cannot take the first step in absolute uncertainty. She must have some intimation as to whether the first step will perchance lead to the desired goal.

And she can ascertain what she wishes to know only in some such way as that in which I am proceeding. I am merely asking you after the manner that one man would ask another in a difficult personal situation. Do you believe that President Wilson would or would not refuse to discuss these proposals, if they should eventually come before him in the formal and regular way? This is all I ask to know now— your honest opinion. If you can express an opinion that is affirmative, then I tell you in all honor that Bavaria will take your word and act.

Let me now repeat that if we can agree as to the disposition of Alsace-Lorraine in some such manner as I have proposed then guaranties in any required form might certainly be given, which would prove the absolute integrity of our intention. To us the principal question is not Alsace-Lorraine, as you think. It is the question of our total future relation to England, and our position in the Society of Nations. You will notice this is the chief question in the speeches of Kühlmann and of the Chancellor. Kühlmann speaks of the colonial question, the Chancellor of the Society of Nations. Kühlmann refers to a conviction that is clearly held in Germany, that England plans to destroy the possibility of a colonial policy on the part of Germany. The Chancellor speaks of the possibility of the Society of Nations becoming an institution that might be used for the suppression of Germany. These are two official questions, which even if they are put in a negative way, I can repeat unofficially.

Now if these two questions are settled clearly and justly for us, I have no doubt that all other questions can be solved very quickly. The rest are secondary questions. But we should like to know the attitude of the Allies on these two fundamental points before we are ready to discuss the general outlines and the many details of peace.

Now I do not see why we should not, some of us, speak clearly and confidentially about these questions, preparatory to a final understanding. If America really wants to create a durable peace in Europe, if America wishes to settle all questions according to her high and noble mission which mission we are coming to truly believe in in Germany, why may we not know what will be done with Germany if Germany reaches out her hand for peace? If Germany knows that she is in no danger of destruction or dismemberment, no danger of economic ostracism if she sues for peace, then I believe she will gladly reach out her hand. I should like to get from you the word that would give me courage to persuade others, give Bavaria courage to persuade the federal states, that in the question of colonies and of the Society of Nations nothing will be demanded which Germany could not concede, nothing which is inconsistent with her self-preservation and her place beside England and America as a great power. As to the rest, the leaven is already fermenting in the dough. And believe me when I tell you that I am working not only for the salvation of Germany, but for the Society of Nations, which I believe in as ardently as you yourself. Moreover, the men who have previously come to you have been politicians, who were ambitious for themselves and had to take count of their own careers, whereas I want nothing whatever but peace, a good peace, a just peace, a durable peace, that shall make it forever impossible for such a catastrophe again to overtake the world. It is for this reason, because I neither expect nor want any position for myself, that I have brought it about that a faithful report of all that you said in our previous conversation has been placed before the eyes of all who are in places of power in Germany. You can depend upon it that I shall act just as faithfully and disinterestedly in the future. Only do not let it be that mere formalities, that diplomatic and official technicalities shall prevent the opening of the door which I am asking you to open. I am not a diplomat, but you remember how the One who is greater than all others taught that the weak things of the world would bring down the things that were great and powerful. I am one of those whose minds are burdened with the woes of their country and of the world, one of those who are weighed with a thousand cares for humanity. But I am of those through whom a new Germany, and a new world will have to come, if they are to come at all. I only ask you to believe me when I tell you that the intentions of the enemy peoples—never mind the Kaiser and the Pan-Germans—are not as bad as you think.

Herron: When I asked if there were not a way by which your King could confidentially ask the question he desires answered,—ask the question of the President directly, I mean,—I was not thinking of any formality or diplomatic technicality. I was thinking only of the value or effectiveness of the answer. Instead of getting a mere personal opinion from me as to the possible attitude of the President, why not find some correct way of getting the President's own word upon the subject? You would thus be standing on certain ground. It was for this reason I raised the question, though I do not raise it again since you have already stated that you cannot answer it without returning to Munich.

184. (d) FOURTH CONVERSATION

De Fiori: Let me now tell you about the report that I hope to make. I shall begin with the beautiful words you spoke of your feelings about Germany in your student days, and of how you told me that in all your early vacations, when you had a choice of where you would go, you would always end by choosing a walking tour, alone or with a friend through some new part of Germany. We are a romantic people, you know, notwithstanding our hard present materialism, and I shall thus touch a tender spot even in the heart of our Hindenburg. I shall say that I came again to you upon the question of peace, and that you told me of your impression that I was the first man who had reported your actual words to persons in authority in Germany, and who had really made clear to them your presentation of America's reasons for entering the war and for continuing it until Germany had repented or was overthrown. I shall also say that if the men who came to you last winter had truthfully and convincingly reported you, then the terrible course of events since then might have been avoided. Certainly the gentlemen in Berlin did not then know the truth about America, but they do know, or will know the truth now. And whatever you tell me about America's spiritual and material and military participation in the war, I shall faithfully report, and I assure you I shall see that it is believed.

Then I shall state exactly how I put the question as to President Wilson's consideration of the tentative terms I proposed, and shall give your answer. I shall also report all that we have spoken together about possible peace conditions.

I want to tell you still more frankly how the matter stands. I shall present two reports, one for Bavaria, in which I tell everything unto the last syllable, and one for Berlin, in which I shall have to use a measure of caution in my mode of presentation, but which shall contain the truth. If I should tell everything in Berlin, then Berlin would intrigue at once among the federal states against Bavaria. It is not impossible that Berlin could create jealousy of Bavaria among the federal states, say in Württemberg for instance, if it was known that the House of Bavaria was planning a great historical deed. Also, if it were known in Berlin that Bavaria were planning such a deed, then everything that we hope for in Bavaria might be lost. My complete report of our present discussions will therefore be very confidential, and will go only to the King and the Crown Prince and the Minister President. And it will be in a much warmer tone than the report that I make to Berlin, as I wish to encourage and urge them to go on with the great thing they have in hand.

Herron: But I want to call your attention to one thing which you seem to have overlooked, that in the tentative peace outlines you have sketched it is England much more than America that is concerned. It seems to me it is the mind of England you would wish to understand primarily. And even before I could form an opinion, after due reflection, as to what might be America's attitude, I should need to know, what England thinks regarding the colonial questions and your place in the Society of Nations. Is there no Englishman to whom you can put your question?

De Fiori: There is no Englishman in Switzerland at present to whom I would wish to put this question, and in any case we must know the attitude of America first, because it is America that must mediate between England and Germany.

Herron: But what is it that Germany wants or expects from England regarding the colonies?

De Fiori: The speech of Kühlmann has been` interpreted as if Germany wanted more colonies wherein to expand,—more than she had before the war, I mean. Nobody in Germany has this impression, and certainly it is not a true impression.

I believe that through America's mediation between England and

Germany a result can be reached that will be satisfactory to both. Of course, if Germany calls to America, America must inform herself as to whether England would accept such mediation, and must come to an understanding with England concerning the matter. If England should agree to America's acting as umpire, the program of mediation could then easily be arranged.

I cannot precisely answer your question as to what Germany expects of England regarding colonies, but I want you to believe that it is possible to clear up completely the supposed differences, which come partly out of jealousy and partly out of misunderstanding. The world is large enough to furnish room for both England and Germany. Already before the war Germany and England were on the way to a complete and perfect understanding. What Lichnowsky has written upon this subject has been confirmed by von Jagow. As you know, Sir Edward Goschen and von Jagow worked long and in perfect harmony to bring about a complete agreement on all outstanding differences or questions between the British and German Governments, and had wonderfully and almost miraculously succeeded. It was at their last meeting, when the document of understanding had received its last touches, that von Jagow exclaimed: "Now if only the Kaiser will remain long enough away and not suddenly return, we shall have secured the peace of the world." But the terrible thing happened, the Kaiser suddenly returned, and Germany did not sign the agreement. I know that in this respect the Kaiser and the Junkers or the Pan-Germans are responsible for having plunged this devastation upon the world. But it was not the fault of the German people. It was the fault of our mad, and now really demented Kaiser, and of the Prussian military Junkers and Pan-Germans who were behind him. The German people did not then know what they were doing, and they do not even yet know what they are doing. They are only beginning, even now, to have doubts and ask questions.

Herron: Suppose I should feel, after due reflection, that I could express an opinion that would accord with your desires. Do you believe that Bavaria could not only persuade the other confederate states of the Empire to compel Prussia to propose peace on the basis you have outlined, but that you could also persuade them at last to a peace based upon the famous four principles laid down by President Wilson? Could Bavaria persuade these confederate states to an unreserved advocacy of the Society of Nations, to an agreement that all questions raised by the war and unsettled by the peace conference should be submitted to the Tribunal of that Society? Would they be willing, without any reservations or prior conditions, to have the German Empire enter that Society on exactly the same footing wherewith America or England or any other nation would enter it?

I would like to remind you, in this connection, that the most important thing to the non-German world is some sure sign of repentance, of a change of purpose on the part of Germany. America, in the person of President Wilson, has made gesture after gesture of great faith concerning the human future. Now some gesture of trust in humanity, some true and righteous reconciliation on the part of Germany with the nations she has assaulted, would do more to prepare the way for a consideration of Germany's peace tentatives than all the guaranties that could be imagined. Remember, as I have previously stated to you, we have no reason for trusting any guaranties you may make in advance. We might be moved by an unconditional and unreserved proposal on your part to become a member of the Society of Nations, and to submit all questions raised by the war to the arbitration of that Society. Is there no one in Germany of sufficient capacity and authority to agitate for this great gesture of faith?

Let me call your attention to something pertinent to my question. At the time when President Wilson first entered upon his office, the distrust of Mexico and of all the South American Republics toward the United States had reached its climax. Each of these South American countries was ripe for German penetration. It was then that the worst conditions of Mexico required some sort of action on our part. Capitalists and politicians, a large part of the public press, such men as Mr. Roosevelt and Senator Beveridge, were clamorous for an American occupation of Mexico. If President Wilson had proceeded to make war upon Mexico, a war inevitably resulting in indefinite occupation, he would have had the public opinion of our country almost unanimously behind him. He stood almost alone for a time, stood out against the nation which had just elected him as President,—in his steady and stalwart refusal to take what the nations of Europe, as well as the public opinion of his own nation, would have declared to have been the justifiable and natural course. He insisted that American action in Mexico should be reduced to the least possible necessity, and should be manifestly a desire to help the Mexican peoples to a solution of their own problems. He made Mexico understand, at last, and he made America and the world understand, that never by his word or will should American occupation of Mexico take place, that never by his word or will should the powers of the American Government be used to serve the great concessionaires who were clamoring for occupation. Mexico must be left free and helped to solve her own internal problems. Consider what a miraculous change this attitude of our President has wrought upon the two American continents. Instead of being, as we formerly were, the object of suspicion and jealousy on the part of the South American Republics, we now have their devoted confidence, their eager and willing co-operation. Here we have the example of a host of lesser nations believing in the actual disinterestedness and friendship and helpfulness of a great nation. Nothing like this has happened before in the history of the world, and it has happened because of the high action of our President, an action which was practically derided throughout the governmental and financial world of that time as utopian. By a great and continued action of determined faith, our President swung the whole history of the western continents into a new path of progress.

Now, why cannot Germany profit by this stupendous example so recently set before her? Instead of bargaining like brokers for this advantage and that, why do not some of those who sit in high places in Germany propose Germany's acceptance of the Society of Nations on equal terms with all other nations and agree with them to submit every outstanding difference between the nations of the world to the constituted Tribunal of this Society. If Germany should propose this now, propose it honestly and unconditionally, she would practically render the world bound to give her the fullest and most generous justice. America would be just as ready then to serve Germany's righteous interest, as she is today ready to spend her last dollar and her last beloved son in fighting for the overthrow and if needs must be, the destruction of Germany. If there are those among you who can force the hand of your military masters and compel this great gesture to be made by Germany to her enemies, you will thereby not only redeem the world from war, but you will redeem yourself from the wrongs which you certainly have perpetrated upon humanity. Do you prefer your own destruction to this great act of faith? For certainly it will come to a choice between these two, and that very soon. Germany will never reach peace by bargaining, by intrigue, by negotiation. She will only reach her own destruction thereby. As I said to you before, every day that you choose to continue the war for the accomplishment of your dominion, you are thereby sealing your own doom, and demanding of God your own destruction and extinction as a power.

Let me say again, if I were able to open the door you have urged me to open, if I could be convinced that it was for the final good of mankind that I should open it, do you believe it possible that Bavaria would go beyond the mere seeking of what you call the peace of understanding? Do you believe that Bavaria could and would seek to bring such pressure upon the federal German states as to finally compel or inspire Germany to take an initiative for peace that would be really great and noble and prophetic?

De Fiori: My dear Professor Herron, you are talking in the terms of a beautiful vision. You forget what manner of world we live in.

Here in Europe we are living among howling wolves. We Germans are surrounded by enemies, even if the enemies are of our own making.

Even so, I honestly believe that if we understood the Society of Nations according to President Wilson's meaning; and if we could be made to understand what he means by the Tribunal of this Society, we on our side would have no difficulty in entering therein.

I am opposed to our politics of power and force, and I believe that not only we Bavarians, but every honest German can be convinced of the falsity and futility of our Prussian politics. We all can be so convinced, and we can enter the Society of Nations, if we are sure we can stand on equal footing with the other powers, with England and America, and with undiminished standing in the world.

Yet I cannot say that we are prepared to enter the Society of Nations if questions of territories that are already parts of the German Empire must come before the Tribunal. Certainly for instance, the injustice done to the Poles of Posen must be rectified. The wrong must be made right. Posen must be given home-rule. But I cannot yet say that Posen should be separated from Prussia. Also with Alsace-Lorraine, I agree with Professor Foerster in saying that Alsace-Lorraine must become an independent confederate state. But Germany will never consent to separation. Alsace-Lorraine is a part of our German racial being, and if it were taken from us that would inevitably mean war in the future. So how can we consent that the question of Alsace-Lorraine be submitted to the Tribunal of the Society of Nations? I might admit it, Professor Foerster might admit it, but not Germany.

Consider the Society of Nations. Will not all countries enter it in their former mental frame? Is it not a Tribunal which these faulty nations will erect? Can you consider that this will be a veritable Tribunal of God amidst humanity? If everyone who had to do with the future were such as Professor Herron, or Professor Foerster, it would be easy even for us Germans to accept the Society. But this is no ideal world, but a blundering world of terrible realities. And you must remember that if once a nation enters this new international régime, that nation cannot separate itself therefrom without grave and irreparable consequences. If I knew that President Wilson and Professor Herron were to live forever, and that the Society of Nations was to be instituted and continue according to their ideal, then I would go back to Germany and immediately tell them to make this great gesture of faith which you speak of. But you American idealists will not live forever, and you cannot tell what will become of your ideals after you.

Even so, I am convinced that if it were possible to give the Germans a clear understanding of President Wilson's idea, if they could be persuaded that the Society of Nations does not touch their national prestige, then the principal difficulty would be removed. So far as Austria is concerned, it goes without saying that the Society of Nations cannot consent to a state of things such as now exists in that unhappy country. There would have to be a change and a reconstitution of that Empire on the lines laid down by Professor Lammasch. But I am convinced, let me repeat, that the greater part of public opinion in Germany would gladly give proof of confidence in America by accepting the four principles proclaimed by President Wilson, and the Society of Nations as the crowning work of peace, if the German people were convinced that this noble program would also be sincerely accepted by England and France.

I believe that at bottom we think in the same way. But I beg you to permit me to continue to formulate the problem in my own way, which means the way in which I must at present put it to my people. If the Society of Nations is constituted with the same rights and duties regarding nations that are granted to individuals by the American Declaration of Independence and the American Constitution—which means that the small and the great have the same rights—and if we Germans were convinced that the charter of the Society of Nations would be so,—then there would be no doubt of our accepting this Society and its international judgments.

It is necessary that we agree about these four principles, and their application, and then the smaller differences will rapidly pass. And it seems to me that in this moment of history, if we are seeking for permanent peace, we must begin by using all that can unify us, before we undertake to eliminate all that is separating us.

The prerequisite for Germany is that she shall keep her integrity untouched. Everything else can be discussed. But Germany cannot admit intervention in her own territorial and commercial and moral questions. But all the questions that lie between her and the other nations must be thoroughly discussed and a mutual agreement reached. First of all, the material questions which have created hatred and division among men must be settled. Then we can proceed to other questions.

I wish to convince not only my fellow-citizens, but our Imperial Government, at last, that the four principles of President Wilson can be accepted without fear that the President means to use them to dismember and destroy Germany.

Herron: There is no intention to destroy Germany, unless her own obduracy and continuance of the war renders that destruction essential to the safety of the world. If Germany is destroyed at last, it will be because Germany herself has compelled that destruction, and because the moral sense of mankind requires it.

But if Germany should unconditionally ask for peace and for entrance into the Society of Nations, agreeing to submit all questions raised by the war to the conference for peace or the Tribunal of the Society, reserving no question which the war has raised for an independent judgment of her own, then you may be sure that President Wilson would be the very first to stand for all the true interests and integrities of the German people.

But let me ask you again, as a conclusion to all the conversation that has passed between us, do you state it as a determined fact that Bavaria will undertake to bring it about that Germany shall propose peace upon the basis of the memorandum you have presented to me, if I should express to you my sincere personal conviction that such action would be favorably considered by the President?

De Fiori: Yes, and my answer is without qualification or reservation or hesitation.

184. (e) FIFTH CONVERSATION

In this final [?] conversation, which lasted from seven o'clock until eleven in the evening, there was little that can be called an addition to what went before. Nearly all the points of our previous discussions were reviewed and concluded. . . . .

184. (f) SIXTH CONVERSATION

Dr. de Fiori came to me Saturday morning, the 13th, with a statement and two questions.

He had just been informed that a copy of his report of his conversations with me had been sent from Berlin to the German Minister in Bern, with instructions to investigate my statements, my motives and myself, to the utmost. (Such a step cannot have been taken by the German Foreign Office, Dr. de Fiori declares, except by the authority of the Kaiser.) Do, or do I not, truthfully present the American mind and intention concerning the war? Do I, or do I not, speak the mind and intention of the President? Since I have no official or diplomatic position, by what right or authority, or from what motive, do I speak upon these subjects, or answer questions put to me by Haussmann, Foerster, Jaffé and others? Am I what Professor Foerster, Jaffé and other German friends represent me as being—an honest and ardent idealist? Or am I what Berlin believes—an omnipresent conspirer against Germany, cleverly ensnaring and deceiving the guileless Germans who come to see me?

Such are the questions Minister Romberg has been instructed to get answers for. . . . .

II. Dr. de Fiori said that he had been especially instructed, an hour before he started, to ask this: If a highly-placed personage in Germany —so highly-placed that he could properly take such action—should present a personal question directly to the President, asking only for a personal and not an executive word in reply, would it be possible for me to convey that question in such a way that it would be kept strictly confidential, and not be made known to the respective diplomatic corps of the Entente countries? My reply was that it was possible the transmission of such a question might be managed, but that I could give absolutely no guess or hope as to its being answered.

He replied that it must not be thought that this question would be of the nature of intrigue or of secret diplomacy. It would be merely for the personal guidance of the highly-placed person who would ask it. . . . .

185. THE FOURTH VISIT OF DR. DE FIORI, SEPTEMBER 10, 1918[15]

For the fourth time Dr. de Fiori, the most confidential and appointed of the German peace agents, has come and gone. This time he presented a credential from the German Foreign Office in the form of a letter addressed to himself, saying that he was authorised to carry on these negotiations, but that Germany could not go into details of what she would do until it was known what propositions the other side—that is the Entente and especially America—had to make. It was noticeable at the outset of our conversations and all through his presentations and appeals, that Dr. de Fiori was this time speaking directly for Berlin; Bavaria did not separately come into the conversations, nor was there any renewal of the former propositions from a Bavarian standpoint.

It seemed, when all was said, that Dr. de Fiori had come with a view to impressing upon me one special point, and of obtaining an answer to one special question. The point was this: *that the moment had now arrived when President Wilson, by proposing definite and reasonable terms of peace to Germany in the name of the Entente, could win a complete moral victory over the German people without the necessity of pursuing the complete military victory;* and the question was this: *is there some way by which Germany may convey official propositions to America, either through a neutral power or through myself; and be sure that these official propositions shall be kept strictly*

[15] Herron Papers, I, Document XXV-G.

confidential, not to be made public unless a favorable result should be reached, when naturally, it would be in order to announce such result to the world.

Before taking up our discussion—(or rather his discussions, for what I said was little)—of the point and the question with which he came, let me present several incidental matters wherewith the discussions were prefaced.

(*a*) On his way to Geneva, Dr. de Fiori was in conference with Scheidemann at Berne, and came directly from Scheidemann to me. Scheidemann authorized him to say to me that Troelstra's attitude and propositions did not represent the Majority Socialists of Germany. Scheidemann had never said that the question of Alsace-Lorraine was undebatable. On the contrary, he believed that an arrangement could be arrived at that would be satisfactory alike to Germany and to France, and that the German Majority Socialists were ready to discuss such an arrangement. Dr. de Fiori added that Scheidemann and Troelstra had a difference at Interlaken, and had had nothing to do with each other since. It is a singular fact, though doubtless Scheidemann would not exactly express it so, *that the separation took place because Troelstra was much too Germanophile for Scheidemann.*

(*b*) I raised the question with Dr. de Fiori of a Professor Hertz, another peace messenger now in Switzerland, whose visit I was expecting. This Dr. Hertz, who is a voluminous writer on economic and sociological subjects, had previously arrived in Bâle, and from there had sent me his request for an interview and credentials showing him to be the chief of a department in the German War Office. (At the same time he is connected with the Austrian War Office. I have not been able to make out the connection between his two positions.) Dr. Hertz, however, before he reached me, fell victim to the "Spanish grippe" which affected him very seriously and sent him to the mountains to convalesce. He had just notified me to expect him, so I inquired of Dr. de Fiori, who answered my inquiry by holding up his hands with what was at least a semblance of horror; and, finally, Dr. de Fiori begged me to be much on my guard against Dr. Hertz.

Apparently, there are two camps of German peace messengers in Switzerland, as well as in Germany itself, one representing the more liberal peace sentiment, and the other representing more distinctly the Prussian idea of peace. I say apparently, for all this may be stage-play and camouflage for my special benefit—or rather in order that I may report fictitious German differences to America. These ostensibly opposite camps may be merely two wings of the peace offensive. Perhaps I can form a clearer opinion of this when I have seen Dr. Hertz. The same thing might be surmised concerning Scheidemann and Troelstra—

though I am somewhat of the opinion that an actual difference *has* taken place between these two men, and that, in one way or another, Troelstra's whole campaign has been a disastrous failure.

(*c*) Dr. de Fiori said that, through an indiscretion somewhere—of which indiscretion he would speak later—rumors of our previous conversations had reached Italy and especially Sonnino, and had also gotten about Germany. But it was Italy of which he wished especially to speak. He begged me to convey to such Italians as I could, especially to Marquis Paulucci, the Italian Minister at Berne, that he (Dr. de Fiori) would under no circumstances favor or promote any propositions which could be considered injurious to Italy. He wanted it known that he was Italy's good friend, and would think of her best future in all efforts he should make for peace.

(*d*) He wanted to warn me that certain Americans—he would not tell me whom—had seen him in Thun, and tried to dissuade him from seeing me again, declaring that I was a person of no consequence or authority whatever—(which may all be true enough),—that it was useless to talk with me, that there were others with whom he had better talk. He intimated that these were Americans of position.* This again may be more camouflage. I do not know; I merely set it down as an incident of his last visit because I wish to make this memorandum inclusive.

(*e*) He dwelt at considerable length upon a desire that I should say to the German Government through him: "I told you so." He related how little belief the German Government formerly had in America's purpose regarding the war, even when he presented my first emphatic and ample statements regarding America's purpose and preparations in June. After the second visit, when Count Hertling had become convinced, and had fifteen or sixteen copies of the report of de Fiori's interview with me made for distribution, then the German Government began to believe and tremble before America's determination to prosecute the war with all her resources of men and materials. But even then the projected offensive was not held back, but was pursued blindly and stubbornly, and to the disaster of Germany. Dr. de Fiori wanted me emphatically to point out that if Germany had asked for peace instead of pursuing this offensive she could have had better conditions than she will now ever again be able to obtain; and that every day she pursues the war is making harder the conditions which her enemies,

* *Were they the American financiers (or their representatives) who are hoping to capture the Bagdad railway concessions through procuring for Bulgaria the separate peace—and permission for further conquests—which Bulgaria is plotting for, and for which the financiers darkly plot also? Or were they a fiction?*—Herron's note.

and above all America, will impose. The German peoples were all against the offensive, so Dr. de Fiori says, and only the military camarilla and the dynasty persisted in it. Now the disaster is so complete that there can be no question of another German offensive. All that Germany can now hope for is a defensive war, making her long retreat as costly and exhaustive as possible to her enemies.

Dr. de Fiori seemed to imagine that if I would dwell much upon this "I told you so," emphasizing and amplifying it, it might have some effect in turning some members of the German Government towards reason now.

I merely listened to Dr. de Fiori's request, but made no response to it beyond telling him that *he* could remind his chiefs of my former statements, and use them as emphatically as possible, but that I did not care to present these reminders myself.

(*f*) Dr. de Fiori stated that the best and most convincing information which they had ever had in Germany concerning American determination and organization for the war had been given them through him as coming from me. I took advantage of this statement to tell him that if Germany did not immediately and unconditionally sue for peace, I feared there would not be a great deal of Germany left to sue, if she waited until American preparations were complete. I informed him that we were making between four and five hundred war-planes a day, well and powerfully equipped; that we should probably have four million American soldiers in France by early spring, amply provided for in every particular; that it would be quite impossible to stop this army, once it was on its march to Berlin; that once our war-planes had all assembled on the Rhine, it would even be doubtful if there should be any Berlin left to march to.

In this connection, Dr. de Fiori raised the question as to why the war-planes were now bombarding Cologne daily and did not fly over Essen. Of course, I did not answer his question.

(*g*) He stated that in all probability Hertling would soon have to go. He was not strong enough to stand against the Great General Staff and the dynasty on one side, nor was he strong enough to take the leadership of a real movement for peace on the other. Hertling will have to go, and probably a military dictatorship will be the early result —*unless* (and I give this with his own emphasis), *unless President Wilson can and will encourage the German people (by some personal message) to believe they can have a reasonable peace if they rise against their government. There is no use in their rising, they have no heart to do so, unless they have some assurance, or at least intimation, that their compulsory action against their own government will not result in the ruin or division or substantial imprisonment of Germany. . . . .*

186. "A LAST APPEAL FROM GERMANY," OCTOBER 25, 1918[16]

Doctor de Fiori returned from Germany, and came to see me yesterday. He stated immediately that he had no commission this time; that all our former discussions had been rendered useless by recent events; and that further discussion would be still more useless. The fact that I had publicly advocated the placing of Germany under international control had now been published abroad in German papers, he said, and this alone, to say nothing of events, rendered the discussion between us an idle pastime.

Nevertheless, he had come; and nevertheless we talked; and it was evident from the first that he had something definite to say or propose. As I shall be presenting another memorandum concerning his visit a few days later, I will only here sum up briefly the points of our conversation, which lasted some three hours.

I. First of all, he brought the *"innigste Grüsse"* from Herr Conrad Haussmann—who is now Secretary of State in the new government—and Haussmann's explanation as to why his December and February interviews with me, with their abundant promises on his part, had failed of the result he expected; and why he apparently did not keep his promise to present to his government my statement of America's principles and purposes concerning the war.

If the State Department would care to refer back to the report of the February interviews, what I said to Haussmann on that somewhat memorable night can there be read, and with it Haussmann's promise faithfully and literally to report the same to his group in the Reichstag and also to Count Hertling. He had expressed, at that time, the opinion that he could command a sufficient majority of the Reichstag to overthrow the government and to demand peace on the terms embodied in the President's Four Principles. Haussmann now says that he returned to Berlin to keep his promise in all good faith. He went first to Chancellor Hertling and presented all that had taken place between us at Gümligen—where the interview took place in the house of Doctor Mühlon. The Chancellor seemed at the time very deeply impressed, and told Mr. Haussmann that he would consider his report carefully and decide what action to take regarding it. Then, a few days later, Count Hertling made his famous speech purporting to accept the Four Principles, but in such a way, says Haussmann, as to practically repudiate them before the Reichstag. Haussmann now confesses that Hertling's speech had no other purpose than to discredit the Four Principles, and to make a mockery of them in the eyes of Germany. He went to Count

[16] Herron Papers, I, Document XXV–L.

Hertling and upbraided him for what he had done. "How can you expect peace now," he exclaimed to the Chancellor, "after speaking in a way that can only cancel the result of all I presented to you concerning America's attitude—the attitude I believe Professor Herron truthfully set forth to me?"

Thus, at this late date, Mr. Haussmann wishes me to know the truth of the matter, just as I have presented it above.

One may form any number of conjectures as to why Haussmann should be sending this explanation and message to me at this time. It may be in part because he wished to set himself right, after his rather solemn covenant with me on that solemn night of our interview. But most likely he hoped that this explanation would reach Washington, and soften somewhat the inevitable severity of the peace terms finally emanating from our President.

Haussmann admitted to Doctor de Fiori that every word I spoke upon that night concerning the future development of America as regards the war, and the final debacle of Germany as a result of that development, had come true, but that nobody in Berlin believed a word of it at the time I spoke.

II. Doctor de Fiori stated that, so far as the German peoples were concerned, Alsace-Lorraine and the Polish Provinces of Prussia were ruled out of any further discussion. The Germans had absolutely given them up, and would be glad to get rid of them if this brought peace any nearer. The German peoples now consider the surrender of Prussian Poland and Alsace-Lorraine a cheap price to pay for peace. They would be quite ready to give up Dantzig, even though it has been for generations German, provided it be made a free city, the Germans having equal rights with the Poles in the port.

It will be seen that this is a complete reversal of the attitude of Doctor de Fiori in our previous conversations. At that time he contended that, under no circumstances, would Germany give up Alsace-Lorraine or consider it as other than an interior question of the German Empire; nor Prussian Poland and Schleswig-Holstein could then be considered as other than German domestic questions.

He also states, now, that Germany is ready absolutely to annul the treaties of Brest-Litovsk and Bucharest. In the previous conversations, these treaties were to be reconsidered and brought into the Peace Congress. Now Germany is ready to treat them as nonexistent.

In fine, Doctor de Fiori says, the German peoples are ready to do anything and everything that President Wilson would probably require. Therefore, he wants to know why Germany cannot have peace.

III. Would America like to see a complete social revolution in Germany? Or, rather social dissolution? Not a change of government, not a political revolution, not even a deliberate or organized revolution of any sort, but a state of complete dissolution and the destruction of every form of social order—that is what threatens Germany, he opines, if peace is not soon obtained. Do the Allies think that such complete social violence and disorganization as he foresees can be confined to Germany? Is it not likely to overflow and deluge the whole of Europe, and even leap across the Atlantic into America? The President, he says, must consider whether he wishes to take some steps to make peace possible, or to take the risk of a German debacle which shall engulf the whole of modern civilization.

IV. Then came what I take to be the real purpose of Dr. de Fiori's visit. The German peoples, he avows, are at last ready for peace on almost any terms short of national annihilation. But they have been kept in ignorance of the mind and intentions of the outer world since the beginning of the war; and now they are in a state of complete confusion regarding what the application of President Wilson's conception of peace would mean to Germany. The German people do not wish to fight longer; but they are utterly in the dark as to the intentions of America and the Entente, and are being hopelessly deceived and driven on by the dynasty. Why will not President Wilson, without delay, state to the German peoples, specifically and detail by detail, what he expects them to give up, what he expects them to do as the price of peace? Let him interpret in plainest language his own principles as applied to Germany. If he means by peace the overthrow of the dynasty, the surrender of Alsace-Lorraine and the reduction of Prussia to the people who are strictly Prussian, if he means the occupation of the Rhine fortresses and Heligoland for a time; if he means disarmament of the German armies,—let him say the whole. Let the President name each particular of what he requires, so that every German of us, the peasants included, may understand just what to expect. Let him tell us also, then, what our future is to be, if we fulfil the conditions that he imposes. Shall we have a right to take equal place with other nations in the Society of Nations? Shall we again have a right to trade with the rest of the world? If the colonies are taken from us and internationalized, shall we have a share in the international administration? . . . .

187. DR. DE FIORI'S LAST APPEAL, NOVEMBER 4, 1918[17]

Dr. de Fiori has again come and gone, probably for the last time; in fact, he meant this indeed for his valedictory word. He came instructed by the Bavarian Prime Minister, and on behalf of the Bavarian King, to say:

[17] Herron Papers, I, Document XXV–O (British Memorandum XXX).

I. That the King of Bavaria would put no obstacle in the way of the abdication of the Emperor and his sons. Indeed, the King was rendering all possible assistance towards the procuring of this abdication. He and other heads of the Federal German States favored a regency composed of a governing council, not of a single person, and the choosing of an infant grandson of the Kaiser as the heir to the Imperial throne. The child would be taken away from the House of the Hohenzollerns, and educated under the care of the regency for a new and constitutional order of things.

Now what would be the effect of such an arrangement, if it could be speedily accomplished, upon our President or upon the American Government's consideration of Germany in the peace settlement? Dr. de Fiori asked this question, he said, on behalf of the Bavarian Prime Minister and his King.

My reply was to the effect that neither he nor his Government had any right to ask the question, at this stage of events, nor had I any right to answer it. The asking of the question was a proof that the German mentality had not changed; and for me to answer or even consider it, would be on my part immoral. If Germany really felt her institutions and political manners to be wrong, to be discordant with the institutions and manners of her fellow-nations, let her change them. But she could not make merchandise of her proposed reforms or revolutions. It was too late for her to think of the Peace Table as a bargain counter whereon she could barter her promises of reform for territorial or economic concessions. As long as she considered her remedial promises as things to be brought to the market, and there exchanged for compromises and advantages, just so long she was in possession of no mind or understanding wherewith to come into accord with our President's world-policy, or with the purpose for which our Allies have made war against her.

II. Dr. de Fiori wished it to be understood that Germany would be in perfect accord with America's plan for Italy and the Jugo-Slavs. Germany, he said, would insist upon the cession of Trieste and the Irredenta, along with whatever else Italy would probably want.

I have puzzled myself not a little in searching for a reason for the gift of this information by Germany—or at least by Bavaria. It seemed brought in by a *tour de force*. On reflection, however, I am of the opinion it is a part of Germany's program to seek every possible chance to divide the Allies, on one question and another, at and before the Peace Conference. If Germany is admitted thereto, we need not be surprised to find her taking the attitude of supporting the President's doctrine as to the right of nations against what she will represent as French and English imperialism.

Nor only because of this incident, let me say in passing, but because of others, I am convinced that this is Germany's intention—henceforth to range herself beside America on every possible occasion, and especially on those occasions where America and the Allies may not seem to be of the same mind.

Another reason for bringing in this statement is Germany's hope to recover her former economic possession of Italy, and her former dominance in Italian politics. She will ostentatiously appear as the friend of Italy as well as the friend of America.

III. Dr. de Fiori stated that they now know in Bavaria, that the reports of German atrocities in Belgium and France are true. He rehearsed to me, in strict confidence, his own experience in compelling the present cessation of these' atrocities. He carried to Berlin from Munich sixty letters from army officers of Bavaria and Württemberg and Baden, complaining bitterly of the outrages they were compelled to perpetrate by the direct order of the Supreme Command. Not only officers, but whole bodies of men in South-German army corps had protested, some had mutinied, and in some instances officers had committed suicide. The things that had been done in France and Belgium had been done by the absolute order of the Great General Staff. Dr. de Fiori carried these letters to Berlin with the sanction of the Bavarian Government, and forced the Imperial Government to take knowledge of the facts, thus bringing about a conflict with Ludendorff. It was then that the Government imperatively ordered that no more outrages be committed, no more villages burnt, no more goods carried away, but that the retreat henceforth be carried out in some sort of moral order.

Dr. de Fiori says that five days before he arrived with the letters, Ludendorff had made the statement that the command had been given to the army to cease all burnings and lootings. Dr. de Fiori confronted him with the letters, all from officers in the army, showing not only they had not ceased, but that no such instructions had been given. It was then that the Government compelled Ludendorff to give the order, and his resignation followed.

IV. But here Dr. de Fiori brings in his strongest plea—in which plea he is supported by so honorable a man as Professor Foerster, as well as by his Government—the plea that the German people have been kept in complete ignorance of the atrocities. The letters from the soldiers and officers to their homes, telling about the monstrous things commanded and carried out, were never allowed to pass the army censorship, and the severest punishment was visited upon the writers. To this day, the German people are in utter ignorance of all the evil their armies have done. It is for this reason that they cannot at all understand the attitude of the rest of the world towards them. They have been hermetically sealed against information from the outside world and the Allies, also against information as to their own Government. Even now, most of the German people think they are still winning victories, and that the retreat is somehow a part of the plan of the Great General Staff.

But how can the German peoples repent, ask Dr. de Fiori and Professor Foerster, when they have no knowledge of the things they are to repent of? All the writings against the German Government have been sequestered during the war. Dr. de Fiori himself knows of five hundred such books. Not once has an honest translation been made of anything said to or about the Germans by the outside world. There had only been paraphrases. Even the President's last reply to Germany's request for an armistice has not been honestly or fully published in Germany. As long as the war government lasts, these men declare, they cannot even tell the German peoples about the infamies that have been perpetrated in their name, and of the changes they must make in both their mind and their government. "We cannot change Germany," he exclaimed, "*until* we have peace; and you demand that we change Germany *before* we have peace. Can you trust us in nothing? Be as considerate with us as you can; give us an opportunity to speak to the German people and to effect the needed changes; then you may be sure that Germany will soon be taking her place in the democratic vanguard, and will never again make an assault upon the world."

I need not go into the details of the discussions which arose from my replies to this plea. I had to say frankly that I felt the whole plea was another species of moral evasion, another shifting of responsibility. Our discussion upon this point lasted for well on to two hours, and reached a stage that was almost violent.

V. Dr. de Fiori admitted, finally, that Germany would not consent to stand before the world humiliated, confessing herself the guilty originator of the war.

I felt obliged to reply that, until she should so stand before the Allies—confessing first, her defeat; second, her guilt; it was useless for her to appeal for any confidence in herself or her promises of reform. Her very manner of asking for an armistice was simply intensifying the distrust which the war and her previous politics had created. The only hope of her salvation lay in her acceptance of this humiliation as her just portion. I affirmed:

a) Germany began the war; she must confess that she began it, and that she is defeated. She must unconditionally surrender.

b) Germany stands before God and in the eyes of men as the most criminal nation of history. She must confess her sins and repent.

c) So long as she tries to avoid these two steps, just so long she

580 FALL OF THE GERMAN EMPIRE

increases the distrust and hardens the heart of the world towards her. But let her confess her defeat and her crimes; let her truly and bitterly repent; let her prove her repentance by requesting and accepting the judgment of the world; then she will find mercy and confidence, and the hope of future fellowship among the nations.

VI. But will the President, will the good American people, do nothing to help us save appearances?

"If we should," was my only possible reply, "we should ourselves thereby destroy the soul of Germany. If we should take the least step, if we should make the least compromise whereby Germany escaped the full knowledge and full confession of her sin—whereby Germany welcomes as just the fulfilment of a complete retribution for those sins— we would thereby participate in Germany's crime and guilt; we would thereby perpetrate against Germany the supreme injustice, degrading ourselves at the same time to Germany's level, and closing the door that is now opening into a nobler future for all mankind; we would thus deliberately bring a long and desperate night upon the world.

"The only salvation for Germany," I concluded, "is in the acknowledgment of her guilt and her repentence. The only salvation for the Allies is in their requirement that Germany shall pay the uttermost farthing that it is mortally possible for her to pay. Only in the rendering of just and complete judgment upon Germany by the Allies, and in the willing acceptance of that judgment by Germany, lies the hope of a new international morality, and of a world that shall pursue a program of good will among nations and among men."

Part III
The Armed Forces of the Empire

CHAPTER X

THE ARMY

INTRODUCTORY NOTE

THE KAISER, as Commander-in-Chief of the armed forces of the Empire, was the final authority in all military matters. Immediately responsible to him in 1905 was Count Schlieffen, Chief of the General Staff, who prepared the plan for the invasion of France through the gateways of Liége and Dutch Limburg. Although the Schlieffen Plan of campaign called for the violation of Belgian neutrality as well as the invasion of the Netherlands, the then Imperial Chancellor, Prince von Bülow, has stated that he was never officially consulted concerning its tremendous political consequences. In fact the Great General Staff was responsible to neither the Chancellor nor the Reichstag. Thus freed from all constitutional responsibility, the Staff staked the fate of the Empire on this surprise offensive against France, and lost. The Allied and Associated Powers at the peace conference of Paris were aware of certain documents in the archives of the Staff and therefore denounced the German power of command as the citadel of that militarism which bears such a large responsibility for the outbreak of the war. *Article 162* of the Treaty of Versailles declares: "The Great German General Staff and all similar organizations shall be dissolved and may not be reconstituted in any form. . . . ."

General Hoffmann has described the great conflict as "The War of Lost Opportunities." The first of these great military problems is the loss of the battle of the Marne, in September 1914, first described accurately by Professor Kircheisen in an anonymous pamphlet, *Die Schlachten an der Marne,* published in January 1916 and promptly suppressed by the censor of the Chief of the General Staff, von Falkenhayn. Then the tragedy of Verdun, the First Battle of the Somme, and the decisive failure in 1915 to annihilate Russia have caused fundamental differences of opinion among military critics.

The appointment of Hindenburg and Ludendorff altered the

583

relationship of the Kaiser to the General Staff. The Chief of Staff and his First Assistant no longer were an advisory and executive organ of the Commander-in-Chief but the actual possessors of decisive military power of command. After the dismissal of Imperial Chancellor von Bethmann-Hollweg, the Supreme Command dominated the civil government of the Empire, and this domination continued even after the Imperial order of January 1918, which restricted the military powers.

The decision of the Supreme Command in favor of the March 1918 offensives, the failure of these in July, and the resultant military collapse form the final tragedy of the Imperial Army. Ludendorff and Hindenburg were confident that the Imperial armies could win a decisive victory which would end the war before the American Expeditionary Force could reach the Western front. After initial victories in March and May the German armies on July 18 were confronted with inevitable defeat, owing to the military superiority of the Entente Powers. Although the Kaiser recognized the necessity of a change to a strategic defensive, he did not demand it until after August 8, when two of his armies were defeated by a surprise tank attack in the salient east of Amiens. As the armies, in September, were retreating on the Western front to defensive positions, Bulgaria and Austria-Hungary collapsed. On September 29 the Supreme Command demanded an immediate armistice to prevent a complete military defeat. The war was lost.

188. THE SCHLIEFFEN PLAN[1]

The plan evolved by Graf Schlieffen, the German Chief of the General Staff, in 1904–5, just before he left office, by which France was to be overwhelmed in a few weeks, and the legend of how by departing from this plan—"watering it down" is the favorite expression—his successor, Moltke, failed to deliver the "knock-out blow," have been frequently discussed in the German military books which have been reviewed in these pages. Only short extracts from it and what purport to be summaries of it, often contradictory, have, however, been given, and it has never been published in its entirety. All writers have, however, been in accord that Moltke made the left or defensive wing in Alsace and Lorraine stronger than Schlieffen designed, and that he did so at the expense of the right wing, the decisive one, which in swinging round was to sweep the French Armies against the back of their eastern fron-

"The Schlieffen Plan," in *The Army Quarterly,* XVIII (1929), pp. 286–91.

tier fortresses and against the Swiss frontier. It has been repeated by
many German authorities (e.g. General Groener) that Schlieffen made
the proportion of one wing to the other 1 to 7, whilst Moltke changed
it to 1 to 3, but how these figures are arrived at, they do not reveal.
According to General Groener in *Das Testament des Grafen Schlieffen,*
the deployment of the troops against France in the 1905 plan and in
1914 were, omitting Landwehr and Ersatz troops, for sieges and L. of
C. purposes:

1905	1914	Army
11 corps 7 Reserve corps	8 corps 5 Reserve corps (line just south of Namur)	First and Second
6 corps ½ Reserve corps	6 corps 3 Reserve corps (line through Mézières)	Third and Fourth
8 corps 5 Reserve corps	3 corps 2 Reserve corps (line through Verdun and Metz)	Fifth
3 corps 1 Reserve corps	4 corps 1 Reserve corps (line through Strassburg)	Sixth
nil	2 corps 1 Reserve corps	Seventh

Total 41½   Total 35

Schlieffen detailed 10 divisions for the Eastern front; Moltke, 8.
Moltke, still less Schlieffen, never had the number of corps and divisions which the Schlieffen plan assumed to exist—the latter's plan was
only a *projet*. But, taking the above figures: in Schlieffen's plan the
defensive wing is to the offensive as 4 to 37½ (1 to 9⅜), in Moltke's
8 to 27 (1 to 3⅜); but Schlieffen's with the forces available in 1914,
would have been 4 to 31 (1 to 7¾).

It has been left to Dr. Bredt, a member of the Reichstag and of the
Parliamentary Committee of Enquiry into the loss of the war, to tell
what was the real nature of the plan, how Moltke altered it, and why

he did so.* His work, which shows a wide acquaintance with war literature, purports to contain portions of the Schlieffen plan of which the public had not yet heard, and which fully justify the reproach that Moltke changed it for the worse, much the worse, but not in the way hitherto imagined. Dr. Bredt, however, points out that Ludendorff was head of the Operations Section of the Great General Staff in 1908–9, at the time of the vital alterations, and from what we know of the First Quartermaster's ruthless methods and ignorance of the world, he probably had more to do with the changes than his courtier chief. . . . .

"Graf Schlieffen," says Dr. Bredt, in discussing the plan, "quite realized that an immediate participation of the British on the side of our opponents was to be reckoned with. He did not estimate the value of the British Expeditionary Force very highly, but all the higher the value of the British activity at sea. He insisted in all circumstances on a rapid decision of the war, before the economic consequences of British hostility made themselves felt. For this reason the Franco-British Army must be rapidly and decisively beaten. In the East Graf Schlieffen proposed to remain on the strategic defensive until after the victories in the West. In Alsace-Lorraine the front was to be held with the minimum number of troops, supported by the fortresses of Strassburg and Metz. Should the French succeed in breaking in, so much the better, and it should not cause alarm, for operations there would only absorb the French troops without their serving any useful purpose, and keep them away from the real decisive theater." . . . .

The reasons for strengthening the left wing are given by Dr. Bredt as follows: Moltke could not abandon Alsace, as Schlieffen designed to do, for the Italians might take part on the German side; General Pollio, the Italian Chief of the Staff, until his death in 1914, had assured him they would. As they were to be brought to Alsace, Moltke considered it necessary to hold that province with two corps. If the Italians did not appear, then the question of the transport of the two corps to the right wing would arise. As we know, the French attack towards Mülhausen fatally delayed this. These two corps, plus the two corps sent from France to Russia, would, if added to the right wing, have made it as strong as Schlieffen intended.

It emerges incidentally that the Schlieffen plan was worked out for war on the Western front only; for when drawn up Russia was still very weak as a result of the Manchurian War. It also contemplated

---

* *Die Belgische Neutralität und der Schlieffensche Feldzugsplan* (Belgian Neutrality and the Schlieffen Plan of Campaign), by J. V. Bredt, "Doctor of Theology, Doctor of Law, Doctor of Philosophy, formerly Professor of Jurisprudence in Marburg University, Member of the Reichstag and of the Parliamentary Committee of Enquiry" (Berlin, Stilke, 10 Marks).

additions to the army that did not take place. There was only a general statement that in the case of Russia intervening, ten divisions should be withdrawn from the Western front and sent to the East, without altering the proportion of the two wings.

More important than the changes in technical details was the alteration of the plan politically. In the Schlieffen plan "there was no ultimatum to Belgium, but the German army, without any notification, was first to deploy on the Dutch-Belgian frontier. As the German plan would be divulged by this, it was assumed that the French would take counter-measures. These, according to Schlieffen's views, could only be the occupation of the natural defensive position in the Meuse valley south of Namur; and thus the French would themselves violate Belgian neutrality. Such a plan must have at least been considered by the French, and in 1914 the German General Staff took it for granted that they would advance to the Meuse.* All this presumed that Belgian neutrality would not be broken by Germany first. Such a step Graf Schlieffen desired, if possible, to avoid. He wished to leave sufficient time so that, in one way or another, the German statesmen would be able to evade the reproach of the violation of Belgian neutrality. "That Liége would always be captured sufficiently soon after the entry of the German army into Belgium, to serve as the railway junction for reinforcements and supply, could be accepted."

This was all changed in the deployment plan of the mobilization year 1908–9, by which Liége was to be captured by a *coup de main,* without artillery preparation, during the mobilization. Dr. Bredt quotes from the mobilization instructions of that year:

"The weakness of the garrison and armament offers the prospect of a successful attack in which the infantry, without waiting for the artillery to open fire, pushes through the intervals between the forts, obtains possession of the heights surrounding the town, cuts off the retreat of the garrison, and hinders the destruction of the railway stations, bridges, and tunnels. The greater the surprise by which it is carried out, and therefore the less time the defenders have been allowed to mobilize the garrison and put the fortress in a state of defense, the better will be the prospects of success by this method of attack. Simultaneously the heavy artillery of the field army should go into position so that it is ready to fire on the night of the break-through. If the infantry columns are detected by the forts, the artillery should draw the fire of the defense as much as possible. It should further prove to

---

* In order to give Germany no excuse to make frontier incidents the cause for war, the French in August 1914 cleared all troops out of a 10-km. zone next the Franco-German boundary; so it seems unlikely that they would have done what Schlieffen hoped.

the enemy, should he delay with surrender, that behind the infantry which has penetrated into the town there is an artillery that is capable of breaking the resistance of the forts. Finally, it should, if the *coup de main* fails, carry out the artillery attack."

There was, Dr. Bredt points out, a further reason in favor of the idea of a *coup de main* against Liége. The German deployment as imagined by Schlieffen would stretch as far north as Crefeld; that is, along the Dutch frontier.

"Schlieffen did not consider it out of the question, in view of the then (1905) political situation, as he judged it, that German diplomacy might succeed on the outbreak of war against England in obtaining from the Netherlands Government by an amicable arrangement (*auf gütlichem Wege*) permission for the German army to cross the Dutch province of Limburg (Maastricht, Roermond). By this means the fortress of Liége would be avoided by passing north of it, and could quickly be brought to surrender by threatening it in rear."

Moltke did not believe that Holland would give permission to traverse her territory, and dropped the idea of an advance of the German right wing by this route. On the other hand he feared that Liége could not be taken quickly enough by an accelerated artillery attack to prevent a delay in the general advance of the right wing. It was most important not to give the Belgians time to put the fortress in a state of defense, and in particular to construct defenses in the intervals between the forts and destroy the important railways passing through Liége. It also appeared to him that it was impossible to march an army between Liége and the Dutch frontier. He therefore decided to take Liége by a *coup de main* carried out by troops on the peace establishment without mobilization immediately on outbreak of war.

"Two days and the following night were allowed for the execution of the *coup de main*."*

It is obvious that the immediate attack on Liége from the point of view of international law immensely changed the Schlieffen plan. Dr. Bredt first quibbles that the German Government had no *official* knowledge of this, claiming that "negociations (*Verhandlung*) with the Imperial Chancellor about it did not then take place, because particularly in peace no organic liaison existed for work in common between the Government and the General Staff." He then, however, admits that the Imperial Chancellor and Herr von Jagow, the Foreign Minister, "knew long before the war that an inroad into Belgium was intended and also that international law was deeply touched by this matter." Nevertheless, he quotes the speech of Jagow in the Reichstag on the 29th

* As the 5th of August was the first day and the last forts fell on the 16th, the disappointment of the Germans must have been considerable.

of April, 1913, when, in reply to a Socialist question, he said: "The neutrality of Belgium is established by international treaties, and Germany is determined to hold to these treaties."

189. SCHLIEFFEN'S ESTIMATE OF FRENCH DEFENSES[2]

. . . . It was generally taken for granted that peaceful Germany constantly thought of a marauding expedition to the laughing fields of the Seine and Loire valleys. If the direct way were barred to her, one could still assume that she would seek to go round the unpleasant barrier either through Switzerland or Belgium.

In order to forestall such a blow against her right wing, France closed all the passes of the Jura with fortifications. On her left, Belgium came to her aid. She cut off the great highway of the nations along the Meuse and the Sambre with concrete emplacements and armored turrets, and behind these set up Antwerp as an impregnable bulwark. The Netherlands endeavored, to the best of their ability, to support the efforts of their neighbor in order to protect themselves as well as France from German attacks.

. . . . Austria must form front to the south, Germany to the west. . . . .

190. ON THE ANNIVERSARY OF THE DEATH OF GENERAL FIELD-MARSHAL COUNT SCHLIEFFEN (JANUARY 4TH), BY GENERAL GROENER[3]

In his campaign letters of March 13, 1915, Lord High Admiral von Tirpitz writes: "The Army Command had no proper understanding of England's significance in war, but absolute confidence in the victory formula of the late Count Schlieffen."

It is apparent that the victory formula of Count Schlieffen was not really understood by the writer of the letter; for at that time not only was the old gentleman dead but also the fundamental principle upon which the conduct of the war on two fronts was to be based. The victory formula had been filed away. Even during his lifetime, the imaginative flights of Schlieffen were not always understood; in fact, there were some very clever people who called him a fool and declared that he should be incarcerated, in order that he might not put foolish ideas into the heads of the young people of the country. On the other hand, it was the opinion of the old gentleman that one or the other

[2] [Graf Schlieffen], *"Der Krieg in der Gegenwart,"* in *Deutsche Revue,* January 1909, pp. 22–24.

[3] *Deutsche Revue,* January 1920; official military translation in (German) *Military Information,* 1919–20.

among these youths might be selected at some time to assist in the leadership of the million-membered German Army at a critical juncture; therefore those youths could not begin early enough in attempting to master the problems the solution of which was required for the proper conduct of a war with modern armies of tremendous size.

The old gentleman died on January 4, 1913, not without uttering his last warning as to the manner in which the German Army should be victorious. Fate had never granted him the honor of leading the German Army, although he had received considerably more than one drop of "Samuel's ointment," and felt himself, as a youthful patriarch, able to take charge of the committee which was to take the place of the military commander. Now he was dead, but his spirit remained vividly before us; it was our task to take hold of his spirit in black and white—in essays, studies and memoirs—to be used as time permitted and the need made itself felt. Not much was necessary; for the thoughts of the old gentleman were simple and clear as the most brilliant crystal. The instructions for striking a decisive blow against the French and for bringing about the most speedy and conclusive decision in one operation were blended in one focus: "Strengthen the right wing."

On March 13, 1915, when Lord High Admiral von Tirpitz wrote his letter, the victory formula of the departed Schlieffen no longer had any validity; the operative thought had been lost on the battlefields in the West; the thought, which could justify the absolute confidence about which Tirpitz wrote. The thought which formed the basis of Count Schlieffen's plan was, at the same time, great and yet immeasurably small. "Make the right wing strong,"—in these few words which could not be misconstrued, lay the instruction and the permanent warning. On every page, almost in every line of Count Schlieffen's works, one could read what he desired. It was his constant fear, which did not leave him even on his deathbed, that his guiding principles, the simplicity of which was only surpassed by its boldness, could be forgotten by those he left behind. "By this sign conquer" is his heritage to the General Staff.

It must be left to the critical investigation of sources on the part of the historian to determine why the victory formula which it was hoped to apply in 1914 remained without the hoped-for success.

The kernel of Schlieffen's plan of operations consisted in directing the massed formation of the German Army against the left flank and rear of the French Army in such a manner that the turning of the flank would be attained by means of powerful forces and that the superiority of the German Army would be assured on the decisive battlefields of Northern France, be it on the lower Somme or Seine. The forces of the German right wing would have to be strong enough, not only to strike a decisive blow against the French left flank, but also to make a showing previously against the Belgian Army and a possible English force landed on the Flemish or French coasts, to say nothing of rendering the hostile troops situated in the Belgian or French fortresses innocuous. The road to the decisive field of battle ran parallel to the coast. The task, the fulfillment of which was contingent upon the success of the great and deciding operation, was to throw all available forces in this direction and not to permit them to be occupied elsewhere, in Alsace, in Lorraine, or in the East. It failed because the task of uniting all available forces at the extreme flank was not carried out; on the other hand, the various forces were occupied at places where no decisive outcome could be expected and where it would not have been sought if the instructions of Count Schlieffen had been followed.

It is because Count Schlieffen clearly recognized the significance of England in the case of a war on two fronts, and at so early a stage, that he emphasized again and again the warning: "Make the right wing strong." Only if *his* plan had been actually carried out, only if the High Command had refrained from weakening the right flank in favor of other fronts, for instance, for the protection of German territory without any tactical necessity for such a step, only if this great operative plan for the disposal of troops had been strictly followed, could the right wing have been so strong that we should have been equal not only to every probable situation but even to unexpected contingencies. In the further execution of Schlieffen's plan, the simplicity, consistency and boldness of which are equally admirable, the French Channel coast was to be seized and the German Army to be pushed like a mighty wedge between the French and their reinforcements from England, to break the connections between the island empire and the French mainland—reaching as far as possible along the coast toward the south.

Had the plan succeeded, not only would the French Army have been decisively beaten and the city of Paris taken in a short time, but all of France would have been so overpowered that it could not count upon a reconstruction of the situation by means of aid from the English, since the latter—in so far as it had not already been rendered harmless—would remain possible only to a slight extent by means of the harbors of Southern France. This English aid came in an entirely different form when the German operations came to a halt in process of execution on the German right flank through lack of men, the Channel coast did not fall into the hands of the Germans, and the connections with England were not broken. Thereby we see that all those military possibilities contained in Schlieffen's plans were those from which Lord High Admiral von Tirpitz drew his deductions concerning the significance of England in the war.

Thus the confidence in the victory formula of Schlieffen was surely justified, from the point of view of the Lord High Admiral; the practical execution of the operations in August and September 1914 was quite different. In this case, the victory formula was not applied to the extent and in the manner in which Count Schlieffen had constructed it and bequeathed it to his successors. It is for the historian to investigate the development of the operative scheme which led to our failure on the Marne in 1914. As a result of this failure, the opinion has been expressed that such gigantic strategic enveloping operations, as they were born in the spirit of Count Schlieffen, could not be carried out with large modern armies; in such cases, frontal operations and the application of brute force would have to be resorted to. This is correct. As soon as the front has become stabilized and the wings have arrived at insuperable obstacles—the sea and the Alps in this case—enveloping operations can be undertaken again only when brute force has succeeded in breaking the hostile front, whereby new flanks have been formed. Such operations of penetration are extremely difficult of execution in the application of modern technical weapons and demand premises which as a rule can be brought to accomplishment only by a numerical superiority of men and material. These premises were not encountered on the western theater of operations. We would call attention to the manner in which Count Schlieffen prophetically laid down his decision concerning frontal attacks in this publication (*Deutsche Revue*, January 1909). In *Present-Day Warfare* he wrote as follows: "The Russo-Japanese War has shown that a direct attack upon a hostile front will very frequently succeed in spite of all difficulties. However, even in the most favorable case, the result of such an attack is but slight. To be sure, the enemy is repulsed but soon regains the temporarily lost power of resistance at another point. The campaign is dragging."

As a matter of fact, that is what occurred; the campaign was stretched out over four years after the great decisive operation, which had been evolved in the mind of Count Schlieffen as a gigantic enveloping movement, had not succeeded. The war thereby took on an aspect which did not bring the best characteristics of our army—leadership, and the spirit of attack in a war of movement—fully into prominence, but gave the personal and material superiority in personnel and material of the hostile organization every assistance; above all, it gave this organization time to subject its available masses of men, far superior to ours in number, to military training, and to form them into effective groups, as well as to draw upon the industries of the whole world— quite apart from the international economic power which this alliance had at its disposal. It was practically impossible to shake these international economic foundations so long as Germany did not succeed in overcoming England's dominance on the seas. Our high seas fleet was too weak for this task. In pursuing this train of thought there was from the beginning no doubt that the contest against England's mastery of the sea would remain an insoluble problem for us so long as we did not succeed, in the execution of Schlieffen's bold plan, in defeating the military power of France so completely that French ground could not be considered as a possible field of battle on land with England, whereas, on the French coast we would obtain the only basis of operations from which the contest against England could be carried on. Thereby the U-boat warfare also gained in importance as a weapon for shattering English sea control.

Whatever problems may have come down to us from the past war, they all lead back to that one problem the successful solution of which Count Schlieffen guaranteed in his plan of operations: the quickest, most thorough annihilation of France in the one way possible. The late Count Schlieffen is not to blame for the fact that things turned out differently. Since we did not follow his instructions in 1914, we were driven to the strategy of attrition in spite of the superhuman efforts of our armies.

"A strategy of attrition can not be carried on when billions are required for the support of millions."

"However, such wars are impossible at a time when the existence of the nation is based upon an uninterrupted life of trade and industry, and, when by a quick decision the machinery which has come to a stop must again be put into motion."

We have every reason to remember General Field-Marshal Count Schlieffen on this, the anniversary of his death.

191. IMPORTANT ITEMS OF MILITARY INTELLIGENCE,
JULY 27–AUGUST 2, 1914[4]

27.VII.14. 12:30 P.M.

Military Attaché in Paris reports: 6:00 P.M. in Paris (95618) no loud excitement. In all barracks (4825) complete Sunday rest. Officials (5996) have orders to be on duty. . . . .

28.VII.14

REPORTS UNTIL 10:00 A.M.

M. Attaché Bern: Swiss General Staff reports Russia ordered mobilization of 12 army corps; French 14 Army Corps maneuvers at Lyon stopped, returned to garrisons.

[4] Collection of German Military Documents, Hoover War Library.

M. Attaché Paris: 27. 4:00 P.M. so far only higher officers recalled from leave. No reports about war preparations received. In Paris barracks [Information Center] all quiet.

N. St. Saarbrücken: Until 27. 4:00 P.M. no signs of tension in intercourse between borders at Avricourt.

N. St. Karlsruhe: Border patrol, customs officials, two agents Ka 1. and 14 report unanimously that in France no mobilization preparations.

N. St. Coblenz: Agent C. 16 reports: right East of Longwy all French conscripts have been listed according to statement of a Luxemburg railroad official. A confidential man confirms prohibition of leaves of absence on East French border. No information that mobilization preparations are in progress in Longwy.

N. St. Saarbrücken: Agent S. 27, found on 26.–27. intercourse at border and Nancy surprisingly quiet. No signs of tension. No Sunday leave of absence after 9:00 P.M.——

Garrison Lunéville ready to march since 27. Officers recalled from leave. Field art. 39 from Mailly already 27. returned to Toul. Railroad communication normal; only railroad bridges at Lunéville militarily guarded at night.

Gendarme Vic reports that troops at Nancy and Lunéville not allowed any more to leave barracks.

N. St. Metz: Traveler R. reports: railroad depot at Pony usually entirely full, empty on 27.; the same at Pont-á-Mousson. Military command to have attached rolling stock of the East Railroad. Telegraph bureaus occupied by officers. Canal tunnel between Commercy and Toul guarded by soldiers. In Toul surprising military life. Soldiers in new uniforms, apparently war equipment; red breeches, short blue jacket, high boots, epaulettes, side arms. Mood of the people earnest and downcast. No war enthusiasm.

Gendarme Rhein reports 27. Test-mobilization of Longwy garrison at 4:00 A.M.; officers carry guns. Field equipment packed.

Agent M. 94 reports: 16 *chasseur* regiment, which was supposed to be in the camp of Châlons, arrival in full numbers in Conflans, 27. evening. Reservists who were to have been called on 28, arrived in Conflans the 27. 28 locomotives with many freight cars left Conflans for Châlons. At depot of Conflans many locomotives under steam.

(Z., O.Q.I., IV, 3)

Postscript

Agent 17 Paris: In Council of Ministers 25.VII evening, a telegram from Viviani communicated, in which ordered to take some precautionary measures before his return, or to instruct French foreign representatives, with whom, moreover, Viviani had placed himself in communication from Stockholm.

The Ministers meanwhile came to agreement to cancel for the time being all leaves of higher officials and officers, to order the Prefects of Departments not to leave their posts, the absent ones to be recalled at once and to take measures toward the immediate recall of furloughed persons. Nearly all bearers of great responsibilities, especially the Ministers and'the leaders of the great parliamentary parties, with exception of the Nationalists, are for the localization of the conflict, and wait with anxious tension for the Russian *môt d'ordre*.

28.VII.14

REPORTS UNTIL 5:30 P.M.

M. Attaché Paris: According to *Figaro* field art. XX. A. C., 42. Infantry Division have been sent back from training grounds to garrisons, ramps at depot detached, transport material made ready. Newspapers however publish little, probably under instruction. No reservists called in Paris. Unrest growing.

N. St. Metz (by letter of 27. 10:00 P.M.): Musicians of a *chasseur* battalion (No. 18 from Stenay), who played at a gymnastic fête in Briey, were recalled to garrison. Trucks for troop transportation supposed to be at Audun, Longuyon, and Longwy. Troops of the reserve of the territorial army who are assigned for border protection are in possession of uniforms (?), and are to receive arms at gendarmery stations. French East Railroad has order to detain cars and not to load; to hurry with repairs.

(The following four messages are from border Gendarmes):

Agent 94 reports that in Conflans there is fear of a sudden attack. At depot there are three cars with sharp munition under guard. Arriving chasseurs supposed to have told that no troops remained in the camp of Châlons on the 27.

A reliable man from Luxemburg tells that Verdun has hardly any food supplies, since everything was sent to Morocco; that on the 26. the French railroad officials had lost their heads.

Agent A. from Nancy reports that the 8th field artillery regiment on return from Mailly interrupted its march in St. Dizier, took the train, and arrived in Nancy the 26. The officers of the *centre d'aviation* on Sunday had to report at what localities they could be reached.

(The line to the fortress Kaiserin was interrupted in the afternoon of the 27., through outside influence it is suspected.)

The journey of confidential man B. resulted: rolling stock is being shipped back, art buildings are being guarded, mood depressed.

N. St. Saarbrücken: Report from Avricourt: railroad crossings at Embermenil, Nancy occupied by cavalry. The same from Chambrey; railroad crossings from Plum west of Chateau-Salins to Pont-á-Mousson and Toul garrisoned with troops. Everyone on furlough wired to return to their regiments. 40 German railroad employees from Lunéville removed to Germany the 28.7.

N. St. Strassburg: Agent Str. 28 confirms the return of garrisons of Nancy, Toul, and St. Nicolas from Mailly. Military guarding of all railroad bridges at Nancy by day and night. Recalling of all on furlough. No reservists called.

Str. 136 reports upon rumor about recall of all on furlough at St. Dié; rumor about calling in reserves not confirmed.

Central Police Station, Strassburg: Banks in Nancy closed.

N. St. Metz: Trustworthy man reports: test mobilization at Longwy went off smoothly, everything ready. Prevailing opinion among population but especially among officers, very depressed. Everyone believes in a surprise attack by the Prussians.

Agent M. 120 confirms, according to a statement of chief of depot at Pompey, the returning of all box-car materials, whether empty or not, to Verdun.

A traveler through Noveant claims to have seen in Toul on the night of 27.–28. trains with field-artillery material.

(Z., O.Q.I., IV^k, 1., 3)

III B   29.VII.14

REPORTS UNTIL 10:00 A.M.

Mil. Attaché Paris: Lieutenant-Colonel Dupont told the Span. Mil. Attaché, that he has exact information about German war preparations, which were important only at Metz, not nearly as advanced as the French. He could not understand, why Russia did not strike the blow. Travelling German officers report transports of non-mobile troops along Havre-Paris, especially at Rouen; these bridges everywhere guarded; empty trains, vehicle transports in different directions. Versailles field vehicles in the yards, Paris ostensibly quiet. Newspapers report railroad transports at Belfort. 11:00 P.M. freight transports entirely discontinued. Impossible to obtain gold. In afternoon field vehicles also in Paris barracks. Newspapers report, trains for transports at all Paris depots; only 40,000 men remain in Morocco. From Herbesthal, through confidential man who was in Paris: Telephone Paris—Germany closed since 12.00 noon, reserved for mil. purposes. Banque de France pays at most 100 francs gold. Firms transfer money to Belgium. Newspapers report concentration VII. A.C., that troops from Belfort being sent to positions. Going through Paris—Herbesthal no preparations noticed. Active officers, also those on leave recalled to colors. No reserves called.

N. St. Metz: Verdun: thereto intercourse slight, in V. livelier. One tractable, two globe balloons filled. Increased troop transport to Verdun and Châlons and M. St. Menehould one comp. chasseurs transferred, with general and higher officers. (Report of traveler from Châlons and M.)

Gendarme Chambrey reports calling of French reserve officers.

Agent 94. reports that recall of all officers on leave ordered through secret *chiffre*-ministerial-order.

M. 94. Garrison Conflans lies in border protection between Batilly and Mars-la-Tour. I.-162 from Verdun was expected 9 evening at Jeandleize west of Conflans. Gendarmes Briey, Conflans with war equipment. Railroad crossings Verdun, Conflans, Longwy guarded nights too by civilians. Great excitement Joeuf, Conflans.

M. 40: The reserves, to be called in August, already 29. called to Verdun. French border places great agitation.

M. 96: Customs officials in France have not yet orders for closing measures.

M. St. Saarbrücken: Avricourt reports: on 25. 80 carloads with munitions were sent to Fort Manonviller. Owners of horses at Igney have received troop designations, which are to collect the horses. Banks at Nancy closed. Border officials not increased, intercourse as usual.

Traveler (very skilled): Returning from Nancy no border patrol noticed. Nowhere seen mobilization placards. Troops Nancy, Essey, St. Nicolas, Lunéville war uniforms. Many empty vehicles at depots, especially Jarville, Blainville.

42. division reports 28. early French border practice at Igney and Blâmont, as well as statement of unknown railroad employee, that French division gathered 28. at Baccarat, border patrol XX. A.C. marched out. (Being verified.)

S. 47. (traveled Vitry-Troyes-Châlons sur M.) : 27. evening, F.A. 8., Jägers 1, pioneer batl. especial trains Mailly-East. More than 20 empty trains 27. to 28. from Nancy via Châlons to Paris. Troops Vitry, Châlons, Nancy consigned. In Troyes 5 trains for back transport; F.A. 60 from Mailly equipped. Railroad bridges Arois. & Aube between Bar-le-Duc and Vitry, St. Nazaire, Pt.-á-Mousson militarily guarded. In Châlons about 25, in Toul 8 locomotives under steam. West of Toul no empty material. Prevailing opinion quiet.

St. 31. reports Nancy war munition and war equipment distributed. J.R. 26.–28. at night railroad protection practice, returned to Nancy. Pagny no border protection. Troops consigned, horse levy prepared. Since last week practice res. rgts. 17 days at fixed time.

III B Nr.   29.VII.14

Reports—West until 3 in the Afternoon

N. St. Munster: On German Belgian border no railroad patrol. Optic telegraph station on church tower at Henri-la-Chapelle (at Herbesthal).

Through travelers at Herbesthal report about the accumulation of cars with military inscriptions at the larger French railroad depots.

Belgian morning papers announce the calling of classes 1910, 1911, 1912, to bring army up to 100,000 (confirmed by Wolff representative, Brussels).

N. St. Coblenz: Traveling man reports on 28., in Longwy no remarkable preparations for mobilization.

Reliable confidential men report, 29. forenoon entire garrison of Liége kept in barracks and forts without leave of absence. Forts are to be supplied with munition. At all bridges in Liége mine chambers are being busily constructed. At border of Herbesthal increased military police posts.

N. St. Saarbrücken: 7 o'clock morning reports available at district director of Chateau-Salins do *not* confirm that border is militarily occupied. In border places are posted placards calling attention to seriousness of the situation and warning for war preparedness.

S. 38. reports: In Lunéville and Nancy all troops in warlike manner with munition in barracks. Patrols going to border. Border patrol is *not. juy. 2* for ten days strengthened with training troops; fort Manonviller strengthened by 1 company and 120 infantry artillerists. Thither for 3 days munition supplies. On forts Guelle, Anance, Dom Basle is being ceaselessly worked.

N. St. Karlsruhe: Boundary Police Commissioner Altmünsterol reports: a train with new artillery went in night of 28.–29. from Châlons S.M. to Nancy. Customs inspector Upper Alsace reports: automobile closures at the border militarily occupied.

Central Police Station Strassburg: (upon inquiry) freight cars so far were not retained in France.

N. St. Saarbrücken: At Chambrey told French fliers sighted. At Neunkirchen 29.7. one landed, being detained.

Opposite district Chateau-Salins mobilization (?) of French border *officials* confirmed.

Central Police Station Strassburg: Written report from Altmünsterol: Garrison Belfort complete before Sunday, 26., no furloughs. The trains from France arrived the 26. more punctually than ever before. A special commissioner from Belfort was called by telegram to Paris 25., returned Sunday. Declarations of the border population: it favors war on the other side of the border: the Belfort narrow-gauge railroad between the forts transports war materials day and night.

From reliable people in Brussels and Antwerp: newspapers report, that troop transports begin depot *Aneonis*.

Firm Vienna-Antwerp sold 25.7. 20,000 tons of wheat to Austria.

Prevailing opinion in Belgium 27. more confiding, but pronounced anti-German.

In Belgium they talk about English intention eventually to land troops in Belgium, allegedly west of Ostend.

N. St. Strassburg: Str. 4. reports from Beauvais: Furloughed 27. back, since 20. only supply work, repairing of vehicles, preparations for their loading. No calling of reserves. Railroad management announced 28.7., that mobilization order "dans les chemins de fers" not given and not impending.

Str. 276. reports from Nancy the occupying of bridges and unloading ramps, artil. munition wagons stand ready loaded. Nancy's powerhouse guarded by soldiers. Mil. ramp Javille vacated, occupied by military. Chief of depot told to take freight cars out of traffic.

N. St. Metz: Border police station Novéant reports, since 28.–29. 2:00 A.M. French customs officials mobilized, customs houses closed.

N. St. Saarbrücken: French border officials according to message gendarme—in Lagarde mobil. Navigation on Rhine-Marne Canal to France discontinued.

Report of Railroad division: Paris' closing of the Dresden Bank: large number of the employed recruits, their automobiles ordered for inspection on 29. Traffic on state railroads restricted. Telegraph and telephone communication still intact. Complete panic on Paris Exchange, 28.7.

III B   29.7.14. 5:00 P.M.
REPORTS FROM "17"

By letter from 27.VIII.: The French Foreign Office has reports since 26.7., which supposedly show, that since 3 weeks ago Austria has firmly decided upon the settlement, in complete understanding with Germany; otherwise the submissive Serbian note should have given material for discussion. This conception originates from St. Petersburg.

The procedure of the Triple Alliance is regarded as most clearsighted and clever; motive and time could not have been better selected. Germany accordingly does not fear war on 2 fronts, whereas in France because of military unpreparedness the maintenance of peace *now* is regarded as imperative to existence for various reasons. The Government fears, Germany regards the moment as exceptionally favorable, to settle thoroughly with France and exerts itself to keep Russia from serious intervention.

Experts in the meantime generally believe that the Russians probably won't shut their big mouth, but also for the time being, won't march.

The cancelling of furloughs and recalling of prefects and higher officers on 26. extended also to Algiers-Tunis. Military preparations not existing. It is avoided, even to carry out normal sending of materials, the size of which could be construed as preparation for mobilization. Thus the shipment of siege materials out of Reims, Langres, and Toul is shifted to the great training camp in Épinal.

The bearers of the responsibility are doubtful and dejected, even Delcassé—about whose sending to London there is talk—expresses with external calmness various apprehensions.

(Z., O.Q.I., IV^k, 3)

III B   31.7.14
REPORTS—WEST UNTIL 4:00 P.M.

From Antwerp: (Reliable confidential man) Belgium called 3 more classes of reserves. Mobilization ordered for Meuse ports. Troop transports began railroad Charleville-Givet.

From Ostend: (Adm. Staff, Confidential man, 29.7.) In Zeebrugge numerous Belgian military and many railroad cars.

Mil. Attaché Paris: 31.7., 9:30 A.M.: 29. evening and today quiet in Paris. Report Capt. Janensch and impressions in Paris confirm yesterday's report that in French military measures temporary termination and no increase. Local safeguarding of art buildings varied extensively according to officials, in and around Paris heavy, because of feared sabotage. Reserves not called. Cuirassiers regiment in barracks. Freight transport at least partly in action. Answer given by Viviani 29. afternoon appears as a whole correct. Expressions of Lieutenant-Colonel Dupont of 28. appear to be boastful.

(Z., O.Q.I., 3)

III B West   A.2.8.14

REPORTS UNTIL 2 O'CLOCK AFTERNOON

Wolff's Dept. Bureau hears from railroad management Nürnberg, that along the distances Nürnberg-Kitzingen and Nürnberg-Ansbach fliers threw bombs, without causing damages.

Foreign Office learns from Paris dispatch via Sofia from 1.8 evening, that after a false border offense through a French patrol the French outposts took their positions everywhere at least 10 km. from the border.

N. St. Münster: Telegram from Essen reports that the artillery commands in Krupp's works did not see anything of the airplanes as reported at night.

N. St. Coblenz: Airship seen tonight at Kerben-Mayen also airplanes at Elsenborn, Kall i. Eiffel, Hohenbudberg at Crefeld, everything with reflectors. Firing followed at Elsenborn and Hohenbudberg. Verification as to whether they were enemy aeroplanes until now not received.

Agent reports that according to travelers yesterday 6 o'clock evening mobilization announced in France.

N. St. Strassburg Els: 31.7. evening. Garrisons Grenoble and Chambéry not yet alarmed. Lyon, Grenoble, and Chambéry no reserves called. At least 2 artillery transports to East border 31.7. passed Chambéry.

Traveler reports from Turin: mobilization garrison Modena 2:00 A.M. 31. for 1.8. ordered. Complete mob. until 1.8. 10:00 A.M. not yet ordered.

(A N Z.3)

192. ORDER FOR CALLING UP THE LANDSTURM[5]

We, Wilhelm, by the Grace of God German Emperor, King of Prussia, etc., in accordance with Article II, Paragraph 25 of the Law concerning certain alterations in the duty of bearing arms of February 11, 1888, order in the name of the Government as follows: In the 1st, 2d, 5th, 6th, 8th, 9th, 10th, 14th, 15th, 16th, 17th, 18th, 20th, and 21st Army Corps Districts, the General Officers concerned will—upon further instruction—call up the Landsturm. This Order comes

---

[5] *Deutscher Reichsanzeiger und Königlich Preussischer Staatsanzeiger,* August 1, 1914, special edition.

into force from the date of publication. As Witness our signature and seal.

WILHELM I. R.

von Bethmann-Hollweg

Done at the Castle, Berlin, August 1, 1914

193. THE REVIVAL OF THE ORDER OF THE IRON CROSS, AUGUST 5, 1914[6]

We, Wilhelm, by the Grace of God King of Prussia, etc., having regard to the serious situation of our dear Fatherland brought about by the war which has been forced upon us, and in thankful remembrance of the deeds of our forebears in the great years of the War for Freedom, the War for the Unification of Germany, decree that this honorable Order of the Iron Cross revived by our revered grandfather shall be again reconstituted. All members of the Army, Navy, or Landsturm, without regard to their rank, members of Volunteer Aid Detachments, and all other persons who serve with the Army or Navy in any official capacity or who are employed in the administration thereof, shall be eligible for it, whether they belong to the German fighting organization, or to those of Germany's allies, as a reward for good service done, whether in the field or at home.

In accordance herewith we order as follows:

1. The revived decoration of the Iron Cross shall now, as formerly, consist of two grades and a Gold Cross. The Cross and riband shall remain unchanged, except that on the face of the Cross the date 1914 shall be placed below the W with the crown.

2. The Cross of the Second Class shall be suspended from a buttonhole by a black riband bordered with white for those who receive it for service on the field; for those who obtain it for service at home, the riband shall be white with a black border. The Cross of the First Class will be worn on the left breast, the Grand Cross suspended round the neck.

3. The First Class can be conferred only on those who are already in possession of the Second Class, and will be worn near it.

4. The bestowing of the Gold Cross is not conditioned by previous winning of the First and Second Class. It will be conferred only on the winner of a decisive battle in which the enemy has been forced to abandon his position, or on the commander of an independent army or fleet which has obtained an important success, or on the commander of an important fortress which has made a long resistance.

---

[6] *Norddeutsche Allgemeine Zeitung,* August 6, 1914, second edition, p. 1.

5. All the advantages given to the holders of the Good Service Badge, both First and Second Class, are to be enjoyed by holders of the First and Second Class of the Iron Cross, with reservation of the question of an allowance until the regulations for the same have been made.

Given under our hand and the Royal Seal.

WILHELM

von Bethmann-Hollweg, von Tirpitz, Delbrück, Beseler, von Breitenbach, Sydow, von Trott zu Solz, Freiherr von Schorlemer, Lentze, von Falkenhayn, von Loebell, Kühn, von Jagow

BERLIN, August 5, 1914

194. PROCLAMATION OF KAISER WILHELM II, AUGUST 6, 1914[7]

After forty-three years of peace, I call upon all Germans capable of bearing arms. We have to defend our most sacred possessions, our Fatherland and our hearths, against wicked attack. Enemies on all sides of us! That is the feature of the situation. A hard fight, great sacrifices, face us. I am confident that the old warlike spirit still lives in the German people—that mighty warlike spirit which attacks the enemy wherever it finds him, regardless of the cost, which already in the past has been the dread and terror of our enemies.

German soldiers! I have confidence in you. The ardent and indomitable will to conquer lives in each and all of you. Every one of you knows how, if need be, to die as a hero. Remember our great and glorious past! Remember that you are Germans! God help us!

WILHELM

BERLIN, the Palace, 6th August 1914

195. THE KAISER'S SPEECH TO THE GUARDS AT POTSDAM[8]

Former generations as well as all those who are standing here today, have hitherto often seen the soldiers of the First Guard Regiment and My Guards at this place. Then it was the oath of allegiance which we swore before God that brought us here together. Today all have gathered to pray for the victory of our weapons, for now it depends upon proving that oath to the last drop of blood. The sword, which for decades I left in the scabbard, shall decide. I expect of My First Guard Regiment on Foot and My Guards that they will add a new leaf of fame to their glorious history. Today's celebration finds us

[7] *Reichsanzeiger,* August 6, 1914.

[8] *Neue Preussische Zeitung,* August 19, 1914, II, 1.

confident in the highest God and remembering the glorious days of Leuthen, Chlum, and St. Privat. Our old fame is an appeal to the German people and its sword. And the whole German people to the last man has grasped the sword. And so I draw the sword which with God's help I have kept for decades in the scabbard. [*Hereupon the Kaiser drew his sword from the scabbard and held it high above his head.*] The sword is drawn, which without victory and without honor I cannot sheathe again. And all of you shall and will see to it that only in honor is it returned to the scabbard. You are my guaranty that I can dictate peace to my enemies. Up and at the foes, and down with the enemies of Brandenburg! Three cheers for our army!

196. THE KAISER'S PROCLAMATION OF AUGUST 22, 1914[9]

The mobilization and the mustering of the army on the frontiers have been accomplished. The German railways have carried out this mighty movement of transportation with unexampled punctuality and security. My thoughts go out first of all in thankfulness to the men whose silent work since the war of 1870–71 has created an organization which has now so splendidly stood this great test. But to all those who, answering to my call, have worked together to hurl the German nation in arms along the iron roads against the enemy, and in particular to the officers commanding the lines and to the railway authorities as well as to the German railway administration, from the highest officials to the humblest workmen, I express my Imperial thanks for their loyal devotion and fulfillment of duty. What has been already accomplished affords me the fullest assurance that in the further course of the great fight for the future of the German nation the railways will prove themselves equal to every demand which the leaders of the army may make upon them.

WILHELM I. R.

GREAT HEADQUARTERS, 22 August 1914 .

197. THE OFFICIAL REPORT OF DEFEAT AT THE MARNE[10]

BERLIN, Sept. 10. (W.T.B.) The German Army divisions, which in pursuing the enemy advanced to and across the Marne to the east of Paris, have been heavily attacked between Paris, Meaux, and Mont-

[9] *Norddeutsche Allgemeine Zeitung,* August 24, 1914, p. 1.

[10] Official War Dispatches, according to the Wolff Telegraphic Bureau, I, 85. Professor Kircheisen published, in January 1916, the first accurate account of the Battle of the Marne in the anonymous pamphlet, *Die Schlachten an der Marne* (Berlin, E. S. Mittler und Sohn). The pamphlet was promptly suppressed.

mirail. In two days' heavy fighting they have checked the enemy and advanced themselves. Their wing was taken back, when it was reported that strong enemy columns were advancing. The enemy did not follow anywhere.

Until now 50 guns and some thousands of prisoners have been captured as spoils of these fights.

The army divisions, which are fighting to the west of Verdun, are engaged in continuous battle. The situation in Lorraine and the Vosges is unchanged.

The battle in East Prussia has been resumed.

QUARTERMASTER-GENERAL V. STEIN

198. MEMORANDUM OF THE CHIEF OF THE GENERAL STAFF OF THE FIELD ARMY, NO. 2229[11]

May 24, 1917

Colonel Hentsch, then Lieutenant-Colonel and head of a section on the staff of the Chief of the General Staff of the Field Army, on the 8th of September 1914 at Great Headquarters received verbal instructions from the Chief of the General Staff of the Field Army (Generaloberst von Moltke), to motor to the Fifth, Fourth, Third, Second, and First Armies and bring back a clear idea of the situation. In case rearward movements had already been undertaken on the right wing, he was instructed so to direct them that the gap between the First and and Second Armies would again be closed, the First Army moving, if possible, in the direction of Soissons.

Lieutenant-Colonel Hentsch was therefore authorized, in the specified circumstances, to give binding instructions in the name of the Supreme Command.

He motored on the 8th of September 1914 to the Headquarters of the Fifth, Fourth, and Third Armies, and spent the night of the 8th-9th of September at Second Army Headquarters. The commander of the Second Army made independently his decision to retire behind the Marne early on the 9th of September.

Lieutenant-Colonel Hentsch agreed with this conclusion and motored on to the First Army. There, after discussion of the situation with the Chief of the Staff on the afternoon of the 9th of September, he gave the order for the retreat in the name of the Supreme Command, quoting the powers conferred on him. He was justified in this, for the case

[11] Quoted in Major-General a. D. Baumgarten-Crusius, "Die Mitwirkung des Oberstleutnants Hentsch von der O.H.L. biem Rückzugsbefehl in der Marneschlacht 1914," in *Militär-Wochenblatt*, No. 12, September 18, 1920, p. 257.

provided for in his instructions—the commencement of rearward movements—had arisen.

Whether the decision of the Second Army Headquarters and the order of Lieutenant-Colonel Hentsch to the First Army Headquarters to retreat were actually necessary from the situation must be decided by historical research in future years.

Colonel Hentsch incurs no personal reproach that he went beyond what he was entitled to do. He acted solely in accordance with the instructions given to him by the then Chief of the General Staff of the Field Army.

I request that this decision may be circulated down to division staffs.

By order: LUDENDORFF

199. THE KAISER'S PROCLAMATION TO THE ARMY AND NAVY, DECEMBER 31, 1914[12]

After five long months of severe and fierce struggling we enter upon a new year.

Brilliant victories have been gained, great successes have been won. Almost everywhere the German armies stand on enemy soil. Repeated attempts by the enemy to overrun German soil with his massed armies have been frustrated.

My ships have covered themselves with glory on every sea; their crews have proved that they not only can fight victoriously but that they know how to die heroically when crushed by superior force.

Behind the army and the fleet the German nation stands in unparalleled unity prepared to give up its best for the holy homely hearth that we are defending against a wicked attack.

Much has happened in the old year; but even now the enemy is not brought down; fresh hosts hurl themselves continuously against our armies and those of our faithful allies.

But their number do not frighten us. Though the times are serious and the task before us difficult, we can look into the future with full confidence.

Next to God's wise guidance I rely on the incomparable bravery of the army and navy and know I have the entire German nation with me.

Let us therefore go forth toward the new year undismayed to fresh deeds and fresh victories for the beloved Fatherland.

WILHELM I. R.

---

[12] *Norddeutsche Allgemeine Zeitung*, January 1, 1915, II, 1.

200. BARON BURIAN TO PRINCE HOHENLOHE, JUNE 21, 1915[13]

VIENNA, June 21, 1915

Telegram in cipher to Prince Hohenlohe
Berlin—513

(In regard to Telegram 278. Strictly confidential)

The agitation of the Chancellor I sincerely regret; however, it is incomprehensible to me.

Upon his wish and with my understanding Count Tisza went to Berlin without even an allusion as to the reason for the call. Naturally he presupposed only the necessity of a discussion and could not expect a merited negotiation about foreign affairs. The meeting that took place, therefore, had only an informational character. Count Tisza, too, regarded it only as such. Accordingly he reported to me his exchange of opinion with Herr Bethmann, which, as far as I am concerned, could only have the quality of a proposition, but to which, of course, the Hungarian Premier had taken an attitude, in so far as it concerned internal political affairs of Hungary.

From the standpoint of my office and on account of my responsibility I had to study carefully the incisive propositions of the Imperial Chancellor and when in so doing I was not in the position—unfortunately—to approve of them without further concern; so that is due not to an underestimate of the question of munitions, but to my justified though naturally different conception regarding the problem of compensation raised thereby. This surely cannot offend the Imperial Chancellor.

The practical justification of my position, as well as of my counterproposal, is contained in the instructions sent to Your Honor this evening.

I beg you to enlighten the Imperial Chancellor in the sense of the above and to calm him.

BURIAN

201. GENERAL VON FALKENHAYN'S ESTIMATE OF THE RUSSIAN ARMY, JUNE 25, 1915[14]

PLESS, 25th of June, 1915

Chief of the General Staff of the Field Army . . . .

In the report concerning the internal conditions in Russia which Your Excellency [the Chief of the Representative General Staff of

[13] Collection of Austrian Documents, Hoover War Library.
[14] Collection of German Military Documents, Hoover War Library.

the Army, Berlin] sent to me with your letter of the 19th instant, there is among other things a reference to the low morale which dominates the Russian Army. Similar descriptions are often received by me here. Nevertheless I believe that I must warn against them so that our people will not accept the view that the Russian Army is already an outworn instrument in the hands of its leaders. A very important number of the Russian regiments have fought remarkably well in the last battles. Where this was not the case with certain troop units it was mostly due to the fact that they lacked arms, equipment, and munitions.

The power of resistance of the Russian Army in its entirety is not yet by any means fully broken.

(*Signed*) v. FALKENHAYN

202. DISMISSAL OF GENERAL VON FALKENHAYN, AUGUST 29, 1916[15]

GREAT HEADQUARTERS
August 29, 1916

To the General of the Infantry, v. Falkenhayn, Chief of the General Staff of the Field Army

MY DEAR GENERAL V. FALKENHAYN: In not wishing to oppose your request for dismissal from your present position, I take the opportunity to thank you with all my heart for the devotion and dutifulness with which for two years you managed your difficult and responsible post. What you especially have done for the Army and the Fatherland in vigorous and farsighted work and never-tiring creative impulse will not be forgotten. The full appreciation of your services obtained in the war at the head of the General Staff, however, will have to be left for a later time. To me personally you have been a true, unselfish counsellor. In gratitude for that my best wishes accompany you for your future and I bestow upon you the cross and star of the Commander of the Knights of the Royal Order of Hohenzollern.

You draw your present salary out of the budget for officers in special position until I have made a decision about using you elsewhere.

(*Signed*) WILHELM R.

[15] *Norddeutsche Allgemeine Zeitung*, August 31, 1916, II, 1.

203. APPOINTMENT OF HINDENBURG AS CHIEF OF THE GENERAL STAFF[16]

To the Field-Marshal General v. Beneckendorf and v. Hindenburg

I appoint you as Chief of the General Staff of the Field Army and am convinced that I could not place that position in better hands. I expect with confidence that you will render my Army and the Fatherland the best of services in this position. Again I make use of the opportunity to express my heartiest thanks to the victorious defender of our East front for everything that he has done for the Fatherland during the two years of the war.

(*Signed*) WILHELM R.

GREAT HEADQUARTERS, August 29, 1916

204. APPOINTMENT OF LUDENDORFF AS FIRST QUARTER-MASTER-GENERAL, AUGUST 29, 1916[17]

To Lieutenant-General Ludendorff

By promoting you to General of Infantry I appoint you as First Quartermaster-General with the pay of that of a commanding general and on this occasion express my warm thanks for the excellent services you have rendered me and the army during two years of war.

(*Signed*) WILHELM R.

GREAT HEADQUARTERS, August 29, 1916

205. THE IMPERIAL ADDRESS TO THE TROOPS AT MÜLHAUSEN, DECEMBER 13, 1916[18]

MÜLHAUSEN, December 13

In Mülhausen on December 13 the Kaiser reviewed in the presence of the Crown Prince the troops of General v. Gündell. At the end of the review the Kaiser spoke to the troops; the content of his speech, as reported by Dr. Wegener, was as follows:

At first, there were beautiful words of gratitude and joy for the valiant troops, stationed here in Alsace as outposts, troops which with

---

[16] *Norddeutsche Allgemeine Zeitung,* August 31, 1916, II, 1.

[17] *Ibid.*

[18] *Kölnische Zeitung,* December 15, 1916, morning edition, p. 1.

their blood had so often defended this country against the French invader who even in peace time had attempted to shatter the loyalty of its inhabitants. Here, too, as in other places of the Western front, the battalions had drawn an iron wall around the Fatherland; for this perseverance, bravery, and self-sacrifice, he expressed his Imperial thanks as well as those of the entire Fatherland to the troops in the Vosges. This holding on in the West had also been largely responsible for making it possible to strike those destructive blows in the East. The Kaiser then expressed his satisfaction for having been able to meet some of these troops on many different occasions previously and for having always been able to praise them with the same satisfaction. Thus he was particularly pleased to meet here again a Pomeranian Regiment to which he had addressed words of thanks last spring and which in the meantime had reaped new glories and shown the enemy "what Pomeranian wedges mean." Then he spoke with words of wrathful contempt of those people in the East who had thought they could stick a dagger in the back of our ally. The judgment of God had therefore fallen on them in the campaign which had been conducted according to the brilliant plans of Field-Marshal von Hindenburg. The Emperor continued: "The Old God of Battles directed. We were his instruments and were proud of it. . . . . Confident that we are completely the victors," the Kaiser continued, "he had yesterday made a proposal to the enemy to discuss with him the question of further war or peace. What would come of it, he did not yet know. But it now was their responsibility whether or not the struggle was to continue. If the enemy still thinks he has not had enough, then I know you will——" Here the Kaiser ended with a military gesture, which produced fierce smiles on the faces of all his men. . . . . In the following meeting with the officers he emphasized the extraordinary importance of formal discipline and drilling, which had proved their value particularly in this war. It had been shown that the personal courage and spiritual fortitude of young people, who were less used to this military training, were less equal to the terrible requirements of the terrific bombardment, than those of a troop trained in strict military discipline. In great detail the Kaiser then talked about the Rumanian offensive, its strategic importance, the economic spoils of the victory, etc. With greater length he dwelt upon the events accompanying the surrender of Bucharest according to the report made to him by Major Lange. He talked about how our troops had been received by the inhabitants of the capital with shouts of welcome and bouquets of flowers. . . . . He also spoke of the irony of fate which had permitted the grain purchased by the English to fall into German hands. "The English paid for it, and we eat it. And that they call a war of starvation."

206. KAISER WILHELM II TO POPE BENEDICT XV, DECEMBER 7, 1916[19]

GREAT HEADQUARTERS . . . .

His Eminence, Cardinal Hartmann, has presented a communication of October 6 from Your Holiness to me, in which Your Holiness has the kindness to express your warm interest in the preservation of the Reims Cathedral and at the same time to suggest the drawing up of an agreement with the French Government which would render it possible to carry out the repairs to the church, which have become urgently necessary for its protection against the roughness of the weather. I beg Your Holiness to be assured that I share most earnestly your interest in the cathedral and that your suggestion meets with my full and sincere appreciation. I have always regretted that my endeavors to preserve the venerable places of worship and monuments of art which I regard as the common property of mankind have not always been crowned with success and that unfortunate circumstances have not allowed this wish to be realized. I have above all regretted that the Cathedral of Reims, one of the most beautiful sanctuaries which Christendom possesses, has been so involved through the military measures adopted by our enemy. May Your Holiness be convinced that the fulfillment of the noble and magnanimous intentions which have caused Your Holiness to make the above suggestions would give me deep satisfaction. Acting in this spirit, I have issued the necessary instructions that the suggestion of Your Holiness be examined with greatest possible good will. There are reasons of a military nature, however, which place certain limits upon the consideration which we are only too ready to take. But I hope that the suggestions contained in the supplement, which aim at a satisfactory solution to the question, will be considered a basis for the agreement with the French Government for the attainment of which Your Holiness has so kindly offered to intercede.

I take advantage of this opportunity to express again to Your Holiness my feelings, feelings of highest esteem and sincerest friendship.

WILHELM I. R.

The German Government declares itself ready to offer assurance for the undisturbed carrying out of the repairs to the Cathedral of Reims which are desired by His Holiness the Pope. Nevertheless a formal binding declaration is dependent upon the acceptance of the following conditions, demanded by military considerations. . . . .

[19] Germany, Paris Peace Conference Delegation Propaganda, Paul Clemen, *Protection of Art during War*, p. 49.

207. HINDENBURG'S SECRET MEMORANDUM ON THE RECENT FIGHTING AT VERDUN, DECEMBER 25, 1916[20]

Chief of the General Staff
    of the Field Army   GENERAL HEADQUARTERS
    II/Ia. No. 42728 Op.   25th December, 1916

(Secret. T. 40. Not to be taken into the trenches)

EXPERIENCE OF THE RECENT FIGHTING AT VERDUN

The serious and regrettable reverses sustained at Verdun during October and December have led me to issue the following orders:

1. *Construction of Defenses.* The principles laid down in the textbook, "Construction of Defenses" (*Stellungsbau*), have proved sound. Single *lines of trenches* do not suffice. *A fortified zone must be constructed, organized in depth,* allowing of a stubborn defense of an area even after the capture of fragments of its lines of defense.

The rearward portion of this zone will therefore consist of a system of strong points, machine-gun nests, etc., merging toward the front into an increasingly closer-meshed network of trenches. The individual trenches, machine-gun nests, etc., must afford each other mutual flanking support.

Deep mined dugouts in the front line trench will be absolutely prohibited. They simply form man traps and will, therefore, be blown up wherever they exist. The place for the majority of the dugouts (which should be of concrete and be well distributed and masked) is in the rearward lines and in the intermediate zones. Vast subterranean accommodation is admissible only for reserves far in rear.

Of greater importance than a wide *obstacle* covering the front line trench, which in any case will always be destroyed in a serious attack, is the construction of a *number of obstacles* within the fortified zone, namely, along the communication and switch trenches, and farther in rear, forming a part of the strong points. These obstacles form the meshes in which an enemy who has broken through is caught, and which prevent him from surrounding the portion of the garrison which has held out in the front line.

Difficulties will be added to the enemy's reconnaissance and artillery work by the construction of the greatest possible number of targets and by making them difficult of recognition (also of dummy defenses).

At Verdun, where there were too many dugouts in the front line trench, a proportion of the infantry did not get out of them quickly enough. A close-meshed network of trenches was lacking, as were also obstacles running perpendicular to the front.

[20] Collection of German Military Documents, Hoover War Library.

2. *Observation.* Observation both for artillery and infantry must be assured even under the heaviest fire. This is not the case when, as at Verdun, observation is mainly carried out from the front line trench. It is preferable to construct a network of observation posts located at points in rear. The view from one post must supplement that from another.

In addition, constant observation of the enemy's activity, from balloons and by artillery and infantry aëroplanes (contact patrols), must, of course, be absolutely guaranteed.

Finally, one must insist that infantry quartered in deep dugouts and shelters protect themselves effectually against surprise attacks by posting lookout men and by frequent visiting rounds. The large number of unwounded prisoners shows that this was not properly done.

3. *Method of Holding the Position, and the Infantry Battle.* As pointed out in the "Defensive Battle" (*Abwehrschlacht,* see more particularly pars. 6, 13, and 15), a stubborn defense alone will not lead to the desired result.

The front line trench cannot be too thinly held. Distribution in depth is essential, even for a company. Each strong point must have its definite garrison which will be responsible for holding it.

Only isolated *machine guns* will be taken into the *front line trench;* they will usually be kept in carefully selected positions behind the front line, concealed and posted checker-wise, frequently in hollows, which are difficult to detect from the air and cannot be reached by the artillery; their main task is to open a surprise flanking fire on an enemy who has broken through. The operation of bringing machine guns into position and relieving them will be specially supervised.

Reserves must also know their way about the sectors of the divisions on their flanks. When fighting conditions permit, a certain tactical situation will be assumed, schemes will be set, and maneuvers carried out over the actual ground. Tactical work in the front line position and tours of inspection must be exacted from senior officers, from the battalion commander to the higher commander or the latter's staff officers. In certain circumstances the regimental commander, just like the battalion commander, must personally lead forward his reserves. No one, from the counter-attacking squads of the front line garrison down to the divisional reserves, is to wait for orders to counter-attack, but each will *act on his own initiative.*

During *training* the following must be practiced and supervised:

The counter-attack, from that of the counter-attacking squads of the front-line garrison to that of the larger reserves.

The measures to be adopted by the front-line garrison, while awaiting the counter-attack of the formations in rear, against an enemy who has broken through and is surrounding this garrison.

The action of the emergency garrisons posted in machine-gun nests and strong points.

At Verdun these arrangements partially broke down. Units in rear showed a lack of offensive initiative. Portions of the foremost fighting-lines which were gallantly holding out, were left in the lurch by those in rear, and fell victims to the enemy.

4. *The Artillery Battle.* As in the preceding case, if proper arrangements are made for the battle, the enemy's attack can be anticipated. Nevertheless, at Verdun, artillery support appears to have been lacking.

It is not quite clear to what extent the enemy's artillery was engaged by our own. To engage the enemy's artillery (with the help of aëroplane observers) is, however, the principal and most effective means of fighting a defensive battle to a successful conclusion. Should this succeed, the enemy's attack is absolutely paralyzed.

When the enemy's infantry attack is imminent, fire must be more and more concentrated on the enemy's infantry as well.

In so doing it is not advisable to direct a destructive fire on successive portions of the enemy's position chosen arbitrarily. Fire will preferably be directed on points where work is in progress and where effect against living targets may be expected. The same holds good for harassing fire, for which, in certain circumstances, gas shells are particularly effective.

For both kinds of fire, observation and supervision are the main factors for obtaining effective results (see above).

The destructive fire to be directed on the enemy's front line trenches will be increased, both as regards the number of batteries engaged and the expenditure of ammunition, in proportion to the increase of the enemy's fire on our infantry lines. It will be increased to annihilating fire as soon as a maximum rate of fire on the part of the enemy, or other signs, denote that the attack is about to be launched. From this time onward, the mass of the artillery, even including the 21 cm. mortars, will concentrate fire of the utmost intensity on the enemy's starting-points and assembly trenches, so as to annihilate the troops held in readiness for the attack before they can move to the assault. Arrangements must be made for annihilating fire to be broken off like barrage fire, but, in any case, only on receipt of an order from a senior officer (battalion commander).

During these short phases of the battle there is to be no thought of economizing ammunition.

This procedure does not debar individual batteries from simultaneously continuing to sweep valleys and ways of approach so as to prevent reserves from being brought up. At such moments, also, it is advisable to neutralize sections of the enemy's artillery by using gas shells.

It is the duty of all artillery commanders to acquire a practiced eye and ear, and to utilize every means of reconnaissance and observation to gauge accurately the moment at which the maximum intensity of fire should commence. In no circumstances should this increase of fire take place only when the infantry ask for barrage fire, as in that case the most effective period for engaging the enemy's infantry, the period of assembly, is missed. On the other hand, the duration of annihilating fire will, naturally, always be strictly limited.

When the enemy's attack is launched, barrage fire will finally be opened automatically. Barrage fire is purely a means to repel an attack. The artillery must, however, assume the offensive not only against the enemy's artillery but also against his infantry. Acting on their own initiative, artillery of all calibers and also the *Minenwerfer* will devote their main strength to seeking and engaging the most favorable targets and not merely to putting up a purely mechanical barrage.

Well-organized barrage fire, important as it is, does not necessarily by itself afford absolute protection. The enemy may either run the gauntlet of our barrage or else draw it before the attack and at the decisive moment endeavor to neutralize it by opening fire with gas or high explosive shells. Or again, he may make a detailed study of the lie of our rather mechanical barrage, with the result that he will find points which are less heavily shelled than others and will make his way through them with few casualties.

It thus follows that the barrage must be flexible, i.e., it must be mobile so as to correspond to the probable movements of the enemy.

Observation and fire control (cf. par. 2) must also be aimed at during the annihilating and barrage fire. This will generally be achieved by transforming automatic and spontaneous unobserved fire as soon as possible into observed fire. For this purpose, it is often possible for the aëroplane observer to fly at a low altitude, far behind our own line and as though perched on a giant observation ladder, and communicate with the batteries in action not only by wireless but by means of the simple signals. Only thus will it be possible to engage fleeting targets and to punish immediately any imprudence on the part of the enemy—batteries moving across the open, infantry advancing or concentrating without cover.

But even making allowances for considerable improvement in our artillery work, the infantry must clearly understand that artillery can relieve them of only a part of the defense, and that, finally, it is the infantryman who has to repulse the enemy at close quarters with machine gun, rifle, hand grenade, and trench mortar.

5. *Artillery Command.* The long ranges, combined with the difficulty of obtaining a general view of the country, necessitate the general

allotment of targets and fire control being carried out by the Higher Command, from the Group of Armies downward, even for artillery under divisional commands. The Higher Commanders must issue precise instructions for the artillery battle and must not hesitate to go into details when it is a question of co-operation between neighboring sectors. The division, for its part, must *daily* define the tasks for its artillery (see par. 23 of the "Defensive Battle"). Fire-control practices must constantly be held. If, in addition to the issue of precise orders, there is a thorough supervision of the work of all grades (down to and including the observers), the artillery will prove equal to its task.

6. *Reliefs.* Timely relief is very important (see the "Defensive Battle," pars. 9 and 18); it can only take place gradually, and requires the most careful preparation. The infantry has frequently, for example, to relieve the unit farthest in rear, and then gradually work forward until the front line is reached. Regiment must hand over to regiment, and battalion to battalion, etc. The outgoing commander may leave the position only with the consent of the commander who is relieving him. This method should insure that during the actual relief there is always one unit in the position which knows the ground, and that the incoming unit gradually obtains a knowledge of the position.

The relief of artillery, other than divisional, demands special attention, and experience shows that this matter often receives less consideration.

During pauses in the fighting, batteries belonging to Armies and Groups of Armies must be withdrawn, which will also give them an opportunity to overhaul their material.

The same principle holds good for pioneers and other auxiliary services.

7. *Morale, Care of Troops, and Supervision of Commanders.* The number of prisoners (which was unusually large for German troops), some of whom evidently surrendered without offering serious resistance and without suffering heavy losses, shows that the morale of some of the troops engaged was low. The reasons for this require most careful investigation. The whole spirit of the German infantry must be revived by means of training and the strictest drill, as well as by educating and instructing the men. It is a matter of vital importance to our army that the proper steps be taken.

This question is closely allied to that of looking after the troops in regard to clothing, food, and quarters, adjustment of work and rest, equitable allotment of leave, as well as the personal example of all ranks. I particularly wish to emphasize the fact that under the extraordinarily difficult fighting conditions at Verdun this latter point is just as important for fighting efficiency as are tactical decisions.

The supervision of officers, particularly of the more senior officers, must be searching, and the matters mentioned above must also be taken into account. Any officer incapable of doing his work will be summarily removed from his post. Long leave, given in time, will frequently suffice to enable officers suffering from nervous strain to recuperate and return to their work.

8. *Troops at Rest.* Troops which have been withdrawn must be given facilities for rest and training. The necessity for bringing them up to dig trenches is an evil which cannot be completely avoided.

Training and inspections alike must reflect the spirit of the foregoing. The attack will also be practiced by higher formations.

As remarked in paragraph 7, training for battle is not sufficient by itself but must be combined with drill. The experience of war confirms the principles of our peace training.

v. HINDENBURG

208. SECRET MEMORANDUM OF EXPERIENCE OF THE FIRST ARMY IN THE SOMME BATTLE, JUNE 24– NOVEMBER 26, 1916[21]

PART I. TACTICAL

First Army H.Q.
Ia-2122. Secret   30th January 1917

A. PRELUDE TO THE BATTLE

1. The Somme battle did not come as a surprise to the Second Army, which, from the 19th July 1916, onward, was divided into the First and Second Armies. As early as February 1916 our aëroplanes reported the construction of numerous new hutments in front of the northern wing of the army on both sides of the Ancre. Shortly afterwards, an increase in the number of divisions on the English front north of the Somme took place. As a result of successful raids and patrol work, we learnt that these divisions were relieved successively after a few weeks in line. Toward the end of April, the number of English divisions north of the Somme had already increased to 12, opposed to only 4 German divisions.

The plan which was formed at that time of meeting the enemy's expected offensive north of the Somme by a counter-offensive could not be carried out owing to lack of sufficient forces. In April one division was placed at the disposal of the army as a reinforcement. This

---

[21] Collection of German Military Documents, Hoover War Library.

division was put into line north of the Ancre River where the English line was most strongly held. Thus on the right wing of the army each division held an average front of 6 kilometers, while on the rest of the army front the divisional sectors amounted to 7–9 kilometers.

In May, 2 divisions were withdrawn from the front of the Second Army and replaced by one division which, during its short period of rest, had not yet been able to replace the losses which it had suffered at Verdun. In addition to this, a considerable number of heavy batteries equipped with modern German guns were replaced by batteries of captured guns.

Up to May it was not considered probable that the French would co-operate in the expected attack.

At the beginning of June the signs of an approaching attack became more evident. Just north of the Somme 2 French divisions took over the sector previously held by the English. The conclusion at first drawn that this measure had a defensive object, with a view to giving greater depth to the English offensive mounted further north, was rejected as soon as the specially good 20th French Corps, known as a "Gladiator Corps," was identified by raids north of the Somme. South of the Somme, also, preparations for a hostile attack became more and more apparent, so that during June the supposed frontage of the enemy's offensive was fairly clearly established as extending from the neighborhood of the Roman road about 8 kilometers south of the Somme, on the south.

In June one division and the field artillery of another division were placed at the disposal of Army Headquarters. Toward the end of June, a further reinforcement of 17 light field howitzer batteries was allotted to the army.

2. On the 22d June the enemy's bombardment began to become intense.

From the 24th June onward the intense bombardment was continuous. This bombardment comprised a large proportion of artillery of the heaviest calibers and of heavy long range guns.

On the 1st July, about 8 A.M., the great English-French infantry assault took place on a front of 40 kilometers between Gommecourt and the west of Vermandovillers, while the artillery bombardment was continued on a sector which considerably overlapped the zone of attack. The assault penetrated our badly damaged defensive front at a great many points. North of the Ancre, by the evening of the 2d July, counter-attacks were successful in recapturing the whole of our line and inflicted heavy losses in killed and prisoners on the English. South of the Ancre also, as far as Thiepval inclusive, the English and French had driven a deep wedge into our defensive front. On this sector our losses were so considerable that there was no available strength with which to carry out the intended counter-attack.

During the following days and weeks, we continued to lose further ground at this broad breach in our front. The engagement of the reinforcements which flowed in to the army from all sides had to be effected under the most unfavorable circumstances. Owing to the overwhelming superiority of the enemy in aircraft, artillery, ammunition, and men, it was possible to stop only the most dangerous gaps which had been made in the German defensive front. Owing to the force of circumstances, the cohesion of the arriving reinforcements had to be broken up in order to avoid the danger of the enemy breaking through.

Under these difficult conditions the whole organization of the defense had to be constituted anew. It was only after the lapse of long weeks that the defense could be put on an equality with the enemy as regards fighting material of every kind.

In spite of this the enemy has not succeeded in achieving the intended breaking through of our Western front. His plans have been shattered by the devoted and untiring courage and loyalty of our army. Every man who has fought on the Somme may be proud that he was there, and that the battle, which is so far the greatest in any war, has, through the failure of the enemy, ended as a German victory.

B. Object and Arrangement of the Lessons Learnt

3. The numerous lessons learnt from the Somme battle have already been dealt with and published in Part 8 of the Chief of the General Staff's instructions for trench warfare entitled "Principles of Command during a Defensive Battle in Trench Warfare." A thorough acquaintance with these instructions is therefore assumed as a preliminary to studying and understanding the following remarks, which have been published by the First Army at the desire of the Crown Prince of Bavaria's Group of Armies. In this memorandum, the "Principles of Command during a Defensive Battle" will be referred to only in so far as the events on the Somme are concerned; the organization, tactical employment, and co-operation of the different arms will be described in the light of the experience gained during a battle in which the forces involved have been on a scale hitherto unknown.

The subject-matter has been divided up in such a way that in Part I (Tactical), the different arms are treated under the following subheadings: (1) The causes of initial failures; (2) The measures by which a gradual improvement was attained; (3) Experiences and lessons.

In this way will be obtained a picture of the development of all details of the fighting during the battle which will perhaps be of use to a commander who may in future find himself engaged in a battle of similar nature.

PART II. ADMINISTRATION AND INTERIOR ECONOMY

C. HIGHER COMMAND; EXPERIENCES AND LESSONS

4. Before the beginning of the Somme battle, the headquarters of the Second Army, as then constituted, had grouped the five divisions north of the Somme and the four divisions south of the Somme under the two Corps Staffs which were available in the area, in order to obtain a uniform system of command throughout the anticipated zone of attack. The battle frontage of the two corps, thus constituted, amounted to 22 miles north of the river and 20 miles south of the river. The initial attack by the enemy astride the river and the consequent re-entrant created in our line increased these frontages considerably. The divisions sent up as reinforcements by the Supreme Army Command were only accompanied very gradually by fresh Corps Staffs, and these staffs were totally unacquainted with the Somme battle front. Their entry into line did indeed reduce the frontages held by formations, but the commanders had to become acquainted with the ground before they could carry out their tasks.

The ever-increasing size of the Second Army prompted the Higher Command to reorganize the troops engaged on the battle front in the First and Second Armies. This change took effect from the 19th July. The First Army took over approximately the same battle front as had been previously held by the northern corps of the Second Army. This sector was gradually divided up among five groups, each under a Corps Headquarters, each group commanding two to four divisions.

It was not till the 1st October that the new First Army was given a separate Lines of Communication Headquarters. Until then its administration was effected by the Lines of Communication Headquarters of the Second Army. . . . .

D. INFANTRY AND MACHINE GUNS

I. CAUSES OF INITIAL FAILURES

16. The reasons for our previous failures arose not so much in the domain of purely infantry considerations as from our inability at the outset to make equivalent reply to the enemy's concentrations, more especially of aircraft and artillery. . . . .

II. EXPERIENCES AND LESSONS

(Based chiefly on reports from the troops)

(a) General

23. *Our infantry is superior to that of the enemy.*—In the Somme battle wherever the enemy gained the upper hand it was chiefly due to the perfected application of technical means, in particular to the employment of guns and ammunition in quantities which had been hitherto inconceivable. It was also due to the exemplary manner in which infantry, artillery, and aëroplanes co-operated. After artillery preparation, wherever the enemy's infantry, following up the last shell, came upon positions that were still held, the attack usually broke down, and if the advance was made against positions already destroyed the infantry could be ejected by determined and rapidly executed counter-attacks.

The duty of every infantry commander is, first, to train and educate the infantry soldier for this hand-to-hand fighting (which should not be a privilege reserved for assault units, but should be a universal one); next, and more difficult, to keep him, both before and during an engagement, physically and mentally fit to fight; and, lastly, the most difficult of all, to get his men out of their shelters and dugouts in time and launch them against the enemy.

(b) Training

24. In this war, which is apparently dominated by science and numbers, individual will-power is nevertheless the ultimate deciding factor. The defense of a position depends more than it ever did before on the unshakable determination of the subordinate commander and of each individual man to hold his position. . . . .

(f) Defense

53. An active conduct of the defense is absolutely essential even against an enemy who is far superior in numbers. Intense activity of patrols, and raids on weak points of the enemy's position, interfere with his preparations for attack and compel him to keep in a condition of continual readiness for our attacks and so to hold his positions more strongly even at times when he is not contemplating an attack himself. . . . .

63. During the battle of the Somme, the methodical evacuation of portions of the position depended on obtaining permission from Army Headquarters, and every evacuation of positions, even to the smallest extent, carried out on the responsibility of the individual commander was forbidden. Every man was obliged to fight at that point at which he was stationed; the enemy's line of advance could lead only over his

dead body. Army Headquarters believes that it was owing to this firm determination to fight, with which every leader was inspired, that the enemy, in spite of his superior numbers, bled to death in front of the serried ranks of our soldiers. . . . .

(h) Equipment

77. The steel helmet has proved thoroughly satisfactory and is very popular. To diminish the polish of the helmet, which remains bright in spite of the gray paint, it has been found useful to smear the helmet with clay and earth.

78. Assault kit must be supplemented by sandbags carried like a rucksack, serving for carrying up rations and ammunition rather than the pack, which is too heavy. It is always advisable to take greatcoats and waterproof sheets. Blankets are necessary only in cold weather.

One hundred fifty cartridges per man are enough. Before the men go into action, it is necessary to issue large numbers of hand grenades in sandbags, and to equip every man with a large spade (every section with a pickaxe, also pioneer and building material) as well as with cold rations for three or four days.

79. On days when there is heavy fighting, the demand for food is not so great as that for something to drink. It is necessary to equip the men with two water bottles full of tea or coffee, and to issue several bottles of mineral water, as well as to avoid all food which causes thirst (no salted or smoked meat). Bacon, sausage which will keep, bread, rusks, biscuits, chocolate, tinned meat, and tinned fat are recommended. No rations must be issued in larger than half packages, so as to make each man independent of the others. Tobacco and cigars in fairly large quantities are a very welcome supplement, as also is alcohol in wet, cold weather. To avoid the misuse of concentrated alcohol, it is advisable to mix rum or red wine with the tea. It has proved very useful to issue solidified methylated spirits for warming up tinned food and the food sent up from the traveling kitchens. It is absolutely necessary to issue illuminating material such as candles, carbide lamps, and electric lamps with spare batteries. . . . .

F. ARTILLERY

I. CAUSES OF INITIAL FAILURES

94. At the beginning of the battle of the Somme, our artillery was far too weak in numbers, in calibers, supply of ammunition, and means of observation to meet the enemy from the outset with the requisite counter-measures. To this may be added the quite noticeable inferiority of our reconnaissance, especially aërial reconnaissance, for which the

enemy produced a very large number of machines, corresponding to his artillery equipment, and which doubtless also were well organized and employed. . . . .

III. EXPERIENCES AND LESSONS

(c) Training

113. The training of the troops, especially in the case of the young officers and battery commanders, no longer reaches the standard formerly required. In particular the results obtained in shooting by officers and acting-officers, some of whom are inexperienced, have been insufficient. It has proved of practical value, when circumstances have permitted it, to discuss the general idea and execution of an important shoot beforehand, as well as subsequently to criticize on the basis of the rounds recorded the shoots that have been carried out.

It is necessary to arrange for further training areas where formations stationed in readiness as a reserve in the hands of the Higher Command can stiffen their training. In these areas, artillery schools and practice with live rounds must be arranged for; individuals belonging to troops in line will be detailed to attend such courses. . . . .

G. COMMUNICATIONS AND AIR RECONNAISSANCE

I. CAUSES OF INITIAL FAILURES

154. The breakdown of the communication service at the beginning of the battle is chiefly attributable to the inadequate provision of means of communication. These were numerically much inferior to those of the enemy. Their increase did not keep pace with the increase in the number of divisions and heavy artillery units engaged. . . . .

II. MEASURES BY WHICH A GRADUAL IMPROVEMENT WAS ATTAINED; INCREASE OF THE MEANS OF COMMUNICATION

165. The wireless detachments proved their value. It was found necessary to control the wireless traffic within groups. For this purpose, group wireless officers were appointed who controlled the whole of the wireless traffic, including aëroplane wireless. Arrangements were made to use wireless for calling for barrage, by employing aëroplane receiving stations (ground stations) for the purpose. . . . .

H. THE FIGHTING TASKS OF AËROPLANES AND ANTI-AIRCRAFT ARTILLERY

I. CAUSES OF INITIAL FAILURES

196. The beginning and the first weeks of the Somme battle were marked by a complete inferiority of our own air forces. . . . .

II. MEASURES BY WHICH A GRADUAL IMPROVEMENT WAS ATTAINED

199. The reinforcement of the air forces, which was gradually effected, and especially the arrival of powerful pursuit machines, was principally responsible for the improvement of the position in the course of the battle. . . . .

III. EXPERIENCES AND LESSONS . . . .

210. The employment of numerous single-seater fighting machines is the best method of destroying the enemy's aircraft. These units are most suitable for offensive work. Their task is to attack and destroy every hostile machine which shows itself. Whether the enemy's machines fall into our hands or not after they have been shot down is immaterial in estimating results. The shooting down of machines beyond the enemy's lines bears equally good testimony to our superiority in the air.

The number of pursuit flights engaged in should be sufficient to gain the mastery in the air from the enemy. Their number is not the only decisive factor but also their success in action. During the Somme battle, the First Army had, attached to it, the 2d Pursuit Flight, which now bears the name of its heroic commander, Captain Boelcke, who unfortunately perished too soon. This pursuit flight shot down 87 machines during the Somme battle, 21 of these having been brought down and crashed by the commander alone. . . . .

I. Effects of Gas and Protection against Gas

EXPERIENCES AND LESSONS

224. The lack of effect of the great British gas attacks at the end of June, which were delivered as a preparation for the infantry attacks in spite of the unfavorable weather, resulted in our troops beginning to underestimate the effects of the enemy's gas. Later gas attacks on a smaller scale, which the enemy delivered successfully owing to the weather conditions being favorable, caused the same troops losses which were partly due to carelessness. . . . .

228. Our own gas shells were employed for counter-battery work against hostile batteries which had been located, and according to prisoners' statements have often proved effective. In methodical attacks a bombardment with "green cross" shell of the enemy's observation posts and barrage batteries, just before the assault, considerably reduced the intensity of his fire.

No experience is yet available as to the effect of combining "green cross" shell with high explosive shell in harassing and annihilating fire.

209. EXTRACT FROM GENERAL ORDER OF THE SUPREME COMMAND, JANUARY 10, 1917[22]

(1) Our task in the West consists now in the organization of the defense and the taking out and training of reserves.

(2) It is not the mass of troops employed in the defense which will see us through, but care in the preparation and training combined with the most careful supervision and the control even of the smallest details.

(3) Reserves can never be too strong. The objection to taking out reserves will disappear the more all ranks are convinced that they will be of value in a crisis. Any premature strategic use of reserves is detrimental to the interests of the troops and their training and is undesirable from the point of view of command. . . . .

210. GENERAL VON MAUR'S MEMORANDUM ON THE ENGLISH TANK ATTACK OF APRIL 11, 1917[23]

I. *Conduct of the tanks:*

a) The tanks are made ready and brought forward in the darkness. The noise of the motors can be heard for kilometers.

b) The tanks at first follow one another, then march up, and finally attack alongside of each other. On the 11.4 distances of 80 yards were ordered. Single tanks for the time being are held back.

c) The speed off the roads is at most 4 km. per hour.

d) The built-in machine guns in the front side of the tank open fire at a distance of 500 to 1,000 meters before approaching our trenches. The guns of the male tanks can shoot only sideways, forward, and sideways. Their range possibility is quite great.

e) After reaching or passing over our trenches the majority of the tanks turn right or left, in order to aid the following infantry in mopping up the trenches. Individual tanks prepare the way for the infantry to break through. The tanks signal to each other and to the infantry by means of colored lights.

Among other things: green means, "Approach" or "Wire is cut"; red means, "Danger" or "Wire is not cut"; red-green means, "Wait a little."

f) The tanks overcome ordinary wire entanglements playfully; but by high, thick, and wide interferences, as we have them at the Siegfried position, came difficulties. The wire winds itself easily around the trans-

[22] Collection of German Military Documents, Hoover War Library.
[23] *Ibid.*

port bands. On the 11.4 one tank was hopelessly stuck in our entanglements.

g) The tanks seem to regard deep trenches of 2.5 m. width as an unpleasant hindrance.

h) The tanks avoid road crossings near the front or behind the German position because there they suspect traps or mines. (This can be seen from the English maps.) The tanks use the roads leading to our position for marching up only as long as they are far away from our trenches. Later on they leave the roads and use them solely for the purpose of orientation, in that they drive parallel to them.

II. *Resisting the tanks:*

a) Ditches of 4 m. depth and width are the tank's destruction. One of the many Siegfried foundation-trenches which was to be filled with concrete became a trap for the tank. Tank-ditches are more profitably placed on both sides of the roads than on the roads. It is by mere chance that a tank gets into one; therefore, it hardly pays to make the effort.

b) The tanks are being fired upon during the daytime by all those batteries which can observe the effect of their fire at long distances and which at the moment do not have more important tasks. All kinds of batteries have on the 11.4 placed tanks out of commission. The independent activity of battery commanders must be left the widest field of play.

c) During the night only fire at the closest range promises success. April 11 has shown that guns and machine guns which fire with S.M.K. munition can put tanks out of commission. The fire upon the sides of the tanks is more effective than upon the front. The greatest danger for the tank is the inflammability of its gasoline and oil supplies. M.G. fire, too, can ignite them.

d) Tank guns cannot be spared; especially for the fighting of tanks which have broken through our positions, and for resisting the infantry which follows the tank they are valuable. As long as the tanks are within our front line, the tank guns endanger their own infantry. On 11.4 seven tanks were destroyed, three of which were destroyed by tank guns.

e) *The most effective weapons against the tanks are small trench cannon operated by infantrymen, which until their use find protection in a depression and which fire from close range.* The cannon must not be much less manageable than machine guns.

f) Also bomb-throwers of all kinds are suitable for fighting the tanks. On the 11.4 a small bomb-thrower put one tank out of commission.

g) The moral effect of the tanks upon the infantry is very great; however, it has somewhat palled in the division after the successful fighting on 11.4.17. Also the actual effect of the tank guns and the tank machine-guns must not be underestimated. Infantry Regiment 124 suffered appreciable losses through them on the 11.4. Equipping the infantry with sufficient K-munition and trench cannon, however, will give the infantry a weapon which must mean practically the end of the tank attacks.

von MAUR

211. THE KAISER'S PROCLAMATION OF AUGUST 1, 1917[24]

To the German Army, the Navy, and the Colonial troops:

The third year of war is at an end. The number of our enemies has increased; not so their prospects of final victory.

You crushed Rumania last year; the Russian Empire trembles once more under your blows. Both countries exposed their lives in the interest of others and are bleeding to death. In Macedonia you have forcibly resisted the enemy onslaught. In mighty battles in the West you have remained masters of the situation. Your lines, guarding our beloved country from the terrors and devastation of war, stand firm.

My Navy has also achieved great results. It has rendered the enemy's command of the sea questionable and threatened the very heart of its existence.

Far from home a small German force holds German Colonial territory against a vastly superior enemy force.

Victory will again be on our side and that of our faithful allies in the coming year of war. And final victory will rest with us.

I thank you with deep emotion in my own name and that of the Fatherland for what you have accomplished in the last year of war. We remember, too, with reverence those who have valiantly fallen in battle or died for the honor and safety of the Fatherland.

The war goes on. It is still forced on us. We are fighting for our existence and our future with steeled resolution and unwavering courage. As the task increases, so our strength increases. We cannot be conquered. We are resolved to conquer. The Lord God be with us.

WILHELM

At the Front, August 1, 1917

[24] *Norddeutsche Allgemeine Zeitung,* August 1, 1917, II, 1.

212. LUDENDORFF'S PREPARATIONS FOR THE MARCH 1918 OFFENSIVE: THE ATTACK IN POSITION WARFARE, JANUARY 1, 1918[25]

Ia-53996.

Manual of Position Warfare for All Arms

Part 14 (Provisional)

The Attack in Position Warfare

1st January 1918

Issued by the Chief of the General Staff of the Field Army. Not to be taken into the front line. Secret. Distribution down to battalions.

A. INTRODUCTION

1. This manual treats of the *attack in position warfare with a limited objective and the offensive battle leading from position warfare to the break-through.*

The manual equally applies to the *methodical counter-attack* in the defensive battle. The *immediate counter-attack,* on the other hand, being an affair of minor tactics, is not dealt with here.

B. GENERAL PRINCIPLES

2. Education of the troops in that spirit of bold attack and will to conquer with which we entered the present war is the first guaranty of success.

The instruction of commanders and troops for the attack cannot be too minute or thorough.

Formations that are going to take part must have rehearsals of the attack against trenches specially constructed for the purpose; the smallest details must be practiced. It is particularly important that the troops who are to be used in an offensive should be rested and kept fit until the moment of attack.

Thorough knowledge of the effect of the arms employed and the capabilities of the various means of warfare, such as trench mortars, artillery, and ammunition, as well as of the modern means of communication, is indispensable.

The principles of training are laid down in the new manuals (compare C.G.S. of the Field Army, No. II 75,424 op., dated 14.1.18) and in special instructions.

[25] Collection of German Military Documents, Hoover War Library.

3. Command.—The attack, no less than the defense, requires that the troops should be *really commanded and that careful and detailed instructions are given to insure the co-operation of all arms* in a particular sector, and with the troops of neighboring sectors, and that the objectives are clearly defined. On the other hand, every attack offers an *opportunity for independent decision and action* even down to the private soldier.

The art of conducting an attack consists in a clear appreciation of the enemy's defensive dispositions and their tactical influence on the execution of the attack, in careful preparation, clear instructions, and consistent direction.

The offensive battle requires, finally, complete mastery of the art of moving large masses of troops in a narrow space and of supplying them with all that they require.

For military success the *influence of commanders of all ranks and all arms is the decisive factor. It is properly used when scope for independent action and initiative* is left even to the private soldier and the exercise of these qualities is required. This is one of the basic principles of the manual.

There is, however, a limit to the *possibilities of commanding and supplying large masses of troops concentrated in a narrow space.* Too close concentration produces congestion. Careful reflection, practical imagination, and personal experience will give the Higher Command some idea of the actual conditions that will arise (cf. par. 6, last sub-par. but five).

4. Liaison.—*The maintenance of close liaison between all arms and all commanders* from the front to the rear, from the rear to the front, and to the flanks, is indispensable. It insures the methodical progress of the attack and prevents surprises, especially from the flanks. Where liaison is good, the Higher Command is always in a position to take measures to suit any emergency, and at the right moment.

5. Center of gravity of attack.—Every attack must have a center of gravity. On this must be calculated the grouping of the forces, the breadth of front (par. 12), the concentration of artillery, trench mortars, and other means of warfare, and the assembly and engagement of reserves.

6. Various kinds of offensives.—*The objective, purpose, and conduct of an attack will vary according to its extent and depth.* In addition to inflicting losses on the enemy, *attacks with limited objective* may be undertaken to improve the position, to relieve the main battle fronts, to mystify and mislead the enemy, or to obtain information. If it is intended that the objective should be permanently held, it should offer more favorable conditions for defense than the "departure" trench.

The object of an attack may, however, be frequently attained when a withdrawal is subsequently made to the "departure" trench. Limited attacks should, as a rule, be carried out in *one* continuous thrust until the objective is attained.

The offensive battle is an effort to obtain a tactical penetration and the ultimate development therefrom of strategical break-through. In the latter case it works up to the *battle for a break-through,* which aims at compelling open warfare. When it becomes possible for the Higher Command to have this important objective in view, all measures for its attainment must from the very first be set in motion.

From the moment of penetration, the attacker will have to reckon with fresh troops being continually put in by the enemy and with hostile counter-attacks. It is in this way that the break-through battle acquires its special characteristics:

Penetration of the enemy's position with the farthest possible objective.

Capture at least of the enemy's artillery on the first day.

Firmness in consolidating gains and in meeting the enemy's counter-strokes and counter-attacks.

Bringing up the mass of artillery and fresh infantry.

New attacks and the counter-measures taken by the enemy, etc.

The break-through battle consists of "devouring" the series of hostile positions for the most part in the face of heavy offensive opposition by the enemy. It must be carried through *rapidly and in depth.*

The first penetration is comparatively easy. The difficulty lies in maintaining the vigor of the attack. The enemy must not be allowed to recover from his surprise. His counter-measures must be rendered useless by the rapid progress of the attack. *It is a question of taking rapid action with the consciousness that protection of flanks and rear, as well as support from artillery, will be provided from behind.*

The danger of slackening in the force of attack is great. The dead center must be overcome by the energy of commanders well forward in the line and by fresh effectives.

Here, less importance should be attached to mass than to the intensity of artillery and infantry fire. Too numerous effectives are a hindrance to themselves and add to the difficulties of command and supply. All depends on rapid and independent local action within the general scheme and on bringing up artillery and supplies of ammunition.

The vital point in the conduct of the attack lies in steady co-operation between the assaulting infantry and the artillery.

Artillery and *trench mortars* are indispensable for breaking the resistance of the enemy, even while the attack is in progress. By skilful and rapid action, they must put the finishing touches to the success of the infantry. If the attack is held up, it is not fresh infantry that is first required but *renewed artillery preparation.*

When the attack has pressed on beyond the range of the mass of our guns, the rapid pushing forward of the artillery and the ammunition supply of this advanced artillery are decisive in securing the success of the attack. This idea is frequently recurring in the manual.

After the first penetration, a few rounds from the *accompanying artillery* (or trench mortars) or even *machine-gun fire*—these make the enemy keep his head down—are often sufficient as a renewal of the fire preparation. The stronger the resistance, the more the *concentrated fire* of numerous pieces, particularly heavy ones, is required. The more powerful artillery, with a good supply of ammunition, that accompanies the advance, the easier will it be possible to keep the attack going.

The *infantry,* on the other hand, should be put in sparingly. Distribution in depth must always be maintained, or if it should be temporarily lost during an attack it should always be restored and that, as far as possible, by pushing forward the most advanced units.

7. Surprise.—The greatest successes in war are to be looked for from measures for which the enemy is least prepared. *Therefore, in all offensive actions, surprise of the enemy is of decisive importance.*

To secure this are necessary: strictest *secrecy* regarding intentions, execution of preparatory measures as inconspicuously as possible, restriction of new works to the indispensable minimum, simulation of intended attack or actual attacks in other sectors, and variations in the details of the attack. In these matters the official manual allows sufficient latitude. It is the business of all commanders to make the proper use of the methods available.

Complete surprise is rarely attainable, nor is it necessary. In important attacks, by skilful mystification and deception at other points, it will generally be possible to arrange that the enemy will be late with his measures of defense even though he may have partly noticed the imminence of an attack. As a rule, the hour of the infantry assault at least will come as a surprise to him. This at any rate will be of some advantage to the attacker.

8. Flanking action.—The great importance of flanking action, even with small forces, especially of artillery and machine guns, has been repeatedly shown in all offensive operations. Flanking movements, therefore, should continue to be methodically planned. Strong defensive works should not be attacked from the front, but from the flanks and rear.

In the break-through battle, the tactical surroundings of whole sectors of a position should be aimed at in the preliminary dispositions for the battle.

9. Study of the ground.—All commanders should be thoroughly instructed in the *tactical exploitation of positions and natural features of the ground.* The study of the field of battle and its tactical detail which is indispensable for the mounting and successful execution of all attacks.

The fight for commanding positions, which has lost its importance in position warfare, will come all the more into prominence the more battles assume the character of a war of movement.

10. Importance of the above principles.—If the principles here briefly laid down receive due attention, we shall be victorious in attack on the Western front also.

C. EFFECTIVES REQUIRED; PREPARATION IN GENERAL

11. Preliminary estimate.—At the very beginning of the contemplation of an attack the necessity will arise for a preliminary calculation of requirements in the means of attack, especially in artillery, trench mortars, and ammunition (par. 18). If they cannot be made available, the objective must be limited or the attack abandoned. An attack with inadequate means invariably fails, entails useless expenditure of blood, and is a flagrant mistake in command.

In *estimating requirements,* the expected resistance of the enemy must be taken into account. The maximum numbers are to be employed only in cases where a strongly fortified position with a numerous garrison is being attacked. Where surprise is aimed at and there is any probability of it succeeding—if only partially—weaker forces will be sufficient.

The principle that on no account should an attack be carried out with insufficient force must not lead to the adoption of exaggerated factors of safety. In order to avoid any unwieldy concentrations, *the minimum of what is required* should not as a rule be exceeded (cf. the last 2 sub-pars. of par. 3 and the last 5 of par. 6).

12. Frontages.—In attacks of considerable depth, a thrust with one and the same formation (division), continued until its strength is used up, is preferable to successive attacks with fresh formations. Accordingly, the fronts of attack should be so chosen that a formation may be capable, without assistance, of maintaining the vigor of its attack for a long period and of fighting its way through the whole depth of the enemy's trenches without a pause.

The idea that in a break-through a division which takes part in the first attack will be relieved on the first or second day as a matter of course should be strongly discouraged.

If the attack has been properly prepared and the artillery pushed on in good time, the attack should succeed without too many casualties.

After the first attack, therefore, an attacking division should have a sufficient fighting strength for the moment. The further advance will depend upon putting in an adequate and powerful artillery rather than fresh infantry (see par. 6).

A change of staffs at this time would affect the continuity and coherence of command injuriously and is therefore extremely undesirable.

The *width of the front of attack,* however, must *not* be made *too narrow* on the grounds of facilitating unity of command. Where it is merely a question of seizing an enemy's front-line system of trenches, *a division may cover as much as 3,300 yards and more.* If, however, it is intended to penetrate an enemy's position in depth, narrower divisional fronts must be allotted; *they can hardly be reduced below* 2,200 yards.

With reference to the statements made in the last portion of paragraph 6, even with present strengths, the width of a divisional sector should be not less than 2,200 yards for divisions of 3 infantry regiments. A greater width facilitates command (especially of the artillery) and the bringing up of reserves and supplies. Giving all divisions the same fixed width of sector is to be avoided.

In attacks on a large scale, fresh formations will be held close up in readiness so that they can be thrown in at once as the attack progresses. Their task is to extend the successes already obtained (cf. par. 6, last sub-par. but five).

13. Considerations of supply.—The conditions necessary for the development of an initial success to a strategic break-through are that strong forces of infantry and a large number of light and heavy guns are able to push on without a pause and that there is no hitch in the sending up of ammunition and other supplies. *Numerous mobile ammunition and supply columns, labor companies,* etc., are therefore necessary. Requirements of this nature, just like the number of fighting troops necessary, must be considered in forming the plans.

14. Preparations.—Every attack requires more or less extensive preparations. The more important the attack, the earlier these must be taken in hand.

The first step in the preparations is an accurate estimate of requirements in troops of all arms, ammunition, equipment, and all kinds of stores. It must be based on a definition of the scope of the attack and of the target sectors for guns and trench mortars.

The following list of preparatory measures will serve as a guide:

(*a*) Reinforcement of all existing staffs and administrative authorities (officials), including those on the lines of communication.

(*b*) Sending forward of staffs and advance parties of the formations to be employed in the attack. (Group—Corps—and divisional headquarters, administrative authorities, special units, etc.)

(*c*) Working out of the whole scheme of operations and supply, commencement of provision of supply of material, stores, etc.

(*d*) The gradual clothing of this "skeleton deployment" by sending forward subordinate staffs and additional advance parties to learn the ground. Moving up of the mass of ammunition and supply columns and material and stores.

(*e*) Deployment of the fighting troops (artillery and trench mortars first). Where a break-through is to be attempted, the contingents of special units necessary for its exploitation (ammunition and supply columns, road construction companies, railway troops, labor companies) are very numerous.

15. Further detailed preparations.—Among other details, attention must be paid to:

(*a*) Settlement of the chain of command.

(*b*) Organization of artillery and trench mortars, siting and construction of command and observation posts, formation of ammunition depots.

(*c*) Reinforcement of the signal service and communications.

(*d*) Organization of the infantry, fixing of battle sectors, command posts, lines of approach, places of assembly, objectives in detail.

(*e*) Assembly of engineer and other material in numerous small depots well forward, and on wagons; allotment of engineers to assist other arms in overcoming obstacles and consolidating captured positions.

(*f*) Reinforcement of air forces (aircraft, balloons, anti-aircraft guns).

(*g*) Production and issue of maps.

(*h*) Improvement of rearward communications, roads, railways, dumps, etc.; provision for the protection of railways.

(*i*) Billets, rations, water supply; the latter is especially important immediately after the attack.

(*j*) Assembly of ample reserves of artillery material (guns of every caliber, gun carriages, spare parts), an increased number of repair shops, with advanced auxiliary shops for fitting spare parts and executing small repairs.

(*k*) Medical arrangements.

The importance of all preparations connected with replenishment of stores and supplies of all kinds must not be underestimated.

16. Necessity for secrecy.—It is an essential condition of success that the *intention of attacking should be kept secret and that the preparatory work should be concealed* from hostile air reconnaissance and ground observation.

It may be expedient for the purpose of concealment of the intention, even from our own troops, to give out that the preparations are being made in view of a threatened hostile attack and to use a code name for the preparatory work which will not excite attention. This secrecy toward our own troops must not lead to their being instructed too late or insufficiently as regards their tasks.

When the preparations for an attack are spread over several weeks, it will be necessary to bind all officers entrusted with work connected with it to special secrecy, to have all the correspondence dealt with by officers only, to prohibit telephone conversations and telegraphing otherwise than in code, to supervise the administrative services (officials) co-operating in the work, and from time to time to examine the post. The use of motor cars by the numerous staffs occupied in reconnaissance work also requires regulating.

All movements of troops will be carried out when the light is too poor for observation or under cover of darkness without the use of lights; captive balloons will be sent up at night to see that this is carried out.

The construction of ammunition dumps in the battery positions will be carried out before the artillery and trench mortars are brought up; it is advisable to obliterate the tracks behind the last vehicles by means of harrows, etc.

The infantry will not for the most part be brought up to their positions of readiness until the last night before the attack.

As soon as our troops are informed of the intended attack, all raids should cease.

As regards the operations as a whole, it will be advisable to assign the duty of seeing that secrecy is observed to selected officers of the higher staffs.

17. Extent of preparations.—Good preparations take time. Too great haste endangers the success of the undertaking and results in heavy casualties. On the other hand, *preparations should be confined to what is strictly necessary,* with the object of obtaining a surprise and avoiding useless expenditure of men and material. Much must be done without for the sake of effecting surprise, but, on the other hand, preparations which can be carried out free from the enemy's observation must be all the more thorough.

18. Requirements after a successful attack.—After a successful attack, a high degree of activity will usually continue for a time on the battle front. This must be taken into account in calculating requirements in men, ammunition, and stores.

19. Higher Command.—According to the number of troops engaged, the direction of the attack is taken over by the commander of a Group of Armies, an Army, a Corps, or a Division.

Even in the case of limited objectives and small infantry forces, direction by a division is desirable, as this formation alone has the necessary forces and means at its disposal for the proper conduct of the fight as a combined operation, especially in the concentration and direction of artillery fire and the co-operation of all arms.

Even *in important attacks, the division is the battle unit.* Special tactical channels, short-circuiting the division, are prejudicial to co-operation.

20. Subordinate commanders.—The attacker has the start in the attack. He has it in his power to *settle beforehand the course that will be taken by the battle, at least in its earliest stages,* down to the smallest detail. He should make full use of this advantage. The limitation of the independence of the subordinate commanders that results from this cannot be avoided.

On the other hand, *full play* must be left to *independence in co-operation.*

21. A plan of attack must next be *drafted,* laying down the general lines of the projected course of the fighting. In particular, the action of the artillery and trench mortars and the arrangement of the replenishment of ammunition and supplies requires to be worked out as a whole from the outset.

In important attacks, on receipt of the plan of attack drafted by the Higher Command, subordinate commanders of formations, down to and including divisions, submit *drafts of orders* for the infantry attack and for the deployment and action of the artillery, etc., based on local reconnaissances.

The *attack order* is then issued, which settles the action of all arms on the whole front as a combined operation, especially in regard to time, and thus definitely fixes the limits of time and space for the whole attack. This is necessary, as all arms must co-operate *exactly to the minute* on the whole front.

22. Fresh formations for the attack.—It is generally necessary before attacks on a large scale to *put fresh formations into the line.* This should be concealed from the enemy as long as possible. The order and time of the arrival of these troops, and their instruction in the nature of the ground, by means of practice trenches and lectures, conferences, sketches, etc., will be carefully arranged. A model of the ground where the attack is to be made, representing its form and natural cover on a greatly reduced scale (say 1–500), made in a back area, may be useful.

23. Second and third line troops must be assembled at the proper time for reliefs and for feeding the attack. The intention to attack must not be revealed to the enemy by premature massing of these troops on the battle front.

24. Employment of reserves.—Even in an attack which it has been possible to plan methodically beforehand in all its details, the Higher Command must come to an early *decision as to the employment of reserves,* and generally on imperfect information. Any weakening on the part of the enemy and any advantages gained must be foreseen and rapidly exploited.

The Higher Command must aim at directing the course of the battle to its wishes by the use of reserves. Their employment is most effective where the attack is gaining ground most quickly; this is also the best method of assisting those parts of the line which are advancing only slowly or are being held up. If the enemy is preparing to make heavy counter-attacks, it is most important to realize whether their effect may be counteracted by carrying the attack forward at other points or whether direct support should be given to certain parts of our line.

From the beginning of the attack the Higher Command must be careful to keep its reserves well forward. At the same time, any over-loading of lines of communication which might lead to their being blocked should be avoided. It is of first importance that the fire power of the fighting troops should be maintained by the uninterrupted and rapid supply of ammunition.

It is an important duty of all commanders to see that this is the case in their area. Notwithstanding this, the higher commands should relieve the lower to as large an extent as possible from having to occupy themselves with replenishment of ammunition and stores. This especially applies to corps staffs. . . . .

E. RECONNAISSANCE; MAPS; TRANSMISSION OF INFORMATION

. . . . 31. Meteorological service.—The final determination of the time of attack is mainly dependent on the weather (e.g., in relation to the use of gas, visibility, effect on artillery, practicability of roads in wet and dry weather). The meteorological service, therefore, should be consulted at an early date.

An attack cannot be completely independent of *weather conditions.* Preparations, artillery action (even with H.E. shell), the advance of all arms in the attack and the pushing up of ammunition, stores, and supplies are seriously influenced by the weather. The weather has forced us to postpone many important attacks (e.g., at Verdun in February 1916, in Rumania in November 1916, at Riga in August 1917, in Italy in October 1917). These experiences will always make it necessary to take the possibility of a *sudden change in the weather* into account. The entire success of an artificially timed sequence of attacks can never, therefore, be relied on with certainty. . . . .

F. THE VARIOUS ARMS

1. Artillery and Trench Mortars

35. The artillery preparation for the attack will vary in character; it is dependent on the nature of the battle ground, the scope of the projected attack, the strength of the enemy's means of defense, and the degree of surprise intended.

A *complete abandonment of artillery preparation* is permissible only in exceptional cases. Against a watchful enemy there is small prospect of success by this means.

In minor and medium operations an *artillery preparation lasting a few minutes* has been found useful. Notes regarding this are given in "The mounting of minor offensive operations in the Vailly Group in May and June, 1917."

The crippling of the enemy's artillery and the practical destruction of his defenses can be effected only by an *artillery preparation lasting several hours.*

36. Battle tasks.—In attacks during position warfare, the following are the usual battle tasks of the artillery in co-operation with trench mortars:

(*a*) The engagement and neutralization of the enemy's artillery and trench mortars.

(*b*) Neutralization of the enemy's trench garrisons and destruction of the enemy's positions in preparation for an assault.

(*c*) Bombardment of reserves and rearward communications, observation and command posts, parks, balloons, and traffic and ammunition supply in the rear of the objective.

(*d*) Support of the infantry attack by a creeping barrage.

(*e*) Accompaniment of the infantry attack with "infantry guns" and field artillery, with the object of breaking down local resistance by shelling at close range over open sights.

(*f*) Protection of the infantry by means of a protective barrage after the attainment of the objective.

(*g*) Repulse of hostile counter-attacks, keeping back of advancing reserves. . . . .

40. Preparatory bombardment of the trenches.—. . . . All kinds of false ideas prevail regarding *artillery preparation for assault.*

The manual requires on an average *one howitzer battery for the destruction of about* 100 *meters of trench.* Naturally, accuracy of fire (the nature of gun and ammunition, observation, range, weather conditions, etc.) and the quantity of ammunition fired (and thus, principally, rapidity of fire and length of bombardment) also play an essential part. *The complete destruction of a trench 100 meters long by one battery in an hour will generally be a very good performance.* Hence it follows that in a short preparatory bombardment (one to two hours and less) the *destruction of all the enemy's fire trenches,* etc., would necessitate the employment of unlimited masses of batteries.

Such complete destruction, however, is not necessary. If the trenches are destroyed, the enemy will occupy the cratered area. It may suffice if the most important works (flanking trenches, the intersection of communication trenches, obstacles at points where the attacker wishes to penetrate, etc.) are destroyed. The weaker the garrison and the more surprise may be relied on, the lighter will be the task of destruction, pure and simple.

The bombardment of the intervening ground also . . . . cannot annihilate all living resistance. It is solely intended to cause loss to the enemy, to make him keep his head down and to shake his morale. It is further intended to deprive him of the power of observation and communication, so that he may finally be surprised by the moment of the infantry attack, thrown into confusion and, having lost touch with his commander, may become incapable of the determination necessary to insure energetic resistance.

Moral effect will therefore be particularly aimed at, especially if the artillery preparation is brief (cf. par. 40*f*). . . . . Success depends on the attacking infantry not allowing the moral effect attained to pass off, but at once taking full advantage of it. *It will rarely happen that the infantry will be entirely spared thereby from hand-to-hand fighting; this will, however, be light if the infantry makes a really determined attack and presses forward so rapidly that the leading men reach the defenders simultaneously* with the last rounds from their own guns (cf. par. 60). . . . .

45. The creeping barrage (par. 36*d*) in front of the attack will be formed by the largest possible number of batteries, so that it may possess the necessary depth. The extent to which Blue Cross ammunition can be used for this purpose depends on local circumstances.

In order that the infantry when it advances may be able to move forward almost into the artillery fire, it is advisable, in order to lessen the danger from splinters, to fire last rounds of the artillery preparation with delay action fuse (if this is available), or to finish by firing some blind rounds from trench mortars. Troops must be trained in advancing behind a barrage.

The lifting of the fire takes place by "bounds," the times and length of which are regulated in the attack orders. The length depends on the ground, the nature of the country, and the probable duration of the attack. The rate of progress of the barrage must be so calculated that the advance of the infantry in the attack continues uninterruptedly.

In order to bring the infantry advance, in attacks with distant objectives, into touch with the progress of the creeping barrage again after long distances (1–2 kilometers) have been covered, it may be advisable to fix certain lines on which the barrage will halt. Lengthening of the range will begin again only when the infantry asks for it by means of an agreed signal. *The advance of the infantry must on no account be checked by a proceeding of this kind.*

The artillery must also be in a position to protect the infantry by shortening its fire in case of any temporary reverse.

If certain areas (strong points, villages, woods) are not to be dealt with by frontal attack, but surrounded after a break-through has been effected in neighboring sectors, artillery fire will be continued on them during the assault, particularly on their edges, and will be switched to a flank or to the rear at carefully fixed hours, or on a previously arranged signal. In certain circumstances, a concentration on the interior of the area to be assaulted will be necessary before fire is withdrawn. . . . .

(*e*) A warning is necessary against expecting too much of the barrage. Fire at definite targets with observation will always prove superior to a barrage, which will always remain to a certain degree inelastic and unadaptable, however skilfully handled. Its effectiveness depends upon succeeding, contrary to the British practice, in making the barrage depend on the infantry, and in training our infantry *to keep immediately behind the barrage in spite of loss from stray "shorts" and injury from our own shell splinters* (cf. par. 60, last sub-par.). . . . .

50. General artillery consideration.—*In ordinary attacks, the depth of the attack is limited by the range of the mass of artillery in position.*

In deep attacks, with a break-through as their objective, careful preparation must be made for moving forward all the mobile artillery and trench mortars, with a sufficient supply of ammunition. This is one of the essential conditions of success in the break-through battle. . . . .

II. Infantry

53. Factors of success.—*In the success of the infantry attack, the numbers of infantry employed is not the decisive factor, but their fighting power (which depends on rest, training, and equipment), the care taken in preparation, and the skill of officers and men, combined with rapid and determined action.*

54. Strength.—The strength necessary for the attack depends on:

(*a*) The distance of the objective.

(*b*) The artillery preparation and support during the assault, as well as on the strength of the enemy's position and its garrison.

(*c*) The possibilities and manner of assembly of the troops for the attack.

(*d*) The equipment (e.g., machine guns, flame projectors, trench mortars) of our own infantry.

As regards (*a*), *the nearer the objective lies the weaker* may be, as a general rule, the attacking infantry. *In deep attacks distribution in depth* is necessary, in order to provide assistance at particular points, to check reverses, to close gaps which may arise, and to protect threatened flanks.

As regards (*b*), assaulting infantry must, especially in deep attacks, possess *sufficient fighting strength* from the outset, in order to be able to break down any unforeseen resistance and the opposition which will become stronger and stronger as the attack progresses. Nevertheless, fighting strength is expressed not only in terms of the number of men with rifles and of bombers but just as much in *intensity of fire* (number of machine guns, fire support).

As regards (*c*), the possibilities and manner of *assembly of the attacking infantry and the choice of approach routes* have a decisive influence on the mounting and course of the attack. Assembly points should be chosen so that the troops in readiness shall be as much as possible withdrawn from artillery fire and that favorable approach routes and lines of attack shall be available.

If the attack is conducted from carefully constructed, permanent positions, the assembly will be possible in the trenches, and partly even in dugouts. As a rule, trenches without dugouts, shell-craters, or natural cover are sufficient. Even in cratered areas, an attempt should at least be made by joining up the craters, to enable subordinate commanders to inspect the assembly, to supervise the men, and to get orders to them. Earthworks which might be recognized as jumping-off trenches must be avoided. It is of the greatest importance to conceal the assembly from air observation.

The difficulties in the way of carrying out the assembly without the enemy noticing it and of effecting a surprise attack increase with the number of troops to be assembled. Endeavors should therefore be made to carry it out with as small a force of infantry as possible. The shorter the distance over which the attack has to pass, the smaller will be the effectives required.

The assembly will be in close formation or more or less distributed in depth, according to local conditions. In the first case, the troops do not open out until the advance begins. In particularly favorable circumstances the assembly may be carried out close in front of the zone of the enemy's barrage fire.

The assembly of the attacking infantry is the crisis of the attack. Of especial importance are strict limitation of its numbers to what is necessary, and avoidance of too extensive concentrations, which make cover for bringing up and assembly very difficult, endanger the chance of a surprise, and may incidentally lead to unnecessary losses, confusion, and panic.

If the whole of the assembly position lies forward of the enemy's barrage zone, distribution in depth must be gained during the advance. Otherwise the infantry will be used up too rapidly without any result (cf. par. 6, last sub-par.).

Similarly, the detailing of reserves in the course of the attack is of very great value (cf. par. 60, last sub-par. but one).

As regards (*d*), *machine guns* are not auxiliary weapons but just as much the *principal weapon of the infantry* as their rifles. Nevertheless, at the present time in break-through attacks, in view of their reduced fighting strengths, infantry companies cannot take more than 4 light machine guns (and one in reserve), and machine-gun companies only 6 heavy machine guns (and 3 in reserve). . . . .

Granatwerfer will be kept in the departure position during break-through attacks. Their detachments, like those of the light *Minenwerfer* of the infantry which remain behind, will join in the attack as riflemen. . . . .

56. Attack formations.—The infantry will attack on the lines laid down in their training manual (*Manual of Infantry Training in War, 1918*). The peculiar nature of the objectives necessitates the attack being generally led by assault detachments. Endeavors must be made to form these assault detachments from groups of riflemen, which will be reinforced or formed as required.

Whether it is better to employ waves formed of lines of skirmishers or waves of assault detachments or a combination of both must be decided according to each particular case. . . . .

60. Method of carrying out the attack.—In the *assault* it is most important to exploit to the full the effects of the artillery preparation and support. *The assaulting infantry must be in the enemy's position simultaneously with the last rounds from their artillery and trench mortars, and during the further course of the attack must follow immediately behind their own barrage,* so that the enemy has no time to come out of the dugouts that may still be intact, or to prepare for action in any other way.

Besides making full use of the weapons at their disposal and exploiting the enemy's known weaknesses, *the troops must have dash* if an assault is to be successful. Success is gained by determined and reckless drive and initiative on the part of every individual man. A check in the attack at one place must not spread to the whole line; infantry which pushes well forward will envelop the parties of the enemy which are standing fast, will sweep them aside, and pave the way for the advance of any of their own detachments which have been held up. Hesitation leads to failure.

The battle sectors are best arranged when the front waves can attack straight to the front. Boundaries should be formed by conspicuous points and lines on the ground, e.g., roads, railways, edges of woods.

Within the battle sectors the attacks must not be carried out uniformly. Strong points, villages, and woods must be neutralized, in certain circumstances by means of smoke clouds. The troops should pass them and, distributed in depth, attack the points which appear likely to offer the least resistance. Rearward waves will capture the strong points, etc., by envelopment.

In order to compel the rapid surrender of nests and strong points which the leading waves have overrun, it may be advisable to detail special mixed detachments—if necessary composed of all arms—under energetic leaders, to deal with them.

The leading infantry should avoid all halts which are not absolutely necessary. The front line is frequently weakened more rapidly by men falling out to rummage through the enemy's dugouts, dumps, and baggage in search of food, etc., than by the enemy's fire and by exhaustion. Strict supervision is therefore necessary. Men shirking and looting must be got hold of by parties from *their own* regiments and brought on immediately.

Attacks conducted on the principle of rolling up the defense by working along the trenches are advisable only in small unimportant operations and minor enterprises, which are more of the nature of retaliation and raids and have not been preceded by an effective fire preparation for assault.

The smaller the attack and the nearer the objective, the more minutely must the routes to be followed by the attacking infantry be marked out and the details of the operation laid down. The deeper and more important the attack, the more frequently do situations occur in which a decision will be brought about by the independent action of individual assault detachments or groups, provided this action properly conforms to the spirit of the whole operation. In this way small advantages gained may at once be developed into great successes. All directions given and measures taken must aim at insuring that the commander's ideas are carried out. Every man must be trained to keep continuously in touch with the commander of his assault detachment. No commander may even for an instant lose sight of co-operation with the unit to which he belongs and the neighboring detachment, as well as with other arms. Signals by means of flares (also flame projectors) should be carefully arranged.

When sections or assault detachments broken up in the attack get bunched together in the enemy's defenses, endeavor must be made, as soon as the situation permits, and in order to avoid being surprised in a formation unsuited to fighting, to extend them in regular lines of skirmishers, as laid down in the *Manual of Infantry Training in War, 1918,* to detail a reserve and flank guards, and to send out patrols to the front and flank.

The principle that in the attack the infantry must advance into their own artillery and trench-mortar fire, which was so successfully taught in the assault battalions, must become general among all infantry. It requires reckless pluck and high morale, as occasional casualties from their own artillery fire must be put up with. By such an advance, on the other hand, close fighting with the enemy's infantry and its machine guns will be made easier. The total casualties will therefore be considerably less. The infantry must be taught by every means to understand this. *It must be possible.* The energy of the infantry attack and its success essentially depend upon it (cf. also par. 40, last sub-par., and par. 45e). . . . .

63. Necessity for relief.—It is a matter of experience that infantry generally suffers less in the attack than in the subsequent bombardment and counter-attacks. The Higher Command must, therefore, make timely provision for the relief of the infantry, or the continuation of the attack, by new formations.

Regarding reliefs in a deep break-through, compare par. 12, 2d–4th sub-pars. . . . .

III. Cavalry

66. Cavalry.—During the attack, all staffs down to and including battalions and artillery *Abteilungen* must be provided with *dispatch riders* and mounted scouts. The more the attack becomes transformed into a war of movement, the more cavalry must be allotted to formations for reconnaissance and dispatch-carrying.

IV. Engineers

67. Mining.—As a preliminary to an attack, mines are often fired. If the explosion takes place at the moment of commencing the attack, it may inflict considerable loss on the enemy. Mines have, moreover, an important moral effect and facilitate the first rush forward. They de-

mand, however, very tedious preliminary work and a considerable amount of labor; their effect does not reach far back. If the enemy notices that mining is going on, he will endeavor to make its success doubtful by countermining.

68. Further tasks allotted to the engineers in the attack are the demolition of our own obstacles and the removal of those placed by the enemy, the blowing up of defended dugouts, concrete pill-boxes, caves, and cellars, if the resistance cannot be broken by flame projectors and the works thereby preserved for our own use. They have also to construct temporary bridges and other means of passage. For these and kindred tasks, detachments of engineers should be detailed and provided with the necessary material. They should be partly allotted to the assault troops and partly used farther back. . . . .

V. Signal Service

71. Signal commanders must be early informed of the intentions of the commander of the troops, especially as to the time and objective of the attack. Careful calculation of time and resources and systematic preparation are necessary for:

(*a*) Construction of the system of communications in the assembly zone.

(*b*) The execution of the attack.

(*c*) Spaces to be crossed if preliminary success is exploited.

These calculations and preparations form an essential part of the preparations for the attack. . . . .

VI. Air Forces

81. Introductory.—The following rules apply to *attacks on a large scale* for which strong air forces of all types are indispensable; naturally they are also applicable to smaller attacks.

82. Principles to be observed when reinforcing the front.—The appearance of strong air forces (aëroplanes, balloons, and anti-aircraft guns) is for the enemy one of the surest signs of an impending attack. *The activity of the air forces must therefore be moderated during preparations.*

It is very difficult to insure an adequate engagement of aëroplanes whilst still observing the demands of secrecy, as reinforcements cannot be brought up till very late. By frequently exchanging aircraft units, by attaching aviators to the reconnaissance and protective flights already present on the front of attack, and by forming instructional centers behind the front, an attempt must be made to insure that the flying personnel possesses the necessary knowledge of the country on the front of the attack without premature transference of forces. Flying at the front must be co-ordinated so that, on the one hand, it will be difficult for the enemy to detect reinforcement, and so that, on the other, the aviators are given sufficient opportunity for learning the country.

In any case, complete *photographic reconnaissance* with no gaps must be insured. This is of decisive importance. Next in importance is the necessity of familiarizing artillery, infantry, and battle aviators with the ground. The main reinforcements in pursuit and protective flights can be brought up last.

The distribution among the attacking divisions of reconnaissance flights and of units detailed for battle flying must be carried out sufficiently early to enable them to take part, behind the front (as far back as possible), in the practice attacks of their divisions. Practice in mutual co-operation is indispensable.

The bringing up, housing, and work of balloons and of anti-aircraft guns are governed by the same principles. . . . .

G. REARGUARD COMMUNICATIONS

103. Importance of rearward communications.—The greater the scale of the attack, the more do *careful maintenance and allotment of road and railway communications* and the employment of a proportionately larger force of men and quantity of materials for the supply of the army and for work of all kinds form the preliminary conditions for success. *When rearward communications fail, especially when ammunition cannot be got up, reverses endangering the success of the whole operation are inevitable.*

104. Rearward roads and railways must be equal to meeting the demands of the most intense traffic. They should be allotted at an early stage to corps and divisions. Extension arrangements must be made at railheads to deal with all possible requirements for unloading and transshipment. For this, and for issue at the dumps, sufficient labor must be made available; careful regulations must be made for traffic control at all dumps.

On narrow roads in the zone nearest the front the construction and marking of passing-places and of diversion roads round villages and the erection of conspicuous sign-posts are a necessary condition for the smooth working of traffic. It will frequently be necessary to order that certain roads must be used in *one* direction only.

During the last few weeks before the attack, all increased activity in construction of railways and roads which might be observed from the air must be desisted from. . . . .

FINAL REMARKS

The great attack for a break-through requires that commanders and troops should free themselves from habits and customs of trench warfare. Methods of warfare and tactics have changed in detail. But the great military principles which formed the backbone of our military training in peace time and to which we owe all great successes of the war are still the old ones. Where they may have been forgotten they must be resurrected.

LUDENDORFF

213. ORDERS FOR THE MAINTENANCE OF SECRECY WITH REGARD TO OPERATIONS JANUARY 23, 1918
GENERAL VON LOSSBERG[26]

Fourth Army, H.Q.
Ia S. No. 410, January

(Secret. Not to be taken into the front line)   23.1.18

The memorandum, "Orders for the Maintenance of Secrecy with Regard to Operations," is intended to prevent the enemy from gaining an insight into our order of battle, intentions, and troop movements.

It is the duty of every individual, whether officer, official, or private soldier, to do everything possible, so far as he is concerned, to make the maintenance of secrecy successful.

It is the duty of commanding officers continually to draw the attention of the officers and men under their command to the necessity of maintaining silence and reserve in conversations and in writing, and to see that they comply with this duty. The memorandum should be discussed with the officers at least once a month. The points which concern the men should be explained to them at pay parades, more especially to those who are on detached duty.

Corps will send in to Army H.Q. by 10.2.18 any experience gained and any wishes with regard to revision of "Orders for the Maintenance of Secrecy with Regard to Operations," whether these are of a general nature, or refer to particular sectors of the front. Requests of an urgent nature should be submitted in every case without delay.

For the Army Commander,

v. LOSSBERG, Maj.-Gen.
C.G.S.

[26] Collection of German Military Documents, Hoover War Library.

Distribution down to battalions and independent units, including foot artillery batteries not organized in battalions, pioneer companies, etc.

A. Regulations for Traffic

1. *The importance of keeping movements and concentrations secret in attack and in defense* makes it a point of honor for every man to do all in his power to contribute to the successful maintenance of secrecy. Every detachment and column, whether on the march or at rest, and every individual must do his best to insure that less movement and fewer lights are seen than even in quiet times. . . . .

B. Instructions for the Use of the Telephone in the Danger Zone and in the Rearward Area

9. *The effective range of the enemy's listening sets* extends as far as 3,300 yards behind our front lines. This area is called the "danger zone." Divisions will fix the rearward boundary of the "danger zones" for their sectors and the command posts which are situated within the "danger zone." In the rearward area, special measures are necessary to render it difficult for the enemy's spies to listen in to conversations.

The maintenance of secrecy as to our order of battle and intentions must be secured by the most rigorous application of discipline in telephone and wireless traffic. Every man who is engaged in the Signal Service must be made to understand that the slightest carelessness in this branch of the service jeopardizes our success.

C. Regulations for Wireless Communication

13. *The employment and traffic stations demand very special caution.* As all receiving stations within the range of the transmitting station can pick up the messages, the enemy is in a position to obtain information as to our order of battle and intentions, if our stations are employed carelessly. . . . .

D. Concealment of All New Construction from Aërial Observation

15. Aëroplane and balloon observers use both the eye and aërial photography for observation. On an air photograph it is often possible to see objects which are not recognizable to the eye. It is therefore necessary to screen from enemy observation not only the traffic on our roads and railways but also our infantry works and battery positions

and the arrangements required for the supply of ammunition, rations, and building material, both during their construction and after completion. . . . .

16. *In the case of all new construction, wherever it is at all possible, it is absolutely essential that camouflage material shall be available beforehand in large quantities, before the building material is brought up and the work begun, so as to make it impossible or difficult, from the beginning, for the enemy to observe what is going on.* . . . .

F. Measures to Render Enemy Espionage Difficult

19. *The enemy's espionage service operates both in the field and in Germany,* through the most varied means, to ascertain the distribution of our forces, our order of battle, troop movements, and intentions.

The most usual means are: By questioning or overhearing the conversation of individual soldiers and the persons on whom they are billeted; by questioning relatives of soldiers in Germany; by recording the notice boards at the headquarters of divisions and other formations or units and at supply depots; by observing troop movements and the units which are taking part in them; by the theft of situation maps, orders, etc.; by tapping telephone wires and listening in.

The information which the enemy's Intelligence Service particularly desires to obtain may be seen from the attached list of questions which has been dropped in large numbers in the occupied territory from aëroplanes or message balloons.

"*What troops are stationed at present in your neighborhood?*

"(No attention need be paid to Landsturm, as that is of no interest.) Inf. Regt. No. ——, Artillery Regt. No. ——, Cavalry Regt. No. ——; Active, Reserve, Ersatz or Landwehr ——; Place ——; Since ——;

"Are these troops resting?

"Have they come from our front? If not, from which?

"Have they come from Russia? If so, when did they detrain, and where?

"The *morale* of the troops is ——.

"The average company strength is —— men.

"The rations of the men are ——.

"The men complain of ——.

"The youngest were born in the year ——.

"We also wish to know the sites of aërodromes and ammunition depots, reports of air raids and their results, assemblies of troops which the Germans are making. All this information should be given with map references so that we can ascertain the exact place easily.

"In the case of air raids, the following information must be given with special accuracy: The *camouflage* used to conceal buildings which contain ammunition, petrol, etc.; the color and some guiding points should be given, e.g., 200 feet from the church, mill, Scheldt, etc."

20. *The means employed by the enemy's spies to transmit their information are:*

Personal reports.—These take much time and usually arrive after the event has occurred.

Transmission by aëroplanes landing in back areas and picking up the reports.

Transmission by carrier pigeons, which are dropped in large numbers from aëroplanes and balloons by means of small parachutes, and by *wireless stations* with a range of 30 miles which spies dropped from aëroplanes carry with them and erect at points not likely to arouse suspicion. *The civilian population of the occupied territory* has been induced on a very large scale to collect and transmit information.

21. *Measures to be taken to counter the enemy's espionage system.*

(*a*) *The precautions ordered to be taken to insure the secrecy of troop movements must be very strictly adhered to. . . . .*

(*b*) *The greatest care must be exercised in intercourse with the inhabitants of the occupied territory.* No officer or man may say where he has come from, or where he is going, in what part of the line he is stationed, how long he is to be in rest billets, or where his unit has been engaged. Social intercourse with the civil population and the carrying of letters for the inhabitants of the occupied territory are forbidden.

(*c*) *Great self-restraint when writing home and in conversation whilst on leave. Other measures to be taken:*

No postal packet from the theater of war, no matter from whom, to whom, or to what place, may contain the following matters: Information as to the units, the places in which they are billeted, their movements, transport by rail, strength, fighting value and condition of the troops, the employment of heavy artillery and other special weapons, intended raids, losses or unusual events, names of commanders, or, in short, any information whatever of a military nature, as a spy can draw important conclusions from information on all these matters if it comes into his possession. The danger of carrying and sending home in letters portions of diaries will be specially emphasized. Army H.Q. will exercise a strict supervision of the letters of officers and men, and all breaches of the above regulations will be dealt with regardless of individuals or their position.

(*d*) *Special attention is to be paid to unusual behavior on the part of hostile aëroplanes and to hostile captive balloons, message balloons, and carrier pigeons.*

214. THE ATTACK BEYOND KEMMEL OF THE FOURTH ARMY UNDER GENERAL SIXT VON ARNIM, APRIL 29, 1918[27]

10:45 (A.M.) General Ludendorff to the Chief of the Army Staff: H. E. Ludendorff has the impression that the attack is not developing favorably.

13:55 Captain von Ilsemann to the Chief of the Army Staff: By order of H. M. the Kaiser, Captain von Ilsemann asks for information concerning the situation. The Chief of the Army Staff replies to him that on account of the solid organization of the enemy's defense, its echelon in depth, the attack of the 29th of April is indeed meeting with greater difficulties than were previously encountered. . . . .

19:55 His Imperial Highness the Crown Prince asks the Chief of the Army Staff for information concerning the situation. [The reply is not recorded.]

21:35 The Chief of the Army Staff to General Ludendorff: Estimate of the situation by the Chief of the Army Staff: He concludes from the information received up to the present time that the attack has resulted in only a minimum advance. Our shock troops have attacked an adversary who is generally echelonned in depth, well prepared for defensive operations, and supported by a powerful artillery and numberless machine-gun nests. In the forces actually at our disposal, our operation does not present any chance of success. It will be best to discontinue it. It is advisable to determine the exact front of the two forces and improve our own front according to our means.

It will then be in order to decide if a methodical renewal of the offensive offers a prospect of success, or if it is preferable to stop the operations.

H. E. Ludendorff approves this manner of estimating the situation.

23:00 The Chief of the Army Staff (von Lossberg, Major-General and General à la suite) to the Chief of Staff of [Crown Prince Rupprecht's] Group of Armies.

The Chief of the Army Staff reports that, except for a slight advance on the right wing, the continuation of the attack has not procured any particular advantage. . . . .

23:30 Telegram transmitted to the 10th Reserve Corps at 23:40 to the 18th Reserve Corps at 23:40 to the Guard Corps at 23:40 to the Guard Reserve Corps April 30 at 0:15 by telephone message, to the VI Army and to the 3d Bavarian Corps, April 30 at 0:15, to the Group of Armies April 30 at 0:50:

[27] "Register of Telephone Conversations, Reports of Conferences, Copies of Operations Orders, April 29, 1918," Collection of German Military Documents, Hoover War Library.

ARMY ORDER FOR THE DAY OF APRIL 30

1. The attack will not be renewed tomorrow April 30; minor operations remain authorized. 2. It is important to hold the front in our possession and for that purpose to organize the defense in depth. (Machine guns, etc.) It is necessary to maintain the reserve nearer, to establish in the rear of our first position a secure position to protect the artillery and enable them to occupy it. 3 . . . 7 . . . IV Army, Ia, No. 742—E.M.

215. ORDER OF THE SIXTH ARMY ON DISCIPLINE, MAY 8, 1918[28]

"The slow but steady deterioration of discipline is undoubtedly due to the long duration of the war. This lack of discipline shows itself primarily in the large number of sentences passed in which the courts-martial too often show signs of a misplaced clemency, and, subsequently, more plainly in the unsoldierly bearing adopted by the men towards their superiors. Non-commissioned officers maintain the correct attitude, but, amongst the great majority of the men, it appears that saluting or other marks of respect (coming to attention) shown to officers whom they meet on foot or in cars are no longer strictly carried out. Even officers appear to forget that it is their duty to return salutes.

"These breaches of discipline are undoubtedly largely due to the fact that superior officers pass by rapidly in cars, as well as to the indifference of officers who shirk the trouble of punishing breaches of discipline.

"If officers will do their duty in this respect, the change will soon be felt. Subordinate officers will drill their men when behind the front in paying those marks of respect the execution of which leaves much to be desired.

"Men must drop the habit, borrowed from the French, of keeping their hands in their pockets.

"Officers and men must be instructed as to the flags carried by staff cars.

"The appearance of the men will be smartened up as soon as they are relieved.

"Instruction and drill will commence immediately.

"I shall hold all officers responsible for this, and particularly the commanders of independent units.

"(*Signed*) VON QUAST
"General of Infantry Commanding the Sixth Army"

[28] *Confidential Summary of Information*, A.E.F., General Staff, No. 126, August 3, 1918, pp. 897–98.

216. LUDENDORFF'S ORDER FOR THE TRAINING OF TROOPS, JUNE 9, 1918[29]

Chief of Staff of the Army
    in the Field   GENERAL HEADQUARTERS
Ia II No. 8.615 Secret Op.   June 9, 1918

The accuracy of the instructions and principles laid down by the Army High Command for the training of troops and the methods of attack has been confirmed to the smallest details since the "Bluecher" offensive [probably the Aisne offensive of May 27, 1918].

Some new ideas which should be considered in the training of troops form the basis of this article:

GENERAL REMARKS AND COMMAND

1. It is necessary to have a firm command without destroying the initiative of the troops making an advance. With this in view, a greater importance will be attached to the preparation of the means of communication for the transmission of information, to the method of forwarding information and to the manner of mutual advice as to the course of events. The time which orders and reports take to reach destination will be taken into consideration. A rapid comprehension of the entire situation, even in the smaller units, has a deciding influence upon the success of the operations. . . . .

6. An attack fulfills its purpose as soon as the losses inflicted upon the enemy become much greater than our own. This is always the case in a successful surprise attack. It is therefore a question of hurling the troops upon the enemy without being influenced by fear of losses and without losing sight of assistance and preparation by artillery fire.

It is the task of the command to anticipate the moment when the action of the enemy's reserves will become more pronounced. The attacks must then be gradually carried on in a more methodical manner; heavy artillery preparation with an increase of expenditure of ammunition will be required more and more up to the moment when it appears that the operation should pass into the defensive stage. When the enemy's reaction and counter-attacks are made without sufficient preparation he will suffer heavy losses in the face of a skilfully conducted defensive, while our own forces will be economized. It is almost never a question of our gaining ground at any price. We must destroy the enemy but economize our forces. From this point of view we must

[29] Confidential Summary of Information, A.E.F., General Staff, No. 124, August 3, 1918, pp. 889–91.

have a clearer military perception; we have still had a tendency during recent fighting to attack with too feeble forces and to fight for gains in ground which were of no importance to the general situation.

On the defensive the tried principles will be observed: an offensive attitude of the artillery and infantry; elasticity; distribution in depth; and no attempt to contest every inch of ground. . . . .

Summary

20. The facts stated above show that an effort was everywhere made to perfect training with zeal and intelligence. Where instruction was still insufficient the fault was due in most cases to the brevity of the period of training. But even a little time is useful if well employed. It is necessary, therefore, to lay particular stress on exercises in minor tactics and drill for specialists in their particular branch. Large maneuvers and reviews will rarely be held, because their preparation takes up too much of the time of the troops.

If we take all opportunities for work according to the orders of the High Command (mainly those contained in Memorandum Ia II No. 7745 of April 17, 1918, and Ia—Ic—II No. 7925, April 29, 1918) we shall maintain the tactical superiority in maneuver which we have acquired, and we shall advance to new and greater successes.

(*Signed*) Ludendorff

217. DIVISIONAL ORDER ON DESERTIONS, JUNE 11, 1918[30]

1st Reserve Division

General Headquarters
June 11, 1918

The present offensive of the XVIIIth Army between Montdidier and Noyon was revealed to the French several days in advance by Germans whom they had taken prisoner and mainly by an infamous deserter. The French were thus prepared five days in advance for the attack. The purpose of the offensive was without doubt achieved, but it cost greater sacrifices than a surprise offensive. The resulting losses are due to the infamous and thoughtless conduct of certain individuals. Through them the number of fathers, mothers, wives, fiancées, brothers, and sisters who mourn the death of a relative is greater than it should have been. Lectures will be given to our troops on this matter.

(*Signed*) Count von Waldersee

[30] *Confidential Summary of Information,* A.E.F., General Staff, II, August 6, 1918, No. 127, p. 899.

218. LUDENDORFF'S GENERAL ORDER ON DESERTIONS, JUNE 23, 1918[31]

General Headquarters of the
Army in the Field
Ia. No. 8915 June 23, 1918

DESERTERS

1. Every man going over to the enemy will be punished with death on his return to Germany.
2. All his property within the country will be seized.
3. He will lose his nationality; his next of kin will not have the right to receive an allowance.
4. If a man is suspected of having betrayed his country, if only of having been admitted into a so-called privileged camp, action will be taken against him for treason to his country.
5. It is useless to reckon on escaping the penalty by remission or by lapse of time. Furthermore, it must be methodically explained to the men that through our offensives and also by other means we almost always succeed in knowing the names and units of prisoners who have given information, as well as the nature and importance of what they have revealed.

On the conclusion of peace these soldiers will be brought before a court-martial as traitors to the country. The severest punishment will be meted out to these men lacking honor and patriotism.

(*Signed*) LUDENDORFF

219. LUDENDORFF'S INSTRUCTIONS ON GAS SHELLING, JULY 9, 1918[32]

Chief of Staff of the Army
in the Field G.H.Q., July 9, 1918

Instructions of the circular of April 25, 1918, II, No. 84.419 Op., on the subject of the properties of ammunition, are replaced by the following:

A knowledge of the principal qualities of guns, ammunition, and fuses is indispensable in order to employ artillery judiciously and know

---

[31] *Confidential Summary of Information,* A.E.F., General Staff, II, August 6, 1918, No. 127, p. 899.

[32] *Confidential Supplement to Summary of Information,* A.E.F., General Staff, September 7, 1918, pp. 1065–67.

what must be expected of it. Errors which seem insignificant, such as, for example, forgetting the plunger of the striker, using delay action on marshy ground, may almost completely nullify its effect.

All higher commanders and officers of the General Staff, as well as infantry regimental commanders who often have artillery under their orders, should acquire the knowledge necessary to enable them to judge to what extent artillery can aid them and in order to avoid asking the impossible of it.

The following hints do not purport to give a complete outline but only to emphasize certain points of capital importance. They may serve as a basis for artillery conferences, which the largest possible number of infantry officers should likewise attend. (See also *Regulations on Artillery Fire*, par. 10.)

I. MORAL EFFECT . . . .

II. MATERIAL EFFECT

The material effect comprises: (1) The effect through fragmentation; (2) explosive effect (mine effect); (3) effect of gases; (4) smoke effect; (5) incendiary effect. . . . .

For gas shelling, the sensitive fuse is suitable, as otherwise the ground absorbs a great part of the effect. It is only when effect in the interior of houses, etc., is sought that the ordinary percussion (M.V.) fuse is preferable to the sensitive fuse. The time-fuse would be very effective in principle, but it is difficult to apply in practice, as the adjustment of the height of burst, which is particularly important in gas shelling, is very difficult. Delay-action or time-fuse gas shells are used only very exceptionally.

The greater part of the gas shells will in the future have a relatively large explosive charge. This has the following advantages:

(*a*) It produces a more favorable expansion of gas, so that, in spite of the diminished gas contents, the gas effect obtained at least equals that of the same number of ordinary gas shells of the same caliber.

(*b*) It produces, in addition to the gas effect, to an appreciable extent, a moral effect, an effect of fragmentation, and an explosive effect, although the latter is, on account of the decrease of the explosive charge, smaller than in firing with ordinary explosive shells.

(*c*) It disguises the gas shelling to some extent. The peculiarity of gas effects explains the fact that gas fatalities or casualties rarely fall into our hands. Nevertheless, there is no doubt about the effect, as shown by our own experiences, captured documents, and our successes.

Proper utilization of gas ammunition presupposes a knowledge of the peculiarity of the gases (see "Regulations on Artillery Gas Shelling"). Many mistakes are still made; the necessity for a sufficient gas density in particular is not always taken into consideration. This depends on: Dispersion of the shells; number of shells; duration of the fire; atmospheric conditions; nature of the ground at point of impact.

Different Kinds of Gas

(*a*) *Green Cross.*—This gas acts rapidly, with fatal effect after several breaths without the mask. Otherwise masks most generally afford protection against this kind of gas. When the adversary can be surprised when not protected by his mask *gas surprises* will be useful in any combat situation. Moreover, it may be necessary to shell certain parts of the terrain (battery or infantry positions) with large quantities of gas. This is not generally effective except immediately before important enterprises (offensive or defensive). As the enemy cannot remain in the gas even with the mask for many hours, he temporarily evacuates the shelled spot, as experience has shown.

It is in this way that Green Cross gas has been successfully used up to the present, in temporarily paralyzing hostile artillery during attacks. The permanent reduction and definite evacuation of the shelled area cannot be counted upon, as the effect of Green Cross gas continues only during a short period; the shelled area can be crossed by our troops about two hours after the shelling. Green Cross gas will hereafter be used in the Green Cross shell proper, and probably also in the H.E. Green Cross shell.

(*b*) *Yellow Cross No. 1 (now Green Cross No. 3).*—Yellow Cross Gas No. 1 resembles Green Cross gas, but is superior to it in several respects. Yellow Cross No. 1 will hereafter be designated Green Cross No. 3, in order to avoid confusion.

(*c*) *Blue Cross.*—Blue Cross gas acts extraordinarily rapidly, almost instantaneously, but creates a casualty for only a short time. When sufficiently dense, it goes completely through the French mask, not so completely in the case of the English mask, and compels the enemy to take off his mask. For this reason the mixing of Blue Cross and Green Cross gas is recommended. When not sufficiently dense, Blue Cross gas will at least compel the adversary to put on his mask and hamper his action.

The effect of the gas disappears with the dispersal of the gas sheet or the smoke detonation, and the gas evaporates rapidly. It may therefore be used when our infantry is relatively very near. If care is used, isolated shots may be fired without hesitation in combat of the accompanying guns against machine-gun nests, even when our infantry is very close.

Blue Cross gas is generally used only in H.E. gas shells. The shell has considerable explosive effect.

(*d*) *Yellow Cross* (not to be confused with Yellow Cross No. 1 ; see *b* above).—It does not at first disturb the enemy. The material effect does not commence to make itself felt until after several hours or days and acts progressively. The mask affords protection against this gas. However, splashing of the liquid penetrates clothing. The effect of the gas persists for a considerable period in dry weather, especially in villages and woods.

Experience proves that the enemy most generally evacuates places which have been shelled with Yellow Cross shell. Documents captured from the enemy show that he especially fears this gas.

Ground which we intend to occupy ourselves should not be contaminated with Yellow Cross during the last two or four days, depending upon the weather. Very light cases of poisoning result from a prolonged stay in the shelled area. After eight days all persistence of the effect has worn off, except in places which are particularly sheltered from fresh air—for example, caved-in cellars or tunnels.

Yellow Cross shell is now used in gas shell, properly so called, and in Yellow Cross H.E. shell. The latter will probably in the future be exclusively manufactured. The combination with the explosive has, in consequence of a very even but dense distribution of the gas in the cloud produced by the burst, the advantage of producing the effect of the Yellow Cross gas more rapidly than with Yellow Cross shell proper, while at the same time the effect is less persistent (approximately three times less). Our infantry can therefore cross shelled open ground a short time after the shelling (a few hours). Contact with objectives such as tree trunks, branches, cadavers, guns, and a prolonged stay in the shelled areas are, however, to be avoided for 24 hours.

220. INSTRUCTIONS AND RULES OF GUIDANCE FOR THE CONDUCT OF EVERY GERMAN SOLDIER WHO IS TAKEN PRISONER[33]

Wytschaete Group,
   Section Ic   July, 1918

(Not to be taken into the front line)

To be issued to the rank and file by companies for perusal, then collected again and filed by regimental staffs for occasional reissue and collection.

[33] Collection of German Military Documents, Hoover War Library.

For a man to allow himself to be taken prisoner without having defended himself to the utmost is a dishonorable act equivalent to treachery.

Capture at the hands of our inhuman foes, in view of their unexampled brutality of treatment, which is now proved beyond question in so large a number of cases, merely means being slowly tortured to death.

Should, however, a man be captured in spite of all his bravery and without its being his fault, even then the soldier still has sacred duties toward his comrades, toward his Commander-in-Chief to whom he took the oath of fealty, and toward his country. It is an easy duty for him to fulfill; he has only to preserve in his captivity the same courage which he has so often shown in the face of the enemy. The first thing suggested to prisoners in the enemy's camp, after their confidence has been gained by stimulating drinks and the best fare, is nothing less than the betrayal of their country. Afterward, when the object is attained, follows the usual meager prisoners' fare and hard work, with the most brutal treatment.

A prisoner is submitted to an examination in which, by cleverly framed questions, insincere promises, or even by threats of every kind, attempts are made to cause him to give away military secrets, such as the order of battle, the strength with which a front is held, intentions and plans for attack, measures for defense, concentrations or movements of troops, the exact condition of his own unit, strength of units, events taking place behind the front and in Germany, rest billets of his comrades, and other matters.

It is regrettable that this war has provided many instances where the statements of a man *without honor,* which unfortunately have often been only too accurate, have been proved to have had disastrous effects for *his own comrades.* How many brave soldiers have lost their lives through this cause?

The success of our attacks and enterprises is also imperiled in this way, and the successful issue of the war may thus be to a great extent jeopardized and the whole Fatherland receive the gravest injury.

It is just now, at the decisive point of the final struggle, that every soldier must feel more than ever the shame and infamy of such unprincipled conduct.

Again and again do prisoners captured by *us* give confirmation of the fact that those German soldiers, no matter to which state they belong, who allow themselves to be pressed under examination into making all kinds of statements, in the idea that they will receive better treatment, have had afterwards a much harder time than those who refused to say anything. For even among our enemies, the soldier who consciously betrays his country and puts his own comrades in danger ranks as a man without honor.

On the other hand, even the enemy invariably respects the German soldier who remains steadfast and refuses to make statements, even in the face of threats, or by a clever answer makes from the start all further questioning useless. Thus, Private Wiegand, of the 3d Company, 60th Infantry Regiment, who pleaded his soldier's oath and refused to make any statements, received full recognition in the Army Orders of the enemy.

If questions are asked about military or other dangerous subjects, there are many answers by which a man can escape further questions or at any rate parry them, e.g.:

"Only joined the unit a few days ago as a reinforcement."

"Just back from leave."

"Have been sick in quarters," or "Have just come out of hospital a few days ago and therefore have no information."

"Was on special duty (forestry, collieries, road construction, production of trench materials, etc.)."

"Accommodation under canvas in a wood, the name and exact location of which I cannot give. Have observed nothing there. Have seen no other troops beyond men of the detachment, or any artillery positions: have seen no transport to or from batteries or single guns, or movements of troops."

If further questions are asked, always repeat the same answer: "I was not there"; "I do not know"; "Am not acquainted with the sector"; "Do not know the flanking units"; "Have seen no artillery, as visiting artillery positions is strictly forbidden"; "Do not know the positions of sentries or machine guns, or their number"; "Know of no plans for attack"; "Know nothing of the relief of the division"; "Do not know the lines of approach to and departure from the position, as I went in at night"; "No work of any consequence in progress in the trenches or behind the front"; "Trenches, rations, and *morale* good."

221. LUDENDORFF'S DEFENSIVE ORDER, AUGUST 4, 1918[34]

Chief of Staff of the Army in the Field
Ia, No. 9670. Operations   August 4, 1918

I am under the impression that on many sides the possibility of a hostile attack is viewed not without some apprehension. This apprehension is wholly unjustified if our troops are watchful and do their duty.

[34] *Confidential Summary of Information*, A.E.F., General Staff, No. 151, August 30, 1918, p. 1020.

In all the operations of open warfare during their great defensive battle between the Marne and the Vesle the French were able to gain only one initial tactical success due to surprise, that of July 18, and they should not have had that success. During the fighting which followed, the enemy in spite of his mass of artillery was unable to obtain the least tactical advantage and, far from occupying prepared positions, our troops fought in open country and only occupied positions which are found at hand at the close of a day's battle. All of the enemy's attacks failed with severe losses. It was not the tactical success of our adversary but rather the requirements of our communications with the rear which caused our withdrawal.

The French and British infantry generally operated with circumspection; the American attacked more boldly but with less skill. It is to the tanks that the enemy owes his success on the first day. But they would not have been formidable if the infantry had not allowed itself to be taken by surprise and if the artillery had had a sufficient distribution in depth. Now we everywhere occupy positions which have been powerfully reinforced, and I am certain that we have judiciously echelonned our infantry and artillery. Henceforth we may await every hostile attack with the greatest of confidence. As I have already stated, nothing could please us more than to have the enemy launch an offensive which cannot but hasten the dissolution of his forces.

Officers and men should be animated with the indomitable will to conquer on the defensive as well as on the offensive. This fact will not be lost sight of during training. In the present situation we should not, therefore, devote our attention too exclusively to the offensive and neglect a co-ordinated defensive, which is generally more difficult. It is the latter, in fact, which frequently most severely tries the morale of the troops.

(Signed) LUDENDORFF

222. EXPERIENCES FROM THE FIGHTING ON THE WEST BANK OF THE MEUSE[35]

Meuse Group East
General Command, 5th Reserve Corps CORPS HEADQUARTERS
Ia No. 3878 op. September 29, 1918

1. American infantry is very unskilful in attack. It attacks with closed ranks in numerous and deep waves, at the head of which come the tanks. Such forms of attack form excellent targets for the activity

[35] Collection of German Military Documents, Hoover War Library.

of our artillery, infantry, and machine guns, if only the infantry does not get scared on account of the advancing masses and lose its nerve. Wherever the troops have made use of their weapons in an appropriate manner the American attacks collapsed with the heaviest losses. For example, Regiment 150 of the 37th Division repulsed yesterday 10 and today 3 American attacks without a loss of territory and with comparatively little loss to itself.

The Americans are very susceptible to artillery fire, particularly to gas shells. A few shots of Blue Cross are sufficient to cause a gas alarm and considerable nervousness. Repeated Blue Cross attacks, above all at night, are therefore advisable.

Having recovered from the first scares (*Schrecken*), the troops have now become very well accustomed to the American tanks. The tanks, therefore, do not any longer possess an appreciable battle-value. The infantry allows them to approach closely and then fires upon them with machine guns, with rifles (in both cases with S.m.K. ammunition), and with artillery. Thereupon, the tanks generally turn back. In case they keep on coming the infantry remains quiet and leaves the disposal of them to the artillery. In repeated cases tanks were also put out of commission when infantrymen threw hand-grenades into the loopholes. The infantry must again and again be made to realize that the tanks hardly deserve a battle-value at all and that their threatening danger is overcome when the infantry does not permit itself to become frightened by them any more.

The American infantry generally allows the tanks to proceed considerably in advance, so that our infantry found time to occupy itself first with the tanks and then with the oncoming infantry.

The general opinion of the troops of *Maas-West* is that the American army is not a dangerous enemy, once one has learned to know its method of fighting.

The divisions have to take care that these experiences are brought *immediately* to the attention of the troops.

(*Signed*) . . . . v. SODEN

223. EXTRACT FROM LUDENDORFF'S TELEGRAM TO BARON VON LERSNER, OCTOBER 8, 1918[36]

1. In the first place it is not to be considered that the retreat will be so extensive as to bring about a violation of Dutch territory.

2. Even if a greater movement eastward should be actually carried out, Dutch territory will not be affected by it.

[36] Collection of German Military Documents, Hoover War Library.

3. Nevertheless, in case this should happen through an unforeseen event, the German Supreme Army Command will, without further discussion, assume that these troops are to be interned in Holland according to prevailing law.

224. REPORT FROM HEADQUARTERS 461ST INFANTRY REGIMENT, OCTOBER 21, 1918[37]

461ST INFANTRY REGIMENT   October 21, 1918

In the sector of the Army Corps the troops have recently again shown a marked tendency to request a barrage by light signals as soon as they perceive the enemy in the advanced zone. This practice not only shows the enemy how much the infantry is frightened by his approach but it also indicates that the infantry lacks confidence in its own means of defense. This idea is apparently tending to become fixed in the companies. I request all commanding officers to take vigorous steps to counteract this state of mind. We shall not always have the good fortune to have such a strong force of artillery at our disposal as at present; we shall surely find ourselves in situations where we shall be forced to defend ourselves by our own means against enemy attacks. Furthermore, the laying down of barrages without any real necessity means the useless consumption of large amounts of ammunition.

I again direct attention to the fact that only company commanders and commissioned platoon leaders are authorized to display colored light signals.

225. THE LAST OFFICIAL WAR BULLETIN, NOVEMBER 11, 1918, 1:46 P.M.[38]

In the course of the repulse of American attacks E. of the Meuse the following troops distinguished themselves particularly by successful counter-attacks: the 207th Brandenburg Reserve Infantry Regiment, commanded by Lieutenant-Colonel Hennigs, and troops of the 192d Saxon Infantry Division, under command of Lieutenant-Colonel von Zeschau, commander of the 183d Infantry Regiment.

In consequence of the signature of the armistice agreement, hostilities were suspended on all fronts today at noon.

(*Signed*) GROENER,
First Quartermaster-General

[37] *Confidential Summary of Information*, A.E.F., General Staff, III, No. 227, November 14, 1918, p. 1450.
[38] *Ibid.*, p. 1451.

CHAPTER XI

THE NAVY

INTRODUCTORY NOTE

THE FINAL naval policy of Imperial Germany was established by the *Novelle* of 1911 which led directly toward a war with Great Britain. The operations order of July 30, 1914, indicates, however, that the Empire's growing strength at sea could not then be used effectively against the greatest naval power. The first phase of submarine warfare was followed by the naval policy for the High Seas Fleet, which led to the battle of Jutland.

At the dramatic conference of Pless, January 9, 1917, Admiral von Holtzendorff expressed the judgment of the naval and military leaders that if unrestricted submarine warfare were resumed no American soldier could set foot on the European Continent. Unrestricted submarine warfare was then commenced and resulted in the entry of America into the war.

The morale of the High Seas Fleet declined after 1916, when the chief naval energies of Germany were directed toward the development of a submarine force. In 1917 a serious mutiny which broke out on the German battleships was suppressed with an iron hand. Nevertheless, revolutionary propaganda permeated the battle fleet, which revolted at the end of October 1918. This naval revolt was the signal for the overthrow of the Bismarckian Empire.

226. OPERATIONS ORDERS FOR THE NAVY, JULY 30, 1914[1]

(a) THE NORTH SEA

His Majesty the Kaiser decrees for the waging of war in the North Sea:

1. The aim of the operations is to be the damaging of the English Navy by means of offensive attacks against the warships that guard or blockade the German Bay as well as through an inconsiderate offensive

---

[1] Collection of German Naval Documents, Hoover War Library.

with mines, and if possible with U-boats, up to the very coast of
England.

2. After a balancing of strengths has been obtained by means of
such a warfare, our entire forces will be concentrated and held ready,
and an attempt shall then be made to send our navy under favorable
conditions into battle. Should a favorable opportunity offer itself prior
to this, it must be taken advantage of.

3. The war against merchant ships is to be conducted according to
the prize rules. To what extent it is to be waged in the home waters
shall be determined by the Chief of the High Seas Forces. The ships,
which are to wage the commercial war outside of the home waters, are
to be sent out as soon as possible.

226. (b) THE BALTIC

His Majesty decrees for the waging of war in the Baltic:

1. Main object of the waging of war is: to hinder as much as possible an eventual offensive of the Russians. Besides that the Kiel Bay
must be protected against the English and Russian Navies, and the
enemy trade in the Baltic must be damaged.

2. Mine undertakings against the Russian coast are to be made as
soon as possible after the outbreak of the war.

3. The temporary dispatch of squadrons of the High Seas Fleet for
the striking of a blow against the Russian Navy remains reserved according to the requirements of the events of the war.

4. The war upon commerce is to be waged according to the prize
rules.

227. THE WAR ZONE AROUND THE BRITISH ISLES,
FEBRUARY 4, 1915[2]

1. The waters around Great Britain and Ireland, including the entire English Channel, are hereby declared a military area. From February 18 every hostile merchant ship found in these waters will be
destroyed, even if it is not always possible to avoid thereby the dangers
which threaten the crews and passengers.

2. Neutral ships also incur danger in the military area because, in
view of the misuse of neutral flags ordered by the English Government
on January 31 and the accidents of naval warfare, it cannot always be
avoided that attacks intended to be made on enemy ships may also involve neutral ships.

[2] *Deutscher Reichsanzeiger und Königlich Preussischer Staatsanzeiger,* February 4, 1915, p. 1.

3. Traffic northward around the Shetland Islands, in the east part of the North Sea, and through a strip of at least thirty sea miles in breadth along the coast of Holland is not endangered.

Chief of the Admiralty Staff,
VON POHL

BERLIN, February 4, 1915

228. ADMIRAL BEHNCKE ON THE NAVAL SITUATION[3]

BERLIN, February 16, 1915

Admiral Behncke, of the Marine Department, has made a statement to Lieutenant-Commander Walter R. Gherardi, Naval Attaché of the American Embassy at Berlin, which is given out officially as the best exposition of the situation with respect to Germany's declaration of the waters around the British Isles as a war zone. Admiral Behncke's statement follows:

"Up to the present time Germany in the war at sea has followed the London Declaration. Great Britain has not followed such Declaration, nor the stipulations of the Paris Treaty, whereon the conduct of war on the sea was based before the London Declaration. In waging this commercial war Great Britain had in view the subjugation of Germany by starvation. Germany has in every way sought to call the attention of the neutral Powers and all others to the necessity that she is under to obtain food for her civil population, which is her right under the laws of war.

"No results could be obtained from her efforts. Since the shutting off of food has now come to a point where Germany no longer has sufficient food to feed her people, it has become necessary for her to bring Great Britain to terms by the exercise of force. Germany knows that by the use of submarines Great Britain can be placed in a position where food will be lacking. Germany has the submarine force to accomplish this. Her life as a nation and the lives of her people depend upon putting this campaign into action, and she must do so. Difficulties lying in the way of this campaign have been largely connected with the care which it is desired to bestow on neutral ships and the lives on board all commercial ships, whether neutral or enemy.

"First, in arming her merchantmen with guns for self-defense Great Britain has adopted a policy against which Germans have strongly protested. The United States took the British point of view. It is impossible for German submarines to approach British merchantmen and make examinations without exposing themselves to gunfire or bomb attack, against which a submarine boat would be helpless.

[3] *New York Times*, February 17, 1915

"Secondly, Great Britain has advised her merchant fleet to fly neutral flags, to cover the names, and to alter funnels and painting so as to escape the consequences of their nationality. (Here Admiral Behncke produced a copy of an English wireless message sent broadcast to ships to this effect.) This plan was designed to bring Germany into conflict with other nations. Germany does not wish in the slightest degree to harm American or other neutral ships or cargoes unless carrying contraband. She is, however, in the position where her life depends upon putting into effect the only means she has of saving herself. She must, and will, use this means. Commanding officers of submarines have been given orders to make every effort to safeguard neutrals. In spite of the precautions which a submarine might take without risking her own destruction, it is possible that neutral ships may be destroyed through error or accident. For this reason a strong warning has been issued. In addition, the British coast is mined by the British themselves for protective reasons, and will be mined by Germans as an act of offensive warfare. Ships are therefore in danger from mines.

"In spite of the great effect that the Admiralty feels that the use of submarines will have in bringing the war to a rapid close, they do not wish to put it into effect to the detriment of neutral commerce and the rights of nations on the high seas. They have therefore stated that if Great Britain will abide by the Declaration of London without modification or by the Treaty of Paris, whereby food supplies necessary for the civil population can be freely brought into Germany, the whole matter of a submarine blockade will be dropped by Germany. This proposal has been transmitted through diplomatic channels, and, if accepted, the matter is no longer one provocative of trouble between America and Germany."

Admiral Behncke called Commander Gherardi's attention to the fact that Great Britain, when by her proclamation she closed the North Sea, did not give free passage to American ships bound for the neutral country of Holland but compelled the ships to pass through certain channels, take an English pilot aboard, and undergo a search for contraband of war at the hands of officers of British warships.

Admiral Behncke then said Germany was prepared to suggest to the United States an even freer and safer method for American ships bound either through the Channel or to English ports, namely, that several American warships should wait in some port on the southwest coast of Ireland, and when communicated with by wireless by an American merchantman one of them should proceed to the place indicated and convoy the merchantman through that portion of the sea which Germany, following the example of Great Britain, had declared to be dangerous.

"Of course," said the Admiral, "ships under convoy, by the rules of international law, are not subject to search, but the country to which they belong is upon its honor, as it were, to see that they do not carry contraband.

"American warships have distinctive masts and are well known to the officers of the German Navy, and either by night or day they and the vessels under their convoy would be respected by German submarines.

"This is a safe method to follow for American ships which desire to enter those portions of the seas proclaimed dangerous by Germany, and differs only from the rule adopted by Great Britain with reference to American ships passing through the Channel in that American ships, instead of being compelled to enter a British port, take a British pilot, and be searched by officers of a British warship, would be permitted to pass unmolested to their destination without being subjected to search, the Imperial German Government being willing, of course, to accept the implied word of honor of the United States that the ships carry no contraband of war."

229. PERSIUS' ACCOUNT OF A SECRET ORDER OF THE KAISER, SEPTEMBER 7, 1915[4]

At first we spoke about the U-boat war. Persius related that the Chancellor had recently assembled all the different party leaders and explained to them the actual state of affairs. . . . . We then came to talk about Tirpitz's personality. . . . . I asked Persius if he had heard that the Kaiser had written a letter to Tirpitz inquiring whether or not we had enough U-boats for the execution of the blockade, that Tirpitz had answered no, and had thereupon obtained his dismissal. Persius had not heard about it, but thought it might be true; however, he could not confirm that.

I then asked him about Tirpitz's successor, Capelle. Persius explained that the latter had accepted the post only in the interest of the Throne. . . . . Asked what that expression "he accepted the post only in the interest of the Throne" meant, Persius replied: "A breakdown of the Fleet; and there is a fear that this might mean an undermining of the position of the dynasty." I expressed my surprise about it, to which Persius said that he was going to read me a writing which was a secret order of the Kaiser to all staff officers of the navy. Thereupon he read it to me. It was as follows:

---

[4] Kanner Papers, III, 73–90.

"Official reports and personal remarks that have come to my cognizance have shown me that in my Navy there exists an erroneous conception of the whole position of the Navy in this war; which conception often leads to a dejected mood. Even if the unexcelled deeds of my Navy, wherever it has come in touch with the enemy, have removed my regrets about such a state of affairs, I must, nevertheless, direct a reminder to the Officers Corps to hold high everywhere the spirit of joyful fulfillment of duty, even where so far there has been no opportunity to get at the enemy or where, according to human comprehension and the whole course of the war, no engagement with the enemy probably ever will take place. It is understandable that the use of my Marines, as conditioned by the state of affairs, has frequently given rise to disappointment and even discontent. But these sentiments must be suppressed and they must not change into expressed doubts as to the importance of the Navy in general or in the expediency of the orders and measures given for the prosecution of the war. In this respect the officers must practice great restraint if they do not wish to injure the spirit of their subordinates and thus become accomplices to almost criminal rumors and denouncements, such as arose, for example, in connection with the skirmish at the Dogger-Bank and which reached my ear. Because of the extremely involved conditions of this war it is necessary to demand the confidence of the officers in the Highest Military Command, which, balancing all military and political factors that more or less escape the view of the general public, decides where an attack is to be made or where quiet is to be observed. I know that that often requires great restraint. This was asked and given by my Army in the West at the time of the great offensive in the East. I had to use it with my Fleet in view of the strategic affairs in the North Sea, where the use of the Fleet under unfavorable conditions known in advance would have been an eventful political mistake, surpassing greatly the probable material losses. Finally, for political considerations I had to place certain temporary restrictions upon the U-boat war upon merchant ships. I know full well that these restrictions were felt severely by the Officers Corps, which is justly proud of the U-boats. I do not contest anyone's right to do so; however, I must reject as a heavy military mistake any disparaging criticism against the Highest Military Command by the Officers Corps, a criticism which, through indiscretions, unfortunately often exert a poisoning effect even beyond the Navy. The U-boat war is not an end in itself, and I demand of the Officers Corps not to usurp judgment as to whether in the sense of the general war aims it is expedient or not to restrict this mode of warfare. Finally, with this I demand of you loyal subordination to my Will as Highest War Lord, who bears the heavy responsibility for the future of the

Reich and of whom the Navy particularly should be convinced that he would be happy to send it unhampered against the enemy.

"This order is . . . .

"September 7, 1915"

I was simply stunned when I heard all that. I told Persius that that was simply unbelievable and the admitted breakdown of the whole navy policy. According to this the whole fleet might just as well be scrapped or sold. Persius assented. However, I seriously questioned the authenticity of this order . . . . whether it was not a fake . . . ., or whether it might not have been deliberately given to him in order to compromise him. Persius rejected those suppositions emphatically and said that during his twenty years of service as a naval officer he had had such secret orders often enough in his hand, that he knew just what such a secret order looks like, and that he knew the Kaiser's signature well. I replied that if this was true then this document was of the greatest importance and that its publication, although absolutely impossible at present, would even in later days create a tremendous impression. . . . .

230. FIRST OFFICIAL STATEMENT OF THE BATTLE OF JUTLAND[5]

BERLIN, June 1, 1916. (W.T.B.) On May 31 our High Seas Fleet encountered during an enterprise directed northward the main part of the English Fighting Fleet, which was considerably superior to our forces. A series of heavy engagements developed during the afternoon between Skagerrak and Horn Reef. The engagements were successful for us and they continued during the whole of the night.

In these engagements, as far as is known up to now, the large battleship "Warspite," the battle cruisers "Queen Mary" and "Indefatigable," two armored cruisers, apparently of the "Achilles" class, a small cruiser, the new flagships of the destroyer squadron, the "Turbulent," "Nestor," and "Alcaster," as well as a large number of torpedo-boat destroyers and one submarine were destroyed by us. Further, according to unquestionable observations, a large number of English battleships suffered heavy damages from our ships' artillery and from the attacks of our torpedo-boat flotillas during the day and night engagements. Among others, the large battleship "Marlborough," too, was hit by a torpedo, as has been confirmed by prisoners. Portions of the crews of the sunken English ships were picked up by several of our ships. Among the rescued there were only two survivors from the "Indefatigable."

[5] *Norddeutsche Allgemeine Zeitung*, June 2, 1916, p. 1.

On our side the small cruiser "Wiesbaden" was sunk by hostile artillery fire during the day's engagement, and the "Pommern" was sunk during the night by a torpedo. Nothing is known, so far, of the fate of the "Frauenlob," which is missing, and of some torpedo boats which have not yet returned.

The High Seas Fleet returned to our ports during the course of today.

THE CHIEF OF THE ADMIRALTY STAFF
OF THE NAVY

231. STATEMENT OF THE CHIEF OF THE ADMIRALTY STAFF OF THE NAVY ON THE BATTLE OF JUTLAND[6]

BERLIN, June 7 (W.T.B.). Official and unofficial British press reports, as well as statements which British missions spread in neutral countries, make a systematic attempt to deny the greatness of the English defeat in the naval battle of May 31 and thus to create the belief that the battle was successful for the British arms. Thus it is being asserted that the German Fleet left the battlefield and that the British Fleet remained in possession of it. As regards this, we state that by the repeated and effective attacks of our torpedo-boat flotillas during the battle, on the evening of May 31, the British Main Fleet was forced to turn round and never again came within sight of our forces and, in spite of its superior speed and reinforcements by a British battle squadron of 12 vessels, which came up from the southern region of the North Sea, never attempted to come again into touch with our forces, to continue the battle, or to effect a junction with this squadron in order to bring about the desired destruction of the German Fleet.

The further British assertion that the British Fleet in vain endeavored to reach the fleeing German Fleet in order to defeat it before reaching its home *points d'appui* is contradicted by the alleged official British statement that Admiral Jellicoe with his Grand Fleet had already reached his base at Scapa Flow (Orkneys), three hundred miles from the battlefield, on June 1.

And so our numerous German torpedo-boat flotillas were sent northward beyond the scene of the day battle to make a night attack, but in spite of a keen search they were unable to find the British Main Fleet. Moreover, our torpedo boats were able to rescue a large number of British survivors of vessels which had been sunk.

As further proof of the fact that the entire British Battle Fleet participated in the battle, it is pointed out that the British Admiralty

6 *Ibid.,* June 8, 1916, p. 1.

report announced that the "Marlborough" was disabled. Furthermore, one of our submarines on June 1 sighted another vessel of the "Iron Duke" class, badly damaged and steering toward the English coast. Both the vessels mentioned belong to the British Main Fleet.

In order to belittle the great German success, the British press also attributes the loss of several British vessels to German mines, submarines, and airships. In this connection it is expressly pointed out that neither mines, which would have been just as dangerous to our own fleet as to that of the enemy, nor submarines were employed by our High Seas Fleet. German airships were used June first exclusively for reconnaissance work.

The German victory was gained by able leadership and by the effect of our artillery and torpedoes.

Until now we refrained from contradicting many of the alleged official British assertions regarding German losses. The latest assertion, again and again repeated, is that the German Fleet lost no less than two vessels of the "Kaiser" class, the "Westfalen," two battle cruisers, four small cruisers, and a great number of destroyers. Moreover, the British indicate that the "Pommern," which was lost, is not a ship of the line of 13,000 tons, built in 1905, but a modern dreadnought of the same name.

We state that the total loss of the German High Seas forces during the battle of May 31 and June 1, and subsequently are: One battle cruiser; one ship of the line of older construction; four small cruisers; five torpedo boats.

Of these losses, the "Pommern," launched in 1905, the "Wiesbaden," the "Elbing," the "Frauenlob," and five torpedo boats have already been reported sunk in official statements.

For military reasons we refrained until now from making public the loss of S.M.S.S. "Lützow" and "Rostock." In view of the wrong interpretation of this measure, and above all in order to frustrate English legends about gigantic losses on our side, these reasons must now be disregarded. Both vessels were lost on their way to repair harbors, after attempts had failed to keep the badly damaged vessels afloat. The crews of both ships, including all severely wounded, are safe.

While the German list of losses is hereby closed, positive indications are at hand that the actual British losses are materially higher than established and made public by us on the basis of our own observations. From British prisoners comes the statement that besides the "Warspite," the "Princess Royal" and the "Birmingham" were also destroyed. According to reliable reports the dreadnought "Marlborough" also sank before reaching port.

The battle of the Skagerrak was, and remains, a German victory, even if the result is judged solely by the losses in ships officially admitted by the British, according to which the total tonnage of German losses is 60,720 tons, against 117,750 tons British losses.

THE CHIEF OF THE ADMIRALTY STAFF
OF THE NAVY

232. AN UNPRECEDENTED OCCURRENCE[7]

Wolff's Bureau sends out the following news which will certainly create a sensation:

"In pursuance of former conferences of a similar nature, a discussion was held today in the Reichstag building with Dr. Paasche, Vice-President of the Reichstag, presiding. The purpose of this meeting, in which leading members of the bourgeois parties participated, was to give expression to the firm desire of these members of the Reichstag, who are doubtlessly backed by the Reichstag and the German nation as a whole, that the nation should do the utmost to exert its fighting strength on sea as well as on land.

"In view of the momentous importance of the resolutions passed at this meeting, the following communication to the Secretary of the Navy was made public as soon as the conference had come to an end:

" 'The undersigned members of the Diet are willing and ready to use their influence within their respective parties as well as in the Reichstag so that all measures of the Department of the Navy made necessary by the war will be approved by the Reichstag so far as budget procedure and accounting are concerned.

" 'In particular they pledge their vote for: 1. The replacement of ships lost; 2. The immediate carrying out of all plans for the navy agreed upon in 1912; 3. The immediate construction of ships due to be started in 1915; 4. The reduction of the life of ships of the navy from 20 to 15 years.

" '(Signed) DR. PAASCHE   DR. WIEMER
FRHR. VON GAMP   GRAF WESTARP
ERZBERGER   SHULTZ-BROMBERG' "

That the leaders of the bourgeois parties representing neither Parliament nor the German nation, usurp the prerogatives of the German Reichstag is unprecedented. If the Government considers it necessary to take legal steps, the Constitution permits but one method: The Reichstag must be summoned.

[7] *Vorwärts,* September 6, 1916, p. 3.

Nor is there any reason why this method could not be carried out. In England Parliament is in session during the war. Members of the Reichstag serving at the front might be granted leave of absence. That leaders of the bourgeois parties, without any authority whatever, attempt to set aside the Constitution and take it upon themselves to decide matters of greatest importance which seriously affect the budget and, as though it were a trifling matter, grant all that the navy demands, is preposterous. How little respect have the parliamentarians for their own Parliament!

It is extremely characteristic that these conferences were held without the Social-Democratic Party having been informed of them or having been invited to take part in them. It has often been stated that during the war all party differences have ceased. We thank these gentlemen for having furnished us considerable enlightenment on this point!

233. THE NAVAL MUTINY IN 1917

(a) ADMIRAL VON CAPELLE'S STATEMENT IN THE REICHSTAG[8]

Admiral Von Capelle, Secretary of State of the Navy Department: Gentlemen, it is rather a sad fact that the Russian Revolution has turned the heads of a few people in our navy and aroused within them revolutionary ideas. [*"Hear, hear!"—Right.*] The mad plan of these few men aimed at winning confidential men on all ships and of inciting the entire crews of the navy to insubordination [*"Hear, hear!"—Right, Center, Left*] in order to cripple the fleet and eventually, by the use of force, to obtain peace. [*Shouts of "Shame!" from the National-Liberals and Left.*] It is a fact that these people had had intercourse with the Independent Social-Democratic Party. [*Renewed shouts of "Shame!" Chairman calls to order.*] Documents now show [*"Well, well!"—Independent Social-Democrats*] that the chief agitator related his plans to Deputies Dittmann, Haase, and Vogtherr here in the Reichstag in the room of the Independent Social-Democratic Party [*stormy shouts: "Hear, hear!"*] and received their approbation. [*Shouts of "Shame!"—Counter-shouts by Independent Social-Democratic Party.*] The deputies, although calling attention to the danger of the enterprise, and warning them to take the greatest caution [*"Hear, hear!"—Right*], yet promised their full support by supplying propaganda material for the incitement of the navy. [*Renewed excitement.*] In view of such a state of affairs it was my first duty to prevent as far as was in my power the seeping through of the propaganda material

[8] *Verhandlungen des Reichstags*, No. 124, October 9, 1917, p. 3773.

as promised by the Independent Social-Democratic Party. [*Shouts of approval from the Right and Left.*] I have, therefore, asked the authorities concerned to prevent the distribution of this material in the navy by every possible means. [*Renewed applause.*]

Gentlemen, I shall not go into further details here about the occurrences in the navy. A few people who forgot their honor and duty have committed grave offenses and received the deserved punishment. However, I should like to state from this tribunal that the rumors spread about are grossly exaggerated. The preparedness of the navy for battle has not been in the least impaired [*applause*] and thus it shall continue to be. [*Renewed applause.*]

233. (*b*) HAASE'S REPLY TO VON CAPELLE[9]

Haase (Königsberg): Gentlemen, the Secretary of the Navy made a sensational statement here today. He has told that condemned sailors pursued a plan of winning over men of confidence to incite the crews to insubordination in order to paralyze the navy and thus to force peace. To this statement he appended the following remark: "It is a fact that the chief agitator related this plan to Deputies Haase, Dittmann, and Vogtherr here in the Reichstag in the room of the Independent Social-Democratic Party. They called his attention to the danger of the plan and advised caution."

There is no need for me to leave any doubt about our political activity. I shall disclose everything that happened, and in regard to the Secretary of the Navy's statement, I have this to state: The sailor in question visited me in our Party room, but it is not true that he related such a plan to me. I beg the Secretary to produce evidence of his assertion to the contrary. [*"Very good!"—Independent Social-Democrats.*] To elucidate the matter still further, I have to add the following: Sailors and men belonging to the land army have often visited me in the Reichstag in order to tell me their complaints about the evil conditions in the army or the navy, particularly regarding complaints about the maltreatment they had personally suffered. On such occasions they have frequently developed a picture of the prevailing sentiment in the army and navy. I received these complaint lodgers just as any other deputy does, whether it be in the lobby, in one of the drawing-rooms, or in the Party room. Therefore, I do not see what significance should be attached to the remark that a sailor had visited me.

In the summer of this year the sailor in question visited me and uttered bitter complaints about the conditions under which he and his comrades were suffering. He also told me of the great discontent and

9 *Ibid.*, p. 3785.

the great exasperation among the sailors. He further complained of the lack of intellectual stimulation, which was felt particularly by those sailors who had been serving for a long period; but now that they had subscribed in very large numbers to the press of the Independent Social-Democratic Party, and had read it eagerly, it had been a stimulant to them. Their plan was to further educate themselves and to foster political discussions in shore meetings. For this purpose he wished to have literature. Gentlemen, although political discussions are permitted on land—in fact of late have been officially conducted with high pressure—I told him that the plan, which in itself was permissible, could be very dangerous owing to the circumstances under which he lived. Therefore I suggested caution and warned him. Accordingly, I charge you, gentlemen, to evaluate the Secretary's statement for what it is worth. I owe it to the memory of this sailor, who gave the impression of being a frank young man with high ideas, to say that, although I had no other relations with him, I was most deeply shocked when I learned that he had been compelled to suffer death for his political ideals. ["*Hear, hear!*"—*Independent Social-Democrats.*]

The Secretary of State spoke of the effect of the Russian Revolution on the sailors. I call your attention to the fact that not only the members of my party, the Independent Social-Democrats, but also the Social-Democratic parties of all views, expressed their enthusiasm and sympathy with the Russian Revolutionists, and that they did here in the Reichstag as well as in the press. ["*Very good!*"—*Independent Social-Democrats.*] It was natural that this greatest event of the century should make a deep impression on all men who thirst for freedom. ["*Bravo!*"—*Independent Social-Democrats.*] But the object of the Secretary's statement is obvious. ["*Quite right!*"—*Independent Social-Democrats.*] In view of the practice of the authorities against my party regarding the right of assembly and association as well as in the press, and particularly after the Chancellor's declarations made yesterday in the Main Committee, I expected nothing else than that the gentlemen should believe they must wave the red flag in order to forge the other parties into a firm bloc for the purpose of supporting the unhappy Government's policy, ["*Quite right!*"—*Independent Social-Democrats*] which has brought our people into ruin and is bound to drag us into even worse ruin.

The Chancellor's declaration, putting us outside the pale of the law, has not surprised me at all. I had been expecting that from the first day of the war, and many in this House will remember that I predicted its coming immediately preceding the decisive session of August 4. ["*Quite right!*"—*Independent Social-Democrats.*] The declaration of the Chancellor only proves that he and the supporters of his policy are

at the end of their tether. [*"Very true!"—Independent Social-Democrats.*] And in this situation, when they do not know how to get out of
all this misery, they belittle the men who from the beginning opposed
this war policy and predicted disaster. [*"Quite right!"—Independent
Social-Democrats.*]

The words of the Chancellor do not sound new to us. We remember them yet from the days of the Socialist Law. [*"Quite right!"—
Independent Social-Democrats.*] Of course the words did not flow as
vigorously or as easily from the lips of the Chancellor as they did from
those of Herr von Puttkamer; but it is the same spirit—that spirit of
Herr von Puttkamer. [*"Very true!"—Independent Social-Democrats.*]
Meanwhile, Herr Chancellor Michaelis, ere long you will see your
policy broken into pieces, just as the attempts of von Puttkamer and
the still greater Bismarck were. And you will see that those policies for
which we fought and are still fighting will find more and more adherents in our country, as well as in other countries in which civilized
people live. [*Hearty applause by the Independent Social-Democrats.
Hissing from the Right.*]

233. (c) VOGTHERR'S REPLY[10]

Deputy Vogtherr: Gentlemen, I have little to add to what my friend
Haase has said, particularly as far as it concerns my own self. The
Secretary of the Navy declared that there had been a plan to incite the
marines to insubordination in order by thus paralyzing the fleet to force
a peace, and, furthermore, that it was an established fact that the
aims could be ascribed to relationships between certain sailors and the
Independent Social-Democratic Party.

Gentlemen, I declare, just as my friend Haase has done, that I too
have spoken with the sailor, who has been honorably mentioned already
in this House, that I have conversed with him about the conditions on
his ship and the conditions in the fleet in general. It is the right of the
sailors concerned to voice their complaints where they have confidence
and where they can hope that the complaints will be relayed to the
proper authority. [*"Quite right!" — Independent Social-Democrats.*]
And, gentlemen, it is the right of the deputies—no, it is more than that,
it is their duty and obligation [*hearty approval by the Independent
Social-Democrats*]—to listen to similar complaints and to exert all
their power to remedy what weighs so heavily upon the poor, pitiable
people. [*"Very true!"—Independent Social-Democrats.*] And let the
gentlemen take notice of it: had those had confidence in you, they
would not have come to us. [*Hearty approval by Independent Social-*

---

[10] *Verhandlungen des Reichstags*, No. 124, October 9, 1917, pp. 3786–87.

Democrats.] They go where they believe they can find a kindly disposed and, above all, a human ear.

But more than that. We heard that they had many grievances. I personally gave them some material. Of course, as we know for thirty years, with this material the attempt is being made to create public opinion whenever courage is lacking to come forth with that material. [*"Very true!"—Independent Social-Democrats.*] Yes, Herr Secretary, from the way you presented the case, the superficial and unconcerned listener must conclude that the plan to incite to insubordination, to paralyze the fleet, and to force a peace, resulted indirectly from the material obtained from us. [*"Quite right!"—Independent Social-Democrats.*] I challenge the Secretary of the Navy to produce a single writing and in that writing show me a single word from which could be drawn the conclusion that between the ill-fated sailors and ourselves there existed, even only indirectly, such a relationship.

Gentlemen, in this connection, as my friend Haase already stated, the champions of the Socialist Law at their time made a better job of it. They, too, confronted us with material which was to prove everything possible that it could not prove. That, too, was material which was supposed to be used against Social-Democracy, but did not originate from it. It is not precluded that the Secretary of the Navy has material which contains similar allegations and provocations, but it is impossible for him to prove any relationship between such material and us. There is no such connection.

The material we gave out can be obtained from us by any one of you. We took care to spread it as widely as possible, since it is legal; we had to care for its distribution, since the system under which we live and the damnable state of siege under which we suffer took away from us the freedom of the press and took away from our followers the possibility of informing themselves on political matters. But, gentlemen, what the Secretary attempts is amateurish. . . . . [*"Oh, oh!"— and laughter on the Right. Bell of the Chairman, who calls them to order.*] What the Secretary mentioned in order to spread distrust and to raise accusations against us—all this is nothing else than a continuation of the policy which the Chancellor announced this morning as his own. The Chancellor said today that my friend Dittmann was the last to have the right to complain here of agitation. The Chancellor is mistaken. We are not here in any official's office. Everyone here has the right to speak, even those who are not acceptable to the Chancellor. What did the Chancellor declare? He probably referred to the speech he made yesterday in the Main Committee, in which he said that any official could belong to any party provided it did not pursue subversive policies. He said that we, the Independent Social-Democrats, were on the outside of the boundary, which he drew with these words. [*"Hear, hear!"—Independent Social-Democrats.*] Let the Chancellor remember this, that if he wishes to stand on the basis of the Constitution he has not the possibility nor the right to restrict in any way our rights in this House. But it matters not about us. We can defend ourselves and will hold our own. However, the Chancellor forgets that therewith he not only insulted us, but also that behind us stand hundreds of thousands of men and women who agree with this policy we defend, although the Chancellor may label it any way he pleases. He forgets that behind us stand hundreds of thousands who at the front are baring their bosoms, so to speak, to the enemies of the Fatherland [*shouts from the Right*]; yes sir, who do not know why they are waging the war [*uproar on the Right*]; not for you, gentlemen, but only for a future, which will not be as you wish it.

Gentlemen, the Chancellor tried to imitate, in the same insufficient way, that which the Secretary of the Navy had aimed at and what we believed to have been forgotten since the time of the Socialist Law. These are the frozen trumpet blares of the deceased Herr von Puttkamer; they are the same tactics and are the same phrases which for a long time have aroused the laughter of all politically mature men. [*"Very true!"—Independent Social-Democrats.*] However, neither the Chancellor, nor a future Chancellor who may be bigger than he, will be able by such methods to camouflage a policy which in its essence, in its presuppositions, and in its aims is destined to complete failure. [*"Quite right!"—Independent Social-Democrats.*] If you, Herr Chancellor, wish to restore the shattered unity of the German people by putting a large section of it in the pillory, which section defends its political convictions with the whole force of its personality, and if you wish thereby to open a new campaign, then you have shown not only the failure of your own policy but also the insufficiency of all that you believed you could defend. [*Hearty applause by the Independent Social-Democrats.*]

233. (d) DITTMAN'S REPLY[11]

Deputy Dittmann: I have little to say after the pointed and striking rejection on the part of my colleagues, Vogtherr and Haase, of von Capelle's attacks. However, since the Secretary has mentioned my name in this connection, I must add a few words.

As far as I personally am concerned I can only confirm what has been said by Haase and Vogtherr regarding their connection with the sailors in question. I, too, have been visited by great numbers of

---

[11] *Verhandlungen des Reichstags,* No. 124, October 9, 1917, pp. 3787–88.

sailors and soldiers in my home, my office, and here in the Reichstag, and they have related their complaints and grievances about the conditions in the navy and the army to me, imploring me, at the same time, to defend them and their interests. In very many cases, I have forwarded their complaints to the appropriate official places; in others, I have told them how to file their own complaints; and in others, I have called the attention of those people to the dangers which might occur under the circumstances if they should give vent to their just anger. I believe that I was justified in so doing. The Secretary of the Navy, however, mentioned this fact in such a way as to insinuate that I and my colleagues, Haase and Vogtherr, had counseled the sailors in question to realize their plans but to be careful about it. Gentlemen, as a Reichstag deputy I shall not allow anyone—the Chancellor and the Secretary of the Navy are not excluded—to deprive me of my right to receive anyone who may come to me with his complaints.

Persecutions are not solely being directed against the Independent Social-Democrats; no, attacks are being made in both the army and the navy against the Majority Socialists. I refer to the list of twenty-three Social-Democratic newspapers, which I recently read to you, and among which there are a number of Majority Socialist papers. Adherents of the Majority Socialist Party have also been arrested on ships. Thus, for example, a man was arrested because the authorities found on him an undispatched letter addressed to *Vorwärts,* which letter contained political allusions. Another was arrested only because he had a print of a peace manifestation. The aim that is being systematically pursued in the army and the navy is to make any manifestation of the desire for peace impossible. [*"Quite right!"—Independent Social-Democrats.*] This is the purpose of this whole procedure. If the statements of Secretary von Capelle are true, then you on the Right should raise complaint against him for not having filed a public accusation against us [*"Quite right!"—Independent Social-Democrats*] who are supposed to have hatched this plan in understanding with the said sailors. [*Renewed approval by the Independent Social-Democrats.*] That has not happened, and it shows that Secretary von Capelle knows on how weak a foundation his accusation against us is based. [*"Quite right!"—Independent Social-Democrats.*] However, they shall not keep us from doing what we regard as our duty in the interest of the German proletariat and the international proletariat and in the interest of a speedy bringing about of peace for the welfare of the entire civilized world. [*"Bravo!"—Independent Social-Democrats.*]

233. (e) ADMIRAL VON CAPELLE'S REPLICATION[12]

Von Capelle, Secretary of the Navy: Gentlemen, Herr Dittmann's first statements left no other way for me than to clear up this matter in accordance with the facts as disclosed at the official inquiry. But Herr Vogtherr made a series of statements which do not coincide with my speech. He said that I had presented the matter in such a way as to imply that the Independent Social-Democrats had created this plan and attributed it to the sailors. I said nothing of the sort. [*He reads extracts from his speech.*]

Gentlemen, I have before me an excerpt from the documents of the official inquiry which fully prove all I have said. [*"Hear, hear!"— Right. Lively shouts from the Independent Social-Democrats. Bell of the Chairman.*] Gentlemen, I shall read only one of the documents. One of the guilty parties states—[*lively shouts by the Independent Social-Democrats. Bell of the Chairman*]—the party concerned states: "I, too, went personally to Herr Dittmann in the Reichstag, after Reichpietsch had visited him. I identified myself by referring to Reichpietsch; I also told him that I came on the same matter. Dittmann, who showed himself conversant with the matter, was pleased and said that we should continue the work, but to exercise great caution. [*"Hear, hear!"— Right. Shouts from the Independent Social-Democrats.*] Reichpietsch told me the following about his interview with the members of the Party: he had not been alone with Dittmann, but that a kind of party conference took place at which Dittmann, Vogtherr, and Haase were present. Reichpietsch then related the plan and the successes of the organization to the three men assembled there, who, according to his report, had been enthusiastic about it. [*"Hear, hear!"—from the Right. Shouts from the Independent Social-Democrats.*]

"After the discussion of the details of the organization, the deputies declared to Reichpietsch that the organization comprised a forbidden and punishable act, that it was a great risk, and that he should be extremely careful. As far as they were concerned, they would support the organization in every way, especially by pamphlets and other printed matter." [*Shouts from the Independent Social-Democrats. "Hear, hear!"—Right.*]

Next comes the accused, Reichpietsch, and states upon questioning: "I, too, now admit of having been not only in the office of Deputy Dittmann, but also in the room of the Independent Social-Democratic Party with Deputies Haase, Vogtherr, and Dittmann. As far as details are concerned I ask to be given time till the afternoon in order to think it over."

[12] *Verhandlungen des Reichstags,* No. 124, October 9, 1917, pp. 3788–89.

In the afternoon, upon the reading to him of the declaration of the accused, Sachse, he said: "As far as the evidence applies to me, it is correct. That means that I have not only thus related the affair, but that is what actually happened in Berlin." [*Excited cries from the Independent Social-Democrats. Counter-shouts from the Right. Bell of the Chairman.*]

233. (*f*) STATEMENTS IN THE REICHSTAG OF TRIMBORN, EBERT, STRESEMANN, AND MICHAELIS[13]

Deputy Trimborn: .... The two speeches of von Capelle's prompt me to the following declaration.

It seems to me rather doubtful and impossible to connect the Independent Social-Democratic Party in its entirety with the accusations which have been made against these three deputies.

I must further assume that the Secretary of the Navy was able to support the charges against the three deputies with sufficiently conclusive evidence; for if that had not been the case he could and should not have raised these accusations. [*Shouts from the Independent Social-Democrats.*]

We certainly expect that if the three deputies have transgressed the law, particularly if their action is a question of high treason, that they shall be dealt with according to the full extent of the law.

Deputy Ebert: .... The Chancellor and the Secretary of the Navy brought the gravest possible charges against individual members of the Independent Social-Democratic Party as well as against the entire Party. The Chancellor even went so far as to draw the gravest political consequences against this Party. The Government should consider the effect of such action on domestic and foreign policy. [*"Quite right!"*] After all, the accusation should have been made only if absolutely reliable and conclusive material was at hand..... The material which Herr Capelle produced did not justify the charge. That the soldiers discuss their complaints with members of Parliament has been increasingly frequent during the war..... Equally invalid is the other charge of Capelle's against the Independent Social-Democratic Party, namely, that of propaganda. Gentlemen, it is open to any party of this House to carry on propaganda for its views and purposes..... The High Army Command itself has carried politics into the army.....

Deputy Stresemann: The Secretary of the Navy made grave charges against members of the Independent Social-Democratic Party, which charges arouse in us the suspicion that these members of that Party

---

[13] *Verhandlungen des Reichstags*, No. 124, October 9, 1917, p. 3789.

should be charged with participation in mutiny. Such a proceeding lies in the interest of Parliament itself, since only in that way can guilt or innocence be established. We expect that the Government will immediately take the necessary steps. [*"Bravo!"*]

Chancellor Michaelis: Herr Dittmann has stated that sentences have been passed on sailors at Wilhelmshaven to the aggregate of two hundred years of hard labor and that even death sentences had been imposed. From his presentation it would have been possible to draw the conclusion that these punishments were excessive and unjust; then the anger which has been voiced by members of the House would be justified.

Now I know the regrettable fact that crimes have been committed by some of our sailors, and I know that these men had cards on which it was stated that they had bound themselves to recognize the principles of the Independent Social-Democratic Party, and that with these cards an agitation on a large scale was carried on, on board of German ships. . . . . Punishment had to be heavy, because it was a question of the principle of military discipline. Resistance had to be broken down, for it was a critical moment. That it had to happen we regret from the bottom of our hearts. But the reason is that the guilty parties were ill advised and acted in a way which was incompatible with fidelity and obedience.

234. THE NAVAL ATTACHÉ IN THE HAGUE TO THE CHIEF OF THE ADMIRALTY STAFF OF THE NAVY, OCTOBER 17, 1918[14]

. . . . Today conference with Chief of Dutch Naval Staff. English preparations for a landing are known to the Dutch Navy. . . . .

[14] Collection of German Naval Documents.

Part IV
War Diplomacy

CHAPTER XII

THE EMPIRE AND BELGIAN RELIEF

INTRODUCTORY NOTE

THE OCCUPATION of Belgium by the German Army in August 1914 created the problem of feeding an entire nation. The Commission for Relief in Belgium was organized under the chairmanship of Herbert Hoover in September 1914 and continued its relief operations until April 1919. It was conducted during the war as a neutral organization or practically a neutral state organized for philanthropy. It was originally begun as a purely philanthropic enterprise, but later secured financial support from the Belgian, British, French, and American Governments. The Commission maintained direct diplomatic relations with belligerent and neutral states, enjoyed immunity from submarine attack and naval interference, flew its own flag over a large fleet of ocean vessels, requisitioned native food supplies, made full provision for the destitute through local organizations, and provided an entire population with its necessary food imports. At one period of the war the Commission fed over four million destitute persons in Belgium and Northern France.

The following documents illustrate the relations between the Imperial Foreign Office, the general government of Belgium, the Supreme Command, and the Commission for Relief in Belgium, as well as the principal guaranties which the German authorities gave to the Commission during the war.

235. FIELD-MARSHAL VON DER GOLTZ TO THE COMITÉ CENTRAL, OCTOBER 16, 1914[1]

General Government in Belgium

To the Comité Central de Secours   BRUSSELS, October 16, 1914
et d'Alimentation, Brussels:

In answer to your esteemed letter of this date, I have the honor to reply that I welcome with keen satisfaction the work undertaken by the Comité Central de Secours et d'Alimentation and that I have no hesitation in giving by the present letter my formal and express assurance that the foodstuffs of all sorts imported by the Comité for the provisioning of the civil population of Belgium are exclusively reserved for the needs of the population of Belgium, that consequently these foodstuffs shall be exempt from requisition on the part of the military authorities and finally that they remain at the exclusive disposal of the Comité.

(*Signed*) BARON VON DER GOLTZ
General Field-Marshal

236. OFFICIAL GERMAN APPROVAL OF THE COMMISSION FOR RELIEF IN BELGIUM[2]

GERMAN FOREIGN OFFICE, BERLIN
23 November 1914

To the Embassy of the United States of America:

The Foreign Office has the honor to inform the Embassy of the United States of America in answer to the verbal note of November 14, F.O. 1105, that the Imperial Government is in complete sympathy with the meritorious efforts of the American Commission in Belgium to provide the population of that country with foodstuffs. The Imperial Government therefore—until further notice and with reservation of any recall which may become necessary at any time—gladly consents that

---

[1] The Commission for Relief in Belgium, "Guarantees and Undertakings from the German Authorities in Belgium," Hoover War Library. Hereafter cited as C.R.B., "Guarantees."

[2] Translation, "Document No. 22, Note, German Foreign Office to Gerard, giving official approval to the C.R.B., and guaranteeing freedom from seizure to non-neutral vessels carrying supplies of the C.R.B. to Dutch ports," in George I. Gay (with the collaboration of H. H. Fisher), *Public Relations of The Commission for Relief in Belgium, Documents* (Stanford University, 1929), I, 25. Hereafter cited as *C.R.B. Documents.*

the transportation of the said foodstuffs to Dutch harbors take place also in other than neutral vessels, and will grant in this case also the same guarantee for the disposition of the foodstuffs, according to agreement, as if the transportation had been made in neutral vessels. In order to obviate seizure by German war vessels at sea, it is advisable that such non-neutral vessels be provided with a certificate of a competent American authority, in which it is stated that the vessel carries foodstuffs which are to be brought through the agency of the American Commission for Relief with the consent of the German Government by way of Dutch harbors into Belgium for the supplying of the population there; and it is furthermore advisable that the non-neutral vessels also carry with them a pass from the Imperial German Ambassador in Washington to be issued on the basis of the aforesaid certificate.

237. CONFIRMATION OF GUARANTY AGAINST REQUISITION IN BELGIUM, DECEMBER 31, 1914[3]

BERLIN, 31 December 1914

His Excellency, Mr. Gerard
Ambassador of the United States of America

The undersigned has the honor to inform His Excellency, Mr. Gerard, Ambassador of the United States of America, with reference to the esteemed note of the 28th instant, that the Imperial Governor-General in Belgium will issue without delay an order prohibiting all the troops under his command from requisitioning food or forage of any kind whatsoever which would require to be replaced by importations by the American Committee for Belgian Relief. The Governor-General will, in addition, authorize the Minister of the United States and the Spanish Minister at Brussels as Honorary Chairmen of the Committee, to convince themselves in any way which may to them appear advisable that the prohibition is observed most scrupulously.

With regard to the desire that non-neutral ships bringing food for Belgium may not be interfered with on their return to British ports, and that assurance to this effect might be given, reference is respectfully made to the Note Verbale of the 24th instant, No. 3 of which contains provisions dealing with this desire.

The undersigned avails himself of the opportunity to renew to the Ambassador the assurances of his most distinguished consideration.

(*Signed*) ZIMMERMANN

---

[3] Translation, "Document No. 321, Letter, Zimmermann to Gerard, confirming, but with important alterations, the guarantee against requisition in Belgium," *C.R.B. Documents*, I, 518.

238. NEGOTIATIONS CONCERNING THE C.R.B., FEBRUARY 4, 1915[4]

BERLIN, 5 February 1915

On Tuesday the 2d of February, Mr. Gerard took myself, Mr. Heineman, Mr. Hulse, and Mr. Gibson to call on Mr. Zimmermann, the Under-Secretary of Foreign Affairs. I presented to him the position in which the Commission found itself and the absolute necessity for assistance in working out its problems for the German Government. I reviewed the work which we had done, the circumstances under which we had begun operations, the volume of the work which we are now handling, and the necessity of government co-operation. I proposed to him the abandonment of the contribution from Belgium to be coupled with a subsidy in gold from the English and French Governments to this Commission. Herr Zimmermann took a great interest in the whole position, and the conversation lasted over one hour. He finally expressed himself as in favor of our proposals and stated that he would assist us to the best of his ability, but remarked that men of peace have but little influence in these times. He asked to have a complete memorandum sent to him, which I agreed to prepare.

239. FURTHER NEGOTIATIONS, FEBRUARY 4, 1915[5]

BERLIN, 6 February 1915

At 6 o'clock I had a meeting, accompanied by Mr. Heineman, with the Finance Minister, Mr. Helfferich. Mr. Heineman, having seen him previously, was well informed as to our proposals. He stated at once, however, that the proposed abandonment of the contribution from Belgium was wholly and absolutely impossible. He stated that Herr Zimmermann could not have understood what we meant. He stated that some other way would have to be found to assist the Commission, and suggested that we go to Brussels and place our requirements before the Local Government, and that he would ask them to assist us in every way possible. I told him that this was a matter which concerned the

---

[4] "Document No. 134, Memorandum, by Hoover, of a conversation with Zimmermann, 2 February 1915, with a memorandum and covering letter dated 4 February 1915, sent by Hoover, describing the problems confronting the C.R.B. in the continuation of Belgian relief," *C.R.B. Documents,* I, 241–42. The memorandum of the conversation only is here quoted.

[5] "Document No. 135, Memorandum, by Hoover, of a conversation with Dr. Karl Helfferich, Imperial Finance Minister, 4 February 1915, concerning the indemnities and the financial proposals of the Minister," *C.R.B. Documents,* I, 245–47.

Imperial Government itself, that the questions of feeding seven millions in Belgium, three millions in France, and ten millions in Poland were all wrapped up in one question, and that was the question as to the control of imported foodstuffs through neutral committees, and that I presumed these committees would have to be, from the nature of things, American, and that it was due to anybody who undertook such a labor that his requests should receive attention from the highest.

I explained the voluntary character of our effort, the philanthropic origin of our funds, the additions which we had had to these funds from Belgian sources, and the absolute vital importance to the German Government from a military point of view that we should continue our action, and stated that unless we could be properly recognized by the Government and helped in our work by them, it would ultimately dwindle down to a service totally inadequate to the millions of people.

The Minister then made a series of suggestions as to other methods. He proposed that the contribution on Belgium should be increased and that we should be handed the increased contribution. To this I replied that this would be nothing but paper and that we must have gold. He then suggested that we might have bills drawn by the people from whom we purchased foodstuffs, and have these bills accepted by the Belgian banks, and that through the friends of the German Government in New York they could arrange to have these bills discounted and even renewed. He explained to me that Mr. Warburg, the head of the banking firm of Warburg and Company of Hamburg, was a brother of Mr. Warburg of Messrs. Kuhn, Loeb and Company of New York, head of the American Government National Reserve Board, and that the National Reserve Board was anxious to set up a large business in bills, diverting especially South American bills from the London to the New York market, and that Mr. Warburg in New York would be in a position to induce the various banks to discount these bills, and he stated that no doubt they would be renewed from time to time until the war was over.

I explained to him that there were two weaknesses in his proposal: The first was that I saw no reason why any Belgian bank should accept these bills, as we had no money to pay any Belgian bank; that although we sold a portion of the foodstuffs the money which we received was dissipated in caring for the destitute and in paying communal officials; and that I could see no more reason why a Belgian bank should accept such bills than any other bank in the world; the other difficulty was that the amount of such bills would run into ten millions of dollars per month and that it would go on for nine months at least. We had some argument on the question and he stuck to his point tenaciously and said we should see Mr. Warburg, with whom he had already discussed the matter. He again repeated that the idea of abandoning the contribution from Belgium was wholly impossible for three reasons: (1) The technical arrangements under which the contributions had been set up requiring the abandonment of the rights of local generals, and other interdepartmental arrangements which could not be broken down; (2) it would be equivalent to the German Government paying for the food of the Belgians; and (3) the English Government could say that it compelled the Germans to do it.

I replied that this was not my view; that the possession of the contribution placed in the hands of the Germans a club which they could use to force the English and French to pay out two million pounds per month in gold to feed the Belgians; and that all it meant to the Germans was the abandonment of forty million francs worth of doubtful paper. He suggested that we might expand the contribution, the Société Générale to discount the provincial bonds as in the old case, and to print similar currency against them, and that the Imperial Government might entertain some method of guaranteeing their exchange value and interesting their friends, Messrs. Warburg and the German agents in New York, to raise money against such guaranteed exchange.

I pointed out that sooner or later this would mean the export of gold from Germany, that in any case it means the inflation of the Société Générale currency to a disastrous point. I informed him that in any event his method was one which required the Americans to loan the money, the Belgians to repay the loan, the Germans hanging on to their indemnity from Belgium; that if I went back to England and replied to questions of the English Government that the Germans had refused to relax the pressure on Belgium, the English must at once give publicity to their offer, and that I did not think any American banker would care to loan money to the Belgians under such circumstances.

We parted in order to see Mr. Warburg at the Adlon Hotel.

240. INDEMNITIES, OTHER RELIEF PROBLEMS, AND PUBLIC
OPINION, NEGOTIATIONS OF FEBRUARY 6, 1915[6]

BERLIN, 7 February 1915

At 4:30 I accompanied Mr. Gerard to call upon Herr von Jagow, Minister of Foreign Affairs. He told me he had had some discussion with Mr. Zimmermann, and also with the Chancellor and with Mr. Helfferich, and that Dr. Helfferich was formulating a plan to solve our

[6] "Document No. 139, Memorandum, by Hoover, of a conversation by Gerard and himself with von Jagow, 6 February 1915, respecting indemnities, other problems of relief, and the attitude of public opinion," *C.R.B. Documents,* I, 250–52.

difficulties. He stated that of course the monthly indemnity on Belgium could not be abandoned, but the matter could be solved in another manner, and stated that we had better continue our negotiations which we were carrying on with Dr. Helfferich. I stated that the proposals outlined by Dr. Helfferich were not agreeable to us, and that I felt that this matter did not lie entirely in the Finance Department, but lay largely in the Foreign Office, because it was a matter which concerned all Germany in relations and its good reputation abroad; that it seemed to me a great deal of a task to continue to feed the Belgians, no matter from what source money might be obtained, so long as the German Government continued to extract from these people a similar amount of money. I told him that as apparently the indemnity was only laid on Belgium after we had become well established in our work, I felt sometimes that we had been the cause of this terrible infliction, because if the people of Belgium had been as desperate as the people in Poland for want of food, it is impossible that the fine would ever have been imposed. He replied that the people of Belgium had enormous resources, and that forty million francs a month was much less than they could really afford to pay; that this was collected merely to support the occupying army under the provisions of the Hague Convention and that none of the money was sent to Germany; and he again affirmed that we should continue our negotiations with Dr. Helfferich, who, he stated, would help us in every possible way, as would the other members of the Government.

I then took up with him the question of passes for the people employed on our work; that it was almost impossible for us to obtain the passes which we needed; that there were great delays; and that the passes very often proved inadequate for the purpose for which they were issued; that we were made to feel most of the time that a favor was being conferred upon us that we were allowed to work in Belgium; and that I did think it was most necessary that the whole of this attitude and method should be revised. I suggested that in the future passes should only be issued on a request signed by Mr. Whitlock or the Chargé d'Affaires at the Embassy, but that a pass should be issued instantly upon sending in such a request; that practically I wanted Mr. Whitlock given the right to issue passes himself for this work.

I then took up the question of our steamers coming up the Channel after the 18th February, the presumable date of the submarine blockade. I pointed out that under the English regulations and the conditions of their charters, it was wholly impossible for these ships to go to Rotterdam by way of North Scotland. After some discussion the Minister promised to have orders issued of the most scrupulous care of our steamers.

I then returned to the discussion of the indemnity question, stating to the Minister that there was one phase of this whole question which Germans obstinately ignored: that the Germans were obviously anxious to win the good feeling of the American people; that they were most severe in their denunciation of our lack of neutrality, and yet they did not take the most essential precautions to win and hold the esteem of the American people; and that if they held at least one-half of the American sentiment, they could be assured of impartiality in national conduct and therefore it was worth while to make some effort. I pointed out to him that America was not nascently pro-British, while at the present time 70 per cent of the American people were extremely pro-English; that this sentiment did not arise from any love of England, but arose out of the fact that the Americans were pro-Belgian, and that it was entirely out of their views as to the treatment of Belgium by the Germans and their belief that the English were fighting the Belgian cause which led their feelings to lean so predominantly toward the English; and that I was absolutely satisfied that in order to win American opinion Germany must mend her methods toward Belgium; that if Germany today would take a generous and grand view and would release the Belgians from their monthly indemnity, I believed it would do more to win American opinion than any other act possible; that therefore this whole problem became one of the Foreign Office, whose duty it is to guard foreign opinion and relations; and that I hoped he would consider the thing as a problem apart from the financial schemes of Dr. Helfferich. These schemes might be of able financial character but they implied that Americans supply the money and that Belgians ultimately repay it; and while it reflected credit on the skill of the Finance Ministry, it did not reflect any particular credit or give cause for gratitude toward Germany.

Mr. Gerard pointed out that he himself had been the vehicle through which the Germans had communicated their offers to the Belgians, after the taking of Liége, offering the Belgians not only guarantees as to their national integrity, but also large indemnities; and that therefore it was not much of a step to say now that when the Belgians are completely conquered they should at least be assured their national integrity, even though they do not receive any indemnities, and that they should be free from themselves paying indemnities to the Germans.

He also reminded the Minister of the Chancellor's speech on the 4th August, in which assurances were given with regard to Belgium which had not yet been withdrawn.

241. FURTHER NEGOTIATIONS CONCERNING INDEMNITIES, FINANCE, AND OTHER PROBLEMS, FEBRUARY 7, 1915[7]

BERLIN, 7 February 1915

At 6 o'clock I accompanied Mr. Gerard to a meeting with the Imperial Chancellor, His Excellency von Bethmann-Hollweg. Mr. Gerard presented to him the essential facts with regard to our position: that the question of the feeding of the Belgians would soon get beyond the resources which we could command by philanthropy or from the assistance of the Belgian Government; that if we were to feed the people of Northern France as well as the Belgians, we should require 40 or 50 million marks per month; and that the Allied Governments had refused to come to our assistance so long as the Germans continued their monetary levies on Belgium. The Chancellor stated at once with emphasis that the Germans would never give up this contribution, reiterating that it was absolutely impossible; that, on the other hand, they recognized the very necessary character of the work and were prepared to find some other method of financial assistance; that Germany wanted no help from the Allies in anything. That in the face of the world and of German public opinion they could not for one moment retreat from an act which they had taken under the full rights confirmed by the Hague Convention. He stated that financial proposals were being drawn up by Mr. Helfferich in consultation with the financial members of the German Civil Government in Belgium and that a method would be worked out which would make our path easy from a financial point of view. I pointed out that we had had discussions with Mr. Helfferich and that all of his proposals revolved around the Belgians undertaking to pay for the foodstuffs ultimately, and that in the meantime the American public or American bankers should furnish the money; and that the first part of the proposal was a matter with which I had nothing to do and must be settled with the Belgians, but I could state at once with regard to the second part of the proposal, that is, the finding of the necessary money in America, that this would meet with the strongest opposition. That I had no doubt that upon my arrival in London the English Government would immediately demand to know whether the Germans had accepted our proposal, and that I would be compelled to inform them that it had not been accepted. Upon this the English would announce to the world that they had offered to pay for the

---

[7] "Document No. 140, Memorandum, by Hoover, of a conversation by Gerard and himself with Herr von Bethmann-Hollweg, Imperial Chancellor, 7 February 1915, with regard to indemnities, finance, and other problems of relief," *C.R.B. Documents,* I, 252–55.

feeding of the Belgians themselves if the Germans would withdraw their forced contributions from Belgium, and that I did not believe that in the face of such an announcement the Americans would be disposed to at all facilitate the matter. Moreover, it might release the English from all feeling of responsibility in the matter. That I felt strongly that this was a matter in which both Governments must meet half way through this Commission. He stated that he could have no negotiations with the English in any shape or form, to which I replied that we were not proposing any such negotiations but merely that each Government should assent to an arrangement with the Commission. Mr. Gerard pointed out that the Commission was absolutely the only way through which the Belgians could be kept from starvation, and that in keeping them from starvation the greatest possible military service was being done to the Germans. The Chancellor replied again that it was utterly impossible that they should give up the contribution and that he could not discuss the matter on this footing; and again affirmed strongly that German public opinion would not stand for it. Mr. Gerard pointed out that he had discussed the matter with the editor of one of the most prominent German papers, who had told him that he thought it was the proper course to take; and Mr. Gerard suggested that if His Excellency would acquiesce, he, Mr. Gerard, would call in a lot of editors and lay the proposal before them and endeavor to formulate public opinion. The Chancellor said this did not suit the occasion, and stated that Germany was fighting with her back to the wall, in a situation for which he could not find an English word to fully express himself—that the word "serious" was not at all adequate as a description of the position in which Germany lay at the present moment. He stated that all Germans were grateful to the Commission for the work they were carrying on, and he would pledge himself to support the Commission in every way; but he could not entertain the proposals which had been made, and begged the Ambassador not to press the point. I stated to him that in pressing this point we were pressing a point which we felt sure was one which gave the Germans a unique opportunity to demonstrate to the world their desire to be fair and generous to the Belgians, and, disregarding all that had happened, the Germans had not turned from the view which they had held from the beginning with regard to Belgium. Mr. Gerard pointed out that the Germans had consistently taken the attitude that they were not conquering Belgium, but had merely entered it as a military necessity, and that it would only be consistent with such an attitude if they did not exercise the rights of conquerors in levying the cost of occupation upon these people. I pointed out it should be the desire of every German to secure the favorable opinion of the United States toward the Germans, and that the first and primary thing necessary to obtain such good opinion was by showing the generous attitude toward Belgium. He stated that American opinion was apparently of little value, as the Americans were supplying arms to the Allies and would probably continue to do so, and that in so doing they were prolonging the war. To this Mr. Gerard replied that the position was akin to two people playing chess, where one, which he might call the Germans, stopped in the middle of the game and asked to have the whole rules of the game altered; that the rules of this game had been set down and practiced by every nation for years, and that if the rules were to be changed it could not be done in the middle of the game.

I told His Excellency that there was one other line of action which I thought that the Germans could take with regard to Belgium, which I thought would be most helpful. That it was vital that industry should be re-established in Belgium as far as it was possible, but that before any such industry revival could take place the Belgians must have a greater freedom of movement, and told him that I sincerely hoped that he would reconsider the present attitude toward the better class of Belgians and see if they could find some method by which these better classes could be allowed to move around the country with greater facility, as it was hopeless to get industry re-established unless this was done. I told him that not only myself but all of my colleagues in the work had been on the most intimate terms with thousands of Belgians and that I could give him my word of honor that neither myself nor they, as far as I could learn, had ever had any suggestions of conspiracy and rebellion since we undertook this work; and that I felt the Germans were perfectly safe in allowing twenty or thirty thousand Belgians of the more important order to have complete freedom of movement within the Occupation Zone. He said, "I wonder if this is really the case"; and stated that he would have the matter looked into and see what could be done.

Mr. Gerard again returned to the question of the indemnity and pressed the point vigorously that the Germans could well afford to, and that it was positively in their interest that they should give way. To this the Chancellor said that it is finally, and once for all, absolutely impossible. I then stated to him that no matter what proposals were brought forward, I hoped that he would bear in mind at all times that these proposals would have to be agreeable to the English, otherwise we could not introduce one pound of foodstuff into Belgium; that the English were in no wise convinced that the work we were carrying on was necessary, and that they certainly considered it was not in the interest of the Allies; and that our whole operations hung on a slender thread of sentiment, a large measure of which toward the Belgians existed in England, but that a breath could blow away this sentiment and the

Germans would be faced with ten million starving people on their hands. Mr. Gerard pointed out that the same situation existed in Poland and that if they were to obtain the establishment of the same system of food introduction, it would entail the satisfaction of the neutral world with the other belligerents over Belgium. The Chancellor replied that they recognized these points and that they would take them into consideration in the proposals which he hoped they would be able to make; and he stated that the Commission need have no fear but that a solution would be found for other monetary necessities, but that it could not be the solution which the Commission had proposed.

242. PERMISSION FOR USE OF CHANNEL ROUTE
BY C.R.B. SHIPS, MARCH 5, 1915[8]

FOREIGN OFFICE, BERLIN
5 March 1915

MY DEAR EXCELLENCY:

Many thanks for your kind letter of the 1st instant enclosing a copy of the telegram of Mr. Hoover. Herr von Bethmann-Hollweg and I retain the most pleasing remembrance of Mr. Hoover and both he and Your Excellency may rest assured that the Imperial Government maintains its former attitude to afford the humanitarian work of the Relief Commission on the part of Germany every possible support.

We had also been informed of Mr. Hoover's anxiety through our Legation at The Hague, and I had thereupon ascertained at once through the Imperial Admiralty that ships of the Relief Commission should also proceed undisturbed by the English Channel route provided that they be recognizable by the customary insignia, which should also be illuminated so as to be plainly visible at night. The German submarines have been instructed accordingly. Herr von Mueller at The Hague will in the meantime have advised Mr. Hoover of this fact through the American Minister at The Hague.

In this connection we must naturally assume that all means will be taken to exclude the possibility of a misuse of the insignia of the Relief Commission. To this end the Imperial Foreign Office will invoke again in an official communication the kind mediation of Your Excellency to obtain from the British Government a declaration containing the assurance that only those ships that are actually in the service of the Relief Commission may carry the insignia of the Commission.

---

[8] Translation, "Document No. 202, Letter, von Jagow to Gerard, granting permission to C.R.B. ships to use the Channel route," *C.R.B. Documents*, I, 317–18.

As Your Excellency will easily understand, we were unable, in view of the existing danger from mines in the war zone, to refrain from declining to issue safe-conducts to the ships of the Commission for the journey to and from England. On the other hand, we will gladly issue safe-conducts, as heretofore, to those ships of the Commission which do not touch at English points, and at the same time urgently recommend them, precisely on account of the danger from mines, to choose the northern route around Scotland indicated in the "Nachrichten für Seefahrer," No. 3161, 1914.

I am happy to avail myself of this opportunity to renew to Your Excellency the assurance of my highest consideration.

(*Signed*) von Jagow

243. GOVERNOR VON BISSING TO THE COMITÉ NATIONAL, REAFFIRMING GUARANTIES OF OCTOBER 1914 AND JANUARY 1915, AND INTERPRETING THAT OF JANUARY 21, 1915[9]

General Government in Belgium

Brussels, March 12, 1915

Comité National de Secours et d'Alimentation, Brussels:

Referring to your letter of the 9th inst. I am quite willing, in order to encourage the humanitarian efforts of the Comité which have always had my warmest sympathies, to confirm herewith the previous declarations which have already been given to the Comité in October 1914 and January of this year.

According to these, the foodstuffs of all kinds imported by the Comité for the feeding of the civil population of Belgium remain exclusively reserved for the population of Belgium, and must remain free from military requisitions. I also repeat, in conformity with my declaration of January, that all troops under my orders in the Occupation Zone are forbidden to take, even against payment, foodstuffs and artificial foods for animals, of any kind whatsoever, which are replaced through importations by the Comité. I attach herewith copy of my instructions of January 21, 1915, to my troops.

I cannot agree with your opinion that "every product obtained from our soil" is already being imported by you, and could therefore no longer be requisitioned. In particular, it is not within my knowledge that oats, straw, hay, potatoes, fresh vegetables, and sugar are imported

[9] C.R.B., "Guarantees."

in such quantities that my prohibition should be extended to these articles also.

If English financial circles demand a more extended declaration in the sense that the Imperial General Government exempt from requisition all foods, without any distinction, necessary for the maintenance of the people and animals, which shall be produced hereafter in the country, I regret that I am not in a position to give such a declaration. On the contrary, adherence must be continued to the principle that the stocks of articles, specified in detail, which were still in the country at the time of the publication of my declaration of January 21, 1915, shall be kept for the country and may not be requisitioned in favor of the troops, even against payment.

Having thus quite clearly explained my point of view to the Comité, I am very willing, by the delivery of a passport, to make possible the trip to London of the Comité's delegate, Monsieur Francqui, for the purpose of negotiations planned by him.

The Governor-General
(*Sgd.*) BARON VON BISSING

244. CONFERENCE REGARDING RELIEF OF NORTHERN FRANCE, MARCH 21, 1915[10]

CONFERENCE

At General Headquarters on the 21st March 1915, morning

Present: Major-General Zoellner, representing the Commander-in-Chief of the Army, and Mr. A. N. Connett, representing the C.R.B. (Commission for Relief in Belgium).

1. Mr. Hoover's telegram, dated London, 18th March 1915, concerning the supervision of the distribution of foodstuffs to the civilian population of the portions of Northern France occupied by the German army was produced and discussed.

2. The German army administration agree in principle that American officials in uniform act in the manner proposed as supervisors for the activities of the C.R.B.

3. The German army administration gives the assurance that in no case will the goods be claimed for the needs of the army, but that they will be solely used for the civilian population of the occupied portions of France.

---

[10] Translation, "Document No. 281, Memorandum, of conference between Major-General Zoellner and Connett, regarding relief of Northern France," *C.R.B. Documents*, I, 412–13.

4. The German army administration has requisitioned and given receipts for the foodstuffs for man and beast existing in Northern France, so that all stocks have passed to the possession of the German army administration. Therefore no stocks whatsoever any longer exist which belong to the French population, with the exception of poultry and vegetables in the gardens. To exclude any misunderstandings, the fact must therefore be stated, that the claiming for army purposes of the stocks now already requisitioned, should not be regarded as a new requisition. The most indispensable foodstuffs for man and beast have hitherto been delivered to the population by the Germans in strictly specified rations.

5. With regard to the utilization of the new crop, the German army administration has a free hand, because, by supplying seed and furnishing labor, horses, motor plows, and so on, the administration itself effects the things essential to the securing of the crop, and furnishes compensation for the use of the land and of French labor.

6. The German army administration assures the C.R.B. of the greatest liberality in regard to freight charges and will grant at least the same concessions as for the provisioning of Belgium.

245. AGREEMENTS AS TO PROVISIONING THE POPULATION IN THE OCCUPIED FRENCH TERRITORY, APRIL 13, 1915[11]

Brussels, 13 April 1915

Main Agreement

1. The German Commander-in-Chief gives his consent for the C.R.B. to undertake the supply of the population of the occupied French territory with foodstuffs.

2. The German Commander-in-Chief gives the assurance that the goods imported for the said purpose will never be called upon for the use of the German Army, but shall be used solely for the French population of the occupied territory. The German Commander-in-Chief will issue strict orders to all the respective subordinate authorities to the effect that these goods must never be seized.

Any goods which may not have been distributed at any time will remain at the exclusive disposal of the C.R.B.

[11] Translation, "Document No. 283, Agreements, between the Supreme Command of the German Army at request of the Quartermaster-General (represented by Major von Kessler) and the C.R.B. (represented by O. T. Crosby and A. N. Connett), regarding the provisioning of the population in the occupied French territory," *C.R.B. Documents*, I, 414–15.

3. The C.R.B. is authorized to appoint in the occupied territory of Northern France, American citizens as its delegates, who may, subject to the supplementary agreement No. 1 attached hereto, satisfy themselves to the carrying out of the assurance given under paragraph 2.

4. The requests to the C.R.B. for, and the distribution of the goods will be effected according to the determinations of the C.R.B., in conjunction with the German military authorities, by French trustees, who are to be nominated by the French communities, subject to the approval of the German military authorities and of the C.R.B. These trustees will represent the French communities in the transactions with the delegates of the C.R.B., more particularly in connection with accounts and payments.

5. The German Commander-in-Chief will afford every facility for the carriage of the goods to the place of destination. The goods will be admitted free of duty, and freight will be charged according to similar principles as may, from time to time, be in force for the supply of Belgium.

The transport is regulated by the supplementary agreement No. 2 attached hereto.

6. In order to eliminate doubts as to origin and destination of the goods supplied, all means of transport and storing rooms will be labeled officially by the German military authorities in such a manner as to make the goods recognizable as those covered by the stipulations of paragraph 2.

7. If military exigencies should so require, this agreement may be canceled by the German Commander-in-Chief at any time without giving any reasons, by a notice to that effect to the C.R.B. However, all goods imported by the C.R.B., then being already within the occupied French territory, shall be disposed of in accordance with the stipulations of this agreement, the American delegates remaining long enough to discharge their duties with respect to such goods, in so far as this is considered practicable for military reasons.

8. The right of the German military authorities to requisition for military purposes against "Bons" the foodstuffs for men or animals still existing in the country is in no way affected by this agreement.

Likewise, the German military authorities reserve to themselves all rights in respect to the new crop.

(S.) von Kessler, Major
(S.) Oscar T. Crosby

246. RESERVATIONS OF FOOD AND INCREASE IN RATIONS, AUGUST 26, 1916[12]

BRUSSELS, 26 August 1916

Major von Kessler declared it to be the intention of the German authorities to increase, from October 1st, 1916, the ration of flour and potatoes of the civil population of the North of France and the Belgian Etappen to 200 grams of flour and 400 grams of potatoes per person per day, this being an increase over the flour ration at present provided of 100 per cent, and over the potato ration of 100 per cent.

Major von Kessler further declared it to be the intention of the German authorities to continue to reserve to the civil population the garden fruit and vegetables and to make certain other reservations to the civil population of poultry, eggs, pigs, rabbits, etc., as will help to insure a supply of fresh meat to the people.

Director Kellogg declared it to be the intention of the Commission for Relief in Belgium to continue the ravitaillement of the North of France and the Belgian Etappen along the lines of the present ravitaillement but with certain changes in the amounts of flour and other food-stuffs in order to make the whole ration, German and C.R.B. combined, the most advantageous one from the point of view of the nutrition of the people.

The increase in the German ration of flour, for example, would allow the C.R.B. flour ration to be somewhat reduced, and the money and tonnage thereby saved devoted to the increase in the amounts of certain other foodstuffs provided, as bacon and lard, dried peas and beans, etc., and especially to the obtaining and providing, if possible, of fresh or preserved meats.

Director Kellogg also declared it to be the intention of the C.R.B. to endeavor to obtain an increase in its funds devoted to the ravitaillement of the North of France in order to meet the additional needs of the people for the coming winter.

These declarations are hereby accepted as the basis of an agreement between the German General Staff of the Great Headquarters and the Commission for Relief in Belgium as to the conditions of the further ravitaillement of the civil population of the North of France and the Belgium Etappen, that is, from October 1st, 1916, until later agreement.

(*Signed*) VON KESSLER
(*Signed*) V. L. KELLOGG

[12] "Document No. 377, Memorandum of a conference and agreement between Major von Kessler and Kellogg of the C.R.B., regarding reservations of food in Northern France and the Belgian Etapes and increase in rations to the civil population," *C.R.B. Documents*, I, 594.

247. RELIEF WORK IN THE BELGIUM ARMY ZONE[13]

[GHENT, 6 July 1915]

1. The Etappen-Inspektion gives the assurance that the goods imported for the said purpose will never be called upon for the use of the German Army, but shall be used solely for the Belgian civil population of the occupied territory. The Etappen-Inspektion will issue strict orders to all the respective subordinate authorities to the effect that these goods must never be seized. Any goods which may not have been distributed at any time will remain at the exclusive disposal of the C.R.B.

2. The Etappen-Inspektion will afford every facility for the carriage of the goods to the place of destination. The goods will be admitted free of duty and freight will be charged according to similar principles as may, from time to time, be in force for the supply of Belgium.

3. In order to eliminate doubts as to origin and destination of the goods supplied, all means of transport and storing-rooms will be labelled officially by the German military authorities in such a manner as to make the goods recognizable as those covered by the stipulation of paragraph 1.

4. If military exigencies should so require, this agreement may be cancelled by the Etappen-Inspektion at any time without giving any reasons, by a notice to that effect to the C.R.B. However, all goods imported by the C.R.B. then being already within the occupied Belgian territory shall be disposed of in accordance with the stipulation of this agreement. In this case the American delegates will be permitted to remain long enough to discharge their duties in so far as this is considered practicable for military reasons.

5. The right of the German military authorities to requisition for military purposes against *bons* the foodstuffs for men and animals still existing in the country is in no way affected by this agreement. Likewise, the German military authorities reserve to themselves all rights in respect to the new crop.

6. The delegates of the C.R.B. are authorized to satisfy themselves that the goods supplied by the C.R.B. are being used in accordance with the guarantees given.

7. The German military authorities will afford them every possible assistance in the carrying out of this duty. On the other hand, for military reasons, they will be expected to limit themselves to such matters as are within the scope of their duties.

---

[13] "Document No. 667, Agreement, 6 July 1915, between the Army Command and the C.R.B., covering the relief work in the Army Zone in Belgium," *C.R.B. Documents,* II, 439–40.

8. The delegates are aware that their activities in the zone of the field army will have to be subjected to certain restrictions. These will be fixed as binding by the military authorities in respect of the military situation at the time being.

9. There will be established in the territory occupied by the Fourth Army:

> A central office (Ghent)
> Three sub-districts with stores (Beernem, Thielt, Courtrai).

10. At the central office two gentlemen of American nationality will be admitted, as selected by the C.R.B. A military motor car will be placed at the disposal of these gentlemen for the journeys necessitated by their duties in the zone of the Fourth Army; for the journeys to Brussels a car of their own with the corresponding passes can be used. Every gentleman will be granted a passport guaranteeing his personal safety and a car permit.

11. To the central office, an officer speaking English and French will be detailed exclusively for this duty. He has to accompany the delegates on their journeys for their personal safety and will generally assist them in every possible way.

12. All correspondence of the C.R.B. relative to ravitaillement has to be handed open to the attached officer who will forward it on by the quickest means, and in the zone of the Imperial Post, free of postage. The use of the military telegraphs and telephones will be allowed through the medium of the said officer. No fees will be charged.

13. On entering upon his position, every delegate will certify by his signature that he has been made acquainted with the above stipulations. At the same time he takes upon himself the obligation to carry out his duties in such a manner as may be expected from an honorable citizen of a neutral state.

14. As far as possible, the transportation shall take place by water. No tolls have to be paid for the use of the waterways. The payment of the freight to the lightermen is a matter of the C.R.B. Special regulations will be fixed for the granting of passes for the lightermen by the Etappen-Bau-Inspektion and the Hafenkommandanturen.

15. For the shipment by rail of foodstuffs for man and beast, the German Railway Administration in Brussels will demand no more than 50 per cent of normal freight rates. The same reduction of rates will apply to the return of empty bags. For cars which are delayed during the loading or unloading, the full demurrage, as specified by the tariffs, must be paid.

16. The waybills accompanying the rail-shipments must contain a regular attestation made in accordance with the decision of the German

Railway Administration and stating that the goods are destined for the Belgian civil population.

17. The railway cars used for the transportation must be provided with labels which show that the contents are the property of the C.R.B.

18. All means of distinguishing the goods, as labels, etc., have to be supplied by the C.R.B. in agreement with the German Railway Administration at Brussels.

19. The loaded cars will be delivered sealed at destination. Delegates of the C.R.B. will not be allowed to accompany cars or trains in transit.

20. Applications for the necessary cars must reach the station master at least two or three days beforehand. The German Railway Administration do not guarantee the supply of the cars. However, they will as far as possible attend to the needs of the C.R.B.

248. VERBAL NOTE OF THE POLITICAL DEPARTMENT OF THE GOVERNOR-GENERAL IN BELGIUM, DECEMBER 3, 1916[14]

J. No. V. 2467

VERBAL NOTE

His Excellency the Minister of the United States has been good enough to verbally inform Count Harrach of the fact that the British Government has advised the United States Embassy in London that exportations of cattle and foodstuffs from the territory administered by the Governor-General are said to have been made, contrary to the agreement entered into last April with the Ministers Protector of the Comité National. His Excellency the Minister of the United States added that the British Government requested urgent information in the matter, considering that the ravitaillement work might be jeopardized by such facts.

In reply to this communication, the Political Department has the honor to set forth the following facts by which it is established that the Governor-General has entirely fulfilled the engagement contracted by him in the interest of the Belgian civil population.

In his letter of April 14th last, Baron von der Lancken among other things advised the Ministers Protector that the Governor-General would give "instructions prohibiting the exportation from the territory of the General Government of foodstuffs (including cattle) provisions and fodder used for human consumption and for that of cattle," as well as that "of the seeds, fertilizers and agricultural supplies." He also wrote that "the Governor-General will give accordingly to the Military Com-

[14] C. R. B., "Guarantees."

missariat (Intendance Militaire) of the General Government orders not to make any further requisitions nor to purchase freely in the occupied territory of Belgium for the wants of the army of occupation any of the products mentioned above." These prohibitions were to be subject to exceptions only in certain cases enumerated in the said letter.

In accordance with these assurances, the Governor-General has immediately issued the instructions cited above and orders to all authorities and troops under him. He then completed them by measures of various kinds as appeared from time to time necessary to assure their execution.

Given the complexity of the conventions concluded with the Ministers Protector and the difficulties of application inherent in them, it is, however, not impossible that infractions of the minute and precise instructions given by the Governor-General may occasionally occur in spite of his efforts to prevent transgression thereof. One of the principal difficulties which oppose themselves to the end aimed at lies in the fact that numerous Belgians engage in smuggling of foodstuffs, cattle, etc., along the frontier, or act as intermediaries for purchases in the interior of the country, attracted by the considerable gain which they can obtain from such traffic. Experience of the last few months has shown that these persons act with such shrewdness that it often becomes extremely difficult to discover them and to prevent them from continuing their operations. In certain cases, the Governor-General can intervene only when precise indications are furnished him in regard to facts of the kind.

Such indications have among others been furnished the Governor-General by the communications which His Excellency the Minister of the United States has from time to time transmitted to the Political Department. All the facts thus pointed out have been examined with great care.

Some among these seem, for various reasons, not to be contrary to the orders given by the Governor-General; for others the informations furnished were not sufficiently precise to permit of the discovery of the authors of the incriminating facts and to take the measures which the situation demanded. In all other cases the Political Department has regularly caused an examination to be made by the competent authorities for the purpose of establishing the facts and, if there is found to be a case, steps are taken for punishing the culprits and for avoiding the repetition of acts which seem contrary to the orders given. The results of these examinations, which often require some time, are communicated to the Ministers Protector as they come to the knowledge of the Political Department.

For the purpose of further preventing as far as possible, any smuggling, the Governor-General has likewise completed and extended the measures previously taken for the surveillance of the frontier between Germany and Belgium in order to prevent the transportation of food-stuffs taking place there. Inspectors recently specially sent for that purpose into the region of Welkenraedt have made detailed reports in the matter of this surveillance. It appears therefrom that the smugglers, generally Belgian subjects, take the foodstuffs destined for exportation from the railway at a station near the frontier and carry them along the road to localities situated thereon. From there they are taken to the frontier in small quantities and during the night. The report says that the German functionaries of the customs service conscientiously fulfill their duty and that they are subjected to frequent control. On the other hand, it appears that the zeal of the Belgian controllers sometimes leaves much to be desired and this especially when the weather is bad. During the month of October fourteen seizures of some importance were effected along this frontier.

The Governor-General has also applied another means for prevent-ing smuggling. He has had seized at Welkenraedt, a locality situated near the German frontier, a certain quantity of foodstuffs which prob-ably were accumulated there for exportation. These foodstuffs will be returned to the Belgian civil population, and the Comité National has been requested to take possession of it for the indigent. The delinquents will be prosecuted. The Governor-General has also caused an order to be given to the commune of Welkenraedt to see to it that the food-stuffs be not exported, and the commune must at all times be able to justify itself for the direction taken by these provisions. The commune has also been notified that it must, under penalty of a fine, keep watch over the inhabitants to prevent them from engaging in smuggling.

Following the verbal communication of the United States Minister mentioned above, the Governor-General had decided to take fresh meas-ures based on the experiences of the last few months and to strengthen the ones previously taken. The Political Department has the honor to state some of these measures below.

The Administration of Railways has been informed that it must make arrangements for stopping all traffic of merchandise of any kind des-tined for Welkenraedt and for Verviers, and this for an undetermined period, except indispensable shipments for the provisioning of the local population. The purpose of this measure is to prevent the despatch of foodstuffs destined for these two stations, to ascertain the addresses of these shipments, and to find out which of these are made with a view to subsequent exportation. The same administration will have to subject to a minute examination all shipments crossing the frontier, especially with a view to establishing a control over possible shipments of foodstuffs. These shipments will be authorized only on the showing of a permit to be issued by an especially designated office and shall be issued exclusively for shipments which do not come under the application of the conventions concluded with the Ministers Protector. A special superintendence must be established for soldiers frequenting railway stations.

The Governor-General, on having learned that the line of vicinal railway which crosses the frontier south of Verviers is used for smuggling, has ordered that the operation of this railway be immediately stopped. One of the lines toward Germany facilitating smuggling will thus be suppressed. Likewise traffic on the line of the electric tramway from Verviers to Stembert, which facilitates transportation of foodstuffs in the direction of the frontier, will be completely stopped.

The Governor-General has likewise ordered a further strengthening of the service of surveillance established along the frontier. The troops charged with this service are to be frequently replaced, and they, as well as the customs employees, have received fresh and precise instructions intended to render this surveillance more efficacious.

Hereafter, and for a certain lapse of time, regular and frequent visitations of the houses of Welkenraedt will be made to ascertain and seize any quantity of meat, etc., exceeding that stipulated in the ordinance of the Governor-General of October 14, 1916 (concerning prohibition to accumulate too important a supply of meat and products having meat as their basis in private households). Delinquents are to be prosecuted in conformity with this ordinance and the foodstuffs seized shall be put at the disposal of the communal administration. This measure aims at limiting the accumulation near the frontier of foodstuffs destined for exportation.

The Governor-General has also determined to bring about the arrest and prosecution of a certain number of intermediaries and merchants whose names have been pointed out to him in various communications of the Ministers Protector as persons engaged regularly in the traffic of cattle and foodstuffs destined for exportation. A list of the names of persons thus committed for trial is attached to the present note. The authorities in the provinces have also been advised that they must exercise a close watch over merchants, brokers, etc., who are manifestly engaged in such traffic and if a case be found to proceed against them.

From this statement, His Excellency the Minister of the United States will be able to take notice that the Governor-General has conscientiously fulfilled and continues to fulfill the obligations which he has assumed by reason of the conventions concluded by him. The Political Department feels sure that the measures taken and thus decided on now by the Governor-General will not fail to attain to a great extent their purpose, which is prevention of the transgression of the instructions given in conformity with these obligations.

The Political Department begs of His Excellency the United States Minister to bring the contents of this note to the knowledge of the Ambassador of the United States in London. The Department trusts that the latter will be good enough to make use of it in replying to the assertions of the British Government and to prevent it from taking measures which would have the effect of compromising the ravitaillement with foodstuffs of the civil population of Belgium. The Governor-General having entirely satisfied the engagements contracted by him considers that he has a right to demand that the British Government do not withdraw from the obligations which on its part it has assumed. He throws on that Government in advance the entire responsibility for the consequences which an interruption, even momentary, in the transportation of foodstuffs destined to assure its alimentation would entail for the civil population of Belgium.

BRUSSELS, December 3, 1916

249. NOTE VERBALE OF THE IMPERIAL MINISTRY OF FOREIGN AFFAIRS CONCERNING THE COMMISSION FOR RELIEF IN BELGIUM, MAY 4, 1917[15]

Political Department
Nr. II U 1574

65021   BERLIN, May 4, 1917

VERBAL NOTE

The Imperial Government regrets to note the information given by the Foreign Office in the "Aide Memoir" of the 2d instant, No. 3824, that the ships of the Relief Commission in England did not sail on the 1st instant, in spite of the security given for safe passage to Holland. In view of the argument that the departure of the ships did not take place on account of the refusal to give them for the return passage a guaranty without reserve, the Foreign Office begs to give below a connected account of the development of the whole question:

England obviously had the intention, immediately after the notice of the ruthless submarine warfare and the danger arising therefrom of a possible warfare and the danger arising therefrom of a possible shortage of foodstuffs, to hold for itself the foodstuffs lying in English

---

[15] Commission for Relief in Belgium, London Office, "Blue Dossiers," Hoover War Library. Hereafter cited as C.R.B., "Blue Dossiers."

ports, and the foodstuffs on the way to English ports on the 1st of February of this year. It has in the first place prevented the Relief Commission from despatching the vessels with foodstuffs lying in English ports, within the days of grace valid up to the 5th February last which was required from the Commission by the General Government in Belgium on the 1st of February last. The English authorities have apparently also prevented the Commission from warning the steamers of the Commission on the way to English ports on the 1st February last against sailing in the blockaded zone.

When the Relief Commission, in reply to their request to the Imperial Government to make it possible subsequently for the ships lying in England to cross safely to Rotterdam, was asked which vessels the request referred to, and in which ports they were, England not only prevented the London Office of the Commission from giving these particulars but even prohibited the Director of the London Office, Kellogg, on a journey to Brussels from verbally giving the details which were known to him. When the English Government then threatened to discharge the ships within a period of a few days and distribute the foodstuffs to their own people, the diplomatic patrons of the Relief Commission were informed on the 27th of February last in a detailed protest note that, notwithstanding all their efforts, no success had been arrived at in obtaining from the Commission the necessary particulars for the granting of safe-conducts for the mentioned Relief ships. After the Spanish Ambassador and the Dutch Ambassador in Berlin had been informed by the Imperial Government of the principle on which the ships would be granted safe passage to Dutch ports, subject to a decision regarding the possibilities of such a passage after receipt of the required particulars, the British Government stated that they would hand these particulars to the Swiss Ambassador in London as soon as the latter would be authorized by the Imperial Government to make out safe-conducts for the ships. In order, however, to render it difficult for the Imperial Government to grant safe-conducts, on account of the hindrance to the naval warfare in the blockaded zone attached thereto, England again required that the ships should be loaded to depart, without their being bound down to a certain channel or to a certain day. Notwithstanding the mentioned statement, made in principle by the Imperial Government, also that the request was made to the Swiss Ambassador in London, on the grounds of this statement, that he ask for the necessary particulars respecting the present position of the ships, the British Government, as before, prohibited the Relief Commission from giving the required information. From the telegrams further exchanged in the matter between the patrons of the Relief work and the offices of the Relief Commission, it clearly appears that England continually seeks for new excuses, in order to prevent the Imperial Government being placed in a position to grant to the ships a safe departure.

Nevertheless the Commission was distinctly informed that the ships would be allowed to leave the English ports on the 1st of May last, and to pass through, safe from attacks, the blockaded zone along a route still to be indicated, if up to the 10th April last England declared itself prepared to allow the vessels with cargo to depart on the 1st of May of this year and provided the Relief Commission stated which ships desired to make use of the offer of passage as well as where they were lying.

The English Government replied thereto with the statement that all steamers—with the exception of four small vessels—had been discharged and departed from the English ports without their cargoes, without safe-conduct pass, and consequently at their own risk. The four ships mentioned, "Brabant," "Comte de Flandres," "Clara," and "Espagne," would also be treated in the same manner, if a safe-conduct pass for immediate departure were not issued for them valid till the 28th of March. As this demand reached the Commission only on March 28th of this year, it was already out of the question for this to be carried out. In spite of this the Patrons of the Relief Commission at Brussels were immediately informed that the Imperial Government would guarantee the possibility of a safe crossing to the Netherlands along the Southwold-Flushing route for the four ships named.

Further, the Commission was informed that in accordance with their desire the other smaller ships mentioned by them, of a total tonnage of 8,000 to 10,000 tons, could also sail in safety from England to Rotterdam. Safe-conduct passes for the Southwold-Flushing-Rotterdam trip on the first of May could be made out in the same manner as heretofore. Further, the Commission was allowed to have, from the 15th of May last, one steamer, provided with the usual Commission markings of these ships, to effect daily the outward and return voyage Flushing-Southwold or Flushing-Lowestoft, in connection with the released Dutch steam paddle-wheel boats.

Against these concessions the British Government made the objection that the loading could practically take place neither at Southwold nor at Lowestoft; that, further, sailing in the company of the steam paddle-boats was not possible, because these latter had a greater speed and no sufficient security existed for the ships.

The ships should therefore be allowed to sail from the Thames mouth to Rotterdam and it would be desirable to have the safe-conduct passes already made out by the Swiss Minister in London for the return trip. In order to eliminate any pretext of a disturbance of the Relief Work by the English Government, the Imperial Government made a further concession, viz., that the Swiss Ambassador in London might issue the safe-conducts for the outward voyage and return, which safe-conduct, however, must contain the express remark that the sailing to the Netherlands should take place either on the 1st of May of this year or in connection with one of the released paddle-wheel steamers and that the return voyage might be carried out only in connection with one of the released paddle-boats.

The fact that the steam paddle-boats travel faster than the freight vessels of the Relief Commission cannot be considered as acceptable excuse, because it would be easy to have the former adopt a lower speed. It would also be possible, if some good will was shown by the English to carry through the freighting of the ships at Southwold or at Lowestoft.

The route Rotterdam-Thames-mouth can, on account of mine danger, certainly not be allowed, for outside of the channel free from mines, no guaranty can be given against mines. An agreement in accordance with the desire of the English would have as a consequence only that the English, with the aid of the ships of the Relief Commission, would have at their disposal an entrance to the Thames remaining permanently free from mines. From these facts it obviously appears that the Imperial Government has always earnestly desired, as far as it was possible, to do away with the difficulties continually raised by the English Government and to observe fully the guaranties given to the Commission for Relief.

The last request of England, which cannot possibly be granted, viz., to allow the ships of the Relief Commission a *garantie sans reserve* for the return voyage, in other words, to allow the vessels to move freely as they like in the blockaded zone, means nothing more nor less than a request to have the declaration of the blockaded zone withdrawn. As to the impossibility of fulfilling this condition, the English Government should not be in doubt for a moment. The desire rather proves that the English Government has systematically worked from the beginning to obtain the foodstuffs belonging to the Commission without consideration of the consequences for the population of their own allies and yet to throw the blame on the Imperial Government for the withdrawal of the foodstuffs still lying in England. The Imperial Government, however, certainly expects that both the Dutch Government and all the neutral countries on the Continent, as well as the French and Belgian Governments, will see the impossible position taken up by the English Government and will do all they can to remove the opposition, emanating only from England, to the undisturbed continuance of the praiseworthy Relief Work.

250. MEMORANDUM OF MEETING BETWEEN BARON VON STUMM OF THE GERMAN LEGATION AND MR. BROWN OF THE COMMISSION FOR RELIEF IN BELGIUM, FEBRUARY 5, 1917[16]

The subject discussed concerning ships which had left leading ports previous to the 1st of February bearing safe-conduct passes which carried no stipulating clauses as to the new German proclaimed war zone. Mr. Brown stated that these ships would be rapidly approaching the war zone, would be travelling in all good faith under the safe-conduct passes as issued by the German Government, and there was no possibility whatever of diverting these ships from their course, as they were not equipped with wireless; that the Commission was powerless to do anything in this matter, and that the torpedoing of any of these ships would be a crime, and that they must be protected in some manner. Baron von Stumm replied that a special provision had been made to cover this circumstance, both for the Commission's ships and for the ships of the Dutch Government, and that a reasonable time would be allowed for such ships to reach English ports, even if they entered the proclaimed war zone subsequent to February 5. He thus anticipated that there would be no liability of any Commission ships being torpedoed under these circumstances, and stated that this was more especially so as there had never been a case of misuse of the Commission's markings, and that therefore the German naval authorities had every reason to respect the Commission's fleet. He further stated that there was absolutely no use in taking up this question with Berlin, as the point was already covered by instructions of the German Admiralty.

251. MEMORANDUM OF MEETING AT THE HAGUE ON FEBRUARY 7, 1917, BETWEEN BARON VON STUMM OF THE GERMAN LEGATION AND MR. BROWN[17]

Mr. Brown stated that while there was a narrow passage approximately 18 miles wide now open between the zones proclaimed dangerous by the British and German Governments, the Dutch had declared this passage to be dangerous and under the circumstances, if it could be arranged to do away with coaling and detention at English ports, would

---

[16] C.R.B., "Blue Dossiers," 84–86.
[17] C. R. B., "Blue Dossiers."

there be any possibility of Relief ships sailing by the southern route through the English Channel under German safe-conducts?

Von Stumm replied that under no circumstances could this be allowed as the German submarines would be working at their utmost power along the southern route, and that the inevitable result would be the sinking of C.R.B. ships. He further states that the area declared dangerous by the Dutch had been so informed, and that they might consider this area relatively safe for the next month and absolutely safe beyond that time, so far as German naval measures were concerned. Explaining the term "Relatively safe for the next month," von Stumm stated that while submarines working in the North Sea zone would undoubtedly have received instructions to consider this passage clear, yet those operating at a long distance from their base and returning to Germany might not have received these instructions, and would therefore be likely to act under the original instructions given them: further, that the time of greatest danger in this section would probably be about the end of this month, and these submarines would then be returning to Germany.

Von Stumm further stated that safe-conduct passes would continue to be issued both from The Hague and from American ports for the northern route, even in the eventuality of war with America, as they could then be issued by the Embassy taking over the German interests in Washington and, if necessary, an arrangement could probably be arrived at for issuing return safe-conduct passes from The Hague.

Mr. Brown requested that arrangements be made to enable C.R.B. shipping now in English ports to reach Rotterdam, and to allow a continuation of shipments from England of purchases made there. Von Stumm stated that he was now negotiating with Berlin on this point, recommending that a mode of operation be arranged, possibly on the lines of all C.R.B. ships now in English ports sailing together on a designated day, when instructions would be given to respect them; further, that for continued shipments from England permission might be given for C.R.B. ships to use the route Flushing-Southwold, when they could then travel to Rotterdam along the 20-mile free strip off the Dutch coast.

252. BARON VON DER LANCKEN TO HIS EXCELLENCY MARQUIS DE VILLALOBAR[18]

BRUSSELS, February 10, 1917

To His Excellency the Marquis de Villalobar
Minister of Spain, Brussels

YOUR EXCELLENCY:

The breach of diplomatic relations between the Imperial Government and the Government of the United States of America might create the impression that a new situation has arisen for the work of ravitaillement of the civil population of the occupied territories of Belgium and Northern France.

To avoid having misunderstandings arise under these circumstances, I want immediately to advise Your Excellency that such an opinion would seem erroneous to me, as this work enjoys the high protection of the Government which Your Excellency represents as well as that of the Netherlands at the same time and to the same extent as that of the Government of the United States. If thus the Government of His Majesty the King of Spain considers that it has to continue to give its high protection to the work of ravitaillement, I have the honor to inform Your Excellency that the Imperial Government and the Governor-General in Belgium will in the future, as they have done in the past, and in conformity with the agreements, give their aid and protection to this work, so necessary for the suffering populations of the occupied territories of Belgium and Northern France.

As to the possibility that certain American members of the Commission for Relief in Belgium might think it necessary to return to their country, I think that Your Excellency will find it useful to replace these by other persons who may seem to Your Excellency to be fit for this mission, the Commission having since its inception been composed of neutral members of different nationalities.

The Governor-General wishes, however, to submit to the appreciation of Your Excellency whether you judge it desirable that certain American members of the Commission for Relief in Belgium continue to exercise their functions with the management of the Commission in Brussels.

If Your Excellency should be of this opinion, the Governor-General would be pleased to see Mr. Brand Whitlock give to the work of the Commission for Relief in Belgium that activity of which I am certain this institution would be deprived only with regret.

[18] C. R. B., "Blue Dossiers."

I would beg Your Excellency in this case to arrange with Mr. Brand Whitlock in what form his collaboration may be maintained to the said Commission.

I beg Your Excellency to let me know the measures which you think of taking in order to assure, as in the past, the smooth operation of the work of which you have been willing to accept the patronage and which has pursued so successfully for nearly two and a half years the humanitarian and exalted aim of alleviating the burden of the war upon the populations of the occupied territories.

I take this opportunity to renew to Your Excellency the assurance of my high consideration.

(*Signed*) BARON VON DER LANCKEN

253. THE CONTINUATION OF THE WORK OF THE COMMISSION FOR RELIEF IN BELGIUM IN FEBRUARY 1917[19]

IMPERIAL FOREIGN OFFICE
No. II U 657

26466

BERLIN, February 18, 1917

To His Excellency Monsieur Luis Polo de Bernabe
Ambassador of Spain in Berlin

MONSIEUR L'AMBASSADEUR:

In reply to your letter of the 8th of this month which Your Excellency was good enough to address to me—No. Reg. 2326—I have the honor to communicate the following:

As I have already had the honor of expressing to you in my letter of the 18th inst., No. II U 642, the Imperial Government also is actuated by a lively desire that the humanitarian work of the Relief Commission of Belgium should continue. Although the Government of the United States has broken off diplomatic relations with Germany, the work of ravitaillement, based on the agreements concluded at the same time with the Governments of Spain and of the Netherlands, can evidently continue its benevolent work. The Imperial Government has no intention of forcing the members of the Commission to suspend their work and to leave the occupied territories. They think, on the contrary, that it would be useful if these gentlemen remained provisionally at their posts, even while considering the possibility of their

[19] *Ibid.*

replacement in case of need by other neutral agents suitable to the work. Further, nothing will prevent certain of the American members from remaining in Brussels for the management of the Commission.

With a view to settling this question negotiations have been set on foot by the General Government in Belgium directly with the Protecting Ministers of the Commission. These negotiations have resulted in the Americans remaining at their posts until further orders; the question of the introduction of other neutral agents into the Commission, in the first place to assist the Americans, and subsequently to replace them, is reserved for the present.

The Minister of the United States, Mr. Whitlock, and the Secretary of the Legation, Mr. Ruddock, have already declared themselves ready to continue their activities in Brussels as private persons.

In the hope that these measures may assure the continuation of the work of Relief without hindrance, I take this opportunity to renew to you, Monsieur l'Ambassadeur, the assurances of my highest consideration.

(*Signed*) ZIMMERMANN

254. THE LEGATION OF THE NETHERLANDS IN BERLIN TO THE IMPERIAL MINISTRY OF FOREIGN AFFAIRS[20]

No. 4254   May 13, 1917

The Royal Legation of the Netherlands has not failed to transmit to its Government the Note Verbale of May 4, No. II U 1547/65021, regarding the vessels of the Relief Commission for Belgium to be loaded, and has the honor to thank the Imperial Government for this communication, of which the mentioned above Commissioner was immediately informed.

Without wishing in any way to criticize the attitude of the belligerents in regard to this question of the departure of the vessels which are at present in England, the Commission begs that the German Government will be good enough to consider the following:

The Commission has the absolute conviction that the British Government will authorize an immediate departure as soon as an unreserved guaranty is granted. This unreserved guaranty will in no way permit the vessels of the Commission to navigate at will in the prohibited zone. The unreserved guaranty is to state that the Imperial Government promises:

1. That the vessels will not be attacked by the German naval forces during their voyage from the Thames to Rotterdam and return, and

[20] C.R.B., "Blue Dossiers."

2. That, once arrived in Holland, the vessels may in a short time return to England without being bound to the paddle-wheel boat service of the Zeeland Company.

The Commission is therefore ready to navigate their vessels on the date and by the route indicated by the German Government and will conform to all the instructions which the German Government may give on the subject.

The Commission asks for no guaranties against danger from mines, and as at present the question in discussion is the voyage from the Thames to Rotterdam and return, agreement does not in any way appear to entail an obligation to leave the free passage always open, to the advantage of the British navigation.

In view of the preceding, the Relief Commission cannot conceive that any military interest of the Germans would be endangered by the requested guaranty and they beg the Imperial Government to reconsider, with as little delay as possible, the decision which is so threatening to the continuance of the work.

As they have the same interests at heart, the Government of the Queen has charged the Royal Legation to support this appeal of the Commission.

255. NOTE VERBALE OF THE IMPERIAL MINISTRY OF FOREIGN AFFAIRS CONCERNING THE SAILING OF RELIEF SHIPS BETWEEN ENGLAND AND HOLLAND, MAY 23, 1917[21]

No. II U 1686
74971

NOTE VERBALE

The Foreign Office has the honor to advise the Royal Dutch Legation that the proposal contained in the esteemed note verbale of the 13th instant, No. 4254, has already reached here from the Relief Commission for the occupied districts of Belgium and the North of France, through the intermediary of the Imperial Legation in The Hague.

The Imperial Government regrets not to be in a position to agree to this proposal in the form in which it is presented. If the Imperial Government were to agree to the desire to permit the ships of the Relief Commission to navigate between England and Holland on certain days, it would be necessary to leave their submarine war quiescent on those days in those districts, because only by that means could the danger of confusion be obviated. The English Government would have

[21] *Ibid.*

also, on these days, the opportunity to allow the transport of foodstuffs between Holland and England to be carried on without danger from submarines or mines. On the contrary, the desired object can easily be attained by other means. As has already been advised in our note verbale of the 29th ultimo, II U 1478, the Relief Commission is offered by the Imperial Government the alternative of chartering for themselves the paddle-boats of the Zeeland Line. As this line has decided to initiate on its own account the voyages of its steamers to Southwold, the Commission is placed in a position to charter the ships and use them, with the painting already prescribed for these ships, to lead their steamers on the outward and homeward voyages over the permitted route between Southwold and Flushing. The former pretext that the paddle-boats travel faster than the Commission's ships would thereby fall to the ground.

By these means foodstuffs for Belgium and the North of France still lying in England would be conveyed to the distressed population without danger and the return of the ships to England be assured.

There would also be no objection to the Relief Commission loading the paddle-boats.

The Imperial Government therefore confidently expects that the Royal Dutch Government will contribute toward rendering possible for the Relief Commission this simple solution of the whole problem.

It is, however, clearly notified that this travelling of the Relief Commission's ships between England and Holland applies only to the permitted route between Flushing and Southwold, the English Government having, as Havas under date the 13th instant advises from London, closed until further notice the port of Lowestoft to all ships except those of England and the Allies. If the Relief Commission, as appears from the esteemed note verbale of the 13th instant, wishes to obtain assurance that the Commission's ships may travel without danger from the mouth of the Thames to Holland and their safe return, it has already been intimated in our note verbale of the 4th instant—II U 1547—that acquiescence in this desire would be equal not only to granting the English an open passage into the Thames, free from mines, with the help of the Commission's ships, but also to making illusory the closing of one of their most important places.

BERLIN, 23d May, 1917

CHAPTER XIII

THE CONTROL OF IMPERIAL FOREIGN AFFAIRS

INTRODUCTORY NOTE

I N THE German Imperial system the highest civil and military authority was combined in the person of the monarch. The actual exercise of civil authority was vested in the Chancellor and the Imperial Government. At the outbreak of the war the Reichstag unanimously supported the foreign policy of the Chancellor and maintained the party truce for three years. During 1916 the Conservatives, Free Conservatives, Centrists, and National-Liberals favored the commencement of unrestricted submarine warfare in opposition to the Chancellor. Bethmann-Hollweg did not resign when this coalition was formed but continued in office until the July 1917 crisis disclosed the failures of submarine warfare. The Reichstag allowed the Chancellor to fall and a few months later overthrew his successor. From the commencement of negotiations with Russia at Brest-Litovsk until the March 1918 offensive on the Western front, the Reichstag took no decisive stand in foreign affairs.

It was the tragic fate of Germany in the World War that the primacy of the political will in the supreme directorate of the German Empire was gradually subordinated to military necessities, whereas among Germany's democratic enemies political dictators assumed control of fundamental war activities. The conduct of German foreign affairs passed during the war into the hands of the military authorities. The parliamentary government of the October 1918 coalition of National-Liberals, Centrists, Progressives, and Social-Democrats was in reality established by the Supreme Military Command.

256. WAR AND DIPLOMACY[1]

Italy's entrance into the great European War, nine months after its beginning, for obvious reasons draws the general attention to the func-

[1] *Vorwärts,* No. 143, May 26, 1915, p. 5.

tion of diplomacy, with which the formal regulation of the relations between the nations rests under present conditions. One cannot say that there is in any country general satisfaction with the achievements of professional diplomacy. The desire for the abolition of secret diplomacy which has been demanded by Social-Democracy now for some time has been aroused in large numbers of the people. Herr v. Gerlach expresses the feeling of large classes in the *Welt am Montag* when he writes, with regard to the breaking up of the Triple Alliance, the following:

"We did not hear of the Triple Alliance until the moment when it was destroyed. For fully thirty-three years it has determined our foreign policy. During all this time only a few chosen persons had an exact knowledge of its provisions. As long as it was in force the people governed by it could only make conjectures about it. Now, when it is no longer in force and only of historical importance, one may glance at the interesting document. . . . . The art of secret diplomacy is the worst survival of the past absolutism. . . . . The people are excluded when a treaty is being made for a period of decades, one which may possibly determine the fate of an entire nation, whether it shall prosper or be destroyed.

"That is the way of the past. But that must not be the case in the future. All peoples should have at least learned this one lesson from the war—all peoples, for all suffer alike from such a state of affairs. All pay with their blood for the mistakes of past diplomacy. . . . ."

257. CONTROL OF FOREIGN AFFAIRS BY THE MAIN COMMITTEE OF THE REICHSTAG[2]

After a two-hour discourse by State Secretary Dr. Helfferich, the Main Committee of the Reichstag recessed for the breakfast recess. Following this, State Secretary von Capelle spoke. The party speakers of the day were from the National-Liberal and Deutsche "Fraktionen." In addition, the Imperial Chancellor spoke. Following his address, the Main Committee adjourned further deliberation until Thursday forenoon.

In the meantime the select Committee will make use of the intermission to secure strictly confidential information from the Government. Two additional resolutions were placed before the Main Committee:

1) a Progressive resolution, relative to the appointment of a standing committee for foreign affairs, in substance the same in meaning as the National-Liberal resolution announced yesterday;

[2] *Norddeutsche Allgemeine Zeitung,* October 1, 1916, II, 3.

2) a Conservative resolution, aiming to bring about an improvement in the condition of the German prisoners in Russia and in France, and advocating the use of all possible means—even, in so far as necessary, the threat and execution of peremptory measures of reprisal.

258. RESOLUTIONS IN THE MAIN COMMITTEE OF THE REICHSTAG CONCERNING THE CONTROL OF FOREIGN AFFAIRS[3]

[October 9, 1916]

After its intermission, the Main Committee of the Reichstag, in its session on Monday, took under consideration the resolutions which had been placed before it.

The National-Liberal resolution calls for the establishment of a standing committee for foreign affairs, empowered to assemble at any time, even when the Reichstag is not in session.

The Progressive resolution demands: (1) the establishment of a standing committee for foreign affairs; (2) a pledge from the Imperial Chancellor that this committee shall have the right to meet even if the Reichstag is not in session.

The resolution of the Center declares: The Reichstag shall empower the Main Committee to meet during an adjournment for deliberation upon matters relating to foreign policy and the war.

A speaker of the National-Liberal "Fraktion" opened the discussion by giving the reasons for the resolution proposed by his group. At the present time, he said, when decisions are being made that concern the future of the Empire and of the nation, it is self-evident that the Reichstag should be informed and that it should have not only the right of deliberation but the right of participation in the making of decisions. The majority of his political friends, he said, are opposed to the parliamentary system. But many doubts concerning this system will have to be put aside after experience with it. In countries with parliamentary government, there now exists a closer unity of action between people and Government than formerly one was inclined to believe possible. The proposed resolution, he said, does not in any way signify lack of confidence in the Government, but a nation of seventy million people cannot place entirely in the hands of the Government the making of decisions which concern questions of such great importance to the lives of all.

A speaker of the Progressive "Fraktion" explained the resolution

[3] *Ibid.,* October 10, 1916, II, 2.

of his group. He did this, in part, by reference to what the preceding speaker had said.

Following this, the resolution of the Center was explained by a member of this "Fraktion." The Main Committee, he said, should prepare a definite plan of action for the Reichstag and should not be looked upon as merely advisory to the Foreign Office. The inclusion of former ministers and of the Imperial Chancellor cannot be sanctioned. The discussion of foreign affairs should proceed, as formerly, in the Main Committee, but with the additional provision that this discussion could be continued during the adjournment of the Reichstag. Beside questions of foreign policy, the Main Committee has to deal with the more important questions of internal policy, with colonial problems, and with matters of taxation and allied subjects. It should have the opportunity, at any time, of consultation with the Government; this is, above all, necessary in time of war. Since a closing of the Reichstag does not occur during the war, constitutional considerations are, in this instance, beside the point. In the event of a closing, the convening of the Committee at any time should be assured by the due process of a motion to that effect. There is no legal basis for leaving to the Imperial Chancellor the right to summon proxies for the parliament.

State Secretary von Jagow responded that he understood perfectly the interest of the parliament in providing for a permanent informative agency in matters of foreign policy. By no means does he regard the various motions as a vote of lack of confidence. In reply to the accusation, evident in a number of the addresses, that the Reichstag does not receive adequate information, he felt it his duty to state, emphatically, that no parliament is better informed concerning the conduct of foreign policy than the Reichstag and its Committee. In the present war period, he said, the Imperial Chancellor is furnishing information to the party leaders continually. In addition, every deputy has ample opportunity to secure information from the Foreign Office. In regard to the demand for the more frequent publication of White Books, consideration ought to be given to the fact that the Imperial Government can act, in this respect, only after reaching an understanding with the other Governments that would be involved in such a procedure. The view taken that in other countries the committees have greater access to information is unjust. The State Secretary pointed to the example of England before and at the outbreak of the war. There the parliamentary system did not prevent the Government from making the most far-reaching settlements without the knowledge of Parliament. It cannot be said that in France either the parliamentary system has stood the test. There the Briand Cabinet is exercising a dictatorship; virtual terrorism holds sway. He was of the opinion that the demand for more complete information would be best met through the agency of the Main Committee. The activity of this Committee is of necessity confined to informative matters; it cannot make the final decisions. The Committee cannot take away from the Government the responsibility for making the final decisions. Indeed, it is not always possible to call the Committee together beforehand when important decisions are to be made. By so doing, the decisions would be reached when it was too late. However, it is the essential duty of the Committee to keep itself informed and to deliberate upon the general outlines of the foreign policy. From this standpoint, he was ready to enter into closer relations with the Committee.

The Secretary of the Interior reviewed the legal aspect of the proposed motions. In the abstract, he said, the Reichstag was, without doubt, free to form a special committee for foreign affairs, in addition to the already existing committees and with similar competence. But in his opinion, there is no purpose at all in taking questions concerning foreign affairs out of the Main Committee. A meeting of Reichstag committees after the close of the session is in contradiction to the Constitution. Moreover, during an adjournment declared by the Emperor, a Reichstag committee cannot meet without the consent of the Emperor, who has declared the adjournment. In practice, a law is drawn up for this contingency, the details of which regulate the question of remuneration. If the Emperor should again cause an adjournment of the Reichstag, then that is the time for reaching an agreement between the Reichstag and the Government whether and in what form adequate expression can be given to the ideas embodied in the motions.

When the vote was taken, the National-Liberal resolution was rejected by all but two votes, and the Progressive resolution was rejected by all but five.

The resolution of the Center was accepted by a large majority. The Conservative vote was against it.

Questions relating to points of order were then brought up for discussion before the Imperial Chancellor. Following this, the session was adjourned until Thursday forenoon. On the same day, at eight o'clock in the evening, another meeting will be held.

259. ZIMMERMANN'S DEFENSE OF HIS NOTE BEFORE THE
MAIN COMMITTEE OF THE REICHSTAG,
MARCH 5, 1917[4]

It is a natural and justifiable act of precaution to look around for allies in the event of war with America. He did not regret the fact that

[4] *Vorwärts,* March 6, 1917, p. 3.

the instructions had become known in Japan through the American publication. The safest way at present available had been chosen for forwarding the instructions. They had still absolutely no idea how the Americans came into possession of the text, which was sent to Washington in an absolutely secret code. That the instructions had fallen into the hands of the Americans was a mishap, but made no difference to the fact that the step was necessary in interest of the Fatherland. Least of all in America had they the right to be excited about our action. It would be a mistake to suppose that the step had made a particularly deep impression abroad. It is taken for what it is, a justifiable measure of defense in the contingency of war.

260. KÜHLMANN'S SPEECH IN THE REICHSTAG ON THE FOREIGN POLICIES OF THE EMPIRE, OCTOBER 9, 1917[5]

Gentlemen, it is a comparatively short time since I had in the Main Committee the honor of expanding on a few points the utterances of the Chancellor on foreign policy. I shall only review in a few words the recent events in foreign affairs and then briefly deal with the speech of the Chancellor on the papal note and the European situation created by it.

Our relations with Peru have come to a crisis in a rather surprising way, so that the breaking off of diplomatic relations is now only a question of a short time. A few months ago a Peruvian ship, the "Northon," was confiscated for carrying contraband and, according to the rules of naval warfare, was sunk after all the crew were saved. The German Prize Court is at present investigating the legality of this incident. The Peruvian Government has abruptly demanded that the case should be withdrawn from the Prize Court and satisfaction and compensation given at once. This attitude of the Peruvian Government is absolutely unjustifiable according to international law, and during the war between Chile and Peru the German Government allowed the case of the German steamer "Luxor" to be dealt with by the Peruvian Prize Court. ["*Hear, hear!*"] A German concession to the Peruvian demand, which is accompanied by a short-dated ultimatum and thus forms a threat unusual to a Great Power, was absolutely impossible, as it would have undermined the whole system upon which our Prize Courts are based. All neutrals would have quoted the case and would have demanded, when occasion arose, that their cases also should not be sent before our Prize Courts. We replied to the Peruvian note very courteously and moderately in a conciliatory tone, but at the same time distinctly em-

---

[5] *Verhandlungen des Reichstags,* No. 124, October 9, 1917, pp. 3811-13.

phasizing the legal point of view upon which we must take our stand. The Peruvian Government then confiscated the German ships lying in Peruvian harbors, and a breach of diplomatic relations is, as I have just said, a matter of the very shortest time. German interests in Peru will be taken over by the Spanish Government if the breach becomes an accomplished fact.

According to a dispatch which has recently reached me the Republic of Uruguay also has decided to break off diplomatic relations with us. In his message to Congress the President said that although he has by no means been directly insulted by Germany, it seems necessary to him to show that he is on the side of justice, democracy, and small nations. [*Great merriment.*]

In contrast to these unpleasant items, the question, which has several times been discussed in the Main Committee, of a coal and credit agreement with Holland has made such progress that only a few formalities are necessary to complete the settlement. [*Applause.*]

I now come, gentlemen, to the real subject of today's discussion. The efforts of the Papal Curia to pave the way for an exchange of views between the belligerents have made no essential progress since the reply of the Central Powers to the papal note, as I must acknowledge with regret. Whether the enemy will decide to answer the note at all and to define their attitude to the clear, straightforward announcement of the Central Powers in favor of peace, cannot yet be ascertained with certainty. One thing, however, can already be said—and I again must express my regret—that the evidence of announcements by more or less responsible enemy statesmen, and the views of enemy newspapers, show hardly any prospect that a reply to the papal note would bring the world one step forward in the sense suggested by his Holiness, in spite of the fact that only quite recently my honored political friend, Count Czernin, Foreign Minister of the Austro-Hungarian Monarchy, in his great speech outlining his program in Budapest, has not only once more emphasized the readiness of the Central Powers and their allies for an honorable peace but has also brilliantly, looking far into the future in a way to which the preceding speaker has paid a well-merited tribute, indicated the foundations on which a new Europe may perhaps one day be built.

When I now proceed to discuss in detail some particularly characteristic utterances of enemy statesmen, I may say that I think the speech which the former First Lord of the Admiralty, Winston Churchill, delivered in London was one in which there was very little trace of the new spirit. The leader of the brilliant expedition to Antwerp [*laughter*] expects an internal collapse of Germany, and says in his speech how thin may be the wall which separates Germany from final collapse.

Statesmen, says Mr. Churchill, ought to learn from experience [*"Hear, hear!"*] ; if they do not do so, it is not only stupidity, but a crime. I shall not be so hard on him. [*Laughter.*] Nevertheless, Winston Churchill ought to have learned in his second brilliant expedition, the objective of which was Constantinople and which found an inglorious end on the peninsula of Gallipoli before the bayonets of our brave Turkish allies, that even a thin partition can transform a victory dreamed of into a great defeat, if this wall is one of men. [*Great applause.*] Between a "rat hole" in the North Sea, which in English means Horns Reef, and the Isonzo there stands the mighty rampart of the German people inspired by a single iron will. It is, God be praised, a very thick and unshakable will, and if Mr. Churchill is expecting its collapse he must possess his soul in patience. [*"Hear, hear!"*]

The speech of the leader of the Liberal Opposition, Mr. Asquith, in the House of Commons, which, when I spoke in the Main Committee was only available in a telegraphed version, reads no better in the complete text than in Reuter's version. The speech must be a lesson to those who thought from Asquith's question, thrown out in the course of a speech in Parliament, about Germany's intentions in Belgium that they could deduce a willingness for peace on the part of this politician, for whom a great Liberal past assures great authority among his people. In his latest speech, as a Liberal paper, the *Manchester Guardian,* rightly points out, Mr. Asquith makes the demand for the return of Alsace-Lorraine of equal importance to that for the restitution of Belgium [*"Hear, hear!"*], and thus, moreover, sums up the situation in the same way as it appears to me with absolutely convincing clearness after a very thorough study of the whole position and of reports from the most varied sources from neutral and enemy countries. The question for which the peoples of Europe are at present fighting and pouring forth their blood is not primarily the Belgian one. The quarrel over which Europe is being gradually transformed into a rubbish heap is the future of Alsace-Lorraine.

According to reliable information which we possess, England has made a diplomatic pledge to France [*"Hear, hear!"*] to champion with all her authority and strength the demand for the return of Alsace-Lorraine so long as France herself holds to this demand.

This, gentlemen, is the real situation, and it seems to me appropriate to state the German attitude calmly, clearly, but firmly, as it is a remarkable fact that not only among the enemy but occasionally among neutrals also doubts have been raised about our attitude on this fundamental question. We have only one answer to the question: "Can Germany make France any concessions in Alsace-Lorraine?" No! Never! [*Great applause on all sides.*] As long as a German hand can hold a rifle the integrity of the Empire which we have received as a glorious heritage from our fathers cannot be the subject of any negotiations or concessions. [*Renewed great applause.*] Alsace-Lorraine is Germany's escutcheon and the symbol of German unity. Everyone from Left to Right will agree, I am sure [*applause*]—I am not one of those who believe that a frank and clear statement of such a fact could in any way injure the growth of a just willingness for peace in the world. [*Great applause.*] On the contrary, I believe that such a righteous will for peace can only flourish on the soil of absolute clearness [*applause*], and therefore I think it necessary to emphasize this point with all possible vigor and distinctness to those at home and still more to those abroad, in contrast to other questions which have recently occupied so much space in public discussion. What we are fighting for—and shall fight for till the last drop of blood—is not fantastic conquests; it is the integrity of the German Empire. [*Applause.*]

In France, when it seemed advisable to adopt the formula of "no annexations" invented in Russia, her statesmen used the transparent artifice of concealing what is really naked, forceful conquest under the name "disannexation." The artifice is really too crude to be worth a reply. One must, however, call the attention of the fathers of this idea to the fact that it is nowhere written what year of the world's history is to be considered the year of *ne varietur* [*"Hear, hear!"—Left*]—and if we Germans look back on history and want to go on the *ne varietur* principle, we come upon fine, pleasant-sounding names like Toul and Verdun. [*"Hear, hear!"*]

One view I must briefly answer, as it frequently crops up in the enemy press. I am thinking especially of an article in the English Liberal paper, the *Manchester Guardian*, in which it is claimed that the political attitude of Germany will become more defined as soon as the military results of the great autumn battles are known. It is an absolutely erroneous conception of German policy to think that we play high or low, become conciliatory or stubborn, according to the results of individual military enterprises. This is absolutely false. The essential lines of our political attitude are defined by all factors after thorough and careful consideration, and as far as I am able to survey the world position there would be no absolute obstacle to peace except French wishes regarding Alsace-Lorraine [*"Hear, hear!"—Left*]—no problem which could not be solved by discussion and give and take in a way which would justify the expenditure of so much blood and wealth before the eyes of the nations and of history. [*Great applause from the Left.*]

A further fundamental mistake made by the enemy, and one which is sometimes made in our discussions at home, is the idea that even at the last stage of this tremendous struggle the political situation could be considerably improved by public declarations from the rostrum. Public announcements have, from their nature, severe defects with respect to the attainment of such an object. They have to be comparatively simple. Just because all questions under discussion are bound up with one another and mutually presume one another and are interdependent, public announcements can only in a limited way do justice to the demands of the moment. Public announcements and the discussion of such questions in open parliament have also the practical disadvantage that the responsible enemy reply is lacking. Public announcements completely bind the side which makes them, but leave the enemy absolute freedom of action. [*"Quite right!"*]

We must not forget the essential point which the enemy have always obscured, with the great tactical skill which is peculiar to them. They have not yet announced their war aims in a way which even approximately agrees with the existing facts. [*"Hear, hear!"*] What they have announced to the world is an absolutely utopian maximum program of conquests which can be carried out only after Germany and her allies are utterly overthrown. We have no inducement to follow them on this path. [*"Hear, hear!"*] The German Government has so far declined to do this and will continue to do so. Our policy is concrete and moderate, and takes facts as they are. If the enemy take the attitude that they can get no clear idea of what the Government and the German people wish and intend, this is hypocrisy. [*"Hear, hear!"*] Our answer to the papal note and the declarations made on it by general agreement of the parties in the parliament, as I would like again to emphasize, can leave no doubts with anyone who wishes to hear and understand as to the essential principles of the German peace program. [*"Hear, hear!"*]

One thing I have emphasized in the Main Committee, and although it perhaps only indirectly lies within the sphere of foreign politics I should like you to allow me once more to emphasize it after the debates we have listened to: foreign policy can be successful only if it is supported by the approval of the great masses of the German people [*applause*]—if it represents and embodies the will of the people, is their essential unity. And therefore the person entrusted with the representation of the Foreign Office must constantly remind the people that however high the waves of domestic political differences may rise in this earnest and fateful hour everyone is called upon to give our foreign policy that weight and unanimity which it requires to attain victory and peace through toil and endurance. [*Great applause from all sides.*]

261. DISCUSSIONS IN THE REICHSTAG ON THE CONTROL OF FOREIGN AFFAIRS, OCTOBER 11 AND 26, 1916

(a) CONTROL OF FOREIGN AFFAIRS, OCTOBER 11, 1916[6]

Deputy Bassermann, Reporter: Gentlemen, the Committee recommends for your consideration, the following motion:

"The Reichstag shall empower the Budget Committee to assemble for deliberation upon matters of foreign policy and the war, during an adjournment. . . . ."

Deputy Bassermann, Reporter: Gentlemen, three motions were placed before the committee. The first motion called for the establishment of a standing committee for foreign affairs, empowered to assemble at any time, even during an adjournment of the Reichstag. A second motion called for the establishment of a standing committee for foreign affairs, and for a pledge from the Imperial Chancellor that this committee might have the right to assemble, even if the Reichstag were not in session. A final motion proposed that the Reichstag empower the Budget Committee to assemble for deliberation upon matters of foreign policy and the war, even during an adjournment.

Gentlemen, the fundamental thought back of these motions is that this fearful war has demonstrated to us the necessity of a more active participation in questions of foreign policy. The terrible consequences of a world war of this kind are such as to show that, in the last analysis, questions relating to the conduct of foreign policy are of greater moment than economic or social questions. . . . .

By those opposed to the motions as a whole it was pointed out that in accepting any of them the first step was being taken in the direction of the parliamentary system, and that it was important *principiis obsta,* that is, to oppose such attempts in their first stages.

Among other things, the idea was stressed by the Government that here in Germany the parliament could not complain of being inadequately informed; on the contrary, there was at hand, here, an exhaustive supply of information, such as not even England and France could show. In reply to this claim, it was then pointed out that one could not draw a parallel from England and France, since in these countries, under parliamentary rule, the Government was a committee of the ruling party, and by this means there was established a connection, between the parliament and the committee of the parliament forming the Government, which naturally resulted in an adequate and constant control over the conduct of matters of foreign policy.

[6] *Verhandlungen des Reichstags,* No. 64, Sitzung, Mittwoch den 11. Oktober 1916, pp. 1741–42.

The committee did not enter into this argument, but in the interest of a better parliamentary orientation resolved to create a control organization, to select for this the Budget Committee, and to give to it the right to assemble even during an adjournment of the Reichstag. In the name of the Budget Committee I recommend for your acceptance the motion that is placed before you.

261. (b) CONTROL OF FOREIGN AFFAIRS, OCTOBER 26, 1916[7]

Deputy Gröber: Gentlemen, the former management of foreign policy in the Reichstag has been unsatisfactory, and, one might well say, inadequate. To be sure, there have been discussions of foreign policy, connected, ordinarily, with the debates on the budget of the Foreign Office or with the debates on the great army bills, in particular on bills dealing with the question of effective forces in time of peace. In addition, of course, the Budget Report of the Imperial Chancellor has always afforded a favorable opportunity for debating, among other things, the particular matter of foreign policy. But what has been lacking is a permanent understanding between the Reichstag and the leaders of the Government upon the general outlines of foreign policy, also a fixed control over the conduct of this foreign policy by the Reichstag. In confining debates on foreign policy to certain occasions, such as the debates on the budget, and other special laws, there has resulted the unpleasant situation that, as long as there was no such special occasion, discussion of foreign policy could be carried on only in an irregular manner. This has been accomplished in part, and in exceptional cases, in the treatment of single questions and of special political situations, through the use of the interpellation.

If we ask ourselves for the real cause for this unsatisfactory treatment of foreign policy in the Reichstag, we shall find, after candid investigation, that the true source is a lack of orderly development and of clearness in the field of foreign relations. It cannot be disputed that during the period of the development of a world policy only little by little and actually only by the experiences of this world war have we arrived at a clear understanding of many questions which, in years past, have not been made sufficiently clear. In this very lack of clarity on questions of foreign relations is found the full explanation of the so-called zigzag course which our foreign policy has taken, and of the part which the Reichstag has played in connection with these matters.

Moreover, indeed, no little part in the unsatisfying management of foreign policy must be assigned to the conduct of the Government itself;

[7] *Verhandlungen des Reichstags*, No. 67, Sitzung, Donnerstag den 26. Oktober 1916, pp. 1808–19.

for the Government, in accordance with the position taken by almost all foreign Governments, has conceived of the conduct of foreign policy as a kind of secret art, I might almost say, a secret art from the management of which it has been sought to keep the common man and his representatives as much excluded as possible.

Quite particularly characteristic of this latter attitude is the stand taken by the Government in response to the wish repeatedly expressed in the Reichstag that a diplomatic White Book might be published. When this wish was first expressed in the Reichstag, April 22, 1869, by National-Liberal Deputy Twesten, it received such a sharp refusal from Bismarck, a refusal couched in language of such biting scorn, that during the whole period of the Bismarck chancellorship no one again dared to give utterance to such a wish. Only after almost forty years did the Reichstag, on May 1, 1907, upon the motion of the Center Party, adopt the resolution that

"A request be presented to the Imperial Chancellor that periodically there be placed before the Reichstag documentary material pertaining to the international relations of the German Empire. . . . ."

Gentlemen, the right of the Reichstag to information concerning foreign policy cannot be contested. It is indisputable of itself and also by virtue of the fact that the Reichstag passes upon the appropriations to support the management of this foreign policy and thus is entitled to know how and in accordance with what principles this policy is conducted. At present we are not so much concerned with proof of the undisputed right of the Reichstag to be informed in matters of foreign policy as with a presentation of the necessity of Reichstag participation in discussions in this field. And if there were ever a time suitable for bringing this necessity clearly before the minds of all, it is the present time of war. A war which like the present one brings suffering to the whole nation demands, with firm insistence, that in this field as in others the representatives of the nation shall give opportune and effective expression to the justifiable interests and desires of the people. ["*Quite true!*"] . . . . It is a natural and thoroughly justifiable wish of the people that vital political decisions, influencing the whole future of the German people, shall be arrived at only through the common action of Government and Reichstag and that for the attainment of this end the Reichstag shall be in constant and close contact with the Government in order that it shall not be presented, suddenly, with accomplished facts, any alteration of which would be impossible. ["*Quite true!*"] . . . . To me, the practical question at issue seems to be: . . . . Do we want to retain deliberation (upon foreign policy) in the Budget Committee, or do we want to establish a separate committee for this purpose? . . . .

It seems to me that there are two convincing arguments for retaining the preparation of questions of foreign policy in the hands of the Budget Committee, where such matters have been dealt with in the past. The first of these arguments arises from the significance of the Budget Committee as a central committee. The Budget Committee differs from other committees . . . . in that its task is to deal permanently with all fundamental problems of Imperial policy, foreign as well as internal, and to control the whole Government policy through the medium of deliberation upon the budget. . . . . I am convinced that a vigorous stand before the Government by the representatives of the people is to be considered only in a central committee. . . . .

Then there is a second consideration: Upon what after all does the political power of the Budget Committee in reality rest? The strength of the Budget Committee lies in its preliminary decisions upon the appropriations. [*"Quite true!"*] . . . .

Every representative body that has an accurate understanding of its problem will devote its most careful attention to this aspect of the matter, and will realize that herein lies the effective pressure which, used here and there, can achieve political results. Not through resolutions alone nor merely by beautiful speeches and decisions will the people's representatives achieve results, but above all by control over the voting of money supplies. "Thumbs upon the purse strings!"—that is the source of the power of the people's representatives. [*"Quite true!"*] It is very often said that cannon are the final argument of kings. I believe that one can much more truly say that in decisions upon the voting of appropriations can be found the final argument of the representatives of the people. [*"Quite true!"*] . . . .

Indeed, we can frequently observe that the organs of the Government are much more amenable to our wishes and decisions in this committee than in any other. That is no mere accident, but rests upon good reasons, and because of it I am convinced that if we hope to accomplish results, even in the sphere of foreign policy, then we must still keep questions dealing with foreign policy in the Budget Committee, which is in possession of the pressure necessary to give effective force to a resolution. [*"Bravo!"—Center.*] . . . .

Von Jagow, Minister of State, Secretary of State for Foreign Affairs, Member of the Bundesrat: I have already declared in the committee that we understand completely the wish of the parliament, called forth by the seriousness of the time, that in matters pertaining to foreign policy, so intimately connected as they are with the great war, we maintain a closer and more permanent contact with the parliament. Out of consideration for this wish, and in order to give it recognition, the Imperial Chancellor, even during the adjournment of the Reichstag, has repeatedly summoned the party leaders to him that he might disclose to them the foreign situation. Moreover, I have already declared in the committee our readiness to comply with the wish of the Reichstag, even to the extent called for in the motion of the Center. . . . .

Deputy Dr. Gradnauer: . . . . In a very particular measure the conditions of foreign policy demand that the rights of the Reichstag be strengthened and that the Reichstag be constituted upon a more independent and more energetic basis; for, in truth, issues are at stake which are of the very utmost concern to the fate of our nation. The settlement of all these matters, involving questions of such great and profound responsibility, is placed, at the present time, exclusively in the hands of a few people; upon the greater or lesser degree of their wisdom rests the fate of the nation. But the Reichstag, the people's representative, was formerly, and at this hour still is, completely excluded from a vote upon these questions, or from making a decision concerning them. . . . .

Now, gentlemen, the achievements and results of our diplomacy constitute a most extensive subject, a detailed discussion of which is not necessary in the present time of war. Ample opportunity will be given later for consideration of the accomplishments of our diplomacy before and during the war; the judgment of history will be passed upon it. But without entering into a further discussion of the subject I must state as my belief . . . . the achievements and results of German diplomacy before and during the war have been by no means of such a character that the German people will have cause to say: "Behold! all was well [*"Very true!"—Social-Democrats*] ; things can go on peacefully in the course that they have been following!" No, gentlemen, such a thing cannot be considered. The German people and its duly elected representatives, the Reichstag, rather have every reason to draw the most solemn lessons from the events of this war, in the very matter of questions of foreign policy, and to see to it that the influence of the Reichstag in this field is increased and that the Reichstag has the opportunity to participate in the molding of foreign policy, not only by taking part in the fullest possible sense in the debates but by having a share in the making of the decisions. [*"Quite true!" — Social-Democrats.*] The World War has brought a realization of this necessity to all ranks and classes of the population.

. . . . There can be no doubt but that the maintenance and guaranty of the rights of the Reichstag in matters of foreign policy must be one of the first and most important problems of the immediate future. Herein lies, undoubtedly, one of the most momentous tasks of the widely proclaimed new orientation. . . . . We have had but few plenary sessions of the Reichstag; . . . . The adjournments have been extremely long, and, in this period of many months, when events of such utmost importance were in progress, when great changes were being made, and crises were occurring, the people's representatives have not been present. . . . . It is my belief that the great unrest and the heated statements which we have heard out among the people in recent months, especially in relation to the submarine question, have in reality been associated with the fact that for so long a period the Reichstag was not assembled and that there was afforded no means of keeping in touch with the Government. . . . .

Therefore, gentlemen, because of these things, my party friends are convinced that it is high time that action be taken in accord with the provision of this motion. The exclusion of the Reichstag, in the manner hitherto in practice, cannot continue. . . . . We hold it to be an inalienable right of the representatives of the German people that, without limitation, they be permitted to participate in the deliberations upon, the formation of, and the decisions concerning the general outlines of foreign policy. If the Reichstag strengthens and increases its right in this direction, then it will but be working to benefit the German people, our position in the world, and our future. [*"Bravo!"—Social-Democrats.*] . . . .

Deputy Haussmann: . . . . The part played by the parliament in matters of foreign policy has been exercised hitherto in a rudimentary fashion, and frequently it has been the tradition to abstain from participation as much as possible and to be constrained from such participation as much as possible. The motions now in question . . . . have brought to expression the fact that, as an *opinio necessitatis,* which, as is well known, is an old source of one's rights, there is felt, by the people's representatives as well as by the people, the need for a stronger share in, a stronger control of, and a more systematic participation in matters of foreign policy by the representatives of the people. . . . .

Deputy Dr. Stresemann: Gentlemen, the motions which were under consideration by the Budget Committee . . . . show, in the first instance, one thing: that the situation, as it has hitherto existed, has been felt by all to be unsatisfactory. The case is not at all altered by reference . . . . to the conferences which, for the time being, have taken place between the Imperial Chancellor and the party leaders, as if to imply that they were a step toward the accomplishment of that which we are here striving to attain. I do not at all understand how one can extol these conferences for any reason whatsoever. [*"Quite true!"*] For, after all, it goes entirely without saying that the statesman at the head of affairs will have need, in peace as well as in war, when great decisions are to be made, to call into conference the leaders of the parties in the Reichstag and engage in an interchange of ideas with them.

261. (c) CONTROL OF FOREIGN AFFAIRS, OCTOBER 27, 1916[8]

Vice-President Dr. Paasche: . . . . we shall . . . . pass to the sixth matter of business for the day:

"Vote upon the motion of the Budget Committee relating to deliberation in the Budget Committee upon matters of foreign policy and of the war, during the adjournment . . . ."

Will the gentlemen who are in favor of the motion of the committee please turn in cards with "Yes," and will those who are opposed to it please turn in cards with "No"? Will the secretary please collect the ballots? . . . .

The provisional result of the vote is as follows: In all, there were 334 ballots cast, of which 302 were in favor of the motion, 31 opposed, with one deputy not voting.

[8] *Verhandlungen des Reichstags,* No. 68, Sitzung, Freitag den 27. Oktober 1916, p. 1857.

Final vote: 335 ballots cast, 303 in favor, 31 opposed, one not voting. *Ibid.,* p. 1866.

CHAPTER XIV

NEGOTIATIONS WITH BULGARIA AND ITALY

INTRODUCTORY NOTE

GERMANY commenced negotiations for an alliance with ·Bulgaria in July 1914. The simultaneous effort of the Entente to secure the aid of Bulgaria failed in the summer of 1915 because of the refusal of Serbia and Greece to cede the Macedonian territory demanded by King Ferdinand and the Radoslavov ministry. After Turkey had agreed to make concessions, Bulgaria signed on September 5–6, 1915, a secret military convention and a treaty of amity and alliance with Germany. The final unconditional offer by the Entente of a part of Macedonia to Bulgaria was not made until September 15, 1915.

After the outbreak of the World War, German diplomatic efforts in Italy were directed toward the maintenance of Italian neutrality. As early as December 1914, Italy demanded compensation from Austria under Article 7 of the Triple Alliance. Prince von Bülow's mission to Rome failed because Austria was not willing to sacrifice the Trentino and Trieste. On April 26, 1915, Italy concluded the secret treaty of London with the Entente. On May 24, 1915, she declared war on Austria and severed diplomatic relations with Germany.

A. BULGARIA

262. EXCERPTS FROM THE DIPLOMATIC CORRESPONDENCE
BETWEEN THE BULGARIAN MINISTERS IN BUCHAREST,
CONSTANTINOPLE, BERLIN, LONDON, AND ATHENS AND
THE BULGARIAN MINISTER OF FOREIGN AFFAIRS[1]

No. 209

The Minister in Bucharest to the Minister of Foreign Affairs
(Sofia), July 25, 1914.—The head of the German Legation here states
that if Russia intervenes in the Serbian-Austrian conflict, Germany will
also—which means an European war. RADEFF.

No. 213

The Minister in Constantinople to the Minister of Foreign Affairs,
July 26, 1914.—This morning the German and Austrian attachés asked
me for a quick understanding between Bulgaria, Turkey, and the *union
of the three countries.* (Troen Soüez.) TOSHEFF.

No. 214

The Minister in Berlin to the Minister of Foreign Affairs, July 27,
1914.—There is talk here of mobilization in case Russia mobilizes. Germany is in sympathy with Austria. MARKOFF.

No. 229

The Minister in London to the Minister of Foreign Affairs, July 28,
1914.—Up to this minute Germany has not accepted the proposal of Sir
Edward Grey for a conference of the representatives in London. MAD-
JAROFF.

No. 231

The Minister in Berlin to the Minister of Foreign Affairs, July 29,
1914.—Germany rejects the idea of a conference of representatives in
London. She wants to treat the question in ordinary diplomatic fashion. MARKOFF.

---

[1] Bulgaria, *Ministerstvo na vunshnite rabote i na izpovedaniiata Diplomati-
cheski dokumenti po namesata na Bulgariia v evropeiskata, voina* 1913–15, I, Nos.
209, 213, 214, 229, 231, 236, 255, 263, 281, 295, 330, 342, 390, 392, 410, 585, 653, 749,
755, 828, 861, 885, 917, 929, 940, 949. Hereafter cited as Bulgaria, *Documents.*

No. 236

The Minister in Berlin to the Minister of Foreign Affairs, July 30, 1914.—I found out that the German Government is going to demand assurances from France and Russia for keeping the peace. MARKOFF.

No. 255

The Minister in Berlin to the Minister of Foreign Affairs, August 1, 1914.—Today at 6:00 P.M. Germany declared the mobilization of the army and the navy. MARKOFF.

No. 263

The Minister in Constantinople to the Minister of Foreign Affairs, August 2, 1914.—Germany insists that Turkey side with her and act in agreement with her. TOSHEFF.

No. 281

The Minister of Foreign Affairs to the Minister in Constantinople, August 4, 1914.—Here we know definitely that Turkey is in alliance with Germany. RADOSLAVOV.

No. 295

The Minister in Constantinople to the Minister of Foreign Affairs, August 6, 1914.—Germany, Austria, and Bulgaria insist that the Turkish Government should allow the "Göben" and other warships to pass the Dardanelles for the Black Sea in order to protect the Bulgarian coast from Russia. TOSHEFF.

No. 330

The Minister in Constantinople to the Minister of Foreign Affairs, August 11, 1914.—Last night at 11:00 P.M. "Göben" and "Breslau" came into the Dardanelles under the German flag. After that they were announced as Turkish ships bought by Turkey for 80 million francs. This is the answer given to France, Russia, and England. TOSHEFF.

No. 342

The Minister in Constantinople to the Minister of Foreign Affairs, August 13, 1914.—Djemal Pasha informed me that Turkey has told Wangenheim that the German warships cannot pass to the Black Sea until Germany has an agreement with Bulgaria.

On the other hand, Turkey wants us to tell Germany that we cannot join Turkey until we have come to an agreement with Rumania. This is only to save time. TOSHEFF.

No. 390

The Minister in Bucharest to the Minister of Foreign Affairs, August 29, 1914.—A German special train has arrived carrying German sailors to Constantinople. RADEFF.

No. 392

The Minister in Constantinople to the Minister of Foreign Affairs, August 30, 1914.—Yesterday 600 German sailors, officers, and engineers arrived. Germany evidently wants to form a little navy in the Black Sea. TOSHEFF.

No. 410

The Minister in Constantinople to the Minister of Foreign Affairs, September 8, 1914.—According to the German Attaché, Germany wants Bulgaria to tell Turkey that she is on her side so that Turkey will fight against Russia without any fear of Bulgaria. This would also scare Serbia from invading Austria-Hungary. TOSHEFF.

No. 585

The Minister in Constantinople to the Minister of Foreign Affairs, December 9, 1914.—Germany and Austria-Hungary ask Turkey to keep up friendly relations with Greece. TOSHEFF.

No. 653

The Minister in Vienna to the Minister of Foreign Affairs, February 4, 1915.—The German Attaché visited me and told me that Bulgaria should not commence war as yet but should arm just several forces of soldiers and send them, together with the Turkish forces in Macedonia, to intercept the passage of war material between Serbia and Saloniki. This would probably not necessitate war between Bulgaria, Rumania, and Greece. In case it does Bulgaria can count on help from Turkey. TOSHEFF.

No. 749

The Minister in Constantinople to the Minister of Foreign Affairs, March 26, 1915.—Germany is very much irritated with Rumania because Rumania does not let war materials for Turkey pass through her territories. Germany wants to send an ultimatum to this untrue friend. KOLOUSHEFF.

No. 755

The Minister in Constantinople to the Minister of Foreign Affairs, March 29, 1915.—Upon the demand of Turkey, Germany is going to

commence operations against Serbia in order to open the pass through
Nish–Sofia–Constantinople. KOLOUSHEFF.

No. 828

The Minister in Athens to the Minister of Foreign Affairs, May 10,
1915.—There is strong competition between Germany and England to
bring Greece on their side. Germany supports the movement for neutrality in view of danger from Bulgaria. Germany has guaranteed
Greece against Turkey as well as against Bulgaria. PASSAOOFF.

No. 861

The Minister in Constantinople to the Minister of Foreign Affairs,
May 31, 1915.—Germany wants to have Bulgaria on her side, which
would be the only way to scare Rumania. After Italy opens war on
Germany and Austria-Hungary, Rumania is likely to follow. KOLOU-
SHEFF.

No. 885

The Minister in Constantinople to the Minister of Foreign Affairs,
June 2, 1915.—Germany had guaranteed the integrity of Turkey; therefore, the Bulgarian demand for Enos-Midia means war against Turkey
and Germany. Germany is sure that Bulgaria could have Maritza and
even Enos-Midia if she would make a *Treaty* with Turkey *for defense
and offense.* KOLOUSHEFF.

No. 917

The Minister in Constantinople to the Minister of Foreign Affairs,
June 18, 1915.—The German Attaché expresses the opinion that the
promises of England and her allies are not trustworthy, for they promise land that is not in their hands. That Bulgaria can only hope to get
territory through a friendly understanding with Turkey! And that one
should not demand without giving something in return. That we should
not want too much but just Maritza and a railroad to Dedeagatch and
in return we should let the war materials for Turkey pass through.
DOBNEFF.

No. 929

The Minister in Constantinople to the Minister of Foreign Affairs,
June 29, 1915.—Germany will keep her word with Bulgaria concerning
Serbian Macedonia whatever happens. KOLOUSHEFF.

No. 940

The Minister in Berlin to the Minister of Foreign Affairs, July 3,
1915.—The German Minister of Foreign Affairs said that Turkey is

in a bad situation because of lack of munitions. Bulgaria should give Turkey her own munitions and thus help Germany, Turkey, and herself, because, if the Dardanelles fall into the hands of the enemies, Germany will leave the Balkan peninsula to its own fate and Bulgaria will not get a thing. But that if Dardanelles and Constantinople remain in the hands of Turkey she may be more inclined to give territory to Bulgaria. Bulgaria should not worry about being left without munitions for Rumania will soon decide to permit the passage of war materials. RIZOFF.

No. 949

The Minister in Berlin to the Minister of Foreign Affairs, July 8, 1915.—The German Minister of the Marine said that after they had occupied Poland and Galicia they would put 500,000 soldiers against Serbia and, if necessary, against Rumania. Germany wants us to give our own arms to Turkey for the defense of the Dardanelles. RIZOFF.

263. FROM THE BULGARIAN MINISTER IN VIENNA TO THE MINISTER OF FOREIGN AFFAIRS[2]

(Sent February 25, 1915; received March 2, 1915)

Yesterday evening I saw the German Ambassador. To him, as to Baron Burian, I explained the reasons why we think that our neutrality deserves a proper compensation. . . . . Von Tschirschky was irritated at this, stating that he did not see why this question should be raised at this moment, for the solution of it in consonance with the Bulgarian wishes would only strengthen Bulgaria in her inactivity. "Should your people learn that the two monarchies have guaranteed you territorial compensations for your inactivity, what Bulgarian would ever want to fight? Besides, at the time of the remission of the loan your policy took a direction which precluded every doubt. The same happened at and prior to Austria's invasion of Serbia. And still you maintain an attitude of indifference. Just because our enemies have given you promises for your neutrality, you now want the same from us. That means that if they promised you the moon tomorrow you would come and demand from us the sun. But it surprises us how you come to think of Enos and Midia as compensation, in view of your relations with Turkey."

I answered every consideration raised by the Ambassador, pointing out that the promises of territorial compensations for her neutrality did not mean at all that Bulgaria was going to neglect an opportunity

---

[2] Bulgaria, *Documents,* I, 409–10, No. 735.

to enter the war if and when the condition and the interests of her people demanded it. . . . . I also added that nothing was farther from us than to give our policy the character of extortion. And in regard to Enos and Midia, that was our suggestion; but it did not mean that we wanted it at any cost.

Having listened to my answers, von Tschirschky said that, after all, the question might be considered in principle but that our Government should communicate directly with the German Government. . . . . If that is done we shall be able to find out for sure whether or not Western Thrace has been promised to Turkey—which I suspect to be the case. . . .

A. TOSHEFF

Notation. This dispatch is a true document, which it is necssary to preserve.

FERDINAND

264. MILITARY CONVENTION BETWEEN GERMANY, AUSTRIA-HUNGARY, AND BULGARIA, SEPTEMBER 6, 1915[3]

1. The three contracting parties are obliged to act together against Serbia, that is, Germany and Austria-Hungary within 30 days and Bulgaria within 35 days, from the date of this treaty and to start an attack against the Serbian frontier with armed forces as follows: Germany and Austria-Hungary with at least 6 infantry divisions each and Bulgaria with at least 4 infantry divisions according to her tables of organization.

2. The Commander-in-Chief of all the armed forces mentioned in Article 1 will be General Field-Marshal von Mackensen, who will be given the following task: to fight the Serbian Army wherever he finds it and to open and insure as soon as possible the connection by land between Hungary and Bulgaria.

3. The orders of General Field-Marshal von Mackensen are unconditionally valid for the armies under him. Also he has the right to order the moving into the place of attack and to give orders for the beginning of military operations after the interval mentioned in Article 1. However the Bulgarian war operations are not to start until the 5th day after the starting of German and Austro-Hungarian military operations.

To the staff of General Field-Marshal are to be attached at least one high officer from Austria-Hungary and at least one high officer from Bulgaria to act as co-workers on regular service and not as attachés.

[3] Bulgaria, *Documents,* I, 684.

4. The Commander-in-Chief of the German forces is obliged, as soon as the passage to Bulgaria is open and in case Bulgaria wishes it, to send soldiers of about one mixed infantry brigade for Varna and Bourgas and to try as far as possible to take care of the moving and transporting of the German submarines. These soldiers will be quartered by the Bulgarian Government, but they are to supply their own provisions.

5. The Commander-in-Chief of the German forces is obliged, as soon as Bulgaria wants it, to make the Turkish Commander-in-Chief give enough soldiers for the defense of Dedeagatch against attempted attacks and when in action together with Bulgaria to put those soldiers under Bulgarian command. As to Turkey's consent there is no doubt.

6. The Commander-in-Chief of the German forces has received assurance from the German Government that it is to give Bulgaria a war subsidy of 200 million francs in the shortest time possible. Details will be worked out by the financial officials of the two countries.

7. Germany declares that she is ready to give Bulgaria war materials of all kinds as far as she can in reference to her own needs. If any misunderstandings come up over it, they will be decided upon by the chief of the staff of the active German Army.

8. From the day of signing this treaty, the three contracting countries look upon any enemy that attacks one of them as a common enemy and will act toward him as such. On the other hand, Bulgaria declares that she will keep unconditional neutrality with Greece and Rumania until the end of war operations against Serbia, if these countries make declarations that they will not arm, that they will remain neutral, and that they do not want to take Serbian territory.

9. Bulgaria is obliged within 15 days from the signing of this treaty to arm the 4 divisions mentioned in Article 1 and to send them forward so that on the 35th day from the signing of this treaty they should be at the Serbian frontier ready for action. Further, Bulgaria is obliged to furnish soldiers, at least one division, also not later than the 35th day after the signing of this treaty, to cross the Serbian frontier and occupy Macedonia.

10. To Turkey is given the right to adhere to this treaty in all respects. The German Commander-in-Chief will at once begin to negotiate. There is no doubt that Turkey is ready, when Bulgaria wishes it, to give Bulgaria military aid against any enemy and to place troops under Bulgarian command for that purpose.

11. Bulgaria is obliged to give full and unobstructed passage of materials and soldiers from Germany and Austria-Hungary to and from Turkey as soon as the pass through Serbia or the Danube or through Rumania shall be opened.

12. This treaty will be signed by the Chiefs of the General Staff of Germany and Austria-Hungary as well as by the military representative from Bulgaria in Pless, and comes into force immediately.

Signed in Pless September 6, 1915

P. GANTCHEFF	CONRAD
General of the General Staff and Delegate from the Royal Bulgarian Government	General, Chief of the Emperor's and King's General Staff

VON FALKENHAYN
General of Infantry, Chief of
the General Staff of the German Field Army

265. FROM THE MINISTER PLENIPOTENTIARY IN BERLIN TO THE MINISTER OF FOREIGN AFFAIRS[4]

(Sent July 7, 1915; received July 9, 1915)

About the question I had a long conversation with the German Minister of Foreign Affairs and separately with the Under-Secretary of State. The Minister of Foreign Affairs reproached us that we have procrastinated by changing our delegates and by daily increasing our claims. He added that at the beginning Turkey was inclined to give up more but when she noticed our behavior she became more unyielding. When I said that I doubted such a policy on our side, the Minister said that you personally have said—probably to the German Minister Plenipotentiary—that from Turkey one has to demand more in order to obtain less, the Turkey of today being not the same in so far as her tactics are concerned as the Turkey of Sultan Hamid's time. I asked the Minister: "Shouldn't Germany take the part of moral arbiter in the affair?" The Minister answered that the German Ambassador in Constantinople had made great efforts to that end but of course Germany cannot force her ally, Turkey, to give up the impossible. Very delicately I reminded the Minister that not long ago Germany caused her ally, Austria, to make big concessions to Italy. The Minister had nothing to say except the compliment that he did not wish to insult Bulgaria by comparing her with Italy. However, he added that one of these days Wangenheim will pass through Sofia and our Government can talk over the question with him. In any case, the Minister said, Bulgaria should send as delegates to Constantinople persons who are more serious and less orientally-inclined than the present ones.

[4] Bulgaria, *Documents,* I, 726, No. 29.

The Under-Secretary of State, who has always been truly friendly to us, promised to take the question in hand after the arrival of Wangenheim and to do everything possible to conclude it in the shortest time possible. But he made me understand that we should be less stubborn and that we should send stronger delegates to Constantinople. He, as well as the Minister, mentioned as such General Savov and Kaltcheff.

After that, very confidentially, the Under-Secretary of State told me the following: "The mission of Hohenlohe in Bucharest was not successful. I am sure that Rumania will pay dearly for that, but right now it is important that you hasten and take the place of Rumania for Germany. I am telling you this as a German and as your friend. Hurry up and send over to our headquarters—of course in secret—one of your high officers, so that we can come to an agreement as to our war operations against Serbia. Thus, you will hasten our invasion of Serbia and will make sure not only of Macedonia but also of the Serbian triangle to Vidin. Your King had already expressed before Hohenlohe his agreement on this question, and has asked him to speak about the same with Radoslavov. But it is necessary to hurry up this question, because the Russian Army will be beaten soon and your envoy should be in our headquarters before they [our headquarters] have decided what to do after beating Russia."

I am of the opinion that we should cease our wavering and craftiness because we might find ourselves abandoned by both sides. Our military envoy to the German Headquarters could be sent immediately— by preference an officer who speaks the German language. With Turkey we should come to agreement as soon as possible. Here they are entirely sure that by the end of the month Russia will be beaten, that the Dardanelles will not fall, and that the enemies will be chased out of them. If Russia is in reality beaten we shall have a hard time obtaining anything from Turkey then, not even what she is offering now. Also, a disagreement with Turkey will put us in an unpleasant position toward Germany. Excuse my daring to express this my opinion, but our situation is so difficult that each opinion may be valuable.

One American correspondent who was in Sofia lately formed the opinion from a conversation with Fitzmorris that a plot against the King and you is not impossible. For goodness sake take care, not forgetting that Fitzmorris organized the plot of Sultan Hamid against me.

The Under-Secretary of State expressed satisfaction over your intervention with one American correspondent.   Rizoff

Notation. Inform that the cabinet council approved of the decision to send a high officer for negotiations. Details will be told to the German Legation.   Radoslavov

266. FROM THE MINISTER PLENIPOTENTIARY IN VIENNA TO THE MINISTER OF FOREIGN AFFAIRS[5]

(Sent August 7, 1915; received August 8, 1915)

According to the information I gathered, the German-Austrian attack against Serbia will be undertaken with 150,000 German soldiers and 100,000 Austrian soldiers on the 20th of this month and from the side of Orshova.

TOSHEW

267. FROM THE MINISTER PLENIPOTENTIARY IN LONDON TO THE MINISTER OF FOREIGN AFFAIRS[6]

(Sent August 22, 1915; received August 25, 1915)

From my talk with Cambon I was able to draw up the following conclusions:

1. Venizelos has abandoned the policy of generosity toward Bulgaria, which is thought of as being a result of the stubbornness of the Greek King, who is sure of Germany's success.

2. Our negotiations with Turkey have made England and her allies mistrust Bulgaria. The unsuccessful outcome of the negotiations is due to Serbian stubbornness. Here, they even know that at the present time there is a special delegate from the German Emperor in Sofia, or on his way there, to negotiate with Bulgaria.

3. Germany still continues to propose peace even to England, but she and her allies have firmly determined not to sign peace but to impose their own wishes. This opinion is shared by all except a few insignificant groups with international interests.

HADJI-MISHEFF

268. SECRET CONVENTION BETWEEN GERMANY AND BULGARIA OF SEPTEMBER 6 (AUGUST 24), 1915[7]

Germany and Bulgaria, having come to an accord in undertaking in common a military action against Serbia, agree to the following:

[5] Bulgaria, *Documents*, I, 600, No. 1023.
[6] *Ibid.*, I, 626, No. 1061.
[7] *Ibid.*, I, 690.

ARTICLE I

Germany guarantees to Bulgaria the acquisition and annexation of the following territories:

(a) Macedonia, which at present belongs to Serbia, uniting the two zones called "contested" and "uncontested" as they were delimited by the Bulgarian-Serbian Treaty of Alliance of February 29 (March 13), 1912, and conforming to the map annexed to the Bulgarian-Serbian Treaty:

(b) Serbian territory situated to the east of the following line: the river Morava, from the point of its departure from the Danube until the place where it unites with the two rivers: the Bulgarian Morava and the Serbian Morava; from there, the line follows the watershed of these two rivers, passing the crest of Jeherna-Gora, traversing the pass near the Katchanik, mounting to the crest of Char-Planina, touching the Bulgarian frontier at San Stefano and thence following this frontier. The line of demarcation has been traced on the map annexed here, which forms an integral part of the present convention.

ARTICLE II

In case Rumania during this conflict should without provocation on the part of the Bulgarian Government attack Bulgaria, its allies, or Turkey, Germany consents to the annexation by Bulgaria of the territories ceded to Rumania by the Treaty of Bucharest, after the manner in which a rectification of the Bulgarian-Rumanian frontier was laid down by the Treaty of Berlin

ARTICLE III

In case Greece during this conflict should without provocation on the part of the Bulgarian Government attack Bulgaria, its allies, or Turkey, Germany consents to the annexation of the territories ceded to Greece by the Treaty of Bucharest.

ARTICLE IV

The two contracting parties reserve for themselves a later agreement on the subject of the conclusion of peace.

ARTICLE V

Germany engages herself, conjointly with Austria-Hungary, to extend to the Bulgarian Government a war loan to the amount of 200,000,000 francs, which is to be placed at the latter's disposal in four instalments on the following dates:

1. The first fifty million francs on the day of mobilization.
2. The second fifty million francs one month after mobilization.
3. The third fifty million francs two months after mobilization.
4. The fourth fifty million francs three months after mobilization.

The details of this loan shall be regulated by special agreement to be concluded between the Financial Administrations of the two countries.

In case the war lasts longer than four months, Germany, conjointly with Austria-Hungary, extends a supplementary loan to the Bulgarian Government, if, upon a prior agreement, that will be found necessary.

ARTICLE VI

The present convention becomes binding at the same time as the military convention.

Made in Sofia, in duplicate form, September 6 (August 24), one thousand nine hundred and fifteen, and signed by the respective plenipotentiaries.

G. MICHARELLES   DR. V. RADOSLAVOV

269. TREATY OF AMITY AND ALLIANCE BETWEEN THE GERMAN EMPIRE AND BULGARIA OF SEPTEMBER 6 (AUGUST 24), 1915[8]

His Majesty the Emperor of Germany and King of Prussia on one side and His Majesty the King of the Bulgars on the other side, being filled with the conviction of the community of interest of their States, have resolved to conclude a treaty of amity and alliance and have named, as their Plenipotentiaries, the following:

His Majesty the Emperor of Germany, King of Prussia: Dr. G. Michahelles, His confidential adviser, His Envoy Extraordinary and Minister Plenipotentiary in Sofia;

His Majesty the King of the Bulgars: Dr. V. Radoslavov, His President of the Council of Ministers, Minister of the Interior, and Minister of Foreign Affairs *par interim;*

who, having presented to each other their full powers, which were found to be in due and proper form, have agreed upon the following points:

[8] Bulgaria, *Documents,* I, 687.

Article I

The two High Contracting Powers pledge each other peace and amity and will not enter any alliance or arrangement directed against one of their States.

They pledge themselves to pursue reciprocally an amicable policy and to give each other mutual help within the bounds of their interests.

Article II

Germany guarantees with all her means the political independence and the territorial integrity of Bulgaria during the life of this treaty against every attack or offense taking place without any provocation on the part of the Bulgarian Government.

If Germany, without any provocation on her part, has been attacked by a State adjacent to Bulgaria, the latter obliges herself to send her military forces against the State in question, as soon as it is demanded of her.

Article III

The present treaty is in force until December 31 (new calendar), 1920. If it has not been denounced six months before this date, it continues in force for another year and afterwards continues to prolong itself always for one year, as long as its denunciation shall not have taken place.

Article IV

The present treaty remains secret until a further preliminary agreement.

Article V

The present treaty shall be ratified and the ratifications are to be exchanged in Sofia not later than eight days after its signing.

In witness whereof the Plenipotentiaries have signed the treaty and affixed their seals.

Made in Sofia in duplicate form on September 6 (August 24), one thousand nine hundred and fifteen.

Dr. V. Radoslavov   G. Michahelles

B. ITALY

270. MEMORANDUM BY DR. KANNER OF A CONVERSATION
WITH BARON BURIAN, MARCH 25, 1915[9]

. . . . Burian informed me that the negotiations now pending were of very important character and it would be injurious should anything become public about them. . . . .

I asked him, whether, once we conceded the Italian demands, ... we could rest assured that Italy would remain neutral. To that he answered that no one could know; but it would be his task, he added with great show of assurance, to watch constantly the future course of events and to draw his own conclusions. Naturally, in such matters there is no absolute guaranty. . . . . I said it seemed that a great deal of distrust prevailed anyway about these negotiations, and that rumor had it that Italy was asking guaranties from us, or even an immediate fulfillment of the promises; this because they fear that after the war we would not keep our promise. Upon this remark he became again more talkative and said, not without a certain show of satisfaction, that the Italians are scratching their heads, not knowing what to do. State papers, he continued, have all depreciated in value, particularly state papers in the best sense of the word. Since I did not understand him at once, I asked which? He said those papers which are called treaties. They have suffered a great loss of prestige. Thereupon he smiled ironically and then embarked upon a philosophical discussion of the fact that a promise given solemnly between two States did not hold nowadays. . . . . Here I interrupted and said that the Italians knew very well how little one can rely upon treaties. I meant the Three-Power Treaty and remarked that Italy's demand for special guaranties was due to her own bad conscience about that Three-Power Pact. He retorted that he did not believe that Italy had any pangs of conscience. We must never assume that things in other States will be seen in the light in which we regard them. What is the conscience of a people? The English give us the best example. Again and again we have fooled ourselves because we did not understand them. . . . . The conscience of the Englishman is a very complicated affair. His public conscience is enveloped, involved, and it is hard to penetrate it. . . . . He thinks himself to be chosen to rule the world and that what is in his interest is right. . . . .

In order to return to the subject of Italy I said that the Italian papers bring apparently very concrete reports about the course of negotiation. Here I produced a clipping which contained an "Avanti" report

[9] Kanner Papers, I, Part II, pp. 54–72.

and read to him: "Cession of the Trentino, re-establishment of the Statute of Fiume, the passing of a similar statute for Trieste." At this point he interrupted me . . . . and said that those were just conjectures. I said then that it was conceivable that the negotiations must be very difficult. He replied: "Of course, I depend continually upon the events at the front. What happens there might at any time disrupt the negotiations. . . . ."

I asked him then what really our war aim was. He said that . . . . one cannot predict war aims, for everything depends upon the situation at the front, that his war aim for the time being is: Victory. Referring again to Italy, I said that were I the Italian Minister I should not have entered into the present negotiations at all, since I regard them as valueless. He looked at me quizzically, and I continued: "If we win, naturally we will be the ones to remake the map and shall then be in the position to refuse to keep our promises made to Italy in the present negotiations, since in such a case Italy would not be strong enough to go against us. On the other hand, if the Entente Powers should be the victors, they might take from Italy what we conceded to them, already on the basis of what the English Secretary of State said in the *Blue Book,* namely, that England had an interest to keep the Austro-Hungarian Monarchy in an unweakened condition." Burian interjected that this interest could be traced as far back as the wars for the Spanish Succession.

Finally he said that the Italians are waiting for the opportune moment to join this or the other side, but that therein it is easy to make a mistake. . . . . The Italians think themselves very smart. (Thereupon he gestured, as if to say: "But there are even smarter people than they.") . . . .

271. TELEGRAM FROM ERZBERGER TO FATHER COUNT ANDLAU[10]

EXTERNAL, GERMAN EMBASSY, VIENNA

Father Count Andlau, University Place I, Vienna

Please accept cordial thanks for your successful efforts. Holy Father thanks you especially cordially. He states that every restriction of the Austrian concessions put forward by the German and Austrian Ambassadors would invariably lead to war and that he should have to regard Austria's withdrawal of these concessions as a personal insult. This because the Holy Father intervened particularly in behalf of this

[10] Collection of German Documents, Hoover War Library.

Austrian offer. From the whole situation it is evident that high pressure must be exerted these days in Vienna. The change of cabinet is no reason at all for withdrawing the concessions; on the contrary, if a new cabinet will not be able to offer more, it must lead to war. That is the opinion of all prudent political circles. For the last two days Rome resembles a city on the verge of revolution. If in Vienna there are still groups who doubt the seriousness of the situation, that can only be ascribed to irresponsible recklessness. At any rate no responsible statesman can hesitate even for a second to carry out this agreement with Italy. If war is to be avoided, then immediate surrender is absolutely necessary. Austria can give this promise. In case of peaceful understanding, all details of the surrender (time period, in what order, etc.) remain open in spite of this promise. The question of immediate surrender today means the decision between war and peace, if the latter can still be maintained at all. I write this as a friend of Austria, and I beseech you, if your work is not to be entirely in vain, to employ with your great skill and enduring energy all means toward an absolutely necessary understanding. The Vienna Cabinet holds this week the fate of Austria and that of its royal house in its hand. There can be no more procrastination; the sooner the understanding comes about, the better for Austria.

ERZBERGER

272. TELEGRAM TO BERLIN ON MAY 7, 1915[11]

Should war break out, then, according to the opinion which I gained here, everything must be done by means of a strict censorship to prevent whatever could further the outbreak of national passions or that would produce a national war against Italy. We must keep open the possibility of concluding a separate peace in case of a change of government, which is easily possible here.

ERZBERGER
BÜLOW

273. OFFICIAL ANNOUNCEMENT OF A STATE OF WAR BE-TWEEN ITALY AND GERMANY, AUGUST 28, 1916[12]

BERLIN, August 27. The note with which the Italian Minister in Bern requested the Swiss Government on August 26 to inform the

[11] Collection of German Documents, Hoover War Library.
[12] *Norddeutsche Allgemeine Zeitung,* August 28, 1916, I, 1.

Imperial German Government that Italy considers herself in a state of war with Germany from August 28, reads in translation as follows:

"Upon instruction from His Majesty's Government I have the honor to bring to the attention of Your Excellency and the Federal Council the following communication:

"'Acts of hostility by the German Government toward Italy follow one another with growing frequency. It suffices to mention the repeated supplying of arms and instruments of land and sea warfare by Germany to Austria, and the uninterrupted participation of German officers, soldiers, and sailors in the different operations of war directed against Italy. It is also only due to the assistance which has thus been lavishly bestowed by Germany in the most various ways and to the greatest degree that Austria-Hungary has recently been able to concentrate all her efforts against Italy. Further, it is necessary to mention the surrender to our enemy of Italian prisoners who had escaped from Austro-Hungarian concentration camps and who had taken refuge in German territory; again, at the instigation of the Imperial Foreign Office, the German bankers and credit establishments demanded that all Italian subjects be considered as alien enemies, that all payments due them be postponed, and the payments owed to Italian workmen be suspended upon the basis of the formal declaration of German law. These are all facts which reveal the true systematic attitude of the Imperial Government toward Italy.

"'In the long run such a state of affairs cannot be tolerated by the Royal Government. It increases, exclusively to the detriment of Italy, the great contrast between the situation *de facto* and the situation *de jure* which has already resulted from the fact that Italy on the one hand and Germany on the other are allied with two groups of Powers at war with one another.'

"For the reasons mentioned above the Italian Government declares in the name of the King, that from August 28 Italy will consider herself in a state of war against Germany, and requests the Swiss Federal Government to convey the above communication to the knowledge of the Imperial German Government."

274. OFFICIAL COMMENT ON ITALY'S DECLARATION OF WAR, AUGUST 28, 1916[13]

Italy's formal declaration of war against Germany makes little change in the existing state of affairs. Last year when Italy declared war against Austria-Hungary the Imperial Government, before Prince

[13] *Ibid.*

Bülow and the Staff of the Germany Embassy left Rome, pointed out to the Italian Government that everywhere German troops were present in Austro-Hungarian units and that therefore an attack against Austro-Hungarian troops would be equally against German troops. Consequently the Italian Government was not for a moment left in doubt that Germany regarded the giving of military assistance to her Austro-Hungarian ally against any enemy as a part of her treaty obligations.

Regarding the surrender of escaped Italian prisoners of war of Austro-Hungary, it is true that about six Italian prisoners of war who escaped from Austro-Hungarian internment camps had been stopped at the German frontier and brought back. This was the act of subordinate customs officials and did not meet with the approval of the Imperial Government. Moreover, the latter, on representations from the Italian Government, made proposals for a satisfactory settlement of the question. The assertion with regard to the encroachment by the German Government upon Italian banking credits in Germany and on Italian workmen's claims to annuities is only a repetition of statements in the Italian press in July of this year which were exhaustively refuted in this paper on July 20.

It would have been more dignified if the Italian Government had refrained from justifying its declaration of war on Germany by sophisticated arguments. The Italian Government thereby will deceive nobody. Her decision was solely a further consequence of her earlier breach of faith and a result of pressure exerted for months past on Italy by England and her allies.

CHAPTER XV

THE KINGDOM OF POLAND

INTRODUCTORY NOTE

AFTER THE conquest of Congress Poland by the Central Powers in the summer of 1915, provisional governments were established at Warsaw by Germany and at Lublin by Austria. Secret negotiations between the allies concerning the organization of a Polish buffer state ended in August 1916, when the German Supreme Command took over the control of the Eastern front. On November 5, 1916, Congress Poland was restored by the Central Powers as a hereditary constitutional monarchy in military, political, and economic alliance with Germany and Austria. A provisional council of state was appointed, which took office in January 1917.

Ludendorff's plan of developing a Polish military force was opposed by Pilsudski, who was thereupon arrested, July 22, 1916. When the provisional government of Poland collapsed, Germany and Austria established a new executive government by the Letters-Patent of September 12, 1917. This regency council, together with a cabinet and a council of state, governed the country subject to the control of the military governors of the Central Powers. Ludendorff's Polish plan proved to be a major disaster for Germany.

275. POLAND'S FATEFUL HOUR, NOVEMBER 5, 1916[1]

Germany and Austria-Hungary have taken a historic decision. They have determined on the formation of the Polish State. A century has passed since at the Congress of Vienna the European Powers removed the chief part of Poland from the sphere of Western civilization, entrusting it to the hands of Russia. It is not the "protectors of the small nations" that now restore this country to its national development, but the two Powers against which the hatred of the whole world has been called forth by a fraudulent appeal in the name of the small nations. The Western Powers have shown plenty of platonic sympathy

[1] *Norddeutsche Allgemeine Zeitung,* November 5, 1916, II, 1.

for Poland. Many a cry of "Vive la Pologne," which, however, carried no obligation to act, has resounded from the West. Whenever the Poles, confident that they would be helped from London, have commenced to fight for their independence, it has been proved that they were building on empty words. Their freedom could not come from this quarter. Had the decision fallen differently today, were the Russian arms victorious in the East, the population of Congress Poland would for another century, without intervention on the part of the Western Powers, have dragged their chains from promise to promise.

The liberation of Poland is bound up with the victory of Germany and her allies. Only they, not Russia nor the Western Powers, have a vital interest of their own in the existence of a free Poland. The recognition of this interest, forced on us by the development of Europe in the twentieth century, has not as yet, we know well, come home to all circles in Germany. It would be misleading to conceal at this hour the many criticisms which prevent many patriotic men among us from welcoming with joy the bold step taken by the issue of this manifesto. Many of our experiences with Poland, which is at present and for the future inextricably bound up with the Prussian State, appear not to be favorable to the great hazard which we now throw.

But above every consideration, for and against, there stands pre-eminent the principle that we ought not, for the sake of our own future, to allow Poland to revert to Russia. Germany's security requires for all future time that Russian armies should be unable to invade the Empire from a Poland consolidated as a military gate of invasion and dividing Silesia from East and West Prussia. Kind fortune will not always provide us with a Hindenburg to check the Russian flood in spite of frontiers like that. Every year the population of the giant Empire in the East increases by three millions. Shorter, strongly fortified frontiers will be the firmest foundation for peaceful relations with our Russian neighbor. It will also be a great gain for us if in the developments and tasks of the coming years of peace we have at our side the Poles, who in civilization, religion, and history belonged to the West in the past, and ought to belong to the West in the future.

To Poland, freed from Russian domination, we offer the opportunity of attaching itself as a separate state to the Central Powers and, in firm alliance with them, of leading a free life in the political, economical, and cultural spheres. In so doing they will have a strong claim, especially for the near future, upon our assistance. Russian domination did not allow Polish officials, Polish teachers, or a Polish army. It knew how to suppress, divide, distract the nation in its effort to rise. The making of railways and of waterways was neglected. Everywhere the first bases for the administration of the state have yet to be created, though much has been done during our occupation with the sympathetic help of the Poles. The Poles, too, have contributed military forces for the cause of liberation from the Russian yoke. The Polish legions have already fought gloriously in many battles against Russia and by the side of the Central Powers. The creation of a Polish army is therefore in itself nothing new. By permitting the Poles to proceed at once to the formation of an armed force of their own, the Central Powers fulfill a burning desire which is particularly easy to understand in the case of a nation of such military talent. Step by step the building of the Polish state will be carried further. Difficult and exhausting work will have to be done. But the ancient state-creating strength of our nation will in the face of all obstacles achieve the great aim and help to establish it. So shall we in time find in the New Poland an able and friendly neighbor, secure Germany in the East, and win for the future of Europe a valuable comrade.

276. KAISER FRANZ JOSEF I TO DR. VON KOERBER, NOVEMBER 4, 1916[2]

DEAR DR. VON KOERBER:

In accordance with the understanding reached between me and the German Emperor, an independent state with a hereditary monarchy and a constitution will be formed of the Polish districts which our brave armies have snatched from Russian rule. On this occasion I recall with deep emotion the many proofs of devotion and loyalty which during my reign I have received from Galicia and the great and heavy sacrifices which this province, exposed in the present war to a fierce enemy assault, had to bear in the interest of the victorious defense of the eastern frontiers of the Empire, sacrifices which secure for it a lasting claim on my warmest fatherly regard.

It is therefore my will at the moment when the new state comes into existence, and coincident with this development, to grant Galicia also the right to manage independently its own internal affairs in as full a measure as this can be done in accordance with its membership in the state as a whole and with the latter's prosperity, and thereby to give the population of Galicia a guaranty for its racial and economic development. In informing you of this my intention, I charge you to prepare suitable proposals for its legal realization and to submit these to me.

FRANZ JOSEF
(*Countersigned*) KOERBER

VIENNA, November 4, 1916

[2] *Norddeutsche Allgemeine Zeitung*, November 5, 1916, II, 3.

277. PROCLAMATION OF THE FORMATION OF THE KINGDOM OF POLAND, NOVEMBER 5, 1916[3]

To the inhabitants of the Government of Warsaw:

His Majesty the German Emperor and His Majesty the Austrian Emperor and Apostolic King of Hungary, sustained by their firm confidence in the final victory of their arms and guided by the wish to lead to a happy future the Polish districts which by their brave armies were snatched with heavy sacrifices from Russian power, have agreed to form from these districts an independent state with a hereditary monarchy and a constitution. The more precise regulation of the frontiers of the Kingdom of Poland remains reserved.

In union with both the Allied Powers the new kingdom will find the guaranties which it requires for the free development of its strength. In its own army the glorious traditions of the Polish Army of former times and the memory of our brave Polish fellow-combatants in the great war of the present time will continue to live. Its organization, training, and command will be regulated by mutual agreement. The Allied Monarchs confidently hope that their wishes for the state and national development of the Kingdom of Poland will now be fulfilled with the necessary regard to the general political conditions of Europe and to the welfare and security of their own countries and peoples.

The great Western neighbors of the Kingdom of Poland will with pleasure see arise again and flourish at the eastern frontier a free and happy state rejoicing in its national life.

Upon orders of His Majesty, the German Kaiser.

THE GOVERNOR-GENERAL

278. THE KAISER'S LETTER OF INSTRUCTION TO THE GOVERNOR-GENERAL OF WARSAW, GENERAL VON BESELER, SEPTEMBER 12, 1917[4]

My illustrious ally, His Imperial and Apostolic Majesty, and I have decided on a wider extension of the Polish Constitution (*Staatswesen*) for which we laid the foundation by the proclamation of November 5, 1916. Unfortunately the hard conditions of war do not yet permit of a King adding fresh luster to the old Polish Crown and of deliberations for the good of the country being carried on by a representative as-

---

[3] *Norddeutsche Allgemeine Zeitung,* November 5, 1916, II, 1.
[4] *Ibid.,* September 15, 1917, II, 1.

sembly of the people elected by universal and direct franchise. On the other hand, we desire even now to put state power in the main into the hands of a National Government, whilst the rights and interests of the people will be entrusted to a new and extended State Council. In essential agreement with the proposals of the country's trustees (*Vertrauensmänner*) the Powers in occupation will reserve only such powers as are required by the war condition.

I trust that the further working of this new step toward the realization of an independent Polish State may prove rich in blessing, and that through the strength of its citizens and their free and self-chosen accession to the Central Powers, who are animated by feelings of faithful friendship toward them, a peaceful and blessed future may be before this country so long forcibly held back by Russian domination in its free intellectual and economic development.

Accordingly, I charge you to issue the annexed letters-patent concerning the executive power in the Kingdom of Poland, jointly with the Imperial Austro-Hungarian Military Governor in Lublin.

(*Signed*) WILHELM, I. R.

To my Governor-General in Warsaw, General of Infantry v. Beseler

HEADQUARTERS, September 12, 1917

279. LETTERS-PATENT OF SEPTEMBER 12, 1917, CONCERNING THE EXECUTIVE POWER IN THE KINGDOM OF POLAND[5]

ARTICLE I

(1) The supreme executive power in the Kingdom of Poland shall be entrusted to a Regency Council subject to the rights in international law of the Powers in occupation until it shall be taken over by a King or Regent.

(2) The Regency Council shall consist of three members, who shall be appointed by the Monarchs of the Powers in occupation.

(3) The acts of the governing Regency Council shall be countersigned by the responsible Prime Minister.

ARTICLE II

(1) The legislative power shall be exercised by the Regency Council with the co-operation of the State Council of the Kingdom of Poland, according to the provisions of these letters-patent and the laws to be issued hereafter.

[5] *Ibid.*

(2) In all matters the administration of which has not yet been transferred to the Polish executive, legislative proposals can be dealt with in the State Council only with the sanction of the Powers in occupation of the Kingdom of Poland. In accordance with paragraph 1, the executive bodies may issue orders with legal power, nevertheless, only after having heard the State Council. Furthermore, the Governor-General shall have legal power to issue orders imperatively necessary for the maintenance of important war interests, and may also provide for the obligatory notification and carrying out of such orders by the executive bodies of the Polish State authority. The orders of the Governor-General can be rescinded or altered only by the same medium through which they were issued.

(3) Laws, as also regulations made by the Polish Executive to establish the rights and duties of the people, must be submitted to the Governor-General of the occupying Power in whose administrative zone they are to come into force, and will obtain binding force only if the said Governor raises no objection within fourteen days of their submission to him.

ARTICLE III

The State Council will be constituted in accordance with a special law, to be issued by the Regency Council with the approval of the Powers in occupation.

ARTICLE IV

(1) The tasks of administering justice, and other administration, in so far as these are transferred to the Polish Executive, will be carried out by Polish Courts of Justice and departmental authorities, otherwise by the representatives of the Powers in occupation, for the duration of the war.

(2) In matters affecting the rights or interests of the Powers in occupation, the Governor-General may call for re-examination of the legitimacy of the decisions and enactments of the Polish law courts or authorities, by successive legal appeals and on the pronouncement of judgment or the decision in the supreme court, or may set forth the rights and interests affected, by means of a representative.

ARTICLE V

The right of the Kingdom of Poland to international representation and to conclude international agreements can be exercised only on the conclusion of the occupation.

ARTICLE VI

These letters-patent come into force with the establishment of the Regency Council.

(*Signed*) VON BESELER (*Signed*) VON SZEPTYCKI

280. THE PROCLAMATION OF THE TWO GOVERNOR-GENERALS TO THE EXECUTIVE COMMISSION OF THE POLISH STATE COUNCIL[6]

The Governments of the German Empire and of Austria-Hungary have submitted to their rulers the proposals of the Provisional State Council of July 3, 1917, concerning the present organization of the Polish Higher State authorities. Following this, their Majesties the German Emperor and the Emperor of Austria, Apostolic King of Hungary, have charged us to issue the letters-patent connected with these proposals, which fix the main lines of the provisional constitutional regulations of the Polish State.

The Allied Governments regard a Regency Council as a suitable means not only of giving the Polish State a recognized representation but also of preparing for the future monarchy. For the Regency Council will act as the supreme representative of the Polish State until the appointment of the head of the state, and will exercise the rights of the head of the state, subject to the rights in international law of the Powers in occupation.

The first task of the Regency Council will be the appointment of a Prime Minister, which the Allies reserve the right to ratify. The Prime Minister will take all necessary steps without delay for the organization of Ministries in those branches of administration which are transferred to the Polish executive, and, further, for obtaining the final organization of the Polish State authorities by negotiation with the occupying authorities.

In order to insure representation of the wishes and interests of all classes of the Polish people, the State Council will be revised in a newly extended form and with increased rights. It is the precursor of a Polish Diet (*Landtag*); its work lies in the sphere of legislation. Whereas the order of November 26–December 1, 1916, allows the provisional State Council only an advisory voice, the State Council will have a deciding voice in matters of legislation. It will be summoned to periodical sittings by the Regency Council. The rights of the State

[6] *Norddeutsche Allgemeine Zeitung,* September 15, 1917, II, 1.

Council and the prerogatives of the occupying Powers are more closely defined in the letters-patent.

The Allied Powers trust that this further extension of Polish government, confirming the Act of November 5, 1916, will have the active sympathy of all classes of the Polish people; they express the hope that the negotiations over all details of the organization will be carried through quickly, and that the further favorable development of conditions will lead to governing power being placed to an increasing extent in Polish hands.

281. THE EASTERN QUESTIONS[7]

N. BERLIN, March 13
(Priv. Tel.)

Hindenburg's presence in Berlin on March 12 and his reception by the Kaiser, who in connection with this also received the Chancellor in a long audience, has aroused disquiet in Conservative and Pan-German papers, which disquiet the *Kreuzzeitung* also considers justified. Once again the "understanding" politicians, as this Conservative paper calls them, are supposed to be trying to bring about peace before a decisive battle in the West has forced the enemy to acknowledge themselves beaten. This very characteristic fear of peace, about which vague rumors have again been actually in circulation, has no foundation. Hindenburg's presence and audience with the Emperor have nothing to do with any such peace negotiations, as even the papers of the tendency specified above now learn but, on the contrary, are connected with the political questions of the East, which have been brought nearer solution by the peace of Brest-Litovsk. Of these questions, which extend from Bucharest to Finland, there are some which, like the construction of the future of Finland, Poland, Lithuania, and the Baltic Provinces, have to be solved with considerable urgency, according to the statements from Courland and Livonia. The Chancellor had confidential conferences yesterday on all these matters with the leaders of the Reichstag parties, and the members of the Präsidium, and next week exhaustive discussions will take place, both in the Main Committee of the Reichstag and in the Plenum, when the peace of Brest-Litovsk and the new War Credit is discussed. The often-quoted conversations and arrangements between members of the Majority parties of the Reichstag, and the three delegates of the Polish activist parties about the future constitution of Poland and her relations to the Central Powers by means of a political and economic alliance and, as one may take for granted, especially by a

[7] *Frankfurter Zeitung,* March 14, 1918, second morning edition, p. 1.

military convention, are much in the foreground of these conferences. These matters also are really confidential. An interparty conference of the Majority parties was busy with them today again, but we have already given the essential information as to the program which was discussed, and in certain of its main lines also agreed upon, while Vienna reports show that the same Polish parties have been negotiating in the same direction in Vienna also. How far the German Imperial Government is in accord with the main lines of such agreements cannot be said with any certainty, as yesterday's conversations were confidential; moreover, negotiations will still be necessary with Austria-Hungary. It is obvious that the High Command is much interested in this question, for it has long considered essential a strategic securing of the Polish frontier, as is known, and as the *Tägliche Rundschau* especially emphasizes in an article today. It is now confirmed that the Polish Regency Council has assented to the main bases which have been agreed upon between the Polish delegates and the Majority parties in the Reichstag, and one can take it for granted, therefore, that these parties have represented their views to the Chancellor accordingly. The question of Courland is also supposed to have been discussed at yesterday's conference with the Chancellor, and the *Vossische Zeitung* professes to know that the Majority, especially Deputy Erzberger, spoke out definitely against a personal union, the desire for which, as is known, the Courland Landesrat expressed by offering the ducal crown to the Kaiser. In the conversation the general opinion is supposed to have been against deciding the problems of the East too rapidly, or piecemeal, before knowing, for instance, what direction the negotiations in Moscow and Rumania would take. The fact that Hindenburg also received the President and Ambassador of the Finnish Republic yesterday is a reminder that there is also a Finnish military question.

The *Kreuzzeitung* again strongly objects to the actions of the Majority parties in the Reichstag, who have been treating with the Polish delegates and have come to an understanding about the future status of Poland in connection with the Central Powers. This paper considers this an action by which Parliament in fact takes the helm of the ship of state into its hand, and would be glad to know why the Government did not prevent this, and if and to what extent there is an understanding between it and the Majority parties. The Conservative paper also thinks that proposals of the Reichstag Majority are compatible with the Polish program of the Majority parties, but not with the interests of the Empire.

CHAPTER XVI

THE PEACE OF BREST-LITOVSK

INTRODUCTORY NOTE

AFTER THE second Russian revolution of November 1917 the Bolshevik Government notified the Central Powers of its willingness to negotiate a treaty of peace. Military operations were accordingly halted December 1 on the Eastern front and an armistice for thirty days was signed at Brest-Litovsk, December 15, 1917.

The first meeting of delegates to the peace conference took place on December 22, Kühlmann and Czernin representing the Central Powers and Joffe representing Russia. On December 28 the Russian Delegation was notified that their principle of a "peace without annexations and indemnities and the recognition of the right of self-determination for all peoples" would be accepted by Germany and Austria provided the Allied and Associated Powers agreed to this principle as the basis for a general peace.

When the Entente ignored the Bolshevik Government's proposal of peace, the Central Powers presented on January 7 the conditions of a separate peace to the Russian Delegation. Trotsky objected to these conditions, left the conference January 18, and did not return until January 30. General Hoffmann, the German military representative at the peace conference, objected to the dilatory tactics of the Russian Delegation and to the Bolshevik revolutionary propaganda. Trotsky withdrew again from the conference, February 10, stating that Russia would not renew hostilities but would not accept the German terms of peace. Thereupon Germany denounced the armistice on February 18 and a German army advanced through Esthonia threatening Petrograd. The next day the Bolshevik Government accepted the previous German conditions, but received a new ultimatum, which was accepted February 24. Sokolnikov, who arrived at Brest-Litovsk February 26, announced that Russia accepted the terms dictated by her enemies. The treaty was signed

March 3, 1918, and received the approbation of the Reichstag on March 18, 1918.

282. REVOLUTION AND WAR[1]

. . . . This uprising of the Russian people against the bureaucracy was not, as has formerly often been the case, a protest of the popular soul of Russia against the continuation of the war. On the contrary, it was a protest against the negligences of a government, which, in the opinion of the nations, ignored the most essential means for bringing the war to a victorious end. Milyukov, Rodzianko, and their colleagues, including a wide following even in the Left of the Duma—for only the extreme Right and Left are fundamentally opposed to the continuance of the war—are against making peace. They not only believe that the campaign is still undecided; they are even convinced that a proper utilization of Russia's resources is bound under any circumstances to assure the victory. It is important for us to realize this, for it is natural that we should interpret such a profound catastrophe in the country of one of the strongest of our enemies too optimistically, in a sense favorable to peace. Whether or not the Russian rebellion is in effect calculated to promote peace is another question, which must be considered later. In any case, the tendency that inspired the revolution is anything rather than friendly to Germany, and we must keep that fact before our eyes if we wish to make a correct estimate of the consequences of what has occurred in the political situation.

On the other hand, it is only natural that such a violent disturbance as we observe in Russia at the present moment could not but influence the war situation even if both warring factions are firmly determined to prosecute the war. The moral equilibrium of this enormously big country has been disturbed, authority and prestige of the political ideals have been shaken to their very foundation, the administration has been confused, and the army, being in intimate contact with the affairs at home, has been robbed of the spirit of conscious security. It is self-evident that under such conditions the morale of the troops, which alone insures success, cannot be maintained at the necessary height. But even here we must not surrender ourselves to too optimistic conclusions, and we rather await what the future has in store with that confidence which, taking full cognizance of all the unfavorable factors, is the better entitled to count upon success.

[1] *Norddeutsche Allgemeine Zeitung,* March 16, 1917, II, 1.

283. LUDENDORFF'S STATEMENT CONCERNING THE RUSSIAN REVOLUTION[2]

If anyone says to me that the Russian Revolution was a happy accident for us, I always protest that the Revolution in Russia was no lucky accident, but the natural and necessary consequence of our conduct of the war. Things happen in a curious way in modern war. Formerly armies made war against each other; now it is a war of peoples. In former times the war was ended by the hostile army being conquered; now the war ends by the hostile people being conquered. Before this war we none of us knew this, and we have simply had to learn it. There are no more decisive battles such as there were in earlier campaigns, or rather, the battles decide, as the battle of Tannenberg decided, not directly but indirectly. Military defeats shake the confidence of the peoples in their governments. The opposition is strengthened and gains power; the government falls, and if, as in Russia, the whole system is rotten and ripe for decay, there is a universal collapse. No, the Russian Revolution is no lucky accident; it is the consequence of our victories.

284. ARMISTICE CONCLUDED AT BREST-LITOVSK, DECEMBER 15, 1917[3]

I. The armistice begins on 17 December, 1917, at noon (4 December, 1917, at fourteen o'clock, Russian time) and extends until 14 January, 1918, noon (1 January, 1918, fourteen o'clock, Russian time). The contracting parties have the right on the twenty-first day of the armistice to give a seven days' notice of termination; such not being done, the armistice automatically remains in force until one of the contracting parties gives such seven days' notice.

II. The armistice applies to all land and air fighting forces of the said Powers on the land front between the Black Sea and the Baltic Sea. In the Russo-Turkish theaters of war in Asia the armistice goes into effect at the same time.

The contracting parties obligate themselves, during the period of the armistice, neither to augment the number of detachments of troops stationed on the said fronts and on the islands of Moon Sound—this

---

[2] *Vorwärts*, No. 331, December 3, 1917, pp. 1–2.

[3] *Deutscher Reichsanzeiger*, December 18, 1917; also United States Department of State, *Texts of the Russian "Peace,"* pp. 1–7, hereafter cited as *Texts of the Russian Peace*.

applies also to their organization and status—nor to attempt any re-groupings in preparation for an offensive.

Further, the contracting parties obligate themselves not to under-take any transfers of troops until 14 January, 1918 (1 January, 1918, Russian time), on the front between the Black Sea and the Baltic Sea, unless such transfers had already been begun at the moment of the signing of the armistice.

Finally, the contracting parties obligate themselves not to assemble any troops in the harbors of the Baltic Sea east of 15 degrees longitude east of Greenwich and in the harbors of the Black Sea during the period of the armistice.

III. The advance entanglements of each party's position will be con-sidered as demarcation lines on the European front. These lines may be crossed only under the conditions noted in IV.

In places where entrenched positions do not exist, the demarcation lines for each side will be a straight line drawn through the most ad-vanced occupied positions. The space between the two lines will be considered neutral ground. Likewise navigable rivers separating the opposing positions will be neutral and closed to navigation, except in case of commercial shipping agreed upon. For sections in which the positions are widely separated it will devolve upon the Armistice Com-mission (VII) to determine and establish the lines of demarcation.

In the Russo-Turkish theaters of war in Asia the lines of demarca-tion, as well as intercourse through them (IV), are to be determined by the agreement of the division commanders of both sides.

IV. For the development and strengthening of the friendly relations between the peoples of the contracting parties, organized intercourse between the troops is permitted under the following conditions:

1. Intercourse is permitted parlementaires and the members of the Armistice Commission (VII) and their representatives. All such must have passes signed by at least a corps commander or a corps committee.

2. In each section of a Russian division organized intercourse may take place at two to three places.

For this purpose, by agreement of the divisions opposed to each other, centers of intercourse are to be established in the neutral zone between the demarcation lines and are to be distinguished by white flags. Intercourse is permissible only by day from sunrise to sunset.

At the centers of intercourse not more than twenty-five unarmed persons belonging to either side may be present at any one time. The exchange of news and newspapers is allowed. Open letters may be passed for dispatch. The sale and exchange of wares of everyday use is permitted at the centers of intercourse.

3. The interment of the dead in the neutral zone is permitted. The

special details in each case are to be agreed upon by the divisional commanders on either side or their ranking officers.

4. The question of the return of dismissed soldiers of one country whose domiciles lie beyond the demarcation lines of the other country can be decided only at the peace negotiations. This applies also to the members of Polish detachments.

5. All persons who—contrary to agreements 1–4 preceding—cross the demarcation lines of the opposing party will be arrested and not released until the conclusion of peace or the denunciation of the armistice.

The contracting parties obligate themselves to bring to the notice of their troops by strict orders and detailed explanation the necessity for the observance of the conditions of intercourse and the consequences of infraction thereof. . . . .

VIII. The treaty concerning cessation of hostilities of 5 December (22 November), 1917, and all agreements concluded up to this time on separate sectors of the front with regard to cessation of hostilities or an armistice are rendered null and void by this Armistice Treaty.

IX. The contracting parties will enter into peace negotiations immediately after the signature of the present Armistice Treaty.

X. Upon the basis of the principle of the freedom, independence, and territorial inviolability of the neutral Persian State, the Turkish and the Russian Supreme Commands are prepared to withdraw their troops from Persia. They will immediately enter into communication with the Persian Government in order to regulate the details of the evacuation and the other necessary measures for the guaranteeing of the principle mentioned above.

XI. Each contracting party is to receive a copy of the agreement in the German and the Russian languages, signed by representatives with plenipotentiary powers.

Brest-Litovsk, the 15th day of December, 1917
(The 2d day of December, 1917, Russian style)

[Signatures follow]

285. VON KÜHLMANN'S STATEMENT IN THE REICHSTAG ON GENERAL HOFFMANN AS A PLENIPOTEN-TIARY AT BREST-LITOVSK[4]

Gentlemen, I will not take up much of your time; I only want to elucidate one point of today's debate which has been touched upon by various speakers.

[4] *Verhandlungen des Reichstags*, No. 130, February 20, 1918, pp. 4042–43.

The question is of General Hoffmann having signed the Brest-Litovsk peace treaty as representative of the Highest Army Command. The question has already been discussed in the Main Committee of the House. I took the liberty of elucidating it on that occasion, but I shall gladly repeat in the plenary assembly what I said then. In considering the composition of the delegation for the peace negotiations in Brest-Litovsk, it was clear to the Imperial Chancellor and to us that in some way or other the Highest Army Command must be represented at the negotiations. There were many reasons for this, of which I shall only give a few. To begin with, the armistice negotiations, in which the military men took the foremost place, and foreign policy was represented by a delegate associated with them, were so intimately connected with the peace negotiations that the further representation of the Highest Army Command at these negotiations, which immediately followed, appeared an absolute necessity. The fact that the negotiations took place in occupied territory, that they took place at a time when the World War continued to rage on a number of other fronts, and that the place where the negotiations took place was separated from the seat of the central Government in Berlin, and again from the quarters of the Highest Field Army Command by great distances, made it absolutely necessary to have a representative of the Highest Army Command at the place of negotiations who could immediately make a direct statement on the attitude of the Highest Army Command as to questions submitted which concerned its department. The organization decided that, at the suggestion of the Imperial Chancellor, his Majesty the Emperor should direct that the Highest Army Command be represented by a plenipotentiary delegate at the Brest peace negotiations. This delegate was to take part in the negotiations with the consent, and only with the consent, of the political head of the negotiations. With the consent of the latter he was to enter into negotiations and, by the All Highest Command, was to be one of the signatories to the more important deeds which should embody the result of the negotiations. From experience with these negotiations I may say that this arrangement worked very well. It is obvious, from what has been said, that General Hoffmann could not be a political plenipotentiary, as has been suggested today. Were he, for instance, to have been in the position of an officer of an allied Power he would simply have had to carry out the instructions of the Imperial Chancellor. He would, therefore, have been unable to fulfill precisely the functions for which his presence was desirable and necessary. For the rest, such an arrangement in the form selected for General Hoffmann is absolutely nothing new. His Majesty the Emperor nominated delegates of the army and navy to attend both the Hague Conferences, and in the final protocol of the Conference they are expressly specified as military and naval delegates. These gentlemen also were not at that time political plenipotentiaries in the sense of being executive representatives. The same course was chosen at that time exactly for the same reasons which have now led to this arrangement. It has been thoroughly justified by experience, and I assume that the Imperial Chancellor intends to propose a similar course to his Majesty in connection with further negotiations.

286. STATEMENT OF UNDER-SECRETARY VON DEM BUSSCHE IN THE REICHSTAG ON THE ULTIMATUM TO THE RUSSIAN DELEGATES, FEBRUARY 26, 1918[5]

The desire has been expressed from various sides to learn the contents of the ultimatum accepted by the Russian delegates. The ultimatum runs as follows: "Germany is ready to resume negotiations with Russia and conclude peace on the following conditions: (1) The German Empire and Russia declare the state of war ended. Both nations are resolved henceforward to live together in peace and friendship. (2) The territories which lie west of the line communicated to the Russian representatives at Brest-Litovsk, and which belonged to the Russian Empire, will no longer be under the territorial sovereignty of Russia. In the vicinity of Dunaburg (Dvinsk) the line is to be shifted to the eastern frontier of Courland. No obligations of any sort toward Russia will arise from the former allegiance of these territories to the Russian Empire. Russia renounces all interference in the internal affairs of these territories. Germany and Austria-Hungary intend to determine the future lot of the territories in agreement with their populations. Germany is ready, as soon as a general peace has been concluded and Russian demobilization has been completely carried out, to evacuate the territory situated east of the line mentioned above, in so far as nothing else results from Article 3. (3) Livonia and Esthonia will without delay be evacuated by Russian troops and Red Guards and occupied by a German policing force until the country's institutions guarantee security and political order is restored. All the residents of the country arrested on political grounds are to be immediately released. (4) Russia shall immediately conclude peace with the Ukrainian People's Republic. Russian troops and Red Guards shall be withdrawn without delay from the Ukraine and Finland. (5) Russia shall do everything in her power to guarantee a speedy and orderly return of the East Anatolian Provinces to Turkey. Russia shall recognize the abolition of the Turkish capitulations. (6) (a) The complete demobilization of the Russian army, including the portions of any army newly formed by the present

[5] *Verhandlungen des Reichstags*, No. 134, February 26, 1918, pp. 4161–62.

government, is to be carried out without delay. (*b*) The Russian warships in the Black Sea, Baltic, and Arctic are either to be taken to Russian ports, there to be left until the conclusion of a general peace, or immediately to be disarmed. The warships of the Entente in the Russian sphere of power are to be treated like Russian warships. (*c*) Commercial navigation in the Black Sea and the Baltic shall be resumed as provided in the armistice treaty. The clearing away of mines for this purpose must begin at once. The barred zone in the Arctic shall remain in existence until the conclusion of a general peace. (7) The German-Russian Commercial Treaty of 1904 shall again come into force as in Article 7, Section 2*a*, of the Peace Treaty with the Ukraine, with the excision of special preferences for Asiatic countries provided in Article 11, Section 3, Sub-section 3, of the Commercial Treaty. In addition the whole of the first part of the final protocol is to be restored. To the above are added the guaranteeing of freedom of export and freedom from export duty for ores, speedy negotiations and conclusion of a new commercial treaty, the guaranteeing of the most-favored-nation treatment until the end of 1925 at the earliest, and also Section 3, Section 4*a*, Sub-section 1, and Section 5 of Article 7 of the peace treaty with the Ukraine. (8) Politico-legal affairs shall be regulated on the basis of the resolutions in the first version of the German-Russian Legal Convention in so far as those resolutions have not yet been adopted, e.g., in particular the indemnification of civil damages on the basis of the German proposals and the indemnification of expenditure for prisoners of war on the basis of the Russian proposal. Russia shall admit and support, according to her ability, German Commissions for the protection of German prisoners of war, civilians, and those returning home. (9) Russia shall undertake to cease all official or officially supported agitation or propaganda against the Four Allied Governments and their state and army institutions, also in the territories occupied by the Central Powers. (10) The foregoing conditions are to be accepted within forty-eight hours. The Russian plenipotentiaries must immediately proceed to Brest-Litovsk and there within three days sign the Peace Treaty, which must be ratified within a further two weeks." [*Loud applause from the Bourgeois Parties.*]

The Russian Delegation, which will include MM. Trotsky and Joffe, has already left Petrograd, but was involuntarily held up north of Pskov owing to the fact that a bridge there had been blown up. They will arrive at Brest-Litovsk in the course of tonight or tomorrow. The German, Austrian, and Hungarian Delegation is already assembled there, and the Turkish and Bulgarian Delegations will arrive there in the course of the day. [*Loud applause from the Bourgeois Parties. Hissing by Independent Social-Democrats.*]

287. DISCUSSION IN THE REICHSTAG OF THE PEACE TREATY
SIGNED IN BREST-LITOVSK ON MARCH 3, 1918,
MARCH 18, 1918

(a) ALTERATION OF THE ORDER OF THE DAY[6]

Vice-President Dr. Paasche: There seems to be no opposition to this; I may take it, therefore, that the House agrees to the alteration of the order of the day. We now begin with the third item of the order of the day.

First discussion: (a) of the Peace Treaty signed in Brest-Litovsk on March 3, 1918, between Germany, Austria-Hungary, Bulgaria, and Turkey on the one hand, and Russia on the other, together with the enclosure regarding Germany; (b) of the additional German-Russian clause to the Peace Treaty signed at Brest-Litovsk on the same day. (No. 1395 of the printed matter.)

Member Fehrenbach will speak regarding the standing orders.

Member Fehrenbach: Mr. President, I beg to ask to have the fourth item of the order of the day brought on at the same time; I think it would be to good purpose.

Vice-President Dr. Paasche: I, too, think that this combination will be best. There is no opposition; we therefore shall combine discussion of the fourth item of the order of the day with that of the third item.

First discussion: (a) of the Peace Treaty between Germany and Finland signed in Berlin on March 7, 1918; (b) of the commercial and navigation agreement between Germany and Finland signed in Berlin on the same date; (c) of the supplementary protocol of March 7, 1918, to the agreements mentioned above; (d) interchange of views of March 7, 1918, with the plenipotentiaries of the Finnish Government. (No. 1396 of the printed matter.)

I herewith open the first discussion. The Imperial Chancellor will speak. Dr. Count von Hertling, Imperial Chancellor.

287. (b) STATEMENT OF CHANCELLOR VON HERTLING IN
THE REICHSTAG ON THE RUSSIAN PEACE[7]

Gentlemen, when I spoke for the first time on this spot, on November 29 of last year, I was able to announce to the Reichstag that the Russian Government had sent a proposal to all the belligerent powers for entering into negotiations regarding an armistice and a general

[6] *Verhandlungen des Reichstags,* No. 142, March 18, 1918.
[7] *Ibid.,* pp. 4425–26.

peace. We, together with our allies, accepted the proposal, and sent delegates to Brest-Litovsk as soon as possible. Those powers which up to that time were Russia's allies kept away.

The course of the negotiations is known to you, gentlemen. You remember the endless speeches, which were intended not so much for the delegates who were gathered there as for the widest publicity, and which pushed further and further off the proper aim of our endeavor, an understanding, and the repeated interruptions, the discontinuance and the resumption of the negotiations. A point had been reached where a clear alternative had to be formulated. On March 3 the conclusion of peace took place at Brest-Litovsk, and on March 16 it was ratified by the competent assembly in Moscow. [*Applause.*]

It is not my intention to dilate on the judgment passed on the peace with Russia by enemy powers. When hypocrisy has become second nature [*"Quite right!"*] and untruthfulness has grown to brutality [*lively assent*], when at the very moment that an oppressive hand is about to be laid on a neutral country, they dare to speak of pursuing an entirely unselfish policy, every attempt at calm discussion and every objective consideration is bound to fail. [*Lively applause.*] If a telegram from Washington thought fit to express to the Congress assembled at Moscow the sympathy of the United States at the moment, as it declares, "when the German power has thrust in to interrupt and frustrate the whole struggle for freedom" [*Haase: "Of course! Finland!" Cries from the Majority: "Quiet! Is he a German?"*], then I put that calmly aside with the rest. [*Chairman calls for order.*] We have not for a moment contemplated, and do not contemplate, opposing the justified wishes and endeavors of Russia liberated from Tsarism. As I said on November 29 we desire for that sorely tried land a speedy return of peaceful and orderly conditions, and we deeply deplore that this still seems remote and that terrible conditions have made their appearance in many places.

I now turn to the treaty itself. As you will immediately perceive, it contains no conditions whatever dishonoring to Russia, no mention of oppressive war indemnities, and no forcible appropriation of Russian territory. [*Shouts from the Independent Socialists.*] That a number of the border states have severed their connection with the Russian state is in accordance with their own will which was recognized by Russia. In regard to these states we adopt the view formerly expressed by me that under the mighty protection of the German Empire they can give themselves a political form (*Staatliche Gestaltung*) corresponding to their situation and the tendency of their *Kultur,* while, of course, at the same time safeguarding our interests.

In Courland this development has gone the farthest. As you know, a few days ago a deputation sent by the Courland Landesrat, the body which is recognized as competent, came and announced the severance of the country from its previously existing political connections, and expressed the desire for a close economic, military, and political connection with Germany. In the reply with which the Kaiser charged me as the lawful representative of the Empire, I recognized the autonomy of Courland and both thankfully and joyfully took cognizance of its desire to lean on the German Empire, which desire, in fact, corresponds to the old cultural relations, which go back for centuries; but I reserved a final decision on the political form until the conditions there have been further consolidated and until the constitutionally competent factors on all sides have decided upon their future attitude in this connection.

As regards Lithuania, a resolution providing for a close attachment (*Anschluss*) to the German Empire by an economic and military connection was arrived at last year. During the next few days I expect a deputation from the National Council there which will announce anew this decision, after which similar recognition of Lithuania as an independent (*unabhängig*) state organism will follow. We calmly await its further political development.

In Livonia and Esthonia, however, things are somewhat different. Both of these provinces lie east of the frontier line agreed upon in the peace treaty. They are, however, as Article 6 of the peace treaty with Russia says, to be occupied by a German policing force until security is guaranteed by their own institutions and until their public order is restored. The moment for a new political orientation will then have come for these countries also. We hope and desire that they, too, will then place themselves in close and friendly relationship with the German Empire, but in such a way that this will not exclude peaceable and friendly relations with Russia.

Now a few words about Poland, which, it is true, is not expressly mentioned in the peace treaty. As is already well known, it was the proclamation of the two Emperors of November 5, 1916, which announced to all the world this country's independence. It follows, therefore, that the further shaping of this new state can take place only on the basis of joint negotiations between Germany and Austria-Hungary on the one hand and Poland on the other. Suggestions for the shaping of our future relationship have recently reached the Government and the members of the Reichstag from political circles in Poland. We shall now gladly examine whether, and to what extent, these proposals are reconcilable with the aims pursued by the two Governments, which are directed toward living permanently in good and neighborly relations with the newly-arisen state whilst at the same time safeguarding our own interests. Further information will be given by Herr von dem Bussche.

I conclude. When, as I do not doubt, you sanction the treaties now laid before you, and when shortly peace with Rumania is also concluded, then what I ventured to predict on February 24 as an impending event will have become an established fact. Then peace will have been restored on the entire Eastern front [*"Bravo!"*] ; but let us indulge in no delusions. World peace is not yet an accomplished fact. In the Entente States not the slightest inclination to terminate the terrible business of war is yet perceptible. Their aim seems still to be to fight on until we are destroyed. We shall not, however, lose courage. [*Loud cheers.*] We are prepared for every contingency, and we are ready to make further heavy sacrifices. [*Renewed loud cheers.*] God, who has been with us until now, will continue to grant us His help. We have confidence in our just cause, in our incomparable army, and also in its heroic leaders and troops. We have confidence also in our steadfast nation. The responsibility, however, for further bloodshed will fall, as I said on February 24, on the heads of all those who desire the continuance of that bloodshed. [*Lively applause from Right, Center, and Left. Shouts from Independent Socialists. Renewed "Bravos!"*]

287. (c) VON DEM BUSSCHE'S STATEMENT IN THE REICHS-TAG ON THE RUSSIAN PEACE[8]

Gentlemen, the allied Governments had recently the honor to submit to you the first peace treaty in this heaviest of all wars, namely the Ukraine Peace Treaty. These Governments submit to you now two further peace treaties with the Russian and the Finnish Governments. These treaties, as the Chancellor already remarked, make an end to the state of war on the Russian front, and when, as we may safely assume, peace will be concluded in the next few days with Rumania, then we shall soon have returned to peace, in principle, on the entire Eastern front. We owe this relief in the military and economic war situation primarily to the incomparable heroism of our troops and to the troops of our allies, as also to the brilliant leadership of our great generals. [*"Bravo!" and "Quite right!"*]

The reason why, after the conclusion of the second phase of the Trotsky period, we adopted a sharper tone and acted with more firmness in order to attain the desired result of peace cannot have been unknown to you. It soon became evident that Trotsky did not desire the conclusion of peace. He primarily desired to instigate our country to

[8] *Verhandlungen des Reichstags,* No. 142, March 18, 1918, pp. 4426–27.

rebellion and he firmly counted on a revolution in Germany and Austria-Hungary to help him to veil the fact of the Russian defeat. He gave clear expression to his disappointment in this connection.

Trotsky never really negotiated at all. That he had no intention of bringing things to a conclusion we did not simply infer from his speeches and his behavior; we had other quite certain information to that effect. No choice was, therefore, left to us but to draw military conclusions from the breaking off of the negotiations by Trotsky and, when the desired effect immediately followed, to put our demands into a form which left no room for further protraction of the negotiations. It cannot therefore be wondered at that, in consequence of such an equivocal attitude on the part of our opponents, our demands should more than ever before aim at securing safeguards for our future and be raised in consequence.

The negotiators, who, this time without M. Trotsky, again arrived at Brest-Litovsk, realized the justice of our action in raising our demands. Our negotiators gained the impression that the Russians expected far more severe demands after they had, by their conduct, forced us to a fresh appeal to arms and to further considerable expenditure. If during the negotiations between March 1 and March 3 the Russians protested against our action and also made a further protest at their conclusion, declaring that they had been forced to accept our demands without sufficient time for the negotiations, that was assuredly done more to save their own faces than from any real conviction. Without doubt they pursued the tactics decided upon in Petrograd before their arrival in order to brand us with the annexationist and militarist stamp and to represent themselves as the champions of peaceful ideas. I must again expressly state that their protest was entirely unfounded. In substance it was a question of our old demands which had been thoroughly discussed since December during long weeks of negotiations. All that was new, after our ultimatum, was the demand regarding Kars, Ardahan, and Batum.

In the plenary session of March 1, Herr von Rosenberg not only submitted to the Russian Delegation a draft of the political agreement and discussed it article upon article but also gave them a Russian translation. Excellency v. Korner, too, explained on the same day the draft for an agreement upon economic relations, and made it clear to them that the demands were held entirely within the scope of the previous negotiations and the ultimatum. He, too, submitted a Russian translation. This was also done by Excellency v. Kriege with regard to the legal question. In submitting to the Russian Delegation the Russian text of the German-Russian supplementary treaty, he stated to them that this draft is based in all essential points upon the results of the pre-

vious negotiations of the Russian-German Legal Commission. All this
shows that the Russian Delegation was well acquainted with the material
of the Treaty. Thus in the discussion on March 2 and 3 they repeatedly
pointed out inexactitudes in the translations supplied by us and otherwise also showed a thorough knowledge of the Peace Treaty. [*"Hear,
hear!"—Right.*] The Russian Delegation's assertion that it had no
time for adequate study of the peace terms is, therefore, quite untenable.
The Russians had no intention of thoroughly examining the draft treaty,
because at the sitting of March 1 the Russian First Delegate, Sokolnikov, without giving any reason, rejected the proposal to form special
commissions for legal and economic matters. Besides, the Russians had
brought no experts with them, as Sokolnikov himself admitted. As
regards details, of both the main political treaty and the economic and
legal supplementary treaties, I may refer you to the memorandum which
is now in your hands, and I may add that in all essentials it agrees with
the provisions of the Ukraine Treaty, except for a few points which
have been changed in our favor.

We had to conclude a separate peace treaty with Finland afterwards,
in consequence of the recognition by the Russian People's Republic that
Finland had left the existing Russian State and that Russia was therefore unable to conclude a peace with us on behalf of Finland. There is
no doubt that Finland was entirely averse to the war forced upon us by
Russia and our other opponents, but as part of the Russian State it
found itself actually in a state of war with us. The negotiations with
Finland took place in Berlin, and were marked by a spirit of conciliation. In this case, too, our interests had been preserved in a thoroughly
advantageous manner by our negotiators, and a series of improvements
was introduced as compared with the former state of affairs.
[*"Bravo!"*]

287. (d) DAVID'S SPEECH[9]

We agree to the motions to refer both the treaties to the Committee.
Otherwise our feelings toward the *Russian treaty* are very mixed.
[*"Quite right!"—S.D.*] We, too, rejoice that all along the Eastern
front fighting has come to an end. . . . . Still, we regret that the *peace
of Brest-Litovsk* is not the result of a process of mutual agreement, but
is obviously imposed *by force.* [*"Very true!"—S.D.*] At Brest-Litovsk
not only the Bolsheviks but also our own diplomatists have given in to
the representatives of armed force. [*"Very true!"—S.D.*] It is not
because the Empire of the Tsars has gone to pieces that we are so
critical of this treaty. When the Revolution broke out we did not im-

[9] *Verhandlungen des Reichstags,* No. 142, March 18, 1918, pp. 4431–40.

agine it to be our mission to preserve the unity of the Russian Empire, built up in centuries by an aggressive policy of the worst kind. [*"Very true!"—S.D.*] . . . . It was enough to remove the oppressive weight of the Tsar's Government for the national movement to come to the surface. This was one opportunity for a change in those districts inhabited by other races, for the people that so desired could make itself free; . . . . another was the intention of the Bolsheviks to permit self-determination to other races—even to the extent of separation from the Empire. Our diplomatists should have achieved this by an agreement; but they failed because they did not understand the Bolshevik motives. . . . . The need for peace was strongly felt throughout Russia.

The Bolsheviks could put up with the loss of the stranger populations of the marches, but not at the hand of Prussian military power, nor in a way that violated democratic principles. . . . . This road was barred by the declaration of the German Delegation on December 27 that self-determination of the marches in the sense of separation from Russia must be accepted as an accomplished fact. The victor's sword, thrown into the scale by General Hoffmann, increased the difficulty.

When Germany has once accepted *"self-determination"* she must also risk its dangers. . . . . But we were not strong enough for that. That is why this treaty has not evoked the expected enthusiasm but, on the contrary, a great uneasiness. . . . . [*"Very true!"—S.D.*] Faith in German political honor is shaken; the name Brest-Litovsk is being used to smother any desire for peace in France and England. . . . . Enemies of the Bolsheviks taunt them with treason toward Russia, and the party of the Bolsheviks has divided. . . . . No future Russian Government will accept this peace with sincerity. Lenin has stated that this peace is not final, was forced upon them, and is only provisional. . . . . There is no security that this peace will last. The war is finished, but not the hostility. The Entente is already engaged in repairing the Eastern break in the ring. We have made our chief task—the break-up of the hostile coalition—not easier, but harder.

. . . . We have even helped the formation of a new coalition. *England's object in the war*—to unite her African colonial empire with India—is made easier by this treaty. . . . . Mitteleuropa is an inland state and, as regards world economics, a small inland state in comparison with the world-wide empires of England, America, and East Asia. . . . . We can rob the Brest-Litovsk treaty of some of its dangers if we follow it up by giving the right of self-determination to the marches [*"Quite right!"—S.D.*] and allow as many of the inhabitants as possible to share in the settlement of their domestic constitution. Thus we should snatch a very forcible argument away from a hostile Great-Russian Government. Afterwards Russia could, in that case, accommodate itself to circumstances, without prejudice to its honor. . . . . The arrangement of the affairs of the marches is, then, the touchstone of German honor. In November the Chancellor himself said, "You cannot push nations to and fro against their will, as if they were pieces in a game." . . . .

Unfortunately it looks as if our actions in the East were not in agreement with these repeated declarations of the Chancellor. [*"Very true!"—S.D.*] We must have security that the actions of the Government fit its words; as yet, that does not seem to be the case. [*"Very true!"—S.D.*] There is a hostile party in Germany whose aims are opposed to those of the Government. [*"Quite right!"—S.D.*] It commands an influential press, the Pan-German, Conservative, Annexationist papers. It desires expansion in the East, not as security for our frontiers but as annexations. It will not hear a word about a popular franchise in the marches. It fears that such a franchise might affect Prussia. . . . . Among its agents are also many officials of the military government in the Baltic lands. . . . . This divergence of views must not be forgotten. We are convinced the civil government is sincere in what it says; but has it the power to carry out its plans? . . . . Through Poland, Lithuania, and Courland the policy of the military is at cross-purposes with that of the Government. The whole wretched tale of our Polish policy from the date of the Kaiser's proclamation is explained by this divergence of opinion. Now it seems that the difficulty about Cholm has been smoothed over in Vienna. But the military party aim at a great annexation on the Polish west frontier on the plea of securing our boundary. But military security that produces enduring enmity in a neighbor is a mockery of military security. [*"Very true!"—S.D.*] . . . .

In Lithuania, also, the exertions of the military party have aroused great distrust and counter movements which we regret. . . . . The Lithuanians desired that a Diet should be convened by a general, equal, and direct vóte. To achieve their own ends the military party actually stopped communications between the Chancellor and the Lithuanians. A letter from the President of the Lithuanian Landesrat that had to pass the military government of the Baltic lands has up to today not reached the Chancellor. [*"Hear, hear!"—S.D.*] Thus the Chancellor's letters are held up by the superior military commandant who does not approve his policy. . . . . They wish to make Lithuania an east-Elbe colony, which is to renounce popular government. Because the Lithuanians refused, the military party has, so far, prevented the recognition of their independence. . . . . That contradicts the promises made to the border peoples at Brest-Litovsk. [*"Quite true!"*] Can anyone believe that Lithuania can exist as an "east-Elbe" military colony beside the republic of the Ukraine? The Lithuanians are threatened with the division of their country. Who knows whether the military party will hold up the Lithuanian deputation that the Chancellor expects, as they did the above letter! There was formerly a permanent representative of the Lithuanian Landesrat in Berlin, but later the army withdrew his passport. . . . .

I deny that the Courland Landesrat is competent to speak in the name of the inhabitants. It relies on privileges granted by the Tsars. . . . . Now it has no legal standing, for in times of revolution the will of the people is the law. [*"Quite right!"—S.D.*] We recognized that in the case of the Ukraine and Russia. . . . . The decree of the Courland Landtag is no more than a deal made by the Prussian Junkers and the Baltic nobles and agreed to by part of the German-Lettish middle classes. . . . . We welcome the Chancellor's statement that this decision is not final, in opposition to the military party, who regard the decree as final and not to be revoked by a more democratic Landtag. . . . . Even under Russian rule Letts and Esthonians fought for independence. . . . . If their hopes are once again disappointed, they will cherish bitter hatred against their new lords and will find support in Great Russia's hostility to us. You must avoid such a policy if you really desire the safety and progress of the German elements in the Baltic lands. Artisans, small manufacturers, and peasants are not represented at all in the Lettish Landtag. . . . . Formerly the Baltic nobles were hand and glove with the worst reactionaries in Russia. The Russian armies that devastated East Prussia were led by Baltic nobles like Rennenkamp. . . . .

Significant was the remark of the Chancellor: "Our relations with Esthonia and Livonia must be so arranged as not to preclude friendship with Russia." That is the ground from which we take off. . . . . Further, the Chancellor refused to interfere in Finland's internal affairs. Here, too, is a glaring contradiction between the words of the civil government and the acts of the military. [*"Quite right!"—S.D.*] . . . . When the press says we must hurry to help the Finns against the Russians it is trying to lead the public astray. It is to be regretted that the Censor forbids the publication of the truth. The Red Guards in Finland are not Russians but Finns. [*"Hear, hear!"—S.D.*] These Finnish Red Guards are the force at the disposal of the Red Government. . . . . It is civil war in Finland, in which both parties claim to be the lawful authority. We hear stories of Red Guard atrocities in Finland, and it is true that the Red Government is doing its best to destroy some robber bands. There are daily in Berlin 300 cases of theft and assault [*"Hear, hear!"—S.D.*]; in the whole country there must be many thousands. What should we say if a foreign Power for this cause arrogated the right to invade us? . . . . [*"Very true!"—S.D.*] The same forces support the Red Government in Finland as support the Ukraine Government which we call our friend. What fierce hatred will be begotten in the working classes if their movement is crushed by German troops! According to the Norwegian press, Germany's object is to establish a monarchy under a German prince. This is denied. But the denial meets little credence; and our purposes with regard to Courland only strengthen the rumor. All along the Eastern front German policy has destroyed the sympathy of the masses for Germany. . . . . This policy is a declaration of war against all popular forces, against those sections of the marches that desire independence. Should the shortsighted brute force of the military party carry the day against the declarations of the Chancellor, the inevitable result would be that the whole district from the Baltic would become a smoldering furnace where all would resist German influence. We refuse to be brought up against such a situation. . . . . It is now clear that the Pan-Slav movement had no root in the people. This policy of brute force would beget a new Pan-Slav movement—with support in Austria—the object of which would be the destruction of the German policy of domination known abroad as Pan-Germanism and at home as Pan-German force policy. By so doing we should authorize the Entente to put themselves at the head of the opposition to such a policy of force. Therefore, the Reichstag and the Government must make head against an irresponsible party which, apparently, is determined to become supreme in the Empire. . . . . Brute force does not win hearts.

Only a freedom-loving policy can bring order in the East; only an agreement on popular lines can lay the foundation of order in the East. In this way a stronger peace will be secured; a peace resting on the power of the sword is the weakest peace known. Germany cannot solve the problems presented in its general policy by the methods and ways of the old Prussian ruling caste. Peace at home, peace abroad can be won only through right and freedom. [*Applause from the S.D.*]

287. (*e*) STRESEMANN'S SPEECH[10]

Gentlemen, yesterday Dr. David criticized the treaty with Russia very sharply as one won by superior force. . . . . The German people, he said, is very uneasy over it and fears that Russia's weakness will only help England by giving free play to its expansion in Asia. . . . .

At once Dr. Naumann showed that this was not so, that Russia's decay was already complete. Dr. David contradicts his own party, which admits that Russia was ruined not by the German arms but because it was impotent even before the war. . . . . What elements are there in Russia today with whom we can make an alliance? Lenin, Trot-

[10] *Verhandlungen des Reichstags,* No. 143, March 19, 1918, pp. 4453–62.

sky and Company are working for a union of nations on the basis of a mutual understanding of the working classes throughout the world. . . . . Is it a restored Tsar? It is possible that the monarchical idea will come to the top again, ... but for the last twenty-five years and more the grand dukes have been the chief fomenters of hatred toward Germany. [*"Quite right!"—S.D.*] . . . . The Cadets or Octobrists? But when the Russian commercial treaties were being renewed this very section of the Russian middle classes fanned passion against Germany and demanded the closing of Russia against us. . . . . We have never exploited the difficulties of other nations for our own political ends. [*"Quite right!"—N.L.*] What thanks had we for our restraint toward Russia during her war with Japan? An alliance with our enemies; the assault of 1914. . . . . The cause of Anglo-German friendship was pushed with warm-hearted eloquence. . . . . Italy absorbed Tripoli and France Morocco, yet we put forward no claims. . . . . Then followed the agreements between England and Russia—the division of Persia and China into spheres of interest—while we, who most covet expansion, yet stopped always in the shade, stood aside. Yet the consequence was the World War. Peace is not to be had by resigning all idea of expansion. We have respected the rights of neutrals, but we have won no friends. . . . . We laid the foundation of Italian unity, but Italy has surrendered Savoy and Nice to France and fights against us. [*"Quite right!"—N.L.*] . . . . Austrian neutrality in 1870 was not the result of the peace of Nikolsburg, but of our speedy victory in the early days of the war. [*Lively applause from Right and N.L.*] . . . . The re-establishment of the Empire with a population of 170 millions is in the cards, but as yet it is only a hope that may prove fallacious. Therefore a great responsibility rests on those who would favor the Tsar as the partner on whom we should rely in the East. . . . .

Another argument against the treaty is the future economic war. . . . . That must come, and United States capital will be used in it. It will hasten the coming of Chamberlain's Greater England; and France will take an enthusiastic part. . . . . I do not believe in an organized boycott of German goods; witness the preliminary treaties. . . . . The United States will not reject our trade, especially our potash. . . . . For its own sake Italy can take no part in such a war, and other states are too small. We must not be influenced by England's policy, which, now that her hope of victory is gone, is putting forward the economic war to frighten us into concessions in her favor. There is no need for fear. In the midst of war our exports might have been valued by thousands of millions had we so desired. We received offers of this kind from Americans and others. During our negotiations in the East we see how every nation desires German goods first.

I cannot approve Dr. David's criticism of the Brest-Litovsk treaty; we were on the horns of a dilemma. . . . . And I do not blame General Hoffmann for reminding the Russians that we were the victors. . . . . Herr Groeber has on this occasion raised no objections to General Hoffmann's signing the treaty; he was, in fact, the plenipotentiary. . . . . His remarks about Courland provoked me seriously. He spoke of an agreement between Prussian and Baltic Junkers. You cannot dismiss a great historical event by a catchword. [*"Quite right!"—Right and N.L.*] Deputies of the Social-Democrats have lately been bargaining with Baron Ronikier and Prince Radziwill, not as peers but as representatives of the Poles; in this case they took no exception to the fact that a Prince and a Count represented Poland. [*"Quite right!"—Right and N.L.*] . . . . We are not dealing with the Baltic barons alone, for the middle class is German in sentiment. . . . . Had the Baltic Germans wished to be absorbed in Russia, this would have happened long ago, as it has so often happened in America. . . . . It is not correct that this treaty has settled the affairs of Courland while another arrangement is in store for Esthonia and Livonia. . . . . Riga, the capital of Livonia, and the Esthonian islands lie inside the sphere of German interests. After the various deliverances of the Baltic peoples, a vote taken on a more popular basis is not—in my opinion—necessary. . . . . These peoples, through no fault of their own, as a whole are not ready for parliamentary institutions. . . . . So existing institutions—with the assistance of Letts and Esthonians—must be allowed to represent the country. . . . .

I view with apprehension the proposal to separate Courland, with Riga, from the rest of Livonia and Esthonia. . . . . Here the right of self-determination does not apply, for the Letts are the fiercest opponents of such a division. If it is intended that Riga and Courland should go with Germany while Livonia and Esthonia go with Russia, then, among other losses to Germany and the Baltic provinces, would be the loss by Riga of much of its importance; . . . . for Russian trade would be deflected to Reval. Livonians and Esthonians, as well as Germans, hold that the Baltic lands are one. May the Government not forget this! . . . .

We agree that Lithuania is to have its own government as soon as it is ready for it. . . . . The difficulty is that the influential people are the Polish landlords, and, in the towns, Poles and Jews, while educated Lithuanians are in the minority and in many cases live abroad. . . . . By an independent Lithuania we mean, of course, close connection with Germany under a military convention, customs union, and one system of money and communications, as the deputies desired. Full autonomy of such little nations belongs to Utopia. Normal development drives them into union with a bigger neighbor. . . . . I do not believe in Wilson's universal league of nations; I believe that, after the conclusion of peace, it will burst like a soap bubble. . . . . I have no objection to make to Lithuania's wish for a Catholic prince; in a Catholic land, Catholic officials also are desirable. One result of the war will be a better feeling between the two Churches in our own country. [*Applause by Center and N.L.*] . . . . There seems to me little hope of a good understanding with the Poles. They do not see that they are the aggressors, not we. [*"Quite true!"*] . . . . It cannot be treated as a question of Poland only recognizing the *status quo* as regards Germany if Germany recognizes the *status quo* of Poland. I must protest against the suggestion—due to enemy politicians—that an international conference may be held to discuss Poland and Alsace-Lorraine. . . . . We cannot discuss whether Posen and West Prussia should belong to Germany. . . . . We do not wish to annex parts of Poland; but if our High Command tells us that we must improve our frontier by removing it farther east to prevent future invasions, no one will take on himself the responsibility of opposing such a need. [*Applause from the N.L.*]

In Finland our military action has not been an intrusion into party politics. Scandinavian Social-Democrats have proved that crowds of Bolsheviks were sent to massacre and pillage, just as in the Ukraine. . . . . If Sweden had sent help there would have been no need for Germany to come to the rescue. . . . . The economic importance of Finland is often underestimated; before the war we exported more goods to Finland than to Turkey. . . . . Unfortunately in the Russian treaty not sufficient attention was paid to our foreign interests. When the Russian Government has confiscated all bank deposits, even those of foreigners, we cannot fulfill its demands in Germany till we have sufficient security for our own demands. . . . . To waive all claim to an indemnity from Russia is not, in my opinion, to wear a halo of reconciliation. Rather it is a poor outlook for the German taxpayers if they alone must bear the crushing weight of this war. [*Lively applause.*] . . . . We owe the Eastern peace to our weapons alone. The solemn exhortation of the Chancellor to the Western Powers was summarily rejected. . . . . By the fault of our enemies two million Germans are dead and 150 billions of debt is piled up; where is the moral obligation to abide by the Reichstag's offer which they spurned? No! Our enemies must bear the full burden of the prolonged war: only in this way is there any prospect of shortening it. [*Applause of Conservatives and N.L.*] When the Chancellor said that our enemies must bear the responsibility of battles to come, I take it to mean they are responsible also for any change in our policy as to territorial questions and indemnities. . . . . The Dwina-Dnieper canal deserves the closest attention. It will shorten the journey from Odessa to Hamburg by 3,559 kilometers. . . . . The

Eastern peace is a great asset in our war balance. Had not the Entente politicians frivolously played with the destiny of their countries, they would have accepted the chance of peace held out to them by the Chancellor. Let them be warned by Russia. [*Lively applause by N.L.*]

287. (*f*) SCHEIDEMANN'S SPEECH[11]

The aim of Social-Democratic policy is to end the war by a true peace of peoples after the country has been successfully defended, a peace—based on understanding—which will exclude the use of armed force in the future. This aim has not been furthered by the treaty submitted. The Central Powers had promised to effect an understanding with Russia as to the right of self-determination of the border peoples. In contradiction to this, they had in advance required Russia to renounce Poland, Lithuania, and Courland. This policy of might (*Machtpolitik*) pursued in the East, did not take into account the interests of the German Empire, which demanded permanent peaceful relations and a close friendship between the German and the Russian peoples. We must demand that the true democratic right of *self-determination of the Poles, Lithuanians, and Courlanders* shall be secured, so that permanent friendly relations with them, as also with the Russian people, may be made possible for Germany.

We cannot express agreement with the way in which the treaty was accomplished, the Reichstag having been excluded, or with material parts of its contents.

But as the state of war has actually been ended in the East by this treaty, we do not propose to reject it. For these reasons we will *abstain from voting*.

We agree to the treaty with Finland.

287. (*g*) HAASE'S SPEECH[12]

. . . . We have nothing to take back from what we said at the first reading, and in the committee, with regard to the peace treaty. Herr David said that his friends regarded it with mixed feelings; my "Fraktion" has only one feeling, that of shame [*disturbance, and stormy interruptions on the Right*] that a peace of the sword should have been ruthlessly forced on our eastern neighbor. [*"Quite right!"—Independent Socialists.*] . . . . Things in the East have been arranged in accordance with the mad wishes of the annexationist politicians. Herr Erzberger is of the opinion that the peace treaty is in accordance with the Reichstag resolution. . . . . Herr Groeber tried to represent the same

[11] *Verhandlungen des Reichstags,* No. 145, March 22, 1918, p. 4536.
[12] *Ibid.,* pp. 4540–44.

thing today by chicanery. [*Vice-President Dr. Paasche: "You should not accuse a colleague of chicanery."*] What do Messrs. Scheidemann, Ebert, and David say to this interpretation of the resolution by their comrades of the "Fraktion"? . . . . But the gentlemen plant hope on the grave of hope. [*Lively shouts from all sides.*] One often heard formerly that Social Democracy was done for; but then it took an unexpected flight. Give us freedom of the press and freedom of assembly, and then you will see. [*Continuous cheering on the Left. Vice-President Dr. Paasche: "I beg you not to interrupt your own speakers." Laughter and "Quite right!"*]

The military party has once more gained an absolute victory, and it will also know how to profit by its victory in the future. [*"Quite right!"—Independent Socialists.*] The military had the upper hand in the negotiations, and they differed very widely from the principles of a democratic peace. . . . . This peace treaty has been very unfavorably received by the neutral press. . . . . This peace is only an armistice, during which great armaments will be collected, and will be followed by a fresh violent war. The Russian peoples are not liberated; they are only under fresh thralldom. . . . . One who knows Lithuania told me that everywhere in the country the peasants and workmen say, "If we were still under the Tsar now, we should kiss his policemen's feet." At the moment when the Courland barons trembled for their landed property they discovered their love for Germany [*laughter and shouts from the Right; "Quite right!"—Independent Socialists*] and sought friendship with those of their own class here. [*Repeated denials from Right.*] Esthonia and Livonia cannot be detached from Russian sovereignty without an understanding with Russia. . . . . Behind the scenes the idea is to separate these countries from Russia and attach them to Germany. The National-Liberal resolution does not show even a spark of democratic spirit. A few more persons were added to the representative body, and that is the "broad basis." The resolution is conceived in the same spirit as that of the peace treaty. . . . . The trade unions and trade associations are oppressed in Poland as never before; that is the "freedom" which has been brought to Poland. . . . . By violating the peace treaty Armenian territory is being attached to Turkey; . . . . if they had the free right of self-determination, the Armenians would resolve anything rather than association with Turkey. We are all sufficiently aware of how the Turks rage against the Armenians and stop at nothing in order to exterminate them. . . . . The peace treaty with Finland is a pure pretext, for we are not at war with Finland. [*"Very true!"—Independent Socialists.*] . . . . Our proposal to withdraw the German troops from Finland, where they are helping to put down the National Government and its troops, was rejected by the

Main Committee. This peace treaty could only have been intended to give a handle for our inroad into Finland. . . . . All those who sanction further war credits are responsible for this unprecedented misuse of them. . . . . Scheidemann's followers announced today that they will refrain from voting on the Russian treaty, but they represent us outside this House as traitors because we voted against the Ukrainian peace treaty. [*"Very true!"—Independent Socialists.*] . . . . Steps are being taken everywhere against supposed remarkable Bolshevist "marauding bands," while at the same time such important treaties are concluded with Bolshevist Governments. The movements of German troops are not directed against marauders but against the Russian Revolution. Who sows the wind must reap the whirlwind.

287. (h) GRÖBER'S SPEECH[13]

Gentlemen, ... There has been opposition to this treaty in several parts of this House on the ground that it is not a peace of understanding. . . . . The practical question is not whether it is a peace of understanding or not a peace of understanding but whether a peace treaty could have been obtained in any other way. [*"Quite right!"*] This I answer in the negative. [*"Quite right!"*] Therefore I say that in the name of my party we approve the treaty unanimously.

The Russian Delegation were obviously not in earnest in wishing to arrive at an understanding [*"Quite right!"*] ; they were trying to gain time in order to spread their Bolshevist propaganda. [*"Quite right!"*] Trotsky even refused to agree to the provision proposing that there should be peace and friendship in the future; while the German negotiators endeavored to further the negotiations with lamb-like patience [*"Quite right!"—Center and Right*] . . . . the Russians were making incendiary speeches, hoping to succeed in lighting a revolution in Germany and thus bringing all efforts at peace into contempt. At the same time the Russian Army had been rendered incapable of fighting. . . . . The Government cannot be blamed, under these circumstances, for having stated their peace conditions plainly rather than be drawn into further indefinitely prolonged negotiations. . . . . Peace negotiations after such a struggle are not a kind of academic discussion [*"Quite right!"*] but serious work [*lively applause*] ; and if the one party has not the moral courage to recognize its position and the consequences of it, the other must come to the rescue and show it exactly the lines on which it must act. [*Lively assent.*] That was done, and thus we obtained peace. If it is not a peace of understanding, the Bolsheviks are alone to blame. [*"Quite right!"*]

[13] *Verhandlungen des Reichstags,* No. 145, March 22, 1918, pp. 4636–39.

. . . . As regards the contents of the treaty, there is not a single provision that can be regarded as hard or unjust. There is not a single annexation in the whole treaty. All the fault that can be found is, perhaps, in the alienation of important, great, and productive portions of territory. But this did not come about through this treaty. The Ukraine was already separated from Russia. [*"Quite right!"*— *Center.*] Poland and the Baltic provinces were as good as separated, and only the recognition of this separation was affirmed in the treaty. The Bolshevist Government has always particularly demanded that these countries should have the right of self-determination; Germany frankly recognized that right and cannot be blamed if these countries separate themselves from Russia. They have a right to attach themselves to Germany if they wish; that does not concern Russia. [*"Very true!"*—*Center and N.L.*] . . . . The importance of the treaty lies in the immense effect the war has had in weakening the Russian Empire, not only through the loss of certain territories but through the colossal internal upheaval caused by the Revolution. This will prevent Russia's undertaking any war against the border countries and us for a generation to come. Nothing can be a better proof that the treaty is a good one than the enemy outcry over it. England has no right to complain that Germany oppresses other nations at a moment when she is laying her robber hand on Dutch shipping. [*"Very true!"*—*Center.*] . . . . The resolution regarding arbitration is not only a guaranty of peace, ... but an example as to how to deal with future peace treaties, and an event of great importance for the extension of international law. . . . . For our part we shall help to further the application of arbitration. . . . . My friends agree to the resolution regarding protection of workmen and social insurance. . . . . Above all we desire the earliest possible recognition of Lithuania's independence. . . . . We also desire a speedy settlement of the Polish question. We simply cannot understand why, from the day of the Imperial proclamation, November 5, 1916, until now, the matter has not been disposed of. It must be settled by agreement with Austria-Hungary. Every day of delay increases the distrust of those concerned, and the difficulty of the pacification so necessary in the interest both of the Poles and Germans. [*"Very true!"*— *Center.*] . . . . The Cholm question seems to be developing favorably. . . . . That will be advantageous for our domestic policy also. There must, once for all, be an end of the administration and legislation based on mistrust of the Poles which complains that the Poles have no confidence in us. . . . . The law with regard to expropriation has been a theoretical apple of discord, without having much practical importance, and should cease to exist as soon as possible. . . . . Exceptional legislation should be done away with altogether. Until this is done we cannot expect the Poles to act as loyal German subjects. . . . . When peace with Rumania is concluded, we shall have peace on the whole East front, and the hope of a lasting peace. When we remember the frightful danger that has been overcome by this, and which a large number of our people did not recognize, we can only shudder at the thought of the awful abyss with which we were confronted in the first year of the war. ["*Quite right!*"—*Center.*] We have every reason to ask in all humility where we should have been without the merciful help of God? [*Lively applause from Center.*] This help, which has been so palpably ours, will still be granted to us. May God give us the final victory, and therewith lasting peace to the benefit of our people and the whole human race. [*Lively applause from Center.*]

288. "K. R." ON "THE PEACE TREATIES IN THE REICHSTAG"[14]

. . . . Every peace treaty is the documentary evidence of a more or less protracted measurement of the strength of opposing forces. If it had been possible, or if there had been any wish to arrive at an understanding, there would not have been any war. When armies were given marching orders, it was precisely arms which should decide. They were not, indeed, to decide which side was right—this possibility had been given up as hopeless—but they, whichever side had the power, were to carry through their idea of right. What other intention could there be in a war but that the victorious party should accomplish that for the sake of which it came into the war? When a nation has fought for its freedom, it will not lay down its arms until it has shaken off its chains. If it has begun the war for the sake of conquests, it will not give up the object aimed at when it is victorious. If the destruction of the economic efficiency of the other nation was the object of the fight, it will insist upon that. Germany had none of these objects. The war was forced on her; she waged it with energy and success in order to keep her enemies at a distance.

The intention of a final peace could not, therefore, be for Germany the destruction of the enemy, but neither could it be to leave everything as before, so that the game might recommence at any time. As things were, the essence of any peace had to be that Germany should obtain the greatest possible security against repetition of wars of such a nature. Therefore, Germany's conclusions of peace had to be, and must be, acts of agreement, exactly as the enemy would have concluded and would conclude forcible peaces if they could realize their objects in a victorious peace. If the English were to seize the German Fleet, intending in this way to destroy German trade; if the French want to wrest

---

[14] *Norddeutsche Allgemeine Zeitung,* March 21, 1918, I, 1.

Alsace-Lorraine from German federation; if the Russians wanted to take their capital from the Turks, those would be conditions of a peace of force (*Gewaltfrieden*). But if we recognize the independence and right of self-determination of the Russian border peoples, and work to bring this new political structure into as good relations with us as to the old Russia; if we nip fresh wars on our borders in the bud, demand security against an economic war after the war, and include a commercial treaty, profitable to both sides, in the peace conditions, then that is certainly a peace of understanding.

In estimating the Russian peace it must not be forgotten that it is no peace in the true sense, such as has been known to history hitherto; that it does not signify the end of the war and the beginning of a state of peace, but that it is, on the one hand, only an instrument of peace, on the other, however, a weapon of war. The Brest peace treaty is, therefore, not only an end in itself, the ratification of a conclusion of peace, but also a means to the end. Those who realize how valuable the cessation of hostilities in the East is for Germany, attacked as she was on all sides, fought with the greatest bitterness, and threatened with economic, political, and military death, must rejoice over this success, regardless of whether or not the peace can be adapted to the theories of peace which are generally held. What we know of this particular peace, of its conditions, and the results it has already had, and will still have, shows that in accomplishing the first object, Russia's withdrawal from the ranks of our enemies, the other, the reconciliation with Russia, has not been lost sight of. Here time will throw light on the situation, and then we shall also have our reward in the East for the self-restraint we have imposed on ourselves in profiting by our victory.

K. R.

289. COMMERCIAL TREATY NEGOTIATIONS AT BREST-LITOVSK[15]

The Main Committee of the Reichstag concluded Monday a brief discussion of the question of the exchange of prisoners and then took up the economic questions. A Social-Democratic speaker, Deputy Ebert, regretted that the pertinent documents were not yet available and requested a report from the Government on the coming negotiations. The director in the Foreign Office, Johannes, replied that the requested memorandum was about to be distributed to the committee and then gave the following summary of the economic negotiations in Brest-Litovsk:

"The economic discussions could not, of course, owing to the cir-

[15] *Norddeutsche Allgemeine Zeitung,* January 8, 1918, I, 1.

cumstances, occupy any large space, as the first seven days were taken up primarily with the discussion of large political questions. Much time was also lost through the fact that the Russian delegates had to negotiate with the German and Austrian representatives and then with those of Bulgaria and of Turkey, and that while some Russians understood German very well and others French there were others who understood Russian only. The result was that Germans spoke only German, and Russians only Russian, and the remarks of both sides had to be interpreted. In unofficial discussions both German and French were used, also Russian. There was the further circumstance that the Russian economic representatives, although exceptionally able and well-informed men, possessed (as they themselves say) little experience in the sphere of practical administration, and therefore had to proceed very cautiously. Economic questions were accordingly not thoroughly discussed; it was in fact quite impossible to discuss them thoroughly. Only provisional arrangements were made, which are not even exhaustive and which can be supplemented at any time. German efforts were directed, in the first instance, to securing the unequivocal admission that the economic war between the two countries must be ended and that there could be no question in the future as to the realization between Germany and Russia of the ideas of the Paris Conference. Complete agreement in this respect was very speedily reached. . . . .

"The second point was the question in respect to the renewal of the Commercial Treaty. The German representatives were naturally exceptionally eager to obtain from Russia a binding assurance of the renewal. We have, unfortunately, up to now achieved no success. It has already been pointed out that on the Russian side there is a deeply-rooted prejudice against the Commercial Treaty of 1894 and 1904. This prejudice is founded on the Russian belief that the treaty was forced upon Russia. In 1894 we obtained the treaty after waging a customs war with Russia and after making Russia conscious that the German market was indispensable for Russia. In 1904, on the lapse of the first period of the treaty, we succeeded in carrying through its renewal on conditions tolerable for us. But it is maintained by the Russians that this renewal was made possible only under the pressure of the defeats which Russia had suffered in the war with Japan and of the internal confusion which was then already observable.

"In Germany we take the view that Russia made no bad bargain in agreeing to this Commercial Treaty. But it is difficult to convince the Russian gentlemen of this. They refer *inter alia* to Russian statistics, according to which the trade of Russia with Germany shows an unfavorable balance. According to our statistics, the opposite is the case;

and after an exact examination of the circumstances one must be convinced that our figures are the only correct ones.

"The Russian statistics do not take into account that in the transit trade to Russia through Germany there pass exceptionally large quantities of raw materials (such as cotton, etc.), which are entered in the Russian accounts as German imports. On the other hand, the Russian statistics take no account of the large quantities of corn which we draw from South Russia and which we obtain through Belgian and Dutch ports. These exports are credited not to Germany but to Belgium and Holland. We used all these arguments and we shall continue to use them. But up to the present we have failed to persuade the Russian representatives to agree even to a short-term extension of the Commercial Treaty. The obvious prejudice and distaste for the Commercial Treaty was also very marked as far as the representatives of the present government were concerned.

"There is another point. These representatives also declared that they have in view the complete transformation of the economic conditions in Russia, and that therefore they cannot tie their hands by a commercial treaty. Their statement means that they are not desirous that a foreign government should intervene in this new ordering of conditions on the strength of a commercial treaty.

"It is well known, of course, to members of the House that the Kerensky Government also adopted an attitude antagonistic to commercial treaties, and that the then Russian Government cancelled last October their treaties even with their allies. This is a difficult situation, which must be taken into account.

"The German delegates will do their best; it remains to be seen how far they will succeed. In any case the Russian delegates declared their readiness to enter forthwith into negotiations concerning a Russian commercial treaty, which would have to take into account the new and altered conditions.

"The most-favored-nation question was then discussed. We argued that surely it was out of the question in peace-time for one state to treat another worse than it does a third state. The Russian delegates readily gave their adherence to this principle. But even in this connection certain difficulties had to be discussed. The principle of general most-favored-nation treatment cannot be realized in so absolute a way. In every treaty certain exceptions are reserved: for example, exceptions for minor frontier trade and for adherence to Customs Unions. Such has always been the case. Thus Russia in the 1894 Treaty reserved certain advantages for the Asiatic frontier countries, for Persia, Afghanistan, Mongolia, etc. It must be a subject for discussion as to how far these advantages will be maintained in the future.

"There is, then, the great question: what is to be the position as regards those areas that separate themselves from the Russian Empire, some of which will become independent, and some of which will remain in more or less close union with the whole body of the Russian Empire? I refer to Finland, the Caucasus, the Ukraine, etc.

"On the other hand, a new factor has also arisen on the German side. We suggested that there must remain reserved the special regulation of our relations to Austria and to other countries which would form a Customs Union with us. This matter also has not been completely explored. But on the whole the Russian delegates agreed to recognize special relations between Germany and Austria-Hungary.

"As regards the period of duration of the most-favored-nation principle, no definite understanding was reached. A period of twenty years was spoken of as a 'considerable' period, but the Russians declared that it was rather too long and that they must consider the matter further. On the German side, the deliberations on this point are not yet terminated. It will be readily understood that Germans also regard twenty years as too long and perhaps consider a shorter term as suitable.

"These are the main points which were discussed at Brest-Litovsk."

The discussion was then declared confidential.

290. THE APPROVAL OF THE RUSSIAN PEACE
BY THE REICHSTAG[16]

The resolution proposed by the Poles was also referred back to the Main Committee on the motion of Dr. Müller-Meiningen.

The remainder of the Russian treaty was adopted without discussion.

The peace treaty with Finland was likewise sanctioned without debate on the second reading, also the trade and shipping agreement with Finland and the appendices. The resolutions not referred back to the Main Committee were adopted.

The petitions reported on by Prince Schoenaich-Carolath will be dealt with according to the proposals of the Main Committee.

On the third reading, which followed immediately, both treaties were finally passed, the Independent Socialists voting against, while the Majority Socialists abstained from voting.

[16] *Verhandlungen des Reichstags,* No. 145, March 22, 1918, pp. 4567-71.

291. THE TREATY OF PEACE BETWEEN GERMANY, AUSTRIA-HUNGARY, BULGARIA, AND TURKEY ON THE ONE PART AND RUSSIA ON THE OTHER PART[17]

Germany, Austria-Hungary, Bulgaria, and Turkey for the one part and Russia for the other part, being in accord to terminate the state of war, and to enter into peace negotiations as speedily as possible, have appointed as plenipotentiaries:

On the part of the Imperial German Government: The Secretary of State for Foreign Affairs, the Actual Imperial Privy Councillor, Herr Richard von Kühlmann; The Imperial Envoy and Minister Plenipotentiary, Dr. von Rosenberg; Royal Prussian Major-General Hoffmann, Chief of the General Staff of the Commander-in-Chief of the East; Naval Captain Horn.

On the part of the Imperial and Royal Joint Austro-Hungarian Government: The Minister of the Imperial and Royal House and for Foreign Affairs, the Privy Councillor of His Imperial and Royal Apostolic Majesty, Ottokar Count Czernin von und zu Chudenitz; The Envoy Extraordinary and Plenipotentiary of His Imperial and Royal Apostolic Majesty, the Privy Councillor, Kajetan Merey von Kapos-Mere; General of Infantry, His Imperial and Royal Apostolic Majesty's Privy Councillor, Maximilian Csicserics von Bacsany.

On the part of the Royal Bulgarian Government: The Royal Envoy Extraordinary and Minister Plenipotentiary in Vienna, Andrea Toscheff; Colonel Peter Gantschew of the General Staff, Royal Bulgarian Military Envoy Plenipotentiary to His Majesty the German Emperor and Aide-de-Camp of His Majesty the King of the Bulgarians; The Royal Bulgarian First Legation Secretary, Dr. Theodore Anastassoff.

On the part of the Imperial Ottoman Government: His Highness Ibrahim Hakki Pasha, former Grand-Vizier, Member of the Ottoman Senate, Envoy Plenipotentiary of His Majesty the Sultan to Berlin; His Excellency, Zeki Pasha, General of Cavalry, Adjutant-General of His Majesty the Sultan, and Military Envoy Plenipotentiary to His Majesty the German Emperor.

On the part of the Russian Federal Soviet-Republic: Gregory Yakovlevich Sokolnikov, Member of the Central Executive Committee of Councillors to the Deputies of the Workingmen, Soldiers, and Peasants; Lew Michailovich Karachan, Member of the Central Executive Committee of Councillors to the Deputies of the Workingmen, Soldiers, and Peasants; Georgy Vassilievich Tchitcherin, Assistant to

[17] *Texts of the Russian Peace,* from *Reichsgesetzblatt,* No. 77, June 11, 1918, pp. 479–90.

the People's Commissioner for Foreign Affairs; Gregory Ivanovich Petrovsky, People's Commissioner for Internal Affairs.

The Plenipotentiaries met in Brest-Litovsk to enter into peace negotiations and after presentation of their credentials and finding them in good and proper form have agreed upon the following stipulations:

ARTICLE I

Germany, Austria-Hungary, Bulgaria, and Turkey on the one part and Russia on the other part declare that the state of war between them has ceased. They are resolved to live henceforth in peace and amity with one another.

ARTICLE II

The contracting parties will refrain from any agitation or propaganda against the Government or the public and military institutions of the other party. In so far as this obligation devolves upon Russia it holds good also for the territories occupied by the Powers of the Quadruple Alliance.

ARTICLE III

The territories lying to the west of the line agreed upon by the contracting parties which formerly belonged to Russia will no longer be subject to Russian sovereignty; the line agreed upon is traced on the map submitted as an essential part of this treaty of peace, Appendix I. The exact fixation of the line will be established by a Russo-German commission.

No obligations whatever toward Russia arising from the fact that they formerly belonged to Russia shall devolve upon the territories referred to.

Russia refrains from all interference in the internal relations of these territories. Germany and Austria-Hungary purpose to determine the future status of these territories in agreement with their population.

ARTICLE IV

As soon as a general peace is concluded and Russian demobilization is carried out completely, Germany will evacuate the territory lying to the east of the line designated in paragraph 1 of Article III in so far as Article VI does not determine otherwise.

Russia will do all within her power to insure the immediate evacuation of the provinces of eastern Anatolia and their lawful return to Turkey.

The districts of Erdehan, Kars, and Batum will likewise and without delay be cleared of the Russian troops. Russia will not interfere in the reorganization of the national and international relations of these districts but will leave it to the population of these districts to carry out this reorganization in agreement with the neighboring states, especially with Turkey.

ARTICLE V

Russia will, without delay, carry out the full demobilization of her army inclusive of those units recently organized by the present government.

Furthermore, Russia will either bring her warships into Russian ports and there detain them until the day of the conclusion of a general peace or will disarm them forthwith. Warships of the states which continue in the state of war with the Powers of the Quadruple Alliance, in so far as they are within Russian sovereignty, will be treated as Russian warships.

The barred zone in the Arctic Ocean continues as such until the conclusion of a general peace. In the Baltic Sea and as far as Russian power extends within the Black Sea removal of the mines will be proceeded with at once. Merchant navigation within these maritime regions is free and will be resumed at once. Mixed commissions will be organized to formulate the more detailed regulations, especially to inform merchant ships with regard to restricted lanes. The navigation lanes are always to be kept free from floating mines.

ARTICLE VI

Russia obligates herself to conclude peace at once with the Ukrainian People's Republic and to recognize the treaty of peace between that state and the Powers of the Quadruple Alliance. The Ukrainian territory will without delay be cleared of Russian troops and the Russian Red Guard. Russia is to put an end to all agitation or propaganda against the Government or the public institutions of the Ukrainian People's Republic.

Esthonia and Livonia will likewise without delay be cleared of Russian troops and the Russian Red Guard. The eastern boundary of Esthonia runs, in general, along the river Narwa. The eastern boundary of Livonia crosses, in general, lakes Peipus and Pskow to the southwestern corner of the latter, then across Lake Luban in the direction of Livenhof on the Dvina. Esthonia and Livonia will be occupied by a German police force until security is insured by proper national institutions and until public order has been established. Russia will liberate at once all arrested or deported inhabitants of Esthonia and Livonia and insure the safe return of all deported Esthonians and Livonians.

Finland and the Aaland Islands will immediately be cleared of Russian troops and the Russian Red Guard, and the Finnish ports of the Russian fleet and of the Russian naval forces. So long as the ice prevents the transfer of warships into Russian ports, only limited forces will remain on board the warships. Russia is to put an end to all agitation or propaganda against the Government or the public institutions of Finland.

The fortresses built on the Aaland Islands are to be removed as soon as possible. As regards the permanent non-fortification of these islands as well as their further treatment in respect to military and technical navigation matters a special agreement is to be concluded between Germany, Finland, Russia, and Sweden; there exists an understanding to the effect that, upon Germany's desire, still other countries bordering upon the Baltic Sea will be consulted in this matter.

Article VII

In view of the fact that Persia and Afghanistan are free and independent states, the contracting parties obligate themselves to respect the political and economic independence and the territorial integrity of these states.

Article VIII

The prisoners of war of both parties will be released to return to their homeland. The settlement of the questions connected therewith will be effected through the special treaties provided for in Article XII.

Article IX

The contracting parties mutually renounce compensation for their war expenses, i.e., of the public expenditures for the conduct of the war, as well as compensation for war losses, i.e., such losses as were caused them and their nationals within the war zones by military measures, inclusive of all requisitions effected in enemy country.

Article X

Diplomatic and consular relations between the contracting parties will be resumed immediately upon the ratification of the treaty of peace. As regards the reciprocal admission of consuls, separate agreements are reserved.

Article XI

As regards the economic relations between the Powers of the Quadruple Alliance and Russia the regulations contained in Appendixes II–V are determinative, namely Appendix II for the Russo-German, Appendix III for the Russo-Austro-Hungarian, Appendix IV for the Russo-Bulgarian, and Appendix V for the Russo-Turkish relations.

ARTICLE XII

The re-establishment of public and private legal relations, the exchange of war prisoners and interned civilians, the question of amnesty as well as that concerning the treatment of merchant ships which have come into the power of the opponent will be regulated in separate treaties with Russia which form an essential part of the general treaty of peace and, as far as possible, go into force simultaneously with the latter.

ARTICLE XIII

In the interpretation of this treaty, the German and Russian texts are authoritative for the relations between Germany and Russia; the German, the Hungarian, and the Russian texts for the relations between Austria-Hungary and Russia; the Bulgarian and the Russian texts for the relations between Bulgaria and Russia; and the Turkish and the Russian texts for the relations between Turkey and Russia.

ARTICLE XIV

The present treaty of peace will be ratified. The documents of ratification shall as soon as possible be exchanged in Berlin. The Russian Government obligates itself, upon the desire of one of the Powers of the Quadruple Alliance, to execute the exchange of the documents of ratification within a period of two weeks. Unless otherwise provided for in its articles, in its annexes, or in the additional treaties, the treaty of peace enters into force at the moment of its ratification.

In testimony whereof the Plenipotentiaries have signed this treaty with their own hand.

Executed in quintuplicate at Brest-Litovsk, 3 March, 1918.

R. v. KÜHLMANN	COLONEL P. GANTCHEW
Bucharest, 7 March, 1918	DR. THEODORE ANASTASSOFF
v. ROSENBERG	I. HAKKY
HOFFMANN	ZEKI
HORN	G. SOKOLNIKOV
CZERNIN	L. KARACHAN
Bucharest, 7 March, 1918	G. TCHITCHERIN
MEREY	G. PETROVSKY
A. TOSCHEFF	

292. NOTIFICATION OF JUNE 7, 1918, REGARDING THE RATIFI-
CATION OF THE PEACE TREATY BETWEEN GERMANY,
AUSTRIA-HUNGARY, BULGARIA, AND TURKEY ON THE
ONE HAND AND RUSSIA ON THE OTHER HAND, SIGNED
MARCH 3–7, 1918, IN BREST-LITOVSK AND BUCHAREST,
AND THE GERMAN-RUSSIAN TREATY SUPPLEMENTARY
TO THE PEACE TREATY, SIGNED MARCH 3–7, 1918, IN
BREST-LITOVSK AND BUCHAREST[18]

The treaties printed above, signed March 3–7, 1918, in Brest-
Litovsk and Bucharest, namely:

1. Peace Treaty between Germany, Austria-Hungary, Bulgaria, and
Turkey on the one hand and Russia on the other hand

2. Russo-German Supplementary Treaty to the Peace Treaty between Germany, Austria-Hungary, Bulgaria, and Turkey on the one
hand and Russia on the other hand have been ratified. The exchange
of ratifications was effected on March 29, 1918, in Berlin.

BERLIN, June 7, 1918

The Imperial Chancellor:
by VON KÜHLMANN

[18] *Texts of the Russian Peace*, from *Reichsgesetzblatt*, No. 77, June 11, 1918,
p. 654.

CHAPTER XVII

THE TREATY WITH THE UKRAINE

INTRODUCTORY NOTE

THE PROVISIONAL GOVERNMENT of the Ukrainian Republic, which was represented at the Brest-Litovsk peace conference by a separate delegation, proclaimed the independence of the Ukraine when the Bolshevik Government refused to accept their national policy. On January 9, 1918, the Central Powers recognized its independence and right to a separate peace. Trotsky protested this decision on January 30, and withdrew from the peace conference after the Ukrainian treaty was signed. After Russia drove the provisional government of the Ukraine out of Kiev, the Central Powers occupied the Ukraine.

The Central Powers ceded by this treaty the district of Cholm, which was claimed by Poland, to the Ukraine. Austria promised to erect the Ruthenian districts of Galicia into an autonomous crown land. The Ukraine agreed to furnish annually 100,000 tons of cereals, grains, and oil-seeds to the Central Powers.

293. THE TREATY OF PEACE BETWEEN GERMANY, AUSTRIA-HUNGARY, BULGARIA, AND TURKEY AND THE UKRAINE. SIGNED AT BREST-LITOVSK FEBRUARY 9, 1918[1]

Whereas the Ukrainian People has, in the course of the present world war, declared its independence, and has expressed the desire to establish a state of peace between the Ukrainian People's Republic and the Powers at present at war with Russia, the Governments of Germany, Austria-Hungary, Bulgaria, and Turkey have resolved to conclude a Treaty of Peace with the Government of the Ukrainian People's Republic; they wish in this way to take the first step towards a lasting world peace, honorable for all parties, which shall not only put an end

---

[1] *Deutscher Reichsanzeiger,* February 10, 1918, evening edition; translation here from United States Department of State, *Texts of the Ukraine "Peace,"* 1918, pp. 9–22, hereafter cited as *Texts of the Ukraine Peace.*

to the horrors of the war, but shall also conduce to the restoration of friendly relations between the peoples in the political, legal, economic, and intellectual spheres.

To this end the Plenipotentiaries of the above-mentioned Governments, viz.:

For the Imperial German Government: Imperial Actual Privy Councillor Richard von Kühlmann, Secretary of State for Foreign Affairs;

For the Imperial and Royal Joint Austro-Hungarian Government: His Imperial and Royal Apostolic Majesty's Privy Councillor Ottokar Count Czernin von und zu Chudnitz, Minister of the Imperial and Royal House and Minister for Foreign Affairs;

For the Royal Bulgarian Government: Dr. Vassil Radoslavov, President of the Council of Ministers; the Envoy M. Andrea Tosheff; the Envoy M. Ivan Stoyanovich; the Military Plenipotentiary, Colonel Peter Gantshew, and Dr. Theodor Anastassoff;

For the Imperial Ottoman Government: His Highness the Grand Vizier, Talaat Pasha; Ahmet Nessimi Bey, Minister for Foreign Affairs; His Highness Ibrahim Hakki Pasha, and General of Cavalry Ahmet Izzet Pasha;

For the Government of the Ukrainian People's Republic: M. Alexander Sevryuk, M. Mykola Lubynski, and M. Mykola Levytski, members of the Ukrainian Central Rada;

have met at Brest-Litovsk, and having presented their full powers, which were found to be in due and proper form, have agreed upon the following points:

ARTICLE I

Germany, Austria-Hungary, Bulgaria, and Turkey on the one hand, and the Ukrainian People's Republic on the other hand, declare that the state of war between them is at an end. The contracting parties are resolved henceforth to live in peace and amity with one another.

ARTICLE II

1. As between Austria-Hungary on the one hand, and the Ukrainian People's Republic on the other hand, in so far as these two Powers border upon one another, those frontiers which existed between the Austro-Hungarian Monarchy and Russia prior to the outbreak of the present war will be preserved.

2. Further north, the frontier of the Ukrainian People's Republic starting at Tarnograd, will in general follow the line Bilgoray, Szozebrzeszyn, Krasnostav, Pugashov, Radzin, Miedzyzheche, Sarnaki, Melnik, Vysokie-Litovsk, Kameniec-Litovsk, Prujany, and Vydonovsk

Lake. This frontier will be delimited in detail by a mixed commission, according to the ethnographical conditions and after taking the wishes of the inhabitants into consideration.

3. In the event of the Ukrainian People's Republic having boundaries coterminous with those of another of the Powers of the Quadruple Alliance, special agreements are reserved in respect thereto.

ARTICLE III

The evacuation of the occupied territories shall begin immediately after the ratification of the present Treaty of Peace.

The manner of carrying out the evacuation and the transfer of the evacuated territories shall be determined by the Plenipotentiaries of the interested parties.

ARTICLE IV

Diplomatic and consular relations between the contracting parties shall commence immediately after the ratification of the Treaty of Peace.

In respect to the admission of consuls on the widest scale possible on both sides special agreements are reserved.

ARTICLE V

The contracting parties mutually renounce repayment of their war costs, that is to say, their State expenditure for the prosecution of the war, as well as payment for war damages, that is to say, damages sustained by them and their nationals in the war areas through military measures, including all requisitions made in enemy territory.

ARTICLE VI

Prisoners of war of both parties shall be released to their homeland in so far as they do not desire, with the approval of the State in whose territory they shall be, to remain within its territories or to proceed to another country. Questions connected with this will be dealt with in the separate treaties provided for in Article VIII.

ARTICLE VII

It has been agreed as follows with regard to economic relations between the contracting parties:

I. The contracting parties mutually undertake to enter into economic relations without delay and to organize the exchange of goods on the basis of the following stipulations:

Until 31 July of the current year a reciprocal exchange of the surplus of their more important agricultural and industrial products, for the purpose of meeting current requirements, is to be effected according to the following provisions:

(a) The quantities and classes of products to be exchanged in accordance with the preceding paragraph shall be settled on both sides by a commission composed of an equal number of representatives of both parties, which shall sit immediately after the Treaty of Peace has been signed.

(b) The prices of products to be exchanged as specified above shall be regulated on the basis of mutual agreement by a commission composed of an equal number of representatives of both parties.

(c) Calculations shall be made in gold on the following basis: 1,000 German Imperial gold Marks shall be equivalent to 462 gold Roubles of the former Russian Empire (1 Rouble = 1-15 Imperial), or 1,000 Austrian and Hungarian gold Kronen shall be equivalent to 393 Karbowanjec 76 Grosh gold of the Ukrainian People's Republic, or to 393 Roubles 78 Copecks in gold of the former Russian Empire (1 Rouble = 1-15 Imperial).

(d) The exchange of the goods to be determined by the commission mentioned under (a) shall take place through the existing Government central offices or through central offices controlled by the Government.

The exchange of such products as are not determined by the above-mentioned commissions shall be effected on a basis of free trading, arranged for in accordance with the conditions of the provisional commercial treaty, which is provided for in the following Section II.

II. In so far as is not otherwise provided for under Section I hereof, economic relations between the contracting parties shall be carried on provisionally in accordance with the stipulations specified below until the conclusion of the final Commercial Treaty, but in any event until a period of at least six months shall have elapsed after the conclusion of peace between Germany, Austria-Hungary, Bulgaria, and Turkey on the one hand, and the European States at present at war with them, the United States of America and Japan on the other hand:

A. For economic relations between the German Empire and the Ukrainian People's Republic, the conditions laid down in the following provisions of the Germano-Russian Commercial and Maritime Treaty of 1894–1904. . . . .

294. MEMORANDUM SUBMITTED TO THE REICHSTAG BY CHANCELLOR VON HERTLING WITH THE TREATY OF PEACE AND THE SUPPLEMENTARY TREATY WITH THE UKRAINE, FEBRUARY 19, 1918[2]

Ukraine bases her national existence which has come to a new life upon the Third Sovereign Manifesto of 20 November, 1917, by which the Central Rada in Kief has announced the establishment of the Ukrainian People's Republic. The national organization which had originally been thought of as part of a Russian Federal Republic had abandoned the federal conception through the Fourth National Sovereign Manifesto of 24 January, 1918, which declared the Ukrainian People's Republic as an independent, free, and sovereign State, dependent on no one. On 1 February, 1918, the Ukrainian People's Republic has been recognized by the authorized representatives of Germany, Austria-Hungary, Bulgaria, and Turkey as an independent, free, and sovereign State which may conclude independent international agreements.

At the beginning of the peace negotiations in Brest-Litovsk, the representatives of the Ukrainian Government formed a part of the Russian delegation. Subsequently, the Government sent its own delegation, with which the peace negotiations were then conducted independently. Thanks to the practical attitude of the Ukrainian delegates, an attitude which was not intended for propaganda, but directed to the object of a real understanding, it was possible, in a short time, to come to an agreement concerning the large number of, in part, very complex and difficult questions resulting from the first conclusion of peace in the present world war.

On 9 February, 1918, the representatives of the Allied Governments signed, with the Plenipotentiaries of the Ukrainian Government, the Treaty of Peace. Thereby the contracting parties, as emphasized in the beginning of the treaty, desired to take the first step to a durable world peace, honorable to all parties, a peace which shall not only bring the horrors of war to an end, but which shall also lead to the reestablishment of the amicable relations between the peoples within the political, legal, economic, and intellectual spheres.

The negotiations were conducted in three commissions: a political, an economic, and a juridical commission. It devolved upon the political commission especially to consider the boundary questions and the future form of the political relations connected therewith between the Ukraine and her neighbors. It was the main task of the economic commission to

2 *Texts of the Ukraine Peace,* pp. 49–52.

prepare the resumption of the commercial relations, to initiate commercial exchange, especially with regard to the transition period, and to establish a preliminary commercial treaty. Finally, the juridical commission considered the inauguration of diplomatic and consular relations, the matter of war damages and war expenditures, the re-establishment of public and private legal relations between the contracting parties, the exchange of war prisoners and interned civilians, the subject of amnesty, the provisions for the repatriated as well as the matter of the treatment of merchant ships that had come into the power of the opponent.

Whilst in the economic and juridical questions special provisions were in many respects deemed necessary for the individual members of the Quadruple Alliance, the political questions, on the other hand, could be regulated only in a manner that would be uniform to all the parties interested, in which respect Austria-Hungary was, as the nearest neighbor of the Ukraine, the power most interested. This consideration resulted in a division of the chief work into a general treaty, that is to say, the real Treaty of Peace which was concluded by the Powers of the Quadruple Alliance with the Ukraine, and four separate supplementary treaties of which the German-Ukrainian treaty was signed on the same day as the chief treaty. But apart from the purely political articles, the chief treaty presents as well the result of the negotiations of the economic commission which, indeed, contains special provisions with regard to the distinct Powers of the Quadruple Alliance, but which in all essential respects could be determined from the point of view of uniformity. On the other hand, in consequence of the diversity of the juridical questions with regard to the individual allied countries and their relations to the former Russian Empire, the negotiations of the juridical commission led to such differences that it seemed advisable to reserve the most of the subjects which it considered for the supplementary treaties.

The entire construction work of this treaty will, in the following explanations, be considered only in so far as it is obligatory as between Germany and the Ukraine, whilst the political significance of the treaty with regard to the other Powers of the Quadruple Alliance must be left unconsidered. Furthermore, the provisions exclusively concerning the German Empire can be considered only in part with regard to the competence of the lawmaking bodies of the Empire; nevertheless, the entire work connected with the construction of the treaty will be submitted for the approval of the Federal Council. For, although, in accordance with Article II of the constitution of the Empire, it is the prerogative of the Emperor to conclude peace, the carrying out of the treaty would still require the promulgation of legal imperial ordinances, in so far as the provisions of the treaty did not receive legal force through the approval of the legislative bodies.

The following is to be observed with regard to the separate provisions of the treaty:

THE MAIN TREATY BETWEEN THE ALLIED POWERS AND THE UKRAINIAN PEOPLE'S REPUBLIC

ARTICLE I

Through the introductory article, the state of war between the Powers of the Quadruple Alliance, on the one hand, and the Ukrainian People's Republic, on the other hand, is contractually terminated; it also declares that in future peace and amity shall exist between the contracting parties. Therein, on the one hand, we find a further solemn recognition of the autonomy and independence of the Ukraine, and on the other hand, the new national entity is expressly admitted into the circle of Powers with which Germany, Austria-Hungary, Bulgaria, and Turkey carry on an exchange of spiritual and economic goods, as is customary between the members of the international community. Amity does not, in this connection, mean alliance; rather, the Ukrainian delegation has let it be known, that the Ukraine no longer desires to take part in the world war, but desires to join the ranks of the Neutral Powers!

ARTICLE II

This article deals with the frontiers of the Ukrainian State, in so far as they concern the Powers of the Quadruple Alliance. The former Austro-Hungarian frontiers, with regard to Russia, shall continue intact as regards the Ukrainian People's Republic. In the agreements concerning the frontier line between the [farther, *weiter Nördlich*] north, an attempt has been made to find a just settlement between the conflicting national and historic viewpoints. In order to obviate all unfairness, the contracting parties have desisted from determining the details of the frontier line and have indicated but general directions to meet the ethnographic conditions, and under consideration of the wishes of the population the frontier line will be determined by a mixed commission. . . . .

ARTICLE V

With regard to the Ukraine, the allied Powers have maintained the peace offer which they made to the whole of Russia on 25 December, 1917; for although the offer was conditioned upon the joining of the former allies of Russia in the peace negotiations and nullified in consequence of their refusal to do so, it seemed best, nevertheless, to impose no severer conditions upon the honest desire for peace on the part of the Ukrainian People's Republic than had been originally proposed. These conditions, however, included the mutual renunciation of compensation for war expenditures and war damages. With regard to the Ukraine, this renunciation rests less heavily upon Germany than upon Austria-Hungary.

The conceptions as to war expenses and war damages are clearly defined in the article. In the war damages are included all requisitions made by one Power within the territory of the other. This results in the fact that upon the resumption of peace relations no contracting party may present international claims arising from requisitions which the latter effected within enemy territory; rather, compensation for requisitions made of the particular nationalism is left to the decision of each contracting party. This provision does not affect the matter of requisitions which each party made within its own territory and for which, of course, it must pay the nationals of the other party who have been affected thereby. . . . .

ARTICLE VII

Regarding the form of economic relations with the Ukraine, Article VII adopts provisions and divides them into several parts. In the first place, Section I regulates the exchange of goods up to 31 July, 1918. It was desired in this respect to provide for a simple and an immediate settlement, as far as possible, with regard to the Ukrainian products of which we were in urgent need, and, on the other hand, with regard to those goods which the Ukraine desires to secure at once from the States of the Quadruple Alliance.

Organized governmental places on both sides shall arrange for the exchange of the most important articles so that, by taking into consideration the economic needs of the interested States and the transportation conditions of the moment, this exchange may take place in accordance with a definite plan. To what products and to what quantities of such products this centralized exchange of goods is to extend, will be determined in common agreement through commissions. In so far as such commissions take no account of a centralized exchange, commerce will be freely exercised in the interval up to 31 July, 1918. The prices of the goods offered for exchange will likewise be determined by commissions composed of members of both parties. . . . .

295. STRESEMANN'S SPEECH IN THE REICHSTAG ON THE TREATY WITH THE UKRAINE, FEBRUARY 20, 1918[3]

Gentlemen, we associate ourselves with the thanks tendered by Herr Gröber to the Imperial Government for the conclusion of the peace with the Ukraine. We are glad to see him amongst us again in full physical and mental vigor. We thank Secretary of State v. Kühlmann and his colleagues for the resolution, tenacity, and diplomatic skill with which they represented our German interests in the Brest negotiations. . . . .

Gentlemen, Herr Gröber and the previous speaker [Dove] disapproved of the fact that the treaty, beside Herr v. Kühlmann's signature, bore also the signature of Herr Hoffmann in the capacity of representative of the German High Command. I presume that we shall still receive an explanation as to the signature, because there exists a certain contradiction in the introduction of the treaty which specifies Secretary of State v. Kühlmann as the sole representative of the Imperial German Government. However, on this occasion, too, I wish to state that it does not seem to me so important in what manner the formal signing of the treaty took place. For I think that if we do not stick to formalities, but to actual facts, then we must in the first place express our thanks to the High Command for our having arrived at a peace with the Ukraine at all. ["Quite right!"—National-Liberals.] . . . . For that reason I regard the formal signing as of little significance. It is the content of the treaty that matters. . . . . I only like to express the wish that if further peace negotiations take place the Imperial German Government must be harmoniously represented by no one but plenipotentiaries of the German Empire as a unit. All wishes and claims of individual states to have any kind of separate representation must be rejected [lively approval by National-Liberals], for what we wish to bring out of this war is to negotiate before the world as the German Empire and not separately as Prussian, Bavarian, or other plenipotentiaries. ["Bravo!"—National-Liberals.] . . . .

Herr Dr. David mentioned the negotiations with Trotsky up to the first phase of the breaking off of the negotiations. . . . . He was completely prejudiced in his criticism of the German Government. He expressly denied—as was natural—any identification of German Social-Democracy with the government of the Bolsheviki in Petersburg. . . . . He said that it [the Bolshevik Government] had aimed at the achievement of a democratic world peace and that the thought of a world revolution had been very distant from it. . . . . We openly heard from the Secretary of State that Herr Trotsky, misled by Herr Radek, be-

[3] *Verhandlungen des Reichstags*, No. 130, February 20, 1918, pp. 4018–24.

lieved until the last moment that some kind of revolutionary movement
would come to his aid. How can one in the face of this deny the aim
of the Russian Government for a world revolution? That has been
the avowed ideal of those gentlemen. . . . . I am therefore exceedingly
glad that Herr Dr. Dove, with whom I am in complete agreement in
this, stated that there are certain conditions which must absolutely be
observed before the German Government and its allies can be expected
to enter into any new peace negotiations with Trotsky. One condition
is the entire evacuation of Livonia and Esthonia [*"Quite right!"—Left,
Center, and Right*] . . . . and the immediate release of all imprisoned
Germans, Esthonians, and Letts. . . . . Another proviso is the unconditional recognition of the independence of Finland and its evacuation
[*"Quite right!"—Left, Center, and Right*], as well as the recognition of
the status of peace with the Ukraine. . . . .

Our negotiators at Brest-Litovsk have had to solve a very difficult
problem and I regret very much that this position was made more difficult by the attitude of a section of the German press. . . . . *Vorwärts*
has objected to my putting it into the category of papers which created
these difficulties. But at the time of Herr von Kühlmann's first trip to
Brest *Vorwärts* wrote a lengthy article which ended with these words:
"Our negotiators must come back with a peace. They will be held responsible for failing to do so." . . . .

Entirely different is the attitude of a whole category of persons
. . . . not belonging to any one party. I mean the whole school of politicians which is of the opinion that we should try to come to an agreement of friendship with a great, unified, and compact Russia which
would give us the possibility to use this agreement as a basis for the
conclusion of a continental league against England. . . . . These persons
are Professor Hoetzsch, Herr Georg Bernhard, and a group of prominent Socialists who have expressed such ideas in the *Sozialistische
Monatshefte*. . . . . I do not understand how it can be held against our
Government for having cleverly played off the Ukraine against Trotsky
[*"Quite right!"—National-Liberals and Center*] and thereby brought
us today's offer of Trotsky [*renewed approval*]. . . . . We do not have
before us any longer the old, compact, and powerful Russia. . . . .
Besides it must be admitted that we really began to undermine the
structure of a united Russia through a policy which had its origin on
November 5, 1916 . . . . and which created an accomplished fact, which
we cannot escape from any more. . . . . Moreover, I believe that the
advocates of this policy imagine the continental league against England
to be a much simpler thing than it really is. It is argued that an alliance
with Russia will bring with it automatically an alliance with France.
It is possible that this alliance with England will leave many a thorn

in France. But, as matter of fact, hostility . . . . and hatred of Germany will remain the determining factors of French policy. The result of this war will not be a Franco-German alliance. For this reason I think it wrong to reproach our Government for having supported the process of liberation of certain alien peoples from Russia—for having concluded a separate peace with the Ukraine.

The representative of the Polish "Fraktion" attacked the treaty most violently. We fully understand that the Polish gentlemen view with great regret the separation of a district which they regard as overwhelmingly Polish. But I may say this . . . . : What would have happened to a statesman who returned to his country with the declaration that we had had the opportunity to conclude peace in one part of the great front, to live in peace and friendship with a nation of thirty millions, and to secure our provisioning with food, but that we destroyed that opportunity by our insistence that Cholm was to remain with Poland? [*"Quite right!"*] Such a statesman would have been stoned in Austria. . . . . I should also like to call the attention of the Polish "Fraktion" to what was pointed out to them yesterday by a member of the Progressive People's Party. They say that they had not expected that Germany would in any way sacrifice Polish interests. But then we must ask what has been done by the Poles to earn a right to German sympathy? [*"Very good!"—National-Liberals.*]

Gentlemen, I call your attention to the fact that we have lived to see the Chairman of the Austrian Polish Club make the following proposals in the Austrian Abgeordnetenhaus on January 22:

1. The Polish Club states that the right of self-determination must apply to all Poles without consideration of political boundaries [*"Hear, hear!"*] ;

2. The only possible solution of the Polish question is the unification of all Polish territories with access to the sea. [*"Hear, hear!"*] . . . . I must say that I do not have at my command a parliamentary expression for this demand of the Austrian Polish Club. [*"Quite right!"*] . . . . We have heard similar things in the Prussian Abgeordnetenhaus. We have heard that in the future the question of the East Mark is not to be any longer a German question, but the subject of an international settlement. How can they demand that in such vital questions we consider other than German interests authoritative? . . . . My political friends are of the opinion that in questions of the strategical securing of our frontiers the decision of our High Command is authoritative. Beyond that I believe that I am sure of the agreement of my party when I say that from the national point of view we have absolutely no interest in increasing the Polish territory in Germany. We have no interest in adding new difficulties to the difficulties we

already have in the East Mark. It will be the business of our Government to determine whether the securing of the frontiers is a vital question to Germany. If that is the case, then we accept it, not because we desire to incorporate new territory into Germany, but for reasons of state necessity.

Herr Gröber referred to the declaration of the Lithuanian Council of State regarding its future independence. . . . . If Lithuania has the intention of separating from Russia . . . . and the leading classes of the country give us assurances that they are willing to enter into a friendly, neighborly, and close relationship with us . . . . , then, I believe, we can accept this basis. Gentlemen, on the Courland question, too, I agree with Herr Gröber that it would be desirable to give a broader basis to the representative body. . . . . However, I am convinced that even a broader basis of this body will not change anything in the decisions already taken by the Courland Landtag. For nothing has had so great an influence on the separation from Russia as the rule of Herr Lenin and Herr Trotsky. [*Approval.*] In these few weeks the eyes of millions have been opened to the contrasts between anarchy and chaos on one side and security and order on the other. [*Renewed approval.*] . . . .

I now come to the question of the economic importance of the Ukrainian treaty. Strangely enough in yesterday's session the treaty was viewed more critically than approvingly. . . . . Herr Ledebour went so far as to deny the right to conclude agreements with a state which had not come into existence in a constitutional way and which as yet had not received recognition in international law. . . . . The view of Herr Ledebour is that of a legitimist who objects to the "revolutionary" part in the development of nations. [*Laughter.*] . . . . I wish to point out that it was no exaggeration when Herr v. Kühlmann said that the Ukraine had been and possibly would continue to be the economic artery of Russia. The Ukraine accounted for 39 per cent of Russia's grain exports and 80 per cent of the sugar exports. It produced 1,300,000 puds of Russia's 1,900,000 puds of coal and 325,000,000 out of 500,000,000 puds of iron. It is therefore a very important economic body which has separated from Russia and which wishes to enter into economic relations with us. . . . .

The advance in Livonia was undertaken in order to relieve the threatened condition of the Ukraine. It was also undertaken—and this seems to me more important—in order to rescue the populations of Livonia and Esthonia. . . . . In many circles it has been doubted whether conditions really were that bad. It has been said that an official propaganda was being conducted. It has even been said that those Esthonian and Livonian landowners only turned to Germany from anxiety lest the land should be divided. . . . . But the material losses are not the most important factor. . . . . We cannot look on passively while those who, in spite of all persecution, have preserved for seven centuries the German speech and German culture are murdered and slaughtered, simply because they are Germans. [*Lively cheers.*] Were we to tolerate it, then we should be a nation without prestige and honor. [*Lively cheers.*] . . . . It does not mean the annexation of these territories. But it means a free Balticum in close relationship with Germany and under our military, political, intellectual, and cultural protection. . . . . We hope that the Ukrainian peace, which we have before us today, will be the first link in the chain of peace treaties with individual nations which eventually will lead us nearer to world peace. . . . .

296. STATEMENT OF VON KÜHLMANN IN THE BUDGET COMMITTEE ON THE PEACE TREATY WITH THE UKRAINE, FEBRUARY 19, 1918[4]

Unfortunately, the unfavorable prognostications regarding the behavior of the Russian Delegation in Brest-Litovsk have proved correct. Their behavior, especially Trotsky's, is without precedent in history. His last announcement was made with a view of extricating himself from a position which had become untenable. Radek's conduct, too, showed what spirit animated the Russian Delegation, for it proved that he had a decisive influence on the attitude of the delegation. Radek had stated his real intentions in the press beforehand and declared that there could be no question of yielding to the Central Powers. The course of the negotiations showed *that Trotsky was also not in earnest with regard to peace.* All that has been thoroughly discussed in the press.

On the expiration of the seven days' grace, a state of war with Russia again came into force on Monday. Conditions in Russia itself have grown worse from day to day. The Bolshevik Government's tendency is to centralism by violence, as their conduct toward Finland, Esthonia, and Livonia shows. Appeals for help reach us daily. We can no longer believe in Russia's peaceful sentiments, and even the hope of leaving things in abeyance proved illusory. We cannot allow violence to be done to Finland; we must rather provide for peace and order in the countries bordering the occupied territories. Our fresh entry into the war will have a sobering effect in Petersburg, and strengthen the inclination for peace. Even now we are still ready to conclude a peace which answers to our interests.

Peace with the Ukraine resulted from our readiness for peace. The national idea has taken a firm hold of the Ukraine, and the Ukrainian

[4] *Berliner Tageblatt,* February 20, 1918, morning edition, pp. 2–3.

pride of race presents a beautiful and elevating picture. The Ukrainian State idea will always remain an influential factor in Russia. The Ukraine is a rich country, and has large supplies of raw material and foodstuffs. These economic points of view were naturally of decisive importance in the conclusion of peace. The fact that the Central Powers were the first to re-establish relations with the new state will be of permanent value for the future. Precisely those who regard the fostering of good relations with the East as right must welcome the understanding with the Ukraine gladly, as a first step in that direction. In fixing the frontiers of the new state territory, difficulties arose as regards the government of Cholm. The Ukrainians urged their claim to this territory with the utmost energy, so that there was a risk of the negotiations breaking down. There is not the smallest occasion to assume that there was any friction between the Central Powers. The Poles felt themselves injured by the solution of the question arrived at, which was to be expected. On the other hand, one could not take the responsibility of letting the negotiations with the Ukraine break down. The Austrian Prime Minister will make an exhaustive statement on the same questions in the Vienna Reichsrat today. He, too, will point out that the provisions of the treaty form an inseparable whole. There are more supplies in the Ukraine than we can transport. Definite agreements have been reached as regards the delivery, so that we shall benefit by the treaty in the current year.

The Prime Minister, v. Seidler, will also point out today that the government of Cholm will not be handed over to the Ukraine forthwith, but that a mixed Commission will fix the frontier, taking the ethnographical conditions and the wishes of the people into consideration. This joint Commission will be composed of representatives of the contracting Powers and of Poland.

297. A SECOND SPEECH OF KÜHLMANN IN THE MAIN COMMITTEE ON THE TREATY OF PEACE WITH THE UKRAINE, FEBRUARY 20, 1918[5]

The Committee has acted so lavishly on the admonition of its chairman to put questions that it will not be easy for me really to answer exhaustively each separate question which has been broached today, although I am far from intending any evasion. I will endeavor to answer each question as accurately as possible from my notes.

Deputy Gröber first of all suggested that our printed copies should be provided with suitable maps. I regret to say that for technical

[5] *Norddeutsche Allgemeine Zeitung,* February 21, 1918, II, 3.

reasons that will probably not be possible. My representatives are, however, quite willing to enter into communication with the gentlemen when the opportunity can be taken of showing maps on which the lines in question are marked in such a way that everyone who is interested in these questions can easily obtain the necessary information from a survey of these maps. Any hand atlas indeed suffices for the points which have been discussed here.

As regards the Polish representation in the negotiations with the Ukraine, that is a point which was considered by the allies. But for the difficulty of bringing Polish representatives into the negotiations with the Russians—the gentlemen were fully informed of the course of this matter by the protocol of the Brest-Litovsk negotiations published in the papers—there would have been no difficulty in also appointing the gentlemen who had been invited to these negotiations to attend the negotiations with the Ukraine. As a matter of fact, there were objections precisely on the Ukrainian side to summoning an official representative of the Polish nation to Brest-Litovsk for the peace with the Ukraine. It is, however, only owing to the comparatively very rapid conclusion of the negotiations that an official exchange of views did not take place between the Ukrainians and the Poles. I believe that private communications did take place between individual members of the Ukrainian Delegations and Polish politicians. I cannot say anything quite definite about that.

A further question put was how we have determined the quantities of wheat which are still in the Ukraine. With regard to this nothing has been determined, and under the existing circumstances it is not possible to ascertain any precise details. In these matters we have relied on the view of experts in the wheat department, who estimate that there must still be considerable surplus stocks in the Ukraine, which Russia had not been able to export owing to the suspension of her exportation since the closing of the Dardanelles. We have further relied upon the statements of the gentlemen of the Ukrainian Delegation, which absolutely gave the impression of honesty, and we further relied on the views existing in the north of Russia as to the commissariat conditions in the Ukraine. The fact that the Bolshevik Government applied such forcible methods to the Ukraine, and acted so vigorously, is undoubtedly to be explained chiefly by the fact that, besides the political motives by which they were impelled, the Bolshevik Government wanted to gain possession of just these supplies which are in existence. It has been pointed out that even in Kiev itself there has been occasional scarcity; that, gentlemen, is no proof that there are not large supplies still actually in the country, for everyone knows that there is often the greatest difficulty in distribution, even in highly organized countries like Germany, and in view of the unfortunately very unsatisfactory transport conditions existing in the Ukraine today such phenomena would be still more sharply manifested. Therefore, it is not possible to give an estimate. On the other hand, however, the means of transport are limited. From the data at our disposal we have calculated approximately what can be transported between now and the next German harvest, and I have not heard a single voice on any side which did not consider it probable or certain that the supplies which we can transport actually exist. Of course, no one can undertake to guarantee that they will reach the collecting depots, and that they can be unloaded and brought in. However, it would be a criminal omission on the part of any government if it neglected any possibility of improving the food supplies in the present state of the commissariat.

It was further pointed out that it should be stated how far the interpretation and the article as to the actual frontier demarcation of the Cholm district were to be understood, as also the announcements I made today. I think that Deputy Gröber's question as to whether or not whole districts could be transferred under these treaty conditions is already answered in the affirmative by the original article. I think that after what I have announced today I may for my own part answer this question in the affirmative. I may also answer in the affirmative the question whether we intend to leave the line of occupation where it is for the present. The maintenance of the present line of occupation is an absolute necessity, for innumerable reasons, of which I will cite only the police regulations for the prevention of epidemics, and the Ukraine agrees to this.

Turning to Herr Seyda's statements, I appeal to what I have just said as to the representation of the Polish Government. Herr Seyda used the expression "my word of honor," but it appeared from the demand of the Ukrainian Delegation for the frontiers which were sanctioned that things were not as I represented them here. If that is an insinuation that, speaking here officially, I have not spoken the truth, I protest most strongly against this insinuation. In giving the historical explanations just now I stated that the Ukrainians disclosed very far-reaching territorial aspirations, and were very exacting in the interpretation of what more they could claim as Ukrainian territory.

I can reply to a question put later on by Herr Naumann by saying that of course the German Delegation knew, and even if Herr Naumann credits the German Delegation with such great political ignorance, the Austro-Hungarian Delegation most certainly knew very well that the line of demarcation, as drawn, would be strongly objected to and opposed by the Poles. That was obvious. Our duty was to consider on which side German interests, as Herr Fischbeck said, and on which side the great interests of the Quadruple Alliance lay, and the greatest care was taken in considering this. Herr Naumann can find the concrete results of this care in the second part of the clause concerning the matter, and in the supplementary clause, which I have just read, and which the Allied Governments were endeavoring to obtain with regard to this from the Ukraine, long before there was such an uproar in Poland, in so far as such a provision was compatible with the success of the treaty. I can assure you quite objectively that the idea that the Ukrainians came like bashful boys, on whom we pressed province after province, is an absolute fiction. Herr Seyda also asked about Vilna; and if my memory does not deceive me, two questions were asked as to the eventual rearrangement of frontiers in the West and Poland of today. No decisions have yet been formed; therefore I cannot at present make any official statement on these questions. Herr Ledebour led me to a sphere, which reminded me in the most agreeable way of the Brest-Litovsk discussion, namely, the very difficult question as to the origin of a state, and the special question as to how the German Government arrived at the conclusion that a state had come into existence in the Ukraine. An absolute rule for the origin of states does not as yet exist. One may perhaps be drawn up later on by the League of Nations. The Ukrainian People's Republic in its last manifesto (Universal) of January 24, 1918, finally renounced the federal idea, as will be seen from our memorandum, and declared the Ukrainian People's Republic an independent, free, and sovereign state. The Ukrainian People's Republic was represented from the very beginning of the negotiations, first of all by one delegate. After the Christmas interval a large delegation came, led by Herr Holubowitsch, who has now an influential position in the Ukrainian Ministry; it took part in the negotiations as an independent delegation, without any opposition or protest. Even Herr Trotsky certainly did not doubt at that time—at all events he did not let this doubt appear—that as regards the Ukraine we were dealing with an independent state. He pointed out that, failing fixed frontiers, this state might appear still in the process of formation. He adopted his severe attitude toward the Ukraine and the Rada Government only when he saw that the Rada had a policy of its own, i.e., Ukrainian and not Great-Russian. As I pointed out, even Entente States had equally recognized the Ukraine, and have sent diplomatic representatives there at a time when they might be considered still allied to North Russia. The Ukrainian Government notified us solemnly of their resolve to be independent. The Ministers appointed there gave their credentials to the negotiators with the customary diplomatic form. The full powers were in order, and just as we recognized the Finnish Republic we recognized the Ukrainian Republic by unanimous resolution of the allies.

Herr Ledebour then asked whether the Ukrainian representatives had asked for the inclusion of certain points in the provisional frontier line which were outside the Russian Government of Cholm. I must confirm this unconditionally. The Ukrainian Government asked for considerably more. I have not the maps here. Their various demands were traced out by them in maps. These maps are with the documents. They went considerably further. What is now sketched as a provisional frontier line is less than the Ukrainians originally asked. The frontier of the old Cholm Government, which Herr Ledebour so aptly compared to a "dying snake," is such that it is useless as a frontier between two states. The Ukrainian delegates asked more, as I have already said. An agreement was reached by means of a compromise.

Herr Naumann asked how peace was brought about in respect to matters of constitutional law. I have already answered this question. Almost as great chaos exists at present in the Ukraine as in Northern Russia. I am not in a position to conceal this for a moment. Fighting is going on in individual towns, to a certain extent in villages also, and the position changes every day, as there is no question of ordered military operations on a single front, but detachments of troops and bands, which often have no intrinsic connection, march from one village to another plundering partly along the railway, partly in the streets. During the whole negotiation we were in telegraphic communication with Kiev and were able to follow the vicissitudes there very closely. When the treaty was signed, Kiev was in the hands of the Rada. There had been risings there which had been suppressed by the Rada. At present— I have no direct recent news—the Rada is not at Kiev, and is not supreme there. It is expected that when the troops which will be released from the front by the conclusion of peace with the Central Powers can be used elsewhere, they will succeed in maintaining the upper hand. The uncertainty as to whether a government will be permanent in times such as we are living in here ought not in any case to prevent our concluding peace with it, if it is actually the government of the country, for otherwise, gentlemen, we should never obtain the peace for which we all wish and long.

The question whether an alliance exists between us and the Ukraine I can answer with a plain "No." No such alliance has been suggested by the Ukraine, nor have proposals been either made or received by us in this respect.

As to the possibility that it may become necessary to take certain measures of order and security on the railways which lead to the Ukraine, with the consent of the Ukrainian authorities, I consider that the emergency has arisen, and I should like to recommend such measures being taken.

The question of establishing regular trade, and particularly exportation, is, as I have just taken the liberty of pointing out, an extraordinarily important question for us, and we and our allies must do everything to facilitate this exportation.

To deal with another matter first: Doubts appear to have arisen, according to newspaper reports, as to whether such action will be undertaken by Austrian or by German troops. In accordance with the agreements we have made with the Austro-Hungarian Government, the undertaking will be carried out by German as well as Austro-Hungarian troops.

Herr Naumann's further question, whether or not there had been any radical change in the Polish policy, inaugurated by the announcement made by the two Emperors, I can equally emphatically and clearly answer in the negative. The newspaper report which has been referred to says: "Decisions as to further developments have not yet been reached." Of course, the attitude liberated Poland proposes to adopt toward Austria-Hungary and Germany will influence the outcome of the final decisions. I can find nothing in this which has not often been said here. I have not the original before me. I have only a short extract. The future of Poland is not decided. We have often debated the individual questions by implication. I will not go into the Polish question more closely, because it is too late, and because the Polish question will give occasion for the most far-reaching discussions. Herr Naumann then asked whether or not the statement of the Austro-Hungarian Prime Minister which I read is a portion of the agreement. It will not be included in the agreements which are concluded. Notwithstanding this, however, it is a diplomatic agreement, valid internationally, which may be regarded as at least a part of the treaty. As regards the hunger riots in Kiev, I have already taken the liberty of saying all that there is to be said.

The rights of German peasants and of the Polish Minorities in the Ukraine have been made the subject of detailed discussions. If it would be of interest, I could read you the statements made by the Ukrainian delegates regarding this from the particulars of the Ukrainian negotiations. The rights of German peasants were frequently a subject of discussion and were fixed by agreement in the legal treaty. I would ask leave to return to this when the question of rights is discussed. The Commissioner will give corresponding particulars.

I have already answered Herr David's question. There is no difference of policy between us and Austria-Hungary with respect to the possible protection of railway transport in the Ukraine. Austro-Hungarian troops are not confronting Bolshevist or Great-Russian troops anywhere. The Austro-Hungarian front almost entirely coincides with the Ukrainian front. There is no occasion to proceed to other operations there now than those which have already been referred to in connection with Ukrainian interests.

Herr Cohn, however, as far as I can remember from a short memorandum, found fault with our having concluded peace with a government comparatively so insecure and whose sphere of influence and power cannot be defined. With regard to this I should like to refer to what I said above, and I also think that the expression Herr Gröber used is extraordinarily appropriate. Purely diplomatically speaking, the conclusion of peace and the breaking through of the iron ring is in itself a valuable asset, and if Herr Cohn has followed the foreign press, particularly the enemy press, over the course of the negotiations or the conclusion of peace, he will have seen that our enemies characterize this as a very injurious and for them a dangerous maneuver, and these gentlemen have a very good inkling of what is to their own advantage. It was an important consideration to create the possibility of providing foodstuffs and wheat. I may confine myself to what I have already said as to this.

As regards the question concerning military camps and classification of prisoners, according to certain points of view, I prefer to leave it to the representatives of the army to deal with these pre-eminently military matters.

The question, which has been touched upon, whether or not our return for possible Ukrainian supplies will be in goods may, in my view, be answered in the affirmative. The only other way in which it could be made would be by payment in gold, and it would be contrary to all national policy to weaken our gold reserves, particularly as the Ukraine urgently requires goods of every kind. Everything that is necessary for the pursuit of agriculture is absolutely lacking, and I can confidently leave it to those quarters which are entrusted with the distribution and supervision of these things in the Empire to allow nothing to go out of the country which is indispensable to the German people themselves.

Count Westarp asked how our Turkish allies were affected by this conclusion of peace. Turkey joined in signing the treaty and regarded this treaty as a great step forward in foreign policy from her point of view also. The territories of the Ukraine embrace the whole northern coast of the Black Sea. The Ukraine does not at present exercise actual sovereignty in all parts there, because there are disturbances in some parts and in other parts some republics have been formed; but the probabilities are that undoubtedly in the future the Black Sea policy will be predominantly Ukrainian. In so far as the other maritime Powers do not perhaps raise the Dardanelles question at other peace negotiations, it should be satisfactorily settled between Turkey and the Ukraine.

298. STATEMENT OF VON KÜHLMANN IN THE REICHSTAG ON THE TREATY OF PEACE WITH THE UKRAINE, FEBRUARY 20, 1918[6]

Gentlemen, the measure which the Federal Governments put before you today for debate and decision concerns the first conclusion of peace in this the mightiest of all wars. It is the treaty of peace between Germany and her allies on the one side and the Ukrainian People's Republic on the other. The negotiations in Brest took on a new character during the Christmas adjournment by the appearance of an official Ukrainian peace mission under the leadership of Minister Holubowitsch. Even during the armistice negotiations representatives of the Ukraine took part. But they were not very conspicuous. Only after they had come into official relations with us did negotiations with them begin as to the possibility of restoring peaceful relations with the Ukrainian People's Republic.

The Ukrainian People's Republic is a young state, one of those structures which have arisen on the site of the former Russian Empire after the decaying edifice of the Tsar's Empire, which shared the principal guilt for the kindling of the World War, had collapsed under the blow of the German armies. I think that it is not too much to say that while Great-Russiandom had its centers of gravity in Moscow and Petrograd, the Ukrainian race was one of the strongest elements composing the Russian Empire. With respect to minerals, coal, and iron, the Ukraine, which roughly includes the whole of South Russia, is very rich. It also possesses elements of an industry of its own.

The constitutional laws are to be found in the printed matter laid before the House. These fundamental laws are the decisions of the Central Rada, the, so far, sole recognized representative body of the Ukrainian People's Republic.

The Great-Russian representatives of the Bolsheviks maintained friendly relations with the Ukraine as long as M. Trotsky could assume that the People's Republic of the Ukraine would primarily direct its policy according to the interests of the Petrograd Cabinet. When, however, the Ukrainians realized that the Petrograd Cabinet was not pursuing a sincere peace policy, the representatives of the Ukraine took the stand of ending the war by peace. They would in no way be responsible for the sins of Tsarism. They said to themselves: "Our people will have peace; and we will try to satisfy their desire for peace in the shortest and most direct way."

[6] *Verhandlungen des Reichstags*, No. 130, February 20, 1918, pp. 4002–4004.

The negotiations were not quite easy. As in most cases with such young peoples, national ideals and desires are not free from exuberance. The representatives of the Ukraine made territorial demands which could hardly be realized. The demarcation of the frontier with Russia had to be left over for a later period, after discussion with the Russian Government that may then be in power. The only thing that concerned us was to lay down the Western frontiers of the new state, in which connection the frontier demarcation as regards Poland received especial attention and has met the liveliest criticism from the Poles.

It would be erroneous to assume that the statesmen entrusted with the discussion and conclusion of the treaty were not aware of the decisive importance of the stipulations in question. I need hardly say that, weighty as the interests in question are for us, they are considerably weightier for the Dual Monarchy. In our case it is chiefly interests of a foreign political nature; in their case it is vital interests of a foreign political nature and momentous interests of an internal political nature which are affected by this question. The fact that the settlement took the form it did arose from the consideration which Dr. Seidler also pointed out yesterday in the Vienna Reichsrat, namely, that in view of the state of the negotiations the fear was justified that a further screwing back of the Ukraine claims to the Cholm frontier would have resulted in the wrecking of the treaty. ["*Hear, hear!*"—*Right. Shouts, "Call to order!*"] Neither Count Czernin nor I could have accepted such a responsibility.

The overwhelming majority of the German people would not have understood such action and would have disapproved most severely, and I think rightly, of the action entailing the sacrifice of the peace so much desired. That we gave very much consideration, indeed, to Polish interests is clear from the form of the stipulations in which the frontier lines are laid down in a general way only for some points, while a more detailed demarcation is reserved for examination by a Commission. As the House has learned from the statements made yesterday in Vienna, further negotiations which the Austro-Hungarian Government, in accord with the German Government, conducted with the Ukraine have had the result of making it clear that the paragraph about the definitive demarcation of the frontier lines can be interpreted in a much ampler manner, and that in this way the ethnographical situation and the desires of the population can receive the most far-reaching consideration.

As the projected Commission will include not only representatives of the Allies but also Polish delegates, we have done everything possible to attain a just demarcation of the frontiers. The question may be asked why the Ukrainian delegation put forward such extensive claims at Brest, of which some will be abandoned; but the proceeding shows in any case that the untiring effort of the Central Powers to satisfy just wishes is still active. The Ukrainian delegation also will probably have gained the conviction, from the course of events and from personal intercourse in Vienna and Berlin, that the maintenance of sincere and cordial relations with the Central Powers would not be bought too dearly even at the price of some territorial sacrifices on this hotly contested frontier. It is obviously possible that the discussion of the Ukraine Peace Treaty may extend to a general discussion of Polish policy. I should not regard that as desirable. Opportunities for such discussion will occur later. It is inadvisable to extend the debate beyond the subjects directly connected with the settlement of the peace treaty.

Besides the political motives there was another factor of decisive importance. According to trustworthy reports, it may be assumed that substantial supplies of bread, grain, and fodder exist in the Ukraine. The restoration of orderly commercial intercourse with the Ukraine, and the exchange of the surplus grain, fodder, and raw materials there for industrial products from our country and Austria, is therefore quite a vital interest both for us and, still more so, for Austria-Hungary. That will lead, in accord with the Ukrainian Government, to facilities, railway facilities particularly, being made the subject of joint examinations and measures.

I prefer not to go in detail into the legal and commercial parts of the treaty with the Ukraine, since these matters by their nature demand discussion by expert commissaries. But I can go so far as to say that in this first treaty, which has a certain significance and importance as a pattern—since experience shows us that in diplomacy instruments already at hand serve more or less as bases for subsequent proceedings —the restoration of legal relations generally is completely secured, and that we can communicate with this important part of the former Russian Empire with complete security of rights, both diplomatical and politico-commercial. The politico-commercial agreements also offer security for the revival of sound trade as soon as the difficulties still existing in the political conditions permit.

Regarding the question whether the conclusion of the Ukrainian Treaty might prejudice the conclusion of peace with the Bolshevik Government at Petrograd, my impression is that that is not so. If any means whatever existed to induce M. Trotsky to sign a satisfactory peace instrument, it was to be found precisely in the Ukrainian peace, and I still consider the conclusion of this peace an important means of arriving at a settlement tolerable for both parties. The events attending the rupture of the negotiations are sufficiently known to the House.

I can be very short in my historical review, for, meanwhile, new developments have occurred which will, in any case, have a considerable influence on our relations with the Bolshevik cabinet.

After the renewed advance of the German armies, the Council of People's Commissioners yesterday addressed a wireless message to the German Government which, after referring to the treatment of the armistice treaty, says: "The Council of People's Commissioners finds itself obliged, in view of the situation as it stands, to declare its willingness to sign peace on the conditions laid down by the Delegation of the Quadruplice at Brest-Litovsk. [*"Hear, hear!" and great excitement.*] The Council of the People's Commissioners declares that the reply to the detailed conditions laid down by the German Government will be given without delay."

After the experiences which we have had with wireless messages, and the frequent denial of the official character of such messages, this wireless message constitutes for us absolutely no binding document. [*"Very good!"*] We therefore informed the Petrograd Government that the message had been received by us and requested written confirmation of its contents to be sent to our lines. The Petrograd Government thereupon replied that the Government of the People's Commissioners would forward a written confirmation forthwith. [*"Hear, hear!"*] After the experiences of our negotiations with M. Trotsky and his Cabinet, I should not like the impression to arise in any way among wide circles of the public that everything is now smooth and clear, and that peace is already in our pockets. [*"Very true."*] My principal reason for that remark is that I should like to spare the honorable and sincere love of peace of the German people, which is fully shared by the Government, disappointments. Events will certainly now develop comparatively rapidly. We have entered upon an exchange of views with our allies on this new fact. In view of the thorough manner in which the material was dealt with at Brest-Litovsk, that can, however, be completed in a very short time.

So far as can at present be seen, there will, therefore, presumably be no essential shifting of the basis of the negotiations. If I may define the situation caused by this communication, as after conscientious consideration I perceive it, I should say the prospects of the conclusion of peace with the People's Commissaries have been considerably improved by the conclusion of peace with the Ukraine and by the military pressure now exercised by us and by the ruin of certain hopes which had doubtless been entertained in Petrograd. The hope can be expressed that we shall now attain our goal [*applause*], but we shall not indulge in joy about the great result of the real conclusion of peace with Russia until the ink of the signatures is dry. [*Loud applause.*] The impression which I got outside in the country was that the public received the conclusion of peace with the Ukraine with relief and joy, and hailed it as the first step toward a better future and the restoration of the general peace for which we all hope and which with calm, clear, firm, and resolute conduct of foreign policy we also hope to attain within measurable time. [*Loud applause.*]

299. GRÖBER'S SPEECH IN THE REICHSTAG ON THE TREATY WITH THE UKRAINE, FEBRUARY 20, 1918[7]

We approve of the policy of the Government with respect to this peace treaty, and all that is connected therewith. [*Hearty applause.*] . . . . It is the first peace treaty, which, we hope, will soon be followed by others. The treaty with the Ukraine forms, in fact, the preliminary condition, the foundation, for the peace treaties to follow; therefore our satisfaction over it is the more justified. . . . .

As for the form of the treaty, I should like to draw the attention of the House to one point which is perhaps in point of fact not of overwhelming significance but which contains something surprising, namely, the fact that the treaty in addition to being signed by the plenipotentiaries of the German Government, whose names have been communicated to us in the printed material, is also signed by the Chief of the General Staff of the High Command in the East, Major-General Hoffmann, and in his capacity as a representative of the German Army Command. [*"Hear, hear!"—Center and Left.*] . . . . Of course, there is not the slightest objection to General Hoffmann signing the treaty as the representative of the Kaiser and the German Government, but the Army Command, as such, should not appear as one of the contracting parties to such a treaty. How is that explained? . . . . That the Army Command has an extraordinarily high and important task no one would deny, but it cannot appear as a contracting party at the conclusion of peace. [*"Quite right!"—Center and Left.*] I therefore ask the Secretary of State for enlightenment on this point. The most surprising thing in the treaty is the provision as regards the Government of Cholm. Not that we could reject the treaty on that account. As this provision was made a *conditio sine qua non* by the other side, we must put up with it, whether we like it or not. . . . . The interest of the German Empire is decisive. But the provision is and remains extraordinary. The Cholm Government has always belonged to Poland: all that can be in doubt is whether, ethnographically, it ranks as Polish or Ukrainian. . . . . Until a few weeks ago it ranked as Polish. [*"Quite right!"—Center and Poles.*] The distribution of the electoral districts for the pending Polish elections has taken place there, ... and the elections were arranged about a week ago, and now we are confronted with the fact that in this treaty the whole government is credited to the Ukraine. . . . . Without attaching too much importance to statistics, ... it must be remembered that individual districts contain 60 to 85 per cent of Poles. [*"Hear, hear!"—Center and Poles.*] These districts, with such large Polish Majorities, should be left to Poland, not added to the Ukraine. . . . . The Poles would complain, and not without justification, of such a proceeding. Now just such a proceeding is provided for, both in the treaty itself and in the statements made here and in Vienna yesterday. . . . . If a Polish representative is added to the Mixed Commission, and the principle of the right of self-determination is taken into account when definitely fixing the frontier, the wishes of the Polish gentlemen will be considered. . . . . Religious freedom must be guaranteed to national minorities. In the Ukraine violence has often been done to those of another faith [*"Quite right!"—Poles*] ; in this Government churches have been forcibly taken. . . . . [*"Hear, hear!"—Center and Poles.*] Guaranties must be created for the Catholic population. The Ukraine has appealed to us for help against the Bolsheviks, who are devastating it; this opportunity must be turned to account to afford these guaranties to the Catholics until the Ukraine is better consolidated, and is itself in a position to answer for the protection and liberty of its subjects and citizens. . . . . Provision for returning refugees is also particularly important. Here care must be taken that those who had returned before this treaty came into force, and whose property is in part seriously injured, shall have their rights. . . . .

In welcoming the conclusion of the treaty with the Ukraine on behalf of my friends I should like to say that we trust consistent efforts will continue to be made to bring about peaceful relations in the remainder of the East, above all, in Lithuania and Courland. . . . . The announcement made by the Lithuanian Representative Assembly that a completely autonomous Lithuanian state will be proclaimed, with Vilna as its capital, is gratifying. . . . . The way in which matters are shaping in Courland is also satisfactory. Only the representation should be on a wider basis so that it may really be a representation of the whole population of Courland. . . . . Thus we may cherish the hope of very soon being able again to cultivate friendly, neighborly relations with the Eastern countries. . . . . If our Government succeeds in this, the whole German people will be grateful to it. We adopt the treaty with the Ukraine with the wish: *Vivat sequens.* [*Hearty applause.*]

300. AGREEMENT FOR THE UKRAINE'S FURNISHING CEREALS, GRAINS, AND OIL-SEEDS; SIGNED AT KIEF, 12 NOON, APRIL 9, 1918[8]

KIEF, 9 April (W.B.). After long and difficult negotiations, there has been signed this day, at the hour of noon, by the Ukrainian, German, and Austro-Hungarian delegates, an agreement concerning the furnishing of sixty million poods of bread cereals, fodder grain, podded grain, and oil-seeds. For the business accomplishment of the great task, Germany and Austria-Hungary have established in Kief a mercantile office. This office, through its commissioners or through Ukrainian subcommissioners, receives the grain from the Ukrainian commercial organization. In April, nine million poods, in May fifteen, in June twenty, and in July nineteen million poods are to be supplied. The existing maximum prices for the Ukrainian producer, that is, 5 rubles for rye and 6 for wheat, may not be increased. Incidentals for expenses of all kinds, for commissions, and for freight rates are fixed to correspond to the high Ukrainian quotations. The operations for furnishing grains have already begun.

[8] *Texts of the Ukraine Peace,* p. 143.

CHAPTER XVIII

NEGOTIATIONS WITH RUMANIA, TURKEY,
AND THE BALTIC STATES

INTRODUCTORY NOTE

THE DIPLOMATIC efforts of the Entente to secure the military support of Rumania were crowned by the treaty of alliance of August 17, 1916. Rumania, which declared war against Austria-Hungary August 27, 1916, was immediately attacked by the Central Powers and her capital occupied December 6, 1916. Rumania concluded an armistice with the Central Powers December 6, 1917, and commenced peace negotiations, which were continued by the Bratianu, Averescu, and Marghiloman ministries until May 7, 1918, when the treaty of Bucharest was signed. The *Vorwärts* account of this unratified treaty reveals the character of the control of the Danube, the national railways, and the oil-fields which reduced Rumania to economic and political vassalage.

Turkey signed a secret treaty of alliance with Germany on August 2, 1914, but maintained her neutrality until October 29, 1914, when she committed definite acts of war against Russia and Great Britain. As early as September 8, 1914, Turkey declared the capitulations abolished, but the formal recognition of this abolition was not secured from Germany until January 1917.

The revolution of 1917 liberated Finland from Russian control. On December 6, 1917, the Diet and Senate of Finland proclaimed the independence of the country, which was later formally recognized in the treaty of Brest-Litovsk and the treaty of peace between Finland and Germany of March 7, 1918. Germany sent an infantry division to Finland under the command of General von der Goltz, which in co-operation with the forces of General Mannerheim liberated the country from the Red Guards. The crown of Finland was then offered to Prince Frederick Charles of Hesse. Ludendorff was planning a military operation against the Allied forces holding the Murman railway when the initiative finally passed to the Allies on the Western front.

The agreements between Germany and Russia of March 3 and August 27, 1918, included Livonia, Esthonia, Courland, and Lithuania, within the German sphere of influence. Several of the following documents illustrate German policies in these former Russian territories.

301. MEMORANDUM BY DR. KANNER OF A CONVERSATION WITH DR. ZIMMERMANN, JUNE 15, 1915[1]

I greeted Zimmermann with the remark that his fears, expressed during my last visit with him, had come true. With an expression of regret he said: "Yes, you mean Italy. But now we must only attempt to prevent Rumania from 'going off' too." The change from Italy to Rumania was so abrupt that I had the impression that he did not like to talk about Italy. He said it was well that Rumania had not declared war simultaneously with Italy and that now everything must be done to prevent her from following the example of Italy. That would not be impossible at all if only Austria-Hungary were willing to grant concessions. Not much was being demanded. I asked what Rumania really demanded of us. His reply was that Rumania really did not demand anything, but that she awaited an offer from us. I then inquired as to the possible nature of the offer. He said that: (1) The districts of the Bukovina, which are inhabited by Rumanians, i.e., the South-Bukovina, must be ceded. No opposition has been raised on your part to this. (2) Rumania further expects that it be given at least a part of Transylvania, but we shall talk them out of that. (3) In regard to the treatment of Rumanians in Hungary, they demand—"Autonomy," I interrupted involuntarily. He said: "No, for God's sake we cannot call that thing autonomy. We must call it statute, amounting, of course, to the same thing, which would grant the Rumanians certain rights." I asked whether the Rumanians would be satisfied with such a statute and reminded him of what Tisza replied to Rumania's demand, shortly before the war, as to the application of the Nationality Law of 1868. Tisza said that that would mean the suicide of Hungary. Zimmermann replied that a mere agreement between the different Governments would satisfy the Rumanians; that the Emperor would have to make a solemn promise that the Rumanians would never be deprived of those rights. I asked what attitude our Government took in this matter. Zimmermann said that that was just the difficulty—it did not want to hear about it. I asked, "Tisza?" He said, "Burian"; and then added with a certain expression of irritation and deprecation that nothing could be done with him.

[1] Kanner Papers, II, 201-15.

"Burian is capable of giving one a two-hour lecture, very learned and interesting, but nothing comes of it. He cannot make a decision. He is no statesman, but a professor who belongs in a university." I asked about Tisza. He said that Tisza, too, was against it. "Nothing can be done with him. But Andrassy is won," he added in a milder tone. "Well," I said, "what then is to happen; shall Andrassy take Tisza's place?" He denied it. "Burian's place?" I asked. He said that that would be the right thing. . . . . I said: "You mean, then, that Rumania would be satisfied with that?" He said that if our operations against Russia continue to be favorable, they hope that we will obtain for them Bessarabia. "That would be nice. And what does Rumania give us?" I queried. He replied that above all Rumania would remain neutral— "A benevolent neutrality." I asked what that would consist in. He replied that they "would at least let munitions and cereals through. . . . . Everything would go well if only on our part (Austria) some concessions were made. The conditions in Rumania were not so bad for us." I asked whether he meant the latest events with Marghiloman of the Conservative Party. He said evasively that the case with Lahovary was not exactly pleasant and that he was surprised that he too was for the Entente. Thereupon I asked him about the attitude of the King of Rumania. He said, "The King is on our side and he would abdicate rather than wage war against you." I was surprised at that, to which Zimmermann replied that he would abdicate rather than fight us; that he would not act like that little brigand Vittorio Emanuele. I said that if he were right, it was hardly possible to assume that Rumania would fight us. Zimmermann, however, said that the King held a very weak position in that country, and that the Rumanians would not feel much concern about the King's abdication. Then, somewhat relieved, he said that Bratianu too is on our side. I expressed a certain surprise at that; to which his reply was: "Well, Bratianu certainly remembers how Russia cheated his father out of Bessarabia and he has not much to say for the Russians."

I told him then of having recently read in the *Berliner Zeitung* that there exists a treaty between us and Rumania which is to run until 1920, and asked him whether there was anything to it. Zimmermann replied: "Yes, that is simply the Triple Alliance Treaty. Rumania at one time joined the Triple Alliance and has the same agreement with us as Italy." "Well," I said, "in that case it is certainly peculiar that they adopt such a hostile attitude toward us, not to mention at all the threats of war." And, as if having to tell me a secret, he said, somewhat softly, "We have told all that to the Rumanians, and they say that the agreement is illegal, since it is not countersigned." "How then was the agreement made?" I asked. Growing still softer, he said: "The old Carol, you know, who in former times—unfortunately he was too old at last—knew how to force through his will, concluded the agreement all by himself, without his ministers knowing anything about it. He told only a few of his Premiers about the existence of this treaty and none of the other ministers knew about it. The present Minister of Foreign Affairs, Porumbaro, for example, was not aware of the existence of this treaty. All in all, probably about five men knew about it: Bratianu, the present Premier, Sturdza, the former Premier, the old Carol, of course, and one or two other men." (He apparently was unable to recall their names.) "Well, who signed it?" I asked. "King Carol," he said, "who would have also forced the matter through had he not been so old, or better, not so sick. With almost moving words he announced at that time in the Crown Council: "I must hold to my word." But only the old Carol supported him, the rest of them all declaring that they knew nothing of an obligation and that Rumania had nothing to do with this obligation." I then asked whether the present King had signed the treaty. He said, "No." I asked whether he knew of it. Zimmermann affirmed this and repeated that the present King too would surely abdicate in case it should come to a war with us.

302. DECLARATION OF WAR AGAINST RUMANIA, AUGUST 28, 1916[2]

BERLIN, August 28. (W.T.B.) Rumania, after having, as already reported, disgracefully broken the treaties she had concluded with Austria-Hungary and Germany, yesterday declared war on our ally. The German Minister in Bucharest has received instructions to demand his passports and to declare to the Rumanian Government that Germany considers herself in a state of war with Rumania also.

303. THE *VORWÄRTS* ACCOUNT OF THE PEACE OF BUCHAREST[3]

The peace with Rumania is the first part of the Balkan peace. Only Greece and Serbia remain for a complete regulation of all the questions pertaining to the Near East. The first is within the sphere of the Entente's power; the second with its land and people is in the hands of the Central Powers, but its government, like that of Belgium, is outside and still hopes for a later opportunity for a favorable peace.

[2] *Norddeutsche Allgemeine Zeitung,* August 29, 1916.
[3] *Vorwärts,* No. 126, May 8, 1918, p. 1.

Thus the Rumanian peace, too, could not be spared the temporary character which characterizes all the Eastern peace contracts. The Balkan questions are so intertwisted that none of them can be solved entirely without its entire complex requiring a new regulation. Final could be the conquest which Austria and Hungary have achieved for the purpose of "strategic guaranties"; final also the conquest of South Dobruja through Bulgaria. But today there is no Balkan state whose boundaries stand definite in all directions—neither the Rumanian boundaries with Russia, nor Bulgaria's boundaries against Serbia and Greece. Equally uncertain are the boundaries of Turkey against Bulgaria.

Even in the territory which is removed from Entente influence three boundary questions are left up in the air—that of Bessarabia; that of North Dobruja; and that of Turkey with respect to Bulgaria. Rumania, reduced at the expense of Bulgaria and Austria-Hungary, is left open to the possibility of compensating itself in Bessarabia without its having been given a right to that country. As is well known, the Ukraine has vigorously protested against the separating of Bessarabia from it. Thus Bessarabia remains an open question and an open wound.

A connection exists between the affair of North Dobruja, north of the Constanza-Cernavoda line, and the Turkish-Bulgarian boundary question. Turkey did not want to agree to the granting of all of Dobruja to Bulgaria, without receiving back the boundary strip at Adrianople, which it had to surrender to Bulgaria in the treaty of September 6, 1915. They helped themselves by leaving this question open and organized temporarily a condominium, i.e., a common government of the Quadruple Powers. A similar condominium existed from 1864–66 between Prussia and Austria with regard to Schleswig-Holstein. Taught by experience, these Powers probably will not let war come on account of the Schleswig-Holsteins of the Black Sea. The apparent intention is later on to leave the entire Dobruja to Bulgaria, and to reconcile Turkey to this arrangement by a means which has not yet been found.

Here too it has been shown that the territorial fight of the World War is being waged primarily about coast lands, and that the defeated country is in danger of being pushed away from the sea. If Rumania does not find compensation in a strip of Bessarabian coast, it will in its recourse to the sea be dependent upon the line to Constanza, which is not to be given entirely into Bulgaria's hands. What finally is to happen to this line belongs also to the many questions left open by the Bucharest peace.

One is not surprised any more to hear that Rumania upon the fulfillment of peace conditions is not to be freed from the military administration of the Central Powers. Field-Marshal v. Mackensen, in a toast with which he celebrated the conclusion of peace, emphasized that with this treaty the war in the East had found its termination. In spite of that, German armies are in Finland, Esthonia, Latvia, Courland, Lithuania, Poland, the Ukraine, Crimea, and Rumania, and at present there is not even talk about their going out of those places. On the contrary, in the army bulletins (East) we still read of their activities there. Let us hope that in Rumania events will not occur after the conclusion of peace such as occurred in Finland and the Ukraine. However, there is no assurance of that, because of the peculiarity of the military peace in the East. . . . .

The Central Powers expect from Rumania grain, cattle, and petroleum. For the sale and transport of grain the experiences gathered so far will suffice. But the furnishing by Rumania of petroleum to the Central Powers had to be placed upon an entirely new basis.

Before the war, on account of the insufficient transport means on the Danube, the Central Powers imported kerosene, gasoline, and lubricating oil chiefly from the United States of America. The enormous use of mineral oil during the war has made their continuous and certain provision a necessity. The new petroleum agreement with Rumania, which, however, comes in force only if between the German, Austro-Hungarian, and Rumanian Governments no new and better treaty is made prior to December 1, 1918, serves that purpose.

A crude oil monopoly is being introduced. For its realization the Rumanian Government transfers the right of exploitation on all Rumanian Government lands, not only in the occupied region but also in Moldavia, to an oil-land lease company, controlled by the German Government, whose right of exploitation is given for the period of ninety years. The Rumanian Government also recognized the legality of the transfer to this company of the valuables coming from the liquidated enemy companies.

The business monopoly itself is being exercised by a second company. Both companies will remain for a long time under German influence, even if participation is granted to Austria-Hungary and Rumania. The company pays the Rumanian Government 4 lei (francs) for every ton of exported crude oil products. From further contributions it is free. The company is obligated to take all of the petroleum produced but may demand that the prospector of oil be held responsible for shipping the oil to the nearest railroad station or the nearest storage place. The company also establishes semiannually the prices of petroleum. For the petroleum producers this prospect is less terrible than it appears, because the German Government will stimulate the demand for petroleum at will through high prices.

If now the newly created economic relation between Rumania and the Central Powers can in no way be regarded as exemplary, it at any rate shows the whole foolishness of a world of conception, in which only conquests and reparations are deemed the appropriate gains of a victor. There are advantages which cannot be expressed in terms of square miles and sums of money and which yet are of decisive importance for the future of a country. Treaty rights are more important than owner rights; economic world position, secured by treaties, is more important than territorial aggrandizement and financial enrichment. If once universal peace has been concluded, one will have to look less upon the geographic map than on the economic agreements, in order to judge who remained the victor.

304. OFFICIAL ANNOUNCEMENT CONCERNING THE END OF THE CAPITULATIONS[4]

BERLIN, January 11, 1917

According to a Wolff dispatch, the plenipotentiaries of the German and Turkish Empires affixed their signatures at the Foreign Office to the following series of agreements: A Consular Agreement, an Agreement securing the Right of Legal Protection, and the Right of Legal Redress in civil actions, for both parties, an Extradition Treaty and a Settlement Treaty, and also a Treaty for the mutual surrender of subjects liable to military service, as well as deserters from land or sea forces. To these must be added five further agreements according to which the provisions contained in these legal treaties are extended to the German Protectorates. At the same time that these treaties were signed there was an exchange of notes which make certain transitory provisions for the execution of the treaties as well as a further exchange of notes concerning the future conclusion of a Commercial Treaty.

The importance of these treaties consists in the fact that they are meant to replace the system of the so-called capitulations, which has hitherto regulated the legal relations between the German and the Turkish Empires, by new provisions corresponding to the principles of modern international law, and based on entire reciprocity. The repeal of the capitulations is one of the most important of the war aims of the Turkish people. The capitulations have often been the cloak for discreditable intrigues on the part of our enemies against the stability of Turkey; they have thus for a long while impeded a healthy development of the economic and financial life of Turkey. The German Empire was therefore unable to refuse the appeal of the Sublime Porte for friendly assistance on this matter.

The negotiations have been conducted in Berlin and have occupied

---

[4] *Norddeutsche Allgemeine Zeitung,* January 15, 1917, I, 1.

exactly a year. The result, however, has been proportionate to the trouble taken, for in spite of the anticipated difficulties the entire legal relations between Germany and Turkey have been drastically and exhaustively reorganized, a work which has never hitherto been achieved between two nations in the course of a single treaty.

The agreements, in which the interests of both sides have been carefully balanced, will as soon as possible be submitted to the Bundesrat and the Reichstag as well as to the Turkish Parliament. It is to be hoped that the legislative bodies of both countries will by acceptance of their provisions give effect to the lofty aims by which they are inspired.

305. THE MAIN COMMITTEE OF THE REICHSTAG ON THE SITUATION IN THE EAST, MARCH 5, 1918[5]

In connection with the resumed discussion in the Main Committee about the situation in the East:

Dr. David (Socialist) said: The occupation of the Aaland Islands is by no means only a military question, but also a very important political affair. It is by no means certain what tendency will get the upper hand in Finland. It is clear that our procedure must arouse a bitter opposition in Sweden. Regarding Bethmann's telegram of July 31, it is well that it only now became known to the French Government. Therefore it does not come into consideration in the matter of fixing the blame for the World War. It would be desirable to hear more details about the basis of the peace negotiations with Rumania.

Dr. Riesser (National-Liberal): The telegram of July 31, 1914, was a private instruction, and was never the subject of negotiations with France. It can have fallen into the hands of France only by theft. In concluding peace with Rumania it is important to decide whether or not King Ferdinand is to be retained.

Gothein (Progressive): Our sympathy goes out to the White Guard in Finland. Since the last election the "White" Government has a legal basis. Was it necessary to provoke Sweden? The telegram to Herr von Schön has a very painful effect on me. It is an unintelligible diplomatic blunder. It was superfluous because the attitude of France was already certain. With regard to the oil interests in Rumania, they should proceed carefully in the matter of the American holdings in order to avoid unpleasant consequences.

Ledebour (Independent Socialist): If Rumania is to cede the Dobruja to Bulgaria, is it to be compensated in Bessarabia? Bethmann's telegram, even if it actually had not done any harm, was evidence of the aggressive intentions of the former Chancellor.

[5] *Norddeutsche Allgemeine Zeitung*, March 5, 1918, I, 3.

Count Westarp (Conservative): The object of the telegram to Ambassador von Schön is not quite intelligible; however, it is wrong to deduce from it the conclusion that we intended to implicate France in the war. Finland is in exactly the same case as the Ukraine. Its independence, although having been recognized by Russia, must now be secured by German troops and thus give the country peace.

Schönaich-Carolath (National-Liberal): Germany should not care about the present Rumanian King Ferdinand; for in view of past events the German people would not understand our supporting the Rumanian dynasty.

Bruhn (German Party): The internal agitation in Russia took place after the peace resolution of the Reichstag. It is therefore a factor contributing to Russia's defeat. Politics and the sword co-operated in the achievement of peace.

Ebert (Socialist): I could not approve the sending of an expeditionary force to the Aaland Islands which, according to a Danish report, is to take place. I do not understand the instruction to Ambassador von Schön. No first-class country could have submitted to it.

Gothein (Progressive): It would be a political mistake on our part to attempt to save the throne for the Rumanian King. That would arouse the animosity of the Rumanian people. It is regrettable that the Jews and other national minorities are not sufficiently protected by the new peace treaties.

Alpers (German Party): The peace concluded with Russia is gratifying. . . . .

Haase (Independent Socialist): How can we conclude peace with Finland when no Finnish soldier has fought against Germany? All that could possibly be done was the regulation of economic relations by a treaty.

Under-Secretary Bussche gave confidential information upon a number of questions, ... after which the discussion about the situation in the East was closed.

306. TREATY OF PEACE BETWEEN FINLAND AND GERMANY, SIGNED AT BERLIN, MARCH 7, 1918[6]

The Imperial German Government and the Finnish Government, inspired by the wish, after the declaration of the independence of Finland and her recognition of the part of Germany, to bring about a condition of peace and amity between both countries on a lasting basis, have

[6] *Deutscher Reichsanzeiger,* March 8, 1918; translation here as in United States Department of State, *Texts of the Finland "Peace,"* pp. 13–26; hereafter cited as *Texts of the Finland Peace.*

resolved to conclude a treaty of peace, and for this purpose have appointed the following plenipotentiaries: For the Imperial German Government, the Chancellor of the German Empire, Dr. Count von Hertling; for the Finnish Government, Edvard Immanuel Hjelt, Ph.D., State Counselor, Vice Chancellor of the University of Helsingfors, and Rafael Waldemar Erich, LL.D., Professor of Civil and International Law at the University of Helsingfors, who, after the mutual presentation of their powers, found in good and due form, have come to an agreement on the following provisions:

Chapter I

Article 1. The contracting parties declare that between Germany and Finland no state of war exists and that they are resolved henceforth to live in peace and amity with each other.

Germany will do what she can to bring about the recognition of the independence of Finland by all the Powers. On the other hand, Finland will not cede any part of her possessions to any foreign Power nor grant a servitude on her sovereign territory to any such Power before first having come to an understanding with Germany on the matter.

Article 2. Diplomatic and consular relations between the contracting parties will be resumed immediately after the confirmation of the Peace Treaty. As regards the widest possible admission of Consuls on both sides, special agreements are reserved.

Article 3. Each of the contracting parties will indemnify the damages which have been caused in its own territory by virtue of the war, or which the local public authorities or the population have occasioned by actions contrary to international law, or which have been caused to consular officials of the other party either in body, liberty, health, or property, or to consular offices of the other party or to their contents.

Chapter II

Article 4. The contracting parties renounce mutually the refunding of war costs, that is to say, state expenses for the carrying on of the war as well as the payment of indemnities for war damages, that is to say, for those prejudices which have been caused them and their nationals in the war zones by reason of military measures, inclusive of all requisitions made in the country of the enemy.

Chapter III

Article 5. The treaties which went out of force as a consequence of the war between Germany and Russia shall be replaced as soon as possible by new treaties for relations between the contracting parties, to meet the changed viewpoint and conditions. Especially, the two parties shall, as soon as possible, enter into negotiations in order to conclude a treaty of commerce and navigation.

In the meantime the trade relations between the two countries will be regulated through an agreement of commerce and navigation which is to be signed at the same time as the Peace Treaty.

Article 6. Treaties in which, apart from Germany and Russia, also third Powers take place, and in which Finland appears together with Russia or in the place of the latter, come into force between the contracting parties on the ratification of the Peace Treaty or, in case the accession takes place later, at that moment.

In connection with collective treaties of political purport, in which other belligerent Powers also participate, the two parties reserve their attitude until after the conclusion of a general peace. . . . .

CHAPTER X

Article 30. The contracting parties are agreed that the forts built upon the Aaland Islands are to be removed as soon as possible, and that the permanent non-fortified character of these islands and also their treatment in a military and technical sense for purposes of shipping shall be settled by agreement between Germany, Finland, Russia, and Sweden; and to these agreements, at the wish of Germany, the other States bordering upon the Baltic Sea shall be invited to assent.

CHAPTER XI

Article 31. This Peace Treaty shall be confirmed. The confirmatory documents shall be exchanged as soon as practicable in Berlin.

Article 32. The Peace Treaty, in so far as is not otherwise stipulated, shall come into force with its confirmation.

To complete the treaty the representatives of the contracting parties shall meet in Berlin within four months of its confirmation.

In faith whereof the plenipotentiaries of both parties have signed the present treaty and affixed their seals to it.

Done in duplicate original at Berlin, 7 March, 1918.

307. TREATY OF COMMERCE AND NAVIGATION BETWEEN GERMANY AND FINLAND, SIGNED AT BERLIN, MARCH 7, 1918[7]

The Imperial Government, and the Finnish Government, being animated by the desire to resume the relations of friendly intercourse be-

[7] *Texts of the Finland Peace,* pp. 27–38; also *Norddeutsche Allgemeine Zeitung,* March 9, 1918.

tween Germany and Finland which were interrupted by the war between Germany and Russia and to render them as advantageous as possible, have decided to conclude a commerce and navigation agreement and for this purpose have appointed as their plenipotentiaries, to wit:

The Imperial German Government—Count von Hertling, Chancellor of the German Empire;

The Finnish Government—Edvard Immanuel Hjelt, Ph.D., Counselor of State, Deputy Chancellor of the Helsingfors University, and Rafael Waldemar Erich, LL.D., Professor of Civil and International Law at the Helsingfors University,

who, after exhibiting to each other their full powers, which were found to be in due and proper form, have agreed upon the following provisions:

Article 1. As no state of war exists between Germany and Finland and the contracting parties are determined to live with each other henceforth in peace and amity, it is self-evident that hostile actions between the two countries in economic and financial matters must also be precluded.

Accordingly, the contracting parties will mutually refrain from participating, directly or indirectly, in any measures which tend toward hostilities in an economic or financial way, and they will also use all means at their disposal to prevent such measures from being taken within their national territory, whether by private parties or otherwise. On the other hand, they will remove any obstacles which may impede the resumption of friendly commercial and business relations, and facilitate mutual commercial exchange as far as possible.

During the transitional period necessary in order to overcome the effects of the war and reorganize conditions, they shall administer all trade restrictions such as export embargoes, regulation of imports, etc., which are indispensable during this period in such a manner that they shall be as little burdensome as possible. On the other hand, they shall, during the same period, burden the supply of necessary goods as little as possible with import duties and therefore, as far as may be, temporarily continue and extend the exemptions from and reductions in customs duties established during the war. . . . .

Article 18. This agreement shall be ratified. The ratification shall be exchanged at Berlin as soon as possible.

In witness whereof the plenipotentiaries of both parties have signed the present agreement and affixed thereto their seals.

Done in duplicate original at Berlin on 7 March, 1918.

308. THE APPLICATION OF THE PROVISIONS OF THE TREATIES OF MARCH 7 TO THE GERMAN PROTECTORATES[8]

(a) FOREIGN OFFICE. Fr. III a 89

BERLIN, 11 March 1918

The undersigned has the honor to communicate the following to Counselor of State Dr. Hjelt and Professor Dr. Erich, Plenipotentiaries of the Finnish Government:

The Imperial German Government attaches importance to having the representatives of the German and Finnish Governments who are to meet for the purpose of supplementing the treaty between Germany and Finland of the 7th instant (Article 32, Par. 2) also charged with regulating the application of the provisions of the peace treaty as well as of the commerce and navigation agreement of the same date to the German protectorates.

While looking forward to favorable answer as to whether the Finnish Government is willing to accede to this desire, the undersigned avails himself of this opportunity to renew to the Plenipotentiaries of the Finnish Government the assurances of his most distinguished regards.

(*Signed*) VON STUMM

The Plenipotentiaries of the Finnish Government,
Counselor of State Dr. Hjelt, Excellency, and Professor Dr. Erich, Excellency.

308. (b) THE PLENIPOTENTIARIES OF THE FINNISH GOVERNMENT

BERLIN, 11 March 1918

The undersigned have the honor to acknowledge the receipt of letter Fr. III a 89 of this date from the Undersecretary of the Foreign Office and at the same time to declare that the Finnish Government will comply with the request made therein regarding the application of the provisions of the Peace Treaty and the Commerce and Navigation Agreement between Germany and Finland to the German protectorates.

The undersigned avail themselves of this occasion to renew to the

---

[8] *Texts of the Finland Peace*, pp. 45–46.

Honorable Undersecretary the assurances of their most distinguished regards.

(*Sgd.*) Hjelt
(*Sgd.*) Erich

His Excellency Herr von Stumm
Undersecretary in the Foreign Office

309. RESOLUTION NO. 1421 TO THE SECOND READING OF THE BREST-LITOVSK PEACE TREATY[9]

The Reichstag, in taking leave of the Russo-German peace treaty, gives expression to the expectations:

That in accordance with the Chancellor's declaration of November 29, 1917, and the declarations of the German peace-negotiators at Brest-Litovsk, the rights of Poland, Lithuania, and Courland to self-determination will be taken into account.

That steps will forthwith be taken to develop their constitutions with a native civilian administration.

That the present representative assemblies will be placed on a broader basis.

And, finally, that an agreement (*Vereinbarung*) with Germany, as desired by the present assemblies, will be concluded as soon as possible.

310. CORRESPONDENCE BETWEEN KAISER WILHELM II AND THE LIVONIAN KNIGHTHOOD AND THE UNIVERSITY OF DORPAT, MARCH 13, 1918[10]

(a) THE LIVONIAN KNIGHTHOOD TO KAISER WILHELM II, MARCH 13, 1918

The Livonian Knighthood begs Your Majesty to accept its most humble thanks for the deliverance of Livonia from misery and distress, and for putting this most ancient German colony under the protection of the powerful German Empire. The Livonian Knighthood renews its vow of unchanging loyalty, and begs Your Majesty to be sure of this, that the Livonians will always be ready to uphold the greatness of the German Fatherland with their life and property.

Signed on behalf of the Livonian Knighthood, by the Landesrat in residence:

Baron Stael von Holstein,
Knighthood Secretary von Samson Himmelstierna

[9] *Verhandlungen des Reichstags,* Anlagen, Band 324, p. 2154.
[10] *Norddeutsche Allgemeine Zeitung,* March 13, 1918, I, 1.

310. (b) KAISER WILHELM II TO BARON STAEL VON HOLSTEIN

Baron Stael von Holstein

Hearty thanks for the greeting I had the pleasure of receiving from the Livonian Knighthood. The German people rejoice with me that our arms have been able to defend the beautiful, sorely-tried country from further misery. May this difficult time result in the resurrection of Baltic Germanism to free and happy development of its energy.

(*Signed*) WILHELM I.

310. (c) THE UNIVERSITY OF DORPAT TO KAISER WILHELM II

From the University of Dorpat

The assembled German Professors, Dozenten, and students of the old German University, beg Your Majesty to accept their heartfelt thanks for the deliverance of Germanism. We pledge Your Majesty our inviolable loyalty and devotion.

(*Signed*) PROFESSORS DEHIO, HAHN,
ZOEGE VON MANTEUFELL

310. (d) KAISER WILHELM II TO PROFESSOR DEHIO, DORPAT

Professor Dehio, Dorpat

Hearty thanks for the friendly greeting! It is a great pleasure to me and to the whole of academic Germany that, thanks to the victory of our arms, the venerable *alma mater Dorpatensis* can resume her historic rôle as the home of German intellectual life. Great memories of the past will thus be awakened to new life. May a rich blessing proceed from her again, for the so sorely tried order-lands and for German erudition, as in olden days.

(*Signed*) WILHELM I.

311. COUNT HERTLING'S REPLY TO THE RESOLUTION OF APRIL 12, 1918, OF THE JOINT LANDESRAT OF LIVONIA, ESTHONIA, RIGA, AND OESEL, PRESENTED AT GENERAL HEADQUARTERS, APRIL 21, 1918[11]

His Majesty, the Emperor and King, has authorized me to express his warmest thanks to the representatives of the Joint Landesrat of

[11] *Ibid.*, April 23, 1918, I, 1.

Livonia, Esthonia, Riga, and Oesel for the confidence shown in his august person by your resolutions.

The victorious advance of the German troops, and the peace treaty of Brest-Litovsk, have freed you, too, from sore affliction, and have at the same time afforded you the possibility of making political arrangements which answer to the wishes and needs of the population.

Inasmuch as the United Landesrat of Livonia, Riga, and Oesel, as the representative assembly of the population of these countries, appointed by the constitutional bodies, has turned to him, full of confidence, His Majesty declares himself prepared to grant these countries the military protection of the German Empire and to give them effective support in carrying out their separation from Russia. His Majesty will then be very ready to recognize the liberated territories formally as autonomous states, in the name of the Empire.

His Majesty welcomes the wish expressed by the Landesrat that Courland, Livonia, Esthonia, the islands off their coast, and the town of Riga should form a uniform, compact, monarchical, constitutional state, with a uniform constitution and administration, and will willingly advise and assist them to bring this about. His Majesty is also quite ready to facilitate the creation of special provincial organization for the administration of Livonia and Esthonia until a political union of the Baltic territories is effected. It gave His Majesty peculiar pleasure and satisfaction that you have expressed the feeling of gratitude of your countries in the wish that the state to be newly formed should be more closely linked to the German Empire by a personal union with the Crown of Prussia. This request will be benevolently examined, and the All-Highest's decision will be transmitted to the Landesrat after the parties competent to co-operate in the matter have been heard.

His Majesty will further be prepared, after the separation of the Baltic provinces from Russia, to give his august consent to the proposal that the necessary military, currency, commercial, customs, weights and measures, and other conventions should be concluded between the German Empire and the state formed from the Baltic territories. His Majesty sends His Imperial greeting to the representatives of the countries, and trusts that their further work for the development of the provinces they represent may be richly blessed.

312. THE RECOGNITION OF LITHUANIA'S INDEPENDENCE, MARCH 23, 1918[12]

We, Wilhelm, by the grace of God, German Emperor, King of Prussia, etc., hereby make known:

[12] *Norddeutsche Allgemeine Zeitung,* May 12, 1918, I, 1.

Seeing that, on December 11, 1917, the Lithuanian Landesrat, recognized as representing the Lithuanian people, announced the re-establishment of Lithuania as an independent state, united to the German Empire by a permanent, firm alliance and by conventions, chiefly relating to military matters, trade, customs, and coinage, and in order to re-establish this state asked for the protection and help of the German Empire; and seeing, further, that Lithuania's former political ties are dissolved, we hereby authorize our Imperial Chancellor, Count v. Hertling, to announce to the Lithuanian Landesrat that on the basis of the announcement of the Lithuanian Landesrat, December 11, 1917, mentioned above, We, in the name of the German Empire, recognize Lithuania as a free and independent state, and are prepared to grant the Lithuanian State the requested protection and assistance in its re-establishment. In so doing we assume that the conventions to be concluded will take the interests of the German Empire into the same account as the Lithuanian, and that Lithuania will share Germany's war expenses, which also served to liberate her.

At the same time, we authorize our Imperial Chancellor, acting in concert with the representatives of the people of Lithuania, to take the necessary steps to re-establish the independent Lithuanian State, and to cause further steps to be taken as regards the establishment of a permanent and firm alliance with the German Empire and the conclusion of the conventions provided for and requisite to that end. In token whereof we have signed and sealed the present with Our Own Hand.

> (*Signed*) WILHELM I. R.
> COUNT V. HERTLING

Given at Great Headquarters, March 23, 1918.

313. THE CHANCELLOR'S RECOGNITION OF COURLAND AS A DUKEDOM, MARCH 16, 1918[13]

His Majesty the Emperor and King has already given expression to his deep and heartfelt thanks for the resolution of March 8 in his reply to the telegram of homage from the Courland Landesrat, and has now deigned to charge me to communicate to you, the representatives of the Courland Landesrat now present, his warmest thanks for the trust expressed in the resolution.

With singular joy and emotion His Majesty has taken cognizance of the request addressed to him to accept the ducal Crown of Courland. His Majesty sees in this a singular sign of the unshakable trust

[13] *Ibid.*, March 16, 1918, I, 1.

of Courland in his person and the House of Hohenzollern and in the German Empire and Prussia. The All-Highest decision of His Majesty will be made after hearing from the parties with whom it is proper to co-operate and will be communicated to the Landesrat. With lively joy and satisfaction His Majesty has moreover seen that the wish of the Landesrat is directed toward a close union (*Verbindung*) of the Dukedom of Courland with the German Empire.

Since the Courland Landesrat has formerly in September last, and now again through the present resolution, declared its will for the re-erection of the independent Dukedom of Courland, and since in the meantime the previous state connections of Courland have been dissolved, nothing stands in the way of the execution of this wish any longer. His Majesty has charged me, in the name of the German Empire, to recognize the re-erected Dukedom of Courland as a free and independent dukedom, and to assure it of the protection and assistance of the German Empire in the establishment of its state existence and the building up of its constitution, which must also provide for a representative body on a broad basis, and in doing what remains to be done in regard to the establishment and formulation of the close connection resolved by the Landesrat. A formal announcement concerning the recognition of Courland will be put before the Landesrat.

Finally His Majesty has charged me to direct the attention of the Landesrat to the fact that the interest of His Majesty and the German Empire in the destiny of the other Baltic territory has been expressed in the Russo-German peace treaty recently concluded, and to assure the Landesrat that the shaping of conditions in these territories will henceforward also be attended by the warmest interest of His Majesty the Emperor and King.

314. SPEECH OF VICE-CHANCELLOR DR. VON PAYER IN THE MAIN COMMITTEE OF THE REICHSTAG ON THE EASTERN QUESTIONS, MAY 7, 1918[14]

Our debates have assumed such a range and such a character of High Policy that it is much to be regretted that the Secretary of State for Foreign Affairs is absent. That cannot be altered now. The conclusion of peace with Rumania and the questions that hinge on the peace, or are being decided in connection with it, have such an importance that the Secretary of State, von Kühlmann, as well as the principal Austrian statesman, cannot be dispensed with at these discussions. Besides, no one could foresee that we should be indulging in such debates here.

[14] *Norddeutsche Allgemeine Zeitung,* May 8, 1918, I, 3.

In the course of the discussion the demand was put forward that our whole Eastern policy should be uniformly regulated. On this account the resignation of the Commissioner for the Eastern areas was regretted, as he was regarded as more or less representing this idea of uniformity. That is a mistake. Generally speaking, this commissioner never had anything to do with Poland. Besides, it has become apparent that a special officer, not merely a personal commissioner of the Imperial Chancellor, must be created, in order to bring the border states into ordered conditions of government and administration. It was first of all intended to create for this task either a fresh Secretary of State or an officer of similar constitutional importance, but on closer investigation it appeared that there were serious objections to the creation of a further imperial office. For this reason an office has to be established, that will be joined on to or incorporated in an existing imperial office. Count Keyserlingk, former Commissioner for the Eastern areas, thought that this new office did not match in importance his former position, and has therefore resigned. The discussions over the new organization can be concluded very shortly, and then it will be possible to embark on the practical work with clearer and more definite vision.

In the desire for a uniform Eastern policy there exists complete agreement between the Government and the members of this Committee. The aim of our policy toward the border peoples, who, owing to the break-up of Russia have separated from the union with this empire and established themselves on their own feet, is to live with them for the future in peace and friendship. It is both to our advantage and to theirs that we should draw near to each other in matters of policy, economics, and *Kultur,* and, so far as is feasible, in military affairs also. It is to the interest not only of these border states but of ourselves also that we should promote cultural and economic relations in these countries. Especially do we hope for advantages with regard to the assurance of our food supply, and what is comprised under the general term of colonization. The adhesion of these states should and must constitute for us a military assurance for our frontiers toward Russia that we cannot renounce. No one can foresee developments in Russia; no one can know whether we shall not some time later on be again involved in a war with Russia.

At the same time there exists also a national sympathy with the Germans in those areas who have for years waged a bitter struggle for the maintenance of their German nationality. This applies particularly to the Baltic peoples. And a certain humane feeling has played a part in our policy toward those peoples which even after their separation from Russia were drawn into the general distress and disorder.

Moreover, as to the path that a uniform Eastern policy ought to take, there exists agreement between the Reichstag and us. It is the way of understanding, not of violence. But conditions in the individual countries are so diverse that it is impossible to treat all alike. Regard must be had to the differences of conditions. Rigid treatment would lead to wrong conclusions. Compare, for example, the conditions of Poland with those in Esthonia and Livonia. Poland is already recognized as a big state. The policy adopted toward her must be quite different from that toward the other two states. With regard to Poland, Germany and Poland alone cannot decide, but Austria-Hungary also must have a voice. The same applies to the Ukraine. In this case the greatest regard must be paid to the neighboring state of Austria-Hungary. The treatment must vary also, according to the size of the states, according to the economic and political importance and their geographical situation, whether or not direct connection with them is possible. The historical development of each state must be regarded, as well as the question how far a Government is already in existence in each. From this it is clear that for each of these peoples a special policy must, of necessity, be adopted.

First of all, Finland. We have been reproached with having gone in there in an endeavor to play the part of policeman and guardian of order throughout half the world. The real reasons are far more natural. We are still in the midst of a great world war, which makes the most immense demands on our population and our army. Consequently, we are nowhere in a position to employ soldiers uselessly. If, nevertheless, the Supreme Army Command, in agreement with the Imperial Government, saw itself obliged to interfere in Finland at a moment when the preparations for the great Western offensive were approaching a conclusion, the inference must be drawn that in this connection only important military and political requirements can have influenced the decision.

We are glad by our interposition to have secured Finland's independence and freedom, but the particular main reason for the step taken has been to bring about in the north, in the military and political sphere, a lasting condition of peace.

That has hitherto, unfortunately, not been the case, for in spite of the recognition of the independent Finnish Government the Russian revolutionary committees of soldiers and sailors have introduced their anarchy into Finland. From Russia—whether with or without the consent of the Russian Government is neither here nor there—weapons, munitions, and troops were sent to Finland to support the Russian forces. The Finnish Landtag and the Finnish Senate have, in order to end the disorder, frequently appealed to the Russian Government and asked for the withdrawal of the Russian troops from independent Finland, or at least for the cessation of violence on the part of these troops. That has availed nothing. Finally, the President of the Russian District Committee actually declared war on the Government of Finland. This declaration of war, whether made with or without the knowledge and consent of the Petrograd authorities, was by no means merely a paper decree. For whence otherwise would come the guns, machine guns, armored trains, and armored motors, and the immense quantities of arms and munitions that have been captured by our troops in Finland? Since the unconstitutional revocation of the Finnish military service law of 1878 by Russia in the year 1901, Finland herself no longer disposes of any military materials. They come from those Russian sailors and soldiers who had united with the Finnish anarchists to form an army of intimidation and have now fallen by thousands into the hands of our troops.

Thus quite recently, according to the reports of our Ambassador in Finland, the whole staff of the 42d Russian Army Corps, numbering twenty officers, were taken prisoner at Rautus. That proves that it is not a question of mere interference in Finland's internal affairs, but of a struggle by Russia with the help of Finnish anarchists to deprive the country of its freedom. That has been expressly recognized even by the Socialists. I refer to the *Hamburger Echo* of April 17 last, in which it is definitely stated that all reports from Finland lead to the conclusion (I quote the wording) "that this civil war was in the main a war of Russians against Finns." The White Guard, so says the *Hamburger Echo,* is the real Finnish levy of the people, consisting mostly of peasants and tenant farmers, of whom many hold Social-Democratic views. In the Red Guard, on the other hand, were assembled principally the soldiers dismissed from the Russian Army, who were frequently reinforced from Petrograd.

We were asked to come by the lawful Finnish Government. This Government was appointed by the Landtag elected in November 1917 by 100 against 80 votes, and this Landtag was elected under the widest franchise in the world. This Government has been recognized by Sweden, Norway, France, Spain, and ourselves, and even in England it has a representative.

Our action was caused by no desire to interfere in the internal affairs of Finland, and just as little was it necessary for us to do so. Whatever form the future development may take is a purely Finnish matter. Our sole desire was to bring about political and military security and peace on the Baltic, and we are glad to be able to state that we have been successful to a not inconsiderable extent. We have concluded agreements with Finland which correspond to the well-understood interest of both parties, and will contribute to strengthen the already existing warm mutual relations of an economic and political nature between Germany and Finland. By the freeing of Finland we think we have rendered Sweden also a very considerable service through the creation of a barrier toward the East. The aim of our Eastern policy will continue to be the extension of our friendly relations with the Finnish and Swedish peoples. Thanks to the successes we have achieved, we shall happily soon be in a position to consider the Finnish expedition as practically concluded.

With regard to Esthonia and Livonia, I can refer substantially to the declaration of the Imperial Chancellor, made at General Headquarters in the name of the Kaiser, to the Esthonian and Livonian deputation. Both countries must first of all clear up their relations to Russia, in which we shall very gladly support them. Then they must, in my opinion, establish their Government and representation of the people on a broad basis. That is, however, an internal affair of these two states in which we shall not interfere. I may take this opportunity of correcting the mistaken impression that we dissolved the lawful Esthonian Landtag. This old Esthonian Landtag can have had no great internal authority, for it held power for only one day, and was no longer in office at the time when we entered the country. In these chaotic conditions, it is impossible to establish order by a stroke of the pen, but there is need for much work, much effort and racking of brains, not to mention a considerable expenditure of time.

In Lithuania also we must pursue the same object as in the other countries. The Lithuanians must create for themselves their own administration and government. We can support them in this with the one reserve that this independence is kept within the limit of the arrangements made or to be made with the German Government. The establishment of this country's administration can be effected only in agreement between the German civil administration and the German military power, as things at present stand. We must, however, seek out the men suited to this heavy task, and these people must be placed in Imperial organizations, or we must create fresh organizations for the purpose. But all this requires time, especially as many other tasks are pressing on the German military and civil administration. In the main, however, the preliminary work has been completed.

To deal with the Ukraine, I regret that we cannot postpone our discussions until next week, as then definite news would have been available, which would, presumably, have spared us a great deal of trouble. We must insist on the correctness of our information. But you reject with a wave of the hand, or an exclamation, what does not coincide with your ideas or conflicts with your views. That affords no adequate basis for discussion. One can but wait until definite facts are at hand. What excitement arose over the field-sowing order of General von Eichhorn, which was first of all incorrectly published, but who will today still seriously deny that some influence on the Government and the population in the sense of the order was really necessary in order that we should obtain the corn guaranteed to us by the treaty? I am also surprised that in connection with the carrying through of the measures in the Ukraine the earlier confidence has not been manifested in the representative of the Reichstag, General Groener. Yet he is the man who should be appointed to such a post by reason of his capacity for grasping the situation, and dealing and negotiating with the population. What has happened was bound to occur, in order really to carry out the arrangements that we had made with the Ukraine. Austria-Hungary and Germany are acting jointly in the Ukraine. That in individual cases certain differences of opinion should arise is unavoidable. It has, however, been already shown to be false that in the matter of the grain deliveries we are the losers. Subsequent investigation has revealed that this claim was founded on a mistake. We are completely agreed that we should not interfere in the internal affairs of the Ukraine. But that obviously has some limits, firstly in view of the object of our entry into the Ukraine, viz., the establishment of order; and, secondly, in regard to the security of our troops. With reference to the grain deliveries, I can only agree with what Herr Stresemann said yesterday. For us, the question whether or not the grain deliveries take place regularly, in accordance with the treaty, is of far more practical importance than the question who is lawful ruler in the Ukraine or what solution will eventually be found for the property question.

So far as concerns the change of government, it is by no means sure as yet whether it is to be considered a misfortune. Just consider the condition of the Ukraine during the past few weeks—what a lamentable political and economic situation, and what insecurity reigned there. The Government was inactive and helpless in the face of this fearful position, and that is no wonder, having regard to its formation partly from young and inexperienced men. Rather it is really surprising that the people have, generally speaking, put up with these conditions for so long. As matters stand in the Ukraine, it is quite impossible to dispense with a military administration. I refer only to the struggles that are still being fought out in the Ukraine with the troops of neighboring countries. We must, however, not now lose ourselves in a dispute over the powers of the military and civil administrations. There are too many practical tasks still awaiting solution there, and I am pleased, therefore, to be able to state that between our political representative in the Ukraine and Field-Marshal von Eichhorn and his Chief of Staff, General Groener, there exists thoroughly good understanding and co-operation, and that this understanding and co-operation correspond with the concord of the Imperial Government and the Supreme Army Command. We do not know whether still further surprises await us in the Ukraine, but quick decision and correct action are possible only if the authorities concerned in place and office can understand one another.

In conclusion, I will refer shortly to the question of the division of power between the Supreme Army Command and the Imperial Government. If matters went in accordance with the statements of Herr Scheidemann, we should all have had to send in our resignations by this time. I imagine that even for Herr Scheidemann and his friends that would not have been exactly a welcome solution. We have, however, simply taken our stand on the ground of our feelings of duty and responsibility. This idea has been for us the sole standard, whenever there was a question of co-operation between us and the Supreme Army Command. I can only say that since I have been in office not a single man has ever attempted to raise any difficulties for us in giving effect to this feeling of duty and responsibility. I think you can safely leave to us the maintenance of the position of the Imperial Government.

315. MATHIAS ERZBERGER, "MY 'OFFENSIVE' IN THE MAIN COMMITTEE," MAY 14, 1918[15]

The mistakes, misrepresentations, and deliberate inventions which have reached the public, through the medium of the press, with regard to the occurrences in the debate on the Eastern question, compel me to say a few words in explanation and self-defense.

Before entering on the debate, the Committee members of the Center "Fraktion" held a conference at which they unanimously agreed to the main principles underlying the statements I made on the first day of the Committee debate. Vice-Chancellor v. Payer was of the opinion, in his speech, that these main principles "forced open doors," whilst the Conservative and National-Liberal leaders said that they partly contained what was a matter of course, but expressed misgivings as to the demand that the decisive word has to be spoken by the Imperial Chancellor in the political and economic questions of the Eastern countries.

I replied to the Vice-Chancellor's statements and the utterances of the individual "Fraktionen" on Wednesday, May 8. According to the official minutes of the proceedings and the notes before me, the substance of my statements was the following:

The reason the Reichstag has so often to occupy itself with the Eastern question is that the Government did not, in the first place,

15 *Vossische Zeitung*, May 14, 1918, II, 4.

occupy a clear position, and that, up to now, measures for the benefit of the great landed proprietors in the Ukraine and Baltic provinces had proved in practice to be the only standard of policy. Vice-Chancellor v. Payer's statements, however, had been satisfactory in creating clarity as to three decisive main principles, to which he agreed:

1. Herr v. Payer spoke of the support and promotion of a nationalities policy in Russia as the aim of the Eastern policy. This implies a clear repudiation of those tendencies which aimed at the creation of a Great Russia but which did not take into consideration that the future Great Russia would be different from the former Tsaristic Russia ruled imperially by the Cadets and that the fundamental idea of the new Russian policy is enmity to Germany. It is in Germany's interest to further the "nationalities" policy; in this he agreed with Herr v. Payer.

2. The Vice-Chancellor spoke of the way to this goal being the way of understanding, not that of oppression. This rejection of a policy of force he (the speaker) doubly underlined.

3. According to the Vice-Chancellor's statement, the Government was resolved to maintain its competence (*Zuständigkeit*) with regard to the Eastern questions. He particularly welcomed this statement which had been now made for the first time in the Main Committee, because, as a rule, in the debates on the Eastern question, no member of the Government had been present to give an answer and accept responsibility for the measures taken.

He entirely agreed with these three principles in the Vice-Chancellor's speech.

But the question arose, how far the actual occurrences were in accord with the aims fixed by the Vice-Chancellor and the path he had indicated. To his regret, he must point out that a succession of measures had recently been adopted which abandoned the path indicated by the Chancellor, and deviated from the aims he had fixed.

Taking the case of Poland first of all, he recalled the speech made by the Prussian Minister for Agriculture in the Herrenhaus, which left little room for an understanding with Poland and bordered on oppression. More of this in the Plenum.

The occurrences in the Ukraine have caused particularly great regret. The Foreign Office has done a lasting service in having recognized the importance of the Ukraine years before and in having consistently pursued and supported the Ukraine policy. Of course it had always been clear that any Government in the young Ukrainian State would be weak. But how had we acted toward the Ukraine? Our negotiator in Brest-Litovsk had done a great service in recognizing at once that the starting-point for a solution of the Eastern question would be a peace treaty with the Ukraine.

Hardly was the peace treaty concluded with the Ukrainian Government when it had to fly from Kiev. It appealed to the Germans for help, and returned to Kiev under German protection. Shortly afterward, German troops imprisoned and deposed the Government with which we had concluded peace and which had appealed to us for help. That could not inspire confidence. Still more disagreeable were the isolated occurrences in connection with these actions, which were clearly prearranged, and which could only be described as a German *coup d'état,* carried out by the military.

General v. Eichhorn's decree was of no practical use, but politically it was very damaging. The conduct of the German authorities concerning the removal of the Ukrainian citizen Dobry was an interference in the internal political affairs of this state: he hoped and trusted the German authorities would not interfere now if the new Hetman got rid of or imprisoned his political opponents, the former Government. The way in which the former Government had been overthrown and a new Government called into existence by the German military was, as the Vice-Chancellor truly said, a mistake. The following description had reached him from a trustworthy eye-witness of the whole occurrence:

All the parties in the Rada opposed the Eichhorn spring decree. Toward three o'clock in the afternoon sitting, German military with armored cars, machine guns, and guns drew up before the Rada building in order to close it. A German officer appeared in the Assembly room, with German soldiers, and gave the order in Russian, "Hands up, in the name of the German Government!" On being repeatedly required to do so, the deputies obeyed this order. The President, Hrushevsky, who did not obey it, was threatened with a revolver. All the deputies were searched. Members of the Rada were not arrested, but members of the Ukrainian Government were. These occurrences were described in detail in the Kiev papers.

That evening all the "Fraktionen" of the Rada held meetings, in order to discuss measures of protection against the German attack.

During the Rada sitting on St. Sophia's day, General Skoropadski was appointed Hetman. The place was surrounded by German soldiers. The attendance of the Ukrainian people was wretched. The Congress of "Breadmakers" (not Peasants' Congress) met in two sections; very few peasant delegates appeared. The remainder consisted of Russian and Polish owners of large estates. The language of the proceedings was Russian, not Ukrainian. The speakers ended by shouting "For Russia and the Ukraine!" An agreement between the two parties of this congress, i.e., between peasants and great landowners, could not be reached.

General Skoropadski is, no doubt, a Ukrainian by birth, but he served in the Russian Army. Good judges call him the "little Boulanger." The Prime Minister, Ustimovitch, is a large landed proprietor, Russian through and through, and in favor of the unconditional attachment of the Ukraine to Russia.

The other day a delegation from the Rada called on the Ambassador, v. Mumm, in order to negotiate with him for the revocation of the communistic decree regarding possession of the land. The Ambassador said it was too late.

The consequences are, however, very regrettable for Germany. A German soldier can no longer show himself unarmed in Kiev. German soldiers have already been shot down. The bitterness against Germany is increasing. The railway men and workmen are planning a general strike. The whole peasant population was in the highest degree dissatisfied because Skoropadski's new decrees were issued to the advantage of the great landowners. The peasants would not deliver any grain, and in the event of requisitioning bloodshed had to be reckoned with. That is not the way to attain the first object of our intervention, namely securing the surplus grain supplies for the German people.

But the political consequences are even worse. The hatred of Germany is increasing. The Russophil elements were very glad that those Ministers who had concluded peace with us were arrested by us. It is further to be feared that the new Government will seek attachment to Russia as quickly as possible. Thus a new Great Russia is taking its rise from Kiev under German protection. The decrees, which Skoropadski issued, were almost word for word copies of the Russian constitution of 1905. The Ministers hitherto nominated were great landowners, and openly Great-Russian in sentiment. The question is now, what can still be got out of the present by no means favorable situation for Germany. There are only two ways of accomplishing anything:

(1) The immediate assembling of the Ukrainian constituent assembly, which had in any case been fixed for May 12.

(2) The formation of a coalition Cabinet of Ukrainians, not of Great Russians. Yesterday's telegram, respecting General Gröner's interview with Socialists, is already a satisfactory proof that the German authorities are acting on these lines. It would be interesting to hear what answer the Socialists gave. He must repudiate all responsibility for the policy in the Ukraine and its prejudicial consequences for Germany. The demand that the surplus grain should be placed at the disposal of the German people, as soon as possible, in exchange for other goods, was quite compatible with a policy of permanent understanding between the Ukraine and Germany. That, indeed, was precisely what true statesmanship had to do.

As to Esthonia and Livonia, it is regrettable that a promise had been given on the part of Germany "effectively" to "support" the efforts to separate these territories from Russia. The Center "Fraktion" had let the Government know their point of view as regards this question, and it was this: according to the peace treaty Esthonia and Livonia were under Russian sovereignty. They had to accomplish their separation from Russia on their own account in a correct way. If this was effected, the Center would then be quite ready to co-operate in what would be necessary for a close relationship with Germany. The Center must adhere to this standpoint, as opposed to other views, so that no one in the world could say that after Easter, and in consequence of the military acquisitions in the West, we put a different construction on the peace treaty from that which we put on it before Easter.

Finally, as regards Lithuania, it is very regrettable that the same complaints have always been made. A week before Easter, Lithuania was recognized as an autonomous and independent state. When the delegation of the Landesrat came to see the Chancellor, they intended to submit a number of wishes. But they were told that they must leave at once, as a great celebration of independence had been planned in Vilna. At the Imperial Chancellor's residence they were most distinctly given to understand that as early as April 4 they would be summoned to Berlin again. The delegation left, the celebration of independence did not take place; to this day the delegation has not been allowed to return to Berlin, not even a delegation of the Landesrat with the object of negotiating with the competent church authorities over urgent church matters. Even deputies had been prohibited from going to Lithuania. The unanimous wish of the whole country was for a Catholic Prince without any personal union. Certain interests are working expressly to drive the Catholic country into a personal union with the German Emperor. The complaints submitted earlier are still valid. The 35,000 Lithuanian prisoners of war were not allowed to return. Doctors and schoolmasters who were in Russia are also not allowed to return.

Requisitions have been continued with great harshness. The Lithuanian peasant only received 5 pfennigs for a liter of milk, and if he did not deliver enough he was punished. Therefore he welcomed with sincere pleasure the Vice-Chancellor's promise that a Lithuanian Government of their own should be formed and a Lithuanian civil administration of their own should be introduced. He hoped and trusted that these most necessary steps would soon be taken.

A strong government must energetically strive for the object recognized as right, by the means recognized as right, without troubling about any influences. His political friends wished that the following principles should be observed in dealing with the Eastern question:

"Decisions on all the political and economic questions concerning the Eastern countries should be taken only with the previous express consent of the Imperial Chancellor.

"The peace treaties of Brest-Litovsk to be maintained in full, in accordance with both the spirit and the letter.

"In order to secure a speedy and adequate delivery of grain the articles of exchange provided for in Article VII, Section I, of the Peace Treaty concluded with the Ukraine at Brest-Litovsk must be put at the disposal of the Ukraine with the utmost possible speed.

"The political and military German authorities are to refrain from all intervention in the domestic affairs of the Ukraine."

So much for the substance of my explanations. I adhere to the criticism they contain as being well founded and, in view of the whole material, moderate. None of the party speakers who followed could dispute my facts. Neither is it the fact that Herr Stresemann made the statements against me which the *National-Liberale Korrespondenz* circulates. Had it been true, I should certainly not have left them unanswered. Everyone judging objectively must admit that there is no attack on Count Hertling or on the Highest Army Command in these statements. But yet more. If there had been such an attack in this speech, Vice-Chancellor v. Payer, whom I have known and esteemed for years, would not have written and could not have been silent. Not a single representative of the Government protested or raised objections to any of my expressions of opinion. This fact in itself shows that the actual occurrence in the Main Committee was essentially other than it has been represented by a number of newspapers. For this reason the President of the Center "Fraktion" has rightly stated that all the representations which speak of an attack on Count Hertling and on the Highest Army Command must be regarded as false.

As regards the malicious imputations to which my relation to the army and its glorious leaders is subjected, I am anxious in this connection to point out emphatically that the Highest Army Command was not in any way included in my criticism; Hindenburg and Ludendorff, to whom our whole nation rightly looks up with gratitude and confidence, are to me as great and revered personages as to any other German. The name of Eichhorn is forever linked with the memory of a succession of great military deeds in the difficult years of the Russian war. But we are no longer at war with Russia, and particularly with the Ukraine we are supposed to be living on "terms of peace and friendship."

Therefore in criticizing the measures recently adopted by military officials in Kiev, I had exclusively in mind the political questions, with which the military have been mainly occupied, in consequence of the existing circumstances in the Ukraine. But measures of a purely political nature, such as those I spoke of on May 8, cannot possibly be immune from all discussion, because they emanate from military quarters. It is the right and duty of every deputy to adopt an attitude toward them. I give place to none in love of our great German Fatherland, but I do not shut my eyes to anything which adds to the burdens of our people. To reproach me with enmity to the military is a deliberate misconstruction of my intentions, which aim no less at the greatness of the German Empire and at bringing about an honorable, lasting peace which will secure Germany's cultural, political, and economic future than do those of any one of my open and secret adversaries.

Now for the so-called Erzberger resolution. The statements made up to now prove that I did not give notice of nor introduce any such resolution, that therefore it was also not withdrawn and notice of it for the Plenum could not have been given.

The true state of affairs is as follows: I was approached on Wednesday by several people and parties wanting to end the long debate with a resolution; for this purpose, they said, the guiding principles which I had already laid down on Saturday would suit excellently. With my political friends in the Committee I drafted a resolution. This draft was signed by all the members of the Committee present belonging to the Center "Fraktion" (Erzberger, Gröber, Nacken, Dr. Pfleger, and Freiherr v. Rechenberg). The draft was submitted to the members of the Volkspartei and of the Socialist Party for signature. The gentlemen signed the resolution.

Thereupon a member of the Volkspartei discussed the resolution itself with Vice-Chancellor v. Payer at a private interview. Herr v. Payer expressed doubts, and wished for a few editorial alterations, which were agreed to. In the further course of the private negotiations with the Vice-Chancellor the latter said that he would rather the resolution were not introduced at all. On this the gentlemen of the Volkspartei withdrew their signatures. When informed of this I said at once: "Then the resolution shall not be brought forward at all." And I requested them to inform the others who had signed it of this. All the gentlemen said they agreed to the resolution not being brought forward.

That is precisely the great advantage of the present Government system in Germany: the Majority parties first try to agree among themselves, and then negotiate with the Government before they bring forward their resolutions. The fact of this resolution not having been brought forward shows most clearly that when an offensive against Count Hertling and the Highest Army Command is spoken of, it is a pure misrepresentation of the whole proceedings for party purposes. It is regrettable that the discussion of such highly important matters takes place in the semi-obscurity of the Committee, whereby, in default of an objective and comprehensive report, certain circles are given an occasion they apparently desire for political well-poisoning.

CHAPTER XIX

THE LEAGUE OF NATIONS

INTRODUCTORY NOTE

THE REICHSTAG RESOLUTION OF 1917," Erzberger wrote, "was an oath of allegiance to the League of Nations." His monograph, *The League of Nations,* published in 1918, summarized the German literature on the League and considered how it was to be established.

The Allied war propaganda had promised that "this League of Nations would unite the belligerents, conquerors as well as conquered, in a permanent system of common rights." Germany had therefore hoped from the beginning of peace to participate in the establishment of the League. Before the armistice the Imperial Government commenced work on a draft for a league of nations, which was later presented to the Allied and Associated Powers at Versailles.

316. MONTGELAS TO HERRON, AUGUST 28, 1918[1]

VILLENEUVE, HOTEL BYRON, Aug. 28th, 1918

As far as I am able to judge, the idea of a League of Nations has of late made great progress in my country. Evidence of this progress seems to be borne out by the speech of Prince Max von Baden at Karlsruhe on the 23rd inst., and the leading articles from Mr. Dernberg (former Colonial Secretary) in the *Berliner Tageblatt* of Sunday 25th inst., No. 433. But there still exists some mistrust on the part of those who think that the economic and colonial development of the German people might be strangled by the establishment of the League. It therefore would be of the highest importance to give Germany the most positively formal assurance that—in exchange for the limitation imposed on the national action of the members of the League—her eco-

---

[1] Herron Papers, I, Document XLIII.

nomic freedom will be guaranteed and her pre-war colonies or some equivalent of them restored to her.

Many thanks for your eloquent poem. Such is the destiny of America "to pronounce universal brotherhood" and no people, I am convinced, is more called than the German to co-operate in this holy undertaking.

317. PROPOSALS OF THE GERMAN GOVERNMENT FOR THE ESTABLISHMENT OF A LEAGUE OF NATIONS[2]

I. Foundation Principles

1. The League of Nations is constituted for the purpose of founding a permanent peace between its members by obligatory settlement of international differences. It is to be based upon the moral power of right and shall serve as an international community working for the intellectual and material advancement of mankind.

It is to be established for all time and shall form a unity for the purpose of a common defense against all opposing powers from without.

The members guarantee to each other their respective territorial possessions and shall mutually refrain from interfering with the internal political affairs.

2. Especial aims of the League of Nations shall be: (a) the prevention of international disputes; (b) disarmament; (c) securing the freedom of traffic and of the general economic equality of rights; (d) the protection of national minorities; (e) the creation of an international Workers' Charter; (f) the regulation of the colonial question; (g) the uniting of existing and future international institutions; (h) the creation of an International Parliament.

3. The League of Nations shall comprise: (a) all belligerent states inclusive of those arising during the war; (b) all neutral states which were included in the Hague World Arbitration League; (c) all others if they are admitted by two-thirds of the already existing members.

The right of the Holy See to entrance into the League of Nations is held in reserve.

4. The members shall pledge themselves to conclude no separate treaty contrary to the aims of the League nor to enter into any secret agreement of any kind whatsoever. Existing treaties of such a kind shall be annulled.

Secret treaties shall be null and void.

[2] Germany, Auswärtiges Amt, *Vorschläge der Deutschen Regierung für die Errichtung eines Völkerbundes* [1918].

II. Constitution

5. The official bodies of the League of Nations shall be: (*a*) the Congress of States; (*b*) the International Parliament; (*c*) the Permanent International Tribunal; (*d*) the International Mediation Office; (*e*) the International Administrative Bureaus; (*f*) the Chancery.

A. The Congress of States

6. The Congress of States is the assembly of the representatives of the states belonging to the League of Nations. Each state shall have from one to three representatives; the representatives of any state, however, shall vote only as a unit.

7. The Congress shall meet at least once every three years.

8. The Congress shall carry on the business of the League of Nations so far as it is not transferred to other official bodies; it shall elect at its first meeting a permanent committee to take charge of the business in the intervals.

9. The resolutions of the Congress, so far as the treaty does not determine otherwise, shall be passed by a majority of two-thirds of the states represented; for the rest the Congress regulates for itself its own order of business.

B. The International Parliament

10. The first International Parliament shall be composed of representatives of the respective parliaments of the states in the League of Nations. Each single parliament shall elect for every million of inhabitants of its state one representative; but no parliament shall send more than ten representatives.

11. The International Parliament with consent of the Congress of States shall decide on the later composition of the International Parliament.

12. The consent of the International Parliament shall be required for: (*a*) changes in the constitution of the League; (*b*) the laying down of generally valid international legal principles; (*c*) the appointment of new bodies of the League; (*d*) the establishing of the budget of the League.

In these matters the International Parliament shall at the same time have the initiative.

13. The International Parliament shall meet at the same time as the Congress of States. For the rest it shall regulate for itself its own methods of business.

C. *The Permanent International Tribunal*

14. The Permanent International Tribunal shall be elected by the Congress of States for the period of nine years, as follows:

Each state shall propose at least one and at most four persons who are suitable for and ready to accept the office of judge.

At least one of the persons proposed must be not of the nationality of the state which proposes his election.

From the total list of the proposed each state shall nominate fifteen persons; the fifteen persons who receive the most votes shall be elected judges.

Upon the retirement of judges their places shall be taken by those persons who have received the most votes after the fifteen who had been elected, and this in the order of the number of votes obtained.

15. The Tribunal shall give its decisions through the representation of three members, of whom each party shall choose one. The Tribunal represented by all its members shall appoint the President in case the parties do not agree upon his nomination.

D. *The International Mediation Office*

16. Each state shall appoint for the International Mediation Office four electors who possess its confidence. The electors shall meet in a session and elect by majority vote fifteen members of the Mediation Office as well as ten substitutes, whose order of succession shall be determined at the election.

17. The Mediation Office shall give its decisions through the representation of five members, of whom each party shall choose two. The President is to be appointed, in case the parties do not agree upon his election, by the Mediation Office sitting in full session.

18. The members of the Mediation Office shall neither stand in a relation of active service to their home country nor be at the same time members of another official body of the League of Nations.

They have to reside at the seat of the League of Nations.

E. *The International Administrative Bureaus*

19. The League of Nations shall further all efforts for the uniting of the common interests of the nations and shall work for the further development of already existing, and the creation of new, international institutions. This applies especially to the domains of law, economics, and finance.

20. The existing unions shall be joined to the League of Nations as far as possible.

21. All international bureaus which have been established previously by collective treaties shall, if the contracting parties are willing, be subject to the control of the League.

22. All international bureaus which may be established in future shall be subject to the supervision of the League.

F. The Chancery of the League

23. The officials of the Chancery shall be appointed by the Permanent Committee of the Congress of States and are placed under its supervision.

24. The Chancery shall form the common bureau of the official bodies of the League of Nations. Its business order shall be decided upon by the Permanent Committee of the Congress of States.

25. The Chancery shall publish in its official organ all resolutions and communications of the official bodies of the League of Nations. The members of the League of Nations shall be obliged to publish in their official organs, in the original text and in the language of the country, the resolutions and communications of the Congress of States and of the International Mediation Bureau, and to submit them to their legislative bodies.

26. The members of the League of Nations shall bind themselves to hand over all international treaties, concluded by them, to the Chancery for publication in the organ of the League of Nations.

G. Position of the Officials of the League

27. All members of the body of international authorities and of the International Parliament, with the exception of those who themselves belong to the state where they reside, shall enjoy there the privileges and immunities of diplomats.

28. Members of the International Parliament shall enjoy in the state to which they belong the same rights as the members of parliament of that state.

III. Pacific Settlements of International Disputes

29. All difficulties between states which could not be settled by diplomacy and for which a special mode of arbitration has not been agreed upon shall be settled either by the Permanent International Tribunal or by the International Mediation Bureau.

30. The International Tribunal shall be the regular official body for the decision of legal disputes between states. Every member of the League of Nations shall have the right to bring here a complaint which

must be answered by the opposite party. The decisions are issued in the name of the League of Nations.

The same shall apply to the proceedings before the Mediation Office.

31. Besides the jurisdiction over disputes between states, the International Tribunal shall be entitled to decide on: (a) complaints of private persons against foreign states and heads of states, when the State Tribunals have declared their incompetency; (b) disputes between subjects of different states which are members of the League of Nations, so far as the interpretation of state treaties forms the object of the dispute.

32. The states concerned reserve to themselves the right of concluding arbitration treaties for single cases of dispute or for certain kinds of controversies. This right, however, shall not be granted to them when the interpretation of general written rules of international law or the interpretation of the ordinances of the League of Nations are concerned.

33. If the defendant in a conflict raises the objection before the International Tribunal that the question concerns merely a conflict of interests or a legal matter of prevailing political significance, the Tribunal must first of all decide on the merits of this objection. Should this objection be well founded, it shall refer the conflict for settlement to the Mediation Office.

If the conflict is brought before the Mediation Office and it is objected that a purely legal question is concerned, the Mediation Office shall transfer the matter first to the International Tribunal, which shall decide whether the conflict shall be referred back to the Mediation Office or remain with the Tribunal.

34. The Tribunal shall draft an order of procedure based upon the Hague Convention of October 18, 1907, concerning the pacific settlement of international disputes; this procedure shall require for its efficiency the consent of the Congress of States.

The procedure before the Mediation Office shall be decided on by this body.

The Tribunal as well as the Mediation Office shall be authorized to settle by a provisional arrangement the relations arising from the dispute for the duration of the proceedings.

35. The decision of the Tribunal is passed according to international agreements, international customary law, and the general principles of law and equity.

36. The decision of the Tribunal or of the Mediation Office shall demand that the state in question carry out its contents in good faith.

IV. Prevention of International Disputes

37. If the Mediation Office shall establish the fact that a tension has arisen in the relations between individual states of the League of Nations, it can offer its services of mediation to the states concerned. These shall then be obliged to discuss the matter before the Mediation Office and to offer to the same the basis for a proposal which will tend toward a settlement of the question.

38. Every state belonging to the League of Nations shall be under obligation to suppress through its legislative and administrative authorities the calumniations of another nation by speech, writing, or illustration. On violation of this duty, the injured state shall have the right to call for a decision of the International Tribunal.

39. The states of the League of Nations shall reciprocally oblige themselves to rectify at any time such actual assertions as have been published by the press of one state to the disadvantage of another. This rectification being refused, the International Tribunal shall decide.

V. Disarmament

40. The members of the League of Nations shall so limit their armaments on land and in the air that only such forces will be maintained by them as are necessary for the safety of the country.

They shall limit their armament at sea to the forces which are necessary for the defense of their coasts.

41. The total expenditure for armament purposes, according to estimates and expenditures, as well as the figures giving the actual number of troops and the amount of war supplies of all kinds, especially of warships, shall annually be reported to the chancery of the League and by it to the organ of the League of Nations for the purpose of publication.

42. For the carrying through of the disarmament, a special agreement shall be made which shall also provide for the international control over the adherence to these arrangements.

The agreement shall form an essential part of the constitution of the League of Nations.

VI. Freedom of Traffic

43. The dominion over the sea shall be placed in the hands of the League of Nations. The League shall exert its power through an International Sea Police, the organization of which shall be decided upon by a special agreement.

The executive means necessary for the policing of the sea shall be divided by the agreement between the various maritime states of the League of Nations.

No other armed vessels except those of the sea police shall navigate the sea.

44. The straits and canals necessary for the international sea traffic shall be open to the ships of all states belonging to the League of Nations.

45. The states of the League of Nations shall not treat the maritime and inland navigation of any other member state less favorably than their own or that of the most-favored nation. This particularly applies to the utilization of the arrangements made for the supply of coal and other necessaries for the ships. Coastal navigation shall be regulated by a separate agreement. With regard to the seaworthiness of ships and the arrangements on board, the laws of the state under whose flag the ship is sailing shall be recognized until a settlement has been arrived at by the League of Nations.

46. The air shall be free for aëronautic traffic to all member states alike. In order to carry out this principle, a separate agreement shall be arrived at, which, among other things, shall regulate the questions of forced landing on the territory of the state flown over and of securities for the payment of duty.

47. No member state shall be restricted in the freedom of communication by cable or wireless.

48. The legal position of the subjects of one member state in the territory of another with regard to personal liberty, liberty of conscience, the rights of residence and settling, as well as judicial protection shall be settled by a separate agreement on the basis of the greatest possible equality with the native residents.

49. Concerning the practice of commerce, trade, and agriculture, the subjects of one member state shall be in a position of equality with the native residents, particularly also in respect to the imposts incumbent thereto.

50. The member states of the League of Nations shall not participate—directly or indirectly—in any measures taken with the object of continuing or resuming the economic war. Forcible measures on the part of the League of Nations shall be reserved to that body.

51. All kinds of goods coming from or directed to the territory of a state in the League of Nations shall be free from all transit duties in the territories of the member states.

52. The mutual traffic between member states shall not be restricted by import, export, or transit prohibitions, except as necessary for reasons of public safety or on account of the Public Health Office or for the carrying through of internal economic legislation.

53. The several member states are at liberty to settle, according to their special requirements, their mutual economic relations by means of special agreements also in respect to relations other than those enumerated above.

They recognize the creation of an International Commercial Treaty to be the aim of their endeavors.

VII. PROTECTION OF NATIONAL MINORITIES

54. The national minorities in the several member states shall be guaranteed their national individuality, particularly with regard to language, school, church, art, science, and public press. The carrying through of this principle shall be decided upon by a separate agreement, which has in the first line to determine the manner in which the right of the minorities can be asserted before the official bodies of the League of Nations.

VIII. LABOR LAW

55. One of the chief objects of the League of Nations is to secure to the workers of all member states an existence in accordance with human dignity and the enjoyment of their professional activities. For this purpose a special agreement shall settle for the workers the questions of freedom of movement, the right of combining, and the position of equality for natives and aliens, in respect to conditions of work, exchange of labor, social insurance, protection of the working classes, home industries, supervision of labor, and the international carrying through and development of these principles.

56. An international Labor Bureau shall be established in the chancery of the League with the object of supervising and further developing the Labor Law.

IX. THE COLONIES

57. The League of Nations shall issue international regulations for the administration of colonies not possessing the right of self-government, on the following subjects: (a) the protection of the natives against slavery, alcohol, arms and munition traffic, epidemics, compulsory labor, and forcible expropriation; (b) promotion of health, education, and well-being of the natives, and the securing of freedom of conscience; (c) securing peace by the neutralization of the colonial territories and by the prohibition of militarization.

58. The recognized religious communities in the states of the League of Nations shall be guaranteed the free practice of their confessions and of missionary work in all the colonies.

59. The subjects of all member states shall be guaranteed freedom of economic activity, taking into consideration the aforesaid general regulations on the freedom of traffic in every colony.

60. For the carrying through and supervision of the above regulations an International Colonial Office shall be established. In every colony the mandatories of the League of Nations shall be obliged to see to the carrying of the above regulations into effect.

61. The fate of territories of a colonial character which are not connected, directly or indirectly, with the League of Nations shall be decided upon in favor of a member by a verdict of the League of Nations only.

X. Execution

62. If a state of the League of Nations refuses to carry out the decisions, resolutions, or orders of any one official body authorized by the League of Nations or in any other way violates a provision of the constitution of the League, the Mediation Office in its full sitting of fifteen members shall come to a decision about compulsory execution.

63. Execution may in particular consist in: (a) the breaking off of the diplomatic relations by all the other states; (b) the limitation of or the breaking off of economic relations, especially by import and export prohibitions, unequal customs treatment, cutting off the traffic in goods or persons, stopping the transmission of news, confiscation of ships; (c) military measures which are enjoined upon the injured state alone in connection with other states.

64. Every state shall have the right upon an attack being made upon its territory not only to make use of the legal means offered by the League of Nations but also to take immediate steps in self-defense.

65. All costs and damages which result to the members of the League of Nations individually or jointly, from the measures taken for the execution of their orders, shall be paid by the state which breaks the peace.

XI. Costs

66. The total costs of the League of Nations shall be provided for by the members according to a fixed standard, which is to be established by the Congress of States in accordance with the standard fixed by the international postal union.